THE PLANTAGENET ROLL

OF THE

𝔅lood 𝔯oyal

Lady Elizabeth Mortimer, widow of Henry Lord Percy, K.G. called "Hotspur," and her second husband Thomas, Lord Camoys, K.G., from a rubbing of the brass in Trotton Church, Sussex, 1419, by F. R. Fairbank, M.D., F.S.A.

THE PLANTAGENET ROLL
OF THE
Blood Royal

BEING A COMPLETE TABLE OF
ALL THE DESCENDANTS NOW LIVING OF
Edward III, King of England

by

The Marquis of Ruvigny and Raineval

AUTHOR OF "THE BLOOD ROYAL OF BRITAIN," "THE JACOBITE PEERAGE, BARONETAGE,
AND KNIGHTAGE," "THE MOODIE BOOK," "THE NOBILITIES OF EUROPE," ETC.

The Mortimer-Percy Volume
CONTAINING THE DESCENDANTS OF LADY ELIZABETH PERCY, *née* MORTIMER

PART I

WITH SUPPLEMENTS TO THE EXETER AND ESSEX VOLUMES

ILLUSTRATED

HERITAGE BOOKS
2011

HERITAGE BOOKS
AN IMPRINT OF HERITAGE BOOKS, INC.

Books, CDs, and more—Worldwide

For our listing of thousands of titles see our website
at
www.HeritageBooks.com

A Facsimile Reprint
Published 2011 by
HERITAGE BOOKS, INC.
Publishing Division
100 Railroad Ave. #104
Westminster, Maryland 21157

Originally published
London, 1911

— Publisher's Notice —
In reprints such as this, it is often not possible to remove blemishes from the original. We feel the contents of this book warrant its reissue despite these blemishes and hope you will agree and read it with pleasure.

International Standard Book Numbers
Paperbound: 978-0-7884-1872-3
Clothbound: 978-0-7884-8834-4

PREFACE

THE Descendants of King Edward IV. and of his brother and sister, George, Duke of Clarence, and Anne, Duchess of Exeter, and of their aunt Isabel, Countess of Essex and Eu, having been given in the preceding volumes, the present volume of the PLANTAGENET ROLL OF THE BLOOD ROYAL treats of those of Lady Elizabeth Mortimer, wife first of Henry, Lord Percy, K.G., called "Hotspur," and, secondly, of Thomas, Lord Camoys, K.G.

The plan followed is identical with that adopted in the Clarence and Exeter Volumes. The lines from the Lady Elizabeth are traced out in a series of Tables until about the beginning of the last century; then in the body of the book the descendants of the various persons last named in the Tables are set out in the order of primogeniture. The full dates of birth, marriage, and death are given, and in the cases of married persons the names of the husband and wife, &c.

In the Tables the dates of birth, marriage, and death are given whenever possible, but as the object of the writer has been merely to trace out the living descendants of Edward III., and in order to keep the work within bounds, he has been obliged to omit (except in some few cases, where it has been thought desirable to show the descent of a title) the names of persons who died without issue, or whose issue subsequently failed, and also the parentage of the wives.

In the case of a person having been married more than once, only the name of the wife or wives (or husband or husbands) by whom he (or she) had issue are given, the figure in round brackets immediately following the marriage mark (=) signifying whether she (or he) is first, second, or third wife (or husband). Similarly, if the figure precedes the marriage mark, it signifies that he (or she) married as first or second wife (or husband), as the case may be. Wherever the compiler has been able to give the dates of birth and marriage, he has considered this sufficient indication of whether the children are by the first or second marriage; but where the dates have not been obtainable, the figure before the names shows of which marriage they are the issue.

When a name in the Tables is in italics, it signifies that they have a previous descent which has been already shown.

In the Roll itself considerations of space have again rendered it necessary to adopt the briefest possible description, and the words "and had issue" must be held to refer only (with the exceptions mentioned above) to those children who are now living, or whose issue now survives, or those concerning whose issue, or possible issue, the author has been unable to obtain particulars.

Each Section is headed by the name of the person last named in the Tables, and their children are 1a, 2a, &c. The issue of the a's, grandchildren of the head of the line, are b's, and the children of these last, great-grandchildren of the head of the line, are similarly c's, and so on, the d's being children of the c's, and great-great-grandchildren of the head of the line, &c.

Preface

The dates of birth and death immediately follow the names of the persons to whom they refer. In the cases of births, marriages, and deaths outside the United Kingdom, the author has endeavoured to give the place as well as the date.

The surnames of noblemen are given in round brackets after their Christian names, and the nationality of their title is indicated by the initials and names within square brackets immediately following them.[1]

The Lady Elizabeth Mortimer, whose descendants are here set out, was the elder daughter[2] of Edmund (Mortimer), 3rd Earl of March, by his wife the Lady Philippa, only child and heir of Lionel (of Antwerp), Duke of Clarence, the eldest of the four sons of King Edward III. of whom issue now survives. Her brother Roger, 4th Earl of March, was declared heir to the crown of England by King Richard II., and was the father of the Lady Anne Mortimer, who by her marriage with Richard (Plantagenet), Earl of Cambridge, transmitted the hereditary right to the throne to the House of York, and was the ancestress of King Edward IV. and of all the successive sovereigns of England (with the exception of Henry VII.) from that day to this, and equally so of all those whose names are recorded in the Tudor Roll and in the Clarence, Exeter, and Essex Volumes of the present series.

Lady Elizabeth was born at Usk, 12 February 1371, and married the famous Henry, Lord Percy, K.G., called "Hotspur," son and heir of Henry, 1st Earl of Northumberland. He was descended in the male line from Josceline of Louvain, brother of Queen Adeliza, second wife of King Henry I., and younger son of Godfrey, sovereign Duke of Lorraine and Count of Brabant, who, marrying Maud, daughter and eventual heiress of William, 3rd feudal Lord Percy, assumed her name but retained his own paternal arms; and was himself of the Royal Blood, Henry, 3rd Lord Percy of Alnwick (father of the 1st Earl of Northumberland), having married the Lady Mary Plantagenet, daughter of Henry, Earl of Lancaster, and granddaughter of Edmund, Earl of Lancaster, the second son of King Henry III.

Lord Percy was born 20 May 1364; was knighted by King Edward III. in April 1377 along with the future Kings, Richard II. and Henry IV., who were almost exactly of his own age; was made a K.G. at the age of 24 in 1388, and won his sobriquet of "Hotspur" owing to the restless activity he displayed as Warden of the Marches in repressing the inroads of the Scottish Borderers.[3] He was the English commander at the famous

---

[1] The initials E., S., I., G.B., U.K., F., H.R.E., and P.S., standing for England, Scotland, Ireland, Great Britain, the United Kingdom, France, the Holy Roman Empire, and the Papal States. With regard to foreign titles of nobility, it was the original intention of the author to give these in the language of their nationality, but it would have appeared absurd to have written *Herzog von Teck*, or to have referred to the *Freiherr Heinrich von Worms, M.P.*; after much consideration, therefore, he decided to give them in English, adding the foreign equivalent in brackets immediately following, so, "3rd Baron of Hugel (Freiherr von Hugel)"—"7th Count of Salis (Graf von Salis)," after the plan recently adopted in the *Almanach de Gotha*. It is to be wished that some settled rule might be adopted by the Press. To take one case, which might be multiplied without end, *Duc d'Orléans* or *Duke of Orléans* are both equally correct, but the *Duke d'Orléans*, which one constantly sees, is certainly a misnomer. The Spanish Minister is nearly always described as "Marquis of Villalobar," while the Italian Ambassador figures as "Marquis de San Giuliano." Surely it should be "Marquis of" or "Marchese di." All the older writers used to translate the names and titles into English, and this appears to be the only way if any uniform plan is to be attempted, and is, moreover, the plan adopted to-day by such high authorities as the compilers of the British Museum Catalogue.

[2] Her younger sister, Lady Philippa, born at Ludlow, 21 November 1375, married. 1st, John (Hastings), Earl of Pembroke; 2ndly, 15 August 1390, Richard (Fitzalan), 11th Earl of Arundel, and 3rdly, after April 1398, John (Poynings), Lord St. John, but *d.s.p.s.* at Halnaker, co. Sussex, 24 September 1401.

[3] Walsingham, ii. p. 144.

Preface

Battle of Otterburn (Chevy Chase), 10 August 1388—"the best-fought and severest of all the battles I have related in my history," says Froissart—where, though Douglas, the Scottish commander, was slain, Percy himself was made prisoner; and of Homildon Hill, 14 September 1402, where he defeated the Scots and captured the Earl of Douglas. He joined his father in supporting Henry of Lancaster's usurpation of the crown, it being the subsequent boast of the Percies that they had placed Henry IV. on the throne; but afterwards taking mortal offence at the King's refusal to allow him to ransom his brother-in-law Sir Edmund Mortimer whilst claiming the prisoners whom he (Percy) had taken at Homildon Hill, he rose in rebellion and was defeated and slain at the Battle of Shrewsbury, 23 July 1403, by an unknown hand, either by a spear or by an arrow which had pierced his brain. After that "sory bataill," the forerunner of the Wars of the Roses, was finished, his body, over which the King is said to have shed tears, was delivered to his kinsman Thomas (Nevill), Lord Furnival, who buried it in his family chapel at Whitchurch, sixteen miles from the battlefield. But a day or two later, in order to prevent any rumour that he was still alive, it was taken up and placed for public exhibition between two millstones near the pillory in Shrewsbury, somewhere near the present site of the Post Office, guarded by armed men, and then beheaded and quartered. His head was placed over the gate of York, "there to remain so long as it can last," and his four quarters were salted and sent in sacks to the Mayors of London, Bristol, Newcastle-on-Tyne, and Chester, the cost of their carriage being £13, 15s.[1] On 3 November following, however, the King ordered that his head and quarters should be delivered to his widow, who buried them in the Northumberland tomb in York Minster. She was put under arrest after Hotspur's death,[2] but was subsequently released, and married, secondly, as his second wife, Thomas (de Camoys), 1st Lord Camoys, K.G., who commanded the left wing of the army at the Battle of Agincourt. She was living 1417/8, and may have been the "Isabel Camoyse, wife of Thomas Camoyse, Knt.," who died 1444, and was buried in the Friars Minors.

Lord Camoys died 28 March 1419, and was buried at Trotton, co. Sussex, where there is a beautiful brass, with the effigies of himself and Lady Elizabeth, a photogravure of which, taken from a rubbing by Dr. Fairbank, is given as a frontispiece to this volume.

She had issue by her first husband a son, Henry, who was restored as 2nd Earl of Northumberland by Henry V., 11 November 1414, and a daughter, Lady Elizabeth, wife first of John, 7th Lord Clifford, K.G., and 2ndly, of Ralph (Nevill), 2nd Earl of Westmorland; and by her second another daughter, the Hon. Alice Camoys, wife of Sir Leonard Hastings, who all three had issue (see Table II.). The statement sometimes made that she was the mother of Sir Richard de Camoys is incorrect.

On the death of the 7th Earl of Northumberland in 1572 the representation of Hotspur and Lady Elizabeth devolved upon his daughters and co-heirs. The elder Lady Elizabeth married Richard Woodruffe of Wolley, co. York, and had issue, but none of her descendants have been traced to the present day (see p. 567). The younger Lady Lucy married Sir Edward

---

[1] "Battlefield Church, Salop, and the Battle of Shrewsbury," by the Rev. W. G. D. Fletcher, M.A., F.S.A., 1903, p. 13.   [2] *Fœdera*, viii. p. 334.

Preface

Stanley, K.B., and her heir of line is Viscount Gage, who is thus the senior known representative of Lady Elizabeth Mortimer and Lord Percy.

The descendants of Lady Elizabeth are very much more numerous than those of her brother the Earl of March. The present part of the Mortimer-Percy Volume deals with those of Henry, 4th Earl of Northumberland, K.G. (d. 1486) and of his sister, Lady Elizabeth Gascoigne, and contains between nine and ten thousand new names. The actual number of their living descendants who are traceable, however, amounts to some thirty or forty thousand, and they have between them 135,520 descents. Owing, however, to the many inter-marriages with descendants of the Earl of March, the great majority of these have already appeared in one or other of the volumes previously published, in right of a senior descent from him; and owing to the ever-increasing number of descendants and descents which naturally occur as the lines are carried further back, the compiler has in the present index been reluctantly compelled to abandon the plan he had hitherto followed of setting out in the index the name of every descendant whether or not they have already appeared in former volumes, and to confine the index to the present part to the names which actually appear in the body of the work. It will be easily understood how this course has been forced upon him when it is pointed out that all the Clarence,[1] and that 14,478 Tudor,[2] 31,752 Exeter, and 12,176 Essex descents repeat in the present part. To prevent any inconvenience, however, a new plan has been adopted of adding an index of the numbers instead of the names which repeat, so that any one can at once see whether he or she is descended from Edward III. through the Mortimer-Percy marriage. This plan will be found fully explained on page 607, and is the plan which will be followed with duplicate descents in all future volumes.

With this part is included a Supplement, containing some further descendants of the Duchess of Exeter and the Countess of Essex, which the compiler has since succeeded in tracing.

Summarising the five volumes already published, it will be found that some fifty thousand descendants[3] of King Edward III. have been traced, and that they have between them over 300,000 descents, all clearly shown by the numbers attached to each name. Included in the Roll are the names of all the crowned heads of Europe, with the exception of the King of Servia and the Prince of Montenegro; of the majority of our hereditary legislators; of the members of all the royal and princely houses of Europe; of many of the higher nobility of France, Germany, Austria, Hungary, Poland, Bohemia, Italy, Spain, Portugal, Russia, Belgium; and of

---

[1] By the marriages respectively of the Hon. Jane Nevill and Henry, Lord Stafford (both descendants through the Mortimer-Percy marriage; see the present Part, Tables XXVI. and XXI.) with Henry (Pole) Lord Montagu and the Lady Ursula Pole, grandchildren of George, Duke of Clarence (see Clarence Vol., Table II.).

[2] Largely in consequence of the marriage of Henry (Clifford), 2nd Earl of Cumberland (a Mortimer-Percy descendant; see Table VIII.), with the Lady Eleanor Brandon, a granddaughter of King Henry VII. (see Tudor Roll, Table XIV.).

[3] As far as the compiler has been able to trace them, the living descendants of King Edward IV. appear to amount to some 12,000; and those of the Duke of Clarence, of the Duchess of Exeter, and the Countess of Essex to some 18,000, 25,500, and 18,000 respectively; while the present instalment of Lady Elizabeth Mortimer's descendants number some 30,000. In consequence of inter-marriages, however, a considerable number, as already mentioned, are descended from all five, while others again are descended from four, or three, or two of them. He has not had time to work out the exact number of these inter-marriages, but a rough estimate fixes the net number of the descendants of Edward III. already traced at the above number.

Preface

the old aristocracy of the Southern States of America, together with many of those of our baronets and county families with their cadets, who so largely go to make up the professional classes; but with some few exceptions, none have descended to or are at least traceable among the trading or labouring classes.

While tracing hundreds of entirely new lines of descent, it has been the duty of the author to discard others which will not stand in the light of modern investigation. This has been especially so in the case of the Mortimer-Percy lines. For instance, the oft-repeated statement that Lady Eleanor Percy, a daughter of the 3rd Earl of Northumberland, married Reginald (West), 6th Lord De La Warr, is demonstratively incorrect, and this would have been at once seen had the old Peerage writers been more careful in comparing their dates. The will of Henry, 3rd Earl of Northumberland, is dated 1 November 1458, and in it he mentions his three daughters, Eleanor, Margaret, and Elizabeth, *all then unmarried*.[1] Lord De La Warr died on the 27 August 1450, not 1451, as stated by Collins and others. The writs issued on his death are dated 1 September, 29 Hen. VI., which is clearly 1450, and the inquisitions in pursuance were taken in various counties within the next few weeks.[2] From these we learn that Richard West, Esq., was his son and heir and over 19 years of age. Richard West was consequently born not later than 1431, in which year his supposed grandfather, the Earl of Northumberland, *was six years of age!* The Lord De La Warr who died in 1450 was, moreover, at least 30 years older than his alleged father-in-law.[3] This of course cuts out the many lines traced through the Wests, several of which have been printed. Equally incorrect are the lines traced through the marriage of Thomas Frewen, M.P., in 1671, with Bridget Laton,[4] and through the alleged marriage of Thomas ap John Vaughan of Plas Thomas, co. Salop, with Joan, said to have been a daughter of Philip Jennings of Dudleston, by Diana, da. of Sir William Bowyer, Bt.[5]

---

[1] Collins ("Peerage of England," vol. ii. p. 373) quotes this will, and yet both at this reference and at vol. v. p. 382, proceeds to marry Eleanor to Lord De La Warr.

[2] *Ex inform.* Sir Henry Maxwell Lyte. The author has also to thank Sir George Armytage, Bt., and Mr. Erskine E. West for assistance in running this statement to earth.

[3] The Editor has not been able to trace the genesis of the statement of the alleged marriage, but Mr. Erskine E. West suggests that possibly Lady Eleanor Percy married Lord De La Warr's grandson, Reginald West, whose name, and nothing more, appears in several MSS. in the British Museum.

[4] See Burke's "Landed Gentry," 1906, p. 635. The statement there is that Bridget was the sister and heir of Charles and the daughter of Sir Thomas Laton by his wife, Bridget Sandford, which Sir Thomas was the son and heir of another Sir Thomas Laton of Laton and Sexhow, by his wife, the Hon. Mary Fairfax, the said Mary Fairfax being a descendant of Edward III., through Mortimer-Percy (see Table XV.). Bridget Sandford was, however, the *second wife of the first-named Sir Thomas Laton.* Sir Thomas married twice, first Mary Fairfax (who died 1636), by whom he had, with others (see Table XV.), a son, Thomas, incorrectly styled *Sir* Thomas in the above pedigree. This Thomas died *s.p.* ("Harl. MS.," p. 2118), having married Anne, daughter of Ambrose Pudsey, who survived him, and married, secondly, Walter Strickland (Whitaker's "Craven," p. 126). Admon. of Thomas Laton, Esquire, of East Laton, Yorks, was granted to Anne Laton, his widow, 20 April 1659. Sir Thomas married, 2ndly, 1637, the said Bridget, widow of Ambrose Pudsey of Bolton, and daughter of Sir Richard Sandford, by whom he had issue Charles, who *d.s.p.*, and Bridget, who married, 1671, Thomas Frewen, M.P., and had issue. The M.I. to the Rev. John Frewen at Sapcote, Leics., recites that his mother, Bridget Frewen, was the only (*sic*) daughter of Sir Thomas Laton of East Laton and Sexhow . . . by Dame Bridget, his second wife, relict of Ambrose Pudsey . . . and daughter of Sir Richard Sandford, and the minutes of the Committee for the advancing money, 1469/60, have a reference to Bridget, wife of Sir Thomas Layton, to the effect that she had a jointure, and that she applied for one-fifth and was refused. The pedigree at the Heralds' College gives Sir Thomas's marriages correctly, but seems itself to need verifying in other particulars.

[5] See Burke's "Royal Descents," ii., xcv., and "Landed Gentry" (1906, p. 1718). According to this pedigree, Philip Vaughan, the *great-grandson* of Thomas ap John Vaughan, was bapt. 10 October 1690, while Diana Bowyer was bapt. 7 October 1680, only ten years and three days before *her great-grandson!*

Preface

The author has, of course, also ignored all the descents traced from Sir William St. Leger, Lord President of Munster, it having been clearly established now for some years that it was not Sir William's father, Sir Warham St. Leger, but his great-uncle, another Sir Warham, who married the Ursula Nevil.[1] The author hopes that those who find themselves omitted in consequence of the above will not consider him personally responsible, and he will hope in some future volume to have the pleasure of restoring their names in right of some other and more correct descent.

The author must himself plead guilty to an unfortunate slip in the Clarence volume. Following Berry and others, he has in Table LXII. made Elizabeth Meux, the third wife (married at St. Dunstan's West, London, 2 May 1710) of Sir John Miller, 3rd Bt., the mother of all his children, whereas she appears to have had only one child to survive, viz. Elizabeth, wife of Sir Edward Worsley of Gatcombe. The other children appear to have all been by the first wife, Margaret, daughter of John Peachy, who died 23, and was buried in Chichester Cathedral, 25 September 1710. Sir Thomas, 4th Bt., was baptized 4 April 1689, and matriculated at Oxford 1706/7, aged 18. This cuts out sections 548 and 549 (pp. 506-515) and 556, 557, and 558 (p. 518), Nos. 21953-22365, a total of 413; but as Nos. 21987-22002 (Chichesters), 22003-22012 (Hortons), 22015-22020 (Carpenter-Garniers), 22041-22095 (Garniers), 22103-22135 (Delmes), and 22136-22365 (Keppels) reappear in right of their descents in the Essex (p. 632), Mortimer-Percy (pt. i. p. 306), Tudor (p. 171), and Exeter (pp. 243, 385, 243) vols. respectively, the actual number of names which come out is only 63. The author is indebted to Arthur E. Garnier, Esq., for calling his attention to this error.

In the next part it is hoped to complete the other descendants of Lady Elizabeth Mortimer, and as this will at the same time finish all the lines from Lionel, Duke of Clarence, a further Supplement will be added, and the Editor will be very glad to hear of any omissions which may have been noticed in order that he may include them in this Supplement.

Future volumes will deal with the descendants of John (Plantagenet, called of Gaunt), Duke of Lancaster; of Edmund (Plantagenet, called of Langley), Duke of York; of Thomas (Plantagenet, called of Woodstock), Duke of Gloucester; and of the Lady Isabel Plantagenet, wife of Ingleram (de Courcy), Earl of Bedford.

There are, of course, many who affect to laugh at any work treating of Royal descents, and a volume which is devoted to setting forth the individual descent of various more or less obscure personages is naturally of purely personal interest to those whose descent it sets forth, but the present series approaches the subject from a totally different point—from the historical, not from the personal, and aims at treating in a fairly exhaustive manner of all the descendants of, and descents from, the greatest of our Plantagenet kings. While preparing this work the author has received some hundreds of letters from persons in every quarter of the globe, descended not only from Edward III., but in many cases our early Norman and Saxon sovereigns, requesting that their descents may be included, and surprise has in some cases been expressed because the writer,

---

[1] See Table XXVII. The compiler refers to this because descents through this alleged marriage figure so often in previously printed works on Royal descents, and he is being constantly referred to them.

Preface

while casting no doubt on the genuineness of the particular descent, has been obliged to explain, either that it did not come within the scope of his work, or else that a descent from, say, John of Gaunt, could not be included in the volume dealing with those from George of Clarence.

The author is always glad to receive copies of all Royal descents. They are all carefully arranged, and those coming from Edward III. will, if found correct, be duly included in their proper order. It is, however, impossible for him to say off-hand whether such and such a descent is correct. The work is not an easy one to prepare, and it is absolutely necessary for him to confine himself to the particular line of descent upon which he may for the moment be engaged.

Others say that a Royal descent is of no interest, since so many enjoy it; but allowing that there are some 80,000 or even 100,000 descendants of Edward III. now living, what is that out of a total of, say, 100,000,000 persons of British descent; and even if Edward I. may be justly termed the father of the British people, it is quite a different thing to *be able to trace the line*. Let it be remembered that while a word from the King can put one in "the Peerage," or a successful financial speculation in the "Landed Gentry," birth alone entitles one to a place in the Plantagenet Roll; for on one side at least there must be a strain of gentle blood, through which it is possible to trace ancestry[1] to the feudal and crusading days.

As the Rev. W. G. D. Fletcher, a well-known authority on the subject, so truly remarks[2]: "The tracing and working out the descent of living persons from kings and princes of England is often of vastly greater interest than tracing their pedigrees back in the direct male line. A family pedigree is too often a string of the names of almost unknown persons, with their place of abode, the dates of baptism and marriage and death, and the date and proof of their will Useful men, no doubt, these ancestors were in their day, but they were for the most part 'unknown to history.' It is given to but few to have in the male line a Marlborough, a Nelson, a Clive, a Wellington, a Fox, a Burke, a Pitt, a Cromwell, a Lely, or a Reynolds for an ancestor. Whereas every Royal descent necessarily implies the possession of distinguished historical personages as ancestors—men and women who meet us in the pages of history, kings, warriors, statesmen, Knights of the Garter, canonised saints, and so forth. And if it be sometimes urged that, after all, the quantity of Royal blood that flows in any person's veins must be infinitesimally small, the same holds true of the blood of our paternal ancestors; we only have one-half of our fathers' blood, one-quarter of our grandfathers', one-eighth of our great-grandfathers', and so on."

Embracing, as this work does, all classes, from the sovereign to the peasant, it serves to unite all in a common interest in the traditions of the past. Who studying history, or visiting the tombs of the Edwards in Westminster Abbey, or reading Lytton's "Last of the Barons," could fail to feel a better citizen, knowing that step by step, and link by link, he is descended in a clear unbroken line from those who built up the foundations of our mighty Empire, and is united by blood to our common sovereign.

But putting on one side the question of the interest or value of a

---

[1] It should be remembered that any one whose name occurs in this Roll can trace an ancestry back in an unbroken line to William the Conqueror and Alfred the Great, to St. Louis and to the Emperor Charlemagne.

[2] See "Notes on some Shropshire Royal Descents," by the Rev. W. G. D. Fletcher, M.A., F.S.A.

Preface

Royal descent, this series forms a valuable means of recording the genealogies of many important families which do not come within the scope of any of the other genealogical works, and of the cadet and colonial branches of those that do. The Peerages, &c. are naturally more concerned with the fortunes of the titled or landed lines, but the Plantagenet Roll aims at making the pedigrees of such families as come within its scope exhaustive; and the Editor ventures to think that the pedigree here given will be found of use to future generations quite apart from Royal descent, and that the recording those branches settled beyond the seas equally with those at home will help to cement the feeling of kinship between the different parts of the Empire, and so help towards that closer union of the British-speaking States which it is the duty of all to promote.

Every effort has been made to make the Roll as complete as possible, and to thoroughly revise and bring the particulars up to date, and for this purpose proofs have been submitted to all those named therein whose addresses the writer was able to ascertain, and he desires to return his most grateful thanks for the courtesy and assistance which have been extended to him on all hands. It is sometimes invidious to particularise, but he must especially acknowledge his indebtedness to the Rev. E. H. Fellowes, the Rev. W. G. D. Fletcher, F.S.A., Sir George Armytage, Bt., Sir Henry Maxwell Lyte, M. Bijlweld, Editor of the *Nederlands Adelsboek*, the Rev. C. Moor, D.D., Sir Robert A. Morris, Bt., Major Raymond Smythies, Erskine E. West, Esq., Charles E. Lamb, Esq., Mrs. Seton, the Baroness Deichmann, Mrs. Lomas, Col. R. V. Riddell, Arthur G. Garnier, Esq., R. E. Elliott-Chambers, Esq., Miss Oswald (formerly Williamson), Miss Marcon, and some scores of others, far too numerous to enumerate, who have not only assisted with particulars concerning their own families, but have gone to considerable trouble in assisting him to trace out other lines of descent, in searching parish registers, and in obtaining dates. Nor must he omit to accord his grateful thanks to Sir James Balfour Paul, the Lord Lyon King of Arms, for his always prompt and ready replies to inquiries addressed to him; to the Editor of *Notes and Queries* for inserting numerous questions; or his indebtedness to works like Burke's "Peerage" and "Landed Gentry," Debrett's "Peerage," &c.

In compiling this work, the author can truthfully say that he has made every effort to make it as complete as possible; each descent is treated on its own merits, and no distinction is made, whether it be that of the peer or the yeoman; *and absolutely no charge or condition has been made for the insertion of any name or descent in this book.*

There are, of course, many lines which the writer has been unable to trace, the very magnitude of the task making all the conclusions arrived at of a more or less tentative nature, and he is only too fully aware of the number of other errors and imperfections which must, almost of necessity, occur in a first attempt of this kind; but he asks for the kind indulgence of his readers, and he will be most grateful to all those who will point out to him omissions or other errors which may come under their notice. They will all be included in a supplementary volume with which the series will close.

31 *January* 1911.

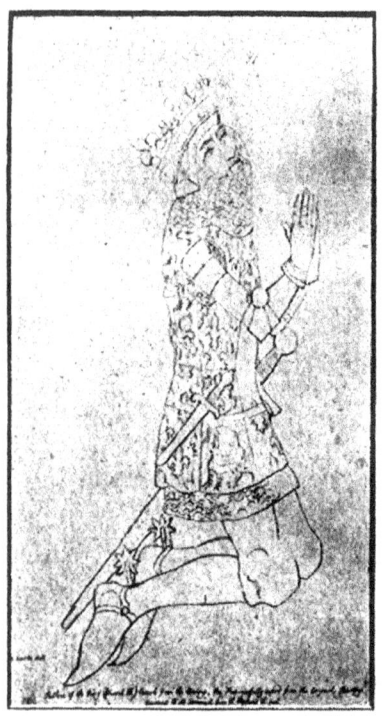 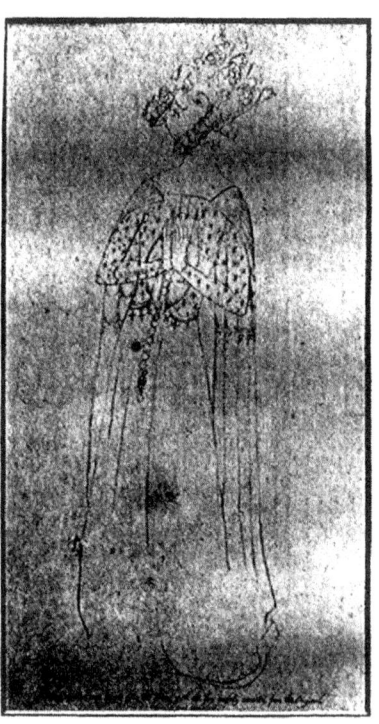

KING EDWARD THE THIRD, 1312-1377, AT THE AGE OF 44.   QUEEN PHILIPPA OF HAINAULT. DIED 1369.

From tracings of the original figures painted about 1356 on the East Wall of St. Stephen's Chapel, Westminster (the old House of Commons).

TABLE I

Genealogical table: Edward III, King of England (1312–1377) = Phillippa of Hainault, d. 1368, and their descendants.

TABLE II

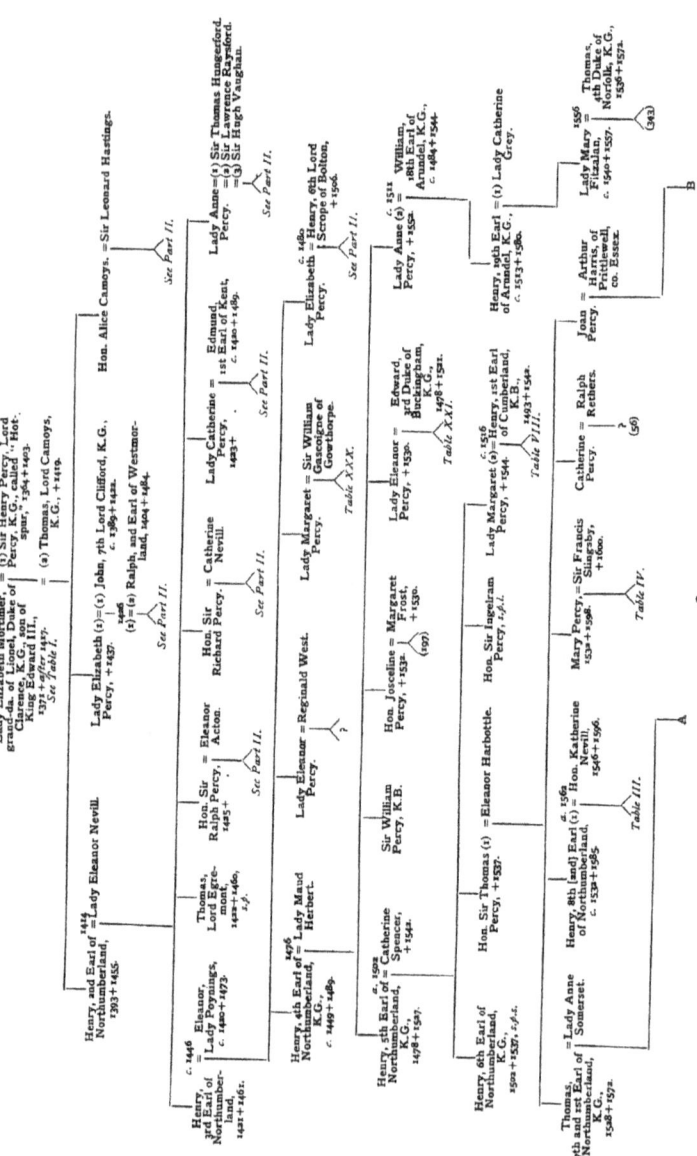

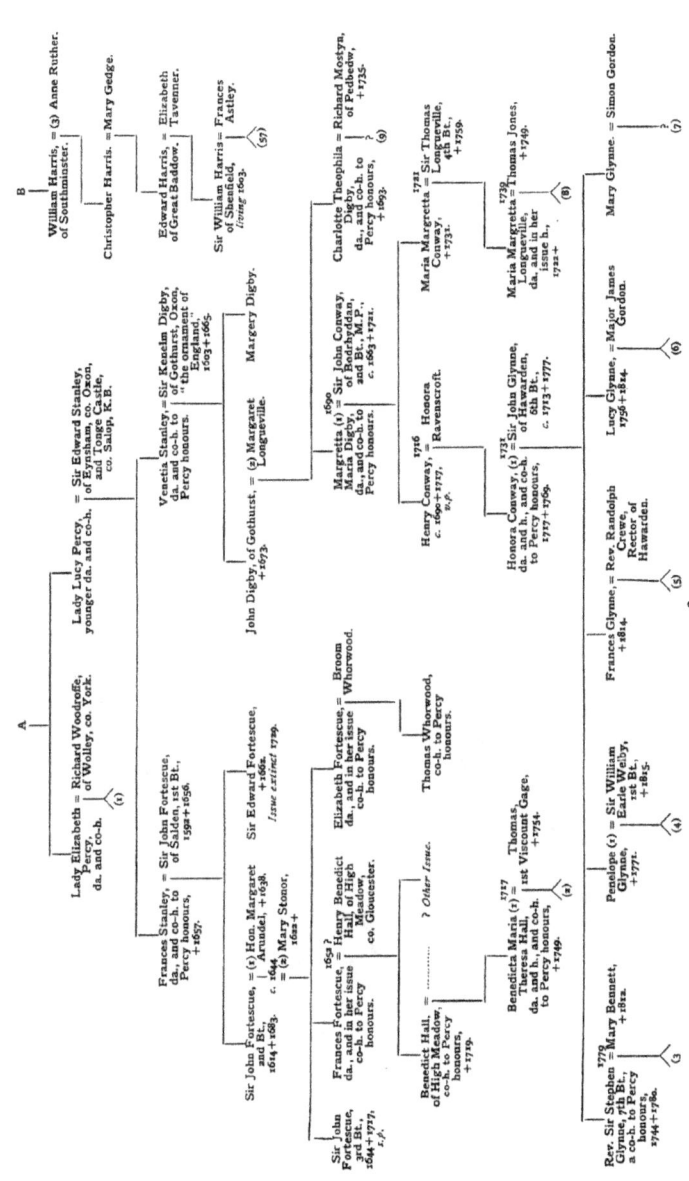

TABLE III

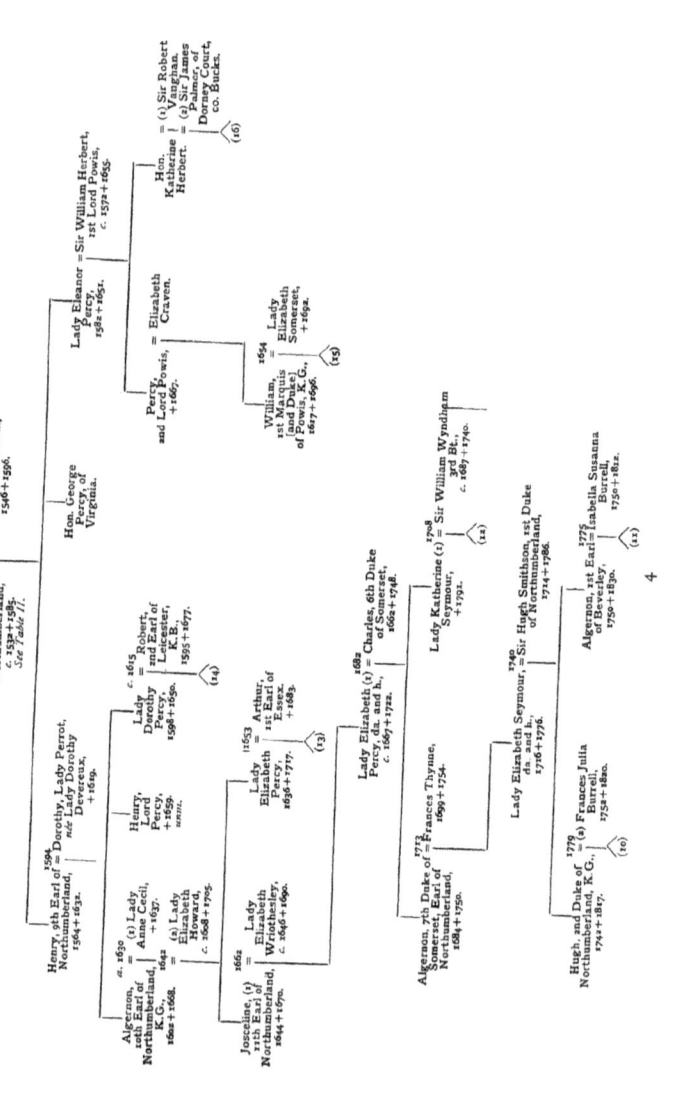

TABLE IV

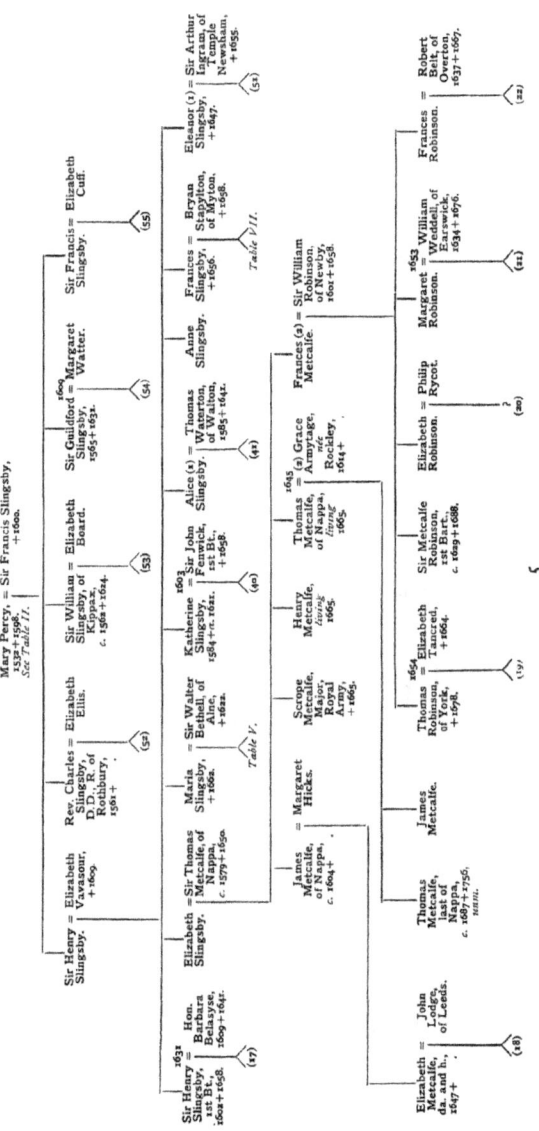

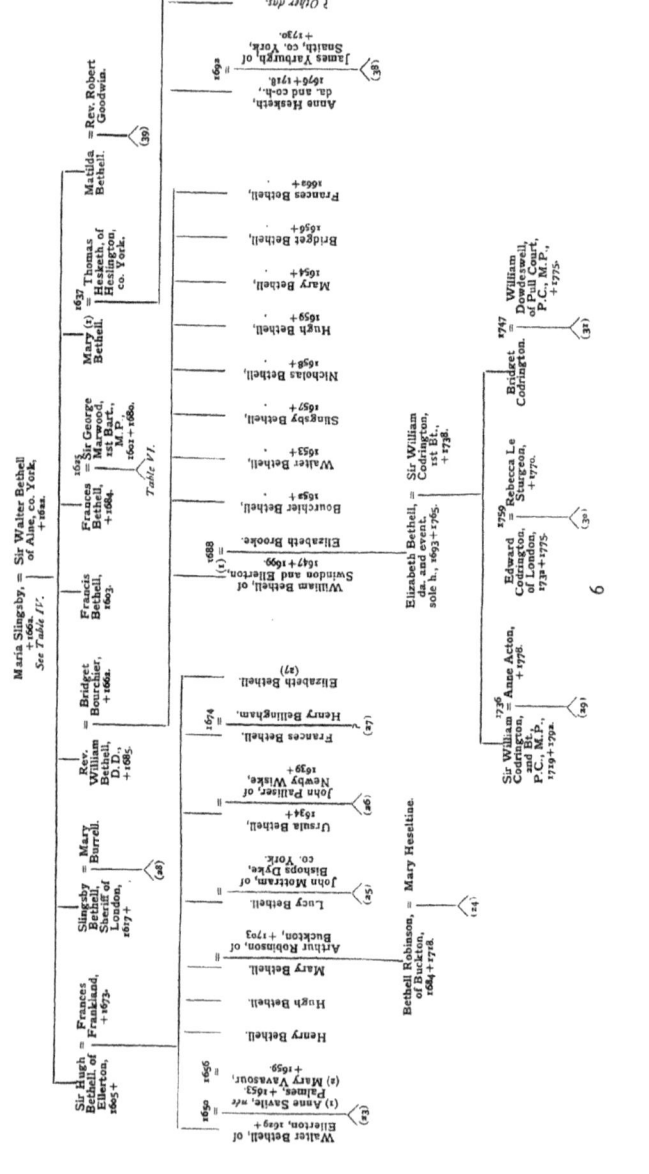

TABLE V

TABLE VI

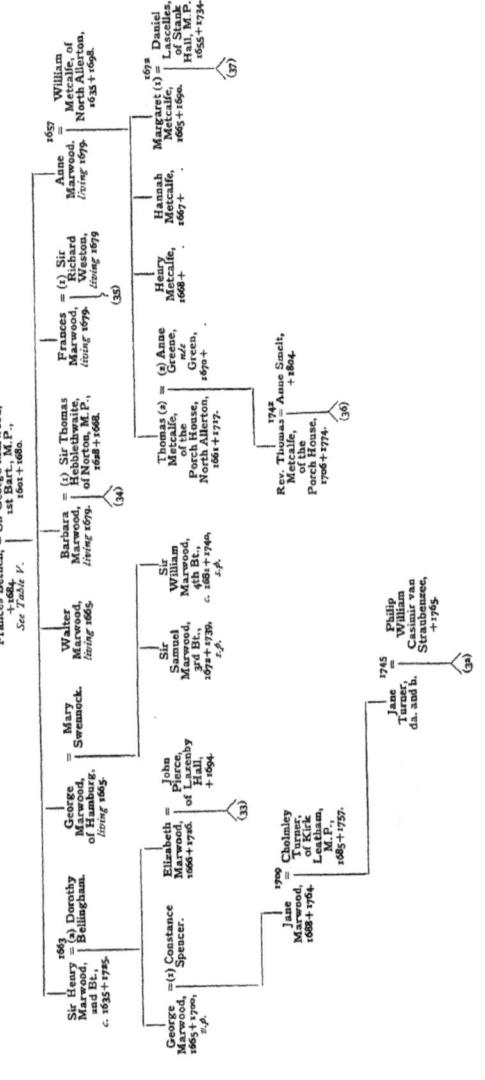

TABLE VII

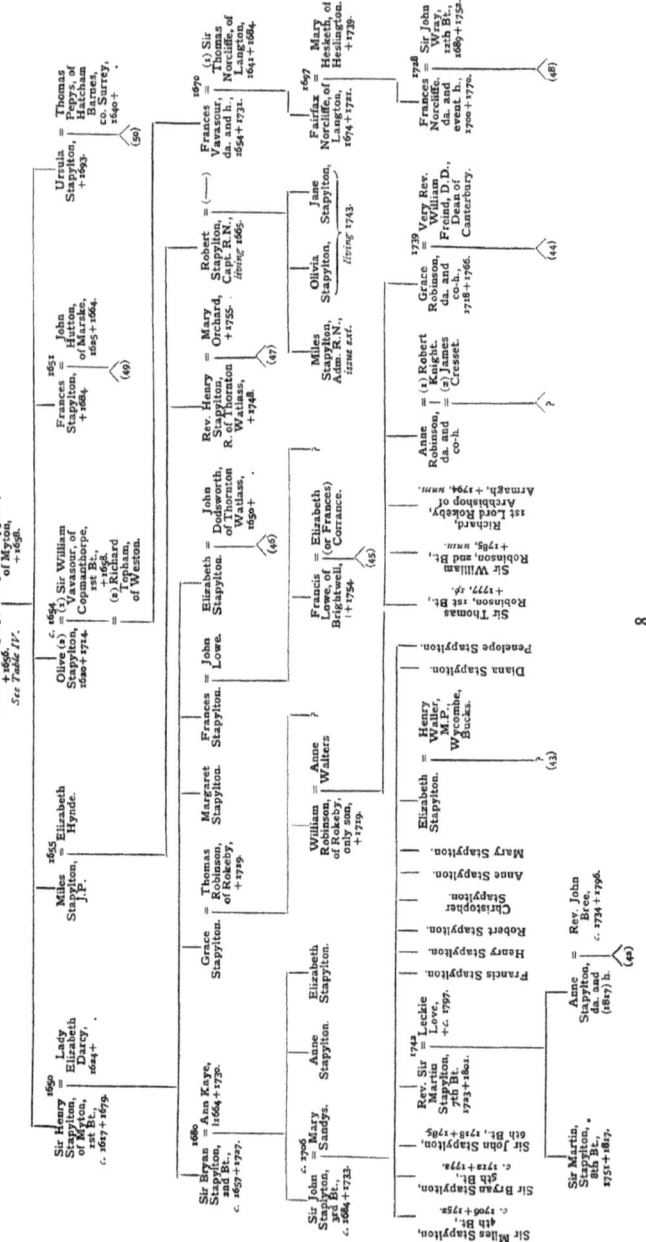

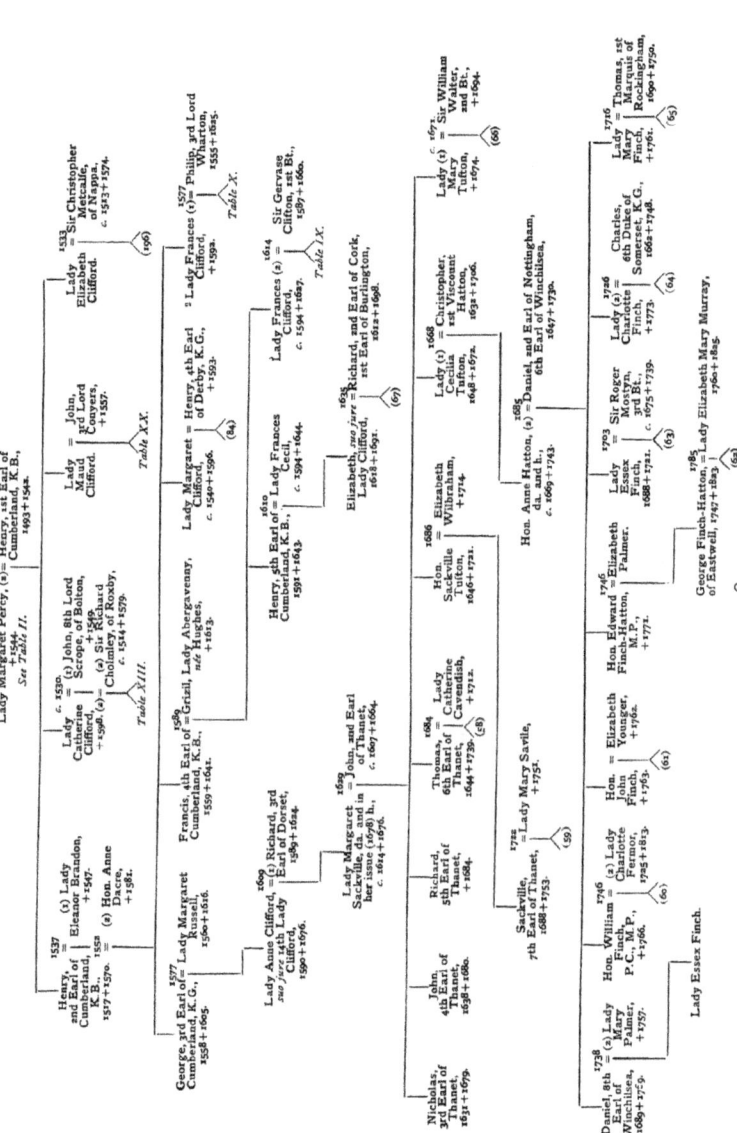

TABLE IX

A genealogical table beginning with Lady Frances Clifford (c. 1504 †1597) = Sir Gervase Clifton of Clifton, 1st Bt., K.B., M.P., 1587 †1666. See Table VIII.

Their descendants include:

- **Margaret Clifton** †1698 = (1) Sir John South, of Kelstern; (2) William Whichcot, of Fotenerby, co. Linc., 1618†; (3) Robert, 6th Lord Hunsden, 1692†, s.p.
- **Frances Clifton** = (1) Robert Tempest, of Bracewell; (2) Anthony Eyre, s.p.
- **Anne Clifton** = Sir Francis Rodes, 2nd Bt., †1651.

Sir Clifford Clifton = Frances Finch, †1670.

Sir John Parsons, and Bt., c. 1656 †1704 = Arabella Clifton, da. and co-h. (1686).

Catharine Clifton, da. and co-h. (1686) = Sir William Clifton, 3rd Bt., 1663 †1686, s.c.m.

Francis South, 1690† — John South, of Kelstern, co. Linc., Kt. of the Royal Oak, 1660 — Elizabeth Tempest — Adm. Sir Francis Wheler.

Sir William Parsons, 3rd Bt., 1686 †1760 = (1) Frances Dutton †1735; 1716 ?

Tempest South, 1669 †1697 — Elizabeth South, 1664† = Leonard Pinkney — Margery Maria South, 1665† — Jane South, 1671† — Sir Christopher Whichcot, 4th Bt., 1728 †1766, c. 1760.

Francis Whichcot, 1651† = Katharine Meres, 1669 †1731; — George Whichcot, of Harpswell, co. Linc., M.P., 1653† = (2) Frances Nelthorpe †1734 — Alice Whichcot, 1659† = Ven. William Bassett, Archdeacon of Stow, 1703 †1765 — Elizabeth Whichcot, 1674 †1774 : 1730 — Elizabeth = John South, of Kelstern, inn. 1660. (83)

Grace Parsons, da. and inber issue (1812), b. — Thomas Lambarde, of Sevenoaks, 1747 — Rev. William Wheler = Jane Smith — Francis Wheler — Sarah Wheler, †1697 = Rev. John Mills, 1712 †1791; 1749 — Jane Whichcot, da. and in issue (1811) = Rev. John Whichcot, 4th Bt., 1738 †1786; c. 1760 — Frances Whichcot, da. and h., 1733 †1813; 1764 — William Hydyard, of Grimsby, †1781; 1764 — George Maddison, of Staunton Vale, 1749 †1807; 1781 — Mary Baugh, †1791; 1757 — James Nelthorpe, of Little Grimsby, 1670 †1735 = Frances Whichcot, †1720 — John Maddison, of Staunton Vale, 1691 †1746; 1723 = Katherine Whichcot, 1701 †1767 — Katherine Maddison, †1744 = John Lawrence, of Putney — Theodosia Maddison, 1735 †1821; 1758 = John, and Lord Monson, 1727 †1774 — Anne Maddison, c. 1728 †1763; 1747 = Rev. Sir William Anderson, 6th Bt., †1785. (80)

Mary Frampton, c. 1741 = Sir Mark Parsons, 4th Bt., c. 1741 †1811, s.p. — William Parsons, 1718 †1751 — Multon Lambarde, of Sevenoaks, 1757 †1826 = Aurea Otway, 1780 †1848 — Mary Lambarde, 1754† = Rev. John Lambarde, of Hallward, †1846; 1784 — Jane Lambarde, 1764 †1856 = John Randolph, Bishop of London, †1813 — Jane Wheler, da. and h., †1847 = Henry, and Viscount Hood, 1753 †1836. (71)

(82), (83), (81), (80a), (79), (78), (77), (76), (75a), (75), (74a), (74), (73), (72), (71), (70), (69), (68)

TABLE X

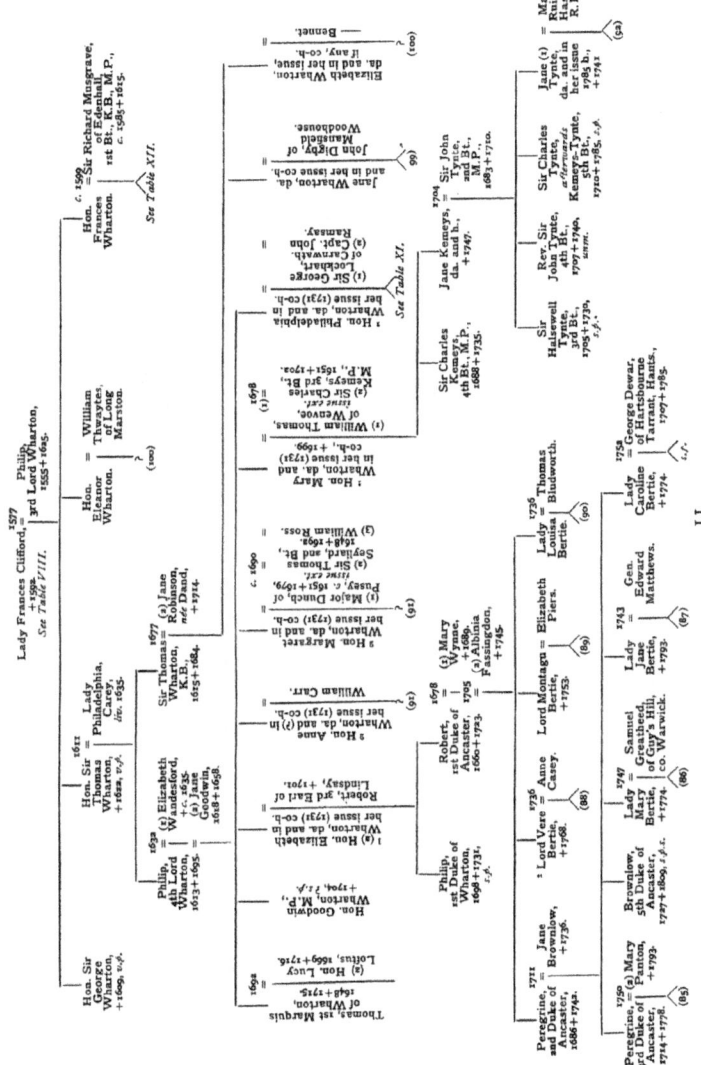

TABLE XI

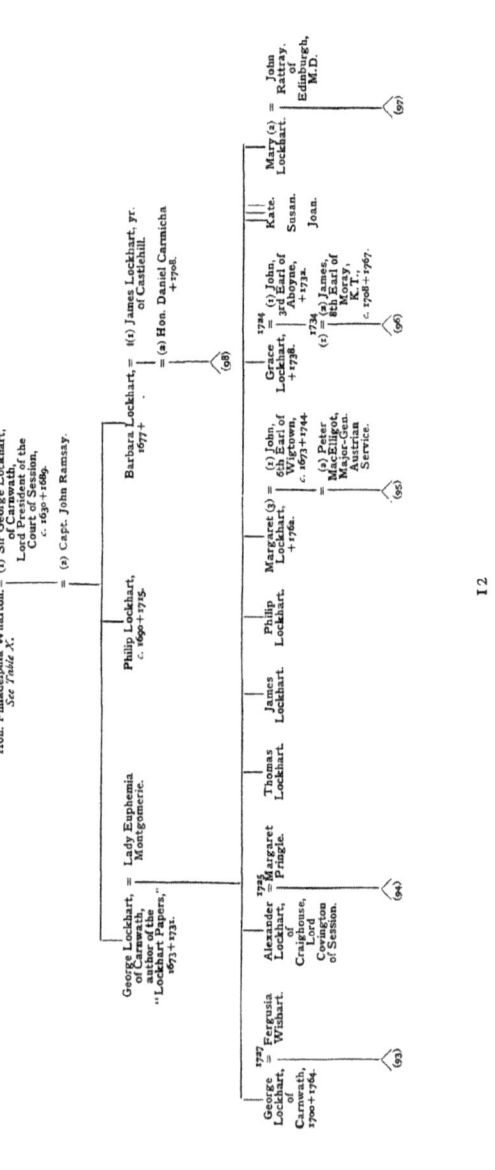

TABLE XII

Hon. Frances = Sir Richard Musgrave, of Edenhall, 1st Bt., K.B. c. 1599 | Juliana Hutton, + 1650.
Wharton. See Table X. | c. 1585 + 1615.

Sir Philip Musgrave, 2nd Bt., 1608 + 1678.

- William Musgrave.
- Rev. Thomas Musgrave, D.D., Dean of Carlisle, c. 1639 + 1686. = (1) Mary Harrison.
- Frances Musgrave = Edward Hutchinson, of Wickham Abbey, co. Yorks.

Sir Christopher Musgrave, 4th Bt., c. 1631 + 1704. = (1) Mary Cogan, c. 1636 + 1664. = (2) Elizabeth Franklin.

George Musgrave, Younger, Keeper of the Ordnance. = Sarah Rosell, née Rosell. (112)

¹Elizabeth Musgrave = John Wyneve, of Brettenham, co. Suffolk. (113)

?Dorothy Musgrave. = James Hawley, of Brentford, co. Middlesex. (113)

Margaret Musgrave, da. and h. = Ralph Shipperdson, of Murton and Pidding Hall, + 1759. (115)

Sir Richard Musgrave, 3rd Bt., +c. 1687. = Margaret Harrison.

¹Philip Musgrave, + 1689, s.p. = Hon. Mary Legge. 1685

Barbara (2) = Thomas Howard, of Corby Castle, + 1740. Musgrave. 1720 (111)

Mary Musgrave, da. and h. = Thomas Davison, of Blackiston, co. Durham.

Sir Christopher Musgrave, 5th Bt., M.P., 1688 + 1735. = Julia Chardin, +c. 1763. 1711

Sir Philip Musgrave, 6th Bt., M.P., 1711 + 1795. = Jane Turton, + 1802. 1742 (101)

Rev. Christopher Musgrave, + 1757. = Perfect, née — ? (102)

Hans Musgrave, Lt.-Col. (103)

Rev. Chardin Musgrave, D.D., Provost of Oriel Coll., Oxon. 1724 + 1768. = Catherine Tipping, c. 1730 + 1793. (104)

Mary Musgrave. = (1) Hugh Lumley. = (2) John Pigott. (105)

Julia Musgrave, + 1778. = Edward Hasell, of Dalemain, Cumberland, 1718 + 1778. (106)

Barbara Musgrave. = (1) John Hogg. = (2) Chief Baron Idle, of Scotland. (107)

Anne Musgrave, + 1780. = Henry Aglionby, of Nunnery, 1715 + 1770. (108)

Elizabeth Musgrave. = (1) Edward Spragge, of Greenwich. = (2) John Johnstone, of London. (109)

Dorothy Musgrave, 1727 + 1799. = Rev. William Wroughton, 1716 + 1776. (110)

13

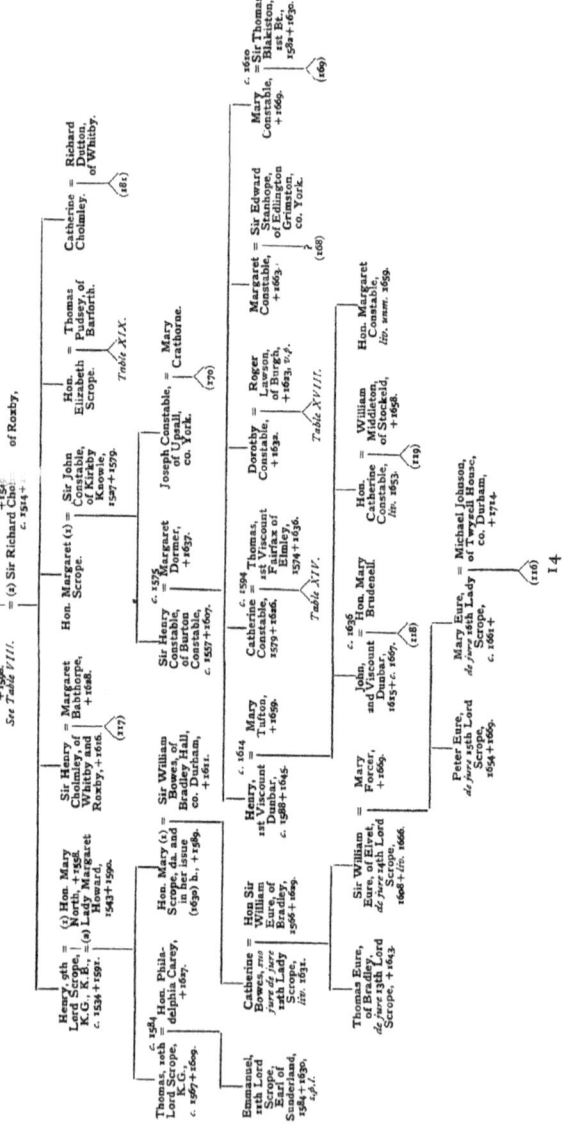

TABLE XIV

Genealogical table of the Fairfax family, descending from Thomas, 1st Viscount Fairfax of Emley (1524†1636) and Catherine Constable. The table traces multiple generations including the Viscounts Fairfax and connections to the Erskine Earls of Buchan.

Key figures include:
- Thomas, 1st Viscount Fairfax, of Emley, 1524†1636 = Catherine Constable (1)
- Thomas, 2nd Viscount Fairfax, c. 1604†1641 = Elizabeth Smith, †1692
- William, 3rd Viscount Fairfax, 1630†1648
- Thomas, 4th Viscount Fairfax, †1651, unm.
- Hon. Alathea Fairfax, da. and h. = Charles, 5th Viscount Fairfax, †1711 (c. 1677)
- Alathea Howard, †1677
- Hon. Henry Fairfax, †1650 = Frances Barker
- Charles, 6th Viscount Fairfax, †1715
- William, Lord Widdington = (1) William, Lord Widdington, †1695
- Hon. William Fairfax, of Lythe, co. York = Mary Cholmley
- Hon. Nicholas Fairfax = Isabel Bickwith, †1657
- Hon. Jordan Fairfax, †1668
- Hon. John Fairfax, liv. 1634
- Hon. Mary Fairfax, †1636 = Sir Thomas Laton, of Saxehowe, 1597†1652 (c. 1615)
- Hon. Catherine Fairfax, †1666 = (1) Robert Stapylton, of Wighill, †1634; (2) Sir Matthew Boynton, 1st Bt., †1647; (3) Sir Arthur Ingram, of Temple Newsham, †1655; (4) William Wickham, 1657
- Hon. Jane Fairfax = Cuthbert Morley
- Hon. Dorothy Fairfax = (1) John Ingram; (2) Sir Thomas Norcliffe (Table XVII)
- Hon. Philip Fairfax = Elizabeth Chaytor, née Davison
- Charles, 7th Viscount Fairfax, †1719, unm.
- Nicholas Fairfax, †1702 = Mary Weld
- William, 8th Viscount Fairfax, †1738 = Elizabeth Gerard
- Alathea Fairfax, da. and h., in her issue (1793) (127)
- Ralph Pigott, of Whitton
- John Fairfax
- Frances Fairfax
- Charles Gregory, 9th Viscount Fairfax, †1772
- Henry Fairfax, of Hurst, co. Berks = (1) — Browne
- David, 9th Earl of Buchan, 1672†1745 = Frances (1) Fairfax, da. and h., †1729
- Lady Frances Erskine, 1700†1774 = Col. James Gardiner, †1745 (1726) (126)
- George Metham, of Metham = Hon. Catherine Fairfax, †1775
- Hon. Alathea Fairfax = John Forcer
- Hon. William Fraser, of Fraserfield, M.P., 1691†1727 = Lady Katherine Erskine, 1697†1733 (1724)
- Henry David, 10th Earl of Buchan, 1710†1767 = Agnes Stewart, †1778 (1739)
- Hon. Henry Erskine, M.P., 1746†1817 = (1) Christian Fullerton, c. 1754†1804 (1772); (2) Sarah Buck, †1805 (123)
- Thomas, 1st Lord Erskine, 1750†1823 = Frances Moore, †1805; (2) Sarah Buck, †1845 (1770) (124)
- William Fraser, of Fraserfield, 1705†1788 = Rachel Kennedy, †1800 (1752) (125)
- David Stewart, 11th Earl of Buchan, 1742†1829, s.p.

15

TABLE XV

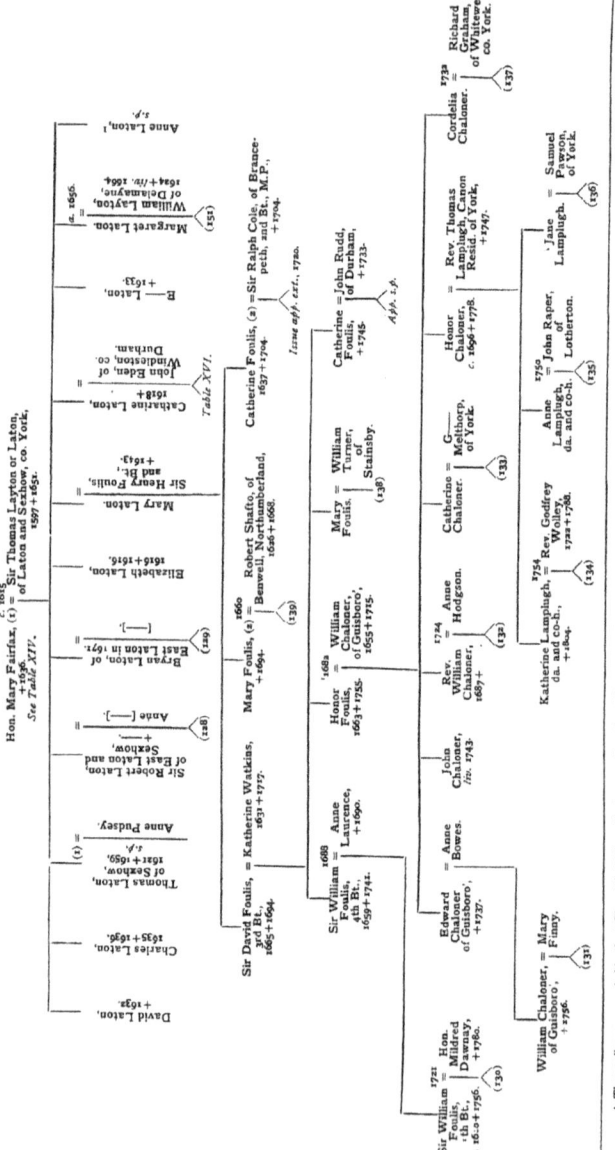

[1] The pedigree recorded in the "Herald's College" gives another da., Alice, m. 1st, Leonard Conyers, of Rudley; 2ndly, J. Ingleby of Lawkland; but the "Visitation" of 1575 makes this Alice the da. of an earlier Thomas Laton.

TABLE XVI

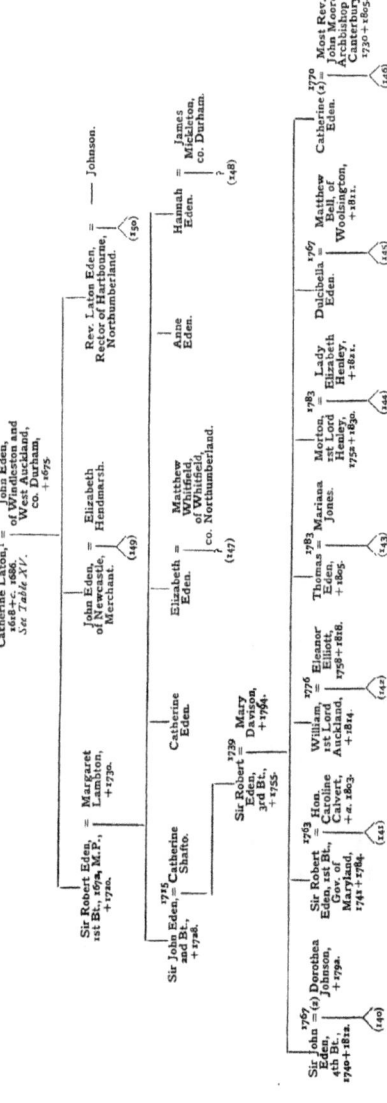

[1] Pedigree in "Herald's College." The Harl. MS. 2118, however, makes Catherine *m.* Thomas ——, *ar.*, and gives her sister Margaret as wife of John Eden

TABLE XVII

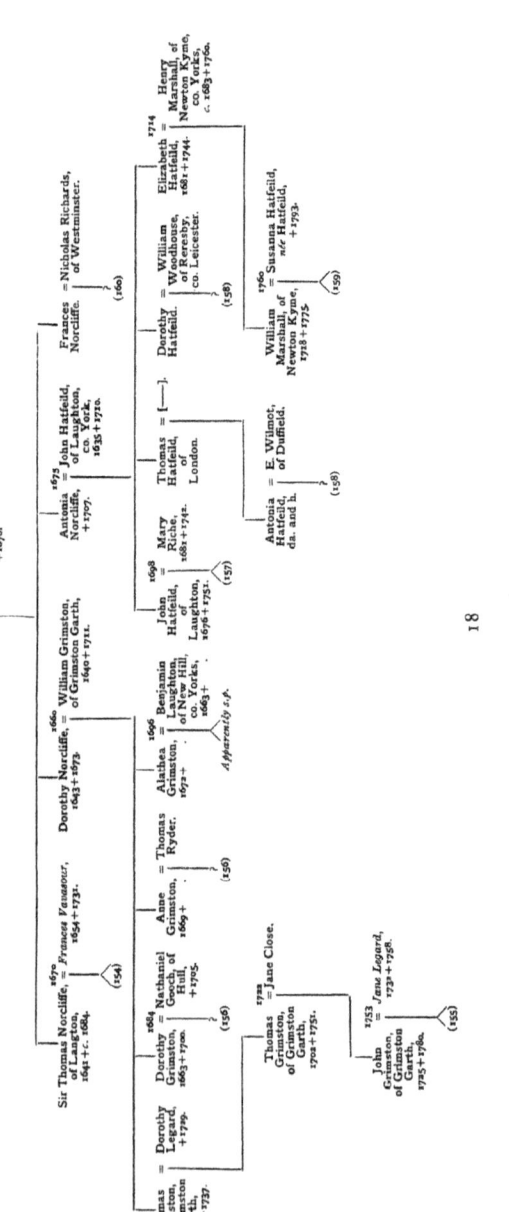

TABLE XVIII

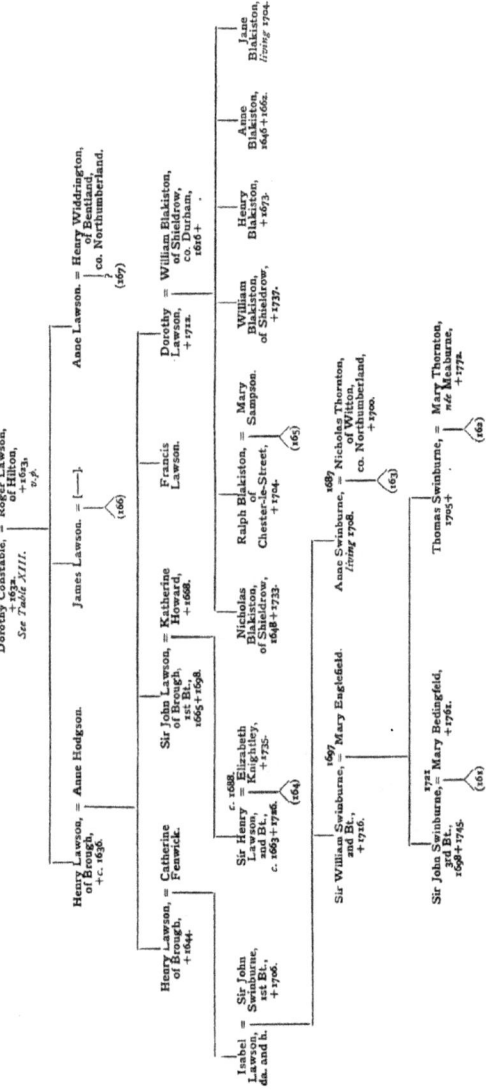

TABLE XIX

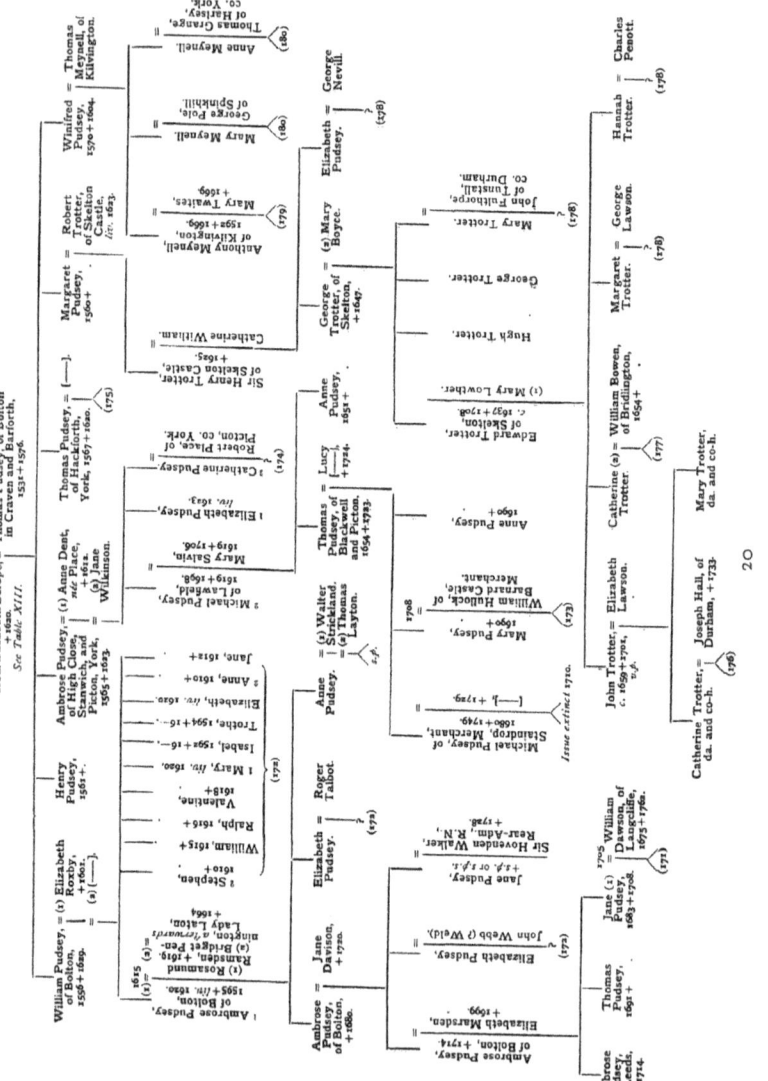

TABLE XX

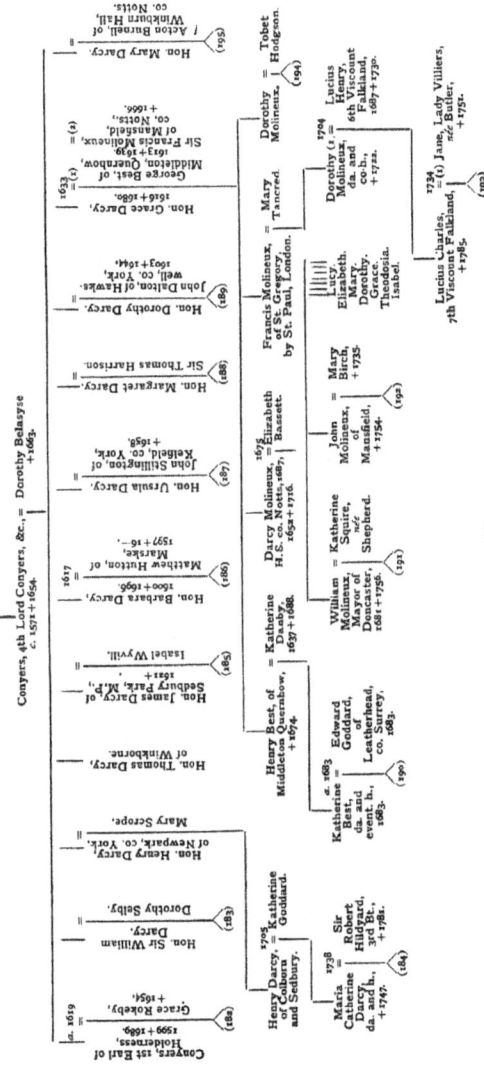

21

TABLE XXI

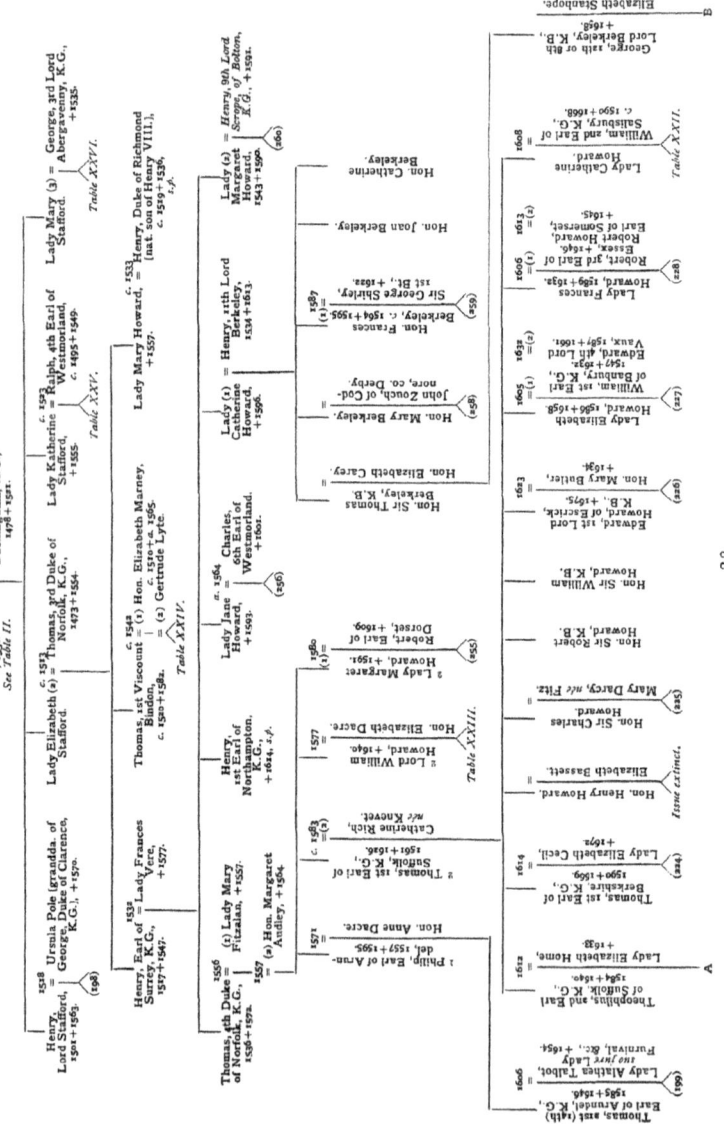

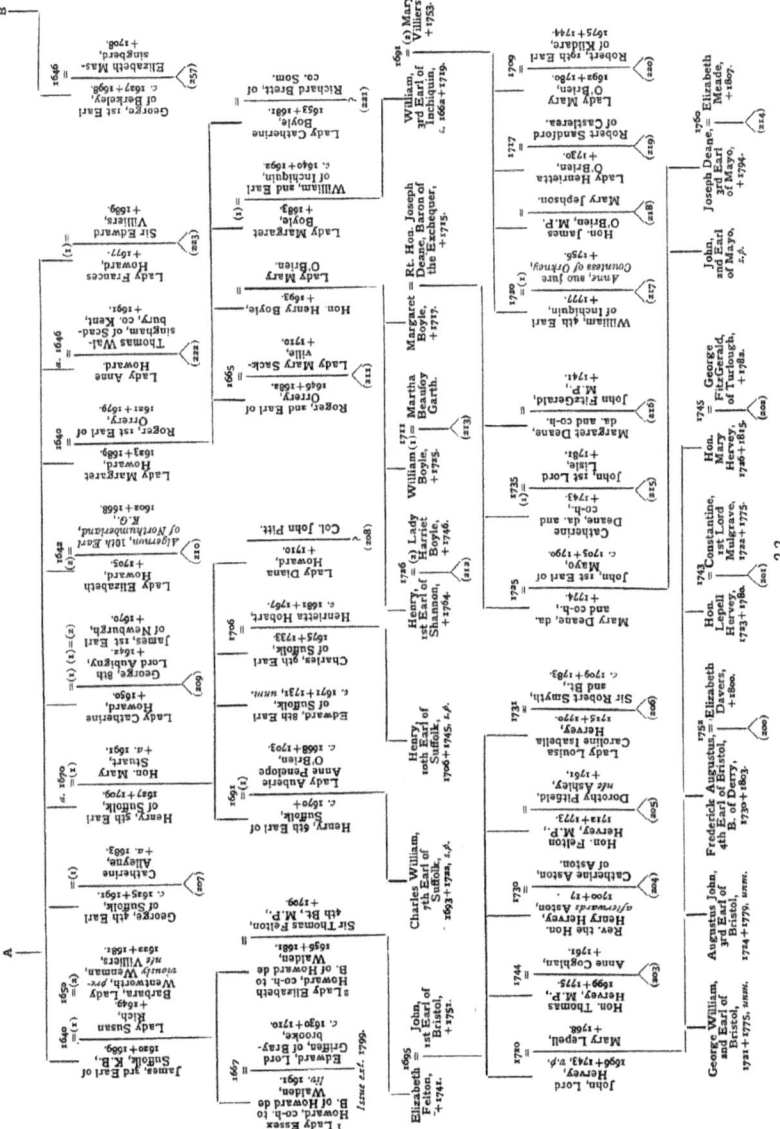

TABLE XXII

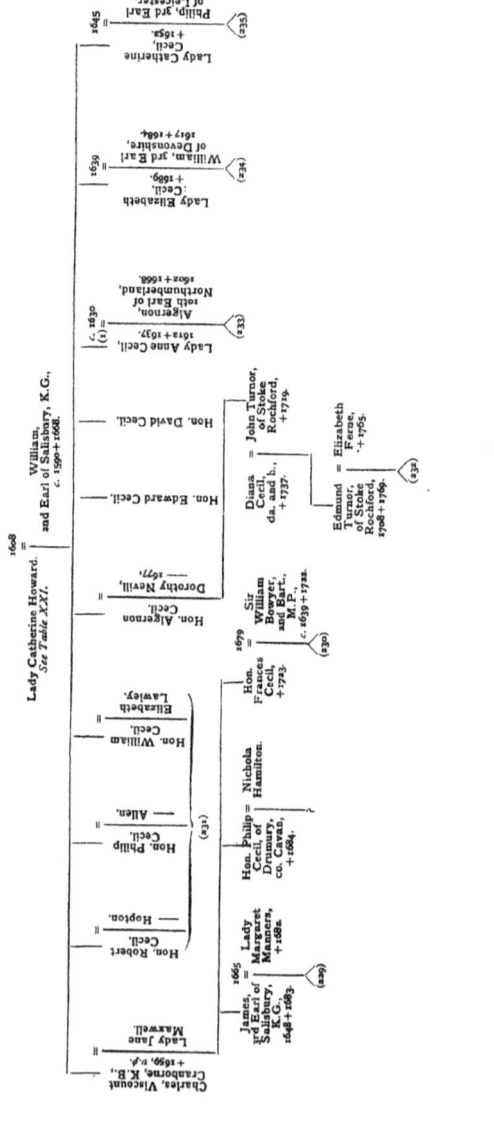

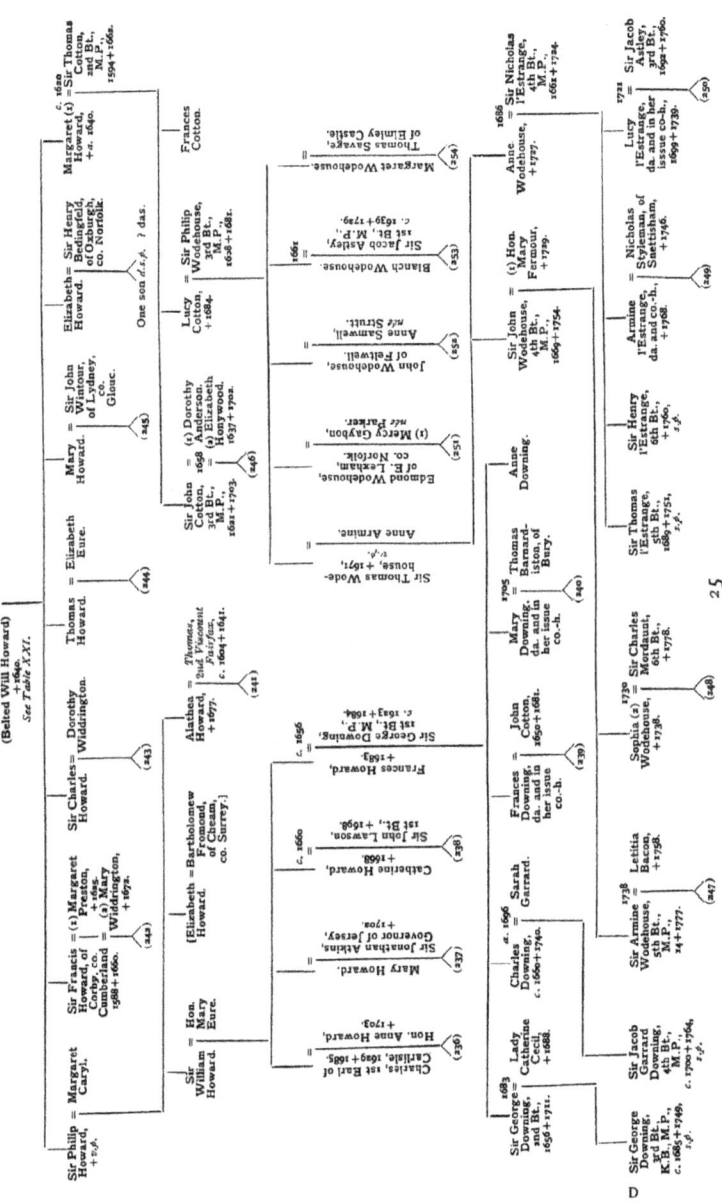

TABLE XXIV

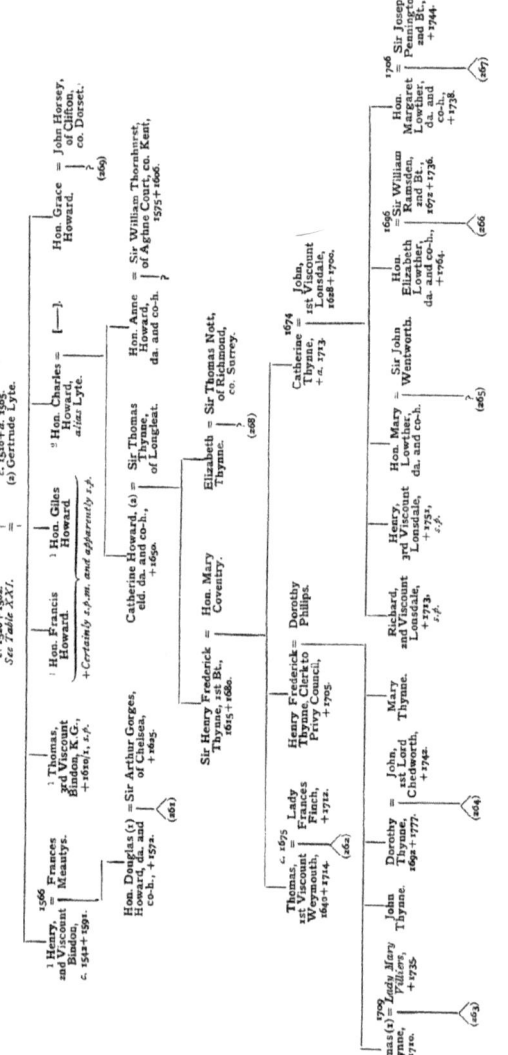

TABLE XXV

c. 1523
Lady Katherine Stafford, + 1555. See Table XXI.
Ralph, 4th Earl of Westmorland, c. 1495 + 1549.
1538
Henry, 5th Earl of Westmorland, K.G., 1525 + 1563.
(1) Lady Anne Manners.
(2) Jane Cholmondeley.
(270)
Hon. Sir Thomas Nevill.
Hon. Edward Nevill.
Hon. Christopher Nevill.
Hon. George Nevill.
Hon. Ralph Nevill.
Hon. Cuthbert Nevill.
Lady Eleanor Nevill.
1536
(1) Lady Dorothy Nevill, + a. 1547.
John, 16th Earl of Oxford, K.B., c. 1512 + 1562.
Lady Mary Nevill, + 1596.
Sir Thomas Danby, + 1590.
(272)
Lady Joan Nevill.
1536
(1)
Lady Margaret Nevill, + 1559.
Henry, 2nd Earl of Rutland, K.G., + 1563.
(273)
(1)
Lady Elisabeth Nevill, + s.p.
Thomas, 4th Lord Dacre, + 1566.
(1)
Lady Eleanor Nevill, + s.p.s.
Sir Bryan Stapylton, of Carlton, + 1606.
Lady Anne Nevill.
Sir Fulke Greville, of Beauchamp Court, co. Warwick.
Lady Ursula Nevill.
Lady Katherine de Vere, + 1599.
Edward, 3rd Lord Windsor, + 1575.
(271)
Sir Fulke, 1st Lord Brooke, + 1628, unm.
Margaret Greville, co-h. to Barony of Willoughby de Broke, + 1631.
Sir Richard Verney, of Compton, M.P., 1563 + 1630.
1618
Sir Greville Verney, de jure 7th Lord Willoughby de Broke, c. 1590 + 1642.
Catherine Southwell.
George Verney.
Lady Tryphena Sheffield.
(278)
Mary (1) Verney.
Sir Richard Samwell, of Upton, co. Northants, 1590 + 1668.
Anne Verney.
John Breton, of Norton, co. Northants.
Margaret Verney.
(——) Shirley.
Greville Verney, de jure 8th Lord, c. 1620 + 1648.
Hon. Elizabeth Wenman, + 1648.
Issue extinct 1683.
a. 1658
Richard Verney, 11th Lord Willoughby de Broke, 1621 + 1711.
(1) Mary Pretyman, + c. 1676.
c. 1677
(2) Francis Dove.
Elizabeth Verney.
William Peyto, of Chesterton, co. Warwick.
(277)
1637
Richard Samwell, of Upton, 1613 + 1662.
Hon. Frances Wenman, + 1677.
Francis Samwell, of Upton, 1616 + 1657.
Rebecca Selsby, + 1708.
(286)
Jane Samwell, 1615 +
Sir Edward Rossiter, of Somerby, co. Linc.
Issue extinct 1706.
1688
¹ George, 12th Lord Willoughby de Broke, 1659 + 1728.
Margaret Heath, + 1729.
¹ Hon. Mary Verney.
Samuel Davenport, of Calverley, co. Chester.
(275)
1684
(2)
² Hon Diana Verney, + 1725.
Sir Charles Shuckburgh, 2nd Bart., M.P., 1659 + 1705.
(276)
1673
(1)
1685
(2)
Sir Thomas Samwell, of Upton, 1st Bart., M.P., + 1694.
Elizabeth Gooday, 1651 + liv. 1678.
Anne Godschalk.
(279)
1665
Margaret Samwell, 1640 + 1727.
Thomas Catesby, of Ecton, + 1700.
(280)
1678
Penelope Samwell, 1641 +
Sir William Yorke, of Lessington, co. Linc.
(281)
Agnes Samwell, + 1717.
Robert Codrington, of Codrington, + 1717.
(282)
1676
Frances Samwell, c. 1658 + 1706.
Sir Thomas Wagstaffe, + 1709.
1682
(1)
(2)
Mary Samwell, 1662 +
Adolphus Oughton, of Fillongby, co. Warwick.
Roger Pope, of Oswestry, co. Salop.
Richard, 13th Lord Willoughby de Broke, + 1752, s.p.s.
Hon. John Verney, Master of the Rolls, c. 1699 + 1741.
Abigail Harley.
1761
John Peyto, 14th Lord Willoughby de Broke, 1738 + 1816.
Lady Louisa North, 1737 + 1798.
(274)
1697
Frances Wagstaffe, da. and h., 1677 + 1714.
(1) Sir Edward Bagot, 4th Bt., + 1712.
(2) Sir Adolphus Oughton, 1st Bt., Brig.-Gen., K.B., M.P., + 1737, s.p.
? other issue.
Frances Pope.
John Neale, M.P., Coventry.
1724
Sir Walter Wagstaffe Bagot, 5th Bt., M.P., 1702 + 1768.
Lady Barbara Legge, + 1765.
(283)
c. 1744
Anne (1) Neale, da. and co-h., 1721 + 1747.
Rev. Sir James Stonehouse, 10th and 7th Bt., 1716 + 1765.
(284)
Catherine Neale, da. and co-h., + (?) s.p.
1742
Frances (2) Neale, da. and co-h., + 1748.
Sir John Turner, 3rd Bt., M.P., 1712 + 1780.
(285)

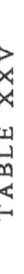

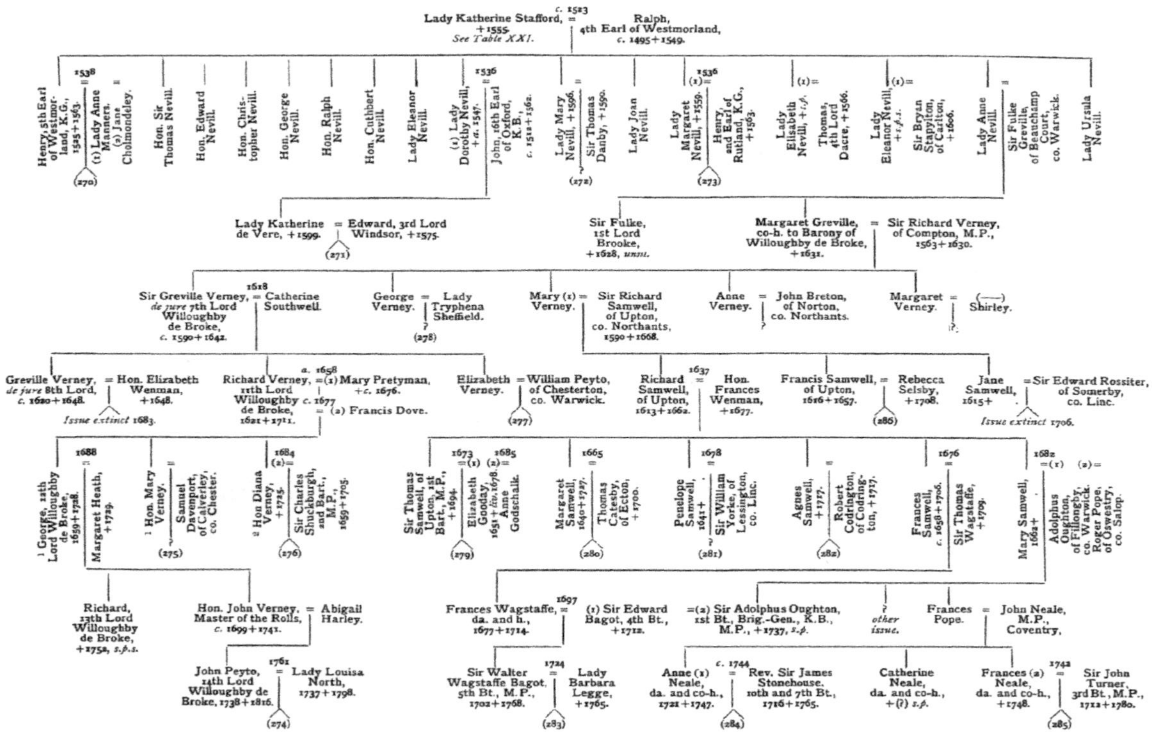

TABLE XXVI

Lady Mary (2) = George, 3rd Lord Abergavenny, K.G., K.B., Stafford. +1535.
See Table XXV.

Children:

- **Henry, 4th Lord Abergavenny**, +1587. = (1) Lady Frances Manners, +1576. (487)
- **Hon. Catherine Nevill.** = **Sir John St. Leger, of Annery, co. Devon.**
- **Hon. (1) Dorothy Nevill**, +1559. = **Hon. William Brooke, 7th Lord Cobham, K.G.**, 1527?–1597.
- **Hon. Jane Nevill.** = **Henry, 1st Lord Montagu, K.G.**, c. 1492 +1539. (312)
- **Hon. (1) Ursula Nevill.** = **Sir Warham St. Leger, of Ulcomb, co. Kent**, +1599. *Table XXVIII.*
- **Hon. Mary Nevill.** = **Thomas, 9th Lord Dacre**, +1541. *Table XXVIII.*

Descendants of Sir John St. Leger = Hon. Catherine Nevill:

- **Mary St. Leger, da. and co-h.**, +1623. = **Sir Richard Granville, of Stow**, +1588.
- **Frances (1) St. Leger, da. and co-h.** = **John Stukeley, of Affeton, co. Devon**, c. 1551 +1611.
- **Eulalia St. Leger, da. and co-h.** = (1) **Edmund Tremayne, of Collacombe**, s.p., +1582. #576 = (2) **Tristram Arscott, of Annery**, +1621. 1583

Children of Sir Richard Granville & Mary St. Leger:

- **Sir Bernard Granville, of Stow**, 1559 +1596. = **Elizabeth Bevill.** A
- **Bridget Granville**, +1597. = (1) **Sir Christopher Harris, of Radford, co. Devon, M.P.**, +1625. = (2) **Rev. John Weekes, Preb. of Bristol.** (393)
- **Mary Granville**, +1608. (399)

Children of John Stukeley & Frances St. Leger:

- **Arthur Tremayne, of Collacombe**, 1553 +1635. #586
- **Sir Lewis Stukeley, or Stucley, of Affeton, Vice-Admiral of Devon and Cornwall**, c. 1580 +1620. = (1) **Frances Monk.** 1596 B
- **Mary Stukeley**, +1632. (308)
- **Simon Weekes, of Brodhurst, co. Devon**, +1646.
- **Gertrude Stukeley**, living 1631. (309)
- **Humphrey Bury, of Colyton, co. Devon**, +1631.
- **Anne Stukeley**, living 1656. = (1) **John Langford, of Coxworthy.** = (2) **William Coode, of Morval, M.P.**, 1573 +1655.
- **Frances Brooke, da. and h.** = (1) **Thomas Coppinger.** = (2) **Edmund Beecher.** *Issue extinct.*
- **Sir Francis Coppinger**, 1579 +1656. = **Hon. Frances de Burgh.** (311)

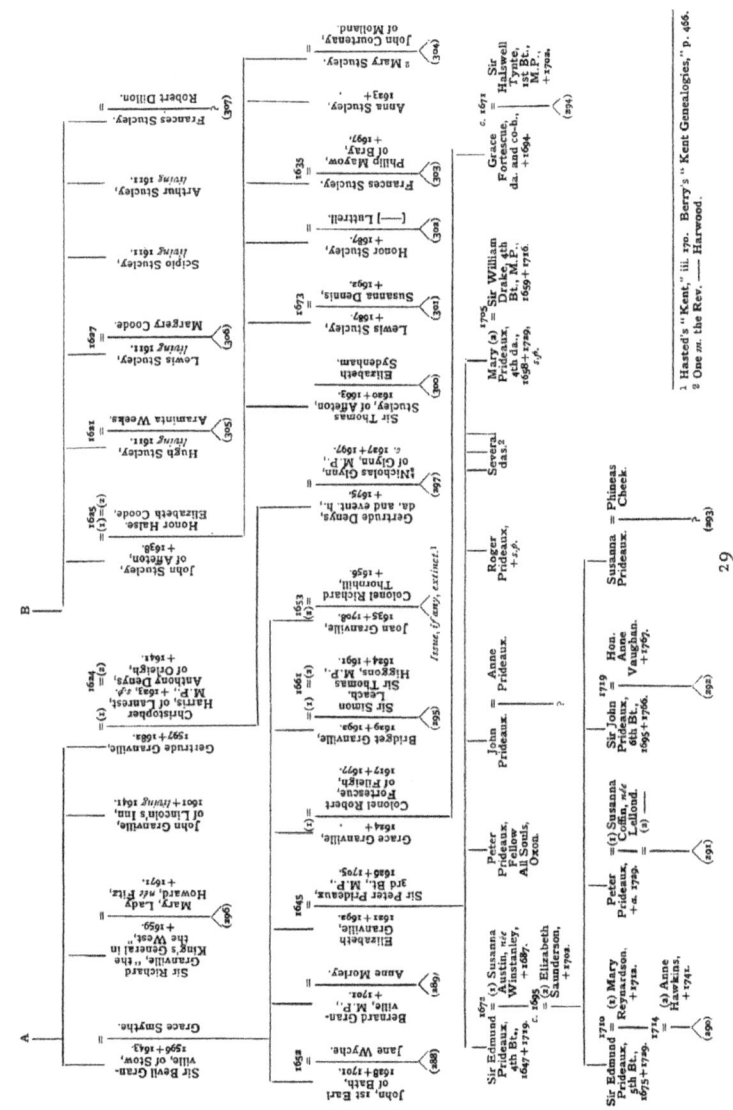

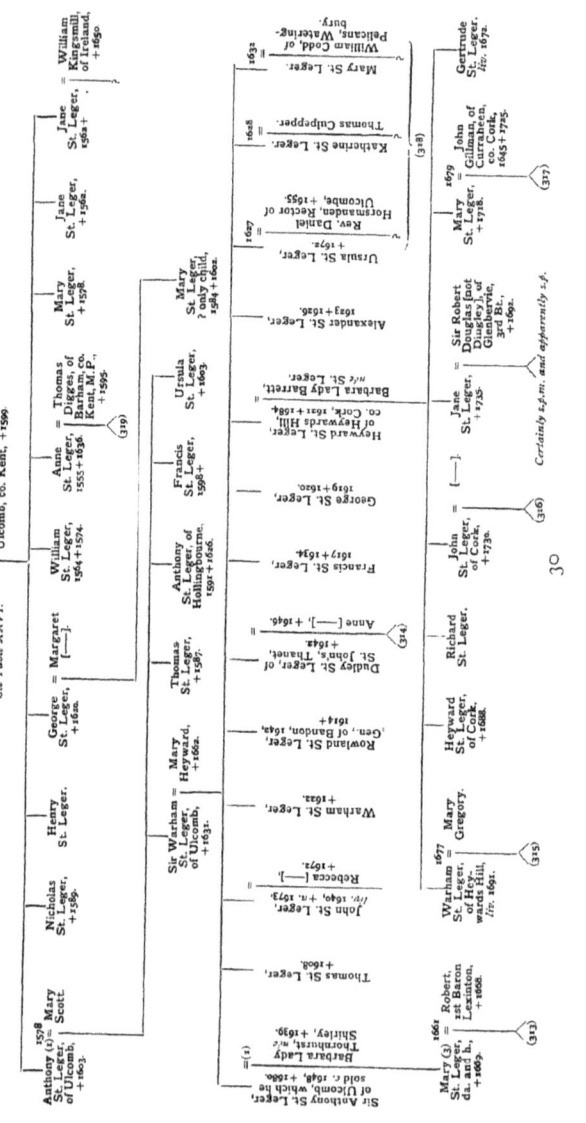

TABLE XXVIII

Hon. Mary Nevill. = Thomas, 9th Lord Dacre, +1541.
See Table XXVI.

Gregory, 10th Lord Dacre, +1594.

Margaret, 11th Lady Dacre, 1541+1611. 1564 = Sampson Lennard, of Chevening, co. Kent, M.P., *c.* 1544+1615.

Henry, 12th Lord Dacre, 1570+1616. 1580 = Chrisogona Baker, +1616.

Hon. Gregory Lennard.

Hon. Thomas Lennard.

Hon. Anne Lennard. = Herbert Morley, of Glynde, co. Sussex, +1611. (334)

Hon. Mary Lennard. = Sir Ralph Bosville, of Sevenoaks, co. Kent. (335)

Hon. Margaret Lennard. = Sir Thomas Waller, of Groombridge, co. Sussex. *Table XXIX.*

Hon. Elizabeth Lennard. 1599 = Sir Francis Barnham, of Boughton, Mounchensea, co. Kent, +1646. (341)

Hon. Frances Lennard. = Sir Robert More, M.P., 1581+1626. (342)

Richard, 13th Lord Dacre, 1594+1630. = (1) Elizabeth Throckmorton, +1622. 1625 (1)=(2) Hon. Dorothy North, +1698.

Hon. Margaret Lennard. = Sir Anthony Wildegoos, of Edridge Court, co. Sussex. (327)

Hon. Philadelphia Lennard, +1660. = Sir Thomas Parker, of Ratton, co. Sussex, +1663.

Hon. (2) Barbara Lennard. 1638 = Sir Philip Stapleton, of Wartre, 1603+1647. *Issue app. extinct.*[1]

Hon. (1) Pembroke Lennard, +*a.* 1638. = Sir William Brooke, of B. [12th Lord Cobham], 1598+1643. *Issue extinct, 1703.*

[1] Francis, 14th Lord Dacre, 1619+1662. = Elizabeth, *afterwards suo jure* Countess of Sheppy, +1686.

2 Hon. Richard Lennard, *afterwards* Barrett, +1696. = Anne Loftus. (325)

Hon. Catherine Lennard. = Chaloner Chute, of the Vine, co Hants. (326)

George Parker, of Ratton, 1620+1673. = Mary Newdigate. (328)

Grace Parker, 1622+ . 1639 = Sir William Campion, of Camberwell.

Philadelphia Parker. 1649 = Samuel Boys, of Hawkhurst, co. Kent, 1617+1688. (330)

Rachel Parker, 1631+1650. 1645 (1) = William Gee, of Bishop Burton, 1625+1678. (331)

Catherine Parker, 1633+1700. = Sir Thomas Nutt, of Mays, co. Sussex.

Anne Parker, 1634+ . 1652 =(1) John Shirley, of Isfield, co. Sussex, 1633+1656, *s.p.* 1667 =(2) Francis Barnham, 1637+1668.

Thomas, 1st Earl of Sussex, *c.* 1653+1715. 1674 = Lady Anne Palmer, *otherwise* Fitzroy, 1662+1722. (320)

Hon. Henry Lennard, 1662-3+1703. = Mary Haddock, +1709. (321)

Hon. Philadelphia Lennard, +1662. = Daniel, 3rd Viscount Clare, +1691.

Hon. Elizabeth Lennard. 1671 = (1) William, 3rd Earl of Meath. *bur.* 1684/5. =(2) Hon. William Moore.

William Campion, of Danny, &c. = Frances Glynde. (329)

Philadelphia Nutt, da. and co-h., *liv.* 1706. *c.* 1695 = Sir Thomas Dyke, 1st Bart., +1706. (332)

Catherine Nutt, da. and co-h., 1662+1708. = Anthony Bramston, of Skreens, co. Essex, 1640+1722. (333)

Daniel, 4th Viscount Clare, +1693.

Charles, 5th Viscount Clare, +1706. = Charlotte Bulkeley.

Lady (2) Elizabeth Brabazon, +1725. =(1) Sir Philips Coote, 1685+1715. =(2) Hon. Philip Bertu, +*s.p.* 1728. (323)

Lady Catherine Brabazon. = Alonso Vere. (324)

Elizabeth Moore. *See Essex Volume*, p. 228.

Charles, 6th Viscount Clare and (1741) 8th Earl of Thomond, K.H.G., Marshal of France, 1699+1761. 1755 = Marie Genevieve Louise, Marchioness of Cheffreville, 1737+1763.

Charles, 9th Earl of Thomond, 1757+*s.p.* 1774.

Lady Charlotte Antoinette Marie O'Brien, 1758+1808. 1775 = Anthony Caesar, 3rd Duke of Praslin, 1756+1808. (322)

[1] See the Exeter Volume, Table XLIX.

TABLE XXIX

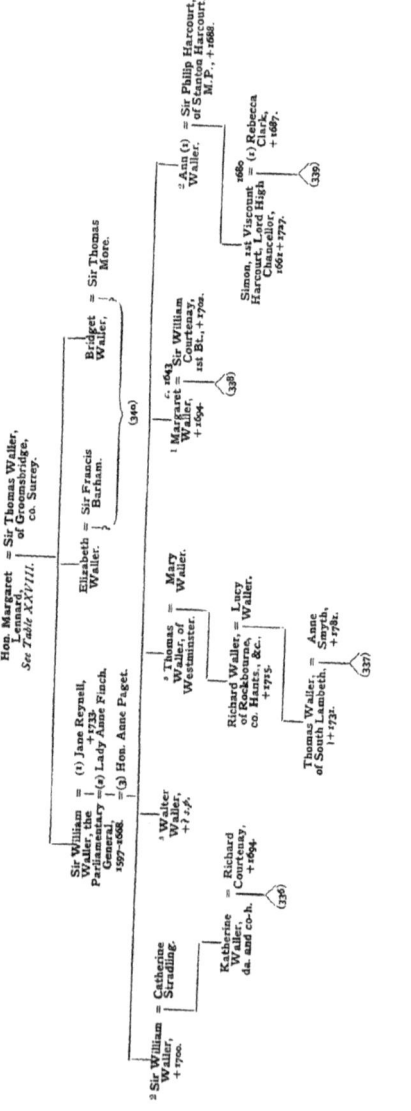

32

TABLE XXX

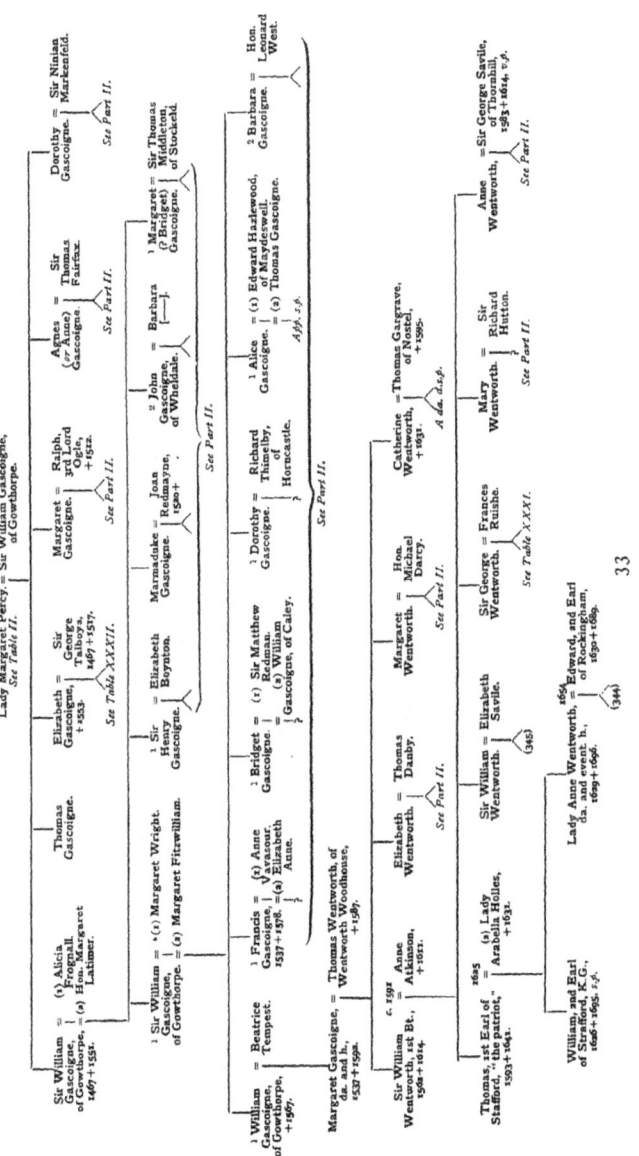

TABLE XXXI

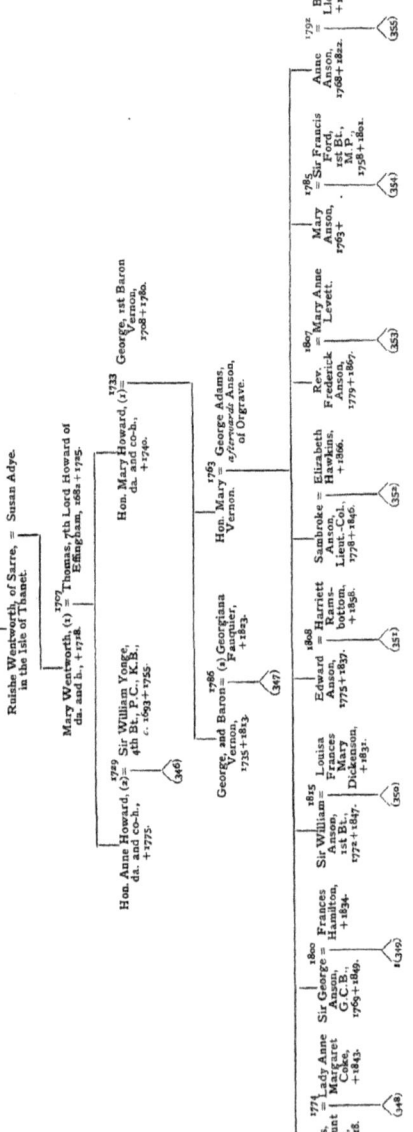

TABLE XXXII

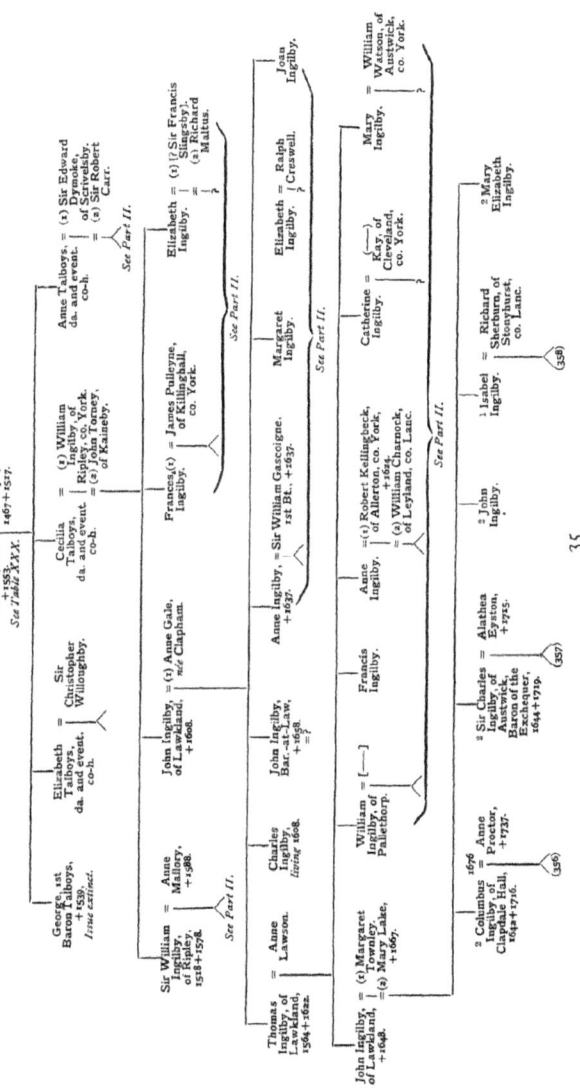

THE PLANTAGENET ROLL

OF THE

BLOOD ROYAL OF BRITAIN

Descendants of Lady Elizabeth Mortimer (grandda. of Lionel (of Antwerp) Duke of Clarence, K.G.), wife 1st of Henry, Lord Percy, called Hotspur, *d.v.p.* (being killed at the Battle of Shrewsbury) 23 July 1403; 2ndly of Thomas, 1st Lord Camoys, K.G.

1. Descendants of Lady ELIZABETH PERCY[1] (Table II.), apparently living and then a widow 19 June 1604,[2] *m.* RICHARD WOODROFFE of Wolley, co. York; and had issue 1*a* to 3*a*.

   1*a*. *Maximilian Woodroffe*, son and h.[2], [3]
   2*a*. *Joseph or Joshua Woodroffe*,[3], [4], [5] d. (-); m. *Magdalene*, da. and h. of *Roger Billings of Marthagare, co. Denbigh*; and had issue 1*b* to 5*b*.
      1*b*. *Charles Woodroffe*,[3], [4], [5] d. *unm.*[3]
      2*b*. *Joseph Woodroffe*.[3], [5]
      3*b*. *Francis Woodroffe*.[3], [5]
      4*b*. *Foljambe Woodroffe of Wakefield, tradesman*,[3], [5], [9] *m. and had issue*[3] 1*c* to 2*c*.
        1*c*. *Francis Woodroffe of Wakefield*,[3] m. *and had issue* (*with a da. who d. young*) 1*d* to 4*d*.
          1*d*. *William Woodroffe*.[3]
          2*d*. *Francis Woodroffe*.[3]
          3*d*. *Charles Woodroffe*.[3]
          4*d*. *Mary Woodroffe*, m. (—) *Wilson of Bedal*.[3]
        2*c*. *William Woodroffe of Wakefield*,[3] m. *and had issue* 1*d*.
          1*d*. *Elizabeth Woodroffe of Wakefield, living there* 1773.[3]
      5*b*. *Mary Woodroffe*.[3], [5]

   3*a*. *Lucy Woodroffe*.[3]

---

[1] See Appendix.
[2] *Mis. Gen. et Her.*, ii. 379.
[3] "Pedigree and Memorials of the Woodroffe Family," by Miss M. S. Woodroffe, 1878.
[4] Harl. MS., 6070, *f*. 123 [144].
[5] Hunter's "Deanery of Doncaster," ii. 387.

The Plantagenet Roll

2. Descendants of BENEDICTA MARIA THERESA HALL, a co-h. to the Baronies of Percy, Poynings, and Fitzpayne [E.] (Table II.), d. 25 July 1749; m. as 1st wife, c. 1717, THOMAS (GAGE), 1st VISCOUNT GAGE [I.], d. 21 Dec. 1754; and had issue 1a to 2a.

1a. *William Hall (Gage), 2nd Viscount Gage [I.], 1st Baron Gage [G.B.]*, b. 1 Jan. 1718; d.s.p. 11 Oct. 1791.

2a. Hon. *Thomas Gage, Governor and Comm.-in-Chief of H.M.'s Forces in North America*, d. 2 Ap. 1788; m. 8 Dec. 1758, *Margaret, da. of Peter Kemble, President of the New Jersey Council*, d. 9 Feb. 1824; *and had issue* 1b to 6b.

1b. *Henry (Gage), 3rd Viscount Gage [I.], 2nd Baron Gage [G.B.]*, b. 4 Mar. 1761; d. 29 Jan. 1808; m. 11 Jan. 1789, *Susannah Maria, da. and h. of Gen. William Skinner*, d. 29 Ap. 1821; *and had issue* 1c to 2c.

1c. *Henry Hall (Gage), 4th Viscount Gage [I.], 3rd Baron Gage [G.B.]*, b. 14 Dec. 1791; d. 20 Jan. 1877; m. 8 Mar. 1813, *Elizabeth Maria [descended from the Lady Isabel Plantagenet* (see Essex Volume, p. 134)], *da. of the Hon. Edward Foley of Stoke Edith*, d. 13 June 1857; *and had issue* 1d to 4d.

1d. Hon. *Henry Edward Hall Gage, Lieut.-Col. Royal Sussex Militia*, b. 9 Jan. 1814; d. 8 Sept. 1875; m. 31 Aug. 1840, *Sophia Selina [descended paternally from George, Duke of Clarence, K.G.* (see Clarence Volume, p. 638), *and maternally from his aunt, the Lady Isabel Plantagenet* (see Essex Volume, p. 59)], *da. of Sir Charles Knightley, 2nd Bart. [G.B.]*; d. 4 May 1866; *and had issue* 1e to 2e.

1e. *Henry Charles (Gage), 5th Viscount Gage [I.] and 4th Baron Gage [G.B.], senior known representative and heir-general of* Henry "Hotspur," Lord Percy, and his wife, Lady Elizabeth, da. of Edmund (Mortimer), 3rd Earl of March, and the Princess Philippa, only child of Lionel (of Antwerp), Duke of Clarence, K.G., the eldest of the sons of King Edward III. of whom issue now survives, and co-h. to the Earldom of Northumberland (1377) and Baronies of Percy (1299) and Poynings (1337) [E.] (*Firle Place, Lewes; Carlton; Bachelors'*), b. 2 Ap. 1854; m. 23 July 1894, *Leila Georgiana [descended from George, Duke of Clarence, K.G.* (see Clarence Volume, p. 605)], *da. of the Rev. Frederick Peel; and has issue* 1f to 4f.

1f. Hon. Henry Rainald Gage, b. 30 Dec. 1895.
2f. Hon. Irene Adelaide Gage.
3f. Hon. Vera Benedicta Gage.
4f. Hon. Yvonne Rosamond Gage.

2e. Selina Elizabeth Gage, m. 1st, 22 July 1862, Henry Cavendish Cavendish (1852), *formerly* Taylor of Chyknell, co. Salop, J.P., D.L. (div. Jan. 1872); 2ndly, 1873, J. White; and has issue 1f to 3f.

1f. Edith Selina Cavendish, m. 24 May 1893, Major Hubert Cornwall Legh, King's Royal Rifle Corps.
2f. Ethel Julia Cavendish.
3f. Elfrida Geraldine Cavendish.

2d. Hon. *Edward Thomas Gage, Lieut.-Gen. and Col. Comdg. R.H.A., C.B.*, b. 28 Dec. 1825; d. 21 May 1889; m. 1st, 17 Jan. 1856, *Arabella Elizabeth* (see p. 40), *da. of the Hon. Thomas William Gage*, d. 8 Nov. 1860; 2ndly, 17 Nov. 1862, *Ella Henrietta* (29 *Clifton Crescent, Folkestone*), *da. of James Maxse [by his wife, Lady Caroline, née Berkeley]*; *and had issue* 1e to 8e.

1e.[1] William Henry St. Quintin Gage, b. 12 Feb. 1858.
2e.[1] Francis Edward Gage, b. 13 Oct. 1860.
3e.[2] *Ella Molyneux Berkeley Gage, Major and Hon. Lieut.-Col. 3rd County of London Imp. Yeo., late* 14th Hussars (*Marlborough; Cavalry*), b. 29 Sept. 1863; m. 30 Oct. 1888, *Ethel Marion, da. of John Lysaght of Springfort, co. Gloucester*; and has issue 1f.

1f. John Fitzhardinge Berkeley Gage, b. 3 June 1901. [Nos. 1 to 13.

HENRY CHARLES, 5TH VISCOUNT GAGE.

THE SENIOR KNOWN REPRESENTATIVE OF THE LADY ELIZABETH PERCY, *née* MORTIMER.

# of The Blood Royal

4e.² James Seton Drummond Gage, *late* Lieut. 5th Dragoons, b. 28 June 1870.

5e.² Moreton Foley Gage, Major 7th Dragoons, served in Uganda 1898-9 and South Africa 1900-2 (*Army and Navy; Marlborough*), b. 12 Jan. 1873; *m*. 1902, Annie Massie, da. of William Everard Strong of New York City, U.S.A.; and has issue 1*f* to 2*f*.

1*f*. Berkeley Everard Foley Gage, b. 27 Feb. 1904.

2*f*. Edward FitzHardinge Feyton Gage, b. 3 July 1906.

6e.¹ Mary Cecil Elizabeth Wilhelmina Gage, *m*. 28 Dec. 1882, the Rev. Henry Stewart Gladstone, *formerly* Vicar of Honingham (*Hazelwood, King's Langley, Herts*); and has issue 1*f* to 2*f*.

1*f*. Thomas Henry Gladstone, b. 21 Mar. 1889.

2*f*. Kathleen Mary Gladstone, b. 15 Mar. 1887.

7e.¹ Georgiana Elizabeth Gage (5 *Eaton Terrace, S.W.*).

8e.² Mabel Maria .Gage, b. 10 *June* 1866; d. 12 *May* 1901; m. 27 *Ap*. 1899, *Lieut.-Col. William Eliot Peyton, D.S.O.*, 15*th Hussars; and had issue.*

3d. Hon. Caroline Harriet Gage, b. 23 *July* 1823; d. 8 *May* 1888; m. 4 *May* 1847, *Standish Prendergast (Vereker), 4th Viscount Gort* [I.], b. 6 *July* 1819; d. 9 *Jan*. 1900; *and had issue* 1e *to* 8e.

1e. *John Gage Prendergast (Vereker), 5th Viscount Gort* [I.], b. 28 *Jan*. 1849; d. 15 Aug. 1902; m. 28 *Jan*. 1885, *Eleanor (East Cowes Castle, I.W.; Hamsterley Hall, co. Durham; 15 Grosvenor Gardens, S.W.*), da. and co-h. of Robert Smith Surtees of Hamsterley Hall (re-m. 2ndly, 27 *June* 1908, Col. Staching Meux Benson); *and had issue* 1*f to* 2*f*.

1*f*. John Standish Surtees Prendergast (Vereker), 6th Viscount Gort [I.] (*East Cowes Castle, I.W.*), b. 10 July 1886.

2*f*. Hon. Standish Robert Gage Prendergast Vereker, b. 12 Feb. 1888.

2e. *Hon. Foley Charles Prendergast Vereker, Capt. R.N.*, b. 21 *June* 1850; d. 24 Oct. 1900; m. 25 *Mar*. 1876, *Ellen Amelia (Hawkridge, Hayward's Heath)*, da. of the Rev. Henry Michael Myddelton Wilshere, Rector of Simon's Town, Cape Colony; *and had issue* 1*f to* 8*f*.

1*f*. Standish Henry Prendergast Vereker, Assist. Resident N. Nigeria, *formerly* Vice-Consul at Cherbourg, served in South Africa with Imp. Yeo., two medals, b. 12 Nov. 1878; *m*. 25 Mar. 1908, Eleanor Elizabeth, da. of Henry Bott of Brentford, M.R.C.S.

2*f*. Leopold George Prendergast Vereker, Lieut. R.N.R., b. 26 Jan. 1881 (H.R.H. the *late* Duke of Albany sponsor).

3*f*. Maurice Charles Prendergast Vereker, b. 21 Aug. 1884.

4*f*. Foley Gerard Prendergast Vereker, Naval Cadet, b. 12 Ap. 1893.

5*f*. Violet Eva Vereker, b. 23 Mar. 1882.

6*f*. Lilian Isolda Vereker, b. 1 May 1883.

7*f*. Muriel Agnes Vereker, b. 19 Oct. 1886.

8*f*. Ivy Mary Vereker, b. 21 Feb. 1888.

3e. Hon. Jeffrey Edward Prendergast Vereker, *formerly* Major R.A. (*Naval and Military*), b. 27 Mar. 1858; *m*. 1902, Deno, da. of Capt. (—) Head.

4e. Hon. Isolda Caroline Vereker, *m*. 23 Nov. 1870, Sir Charles William Frederick Craufurd, 4th Bart. [G.B.] (*see p*. 41) (*Annbank House, co. Ayr; United Service*); and has issue 1*f* to 9*f*.

1*f*. George Standish Gage Craufurd, D.S.O., Capt. 1st Batt. Gordon Highlanders and Staff Officer W. African Frontier Force, has Chitral medal with clasps, and Queen's medal with five clasps and King's medal with two clasps for South African War, where he comm. Batt. Mounted Inf. with rank of Major, b. 19 Nov. 1872.

2*f*. Quentin Charles Alexander Craufurd, Lieut. R.N., b. 11 Feb. 1875; *m*. 1 Oct. 1899, Ann, da. of Thomas Blackwell.

3*f*. Alexander John Fortescue Craufurd, b. 22 Mar. 1876.   [Nos. 14 to 36.

The Plantagenet Roll

4f. Charles Edward Vereker Craufurd, Lieut. R.N., b. 17 July 1885.
5f. Hester Jane Laline Craufurd.
6f. Laline Isolda Craufurd.
7f. Isolda Mabel Cecil Craufurd, m. 9 Nov. 1909, Hugh Walter Wilson [only surviving son of John Walter Wilson of Shotley Hall].
8f. Eleanor Mary Dorothea Craufurd.
9f. Margaret Elizabeth Maria Craufurd.

5e. Hon. Mabel Elizabeth Vereker (10 *Wilton Street, S.W.*).
6e. Hon. Laline Maria Vereker.
7e. Hon. Elizabeth Maria Vereker, m. 1st, 7 Dec. 1886, William Harvey Astell of Woodbury Hall, co. Beds, J.P., D.L., b. 26 Nov. 1860; d. 20 Ap. 1896; m. 2ndly, 12 June 1902, Philip (Sydney), 3rd Baron de L'Isle and Dudley [U.K.], representative and heir-general of the Lady Anne, sister of Kings Edward IV. and Richard III. (*Penshurst Place, Tonbridge; Ingleby Manor, Middlesbrough*); and has issue 1f to 3f.

1f. Richard John Vereker Astell (*Woodbury Hall, Sandy, co. Beds; 16 Sloane Gardens, S.W.*), b. 7 Sept. 1890.
2f. Laline Annette Astell, b. 1 Oct. 1888.
3f. Cynthia Elizabeth Violet Astell, b. 10 Aug. 1893.

8e. Hon. Corinna Julia Vereker.

4d. *Hon. Fanny Charlotte Gage*, b. 8 Nov. 1830; d. 23 Jan. 1883; m. 15 Feb. 1853, *Capt. William Tomline, late 10th Hussars.*

2c. *Hon. Thomas William Gage of Westbury, co. Hants*, b. 4 Aug. 1796; d. 25 Jan. 1855; m. 12 June 1824, *Arabella Cecil, da. of Thomas William St. Quintin of Scampston Hall, co. York*, d. 25 Feb. 1840; *and had issue 1d.*

1d. *Arabella Elizabeth Gage*, d. 8 Nov. 1860; m. *as 1st wife*, 17 Jan. 1856, *Gen. the Hon. Edward Thomas Gage, C.B.*, d. 21 May 1889; *and had issue.*

See pp. 38–39, Nos. 10–11 and 18–21.

2b. *John Gage of Rogate, co. Hants*, b. 23 Dec. 1767; d. 24 Dec. 1846; m. 20 May 1793, *Mary, da. and h. of John Milbanke*, d. 9 Nov. 1846; *and had issue 1c to 3c.*

1c. Rev. *Thomas Wentworth Gage*, d. 19 Mar. 1837; m. 17 Feb. 1831, *Lady Mary Elizabeth, da. and co-h. of Charles (Douglas), 5th Marquis of Queensberry [S.]*, b. 4 Nov. 1807; d. 16 May 1888; *and had issue 1d to 2d.*

1d. *Charles Wentworth Gage*, b. 28 Feb. 1832; d. 17 May 1868; m. June 1862, *Georgina (Woodlands, Peterborough, Canada West), da. of C. Toker of Montreal*; *and had issue 1e.*

1e. Charles Wentworth Gage, b. 1 June 1868.

2d. Fanny Gage (2 *Downe Terrace, Richmond Hill*).

2c. *Charlotte Margaret Gage*, d. 9 Sept. 1855; m. 20 Oct. 1825, *John Hodgetts Foley, afterwards Hodgetts-Foley of Prestwood, M.P., J.P., D.L.* [*descended from the Lady Isabel Plantagenet* (see Essex Volume, p. 134)], b. 17 July 1797; d. 13 Nov. 1861; *and had issue 1d.*

1d. *Henry John Wentworth Hodgetts-Foley of Prestwood, M.P., J.P., D.L.*, b. 9 Dec. 1828; d. 24 Ap. 1894; m. 12 Dec. 1854, *the Hon. Jane Frances Anne, da. of Richard (Vivian), 1st Baron Vivian [U.K.]*, b. 20 May 1824; d. 2 Dec. 1860; *and had issue 1e.*

1e. Paul Henry Hodgetts-Foley, now Foley, J.P., D.L., F.S.A. (*Prestwood, Stourbridge; Stoke Edith, Hereford*), b. 19 Mar. 1857; m. 9 Feb. 1904, Dora, da. and h. of Hamilton W. Langley.

3c. *Louisa Henrietta Gage*, b. 21 Dec. 1809; d. (–); m. 16 Nov. 1847, *Ernst Rodolph (de Bertouch), 1st Baron de Bertouch [Denmark, 23 Jan. 1839], Councillor of the Danish Legation in London*, b. 20 Feb. 1808; d. 8 July 1869; *and had issue 1d.*

[Nos. 37 to 58.

# of The Blood Royal

1*d*. Montagu William Ferdinand (de Bertouch), 2nd Baron de Bertouch [Denmark], Master of the Hunt to the King of Denmark (*Las Palmas*), *b.* 24 Aug. 1851 ; *m.* 31 July 1882, Beatrice Caroline, da. of James Elmslie; and has issue 1*e*.

1*e*. Baron Ernst Rudolph Ferdinand Julian de Bertouch (27 *Scarsdale Villas, London, W.*), *b.* 1 July 1884; *m.* 8 Jan. 1907, Gladys Zara Mary, da. of Thomas Barns of Tilworth, Axminster, Capt. King's Own Scottish Borderers; and has issue 1*f*.

1*f*. Baron Ernst Rudolph Anton Gauthier de Bertouch, *b.* 17 Jan. 1908.

3*b*. Maria Theresa Gage, d. 21 *Ap*. 1832 ; m. 2 *Mar.* 1792, *Sir James Craufurd, afterwards* (R.L. 25 *June* 1812) *Cregan-Craufurd, 2nd Bart.* [G.B.], *b.* 11 *Oct.* 1861 ; d. 9 *July* 1839 ; *and had issue* 1*c to* 2*c*.

1*c. Rev. Sir George William Craufurd, 3rd Bart.* [G.B.], [*descended from King Henry VII.* (see Tudor Roll, p. 283)], *b.* 10 *Ap.* 1797; d. 24 *Feb.* 1881 ; m. 1*st,* 15 *Feb.* 1843, *the Hon. Hester, sister to William,* 1*st Earl of Lovelace* [*U.K.*], *da. of Peter* (*King*), 7*th Baron King* [G.B.], b. 2 *May* 1806; d. (*at Pisa*) 18 *Mar.* 1848 ; *and had issue* 1*d*.

1*d*. Sir Charles William Frederick Craufurd, 4th Bart. [G.B.], Lieut. (ret.) R.N. (*Annbank House, co. Ayr ; United Service*), *b.* 28 Mar. 1847 ; *m.* 23 Nov. 1870, the Hon. Isolda Caroline (see p. 39), da. of Standish Prendergast (Vereker), 4th Viscount Gort [I.] ; and has issue.

See pp. 39-40, Nos. 34-42.

2*c. Jane Craufurd,* d. 25 *May* 1884 ; m. 1*st,* 12 *Oct.* 1823, *Gen. Christopher Chowne* (*R.L.* 3 *Dec.* 1811), *formerly Tilson,* d. 15 *July* 1834 ; 2*ndly,* 29 *Aug.* 1836, *the Rev. Sir Henry Richard Dukenfield, 7th Bart.* [*E.*], d.s.p. 24 *Jan.* 1858.

4*b. Louisa Elizabeth Gage,* d. 21 *Jan.* 1832 ; m. 13 *Feb.* 1794, *Sir James Henry Blake, 3rd Bart.* [G.B.], d. 21 *Feb.* 1832 ; *and had issue* 1*c to* 6*c*.

1*c. Sir Henry Charles Blake, 4th Bart.* [G.B.], b. 23 *Mar.* 1794 ; d. 20 *Ap.* 1841 ; m. 1*st,* 2 *Aug.* 1819, *Mary Anne, da. of William Whitter of Midhurst,* d. 20 *Ap.* 1841 ; *and had issue* 1*d to* 2*d*.

1*d. Rev. Henry Bunbury Blake, Rector of Hessett,* b. 14 *May* 1820 ; d.v.p. 20 *Ap.* 1873 ; m. 1 *July* 1847, *Frances Marion, da. of Henry James Oakes of Nowton Court; and had issue* 1*e to* 5*e*.

1*e*. Sir Patrick James Graham Blake, 5th Bart. [G.B.] (*Bardwell Manor, Bury St. Edmunds*), *b.* 23 Oct. 1861 ; *m.* 18 Oct. 1883, Emma Gertrude, da. of Thomas Pilkington Dawson of Groton House, co. Suffolk; and has issue 1*f* to 2*f*.

1*f*. Cuthbert Patrick Blake, Lieut. R.N., *b.* 2 Jan. 1885.

2*f*. Veronica Blake.

2*e*. Marion Louisa Blake.

3*e*. Emma Gage Blake, *m.* 24 Aug. 1892, George Henry Fillingham (*Syerston Hall, Newark*); and has issue 1*f*.

1*f*. George Augustus Fillingham, *b.* 23 Oct. 1893.

4*e*. Julia Porteus Blake.

5*e*. Mary Anne Thellusson Blake.

2*d. William Gage Blake of Nowton Hall,* b. 14 *Nov.* 1821; d. 1889; m. 16 *June* 1859, *Mary, da. of the Rev. James T. Bennet of Cheveley; and had issue* 1*e to* 3*e*.

1*e*. Constance Gage Blake, *m.* 1883, Edward Charles Harrison Bennet, *formerly* of Copdock, Ipswich; and has issue 1*f* to 2*f*.

1*f*. Judith Harrison Bennet.

2*f*. Bridget Mary Bennet.

2*e*. Evelyn Gage Blake.

3*e*. Henrietta Lillie Gage Blake.

2*c. Rev. William Robert Blake, Vicar of Great Barton, co. Suffolk,* b. 1800; d. (? s.p.) 6 *Dec.* 1868. [Nos. 59 to 84.

The Plantagenet Roll

3c. *James Bunbury Blake of Thurston House, co. Suffolk*, b. 1802; d. *July* 1874; m. 1 Nov. 1831, *Catherine, da. and co-h. of Sir Thomas Pilkington, 7th Bart.* [S.], d. *July* 1899; *and had issue* 1d.

1d. George Pilkington Blake, J.P., Col. Comdg. Suffolk Imp. Yeo., *formerly* 84th Regt., served in Indian Mutiny 1857–58 (*Willesboro', Ashford, Kent*), b. 23 Ap. 1835; m. 1st, 15 May 1860, Adeline, da. of James King King of Staunton Park, M.P., d. Ap. 1890; 2ndly, July 1893, Adela Mary, widow of Thomas Duffield, da. of Theobald Theobald of Sutton Courtney Abbey, J.P.; and has issue 1e to 4e.

1e. Eustace James Pilkington Blake (*St. Leonards, East Sheen*), b. 26 Mar. 1865; *m.* 1889, Ethel Minna, da. of Col. P. B. Schrieber, Royal Scots; and has issue 1f to 2f.

1f. Norman Pilkington Blake, } b. (twins) 1890.
2f. Violet Hilda Blake,

2e. Adeline Annie Blake, m. 1884, Hardinge Hay Cameron, Ceylon C.S.

3e. Kathleen Mary Blake, *m.* 1888, Francis Millett Rickards (*Ashtead, near Epsom*); and has issue 1f.

1f. Thomas Millett Rickards, b. 1889.

4e. Geraldine Blake, *m.* 1907, Edward Thomas of Ceylon.

4c. *Thomas Gage Blake*, b. 1805; d. (? *unm.*).

5c. *Louisa Annabella Blake*, d. (–); m. *May* 1827, *Francis King Eagle, Bencher M.T., County Court Judge*, d. 8 *June* 1856; *and had issue* 1d.

1d. *Francis Blake Eagle, 14th Light Dragoons*, b. 6 *Dec.* 1833; d. 3 *Feb.* 1879; m. 1 Nov. 1865, *Emma Ellen, da. of Lieut. Henry Bond; and had issue* 1e to 8e.

1e. Francis Elwyn Burbury Eagle, Major R.M.L.I., ret., b. 29 Aug. 1866.
2e. Maude Campbell Eagle.
3e. Rose Eagle.
4e. Violet Eagle.
5e. Lilian Dundas Eagle.
6e. Kathleen Emma Louisa Eagle.
7e. Cecil Mary Eagle.
8e. Evelyn Gage Wing Eagle.

6c. *Emily Eliza Blake*, d. 26 *Jan.* 1859; m. *Michael Edwards Rogers*, d. 21 *Ap.* 1832; *and had issue* 1d.

1d. Emily Louisa Merilena Rogers, *m.* 1863, the Rev. J. H. Marshall of New Zealand; and has issue (5 children).

5b. Charles Margaret Gage, d. *Sept.* 1814; m. *as 1st wife*, 22 *Ap.* 1802, *Adm. Sir Charles Ogle, 2nd Bart.* [U.K.], b. 24 *May* 1775; d. 16 *June* 1858; *and had issue* 1c to 3c.

1c. *Sir Chaloner Ogle, 3rd Bart.* [U.K.], b. 18 *July* 1803; d. (*at Brussels*) 3 Feb. 1859; m. 5 *Ap.* 1842, *Eliza Sophia Frances, da. and h. of William Thomas Roe of Withdean Court, co. Sussex*, d. 12 *May* 1886; *and had issue* 1d to 2d.

1d. *Sir Chaloner Roe Majendie Ogle, 4th Bart.* [U.K.], b. 2 *June* 1843; d. *unm.* 29 Nov. 1861.

2d. Hebe Emily Maritana Ogle, d. 28 *May* 1889; m. 19 *July* 1865, *Eldred Vincent Morris Curwen, J.P.* (*Withdean Court, co. Sussex*); *and had issue* 1e to 2e.

1e. Chaloner Frederick Hastings Curwen, b. 20 *July* 1866; d. 3 *Mar.* 1897; m. Elizabeth, da. of Sir William Gordon Cameron, K.C.B.; *and had issue* (2 children).

2e. Edith Margaret Spence Curwen.

2c. *Charlotte Arabella Ogle*, d. 22 *July* 1840; m. (*at Paris*) 15 *Ap.* 1836, *Jules, Baron de Briedenbach, of Darmstadt*.

3c. *Sophia Ogle*, d. 23 *Ap.* 1896; m. 17 *Aug.* 1830, *the Rev. Edward Chaloner*
[Nos. 85 to 102.

# of The Blood Royal

Ogle of Kirkley Hall, Preb. of Salisbury, b. 7 Aug. 1798; d. 7 Nov. 1869; and had issue 1d to 5d.

1d. Newton Charles Ogle, J.P., D.L. (*Kirkley Hall, near Newcastle-on-Tyne*), b. 19 Feb. 1850; m. 26 Nov. 1895, Lady Lilian Katharine Selina [descended from King Henry VII. (see the Tudor Roll, p. 303)], da. of William (Denison), 1st Earl of Londesborough [U.K.], d. 31 July 1899; 2ndly, 12 Oct. 1903, Beatrice Anne [descended from George, Duke of Clarence, K.G. (see Clarence Volume, p. 426)], da. of Sir John William Cradock-Hartopp, 4th Bart. [G.B.]; and has issue 1e to 3e.

    1e. John Francis Chaloner Ogle, b. 1 Dec. 1898.

    2e. Hester Mary Ogle, b. 31 July 1904.

    3e. Bridget Catherine Ogle, b. 1908.

2d. Annie Charlotte Ogle.

3d. Sophia Henrietta Ogle, m. as 2nd wife, 24 June 1879, the Most Rev. Hugh Willoughby Jermyn, D.D., Lord Bishop of Brechin 1875–1903, and Primus of Scotland 1886–1901, d. 1903.

4d. Isabel Ogle (*Chesters, Humshaugh, co. Northumberland*), m. 12 Dec. 1860, Nathaniel George Clayton of Chesters and Charlwood Park, J.P., D.L., b. 20 Sept. 1833; d. 5 Sept. 1895; and has issue 1e to 6e.

    1e. *John Bertram Clayton of Chesters and Charlwood Park*, b. 9 Oct. 1861; d. 8 Ap. 1900; m. 26 Jan. 1886, *Florence Octavia* (*Chesters, Humshaugh, co. Northumberland; Charlwood Park, Surrey*), *da. of Cadogan Hodgson Cadogan of Brinkburn Priory; and had issue 1f to 2f.*

        1f. Eleanor Clayton.

        2f. Diana Pauline Clayton.

    2e. Edward Francis Clayton, Major Scots Guards (78 *Portland Place, W.*), b. 21 Aug. 1864; m. 24 Feb. 1900, Jeanne Marie Renée, da. of Alexandre Leon Raymond Crublier de Fougéres, Councillor-General of the Canton of Ardentes.

    3e. George Savile Clayton, b. 20 Oct. 1869.

    4e. Mary Sophia Clayton, m. 18 Jan. 1883, Mark Fenwick (*Abbotswood, Stow-on-the-Wold*).

    5e. Isabel Evelyn Clayton, m. 14 July 1891, Robert Lancelot Allgood (*Nunwick, co. Northumberland*).

    6e. Alice Pauline Clayton, m. 20 Sept. 1905, Hubert Swinburne, LL.B. Camb. [son and heir of Sir John Swinburne, 7th Bart. [E.] (see p. 294)] (*Wellington; Brooks'*); and has issue 1f.

        1f. Joan Swinburne.

5d. Alice Katherine Ogle, m. 21 Feb. 1874, George A. Fenwick; and has issue.

6b. *Emily Gage*, b. 25 Ap. 1776; d. 28 Aug. 1838; m. *as 1st wife*, 27 Aug. 1807, *Montagu (Bertie), 5th Earl of Abingdon* [E.], b. 30 Ap. 1784; d. 16 Oct. 1854; *and had issue.*

See the Exeter Volume, pp. 78–79, Nos. 146–177.   [Nos. 103 to 150.

3. Descendants of the Rev. Sir STEPHEN GLYNNE, 7th Bart. [E.], Rector of Hawarden, and a co-h. to the Earldom of Northumberland (1377), Baronies of Percy (1299) and Poynings (1337) [E.] (Table II.), b. c. 1744; d. 1 Ap. 1780; m. Aug. 1779, MARY, da. of Richard BENNETT of Farmcot, co. Salop, d. 1 June 1812; and had issue 1a.

1a. *Sir Stephen Richard Glynne, 8th Bt., and a co-h. to the Earldom of Northumberland* (1377), *Baronies of Percy* (1299) *and Poynings* (1337) [E.], b. *posthumous* May 1780; d. (*at Nice*) 5 *Mar.* 1815; m. 11 Ap. 1806, *the* Hon. *Mary, da. of Richard* (*Aldworth-Neville-Griffin*), *2nd Baron Braybrooke* [G.B.], b. 5 Aug. 1786; d. 13 May 1854; *and had issue 1b to 4b.*

43

The Plantagenet Roll

1b. Sir **Stephen Richard Glynne**, 9th and last Bt., a co-h. to the Earldom of Northumberland (1377) and Baronies of Percy (1299) and Poynings (1337) [E.], b 22 Sept. 1807; d. *unm*. 17 *June* 1874.

2b. Rev. **Henry Glynne**, M.A., Rector of Hawarden, b. 9 Sept. 1810; d. 30 *July* 1872; m. 13 Oct. 1843, the Hon. Lavinia, da. of William Henry (Lyttelton), 3rd Baron Lyttelton [G.B.], d. 3 Oct. 1850; *and had issue* 1c to 2c.

1c. **Mary Glynne**, a co-h. to the Earldom of Northumberland (1377) and Baronies of Percy (1299) and Poynings (1337) [E.], *unm*.

2c. **Gertrude Jessy Glynne**, a co-h. to the Earldom of Northumberland (1377) and Baronies of Percy (1299) and Poynings (1337) [E.] (37 *Lennox Gardens, S.W.*), *m*. as 2nd wife, 21 Oct. 1875, George Sholto (Douglas-Pennant), 2nd Baron Penrhyn [U.K.], b. 30 Sept. 1836; d. 10 Mar. 1907; *and has issue* 1d to 8d.

1d. Hon. **George Henry Douglas-Pennant**, Capt. Reserve of Officers, *late* Grenadier Guards, b. 26 Aug. 1876.

2d. Hon. **Charles Douglas-Pennant**, *late* Coldstream Guards (*Soham House, Newmarket*), b. 7 Oct. 1877; *m*. 28 Jan. 1905, Lady Edith Anne, da. of Vesey (Dawson), 2nd Earl of Dartrey [U.K.].

3d. Hon. **Gwynedd Douglas-Pennant**, *m*. 18 Nov. 1899, William Eley Cuthbert Quilter, J.P. [son and h. of Sir Cuthbert Quilter, 1st Bart. [U.K.], M.P.] (*Methersgate Hall, Woodbridge*); and has issue 1e to 3e.

1e. George Eley Cuthbert Quilter, b. 23 Nov. 1900.

2e. John Raymond Quilter, b. 25 Feb. 1902.

3e. Inez Quilter, b. 22 Jan. 1904.

4d. Hon. **Lilian Douglas-Pennant**.

5d. Hon. **Winifred Douglas-Pennant**.

6d. Hon. **Margaret Douglas-Pennant**, *m*. 29 July 1909, Andrew Francis Augustus Nicol Thorne.

7d. Hon. **Nesta Douglas-Pennant**.

8d. Hon. **Elin Douglas-Pennant**.

3b. **Catherine Glynne**, b. 6 *Jan*. 1813; d. 14 *June* 1900; m. 25 *July* 1839, the Right Hon. **William Ewart Gladstone**, P.C., M.P., D.C.L., *four times* (1868–74, 1880–85, 1886, *and* 1892–94) *Prime Minister*, b. 29 Dec. 1809; d. 19 *May* 1898; *and had issue* 1c to 7c.

1c. **William Henry Gladstone**, M.P., D.L., b. 3 *June* 1840; d. 4 *July* 1891; m. 30 Sept. 1875, *the Hon*. Gertrude (41 *Berkeley Square, W.*), *da. and co-h. of* Charles (Stuart), 12th *and last Lord Blantyre* [S.]; *and had issue* 1d to 3d.

1d. William Glynne Charles Gladstone of Hawarden Castle (*Hawarden Castle, co. Flint*), b. 14 July 1885.

2d. Evelyn Catherine Gladstone.

3d. Constance Gertrude Gladstone.

2c. Rev. **Stephen Edward Gladstone**, M.A. (Oxford), Rector of Barrowby, *formerly* of Hawarden (*Barrowby Rectory, Grantham*), b. 4 Ap. 1844; *m*. 29 Jan. 1885, Annie Crosthwaite, da. of Charles Bowman Wilson of Liverpool, M.D.; and has issue 1d to 6d.

1d. Albert Charles Gladstone, b. 28 Oct. 1886.

2d. Charles Andrew Gladstone, b. 28 Oct. 1888.

3d. Stephen Deiniol Gladstone, b. 9 Dec. 1891.

4d. William Herbert Gladstone, b. 8 Aug. 1898.

5d. Catherine Gladstone.

6d. Edith Gladstone.

3c. **Henry Neville Gladstone**, J.P. (78 *Eaton Square, S.W.*; *Burton Manor, Cheshire*), b. 2 Ap. 1852; *m*. 30 Jan. 1890, the Hon. Maud Ernestine, da. and co-h. of Stuart (Rendel), 1st Baron Rendel [U.K.].

4c. **Herbert John** (Gladstone), 1st Viscount Gladstone of Lanark, P.C., M.P.,

[Nos. 151 to 175.

of The Blood Royal

M.A., Oxford, 1st Governor-General of South Africa (9 *Buckingham Gate, S.W.; Sandycroft, Littlestone, Kent*), b. 7 Jan. 1854; m. 2 Nov. 1901, Dorothy Mary, da. of the Right Hon. Sir Richard Horner Paget, 1st Bart. [U.K.], P.C.

5c. Agnes Gladstone, m. 27 Dec. 1873, the Very Rev. Edward Charles Wickham, D.D., Dean of Lincoln, *formerly* Head Master of Wellington College (*The Deanery, Lincoln*), d. 18 Aug. 1910; and has issue 1d to 5d.

1d. William Gladstone Wickham, B.A., b. 3 Jan. 1877.

2d. Rev. Edward Stephen Gladstone Wickham, M.A., Curate of St. Simon Zelotes, Bethnal Green, E., b. 2 Mar. 1882.

3d. Catherine Mary Lavinia Wickham, Head of Bishop Creighton House, Lillie Road, Fulham, S.W.

4d. Lucy Christian Wickham.

5d. Margaret Agnes Wickham.

6c. Mary Gladstone, m. 2 Feb. 1886, the Rev. Henry Drew, Rector of Hawarden and Canon of St. Asaph (*Hawarden Rectory, Flints*), d. 1910; and has issue 1d.

1d. Dorothy Mary Catherine Drew.

7c. Helen Gladstone, *late* Warden of the Women's University Settlement, Blackfriars, and *formerly* Vice-Principal Newnham College, Cambridge (*Sundial, Hawarden*).

4b. Mary Glynne, b. 1813; d. 17 *Aug.* 1857; m. *as* 1st *wife*, 25 *July* 1839, *George William* (Lyttelton), 4th *Baron Lyttelton* [G.B.] *and Baron Westcote* [I.], *and a Baronet* [E.], *P.C., K.C.M.G.*, b. 31 *Mar.* 1817; d. 19 *Ap.* 1876; *and had issue* 1c *to* 11c.

1c. Charles George (Lyttelton), 8th Viscount Cobham and 5th Baron Lyttelton, &c. [G.B.], 5th Baron Westcote [I.] and 11th Baronet [E.], &c., &c. (*Hagley Hall, Stourbridge*), b. 27 Oct. 1842; m. 19 Oct. 1878, the Hon. Mary Susan Caroline [descended from King Henry VII. through five different lines; from George, Duke of Clarence, through five; from Anne (Plantagenet), Duchess of Exeter, through nine; and from Isabel (Plantagenet), Countess of Essex, through nineteen], da. of William George (Cavendish), 2nd Lord Chesham [U.K.]; and has issue 1d to 7d.

1d. Hon. John Cavendish Lyttelton, Assist. Private Secretary to High Commr. for South Africa (Earl Selborne) since 1905, *formerly* Lieut. Rifle Brigade, b. 23 Oct. 1881; m. 30 June 1909, Violet Yolande, da. of Charles Leonard of 18 Kensington Palace Gardens, W., and Gloria, Cape Colony; and has issue 1e.

1e. Charles John Lyttleton, b. 8 Aug. 1909.

2d. Hon. George William Lyttelton, b. 6 Jan. 1883.

3d. Hon. Charles Frederick Lyttelton, b. 25 Jan. 1887.

4d. Hon. Richard Glynne Lyttelton, b. 16 Oct. 1893.

5d. Hon. Maud Mary Lyttelton, m. 25 Feb. 1908, the Hon. Hugh Archibald Wyndham (*Kroomdrai, Standerton, S. Africa*).

6d. Hon. Frances Henrietta Lyttelton.

7d. Hon. Rachel Beatrice Lyttelton.

2c. Rev. the Hon. Albert Victor Lyttelton, M.A., Curate in Charge of St. John's, Hawarden, *formerly* Priest Vicar of Bloemfontein Cathedral (*St. John's Parsonage, near Mold*), b. 29 June 1844.

3c. Hon. Sir Neville Gerald Lyttelton, K.C.B., Gen. and Gen. Officer Comdg.-in-Chief in Ireland, *formerly* Comm.-in-Chief in Transvaal, &c. (*Royal Hospital, Dublin*), b. 28 Oct. 1845; m. 1 Oct. 1883, Katharine Sarah, da. of the Right Hon. James Archibald Stuart Wortley; and has issue 1d to 3d.

1d. Lucy Blanche Lyttelton, m. 2 June 1908, Charles Frederick Gurney Masterman, M.P., Parl. Under Sec. of State for Home Affairs (46 *Gillingham Street, Eccleston Square, S.W.*).

2d. Hilda Margaret Lyttelton, m. as 2nd wife, 23 Feb. 1909, Arthur Morton Grenfell (25 *Great Cumberland Place, S.W.*).

3d. Mary Hermione Lyttelton.

The Plantagenet Roll

4c. Hon. George William Spencer Lyttelton, C.B., M.A., F.R.G.S., &c., Private Sec. to the Premier (Rt. Hon. W. E. Gladstone) 1892-4 (49 *Hill Street, Berkeley Square, W.*), b. 12 June 1847.

5c. Right Rev. the Hon. *Arthur Temple Lyttelton, D.D., Lord Bishop of Southampton*, b. 7 Jan. 1852; d. 19 Feb. 1903; m. 3 Aug. 1880, *Kathleen Mary*, da. of George Clive of Perrystone, co. Hereford, d. 13 Jan. 1907; *and had issue* 1d to 3d.

   1d. Archer Geoffrey Lyttelton, Lieut. 2nd Batt. Welsh Regt., b. 7 May 1884.
   2d. Stephen Clive Lyttelton, Sub-Lieut. R.N., b. 17 June 1887.
   3d. Margaret Lucy Lyttelton (21 *Carlton House Terrace, S.W.*).

6c. Hon. Robert Henry Lyttelton, M.A., a Solicitor and member of the firm of Stow, Preston, & Lyttelton, of Lincoln's Inn Fields (85 *Vincent Square, S.W.*), b. 18 Jan. 1854; m. 14 July 1884, Edith, da. of Sir Charles Santley.

7c. Rev. the Hon. Edward Lyttelton, M.A., Headmaster of Eton since 1905, *formerly* of Haileybury College and Hon. Canon of St. Albans, &c. (*Eton College, Windsor*), b. 23 July 1855; m. 21 Dec. 1888, Caroline Amy, da. of the Very Rev. John West, D.D., Dean of St. Patrick's, Dublin; and has issue 1d to 2d.

   1d. Nora Joan Lyttelton.
   2d. Delia Lyttelton.

8c. Right Hon. the Hon. Alfred Lyttelton, Bar.-at-Law, P.C., K.C., M.P., Member Gen. Council of the Bar, Dep. High Steward Cambridge University, &c., *formerly* Secretary of State for the Colonies (16 *Great College Street, Westminster, S.W.*), b. 7 Feb. 1857; m. 1st, 21 May 1885, Octavia Laura, da. of Sir Charles Tennant, 1st Bart. [U.K.], d. 24 Ap. 1886; 2ndly, 18 Ap. 1892, Edith Sophy, da. of Archibald Balfour; and has issue 1d to 2d.

   1d. Oliver Lyttelton, b. 15 Mar. 1893.
   2d. Mary Frances Lyttelton.

9c. Hon. Meriel Sarah Lyttelton, m. 19 July 1860, the Right Hon. John Gilbert Talbot, P.C., M.P., J.P., D.L. [E. of Shrewsbury Coll., a descendant of Anne (Plantagenet), Duchess of Exeter] (*Falconhurst, Eden Bridge, Kent; 10 Great George Street, S.W.*); and has issue 1d to 9d.

   1d. George John Talbot, K.C., M.A., Bar.-at-Law, Chancellor of the Dioceses of Lincoln, Ely, Lichfield, and Southwark (36 *Wilton Crescent, S.W.; 4 Paper Buildings, Temple, E.C.*), b. 19 June 1861; m. 3 June 1897, Gertrude Harriot, da. of Albemarle Cator of Woodbastwick Hall, co. Norfolk; and has issue 1e to 3e.

      1e. John Bertram Talbot, b. 10 June 1900.
      2e. Thomas George Talbot, b. 21 Dec. 1904.
      3e. Mary Meriel Gertrude Talbot.

   2d. Bertram Talbot, *formerly* Clerk to House of Commons (*Monteviot, Ancrum, co. Roxburgh*), b. 27 Ap. 1865; m. 21 Feb. 1903, Victoria Alexandrina, Dowager Marchioness of Lothian [S.] [a descendant of King Henry VII., &c.], da. of Walter Francis (Scott), 5th Duke of Buccleuch, &c. [S.], K.G.

   3d. John Edward Talbot, B.A. (Oxon.), Senior Examiner in Board of Education (12 *Stanhope Gardens, S.W.*), b. 14 Mar. 1870; m. 27 Ap. 1898, Mabel, da. of Archibald Balfour; and has issue 1e to 4e.

      1e. Evan Arthur Christopher Talbot, b. 31 May 1903.
      2e. Richard Eustace Talbot, b. 11 Feb. 1907.
      3e. Anne Meriel Talbot.
      4e. Joan Ankaret Talbot.

   4d. Mary Talbot, b. 14 July 1862; d. 25 May 1897; m. 14 Ap. 1896, the Ven. Winfrid Oldfield Burrows, *Archdeacon of Birmingham*; and had issue 1e.
      1e. Hilda Mary Burrows.

   5d. Caroline Agnes Talbot, m. 13 Oct. 1891, Talbot Baines (*Westwood Lodge, Leeds*); and has issue 1e to 4e.

[Nos. 199 to 222.

of The Blood Royal

1*e.* Frederick John Talbot Baines, *b.* 25 July 1892.
2*e.* Edward Russell Baines, *b.* 28 Oct. 1899.
3*e.* Henry Wolfe Baines, *b.* Feb. 1905.
4*e.* Susan Meriel Talbot Baines.
6*d.* Meriel Lucy Talbot.
7*d.* Evelyn Talbot, twin.
8*d.* Gwendolen Talbot, *m.* 6 Dec. 1905, Guy Stephenson, Bar.-at-Law, Assist. Director of Public Prosecutions [a descendant both paternally and maternally from George (Plantagenet), Duke of Clarence, K.G.] (41 *Egerton Gardens, S.W.*); and has issue 1*e.*

1*e.* Augustus William Stephenson, *b.* 1 Mar. 1909.

9*d.* Margaret Isabel Talbot, *m.* 2 July 1904, Randall Mark Kerr McDonnell, Viscount Dunluce [son and h. of the 6th Earl of Antrim [I.], and a descendant of George (Plantagenet), Duke of Clarence, K.G.] (*Walney Old Vicarage, Barrow-in-Furness*); and has issue 1*e.*

1*e.* Hon. Rose Gwendolen Louisa McDonnell, *b.* 23 May 1909.

10*c.* Hon. Lucy Caroline Lyttelton, Hon. LL.D. (Leeds), *formerly* Maid of Honour to Queen Victoria (21 *Carlton House Terrace, S.W.*), *m.* 7 June 1864, Lord Frederick Charles Cavendish, M.P., *d.s.p.*, being murdered 6 May 1882.

11*c.* Hon. Lavinia Lyttelton, *m.* 29 June 1870, the Right Rev. Edward Stuart Talbot, D.D., 1st Lord Bishop of Southwark, *formerly* (1895-1905) 100th Lord Bishop of Rochester, &c. [E. of Shrewsbury Coll., a descendant of Anne (Plantagenet), Duchess of Exeter] (*Bishop's House, Kensington, S.W.*); and has issue 1*d* to 5*d.*

1*d.* Rev. Edward Keble Talbot, a Member of the Community of the Resurrection, Mirfield, *b.* 31 Dec. 1877.
2*d.* Rev. Neville Stuart Talbot, Curate of Armley, Leeds, *formerly* Lieut. 1st Batt. Rifle Brigade, *b.* 21 Aug. 1879.
3*d.* Gilbert Walter Lyttelton Talbot, *b.* 1 Sept. 1891.
4*d.* Mary Catherine Talbot, *m.* 6 Ap. 1904, the Rev. Lionel George Bridges Justice Ford, Headmaster of Repton (*Repton Hall, Derbyshire*); and has issue 1*e* to 3*e.*

1*e.* Arthur Edward Ford, *b.* 23 Mar. 1905.
2*e.* Neville Montague Ford, *b.* 18 Nov. 1906.
3*e.* Richard Lionel Ford, *b.* 30 Aug. 1908.
5*d.* Lavinia Caroline Talbot.

[Nos. 223 to 242.

4. Descendants of PENELOPE GLYNNE (Table II.), *d.* Feb. 1771; *m.* as 1st wife, Sir WILLIAM EARLE WELBY of Denton, 1st Bt. [U.K.], *d.* 6 Nov. 1815; and had issue 1*a* to 2*a.*

1*a.* Sir William Earle Welby, 2nd Bt. [U.K.], M.P., *b.* 14 Nov. 1768; *d.* 3 Nov. 1852; *m.* 30 Aug. 1792, *Wilhelmina, da. and h. of William Spry, Governor of Barbadoes, d.* 4 Feb. 1847; *and had issue* 1*b* to 7*b.*

1*b.* Sir Glynne Earle Welby, *afterwards* (R.L. 5 July 1861) *Welby-Gregory,* 3rd Bt. [U.K.], *b.* 26 June 1806; *d.* 23 Aug. 1875; *m.* 6 Mar. 1828, *Frances, da. of Sir Montague Cholmeley, 1st Bt.* [U.K.], *d.* 9 Oct. 1881; *and had issue* 1*c* to 6*c.*

1*c.* Sir William Earle-Welby, *afterwards* (R.L. 27 Dec. 1875) *Welby-Gregory,* 4th Bt. [U.K.], M.P., *b.* 4 Jan. 1829; *d.* 26 Nov. 1898; *m.* 4 July 1863, *the Hon. Victoria Alexandrina Maria Louisa, formerly Maid of Honour to Queen Victoria, da. of the Hon. Charles Stuart-Wortley; and had issue* 1*d* to 2*d.*

1*d.* Sir Charles Glynne Earle Welby, 5th Bt. [U.K.], C.B., J.P., D.L., *formerly* (1900-6) M.P. for Newark and (1900-2) Assist. Under-Secretary of State for

[No. 243.

The Plantagenet Roll

War (*Denton Manor, Grantham ; Carlton, &c.*), *b.* 11 Aug. 1865; *m.* 24 Nov. 1887, Lady Maria Louisa Helena, da. of Lord Augustus Hervey; and has issue 1*e* to 5*e*.

 1*e*. Richard William Gregory Welby, *b.* 6 Oct. 1888.
 2*e*. Oliver Charles Earle Welby, *b.* 26 Jan. 1902.
 3*e*. Dorothy Geraldine Welby.
 4*e*. Katherine Amothe Welby.
 5*e*. Joan Margaret Welby.

2*d*. Emmeline Mary Elizabeth Welby, *m.* 11 Oct. 1893, Henry John Cockayne-Cust, J.P., D.L., *formerly* M.P. and Editor *Pall Mall Gazette*, heir-presumptive to the Barony of Brownlow [G.B.] (*St. James' Lodge, Delahay Street, S.W.; Carlton, &c.*).

2*c*. Rev. Walter Hugh Earle Welby, J.P., M.A. (Oxon.), *late* Rector of Harston (*St. George's Lodge, Ryde, I.W.*), *b.* 19 Aug. 1833; *m.* 1st, 1 Oct. 1861, Frances, da. of the Right Rev. Alfred Ollivant, Lord Bishop of Llandaff, *d.* 3 Jan. 1875; 2ndly, 8 Oct. 1878, Florence Laura, da. of the Rev. George Sloane Stanley, Rector of Branstone; and has issue 1*d*.

 1*d*.¹ Frances Alice Welby.

3*c*. Edward Montague Earle Welby, J.P., M.A. (Oxon.), Bar.-at-Law, now Police Magistrate for Sheffield (*Norton House, near Sheffield*), *b.* 12 Nov. 1836; *m.* 3 Feb. 1870, Sarah Elizabeth, da. and h. of Robert Everard of Fulney House, co. Lincoln, *d.* 25 Feb. 1909; and has issue 1*d* to 5*d*.

 1*d*. Edward Everard Earle Welby, now (R.L. 6 Ap. 1894) Welby-Everard, J.P., B.A. (Oxon.), Bar.-at-Law (9 *Eccleston Square, S.W.; Gosberton House, near Spalding*), *b.* 22 Dec. 1870; *m.* 27 June 1899, Gwladys Muriel Petra, da. of the Rev. George Herbert; and has issue 1*e* to 3*e*.

  1*e*. Philip Herbert Earle Welby-Everard, *b.* 7 May 1902.
  2*e*. Christopher Earle Welby-Everard, *b.* 9 Aug. 1909.
  3*e*. Clemence Penelope Olga Welby-Everard.

 2*d*. Glynne Everard Earle Welby, Capt. 1st Batt. South Wales Borderers, *b.* 24 Nov. 1872.
 3*d*. Hugh Robert Everard Earle Welby, *b.* 27 July 1885.
 4*d*. Cicely Elizabeth Welby.
 5*d*. Margaret Sarah Welby.

4*c*. Alfred Cholmeley Earle Welby, Lieut.-Col. (ret.) 2nd Dragoons, J.P., C.C. for East Finsbury, *formerly* M.P. for Taunton (26 *Sloane Court, S.W.; Carlton*), *b.* 22 Aug. 1849; *m.* 14 Feb. 1898, Alice Désirée, da. of A. E. Copland-Griffiths; and has issue 1*d* to 3*d*.

 1*d*. Rannulf Alfred Earle Welby, *b.* 23 Nov. 1902.
 2*d*. Amyse Mary Welby.
 3*d*. Eda Désirée Welby.

5*c*. Mary Elizabeth Welby, *m.* 1st, 22 Mar. 1860, John Richards Homfray of Penllyn Castle, co. Glamorgan, *d.* 8 Aug. 1882; 2ndly, 13 Nov. 1893, Col. George Shirley Maxwell (*Penllyn Castle, Cowbridge*); and has issue 1*d* to 2*d*.

 1*d*. John Glynne Richards Homfray of Penllyn Castle, J.P., *late* Capt. 1st Life Guards (8 *Grand Avenue Mansions, Hove*), *b.* 13 June 1861; *m.* 1893, Rose Ellen, da. of Charles Henry Simmons.

 2*d*. Herbert Richards Homfray, J.P., *late* Lieut.-Col. Comdg. and Hon. Col. 2nd Vol. Batt. Welsh Regt., *formerly* 1st Life Guards, *b.* 23 Sept. 1864; *m.* 13 June 1889, Blanche Jessie, da. of Charles Henry Williams of Roath Court, Cardiff; and has issue 1*e* to 4*e*.

  1*e*. Herbert Charles Richards Homfray, *b.* 22 Sept. 1890.
  2*e*. John Richards Homfray, *b.* 18 Oct. 1893.
  3*e*. Francis Richards Homfray, *b.* 23 Dec. 1897.
  4*e*. Gwenllian Mary Homfray.

[Nos. 244 to 271.

# of The Blood Royal

6c. Alice Welby, m. as 2nd wife, 19 Sept. 1860, George Troyte Bullock, *sometime* (R.L. 31 Dec. 1852) Troyte-Bullock, and now (R.L. 5 May 1892) Troyte-Chafyn-Grove, of Zeals and North Coker House, F.S.A., J.P., D.L., High Sheriff co. Dorset 1888 (*Zeals House, near Mere, Wilts; North Coker House, Yeovil*); and has issue 1d to 6d.

    1d. Edward George Troyte-Bullock, J.P., Lieut.-Col. Dorset Yeo. Cav., *late* Capt. Royal Dragoons (*Silton Lodge, Dorset*), b. 17 Sept. 1862; m. 6 Jan. 1898, Grace Amy Margaret, da. of Col. John Mount Batten of Upcerne Manor, C.B.; and has issue 1e to 4e.

        1e. George Victor Troyte-Bullock, b. 1900.
        2e. Elizabeth Grace Troyte-Bullock.
        3e. Mary Winifred Troyte-Bullock.
        4e. Cicely Violet Troyte-Bullock.

    2d. Hugh Ambrose Troyte-Bullock (*Wolfville, Nova Scotia*), b. 27 July 1867; m. 16 Sept. 1891, Rosa Margaret, da. of John Caulfield; and has issue 1e.

        1e. Margaret Troyte-Bullock.

    3d. Cecil John Troyte-Bullock, Capt. Somerset L.I., b. 17 May 1869; m. 1904, Joan Acland, da. of Leonard Harper of Jersey.

    4d. Mabel Cicely Troyte-Bullock.
    5d. Evelyn Mary Troyte-Bullock.
    6d. Alice Christine Troyte-Bullock.

2b. Right Rev. Thomas Earle Welby, D.D., *Bishop of St. Helena*, b. 11 July 1810; d. 6 Jan. 1899; m. 1837, Mary Ann, da. of A. Browne, d. 1896; *and had issue* 1c to 10c.

    1c. Henry Earle Welby, b. 1838; d. 16 June 1869; m. 1866, Cecilia, da. of T. Bland of Georgetown, Cape Colony; and had issue 1d.

        1d. Hugh Earle Welby, b. 1867.

    2c. Charles Earle Welby, Hon. Fellow Allahabad Univ., and Capt. Agra Vol. Rifles, *formerly* Inspector of Schools in Indian Educational Service (Allahabad), b. 26 Dec. 1850; m. 21 June 1880, Annie Williams, widow of Walter Conroy, C.E., da. of (———); and has issue 1d.

        1d. Thomas Earle Welby, Sub-Editor *Madras Mail*, b. 18 July 1881.

    3c. Arthur Thomas Earle Welby, Gen. Manager Rio Denver Railroad, U.S.A., b. 15 Feb. 1855; d. 8 Aug. 1909; m. 1st, 1874, Phœbe, da. of Capt. de Cew, d. 1895; 2ndly, 1898, Maria (*Denver, U.S.A.*), da. of J. F. Mitchell; *and had issue* 1d to 5d.

        1d.[2] Alfred Earle Welby, b. 1899.
        2d.[2] Charles Earle Welby, b. 1901.
        3d.[1] Wilhelmina Cecilia Welby.
        4d.[1] Helena Beatrice Welby.
        5d.[2] Muriel Welby.

    4c. Frederick Earle Welby, F.R.C.S.E., b. 1858; d. 21 Oct. 1900; m. 1883, Janet Anne, da. of F. Henderson of Wick; *and had issue* 1d to 4d.

        1d. Francis Thomas Glynne Earle Welby, b. 1888.
        2d. Mary Caroline Welby.
        3d. Edith Jessie Welby.
        4d. Gladys Welby.

    5c. Penelope Welby (*Haughton, Falmouth*), m. 2 July 1863, Major-Gen. John Haughton, R.A., d. 26 Aug. 1889; and has issue 1d to 2d.

        1d. John Welby Haughton, L.R.C.P. (*Falmouth*), b. 16 Ap. 1866; m. 9 June 1896, Florence Maud Audrey, da. of Lieut.-Col. Shonbridge; and has issue 1e to 4e.

            1e. Wilfrid John Haughton.
            2e. Florence Penelope Audrey Haughton.
            3e. Joan Astor Haughton.
            4e. Mary Patricia Haughton.

[Nos. 272 to 301.

The Plantagenet Roll

2d. Hugh Latimer Haughton, Capt. 92nd Punjaubis, b. 18 Sept. 1870; m. 29 Dec. 1903, Kathleen Elizabeth, da. of T. Paterson of Dublin.

6c. Wilhelmina Welby (155 *Coleherne Court, South Kensington, S.W.*), m. 14 Jan. 1864, Major-Gen. Robert Barton, R.E., d.s.p. 11 Aug. 1894.

7c. Elizabeth Welby (*Bradford Peverill, Dorchester*).

8c. Caroline Welby (6 *Bishop Ward's College, The Close, Salisbury*), m. 1st, 17 Aug. 1867, Charles Henry Fowler, M.D., d. 7 Ap. 1877; 2ndly, 25 June 1884, the Rev. Francis William Carré, Vicar of St. Katherine's, Marlborough, d. 2 July 1901; and has issue 1d to 3d.

1d. Charles William Henry Fowler, D.S.O., *late* Capt. S.A. Constabulary, *formerly* Imp. L.H., served through Boer War 1899-1902, mentioned in despatches, medal and six clasps, b. 13 July 1869; m. July 1903, Florence, da. of John Becker of Cape Town; and has issue 1e.

1e. Florence Beatrice Fowler.

2d. Cecil Welby Fowler, b. Nov. 1870; m. 1896, Isobel Mounsey, da. of Capt. Gilfillan of Cape Town, s.p.

3d. Frances Beatrice Caroline Carré.

9c. Katherine Welby (*Mentone, Petworth, Sussex*), m. at St. Paul's Cathedral, St. Helena, 7 Aug. 1873, Saul Solomon of St. Helena, d. 10 Ap. 1896; and has issue 1d to 4d.

1d. Arthur Francis Welby Solomon, Bar.-at-Law, b. 30 Ap. 1874.

2d. Cyril Welby Solomon, b. 29 Oct. 1875; m. and has issue a son and 3 das.

3d. Homfray Welby Solomon, Merchant, b. 3 Ap. 1877; m. and has issue a da.

4d. Mary Jessica Solomon, Actress and Novelist.

10c. Edith Frances Welby (*Bradford Peverill, Dorchester*), m. 19 Feb. 1884, Surgeon Lieut.-Col. Robert Mark Bradford.

3b. Rev. Arthur Earle Welby, *Rector of Holy Trinity, Hulme, Manchester*, b. 22 Aug. 1815; d. 1884; m. 13 *May* 1843, *Julia*, da. *of Capt. George Macdonald, 68th Regt.*, d. 18 Oct. 1892; *and had issue* 1c *to* 7c.

1c. *William Macdonald Earle Welby*, b. 22 Nov. 1845; d. 4 *Oct.* 1885; m. 2ndly, 3 Feb. 1878, *Jessie* (391 *Commissioner Street, Johannesburg*), da. *of Frederick Lucas of Grahamstown, Cape Colony; and had issue* 1d *to* 4d.

1d. Spencer Earle Welby, b. 8 Mar. 1879.

2d. Glynne Earle Welby, b. 14 Nov. 1881.

3d. Isabel Florence Welby.

4d. May Welby.

2c. George Henry Francis Earle Welby, b. 31 Dec. 1846.

3c. Charles Earle Welby, b. 12 May 1848.

4c. Richard Earle Welby, *late* Capt. 5th Batt. Rifle Brigade, &c. (*Naish Priory, North Coker, Yeovil*), b. 3 Jan. 1854; m. 1st, 1886, Mary Isabella, da. of Thomas Paget of Forton, near Lancaster, d.s.p.s. 1892; 2ndly, 1899, Alice Frances, widow of Vice-Adm. Frederick Charles Bryan Robinson, da. of Lieut.-Col. Cyril Blackburne Tew.

5c. Julia Gertrude Welby, m. 21 June 1894, Richard John Linton (12 *Augusta Gardens, Folkestone*).

6c. Caroline Charlotte Welby, d. (-); m. 12 Aug. 1874, Richard Evans; and had issue.

7c. Sarah Wilhelmina Mary Welby (*Barrowby, Lincolnshire*).

4b. *Wilhelmina Welby*, d. 1874; m. 17 *May* 1825, *the Rev. Frederick Browning*, Preb. *of Salisbury*, d. 3 *Dec.* 1858.

5b. *Penelope Welby*, d. 5 *June* 1834; m. 8 *May* 1825, *Clinton James Fiennes-Clinton, M.P.* [*Duke of Newcastle Coll.*], b. 13 *May* 1792; d. 11 *Ap.* 1833; *and had issue* 1c *to* 2c.

[Nos. 302 to 324.

# of The Blood Royal

1c. Rev. Henry Fiennes-Clinton, M.A. (Durham), Rector of Cromwell (*Cromwell Rectory, Nottingham*), b. 5 Feb. 1826; m. 9 July 1850, Sarah Katherine, da. of the Rev. John B. Smith, D.D., d. 23 Mar. 1898; and has issue 1d to 8d.

1d. Rev. Henry Glynne Fiennes-Clinton B.A. (Oxford), Rector of St. James', Vancouver, British Columbia, b. 31 Jan. 1854.

2d. Charles Edward Fiennes-Clinton, b. 24 *July* 1855; d. 11 *Jan.* 1888; m. 5 *Ap.* 1885, *Alice Gertrude, da. of William Waring, M.D.; and had issue* 1e.

1e. Edward Henry Fiennes-Clinton, b. 4 Ap. 1886.

3d. Clement Walter Fiennes-Clinton, a Solicitor, b. 3 Dec. 1856; *m.* 1885, Lucy Eleanor, da. of Henry J. Hassell; and has issue 1e to 2e.

1e. Henry Fiennes-Clinton, b. 1885.

2e. Eleanor Clement Fiennes-Clinton.

4d. Eleanor Katherine Fiennes-Clinton, *m.* 15 Oct. 1872, the Rev. Seymour Bentley, *late* Vicar of Markham Clinton, Tuxford (*Bute, Whitby*); and has issue 1e to 3e.

1e. Seymour Rothwell Bentley, b. 27 Sept. 1873.

2e. Frank Middleton Bentley, b. 23 Oct. 1876.

3e. Agnes Mary Bentley.

5d. Ida Mary Fiennes-Clinton, *m.* 31 Dec. 1878, A. Swainson Allen of Bromyard, co. Hereford.

6d. Susan Charlotte Catherine Fiennes-Clinton, *m.* 7 Aug 1884, Alfred Temple Roberts; and has issue 1e to 2e.

1e. Katherine Helen Temple Roberts.

2e. Gwendoline Roberts.

7d. Madeline Isabella Fiennes-Clinton, *m.* 20 Aug. 1889, the Rev. Cecil Warburton Knox (see below); and has issue 1e.

1e. Madeline Fiennes-Clinton Knox.

8d. Adela Rachel Fiennes-Clinton, *m.* 23 July 1891, Henry Mitchell Hull, C.M.G. (*Cromwell, Shortheath, Farnham*).

2c. Mary Katherine Fiennes-Clinton, b. 26 Dec. 1830; d. 1 *Feb.* 1873; m. 12 Dec. 1855, *Gen. Thomas Knox, R.A.*, d. 29 *Oct.* 1878; *and had issue* 1d *to* 4d.

1d. Welby Francis Knox, b. 15 Dec. 1859.

2d. Henry Fiennes-Clinton Knox, b. 15 Mar. 1861.

3d. Arthur Rice Knox, D.S.O., Major R.A., b. 8 Mar. 1863.

4d. Rev. Cecil Warburton Knox, Curate of St. Margaret's, Westminster, *formerly* Rector of Harston, b. 2 Nov. 1865; *m.* 20 Aug. 1889, Madeline Isabella, da. of the Rev. Henry Fiennes-Clinton (see above); and has issue. See above, No. 340.

6b. *Katherine Welby*, d. 11 *May* 1869; m. 13 *May* 1822, *the Rev. Thomas Welby Northmore* (*see p.* 52), d.v.p. 16 *July* 1829; *and had issue* 1c *to* 2c.

1c. Rev. Thomas Welby Northmore of Cleve (which he resigned to his younger brother), Vicar of Kirk Hammerton and Weston, b. 20 Aug. 1823; d. 12 *Sept.* 1908; m. 5 *June* 1865, *Elizabeth, da. of William Moore; and had issue* 1d *to* 3d.

1d. Thomas Welby Northmore, b. 22 June 1866; *m.* 5 Sept. 1903, Margaret Ainsworth, da. of Lieut.-Col. Gritton, R.M.; and has issue 1e.

1e. Thomas William Welby Northmore, b. 18 Sept. 1906.

2d. Geoffrey Northmore, b. 28 Ap. 1868.

3d. Evelyn Lydia Margaret Northmore, *m.* 29 Aug. 1904, Arthur Cecil Allanson Bailey (*Hornapark, Lifton, Devon*); and has issue 1e to 2e.

1e. Thomas Noel Allanson Bailey, b. 5 Jan. 1909.

2e. Cicely Evelyn Bailey.

2c. John Northmore of Cleve, co. Devon, J.P. (4 *Abbey Mead, Tavistock*), b. 1 June 1826; *m.* 1st, 25 Aug. 1863, Jemima Hayter, da. of the Rev. William

[Nos. 325 to 353.

The Plantagenet Roll

Hames, *d.s.p.* 7 Ap. 1869; 2ndly, 20 Feb. 1873, Harriet Olympia Morshead, da. of Northmore Herle Pierce Lawrence of Launceston, *d.* 1 Sept. 1875; 3rdly, 16 Feb. 1899, Sarah Selina Persse, widow of the Rev. Richard Henry Donovan, R.N., da. of Stephen William Creaghe of Castle Park, Golden, co. Tipperary; and has issue 1*d* to 2*d*.

 1*d*. John Northmore of Cullompton, *b*. 3 Sept. 1874; *m*. 5 Sept. 1903, Marion Colquhoun, da. of Hay Macdowell Grant; and has issue 1*e* to 2*e*.

  1*e*. John Grant Lawrence Northmore, *b*. 18 June 1904.

  2*e*. Judith Marion Northmore.

 2*d*. Olympia Northmore, *m*. 21 Dec. 1899, the Rev. Richard Henry O'Donovan, Chaplain R.N.; and has issue 1*e* to 3*e*.

  1*e*. Terence O'Donovan, *b*. 5 Mar. 1907.

  2*e*. Norah Katherine O'Donovan.

  3*e*. Mary O'Donovan.

7*b*. **Elizabeth Welby**, *b*. 1804; *d*. 18 Nov. 1888; *m*. 17 Feb. 1829, Thomas James Ireland of Ousden Hall, co. Suffolk, *d*. 2 July 1863; *and had issue* 1*c* to 5*c*.

 1*c*. Elizabeth Mary Ireland, *m*. as 3rd wife, 29 Aug. 1856, Welby Brown Jackson, Judge of the Sudder Court, Calcutta [Bt. (1815) Coll.], *d*. 17 Nov. 1890; and has issue 1*d*.

  1*d*. Cecil Welby Jackson, M.F., *late* Major 3rd Bengal Cav., *b*. 2 June 1861; *m*. 24 July 1894, Violet Emily Caroline, da. of Col. Richard George Bolton, R.H.G. (see below); and has issue (2 children).

 2*c*. Agnes Ireland, *m*. 8 June 1852, the Rev. Henry Warburton, Rector of Sible Hedingham, Essex, *d*. (–); and has issue (3 sons living, 1 a clergyman).

 3*c*. Beatrice Ireland, *m*. 1st, Lieut.-Col. Richard George Bolton, 2nd Lancashire Mil., *previously* R.H.G. [son of Richard Bolton of Silliott Hill and Ballyshoonock, co. Waterford], *d*. 1889; 2ndly, 1896, Lieut.-Col. Frowd Walker (81 *Queen's Gate, S.W.*); and has issue 1*d* to 5*d*.

  1*d*. Richard George Ireland Bolton, Major Scots Guards, *b*. 15 Jan. 1865.

  2*d*. Alice Bolton, *m*. Capt. Dudley Loftus, *late* Gren. Guards; and has issue (1 child).

  3*d*. Violet Emily Caroline Bolton, *m*. 24 July 1894, Major Cecil Welby Jackson, M.F.; and has issue
See above.

  4*d*. Maud Bolton, *m*. 1st, A. Bradshaw, *d*. (–); 2ndly, Henry Harris; and has issue (2 children).

  5*d*. Amy Bolton, *m*. 5 Aug. 1896, Lionel Beresford Bethell [B. Westbury Coll.] (*Charwelton Lodge, Byfield, Northants*); and has issue 1*e* to 2*e*.

   1*e*. Vivian Lionel Slingsby Bethell, *b*. 5 June 1897.

   2*e*. Rupert Patrick Bethell, *b*. 9 Sept. 1902.

 4*c*. Emily Ireland, *m*. 9 Nov. 1869, Sir William Algernon Kay, 5th Bt. [U.K.], Lieut.-Col. (ret.) 68th Regt. (*St. Lawrence House, Canterbury; Naval and Military*); and has issue 1*d* to 2*d*.

  1*d*. William Algernon Ireland Kay, Capt. King's Royal Rifle Corps, *b*. 21 Mar. 1876.

  2*d*. Annie Evelyn Ireland Kay.

 5*c*. Caroline Charlotte Ireland (*Owsden House, Lewes*), *m*. as 2nd wife, 10 Aug. 1880, Sir Alexander Entwisle Ramsay, 4th Bart. [U.K.], *d*. 1 Oct. 1902, *s.p.s.*

2*a*. **Penelope Welby**, *d*. 7 Nov. 1792; *m. as 1st wife, Thomas Northmore of Cleve, co. Devon, M.A., F.R.S.* (*see p*. 269), *b*. 1766; *d*. May 1851; *and had issue* 1*b*.

 1*b*. Thomas Welby Northmore, *M.A., Capt. Scots Fusilier Guards, afterwards in Holy Orders and Rector of Winterton, b*. 10 July 1791; *d.v.p*. 16 July 1829; *m*. 13 May 1822, Katherine, da. of Sir William Earle Welby, 2nd Bart. [U.K.], M.P., *d*. 11 May 1869; *and had issue*.

See pp. 51–52, Nos. 347–360.   [Nos. 354 to 389.

# of The Blood Royal

5. Descendants of FRANCES GLYNNE (Table II.), d. 25 Nov. 1814; m. the Rev. RANDOLPH CREWE, LL.B., Rector of Hawarden, d. (-); and had issue 1a to 2a.[1]

1a. Anne Crewe.
2a. Mary Crewe, d. (-); m. (—) Chorley.

6. Descendants of LUCY GLYNNE (Table II.), b. 26 Jan. 1756; d. 24 May 1814; m. at Bath, Major JAMES GORDON, — Regt., d. (-); and had issue (with a son d. young) 1a to 2a.

1a. Lucy Wheler Gordon, da. and co-h., b. 30 Nov. 1781; d. 14 Aug. 1866; m. 11 Sept. 1806, Richard Bateson of Newlands, Wallasey, co. Chester, b. 25 Dec. 1770; d. 24 Feb. 1863; and had issue (with 4 sons and 4 das. d.s.p.) 1b to 3b.

    1b. James Glynne Bateson of Wallasey, co. Chester, b. 20 June 1808; d. 2 July 1866; m. 21 Jan. 1840, Anna, da. of the Rev. R. Phillips of Bettws-yn-Rhos, d. 1908; and had issue (with 5 children d. young) 1c to 5c.

        1c. Arthur William Bateson, b. 28 Nov. 1852.
        2c. Herbert Glynne Bateson, b. 23 Feb. 1855.
        3c. Constance Anne Bateson, m. 15 Ap. 1873, Capt. Thomas Sidney St. Clair Smith, now (1874) St. Clair, 49th Royal Berkshire Regt., d. 14 Ap. 1899; and has issue (with a son d. young) 1d to 6d.

            1d. James Sidney St. Clair, on Staff of Egyptian State Railway, b. in India 17 Oct. 1874.
            2d. Percy Raymond St. Clair, on Staff of *Daily Journal*, Chicago, b. 15 July 1880; m. 26 July 1909, Virginia, da. of (—) Corse-Hunt, U.S. Army.
            3d. Constance St. Clair.
            4d. Adah Johnes St. Clair.
            5d. Lilian St. Clair.
            6d. Norah Gladys St. Clair.

        4c. Amy Charlotte Bateson.
        5c. Ethel Bateson.

    2b. Rev. William Henry Bateson, D.D., Master of St. John's College, Cambridge, b. 3 June 1812; d. 27 Mar. 1881; m. 11 June 1857, Anna, da. of James Aikin of Liverpool; and had issue (with a da. d. young) 1c to 6c.

        1c. William Bateson, M.A., F.R.S., Professor of Biology, Cambridge University (Merton House, Grantchester, Cambridge), b. 8 Aug. 1861; m. 16 June 1896, Beatrice, da. of Arthur Durham, Senior Surgeon Guy's Hospital; and has issue 1d to 3d.

            1d. John Bateson, b. 22 Ap. 1898.
            2d. Martin Bateson, b. 1 Sept. 1899.
            3d. Gregory Bateson, b. 9 May 1904.

        2c. Edward Bateson, a Judge in Egyptian Native Tribunal (Zagazig, Egypt), b. 29 Sept. 1868; unm.
        3c. Margaret Bateson, Editor Public Work and Women's Employment Dept. *Queen* Newspaper, and writer on various subjects connected with women, m. 1901, William Emerton Heitland, M.A., Fellow of St. John's College, Cambridge (Carmefield, Newnham, Cambridge). [Nos. 390 to 406.

---

[1] Burke's "Landed Gentry," 1906, p. 1407. Mr. G. C. Chambers says there were also four sons, and adds: "In a subscription list of 1818 in a neighbouring parish I find the Rev. Offley Crewe for £20; and among the subscribers to a History of Hawarden, published in 1822, occur the Rev. Charles Crewe of Longdon, Worc., and Richard Glynne Crewe of Tamworth, Staff., Esq. I think these may without error be taken as three of the four sons, who, however, are all supposed to have died s.p."

The Plantagenet Roll

4c. Anna Bateson, Market Gardener (*New Milton, Hants*), unm.

5c. Mary Bateson, Fellow of Newnham College, Cambridge, and Historical Writer, b. 12 *Sept.* 1865; d. *unm.* 30 Nov. 1906.

6c. Edith Bateson, Artist, R.A. Exhibitor, &c., unm.

3b. Frederick Septimus Bateson, b. 24 *Mar.* 1820; d. 21 *May* 1900; m. *at St. Petersburg*, 3 *Sept.* 1849, Eliza, da. of Thomas Frost, d. 23 *Ap.* 1909; and had issue (*with a son d. unm.*) 1c to 4c.

1c. Gordon Bateson (*Church Stretton, Salop*), b. 8 Ap. 1853; *m.* 15 Sept. 1888, Ellen Tindal, da. of John Stevens, Bar.-at-Law.

2c. Frederick Bateson (*Sandhurst, near Gloucester*), b. 22 Aug. 1858; *m.* 4 Mar. 1885, Agnes, da. of Frederick William Ormerod; and has issue 1d to 2d.

1d. Glynne Bateson, b. 5 Feb. 1886.

2d. Dorothy Bateson.

3c. Alfred Bateson (*Pheasants Hill, Hambledon, Henley; Engstuen, Dröbak, Norway*), b. 20 Nov. 1860; *m.* 6 Feb. 1901, Helga, da. of Capt. Lauritz Marius Wilse, Christiansand Brigade, Norwegian Army; and has issue 1d to 2d.

1d. Frederick Noel Wilse Bateson, b. 25 Dec. 1901.

2d. Richard Gordon Bateson, b. 16 Nov. 1903.

4c. Emily Bateson, *m.* 8 June 1882, Robert Wood Williamson [eldest son of Professor William Crawford Williamson, D.C.L., F.R.S.] (*The Croft, Didsbury*); *s.p.*

2a. Mary Anne Gordon, da. and co-h., d. 1859; m. 2 Dec. 1817, William Chambres Chambres of Plas Chambres, d. 27 *Sept.* 1861; *and had issue* (*with a da.*, Mrs. Hughes, d.s.p.) 1b to 8b.

1b. William Chambres of Wallasey Grange, co. Chester, J.P., D.L., High Sheriff co. Denbigh and an Alderman of Liverpool, b. 9 *Mar.* 1820; d. 26 *Aug.* 1893; m. 2 *Oct.* 1849, Louisa Mellis, da. of Lieut.-Col. Maddock, 10th Bengal N.I., d. 23 *Mar.* 1905; *and had issue* 1c to 7c.

1c. Reginald Gordon Chambres of Pentre, formerly Hon. Major 3rd Batt. Loyal North Lancashire Regt. (*Pentre, Kempsford, near Fairford, Gloucester*), b. 8 Aug. 1854; *m.* 27 July 1881, May, da. and h. of Markland Barnard of Galley Dean, co. Essex, formerly of the Hon. Body Guard; and has issue 1d.

1d. Gwendolen May Gordon Chambres.

2c. Algernon Dennel Chambres, Stockbroker (*Wold House, Hawarden, Chester*), b. 16 Mar. 1856; *m.* 3 Jan. 1889, Annie, da. of Thomas Burton Hassall; and has issue 1d.

1d. Madeline Chambres.

3c. Louisa Chambres (*Wern Cottage, Mochdre, near Colwyn Bay*), unm.

4c. Florence Chambres, *m.* 16 May 1896, as 2nd wife, John Wood (see p. 55) (*Bramerton Lodge, Carlisle*); *s.p.*

5c. Ethel Chambres (*Wern Cottage, Mochdre, near Colwyn Bay*), unm.

6c. Blanche Chambres (*The Mount, Boughton, Chester*), m. 14 June 1883, Alfred Shaw of Hoole, Cheshire, d. (-); and has issue 1d.

1d. Phyllis Shaw.

7c. Gwendolen Chambres, *m.* 16 Oct. 1885, Edward Cazenove, Stockbroker, Major Northamptonshire Imp. Yeo. (*Cottesbrooke Cottage, Northampton*); and has issue 1d to 2d.

1d. Ralph de L'Hérisson Cazenove, b. 11 July 1892.

2d. Philip Henry de L'Hérisson Cazenove, b. 21 Dec. 1901.

2b. Philip Henry Chambres of Llysmeirchion, J.P., D.L., High Sheriff co. Denbigh 1867, b. 29 *Sept.* 1822; d. 31 *Aug.* 1909; m. 1st, 7 Sept. 1848, Mary, da. of the Rev. Robert Chambres Chambres, d. 21 *Mar.* 1860; 2ndly, 2 Oct. 1862, Louisa, da. of Richard Lloyd Williams of Denbigh, M.D.; *and had issue* (*with others* d.s.p.) 1c to 7c.

1c. Henry Chambres Chambres (*Carlett Cottage, Eastham, Cheshire*), b. 24 Nov.

[Nos. 407 to 429.

of The Blood Royal

1849; *m.* 2 Sept. 1876, Maria Josephine, da. of Thomas Langton Birley of Carr Hill, co. Lanc.; and has issue (with a son *d.* young) 1*d* to 2*d*.
    1*d*. Josephine Chambres.
    2*d*. Maria Chambres.

    2*c*. Robert Chambres Chambres, b. 10 *Jan.* 1851; d. 17 *July* 1897; m. 11 Dec. 1879, *Martha Ann* (*Huntington Court, Kington, co. Hereford*), da. of George Hamerton Crump of Chorlton Hall, co. Chester, *J.P.* ; and had issue 1*d* to 5*d*.
    1*d*. Robert Noel Chambres, b. 11 Mar. 1882.
    2*d*. Philip Chambres, b. 15 Dec. 1885.
    3*d*. John Hamilton Chambres, b. 24 May 1887.
    4*d*. Winifred Chambres.
    5*d*. Harriet Gladys Chambres.

    3*c*. Edward Lloyd Chambres (*Canada*), b. 10 May 1868; *m*. 24 Feb. 1897, Winifred Ellen, da. of George Banner; and has issue 1*d* to 2*d*.
    1*d*. Eileen Chambres, b. 26 May 1903.
    2*d*. Dorothea Grace Chambres, b. 6 May 1907.

    4*c*. Caryl Lloyd Chambres (176 *Warwick Road, Carlisle*), b. 20 Dec. 1871; *m*. 15 July 1896, Madge, da. of Francis Reading of Rugby, co. Warwick; and has issue 1*d* to 3*d*.
    1*d*. Mona Chambres, b. 24 May 1896.
    2*d*. Betty Glynne Chambres, b. 6 Jan. 1905.
    3*d*. Gwendoline Maud Lloyd Chambres, b. 17 Aug. 1907.

    5*c*. Hugh Lloyd Chambres, b. 24 Aug. 1874; *m*. 3 Ap. 1907, Susanna Langford, da. of Hercules E. Brown of Barton Hall, Kingskerswell, co. Devon; and has issue 1*d*.
    1*d*. Cora Langford Chambres, b. 17 Dec. 1909.

    6*c*. Mary Chambres, *unm*.

    7*c*. Maud Chambres (*Great Saughall, near Chester*), *m*. 12 Jan. 1886, Thomas Edward Hassell, *d*. (being drowned off Port Erin, Isle of Man) 21 Oct. 1899; and has issue (with an elder son, Lionel, drowned with his father) 1*d*.
    1*d*. Alexander Burton Hassell, b. 22 July 1896.

    3*b*. *Charles Crewe Chambres of the Eyrie, Wallasey, co. Chester*, b. 4 *Ap*. 1828; d. 26 Feb. 1866; m. 6 *June* 1860, *Lucy, da. of John Bewley of the Slopes, Wallasey;* and had issue (with a son, Austin, d. *unm*.) 1*c* to 2*c*.
    1*c*. Rev. Gordon Crewe Chambres, M.A. (Oxon.), Headmaster, Wigan Grammar School, b. 26 Ap. 1861; *unm*.
    2*c*. Huldah Crewe Chambres.

    4*b*. *Lucy Chambres*, b. 3 Sept. 1818; d. *at Mold* 7 *Oct.* 1871; m. *at Liverpool* 30 *May* 1839, *Charles Hughes Ingleby*, Bar.-at-Law, d. 9 *May* 1849; *and had issue* (with a son, Charles, d. *unm*.) 1*c*.
    1*c*. Fanny Ingleby, b. 19 Nov. 1842; d. 3 *Jan*. 1893; m. *as 1st wife*, 18 *May* 1870, *John Wood, C.E.* (see p. 54) (*Bramerton Lodge, Botcherby, Carlisle*); *and had issue* (with 2 sons d.s.p.) 1*d* to 2*d*.
    1*d*. John Crewe Wood (53 *Bath Road, Swindon, Wilts*), b. 31 Aug. 1873.
    2*d*. Florence Margaret Wood, *unm*.

    5*b*. Penelope Chambres (*Tycroes, Llandulas, Abergele*).

    6*b*. Emma Chambres (*Lystonville, Porthill, Shrewsbury*), *m*. 23 Jan. 1849, the Rev. Hugh George Robinson, Canon of York, *d*. 16 June 1882; and has issue 1*c* to 9*c*.
    1*c*. Hugh Malcolm Robinson, Dep. Chief Inspector of Factories (*Home Office, S.W.*), b. 12 Feb. 1857; *m*. 2 Ap. 1884, Annie Elizabeth Helen, da. of Major Hugh Henry Christian; and has issue 1*d* to 3*d*.
    1*d*. Hugh George Robinson, b. 11 May 1886.
    2*d*. Helen Gertrude Robinson.
    3*d*. Annie Cloberry Robinson.

[Nos. 430 to 458.

The Plantagenet Roll

2c. William Christian Robinson (*New Zealand*), b. c. 1859; m. and has issue 3 das.

3c. Frederick Hampden Robinson (*Fall Hill, Fredericksburg, Virginia*), b. 14 Jan. 1864; m. 1897, Elizabeth, da. of Capt. Murray Lee Taylor; and has issue 1d to 2d.

1d. Frederick Robinson, b. 1903.
2d. Butler Braine Thornton Robinson, b. Feb. 1899.

4c. Alfred Falkland Robinson (*Johannesburg*), b. 6 Aug. 1865; m. 1895, Helena, da. of (—) van Eysen; and has issue 1d.

1d. Hugh Falkland Robinson, b. 23 Jan. 1896.

5c. Emma Chambres Robinson (*London and Church Stretton*), m. 19 Sept. 1882, Henry David Boyle; and has issue 1d.

1d. David Hugh Montgomerie Boyle, b. 1 Sept. 1883.

6c. Gertrude Robinson, m. 27 Oct. 1882, Augustus Walter Francis Warde (*Ouray, Colorado, U.S.A.*); and has issue 1d.

1d. Doris Warde.

7c. Mary Jane Robinson, } *unm.*
8c. Edith Robinson.

9c. Charlotte Emily Robinson, m. 1894, Hugh Bovill (*Bovill, Idaho, U.S.A.*); and has issue 1d to 2d.

1d. Dorothy Bovill.
2d. Gwendoline Bovill.

7b. Mary Anne Chambres } (*Tycroes, Llandulas, Abergele*). [Nos. 459 to 475.
8b. Grace Chambres

7. Descendants, if any, of MARY GLYNNE (see Table II.), d. (–); m. SIMON GORDON, *living* 1802.[1]

8. Descendants of MARIA MARGRETTA LONGUEVILLE [eldest da. and in her issue sole h. of Sir Thomas Longueville, 4th Bart. [E.]] (Table II.), b. 1722; d. (–); m. 1st, 1739, THOMAS (sometimes called JOHN) JONES, d. 29 Sept. 1749; and had with other issue 1a.

1a. Thomas Jones of The Court, Wrexham, Lieut. 104th Regt. and afterwards Capt. Denbigh and Merioneth Militia, b. 1740; d. (*being shot in a duel by his Guardian, R. S. Manning*) 26 Oct. 1799; m. 1st, at Wrexham, 4 May 1767, Jane, da. of John Jones of Aberkin, co. Carnarvon, d. 1 Oct. 1768; 2ndly, Anne, da. of (—) Lloyd, d. 27 June 1796; *and had issue* 1b *to* 6b.

1b. Thomas Longueville Jones, afterwards Longueville of Prestatyn, b. 18 Sept. 1768; d. 21 Dec. 1831; m. 30 Nov. 1796, Anne, da. of John Gibbons of Oswestry, d. 13 June 1861; *and had issue* 1c *to* 2c.

1c. Thomas Longueville Longueville of Penyllan, co. Salop, b. 7 July 1803; d. 27 Oct. 1888; m. 9 Oct. 1838, Anne, da. of Charles Thomas Jones of Oswestry (see p. 63), d. 8 Feb. 1884; *and had issue* 1d *to* 2d.

1d. Thomas Longueville of Penyllan, J.P. (*Llanforda Hall, Oswestry*), b. 29 Ap. 1844; m. 29 June 1868, Mary Frances, da. and h. of Alexander Robertson of Balgownie Lodge, co. Aberdeen; and has issue 1e to 4e. [No. 476.

---

[1] Betham's "Baronetage," 1802, ii. 264. They apparently had no issue in 1822 and presumably *d.s.p.*

# of The Blood Royal

1e. Reginald Longueville, Major Coldstream Guards, b. 26 Mar. 1869.
2e. Edward Longueville, Lieut. Coldstream Guards, b. 22 Dec. 1877.
3e. Francis Longueville, b. 23 Dec. 1892.
4e. Mary Margaret Anne Isabel Longueville.
2d. Anna Maria Longueville (*Penyllan, Oswestry*).

2c. Rev. John Gibbons Longueville, b. 18 Sept. 1810; d. 14 July 1882; m. 29 Mar. 1836, *Agnes Frewin*, da. of John Timothy Swainson of Elm Grove, co. Lanc., Comptroller of H.M.'s Customs for the Port of Liverpool, d. 11 Jan. 1904; and had issue 1d to 2d.
  1d. Edith Longueville (2 *Park Place, Torquay*).
  2d. Cecile Longueville, m. Frank Parker of Chester.

2b.² *Edward Jones*, b. 17 Ap. 1774, d. (—); m. *Charlotte*, da. of (—) Stevens; and had issue 1c to 3c.
  1c. Rev. Harry Longueville Jones, M.A., Fellow Magdalen Coll., Oxon., living 28 Jan. 1858.
  2c. Charlotte Jones, *unm*.
  3c. (—) Jones, m. (—) Naylor, living in Italy.

3b. Hugh Jones of Larkhill, co. Lancaster, b. 20 Sept. 1776; d. 1842; m. 24 Mar. 1806, *Elizabeth*, of Larkhill, da. of Benjamin Heywood of Stanley Hall, Wakefield, co. York, d. 1848; and had issue 1c to 6c.
  1c. Richard Heywood Jones of Babsworth Hall, co. York, J.P., b. 20 Oct. 1810; d. 6 Jan. 1874; m. 11 Oct. 1836, *Margaret*, da. of John Harrison of Ambleside, d. 9 Sept. 1877; and had issue 1d to 4d.
    1d. Richard Heywood Jones, afterwards (R.L. 22 Jan. 1891) *Heywood-Jones of Babsworth Hall*, J.P., Major and Hon. Lieut.-Col. Yorkshire Dragoons Yeo. Cavalry, b. 28 July 1853; d. 11 June 1900; m. 17 July 1888, *Caroline Margaret* (*Babsworth Hall, near Pontefract*), da. of Francis John Johnston of Dunsdale, Westerham [by his wife Caroline, da. of Sir Hardman Earle, 1st Bart. [U.K.]]; and had issue 1e to 4e.
      1e. Margaret Heywood Heywood-Jones.
      2e. Violet Mary Heywood-Jones.
      3e. Caroline Earle Heywood-Jones.
      4e. Cicely Longueville Heywood-Jones.
    2d. Katherine Jones.
    3d. Mary Venetia Jones, *m*. 18 June 1868, the Rev. Clarke Watkins Burton, M.A., Rural Dean and Hon. Canon of Carlisle, Rector of Cliburne (*Templesowerby, near Penrith*); and has issue 1e to 4e.
      1e. Katherine Venetia Burton.
      2e. Florence Burton, *m*. 20 Jan. 1898, Charles Willding Willding-Jones, late Rifle Brigade (see p. 61) (*Hampton Hall, Malpas*); and has issue 1f to 4f.
        1f. Conway Willding-Jones, b. 28 Oct. 1901.
        2f. Charles Longueville Willding-Jones, b. 28 Jan. 1905.
        3f. Rona Mary Willding-Jones.
        4f. Diana Anne Willding-Jones.
      3e. Mary Burton.
      4e. Angela Margaret Burton.
    4d. Elizabeth Jones.
  2c. *Benjamin Heywood Jones of Larkhill*, J.P., D.L., High Sheriff co. Lancaster 1869; b. 1812; d. 1872; m. 1848, *Louisa Elizabeth*, da. of Hugh Hornby of Sandown, Liverpool; and had issue 1d to 5d.
    1d. Arthur Heywood Jones of Larkhill (*Larkhill, West Derby, Lancashire*), b. 1851.
    2d. Oliver Heywood Jones. [Nos. 477 to 502.

The Plantagenet Roll

3*d.* Llewellyn Heywood Jones.

4*d.* Benjamin Noel Heywood Jones.

5*d.* Annie Louisa Heywood Jones (*Frampton Hall, Boston, Lincolnshire*), *m.* 14 July 1874, Francis Foljambe Anderson, J.P. [2nd son of Sir Charles Henry John Anderson, 9th Bart. [E.], and a descendant of George (Plantagenet), Duke of Clarence, K.G. (see Clarence Volume, p. 608)], *d.v.p.* 15 Sept. 1881; and has issue 1*e* to 3*e*.

1*e.* Margaret Louise Anderson, *m.* 7 June 1905, Wilfred Arthur Duncombe, now (R.L. 6 June 1905) Duncombe-Anderson, Lieut. Reserve of Officers, *formerly* 6th Dragoon Guards [E. of Feversham Coll. and a descendant of the Lady Anne, sister of King Edward IV., &c. (see Exeter Volume, pp. 205, 647) (*Lea Hall, Gainsborough*); and has issue 1*f* to 2*f*.

1*f.* Antony John Duncombe-Anderson, *b.* 4 Feb. 1907.

2*f.* Roland Frederick Duncombe-Anderson, *b.* 18 Ap. 1908.

2*e.* Katharine Helen Anderson, *m.* 9 Mar. 1904, Richard Coningsby Sutton [Bt. of Norwood (1772) Coll.], *d.* 12 Sept. 1905; and has issue 1*f* to 3*f*.

1*f.* Francis Richard Heywood Sutton, *b.* 9 Feb. 1905.

2*f.* Olinda Margaret Sutton,
3*f.* Olivia Katharine Sutton, } *b.* (twins) posthumous 4 Mar. 1906.

3*e.* Frances Olive Anderson.

3*c. Elizabeth Anne Jones*, *d.* 16 *Jan.* 1880; *m.* 10 *Sept.* 1828, *Samuel Bright of Sandheys, Liverpool, and Ashfield, co. Lancaster, J.P.*; *b.* 25 *Sept.* 1799; *d.* 28 *Jan.* 1870; *and had issue* 1*d* to 7*d*.

1*d. Henry Arthur Bright of Ashfield, J.P., b.* 9 *Feb.* 1830; *d.* 5 *May* 1884; *m.* 26 *June* 1861, *Mary Elizabeth* (26 *Gloucester Square, London*), *da. of Samuel Henry Thompson of Thingwall Hall, Liverpool, D.L.; and had issue* 1*e* to 5*e*.

1*e.* Allan Heywood Bright, J.P., M.P. for Oswestry 1904-6 (*Ashfield, Knotty Ash, Liverpool; Gorse Hey, Moss Lane, West Derby, Liverpool; Brookside, Weston Rhyn, Salop*), *b.* 24 May 1862; *m.* 10 June 1885, Edith, da. of Alfred Turner, J.P.; and has issue 1*f*.

1*f.* Edith Honora Bright.

2*e.* Henry Yates Bright (*Lima, Peru; 26 Gloucester Square, W.*), *b.* 21 Aug. 1865; *m.* 14 Sept. 1904, Elena, da. of Capt. Manuel Ferreyros, Peruvian Navy; and has issue 1*f*.

1*f.* Henry Edward Yates Bright, *b.* 19 Feb. 1906.

3*e.* Rev. Hugh Bright, M.A. (Camb.), Vicar of King Cross, Halifax, *b.* 4 May 1867.

4*e.* Elizabeth Phœbe Bright, *m.* 18 Dec. 1889, Charles Merivale [son of Dean Merivale] (18 *Norfolk Crescent, London, W.*); and has issue 1*f* to 2*f*.

1*f.* Alexander Merivale, *b.* 2 Dec. 1901.

2*f.* Phœbe Merivale, *b.* 2 Jan. 1891.

5*e.* Mary Honora Bright.

2*d. Heywood Bright of Sandheys, J.P., b.* 20 *Oct.* 1836; *d. Mar.* 1897; *m.* 4 *Nov.* 1884, *Dorothea Anne* (*The Danes, Little Berkhamsted, Herts*), *da. of Col. John Ireland Blackburne of Hale Hall; and had issue* 1*e*.

1*e.* Ursula Dorothea Elizabeth Bright.

3*d.* Samuel Bright (5 *Huskisson Street, Liverpool*), *b.* 15 Jan. 1843.

4*d.* Sarah Elizabeth Mesnard Bright (90 *Chatham Street, Liverpool*), *m.* 20 Nov. 1852, George Melly, J.P., D.L., M.P. for Stoke-on-Trent 1868-75, *d.* 1894; and has issue 1*e* to 7*e*.

1*e.* George Henry Melly, Shipowner (90 *Chatham Street, Liverpool*), *b.* 5 Mar. 1860.

2*e.* Hugh Mesnard Melly, Wool Broker (*The Quinta, Greenhayes Road, Liverpool*), *b.* 23 July 1863; *m.* 1st, 11 Aug. 1886, Cicely Anne, da. of William Durning

[Nos. 503 to 527.

of The Blood Royal

Holt of Liverpool, d. 23 Mar. 1890; 2ndly, 4 Dec. 1895, Eleanor Lawrence, da. of Peter Owen of Capenhurst, co. Chester; and has issue 1ƒ to 5ƒ.

    1ƒ. Hugh Peter Egerton Mesnard Melly, b. 6 Oct. 1896.
    2ƒ. André John Mesnard Melly, b. 9 Oct. 1898.
    3ƒ.¹ Margaret Mesnard Melly.
    4ƒ.¹ Joan Mesnard Melly.
    5ƒ.² Eleanor Mesnard Melly.

    3e. William Rathbone Melly, Merchant (*Liverpool*), b. 30 Mar. 1867.
    4e. Samuel Heywood Melly (15 *Parkfield Road, Liverpool, S.*), b. 31 May 1871; m. 7 July 1898, Edith Matilda, da. of John Roylance Court of Birkdale; and has issue 1ƒ to 2ƒ.

        1ƒ. Francis Heywood Melly, b. 27 Dec. 1899.
        2ƒ. Dorothy Heywood Melly.

    5e. Mary Eveline Melly.
    6e. Florence Elizabeth Melly.
    7e. Ellen Beatrice Melly, m. 13 July 1881, F. Rawdon Smith, J.P., Encaustic Tile Manufacturer; and has issue 1ƒ to 4ƒ.

        1ƒ. George Francis Rawdon Smith, M.B., b. 8 May 1882.
        2ƒ. William Herbert Rawdon Smith, b. 24 Oct. 1887.
        3ƒ. Edward Rawdon Smith, b. 2 July 1890.
        4ƒ. Beatrice Emma Rawdon Smith.

   5d. Elizabeth Bright (*Sudley, Mossley Hill, Liverpool*), m. 1 Dec. 1853, George Holt, d. 3 Ap. 1896; and has issue 1e.

    1e. Emma Georgina Holt.

   6d. Harriette Bright.
   7d. Anna Maria Bright, d. 22 *May* 1904; m. 15 *Sept.* 1874, *Archibald Weir of St. Munghos, Malvern, M.D.*, d. 17 *May* 1894; *and had issue* 1e to 3e.

    1e. Hugh Heywood Weir, M.A., M.B. (Camb.), M.R.C.S. (Eng.), L.R.C.P. (Lond.) (*St. Luke's Hospital, Chemulpo, Korea*), b. 29 Aug. 1875; m. 13 Feb. 1904, Margaret, da. of the Rev. Frederic Charles Skey of Weare.
    2e. George Alexander Weir, Capt. 3rd Dragoon Guards, B.A. (Camb.), b. 31 Dec. 1876.
    3e. Henry Bright Weir, M.A. (Camb.), M.R.C.S., L.R.C.P. (Lond.) (*St. Thomas' Hospital, London*), b. 23 June 1880.

  4c. Mary Ellen Jones, d. 23 *Sept.* 1865; m. 28 *Jan.* 1836, *Robertson Gladstone of Court Hey, Liverpool, J.P.* [*Bt. of Fasque Coll. and brother of the Right Hon. W. E. Gladstone*], b. 15 Nov. 1805; d. 23 *Sept.* 1875; *and had issue* 1d to 3d.

   1d. Walter Longueville Gladstone, heir-presumptive to Baronetcy [U.K.] (*Court Hey, Broad Green, Liverpool*), b. 30 Sept. 1846.
   2d. *Mary Ellen Gladstone*, d. 17 *Sept.* 1895; m. 16 *Feb.* 1860, *Robert Gladstone, J.P.* (*Woolton Vale, near Liverpool*); *and had issue* 1e to 11e.

    1e. Arthur Steuart Gladstone, b. 27 Nov. 1860.
    2e. John Steuart Gladstone, b. 13 Aug. 1862.
    3e. Robert Gladstone, b. 6 May 1866.
    4e. Ernest Steuart Gladstone, b. 6 July 1867.
    5e. Mary Ellen Gladstone.
    6e. Katherine Steuart Gladstone.
    7e. Flora Steuart Gladstone.
    8e. Edith Steuart Gladstone.
    9e. Margaret Steuart Gladstone.
    10e. Helen Steuart Gladstone.
    11e. Lilian Steuart Gladstone.

[Nos. 528 to 561.

The Plantagenet Roll

3d. **Anna Maria Heywood Gladstone**, d. 14 May 1901; m. 14 Dec. 1870, Edward John Thornewill of Dove Cliff, Burton-on-Trent, d. 22 Mar. 1901; and had issue 1e to 4e.

1e. Edward Noel Thornewill, b. 25 Dec. 1874.
2e. Hugh Pearson Thornewill, b. 25 Feb. 1876.
3e. Arthur Basil Thornewill, b. 2 Dec. 1877.
4e. Hilda Mary Thornewill.

5c. **Harriette Jones**, d. 1855; m. Daniel Neilson of Hundhill, Pontefract.
6c. **Emma Jones**, d. 2 Jan. 1904; m. 28 Oct. 1840, the Hon. Richard Denman (see p. 166) [B. Denman Coll.], d. 19 Mar. 1887; and had issue 1d to 6d.

1d. **Richard Denman**, b. 3 Jan. 1842; d.v.p. 5 Ap. 1883; m. 31 May 1871, Helen Mary, da. of Gilbert M'Micking of Miltonise, co. Wigtoun; and had issue 1e to 3e.

1e. **Thomas (Denman), 3rd Baron Denman** [U.K.], P.C., K.C.V.O., a Lord in Waiting to King Edward VII. 1905–1907, and Capt. Comdg. 35th Squadron Imp. Yeo. in South Africa 1900–1901 (Balcombe Place, Sussex; Stony Middleton, Derby), b. 16 Nov. 1874; m. 26 Nov. 1903, Gertrude Mary, da. of Sir Weetman Dickinson Pearson, 1st Bt. [U.K.], M.P.; and has issue 1f to 2f.

1f. Hon. Thomas Denman, b. 2 Aug. 1905.
2f. Hon. Anne Judith Denman.

2e. **Hon. Richard Douglas Denman**, Private Sec. to Postmaster-Gen. (9 Swan Walk, Chelsea, S.W.), b. 24 Aug. 1876; m. 11 Feb. 1904, Helen Christian, da. of Sir Thomas Sutherland, G.C.M.G., LL.D.

3e. **Hon. Anna Maria Heywood Denman**, m. 13 July 1895, Sir John Emmott Barlow, 1st Bart. [U.K.], M.P., J.P. (Torkington Lodge, Hazelgrove, near Stockport; Bryn Eirias, Colwyn Bay, &c.); and has issue 1f to 4f.

1f. John Denman Barlow, b. 15 June 1898.
2f. Thomas Bradwall Barlow, b. 7 Mar. 1900.
3f. Nancy Mary Emmott Barlow.
4f. Anna Elizabeth Barlow.

2d. **Thomas Hugh Anderson Denman**, Barrister, Lincoln's Inn (Lavant, Chichester), b. 16 Jan. 1855; m. 28 Jan. 1890, Margaret Evelyn [descended from King Henry VII. (see Tudor Roll, p. 313)], da. of Charles Watson Townley of Fulbourn Manor, Cambridge; and has issue 1e to 3e.

1e. Richard Charles Denman, b. 16 Aug. 1896.
2e. John Evelyn Thomas Denman, b. 21 Dec. 1901.
3e. Margaret Cecil Denman.

3d. **Emma Sophia Georgiana Denman**, m. 1st, 31 Oct. 1872, Capt. Oswin Cumming Baker-Cresswell of Cresswell, J.P., d. 26 Feb. 1886; 2ndly as 2nd wife, 7 Sept. 1892, Henry George (Liddell), 2nd Earl of Ravensworth [U.K.], d.s.p.m. 22 July 1903; 3rdly, 30 Ap. 1904, James William Wadsworth; and has issue 1e to 4e.

1e. **Addison Francis Baker-Cresswell of Cresswell and Harehope**, Capt. Northumberland Imp. Yeo., late Scots Guards (Cresswell, Morpeth; Harehope, Alnwick), b. 8 Nov. 1874; m. 2 Feb. 1899, Idonea, da. of S. F. Widdrington of Newton Hall, co. Northumberland; and has issue 1f to 3f.

1f. John Baker-Cresswell, b. 7 Dec. 1899.
2f. Addison Joe Baker-Cresswell, b. 2 Feb. 1901.
3f. Cynthia Mary Baker-Cresswell.

2e. **Henry Baker-Cresswell**, Capt. late 15th Hussars, b. 17 Mar. 1876.
3e. **Susan Elizabeth Baker-Cresswell**, m. 13 July 1896, Frederick P. Barnett; and has issue.
4e. **Mary Emma Baker-Cresswell**, m. 16 Oct. 1897, Col. Frederick Charlton Meyrick [s. and h. of Sir Thomas Meyrick, 1st Bart. [U.K.], C.B., and a descendant

[Nos. 562 to 586.

# of The Blood Royal

of King Henry VII., &c. (see the Essex Volume, Tudor Supplement, p. 486)] (*Bush, Pembroke*); and has issue 1*f* to 3*f*.

    1*f*. Thomas Frederick Meyrick, *b*. 29 Nov. 1899.

    2*f*. Mary Cicely Meyrick.

    3*f*. Rachel Eva Meyrick.

    4*d*. Elizabeth Margaret Denman (44 *St. George's Road, S.W.*), *m*. 20 Jan. 1870, Sir Peniston Milbanke, 9th Bart. [E.], J.P., D.L., *b*. 14 Feb. 1847; *d*. 30 Nov. 1899; and has issue 1*e* to 2*e*.

    1*e*. Sir John Peniston Milbanke, 10th Bart. [E.], V.C., Major 10th Hussars (19 *Eaton Terrace, S.W.*), *b*. 9 Oct. 1872; *m*. 6 Dec. 1900, Amelia (Leila), da. of the Hon. Charles Frederick Crichton; and has issue 1*f* to 2*f*.

    1*f*. John Peniston Charles Milbanke, *b*. 9 Jan. 1902.

    2*f*. Ralph Mark Milbanke, *b*. 11 Ap. 1907.

    2*e*. Mark Richard Milbanke (*Bath*), *b*. 17 Mar. 1875.

    5*d*. Anna Maria Denman, *m*. 16 July 1867, Reginald Garton Wilberforce, J.P., D.L. [a son of the Lord Bishop of Winchester, and a descendant of the Lady Anne, sister of Kings Edward IV. and Richard III.] (*Bramlands, Hensfield, Sussex*); and has issue.

See the Essex Volume, Exeter Supplement, p. 660, Nos. 56226/216-229.

    6*d*. Eleanora Denman, *m*. 11 Feb. 1907, Richard Patrick Boyle Davey (200 *Ashley Gardens, S.W.*).

    4*b*. Charles Thomas Jones *of Oswestry*, *b*. (twin) (at *Wrexham*) 28 Aug. 1777; *d*. 16 Oct. 1857; m. (at *St. Thomas', Liverpool*) 27 Dec. 1802, *Maria*, da. of (—) *Welsh*, *d*. (-); and had issue (with 3 sons who d.s.p.) 1*c* to 3*c*.

    1*c*. Charles Willding Jones *of the Dingle, Liverpool*, *b*. 2 Feb. 1805; *d*. 11 *Jan*. 1849; *m*. 1st, 27 *Ap*. 1831, Mary, da. *of William Preston of Birchfield*, *d*. 1 *Jan*. 1833; 2ndly (in *Chester Cathedral*) 21 Aug. 1843, Elizabeth, da. *of John Hassall of Chester*, *d*. 27 *May* 1902; *and had issue* 1*d* to 3*d*.

    1*d*. Willding Jones, now (R.L. 28 July 1891) Willding-Jones of Hampton Hall, M.A. (Oxon.) (*Hampton Hall, Malpas, Cheshire*), *b*. 27 May 1832; *m*. 17 June 1863, Catherine Anne, da. of James Thomas Murray of Edinburgh, W.S.; and has issue 1*e* to 3*e*.

    1*e*. Charles Willding Willding-Jones, *late* Rifle Brigade, *b*. 14 Ap. 1864; *m*. 20 Jan. 1898, Florence, da. of the Rev. Canon Clarke Watkins Burton; and has issue.

See p. 57, Nos. 494-497.

    2*e*. Murray Willding Willding-Jones, *b*. 11 June 1867.

    3*e*. Venetia Marie Willding Willding-Jones.

    2*d*. Charles Digby Jones (12 *Chester Street, Edinburgh*), *b*. 4 Nov. 1844; *m*. 3 Sept. 1872, Aimée Susanna, da. of Surgeon Major Robert Christie, 3rd Bengal Cav.; and has issue 1*e* to 3*e*.

    1*e*. Charles Kenelm Digby Jones, F.G.S., Mining Engineer (*Mazoe, Rhodesia*), *b*. 28 June 1873; *m*. 18 Mar. 1896, Lily Christine, da. of Col. Joseph Beauchamp Leggett, 10th Madras Inf.; and has issue 1*f* to 2*f*.

    1*f*. Philip Kenelm Digby Jones, *b*. 10 Mar. 1897.

    2*f*. Mary Elizabeth Digby Jones, *b*. 4 June 1901.

    2*e*. *Robert James Thomas Digby Jones*, V.C., *Lieut*. R.E., *b*. 27 *Sept*. 1876; *d*. *unm*. (*being killed in defence of Wagon Hill, Ladysmith*) 6 *Jan*. 1900.

    3*e*. Owen Glyndwr Digby Jones, Capt. R.E., *b*. 8 Jan. 1880; *m*. 2 July 1907, Gwenllian Cecil, da. of the Rev. George Philipps.

    3*d*. Richard Everard Jones (*Fassfern, Kinlocheil, R.S.O. Inverness-shire*), *b*. 12 Dec. 1848; *m*. 25 June 1872, Louisa Mary Anne, da. of Major Hector Macneil, one of H.M. Corps of Gentlemen-at-Arms to Queen Victoria; and has issue 1*e* to 3*e*. [Nos. 587 to 624.

The Plantagenet Roll

1e. Willding Everard Jones, Capt. Lovat Scouts, Imp. Yeo., b. 13 Sept. 1884.
2e. Lilly Everard Jones, *unm.*
3e. Eva Conway Everard Jones, m. 4 Feb. 1903, Capt. Edward Sinclair Gooch, Berkshire Yeo., *formerly* 7th Hussars [nephew of Sir Daniel Gooch, 1st Bart. [U.K.], M.P.]; and has issue 1f.
1f. Bridget Mary Gooch, b. 3 Mar. 1904.

2c. Maria Diana Jones, b. 25 Oct. 1809; d. 20 Oct. 1894; m. 6 Ap. 1831, *the Rev. Thomas Griffith Roberts*, Rector of Llanrwst, d. 28 Aug. 1852; and had issue 1d to 6d.
1d. Thomas Vaughan Roberts, b. 31 Jan. 1832; d. 29 June 1903; m. 13 Dec. 1865, Julia, da. of Capt. William Way Baker, 32nd Madras N.I.; and had issue 1e to 3e.
1e. Hugh Alexander Roberts, Solicitor, b. 13 Sept. 1866; m. 10 Sept. 1908, Eleanor (see p. 90), da. of John Henville Hulbert of Stakes Hill, co. Hants.
2e. Ada Charlotte Roberts, m. 29 July 1899, Francis Adolphus Jones; and has issue 1f to 3f.
1f. Humphrey Charles Vaughan Jones, b. 27 July 1900.
2f. Philip Sydney Jones, b. 4 July 1902.
3f. Barbara Winifred Jones, b. 24 Jan. 1907.
3e. Winifred Roberts, *unm.*

2d. Susan Ellen Roberts (1 *Great Bedford Street, Bath*), m. 6 Aug. 1867, *the Rev. Abraham Matchett*, Rector of Trimingham, co. Norfolk, d. 17 Sept. 1883; and has issue 1e to 4e.
1e. Anwyl Charles Matchett, M.B. (Edin.), Surgeon (*Nether Stowey, Bridgwater*), b. 25 July 1868; m. (at Marseilles) 3 Aug. 1905, Céline Celestine Raphael, da. of Paul A. d'Ondats of Hellette, Basse Pyrenees.
2e. Rev. James Trevor Matchett, M.A. (Camb.), Vicar of St. Michael-at-Thorn (2 *Wood Street, Norwich*), b. 15 Jan. 1871; m. 9 July 1907, Cicely Mary, da. of Albert Ketteringham of Norwich; and has issue 1f.
1f. Charles Paul Trevor Matchett, b. 24 Jan. 1909.
3e. Ethel Susan Matchett.
4e. Mabel Katharine Matchett, m. 10 Ap. 1901, Sidney Herbert Hayes, Tea Planter (*Lethenty Hatton, Ceylon*); and has issue 1f to 3f.
1f. Trevor Sidney Hayes, b. (in Ceylon) 21 May 1903.
2f. Herbert Leonard Hayes, b. (in Ceylon) 5 Sept. 1905.
3f. John Douglas Hayes, b. 22 May 1909.

3d. Maria Roberts (9 *West Cromwell Road, S.W.*), m. 15 Aug. 1861, Henry Vallings, d. 30 Sept. 1901; and has issue 1e to 3e.
1e. Henry Alan Vallings, Major 29th Punjabis, b. 24 Ap. 1866; m. 25 Nov. 1899, Gertrude, da. of (—) Whitchurch; and has issue 1f to 2f.
1f. Doris Gwendolen Vallings, b. (in India) 18 Jan. 1902.
2f. Gertrude Colleen Vallings, b. (in India) 7 Mar. 1907.
2e. Gertrude Maria Vallings.
3e. Gwynedd Maud Vallings, m. 7 June 1894, Walter Frerich Dunsterville (*Lushill, Stock, Essex*); and has issue 1f.
1f. Marie Iseult Dunsterville.

4d. Margaret Anne Roberts, *unm.*
5d. Louisa Roberts, m. 23 June 1863, Alexander Brooke (*Handford, Cheshire*); and has issue 1e to 8e.
1e. Alexander Trafford Brooke, Merchant (34 *Craven Hill Gardens, W.*), b. 14 May 1864, *unm.*
2e. Richard Hadden Brooke, J.P., Merchant (*Bombay*), b. 30 Mar. 1878, *unm.*
3e. Eleanor Mary Brooke, *unm.* [Nos. 625 to 655.

of The Blood Royal

4e. Louisa Beatrice Helen Brooke, m. 31 July 1890, Harcourt Augustine Francis Chambers, Accountant, Merchant Taylors Company (*Herongate, Brentwood*), s.p.

5e. Florence Brooke, m. 14 Oct. 1890, John Anderson (*Ceylon*); and has issue 1f to 5f.

    1f. Alexander Bruce Anderson, b. in Ceylon 25 Sept. 1899.
    2f. Elsie Florence Anderson, b. in Ceylon.
    3f. Hilda Eleanor Anderson, b. in Ceylon.
    4f. Margaret Doris Anderson, b. in Ceylon.
    5f. Janet Beatrice Anderson.

6e. Elsie Frances Brooke, m. (at Bombay) 7 Ap. 1903, Major Joseph George Hulbert, I.M.S. (see pp. 89–90); and has issue 1f.

    1f. Richard Carson Hulbert, b. (in India) 10 July 1907.

7e. Constance Brooke, m. 18 Ap. 1900, Thomas Todd (*Elmfield, Hartford, Cheshire*); and has issue 1f.

    1f. Dorothy Annie Todd, b. 24 Jan. 1907.

8e. Margaret Brooke, *unm.*

6d. Elizabeth Roberts, *unm.*

3c. *Anne Jones*, d. 8 Feb. 1884; m. 9 Oct. 1838, *her cousin, Thomas Longueville Longueville, formerly Jones of Penyllan*, d. 27 Oct. 1888; *and had issue.*

See p. 56, Nos. 476–481.

5b. *Harriette Jones*, b. 4 Dec. 1780; d. 17 Feb. 1846; m. 26 Feb. 1802, *Francis Edge Barker of Llyndir, co. Denbigh*, d. 10 June 1827; *and had issue (with 2 other sons and 2 das. who died unm.)* 1c to 4c.

1c. *Richard Barker of Chester and Llyndir, co. Denbigh*, b. 2 Sept. 1808; d. 20 Dec. 1877; m. 27 June 1833, *Sarah, da. of Henry Potts of Chester and Glanyrafon, co. Flint*, d. 12 Nov. 1881; *and had issue (with 2 other sons who died young)* 1d to 4d.

1d. *Francis Henry Barker of Llyndir*, b. 8 June 1834; d. 11 Mar. 1903; m. 14 Jan. 1858, *Elizabeth Anne, da. of John Henry Yates of Preston Brook, co. Chester*, d. 20 Dec. 1901; *and had issue (with an eldest son who d. unm.)* 1e to 8e.

1e. Harry Yates Barker (*Chester; Llyndir, co. Denbigh*), b. 1 Ap. 1861; m. 17 Ap. 1888, Amelia, da. of Benjamin Dodsworth of York; and has issue 1f to 2f.

    1f. Francis Brock Barker, b. 30 Mar. 1893.
    2f. Winefride Mary Barker, b. 5 July 1895.

2e. Ernest Longueville Barker, Bank Manager (*Dulverton, Somerset*), b. 17 July 1862; m. Oct. 1901, Grace Alice, da. of (—) McOstrich, of London.

3e. Walter Hugh Barker, Architect (*Plymouth*), b. 19 June 1865; m. 1 Aug. 1903, Lilian, da. of (—) Turner; and has issue 1f.

    1f. Edward Yates Barker, b. 18 Ap. 1905.

4e. Geoffrey Lionel Barker, Land Agent (*Newton Abbot, Devon*), b. 6 Nov. 1869; m. 20 Feb. 1908, Mabel Annie, da. of Thomas Rees; and has issue 1f.

    1f. Lionel Rees Barker, b. 28 June 1909.

5e. Francis Guy Barker (*Lower Whitcroft, Hereford*), b. 25 Aug. 1875; m. 16 Oct. 1907, Ethel, da. of Col. Carre Fulton, *late* Durham L.I.

6e. Ethel Barker, *unm.*

7e. Mabel Barker, m. 4 June 1903, George Henry Rogerson, Solicitor (*Chester*); and has issue 1f.

    1f. Elizabeth Mabel Rogerson, b. 16 July 1905.

8e. Maud Elizabeth Barker (*Southsea*), m. 8 Jan. 1895, Capt. Augustus Frederick Cooper, Royal Welsh Fusiliers, d. (—); and has issue 1f to 2f.

    1f. Frederick Augustus Cooper, b. 14 Jan. 1899.
    2f. Jane Cooper.

[Nos. 656 to 689.

The Plantagenet Roll

2d. Richard Longueville Barker, Land Agent (10 *Eaton Road, Chester; St. Werburgh Chambers, Chester*), b. 14 Mar. 1837; m. 1 Nov. 1860, Rosabel Charlotte, da. of the Rev. George Heywood, Rector of Ideford, Devon, d.s.p. 29 Jan. 1886.

3d. Frederick Barker, b. 28 *July* 1840; d. 4 *Dec.* 1908; m. 18 June 1872, *Phœbe Susannah*, da. of *Col. Vincent Williams, Royal Welsh Fusiliers;* and had issue (with a da. who died young) 1e to 4e.

1e. Philip Longueville Barker, I.C.S. (*Amritsar, Punjab*), b. 19 Dec. 1874; m. 24 Dec. 1900, Edith Agnes Frances Maria, da. of the Rev. Henry Atkinson Gibson, M.A.; and has issue 1f to 3f.

1f. Phœbe Sybil Barker.
2f. Gwynedd Mary Barker.
3f. Ursula Gladwyn Barker.

2e. Richard Vincent Barker, Royal Welsh Fusiliers, b. 13 June 1880, *unm.*

3e. Sybil Margaret Barker, m. 1st, Charles Frederick Balfour, I.C.S., d. 1907; 2ndly, 2 Sept. 1908, Major James Craik, Indian Cavalry; and has issue (with a da. who died young) 1f to 2f.

1f. Philip Maxwell Balfour, b. 10 Mar. 1898.
2f. Ronald Hugh Balfour, b. 6 Nov. 1901.

4e. Winifred Mary Barker, m. 1908, Nigel Fosberry.

4d. Henrietta Barker, m. 17 Ap. 1873, Hugo Rice-Wiggin, one of H.M.'s Inspectors of Schools (*Bourton-in-the-Water, Glos.*); and has issue 1e.

1e. Cecil Frances Sarah Rice-Wiggin.

2c. *Thomas Francis Barker*, b. 29 *Oct.* 1810; d. 25 *Ap.* 1878; m. 13 *Sept.* 1836, *Eliza Anne*, da. of (—) *Booth;* and had issue (with 3 other sons and a da. who d.s.p.) 1d to 5d.

1d. Henry Barker (*Chester*), b. 17 Nov. 1843; m. 12 Ap. 1887, Emily, widow of Col. Brownrigg, da. of (—) Tottenham, *s.p.*

2d. *Francis Barker*, b. 1 *June* 1844; d. 2 *Nov.* 1878; m. 14 *Oct.* 1874, *Elizabeth*, da. of (—) *Lord of Rawtenstall, co. Lanc.;* and had issue 1e.

1e. Ethel Barker, m. 19 Feb. 1903, John Howarth Massey (*Clitheroe*).

3d. Eliza Harriette Barker, *unm.*

4d. Annie Barker, m. 17 July 1867, Charles Edward Ashburner, *late* Indian Army; and has issue 1e to 4e.

1e. Charles Edward Ashburner.
2e. Lionel Ashburner.
3c. Arthur Ashburner.
4e. Violet Ashburner.

5d. Mary Barker, m. 8 Aug. 1877, James Henry Ewart, *late* Seaforth Highlanders (*The Lodge, Weston Underwood, Olney, Bucks*); and has issue 1e to 3e.

1e. John Murray Ewart, b. 23 Sept. 1884.
2e. James Alan Ewart, b. 16 Nov. 1887.
3e. Monica Mary Ewart, b. 4 Dec. 1885.

3c. *Harriette Barker*, b. 9 *Ap.* 1805; d. 27 *May* 1861; m. *the Rev. Francis Bryans*, d. 3 *May* 1877; and had issue 1d to 3d.

1d. *Rev. Francis Richard Bryans*, *formerly Rector of Greatham*, b. 2 *Feb.* 1835; d. 7 *Jan.* 1909; m. 18 *Oct.* 1864, *Anna Maria* [*descended from King Henry VII., &c.* (see Tudor Roll, p. 513)] (*Clevelands, Babbacombe, Torquay*), da. of *Gibbs Crawford Antrobus of Eaton Hall, co. Chester, J.P., D.L.* [*Bt. Coll.*]; and had issue 1e to 2e.

1e. Edith Anna Bryans.
2e. Bessie Bryans, m. 1901, S. Wood.

2d. Edward de Villars Bryans, b. 17 Sept. 1846, *unm.*

3d. Harriette Bryans, b. 4 Nov. 1836; d. 19 *May* 1906; m. 31 *Mar.* 1869, *Patrick Robertson Buchanan;* and had issue 1e.

1e. Nora Harriette Buchanan, b. 26 Nov. 1874.

[Nos. 690 to 717.

# of The Blood Royal

4c. Mary Anne Barker, b. 12 June 1812; d. 1 Oct. 1882; m. 21 Jan. 1834, Charles Townshend [7th son of John Stanislaus Townshend of Trevallyn, co. Denbigh, J.P.], d. 24 July 1893; and had issue 1d to 2d.

1d. Harriette Dorothea Townshend, b. 29 Nov. 1836; d. 27 Mar. 1878; m. 5 July 1859, the Rev. Latham Wickham [son of Archdeacon Wickham], d. 3 Sept. 1901; and had issue 1e to 6e.

1e. Robert Townshend Wickham (Chester), b. 28 Ap. 1860; m. 22 Feb. 1898, Elinor [a descendant of the Lady Anne, sister of King Edward IV. (see the Exeter Volume, p. 378)], da. of James George Edwards of Broughton, co. Hants; and has issue 1f to 3f.

1f. Lance Townshend Wickham, b. 15 July 1902.
2f. Robert George Wickham, b. 14 June 1905.
3f. Hugh Charles Wickham, b. 23 Ap. 1908.

2e. Charles Townshend Wickham (Twyford School, Winchester), b. 11 June 1862; m. 8 Ap. 1891, Flora Millicent, da. of Col. William Parker of Hanthorpe Hall, Bourne, co. Linc.

3e. Harry Townshend Wickham (The Close, Newport-Pagnell, Bucks), b. 5 Jan. 1866; m. 20 Ap. 1893, Elizabeth Caroline, da. of W. Soutar of Dundee.

4e. John Herbert Townshend Wickham (Westwood, Wanganui, New Zealand), b. 10 Oct. 1868; m. 14 Ap. 1898, Jessica Clarice, da. of George Buckland Worgan of Wanganui; and has issue 1f.

1f. Philip Latham Wickham, b. at Wanganui 1 June 1904.

5e. Dorothea Gladwyn Wickham, m. 2 July 1885, George William Palmer, formerly of Greenwood, co. Hants (Wanganui, New Zealand); and has issue 1f to 4f.

1f. George Palmer, b. 21 June 1888.
2f. Harry Mark Palmer, b. 21 Oct. 1889.
3f. Frederick Ralph Palmer, b. 7 Jan. 1891.
4f. Richard Hugh Palmer, b. 13 Ap. 1893.

6e. Susan Harriette Latham Wickham, m. Sept. 1906, the Rev. Ernest Henry St. Aubyn Trenow, Curate of All Saints, Leamington Spa.

2d. Susan Marian Townshend, m. 10 Nov. 1864, Hugh Robert Hughes of Ystrad, co. Denbigh, d. 8 Feb. 1895; and has issue (with a da. who died young) 1e to 5e.

1e. Marian Margaret Hughes, m. 30 Ap. 1900, the Rev. Edward James Davies, B.A., Rector of Nantglyn (Nantglyn Rectory, Denbigh); and has issue 1f to 3f.

1f. Hugh Edward Townshend Davies, b. 9 Ap. 1907.
2f. Marian Margaret Davies, b. 22 July 1901.
3f. Katharine Mildred Davies, b. 7 Dec. 1903.

2e. Susan Gladwyn Hughes, m. 30 Ap. 1895, Guy Francis, Solicitor (Denbigh).
3e. Katherina Christina Hughes, unm.
4e. Muriel Hester Hughes, unm.
5e. Vera Hughes, m. M. Guy Thompson (The Old Bank, Oxford).

6b. Maria Jones, b. 17 Ap. 1782; d. (at Hamburg) 7 Dec. 1816; m. as 1st wife (at Llanraidr) 23 Aug. 1802, Thomas Lowndes, d. 4 May 1836; and had issue (with 2 sons and a da. who d.s.p.) 1c.

1c. Maria Lowndes, b. 20 Jan. 1811; d. 1 Dec. 1877; m. 1842, her cousin, Thomas John Lowndes, d. 2 Dec. 1855; and had issue 1d to 4d.

1d. Hugh Lowndes, b. 12 Jan. 1843; d. 8 Ap. 1907; m. 1st (at West Derby Parish Church), 2 June 1870, Lydia Jane, da. of William Kenney Tyrer, d. (–); 2ndly (at Chester), 22 Oct. 1901, Amy, widow of Frederick Eaton, da. of G. S. Chapman of Manchester and Monte Video; and had issue (with 2 das. who d. in infancy) 1e to 2e.

1e. Amy Frances Lowndes, m. (at West Kirby) 8 Oct. 1902, Walter MacIver; and has issue 1f to 2f.

1f. Peter Græme MacIver.
2f. Eleanor Audrey Græme MacIver.   [Nos. 718 to 743.

The Plantagenet Roll

2e. Ella Constance Lowndes, m. (at Gresford) 21 Ap. 1896, James Allan Macfie; and has issue 1f.

1f. Ellaline Lydia Joan Macfie.

2d. Thomas Lowndes, b. (—); m. 1900, C. M. E., da. of (—) Devey.

3d. Jane, called Lilly, Lowndes, b. in New Zealand.

4d. Maria Lowndes. [Nos. 744 to 748.

9. Descendants, if any, of CHARLOTTE THEOPHILA DIGBY (Table II.), d. 17 Mar. 1693; m. the Rev. RICHARD MOSTYN of Pedbedw, d. 1735.[1]

10. Descendants of HUGH (PERCY), 2nd DUKE OF NORTHUMBERLAND [G.B.], K.G. (Table III.), b. 14 Aug. 1742; d. 10 July 1817; m. 2ndly, 23 May 1779, FRANCES JULIA, da. of Peter BURRELL of Beckenham, co. Kent., d. 28 Ap. 1820; and had issue 1a to 3a.

1a. Hugh (Percy), 3rd Duke of Northumberland [G.B.], K.G., b. 20 Ap. 1785; d.s.p. 11 Feb. 1847.

2a. Algernon (Percy), 4th Duke of Northumberland [G.B.], K.G., P.C., b. 15 Dec. 1792; d.s.p. 12 Feb. 1865.

3a. Lady Emily Percy, b. 7 Jan. 1789; d. 20 June 1844; m. 19 May 1810, James (Murray), 1st Baron Glenlyon [U.K.], K.H. [2nd son but in his issue (14 Sept. 1846) heir of the 4th Duke of Atholl [S.], K.T.], d. 12 Oct. 1837; and had issue 1b to 2b.

1b. George Augustus Frederick John (Murray), 6th Duke of Atholl [S.], 3rd Earl of Strange [G.B.], 10th Baron Strange [E.], 2nd Baron Glenlyon [U.K.], &c., &c., K.T., b. 20 Sept. 1814; d. 16 Jan. 1864; m. 29 Oct. 1839, Anne, V.A., da. of Henry Home Drummond of Blair Drummond, co. Perth, d. 18 May 1897; and had issue 1c.

1c. John James Hugh Henry (Stewart-Murray), 7th Duke of Atholl [S.], 4th Earl Strange [G.B.], 11th Baron Strange [E.] and 3rd Baron Glenlyon [U.K.], &c., also 6th Baron Percy [G.B.], K.T. (Blair Castle, Blair Atholl, Perthshire; Dunkeld House, Dunkeld; 84 Eaton Place, S.W.), b. 6 Aug. 1840; m. 29 Oct. 1863, Louisa, da. of Sir Thomas Moncreiffe, 7th Bt. [S.], d. 8 July 1902; and has issue 1d to 6d.

1d. John George Stewart-Murray, Marquis of Tullibardine, M.V.O., D.S.O., Capt. and Brevet-Major Royal Horse Guards and Col. Comdt. Scottish Horse Yeo. (Marlborough, &c.), b. 15 Dec. 1871; m. 20 July 1899, Katharine Marjory, da. of Sir James Henry Ramsay, 10th Bt. [S.].

2d. Lord George Stewart-Murray, Capt. 1st Batt. Black Watch, b. 17 Feb. 1873.

3d. Lord James Thomas Stewart-Murray, Lieut. Queen's Own Cameron Highlanders, b. 18 Aug. 1879.

4d. Lady Dorothea Louisa Stewart-Murray, m. 5 Feb. 1895, Lieut.-Col. Harold Goodeve Ruggles-Brise, Grenadier Guards.

5d. Lady Helen Stewart-Murray.

6d. Lady Evelyn Stewart-Murray.

2b. Lord James Charles Plantagenet Murray, b. 8 Dec. 1819; d. 3 June 1874; m. 6 Nov. 1851, Elizabeth Marjory, da. of George Fairholme of Greenknow, co. Berwick [by his wife the Hon. Caroline Elizabeth, née Forbes], d. 11 Oct. 1888; and had issue 1c.

1c. Caroline Frances Murray (8 Royal Crescent, Bath). [Nos. 749 to 756.

---

[1] The Topographer, London, 1790, ii. 212.

# of The Blood Royal

11. Descendants of ALGERNON (PERCY), 1st EARL OF BEVERLEY [G.B.] (Table III.), b. 21 Jan. 1750; d. 21 Oct. 1830; m. 8 June 1775, ISABELLA SUSANNAH, da. of Peter BURRELL of Beckenham, co. Kent. d. 24 Jan. 1812; and had issue 1a to 5a.

1a. *George (Percy), 2nd Earl of Beverley and* (1865) *5th Duke of Northumberland* [G.B.], b. 22 *June* 1778; d. 22 *Aug.* 1867; m. 22 *June* 1801, *Louisa Harcourt, da. of the Hon. James Archibald Stuart-Wortley,* d. 30 *June* 1848; *and had issue* 1b *to* 3b.

1b. *Algernon George (Percy), 6th Duke of Northumberland* [G.B.], *&c., K.G., P.C.,* b. 2 *May* 1810; d. 2 *Jan.* 1899; m. 26 *May* 1845, *Louisa, da. and h. of Henry Drummond, M.P.* [*E. of Perth Coll.*], d. 18 *Dec.* 1890; *and had issue* 1c *to* 2c.

1c. Henry George (Percy), 7th Duke of Northumberland, &c. [G.B.] and 11th Bt. [E.], K.G., P.C., D.C.L., LL.D., *formerly* Treasurer of H.M. Queen Victoria's Household (*Alnwick Castle, Northumberland; Albury Park, Guildford;* 2 *Grosvenor Place, W.; Carlton, &c.*), b. 29 May 1846; m. 23 Dec. 1868, Lady Edith, da. of George Douglas (Campbell), 8th Duke of Argyll [S.], K.G., K.T.; and has issue 1d to 9d.

1d. Henry Algernon George, Earl Percy, M.P., *formerly* Under-Sec. of State for Foreign Affairs, &c. (64 *Curzon Street, W.; Carlton*), b. 21 Jan. 1871.

2d. Lord Alan Ian Percy, Capt. Grenadier Guards, b. 17 Ap. 1880.

3d. Lord William Richard Percy, Barrister I.T., b. 17 May 1882.

4d. Lord Eustace Sutherland Campbell Percy, b. 21 Mar. 1887.

5d. Lady Edith Eleanor Percy.

6d. Lady Margaret Percy.

7d. Lady Victoria Alexandrina Percy.

8d. Lady Mary Percy.

9d. Lady Muriel Evelyn Nora Percy.

2c. Lord Algernon Malcolm Arthur Percy, J.P., D.L., a Mil. A.D.C. to H.M. the King and Col. Comdg. 3rd Batt. Northumberland Fusiliers (*Guy's Cliffe, Warwick*), b. 2 Oct. 1851; m. 3 Aug. 1880, Lady Victoria Frederica Caroline, da. of William Henry (Edgcumbe), 4th Earl of Mount Edgcumbe [G.B.], P.C., G.C.V.O.; and has issue 1d to 2d.

1d. Algernon William Percy, J.P., Lieut. 3rd Batt. Northumberland Fusiliers (*Travellers'; Bath, &c.*), b. 29 Nov. 1884.

2d. Katharine Louisa Victoria Percy, m. 15 Sept. 1904, Josceline Reginald Heber-Percy (see p. 68) (*Chesford Grange, Kenilworth*); and has issue 1e to 2e.

1e. David Josceline Algernon Heber-Percy, b. 10 June 1909.

2e. Mary Katharine Victoria Heber-Percy.

2b. *Lord Josceline William Percy,* b. 17 *July* 1811; d. 25 *July* 1881; m. 8 *Aug.* 1848, *Margaret, widow of the Right Hon. Sir Robert Grant, P.C., M.P., da. of Sir David Davidson of Cantry; and had issue* 1c.

1c. George Algernon Percy, *formerly* Lieut.-Col. Grenadier Guards, b. 17 May 1849.

3b. *Lady Margaret Percy,* b. 16 *May* 1813; d. 15 *Oct.* 1897; m. 23 *Sept.* 1841, *Edward Richard (Littleton), 2nd Baron Hatherton* [U.K.], d. 3 *Ap.* 1888; *and had issue.*

See the Tudor Roll, pp. 187-188, Nos. 20969-20996; also the Essex Volume, pp. 241-242, Nos. 30328-30364.

2a. *Right Rev. the Lord Hugh Percy, D.D., Lord Bishop of Carlisle,* b. 29 *Jan.* 1784; d. 5 *Feb.* 1856; m. 1*st,* 19 *May* 1806, *Mary, da. of the Most Rev. Charles Manners-Sutton, Archbishop of Canterbury* [*D. of Rutland Coll. and a descendant of Anne (Plantagenet), Duchess of Exeter*], d. 4 *Sept.* 1831; *and had issue* 1b *to* 7b.

[Nos. 757 to 809.

The Plantagenet Roll

1b. *Algernon Charles Percy, afterwards* (R.L. 4 Feb. 1847) *Heber-Percy of Hodnet Hall, co. Salop, and Airmyn Hall, co. York, J.P.*, b. 29 *June* 1812; d. 24 *Jan.* 1901; m. 29 *July* 1839, Emily [*descended paternally from Isabel* (*Plantagenet*), *Countess of Essex, and maternally from George* (*Plantagenet*), *Duke of Clarence, K.G., and his sister Anne, Duchess of Exeter*], da. and h. *of the Right Rev. Reginald Heber, Lord Bishop of Calcutta*, d. 8 *Nov.* 1902; *and had issue* 1c to 11c.

1c. Algernon Heber-Percy of Hodnet and Airmyn, J.P., D.L., C.A., and High Sheriff (1908) co. Salop, Capt. and Hon. Major Shropshire Yeo. Cav. and 2nd Vol. Batt. Shropshire L.I., *formerly* Lieut. R.N. (*Hodnet Hall, Salop; Airmyn Hall, Goole, Yorks; Carlton, &c.*), b. 23 Feb. 1845; m. 25 Jan. 1867, Alice Charlotte Mary, da. and h. of the Rev. Frederick Vernon Lockwood [by his wife Mary Isabella, *née* Percy, descended also from King Henry VII., Anne (Plantagenet), Duchess of Exeter, &c.]; and has issue 1d to 2d.

1d. Algernon Hugh Heber-Percy, *formerly* Lieut. Shropshire Yeo. Cav., b. 13 July 1869; m. 15 July 1903, Gladys May, da. of William Edward Montagu Hulton-Harrop of Lythwood Hall, Shrewsbury; and has issue 1e to 3e.

1e. Algernon George William Heber-Percy, b. 27 Ap. 1904.

2e. Cyril Hugh Reginald Heber Percy, b. 18 Dec. 1905.

3e. Alan Charles Heber-Percy, b. 4 May 1907.

2d. Josceline Reginald Heber-Percy (*Chesford Grange, Kenilworth, Warwick*), b. 2 Sept. 1880; m. 15 Sept. 1904, Katharine Louisa Victoria, da. of Lord Algernon Percy (see above); and has issue.

See p. 67, Nos. 770-771.

2c. Reginald Josceline Heber-Percy, Lieut.-Col. *late* 4th Batt. Rifle Brigade (*Chineham, Basingstoke*), b. 2 May 1849; m. 28 Nov. 1894, Gundreda, da. of Hardy Eustace of Castlemore, co. Carlow.

3c. Hugh Louis Heber-Percy, F.R.G.S. (*Ferney Hall, Onibury, Salop*), b. 7 Jan. 1853; m. 10 June 1899, Harriet, da. of Henry S. Earp of Dunstall, Wolverhampton.

4c. Rev. Henry Vernon Heber-Percy, M.A. (Camb.), Rector of Leasingham (*Leasingham Rectory, Sleaford*), b. 16 Ap. 1858; m. 5 Oct. 1886, Judith Elizabeth, da. of Sir Vincent Rowland Corbet, 3rd Bt. [U.K.]; and has issue 1d to 5d.

1d. Neville Henry Heber-Percy, b. 6 Feb. 1890.

2d. Hermione Constance Heber-Percy.

3d. Aleen Judith Heber-Percy.

4d. Rachel Joan Heber-Percy.

5d. Hilda Bridget Heber-Percy.

5c. Alan William Heber-Percy, J.P. (*Durweston, Blandford*), b. 27 Mar. 1865; m. 8 Aug. 1893, the Hon. Susan Alice, da. of William Henry Berkeley (Portman), 2nd Viscount Portman [U.K.]; and has issue 1d to 6d.

1d. Hugh Alan Heber-Percy, b. 5 Dec. 1897.

2d. Bryan Heber-Percy, b. 29 Nov. 1903.

3d. Peter Heber-Percy, b. 3 Nov. 1908.

4d. Margaret Eleanor Heber-Percy.

5d. Ida Mary Heber-Percy.

6d. Constance Emily Heber-Percy.

6c. Ethel Cecilia Heber-Percy, m. 7 June 1870, the Hon. Alexander Frederic Hood (see p. 143) [V. Hood Coll.] (*Airmyn Hall, Goole, Yorks*); and has issue.
See the Tudor Roll, p. 188, Nos. 21015-21019.

7c. Agnes Katherine Heber-Percy.

8c. Maude Ellen Heber-Percy, m. 12 Aug. 1880, Col. Sir Edward Law Durand, 1st Bart. [U.K.], C.B. (35 *Ennismore Gardens, S.W.*); and has issue.
See the Tudor Roll, p. 188, Nos. 21022-21028. [Nos. 810 to 847.

# of The Blood Royal

9c. Gertrude Amelia Heber-Percy, m. 5 Sept. 1895, John James Hardy Rowland Eustace (*Castlemore, co. Carlow*); and has issue.
See the Tudor Roll, p. 189, Nos. 21030-21033.

10c. Evelyn Mary Heber-Percy, m. 16 July 1889, Francis Monckton (*Stretton Hall, Stafford; Somerford Hall, Brewood*); and has issue.
See the Tudor Roll, p. 189, Nos. 21035-21040.

11c. Isabel Harriet Heber-Percy, m. 2 Sept. 1891, Andrew Greville Rouse-Boughton-Knight, J.P. [Bt. of Lawford (E. 1641) and of Downton (G.B. 1791) Coll.] (38 *Norfolk Square, Hyde Park, W.; Wormesley Grange, Hereford*); and has issue.
See the Tudor Roll, p. 189, Nos. 21042-21044.

2b. Rev. Henry Percy, Rector of Greystoke, Canon of Carlisle, b. 5 *June* 1813; d. 6 *Sept.* 1870; m. 1 Feb. 1841, *Emma Barbara*, da. of Capt. Benjamin Baker Galbraith of Olderigg, Queen's Co., d. Nov. 1877; *and had issue* 1c *to* 5c.

1c. *Alfred Percy*, b. 5 May 1850; d. 20 Aug. 1907; m. 2ndly, 14 Feb. 1899, *Mary (Burlington Street, North Walkerville, South Australia*), da. of James Hyland; and had issue 1d to 2d.

1d. Henry Percy, b. 13 Ap. 1901.
2d. Mary Percy.

2c. Edward Galbraith Henry Percy, b. 1854.

3c. Josceline Hugh Percy, *formerly* Capt. 1st Vol. Brig. W. Div. R.A. (49 *Talbot Road, Highgate, N.*), b. July 1856; m. 12 Oct. 1892, Grace Anne, da. of Edward Percy Thompson (see p. 70); and has issue 1d to 4d.

1d. Henry Edward Percy, b. 6 Aug. 1893.
2d. Josceline Richard Percy, b. 1894.
3d. Margaret Percy.
4d. Constance Percy.

4c. Elizabeth Mary Percy, m. 25 May 1871, the Rev. John Adams, *formerly* Vicar of Offchurch (3 *Reddington Road, Hampstead*); and has issue 1d to 6d.

1d. Rev. Henry Theophilus Adams, Vicar of Newbold Pacey (*Newbold Pacey Vicarage, Warwick*), b. 1872; m. 1900, May, da. of Charles Chapman of Carlecotes Hall, York; and has issue 1e to 3e.

1e. John Simon Leslie Adams, b. 1901.
2e. Hugh Adams, b. 1906.
3e. Isabel Adams.

2d. John Cadwallader Adams, *formerly* Lieut. R.M.L.I. (*Junior Naval and Military*), b. 1873.

3d. Hugh Geoffrey Coker Adams, b. 1880; m. and has issue a da.
4d. Edward Josceline Percy Adams, b. 1888.
5d. Elsie Emma Mary Adams, m. 1898, Thomas Owen Lloyd (*The Priory, Warwick*); and has issue.

6d. Kathleen Alice Georgina Adams, m. 1905, Fulwar Estoteville Skipwith, Lieut. Bombay, Baroda, and Central India Railway Vol. [Bt. of Prestwould (1622) Coll.]; and has issue 1e to 2e.

1e. Grey Henry Skipwith, b. 1908.
2e. Elizabeth Kathleen Skipwith.

5c. Emma Annie Isabel Percy, m. 16 Ap. 1884, Herbert Cranstoun Adams, *formerly* Lieut.-Col. 1st Devonshire R.G.A. (Vol.), V.D. (*Exmouth*); and has issue 1d to 6d.

1d. Henry Launcelot Elford Adams, b. 4 Mar. 1885.
2d. John Percy Fitzherbert Adams, b. 16 Ap. 1891. [Nos. 848 to 886.

The Plantagenet Roll

3d. Alan St. George Adams, b. 23 Ap. 1894.
4d. Alice Barbara Adams.
5d. Margaret Hyale Adams.
6d. Norah Roberta Adams.

3b. Hugh Josceline Percy of Eskrigg, co. Cumberland, J.P., D.L., b. 9 Dec. 1817; d. 9 Feb. 1882; m. 24 Oct. 1859, Anne, da. of Joseph Story, d. 25 Mar. 1904; and had issue 1c to 2c.

1c. Edward Josceline Percy (Eskrigg, Wigton, Cumberland), b. 30 Nov. 1864; m. 23 Jan. 1907, Nellie, da. of John Jarvie.

2c. Agnes Ellen Josceline Percy, m. 6 Sept. 1888, Frederic George Mather; and has issue 1d to 2d.

1d. Marjorie Helen Mather.
2d. Phyllis Mather.

4b. Mary Isabella Percy, b. 18 Feb. 1808; d. Mar. 1878; m. 21 July 1840, the Rev. Frederick Vernon Lockwood, Preb. of Canterbury, d. 1 July 1851; and has issue.

See the Tudor Roll, p. 190, Nos. 21073–21075.

5b. Lucy Percy, b. 28 Ap. 1811; d. Jan. 1887; m. 13 Feb. 1832, Henry William Askew of Glenridding and Conishead Priory, d. 1890; and had issue.

See the Tudor Roll, p. 190, Nos. 21076–21093.

6b. Gertrude Percy, b. 30 Aug. 1814; d. 27 Ap. 1890; m. 12 July 1834, William Pitt (Amherst), 2nd Earl [U.K.] and 3rd Baron [G.B.] Amherst, d. 26 Mar. 1886; and had issue.

See the Tudor Roll, pp. 190–191, Nos. 21094–21113.

7b. Ellen Percy, b. 7 Nov. 1815; d. 1899; m. 5 Ap. 1836, the Rev. Edward Thompson, d. 3 Ap. 1838; and had issue.

See the Tudor Roll, p. 191, Nos. 21114–21121.

3a. Lord Josceline Percy, C.B., Vice-Admiral R.N., b. (twin) 29 Jan. 1784; d. 19 Oct. 1856; m. 9 Dec. 1820, Sophia Elizabeth, da. of Moreton Walhouse of Hatherton, co. Stafford, d. 13 Dec. 1875; and had issue 1b to 3b.

1b. Sophia Louisa Percy, b. 24 Dec. 1821; d. 7 Nov. 1908; m. 7 July 1846, Col. Charles Bagot [B. Bagot Coll.], d. 20 Feb. 1881; and had issue.

See the Tudor Roll, pp. 191–192, Nos. 21123–21129.

2b. Emily Percy, m. 17 July 1852, Gen. Sir Charles Lawrence D'Aguilar, G.C.B. (4 Clifton Crescent, Folkestone); and has issue 1c.

1c. Emily Gertrude D'Aguilar.

3b. Charlotte Alice Percy, m. 13 Ap. 1858, Edward Percy Thompson (16 St. Andrew's Road, Southsea); and has issue 1c to 5c.

1c. Henry Thompson, Lieut. R.N., b. 1864.
2c. Alexander Maurice Thompson, b. 1869.
3c. Grace Anne Thompson, m. 12 Oct. 1892, Capt. Josceline Hugh Percy (49 Talbot Road, Highbury, N.); and has issue.

See p. 69, Nos. 896–899.

4c. Gertrude Thompson.
5c. Constance Thompson.

4a. Lady Charlotte Percy, b. 3 June 1776; d. 26 Nov. 1862; m. as 2nd wife, 25 July 1795, George (Ashburnham), 3rd Earl of Ashburnham [G.B.], K.G., d. 27 Oct. 1830; and had issue.

See the Tudor Roll, pp. 192–94, Nos. 21141–21184.

5a. Lady Emily Charlotte Percy, b. 9 Nov. 1786; d. 22 May 1877; m. 25 July 1808, Andrew Mortimer Drummond [E. of Perth Coll.], d. 1 June 1864; and had issue.

See the Tudor Roll, pp. 194–195, Nos. 21185–21229.   [Nos. 887 to 1051.

of The Blood Royal

12. Descendants of Lady KATHERINE SEYMOUR (Table III.), *d.* 9 Ap. 1791; *m.* as 1st wife, 15(21) July 1708, Sir WILLIAM WYNDHAM of Orchard Wyndham, 3rd Bart. [E.], *b. c.* 1687; *d.* 17 July 1740; and had issue.
   See the Tudor Roll, Table L., &c., and pp. 263–292, Nos. 24402–25349.
   [Nos. 1052 to 1999.

13. Descendants of Lady ELIZABETH PERCY (Table III.), *b.* 1 Dec. 1636; *d.* 5 Feb. 1717; *m.* 19 May 1653, ARTHUR (CAPEL), 1st EARL OF ESSEX [E.], *d.* 13 July 1683; and had issue.
   See the Exeter Volume, Table XXVII., and pp. 374–386, Nos. 26747–28169.
   [Nos. 2000 to 3422.

14. Descendants of Lady DOROTHY PERCY (Table III.), *bapt.* 20 Aug. 1598; *d.* 19 Aug. 1650; *m. c.* Jan. 1615, ROBERT (SYDNEY), 2nd EARL OF LEICESTER [E.], K.B., *b.* 1 Dec. 1595; *d.* 2 Nov. 1677; and had issue.
   See the Essex Volume, Table VI., and pp. 88–102, Nos. 9363–13712.
   [Nos. 3423 to 7772.

15. Descendants of WILLIAM (HERBERT), 1st [DUKE and] MARQUIS OF POWIS [E.], K.G. (Table III.), *b. c.* 1617; *d.* 2 June 1696; *m.* 2 Aug. 1654, Lady ELIZABETH, da. of Edward (SOMERSET), 2nd Marquis of Worcester [E.], *d.* Mar. 1692; and had issue.
   See the Clarence Volume, Table XXXV., and pp. 382–392, Nos. 14421–15000.
   [Nos. 7773 to 8352.

16. Descendants, if any, of the Hon. KATHERINE HERBERT (Table III.), *d.* (–); *m.* 1st, Sir ROBERT VAUGHAN of Llwydiarth and Llangedwyn, co. Montgomery; 2ndly, Sir JAMES PALMER of Dorney Court, co. Bucks; and had (with possibly other issue by 2nd husband) 1*a*.[1]

   1*a. Eleanor Vaughan, da. and eventual h.*, d. (–); m. *John Purcell of Nantcribba, co. Montgomery, M.P., J.P., living* 1662; *and had issue* 1b *to* 2b.
   1*b. Mary Purcell, da. and co-h.*, d. (–); m. 1672, *Edward Vaughan of Glanllyn; and had issue* 1c.
   1*c. Anne Vaughan of Llydiarth and Llangedwyn,* d.s.p.s. 14 *Mar.* 1748; m. *as* 1st *wife, Sir Watkin Williams-Wyn,* 3rd *Bart.* [E.], *M.P.*; d. 23 *Sept.* 1749.
   2*b. Catherine Purcell,* d. (–); m. *Sir John Copley.*

17. Descendants of Sir HENRY SLINGSBY, 1st Bart. [E.] (Table IV.), *b.* 14 Jan. 1602; *d.*, being judicially murdered on Tower Hill, 8 June 1658; *m.* 7 July 1631, the Hon. BARBARA, da. of Thomas (BELASYE), 1st Viscount Fauconberg[1] [E.], *bapt.* 11 Oct. 1609; *d.* 31 Dec. 1641; and had issue.
   See the Exeter Volume, Table LXII., and pp. 645–657, Nos. 55517–56278.
   [Nos. 8353 to 9114.

---

[1] Lloyd's "Sheriffs of Montgomeryshire," pp. 225, 489.

The Plantagenet Roll

18. Descendants, if any surviving, of ELIZABETH METCALFE (Table IV.), b. 1647, being aged 18 in 1665, and then unm.; d. (−); m. JOHN LODGE; and had issue 1a to 2a.

1a. *John Lodge of Ripon*, d. 1789; m. 1755, Elizabeth, da. of Matthew Ellerton of London; and had issue 1b to 3b.
1b. *John Lodge*, d. (? s.p.) 1801; m. Margaret, da. of the Rev. Richard Owen of Bodsilin, co. Carmarthen.
2b. *Francis Lodge*, d. (? s.p.) 1826.
3b. *Adam Lodge*, d. 5 Ap. 1837; m. Mary, da. of the Rev. Richard Owen of Bodsilin afsd.; and had issue (with a son, Richard Owen, d. young) 1c to 3c.
1c. *John Lodge, afterwards Ellerton, of Bodsilin*, d. (? s.p.); m. 24 Aug. 1837, Lady Henrietta Barbara [descended from the Lady Anne Plantagenet (see the Exeter Volume, p. 633), widow of the Rev. Frederick Manners-Sutton, da. of John (Lumley-Savile), 7th Earl of Scarborough [E.], d. 27 July 1864.
2c. *Adam Lodge, Bar.-at-Law, M.T.*, d. (? s.p.).
3c. *Mary Catherine Lodge*, d. (? s.p.); m. T. G. Hindle of Woodfold Park, co. Lanc.

2a. *Francis Lodge*, m. (——).

19. Descendants of THOMAS ROBINSON of York, Turkey Merchant (Table VI.), bur. 16 July 1678; m. 31 Dec. 1654, ELIZABETH, da. of Charles TANCRED of Arden, co. York, bur. 15 May 1664; and had issue 1a to 3a.

1a. *Sir William Robinson of Newby, 1st Bt.* [G.B.], M.P., b. c. 1656; d. 22 Dec. 1736; m. 8 Sept. 1679, Mary, da. of George Aislabie of Studley Royal, co. York; and had issue 1b to 4b.
1b. *Sir Metcalfe Robinson, 2nd Bt.* [G.B.], b. c. 1683; d. unm. 26 Dec. 1736.
2b. *Sir Tancred Robinson, 3rd Bt.* [G.B.], Rear-Admiral R.N., b. c. 1685; d. 3 Sept. 1754; m. again 1713, Mary (see p. 73), da. of Rowland Norton of Dishforth, bur. 26 July 1748; and had issue 1c to 4c.
1c. *Sir William Robinson, 4th Bt.* [G.B.], b. 1713; d.s.p. 4 Mar. 1770.
2c. *Sir Norton Robinson, 5th Bt.* [G.B.], b. 1715; d. unm. Feb. 1792.
3c. *Mary Robinson*, b. c. 1716; d. 4 Ap. 1790; m. Thomas Peirse (or Pierce) of Pierseborough, co. York.
4c. *Margaret Robinson*.

3b. *Thomas (Robinson), 1st Baron Grantham* [G.B.], P.C., K.B., one of the Regents of the Realm, 1755, &c., b. c. 1693; d. 30 Sept. 1770; m. 13 July 1737, Frances [a descendant of the Lady Anne, sister of King Edward IV., &c.], da. of Thomas Worsley of Hovingham, co. York, bur. 6 Nov. 1750; and had issue. See the Exeter Volume, pp. 642-643, Nos. 54166-54395.

4b. *Anne Robinson*, d. 15 Jan. 1768; m. as 2nd wife, Thomas Worsley of Hovingham, co. York, b. 16 Nov. 1686; bur. 2 Mar. 1750; and had issue 1c.
1c. *Anne Worsley*, d. 1765; m. in or before 1756, William Bastard of Kitley, co. Devon, who was gazetted a Baronet [G.B.], 4 or 24 Sept. 1779, but took no steps to obtain the Patent,[2] b. 1 Sept. 1727; d. 1782; and had issue 1d to 2d.
1d. *John Pollexfen Bastard of Kitley*, M.P., Col. Devon Militia, d.s.p. (at Leghorn) 4 Ap. 1816. [Nos. 9115 to 9344.

---

[1] Burke's "Royal Descents and Pedigrees of Founder's Kin," p. 75, and Foster's "Yorkshire Pedigrees," under Metcalfe.
[2] See G. E. C.'s "Complete Baronetage."

of The Blood Royal

2d. *Edmund Bastard of Kitley, M.P., Lieut.-Col. Devon Militia,* b. 7 *Feb.* 1758; d. *(at Sharpham) June* 1816; m. *Jane, da. and h. of Capt. Philemon Pownall of Sharpham, co. Devon,* d. *(at Exmouth)* 7 *Mar.* 1822; *and had issue* 1e *to* 3e.

1e. *Edmund Pollexfen Bastard of Kitley, M.P.,* b. 12 *July* 1784; d. 8 *June* 1838; m. 22 *Jan.* 1824, *the Hon. Anne Jane, da. of George (Rodney),* 2nd *Baron Rodney* [G.B.], d. 25 *Ap.* 1833; *and had issue.*
See the Clarence Volume, pp. 202–203, Nos. 3998–4019.

2e. *John Bastard of Sharpham, M.P., Capt. R.N.,* b. 1787; d. 11 *Jan.* 1835; m. 7 *Oct.* 1817, *Frances, da. and co-h. of Benjamin Wade of the Grange, co. York,* d. 23 *May* 1870; *and had issue (with* 2 *sons who d.s.p.)* 1f *to* 2f.

1f. *John Pownall Bastard of Sharpham, a Capt. in the Army,* b. *June* 1818; d. 14 *Nov.* 1886; m. 10 *Nov.* 1841, *Anne Esther, da. of Jacob L. Ricardo,* d. 14 *June* 1889; *and had issue (with an elder son who died young)* 1g *to* 2g.

1g. *John Algernon Bastard,* b. *Oct.* 1844; d. 20 *Nov.* 1908; m. 2 *Sept.* 1879, *Olivia Gertrude Louisa, da. of Gen. E. S. Claremont, C.B.; and had issue* 1h *to* 2h.

1h. Reginald Bastard, Lincolnshire Regt., *b.* 2 Oct. 1880.

2h. Violet Lilian Bastard, *b.* 13 Mar. 1884.

2g. Emmeline Laura Bastard, *m.* 1st, as 2nd wife, 26 June 1873, Horace (Pitt), 6th Baron Rivers [U.K.], *d.s.p.* 31 Mar. 1880; 2ndly, 2 July 1881, Montague George Thorold, *late* R.N. [second son of Sir John Charles Thorold, 11th Bt. (see p. 310)] (*Honington Hall, Grantham; 1 Abbot's Court, Kensington Square, W.*).

2f. *Frances Bastard, V.A., Bedchamber-Woman to Queen Victoria,* d. 11 *Ap.* 1902; m. 2 *July* 1850, *William Frederick Waldegrave, Viscount Chewton [s. and h. of 8th Earl Waldegrave* [G.B.], *C.B.*], d. *of wounds received at the Alma,* 7 *Oct.* 1854; *and had issue.*
See the Exeter Volume, p. 179, Nos. 6402–6413.

3e. *Rev. Philemon Pownall Bastard,* d. (?*s.p.*); m. *Mary, da. of Mr. Justice Park.*

2a. *Tancred Robinson, M.D., second son in* 1665; d. (-); m. *Alathea, da. of (——) Morley; and had issue* 1b.

1b. *William Robinson,* d. (-); m. *Dorothy, da. of Dr. Cook of Derby.*[1]

3a. *Margaret Robinson,* d. (-); m. *Rowland Norton of Dishforth, co. York,* d. (-); *and had issue* 1b.

1b. *Mary Norton,* bur. 26 *July* 1748; m. c. 1713, *Sir Tancred Robinson,* 3rd Bt. [G.B.], *Rear-Admiral R.N.,* d. 3 *Sept.* 1754; *and had issue.*
See p. 72.   [Nos. 9345 to 9381.

20. Descendants of ELIZABETH ROBINSON (Table IV.), *d.* (-); *m.* PHILIP RYCOT, East India Merchant.

21. Descendants, if any surviving, of MARGARET ROBINSON (Table IV.), living a widow 1698; *m.* (settlements dated 15 Aug.) 1653, WILLIAM WEDDELL of Earswick, co. York, Lord of the Manor of Wigginton, *b. c.* 1634; will dated 28 May 1676; and had issue 1a to 3a.[2]

1a. *Margaret Weddell, da. and in her issue co-h.,* d. (-); m. *Alexus Elcock of York, Merchant,* bur. 22 *Ap.* 1700; *and had issue, who took the name of Weddell and became extinct sometime after Ap.* 1792.

---

[1] Foster's "Yorkshire Pedigrees."
[2] Whitaker's "Richmond," ii. 122.

The Plantagenet Roll

2a. *Dorothy Weddell, da. and in her issue co-h.,* d. (-); m. 3 *May* 1688, *Joseph Tomlinson of York, living* 1712; *and had issue* 1b.

1b. *Frances Tomlinson, da. and whose issue, if surviving after* 1792, *became h.,* b. c. 1699; d. 12 *June* 1751; m. *Major Charles Weddell,* b. c. 1691; d. 1768; *and had issue* 1c.

1c. *Thomas Weddell of York,* d. (-); m. 1777, *Jane, da. of Henry Briggs of Pendleton, co. Lancaster.*

3a. *Joan Weddell,* d. (-); m. (—) *James; and had issue.*

22. Descendants, if any surviving, of FRANCES ROBINSON (Table IV.), d. (-); m. ROBERT BELT of Overton, co. York, bapt. 2 May 1637; bur. 26 Mar. 1667; and had issue 1a to 3a.[1]

    1a. *Frances Belt,* } both b. *before* 13 *Sept.* 1665, *named in father's will*
    2a. *Margaret Belt,* } 22 *Mar.* 1667.
    3a. *Mary Belt,* bapt. 5 *Aug.* 1667.

23. Descendants, if any surviving, of WALTER BETHELL of Ellerton, co. York (Table V.), bapt. 28 July 1629; living, aged 37, 9 Sept. 1665; m. 1st, 10 Mar. 1650, ANN, widow of (—) Savile of Copley, da. of Sir George PALMES of Naburn, bur. 22 Mar. 1653; 2ndly, 29 Jan. 1656, MARY (? ANNE), da. of Peter VAVASOUR of Spalding Moor, bur. 23 Dec. 1659; and had issue 1a to 2a.[2]

    1a.[1] *Hugh Bethell,* b. 1658, *living, aged* 7, 1665.
    2a. *Mary Bethell* (? bur. 21 *Ap.* 1687).

24. Descendants of BETHELL ROBINSON of Buckton, co. York, Solicitor (Table V.), bapt. 24 Jan. 1684; bur. 1718; m. MARY, da. of Thomas HESELTINE; and had issue surviving in 1874.[3]

25. Descendants of LUCY BETHELL (Table V.), d. (-); m. JOHN MOTTRAM of Bishop Dyke Hall, Kirk Fenton, co. York, who was living and aged 36, 21 Mar. 1665; and had then issue 1a.[4]

    1a. *Bethell Mottram, son and h., living and aged* 6, 21 *Mar.* 1665.

26. Descendants of URSULA BETHELL (see Table V.), bapt. 13 Jan. 1634; d. (-); m. JOHN PALLISER of Newby Wiske, b. 1639; and had issue 1a to 4a.

    1a. *Thomas Palliser of Portobello and the Great Island, co. Wexford, High Sheriff* 1700, b. 1661; d. 1756; m. *Katherine, da. of* (—) *Wogan; and ha dissue* 1b *to* 2b.

---

[1] Dugdale's "Visitation of Yorkshire," 1665, with additions by J. W. Clay, F.S.A. *The Genealogist,* N.S., xvi. 171.
[2] Foster's "Yorkshire Pedigrees."   [3] *Ibid.*
[4] Dugdale's "Visitation of Yorkshire."

# of The Blood Royal

1b. *William Palliser*, b. 24 June 1699; d.v.p. before Nov. 1756; m. *Mary*, da. of *Philip Savage of Kilgibbon*; and had issue 1c.[1]

1c. *Katherine Palliser of the Great Island*, co. *Wexford*, da. and event. h., d. (-); m. *John Wilson of Scarr*, d. (-); and had issue 1d to 2d.

1d. *Christian Wilson of Scarr*, d. (-); m. *Elizabeth*, da. of *Matthew Redmond of Kilgowan*, co. *Wexford*; and had issue 1e to 2e.

1e. *John Wilson of Scarr*, d.s.p.m.

2e. *Matthew Wilson, afterwards Palliser of the Great Island*, d. (-); m. 12 Aug. 1812, *Jane*, da. of *Christian Wilson of Sledagh*, d. (-); and had issue 1f to 2f.

1f. *Christian Palliser of Begerin*, J.P., d. (-); m. *Mary*, da. of *Rudolphus William Ryan, Crown Prosecutor for co. Wexford*; and had issue 1g.

1g. [da.] Palliser, b. 27 June 1877.

2f. Rev. *Matthew Palliser*, Rector of White Church, m. 1855, *Sophia*, da. of the Rev. Thomas Ottiwell Moore, Rector of Leskinfere, d. 18 Ap. 1856; and had issue 1g.

1g. *Frederick Palliser*, b. Ap. 1856.

2d. *Anne Wilson*, d. (-); m. as 1st wife, 1 Feb. 1785, *Richard Waddy of Cloughheast Castle*, co. *Wexford*, M.D., b. 13 Ap. 1758; d. 21 July 1819; and had issue 1e.[2]

1e. *Frances Waddy*, b. 1789.

2b. *Juliana Hyde Palliser*, d. (-); m. 12 Ap. 1732, *Capt. John Orfeur*, d. (-); and had issue 1c to 3c.

1c. *Dorothea Orfeur*, d. (-); m. (—) *Weston*.

2c. *Mary Orfeur*, d. (-); m. *George Robinson Walters* (see below), *Capt. R.N.*, d. 9 Dec. 1789; and had issue 1d to 3d.

1d. *Sir Hugh Palliser Walters, afterwards* (R.L. 13 Dec. 1798) *Palliser, 2nd Bart.* [G.B.], b. 27 Oct. 1768; d. (at Troyes) 17 Nov. 1813; m. 18 Jan. 1790, *Mary*, da. and co-h. of *John Yates of Oldham*, co. *Essex*, d. 5 Aug. 1823; and had issue 1e to 2e.

1e. *Sir Hugh Palliser, 3rd and last Bart.* [G.B.], b. 8 Mar. 1796; d. (unm.) 3 Aug. 1868.

2e. *Mary Jane Palliser*, d. Oct. 1881; m. 1st, 16 Ap. 1822, *William Lockhart of Gormiston*, co. *Lanark*, d. (-); 2ndly, 11 May 1848, *John Manley Arbuthnot, Lord Keane*, d.s.p.

2d. *Alice Walters*, d. (-); m. *John Clough of York*.

3d. *Ursula Walters*, d. (-); m. *John Fletcher*.

3c. *Catherine Hyde Orfeur*, d. 1814; m. *Matthew Cavendish of Graigue*, d. 1819; and had (with other) issue 1d.

1d. *James Gordon Cavendish*, m. *Ann*, da. of *Odiarne Coates of Green Court*, co. *Herts*; and had issue.

2a. *Hugh Palliser of North Deighton*, co. *York*, a Capt. in the Army, b. 1663; d. (-); m. *Mary*, da. of *Humphrey Robinson of Thicket Priory*, co. *York*; and had issue 1b to 2b.

1b. *Sir Hugh Palliser, 1st Bart.* [G.B.], so cr. 6 Aug. 1773 with a spec. rem., M.P., b. 26 Feb. 1723; d. unm. 18 Mar. 1796.

2b. *Rebecca Palliser*, d. (-); m. *Major William Walters*, d. 28 Feb. 1789; and had issue 1c.

1c. *George Robinson Walters*, Capt. R.N., d. 9 Dec. 1789; m. *Mary* (see above), da. and co-h. of Capt. *John Orfeur*; and had issue.

[Nos. 3982 to 3984.

---

[1] Burke's "Landed Gentry of Ireland," 1904.
[2] Burke's "Landed Gentry," 7th ed. 1886, ii. 1901.

The Plantagenet Roll

3a. *Walter Palliser of North Deighton*, d. (-) ; m. *Elizabeth, da. of (—) Sterne;* and had issue 1b to 2b.

1b. *Rev. Walter Palliser, Rector of Stokenham, and Vicar of Great Drayton and Askham, co. Notts,* d. 1778.

2b. *Alice Palliser,* d. (-) ; m. *Robert Cooper.*

4a. *Frances Palliser, living* 1665.[1]

27. Descendants, if any, of FRANCES BETHELL (Table V.), d. (-); m. 8 Feb. 1674, HENRY BELLINGHAM; and of her sister ELIZABETH.

28. Descendants, if any, of SLINGSBY BETHELL, Merchant and Sheriff of London (Table V.), *bapt.* 27 Feb. 1617 ; d. (-) ; m. MARY, da. of (———) BURRELL of co. Hunts.

29. Descendants of Sir WILLIAM CODRINGTON, 2nd Baronet [G.B.], P.C., M.P. (Table V.), b. 26 Oct. 1719 ; d. 11 Mar. 1792 ; m. 22 Feb. 1736, ANNE, da. of (—) ACTON of Fulham, d. Sept. or Nov. 1778 ; and had issue 1a to 2a.

1a. *Sir William Codrington, 3rd Bt.* [G.B.], b. c. 1737; d. *(at Rennes)* 5 *Sept.* 1816; m. *2ndly or 3rdly,*[2] 1804, *Eleanor, da. of Godfrey Kirke of London,* d. *(at Rennes)* 13 Feb. 1816 ; *and had issue* 1b *to* 2b.

1b. *Sir William Raymond Codrington, 4th Bart.* [G.B.], b. *(at Rennes)* 25 *Jan.* 1805 ; d. *(at the Château de la Boullaye, Brittany)* 17 *Dec.* 1873 ; m. *(at St. Servand Bosc, Ille et Vilaine)* 20 May 1828, *Anne Mary, da. of Joseph Raphael Agrippin Le Fer de Bonaban of Bonaban, near St. Malo,* d. 27 *Oct.* 1876 ; *and had issue* 1c *to* 4c.

1c. *Sir William Mary Joseph Codrington, 5th Bt.* [G.B.], b. *(at St. Malo)* 13 *Mar.* 1829 ; d. *(at Rennes)* 1 *Mar.* 1904 ; m. 12 *Ap.* 1856, *Mary (Château de la Boullaye, near Montfort, Brittany), da. of Robert Roskell of Park House, Fulham ;* and had issue 1d to 3d.

1d. Sir William Robert Codrington of Dodington, 6th Bt. [G.B.], Capt. and Brevet-Major, *late* 11th Hussars *(Standerton, Transvaal),* b. 18 Ap. 1867 ; m. 25 Ap. 1903, Joan, da. of Henry Adams Rogers of Johannesburg; and has issue 1e to 2e.

1e. William Richard Codrington, b. 22 Ap. 1904.

2e. Frank Christopher Codrington, b. 8 May 1908.

2d. George Raimond Codrington, b. 14 Aug. 1868.

3d. Alexander Joseph Codrington, b. 9 Aug. 1870 ; *m.* 24 July 1905, Mary, da. of Nicholas Roskell of 2 Warwick Gardens, Kensington.

2c. *Nancy Mary Codrington,* d. (-) ; m. 29 *Jan.* 1856, *Alexandre Amaury de La Moussaye,* —*th* (17—) *und* 3*rd* (1819) *Marquis of La Moussaye* [F.], b. *(at La Poterie)* 16 *Sept.* 1820 ; d.s.p.

3c. *Emilia Mary Caroline Codrington,* d. (-) ; m. 29 *July* 1861, *Lieut.-Col. James Pollock Gore, late* 1st *Royals.*

4c. *Sophia Mary Codrington,* d. (-) ; m. 2 *June* 1857, *Gustave Bernard de La Gatinais of Valle, near Lamballe.*

2b. *Mary Anne Eleanor Codrington,* d. 1834; m. 1826, *Charles Magon, an Officer 6th Hussars, in the French Army.*

2a. *Mary Codrington,* d. (-) ; m. *George Bernard.* [Nos. 9385 to 9389.]

---

[1] Dugdale's " Visitation of Yorkshire," 1665. Surtees Soc. Pub., xxxvi. 94.

[2] See G. E. C.'s "Complete Baronetage," v. 55, note b.

Of The Blood Royal

30. Descendants of EDWARD CODRINGTON of London, Merchant (Table V.), b. 22 June 1732; d. (at Dijon) Feb. 1775; m. 4 May 1759, REBECCA, da. of (—) LE STURGEON, d. 1770; and had issue 1a to 3a.

1a. Sir Christopher Codrington, afterwards (R.L. 17 Nov. 1795) Bethell-Codrington, styled 4th Bt. [G.B.],[1] M.P., b. Oct. 1764; d. 4 Feb. 1843; m. 16 Aug. 1796, the Hon. Caroline Georgiana Harriet, da. of Thomas (Foley), 2nd Baron Foley [G.B.], d. 1 Jan. 1843; and had issue.
See the Clarence Volume, pp. 354–355, Nos. 11571–11594.

2a. Sir Edward Codrington, G.C.B., M.P., Admiral of the Red, d. 28 Ap. 1851; m. 27 Dec. 1802, Jane, da. of Jaspar Hall of Otterburn, Hexham, d. 21 Jan. 1837; and had issue 1b to 3b.

1b. Sir William John Codrington, G.C.B., M.P., Gen. and Com.-in-Chief of the British Forces in the Crimea, 1855, &c., b. 26 Nov. 1804; d. 6 Aug. 1884; m. 7 May 1836, Mary, V.A., Bedchamber Woman to Queen Victoria, da. of Levi Ames of the Hyde, Herts, d. 28 June 1898; and had issue 1c to 3c.

1c. Alfred Edward Codrington, C.V.O., C.B., Major-Gen. Comdg. 1st London Div. Territorial Force, formerly Comdg. Coldstream Guards (Preston Hall, Uppingham; 110 Eaton Square, S.W.), b. 4 May 1854; m. 20 May 1885, Adela Harriet, da. of Melville Portal of Laverstoke, co. Hants; and has issue 1d to 4d.

1d. Geoffrey Ronald Codrington, Lieut. Leicestershire Imp. Yeo., b. 13 May 1888.
2d. William Melville Codrington, b. 16 Dec. 1892.
3d. John Alfred Codrington, b. 28 Oct. 1898.
4d. Mary Adela Codrington.

2c. Jane Emily Codrington, m. 13 Sept. 1867, Sir Robert Uniacke-Penrose-FitzGerald, 1st Bt. [U.K.], J.P., D.L., formerly M.P. (Corkbeg Island, Whitegate, co. Cork; 35 Grosvenor Road, S.W.).

3c. Mary Codrington (2 Lowndes Square, S.W.), m. 21 July 1864, Major-Gen. William Earle, C.B., C.S.I. [Bt. of Allerton (1869) Coll.], b. 18 May 1833; d. (being killed at Kirbekan, Soudan) 10 Feb. 1885; and had issue 1d to 2d.

1d. Rachel Mary Earle.
2d. Grace Elizabeth Earle, m. 19 Ap. 1893, John Russell Villiers [E. of Clarendon Coll.] (49 Hans Place, S.W.); and has issue 1e to 4e.

1e. Arthur Henry Villiers, b. 27 Mar. 1894.
2e. William Earle Villiers, b. 6 Jan. 1897.
3e. John Michael Villiers, b. 22 Oct. 1899.
4e. Richard Montague Villiers, b. 10 Sept. 1905.

2b. Sir Henry John Codrington, K.C.B., Adm. of the Fleet, b. 17 Oct. 1808; d. 4 Aug. 1877; m. 1st, 9 Ap. 1849, Helen Jane, da. of C. Webb Smith of Florence, d. 1876; and had issue 1c to 2c.

1c. Anne Jane Codrington, m. 12 Jan. 1882, Henry Stormont (Finch-Hatton), 13th Earl of Winchilsea and 8th Earl of Nottingham [E.], &c. [also a descendant of King Edward III. through Mortimer-Percy (see p. 129)] (Harlech, co. Merioneth); and has issue 1d to 3d.

1d. Guy Montagu George Finch-Hatton, Viscount Maidstone, Lieut. Royal East Kent Yeo., b. 28 May 1885.
2d. Hon. Denys George Finch-Hatton, b. 24 Ap. 1887.
3d. Lady Gladys Margaret Finch-Hatton.

2c. Ellen Codrington, m. 27 July 1878, Sir John Roche Dasent, C.B. (26 Elvaston Place, S.W.; Montrose House, St. Vincent, W.I.); and has issue 1d to 2d. [Nos. 9390 to 9431.

---

[1] He and his son assumed the baronetcy under the assumption that the 3rd Bart. had d.s.p.l. See G. E. C.'s "Complete Baronetage," v. 56.

The Plantagenet Roll

1*d*. Manuel Dasent, Lieut. R.N., *b*. 13 May 1879.

2*d*. Walter Dasent, Lieut. R.N., *b*. 15 Nov. 1880.

3*b*. Jane Barbara Codrington, d. 3 *Ap*. 1884; m. *Capt. Sir Thomas Bourchier*, R.N., K.C.B.

3*a*. Caroline Codrington, d. (-); m. 28 Dec. 1797, Joseph Lyons (*Walrond*), 6*th Marquis of Vallado* [Spain], &c., of Antigua and Dulford House, co. Devon, b. 1752; d. 13 *Jan*. 1815; and had issue 1*b* to 2*b*.

1*b*. Lyons (*Walrond*), 7*th Marquis of Vallado* [Spain], b. 21 *Ap*. 1800; d. (unm.) 21 May 1819.

2*b*. Bethell (*Walrond*), 8*th Marquis of Vallado* [Spain] and a co-h. to the Barony of *Welles* [E.], M.P., J.P., D.L., b. 10 Aug. 1802; d. 1876; m. 10 Nov. 1829, Lady Janet, da. of James (St. Clair), 2nd Earl of Rosslyn [U.K.], G.C.B., d. Nov. 1880; and had issue 1*c*.

1*c*. Henry (*Walrond*), 9th Marquis of Vallado and a Grandee of the 1st Class [Spain] and a co-h. to the Barony of Welles [E.], J.P., late Lieut.-Col. and Hon. Col. 4th Batt. Devon Regt. (21 *Bloomfield Street, W.*), b. 9 Nov. 1841; *m*. 1861, Caroline Maud, da. of William John Clarke of Buckland Tous-saints, co. Devon, J.P., D.L.; and has issue 1*d* to 10*d*.

1*d*. Henry Humphrey Walrond, B.A. (Oxon.) (28 *Pennsylvania Road, Exeter*), b. 14 July 1862; *m*. 31 July 1901, Gertrude Gordon, da. of Col. Sir Stephen Hill, G.C.M.G., C.B., s.p.

2*d*. Ernest Adolphus Walrond, b. 22 Oct. 1863; *m*. Oct. 1894, Fannie Jane Helen, da. of William Helm of Fresno, California; and has issue 1*e* to 3*e*.

1*e*. Ernest Henry Walrond, b. 31 July 1896.

2*e*. George Osmund Walrond, b. 25 Aug. 1898.

3*e*. Frank Helm Walrond, b. 25 Oct. 1895.

3*d*. Francis Arthur Walrond (50 *Addison Gardens, W.*), b. 8 Feb. 1866; m. 24 Ap. 1895, Muriel Gwendoline, da. of Frederick J. Methwold of Thorne Court, Bury St. Edmunds, J.P., F.S.A.; and has issue 1*e* to 4*e*.

1*e*. Henry Humphrey Richard Methwold Walrond, b. Oct. 1904.

2*e*. Beryl Methwold Walrond, b. 13 Feb. 1896.

3*e*. Irene Fay Methwold Walrond, b. 4 July 1897.

4*e*. Muriel Joan Methwold Walrond, b. 11 Nov. 1898.

4*d*. Herbert William James Walrond, b. 9 Aug. 1868; *unm*.

5*d*. Conrad Montague Walrond, b. 16 Aug. 1869; m. 3 Aug. 1908, Kate Dalrymple, da. of F. Woollven of Glasgow.

6*d*. George Stewart Basil Walrond, b. 15 May 1876; *m*. 23 Dec. 1903, Mabel, da. of the Rev. W. H. Bloxame, M.A.

7*d*. Edith Maud Walrond, *m*. 6 July 1887, the Rev. Charles Francis Long Sweet, M.A., Vicar of Stourpane (*Stourpane Vicarage, Dorset*); and has issue 1*e* to 3*e*.

1*e*. George Charles Walrond Sweet, b. 4 Dec. 1889.

2*e*. Leonard Herbert Walrond Sweet, b. 15 June 1893.

3*e*. Dorothy Maud Walrond Sweet, b. 7 Oct. 1891.

8*d*. Beatrice Paulina Mabel Walrond, *m*. 28 Nov. 1900, Charles Christopher Davie (see Supplement) (21 *Selborne Road, Hove*); and has issue 1*e* to 2*e*.

1*e*. Paul Christopher Davie, b. (?) 31 Sept. 1901.

2*e*. Ethel Margery Davie, b. July 1904.

9*d*. Kate Gwendoline Walrond, *m*. 7 Oct. 1903, William Hatton Stansfeld (*The Larches, Iver Heath, Bucks*), s.p.

10*d*. Sybil Mary Walrond, *m*. 16 June 1903, Edward Frank Lumley Hopkins; and has issue 1*e* to 3*e*.

1*e*. Writh Sybil Annette Hopkins, b. 4 Dec. 1904.

2*e*. Sylvia Gwendoline Alice Hopkins, b. 6 July 1906.

3*e*. Janet Muriel Ada Hopkins, b. 3 Jan. 1909.   [Nos. 9432 to 9459.

# of The Blood Royal

31. Descendants of BRIDGET CODRINGTON (Table V.), *d.* (-) ; *m.* 1747, the Right Hon. WILLIAM DOWDESWELL (see p. 503) of Pull Court, co. Worcester, P.C., M.P., Chancellor of the Exchequer 1765-66, *d.* (at Nice) 6 Feb. 1775 ; and had issue (with 9 others who *d.s.p.*) 1*a* to 2*a*.

1*a. John Edmund Dowdeswell of Pull Court, M.P., Recorder of Tewkesbury* 1798-1833, *and a Master in Chancery* 1820-50; b. 3 *Mar.* 1772; d. 11 *Nov.* 1851; m. 4 *Sept.* 1800, *Carolina, da. of Charles Brietzcke*, d. 6 *May* 1845 ; *and had issue* 1*b to* 2*b*.
1*b. William Dowdeswell of Pull Court, M.P., J.P., D.L., High Sheriff cc. Worcester* 1855, b. 18 *Oct.* 1804 ; d. 6 *Feb.* 1887 ; m. 19 *Mar.* 1839, *Amelia Letitia, da. of Robert Graham of Cossington House, co. Somerset,* d. 24 *Jan.* 1900 ; *and had issue* 1*c to* 2*c.*
1*c. William Edward Dowdeswell of Pull Court, M.P.,* b. 13 *June* 1841 ; d.s.p. 12 *July* 1893.
2*c.* Rev. Edmund Richard Dowdeswell of Pull Court, M.A. (Oxon.), *formerly* (1881-98) Vicar of Bushley (*Pull Court, Tewkesbury*), *b.* 14 Jan. 1845; *unm.*

2*b. Catharine Dowdeswell,* b. 8 *Sept.* 1801 ; d. 5 *Aug.* 1878 ; m. 10 *Jan.* 1833, *Richard Beauvoir Berens of Kevington, co. Kent,* d. 25 *Feb.* 1859 ; *and had issue* 1*c to* 2*c.*
1*c.* Richard Berens of Kevington, J.P., D.L., High Sheriff co. Kent 1893 (*Kevington, St. Mary Cray, Kent*), *b.* 15 Mar. 1834; *m.* 13 June 1860, Fanny Georgina, da. of Alexander Atherton Park, Master of the Court of Common Pleas.
2*c. Catharine Frances Carolina Berens,* d. 4 *Oct.* 1892 ; m. *Aug.* 1880, *Lieut.- Col. Grant, late Rifle Brigade.*

2*a. Elizabeth Dowdeswell,* d. 21 *Oct.* 1830 ; m. 24 *June* 1777, *Sir William Weller Pepys,* 1st Bart. [U.K.], *a Master in Chancery,* b. 1 *Jan.* 1741 ; d. 2 *June* 1825 ; *and had issue* 1*b to* 3*b*.
1*b. Charles Christopher* (*Pepys*), 1st *Earl of Cottenham* [U.K.], *Lord High Chancellor of Great Britain,* b. 29 *Ap.* 1781; d. 29 *Ap.* 1851 ; m. 30 *June* 1821, *Caroline Elizabeth, da. of William Wingfield Baker* [*by his wife, Lady Charlotte Maria,* née *Digby*], b. 6 *Ap.* 1868 ; *and had issue.*
See the Essex Volume, pp. 163-164, Nos. 20495-20541.

2*b. Right Rev. Henry Pepys, D.D., Lord Bishop of Worcester* (1841-60), b. 18 *Ap.* 1783 ; d. 13 *Nov.* 1860 ; m. 27 *Jan.* 1824, *Maria, da. of the Right Hon. John Sullivan* [*by his wife, Lady Harriet,* née *Hobart*], d. 17 *June* 1885 ; *and had issue.*
See the Clarence Volume, p. 595, Nos. 26139-26185.

3*b. Isabella Sophia Pepys,* d. 21 *Ap.* 1870 ; m. 12 *Jan.* 1813, *the Rev. Thomas Whateley, Rector of Chetwynd, Salop ;* d. 10 *May* 1864 ; *and had* (*with possibly other*) *issue* 1*c.*
1*c.* Arthur Whateley (4 *Southwick Crescent, Hyde Park, W.*).
[Nos. 9460 to 9556.

32. Descendants of JANE TURNER of Kirk Leatham, co. York (Table VI.), *d.* (-) ; *m.* 1745, PHILIP WILLIAM CASIMIR VAN STRAUBENZEE, Capt. Dutch Guards, *d.* 1765 ; and had issue.

See the Essex Volume, Exeter Supplement, pp. 640-642, Nos. 52020/1-58.
[Nos. 9557 to 9614.

The Plantagenet Roll

33. Descendants, if any surviving, of ELIZABETH MARWOOD (Table VI.), bapt. 7 Mar. 1666; d. 26 Mar. 1726; m. 7 May 1685, JOHN PIERCE of Lazenby Hall [son and h. of Richard Pierce of Hutton Bonville], co. York, d. 5 Oct. 1694; and had issue.[1]

34. Descendants of BARBARA MARWOOD (Table VI.), living 1679; m. 1st, Sir THOMAS HEBBLETHWAITE of Norton, co. York, M.P., bapt. 19 June 1628; bur. 21 June 1668;[2] 2ndly, as 2nd wife, Sir FRANCIS COBB of Ottringham;[3] and had issue 1a to 8a.

1a. *James Hebblethwaite*, b. c. 1652; bur. 10 Dec. 1729; m. *Bridget*, da. of Sir William Cobb of Ottringham, d. 13 June 1720; and had issue 1b to 3b.

1b. *Frances Hebblethwaite*, da. and co-h., b. c. 1677; d. 1 Ap. 1720; m. 8 Ap. 1703, Sir Francis Boynton of Burton Agnes, 4th Bt. [E.], M.P., bapt. 17 Nov. 1677; d. 16 Sept. 1739; and had issue 1c to 3c.

1c. *Sir Griffith Boynton*, 5th Bt. [E.], b. 24 May 1712; d. 18 Oct. 1761; m. 5 Ap. 1742, Anne or Amy, da. of Thomas White of Walling Wells, co. Notts, M.P., d. 27 Feb. 1745; and had issue 1d.

1d. *Sir Griffith Boynton*, 6th Bt. [E.], M.P., F.S.A., b. 22 Feb. 1745; d. 6/12 Jan. 1778; m. 1 Aug. 1768, Mary, da. of James Hebblethwaite of Norton and Bridlington [2ndly, 24 July 1798, George John Parkhurst of Hutton Ambro, co. York, and Catesby Abbey, co. Northants, by whom, who d. June 1823, she had also issue and], d. 13 May 1815; and had issue.

See the Exeter Volume, pp. 547-549, Nos. 49541-49587.

2c. *Francis Boynton of Otteringham*, b. 10 Jan. 1718; d. (-); m. 26 July 1762, Charlotte, da. of Sir Warton Pennyman-Warton, 5th Bt. [E.]; and had issue 1d.

1d. *Francis Boynton*, b. 27 Ap. 1764; bur. 9 Oct. 1816; m. at York before 1785; and had issue a son and a da.[4]

3c. *Constance Boynton*, b. 15 Feb. 1704; bur. 9 Dec. 1785; m. 28 Ap. 1741, *Ralph Lutton of Knapton, co. York*.

2b. *Bridget Hebblethwaite*, da. and co-h., bapt. 6 Jan. 1686; bur. 26 Aug. 1720; m. (——) *Bushell*.

3b. *Barbara Hebblethwaite*, da. and co-h., bapt. 11 May 1695; d. (-); m. (——) *Cartwright of Malton*.

2a. *Thomas Hebblethwaite*, bapt. 2 Oct. 1657.

3a. *Charles Hebblethwaite*, bapt. 20 Aug. 1660; bur. 11 Feb. 1727; m. *Margaret*, da. of William St. Quintin of Muston [son and h.-app. of 2nd Bt. [E.]], bur. 19 June 1723; and had issue.

See the Exeter Volume, pp. 547-549, Nos. 49541-49587.

4a. *Mountayne Hebblethwaite*, bapt. (at Norton) 11 Aug. 1662.

5a. *Frances Hebblethwaite*.

6a. *Barbara Hebblethwaite*, d. 15 July 1735; will as of Swanbourne, co. Bucks, widow, prov. by son-in-law, the Rev. Benjamin Reynolds; m. the Rev. Thomas Gataker, Rector of Hoggerston, co. Bucks, bapt. 8 Oct. 1650; d. 10 Nov. 1701; and has issue 1b to 7b.   [Nos. 9615 to 9708.

---

[1] Foster's "Yorkshire Pedigrees."

[2] Dugdale's "Visitation of Yorkshire," 1666, ed. by J. W. Clay, F.S.A. *The Genealogist*, N.S., xiv. 48.

[3] Presumably the Sir Francis Cobb of Ottringham, aged 60, 15 Sept. 1666. See Dugdale's "Visitation of Yorkshire," 1666, Surtees Soc. Pub., xxxvi. 332; but this marriage is not noted there.

[4] Foster's "Yorkshire Pedigrees."

of The Blood Royal

1b. Rev. Edward Gataker, Rector of Mursley-cum-Salden, co. Bucks, b. 24 Jan. 1684; d. 16 Sept. 1729; m. Elizabeth, da. of (—), d. 24 Oct. 1781, in 87th year; bur. in St. Andrews, Hertford; and had issue (with 5 others) 1c to 2c.

1c. Thomas Gataker, Surgeon Extraordinary to George III., d. 17 Nov. 1768; m. Anne, da. of Thomas Hill of Court of Hill, co. Salop, d. 22 July 1797; and had issue 1d to 2d.

1d. Thomas Gataker of Mildenhall, co. Suffolk, b. 1749; d. 16 Nov. 1841; m. Mary, da. of John Swale of Mildenhall, d. at Worlington 4 Nov. 1839, aged 92; and had issue (with a son d.s.p.) 1e.

1e. George Gataker of Mildenhall, co. Suffolk, and White Knight's Park, co. Berks, J.P., D.L., b. 30 Mar. 1792; d. 30 Ap. 1872; m. 1st, 5 Nov. 1825, Elizabeth Harrison, da. of Thomas Wilkinson of Nether Hall, co. Suffolk, d. 1 Jan. 1827; 2ndly, 29 Aug. 1829, Sophia Sarah, da. of Henry Samuel Partridge of Hockham Hall, d. 28 July 1861; and had issue (with a son and 2 das. d. unm.) 1f to 5f.

1f. Melmoth William Gataker, late of Mildenhall, formerly.I.S.C. (5 Marlborough Street, Bath), b. 23 Jan. 1841; m. 30 Jan. 1873, Jemima, da. of Benjamin Wood of Long Newnton, co. Wilts; and has issue 1g to 2g.

1g. Melmoth Leicester Swale Gataker (Branksome Manor, Bournemouth), b. 4 Jan. 1874; m. 14 Feb. 1899, Annie Madeline, da. of George W. Young, of Branksome Manor; and has issue 1h to 2h.

1h. Violet Louisa de Morel Gataker, b. 30 Ap. 1900.

2h. Muriel Elaine Georgina Gataker, b. 19 Oct. 1904.

2g. Reginald Henry Winchcombe Gataker (Boisdale, Wooroolin, Queensland), b. 8 June 1875; m. 26 Nov. 1904, Christian Esson, da. of George Gordon of Ellangowan, Banchory, co. Kincardine; and has issue 1h to 2h.

1h. Reginald Melmoth Gordon Gataker, b. 14 Sept. 1905.

2h. Godfrey George Ormond Gataker, b. (—).

2f. Charles Frederick Gataker (Milden, Maryborough, Queensland), b. 22 Ap. 1843; m. 20 Sept. 1869, Fanny Gulliver, da. of William Barns of Maryborough, afsd.; and has issue 1g to 5g.

1g. Melmoth Leofric Gataker, b. 31 Mar. 1872; m. 5 Nov. 1896, Clara, da. of Josiah Mason Illidge of Gympie, Queensland; and has issue 1h to 3h.

1h. Melmoth Leofric Gataker, b. 2 Nov. 1903.

2h. Minnie Lucy Gataker, b. 22 Ap. 1899.

3h. Amy Maud Gataker, b. 27 Feb. 1901.

2g. George William Frank Gataker, b. 13 Sept. 1873.

3g. Charles James Gataker, b. 9 Oct. 1876.

4g. Walter Reynardson Gataker, b. 26 Oct. 1878; m. 21 Feb. 1904, Sarah Kathleen, da. of James Milles of Nanango, Queensland; and has issue 1h to 2h.

1h. Doris Marian Gataker, b. 13 Sept. 1904.

2h. Kathleen Elsey Gataker, b. Sept. 1905.

5g. Minnie Georgina Elizabeth Gataker, m. 22 Ap. 1905, Reginald Julius (Brisbane, Queensland).

3f. Frank Anthony Gataker, late Lieut. R.N., b. 24 Dec. 1844; m. 30 Oct. 1873, Margaret, da. of Benjamin Harding, of Wadhurst Castle, co. Sussex.

4f.[1] Elizabeth Mary Gataker, m. as 2nd wife, 2 Feb. 1858, the Rev. Walter John Partridge, M.A., Rector of Caston, d. 28 Dec. 1891 s.p.

5f.[2] Louisa Sopdia Gataker.

2d. Annie Gataker, d. (-); m. 19 Dec. 1771, Stamp Brooksbank, of Chesterfield St., Mayfair [2nd son of Stamp Brooksbank of Healaugh Manor, co. Yorks, and Hacknay House, co. Midx.], d. 1802; and had issue (with 2 sons d.s.p.) 1e.

1e. Annie Brooksbank, d. (-); m. 10 Dec. 1795, the Rev. William Villiers Robinson [2nd son of Sir George Robinson, 5th Bt. [E.], M.P.], d. 14 Jan. 1829; and had issue 1f to 3f.   [Nos. 9709 to 9729.

The Plantagenet Roll

1*f*. Rev. Sir George Stamp Robinson, 7th Bt. [E.], *Rector of Cranford and Hon. Canon of Peterborough*, b. 29 Aug. 1797; d. 9 Oct. 1873; m. 24 May 1827, *Emma, da. of Robert Willis Blencowe, of Hayes, co. Midx.*, d. 20 Jan. 1874; *and had issue (with 3 sons and 3 das. who d.s.p.)* 1g to 2g.

1*g*. Sir John Blencowe Robinson, 8th Bt. [E.], b. 20 May 1830; d.s.p. 10 Aug. 1877.

2*g*. Rev. Sir Frederick Laera Robinson, 9th Bt. [E.], J.P., *Rector of Cranford*, b. 28 June 1843; d. 6 Feb. 1893; m. 14 Dec. 1870, *Madeline Caroline, da. of Frederick Sartoris of Rushden Hall, co. Northants*; *and has issue* 1h to 4h.

1*h*. Sir Frederick Villiers Daud Robinson, 10th Bt. [E.], Lt. 2nd Batt. Northamptonshire Regt. (*Cranford Hall, near Kittering*), b. 4 Dec. 1880; *unm.*

2*h*. Evelyn Dorothy Robinson, m. 31 Jan. 1900, Lindsay Ralph Bagnall.

3*h*. Margery Sybil Robinson.

4*h*. Sylvia Joan Robinson, m. 27 Ap. 1903, Major Charles Edward Bagnall, a collector in Uganda.

2*f*. Caroline Penelope Robinson, d. (-); m. 29 Oct. 1834, *Herman Merivale, C.B., Bar.-at-Law, I.T., permanent Under Sec. of State for India*, d. (-); *and had issue (with a da. who d.s.p.)* 1g to 2g.

1*g*. Herman Charles Merivale, b. 27 Jan. 1839; m. 13 May 1878, Elizabeth, da. of John Pitman.

2*g*. Isabel Frances Merivale, m. 16 Ap. 1863, *William Peere Williams-Freeman, of Clapton, co. Northants, Sec. H.M. Diplo. Ser.*, d. 18 Sept. 1884; *and had issue (with 2 sons and a da. d.s.p.)* 1h to 3h.

1*h*. Rev. Lionel Peere Williams-Freeman of Clapton, M.A. (Camb.), *Vicar of Exwick* (*Exwick Vicarage, Exeter*), b. 18 May 1867; m. 23 Ap. 1896, *Louisa, da. of Charles Hope, of Gorleston Priory*; *and has issue* 1i to 5i.

1*i*. William Peere Williams-Freeman, b. 8 Oct. 1909.

2*i*. Mary Leonora Williams-Freeman, b. 17 Nov. 1898.

3*i*. Dorothy Francis Williams-Freeman, b. 29 Dec. 1899.

4*i*. Cecilia Williams-Freeman, b. 25 Oct. 1901.

5*i*. Violet Williams-Freeman, b. 19 Mar. 1906.

2*h*. Agnes Caroline Williams-Freeman.

3*h*. Violet Mary Williams-Freeman, m. as 2nd wife, 15 Ap. 1902, *Arthur Charles Hammersley, Banker* (see p. 281) (*56 Princes Gate, S.W.*); *and has issue* 1i to 3i.

1*i*. Christopher Ralph Hammersley, b. 4 Jan. 1903.

2*i*. David Frederick Hammersley, b. 15 July 1904.

3*i*. Monica Violet Hammersley.

3*f*. Emma Robinson, d. 9 June 1902; m. 12 Nov. 1834, *the Rev. William Duthy, Rector of Sudborough, co. Northants, J.P.*, b. 18 Aug. 1796; d. 29 Sept. 1889; *and had issue* 1g to 6g.

1*g*. Archibald Edward Duthy, Col. R.H.A., b. 4 Jan. 1848; d. 10 Nov. 1906; m. 4 Nov. 1891, *Madeline Alice, da. of James Price*; *and had issue* 1h to 3h.

1*h*. Archibald Elder Desmond Campbell Duthy.

2*h*. Reginald Edward Athelstan Duthy.

3*h*. Humphrey William Gilbert Duthy.

2*g*. John Walter Brand Duthy, *formerly Indian Telegraph Dept.* (*Islip Grange, Thrapston*), b. 31 Jan. 1848; m. 6 June 1883, *Georgina Penelope, da. of George Rooper*; *and has issue* 1h.

1*h*. George Duthy, b. 24 May 1885.

3*g*. Rev. Reginald Henry Duthy, B.A. (Oxon.) (*All Hallows Presbytery, Orange St., Borough*), b. 10 Nov. 1850; *unm.*

4*g*. Georgina Caroline Duthy, m. 26 Mar. 1856, the Rev. Charles William

[Nos. 9730 to 9753.

# of The Blood Royal

Sillifant, Rector of Weare Gifford and Rural Dean (*Hughenden, Parkstone*); and has issue 1*h* to 7*h*.
    1*h*. Charles Herbert Sillifant, b. 12 Dec. 1866.
    2*h*. Gertrude Caroline Emma Sillifant.
    3*h*. Emily Harriet Sillifant.
    4*h*. Georgina Francis Sillifant.
    5*h*. Mabel Sillifant.
    6*h*. Edith Sillifant.
    7*h*. Beatrice Charlotte Sillifant.

    5*g*. Caroline Anna Duthy.
    6*g*. Edith Mary Duthy, *m*. 21 Aug. 1867, Major John William Bain Hawkesworth, J.P. (*Watlington, Oxon.; Stokeford, Wareham*); and has issue 1*h* to 2*h*.
        1*h*. Charles Edward Mackenzie Hawkesworth, b. 25 June 1868.
        2*h*. Thomas Ayscough Fitzwilliam Hawkesworth, b. 8 Sept. 1870.

    2*c*. *Elizabeth Gataker*, b. 1725; d. *at St. Albans* 4 *July* 1790; m. *the Rev. Edward Bourchier, M.A., J.P., Rector of Bramfield* 1740-75, *and Vicar of All Saints and St. John's, Hertford,* 1740-71 [*descended from King Edward I. through Harrison, Villiers, St. John, Scrope, Welles, and Segrave*], b. 7 Aug. 1707; d. 17 Nov. 1775; *and had issue* 1*d to* 9*d*.
        1*d*. Rev. *Edward Bourchier, M.A., Vicar of All Saints and St. John's, Hertford,* 1771-85, *Rector of Bramfield* 1775-85, b. 6 *Sept.* 1738; d. 14 *Dec.* 1785; m. *Catherine,* da. *of William Wollaston of Finborough,* co. *Suffolk, M.P.,* d. 4 Feb. 1801; *and had issue* (*with* 3 *das.* d. *young*) 1*e to* 2*e*.
        1*e*. Rev. *Edward Bourchier, M.A., Rector of Bramfield*, b. 13 *July* 1776; d. 21 *Ap.* 1840; m. 7 Feb. 1804, *Harriet*, da. *of Robert Jenner of Lincoln's Inn Fields,* d. 18 *Jan.* 1864; *and had issue* 1*f to* 9*f*.
            1*f*. *Edward Bourchier*, b. 6 *July* 1810.
            2*f*. *Francis Bourchier*, b. 10 *Aug.* 1812.
            3*f*. *Robert Jenner Bourchier*, b. 2 *Oct.* 1818; d. (? s.p.) 1 *Oct.* 1883.
            4*f*. *Sir George Bourchier, K.C.B., Major-Gen. R.A.;* b. 23 *Aug.* 1821; d. (-); m. 1st, 16 *July* 1854, *Georgiana Clemenson*, da. *of John Graham Lough of London,* d. 2 *Mar.* 1868; 2ndly, 23 *May* 1872, *Margaret Murchison*, da. *of Col. Bartleman*, d. 13 *July* 1881; *and had issue* 1*g to* 5*g*.
                1*g*. George Lough Bourchier, b. 29 July 1855; *m*. 11' Oct. 1879, Mary Catherine, da. of the Rev. Barcroft Boake, Principal of Colombo Academy.
                2*g*. Edward Herbert Bourchier, b. 24 Nov. 1856.
                3*g*. Arthur Charles Francis Bourchier, M.A. (Oxon.), Actor Manager (*The Albany, Piccadilly, W.; Otway Cottage, Bushy Heath*), b. 15 Aug. 1864; *m*. 9 Dec. 1894, Violet Augusta Mary, commonly called " Violet Vanbrugh," the well-known actress [descended from the Lady Anne, sister of Kings Edward IV. and Richard III. (see Exeter Volume, p. 118)], da. of the Rev. Reginald Henry Barnes, Prebendary of Exeter, s.p.
                4*g*. Herbert Eustace Bourchier, b. 13 Jan. 1874.
                5*g*. Ina Maude Mary Bourchier.

            5*f*. *Harriet Jenner Bourchier*, b. 29 Nov. 1804; d. 11 *Ap.* 1883; m. *the Rev.* W. *Harris*.
            6*f*. *Catherine Anne Jenner Bourchier*, d. 7 *Aug.* 1849.
            7*f*. *Elizabeth Jenner Bourchier*, d. 7 *June* 1860; m. *the Rev.* G. *North*.
            8*f*. *Louisa Jenner Bourchier*, b. 26 *Jan.* 1809; d. (-).
            9*f*. *Emma Jenner Bourchier*, b. 9 *Ap.* 1814; d. (-).
        2*e*. *Blanch Maria Bourchier*, d. (-).

    2*d*. *Charles Bourchier, a Member of Council of Bombay*, b. 13 *May*. 1739;
[Nos. 9744 to 9771.

The Plantagenet Roll

d. 28 Nov. 1818; m. 1st, 7 Oct. 1773, *Barbara, da. of James Richardson of Knockshinnock, co. Dumfries,* d. 18 Nov. 1784; 2ndly, 25 Jan. 1787, *da. of the Rev. Benjamin Preedy, D.D.,* d. 27 Ap. 1822; *and had issue* (with 3 sons d. young) 1e to 6e.

1e. **Samuel Bourchier**, H.E.I.C.S., b. Oct. 1781; d. *in Bombay* 1813; m. *Harriet, da. of Major-Gen. Robert Lewis,* H.E.I.C.S., d. 1850; *and had issue* (with 4 sons d. young) 1f to 3f.

1f. **Robert Francis Bourchier**, Capt. 4th Bombay N.I., d. 1837; m. 21 July 1832, *Antoinette Anna Louisa, da. of Capt. the Hon. John Rodney* [B. Rodney Coll.], d. (-); *and had issue* 1g to 2g.

1g. **Robert Lennox Bourchier**, Lt.-Col. R.M.A., b. 1838; d. 12 May 1882; m. 14 Oct. 1859, *Mary, da. of Philips Hast, Lieut. R.N.,* d. (-); *and had issue* 1h to 5h.

1h. Philip Lennox Walter Bourchier, b. 13 Aug. 1870.
2h. Rodney Lewis Bourchier, b. 24 Jan. 1875.
3h. Raymond Walter Harry Bourchier, b. 26 Feb. 1880.
4h. Mary Bourchier.
5h. Amabel Bourchier.

2g. Harriet E. Lennox Bourchier (26 *Taswell Road, Southsea*).

2f. *Harriet Bourchier*, d. (-); m. 1827, *John Burnett, Bombay C.S.;* *and had issue* 1g.

1g. Marianne Burnett.

3f. *Jane Bourchier*, d. (-); m. 1829, *Capt. William Chambers, Bombay N.I.;* *and had issue* 1g.

1g. Jane Chambers, m. 1853, Capt. George Geach; *and had issue* 1h.
1h. George Chambers Geach.

2e. **Rev. Charles Spencer Bourchier**, M.A., *Rector of Great Hallingbury, co. Essex,* b. 22 Feb. 1791; d. 22 July 1872; m. 13 Ap. 1814, *Eliza, da. of Samuel Harman, of Hadley, Barnet,* d. 22 Jan. 1880; *and had issue* (with a son d. young) 1f to 4f.

1f. **Legendre Charles Bourchier**, Col. 98th Regt. and Comdt. of Kurrachee *during the Mutiny,* b. 13 Mar. 1815; d. 27 Ap. 1866; m. 22 Aug. 1850, *Margaret, da. of the Rev. Thomas Beane Johnstone, Rector of Chilton;* *and had issue* (with a da. d. young) 1g to 3g.

1g. **Charles Legendre Johnstone Bourchier**, Capt. Cape Colonial Forces, *formerly* 35th and 65th Regts., b. Aug. 1851; m. 18 Ap. 1873, *Annie Werge, widow of A. Kaye, da. of E. H. Howey of Tynemouth,* d. 25 May 1874; *and had issue* 1h.

1h. Charlie Heumphrey Johnstone Bourchier, b. 25 Mar. 1874.

2g. Helen Johnstone Bourchier.

3g. Margaret Georgiana Johnstone Bourchier, m. 31 May 1881, Peter Purves of Brampson; *and had issue* 1h to 2h.

1h. Douglas Bourchier Johnstone Purves, b. 21 May 1883.
2h. Helen Georgiana Johnstone Purves.

2f. *Georgiana Anne Bourchier*, d. (-); m. *Richard Weller Chadwick;* *and had* (with other) *issue* 1g.

1g. Edward Frederick Chadwick, *late* 33rd Regt., b. (—); m. 20 Sept. 1882, Anna Louisa (? Amy) (see p. 85), da. of the Rev. Charles Torkington.

3f. Marianne Frances Bourchier, twin.
4f. Emily Dorothy Bourchier.

3e. **Richard James Bourchier** *of Malta and 67 Victoria Street, Westminster,* b. 16 June 1793; d. (-); m. 1st, (—), *da. of* (—) *Lander;* *and had issue* (a son and 3 das.).

4e. *Elizabeth Bourchier*, d. Nov. 1856; m. 22 Oct. 1779, *James Torkington* (see p. 91) *of Great Stukeley, co. Hunts, Bar.-at-Law,* d. 7 May 1828[1] or 6 Feb. 1852[2]; *and had issue* (with 12 others who d. unm.) 1f to 2f.   [Nos. 9772 to 9789.

---

[1] Foster's "Noble and Gentle Families," ii. 609. [2] Ibid., ii. 606.

# of The Blood Royal

1f. Laurence John Torkington of Great Stukeley, Lieut. 4th Light Dragoons, b. 27 Sept. 1809; d. 7 May 1874; m. 26 Sept. 1839, Mary Anne, da. of Lieut.-Col. Walker, R.A., d. 1874; and had issue (with a son d. unm.) 1g to 5g.

1g. Charles Torkington of Great Stukeley, co. Hunts, and Stukeley, The Leven, Tasmania, Capt. 41st Regt. (Roslyn, Salisbury Road, Seaford, Sussex), b. 20 July 1847; m. 3 Aug. 1875, Florence Elizabeth Caroline [descended from George, Duke of Clarence, K.G. (see Clarence Volume, p. 185)], da. of Richard George Coke of Brimington Hall, co. Derby; and has issue 1h to 4h.

1h. Gerard Stukeley Torkington, I.S.C., 69th Punjabis, b. 23 Sept. 1878.

2h. Charles Coke Torkington, Welsh Regt., b. 7 Mar. 1881.

3h. John Elmsley Bourchier Torkington, Manchester Regt., b. 19 Nov. 1884.

4h. Dorothy Mary Torkington.

2g. Mary Dorothy Torkington.

3g. Alice Torkington.

4g. Isabella Torkington.

5g. Gertrude Torkington, m. 1 Oct. 1868, the Rev. John Allen, M.A., D.D. (Oxon.), Vicar of St. Mary's, Lancaster, and Hon. Canon of Manchester, d. (-).

2f. Rev. Charles Torkington, Rector of Almer, co. Dorset, b. 13 Dec. 1817; d. (-); m. 1st, 1842, Anna, da. of James Powell, of Clapton, co. Midx., d. 8 Nov. 1847; 2ndly, Nov. 1848, Ellen Eliza, da. of the Rev. W. Cookson; and had issue (with a son and 2 das. d. young) 1g to 6g.

1g. Henry Torkington, Lieut.-Col. and Hon. Col. late R.A., b. 26 May 1843; m. Oct. 1875, Annie Ibbetson, da. of William G. Browne; and has issue 1h to 3h.

1h. Richard Humphrey Torkington, b. 1 May 1878.

2h. Oliver Miles Torkington, Capt. Scottish Rifles, b. 29 Aug. 1880.

3h. Mary Catherine Torkington.

2g. Edward Torkington, b. 15 Jan. 1856.

3g. Charles Richard Torkington, b. 26 Mar. 1860.

4g.[1] Catherine Torkington.

5g.[2] Georgina Torkington.

6g.[2] Amy (? Anna Louisa) Torkington, m. 30 Sept. 1882, Col. Edward Frederick Chadwick of Chetnole, Sherborne, Dorset (see p. 84).

5e.[2] Georgiana Bourchier, b. 1787; d. 8 Mar. 1862; m. James Garden Seton, of the Hanaper Office, in the Court of Chancery; and had issue.

6e.[2] Caroline Bourchier, b. 16 Feb. 1792; d. 1820; m. as 1st wife, 31 Mar. 1814, the Rev. Theodore Dury, Rector of Westmill, co. Herts, d. 2 Oct. 1850; and had issue (who all d.s.p.).

3d. George Bourchier, b. 11 May 1741.

4d. John Bourchier, Capt. R.N., Lieut.-Gov. of Greenwich Hospital, b. 26 Sept. 1747; d. 30 Dec. 1808; m. 1st, Mary, da. of the Rev. Richard Walter, Chaplain R.N., d. 26 Nov. 1789; 2ndly, Dec. 1789, Charlotte, da. of Thomas Corbett of Darnhall, co. Chester, Bar.-at-Law [who m. 2ndly, 27 July 1810, Capt. Platt, S. Linc. Mil.; 3rdly, F. J. Sandars Lang of Keaton, co. Devon, and], d. 5 Jan. 1839; and had issue (with 2 sons and 3 das. d.s.p.) 1e to 9e.

1e. Henry Bourchier, Rear-Adm. of the Blue, b. Oct. 1787 at Lille; d. 14 Oct. 1852; m. Mary, da. of Lieut.-Col. John Macdonald, d. at Ostend 9 Feb. 1852; and had issue 1f to 2f.

1f. Macdonald Bourchier, Comm. R.N., b. 6 Aug. 1814; d. (-); m. 1st, 5 Dec. 1843, Mary Eliza, da. of Rear-Adm. John Hancock, C.B., d. 19 June 1872; 2ndly, 12 May 1874, Charlotte Brumby, da. of John Holland, Lieut. R.N.; and had issue (with a son d. young) 1g to 3g.

1g. Seton Longuet Bourchier, b. (twin) 19 Oct. 1844; m. 25 July 1877, Georgiana Marian, da. of James N. Merriman, M.D., Apothecary Extraordinary to Queen Victoria; and has issue (with a da. d. young) 1h to 2h.

[Nos. 9790 to 9808.

The Plantagenet Roll

1*h*. Olive Longuet Bourchier.
2*h*. Emily Marion Bourchier, twin.
2*g*. Mary Eliza Sophia Bourchier.
3*g*. Alice Gertrude Bourchier.

2*f*. Henry Prescott Pellew Bourchier, *Capt. P. & O. Service*, b. 9 *Nov.* 1816; d. 1 *Aug.* 1856; m. *Ap.* 1851, *Mary Jane, da. of the Rev. Edward Ince, Vicar of Wigtoft*, d. 13 *Mar.* 1856; *and had issue* 1*g to* 4*g*.

1*g*. Henry Edward Bourchier, Comm. R.N. (*Highfield House, Steep, Petersfield*), *b.* 5 Mar. 1852; m. 16 Oct. 1878, Jane Burnett, da. of J. Williamson; and has issue 1*h*.

1*h*. Lily McDonald Bourchier.

2*g*. Mary Jane Bourchier (*Grove Villa, High Street, Feltham, Midx.*).

3*g*. Henrietta Catherine Bourchier, *m.* 21 Sept. 1881, William Booth Williamson (*Grove Villa, High Street, Feltham, Midx.*); and has issue 1*h* to 6*h*.

1*h*. Owen McDonald Williamson, *b.* 11 Ap. 1886.
2*h*. Jack Cecil Bourchier Williamson, *b.* 15 May 1891.
3*h*. Kenneth Bourchier Williamson, *b.* 27 Aug. 1898.
4*h*. Mary Sophia Williamson, *m.* 8 Ap. 1908, the Hon. John Morgan-Owen.
5*h*. Charlotte Dorothy Williamson.
6*h*. Alice Marguerite Williamson.

4*g*. Alice Bourchier (*Grove Villa, High Street, Feltham, Midx.*).

2*e*. *William Bourchier, Comm. R.N.*, b. 1791; d. *in Canada* 22 *Jan.* 1844; m. 1*st, in Canada*, 8 *Ap.* 1821, *Amelia, da. of John Mills Jackson of Downton, co. Wilts.*; 2*ndly*, c. 1834/5, *Laura, previously wife of Lieut. Robert Wrangham Lukin, da. of Robert Preston of London*, d. 29 *Ap.* 1898; *and had issue* 1*f to* 4*f*.

1*f*.[1] Eustace Fane Bourchier, *Lieut.-Gen. R.E., C.B., K.L.H.*, b. 25 *Aug.* 1822; d. 16 *Jan.* 1902; m. 1*st, Anne Jane, da. of Charles Stuart Pillans of Rosebank, Rondebosch*, d. 6 *Ap.* 1868; 2*ndly*, 25 *Aug.* 1869, *Maria, widow of Wilmot Seton of the Treasury, da. of* (—), d.s.p. *by him* 6 Feb. 1882; *and had issue (with* 5 *das.)* 1*g to* 2*g*.

1*g*. Charles Edward Stewart Bourchier, d. (*in Pietermaritzburg*) *May* 1904.
2*g*. Alfred Heseltine Bourchier.

2*f*.[2] Henry Seton Bourchier, *Lieut.-Col. R.M.L.I.*, sometime British Resident at Lukoja on the Niger (*Wayside, South Brent, S. Devon*), *b.* 17 Feb. 1842; *m.* 28 May 1868, Jessie Caroline, da. of Col. Robert Hawkes, 80th Regt.; and has issue 1*g* to 2*g*.

1*g*. Charles Bourchier, Tea Planter, Ceylon, *b.* 8 Dec. 1886.
2*g*. Mabel Jessie Bourchier.

3*f*.[2] Georgina Fanny Bourchier, b. 2 Oct. 1836; d. (*at Brisbane*) 12 *Aug.* 1893; m. at St. Mary's, The Boltons, South Kensington, 23 May 1865, *Edward Raven Priest of Cromer, Chemist*, d. (*at Brisbane*) 9 Nov. 1885; *and had issue* (see Appendix).

4*f*.[2] Laura Ellen Bourchier (7 *Huggen's College, North Fleet, Kent*), *unm.*

3*e*. *Thomas Bourchier*, twin with 4*e*, d. (—); m. *Anne, da. of Morris Graham, of Deal; and had issue (with a son* d. *young)* 1*f* to 2*f*.

1*f*. *William Sutherland Bourchier, Staff Comm. R.N.*, b. 15 Nov. 1823; d. *June* 1904; m. 1*st*, 8 *Sept.* 1850, *Mina Glover, da. of John Aldrich, Master R.N.*, d. 1852; 2*ndly*, 1 *May* 1856, *Mary, da. of Isaac Halse of Sloane Street, Chelsea*, d. 1893; *and had issue* 1*g to* 4*g*.

1*g*.[1] Mina Mary Bourchier, *m.* 1874, Frederick D'Iffanger (85 *Gloucester Terrace, Hyde Park, W.*); s.p.

2*g*.[1] Florence Anne Bourchier, *m.* 1878, William Cooper Keates, L.R.C.P., M.R.C.S. (20 *East Dulwich Road, S.E.*); and has issue 1*h* to 3*h*.

1*h*. Courtnay Cooper Keates.
2*h*. Bransby Cooper Keates.
3*h*. Florence Mina Mary Keates, *m.* (—) Wild.

[Nos. 9809 to 9833.

# of The Blood Royal

3g.² Emily Halse Bourchier, d. 1907; m. 1886, F. Thomas; and had issue 1h to 2h.

1h. Leeson Thomas.
2h. Donald Thomas.

4g.² Ethel Annie Bourchier, *unm.*

2f. Thomas Bourchier, Lieut. R.N., took part in the searches for Sir John Franklin, b. 10 Sept. 1827; d. 9 July 1866; m. 22 Jan. 1853, Anne Bourchier, da. of John Aldrich, Master R.N., d. 1 Mar. 1909; and had issue (with 2 sons and a da. d. unm.) 1g to 4g.

1g. William Thomas Bourchier, New South Wales C.S., b. 9 Oct. 1857; *unm.*
2g. Alfred Eustace Bourchier, Fleet Paymaster, R.N. (ret.), b. 1 June 1859; *unm.*
3g. Annie Undine Bourchier ⎫
4g. Mary Bedford Bourchier ⎭ (97 Victoria Road, Southsea).

4e. James O'Brien Bourchier, J.P., settled in Canada, b. (twin with 3e) c. 1797; d. 28 Aug. 1872; m. Jeanne, da. of James Lyall of Canada, West; and had issue (with 6 das.) 1f to 2f.

1f. William Bourchier, m. and has issue.[1]
2f. John Raines Bourchier, m. and has issue.[1]

5e. John Bourchier, M.D., b. 4 Mar. 1802; d. 11 Feb. 1842; m. 23 Ap. 1836, Sophia, da. of Edward Phillips of Winchester, M.D., d. 18 Ap. 1859; and had issue 1f.

1f. Rev. Walter Bourchier, M.A. and Fellow of New College (Oxon.), Vicar of St. Olave's, E., *formerly* of Steeple Morden (*St. Olave's Vicarage, Hanbury St., E.*), b. 20 Dec. 1837; m. 20 Ap. 1876, Harriet Louisa Eliza, da. of John Peach MacWhirter, Bengal C.S.; and has issue 1g to 5g.

1g. Walter John Majendie Bourchier, b. 26 Feb. 1877.
2g. Rev. Basil Graham Bourchier, M.A. (Camb.), *formerly* Curate of St. Ann's, Soho (*The Vicarage, Garden Suburb, Hampstead, N.W.*); b. 13 Feb. 1881.
3g. Philip Claud Walter Bourchier, b. 28 Oct. 1891.
4g. Constance Corbett Bourchier, m. 26 Dec. 1907, Horace R. Brown, M.D.
5g. Sybil Audrey Bourchier, m. 23 June 1908, Capt. Maurice Capel Miers, Somerset Light Infantry.

6e.¹ Mary Sophia Bourchier, b. 11 Aug. 1786; d. 9 May 1884; m. 21 Aug. 1822, the Rev. Edward Ince, M.A., Vicar of Wigtoft-with-Quadring, co. Linc., d. 6 Aug. 1840; and had issue 1f to 2f.

1f. Rev. Edward Cumming Ince, of Sunbury House, Watford, and Marrick Abbey, co. York, M.A. (Camb.), Vicar of Christ Church, Battersea, 1867–77, b. 17 Mar. 1825; d. 7 Dec. 1899; m. 14 Aug. 1850, Elizabeth Margaret Caroline, da. of John Gason, of co. Wicklow, M.D., d. 10 June 1902; and had issue (with 2 sons and a da. d. young) 1g to 4g.

1g. Rev. Edward John Cumming Ince, now (R.L. 11 Aug. 1893) Whittington-Ince, M.A. (Camb.), Rector of Wormington (*Wormington Rectory, Broadway R.S.O., Worcestershire*), b. 4 Feb. 1852; m. 23 Jan. 1884, Annie Nora, da. of Josceline Frederic Watkins, of Watford, J.P.; and has issue 1h to 9h.

1h. Edward Watkins Whittington-Ince, b. 3 Oct. 1886.
2h. William Berkeley Whittington-Ince, b. 22 Feb. 1889.
3h. Charles Henry Whittington-Ince, b. 27 Mar. 1892.
4h. Ralph Piggott Whittington-Ince, b. 19 Mar. 1898.
5h. Nora Marjorie Whittington-Ince.
6h. Elinor Gladys Whittington-Ince.
7h. Anna Louisa Whittington-Ince.
8h. Mary Elizabeth Whittington-Ince.
9h. Annie Caroline Whittington-Ince. [Nos. 9834 to 9858.

---

[1] Foster's "Noble and Gentle Families."

The Plantagenet Roll

2g. Rev. Henry Gason Ince, M.A. (Oxon.), Vicar of Stanley 1888-1902 (*Maesbury, Cavendish Road, Bournemouth*), b. 24 Sept. 1857; m. 20 July 1887, Margaret, da. of William Fellows Sedgwick of Cashio Bridge, Watford; and has issue 1h to 4h.

   1h. Cecil William Gason Ince, b. 1 Aug. 1888.
   2h. Henry Montague Ince, b. 26 Sept. 1889.
   3h. Douglas Edward Ince, b. 10 Nov. 1890.
   4h. Norman Sedgwick Ince, b. 9 Feb. 1892.

3g. Rev. James Berkeley Cumming Ince, M.A. (Camb.) (34 *Laurence Road, Hove, Sussex*), b. 26 Nov. 1862; m. 1st, 19 Ap. 1893, Emma Augusta, da. of William Edward Parry Hooper of the Admiralty; 2ndly, 4 May 1905, Ethel, da. of Russell Oates of Knaresborough; and has issue 1h to 5h.

   1h. Gordon Bourchier Ince, b. 5 Feb. 1896.
   2h. Berkeley Russell Ince, b. 5 Feb. 1906.
   3h. Margaret Cumming Ince, b. 5 Feb. 1894.
   4h. Violet Berkeley Ince, b. 21 Mar. 1901.
   5h. Ethel Grace Gason Ince, b. 23 Jan. 1908.

4g. Anna Elizabeth Ince, m. 29 June 1904, Frederick Dru Drury [youngest son of Henry Dru Drury of Blackheath] (*Woolsery, Portchester Road, Bournemouth*); s.p.

2f. Mary Jane Ince, d. 13 Mar. 1856; m. Ap. 1851, Capt. Henry Prescott Pellew Bourchier, d. 1 Aug. 1856; *and had issue.*

See p. 86, Nos. 9813-9823.

7e. Charlotte Margaret Bourchier, d. 21 July 1852; m. 1819, Capt. Edward Parke, R.M., d. 14 Nov. 1835; *and had issue (with 2 das. who d. unm.)* 1f to 3f.

   1f. Richard Parke, C.B., Col. R.M., b. 21 Mar. 1821; d. 2 Mar. 1892; m. 8 May 1862, Louisa, da. of Right Rev. the Hon. Edward Grey, Lord Bishop of Hereford [*E. Grey Coll.*], d. 16 May 1904; *and had issue* 1g to 2g.

     1g. Edward Parke, B.A. (Oxon.), of the Dept. of the Official Receiver in Bankruptcy, b. (—); unm.
     2g. Annie Louisa Parke, *unm.*

   2f. Frederick Parke, Capt. R.N., b. 18 May 1828; d. 22 Nov. 1900; m. 27 Mar. 1856, Lucy Anne, da. of William John Wickham of Winchester, d. 7 Jan. 1906; *and had issue* 1g to 6g.

     1g. Charles Parke, b. 7 July 1857; m. Evelyn, da. of (—) Lewis; and has issue 1h to 4h.

        1h. Frederick Parke, b. 1886; m. 8 Feb. 1910, Clara, da. of (—) Barber.
        2h. Ethel Parke, m. 1905, J. van Norman; and has issue (2 das.).
        3h. Louise Parke, *unm.*
        4h. Gertrude Parke, *unm.*

     2g. William Parke, b. 1859; *unm.*
     3g. Ernest Richard Parke, b. 1861; m. July 1890, Maude, da. of (——) Brown.
     4g. Arthur Fiennes Wickham Parke, b. 1865; m. 1901, J——, da. of (—) McCormac; and has issue 1h to 2h.

        1h. Richard Philip Wickham Parke, b. 28 July 1906.
        2h. Gwendolin Maude Parke, b. 28 Aug. 1902.

     5g. Gertrude Mary Parke, *unm.*
     6g. Mabel Lucy Parke, m. 25 Feb. 1891, William Henry Christopher Macartney, M.D. (*Riverhead House, Sevenoaks*), s.p.

   3f. Caroline Mary Parke, d. 8 Mar. 1901; m. 6 Jan. 1842, the Rev. Isaac Philip Prescott, M.A. (Oxon.), Rector of Kelly, co. Devon [son of Admiral Sir Henry Prescott, G.C.B.], d. 30 Aug. 1898; *and had issue (with a son and da. d. unm.)* 1g to 4g.

[Nos. 9859 to 9895.

of The Blood Royal

1g. *Arthur Edward Prescott,* b. 8 *Mar.* 1852; d. 6 *Mar.* 1888; m. 20 *Nov.* 1877, *Kathleen* (18 *College Court Mansions, Hammersmith, W.*), *da. of the Rev. Henry Clarke, Rector of Guisborough; and has issue* 1h *to* 4h.

1h. Henry Cecil Prescott, b. 1 Mar. 1882.

2h. Arthur Robert Prescott, b. 23 June 1886; m. 1906, E. Cynthia, da. of George Betts; and has issue 1i.

1i. Constance Cynthia Prescott, b. 19 Jan. 1908.

3h. Kathleen Mary Prescott, m. 28 Dec. 1904, Eng.-Lieut. George Henry Starr, R.N.; and has issue 1i.

1i. Mary Cecilia Starr.

4h. Constance Alice Prescott.

2g. *Charlotte Alice Prescott,* d. 20 *Aug.* 1865; m. 25 *July* 1864, *Joseph Kaye, a Master of the Supreme Court of Judicature; and had issue* 1h.

1h. Alice Mary Kaye.

3g. *Mary Prescott,* m. 25 July 1877, Capt. Hardy McHardy, R.N., Chief Constable of Ayrshire (*Ayr*); and has issue (with a son d. young) 1h to 5h.

1h. Robert Prescott McHardy, b. 18 Aug. 1882.

2h. Graham Goodenough McHardy, b. 31 Oct. 1889.

3h. Mary Alice McHardy.

4h. Emily Lees McHardy.

5h. Edith Margaret McHardy.

4g. Beatrice Jane Prescott.

8e. *Anne Bourchier,* d. 29 *Ap.* 1877; m. 5 *July* 1826, *John Spice Hulbert of Stakes Hill Lodge, co. Hants, J.P.,* d. 21 *Feb.* 1844; *and had issue (with 2 sons and a da. d. unm.)* 1f *to* 4f.

1f. *John Henville Hulbert,* b. 2 *June* 1831; d. 8 *May* 1908; m. 1*st,* 20 *June* 1854, *Anna Maria, da. of David John Day of Rochester,* d. 22 *Sept.* 1864; 2*ndly,* 26 *Oct.* 1865, *Harriet, da. of the Rev. Joseph Carson, D.D., Vice-Provost of Trinity College, Dublin,* d. 14 *Dec.* 1884; *and had issue (with a da. d. young)* 1g *to* 15g.

1g. Walter Hulbert, B.A. (Camb.) (*Stakes Hill Lodge, Waterlooville, Hants*), b. 4 June 1856; m. 4 Oct. 1894, Ella Millicent, da. of John Crawford Dodgson, Bengal C.S.; and has issue 1h to 2h.

1h. George Dodgson Hulbert, b. 13 May 1898.

2h. Winifred Beatrice Agnes Hulbert, b. 18 Feb. 1896.

2g. Henry Hulbert, Hop Planter (*Sardis, British Columbia*), b. 5 June 1858; m. in Vancouver, B.C., 11 Oct. 1899, Alice Margaret Victoria, da. of Thomas George Askew, of Victoria, B.C.; and has issue 1h to 5h.

1h. Walter Andrew Bourchier Hulbert, b. 28 Aug. 1902; d. 10 Jan. 1903.

2h. John Eric Bourchier Hulbert, b. 21 Oct. 1906.

3h. Audrey Margaret Ella Hulbert, b. 4 Jan. 1904.

4h. Anna Imogen Hulbert,⎫
5h. Ethel Muriel Hulbert, ⎬ twins, b. at Sardis, 3 Oct. 1909.

3g. Charles Hulbert, a Master in Chancery (*Hillfield, Harrow, Midx.*), b. 5 Feb. 1860; m. 22 June 1887, Frances Mary, da. of William Richardson Jolly; and has issue 1h to 4h.

1h. Charles Geoffrey Keith Hulbert, b. 22 Mar. 1888.

2h. Henry Bourchier Hulbert, b. 16 May 1892.

3h. Frances Sarah Nancy Hulbert, b. 29 Aug. 1893.

4h. Margaret Joan Hulbert, b. 27 Nov. 1894.

4g. John Hulbert, of Messrs. Metcalfe, Hussey & Hulbert of Lincoln's Inn, Solicitors (3 *Campden House Road, London, W.*), b. 12 Sept. 1866; *unm.*

5g. Joseph George Hulbert, M.B. (Camb.), M.R.C.S., L.R.C.P. (Lond.), Major

[Nos. 9896 to 9924.

The Plantagenet Roll

Indian M.S., b. 14 Sept. 1867; m. at Bombay 7 Ap. 1903, Elsie Frances [also descended from King Edward III. through Mortimer Percy (see p. 63)], da. of Alexander Brooke of Handford, co. Chester; and has issue (with an elder son, Alexander Joseph, d. in infancy) 1h.

1h. Richard Carson Hulbert, b. in India 10 July 1907.

6g. William Henville Hulbert (3 *Campden House Road, London, W.*), b. 29 Aug. 1869.

7g. Thomas Ernest Hulbert, Capt. Skinner's Horse, Indian Army, b. 13 July 1879; m. 2 Ap. 1907, Kathleen Beatrice, da. of Thomas H. Harvey, of Blackbrook Grove, Fareham.

8g.[1] Agnes Hulbert, *unm.*

9g.[1] Ethel Hulbert, m. 9 Mar. 1887, Duncan Bell-Irving [2nd son of Henry Bell-Irving of Millbanke, Lockerbie] (*Vancouver, British Columbia*); and has issue 1h to 4h.

1h. Duncan Peter Bell-Irving, b. 3 Jan. 1888.
2h. Robert Bell-Irving, b. 30 July 1893.
3h. Agnes Bell-Irving, b. 26 Jan. 1889.
4h. Dorothy Ethel Bell-Irving, b. 13 May 1890.

10g. Anna Hulbert, m. 27 June 1891, Andrew McCreight Creery [3rd son of the Rev. (—) Creery, Rector of Kilmore, co. Down] (*Vancouver, British Columbia*); and has issue 1h to 6h.

1h. Kenneth Andrew Creery, b. 11 Feb. 1894.
2h. Cuthbert John Creery, b. 11 Ap. 1895.
3h. Ronald Hulbert Creery, b. 12 Feb. 1897.
4h. Leslie Charles Creery, b. 9 Dec. 1898.
5h. Wallace Bourchier Creery, b. 22 Feb. 1900.
6h. Irene Anna Creery, b. 10 Mar. 1892.

11g.[1] Ella Hulbert, *unm.*

12g.[2] Fanny Hulbert, *unm.*

13g.[2] Eleanor Hulbert, m. 10 Sept. 1908, Hugh Alexander Roberts, Solicitor, [also descended from King Edward III. through Mortimer-Percy (see p. 62)] (35 *Brunswick Gardens, Kensington, W.*).

14g.[2] Caroline Edith Hulbert (*Geneva*), *unm.*

15g.[2] Olivia Mary Hulbert (3 *Campden Hill Gardens, London, W.*); *unm.*

2f. Mary Hulbert (*The Elms, Ringwood, Hants*), b. 12 May 1829; m. 22 Aug. 1850, Henry Geldart Metcalfe, of Ringwood, co. Hants, M.A. (Oxon.), b. 22 May 1824; d. 29 Oct. 1899; and had issue (with 2 sons d. young) 1g to 7g.

1g. Henry Hulbert Metcalfe, M.I.C.E. (47 *Queen Street, Auckland; Bridgwater Road, Parnell, New Zealand*); b. 30 Oct. 1851; m. 25 Mar. 1878, Jessie Alexandra, da. of M. Hamilton, of Cheltenham; and has issue 1h to 6h.

1h. Henry Ernest Metcalfe, A.M.I.C.E., b. 29 Dec. 1879.
2h. George Hamilton Metcalfe, b. 23 Ap. 1887.
3h. Ellen Mary Metcalfe, b. 29 Mar. 1881.
4h. Marion Sarah Metcalfe, b. 13 July 1882.
5h. Dorothy Caroline Metcalfe, b. 2 Nov. 1884.
6h. Phyllis Metcalfe, b. 17 Mar. 1889.

2g. John Greetham Metcalfe, Senior Partner in the firm of Metcalfe, Hussey & Hulbert, of 10 New Square, Lincoln's Inn, Solicitors (*Bramleigh, Richmond, Surrey*); b. 8 Jan. 1855; m. 21 June 1890, Elizabeth Rose, da. of Edward Walter Williamson, Sec. to the Law Society; and has issue 1h to 3h.

1h. Percy Hulbert Metcalfe, b. 26 Jan. 1892.
2h. Isabella Brenda Metcalfe, b. 5 Mar. 1894.
3h. Eileen Mary Metcalfe, b. 6 Aug. 1902.

[Nos. 9925 to 9957.

# of The Blood Royal

3g. Arthur Henry Metcalfe, b. 31 Mar. 1859; m. 6 Oct. 1896, Agnese, da. of (—) Doyle; and has issue 1h to 3h.
    1h. Rolland Metcalfe, b. 15 Sept. 1897.
    2h. Fanny Metcalfe, b. 28 Dec. 1898.
    3h. Vera Metcalfe, b. 18 Nov. 1900.
4g. Mary Georgina Metcalfe, m. 18 Sept. 1890, Jeffrey Gott.
5g. Clara Warren Metcalfe, *unm.*
6g. Constance Alice Metcalfe, m. 4 Mar. 1890, Alfred Mason Hayes, P.W.D., Madras*; d. Feb. 1897; and has issue (with an elder da., Constance Mary, d. 24 May 1894) 1h.
    1h. Amy Evelyn Hayes, b. 27 Mar. 1892.
7g. Florence Charlotte Metcalfe, *unm.*

3f. *Annie Caroline Hulbert*, d. 6 Aug. 1857; m. *as 1st wife, 21 Mar. 1855, Major Henry Leslie Hunt, 67th Regt.;* d. 17 Dec. 1880; *and had issue* 1g.
    1g. Rev. Henry de Vere Hunt, B.A. (Camb.), Rector of Ahascragh (*Ahascragh Rectory, Ballinasloe*), b. 12 Mar. 1856; m. 20 July 1882, Mary Catherine Caroline, da. of the Rev. Peter William Browne of Blackrod, co. Lanc.; and has issue 1h to 4h.
        1h. Henry Leslie Hunt, b. 21 Ap. 1890.
        2h. Alice Kathleen Hunt, b. 15 Sept. 1883.
        3h. Eleanor Caroline Hunt, b. 21 July 1885.
        4h. Vera Mary Hunt, b. 11 Dec. 1886.
    4f. Fanny Hulbert.

9e. *Susanna Bourchier*, b. 13 *Ap.* 1800; d. 9 *Nov.* 1875; m. 24 *Mar.* 1827, *John Cole of Easthorpe Court, co. Linc., who became,* 27 *July* 1854, *de jure 4th Duke of Polignano (Duca di Polignano) [Naples],* d. 12 *Ap.* 1855; *and had issue* (with a da. d.s.p.) 1f to 2f.
    1f. *John Charles (Cole), 5th Duke of Polignano [Naples], of Easthorpe Court,* d.s.p. 14 *Ap.* 1897.
    2f. James (Cole, now Edwin-Cole), 6th Duke of Polignano (Duca di Polignano) [Naples, 26 Aug. 1730], &c., J.P., Bar.-at-Law (*Swineshead Hall, via Boston, co. Linc.*), b. 27 Ap. 1835; m. 7 Dec. 1880, Mary Barbara, da. of Gent Huddleston, s.p.

5d. Richard Bourchier, b. 11 *May* 1749.
6d. *Mary Bourchier*, b. 1 *Oct.* 1737; d. 1813; m. *the Rev. James Torkington, of Stukeley Hall and Rector of Little Stukeley, co. Hunts* [descended from the Lady Anne, sister of Edward IV. (see the Exeter Volume, p. 662)], d. (–); *and had issue* 1e to 4e.
    1e. *James Torkington, of Great Stukeley,* d. 7 *June* 1828; m. 22 Oct. 1799, *Elizabeth, da. of Charles Bourchier; and had issue.*
    See pp. 84–85, Nos. 9790–9807.
    2e. *Edward Torkington.*
    3e. *Mary Torkington.*
    4e. *Dorothy Torkington.*

7d. *Elizabeth Bourchier*, b. 6 *June* 1745; d. 18 Feb. 1791; m. *the Rev. William Lloyd, Preacher of the Charter House, and of Much Hadham; and had issue.*
8d. *Frances Bourchier*, b. 6 Sept. 1746; d. (–); m. *John Howell (?) of Ross.*
9d. *Julia Charlotte Bourchier*, b. 11 Feb. 1752; d. (–); m. (—) *Tonge of London.*

2b. *Charles Gataker.*
3b. *Thomas Gataker.*
4b. *George Gataker*, d. (–); m. (—), *da. of* (—) *Nash; and had issue.*
5b. *William Gataker*, b. 1691; d. (–); m. *Ann, da. of James Willett.*
6b. *Barbara Gataker*, b. (–); m. 1st, *John Pitcairn of London, Merchant;* 2ndly (—) *Withers of co. Kent; and had issue* 1c.
    1c. *Barbara Pitcairn*, d. (–); m. *Thomas Carter of Dunton, co. Bucks.*

[Nos. 9974 to 9991.

91

The Plantagenet Roll

7*b.* Frances Gataker, b. c. 1678; d. 1715; m. the Rev. Benjamin Reynolds, Rector of Hoggeston, d. 18 Dec. 1758, *in his 82nd year; and had issue* 1c.
   1*c.* Rev. Benjamin Reynolds, Rector of Hoggeston, b. c. 1703; d. 1 Nov. 1781.
7*a.* Theodosia Hebblethwaite, bapt. 4 Dec. 1658.
8*a.* Margaret Hebblethwaite, bapt. 10 *June* 1665.

35. Descendants, if any, of FRANCES MARWOOD (Table VI.), b. c. 1642; living 1679; *m.* 1st, Sir RICHARD WESTON of Gray's Inn, Bar.-at-Law, living 1679; 2ndly, as 2nd wife (lic. 4 May), 1682, Sir EDWARD SMITH, 1st Bart. [E.], K.B., d. (*s.p.* by her) 1707.

36. Descendants of the Rev. THOMAS METCALFE of Northallerton and Sand Hutton, co. York, M.A. (Table VI.), *bapt.* 28 Mar. 1706; *d.* 10 Feb. 1774; *m.* Ascension Day, 1742, ANNE, da. of William SMELT of Kirkby Fleetham, co. York, M.D., *d.* 10 Feb. 1804; and had issue 1*a* to 3*a.*

   1*a.* Rev. George Metcalfe, *afterwards Marwood, of Northallerton and Little Busby Hall, Canon Residentiary of Chichester,* b. 28 Nov. 1746; d. 1 Dec. 1827; m. 1st, 1780, *Margaret,* da. *of Francis Peirson of Mowthorpe Grange, co. York;* 2ndly, *Lucy,* widow *of Capt. Charles Dodgson,* da. *of James Hume; and had issue* 1*b* to 3*b.*
   1*b.* George Metcalfe Marwood *of Busby Hall,* b. 29 *June* 1781; d. 9 *Jan.* 1842; m. 1 *Aug.* 1804, *Mary,* da. *of Capt. John Quantock of Norton House, co. Somerset,* d. 23 *May* 1838; *and had issue* 1*c* to 3*c.*
   1*c.* George Metcalfe Marwood *of Busby Hall,* J.P., D.L., b. 31 Dec. 1808; d. 8 *Ap.* 1882; m. 28 Oct. 1854, *Frances Anne,* da. *of the Rev. Frederick Peel, Preb. of Lincoln,* d. 19 Oct. 1886; *and had issue* 1*d* to 1*ld.*
   1*d.* George Frederick Marwood *of Busby Hall, &c.,* J.P., b. 8 *Ap.* 1858; d.s.p. 23 *May* 1898.
   2*d.* William Francis Marwood of Busby Hall, J.P., Hereditary Lord and Chief Bailiff of Langburgh Wapentake (*Busby Hall, Carlton in Cleveland, York*), *b.* 1 Feb. 1863.
   3*d.* Henry Marwood, Lieut.-Col. Comdg. 2nd Batt. North Staffordshire Regt. (*Multan, India*), *b.* 6 July 1864; *m.* 14 May 1898, Ethel Mary J., da. and h. of Henry G. Piggott of Sheffield Gardens, Kensington; and has issue 1*e* to 2*e.*
   1*e.* George Henry Marwood, *b.* 31 Aug. 1901.
   2*e.* Ethel Mary Marwood, *b.* 4 Mar. 1899.
   4*d.* Arthur Pierson Marwood (*Winchelsea*), *b.* 21 Aug. 1868; *m.* 4 Feb. 1903, Caroline, da. of Matthew Cranswick of Hunmanby, co. York, *s.p.*
   5*d.* Frances Mary Marwood (3D *The Mansions, Earl's Court Road, S.W.*).
   6*d.* Emily Caroline Marwood, *m.* as 2nd wife, 24 Feb. 1876, Edward Heneage Wynne-Finch, J.P., Bar.-at-Law (*Stokesley Manor, York*); and has issue 1*e* to 3*e.*
   1*e.* Arthur Wynne-Finch, *b.* 15 Oct. 1878.
   2*e.* Griffith Wynne-Finch, Lieut. King's Royal Rifle Corps, *b.* 16 Oct. 1880.
   3*e.* Helen Wynne-Finch.
   7*d.* Lucy Susanna Marwood, *m.* 24 Feb. 1881, Charles Napier Kennedy (*Bigfrith End, Cookham Dean*); and has issue 1*e* to 3*e.*
   1*e.* George Lawrence Kennedy, *b.* 24 Nov. 1881.
   2*e.* John Pitt Kennedy, Lieut. Scottish Rifles, *b.* 12 Aug. 1883.
   3*e.* Horace Tristram Kennedy, *b.* 25 Nov. 1887. [Nos. 9992 to 10005.

of The Blood Royal

8d. Elinor Edith Marwood, m. 4 June 1891, Charles Moore Kennedy, B.L. [son of John Pitt Kennedy, Judge Advocate, Calcutta High Court] (*Leaves Green, Keston, Hayes, Kent*); and has issue 1e to 4e.

    1e. Tristram Gervais Kennedy, b. 14 June 1897.
    2e. David Kennedy, b. (twin) 20 Oct. 1901.
    3e. Margaret Kennedy, b. 23 Ap. 1896.
    4e. Virginia Kennedy, b. (twin) 20 Oct. 1901.

9d. Clara Charlotte Marwood.
10d. Lilian Marwood.
11d. Rose Marwood.

2c. *Margaret Marwood*, b. 12 Mar. 1809; d. 2 Nov. 1877; m. 13 Dec. 1842, *Rear-Adm. Colson Festing, R.N.*, b. 12 Sept. 1795; d. 12 Oct. 1870; *and had issue (with a son d. unm.)* 1d to 3d.

    1d. Henry Marwood Colson Festing, Comm. R.N.*(ret.) (*Glencree, Paignton, Devon*), b. (—); m. (—).

    2d. Michael Morton Metcalfe Festing, Capt. (ret.) 20th Foot (21 *Park Crescent, Oxford*), b. 28 Jan. 1851; m. 27 Ap. 1881, Mary Elizabeth, da. of Thomas Hicks of Stanghow, Cleveland; and has issue 1e to 2e.

        1e. Michael Colson Festing, b. 15 Sept. 1885.
        2e. Margaret Vera Festing, b. 18 July 1882.

    3d. Mary Georgina Festing, *unm.*

3c. *Anne Frederica Marwood*, b. 1823; d. 12 Sept. 1884; m. (*at Stokesley, co. York*), 1845, *the Rev. Henry Boyick Scougall, Vicar of Rudgeley, co. Stafford*, b. (*at Tawstock, co. Devon*) 1822; d. (*at Ilfracombe*) 8 Oct. 1865; *and had (with another son and da. who d. unm.) issue* 1d to 5d.

    1d. Henry Scougall.
    2d. John Hearnage Scougall.
    3d. Charles Scougall.
    4d. Hugh Boyick Watkin Scougall.
    5d. Frederica Elizabeth Scougall, m. 6 July 1875, the Rev. Alfred Henry Malan [grandson of Dr. César Malan of Geneva] (*Altarnon Sanctuary, Launceston, Cornwall*); and has issue (with a da. who died in infancy) 1e to 2e.

        1e. Francis Malan, b. 30 May 1877.
        2e. Lionel de Mérindol Malan, b. 16 Mar. 1884.

2b.¹ *Margaret Metcalfe*, b. 1795; d. (-); m. 1822, *the Rev. Charles Hutchinson of Firle, co. Sussex, Canon of Chichester*, d. (-); *and had issue.*

3b.² *Mary Anne Marwood*, b. 1813; d. 22 Mar. 1870; m. *William Wilcox, Collector of H.M. Customs, Sunderland*, d. (-); *and had issue.*

*2a. *Cornelius Metcalfe of Manchester and London, Merchant*, b. 6 Oct. 1749; d. *after* 1795; m. *Dec.* 1773, *Sarah, da. of Samuel Bayley of Manchester; and had issue* 1b to 3b.

    1b. Thomas Metcalfe *of Lincoln's Inn and Portland Place, London, and Regency Square, Brighton*, b. 16 *Oct.* 1781; d. (-); m. *Christiana Brisbane, da. and h. of Henry Kerr Cranstoun* [eldest son of the Hon. George Cranstoun, 4th son of William, 5th Lord Cranstoun [S.]], d. (-); *and had issue* 1c to 6c.

        1c. Thomas M*etcalfe*, b. 31 *Aug.* 1809; d. 1843; m. *Grace, da. of William Shepperd, London, Banker*, d. (-); *and had issue* 1d.

            1d. William Marwood Metcalfe, Capt. Royal Elthorne L.I., b. 1839.

        2c. *Henry Cranstoun Metcalfe, Civil and Sessions Judge at Tipperah, Bengal*, b. 20 *Sept.* 1810; d. (-); m. (—), *da. of* (—); *and had issue* 1d.

            1d. Henry Howe Metcalfe, *late B.C.S.*, b. (—); *m.* and has issue.

        3c. *Ernest Metcalfe, Major 48th Madras Native Infantry, Assist. Resident Counsellor, Prince of Wales Island*, b. 5 *Jan.* 1823; d. 1866; m. 1861, *Julia Catherine, da. of John Shaw of London and Crayford, co. Kent*, d. (-); *and had issue* 1d to 2d.

[Nos. 10006 to 10027.

The Plantagenet Roll

1*d*. Hope Cranstoun Metcalfe (*Dearbrook, Hersham Road, Walton-on-Thames*), *b.* (at Penang, Strait Settlements) 22 Feb. 1866; *m.* 1894, Edith, da. of (—) Kirkpatrick; and has issue (with one other) 1*e* to 2*e*.
    1*e*. Frances Hope Metcalfe.
    2*e*. Sylvia Metcalfe.
  2*d*. Katharine Mary Metcalfe, *b.* at Harryhur, Mysore; *m.* (—).

4*c*. Christiana Metcalfe, d. (–); m. George Clutterbuck Tugwell *of Bath, Banker*, d. (–); *and had issue* 1*d to* 2*d*.
  1*d*. Rev. George Tugwell, M.A. (Oxon.), Rector of Bathwick, Bath, 1871–1894, author of various well-known works (*Southcliffe, Lee, Ilfracombe*), *b.* (—); *s.p.*
  2*d*. Henry William Tugwell (*Crowe Hall, Bath*), *b.* (—); *m.* and has issue (2 das.).

5*c*. *Julia Henrietta Metcalfe*, d. (–); m. *Francis Ommanney of Platt House, Putney; and had issue.*
6*c*. *Emily Metcalfe*, d. (–); m. *Francis Orme; and had issue.*

2*b*. *Anne Metcalfe*, d. (–); m. *James Currie of London; and had issue.*
3*b*. *Dorothy Metcalfe*, d. (–); m. *George William Babington, Surgeon 3rd Dragoons*, d. (–); *and had (with possibly other) issue* 1*c*.
  1*c*. *Cornelius Metcalfe Stuart Babington of Hertford Street, Mayfair, Physician.*

3*a*. Rev. Francis Metcalfe, M.A. (Camb.), Rector *of Kirkbride, &c.,* b. 30 *Ap.* 1752; d. 11 *Nov.* 1822; m. 12 *Nov.* 1785, *Harriett*, da. *of John Clough of York*, d. 9 *June* 1803; *and had issue* 1*b*.
  1*b*. Henry Metcalfe, Lieut. 32nd Regt., b. 10 *Feb.* 1794; bur. 7 *Oct.* 1828; m. *Mary*, da. *of* (———) *Gibson of Guernsey; and had issue* 1*c to* 2*c*.
    1*c*. Anne Metcalfe, living *unm.* 1873.
    2*c*. Harriet Metcalfe, living a widow *s.p.* 1873; *m.* (—).
  2*b*. *John Metcalfe, Capt. H.E.I.C.S.*, b. 9 *Mar.* 1795; d. (at *Madras*) 18 *June* 1833; m. 2*ndly*, 30 *Sept.* 1828, *Keturah, widow of the Rev. John Jeffreys, da. of George Yarnold of Worcester*, d. 5 *Jan.* 1858; *and had issue* 1*c*.
    1*c*. *John Henry Metcalfe of Crayke Castle, co. York, a well-known Antiquary*, d. *unm.*
  3*b*. *Thomas Metcalfe*, b. 28 *Dec.* 1796; d.s.p.m. 1879; *m. and had issue.*

[Nos. 10028 to 10035.

37. Descendants of MARGARET METCALFE (Table VI.), *b.* 1665; *bur.* 20 Dec. 1690; *m.* as 1st wife, 1672, DANIEL LASCELLES of Stank and North Allerton, M.P., High Sheriff co. York 1719, *b.* 6 Nov. 1655; *d.* 5 Sept. 1734; and had issue 1*a* to 2*a*.

1*a*. Mary Lascelles, bapt. 13 *Sept.* 1683; d. 25 *Ap.* 1727; m. 27 *Aug.* 1706, *Cuthbert Mitford of North Allerton.*
2*a*. *Elizabeth Lascelles*, d. (–); m. 10 *Sept.* 1713, *George Ord of Longridge, co. Northumberland*, d. 25 Feb. 1745.

38. Descendants of ANNE HESKETH of Heslington, co. York (see Table V.), *b.* 2 Ap. 1676; *d.* 19 Ap. 1718; *m.* (lic. dated 31 Oct.) 1692, Lieut.-Col. JAMES YARBURGH of Snaith Hall, co. York, a godson of King James II., *bur.* 9 Mar. 1730; and had issue 1*a*.

1*a*. *Charles Yarburgh of Heslington and Snaith Hall, event. sole h.,* b. 10 *May* 1716; d. 6 *Aug.* 1789; m. 2*ndly, Sarah, da. of Sylvanus Griffin of Wirksworth; and had issue* 1*b*.

of The Blood Royal

1b. Sarah Yarburgh, da. and in her issue (1852) sole h., bapt. 18 Mar. 1761; d. 21 Oct. 1785; m. as 1st wife, 1 Aug. 1782, John Græme of Sowerby House, co. York, J.P., D.L., b. 7 Aug. 1759; d. 24 Feb. 1841; and had issue 1c.

1c. Alicia Maria Græme, da. and event. h., b. 1784; d. 3 Jan. 1867; m. 17 May 1810, George Lloyd of Stockton Hall, near York, b. 21 May 1787; d. 12 Mar. 1863; and had issue 1d to 4d.

1d. George John Lloyd, afterwards (R.L. 15 Ap. 1875) Yarburgh, of Heslington Hall, J.P., b. 28 July 1811; d. 16 Mar. 1875; m. 23 July 1840, Mary Antonia, da. of Samuel Chetham Hilton of Pennington Hall, co. Lancaster, d. Jan. 1868; and had issue 1e to 2e.

1e. Mary Elizabeth Yarburgh, d. 22 Oct. 1884; m. 8 May 1862, George William (Bateson, sometime (R.L. 15 Ap. 1876) Bateson de Yarburgh, and finally de Yarburgh-Bateson), 2nd Baron Deramore [U.K.], d. 29 Ap. 1893; and had issue 1f to 5f.

1f. Robert Wilfred (de Yarburgh-Bateson), 3rd Baron Deramore and a Bart. [U.K.], J.P., D.L., C.C., Major Yorkshire Hussars, &c. (*Heslington Hall, Yorkshire; Belvoir Park, Belfast*), b. 5 Aug. 1865; m. 1st, 15 July 1897, Lucy Caroline, da. of William Henry Fife of Lee Hall, Northumberland, d. 26 Oct. 1901; 2ndly, 26 June 1907, Blanche Violet, da. of Col. Philip Saltmarshe of Daresbury, J.P.; and has issue 1g.

1g. Hon. Moira Faith Lilian de Yarburgh-Bateson.

2f. Hon. George Nicholas de Yarburgh-Bateson, J.P. (*North Cliff, Filey; Carlton*), b. 25 Nov. 1870; m. 12 Dec. 1900, Muriel Katharine, da. of Arthur Grey (formerly Duncombe) of Sutton Hall, Easingwold; and has issue 1g to 2g.

1g. Stephen Nicholas de Yarburgh-Bateson, b. 18 May 1903.

2g. Judith Katharine de Yarburgh-Bateson, b. 22 Mar. 1909.

3f. Hon. Eustace de Yarburgh-Bateson, b. 13 Oct. 1884.

4f. Hon Mary Lilla de Yarburgh-Bateson.

5f. Hon. Katherine Hylda de Yarburgh-Bateson.

2e. Susan Anne Yarburgh, d. 21 May 1908; m. 25 Jan. 1865, Charles Lethbridge, J.P., High Sheriff co. Hants 1895 [Bt. [U.K.] 1804 Coll.] (*Heytesbury, Wilts; Carlton*); and had issue 1f to 6f.

1f. Ambrose Yarburgh Lethbridge, late Lieut. Grenadier Guards, b. 2 Nov. 1874; d. 11 Sept. 1909; m. 4 Feb. 1898, Violet (*Trevissome, Flushing, Falmouth*), da. of Charles Townsend Murdoch, M.P.; and has issue 1g to 3g.

1g. Thomas Charles Lethbridge, b. 23 Mar. 1901.

2g. Ambrose William Speke Lethbridge, b. 6 Ap. 1907.

3g. Jacintha Lethbridge, b. 7 June 1904.

2f. Mary Lethbridge, m. 19 Ap. 1888, the Rev. Herbert Barnett, Vicar of Bracknell (*Bracknell Vicarage, Berks*); and has issue 1g to 3g.

1g. John Canning Lethbridge Barnett, b. 27 May 1894.

2g. Avice Mary Barnett.

3g. Bridget Susan Barnett.

3f. Dorothea Lethbridge, m. 17 Nov. 1892, Arthur Finch Charrington (*East Hill, Oxted, Surrey; Oxford and Cambridge*); and has issue 1g to 4g.

1g. Peter Ronald Lethbridge Charrington, b. 27 June 1897.

2g. John Arthur Pepys Charrington, b. 17 Feb. 1905.

3g. Lettice Mary Charrington, b. 28 June 1906.

4g. Susan Auriol Charrington, b. 26 Sept. 1908.

4f. Ellinor Lethbridge.

5f. Ruth Lethbridge, m. 14 Jan. 1904, Willoughby Arthur Pemberton (11 Lower Belgrave Street, S.W.; White's; St James'); and has issue 1g to 2g.

1g. Mordaunt Ashington Sigerist Pemberton, b. 15 Mar. 1907.

2g. Camilla Lethbridge Pemberton, b. 5 Oct. 1905.

6f. Rachel Lethbridge.

[Nos. 10036 to 10060.

The Plantagenet Roll

2d. Rev. *Yarburgh Gamaliel Lloyd, afterwards Lloyd-Greame of Sewerby House*, co. York, J.P., b. 18 *July* 1813 ; d. 30 *May* 1890 ; m. 7 *May* 1839, *Editha Christian, da. of William Augustus Le Hunte of Astramount, co. Wexford*, d. 1900 ; *and had issue* 1e.

1e. Yarburgh George Lloyd-Greame of Sewerby House, M.A. (Camb.), J.P., Lieut.-Col. (*ret.*) Yorkshire Artillery Militia (*Sewerby House, Bridlington*), b. 15 June 1840 ; *m.* 6 Aug. 1867, Dora Letitia, da. of the Right Rev. James Thomas O'Brien, Lord Bishop of Ossory ; and has issue 1f to 4f.

1f. Yarburgh Lloyd-Greame, *late* Lieut. Yorkshire Artillery, b. 19 May 1872 ; *m.* 11 Jan. 1898, Alice Mary, da. of Major George Mark Leycester Egerton of The Mount, York ; and has issue 1g to 2g.

1g. Yarburgh Derek Lloyd-Greame, b. 1902.

2g. Nancy Lloyd-Greame.

2f. Philip Lloyd-Greame.

3f. Editha Lloyd-Greame.

4f. Dora Lloyd-Greame, *m.* 1904, Capt. George Martin Hannay, *formerly* King's Own Scottish Borderers.

3d. Rev. *Henry Lloyd*, M.A. (Camb.), *Rector of Yarburgh*, b. 31 *Dec.* 1815 ; d. 17 *Nov.* 1862 ; m. 30 *Sept.* 1857, *Anne Eliza, da. of the Rev. William Roy, D.D.*, d. 27 *May* 1903 ; *and had issue* 1e to 3e.

1e. George William Lloyd of Stockton Hall, J.P., M.A. (Camb.) (*Stockton Hall, near York*), b. 4 Mar. 1861 ; *unm.*

2e. Henry John Greame Lloyd, Major Cornwall Militia, *late* Duke of Cornwall's L.I. (*Byams, Marchwood, Hants*), b. 6 June 1862 ; *m.* 9 Dec. 1886, Caroline Emily, da. of John Harris Peter-Hoblyn of Colquite, co. Cornwall ; and has issue 1f to 5f.

1f. Cyril Gascoigne Lloyd, b. 11 Sept. 1887.

2f. John Rodney Lloyd, b. 21 June 1890.

3f. Henry Greame Lloyd, b. 2 Dec. 1892.

4f. Caroline Doris Lloyd.

5f. Kathleen Anne Lloyd.

3e. Alicia Margaret Lloyd.

4d. *Edward Lloyd of Lingcroft, near York*, b. 27 *May* 1823 ; d. 4 *Feb.* 1869 ; m. 21 *Sept.* 1854, *Rosabella Susan, da. of George Lloyd of Cowsby Hall, co. York*, d. 20 *July* 1909 ; *and had issue* 1e to 3e.

1e. Georgina Rosabella Lloyd, *m.* 15 July 1879, George St. Maur Palmes, *late* 14th Hussars [himself a descendant of King Edward III.] (*Lingcroft, near York*) ; and has issue 1f to 5f.

1f. Geoffrey St. Maur Palmes, b. 26 Dec. 1881.

2f. Edward William Eustace Palmes, b. 23 Aug. 1884.

3f. Bryan Wilfrid Palmes, b. 3 June 1891.

4f. Cecil Muriel Palmes, *m.* 1908, Alick May Cunard, Lieut. 5th Royal Irish Rifles ; and has issue 1g.

1g. [son] Cunard.

5f. Joan Mary Georgina Palmes.

2e. Edith Maria Greame Lloyd, *m.* 22 Ap. 1879, Frederick Reynard of Sunderlandwick and Hobgreen, J.P., D.L. (*Sunderlandwick, Driffield ; Hobgreen, Ripley*) ; and has issue 1f to 2f.

1f. Claude Edward Reynard, b. 9 Feb. 1880.

2f. Charles Frederick Reynard, b. 14 Jan. 1889.

3e. Cecil Mary Lloyd, *m.* 9 Nov. 1887, Henry Charles Talbot Rice, *late* Capt. 4th Batt. Gloucester Regt. [B. Dynevor Coll.] (*North Cerney House, Cirencester*) ; and has issue 1f to 3f.

1f. Harry Talbot Rice, b. 27 July 1889.

2f. John Arthur Talbot Rice, b. 3 Jan. 1892.

3f. David Talbot Rice, b. 11 July 1903.

[Nos. 10061 to 10089.

# of The Blood Royal

39. Descendants, if any, of MATILDA BETHELL (Table V.), d. (–) ; m. the Rev. ROBERT GOODWIN.

40. Descendants, if any surviving, of KATHERINE SLINGSBY (Table IV.), bapt. 31 July 1584; d. a. 1621; m. as 1st wife (lic. dated) 1603, Sir JOHN FENWICK of Fenwick, 1st Bart. [E.], d. 1658; and had issue (with a son who d.s.p.v.p.) 1a to 2a.

   1a. Catherine Fenwick.
   2a. Elizabeth Fenwick.

41. Descendants of ALICE SLINGSBY (Table IV.), d. (–) ; m. as 1st wife, THOMAS WATERTON of Walton Hall, co. York, b. c. 1585 ; d. 1641; and had issue 1a to 7a.

   1a. Thomas Waterton of Walton Hall, d. (–); m. Alice, widow of Edward Clarke of Winterset, da. of (—) Wetherby ; and had issue 1b to 4b.
   1b. Thomas Waterton of Walton Hall, d. (–); m. Catherine, da. of Nicholas Fairfax of Gilling ; and had issue 1c.
   1c. Charles Waterton of Walton Hall, bur. 25 Jan. 1726; m. 1st, Anne, da. of Sir William Gerard, 4th Bart. [E.]; 3rdly Anne, da. of William Poole [Bt. of Poole Coll.], living 1726 ; and had issue 1d to 4d.
   1d. Charles Waterton of Walton Hall, imprisoned at York, 1746, as a Jacobite, d. (–) ; m. 1733, Mary, da. of Cresacre More of Bamborough [6th in descent from Sir Thomas More] ; and had issue 1e to 4e.
   1e. Thomas Waterton of Walton Hall, bur. 19 Mar. 1805; m. Anne, da. and h. of Edward Bedingfield [Bt. Coll.]; and had issue 1f to 2f.
   1f. Charles Waterton of Walton Hall, Author of "Wanderings in South America," &c., b. 3/12 June 1782 ; d. 27 May 1865; m. (at Bruges) 11 May 1829, Anne, da. of Charles Edmonstone of Cardress Park, co. Dumbarton, d. 27 Ap. 1830 ; and had issue 1g.
   1g. Edmund Waterton of Walton Hall and afterwards of Deeping Waterton, Knight of the Order of Christ, Private Chamberlain to H.H. Pope Pius IX., J.P., D.L., F.S.A., &c., b. 7 Ap. 1830; d. 1887; m. 1st, 20 Aug. 1862, Margaret Alicia Josephine, da. and co-h. of Sir John Ennis, 1st Bt. [U.K.], d. (at Cannes) 26 Dec. 1879 ; 2ndly, 15 Nov. 1881, Helen, da. and h. of John Mercer of Alston Hall, co. Lancaster, J.P. ; and had issue 1h to 7h.
   1h. Charles Edmund Maria Joseph Aloysius Waterton of Deeping Waterton, co. Lincoln, b. 10 June 1863 ; d. 23 Feb. 1897 ; m. 1890, Josephine, da. of John Rock of Northbank, Shepton Mallet ; and had issue 1i to 4i.
   1i. Joseph Waterton (Deeping Waterton Hall, Market Deeping), b. 18 Nov. 1893.
   2i. Charles Waterton.
   3i. Edmond Waterton.
   4i. John Waterton.

   2h. Thomas More Mary Joseph Pius Waterton (Johnstone, Enfield ; Martinstown, co. Meath), b. 8 July 1876.
   3h.[1] Mary Paula Pia Waterton, a Canoness Regular of St. Augustine's, Bruges.
   4h.[1] Agnes Mary Pia Waterton.
   5h.[1] Josephine Mary Everilda Pia Waterton.
   6h.[2] Monica Mary Colette Paula Waterton.
   7h.[2] Ethelburga Mary Magdalen Pega Waterton.   [Nos. 10090 to 10099.

The Plantagenet Roll

2*f*. *Isabel Waterton*, d. (-); m. *John Philips Steel of Wakefield*.[1]

2*e*. *Christopher Waterton of Woodlands, co. York, and Demerara*, d. 10 Oct. 1809; m. *Anne*, widow of *Edward Bermingham, da. of John Waddell, M.D.*; d. 29 Aug. 1821; *and had issue 1f to 3f*.

1*f*. *George Waterton of Woodlands, and afterwards* (1851) *of Hunslett and of Dublin in* 1865,[2] *an Officer in the Austrian Service*, d. (-); m. 185–, *the Baroness Matilda*, widow of *Maurice, Baron Mack von Leiberich* (d. 28 Feb. 1851), da. of *Joseph Felix William Dominic (von Barco), Baron Barco* [H.R.E. 1745], b. 27 Dec. 1805; d. (-).

2*f*. *Henry Waterton of Winsford Lodge, co. Chester, in* 1843, d. (-); m. *Isabella*, da. of *William Wallace Ogle of Cawsey Park, Northumberland*, d. 1889; *and had issue 1g to 4g*.

1*g*. Charles Waterton, *b*. (—);
2*g*. Bertram Robert Waterton, *b*. (—); } settled in New Zealand.

3*g*. Rev. Canon George Webb Waterton (*Durran-hill, Carlisle*), *b*. (—).

4*g*. *Frances Waterton*, d. 12 Feb. 1890; m. 1*st*, 4 *June* 1860, *Edward Seymour-Ball-Hughes*, d. 1866/7; 2*ndly*, 24 *June* 1872, *Sir Maurice Duff-Gordon*, 4*th Bt*. [U.K.], d. 5 *May* 1896; *and had issue 1h to 3h*.

1*h*. *Charles Ball-Hughes*, b. Dec. 1862; d. *Mar*. 1897.

2*h*. Marie Louise Ball-Hughes (22 *Royal Avenue, Sloane Square, S.W.*), *m*. 12 Aug. 1885, Henry Arthur Tennent, *d*. 6 Nov. 1905; and has issue 1*i* to 5*i*.

1*i*. Marguerite Lucy Tennent, *b*. 1 July 1886.
2*i*. Violet Frances Tennent, *b*. 24 Sept. 1887.
3*i*. Myrtle Marie Ida Tennent, *b*. 10 Oct. 1888.
4*i*. Olive Cecilia Tennent, *b*. 21 Nov. 1889.
5*i*. Iris Veronica Tennent, *b*. 18 Nov. 1890.

3*h*. Caroline Lucie Duff-Gordon, *m*. 1 July 1902, Aubrey William Waterfield (*Northbourne Abbey, Eastry, R.S.O.*); and has issue 1*i*.

1*i*. Henry Gordon Ottiwell Waterfield, *b*. 24 May 1903.

3*f*. *Matilda Waterton*, d. 14 *July* 1865; m. 25 *July* 1829, *Edmund William Jerningham* [B. Stafford Coll.], d. 2 Nov. 1860; *and had issue*.

See the Clarence Volume, pp. 448–449, Nos. 19067–19104.

3*e*. *Mary Waterton*, b. 1733; d. (? *unm*.).[3]
4*e*. *Anne Waterton*, d. (-); m. [——] *Daly*.[3]
2*d*. *Robert Waterton*.[3]
3*d*. *Joseph Waterton*.[3]
4*d*. *Catherine Waterton*.[3]
2*b*. *John Waterton*.[3]
3*b*. *Alice Waterton*.[3]
4*b*. *Anne Waterton*.[3]

2*a*. *Priscilla Waterton*, bur. 10 *Sept*. 1638 s.p.s.; m. *as 1st wife*, Thomas Beckwith *of Aickton*.

3*a*. *Elizabeth Waterton*, d. (-); m. *as 2nd wife*, Francis Malham *of Elslack in Craven*, b. 22 May 1660; d. (-); *and had issue 1b*.[4]

1*b*. Francis Malham, aged 16, May 1666.

4*a*. *Mary Waterton*, d. (-); m. 1*st*, *William Ramsden of Lascelles Hall, co. York*, d. shortly before 30 *Sept*. 1639; 2*ndly*, Sir *Thomas Smith of Broxton* [brother to 1*st* Lord Carrington [5]]; *and had (with possibly others by 2nd husband) issue 1b*.

[Nos. 10100 to 10148.

---

[1] Foster's "Yorkshire Pedigrees." [2] Freih. Taschenbuch, 1865, p. 22.
[3] Foster's "Yorkshire Pedigrees." [4] Whitaker's "Craven," p. 91.
[5] She was possibly his second wife. In Nichol's "Leicester" (iii. 29) he is said to have married the daughter and heiress of Sir Thomas Blackston [Blakiston, 1st Bart., see p. 299], and no issue is mentioned.

# of The Blood Royal

1b. John Ramsden, h. to father, and aged 51 years and 2 months 30 Sept. 1639.

5a. Rosamund Waterton.

6a. Anne Waterton, m. Francis Middelton.

7a. Frances Waterton.

42. Descendants of ANNE STAPYLTON [sister and h. of Sir Martin Stapylton of Myton, 8th and last Bart. [E.]] (Table VII.), d. (–); m. 1770, the Rev. JOHN BREE, M.A., and Fellow of Balliol College, Oxford, and Rector of Marks Tey, co. Essex, d. 1796; and had issue 1a to 3a.

1a. Martin Bree, afterwards (R.L. 13 July 1811) Stapylton of Myton, b. Sept. 1771; d. 7 Mar. 1842; m. 1st, Sophia, da. of William Parsons of Plymouth ; 2ndly, Anne, da. of William Curtis of Chiswick; and had issue 1b to 4b.

1b. Stapylton Stapylton of Myton, b. 22 Jan. 1798; d. 8 July 1864; m. 2ndly, 5 Aug. 1830, Margaret, da. of Thomas Tomlinson of York, d. 29 Nov. 1883; and had issue 1c to 2c.

1c. Henry Miles Stapylton of Myton, J.P., D.L., b. 8 July 1831; d.s.p. 25 Mar. 1896.

2c. Martin Bryan Stapylton, M.A. (Oxon.), J.P., Bar.-at-Law, b. 23 Nov. 1832; d. 2 Jan. 1894; m. 11 Dec. 1860, Mary Jane, da. of John Brymer of Islington House, Dorset, d. 1 Jan. 1885; and had issue 1d to 4d.

1d. Miles John Stapylton of Myton, Lord of the Manor of Eston, co. York, J.P., D.L., Major late Yorkshire Hussars and 21st Lancers (Myton Hall, Helperby), b. 28 Mar. 1869; m. 14 Feb. 1900, Norah Evelyn, da. of J. H. Love of Hawkhills, Easingwold; and has issue 1e to 3e.

1e. Miles Henry Stapylton, b. 29 Jan. 1901.

2e. Ursula Evelyn Mary Stapylton.

3e. Norah Cecilia Stapylton.

2d. Martin Frederick Stapylton, late R.N., b. 1 Oct. 1873; m. 3 Sept. 1901, Ethel Horatia, da. of J. H. Love of Hawkhills, Easingwold; and has issue 1e.

1e. Olive Love Stapylton.

3d. Laura Mary Stapylton, m. 1st, 19 Dec. 1882, Col. Huntly Bacon of Apton Hall, co. Essex, d. 9 June 1897; 2ndly, Aug. 1898, James Leslie Wanklyn, formerly M.P. Central Bradford (75 Chester Square, S.W.; Aasleagh House, Leenane, Galway); and has issue 1e.

1e. Vera Marguerite Bacon, m. Arthur T. Hodgson of Smallwood, co. Staff., late 60th Rifles.

4d. Violet Louise Stapylton, m. 11 Ap. 1894, Edmund Clerke Schomberg of Seend House, J.P., D.L., High Sheriff co. Wilts 1902 (Seend House, Melksham).

2b. Rev. Martin Stapylton, Rector of Barlborough, d. 1869; m. 17 July 1828, Elizabeth Henrietta Stote, da. of the Rev. James Watson Stote Donnison of Feliskirk, co. York, d. 1887; and had issue 1c to 8c.

1c. Rev. Martyn Stapylton, M.A. (Durham), Rector of Barlborough, b. 12 June 1830; d. (–); m. June 1866, Esther, da. of the Rev. Robert Cock, d. 30 Dec. 1869; and had issue 1d to 2d.

1d. John Stapylton, b. 21 Ap. 1867; m. 1891, Annie Mathilde, da. of Henry Carter Moore; and has issue 1e to 2e.

1e. Henry Bryan Stapylton, b. 8 Ap. 1892.

2e. Elizabeth Olive Stapylton.

2d. Hilda Stapylton.

2c. Harriet Elizabeth Stapylton.

[Nos. 10149 to 10161.]

The Plantagenet Roll

3c. *Jane Emma Stapylton*, d. 7 Dec. 1865; m. *as 1st wife*, 16 Nov. 1854, *Richard Laurence Pemberton of The Barnes and Bainbridge Holme, co. Durham, J.P., D.L.*, b. 12 Oct. 1831; d. 21 June 1901; *and had issue* 1d *to* 6d.

1d. John Stapylton Grey Pemberton of The Barnes and Bainbridge Holme, *formerly* (1900-1906) M.P. for Sunderland (*The Barnes, Sunderland; Bainbridge House, near Sunderland; Belmont Hall, near Durham, &c.*), b. 23 Dec. 1860; m. 1st, 11 June 1890, Janet Maud (see p. 102), da. of Lieut.-Col. Sir Thomas Horatio Marshall, C.B., d. 20 Oct. 1892; 2ndly, 22 Ap. 1895, Nira, da. of Hercules Grey Ross, B.C.S.; and has issue 1e to 3e.

1e. Richard Laurence Stapylton Pemberton, b. 10 Ap. 1891.
2e.² Nira Penelope Pemberton.
3e.² Eleanor Mary Pemberton.

2d. Ralph Hylton Pemberton, b. 17 July 1864.
3d. Ellen Pemberton, m. 14 June 1883, Col. Emilius Clayton, R.A.; and has issue (3 sons and 2 das.).
4d. Mary Laurence Pemberton.
5d. Laura Penelope Pemberton.
6d. Jane Emma Stapylton Pemberton, m. 12 Sept. 1894, Edmund Robert Durnford (*Fagoo, Bengal*); and has issue (a da.).

4c. *Laura Anne Stapylton*, d. 13 Dec. 1858; m. *as 1st wife*, 16 Dec. 1857, *Lieut.-Col. Sir Thomas Horatio Marshall, C.B., J.P.* (*Bryn-y-Coed, Bangor*); *and had issue* 1d.

1d. Henry Stapylton Marshall, b. 4 Nov. 1858.

5c. Susan Mary Roper Stapylton.
6c. Margaret Monica Stapylton, m. 14 Ap. 1863, George Thomas John Bucknall (Sotheron-Estcourt), 1st Lord Estcourt [U.K.], J.P., D.L. (*Estcourt, near Telbury; Darrington, W.R. Yorks*).
7c. *Frances Blanche Stapylton*, d. 2 June 1861; m. 9 Ap. 1860, *Rudolph Zwilchenbart of Liverpool; and had issue* 1d.

1d. Blanche Zwilchenbart, m. Col. de Courcy Daniell, *late* R.A.; and has issue (3 das.).

8c. *Octavia Constance Stapylton*, d. (-); m. *the Cavaliere F. F. Figulelli* (*Rome*); *and had issue* 1d.

1d. Francesca M. S. Figulelli, now living in Italy.

3b. *Bryan Stapylton*, d. (-); m. *Lucy, da. of the Rev. A. Johnson, Rector of South Stoke, near Bath; and had issue.*

4b. *Laura Anne Stapylton*, b. 1809; d. 23 Oct. 1894, aged 86, bur. *at Brompton;* m. 1829, *Thomas Vardon of Esher, formerly Librarian to the House of Commons,* b. 1799; d. 12 Ap. 1867; *and had* (*with a son, Capt. Noel Hasenden Bryan Vardon, who* d.s.p. *Dec.* 1883) *issue* 1c *to* 2c.

1c. *Eva Dora Anne Vardon*, b. 20 Dec. 1831; d. 8 Dec. 1881; m. 1852, *Charles James Durant*, b. June 1829; d. (*at Sidmouth*) 14 Jan. 1903; *and had* (*with* 2 *younger sons who* d.s.p.) *issue* 1d.

1d. Charles Richard Durant, educ. at Eton (13 *Egerton Gardens, S.W.; The Manor House, White Waltham*), b. 20 Sept. 1853; m. 27 Sept. 1887, the Hon. Nora Augusta Maud [descended from the Lady Anne, sister to King Edward IV., &c. (see Exeter Volume, p. 239)], widow of Alexander Kirkman Finlay, da. of Hercules George Robert (Robinson), 1st Baron Rosmead [U.K.], P.C., G.C.M.G.; and has issue 1e.

1e. Noel Henry Colin Fairfax Durant, b. July 1888.

2c. *Laura Emily Bethune Vardon*, d. (-); m. *Capt. F. Walker, 7th Dragoon Guards.* [Nos. 10162 to 10177.

# of The Blood Royal

2a. *John Bree of Emerald, Keswick,* d. (-); m. *Eliza, da. of* (—) *Bearcroft;* and had issue 1b to 6b.

1b. *John Bree,* d. *in India.*

2b. *Henry Bree,* d. 1837.

3b. *Charles Robert Bree of Colchester, M.D., F.Z.S., J.P., Author of "Birds of Europe not observed in the British Isles,"* d.s.p. Oct. 1886 ; m. 19 Dec. 1845, *Frances Elizabeth, da. of Sir Augustus Brydges Henniker,* 3rd Bart. [U.K.], d. 19 Nov. 1906.

4b. *Stapylton Bree,* d. *at sea.*

5b. *Right Rev. Herbert Bree, Lord Bishop of Barbados* 1882-1899, *formerly Vicar of Brampton,* d. (-); m. 1st, *July* 1860, *Jane Sarah, da. of Edgar Rust d'Eye, Rector of Drinkstone,* d. 18 *June* 1863 ; 2ndly, Nov. 1865, *Mary Harriet, da. of W. Newland of Bramley, co. Surrey,* d. (-) ; *and had issue* 1c *to* 7c.

1c. Charles Herbert Bree, b. 20 May 1851.

2c. Edward Henry Bree, b. Oct. 1852.

3c. Arthur Stapylton Bree, b. 1854.

4c. John Bree, b. 1858.

5c.[1] Janet Bree, m. 22 June 1887, Robert Michael Nowell-Usticke of Polsue Philleigh, J.P. (*Polsue Philleigh, near Grampound Road, Cornwall*) ; and has issue.

See below, Nos. 10190-10191.

6c.[2] Mabel Eleanor Bree.

7c.[2] Evelyn Mary Bree.

6b. *Emily Bree,* d. (-); m. *the Rev. George Thomas Hall, M.A.* (*Camb.*), *Vicar of Albrighton* 1899-1908 (*Kingsland, Shrewsbury*).

3a. *Rev. Robert Francis Bree of Sydenham, M.A.,* d. (-); m. 2ndly, (—), *da. of* (—) *Richards of Ireland ; and had issue* 1b *to* 4b.

1b. *Rev. Robert Stapylton Bree, M.A., Rector of Tintagel, co. Cornwall,* d. 1851 ; m. 1st, *Fanny, da. of the Rev. J. Bindlass of York,* d. (-) ; 2ndly, 5 Nov. 1838, *Philippa Allen, da. and co-h. of Sir Edwin Bayntun Sandys,* 1st Bart. [U.K.], d. (-) ; *and had issue* 1c *to* 5c.

1c.[2] Robert Bree.

2c.[2] Miles Bree, b. 1845.

3c. *Emma Charlotte Sophia Bree,* d. (-); m. 10 Ap. 1844, *the Rev. Edwin Montfort Stephen Sandys,* d. 14 Dec. 1854 ; *and had issue.*

4c. *Lucy E. Marianne Bree,* d. (-); m. 20 Ap. 1858, *Stephen Usticke Nowell-Usticke* (R.L. 23 Feb. 1852), *previously Beauchant, of Falmouth, J.P.,* b. May 1818 ; d. Mar. 1875 ; *and had issue* 1d *to* 6d.

1d. Robert Michael Nowell-Usticke of Polsue Philleigh, J.P., Capt. Cornwall and Devon Miners Art., &c. (*Polsue Philleigh, near Grampound Road, Cornwall*), b. 20 Oct. 1859 ; m. 22 June 1887, Janet (see above), da. of the Right Rev. Herbert Bree, D.D., Lord Bishop of Barbados ; and has issue 1e to 2e.

1e. Robert Stapylton Nowell-Usticke, b. 2 Mar 1892.

2e. Phyllis Evelyn Nowell-Usticke.

2d. Michael Stanley Nowell-Usticke, b. 1864.

3d. William G. Stapylton Nowell-Usticke, b. 1866 ; m. 1889, Elizabeth, da. of Charles Wright of Wirksworth ; and has issue 1e to 3e.

1e. Gordon Wright Nowell-Usticke, b. 9 Sept. 1894.

2e. Claude Stapylton Nowell-Usticke, b. 20 July 1898.

3e. Robert Stanley Nowell-Usticke, b. 25 Ap. 1901.

4d. Charles Michael Nowell-Usticke, b. 1869 ; m. 14 June 1900, Margaret de Visme, da. of Charles Wright of Wirksworth ; and has issue 1e.

1e. Charles de Visme Nowell-Usticke, b. 30 May 1902.

[Nos. 10178 to 10198.

The Plantagenet Roll

5d. Lucy Elizabeth Nowell-Usticke, d. 5 June 1888; m. 2 June 1881, Capt. George Hewat, King's Own Scottish Borderers; and had issue 1e to 2e.

    1e. Dora Lucy Hewat.

    2e. Frances Hewat.

6d. Minna Georgiana Nowell-Usticke, m. 11 Jan. 1905, David Pearson (*Edinburgh*).

5c. Laura Bree, d. (-); m. T. Watson Chapman, Lieut. R.N.

2b. Rev. Edward Nugent Bree of Auckland, New Zealand, M.A., d. (-); m. 1st, Hanna, da. of (—) Fox of St. Bees, co. Cumberland, d. (-); 2ndly, E., da. of (—) King of Hereford, d. (-); and had issue 1c to 4c.

    1c. Miles Reginald Bree, b. 2 Oct. 1849; d. 30 Ap. 1899; m. 1st, at Auckland, N.Z., 5 Nov. 1873, Louisa, da. of Col. Balneavis, 58th Regt., d. (-); 2ndly, at Gore, 7 July 188-, Sarah Eliza (Gore, New Zealand), adopted da. of Judge Mansford of Port Chalmers, N.Z.; and had issue 1d to 6d (*with 2 sons and a da.*, d.s.p.).

        1d.² Brian Stapylton Bree, b. 21 June 1885.

        2d.² Reginald Nugent Stapylton Bree, b. 30 Nov. 1890.

        3d.² Edward Nugent Stapylton Bree, b. 16 Oct. 1893.

        4d.¹ Ethel Balneavis Bree, b. 1 Oct. 1876; m. A. Jordan (*Dunedin, New Zealand*).

        5d.² Monica Louisa Stapylton Bree, b. 10 June 1884; d. 20 Jan. 1907.

        6d.² Adela Lucy Stapylton Bree, b. 4 Aug. 1887; m. at Wellington, N.Z., 17 June 1908, Guy Hardy Scholefield [son of John Hoick Scholefield] (88 *Gleneldon Road, Streatham, S.W.*); and has issue 1e.

            1e. Jack Hardy Bree Scholefield, b. 10 Oct. 1909.

    2c. Eleanor Annie Bree, m. George Burnett (*Wangarei, New Zealand*).

    3c. Lucy Martina Bree, m. as 2nd wife, 28 Nov. 1862, Col. Sir Thomas Horatio Marshall, C.B., J.P., late 3rd Mil. Batt. Cheshire Regt. (*Bryn-y-Coed, Bangor; Hartford Beach, Cheshire*); and has issue 1d to 7d.

        1d. Thomas Edward Marshall, Major R.A. (*Malta*), b. 28 July 1865.

        2d. John Marshall, Lieut. R.N. (*Brynhild, Festing Grove, Southsea*), b. 12 Nov. 1868; m. 21 Aug. 1897, Hilda Renée, da. of Capt. Herbert Lemprière, late Hants Regt.; and has issue 1e to 2e.

            1e. George Herbert Lemprière Marshall, b. 23 Feb. 1901.

            2e. Renée Marshall.

        3d. Reginald Marshall, b. Dec. 1870.

        4d. Rev. Charles Cecil Marshall, Vicar of St. Chad's (*St. Chad's Vicarage, Far Headingley, Leeds*), b. 26 May 1872; m. 2 Aug. 1905, Ethelred Hope, da. of Charles Havelock; and has issue 1e.

            1e. Mary Havelock Marshall.

        5d. Agnes Bertha Marshall, m. 24 Sept. 1884, Sydney Platt [youngest son of John Platt of Werneth Park, Oldham, M.P., J.P., D.L.] (24 *Lowndes Square, S.W.*); and has issue 1e to 2e.

            1e. Lionel Sydney Platt, 17th Lancers, b. 1 Oct. 1885.

            2e. Eira Guendolen Platt.

        6d. Janet Maud Marshall, d. 20 Oct. 1892; m. as 1st wife, 11 June 1890, John Stapylton Grey Pemberton of The Barnes and Bainbridge House, late M.P. (*The Barnes, near Sunderland, &c.*); and had issue.

        See p. 100, No. 10163.

        7d. Everilda Lucy Marshall, m. 21 Ap. 1906, Major Robert Warren Hastings Anderson, Highland Light Infantry [2nd son of Col. J. W. Anderson of Bourhouse, Dunbar].

4c. Alice Bree, b. c. 1852; d. at Napier, N.Z., 21 Ap. 1895; m. at All Saints Church, Ponsonby, Auckland, N.Z., Horace William Baker of Napier; and had issue 1d to 3d.

[Nos. 10199 to 10221.

of The Blood Royal

1d. Tudor Nugent Baker, b. 9 Aug. 1881; m. Dec. 1906, Elsie, da. of (—) Bayley of Taranake, N.Z.; and has issue 1e.
    1e. Horace Holland Baker, b. 3 Jan. 1909.
2d. Horace Mathias Baker, b. 23 Feb. 1887; unm.
3d. Adèle Gwendoline Baker, m. at St. John's Cathedral, Napier, N.Z., 21 Nov. 1896, Walter Menzies Fulton (see p. 212) (Box 5465, Johannesburg); s.p.s.
3b. Mary Anne Bree, d. (-); m. N. Smith.
4b. Julia Bree, d. (-); m. Charles Douglas, Capt. in the Guards.
[Nos. 10222 to 10225.

43. Descendants, if any, of ELIZABETH STAPYLTON (Table VII.), d. (-); m. HENRY WALLER, M.P. for Wycombe, co. Bucks.

44. Descendants of GRACE ROBINSON (Table VII.), b. 5 Jan. 1718; d. 26 Nov. 1766; m. Ap. 1739, the Very Rev. WILLIAM FREIND, D.D., Dean of Canterbury, d. (-); and had issue 1a to 4a.

1a. Robert Freind, b. 1740; d. (? s.p.) 20 Jan. 1780.
2a. Rev. William Maximilian Freind, Rector of Chinnor, co. Oxon., d. 11 June 1804; m. 25 Feb. 1778, Deborah, da. and h. of Thomas Walker of Woodstock, co. Oxon., d. 13 June 1781; and had issue 1b.
    1b. Deborah Susannah Freind, da. and event. (1795) h., d. 24 Mar. 1810; m. as 1st wife, 26 May 1802, Henry Jeffrey (Flower), 4th Viscount Ashbrook [I.], b. 6 Nov. 1776; d. 4 May 1847; and had issue 1c to 3c.
        1c. Henry (Flower), 5th Viscount Ashbrook [I.], b. 17 June 1806; d. 3 Aug. 1871; m. 7 June 1828, Frances (see p. 108), da. of the Ven. Sir John Robinson, previously Freind, 1st Bt. [U.K.], d. 15 June 1886; and had issue 1d to 6d.
            1d. Henry Jeffrey (Flower), 6th Viscount Ashbrook [I.], b. 26 Mar. 1829; d.s.p. 14 Dec. 1882.
            2d. William Spencer (Flower), 7th Viscount Ashbrook [I.], b. 23 Mar. 1830; d.s.p.s. 25 Nov. 1906.
            3d. Robert Thomas (Flower), 8th Viscount Ashbrook [I.], formerly Lieut.-Col. Royal Canadian Regt. (Castle Durrow, Durrow, Queen's Co.; Knockatrina House, Durrow, Queen's Co.; Carlton), b. 1 Ap. 1836; m. 18 July 1866, Gertrude Sophia (see p. 108), da. of the Rev. Sewell Hamilton of Bath; and has issue 1e to 5e.
                1e. Hon. Llowarch Robert Flower (Knockatrina House, Durrow, Queen's Co.), b. 9 July 1870; m. 14 Feb. 1899, Gladys Lucille Beatrice [descended from the Lady Isabel Plantagenet (see the Essex Volume, p. 289)], da. of Gen. Sir George Wentworth Alexander Higginson, K.C.B.
                2e. Hon. Reginald Henry Flower, b. 15 June 1871; m. 10 May 1901, Kate, da. of Col. Cuming of Crovar, co. Cavan.
                3e. Hon. Frances Mary Flower, m. 2 Sept. 1893, Harry Ernest White [2nd son of Gen. Sir Robert White of Aghavoe, K.C.B.] (Aghavoe, Queen's Co.); and has issue 1f.
                    1f. Robert Llowarch White, b. 19 Jan. 1896.
                4e. Hon. Eva Constance Gertrude Flower.
                5e. Hon. Gertrude Flower.
            4d. Hon. Mary Sophia Flower, b. 17 June 1832; d. 17 Ap. 1886; m. 2 Oct. 1860, Major Robert Blakeney, 48th Regt., d. 20 June 1902; and had issue (with a younger da. d. unm.) 1e to 4e.
                1e. Henry Ross Blakeney, b. 2 Ap. 1862.
                2e. Frederick Robert Blakeney, b. 16 May 1863.
                3e. Ernest Charles Cecil Blakeney, b. 27 Jan. 1869.
                4e. Frances Alice Blakeney.
[Nos. 10226 to 10236.

The Plantagenet Roll

5d. Hon. *Frances Esther Flower*, b. 17 Mar. 1834; d. 21 May 1881; m. 14 July 1857, *John Capel Philips of the Heath House, co. Staffs., and Newlands, co. Glouc.*, J.P., D.L., d. (-); and had issue (with a son d. young) 1e to 4e.

 1e. Burton Henry Philips (see below), C.M.G., Lieut.-Col. Reserve of Officers, formerly Royal Welsh Fusiliers (*The Heath House, Teane, co. Stafford*), b. 1 Oct. 1858; m. 10 Feb. 1904, Lucy Madeline, da. of Col. George Blucher Heneage Marton of Capernwray; and has issue 1f.

  1f. Audrey Adelaide Philips.

 2e. John Augustus Philips, b. 1 Jan. 1861; *unm.*

 3e. Frances Margaret Philips, m. 1885, Ernest Capel Cure [youngest son of Robert Capel Cure of Blake Hall, co. Essex, and a descendant maternally of King Henry VII.] (see Tudor Roll, p. 451)].

 4e. Bertha Mary Philips.

6d. Hon. *Caroline Gertrude Flower* (*Capernwray Hall, Burton, Westmorland*), m. 1 May 1866, George Blucher Heneage Marton of Capernwray, J.P., D.L., and High Sheriff co. Lancaster 1877, M.P. Lancaster 1885-86, Hon. Col. 3rd and 4th Batt. R. Lancaster Regt., d. 18 Aug. 1905; and has issue 1e to 10e.

 1e. George Henry Powys Marton of Capernwray (*Capernwray, co. Lancaster; White's*), b. 11 Ap. 1869.

 2e. Richard Oliver Marton, D.S.O., Capt. R.A., is 1st Assist. Sup. of Experiments at School of Gunnery, b. 24 Aug. 1872; m. 4 Ap. 1899, Margaret Elizabeth [descended from King Henry VII. (see Tudor Roll, p. 404)], da. of Egerton Leigh of Jodrell Hall [by his wife, Lady Elizabeth, *née* White]; and has issue 1f to 2f.

  1f. Oliver Egerton Christopher Marton, b. 25 May 1903.

  2f. Guy Burton Heneage Marton, b. 5 Nov. 1904.

 3e. Rev. Lancelot Edward Marton, b. 25 July 1878.

 4e. Lionel Marton, Lieut. Royal Berks. Regt., b. 7 Aug. 1879.

 5e. Augusta Adelaide Cecily Marton, m. 20 Oct. 1896, Stanley Hughes Le Fleming, J.P., D.L., High Sheriff co. Westmorland, Hon. Major Westmorland and Cumberland Yeo., Lord of the Manors of Backermet, Skeriwith, Kirkland, and Brathmuire, co. Cumberland, Coniston, co. Lancaster, and Rydal, co. Westmorland (*Rydal Hall, Ambleside; Carlton*); and has issue 1f to 3f.

  1f. Michael George Le Fleming, b. 17 July 1900.

  2f. Richard Cumberland Le Fleming, b. 22 July 1901.

  3f. [da.] Le Fleming, b. 27 May 1905.

 6e. Lucy Madeline Marton, m. 10 Feb. 1904, Lieut.-Col. Burton Henry Philips, C.M.G. (*The Heath House, Teane*); and has issue.
See above, No. 10238.

 7e. Florence Augusta Marton, m. 16 Feb. 1901, John Ralph Aspinall [son and h. of Ralph John Aspinall of Standen Hall, co. Lanc., J.P., D.L.] (*30 Queen's Gate Terrace, S.W.*).

 8e. Alice Caroline Marton.

 9e. Adelaide Esther Marton.

 10e. Georgina Mary Marton.

2c. Hon. *Susannah Sophia Flower*, b. 5 July 1803; d. 6 Nov. 1864; m. 1st, 21 May 1824, the Rev. William Robinson [2nd son of the Ven. Sir John Robinson, 1st Bt. [U.K.] (see p. 107)], d. Dec. 1834; 2ndly, 26 Dec. 1836, William Wilson Campbell of Dublin, M.D., d. 1856; and had issue (with possibly others by 2nd husband) 1d to 2d.

 1d. Caroline Susannah Robinson, d. (-); m. Aug. 1854, Major-Gen. Arthur J. Macan Rainey of Trowscoed Lodge, Leckhampton Road, Cheltenham; and had issue.

 2d. Helena Robinson, d. June 1899; m. 21 Sept. 1880, Sewell Hamilton (see p. 108).

3c. Hon. *Caroline Flower*, b. 30 July 1807; d. 17 Ap. 1840; m. *as 1st wife*,

[Nos. 10237 to 10258.]

# of The Blood Royal

26 *Mar.* 1829, Henry Every (see p. 107), 1*st Life Guards [son and h.-app. of Sir Henry Every, 9th Bt.* [*E.*]], d.v.p. 27 *Feb.* 1853 ; *and had issue* 1*d to* 5*d.*

1*d.* Sir Henry Flower Every, 10th Bt. [*E.*], D.L., b. 23 Dec. 1830 ; d. 26 Feb. 1893 ; m. 2*ndly,* 12 *Oct.* 1859, *Mary Isabella* (18 *Montagu Street, W.*), *da. of the Rev. Edmund Hollond of Benhall Lodge, Saxmundham* (see p. 108) ; *and had issue* 1*e to* 8*e.*

1*e.* Henry Edmund Every, Capt. South Wales Borderers, b. 9 *Oct.* 1860 ; d.v.p. 1 Dec. 1892 ; m. 18 *Nov.* 1884, *Leila Frances Harford, da. of the Rev. Henry Adderley Box, M.A., d.* 4 *Feb.* 1890 ; *and had issue* 1*f.*

1*f.* Sir Edward Oswald Every, 11th Bt. [*E.*] (*Egginton Hall, Burton-upon-Trent*), *b.* 14 *Jan.* 1886 ; *m.* 17 Aug. 1909, Ivy Linton, da. of Major Alfred Meller of Rushmere, co. Suffolk.

2*e.* Right Rev. Edward Francis Every, D.D., M.A. (Camb.), Lord Bishop of the Falkland Islands (*Calle Industria, Buenos Aires*), b. 3 Ap. 1862.

3*e.* Ernest Hollond Every (*Colorado Springs, U.S.A.*), b. 10 July 1870 ; *m.* 20 Dec. 1902, Beatrice May, da. of Harvey Young of Colorado Springs ; and has issue 1*f* to 2*f.*

1*f.* Ernest Henry Every, *b.* 14 Feb. 1906.
2*f.* Patricia Every, *b.* 26 *Mar.* 1904.

4*e.* Alice Vere Every.
5*e.* Eleanor Maude Every (18 *Montague Street, W.*).
6*e.* Constance Margaret Every.

7*e.* Clara Helen Every, *m.* as 2nd wife, 11 Oct. 1899, the Rev. Edward Digby Stopford Ram of Clonattin, co. Wexford, Rector of Oxted [descended from King Henry VII. (see the Tudor Roll, p. 161)] (*Oxted Rectory, Surrey*) ; and has issue 1*f* to 2*f.*

1*f.* Abel James Ram, *b.* 3 Nov. 1902.
2*f.* Andrew Ram, *b.* 26 Mar. 1908.

8*e.* Agnes Mabel Every.

2*d.* Oswald Every, Capt. 75th Foot, *b.* 26 *June* 1835 ; d. 26 *Jan.* 1892 ; m. 1*st,* 3 *June* 1862, *Cecilia Charlotte, da. of Henry Charles Burney, LL.D., d.* 1882 ; 2*ndly,* 1885, *Florence Amy* (4 *Westerfield Terrace, Weetens Lane, Liscard*), *da. of William Sheridan of Fawsley, co. Devon ; and had issue* 1*e to* 9*e.*

1*e.* Edward Every, *b.* 1865.

2*e.* Oswald Every, J.P., Lieut. *late* West India Regt., *formerly* Sergeant 21st Lancers, has West Africa Medal and Clasp 1898-1899 (*Hampton Hall, Worthen, Salop*), *b.* 25 May 1872 ; *m.* 11 Feb. 1902, Edith, da. of James Whitaker of Hampton Hall, co. Salop, J.P.

3*e.* Victor George Every, *b.* 1886.
4*e.* John Every, *b.* 1888.
5*e.* Francis Flower Every, *b.* 1890.

6*e.*[1] Florence Every, b. 29 *May* 1863 ; d. 14 *May* 1908 ; m. 23 *Sept.* 1886, *the Rev. Alexander Frederick de Gex, J.P., Rector of Meshaw and Creacombe* (*Meshaw Rectory, South Molton, Devon*) ; *and had issue* 1*f.*

1*f.* Ruthven Gore de Gex, *b.* 4 July 1887.

7*e.*[1] Beatrice Every, b. 29 *May* 1865 ; d. 5 Dec. 1893 ; m. 13 Dec. 1887, *Thomas Husband Gill, Solicitor* (3 *St. Aubyn Street, Devonport*) ; *and had issue* 1*f to* 3*f.*

1*f.* Eric Every Gill, *b.* 16 Sept. 1888.
2*f.* Oswald Tom Every Gill, *b.* 15 Aug. 1891.
3*f.* Basil Every Gill, *b.* 24 Nov. 1893.

8*e.*[1] Cissy Vere Every.
9*e.*[1] Mabel Every.

3*d.* Caroline Penelope Every (*Avenue Lodge, Eastbourne*), *m.* 29 Ap. 1852, Sir George Ebenezer Wilson Couper, 2nd Bt. [U.K.], K.C.S.I., C.B., C.I.E., *d.* 5 Mar. 1908 ; and has issue 1*e* to 7*e.*   [Nos. 10259 to 10282.

The Plantagenet Roll

1*e*. Sir Ramsay George Henry Couper, 3rd Bt. [U.K.], *formerly* Lieut. King's Royal Rifle Corps, Afghan Medal with two clasps and Bronze Star, *b*. 1 Nov. 1855; *m*. 1884, Nora Emma S., da. of Horatio Willson Scott of Hampstead; and has issue 1*f* to 3*f*.

1*f*. Guy Couper, *b*. 12 Mar. 1889.
2*f*. Sybil Couper.
3*f*. Evelyn Couper.

2*e*. Victor Arthur Couper, Lieut.-Col. 4th Batt. the Rifle Brigade, has Burmese and Punjab Medals (*Naval and Military*), *b*. 4 Ap. 1859.

3*e*. Edward Edmonston Couper, Lieut.-Col. Comdg. 9th Gurkha Regt., has Indian Frontier Medal (*East India United Service*), *b*. 15 Dec. 1860; *m*. 28 June 1899, Daisy Ethel Aylmer, da. of Henry E. Rose of Whiteshools, Bourton-on-the-Water; and has issue 1*f*.

1*f*. John Victor Hay Couper, *b*. 1902.

4*e*. James Robert Couper (*Mansfield House, Moffat*), *b*. 24 June 1863; *m*. 27 Oct. 1897, Jessie, da. of John Kissock of Drummore, co. Kirkcudbright; and has issue 1*f* to 4*f*.

1*f*. George Robert Cecil Couper, *b*. 15 Oct. 1898.
2*f*. John Every Couper, *b*. 15 Nov. 1900.
3*f*. Jem Ramsay Couper, *b*. 13 Mar. 1904.
4*f*. Doris Helen Couper, *b*. 14 Mar. 1907.

5*e*. Caroline Georgiana Jane Elizabeth Couper, *m*. 6 Sept. 1881, Major-Gen. Frederick William Benson, C.B., is in charge of Administration, Southern Command, has South African Medal with 3 clasps, &c. (*Salisbury; Army and Navy*).

6*e*. Ada Lucy Couper.
7*e*. Maude Madeline Couper.

4*d*. Jane Charlotte Rose Every, *d*. 5 July 1874; *m*. 23 Nov. 1858, the Rev. Rowland Mosley, Rector of Egginton [Bt. Coll.], *d*. 24 July 1888; *and had issue* 1*e* to 8*e*.

1*e*. Arthur Rowland Mosley, J.P., Major *formerly* 6th Dragoons, has Queen's Medal with 3 clasps and King's with 2 clasps for South African War (*The Hollies, Linslade, Leighton Buzzard; Cavalry, &c.*), *b*. 8 May 1862; *m*. 16 Oct. 1899, Henrietta, da. of Henry Bolden.

2*e*. Godfrey Mosley, of Messrs. Taylor, Simpson & Mosley, 35 St. Mary's Gate, Derby, Solicitors, B.A. (Oxon.), Major 5th Batt. Sherwood Foresters (*35 St. Mary's Gate, Derby*), *b*. 15 June 1863.

3*e*. Ashton Edward Mosley (*Peterborough, Ontario*), *b*. 24 Oct. 1868.

4*e*. Wilfred Rowland Mosley, Architect (*Windsor Road, Slough*), *b*. 25 Ap. 1872.

5*e*. Theresa Jane Mosley
6*e*. Mildred Isabel Mosley
7*e*. Sybil Georgiana Rose Mosley } (*Glenbrook, Duffield Road, Derby*).
8*e*. Jane Agnes Muriel Mosley

5*d*. Maria Georgiana Every (*104 Beaufort Street, S.W.*), *m*. 21 Oct. 1863, the Rev. William Mills Parry Pym, Vicar of Corsham, *d*. 19 July 1872; and has issue 1*e* to 3*e*.

1*e*. Paul John Every Pym, *b*. 28 Ap. 1870; *unm*.

2*e*. Guy William Every Pym (*Malahiwi, Geraldine, New Zealand*), *b*. 9 July 1871; *m*. 2 Mar. 1905, Elsie, da. of Robert George Alcorn of West Maitland, Australia, M.D.; and has issue 1*f* to 3*f*.

1*f*. Guy Pym, *b*. 2 May 1906.
2*f*. Jack Pym, *b*. 7 Nov. 1907.
3*f*. Vere Pym, *b*. 19 Aug. 1909.

3*e*. Caroline Vere Pym, *m*. 4 Oct. 1883, Alfred Edward Flood (*Rowborough, Cookham, Berks*); *s.p.*

[Nos. 10283 to 10312.

of The Blood Royal

3*a*. *Ven. Sir John Robinson* (*R.L.* 29 Nov. 1793), *previously Freind*, 1st Bt. [*U.K.*], so cr. 14 Dec. 1819, *Archdeacon of Armagh*, b. 15 Feb. 1754; d. 16 *Ap.* 1832; m. 1786, Mary Anne, da. of James Spencer of Rathangan, co. Kildare, d. 19 Jan. 1834; *and had issue* 1b to 9b.

1*b*. Sir *Richard Robinson*, 2nd Bt. [*U.K.*], b. 4 Mar. 1787; d. 2 Oct. 1847; m. 25 Feb. 1813, *Lady Helena Eleanor, da. of Stephen* (*Moore*), 2nd *Earl of Mount Cashell* [*I.*], d. at Paris 23 Sept. 1859; *and had issue* 1c to 4c.

1*c*. Sir *John Stephen Robinson*, 3rd Bt. [*U.K.*], *C.B., Hon. Col. 6th Batt. Royal Irish Rifles*, b. 27 Sept. 1816; d. 21 May 1895; m. 2 Sept. 1841, Sarah Blackett, da. of Anthony Denny of Barham Wood, co. Herts [*Bt. of Tralee Coll.*], by his wife the Hon. Mary Patience, née Collingwood, d. 26 Oct. 1875; *and had issue* 1d to 2d.

1*d*. Sir *Gerald William Collingwood Robinson*, 4th Bt. [*U.K.*], b. 11 Feb. 1857; d. *unm.* 31 May 1903.

2*d*. Maud Helena Collingwood Robinson of Rokeby, m. 26 Mar. 1890, Richard Johnston Montgomery of Beaulieu (*Beaulieu, co. Louth; Killineer House, co. Louth; Rokeby Hall, co. Louth*); *s.p.*

2*c*. Sir *Richard Harcourt Robinson*, 5th Bt. [*U.K.*], *formerly* Lieut.-Col. 60th Rifles (3 *Harley Gardens, S.W.; Army and Navy*), b. at Pisa, 4 Feb. 1828; *unm.*

3*c*. *Helena Esther Florence Robinson*, b. at Florence 1817; d. 22 Dec. 1900; m. *as 2nd wife*, 10 Jan. 1849, *Lieut.-Col. Baron Knut Philip Bonde, K.N.S.* (*R.N.O.*), *K.C.N.* (*R.N.Ekk.*), *K.L.H.* (*R.F.H.L.*) [*B. Bonde* [*Sweden*, No. 20, 1802] *Coll.*], b. 1815; d. Oct. 1871; *and had issue* 1d to 3d.

1*d*. *Baron Carl Bonde, Lord of the Manors of Fituna, &c.*, b. 1853; d. (*apparently s.p.*) *a.* 1890.

2*d*. *Baroness Ingeborg Helena Bonde*, b. 1849; d. (? *unm.*) *a.* 1880.

3*d*. *Baroness Florence Charlotte Lucie Bonde*, b. 1851; d. (-); m. 1870, *Kammarherren John Henning von Horn, K.D.D.* (*R.D.D.O.*).

4*c*. *Elizabeth Selina Robinson*, b. at Paris; d. 16 June 1891; m. 26 Oct. 1843, Adolphe, Viscount de St. Geniez; *and had issue* (a son and da.).

2*b*. *Rev. William Robinson, Rector of Bovevagh, co. Derry*, b. 20 Dec. 1793; d. Dec. 1834; m. 21 May 1824, *the Hon. Susannah Sophia, da. of Henry Jeffrey* (*Flower*), *4th Viscount Ashbrook* [*I.*]; *and had issue.*

See p. 104.

3*b*. Sir *Robert Spencer Robinson, K.C.B., F.R.S., Admiral R.N., Comptroller of the Navy* 1861–1871, b. 6 Jan. 1809; d.s.p. 27 July 1889.

4*b*. *Jane Robinson*, d. 31 Aug. 1860; m. 1st, 2 Aug. 1825, *George Powney*, d. (? s.p.) 1827; 2ndly, *as 2nd wife*, 20 Feb. 1844, *Henry Every* [son and h.-app. of the 9th Bt., see p. 104], d. (? s.p. by her) 27 Feb. 1853.

5*b*. *Louisa Robinson*, d. 24 Dec. 1849; m. *as 2nd wife*, 20 Dec. 1821, *the Rev. William Knox* [*E. of Ranfurly* [*I.*] *Coll.*], d. 26 Feb. 1860; *and had issue* 1c to 2c.

1*c*. *Anne Eliza Knox*, d. (-); m. 25 Sept. 1856, *the Ven. James Gaspard le Marchant Carey, Archdeacon of Essex*, d. 1885; *and had issue* 1d.

1*d*. Gaspard William Carey, b. 9 Aug. 1864.

2*c*. *Frances Emily Knox*, d. 26 May 1863; m. *as 1st wife*, 7 Nov. 1858, *Robert Vesey Truell of Ballyhenny, co. Wicklow*, d. 27 Feb. 1867; *and had issue* 1d to 2d.

1*d*. Louisa Anne Truell.

2*d*. Phœbe Editha Truell, m. *as 2nd wife*, Feb. or July 1896, *Robert Vesey Stoney of Rosturk Castle, &c., J.P., D.L., High Sheriff co. Mayo* 1884 (*Rosturk Castle, co. Mayo; Inaskerkin, co. Mayo; Knockadoo, co. Roscommon*); *and has issue* 1e to 2e.

1*e*. Thomas Samuel Vesey Stoney, b. 23 Aug. 1898.

2*e*. Robert Vesey Stoney, b. 24 Sept. 1903. [Nos. 10313 to 10319.

The Plantagenet Roll

6b. Caroline Robinson, b. 1801; d. 4 May 1886; m. 2 Nov. 1822, John James (Pomeroy), 5th Viscount Harberton [I.], b. 29 Sept. 1790; d. 5 Oct. 1862; and had issue 1c.

1c. James Spencer (Pomeroy), 6th Viscount Harberton [I.], J.P. (3 *Ashburn Place, S.W.; 19 Albert Road, Great Malvern*), b. 23 Nov. 1836; m. 2 Ap. 1861, Florence Wallace, da. of William Wallace Legge of Malone House, co. Antrim, D.L.; and has issue 1d to 3d.

1d. Hon. Ernest Arthur George Pomeroy, *formerly* Capt. 3rd Batt. Royal Dublin Fusiliers, has S. African Medal (6 *Camden House Chambers, Kensington, W.*), b. 1 Dec. 1867.

2d. Hon. Ralph Legge Pomeroy, *formerly* Capt. 5th Dragoon Guards, served in S. Africa 1899–1902 (*Heyford Manor, Weedon; Isthmian; Cavalry*), b. 31 Dec. 1869; m. 25 June 1907, Mary Katherine, da. of Arthur William Leatham of Miserden Park, co. Glos, J.P.; and has issue 1e.

1e. Henry Ralph Mostyn Pomeroy, b. 12 Oct. 1908.

3d. Hon. Hilda Evelyn Pomeroy (*Juniper Hill, Rickmansworth, Herts*), m. 5 Oct. 1892, Thomas Arthur Carless Attwood of Sion Hill, Wolverley, F.S.A., from whom she obtained a decree of nullity of marriage 1902.

7b. Frances Robinson, b. 1803; d. 15 *June* 1886; m. 7 *June* 1828, Henry (Flower), 5th Viscount Ashbrook [I.], d. 3 Aug. 1871; and had issue.
See p. 103, Nos. 10226–10258.

8b. Selina Robinson, d. 30 Aug. 1873; m. Nov. 1833, the Rev. Sewell Hamilton of Bath, d. (–); and had issue 1c to 2c.

1c. Sewell Hamilton, b. (—); m. 21 Sept. 1880, Helena, da. of the Rev. William Robinson (see p. 104), d. June 1899.

2c. Gertrude Sophia Hamilton, m. 18 July 1866, Robert Thomas (Flower), 8th Viscount Ashbrook [I.], &c. (*Castle Durrow, Durrow, Queen's Co.*); and has issue.
See p. 103, Nos. 10227–10232.

9b. Isabella Robinson, d. 23 Jan. 1848; m. *as 1st wife*, 6 Feb. 1839, the Rev. Edmund Hollond of Benhall Lodge, co. Suffolk, d. 19 May 1884; and had issue 1c to 5c.

1c. Edmund William Hollond of Benhall Lodge, M.A., Bar.-at-Law, b. 18 Ap. 1841; d. 2 Jan. 1900; m. 20 Jan. 1876, Ada (*Benhall Lodge, Saxmundham*), da. of Robert Rygate of Wellington, N.S.W.; and had issue 1d.

1d. Edmund Robert Hollond of Benhall, B.A., J.P. (*Benhall Lodge, Saxmundham, Suffolk*), b. 24 Nov. 1876.

2c. John Robert Hollond, J.P., D.L., M.A., Bar.-at-Law, *formerly* (1883–1885) M.P. for Brighton (*Wonham, Devon*), b. 2 Nov. 1843; m. 17 Aug. 1870, Fanny Eliza, da. of Frederick Keats of Braziers, co. Oxon.; and has issue 1d to 6d.

1d. Robert Edward Hollond, b. 21 July 1871.

2d. Spencer Edmund Hollond, Capt. Rifle Brigade (41 *Princes Gate, S.W.*), b. 19 Mar. 1874; m. 5 Oct. 1905, Lula, da. of Charles Pfizer of New York; and has issue 1e.

1e. Christopher Arthur Spencer Hollond.

3d. Ellen Fanny Hollond, m. 13 Sept. 1899, Edward Cornwall Nicholetts (*The Manor House, Brent Knoll, Somerset*); and has issue 1e to 2e.

1e. Gilbert Edward Nicholetts, b. 9 Nov. 1902.

2e. Nina Joyce Nicholetts.

4d. May Beatrice Hollond.

5d. Florence Nina Hollond, m. 10 Oct. 1905, Capt. Edward Lisle Strutt [B. Belper Coll.] (*Travellers'; White's; Alpine*).

6d. Monica Hollond.

3c. Mary Isabella Hollond (18 *Montagu Street, W.*), m. 12 Oct. 1859, Sir Henry Flower Every, 10th Bt. [E.], d. 26 Feb. 1893; and has issue.
See p. 105, Nos. 10259–10270. [Nos. 10320 to 10389.

# of The Blood Royal

4c. Esther Harriett Hollond, m. 24 Ap. 1867, the Rev. Basil Kilvington Woodd, L.L.M. [son and h.-app. of Basil Thomas Woodd of Conyngham Hall, M.P.], d.v.p. 16 Ap. 1886 ; and has issue 1d to 4d.

1d. Basil Aubrey Woodd of Conyngham Hall, J.P., B.A. (Camb.), Bar.-at-Law, Lieut. Yorks Hussars Imp. Yeo. (*Conyngham Hall, Knaresborough ; 35 Tite Street, Chelsea*), b. 1869 ; m. 12 Dec. 1895, Rosalie, da. of John Dyson of Moorlands, near Crewkerne; and has issue 1e to 2e.

1e. Iris Rosalie Woodd, b. 10 *May* 1897 ; d. 9 *Ap*. 1906.
2e. Elaine Jane Woodd, b. 24 Jan. 1899.

2d. Evelyn Anthony Woodd, b. 13 Dec. 1870.

3d. Dorothy Eugenia Woodd, m. 10 Jan. 1900, Hugh Roubiliac Roger-Smith, M.D., M.R.C.S. (Eng.), L.R.C.P. (Lond.) (1 *College Terrace, Fitzjohn's Avenue, N.W.*); and has issue 1e to 3e.

1e. Raymond Roger-Smith, b. 21 Nov. 1902.
2e. Basil Hugh Roger-Smith, b. 5 May 1909.
3e. Barbara Roger-Smith, b. 6 Ap. 1904.

4d. Gertrude Frances Woodd, m. 7 Sept. 1907, Thomas Walter Breed (*Tetlham Hill, Battle, Sussex*); and has issue 1e.

1e. Nancy Gertrude Breed, b. 13 Aug. 1908.

5c. Fanny Louisa Hollond, m. Oct. 1884, John Dyson, *formerly* Judge at Feyzabad, Oude.

4a. *Grace Freind*, d. 1809 ; m. 1765, *Lieut.-Gen. Campbell, R.M.*, d. 1812 ; *and had issue.* [Nos. 10390 to 10400.

45. Descendants of FRANCIS LOWE of Baldwyn Brightwell, co. Oxon. (Table VII.), d. June 1754 ; m. ELIZABETH or FRANCES, da. of John CORRANCE of Parham, d. (−) ; and had issue 1a.

1a. Catherine Lowe, da. and event. sole h., d. 1789 ; m. 1747, *William Lowndes of Astwood Bury, co. Bucks*, b. 1712 ; d.v.p. 1773 ; *and had issue* 1b *to* 2b.

1b. William Lowndes, *afterwards* (1789) *Lowndes-Stone of Astwood Bury, co. Bucks, and Baldwyn Brightwell, co. Oxon.*, b. 1750 ; d. *May* 1830 ; m. 15 *July* 1775, *Elizabeth, da. and co-h. of Richard Garth of Morden, co. Surrey*, d. *Feb.* 1837 ; *and had issue* 1c *to* 7c.

1c. William Francis Lowndes-Stone of Brightwell Park, J.P., D.L., D.C.L., High Sheriff co. Oxon. 1834, b. 27 Oct. 1783 ; d. 1858 ; m. 3 Oct. 1811, *Caroline, da. of Sir William Strickland of Boynton, 6th Bart.* [E.], d. 11 *Ap*. 1867 ; *and had issue*.
See the Clarence Volume, pp. 233–235, Nos. 4817–4865.

2c. Rev. Richard Lowndes, *afterwards* (R.L. 20 Mar. 1837) *Garth, of Morden*, b. 1790 ; d. 1862 ; m. *Mary, da. of the Rev. Robert Douglas of Salwarpe*, d. 1849 ; *and had issue* 1d *to* 3d.

1d. Hon. Sir Richard Garth of Morden, Q.C., M.P., Chief Justice of Bengal 1875, b. 11 *Mar.* 1820 ; d. 23 *Mar.* 1903 ; m. 27 *June* 1847, *Clara, da. of William Loftus Lowndes, Q.C.*, d. 15 *Jan.* 1903 ; *and had issue* 1e *to* 7e.

1e. Richard Garth (*Birse, Rugby Road, Brighton*), b. 2 June 1848 ; *unm.*

2e. George Douglas Garth, b. 15 *May* 1852 ; d. 6 *Jan.* 1900 ; m. 12 Oct. 1878, *Mildred (Morden, Iffley Road, Oxford), da. of Arthur Noverre of London* ; *and had issue* 1f *to* 5f.

1f. George Douglas Garth, Brewer,
2f. Arthur Douglas Garth, Jute and Gunny Broker } b. (twins) 26 Jan. 1880.
Calcutta),
3f. Humphrey Garth, B.A., Chartered Accountant, b. 8 Oct. 1881.
4f. Margaret Garth.
5f. Primrose Garth. [Nos. 10401 to 10455.

The Plantagenet Roll

3e. William Garth, Bar.-at-Law (*Russell Street, Calcutta*), b. 26 Aug. 1854.

4e. Charles Garth, b. 10 July 1870; m. Mabel, da. of George Day Harrison; has a da.

5e. Mary Eliza Garth (6 *Alfred Place West, S.W.*), m. 20 Ap. 1869, Henry Leigh Pemberton [youngest son of Edward Leigh Pemberton of Torry Hill, Sittingbourne], b. 1835; d. 29 Mar. 1895; and has issue (with 2 sons and a da. d. unm.) 1f to 5f.

1f. Cyril Leigh Pemberton, b. 6 May 1873; m. 15 June 1909, Mary Evelyn, da. of Matthew Megaw of Pont Street, S.W.

2f. Norman Leigh Pemberton, b. 31 July 1874.

3f. Harry Leigh Pemberton, b. 3 Feb. 1878.

4f. Guy Leigh Pemberton, b. 23 June 1883.

5f. Dorothy Leigh Pemberton.

6e. Helen Frances Garth, m. 5 May 1881, Capt. Alexander Evans-Gordon, B.S.C.; and has issue 1f to 5f.

1f. Kenmure Alick Garth Evans-Gordon, b. 20 Aug. 1885.

2f. Marjorie Evans-Gordon, m. (—).

3f. Madeline Evans-Gordon, m. (—).

4f. Jean Evans-Gordon, } twins.
5f. Joan Evans-Gordon, }

7e. Evelyn Selina May Garth, m. 3 July 1887, Herbert Tyrrell Griffiths of 5 Kensington Square, W., M.D., d. 1905; and has issue (with a son, Leslie Valentine, d. young) 1f to 3f.

1f. Richard Evelyn Griffiths, b. 8 Ap. 1888.

2f. Ivor Herbert Griffiths, b. 11 Ap. 1891.

3f. Joyce May Griffiths, b. 16 Dec. 1901.

2d. Elizabeth Garth, b. 1827; m. George Cecil Henry, Col. R.A.; and has issue 1e to 2e.

1e. Charles Cecil Henry, b. 1865; m. 24 Sept. 1901, Mary, eldest da. of the Rev. Frank Kewley; and has issue 1f to 2f.

1f. John Charles Henry, b. 1907.

2f. Barbara Henry.

2e. Mabel Mary Henry.

3d. Frances Garth (*Brightwell, Farnham, Surrey*), b. 12 July 1833; m. 23 Oct. 1855, Patrick Lewis Cole Paget, Col. Scots Guards, d. 17 July 1879; and has issue 1e to 4e.

1e. Gertrude Frances Paget, m. 1884, Phelips Brooke Hanham, Col. *late* R.A.; and has issue 1f to 2f.

1f. Esmond Henry Paget Hanham, b. 12 Mar. 1887.

2f. Patrick John Hanham, b. 15 Oct. 1893.

2e. Florence Mary Emily Paget.

3e. Violet Evelyn Paget, m. 27 Nov. 1906, the Rev. George Harvey Ranking (135 *Lambeth Road, S.E.*).

4e. Mildred Eileen May Paget, m. 12 Oct. 1889, Henry Lloyd Powell, Major R.H.A. (*Burton Hall, Christchurch, Hants*); and has issue 1f to 3f.

1f. Ivor Powell, b. 1893.

2f. Gladys Powell.

3f. Dorothy Mary Powell.

3c. Henry Owen Lowndes, b. 1795; d. (—); m. 1827, *Sarah Anne, da. of Augustus Turnbull of* (—), *America;* and had issue 1d to 2d.

1d. Kate Lowndes, d.s.p.; m. (—).

2d. Mary Lowndes, m. (—) Stevens of Boston, U.S.A.; and has issue.

[Nos. 10456 to 10489.

of The Blood Royal

4c. *Elizabeth Lowndes*, d. 20 Nov. 1865; m. 6 *June* 1802, *John Fane of Wormsley* [*E. of Westmorland Coll.*], d. 4 Oct. 1850; *and had issue.*
See the Exeter Volume, pp. 356-358, Nos. 25861-25927.

5c. *Catherine Lowndes*, d. (-); m. 1812, *the Rev. John Holland, Vicar of Aston Rowant*, co. *Oxon*, d. 13 Nov. 1844; *and had issue (? an only child)* 1d.

1d. Catherine Holland, d. *unm.* 23 May 1843.

6c. *Anne Lowndes*, d. 21 *Aug.* 1864; m. 13 *July* 1822, *William Henry Sharp*, b. 27 *May* 1782; d. 13 Oct. 1844; *and had issue* 1d.

1d. Anne Sharp (*Balmore, Caversham, Reading*), *m.* 3 Sept. 1861, Robert Parker Radcliffe, Major-Gen. R.A., *d.* 29 Mar. 1907; and has issue 1e to 5e.

1e. Robert Edmund Lowndes Radcliffe (*Egmont, Binfield, Bracknell*), b. 16 Ap. 1865; *m.* 7 June 1894, Gertrude, da. of Charles Combe of Cobham Park, co. Surrey, J.P., D.L., High Sheriff 1885; and has issue 1f.

1f. Joyce Naomi Aileen Radcliffe.

2e. William Scott Warley Radcliffe, Major Shropshire Light Infantry, b. 3 July 1866; *m.* 14 June 1906, Cecily Mary, youngest da. of the Hon. Cecil Parker of Eccleston Paddocks, co. Chester; and has issue 1f to 2f.

1f. Cynthia Alice Radcliffe.
2f. Meriel Margaret Radcliffe.

3e. Annie Elsie Radcliffe.

4e. Mabel Maud Radcliffe, *m.* 2 June 1897, the Rev. Bertram Long, M.A. (Camb.), Rector of Wokingham (*The Rectory, Wokingham*); and has issue 1f to 3f.

1f. Frederick Kenneth Radcliffe Long, b. 20 May 1900.
2f. Monica Elsie Long.
3f. Doris Mary Long.

5e. Evelyn Mary Radcliffe, *m.* 25 Ap. 1900, the Rev. Walter Alexander Thackeray (*Nidd Vicarage, Ripley, Yorks*); and has issue 1f to 4f.

1f. Guy St. Vincent Radcliffe Thackeray, b. 22 Jan. 1902.
2f. Colin Michael Carnegie Thackeray, b. 12 May 1903.
3f. Bernard John Martin Thackeray, b. 6 Oct. 1905.
4f. Una Madeline Agatha Thackeray.

7c. *Mary Lowndes*, b. 4 Feb. 1793; d. 10 Nov. 1863; m. 8 *Oct.* 1812, *Edward Jodrell*, b. 19 *Nov.* 1785; d. 14 *Sept.* 1852; *and had issue* 1d to 3d.

1d. Edward Jodrell, Capt. 18th(?) 10th Royal Irish, b. 9 Aug. 1813; d. 27 Jan. 1868; *m.* 4 *July* 1843, Adela Monckton, da. of the Rev. *Sir Edward Bowyer-Smijth of Hill Hall*, co. *Essex*, 10*th Bt.* [E.], b. 11 Oct. 1823; d. 23 Sept. 1896; *and had issue* 1e to 3e.

1e. Sir Alfred Jodrell, 4th Bt. [G.B.] (*Bayfield Hall, Holt, Norfolk*), b. 13 Aug. 1847; *m.* 25 Feb. 1897, Lady Jane, da. of James Walter (Grimston), 2nd Earl of Verulam [U.K.].

2e. Adela Jodrell, *m.* as 2nd wife, 2 June 1885, Sir John Henry Seale, 3rd Bt. [U.K.] (*Wonastow Court, Monmouth*); *s.p.*

3e. Marianne Jodrell (*Glaven, Harvey Road, Guildford*), *m.* 5 Nov. 1868, Frederick John Nash Ind, Major *late* 37th Regt., b. 2 Jan. 1832; *d.s.p.* 11 Mar. 1906.

2d. Rev. Henry Jodrell, *Rector of Gisleham*, co. *Suffolk*, b. 28 *Jan.* 1817; d. 16 Dec. 1896; m. 19 *Oct.* 1843, *Eloisa Fanny Harriet, 2nd Countess of Cape St. Vincent* (*Condessa de Cabo de San Vincent*) [*Portugal*], *da. of Adm. Sir Charles Napier, 1st Count of Cape St. Vincent* (*Conde de Cabo de San Vincent*) [*Portugal*], *K.C.B.* ; *and had issue* 1e to 5e.

1e. Eloisa Napier Jodrell, *m.* 15 Oct. 1870, David John Dickson Safford, Col. Royal West Kent Regt., b. 26 Aug. 1837; *d.* 7 Ap. 1901; and has issue 1f to 4f.

1f. Charles John Napier Safford, Capt. South Wales Borderers, b. 22 June 1871; *d.* 1910; *unm.* [Nos. 10490 to 10577.

The Plantagenet Roll

2*f*. Napier Edward Frederick Safford, Capt. West India Regt., *b*. 24 July 1872; *m*. 5 June 1901, Louisa Annie Margaret, da. of (—) Jewell; and has issue 1*g* to 2*g*.

1*g*. John Charles Safford, *b*. 15 June 1905.
2*g*. Violet Heloise Dorothea Safford.
3*f*. Maude Heloise Safford, *m*. Frank Cox; and has issue 1*g* to 2*g*.
1*g*. Eileen Marjorie Cox.
2*g*. Mavis Heloise Cox.
4*f*. Stella Fanny Safford.

2*e*. Fanny Jodrell (11 *St. Andrews Road, W.*), *m*. 3 June 1879, Henry Hope of Marland Place, co. Hants, *d.s.p.* 12 Ap. 1900.

3*e*. Mary Campbell Jodrell, *m*. 28 June 1881, the Rev. Philip Sherlock Gooch, Rector of Benacre, co. Suffolk, *d.s.p.* 29 Ap. 1909.

4*e*. Celia Cator Jodrell, *m*. 10 July 1872, the Rev. Lewis Richard Charles Bagot, Vicar of Stanton Lacy [B. Bagot Coll., and a descendant of King Henry VII. (see the Tudor Roll, p. 369)] (*Stanton Lacy Vicarage, Bromfield, Salop*); and has issue 1*f* to 4*f*.

1*f*. Caryl Ernest Bagot, *b*. 9 Mar. 1877; *unm*.
2*f*. Ysolde Cicely Bagot, *m*. 1899, B. Gordon Snell; *s.p.*
3*f*. Gladys Mary Beatrice Bagot, *m*. 18 Jan. 1905, Frank Herbert Leake (*Lee Mills House, Cork*); and has issue 1*g* to 2*g*.
1*g*. Maureen Avice Leake.
2*g*. Merrell Gladys Leake.

4*f*. Enid Avice Bagot, *m*. Sept. 1905, Reuben James Charles Jewitt (*Exning, Newmarket*); and has issue 1*g*.
1*g*. Dermod James Boris Jewitt, *b*. 13 Oct. 1908.

5*e*. Madeleine Jane Jodrell, *m*. 3 Sept. 1879, Arthur Keane Tharp (112 *St. James' Court, Buckingham Gate, S.W.; Eaglehurst, Southampton*).

3*d*. Mary Jodrell, *b*. 2 Aug. 1828; *d*. 29 Mar. 1875; m. 30 *May* 1854, *Charles Bishop of Marston Lodge, co. Oxon, b*. 9 *Dec*. 1833; *d*. 26 *Oct*. 1866; *and had issue* 1*e*.

1*e*. Mary Louisa Jodrell Bishop, *m*. 8 Sept. 1880, Frederick Marcus Worsley; *s.p.*

2*b*. Catherine Lowndes, d. (? *unm*.). [Nos. 10578 to 10596.

46. Descendants of ELIZABETH STAPYLTON (Table VII.), *d*. (–); *m*. JOHN DODSWORTH of Thornton Watlass, co. York, D.L., *b*. *c*. 1650; *d*. (–); and had issue 1*a* to 2*a*.

1*a*. *John Dodsworth of Thornton Watlass,* d. (–); m. 8 *Feb*. 1719, *Henrietta, sister of Matthew Hutton, Archbishop of Canterbury, da. of John Hutton of Marske* [*also a descendant of King Edward III.* (see *p*. 120)], d. 1797; *and had issue* 1*b* *to* 2*b*.

1*b*. *Henrietta Maria Dodsworth, da. and co-h.,* d. (–); m. 20 *July* 1761, *Sir Silvester Smith of Newland Park, co. York,* 1st *Bt*. [*G.B.*], *so cr*. 22 *Jan*. 1784; d. 15 *June* 1789; *and had issue* 1c *to* 2c.

1*c*. *Sir Edward Smith, afterwards* (R.L. 21 *May* 1821) *Dodsworth*, 2nd *Bt*. [*G.B.*], b. 13 *Aug*. 1768; d.s.p. 31 *Dec*. 1845.

2*c*. *Sir Charles Smith, afterwards* (R.L. 12 *Mar*. 1846) *Dodsworth*, 3rd *Bt*. [*G.B.*], b. 22 *Aug*. 1775; d. 28 *July* 1857; m. 8 *June* 1808, *Elizabeth, da. and h. of John Armstrong of Lisgoole, co. Fermanagh, by his wife, the Hon. Sophia, née Blayney,* d. 12 *June* 1853; *and had issue*.

See the Exeter Volume, p. 286, Nos. 11625–11646. [Nos. 10597 to 10618.

# of The Blood Royal

2b. Elizabeth Dodsworth, da. and co-h., b. c. 1723; d. 5 Dec. 1772; m. c. 1750, the Rev. James Tunstall, D.D., Canon Residentiary of St. David's, d. 28 Mar. 1762; and had issue (of whom 7 das. at least survived him;[1] only 3, however, were living in 1772, viz.) 1c to 3c.

1c. Henrietta Maria Tunstall, d. (-) ; m. 14 June 1775, John Croft of Oporto, Merchant, d. (-) ; and had issue 1d.

1d. Sir John Croft of Doddington Hall, co. Kent, 1st Bt. [U.K.], so cr. 3 Oct. 1818, and 1st Baron da Serra da Estrella [Portugal], so cr. 14 Dec. 1853, K.T.S., D.C.L., F.R.S., &c., b. (at Oporto) 21 Mar. 1778; d. 5 Feb. 1862; m. 1st, 1 Aug. 1816, Amelia Elizabeth, da. of James Warre, d. 20 Oct. 1819 ; 2ndly, 24 July 1827, Anne Knox, da. of the Rev. John Radcliffe, Rector of Limehouse, d. 5 Mar. 1887 ; and had issue 1e to 2e.

1e. Sir John Frederick Croft, 2nd Bt. [U.K.], 2nd Baron da Serra da Estrella [Portugal], b. 31 Aug. 1828 ; d. 24 May 1904; m. 4 June 1856, Emma, da. of John Graham of Skelmorlie Castle, co. Ayr ; and had issue 1f to 12f.

1f. Sir Frederick Leigh Croft, 3rd Bt. [U.K.], and Baron da Serra da Estrella [Portugal] (Doddington Place, Sittingbourne), b. 14 Feb. 1860.

2f. Francis Edgar Croft, b. 19 Oct. 1861; m. 1891, Zoë, da. of (—) Bromley; and has issue 1g to 3g.

    1g. Lilian Mary Croft.
    2g. Cynthia Croft.
    3g. Eleanor Croft.

3f. William Graham Croft, b. 26 Dec. 1862.
4f. Percy Hutton Croft, b. 27 Oct. 1872.
5f. Tom Radcliffe Croft, b. 1878.

6f. Constance Margaret Graham Croft, m. 14 July 1887, Gilbert Charles Bourne of Cowarne Court, D.L. (Cowarne Court, Ledbury ; Savile House, Oxford) ; and has issue 1g to 2g.

    1g. Robert Croft Bourne, b. 15 July 1888.
    2g. Cecily Radcliffe Bourne.

7f. Gertrude Mary Croft, m. 31 Aug. 1893, Arthur John Chitty, Bar.-at-Law [eldest son of the Right Hon. Sir Joseph Chitty, P.C.] (27 Hereford Square, S.W. ; Huntingfield, Faversham, Kent) ; and has issue 1g to 3g.

    1g. James Malcolm Chitty, b. 1898.
    2g. Margaret Hyacinth Chitty.
    3g. Violet Ada Pamela Chitty.

8f. Elinor Violet Croft, m. 13 Oct. 1896, Walter Graham Crum (Dalmottar House, Old Kirkpatrick); and has issue 1g.

    1g. Joscelyn Margaret Campbell Crum.

9f. Ethel Mary Croft, m. 1st, 17 Ap. 1890, Hubert Hedworth Grenville Wells, d. 17 Ap. 1904; 2ndly, 1906, Alfred Benjamin (Holly Lodge, Cookham, Berks); and has issue 1g to 2g.

    1g. Yvo Hedworth Fortescue Grenville Wells, b. 6 Sept. 1893.
    2g. Rose Allada Grenville Wells.

10f. Editha Croft, m. 6 Mar. 1906, Bateman Lancaster Rose, a Member of the London Stock Exchange and Partner in the firm of Linton, Clarke, & Co. [5th son of Sir Philip Rose, 1st Bt. [U.K.]] (1 Cromwell Road, S.W.); and has issue 1g.

    1g. Ronald Paul Lancaster Rose, b. 1907.

11f. Lucy Croft, m. 17 Oct. 1905, Donald Hatt Noble Graham, Cadet of Airthrey ; and has issue.

12f. Mildred Jessie Graham Croft.   [Nos. 10619 to 10642.

---

[1] "Dict. Nat. Biog.," lvii. p. 315. Foster ("Yorkshire Pedigrees, Dodsworth") calls him Dean of St. Paul's, and only mentions the 3 das., so presumably the others died unm.).

The Plantagenet Roll

2e. Elizabeth Anne Croft (*Holme Priory, Wareham*), m. 26 Aug. 1843, Sir Harry Stephen Meysey-Thompson of Kirkby, 1st Bt. [U.K.], so cr. 26 Mar. 1874, M.P., J.P., D.L., b. 11 Aug. 1809; d. 17 May 1874; and has issue 1f to 9f.

1f. Henry Meysey (Meysey-Thompson), 1st Baron Knaresborough [U.K.], so cr. 26 Dec. 1905, 2nd Bt., J.P., D.L., *formerly* M.P. for Handsworth, &c. (*Kirkby Hall, York*), b. 30 Aug. 1845; m. 21 Ap. 1885, Ethel Adeline (see p. 218), da. of Sir Henry Pottinger, 3rd Bt. [U.K.]; and has issue 1g to 5g.

1g. Hon. Claude Henry Meysey Meysey-Thompson, Lieut. Rifle Brig., b. 5 Ap. 1887.

2g. Hon. Violet Ethel Meysey-Thompson.

3g. Hon. Helen Winifred Meysey-Thompson.

4g. Hon. Doris Mary Pottinger Meysey-Thompson.

5g. Hon. Gwendolen Carles Meysey-Thompson.

2f. Richard Frederick Meysey-Thompson, Lieut.-Col. Reserve of Officers, *formerly* Lieut.-Col. and Hon. Col. 4th Batt. W. Yorkshire Regt., &c. (*Nunthorpe Court, York*), b. 17 Ap. 1847; m. 14 July 1879, Charlotte, da. of Sir James Walker of Sand Hutton, 1st Bt. [U.K.]; and has issue 1g to 2g.

1g. Algar De Clifford Charles Meysey-Thompson, b. 9 Nov. 1885.

2g. Violet Ileene Cassandra Meysey-Thompson, m. 17 Oct. 1905, Major Charles William Cuffe-Knox, 4th Batt. Rifle Brigade (*Creagh, co. Mayo*).

3f. Albert Childers Meysey-Thompson, Q.C., Bar.-at-Law, b. 13 *July* 1848; d. 20 Mar. 1894; m. 19 *Aug.* 1882, *Mabel Louisa* [a descendant of *King Henry VII.*], da. of Rev. the Hon. *James Walter Lascelles* [*E. of Harewood Coll.*]; *and had issue* 1g.

1g. Hubert Charles Meysey-Thompson, B.A. (Camb.), Bar.-at-Law (*Broxholme, Ripley*), b. 9 June 1883.

4f. Rev. Charles Maude Meysey-Thompson, M.A., Rector of Claydon, b. 5 Dec. 1849; d. 12 Sept. 1881; m. 28 *Ap*. 1874, *Emily Mary* (*Hillthorpe House, Scarborough*), da. of Sir James Walker of Sand Hutton, 1st Bt. [U.K.]; and had issue 1g.

1g. Harold James Meysey-Thompson, Capt. 4th Batt. Rifle Brig. (*Army and Navy; Bachelors'*), b. 24 Sept. 1876.

5f. Arthur Herbert Meysey-Thompson, *late* Lieut. Yorkshire Hussars (*Scarcroft, Yorks*), b. 5 Oct. 1852; m. 1 June 1896, Horatia Dorothy, da. of Sir Hedworth Williamson, 8th Bt. [E.]; and has issue 1g to 3g.

1g. Guy Herbert Meysey-Thompson, b. 21 Sept. 1901.

2g. Sylvia Dorothy Meysey-Thompson.

3g. Diana Elizabeth Meysey-Thompson.

6f. Ernest Claude Meysey-Thompson, M.P., J.P., Major Yorkshire Hussars (*Spellow Hill, Staveley, Knaresborough*), b. 18 Feb. 1859; m. 1 Nov. 1894, Alice Jane Blanche, da. of Col. John Joicey of Newton Hall, M.P.; and has issue 1g to 2g.

1g. Onslow Victor Claud Meysey-Thompson, b. 1 June 1897.

2g. Alice Hildegarde Eva Meysey-Thompson.

7f. Elizabeth Lucy Meysey-Thompson, m. 23 Sept. 1868, Walter Stafford (Northcote), 2nd Earl of Iddesleigh [U.K.], 9th Bart. [E.], C.B., &c. (*Pynes, near Exeter*); and has issue 1g to 3g.

1g. Stafford Henry Northcote, Viscount St. Cyres (*Brooks'; Athenæum*), b. 29 Aug. 1869.

2g. Lady Rosalind Lucy Northcote.

3g. Lady Elizabeth Mabel Northcote.

8f. Mary Caroline Meysey-Thompson, m. 2 July 1878, William Henry Bond, *late* Royal Scots (*Tyneham, Wareham*); and has issue 1g to 5g.

1g. Algernon Arthur Garneys Bond, Capt. and Adj. 4th Batt. Rifle Brig., b. 21 July 1879. [Nos. 10643 to 10667.

# of The Blood Royal

2g. William Ralph Garneys Bond, Sudan C.S., b. 12 Dec. 1880.
3g. Edith Cicely Garneys Bond.
4g. Lilian Mary Garneys Bond.
5g. Margaret Helen Garneys Bond.
9f. Amelia Annie Meysey-Thompson.

2c. *Catherine Tunstall* (6th da.), d. 18 *May* 1807; m. 1*st, the Rev. Edward Chamberlayne, Rector of Charlton;* 2*ndly, as* 2*nd wife,* 28 *July* 1806*, Horatio* (*Walpole*), 2*nd Earl of Orford* [*U.K.*]*,* d. (s.p. *by her*) 15 *June* 1822.

3c. *Jane Tunstall,* d. 26 *May* 1841; m. 1*st, Stephen Thompson,* d.(-); 2*ndly,* 3 *Nov.* 1792*, Sir Everard Home,* 1*st Bt.* [*U.K.*]*, F.R.S., President R.C.S. and Sergeant-Surgeon to King George III.,* b. 6 *May* 1746; d. 31 *Aug.* 1832; *and had issue* 1d *to* 3d.

1d. *Sir James Everard Home,* 2*nd Bt.* [*U.K.*]*,* b. 25 *Oct.* 1798; d.s.p.

2d. *Mary Elizabeth Home,* b. c. 1795; d. 9 *Ap.* 1841; m. 28 *Oct.* 1815*, Charles Powlett Rushworth* [*son of Edward Rushworth of Farringford Hill, I.W., by his wife, the Hon. Catharine, da. and co-h. of Leonard* (*Troughear*), 1*st Lord Holmes of Kilmallock* [*I.* 1797]*,* b. c. 1790; d. 15 *Oct.* 1854; *and had* (*with* 2 *other sons and* 4 *das who* d.s.p.) *issue* 1e *to* 4e.

1e. *Edward Everard Rushworth, C.M.G., D.C.L., Colonial Secretary and Lieut.- Governor of Jamaica,* b. 23 *Aug.* 1818; d. *of yellow fever in Jamaica* 10 *Aug.* 1877; m. 1*st,* 13 *Jan.* 1855*, Amelia Adelaide, da. of Horatio Nelson de les Derniers of Vaucheuil, Lower Canada,* d. (-); *and had* (*with a son and* 2 *das. who* d. *unm.*) *issue* 1f *to* 4f.

1f. Edward Henry Rushworth, b. 2 Dec. 1864, *unm.*

2f. William Arthur Rushworth (*United States*), b. 3 Nov. 1866; *m.* and has issue a son and da.

3f. Harriet Jane Rushworth, m. 21 Jan. 1875, Gilbert Robertson Sandbach [son of the Rev. Gilbert Sandbach of Woodlands, co. Lancaster] (*Stoneleigh, Rossett, Denbigh*); and has issue 1g to 6g.

1g. Gilbert Robertson Sandbach, b. 22 Aug. 1892.
2g. Adelaide Mary Sandbach, b. 1 July 1878.
3g. Doris Annette Sandbach, b. 10 Jan. 1883.
4g. Eleanor Katherine Sandbach, b. 6 Jan. 1884.
5g. Violet Marion Sandbach, b. 10 Aug. 1885.
6g. Margaret Elizabeth Sandbach, b. 3 Aug. 1895.

4f. Rosamond Linda Rushworth, m. 16 Ap. 1884, the Rev. Cecil Evan Smith, Rector of Titsey (*Titsey Rectory, Limpsfield, Surrey*); and has issue 1g to 4g.

1g. Everard Cecil Smith, Lieut. 3rd Batt. Royal Fusiliers 1908, educ. Winchester Coll. 1897-1903, and Sandhurst 1904-1905, b. 3 Feb. 1885.
2g. Charles Home Cecil Smith, educ. Winchester Coll. 1902-1906 and Trinity Coll., Camb., 1907, b. 8 May 1889.
3g. Rosamond Mary Cecil Smith, b. 21 Dec. 1885.
4g. Linda Katharine Cecil Smith, b. 27 Jan. 1894.

2e. *Horatia Ann Rushworth,* b. 21 *July* 1823; d. 5 *Mar.* 1859; m. 12 *July* 1851*, Marcus Staunton Lynch-Staunton of Clydagh, co. Galway, Bar.-at-Law,* d. 19 *Oct.* 1896; *and had issue* 1f *to* 2f.

1f. Charles Rushworth Lynch-Staunton of Clydagh, Inspector Local Government Board, Ireland, 1892 (*Clydagh, Headford, Tuam*), b. 1854.

2f. Alice Lynch-Staunton.

3e. *Rosamond Rushworth,* b. 17 *Oct.* 1830; d. 24 *June* 1904; m. 3 *Oct.* 1861*, Sir Arthur Townley Watson,* 2*nd Bt.* [*U.K.* 1866]*, K.C.,* d. 15 *Mar.* 1907; *and had issue* 1f *to* 4f.

1f. Sir Charles Rushworth Watson, 3rd Bt. [U.K.] (*Reigate Lodge, Reigate ; K5 The Albany, Piccadilly; The Elms, Prior's Hardwick, &c.; Travellers'*), b. 21 Sept. 1865. [Nos. 10668 to 10689.

The Plantagenet Roll

2f. Arthur Watson, now Cotton-Watson, Capt. 4th Batt. Royal Irish Rifles (*Isthmian*), b. 3 Aug. 1870.

3f. Mabel Frederica Watson, m. 11 Aug. 1887, the Rev. Reginald Fitz-Hugh Bigg-Wither, Rector of Wonston (*Wonston Rectory, Micheldever, Hants*); and has issue 1g to 2g.

    1g. Olga Mary Bigg-Wither.

    2g. Joan Gertrude Bigg-Wither.

4f. Amy Catherine Rose Watson.

4e. Frederica Rushworth, b. 13 Dec. 1836; m. 4 Oct. 1855, the Rev. William Birkett, d. (-) ; and has issue 1f to 4f.

    1f. Trevor Birkett.

    2f. Mary Birkett,

    3f. Leonora Birkett,   } all m. to Germans and residing abroad.

    4f. Frederica Birkett,

3d. Charlotte Home, b. 26 Dec. 1802; d. 21 Jan. 1878; m. 1823, *Capt. Bernard Yeoman, R.N.* [also descended from King Edward III. through the Mortimer-Percy marriage (see p. 252)] ; d. 23 Ap. 1836; *and had* (*with an elder son, Henry Everard, who d.s.p.*) issue 1e to 3e.

1e. Constantine Laurence Yeoman, Capt. R.H.A. and Lieut.-Col. Turkish Army (25 *Orchard Street, Brentford, Middlesex*), b. 1828 ; *unm.*

2e. Linda Constantia Yeoman, m. 4 Aug. 1857, Francis Rowden of the Inner Temple, Bar.-at-Law (72 *Braybrooke Road, Hastings*); and has (with a son and a da. who *d.s.p.*) issue 1f to 6f.

    1f. Francis Constantine Bernard Rowden, b. 22 Ap. 1860; *unm.*

    2f. Linda Everardina Rowden, *unm.*

    3f. Rosa Charlotte Rowden, m. 25 Mar. 1904, John Richards Orpen, Bar.-at-Law (*Dublin*); and has issue 1g.

        1g. Dorothy Esther Penelope Orpen.

    4f. Dora Rowden, *unm.*

    5f. Eva Rowden, *unm.*

    6f. Maud Octavia Rowden, m. 14 Nov. 1906, Frederick Oddin-Taylor, D.L. (*Norwich*); *s.p.*

2e. Rosa Charlotte Yeoman, b. 12 May 1831; d. 21 May 1908; m. 18 Feb. 1857, the Rev. Edward Woodyatt, M.A. (Oxon.), Vicar of Over (*St. John's Vicarage, Over, Cheshire*); *and had issue* 1f *to* 8f.

    1f. Nigel Gresley Woodyatt, Col. Ghurka Rifles, b. 30 Mar. 1861; m. 12 Nov. 1887, Florence Emily Stewart, da. of Arthur Blakeley Patterson, C.S.I.; and has issue 1g.

        1g. Reginald Nigel Gresley Woodyatt, b. 1890.

    2f. Edward Woodyatt (*Trunch, North Walsham, Norfolk*), b. 23 Dec. 1867; m. Oct. 1903, Lillian, da. of James Blanchflower of Norfolk, d. 1907; and has issue 1g.

        1g. Gwendolen Yeoman Woodyatt.

    3f. Bernard Hale Woodyatt, M.R.C.S., Surg. Albert Infirmary, Winsford (*Over, Winsford*), b. 1 June 1869 ; *unm.*

    4f. George Everard Staples Woodyatt, Capt. 7th Batt. Royal Fusiliers (86 *Eaton Terrace, S.W.*), b. 27 Mar. 1873; m. 3 Oct. 1894, Rosalie Frances Helen, da. of Capt. Luxmoore Brooke of Ashbrook Towers, co. Chester; and has issue 1g.

        1g. Henry Luxmoore Brooke Woodyatt, b. 19 Sept. 1897.

    5f. Henry Constantine Woodyatt, M.R.C.S., Staff Surgeon R.N., b. 18 May 1875, *unm.*

    6f. Florence Woodyatt, *unm.*

    7f. Rosa Louisa Woodyatt, m. 24 Ap. 1895, James Henry Wakeman Best [son

[Nos. 10690 to 10718.

# of The Blood Royal

of James Best of Holt Castle, co. Worcester] (*The Stocks, Suckley, Worcester*); and has issue 1g to 4g.

 1g. James Edward Best, b. 1 Jan. 1905.
 2g. Violet Rosalie Best, b. 8 Ap. 1896.
 3g. Florence Beatrice Best, b. 5 July 1898.
 4g. Doris May Best, b. 17 May 1902.

 8f. Edith Beatrice Woodyatt.

 2a. *Dorothy Dodsworth*, d. (-) ; m. (—) *Barilet of Nutwitheral, in the parish of Masham*. [Nos. 10719 to 10723.

47. Descendants of the Rev. HENRY STAPYLTON, M.A. (Oxon.), Rector of Thornton Watlass and Marske, co. York (Table VII.), d. 9 Feb. 1748 ; m. MARY, da. and h. of the Rev. (—) ORCHARD, bur. 22 Dec. 1755 ; and had issue 1a to 5a.

 1a. Rev. *John Stapylton, M.A., Rector of Thornton Watlass*, bapt. 19 Sept. 1707 ; d. 3 Oct. 1767 ; m. 2ndly, 4 Feb. 1754, *Lucy, da. of Thomas Wycliffe of Gailes, co. York ; and had issue* 1b.
 1b. *Henry Stapylton of Norton, co. Durham, J.P.*, d. Aug. 1835 ; m. 3 Jan. 1786, *Mary Ann, da. and h. of Capt. Robert Gregory, R.N.* [*by his wife*, (—), *da. and event. h. of Rear-Adm. Polycarpus Taylor of Norton*], d. (-) ; *and had issue* 1c to 3c.
 1c. *Robert Martin Stapylton, Army Pay Office*, b. 21 Sept. 1793 ; d. 17 Jan. 1864 ; m. 16 Ap. 1818, *Martha Eliza, da. of John Bockett of Southcote Lodge, co. Berks*, d. (-) ; *and had issue* 1d to 4d.
 1d. *Robert George Stapylton, Bar.-at-Law*, b. 13 Aug. 1820 ; d. 6 Jan. 1873 ; m. 24 May 1855, *Madalina Clementina, da. of the Rev. George Hull Bowers, D.D., Dean of Manchester*, d. (-) ; *and had issue* 1e to 3e.
 1e. Rev. Robert Miles Stapylton, b. 15 Ap. 1864 ; m. 1892, Margaret, da. of the Rev. T. Sharpe, Rector of Little Downham and Canon of Ely ; and has issue 1f.
  1f. John Miles Stapylton, b. 18 Nov. 1896.
 2e. Olive Harriet Stapylton, *unm.*
 3e. Mary Ursula Stapylton, m. Walter H. Thorley.

 2d. *Henry Stapylton, emigrated to Australia* 1852, b. 15 Aug. 1834 ; d. 6 May 1902 ; m. *at St. Andrew's Church, Braidwood*, 6 Jan. 1859, *Margaret, da. of Edward O'Conor of Dublin ; and had issue* 1e to 3e.
 1e. Robert Miles Stapylton (*Norton, Wardell Road, Dulwich Hill, Sydney, N.S.W.*), b. 20 Oct. 1859 ; m. 24 Jan. 1885, Elizabeth, da. of William McCann of Sydney, N.S.W.
 2e. Edward Stapylton, Justice Dept., b. 9 Nov. 1862 ; m. Jane, da. of Henry Underhill, J.P. ; and has issue 1f.
  1f. Edward Stapylton.
 3e. Henry Miles Stapylton, Postal Telegraph Dept., b. 25 Oct. 1865 ; m. Caroline, da. of C. Womsen ; and has issue 1f to 4f.
  1f. Alan Stapylton.
  2f. Miles Stapylton.
  3f. Robert Stapylton.
  4f. Margaret Stapylton.

 3d. Miles Stapylton (20 *Mortlake Road, Kew, Surrey*), b. 9 Feb. 1836 ; m. 1 Feb. 1868, Sarah Dorcas, da. of the Rev. Benjamin Bradney Bockett, M.A., Vicar of Epsom ; and has issue 1e to 5e. [Nos. 10724 to 10736.

The Plantagenet Roll

1e. Bryan Stapylton, *Vol. Paget's Horse*, b. 23 Nov. 1870; d. *of wounds in South Africa* 13 *Mar.* 1901.

2e. Alan Stapylton, M.I.C.E., b. 16 May 1872; m. 27 Oct. 1904, Beatrice, da. of the Rev. S. Goldney, M.A.; and has issue 1f.

1f. Mabel Grace Stapylton, b. 26 July 1905.

3e. Ella Mary Stapylton, *unm.*

4e. Mabel Dorcas Stapylton, *unm.*

5e. Kathleen Eliza Stapylton, m. 16 Sept. 1905, Horatio John Nelson Hawkins, C.E.; *s.p.*

4d. Mary Jane Stapylton, *unm.*

2c. Mary Frances Stapylton, d. 18 May 1878; m. 2 Dec. 1824, *Marshall Robinson, afterwards (R.L. 19 Aug. 1828) Fowler, of Preston Hall, co. Durham* [*Robinson of Herrington Coll.*]. d. 28 Feb. 1874; *and had issue* (*with* 2 *sons d.s.p.*) 1d *to* 2d.

1d. Robinson Fowler, Bar.-at-Law, *Stip. Mag. at Manchester*, b. 15 *Mar.* 1828; d. 16 *Jan.* 1895; m. 1st, 18 *June* 1849 (*dissolved* 1 Feb. 1859), *Olivia Stapylton* (see p. 119), da. *of George William Sutton of Elton Hall, co. Durham*; 2ndly, 29 *Aug.* 1859, *Anne Agnes Erskine*, da. *of Very Rev. the Hon. Henry David Erskine, Dean of Ripon* (see p. 227); *and had issue* 1e *to* 3e.

1e. Marshall Robinson Fowler, *afterwards* (D.P. 1878) *Stapylton*, b. 2 May 1850; d. 21 *Ap.* 1894; m. 28 *Dec.* 1878, *Alice Edith*, da. *of* (—) *Attwood*, d. 17 Dec. 1881; *and had issue* 1f.

1f. Algernon Marshall Stapylton, *formerly in the Army* (*Australia*), b. 17 Sept. 1881; *unm.*

2e. George Stapylton Fowler, b. 30 Mar. 1851; *unm.*

3e. Florence Mary Fowler, *unm.*

2d. Marshall Fowler of Preston, J.P., cos. Durham and York (*Otterington House, Northallerton*), b. 3 May 1834; m. 19 Dec. 1893, Emily Hindman, widow of Robert Walton, da. of Capt. James William Armstrong, R.N.; *s.p.*

3c. Olivia Stapylton, b. 13 *Ap.* 1793; d. *Feb.* 1883; m. 21 *Ap.* 1824, *George William Sutton* (R.L. 17 *Oct.* 1822), *previously Hutchinson, of Elton Hall, co. Durham*, d. 1852; *and had issue* (*with a son and da. d. unm.*) 1d *to* 3d.

1d. John Stapylton Sutton (*Faceby, Northallerton*), b. 23 Nov. 1832; m. 1855, Sarah Jefferson, da. of John Charles Maynard of Harlsey Hall, Northallerton; and has issue 1e to 3e.

1e. George William Sutton, Land Agent (*Eaglescliffe, Yarm.*), b. Dec. 1857; m. 1900, Laura, da. of (—) Johnson, d. 1902; and has issue 1f.

1f. Eric John Stapylton Sutton, b. 28 Dec. 1901.

2e. Catherine Olivia Sutton, *unm.*

3e. Laura Eugenie Sutton (*Faceby Manor, Northallerton*), m. 19 Ap. 1886, Martin Morrison of Faceby Manor, d. Feb. 1900; and has issue 1f to 6f.

1f. Ronald John Martin Morrison, b. 10 Aug. 1884.

2f. Martin James Morrison, l. 20 Aug. 1893.

3f. James William Sutton Morrison, b. 11 Dec. 1897.

4f. Hilda Olive Eugenie Morrison.

5f. Riva Sarah Mary Morrison.

6f. Florence Beryl Morrison.

2d. Grace Sutton, b. 12 *Aug.* 1826; d. 17 Dec. 1894; m. 4 *June* 1850, *the Rev. Henry Maister, Vicar of Skeffling, co. Yorks*, b. *at Winestead, Hull*, 20 *June* 1813; d. 18 *June* 1898; *and had issue* 1e *to* 6e.

1e. Reginald Henry Maister, b. 19 June 1851; *unm.*

2e. George Sutton Maister (*New Zealand*), b. 11 July 1855; m. Rose, da. of (—) Andrewes of Hull; and has issue (4 sons and 3 das.).

[Nos. 10737 to 10759.

of The Blood Royal

3e. Rev. Arthur Gerald Maister, Vicar of Mumby (*Mumby Vicarage, Alford*) b. 20 Feb. 1862; m. 19 Sept. 1899, Edith Jane, da. of John Reed; s.p.

4e. Henrietta Grace Maister, *unm.*

5e. Olivia Lucy Maister (*Ravenser, Easington, Hull*), *unm.*

6e. Edith Everild Maister, m. May 1888, the Rev. John Thomas, Vicar of Cutcombe (*Cutcombe Vicarage, Dunster, Somerset*); and has issue 1f.

1f. Henry Evan Eric Thomas, b. 26 May 1900.

3d. Olivia Stapylton Sutton, b. 2 May 1830; d. 20 Oct. 1872; m. *as 1st wife*, 18 June 1849, Robinson Fowler of London, Bar.-at-Law, d. 16 Jan. 1895; and had issue.

See p. 118, Nos. 10743–10745.

2a. Elizabeth Stapylton, bapt. 26 Aug. 1698; d. (–); m. Richard Tennant.

3a. Sarah Stapylton, bapt. 19 Feb. 1703; d. 29 Sept. 1783; m. 8 Aug. 1733, Thomas Raisbeck of Stockton and Durham, Solicitor, Mayor of Stockton 1737–1738, 1747–1757, d. Feb. 1765; and had issue 1b to 2b.[1]

1b. Thomas Stapylton Raisbeck of Stockton, Solicitor, Mayor of that town 1769, 1770, and 1788, b. c. 1740; d. 4 Dec. 1794; m. Sarah, da. of Leonard Robinson of Stockton, d. 5 Mar. 1813; and had issue 1c.

1c. Leonard Raisbeck of Stockton, Solicitor, d.s.p. 1845.

2b. William Raisbeck of Newcastle-on-Tyne, living 1768; m. Mary, da. of (—) Gunn; and had issue (a son who d.s.p. and) 1c to 2c.

1c. Sarah Raisbeck, } d. (? *unm.*).
2c. Mary Raisbeck, }

4a. Olivia Stapylton, bapt. 19 Sept. 1707; d. (–); m. 13 Ap. 1738, *the Rev. Thomas Robinson, M.A., Rector of Wycliffe, co. York*; and had issue 1b.

1b. Mary Robinson, d. 19 July 1815; m. 1771, Joshua Greenwell of Kibblesworth, co. Durham, d. 26 Aug. 1797; and had issue 1c.

1c. Robinson Robert Greenwell of Newcastle, b. 3 Ap. 1778; d. Nov. 1841; m. 2 Feb. 1819, Elizabeth, da. of John Mellar of Whitby, d. 7 Jan. 1822; and had issue 1d.

1d. Rev. William Greenwell of Carr Mount, co. York, M.A., b. 5 Nov. 1819; d. 30 Mar. 1899; m. 15 May 1851, Jane, da. of the Rev. William Blow, M.A., Rector of Goodmanham, d. 22 Dec. 1879; and had issue 1e to 5e.

1e. Leonard William Greenwell, b. 26 June 1853.

2e. Harold Stapylton Greenwell, b. 10 Jan. 1857.

3e. Augusta Isabella Greenwell, m. 22 Oct. 1878, Alan Greenwell (*34 Old Elvet, Durham*); and has issue 1f to 2f.

1f. Alan Leonard Stapylton Greenwell, b. 29 Jan. 1880.

2f. William Basil Greenwell, Lieut. Durham L.I., b. 29 Oct. 1881.

4e. Olivia Greenwell.

5e. Ethel Edith Mary Greenwell.

5a. Henrietta Stapylton, bapt. 3 Sept. 1714; d. (–); m. 14 Feb. 1740, *John Soux of London*. [Nos. 10760 to 10774.

48. Descendants of FRANCES NORCLIFFE of Heslington (Table VII.), b. 16 Sept. 1700; d. 15 July 1770; m. 4 Mar. 1728, Sir JOHN WRAY of Sleningford, 12th Bt. [E.], b. 24 Oct. 1689; d. 26 Jan. 1752; and had issue.

See the Clarence Volume, pp. 574–581, Nos. 24241–24443.

[Nos. 10775 to 10977.

---

[1] Nichol's "Topographer and Genealogist," ii. 91.

The Plantagenet Roll

49. Descendants of FRANCES STAPYLTON (Table VII.), *bur.* 5 May 1684; *m.* (settlement dated 13 Sept.) 1651, JOHN HUTTON (see p. 310) of Marske, co. York, *b.* 6 Oct. 1625; *d.* 21 Mar. 1664; and had issue 1a to 3a.

1a. *John Hutton of Marske,* b. 14 *July* 1657; bur. 2 *Mar.* 1731; m. (*settlement dated* 24 *Nov.*) 1680, *Dorothy, da. and co-h. of William Dyke of Frant, co. Sussex,* bur. 7 *Jan.* 1743; *and had issue* 1b *to* 4b.
    1b. *John Hutton of Marske,* bapt. 18 *Nov.* 1691; d. 16 *Jan.* 1768; m. 2*ndly,* 5 *Mar.* 1726, *the Hon. Elizabeth, da. and co-h. of James (Darcy),* 1st *Lord Darcy of Navan* [*G.B.*], bapt. 13 *Oct.* 1706; bur. 10 *June* 1739; *and had issue.*
    See the Exeter Volume, pp. 555–558, Nos. 49684–49747.
    2b. *Most Rev. Matthew Hutton, D.D., Lord Bishop of York* 1747–1757, *and of Canterbury* 1757–1758, b. 3 *Jan.* 1692; d. 19 *Mar.* 1758; *leaving issue now extinct.*
    3b. *Timothy Hutton,* bapt. 31 *Mar.* 1696.
    4b. *Henrietta Hutton,* bapt. 23 *Oct.* 1701; d. 1797; m. 8 *Feb.* 1719, *John Dodsworth of Thornton Watlass, co. York; and had issue.*
    See p. 112, Nos. 10597–10723.
2a. *Frances Hutton,* b. 7 *Mar.* 1653; d. (–); m. *Andrew Wanley of Eyford, co. Gloucester.*
3a. *Olive Hutton,* b. 30 *Nov.* 1656; d. (–); m. *Thomas Alcock of Chatham,* bur. (*at Marske*) 15 *Dec.* 1698. [Nos. 10978 to 11168.

50. Descendants, if any surviving, of URSULA STAPYLTON (Table VII.), *d.* (admon. to da. 21 Ap.) 1693; *m.* THOMAS PEPYS of Hatcham, Barnes, and Merton Abbey, co. Surrey, Master of Jewel Office to Kings Charles II. and James II. and VII., *bapt.* 16 Jan. 1640; *d.* (–); and had (with possibly other) issue 1a.

1a. *Olivia Pepys,* m. *before* 21 *Ap.* 1693, *Sir Edward Smith of Edmondthorp, co. Leicester.*[1]

51. Descendants of ELEANOR SLINGSBY (Table IV.), *d.* 1647; *m.* as 1st wife, Sir ARTHUR INGRAM of Temple Newsham (Table IV.), *d.* 1655; and had issue 1a to 2a.

1a. *Henry (Ingram),* 1st *Viscount Irvine* [*S.*], bapt. 8 *Ap.* 1641; bur. 13 *Aug.* 1666; m. (*lic. dated* 7 *June*) 1661, *Lady Essex, da. of Edward (Montagu),* 2nd *Earl of Manchester* [*E.*], d. (*will dated* 4, *prov.* 13 *Oct.*) 1677; *and had issue.*
    See the Essex Volume, Table X., and pp. 149–152, Nos. 17211–17285.
2a. *Arthur Ingram of Barrowby, co. York,* d. 13 *Sept.* 1713; m. *Jane, da. of Sir John Mallory of Studley, co. York,* bur. 3 *Aug.* 1693; *and had issue* 1b *to* 6b.
    1b. *Thomas Ingram,* d. 19 *Feb.* 1703; m. *Frances, da. and h. of John Nicholson of York, M.D.* [m. 2*ndly, John Wood of Copmanthorpe, Bar.-at-Law, and*] d. 23 *Mar.* 1740; *and had issue* (*with* 2 *sons who d. in infancy*) 1c.
    1c. *Frances Ingram, presumably dead s.p. before* 1708.
    2b. *Arthur Ingram, a Turkey Merchant, heir to his nephew Arthur, May* 1708; [Nos. 11169 to 11243.

---

[1] "Genealogy of the Pepys Family, 1273–1887," by W. C. Pepys. London, 1887. Pedigree V.

of The Blood Royal

d. (-); m. *Elizabeth, da. of (—) Barns; and had issue which became extinct* 22 *May* 1830.

3b. *Mallory Ingram.*
4b. *Mary Ingram.*
5b. *Katherine Ingram.*
6b. *Elizabeth Ingram*, d. *Ap.* 1717;[1] m. *as* 1st *wife*, 1709, *Anstrupus Danby of Swinton and Farnley, co. York*, b. 1680; d. 12 *Mar.* 1750; *and had issue which became extinct* 4 *Dec.* 1833.

52. Descendants, if any surviving, of the Rev. CHARLES SLINGSBY, Rector of Rothbury (Table IV.), *bapt.* 22 Nov. 1561; *d.* (-); *m.* ELIZABETH, da. of John ELLIS of Barnborough, co. York; and had issue 1α to 3α.[2]

   1a. *Thomas Slingsby, aged* 17 *and unm.* 1617; bur. 10 *Feb.* 1670.
   2a. *Margaret Slingsby*, m. *Thomas Barret of York.*
   3a. *Mary Slingsby, aged* 20, 1617.

53. Descendants, if any surviving, of Sir WILLIAM SLINGSBY of Kippax, co. Midx., D.L., Carver to Queen Anne of Denmark (Table IV.), *d.* Aug. 1624; *m.* ELIZABETH, da. of Sir Stephen BOARD of Boardshill, co. Sussex; and had issue 1α to 2α.[3]

   1a. *Henry Slingsby, Master of the Mint to King Charles I., and as such author of the motto* "Decus et Tutamen" *which appears on the coinage*, b. c. 1620; d. (-); m. *according to some,* (—), *da. of Sir* (—) *Cage, and to others, Catherine, da. of Sir William Lowther of Great Preston; and who had issue* 1b.
   1b. *Elizabeth Slingsby, da. and in* 1697 *sole h.*, d. (-); m. *Adlard Cage of Thavies Inn, Midx.*

   2a. *Elizabeth Slingsby, aged* 8 *in* 1627.

54. Descendants, if any surviving, of Sir GUILDFORD SLINGSBY, Comptroller of the Navy (Table IV.), *bapt.* 7 Oct. 1565; *d.* at sea 1631; *m.* 1609, MARGARET, da. of William WATTER of Cundall, Lord Mayor of York in 1620; and had issue 1α to 11α.

   1a. *Guildford Slingsby, Lieut. of the Ordnance Office and Sec. to the great Earl of Stafford*, bur. 26 *Jan.* 1642.
   2a. *Sir Robert Slingsby of Newcells,* 1st *Bt.* [E.], *so cr.* 16 *Mar.* 1661; b. c. 1611; d.s.p. 26 *Oct.* 1661.
   3a. *Percy Slingsby.*
   4a. *Walter Slingsby.*
   5a. *George Slingsby.*
   6a. *Francis Slingsby of St. Martin's in the Fields, will proved* 1670.
   7a. *Sir Arthur Slingsby of Bifrons,* 1st *Bt.* [E.], *so cr.* 19 *Oct.* 1657; b. c. 1623; bur. 12 *Feb.* 1666; m. (—), *a Flemish lady who was living* 26 *Ap.* 1666; *and had issue* 1b *to* 4b.

---

[1] J. Fisher's "History of Masham," p. 244.
[2] Foster's "Yorkshire Pedigrees."
[3] Ibid.

The Plantagenet Roll

1b. *Sir Charles Slingsby of Bifrons*, 2nd Bt. [E.], *living abroad* 1670; *sold Bifrons* 1677, *after which nothing is known of him.*

2b. *Peter Slingsby, living abroad with brother* 1670.

3b. *Anna Charlotte Slingsby*, bapt. 4 *Jan.* 1664; d. (–); m. *Sir Edward Nightingale, de jure 5th Bt.* [E.], bapt. 27 *Aug.* 1658; d. 2 *July* 1723; *and had issue.* See the Exeter Volume, Table XXXIII. and pp. 428–433, Nos. 34734–34997.

4b. *Mary Slingsby*, b. *posthumous and* bapt. *at Patrixbourne* 26 *Ap.* 1666.

8a. *Dorothy Slingsby*, d. (–); m. *Jeffrey Nightingale of Kneesworth, co. Camb.*

9a. *Margaret Slingsby.*   10a. *Mary Slingsby.*   11a. *Anne Slingsby.*

[Nos. 11244 to 11507.

55. Descendants, if any surviving, of Sir FRANCIS SLINGSBY of Kilmore, co. Cork (Table IV.), d. (–); m. ELIZABETH, da. of Hugh CUFF of Cuff Hall, co. Somerset; and had issue 1a to 7a.[1]

1a. *Francis Slingsby.*   4a. *Catherine Slingsby.*   6a. *Elizabeth Slingsby.*
2a. *Henry Slingsby.*   5a. *Anne Slingsby.*   7a. *Jane Slingsby.*
3a. *Mary Slingsby.*

56. Descendants, if any, of CATHERINE PERCY, sister to the 7th and 8th Earls of Northumberland [E.] (Table II.), d. (–); m. RALPH [RITHER] RETHERS.

57. Descendants of Sir WILLIAM HARRIS of Shenfield Manor, in Margarelting, co. Essex, Knighted at the Coronation of King James I., 23 July 1603 (Table II.); d. (–); m. FRANCES, da. of Thomas ASTLEY of Writtle; and had (with possibly other) issue 1a.

1a. *Frances Harris*, bur. *at Walter Belchamp*, 1678; m. *Oliver Raymond of Belchamp Hall, co. Essex, M.P. for Essex in Cromwell's Parliaments*, 1653 *and* 1656; d. (–); *and had issue* 1b *to* 2b.

1b. *St. Clere Raymond, disinherited on account of marriage, became Steward to Duke of Rutland*, d. (–), bur. *at Grantham*; m. *Anne, da. of Lawrence Warkham; and had issue* 1c *to* 9c.

1c. *John Raymond, M.A. (Emmanuel College, Camb.) and of Gray's Inn*, bur. *in Walter Belchamp Church*, 1690; m. *Anne, da. of Sir Roger Burgoyne*, 2nd Bt. [E.]; *and had issue a son, John, who d.s.p.* 1720.

2c. *William Raymond of Belchamp Hall, after his nephew*, d.s.p. 1732; *will dated* 20 *Oct.* 1727, *proved P.C.C.* 9 *July* 1733.

3c. *Samuel Raymond*, d. (–), *being blown up in a ship*; m. *and had issue* 1d.

1d. *William Raymond, living* 20 *Oct.* 1737; d. (–); m. *and had issue* 1e.

1e. *Rev. Samuel Raymond of Belchamp Hall, co. Essex, inherited the family estates on the death of his great-uncle*, 1732; d. 5 *Jan.* 1767; m. *Isabella, da. of Richard Child of Lavenham, co. Suffolk, M.D.*, d. (–); *and had issue* 1f *to* 2f.

1f. *Rev. Samuel Raymond of Belchamp Hall, Rector of Belchamp and Middleton and Vicar of Bulmer, co. Essex*, b. 1744; d. 18 *Jan.* 1825; m. 1780, *Margaretta, da. of the Rev. Nathaniel Brook Bridges, Rector of Orlingbury* [*by his wife Ann,* née *Smythies*], d. 29 *Sept.* 1849; *and had issue* 1g *to* 3g.

1g. *Samuel Milbank Raymond of Belchamp Hall, J.P.*, b. 6 *Feb.* 1787; d. 18 *Jan.* 1863; m. 7 *Mar.* 1808, *Sarah, da. of the Rev. William Cooke, Rector of Preston; and had issue* 1h *to* 3h.

---

[1] Foster's "Yorkshire Pedigrees."

of The Blood Royal

1*h*. Rev. John Mayne St. Clere Raymond of Belchamp Hall, sometime Vicar of Dinnington, &c., b. 23 July 1814; d. 1 Dec. 1893; m. 12/13 May 1857, Louisa Anne, da. of the Rev. Charles Fisher, Rector of Ovington-cum-Tilbury, d. 7 Feb. 1895; and had issue 1*i*.

    1*i*. Samuel John St. Clere Raymond of Belchamp Hall, J.P., b. 11 July 1859; d. 9 Ap. 1900; m. 22 Oct. 1884, Margaret Charlotte Montague (The Rectory House, Great Yeldham, Essex), da. of Francis Smythies of Headgate House, Colchester; and had issue 1*j*.

    1*j*. Samuel Philip St. Clere Raymond of Belchamp Hall, Lord of the Manor of Belchamp Walter and Patron of Belchamp-cum-Bulmer, &c. (*Belchamp Hall, near Sudbury, Suffolk*), b. 26 Ap. 1886.

2*h*. Isabella Raymond, b. at Belchamp, 19 Mar. 1810; d. at Bury St. Edmunds, 18 Ap. 1848; m. Rowland Dalton of Bury St. Edmunds, Surgeon, b. 10 Jan. 1801; d. at Bury St. Edmunds, 21 Aug. 1890; and had issue 1*i* to 7*i*.

    1*i*. Henry Dalton, Naturalist (82 *Boulevard du Port Royal, Paris*), b. 18 Mar. 1836; m.

    2*i*. Oliver Dalton, Clerk in the Custom House, London, b. 8 May 1842; d. 11 Oct. 1881; m.

    3*i*. Walter Dalton, emigrated to the United States, where he is still living, b. 11 Feb. 1844; m.

    4*i*. Alfred Dalton, emigrated to the United States, where he is still living, b. 11 Oct. 1846; m.

    5*i*. Isabella Dalton, m. 20 Sept. 1859, Francis Winter Clarke, Surgeon (*Wrentham, Foxenden Road, Guildford*).

    6*i*. Margaretta Dalton (*Aingarth, Parkstone Avenue, Parkstone*), m. 31 Oct. 1870, Francis Reginald Statham of Liverpool, Author, d. 4 Mar. 1908; and has issue (with a 3rd son, Gilbert, who d. 19 Sept. 1894) 1*j* to 4*j*.

    1*j*. Paul Bernard Statham, Draughtsman and Surveyor, b. 22 Aug. 1871.

    2*j*. Claude Oliver Statham, Electrical Engineer, b. 5 Feb. 1877.

    3*j*. Margaret Lilian Statham.

    4*j*. Violet Statham, m. 7 June 1905, John Henry Crake Vaughan [eldest son of Prebendary Vaughan of Wraxall, near Bristol]; and has issue 1*k*.

    1*k*. Margaret Christine Vaughan, b. 21 July 1908.

    7*i*. Octavia Dalton, *unm*.

3*h*. Emma Brereton Raymond, m. 16 Feb. 1858, Frederick Perry, d. 24 Dec. 1885; and has issue 1*i*.

    1*i*. Rev. Clement Raymond Perry, D.D. (Oxford), Rector of Mickfield (*Mickfield Rectory, Suffolk*), b. 8 Dec. 1858; m. 25 July 1888, Florence Kathleen, da. of Henry John Thorp, M.D.; and has issue 1*j* to 3*j*.

    1*j*. Arthur Stanley Raymond Perry, b. 26 Sept. 1892.

    2*j*. Edward John St. Clere Perry, b. 21 June 1901.

    3*j*. Winifred Eleanor Victoria Perry, b. 21 Oct. 1896.

2*g*. Rev. Oliver Raymond, LL.B., Rural Dean, Rector of Middleton and Vicar of Belchamp, b. 9 Jan. 1794; d. 15 Sept. 1889; m. 4 Feb. 1817, Anne, da. of the Rev. Charles Andrewes, Rector of Flempton, d. 1 June 1863; and had issue 1*h* to 7*h*.

    1*h*. Rev. Oliver Edward Raymond, M.A. (Camb.), Rector of Middleton (*Middleton Rectory, Sudbury, Suffolk*), b. 22 Nov. 1825; m. 1st, 30 Jan. 1851, Ellen Jane, da. of William Foster, d. 23 May 1876; 2ndly, 6 Ap. 1880, Frances Elizabeth (see p. 126), da. of John Greene; and has issue 1*i* to 6*i*.

    1*i*. Oliver John Raymond, b. 23 Ap. 1853; m. 27 Nov. 1880, Clara Catherine, da. of (—) Robson, d. 30 May 1900; and has issue 1*j* to 4*j*.

    1*j*. John Raymond, b. 5 Feb. 1890.

    2*j*. Katharine Margaret Raymond, b. 9 Oct. 1881.

    3*j*. Ellen Gertrude Raymond, b. 11 June 1883.

    4*j*. Olive Mary Raymond, b. 8 Mar. 1886. [Nos. 11508 to 11530.

The Plantagenet Roll

2*i*. Rev. Philip Foster Raymond, Senior Chaplain to the Forces (*Aldershot*), *b*. 11 July 1855; *m*. 19 Jan. 1881, Christine Louisa, da. of Thomas Ruggles Fisher; and has issue 1*j* to 4*j*.

1*j*. Hugh Philip Raymond, *b*. 15 Feb. 1889.
2*j*. Cicely Raymond, *b*. 22 Nov. 1881.
3*j*. Eva Christine Raymond, *b*. 3 Ap. 1884.
4*j*. Lois Raymond, *b*. 8 Feb. 1891.

3*i*. Percy Algernon Raymond, *b*. 22 Sept. 1860; *m*. 17 July 1886, Amy, da. of (—) Turner; and has issue 1*j* to 3*j*.

1*j*. Harry Turner Raymond, *b*. 11 Feb. 1893.
2*j*. Ada Louisa Raymond, *b*. 24 Ap. 1887.
3*j*. Mildred Mary Raymond, *b*. 23 Oct. 1905.

4*i*. Lionel Charles Raymond, Assist. Manager Colonial Sugar Refining Coy. (*Fiji*), *b*. 20 Mar. 1868; *m*. 13 Feb. 1895, Edith, da. of (—) Dornwell; and has issue 1*j* to 2*j*.

1*j*. Oliver Claude Raymond, *b*. 2 Dec. 1895.
2*j*. Rowland Lionel Raymond, *b*. 12 Jan. 1899.

5*i*. Ellen Margaret Isabella Raymond, *m*. 10 Oct. 1883, Robert George Hallowell-Carew, *formerly* a Tea Planter in Assam (see p. 125) (8 *Raleigh Villas, Exmouth*); and has issue 1*j* to 2*j*.

1*j*. Robert Raymond Hallowell-Carew, Lieut. R.N., *b*. 6 Sept. 1884.
2*j*. Margaret Maude Hallowell-Carew, *b*. 27 Aug. 1886.

6*i*. Mary Louisa Raymond, *unm*.

2*h*. Rev. Charles Andrewes Raymond, M.A., Vicar of Bray (*Bray Vicarage, Maidenhead*), *b*. 16 Oct. 1833; *m*. 5 Ap. 1864, Elizabeth, da. of the Rev. John Maynard, Rector of Sudbourne; and has issue 1*i* to 3*i*.

1*i*. Rev. William Maynard Raymond, Vicar of SS. Peter and Paul, Upper Teddington (*Upper Teddington, Midx.*), *b*. 23 Feb. 1868; *m*. 27 Jan. 1898, Julia May, da. of the Rev. Charles Cooke of Alverley Hall, Doncaster; and has issue 1*j* to 5*j*.

1*j*. Oswald William Edward Raymond, *b*. 22 May 1902.
2*j*. Hugh Medlicott Raymond, *b*. 17 Oct. 1903.
3*j*. Monica Raymond.
4*j*. Nancy May Raymond.
5*j*. Audrey Mary Raymond.

2*i*. Anne Maynard Raymond, *m*. 3 Jan. 1895, the Rev. Thomas Henry Wrenford, Vicar of Littlewick (*Littlewick Vicarage, Maidenhead*); and has issue 1*j*.

1*j*. Cecil Raymond Brookes Wrenford, *b*. 23 May 1896.

3*i*. Katharine Elizabeth Raymond, *m*. 18 Nov. 1896, the Rev. Robert Perceval Newhouse, Vicar of St. Laurence's, Reading (*St. Laurence's Vicarage, Reading*); and has issue 1*j* to 3*j*.

1*j*. Katharine Raymond Newhouse.
2*j*. Clare Maynard Newhouse.
3*j*. Mary Perceval Newhouse.

3*h*. Margaretta Lyon Raymond, *b*. 22 Nov. 1817; *d*. 23 *Jan*. 1852; *m*. 9 *Oct*. 1845, *George Ure Skinner* [*son of Dean John Skinner of Forfar and grandson of John Skinner, Lord Bishop of Aberdeen*], *d*. 9 *Jan*. 1867; *and had issue* (*with a son and da. d. in infancy*) 1*i* to 2*i*.

1*i*. Margaretta Raymond Skinner (30 *Gordon Road, Ealing*), *m*. 30 Ap. 1872, the Rev. George Ruggle Fisher, Chaplain to H.M. Forces, *previously* 102nd Regt., Medal and Clasps for Pegu, 1852–1853, *d*. 22 Oct. 1894; and has issue 1*j* to 2*j*.

1*j*. Mary Agnes Fisher.
2*j*. Margaret Eleanor Fisher.

[Nos. 11531 to 11562.

of The Blood Royal

2*i*. Mary Elizabeth Skinner (*Inchgarth*, 31 *Broad Park Avenue, Ilfracombe*). *m.* 12 Jan. 1875, Lieut.-Col. Edward Staines Daniell, 102nd Regt., medal and clasps for Pegu 1852-1853 and Lucknow, *b.* 20 July 1828; *d.* 19 Nov. 1906; and has issue 1*j* to 6*j*.

1*j*. George Edward Staines Daniell (*Omata Valley, Waitotara, New Zealand*), *b.* 31 Dec. 1875.

2*j*. William Raymond Daniell, Capt. 123rd Outram's Rifles, *formerly* Devon Regt., South African medal and 4 clasps, *b.* 15 Dec. 1878.

3*j*. James Skinner Daniell (*New Zealand*), *b.* 17 Nov. 1883.

4*j*. Charles John Williamson Daniell, Electrical Engineer, *b.* 1 Dec. 1885.

5*j*. Agnes Katharine Raymond Daniell, *m.* 17 Ap. 1906, Charles Orpen Tuckey, Mathematical Master at Charterhouse School (*Godalming*); and has issue 1*k*.

    1*k*. Richard Edward Orpen Tuckey, *b.* 16 Feb. 1907.

6*j*. Margaret Swayne Daniell.

4*h*. Agnes Raymond, *b.* 14 *Oct.* 1819; d.s.p.s. 8 *July* 1904; m. 18 *July* 1848, the Rev. James Skinner, M.A., Vicar of Newland, co. Worcester, d.s.p.

5*h*. Katharine Raymond, b. 19 *Mar*. 1822; d. 27 *Oct*. 1874; m. *as 2nd wife,* 14 *June* 1855, *John Greene of Bury St. Edmunds* (see p. 126), d. 29 *Jan*. 1867; *and had issue (with a son and da. who* d. *unm.*) 1*i* to 3*i*.

1*i*. Edith Anne Greene (12 *Oakfield Road, Clifton, Bristol*).

2*i*. Mary Beatrice Greene, *m.* 6 Aug. 1879, Reginald John Lake of Lincoln's Inn, Bar.-at-Law (*Beodricesworth, Alexandra Road, Watford*); and has issue 1*j* to 8*j*.

1*j*. John Stephen Raymond Lake, Capt. 3rd South Wales Borderers, served in South Africa Feb. 1900-Ap. 1902, *b.* 3 Dec. 1881.

2*j*. Reginald St. George Lake, Lieut. Bedfordshire Regt., *b.* 4 Dec. 1887.

3*j*. Michael Neville Lake, *b.* 3 Oct. 1890.

4*j*. Helen Mary Beatrice Lake.

5*j*. Edith Carleton Lake.

6*j*. Margaretta Eunice Lake.

7*j*. Beatrice Victoria Lake.

8*j*. Katherine Madeline Lake.

3*i*. Madeline Greene (15 *Alexandra Road, Clifton, Bristol*), *m.* 19 Ap. 1899, Wilfred Martin Barclay of Clifton, F.R.C.S., L.R.C.P., *d.s.p.* 9 May 1903.

6*h*. Anne Ryecroft Raymond (1 *Carlton Hill, Exmouth*), *m.* 1st, 24 Sept. 1846, Walter Tyson Smythies, *d.s.p.* 23 Oct. 1848; 2ndly, 17 July 1851, Capt. Robert Hallowell-Carew, 36th Regt., *d.* 18 Ap. 1903; and has issue 1*i* to 2*i*.

1*i*. Robert George Hallowell-Carew, *formerly* Tea Planter in Assam (8 *Raleigh Villas, Exmouth*), *b.* 9 May 1852; *m.* 10 Oct. 1883, Ellen Margaret Isabella, da. of the Rev. Oliver Edward Raymond; and has issue.

See p. 124, Nos. 11544-11545.

2*i*. Walter Raymond Hallowell-Carew, b. 12 *Sept.* 1853; d. 22 *Oct.* 1896; m. 1 *May* 1889, *Edith May, da. of A. Porch; and had issue* 1*j*.

1*j*. Marjorie Hallowell-Carew, *b.* 31 Mar. 1891.

7*h*. Juliana Raymond (*Bray Vicarage, Berks*), *unm.*

3*g*. *Isabella Raymond, b. at Belchamp Hall* 3 *Mar*. 1784; *d.* 8 *Sept.* 1858; m. 14 *Nov.* 1809, *the Rev. Henry Yeats Smythies, M.A., B.D., Fellow of Emmanuel Coll.* (*Camb.*), *Vicar of Stanground-cum-Farcett, co. Hunts, J.P., b. at South Moreton, co. Berks,* 15 *Feb.* 1765; *d. at Stanground* 20 *June* 1842; *and had issue* (*with* 6 *other children who* d.s.p.) 1*h* to 3*h*.

1*h*. Rev. Raymond Brewster Smythies, M.A. (*Camb.*), *&c., b.* 18 *June* 1824; d. *at Brighton* 19 *Jan.* 1861; m. *at Rugby* 27 *Dec.* 1859, *Isabella Jane* [a descendant *of the Lady Isabel Plantagenet* (see Essex Volume, p. 306)], *da. of the Rev.*

[Nos. 11563 to 11587.

The Plantagenet Roll

Charles Alleyne Anstey, M.A. [*grandson of Christopher Anstey of Trumpington Hall, co. Camb.*] [*who re-m. 2ndly, 1868, Major-Gen. Robert Yeld Chambers, and*] d. 28 *July* 1903; *and had issue* 1*i*.

1*i*. Raymond Henry Raymond Smythies, Major *late* 40th Regt., served in South African War 1900–1901, medal with three clasps, author of "Historical Records of 40th Regt." (20 *Addison Court Gardens, W.; Army and Navy*), b. at Rugby, 19 Nov. 1860; *unm.*

2*h*. Margaretta Smythies, b. 26 Feb. 1812; d. 20 Ap. 1853; m. *as* 1*st wife*, 12 Ap. 1836, *John Greene of the Abbey Ruins, Bury St. Edmunds* (see p. 125), b. 15 Aug. 1810; d. 29 Jan. 1867; *and had issue* (*with* 2 *elder das. who d. unm.*) 1*i to* 3*i*.

1*i*. John Smythies Greene of the Panels, Bury St. Edmunds, Solicitor, b. 5 Aug. 1842; d. 17 Oct. 1884; m. 4 *July* 1867, *Eleanor Annie, da. of the Rev. Charles Buchanan Wollaston, Preb. of Chichester*, d. 6 Aug. 1895; *and had issue* 1*j* to 6*j*.

1*j*. John Wollaston Greene, Solicitor (*The Panels, Bury St. Edmunds*), b. 1 Sept. 1869.

2*j*. Cecil Wollaston Greene, b. 13 Nov. 1872; d. 16 Feb. 1909; m. 31 *Jan.* 1905, *Lucy Gertrude, da. of Surg.-Major Isaac Newton; and had issue* 1*k*.

1*k*. John Cecil Wollaston Greene, b. 15 June 1908.

3*j*. Kenneth Wollaston Greene, Solicitor (*Bury St. Edmunds*), b. 10 Jan. 1880; m. 9 Sept. 1909, Constance Agnes, da. of Robert Jackson of Ormesby House, Huddersfield.

4*j*. Ella Wollaston Greene (*The Panels, Bury St. Edmunds*).

5*j*. Hilda Wollaston Greene, *m.* 27 Aug. 1907, R. C. F. Maugham, H.B.M.'s Consul-Gen. for Portuguese East Africa.

6*j*. Rhona Wollaston Greene (*The Panels, Bury St. Edmunds*).

2*i*. Rev. Carleton Greene, Vicar of Great Barford (*Great Barford Vicarage, St. Neots*), b. 26 Jan. 1844; *m.* 4 Oct. 1870, Jane Elizabeth, da. of Col. John Alexander Wilson, d. 5 Mar. 1903; *and has issue* 1*j* to 4*j*.

1*j*. Francis Carleton Greene, B.A. (Camb.), b. 18 May 1881.

2*j*. Marion Raymond Greene, *m.* 31 Dec. 1895 her cousin-german once removed, Charles Henry Greene (*St. John's, Berkhamsted, Herts*); *and has issue* 1*k* to 4*k*.

1*k*. William Herbert Greene, b. 25 Ap. 1898.
2*k*. Charles Raymond Greene, M.A. (Oxon.), b. 17 Ap. 1901.
3*k*. Henry Graham Greene, b. 2 Oct. 1904.
4*k*. Alice Marion Greene, b. 30 Dec. 1896.

3*j*. Maud Churchill Greene.
4*j*. Nora Carleton Greene.

3*i*. Frances Elizabeth Raymond Greene, *m.* as 2nd wife, 6 Ap. 1880, the Rev. Oliver Edward Raymond, Rector of Middleton (see p. 123).

3*h*. Emily Smythies, b. 17 Sept. 1820; d. 3 Feb. 1848; m. *as* 1*st wife*, 4 Feb. 1840, *Edward Greene of Nether Hall, Bury St. Edmunds, M.P.* [*younger brother of the above-named John Greene*], b. 17 Aug. 1815; d. 15 Ap. 1891; *and had issue* 1*i to* 4*i*.

1*i*. Sir (Edward) Walter Greene of Nether Hall, 1st Bt. [U.K.], so cr. 21 June 1900, J.P., D.L., High Sheriff co. Suffolk 1897, Hon. Col. 3rd Batt. Suffolk Regt. and Major and Hon. Lieut.-Col. Suffolk Imp. Yeo., M.P. for Bury St. Edmunds 1900–1906 (*Nether Hall, Thurston; Westgate House, Bury St. Edmunds; Carlton; Royal Yacht Squadron*), b. 14 Mar. 1842; *m.* 16 June 1864, Annie Elizabeth, da. of the Rev. Charles S. Royds, Preb. of Lichfield; *and has issue* 1*j* to 6*j*.

1*j*. Walter Raymond Greene, B.A. (Oxon.), M.P., J.P., and *formerly* C.C. London, Hon. Lieut. in the Army, and Lieut.-Col. Comdg. Royal Suffolk Hussars Yeo., and *formerly* (1895–1906) M.P. for Chesterton Div. of co. Camb. (*Nether Hall, Thurston;* 113 *Mount Street; Carlton, &c.*), b. 4 Aug. 1869.

2*j*. Edward Allan Greene, Lieut. Royal Suffolk Hussars Yeo., b. 12 Sept. 1882.

[Nos. 11588 to 11607.

# of The Blood Royal

3j. Agatha Royds Greene, m. 17 Jan. 1907, Major Harry Trevor Trevor, *late* Indian Army (*Larpool Hall, near Whitby, Yorks*); and has issue 1k.

    1k. Raymond Salusbury Rose Trevor, b. 26 Dec. 1907.

4j. *Annie Mabel Greene*, d. 5 Ap. 1905; m. 18 Feb. 1890, *Arthur James Taylor of Strensham Court, J.P., late 3rd Dragoon Guards* (*Strensham Court, near Tewkesbury*); *and had issue* 1k *to* 5k.

    1k. John Walter Taylor, b. 14 Aug. 1891.
    2k. Charles Taylor, b. 26 July 1892.
    3k. Arthur Taylor, b. 2 Dec. 1902.
    4k. Angelica Taylor, b. 14 Oct. 1895.
    5k. Philippa Mabel Taylor, b. 21 Aug. 1901.

5j. Catharine Marion Greene, m. 17 June 1897, Albert Julian Pell of Wilburton Manor, J.P., D.L., Chairman Quarter Sessions, Capt. and Hon. Major 4th Batt. Suffolk Regt. (*Wilburton Manor, near Ely*); and has issue 1k to 2k.

    1k. Angela Lilian Adelaide Pell, b. 29 Sept. 1899.
    2k. Barbara Katharine Pell, b. 16 Oct. 1903.

6j. Helen Lilian Royds Greene, m. 6 June 1891, Basil Arthur Charlesworth, Bar.-at-Law (*Gunton Hall, near Lowestoft*); and has issue 1k to 3k.

    1k. Frederick Raymond Charlesworth, b. 1894.
    2k. Julian Basil Charlesworth, b. 1899.
    3k. Kathleen Agatha Charlesworth, b. 1892.

2i. Emily Smythies Greene, m. 26 Sept. 1864, Frederic Machell Smith (*Tichton Hall, Beverley, Yorks*); and has issue 1j.

    1j. Kathleen Machell Smith, m. 12 Mar. 1903, Francis Edward Bradshaw-Isherwood, Capt. York and Lancaster Regt. [2nd son of John Henry Bradshaw-Isherwood of Marple Hall, co. Chester, J.P.]; and has issue 1k.

        1k. Christopher William Bradshaw-Isherwood, b. 26 Aug. 1904.

3i. Julia Isabella Greene, m. 27 July 1876, the Very Rev. Thomas Charles Fry, D.D., Dean of Lincoln, *formerly* Head Master, Berkhamsted School (*The Deanery, Lincoln*); and has issue 1j to 2j.

    1j. Rev. Charles Edward Middleton Fry, M.A. (Oxon.), b. 14 July 1882.
    2j. Basil Homfray Fry, B.A. (Oxon.), b. 17 Mar. 1884.

4i. *Helen Emily Greene*, d. 25 Oct. 1880; m. *as* 1st *wife*, 13 *Sept.* 1870, *the Rev. Thomas Holt Wilson, M.A.* (*Camb.*), *Rector of Brayesworth, formerly Rector of Redgrave* (*Briarfield, Great Malvern*); *and had issue.*

See p. 459, Nos. 95383–95385 and 95388–95394.

2f. *Isabella Raymond*, d.s.p. *Dec.* 1808; m. 1st, *John Mayne of Telfont, co. Wilts;* 2ndly, *as* 2nd *wife,* 12 *Ap.* 1788, *Archibald* (*Cochrane*), *9th Earl of Dundonald* [S.], d. 1 *July* 1831.

    4c. Edward Raymond.[1]
    5c. James Raymond.[1]
    6c. *Joseph Raymond*,[1] d. *before* 20 *Oct.* 1727, *leaving issue, who had* £50 *each under the will of their uncle, William Raymond of Belchamp.*
    7c–9c. 1 *other son and* 2 *das.*[1]

    2b. Oliver Raymond of London, Silk Merchant.
    3b. **William Raymond.**
    4b. *Anne Raymond*, m. 1st, *John Lawrence;* 2ndly, *John Eden.*
    5b. *Frances Raymond*, m. *John Darcy.*
    6b–21b. 16 other children.   [Nos. 11608 to 11637.

---

[1] One of these was presumably the father or mother of the Mrs. Anne Watkins who inherited £1500 under the will of her uncle, William Raymond of Belchamp, 9 July 1733.

The Plantagenet Roll

58. Descendants of THOMAS (TUFTON), 6th EARL OF THANET [E.] (Table VIII.), *b.* 30 Aug. 1644; *d.* 30 July 1729; *m.* 14 Aug. 1684, Lady CATHERINE, da. and co-h. of Henry (CAVENDISH), 2nd Duke of Newcastle [E.], *d.* 20 Ap. 1712; and had issue 1*a* to 3*a*.

    1*a. Lady Catherine Tufton, da. and co-h.*, b. 24 *Ap.* 1691; d. 13 *Feb.* 1734; m. 23 *Jan.* 1708, *Edward Watson, Viscount Sondes, M.P.*, d.v.p. 20 *Mar.* 1722; *and had issue.*
    See the Exeter Volume, Table XIII., and pp. 242–243, Nos. 8843–9108.

    2*a. Lady Anne Tufton, da. and co-h.*, b. 9 *Aug.* 1693; d. 22 *Mar.* 1757; m. 12 *Feb.* 1709, *James (Cecil), 5th Earl of Salisbury* [E.], d. 9 *Oct.* 1728; *and had issue.*
    See the Exeter Volume, Table XI., and pp. 216–219, Nos. 7652–7738.

    3*a. Lady Mary Tufton, da. and co-h.*, b. 6 *July* 1701; d. 12 *Feb.* 1785; m. 1*st*, 17 *Feb.* 1718, *Anthony (Grey), 3rd Lord Lucas* [E.], *styled Earl of Harold*, d.s.p.v.p. 21 *July* 1723; 2*ndly, as 3rd wife*, 16 *May* 1736, *John (Leveson-Gower), 1st Earl Gower* [G.B.], d. 25 *Dec.* 1754; *and had issue*
    See the Exeter Volume, Table VIII., and pp. 172–175, Nos. 5449–5574.

[Nos. 11638 to 12116.

59. Descendants of SACKVILLE (TUFTON), 7th EARL OF THANET [E.] (Table VIII.), *b.* 11 May 1688; *d.* 4 Dec. 1753; *m.* 11 June 1722, Lady MARY, da. and co-h. of William (SAVILE), 2nd Marquis of Halifax [E.], *d.* 30 July 1751; and had issue.

See the Exeter Volume, Table XXI., and p. 321.

60. Descendants of the Right Hon. and Hon. WILLIAM FINCH, P.C., M.P. (Table VIII.), *d.* 25 Dec. 1766; *m.* 2ndly, 26 Aug. 1746, Lady CHARLOTTE, da. of Thomas (FERMOR), 1st Earl of Pomfret [G.B.], *b.* 16 Feb. 1725; *d.* 11 July 1813; and had issue 1*a* to 2*a*.

    1*a. George (Finch), 9th Earl of Winchilsea and 3rd Earl of Nottingham* [E.], K.G., b. 4 *Nov.* 1752; d.s.p. 2 *Aug.* 1826.
    2*a. Sophia Finch, da. and (herself or in her issue) co-h.*, d. (–); m. *July* 1772, *Capt. Charles Feilding, R.N.* [E. *of Denbigh* [E.] *and Desmond* [I.], *Coll.*], d. (–); *and had issue* 1*b* to 3*b*.
    1*b. Charles Feilding, Rear-Adm. R.N.*, b. 1780; d. 2 *Sept.* 1837; m. 24 *Ap.* 1804, *Lady Elizabeth Theresa, widow of William Davenport Talbot of Lacock, da. of Henry Thomas (Fox-Strangways), 2nd Earl of Ilchester* [G.B.], d. 12 *Mar.* 1846; *and had issue.*
    See the Exeter Volume, p. 706, Nos. 58365–58390.

    2*b. Sophia Charlotte Feilding*, d. 19 *Sept.* 1834; m. 22 *July* 1792, *Lord Robert Stephen FitzGerald, M.P.* [D. *of Leinster Coll.*], d. 2 *Jan.* 1833; *and had issue.*
    See the Exeter Volume, pp. 475–476, Nos. 41754–41759; and Essex Volume, Exeter Supplement, p. 639, Nos. 41759/1 to 41759/19.

    3*b. Augusta Sophia Feilding*, d. (–); m. 8 *Mar.* 1813, *George Hicks*, d. 1 *Aug.* 1820.

[Nos. 12117 to 12168.

# of The Blood Royal

61. Descendants of the Hon. JOHN FINCH, M.P., K.C., Solicitor-General to George II. when Prince of Wales (Table VIII.), d. 12 Feb. 1763; m. ELIZABETH, da. of (—) YOUNGER, d. 24 Nov. 1762; and had issue 1a.

1a. *Elizabeth Finch, da. and h., d. (-); m. 2 June 1757, John Mason of Greenwich.*

62. Descendants of GEORGE FINCH HATTON of Eastwell Park, co. Kent (Table VIII.), b. 1747; d. 17 Feb. 1823; m. 10 Dec. 1785, Lady ELIZABETH MARY, da. of David (MURRAY), 2nd Earl of Mansfield [G.B.], d. 1 June 1825; and had issue 1a to 2a.

1a. *George William (Finch-Hatton), 10th Earl of Winchilsea and 5th Earl of Nottingham [E.], b. 19 May 1791; d. 8 Jan. 1858; m. 1st, 26 July 1814, Lady Georgiana Charlotte, da. of James (Graham), 3rd Duke of Montrose [S.], d. 13 Feb. 1835; 3rdly, 17 Oct. 1849, Fanny Margaretta (Halton, Sevenoaks), da. of Edward Royd Rice of Dane Court, co. Kent; and had issue 1b to 5b.*
1b. *George James (Finch-Hatton), 11th Earl of Winchilsea and 6th Earl of Nottingham [E.], b. 31 May 1815; d. 9 June 1887; m. 1st, 6 Aug. 1846, Lady Constance Henrietta [a descendant of King Henry VII.], da. of Henry (Paget), 2nd Marquis of Anglesey [U.K.], d. 5 Mar. 1878; and had issue 1c to 2c.*
1c. Lady Constance Eleanor Caroline Finch-Hatton (9 *St. George's Road, S.W.*), m. 3 June 1871, the Hon. Frederick Charles Howard [E. of Effingham, &c., Coll.], d. 26 Oct. 1893; and has issue 1d to 2d.
1d. Gordon Frederick Henry Charles Howard, heir-presumptive to the Earldom of Effingham [U.K.], &c., b. 18 May 1873; m. 26 Jan. 1904, Rosamond Margaret, da. of Edward H. Hudson of Scarborough; and has issue 1e to 2e.
1e. Mowbray Henry Gordon Howard, b. 29 Nov. 1905.
2e. John Algernon Frederick Charles Howard, b. 29 Dec. 1907.
2d. Algernon George Mowbray Frederick Howard, *late* Capt. 3rd Batt. King's Own (*White's*), b. 15 Sept. 1874.
2c. *Lady Hilda Jane Sophia Finch-Hatton. b. 3 Mar. 1856; d. 8 Feb. 1893; m. as 1st wife, 23 Ap. 1877, Henry Vincent Higgins, C.V.O., a Solicitor and member of the firm of Treherne, Higgins & Co., formerly 1st Life Guards (1 Upper Berkeley Street, S.W.); and had issue.*
2b. *Murray Edward Gordon (Finch-Hatton), 12th Earl of Winchilsea and 7th Earl of Nottingham [E.], b. 28 Mar. 1851; d. 7 Sept. 1898; m. 27 Oct. 1875, Edith [a descendant of Kings Henry VII. and Edward IV., George, Duke of Clarence, K.G., Lady Anne Plantagenet, &c.] (Haverholme Priory, Sleaford), da. of Edward William Harcourt of Stanton Harcourt, M.P.; and had issue 1c.*
1c. Lady Muriel Evelyn Vernon Finch-Hatton, m. 31 May 1897, Sir Richard Arthur Surtees Paget, 2nd Bt. [U.K.] (*Cranmore Hall, near Shepton Mallet; Clive House, Roehampton, &c.*); and has issue 1d to 3d.
1d. Sylvia Mary Paget.
2d. Pamela Winefred Paget.
3d. Angela Sibell Paget.

3b. Henry Stormont (Finch-Hatton), 13th Earl of Winchilsea and 8th Earl of Nottingham [E.], &c. (*Harlech, co. Merioneth; Carlton*), b. 3 Nov. 1852; m. 12 Jan. 1882, Anne Jane [also a descendant of King Edward III. through Mortimer-Percy], da. of Admiral of the Fleet Sir Henry John Codrington, K.C.B. [Bt. Coll.]; and has issue.

See p. 77, Nos. 9428-9430. [Nos. 12169 to 12181.

The Plantagenet Roll

4b. *Lady Caroline Finch-Hatton*, b. 6 July 1816; d. 13 Mar. 1888; m. 2 Feb. 1837, *Christopher Turnor* (see p. 392) *of Stoke Rochford, M.P., J.P., D.L., High Sheriff co. Lincoln* 1823, b. 4 Ap. 1809; d. 7 Mar. 1886; *and had issue* 1c *to* 7c.

    1c. *Edmund Turnor of Stoke Rochford, M.P., J.P., D.L.*, b. 24 Mar. 1838; d.s.p. 15 Dec. 1903.

    2c. *Christopher Hatton Turnor*, b. 16 Dec. 1840; d. (-); m. *at Toronto, Alice, da. of the Hon. Hamilton H. Killaly; and had issue* 1d.

        1d. Christopher Hatton Turnor of Stoke Rochford (*Stoke Rochford, Grantham; Panton Hall, co. Lincoln*), b. 23 Nov. 1873; m. 7 Aug. 1907, Sarah Marie Talbot [descended from George, Duke of Clarence, K.G. (see the Clarence Volume, p. 81)], d. and h. of Admiral the Hon. Walter Cecil Carpenter, *formerly* Talbot, R.N.

    3c. Algernon Turnor, C.B., J.P. (*Goadby Hall, Melton Mowbray;* 37 *Pont Street, S.W.*), b. 14 Nov. 1845; m. 3 Aug. 1880, Lady Henrietta Caroline [a descendant both paternally and maternally of King Henry VII. (see Tudor Roll, p. 498)], da. of Randolph (Stewart), 9th Earl of Galloway [S.]; and has issue 1d to 5d.

        1d. Herbert Broke Turnor, b. 22 Aug. 1885.

        2d. Christopher Randolph Turnor, b. 16 Aug. 1886.

        3d. Marjorie Caroline Isabel Turnor.

        4d. Algitha Blanche Turnor.

        5d. Verena Henrietta Turnor.

    4c. Graham Augustus Turnor, b. 13 Sept. 1853; m. 1st, Annie, da. of (—) Riddle; 2ndly, Beatrice, da. of (—) Cranstone; and has issue 1d to 6d.

        1d. Edmund Turnor.

        2d. Effie Caroline Turnor.

        3d. Constance Yolande Turnor.

        4d. Charlotte Octavia Turnor.

        5d. Bertha Kathleen Turnor.

        6d. Edmunda Turnor.

    5c. Edith Georgina Turnor, m. 16 Sept. 1868, Frederick Archibald Vaughan (Campbell), 3rd Earl [U.K.], and 4th Baron [G.B.] Cawdor, P.C., a Member of the Council of H.R.H. the Prince of Wales, &c. [descended from King Henry VII. (see Tudor Roll)] (*Stackpole Court, Pembroke; Cawdor Castle, Nairn;* 7 *Princes' Gardens, S.W.*); and has issue.

See the Tudor Roll, pp. 214-215, Nos. 21735-21746.

    6c. Bertha Kathleen Turnor.

    7c. *Dora Agnes Caroline Turnor*, d. 7 Ap. 1899; m. 27 July 1889, Benjamin Bloomfield Trench *of Loughton Moneygall, King's Co.* (41 *Onslow Square, S.W.*); *and had issue* 1d *to* 2d.

        1d. Sheelah Georgiana Bertha Trench.

        2d. Theodora Caroline Trench.

5b. Lady Evelyn Georgiana Finch-Hatton, m. 28 Feb. 1883, Henry Edward Montagu Dorington Clotworthy (Upton), 4th Viscount Templetown [I.], and a Rep. Peer (*Castle Upton, Templepatrick, co. Antrim, &c.*); and has issue 1c to 3c.

    1c. Hon. Eric Edward Montagu John Upton, Lieut. 2nd Batt. King's Royal Rifle Corps, b. 8 Mar. 1885.

    2c. Hon. Henry Augustus George Mountjoy Heneage Upton, b. 12 Aug. 1894.

    3c. Hon. Margaret Evelyn Upton.

2a. *Rev. Daniel Heneage Finch-Hatton, Chaplain to Queen Victoria*, b. 1795 d. 3 Jan. 1866; m. 15 Dec. 1825, *Lady Louisa*, da. *of the Hon. Robert Fulke Greville, by his wife Louisa*, suo jure **2nd Countess of Mansfield** [G.B.], d. 11 Ap. 1883; *and had issue*.

See the Tudor Roll, pp. 199-200, Nos. 21327-21341.   [Nos. 12182 to 12230.

# of The Blood Royal

63. Descendants of Lady ESSEX FINCH (Table VIII.), b. c. 1688; d. 23 May 1721; m. 20 July 1703, Sir ROGER MOSTYN of Mostyn, 3rd Bt. [E.], M.P., d. 5 May 1739; and had issue 1a.

1a. Sir Thomas Mostyn of Mostyn, 4th Bt. [E.], M.P., b. c. 1704; d. 24 Mar. 1758; m. c. 1735, Sarah, da. and co-h. of Robert Western of St. Peter's, Cornhill, and of Rivenhall, co. Essex, d. 28 May 1740; and had issue 1b to 4b.

1b. Sir Roger Mostyn of Mostyn, 5th Bt. [E.], M.P., b. c. 1735; d. 26 May 1796; m. 19 May 1776, Margaret, da. and h. of the Rev. Hugh Wynne, LL.D., Preb. of Salisbury, d. 14 Oct. 1792; and had issue 1c to 2c.

1c. Sir Thomas Mostyn of Mostyn, 6th and last Bt. [E.], M.P., b. c. 1776; d. (unm.) 17 Ap. 1831.

2c. Elizabeth Mostyn, da. and in her issue (29 Ap. 1859) sole h., d. 26 Nov. 1842; m. 11 Feb. 1794, Sir Edward Pryce Lloyd, 2nd Bart. [G.B.], afterwards (10 Sept. 1831) 1st Baron Mostyn [U.K.], d. 3 Ap. 1854; and had issue 1d.

1d. Edward (Lloyd, afterwards (R.L. 9 May 1831) Mostyn), 2nd Baron Mostyn [U.K.], b. 13 Jan. 1795; d. 17 Mar. 1884; m. 20 June 1827, Lady Harriet Margaret [a descendant of King Henry VII.], da. of Thomas (Scott), 2nd Earl of Clonmell [I.], d. 27 May (or 3 June) 1891; and had issue.

See the Tudor Roll, pp. 197–198, Nos. 21274–21294.

2b. Thomas Mostyn, certainly dead s.p.m. before 17 Ap. 1831.

3b. Anne Mostyn, d. 1802; m. as 2nd wife, 1777, Thomas Pennant of Downing, co. Flint, D.C.L., the well-known Naturalist and Author, d. 16 Dec. 1798, leaving a son who d.s.p. 1846.[1]

4b. Frances Mostyn, d. (? unm.). [Nos. 12231 to 12251.

64. Descendants of Lady CHARLOTTE FINCH (Table VIII.), d. 21 Jan. 1773; m. as 2nd wife, 4 Feb. 1726, CHARLES (SEYMOUR), 6th DUKE OF SOMERSET [E.], K.G., "the Proud Duke," d. 2 Dec. 1748; and had issue.

See the Tudor Roll, Table L., &c., and pp. 263, 292–311, Nos. 24118–24401, 25350–26006. [Nos. 12252 to 13192.

65. Descendants of Lady MARY FINCH (Table VIII.), d. 30 May 1761; m. 22 Sept. 1716, THOMAS (WATSON), 1st MARQUIS [G.B.], and 6th BARON [E.] OF ROCKINGHAM, K.G., d. 14 Dec. 1750; and had issue.

See the Exeter Volume, Table XIII. and pp. 253–261, Nos. 9608–9890.
[Nos. 13193 to 13475.

66. Descendants, if any surviving, of Lady MARY TUFTON (Table VIII.), bur. 7 Feb. 1674; m. as 1st wife, c. 1671, Sir WILLIAM WALTER of Sarsden, 2nd Bt. [E.], d. 5 Mar. 1694; and had issue 1a to 2a.

1a. Sir John Walter, 3rd Bt. [E.], b. c. 1673; d.s.p. 11 June 1722.

2a. Mary Walter, da. and (either herself or in her issue) heir after the death s.p. 20 Nov. 1731, of her half-brother Sir Robert, 4th and last Bt.; living 1741; m. 7 May 1698, Sir Robert Rich of Sunning, 3rd Bt. [E.]; d. 9 Nov. 1724; and had issue 1b to 7b.

---
[1] "Dict. Nat. Biog.," xliv. 322.

The Plantagenet Roll

1b. Sir William Rich, 4th Bt. [E.], d. 17 July 1762; m. Elizabeth, da. of William Royal of Minstead, d. 27 Ap. 1771; and had issue 1c.

1c. Sir Thomas Rich, 5th and last Bt. [E.], Adm. R.N., d.s.p.l. 6 Ap. 1803.

2b. Thomas Rich of Bombay, living 1741,
3b. Charles Rich,
4b. James Rich,
5b. Daniel Rich, Matric. St. John's Coll., Oxon., aged 17, a Student of the Middle Temple 1734,
} all presumably d.s.p.m., and apparently also s.p. before 6 Ap. 1803.

6b. [da.] Rich, m. Capt. Wilson of the Guards.
7b. [da.] Rich, m. Walter Knight of Buscomb, co. Berks.

67. Descendants of Lady ELIZABETH CLIFFORD, *suo jure de jure*, 2nd BARONESS CLIFFORD [E.] (Table VIII.), b. 18 Sept. 1618; d. 6 Jan. 1691; m. 8 July 1635, RICHARD (BOYLE), 2nd EARL OF CORK [I.] and 1st EARL OF BURLINGTON [E.], d. 15 Jan. 1698; and had issue 1a to 4a.

1a. Charles (Boyle), Lord Clifford of Lanesborough [E.] and Viscount Dungarvan [I.], bapt. 12 Dec. 1639; d.v.p. 12 Oct. 1694; m. 1st, Lady Jane [a descendant of King Henry VII.], da. of William (Seymour), 2nd Duke of Somerset [E.], d. 23 Nov. 1679; 2ndly, Lady Arethusa, da. of George (Berkeley), 1st Earl of Berkeley [I.], d. 11 Feb. 1743; and had issue 1b to 3b.

1b. Charles (Boyle), 3rd Earl of Cork [I.] and 2nd Earl of Burlington [E.], b. about 1674; d. 9 Feb. 1704; m. 26 Jan. 1688, Juliana, Mistress of the Robes to Queen Anne, da. and h. of the Hon. Henry Noel, d. 17 Oct. 1750; and had issue.
See the Tudor Roll, Table XLI. and pp. 240-260, Nos. 22551-23494.

2b. Hon. Mary Boyle, b. c. 1670; d. 2 Oct. 1709; m. 1 Dec. 1685, James (Douglas), 2nd Duke of Queensberry [E.] and 1st Duke of Dover [E.], K.G., d. 6 July 1711; and had issue.
See the Tudor Roll, Table XLIX. and pp. 263, Nos. 23605-24117.

3b.² Hon. Arethusa Boyle, d. (-); m. James Vernon.

2a. Lady Frances Boyle, d. about 1674; m. 1st, Col. Francis Courtenay; 2ndly, Ap. 1662, Wentworth (Dillon), 4th Earl of Roscommon [I.], d.s.p. 18 Jan. 1685.

3a. Lady Anne Boyle, d. (-); m. Jan. 1668, Edward (Montagu), 2nd Earl of Sandwich [E.], d. in France shortly before 8 Dec. 1688; and had issue 1b.

1b. Edward (Montagu), 3rd Earl of Sandwich [E.], b. c. Dec. 1670; d. 20 Oct. 1729; m. (a. 11) July 1689, Lady Elizabeth, da. and event. co-h. of John (Wilmot), 2nd Earl of Rochester [E.], d. in Paris 2 July 1757; and had issue 1c.

1c. Edward Richard Montagu, Viscount Hinchinbroke, M.P., b. c. 1690; d.v.p. 3 Oct. 1722; m. 12 Ap. 1707, Elizabeth [a descendant of Isabel (Plantagenet), Countess of Essex], da. and h. of Alexander Popham of Littlecote [m. 2ndly, 30 July 1728, Francis Seymour of Sherborne, M.P., and], d. 20 Mar. 1761; and had issue.
See the Essex Volume, Table XIV. and pp. 191, 192-193, Nos. 26449-26468 and 26506-26809.

4a. Lady Henrietta Boyle, d. 12 Ap. 1687; m. 1665, Lawrence (Hyde), 1st Earl of Rochester [E.], K.G., d. 2 May 1711; and had issue 1b to 3b.

1b. Henry (Hyde), 2nd Earl of Rochester and (12 Feb. 1713) 4th Earl of Clarendon [E.], b. 1672; d.s.p.m.s. 10 Dec. 1753; m. (lic. 2 Mar. 1692), Jane, da. of Sir William Leveson-Gower, 4th Bt. [E.], d. 24 May 1725; and had issue 1c.

1c. Lady Jane Hyde, da. and eventual sole h., d. 30 Jan. 1724; m. as 1st wife,
[Nos. 13476 to 15256.

of The Blood Royal

27 *Nov.* 1718, *William (Capel), 3rd Earl of Essex* [E.], K.G., K.T., d. 8 *Jan.* 1743; *and had issue.*
See the Exeter Volume, pp. 379–384, Nos. 26875–27087.

2b. *Lady Henrietta Hyde,* b. c. 1677; d. 30 *May* 1730; m. 2 *Jan.* 1694, *James (Scott), Earl of Doncaster and Dalkeith,* K.T. [*son and h.-app. of the 1st Duke and Duchess of Monmouth* [E.] *and Buccleuch* [S.], d.v.p. 14 *Mar.* 1705; *and had issue* 1c.

1c. *Francis (Scott), 2nd Duke of Buccleuch* [S.] *and Earl of Doncaster* [E.], K.T., b. 11 *Jan.* 1695; d. 22 *Ap.* 1751; m. 1st, 5 *Ap.* 1720, *Lady Jane* [*a descendant of King Henry VII.*], *da. of James (Douglas), 2nd Duke of Queensberry* [S.] *and 1st Duke of Dover* [E.], d. 31 *Aug.* 1729; *and had issue.*
See the Tudor Roll, Table XLIX. and p. 263, Nos. 23605–24117.

3b. *Lady Mary Hyde,* d. 25 *Jan.* 1709; m. *as 1st wife,* 17 *Feb.* 1704, *Francis (Seymour, afterwards* (1699) *Seymour-Conway), 1st Baron Conway of Ragley* [E.] *and Baron Conway and Killultagh* [I.], d. 3 *Feb.* 1732; *and had issue* 1c.

1c. Hon. *Mary Seymour Conway,* d. (-); m. *as 1st wife, Nicholas Price of Saintfield, co. Down,* M.P., d. 1742; *and had issue* 1d.

1d. *Francis Price of Saintfield,* M.P., d. 1794; m. *Charity, da. of Matthew Forde of Seaforde, co. Down; and had issue* 1e.

1e. *Nicholas Price of Saintfield,* J.P., D.L., *High Sheriff co. Down* 1801, b. 1 *Oct.* 1754; d. (-); m. *Nov.* 1779, *Lady Sarah, da. of Charles (Pratt), 1st Earl of Camden* [G.B.], d. 7 *Ap.* 1817; *and had issue* 1f.

1f. *Elizabeth Anne Price of Saintfield, da. and h.,* d. 6 *Feb.* 1867; m. 17 *June* 1804, *James Blackwood, afterwards Price, of Strangford, co. Down,* d. 5 *June* 1855; *and had issue* 1g *to* 7g.

1g. *James Charles Price of Saintfield,* J.P., D.L., *High Sheriff co. Down* 1859, b. 17 *June* 1807; d. 23 *May* 1894; m. 18 *Mar.* 1840, *Anne Margaret, da. of Major Patrick Savage of Portaferry,* d. 14 *Mar.* 1877; *and had issue* 1h *to* 3h.

1h. James Nugent Blackwood Price of Saintfield, J.P., D.L., High Sheriff co. Down 1902, Brevet-Major *late* 60th Rifles, &c. (*Saintfield House, Saintfield, co. Down; Army and Navy*), b. 13 Oct. 1844; *m.* 5 Jan. 1869, Alice Louisa [a descendant of George (Plantagenet), Duke of Clarence, K.G. (see Clarence Volume, p. 279)], da. of William Robert Ward, Diplo. Service [V. Bangor Coll.]; and has issue 1i to 3i.

1i. Conway William Blackwood Price (*United University*), b. 28 July 1872.

2i. Rev. Edward Hyde Blackwood Price, M.A., Rector of St. Nicholas' and Vicar of St. Peter's, Droitwich, b. 5 Feb. 1875.

3i. Ethelwyn Mary Blackwood Price, *m.* 27 Aug. 1901, Richard Douglas Perceval, C.E., J.P. (*Downpatrick, co. Down*); and has issue 1j to 2j.

1j. Richard John Perceval, b. 26 July 1902.

2j. Michael Charles Perceval, b. 16 Feb. 1907.

2h. Francis William Price, b. 27 Dec. 1847.

3h. Catherine Anne Price.

2g. *William Robert Arthur Price,* b. 22 *Jan.* 1813; d. (-); m. 1st, *May* 1843, *Anna Eliza, da. of the Rev. William Jex-Blake of Swanton Abbots, co. Norfolk,* d. (-); 2ndly, *Henrietta, da. of George Kenyon of Cefn, co. Denbigh; and had issue* 1h.

1h.[1] Anna Maria Frances Price.

3g. *Rev. Townley Blackwood Price,* b. 5 *Jan.* 1815; d. 1902; m. 1st, *Feb.* 1841, *Maria Catherine, da. of the Rev. William Jex-Blake of Swanton Abbots,* d. (-); 2ndly, *Anne, da. of the Rev. the Hon. Henry Ward* [V. Bangor Coll.], d. 6 *June* 1852; 3rdly, *Sarah Olivia, da. of Henry Lyle of Knoctarna, co. Derry; and had issue.*

4g. *Richard Blackwood Price, Lieut.-Col.* R.A., b. 12 *May* 1818; d. (-); m. *Anne, da. of Robert Wade of Clonebrancy; and had issue.*

5g. Mary Georgiana Price.   [Nos. 15257 to 15992.

The Plantagenet Roll

6g. Sarah Elizabeth Price, m. 15 June 1848, the Rev. Henry Montgomery Archdale of Thornhill, co. Fermanagh, M.A., b. 28 Ap. 1818; d. 14 Feb. 1898; and has issue 1h to 10h.

 1h. Edward Archdale of Castle Archdale, B.A. (Oxon.), J.P., D.L., High Sheriff co. Fermanagh 1902 (*Castle Archdale, Irvinestown, co. Fermanagh; Trillick Lodge, co. Tyrone*), b. 22 Mar. 1850.

 2h. Henry Dawson Archdale, b. 1851.

 3h. James Blackwood Archdale, Major *late* R.A. and Army Ordnance Dept. (*Lansdown, Camberley*), b. 17 July 1853; m. Feb. 1886, Elizabeth, da. of George May of Cambridge; and has issue 1i.

  1i. Henry Blackwood Archdale, b. 15 Mar. 1887.

 4h. Audley Mervyn Archdale (*Parkside, Woodville Road, Bexhill-on-Sea*), b. 1 Oct. 1855; m. 17 Sept. 1895, Mary Scott, da. of George Elphinstone of Oakfield House, Streatham; and has issue 1i to 3i.

  1i. George Mervyn Archdale, b. 14 Aug. 1896.

  2i. Margaret Helen Archdale.

  3i. Beatrice Mary Archdale.

 5h. Montgomery Archdale, b. 1858.

 6h. George Archdale, *late* Capt. 5th Batt. Royal Irish Rifles (*Dromard, Kesh, co. Fermanagh*), b. 27 Jan. 1860; m. 28 Dec. 1894, Mary, da. of John Graham of Parade House, Cowes; and has issue 1i to 6i.

  1i. Mervyn Henry Dawson Archdale, b. 11 Mar. 1904.

  2i. George Montgomery Archdale, b. 6 July 1907.

  3i. Helen Audley Archdale.

  4i. Mary Blackwood Archdale.

  5i. Sarah Matilda Archdale.

  6i. Joan Archdale.

 7h. Elizabeth Price Archdale.

 8h. Sarah Blackwood Archdale, m. 10 Nov. 1886, the Rev. Edward Blanchard Ryan, Rector of Strangford (*Strangford Rectory, co. Down*); and has issue.

 9h. Matilda Humphries Archdale.

 10h. Richmal Magnell Archdale.

7g. *Elizabeth Catherine Price*, d. (-); m. Oct. 1841, *the Rev. Alexander Orr*, d. (-); *and had issue.* [Nos. 15993 to 16013.

68. Descendants of MULTON LAMBARDE of Sevenoaks, co. Kent (Table IX.), b. 29 July 1757; d. 19 Mar. 1836; m. 22 Sept. 1789, AUREA, da. and co-h. of Francis OTWAY of Ashgrove, Sevenoaks, d. 10 Mar. 1828; and had issue 1a to 3a.

 1a. *William Lambarde of Beechmont, co. Kent*, b. 18 *Nov.* 1796; d. 1 *June* 1866; m. 1 *Oct.* 1818, *Harriet Elizabeth, da. of Sir James Naesmyth, 3rd Bt.* [S.], d. 25 *Ap.* 1879; *and had issue* 1b *to* 9b.

  1b. *Multon Lambarde of Beechmont, co. Kent*, b. 31 *Oct.* 1821; d. 21 *Dec.* 1896; m. 27 *Mar.* 1848, *Marianne Teresa Livesey, da. of Edmund Turton of Brasted, co. Kent, and of Larpool Hall, co. Yorks; and had issue* 1c *to* 7c.

   1c. William Gore Lambarde (*Bradbourne Hall, Riverhead, Kent; Beechmont, Sevenoaks*), b. 22 May 1864; m. 10 Oct. 1888, Florence Lucy, da. of Howard Fetherstonhaugh of Bracklyn, co. Westmeath; and has issue 1d to 2d.

    1d. Bridget Aurea Teresa Lambarde.

    2d. Deborah Silversten Fane Lambarde.

   2c. Mary Teresa Louisa Lambarde, m. 24 Ap. 1890, Adam Young.

   3c. Ellen Grace Lambarde, b. 20 Feb. 1887. [Nos. 16014 to 16018.

# of The Blood Royal

4c. Maude Eleanor Lambarde, b. 1 Sept. 1889.

5c. Harriet Beatrice Aurea Lambarde, m. 8 June 1886, Percy Francis Battiscombe of Shaw Well, J.P. (see below) (*Shaw Well, Sevenoaks*); and has issue 1d to 5d.

    1d. Percival Ralph Battiscombe, b. 18 Sept. 1891.

    2d. Gwendoline Aurea Battiscombe, b. 15 May 1887.

    3d. Ruby Cicely Teresa Battiscombe, b. 3 May 1888.

    4d. Violet Battiscombe, b. 12 Ap. 1889.

    5d. Sylvia Battiscombe, b. 1 June 1890.

6c. Ethel Julia Lambarde, m. 10 Jan. 1893, Joseph William Underwood, 4th Hussars (*Belle Vue, Sevenoaks*); and has issue 1d to 2d.

    1d. Gerald Joseph Underwood, b. 3 June 1897.

    2d. Keene Sybil Underwood, b. 22 May 1894.

7c. Edith Gwendoline Lambarde, b. 12 Feb. 1868.

2b. *John Lambarde, E.I.C.S., b. 28 Feb.* 1823; d. 8 *July* 1848; m. 16 *Aug.* 1847, *Mary Anne Priscilla, da. of Thomas Haslam, Capt. 25th Regt. N.I.; and had issue* 1c.

1c. Harriet Charlotte Lambarde, m. 28 Oct. 1879, William Henley Dodgson (*Forest Lodge, Keston, Kent*); and has issue 1d to 6d.

    1d. William Lambarde Dodgson, Lieut. R.N., b. 29 May 1880.

    2d. John Henley Dodgson, b. 16 Oct. 1881.

    3d. Raymond Charles Dodgson, b. 11 Dec. 1882.

    4d. Arthur Douglas Dodgson, b. 22 Aug. 1884.

    5d. Richard Heathfield Dodgson, b. 4 July 1887.

    6d. Cicely Charlotte Dodgson, b. 17 Sept. 1889.

3b. Francis Lambarde, J.P. (*Manor House, Ash, Sevenoaks*), b. 24 Ap. 1830; m. 1 Nov. 1866, Sophia Katharine Gambier, widow of John Barry Gurdon of Assington Hall, co. Suff., da. of Charles Douglas Halford of West Lodge, East Bergholt, co. Suff., d. 16 May 1903; and has issue 1c to 3c.

1c. Francis Fane Lambarde, Capt. R.A. (*Manor House, Ash, Sevenoaks*), b. 24 Dec. 1868; m. 18 Oct. 1902, Marian Ethel, da. of Joseph Hinks of Warwick.

2c. John Barrett Lambarde (*Alix, Alberta, Canada*), b. 20 Dec. 1874.

3c. Florence Edith Lambarde, b. 11 Feb. 1877.

4b. Rev. Charles James Lambarde (*Ash Rectory, Sevenoaks*), b. 28 Aug. 1833.

5b. *Eleanora Lambarde, b. 20 Sept. 1819; d. 23 Ap. 1884;* m. 5 *Jan.* 1854, *Percival Battiscombe of Shaw Well, Sevenoaks, d. 30 July* 1885; *and had issue* 1c to 4c.

1c. Percy Francis Battiscombe, J.P. (*Shaw Well, Sevenoaks*), b. 15 Mar. 1857; m. 8 June 1886, Harriet Beatrice Aurea, da. of Multon Lambarde of Beechmont, co. Kent; and has issue.

See above, Nos. 16021–16025.

2c. Christopher William Battiscombe (*The Retreat, Canterbury*), b. 30 Mar. 1858; m. 24 Ap. 1889, Beatrice Lucy, da. of Capt. Baird Smith; and has issue 1d to 2d.

    1d. Christopher Francis Battiscombe, b. 4 Ap. 1890.

    2d. Marjory Eleanor Battiscombe, b. 2 May 1891.

3c. Eleanor Teresa Battiscombe (*Arundel, West Byfleet, Surrey*), b. 30 July 1860; m. 1 Sept. 1885, the Rev. Harold Brierley, Vicar of Birdstow, Ross, *d.s.p.* 10 June 1906.

4c. Emily Harriet Battiscombe, b. 7 July 1859.

6b. *Juliana Lambarde,* b. 20 *Dec.* 1828; d. 10 *Nov.* 1906; m. 1857, *James Christie Traill of Hobbister, Orkney, and of Ratter, co. Caithness, J.P., D.L., d. 6 Feb.* 1899; *and had issue* 1c to 4c.   [Nos. 16019 to 16052.

The Plantagenet Roll

1c. James William Traill of Hobbister (*Castle Hill, co. Caithness*), b. July 1858; m. 1887, Ethel, da. of T. J. Sumner of Melbourne, South Australia; and has issue 1d to 2d.

1d. Cecil James Traill, b. Oct. 1888.

2d. Sinclair George Traill, b. May 1890.

2c. Rev. Randolph Richard William Traill (*Orcott College, Birmingham*), b. Sept. 1863.

3c. John Murray Traill, Bedfordshire Regt., b. Oct. 1865.

4c. Minna Harriet Traill, b. Ap. 1862.

7b. Harriet Lambarde, b. 27 Mar. 1835.

8b. *Jane Aurea Lambarde*, b. 10 Feb. 1841; d. 30 Dec. 1882; m. 17 Feb. 1864, *Capt. Henry Lumsden Battiscombe; and had issue 1c to 2c.*

1c. Charles Battiscombe, Major R.A., b. 13 Aug. 1865; m. 13 Mar. 1899, Maria Isabella, da. of (—) Mills; and has issue 1d.

1d. Christopher Robert Battiscombe, b. 8 Nov. 1902.

2c. Maude Aurea Battiscombe, b. 11 Jan. 1871.

9b. *Alice Mary Lambarde*, b. 28 Aug. 1846; d. 21 Ap. 1900; m. 29 Mar. 1880, *Thomas Graham Jackson, R.A.; and had issue 1c to 2c.*

1c. Hugh Nicholas Jackson, Royal Welsh Fusiliers (*Eagle House, Wimbledon*), b. 21 Jan. 1881.

2c. Basil Hippisley Jackson, b. 4 Feb. 1887.

2a. *Bridget Aurea Lambarde*, b. 16 Oct. 1792; d. 1 June 1826; m. *as 1st wife*, 1 July 1823, *John Gurdon of Assington Hall, co. Suff., J.P.,* d. 1869; *and had issue 1b.*

1b. John Barry Gurdon, b. 15 Ap. 1825; d. 28 Jan. 1863; m. 24 Feb. 1857, Sophia Katharine Gambier, da. of Charles Douglas Halford of West Lodge, East Bergholt, co. Suff. [re-m. 2ndly, 1 Nov. 1866, Francis Lambarde, J.P., of Manor House, Ash, co. Kent (see p. 135)]; and had issue 1c to 3c.

1c. Philip Gurdon (*Conduit Road, Bedford*), b. 2 Dec. 1857; m. 4 Nov. 1885, Edith, da. of the Rev. Charles Holland, Rector of Petworth, co. Sussex; and has issue 1d to 3d.

1d. John Gurdon, b. 21 Ap. 1887.

2d. William Nathaniel Gurdon, b. 22 Oct. 1890.

3d. Eleanor Joyce Gurdon.

2c. *Edward Barry Gurdon*, b. 26 Ap. 1860; d. 18 Sept. 1885; m. 1882, *Julia, da. of (—) Chandler of Sydney, N.S.W.; and had issue 1d.*

1d. Augustus Edward Philip Gurdon (*Sydney, New South Wales*), b. 11 June 1883.

3c. William Gurdon, Major R.A., b. 16 Ap. 1862.

3a. *Mary Lambarde*, b. 17 Nov. 1801; b. 2 Oct. 1848; m. 26 Nov. 1835, *the Rev. Richard Salwey, Rector of Ash, near Fawkham, co. Kent* [*descended from the Lady Isabel Plantagenet* (see Essex Volume, p. 318)], d. 6 Feb. 1895; *and had issue 1b to 2b.*

1b. *Edward Richard Salwey, C.E.,* b. 13 Ap. 1843; d. 5 May 1902; m. 9 Ap. 1874, *Ellen Isabel, da. of Edward Burges of The Ridge, co. Gloucester; and had issue 1c.*

1c. Ellen Isold Salwey, m. 17 Jan. 1906, the Rev. Edward Parry Liddon, Rector of Staverton (*Staverton Rectory, Northants*).

2b. Harriet Laura Salwey, m. 28 Aug. 1872, Matthew Edward Howard; and has issue 1c to 6c.

1c. Arthur Edward Howard, b. 6 Jan. 1874; m. 11 June 1896, Lucy, da. of (—) MacSwiney of Dublin, M.D.; and has issue 1d.

1d. Thelma Howard, b. 24 Feb. 1898.

[Nos. 16053 to 16074.

of The Blood Royal

2c. Cecil William Howard, b. 26 May 1875.
3c. Henry Bernard Howard, b. 22 Mar. 1877.
4c. Kenneth Salwey-Howard, } b. (twins) 14 Dec. 1879.
5c. Kathleen Philippa Howard,
6c. Clara Millicent Howard, b. 13 Jan. 1883.   [Nos. 16075 to 16079.

69. Descendants of MARY LAMBARDE (Table IX.), b. 17 Jan. 1752; d. (-); m. 31 Aug. 1784, the Rev. JOHN HALLWARD, Vicar of Assington, co. Suffolk, d. 24 Dec. 1826; and had issue 1a to 2a.

1a. Rev. *John Hallward, Rector of Easthorpe, co. Essex, and later of Swepstone, co. Leicester*, b. 1791; d. 6 *June* 1865; m. *Emily Jane, da. of Charles Powell Leslie of Glasslough, co. Monaghan*, d. (-); *and had issue* 1b *to* 4b.
1b. Rev. *John Leslie Hallward, Rector of Gilston, co. Herts*, b. 29 *Jan.* 1823; d. 3 *Oct.* 1896; m. 22 *Aug.* 1854, *Martha Clementina, da. of the Rev. Robert Govett, Vicar of Staines, co. Middx.*, d. 22 *Feb.* 1907; *and had issue* 1c *to* 5c.
1c. Norman Leslie Hallward of the Indian Educational Service (*United Service Club, Calcutta*), b. 3 Mar. 1859; m. 14 Sept. 1897, Evelyn Alice, da. of Major-Gen. Evelyn Pulteney Gurdon; and has issue 1d to 2d.
1d. Bertrand Leslie Hallward, b. 24 May 1901.
2d. Philip Norman Romaine Hallward, b. 1 Feb. 1903.
2c. Herbert Romaine Hallward, b. 21 Oct. 1860.
3c. Rev. Lancelot William Hallward (*Cala Rectory, Tembuland, Kaffraria*), b. 4 July 1867.
4c. Clement Govett Hallward, b. 30 June 1870.
5c. Constance Maude Hallward (21 *Pembroke Gardens, S.W.*), b. 15 Feb. 1865.
2b. *Charles Berners Hallward*, b. 2 *Aug.* 1825; d. 6 *Jan.* 1896; m. 2 *Oct.* 1850, *Elizabeth Anne, da. of Peter Morgan of H.M. Dockyard, Woolwich*, d. *Nov.* 1874; *and had issue* 1c *to* 8c.
1c. *Charles Morgan Leslie Hallward*, b. 8 *Oct.* 1852; d. *July* 1907; m. *Kate, da. of James Southerton; and had issue* 1d *to* 2d.
1d. Dorothy Hallward.
2d. Muriel Hallward.
2c. Cyril Randolph Hallward (25 *Hogarth Road, S.W.*), b. 27 Jan. 1857; m. 1902, Mary, da. of J. Muggliston of Lytham, co. Lanc.
3c. William Lambarde Hallward (98A *Lexham Gardens, Kensington*), b. 9 Oct. 1854; m. 23 Aug. 1888, Grace, da. of William James Murray of Wolverton, co. Norfolk; and has issue 1d to 3d.
1d. Basil Murray Hallward, b. 17 Nov. 1891.
2d. Iola Leslie Hallward, b. 19 July 1889.
3d. Clare Joyce Hallward, b. 9 June 1899.
4c. Reginald Francis Hallward (*Woodlands, Shorne, near Gravesend*), b. 18 Oct. 1859; m. 2 June 1886, Adelaide Caroline, da. of Robert William Bloxam of Ryde, I.W.; and has issue 1d to 5d.
1d. Reginald Michael Bloxam Hallward, b. 2 Oct. 1889.
2d. Christopher John Hallward, b. 6 Jan. 1898.
3d. Faith Margaret Hallward.
4d. Patience Mary Hallward.
5d. Priscilla Evelyn Gabrielle Jeanette Hallward.
5c. Arthur Wellesley Hallward (*Milton House, Bedford Park, W.*), b. 4 Mar. 1860; m. 21 Sept. 1887, Caroline Sarah, da. of John Marley of Darlington; and has issue 1d to 2d.   [Nos. 16080 to 16100.

The Plantagenet Roll

1*d*. Kenneth Leslie Hallward, *b*. 1 Nov. 1888.

2*d*. Marjorie Hallward, *b*. 7 June 1890.

6*c*. Evelyn Elizabeth Hallward, *m*. 9 Ap. 1878, William Mackinlay (*Meppadi, South Wynaad, S. India*); and has issue 1*d*.

1*d*. Maud Mackinlay, *b*. 19 Oct. 1882.

7*c*. Eleanor Frances Graeme Hallward, *m*. 11 Mar. 1902, Col. James Ridgeway Dyas, Royal Warwickshire Regt. (*Brook House, Woodbridge, co. Suffolk*); and has issue 1*d* to 2*d*.

1*d*. John Hallward Dyas, *b*. 26 Feb. 1907.

2*d*. Eleanor Josephine Sprye Dyas, *b*. 6 Oct. 1909.

8*c*. Lilian Berkeley Hallward (112 *Cromwell Road, S.W.*).

3*b*. Rev. Thomas William Onslow Hallward, *Vicar of Frittenden, co. Kent*, b. 9 Aug. 1827; d. 24 *June* 1899; m. 1 *May* 1863, *Mary Sophia* [a descendant of King Henry VII., &c.] (*Maplehurst Farm, Staplehurst, Kent*), da. of *Henry Hoare* of *Iden Manor, Staplehurst, co. Kent*; *and had issue.*

See the Tudor Roll, p. 274, Nos. 24735-24746; and the Exeter Volume, p. 197, Nos. 7100-7110.

4*b*. Emily *Jane Hallward*, b. 31 *Mar.* 1824; d. 9 *June* 1906; m. 22 *June* 1853, *the Rev. James Bradby Sweet, Vicar of Otterton, co. Devon*, d. 3 *Jan.* 1897; *and had issue* 1*c* to 5*c*.

1*c*. James Leslie Sweet (2 *Bedford Row, London, W.C.*), *b*. 25 Jan. 1857; *m*. 15 Oct. 1885, Ellen Caroline, da. of John Barclay, M.D.; and has issue 1*d* to 5d.

1*d*. John Laxon Leslie Sweet, *b*. 21 July 1886.

2*d*. Gerald Herbert Leslie Sweet, *b*. 13 May 1892.

3*d*. Cyril Vincent Leslie Sweet, *b*. 19 July 1900.

4*d*. Margaret Leslie Sweet, *b*. 24 June 1888.

5*d*. Winifred Mary Leslie Sweet, *b*. 1 June 1897.

2*c*. William MacMurdo Sweet, I.P.W.D., Superintending Engineer, Dacca (*Dacca, E. Bengal*), *b*. 14 Feb. 1860; *m*. Feb. 1895, May, da. of John Francis Hunnard; and has issue 1*d* to 3*d*.

1*d*. Jack Sweet, *b*. 20 Dec. 1895.

2*d*. Richard MacMurdo Sweet, *b*. 10 Nov. 1899.

3*d*. Beryl Sweet, *b*. 8 June 1898.

3*c*. Edward Hoare Sweet, M.D. (*Uckfield, Sussex*), *b*. 6 Aug. 1861; *m*. 28 Jan. 1904, Hilda Mary, da. of the Rev. Edward Sanderson; and has issue 1*d*.

1*d*. Enid Marjorie Sweet, *b*. 15 Aug. 1905.

4*c*. Florence Emily Caroline Sweet, *m*. 12 Jan. 1909, the Rev. George Peregrine Barber Viner, Rector of Mottingham (*Mottingham Rectory, Kent*).

5*c*. Mary Beatrice Sweet (*Church Lodge, Fleet, Hants*).

2*a*. Rev. *Nathaniel William Hallward, Rector of Milden, co. Suffolk*, d. *Oct.* 1884; m. *Harriet, da. of Charles Powell Leslie of Glasslough, co. Monaghan, M.P.; and had issue* 1*b to* 2*b*.

1*b*. Rev. *John William Hallward, Chaplain of Wandsworth Gaol*, d. 5 *May* 1874; m. 7 *Dec.* 1859, *Eliza* (8 *Ashley Gardens, S.W.*), *da. of William Henning of Frome, co. Dorset; and had issue* 1*c to* 2*c*.

1*c*. Frederick Charles Leslie Hallward (4 *Ashley Gardens, S.W.*), *b*. 16 Dec. 1862; *unm.*

2*c*. Mary Augusta Leslie Hallward, *m*. FitzPatrick Mackworth-Praed.

2*b*. Harriet Christina Hallward, *m*. 1856, Arthur William Saunders of Tullig, co. Kerry; and has issue 1*c* to 2*c*.

1*c*. Arthur Leslie Saunders, I.C.S. (*Lucknow*), *b*. 1862; *m*. 1896, Edith Lilian, da. of (—) Hughes-Hallett.

2*c*. William St. Lawrence Saunders, Capt. (ret.) Suffolk Regt., *b*. 13 June 1863.

[Nos. 16101 to 16138.

# of The Blood Royal

70. Descendants of JANE LAMBARDE (Table IX.), *b.* 3 Oct. 1764; *d.* 14 Feb. 1836; *m.* 13 Sept. 1785, the Right Rev. JOHN RANDOLPH, D.D., Lord Bishop of London, *d.* 28 July 1813; and had issue 1*a* to 3*a*.

1*a*. Rev. Thomas Randolph, *Rector of Much Hadham, co. Herts*, b. 9 *Nov.* 1788; d. 2 *May* 1875; m. 28 *May* 1813, *Caroline Diana, da. of the Right Hon. Sir Archibald Macdonald,* 1*st Bt.* [G.B.] [*a descendant of King Henry VII.* (see Tudor Roll, Table LXXXIV.)]; *and had issue* 1*b to* 3*b.*

1*b*. Rev. Edward John Randolph, *Rector of Dunnington and Chancellor and Prebendary of York*, b. 17 *Ap.* 1814; d. 9 *Dec.* 1898; m. 5 *July* 1843, *Catharine, da. of Sir George Rich,* d. 24 *June* 1899; *and had issue* 1*c to* 11*c.*

1*c*. Rev. Edward Seymour Leveson Randolph (17 *Trinity Gardens, Folkestone*), b. 30 May 1849; *m.* 23 Ap. 1881, Agnes Katharine, widow of William Garforth of Wiganthorpe, co. York, da. of Major George Duff, 19th Lancers.

2*c*. Granville Walter Randolph (24 *Shaftesbury Avenue, Bradford*), b. 10 Feb. 1851; *m.* 8 June 1881, Mildred Casandra [a descendant of Anne of Exeter, sister to Kings Edward IV. and Richard III.], da. of Rev. the Hon. Charles James Willoughby; and has issue 1*g* to 4*g*.

1*g*. Charles Edward Randolph, *b*. 1 Jan. 1883.

2*g*. Thomas Granville Randolph, *b*. 31 Oct. 1886.

3*g*. George Algernon Randolph, *b*. 2 Ap. 1890.

4*g*. Hylda Mary Randolph.

3*c*. Charles James Randolph (*Saham Hall, Watton, Norfolk*), b. 28 Dec. 1858; *m.* 16 July 1890, Richmond Emmeline Mary, da. of E. W. H. Scheuley, 60th Rifles.

4*c*. Rev. William Frederick Herbert Randolph (*The Vicarage, Frome Selwood, Somerset*), b. 8 Nov. 1862; *m.* 27 July 1898, Dorothy, da. of the Rev. Henry Montagu Villiers [E. of Clarendon Coll., and a descendant of the Lady Anne, sister of King Edward IV. (see the Exeter Volume, p. 381)], Vicar of St. Paul's, Knightsbridge, and Prebendary of St. Paul's Cathedral, by his wife the Lady Victoria [a descendant of Kings Henry VII. and Edward IV. (see Tudor Roll, p. 427)], da. of John (Russell), 1st Earl Russell [U.K.], K.G.

5*c*. Algernon Forbes Randolph, Col. in the Army (ret.) (*Army and Navy*), b. 12 Ap. 1865.

6*c*. Jane Caroline Randolph, *b*. 5 May 1844.

7*c*. Agnes Catharine Randolph (*St. John's Road, Newbury*), *m*. 16 Oct. 1879, Charles Howard, *d*. 24 July 1907, *s.p.*

8*c*. Caroline Flora Macdonald Randolph, *b*. 30 Sept. 1853.

9*c*. Mary Elizabeth Randolph, *m*. 13 Oct. 1881, James Frederick Digby Willoughby (*Southwell, Notts*) [B. Middleton Coll., and a descendant of Anne of Exeter, sister to Kings Edward IV. and Richard III.]; and has issue 1*d* to 4*d*.

1*d*. Ronald James Edward Willoughby, Mid. R.N., *b*. 7 May 1884.

2*d*. Archibald Macdonald Willoughby, Mid. R.N., *b*. 20 May 1887.

3*d*. Bernard Digby Willoughby, *b*. 8 Ap. 1896.

4*d*. Katherine Mary Seymour Willoughby.

10*c*. Emily Ann Randolph (16 *Herbert Crescent, S.W.*), *m*. 29 Jan. 1885, Charles Edward Farmer; and has issue 1*d* to 5*d*.

1*d*. Charles George Edgar Farmer, *b*. 28 Nov. 1885.

2*d*. Harry Gamul Farmer, *b*. 12 Mar. 1887.

3*d*. Hugh Robert Macdonald Farmer, *b*. 3 Dec. 1907.

4*d*. Olive Agnes Emmeline Farmer, *b*. 16 July 1895.

5*d*. Ruth Alice Farmer, *b*. 10 Aug. 1896.

11*c*. Augusta Margaret Randolph, *b*. 30 Dec. 1860. [Nos. 16139 to 16162.

The Plantagenet Roll

2b. Sir George Granville Randolph, K.C.B., Adm. R.N., b. 26 Jan. 1818; d. 16 May 1907; m. 4 Feb. 1851, Eleanor Harriet, da. of Joseph Arkwright of Mark Hall, co. Essex, d. 5 Ap. 1907; and had issue 1c to 3c.

1c. Rev. Rodney Granville Randolph (*Moray Lodge, Duston, Northants*), b. 23 Nov. 1851; m. Oct. 1884, Frances Charlotta, da. of John Christopher Mansel of Cosgrove, co. Northants.

2c. Rose Caroline Randolph, m. 28 Ap. 1885, the Rev. Alfred George Lovelace Bowling, *formerly* Vicar of St. Barnabas, Hove (*Moreton End House, Harpenden*); and has issue 1d to 6d.

   1d. Charles Randolph Bowling, b. 18 Feb. 1886.
   2d. Edwyn Randolph Bowling, b. 27 Sept. 1892.
   3d. Harold Randolph Bowling, b. 4 Jan. 1894.
   4d. Geoffrey Randolph Bowling, b. 30 Aug. 1898.
   5d. Rose Mary Bowling, b. 2 Mar. 1887.
   6d. Margaret Mary Bowling, b. 4 June 1896.

3c. Violet Mary Randolph.

3b. Rev. Leveson Cyril Randolph, *Vicar of St. Luke's, Lower Norwood*, b. 1828; d. 1 Mar. 1876; m. 13 July 1854, Anne [a descendant of Anne of Exeter, sister to King Edward IV., &c. (see Exeter Volume, p. 240)], da. of Rev. the Hon. John Evelyn Boscawen, *Rector of Wootton, co. Surrey, Canon of Canterbury*, d. 27 Feb. 1899; and had issue 1c to 4c.

1c. George Boscawen Randolph, J.P. (*Steeple Aston, Oxon.*), b. 28 Oct. 1864.

2c. Right Rev. John Hugh Granville Randolph, D.D., Lord Bishop of Guildford (*Guildford*), b. 28 Jan. 1866; m. 31 Jan. 1895, Beatrice Mary, da. of the Rev. Samuel Back, Vicar of Maxstoke; and has issue 1d to 3d.

   1d. Joan Mary Randolph, b. 14 Oct. 1898.
   2d. Margaret Ann Randolph, b. 22 Ap. 1899.
   3d. Frances Edith Randolph, b. 15 Oct. 1901.

3c. Margaret Catherine Randolph, b. 30 Dec. 1860.

4c. Annie Eveline Randolph, b. 28 Feb. 1863.

2a. Rev. John Honywood Randolph, *Rector of Saunderstead, co. Surrey*, b. 8 Mar. 1791; d. June 1868; m. 1814, Sarah, da. of Richard Wilson of Bildeston; and had issue 1b to 3b.

1b. Rev. John Randolph, *Rector of Saunderstead*, b. 15 May 1821; d. 11 July 1881; m. 29 Ap. 1851, Harriet, da. of John Robert Bell; and had issue 1c to 3c.

1c. Percy John Charles Randolph (*Erdington, Worcestershire*), b. 11 Sept. 1858; m. 16 Nov. 1897, Constance, da. of Richard Shaw.

2c. Evelyn Sarah Frances Randolph } (7 *Haldon Terrace, Dawlish,*
3c. Leila Frances Atwood Randolph }   *S. Devon*).

2b. Hannah Georgiana Randolph, m. 8 Jan. 1857, the Rev. Frederick John Coleridge, M.A., Rector of Cadbury 1855–1906 and R.D. 1873–97, b. 4 Dec. 1826; d. 20 Jan. 1906; and has issue 1c to 5c.

1c. Rev. George Frederick Coleridge, *Vicar of Crowthorne* (*Crowthorne Vicarage, Berks*), b. 10 Nov. 1857; *unm.*

2c. Hugh Fortescue Coleridge, D.S.O., Lieut.-Col. Loyal N. Lancashire Regt., served in S. Africa 1899–1900 (*Naval and Military; Gough Barracks, the Curragh, co. Dublin*), b. 11 Jan. 1858; m. 12 Sept. 1906, Kathleen Grace Fane, da. of Rear-Adm. John Hugh Bainbridge of Elfordleigh, Plympton.

3c. James Duke Carmichael Coleridge, b. 14 Jan. 1860; *unm.*

4c. Flora Augusta Townsend Coleridge, *unm.*

5c. Constance Georgiana Randolph Coleridge, m. 12 Ap. 1894, John Henry Cann (*Gothelney Hall, Bridgewater*); and has issue 1d to 2d.

   1d. Hugh John Cann, b. 19 Sept. 1896.
   2d. Constance Nancy Coleridge Cann, b. 7 Sept. 1900.   [Nos. 16163 to 16189.

# of The Blood Royal

3b. Sarah Augusta Randolph, m. 2 Nov. 1848, Francis James Coleridge of the Manor House, Ottery St. Mary, b. 26 May 1825; d. 5 June 1862; and has issue 1c to 7c.

    1c. *Percy Duke Coleridge, Lieut. R.M.L.I.*, b. 1 *Sept.* 1850; d. 29 *Mar.* 1881; m. 27 *June* 1877, *Edith Laura Matilda* [*descended from King Henry VII.* (see Tudor Roll, p. 201)], *da. of Capt. Lovell Stanhope Richard Lovell; and had issue* 1d to 2d.

        1d. John Coleridge, b. 25 Ap. 1878; m.

        2d. Percy Coleridge, b. 20 July 1880; m.

    2c. Francis Randolph Cyril Coleridge, Chief Constable of Devon 1891–1907, b. 27 Nov. 1854; m. 1 Aug. 1903, Alice Gertrude, widow of Capt. Hayhurst France, da. of R. N. Hawks of Dolcorsllwyn, co. Montgomery, *s.p.*

    3c. Frances Augusta Coleridge, m. at Colombo, 20 Feb. 1878, Robert Holme Sumner Scott.

    4c. Harriet Georgiana Coleridge, m. 26 Jan. 1882, William Nicholas Connock Marshall, J.P. (*Treworgey, Liskeard, Cornwall*); and has issue 1d to 2d.

        1d. Coleridge Connock Marshall, b. 15 Mar. 1883.

        2d. Monica A. Connock Marshall.

    5c. Emily Joanna Coleridge, *unm.*

    6c. Dorothy Helen Coleridge, m. 26 Jan. 1882, Reginald Philip Sumner [yst. son of Charles Sumner of Hempsted, co. Glos., a County Court Judge].

    7c. Celia Elizabeth Coleridge, *unm.*

3a. *Rev. George Randolph*, b. 16 *Feb.* 1797; d. 1880; m. 20 *Aug.* 1822, *Catharine Elizabeth* [*a descendant of King Henry VII.* (see Tudor Roll, p. 536)], *da. of the Rev. Henry Roger Drummond, Rector of Fawsley, co. Hants; and had issue* 1b.[1]

    1b. Rev. Cyril Randolph (*Chartham Rectory, Canterbury*), b. 6 Feb. 1826; m. 30 Sept. 1851, Frances Selina, da. of Lionel Charles Hervey; and has issue 1c to 7c.

        1c. *Felton George Randolph*, b. 4 *Ap.* 1854; d. 29 *Dec.* 1906; m. 14 *Jan.* 1896, *Emily Margaret, da. of Sir Evan Colville Nepean, C.B.; and had issue* 1d to 7d.

            1d. John Hervey Randolph, b. 3 Mar. 1897.

            2d. Cyril George Randolph, b. 26 June 1898.

            3d. Thomas Berkeley Randolph, b. 15 Mar. 1904.

            4d. Mary Frances Elizabeth Randolph, b. 24 Nov. 1896.

            5d. Susan Emily Randolph, b. 6 Aug. 1900.

            6d. Margaret Isobel Randolph, b. July 1902.

            7d. Barbara May Randolph, b. 6 Mar. 1906.

    2c. Rev. Berkeley William Randolph, D.D., Hon. Canon of Ely (*Theological College, Ely*), b. 10 Mar. 1858.

    3c. Hugh Lionel Randolph (140 *Reconquista, Buenos Ayres, Argentina*), b. 20 July 1868; m. 20 June 1899, Lily Constance, da. of Charles Y. Fell, of St. John's, Nelson, N.Z.; and has issue 1d to 2d.

        1d. Bernard Nolan Randolph, b. 1900.

        2d. Richard Seymour Randolph, b. 1904.

    4c. Gertrude Frances Randolph, b. 25 Sept. 1853.

    5c. Selina Catharine Randolph, b. 13 Ap. 1859.

    6c. Agnes Susan Randolph, b. 2 Nov. 1861.

    7c. Florence Mary Randolph, b. 23 Dec. 1862.   [Nos. 16190 to 16216.

---

[1] *N.B.*—These should be in Tudor Roll, p. 536, between Nos. 35767–35768.

The Plantagenet Roll

71. Descendants of JANE WHELER (Table IX.), d. 6 Dec. 1847; m. 10 Sept. 1774, HENRY (HOOD), 2nd VISCOUNT [G.B.] and BARON [G.B. and I.] HOOD, b. 25 Aug. 1753; d. 25 Jan. 1836; and had issue 1a to 4a.

1a. Hon. Francis Wheler Hood, Lieut.-Col. in the Army, b. 4 Oct. 1781; d. (being killed in action on the heights of Aire) 2 Mar. 1814; m. 11 Oct. 1804, Caroline, da. of Sir Andrew Snape Hamond, 1st Bt. [G.B.], d. 11 Mar. 1858; and had issue 1b to 2b.

1b. Samuel (Hood, afterwards (R.L. 12 Feb. 1840) Hood-Tibbits), 3rd Viscount [G.B.] and Baron [G.B. and I.] Hood, b. 10 Jan. 1808; d. 8 May 1846; m. 27 June 1837, Mary Isabella, da. and h. of Richard John Tibbits of Barton Seagrave Hall, co. Northants [by his wife Horatia Charlotte, da. of Thomas Lockwood and Charlotte, da. of Lord George Manners-Sutton, a descendant of the Lady Anne, sister of King Edward IV. (see Exeter Volume, p. 165)] [m. 2ndly, 5 May 1849, George Hall of Brighton, M.D.; 3rdly, 17 June 1858, Capt. John Borlase Maunsell], and d. (-); and had issue 1c to 3c.

1c. Francis Wheler (Hood), 4th Viscount [G.B.] and Baron [G.B. and I.] Hood, b. 4 July 1838; d. 27 Ap. 1907; m. 18 July 1865, Edith Lydia Drummond, da. of Arthur W. Ward of Calverley, Tunbridge Wells; and had issue 1d to 6d.

1d. Grosvenor Arthur Alexander (Hood), 5th Viscount [G.B.] and Baron [G.B. and I.] Hood, late Major Grenadier Guards (Barton Seagrave, Kettering; 17 Hertford Street, Mayfair, W.), b. 13 Nov. 1868.

2d. Hon. Horace Lambert Alexander Hood, M.V.O., D.S.O., Capt. R.N., b. 4 Oct. 1870.

3d. Hon. Neville Albert Hood, Capt. R.A., b. 4 Oct. 1872; m. 1908, Eveline Mary, da. of Herman Usticke Broad of Trisilian, Falmouth; and has issue 1e.

1e. Edith Rosemary Hood.

4d. Hon. Francis George Hood, b. 28 Mar. 1880; m. 20 Oct. 1904, Helen Kendell Mouncey, da. of Lieut.-Col. the Hon. Edward Gawler Prior of Victoria, B.C., P.C., Canada; and has issue 1e.

1e. Francis Basil Hood, b. 5 Sept. 1904.

5d. Hon. Mabel Edith Hood, b. 26 May 1866; d. 18 Jan. 1904; m. 25 July 1889, Francis Denzil Edward (Baring), 5th Baron Ashburton [U.K.] [descended from King Henry VII.] (The Grange, Alresford, Hants); and had issue.
See the Tudor Roll, p. 454, Nos. 31825-31829.

6d. Hon. Dorothy Violet Hood.

2c. Hon. Albert Hood, late Rifle Brigade (Upham House, Bishop's Waltham; The Hook, Titchfield), b. 26 Aug. 1841; m. 2 June 1868, Julia Jane, da. of Thomas Wynn Hornby of Upham House, co. Hants, d. 20 Aug. 1906; and has issue 1d to 7d.

1d. Samuel Wynn Hornby Hood (Curdridge, Bothy, Hants), b. 30 Mar. 1869; m. 29 Oct. 1906, Ethel Norah, da. of Lionel Smith.

2d. Albert Oscar Hood, late Lieut. 5th Batt. Rifle Brigade, b. 2 Ap. 1870.

3d. Edward Hood (Dromore, co. Kerry), b. 18 July 1872; m. 27 Oct. 1900, Nora Eveleen, da. of Richard Mahony of Dromore Castle, co. Kerry, D.L.

4d. Alexander Frank Hood, formerly Capt. 3rd Vol. Batt. E. Surrey Regt., b. 27 Jan. 1874; m. 21 June 1905, Gladys Ursula, da. of Edward C. Youell of Galatz, Roumania; and has issue 1e.

1e. Albert Edward Hood, b. 23 Mar. 1906.

5d. Robert Valentine Hood, b. 5 Feb. 1876.

6d. Emily Beryl Sissy Hood, m. 19 Sept. 1893, Edward (Digby), 10th Baron Digby [G.B.] [a descendant of King Henry VII. (see the Tudor Roll, p. 454)] (Minterne House, Cerne Abbas, Dorset; 16 Grosvenor Place, S.W.); and has issue 1e to 5e. [Nos. 16217 to 16236.

# of The Blood Royal

1e. Hon. Edward Kenelm Digby, b. 1 Aug. 1894.
2e. Hon. Robert Henry Digby, b. 24 Nov. 1903.
3e. Hon. Lettice Theresa Digby.
4c. Hon. Geraldine Margot Digby.
5e. Hon. Venetia Jane Digby.
7d. Marguerite Jenny Hood, b. 20 May 1881.

3c. Hon. Alexander Frederick Hood (*Airmyn Hall, Goole, Yorks*), b. 20 May 1843; m. 7 June 1870, Ethel Cecilia [a descendant of King Henry VII., and also through Mortimer-Percy, &c.], da. of Algernon Charles Heber-Percy of Hodnet Hall, co. Salop; and has issue.
See p. 68, Nos. 834–838.

2b. Hon. Caroline Hood, b. 16 Oct. 1805; d. 9 May 1890; m. 25 Feb. 1834, *Arthur Francis Gregory of Styvechale Hall, co. Warwick, D.L.,* d. 27 Feb. 1853; and had issue 1c.

1c. Francis Hood Gregory of Styvechale, J.P., M.A. (Oxon.), *formerly* Major 15th Hussars and A.D.C. to Duke of Abercorn when Lord-Lieut. of Ireland, to Lord Mayo when Viceroy of India, &c. (*Styvechale Hall, Coventry*), b. 29 Oct. 1836.

2a. Samuel (Hood), 2nd Baron Bridport [I.], b. 7 Dec. 1788; d. 6 Jan. 1868; m. 3 July 1810, Charlotte Mary, suo jure 3rd Duchess of Bronté [Sicily], da. and h. of William (Nelson), 1st Earl Nelson [U.K.] and 2nd Duke of Bronté [Sicily], b. 20 Sept. 1787; d. 29 Jan. 1873; and had issue 1b to 5b.

1b. Alexander Nelson (Hood), 3rd Baron [I.] and 1st Viscount [U.K.] Bridport and 4th Duke of Bronté [Sicily], b. 23 Dec. 1814; d. 4 June 1904; m. 2 Aug. 1838, Mary [*a descendant of Anne of Exeter, sister to King Edward IV., &c.*], da. of Arthur Blundell Bandys Trumbull (Hill), 3rd Marquis of Downshire [I.], d. 15 July 1884; and had issue.
See the Exeter Volume, pp. 323–324, Nos. 23985–24031.

2b. Hon. Mary Sophia Hood, b. 1 Dec. 1811; d. 29 Jan. 1888; m. *as 2nd wife*, 17 Aug. 1841, *John Lee Lee of Dillington, co. Somerset,* d. 16 Aug. 1874; and had issue 1c to 3c.

1c. Edward Hanning Lee (now D.P. 13 June 1876) Hanning-Lee, J.P., Col. *formerly* Comdg. 2nd Life Guards (*Old Manor House, Bighton, Alresford*), b. 26 Aug. 1845; m. 1872, Georgiana Emma, da. of Edward Marjoribanks of the Hall, Bushey, co. Herts; and has issue 1d to 4d.

1d. Vaughan Alexander Hanning-Lee, Comm. R.N., b. 1 Oct. 1878.
2d. Francis Charles Hanning-Lee, Lieut. R.N., b. 29 Sept. 1880.
3d. Hazel Hanning-Lee, b. 15 Aug. 1877.
4d. Robinia Marion Hanning-Lee, m. as 2nd wife, 5 Feb. 1902, Henry Edmund (Butler), 14th Viscount Mountgarret [I.] [a descendant of King Henry VII., &c.] (*Ballyconra, co. Kilkenny, &c.*); and has issue 1d.

1d. Hon. Piers Henry Augustine Butler, b. 28 Aug. 1903.

2c. William Hanning-Lee, *late* Col. Comdg. 2nd Dragoon Guards (*Old Catton, Norwich*), b. 9 Dec. 1846; m. 31 Oct. 1877, Emilie Georgiana, da. of the Rev. Alfred Bond; and has issue 1d.

1d. Seymour Hanning-Lee, b. 25 Sept. 1881.

3c. Emily Mary Lee, d. *Mar.* 1893; m. 1st, *Thomas Spragging Godfrey of Balderton Hall, co. Notts,* d. (–); 2ndly, 28 Dec. 1882, *Major-Gen. Henry Lowther Balfour, R.A.* ; and had issue 1d to 4d.

1d. Edward Lee Godfrey, b. 1868.
2d. Alice Sophia Godfrey, b. 2 Jan. 1865; d. 12 May 1886; m. *as 1st wife*, 21 Ap. 1885, *the Hon. Francis Albert Rollo Russell* (*Steep, Petersfield*); and had issue 1e.

1e. Arthur John Godfrey Russell, b. 11 Mar. 1886.
3d. Violet Lucy Godfrey.
4d. Edith Mary Adelaide Godfrey.

[Nos. 16237 to 16308.

The Plantagenet Roll

3b. Hon. *Charlotte Hood*, b. 8 *Aug.* 1813; d. 21 *Aug.* 1906; m. as 2nd wife, 4 *Sept.* 1845, Horace William Noel Rochfort of *Clogrenane, co. Carlow*, d. 16 *May* 1891; *and had issue.*
See the Exeter Volume, p. 202, Nos. 7263-7269.

4b. Hon. *Catharine Louisa Hood*, b. 25 *Mar.* 1818; d. 6 *Oct.* 1893; m. 18 *Ap.* 1837, Henry Hall of *Barton Abbey, co. Oxon.*, d. 17 *Nov.* 1862; *and had issue* 1c to 9c.

1c. Alexander William Hall, M.P., J.P., D.L., High Sheriff co. Oxford 1867 (*Barton Abbey, Steeple Aston, Oxon.*), b. 20 June 1838; m. 27 Aug. 1863, Emma Gertrude, da. of Edward Jowett of Eltofts, co. York; and has issue 1d to 7d.

1d. Alexander Nelson Hall (*Cornwall Manor, Chipping Norton*), b. 25 July 1865; m. 4 Aug. 1891, Susan Isabel, da. of Col. G. C. Porter of Fairford Park, co. Gloucester, *s.p.*

2d. Robin Henry Edward Hall (*The Priory, Prior's Marston, Byfield, R.S.O., Warwickshire*), b. 29 Jan. 1882; *unm.*

3d. Marion Alexandra Gertrude Hall, m. 1889, Lieut.-Col. Malcolm Stewart Riach, 2nd Batt. Cameron Highlanders (*Tientsin, North China*); and has issue 1e to 3e.

1e. Stewart Malcolm Alexander Riach, b. Jan. 1892.
2e. Ronald Riach.
3e. Nigel Riach.

4d. Muriel Hall, m. 1890, the Rev. Frank Langley Appleford, Rector of Castle Combe (*Castle Combe Rectory, near Chippenham*); and has issue 1e to 2e.

1e. Walter Alexander Nelson Appleford, b. 5 Mar. 1891.
2e. Doreen Langley Appleford, b. 27 Nov. 1901.

5d. Amabel Hall, m. 15 Oct. 1896, the Rev. Spencer Henry Harrison, Rector of Aswarby (*Aswarby Rectory, Folkingham, Lincolnshire*); and has issue 1e.

1e. Rosaleen Verena Harrison, b. 23 June 1907.

6d. Mary Verena Hall, m. 26 July 1899, Alfred Hewston Holmes, M.D. (*Down Hall, Rippingill, Lincolnshire*); and has issue.

7d. Monica Hall, m. 2 July 1902, James Frederick Farquharson; and has issue 1e to 2e.

1e. William James Farquharson, b. 26 Feb. 1904.
2e. Ellen Constance Lorraine Farquharson, b. 30 Dec. 1906.

2c. Henry Samuel Hall, C.B., V.D. (25 *Longridge Road, South Kensington, S.W.*), b. 17 Oct. 1839; m. Jan. 1874, Eleanor Elizabeth Mary, da. of Gen. Edward Boxer, R.A., F.R.S., *s.p.*

3c. Herbert Lee Hall, *late* 61st Regt., b. 20 Nov. 1841; *unm.*

4c. Hugh Hall, D.C.L., Bar.-at-Law (100 *Holywell Street, Oxford*), b. (—); m. 9 Dec. 1880, Elinor Mildred, da. of the Rev. John Wright Hopkins, Vicar of Aghern, co. Cork; and has issue 1d.

1d. Hugh Frederick Gethin Hall, b. 24 Oct. 1881.

5c. Horatio Nelson Hall, b. 11 Mar. 1852; *unm.*
6c. Arthur Yonge Hall, b. 23 Oct. 1856; *unm.*
7c. Hilare Charlotte Hall, m. 29 Dec. 1863, John de Burgh Rochfort (*Clogrenane, co. Carlow*); and has issue.
See the Exeter Volume, p. 202, Nos. 7271-7277.

8c. Frances Caroline Hall.

9c. Catharine Hester Hall, m. 1st, 16 May 1865, Stafford Majendie Brown, d. 29 Ap. 1892; 2ndly, 13 Aug. 1892, George Ffrench (*Adderbury, near Banbury, Oxon.*); and has issue 1d to 7d.

1d. Stafford Brown, b. 1 Nov. 1866; m. Emily Ella, da. of (—); and has issue 1e.

1e. Stafford Meredith Brown, b. 22 Ap. 1898. [Nos. 16309 to 16349.

# of The Blood Royal

2*d*. Majendie Brown, *b*. 17 Jan. 1871; *m*. 8 June 1903, Geraldine May, da. of Richard Berridge; and has issue 1*e* to 4*e*.

    1*e*. Richard Majendie Brown, *b*. 19 Aug. 1907.

    2*e*. Frances Helen May Brown, *b*. 14 Oct. 1903.

    3*e*. Catharine Joan Brown, *b*. 30 Dec. 1904.

    4*e*. Nora Ena Brown, *b*. 9 Ap. 1906.

3*d*. Horatio Nelson Brown, *b*. 15 Oct. 1876; *m*. 18 Oct. 1897, Annie Kate, da. of Edward William May; and has issue 1*e* to 2*e*.

    1*e*. Guy Nelson Brown, *b*. 13 July 1901.

    2*e*. Lorna Brown, *b*. 14 Oct. 1898.

4*d*. Nicholas George Ffrench, *b*. 26 Oct. 1893.

5*d*. Ethel Maud Brown, *m*. 6 Feb. 1895, Thomas Oates Halliwell; and has issue 1*e* to 2*e*.

    1*e*. Eric Oates Halliwell, *b*. 31 Dec. 1903.

    2*e*. Marjorie Halliwell, *b*. 30 Oct. 1895.

6*d*. Hilaire Katharine Esme Brown, *m*. 19 Jan. 1899, Edward Theodore Sandys; and has issue 1*e* to 3*e*.

    1*e*. Edith Mary Sandys, *b*. 17 Dec. 1899.

    2*e*. Sybil Esme Sandys, *b*. 17 Nov. 1900.

    3*e*. Hilare Mina Sandys, *b*. 16 June 1903.

7*d*. Hester Sybil Alexandra Brown, *m*. 30 July 1902, Edward Henry Hodge.

5*b*. Hon. *Fanny Caroline Hood*, b. 29 *Mar*. 1821; d. 2 *Oct*. 1903; m. 20 *May* 1845, *Sir John Walrond Walrond, 1st Bt*. [*U.K.*], d. 23 *Ap*. 1889; *and had issue.*
See the Exeter Volume, pp. 119-120, Nos. 1455-1497.

3*a*. Hon. *Susannah Hood*, b. 17 *May* 1779; d. 1 *Nov*. 1823; m. *the Rev. Richard George Richards, Vicar of Hambledon, Hants*, bur. 25 *June* 1841; *aged* 68; *and had (with possibly other) issue (a son, Major Hood Richards, who had a son and da. who* d. *unm.*).

4*a*. Hon. *Selina Hood*, b. 16 *Nov*. 1782; d. 17 *Jan*. 1863; m. 16 *Ap*. 1805, *Vice-Admiral Sir Francis Mason, K.C.B.*, d. 27 *May* 1853; *and had issue* 1*b* to 4*b*.

    1*b*. *Francis John Mills Mason*, b. 4 *May* 1821; d. 14 *July* 1899; m. 7 *Aug*. 1851, *Jane, da. of William Morton of Kent's Green, co. Worcester*, d. *June* 1852; *and had issue* 1*c* to 2*c*.

        1*c*. Rev. Francis Wheler Randall Mason, M.A. (Oxon.), Chaplain of Wroxall Abbey (*The Firs, Warwick*), *b*. 11 *July* 1852; *m*. 5 *Oct*. 1887, Amy, da. of the Rev. Lester Lester of Swanage; and has issue 1*d*.

        1*d*. Rachel Lois Mason.

        2*c*. Rev. Charles Arthur Mason, M.A. (Oxon.), Vicar of Otterbourne, *formerly* Canon of Allahabad (*Otterbourne Vicarage, Winchester*), *b*. 27 Nov. 1858; *m*. 15 Feb. 1890, Laura Kate, da. of Dr. S. Plumbe; and has issue 1*d* to 5*d*.

            1*d*. Arthur Samuel Mason, *b*. 27 Mar. 1893.

            2*d*. Gerald Francis Mason, *b*. 30 Dec. 1897.

            3*d*. John Oscar Lawrence Mason, *b*. 12 Sept. 1899.

            4*d*. Winifred Kate Mason.

            5*d*. Ada Doris Hood Mason.

    2*b*. *Charles Crawfurd Mason*, b. 1826; d. *in California* 1904; m. 1854, *Lucy Ella* (*Box* 720, *Post Office, Sherman, Los Angeles, California*), *da. of* (—) *Holmes; and had issue* 1*c* to 5*c*.

        1*c*. William Robert Mason (*America*), *b*. 186- ; *m*. 1906, Violet, da. of (—), *d*. 1907.

        2*c*. Hugh Francis Mason (*America*), *b*. 1873.

        3*c*. Edith Mary Mason, *m*. Donald Grant; and has issue (3 children).

[Nos. 16350 to 16420.

The Plantagenet Roll

4c. Ethel Mason, m. 1907, Ernest Cox.
5c. Sybil Mason, m. Elliott Cox; and has issue (4 children).
3b. Mary Sophia Mason (*Braunston, Rugby*), b. 16 Mar. 1816; m. the Rev. Charles Bucknill, *d.s.p.* 1866.
4b. *Selina Ruth Ann Mason*, b. 1 Dec. 1818; d. 29 May 1909; m. *the Rev. James William Knight*, d. 28 Aug. 1878; *and had issue* 1c to 2c.
  1c. Selina May Knight, *unm.*
  2c. Edith Mary Knight, m. 17 Jan. 1878, Alfred James Riley, Major 4th Batt. Somerset L.I. (*Grove House, Kidlington, Oxon.*); and has issue 1d to 5d.
    1d. Gerard Brook Riley, Lieut. R.N., b. 5 Ap. 1881.
    2d. Denys Linzee Brook Riley, b. 5 Dec. 1898.
    3d. Agnes Muriel Riley.
    4d. Elsie Mary Riley.
    5d. Edith Marjorie Riley, m. 2 Aug. 1906, the Rev. George Duncan (*Shipton-on-Cherwell Rectory, Kidlington, Oxon.*); and has issue 1e to 2e.
      1e. John Hugh Banchory Duncan, b. 19 Oct. 1907.
      2e. David Lionel Crawfurd Duncan, b. 30 Ap. 1909.   [Nos. 16421 to 16432.

72. Descendants of SARAH WHELER (Table IX.), d. 25 Oct. 1807; m. 17 Nov. 1749, the Rev. JOHN MILLS, Rector of Barford and Oxhill, co. Warwick, b. 10 May 1712; d. 21 Mar. 1791; and had issue 1a to 4a.

1a. *William Mills of Bisterne, Southampton, M.P.*, b. 10 Nov. 1750; d. 20 Mar. 1820; m. 7 Ap. 1786, Elizabeth, da. of the Hon. Wriothesley Digby, d. 27 Dec. 1828; *and had issue.*
See the Essex Volume, pp. 53–56, Nos. 5513–5619.

2a. *Rev. Francis Mills, Rector of Barford, co. Warwick*, b. 29 June 1759; d. 23 Ap. 1851; m. 26 Oct. 1811, Catharine (see p. 410), da. of Sir John Mordaunt, 7th Bt. [E.], d. 7 May 1852,; *and had issue* 1b to 2b.
  1b. *Rev. Henry Mills of Pillerton Manor, Kineton, co. Warwick*, b. 1 Ap. 1815; d. 14 Nov. 1906; m. 9 Dec. 1841, Mary, da. of the Rev. Henry Hippisley of Lambourne Place, co. Berks, d. 3 Sept. 1892; *and had issue* 1c to 3c.
    1c. Francis Mills (*Manor House, Pillerton, near Warwick*), b 18 Jan. 1844; m. 27 Dec. 1877, Selina Mary, da. of the Rev. Henry Charles Knightley [cadet of Fawsley, and a descendant of the Lady Anne Plantagenet, sister to King Edward IV., &c. (see Exeter Volume, p. 518)]; and has issue 1d to 4d.
      1d. Henry Valentine Mills, b. 23 Nov. 1881.
      2d. Mabel Frances Mills.
      3d. Phœbe Mills.
      4d. Esther Mary Mills.
    2c. Catharine Mills (*Carfax House, Barrow-on-Humber; Clyde House, Ventnor, I.W.*), m. 20 Ap. 1882, the Rev. Alfred Freeman, Vicar of Burgh-on-Bain, co. Lincoln, d. 31 July 1895; and has issue 1d to 3d.
      1d. Henry Alfred Freeman, C.E., b. 31 Jan. 1883.
      2d. Katharine Mary Freeman.
      3d. Emma Sophia Freeman.
    3c. Fanny Mills.

2b. *Arthur Mills of Budchaven, co. Cornwall*, b. 20 July 1816; d. 12 Oct. 1898; m. 3 Aug. 1848, Agnes Lucy, da. of Sir Thomas Dyke Acland, 10th Bt. [E.], d. 23 May 1895; *and had issue* 1c to 2c.
  1c. Rev. Barton Reginald Vaughan Mills (12 *Cranley Gardens, S.W.*), b. 29 Oct. 1857; m. 1st, 10 July 1886, Lady Catharine Mary [a descendant of George   [Nos. 16433 to 16550.

# of The Blood Royal

(Plantagenet), Duke of Clarence, K.G. (see the Clarence Volume, p. 591)], sister of Sydney (Hobart), 7th Earl of Buckinghamshire [G.B.], da. of Frederick John Hobart, Lord Hobart, d. 25 Sept. 1889; 2ndly, 10 Jan. 1894, Elizabeth Edith, da. of Sir George Dalhousie Ramsay, C.B.; and has issue 1d to 4d.

    1d. Arthur Frederick Hobart Mills, b. 12 July 1887.
    2d. George Ramsay Acland Mills, b. 1 Oct. 1896.
    3d. Agnes Edith Mills.
    4d. Violet Eleanor Mills.

    2c. Dudley Acland Mills, Col. R.E. (*Broadlands, Jersey*), b. 24 Aug. 1859; m. Feb. 1896, Ethel, da. of Sir Henri Joly de Lotbinière, K.C.M.G.; and has issue (a son and 2 das.).

    3a. *Selina Mills*, d. 1825; m. 1780, *James Molony of Kiltanon, co. Clare*, d. 12 Oct. 1823; *and had issue* 1b to 2b.

    1b. *James Molony of Kiltanon*, b. 18 Aug. 1785; d. 7 July 1874; m. 1st, 17 Feb. 1820, *Harriet, da. of William Harding of Baraset, co. Warw.*, d. 8 Oct. 1826; 2ndly, 15 Ap. 1828, *Lucy, da. of Sir Trevor Wheler, 8th Bt.* [E.], d. 14 May 1855; *and had issue* 1c to 7c.

    1c. *William Mills Molony of Kiltanon*, Major 22nd and 83rd Regts., b. 24 Ap. 1825; d. 7 Sept. 1891; m. 8 Nov. 1865, *Marianne Marsh, da. and co-h. of Robert Fannin of Leeson Street, Dublin*, d. 27 Jan. 1880; *and had issue* 1d to 3d.

    1d. William Beresford Molony, *late* Capt. King's Own Royal Lancashire Regt. (*Kiltanon, near Tulla, co. Clare*), b. 25 Aug. 1875; m. 22 Feb. 1905, Lena Annie Maria, da. of George Wright of Heysham Lodge, co. Lanc., s.p.

    2d. Henrietta Mary Molony, m. 28 July 1903, Marcus Thomas Francis Keane (*Beech Park, Ennis, co. Clare*); and has issue 1e to 2e.

    1e. Marcus William Keane, b. 2 Jan. 1906.
    2e. Helen Louise Keane, b. 17 Jan. 1905.

    3d. Iva Kathleen Molony, m. 10 June 1896, Capt. John Raynsford Longley, East Surrey Regt. (*Devonport; Widey Grange, Crownhill, South Devon*); and has issue 1e to 2e.

    1e. Charles Raynsford Longley, b. 21 Dec. 1897.
    2e. John Molony Longley, b. 21 Sept. 1906.

    2c. Rev. *Francis Wheler Molony*, b. 5 Ap. 1829; d. 27 Feb. 1860; m. 19 Oct. 1853, *Harriet, da. of Capt. G. Baker, R.N.*, d. 11 Ap. 1910; *and had issue* 1d.

    1d. James Arthur Molony (*Enon Valley, Lawrence Co., Penn., U.S.A.*), b. 29 Aug. 1854; m. 14 Dec. 1876, Annie, da. of J. W. Hague of Enon Valley, Pennsylvania; and has issue (with a son and da. d. unm.) 1e to 5e.

    1e. Harriet Eliza Molony, m. 15 Mar. 1900, Frank Chestney of New Castle, Pa.; and has issue 1f to 3f.

    1f. Francis Edwin Chestney, b. 21 Ap. 1902.
    2f. James Chestney, b. 29 July 1904.
    3f. Mabel Evelyn Chestney, b. 18 Sept. 1907.

    2e. Lucy Molony, m. 25 Ap. 1900, William J. Buchanan of Grove City, Pa.; and has issue 1f to 4f.

    1f. Arthur Vandeleur Buchanan, b. 18 Jan. 1901.
    2f. William Leo Buchanan, b. 17 Sept. 1903.
    3f. Grace Heyne Buchanan, b. 27 May 1905.
    4f. Marion Louise Buchanan, b. 30 Aug. 1908.

    3e. Anna Kathleen Molony, m. 6 Dec. 1904, Allen Goodhart of Shippensbury, Pa.; and has issue 1f to 2f.

    1f. Harry Allen Goodhart, b. 8 June 1906.
    2f. Anna H. Goodhart, b. 28 Aug. 1907.

    4e. Henrietta Charlotte Molony, m. 13 Aug. 1907, Albert Weaver of Tarentum, Pa., s.p.s.
    5e. Iva Molony.

[Nos. 16551 to 16577.

The Plantagenet Roll

3c. *Edmund Weldon Molony*, H.E.I.C.S., b. 27 Mar. 1830; d. 30 Jan. 1888; m. 29 *July* 1863, *Frances Selina* (13 *West Cliff Terrace, Ramsgate*), da. of (*Conway*) *Arthur Edward Gayer*, LL.D., Q.C. (see p. 149); *and had issue 1d to 6d.*

1d. Edmund Alexander Molony, Assist. Commissioner at Benares (*Benares, India*), b. 17 Jan. 1866; *m.* in India, 29 Nov. 1898, Ethel Blanche, da. of Herbert Smith of Barla, Aligarh, U.P., India, *s.p.*

2d. Frederick Arthur Molony, C.E., b. 11 Feb. 1875.

3d. Eleanor Mary Molony, *m.* 2 July 1904, George Whitty Gayer, Central Provinces Police, India, *s.p.*

4d. Lucy Selina Molony.

5d. Alice Helen Molony.

6d. Lilian Edith Molony.

4c. *Frederick Beresford Molony*, H.E.I.C.S., b. 15 *June* 1833; d. 13 *Nov.* 1868; m. 13 *Oct.* 1858, *Eleanor Jane* (*Clare Cottage, West Byfleet, Surrey*), da. of (*Conway*) *Arthur Edward Gayer*, LL.D., Q.C. (see p. 149); *and had issue 1d to 5d.*

1d. Francis Arthur Molony, Major R.E., b. 17 May 1863; *m.* 8 Nov. 1888, Katharine Mary, da. of John Williams Grigg of Tamerton Foliot, co. Devon; and has issue 1e to 4e.

1e. Arthur Williams Molony, b. 4 Oct. 1892.

2e. Edward Frederick Molony, b. 16 Mar. 1899.

3e. Dorothy Katherine Molony.

4e. Margery Eileen Molony.

2d. Rev. Herbert James Molony, D.D., Bishop in Mid-China 1908 (*Ningpo, China*), b. 2 June 1865; *m.* 1st, 17 Sept. 1895, Eva, da. of the Rev. Matthew Anderson, d. at Mandla, C.P., India, 12 Sept. 1897; 2ndly, 6 Aug. 1908, Gertrude Elizabeth, da. of the Rev. Stewart Dixon Stubbs.

3d. Mary Selina Molony, *unm.*

4d. Eleanor Florence Molony, *m.* 1st, 6 July 1892, Horatio Scott, M.D., *d.s.p.* 2 June 1895; 2ndly, 25 Aug. 1906, Francis Mackenzie Ogilvy (*Blackthorns, West Byfleet, Surrey*), *s.p.*

5d. Agnes Freda Molony, *m.* 1 Feb. 1908, Edward Millington Synge (*Clare Cottage, West Byfleet, Surrey*).

5c. *Charles Mills Molony of St. Catherine's Priory, Guildford*, Col. in the Army, C.B., b. 26 *Jan.* 1836; d. 14 *Aug.* 1901; m. 2 Aug. 1866, *Eliza*, da. of *Andrew Hamilton of Streatham*; *and had issue 1d to 3d.*

1d. James Rowland Hamilton Molony, Solicitor (*Shenfield, The Drive, Wimbledon; 28 Lincoln's Inn Fields, W.C.*), b. 28 Ap. 1867; *m.* 12 Jan. 1895, Emma Charlotte, da. of Arthur Wienholt of Fassifern, Queensland; and has issue 1e to 4e.

1e. Trevor James Molony, b. 7 July 1897.

2e. Marcus Vandeleur Molony, b. 18 Dec. 1898.

3e. Rowland Hutton Molony, b. 10 Oct. 1906.

4e. Clare Elizabeth Molony, b. 7 Aug. 1902.

2d. Trevor Charles Wheler Molony, D.S.O., Major R.F.A. (*Shalazan, Bergholt Road, Colchester*), b. 28 July 1868; *m.* 31 Oct. 1899, Beatrice Annie, da. of Major-Gen. W. H. Beynon; and has issue 1e to 4e.

1e. Trevor St. Patrick Molony, b. 6 Sept. 1900.

2e. Charles Beynon Molony, b. 15 Jan. 1906.

3e. Norman Molony, b. 14 Ap. 1907.

4e. Pearl Molony, b. 21 July 1903.

3d. Charles Vandeleur Molony, Capt. *late* West Kent Regt., b. 19 July 1870; *unm.*

6c. *Mary Molony* (*Kiltanon*), m. 3 Jan. 1856, *Arthur Vandeleur*, Major R.A., of *Rathlahine, co. Clare*, b. 27 Ap. 1829; d. 6 June 1860; and has issue 1d to 2d.

[Nos. 16578 to 16604.

# of The Blood Royal

1d. Lucy Vandeleur, m. 1881, Arbuthnot Butler Stoney, LL.D., Bar.-at-Law (*Rathlahine, Newmarket-on-Fergus, co. Clare*); and has issue 1e to 3e.

  1e. James Butler Stoney, b. 30 Jan. 1885.
  2e. Arthur Vandeleur Stoney, b. 8 Nov. 1886.
  3e. Mary Evelyn Stoney.

2d. *Emily Harriet Vandeleur*, d. 27 Nov. 1886; m. *as 1st wife*, 29 Ap. 1884, *Lord George Herbert Loftus, heir-presumptive to the Marquisate of Ely* [I.] *and Barony of Loftus* [U.K.], *&c.* (4 *Alexandra Villas, Brighton*); *and had issue* 1e.

  1e. Anna Mary Kathleen Loftus.

7c. Harriet Selina Molony (9 *Dartmouth Square, Dublin*), m. 28 June 1859, the Ven. Thomas Fitzgerald French, Rector of Castle Connell and Archdeacon of Killaloe, d. 30 Dec. 1884; and has issue 1d to 8d.

  1d. Fitzgerald Charles French, b. 1 May 1861; *unm.*
  2d. Riversdale Sampson French, b. 28 Dec. 1862; m. 6 Aug. 1908, Lilian Elizabeth, da. of Henry Morgan Earbery Crofton of Inchinappa, co. Wicklow, J.P. [Bt. of Mohill Coll.].
  3d. Deane French (*Australia*), b. 28 May 1864; m. Sept. 1903, Emily [da. of (—) Crooke of Coonamble, Australia; and has issue 1e to 2e.
    1e. Thomas FitzGerald French, b. 16 Jan. 1906.
    2e. Isabel Harriet French, b. 2 Aug. 1904.
  4d. Arthur James Pascoe French, b. 3 Oct. 1865; *unm.*
  5d. Raymond William French, b. 11 May 1867; m. 11 Feb. 1903, Sophia Rebecca MacMurrogh, widow (with issue) of Francis Richard Wolfe, da. of Arthur MacMurrogh Murphy of Monamolin, "The O'Morchoe of Oulartleigh"; and has issue 1e to 2e.
    1e. Mary Dring French, b. 3 Aug. 1905.
    2e. Sheela O'Morchoe French, b. 3 Nov. 1907.
  6d. Harry O'Donovan French, b. 12 Ap. 1872; *unm.*
  7d. Lucy Selina French, b. 10 Ap. 1860; *unm.*
  8d. Agnes Melian French, b. 21 Oct. 1868; *unm.*

2b. *Edmund Molony, H.E.I.C.S., Secretary to Government of Bengal*, b. 27 *July* 1794; d. *in India* 1830; m. 27 Oct. 1815, *Frances Rosina, da. of Henry Creighton of Goamalty, East Indies*, b. 9 *Aug.* 1795; d. 7 *Aug.* 1864; *and had issue* 1c to 2c.

1c. *Rev. Charles Arthur Molony, Vicar of St. Lawrence, Ramsgate*, b. 22 *Sept.* 1826; d. 13 *May* 1894; m. 4 *Ap.* 1872, *Mary Emily Jane* (*Winton, Barton Fields, Canterbury*), *da. of Robert Deane Parker, H.E.I.C.S.; and had issue* (*with a son, Francis Robert*, b. 14 *Ap.* 1881; d. 18 *Mar.* 1882) 1d *to* 7d.

  1d. Edmund Parker Molony (*Sault Ste. Marie, Canada*), b. 16 Feb. 1873; m. 19 Aug. 1902, Charlena Jean, da. of Charles Murray Gibson of Ontario; and has issue 1e to 3e.
    1e. Charles Edmund Gibson Molony, b. 17 Nov. 1903.
    2e. James Robert Percy Molony.
    3e. Mary Molony.
  2d. Henry James Creighton Molony, Indian Police, b. 2 July 1876.
  3d. John Charles Molony, C.E., b. 23 June 1877.
  4d. Arthur Deane Molony, Capt. 7th Gurhka Rifles, b. 7 Ap. 1879.
  5d. Percy William Molony, b. 2 Jan. 1883.
  6d. Rosina Mary Molony, m. 10 June 1908, Frank Mainwaring Furley.
  7d. Katharine Grace Molony, *unm.*

2c. *Frances Molony*, b. 10 *Sept.* 1817; d. 5 *Jan.* 1908; m. *as 2nd wife*, 9 *Aug.* 1845, (*Conway*) *Arthur Edward Gayer, LL.D., Q.C.*, b. 6 *July* 1801; d. 12 *Jan.* 1877; *and had issue* 1d *to* 4d.

  1d. Rev. Edmund Richard Gayer, M.A., Vicar of Snitterfield (*Snitterfield* [Nos. 16605 to 16633.

The Plantagenet Roll

Vicarage, Stratford-on-Avon), b. 23 Mar. 1847; m. 7 Aug. 1873, Frances Sophia, da. of the Rev. Thomas D'Oyly Walters; and has issue 1e to 2e.

    1e. Hugh Walters Gayer, late Capt. Royal Garrison Artillery, b. 13 May 1876; m. 16 Nov. 1899, Beatrice Ellen Mary, da. of William Bull of 75 St. Aubyns, Hove; and has issue 1f.

        1f. Eric Hugh Trelawny Gayer, b. 10 Oct. 1900.

    2e. Echlin Philip Gayer, b. 11 Sept. 1877.

    2d. Rev. Arthur Cecil Stopford Gayer, M.A., Vicar of Chart Sutton (*Chart Sutton Vicarage, near Maidstone*), b. 26 Aug. 1856; m. 21 Nov. 1899, Ellen Marian, da. of John Hart Sankey, J.P.; and has issue 1e to 2e.

        1e. Charles Murray Acworth Gayer, b. 27 July 1904.

        2e. Dorothy Mabel Gayer, b. 24 Ap. 1902.

    3d. Lucy Harriette Gayer, *unm.*

    4d. Edith Mary Gayer, *unm.*

    4a. *Frances Mills*, d. (? s.p.) 3 *Mar.* 1795; m. 13 *Dec.* 1793, *the Rev. Thomas Cattell, Rector of Berkeswell, co. Warwick.* [Nos. 16634 to 16641.

73. Descendants, if any, of FRANCIS SOUTH, bapt. 3 Sept. 1639; and of his nephew and nieces, TEMPEST SOUTH, bapt. 25 Nov. 1669; ELIZABETH SOUTH, Maid of Honour to Queen Mary of Modena, bapt. 30 Aug. 1664, wife of LEONARD PINKNEY, Verderer of Sherwood Forest; MARGERY MARIA SOUTH, bapt. 25 Ap 1665; and JANE SOUTH, bapt. 12 Jan. 1671 (Table IX.).

74. Descendants of JANE WHICHCOT (Table IX.), d. 30 Jan. 1812; m. 1762, Sir CHRISTOPHER WHICHCOTE of Aswarby Park, 4th Bt. [E.], bapt. 15 Mar. 1738; d. 9 Mar. 1786; and had issue 1a to 2a.

    1a. *Sir Thomas Whichcote, 5th Bt.* [E.], b. 5 *Mar.* 1763; d. 22 *Sept.* 1828; m. 24 *June* 1785, *Diana* [also descended from Edward III. through Mortimer-Percy (see p. 397)], *da. of Edmund Turnor of Panton and Stoke Rochford, co. Lincoln*, d. 4 *Feb.* 1826; and had issue 1b to 6b.

        1b. *Sir Thomas Whichcote, 6th Bt.* [E.], b. 10 *Aug.* 1791; d. 23 *Aug.* 1829; m. 9 *Ap.* 1812, *Lady Sophia* [a descendant of the Lady Anne, sister to King Edward IV., &c. (see the Exeter Volume, p. 660)], *da. of Philip* (Sherard), *5th Earl of Harborough* [G.B.] [re-m. 2ndly, 23 *Ap.* 1840, *the Hon. William Charles Evans Freke and*] d. 23 *Sept.* 1851; *and had issue* 1c *to* 3c.

            1c. *Sir Thomas Whichcote, 7th Bt.* [E.], b. 23 *May* 1813; d. 17 *Jan.* 1892; m. 2ndly, 25 *Mar.* 1856, *Isabella Elizabeth, da. of Sir Henry Conyngham Montgomery*, 1st Bt. [U.K.], M.P., d. 29 *Aug.* 1892; *and had issue* 1d.

                1d. Isabella Whichcote (*Deeping St. James' Manor, Market Deeping*; 114 *Ashley Gardens, S.W.*), m. 7 Sept. 1875, Brownlow (Cecil), 4th Marquis [U.K.] and 13th Earl [E.] of Exeter [descended from King Henry VII., &c.], d. 9 Ap. 1898; and has issue 1e.

                      1e. William Thomas Brownlow (Cecil), 5th Marquis [U.K.] and 14th Earl [E.] of Exeter, Hereditary Grand Almoner, &c. (*Burghley House, near Stamford;* 114 *Ashley Gardens, S.W.*), b. 27 Oct. 1876; m. 16 Ap. 1901, the Hon. Myra Rowena Sibell [descended from King Henry VII., &c.], da. of William Thomas (Orde-Powlett), 4th Lord Bolton [G.B.]; and has issue 1f to 2f.

                            1f. David George Brownlow Cecil, Lord Burghley, b. 9 Feb. 1905.

                            2f. Lady Letitia Sibell Winifred Cecil. [Nos. 16642 to 16645.

# of The Blood Royal

2c. Sir George Whichcote, 8th Bt. [E.], b. 31 May 1817; d. 14 Ap. 1893; m. 10 Ap. 1866, Louisa Day, da. of Thomas William Clagett of Fetcham; and had issue 1d to 3d.

    1d. Sir George Whichcote, 9th Bt. [E.], J.P., D.L. (*Aswarby Park, Folkingham, Lincoln*), b. 3 Sept. 1870.

    2d. Hugh Christopher Whichcote, b. 18 Ap. 1874.

    3d. Louisa Mary Whichcote (*Brooklyn House, Towcester*).

3c. Sophia Whichcote, d. 1 Aug. 1868; m. 9 Jan. 1840, the Rev. Algernon Turnor (see p. 392), d. Aug. 1842.

2b. Diana Whichcote, d. 2 May 1853; m. 1st, 11 Ap. 1810, Herman Gerhard Hilbers, b. at Colmax, Oldenburg, 9 May 1777; d. 24 Dec. 1822; 2ndly, as 1st wife, 24 Feb. 1829, the Rev. George Hambleton of Wallingford (who m. 2ndly and had 2 das.); and had issue (with 3 elder sons and 2 das. who d. unm.) 1c to 2c.

    1c. George James Hilbers of Brighton, Consulting Physician, b. 16 June 1818; d. 30 Oct. 1883; m. 1842, Louisa Susannah, da. of Robert Bates Mathews, R.N., d. 7 Ap. 1906, aged 87; and had issue (with a son and 2 das. who d. in infancy) 1d to 10d.

        1d. Rev. George Christopher Hilbers, M.A. (Exeter Coll., Oxon.), Rector of St. Thomas', Haverfordwest, *formerly* Archdeacon of St. David's (*St. Thomas' Rectory, Haverfordwest*), b. 24 Jan. 1844; m. 14 Oct. 1875, Maria Frances Knowles, da. of the Rev. John Posthumous Parkinson, *formerly* Wilson, of Ravendale Hall, D.C.L., F.S.A.

        2d. William Hilbers, Engineer (*Kaiapoi, Heene Road, West Worthing*), b. 16 July 1847; m. 5 June 1883, Alice Maria, da. of Peter Stevens of Lympsham, co. Somerset.

        3d. Herman Gerhard Hilbers, M.D., B.A. (St. John's, Camb.) (49 *Montpelier Road, Brighton*), b. 30 Sept. 1854; m. 19 Aug. 1886, Grace, da. of H. Mathias of Haverfordwest, J.P.

        4d. Diana Frances Turnor Hilbers.

        5d. Louisa Hilbers.

        6d. Frances Henrietta Hilbers, m. 12 Oct. 1891, the Rev. Daniel Davies (*Ystradyfodwg, Pentre, Rhondda, Glam.*).

        7d. Emily Hilbers, m. as 2nd wife, 12 June 1888, James Balleny Elkington, J.P., co. Carmarthen (*East Lodge, Leatherhead*).

        8d. Marian Hilbers, m. 10 Aug. 1880, Lindsay Stevenson Gresley Young (*East Lodge, Leatherhead*); and has issue 1e to 8e.

            1e. Lindsay Loraine Young, b. 12 Feb. 1883.

            2e. Ronald Hilbers Young, b. 11 Feb. 1885,

            3e. Nigel Bellairs Young, b. 4 Jan. 1887,

            4e. Cranstoun Ridout Young, b. 11 Mar. 1890,   *unm.*

            5e. Eric Herbert Young, b. 2 Dec. 1891,

            6e. Kathleen Marian Young,

            7e. Elsie Helen Young,

            8e. Eileen Violet Young,

        9d. Edith Agnes Hilbers, m. 23 June 1885, Herbert John Pulling, M.R.C.S., L.R.C.P. [son of the Rev. Preb. Pulling of Eastnor, Ledbury] (11 *Old Steine, Brighton*); and has issue 1e to 2e.

            1e. John Bernard Pulling, B.A. (Christ's Coll., Camb.); entered St. Bartholomew's Hospital Oct. 1907; b. 13 Sept. 1887.

            2e. Virginia Edith Pulling, B.A., London.

        10d. Alice Mary Hilbers.

2c. Margaret Sophia Hilbers, d. 1896; m. as 2nd wife, the Rev. Frederick Tryon of Bulwick, d. 1903; and had issue 1d to 3d.

    1d. Manasseh Tryon, b. (—); m. and has issue several children.

[Nos. 16646 to 16669.

The Plantagenet Roll

2d. Stephen Tryon (*Hallen Lodge, Henbury, near Bristol*), b. (—); m. and has 6 children.

3d. John Tryon (*Down Hall, Epsom*), b. (—); m. and has issue 3 children.

3b. Henrietta Whichcote, d. 30 May 1810; m. *as 1st wife*, 28 Nov. 1807, James Atty *of Pinchbeck, co. Lincoln*, d. 17 Oct. 1815; *and had issue* 1c.

1c. James Atty *of Rugby, co. Warwick, and Pinchbeck, co. Lincoln*, J.P., D.L., Major Warwickshire Mil., *previously* 52nd Regt., b. 12 Ap. 1810; d. 14 July 1877; m. 31 May 1831, Catharine Adeline, da. *of Adlard Welby of North Rauceby, co. Linc.*, d. 22 Oct. 1889; *and had issue* (with others d.s.p.) 1d to 5d.

1d. Edward Arthur Atty *of Pinchbeck*, b. 16 Mar. 1847; d. 12 Oct. 1882; m. Florence Laura, da. *of* (—) *Kelson*; *and had issue* 1e to 4e.

1e. James Edward Atty, b. 27 Jan. 1869.

2e. Grace Catherine Atty.

3e. Florence Atty.

4e. Edith Marion Atty.

2d. Robert Atty, b. 19 May 1849; m. 21 Ap. 1870, Gertrude, da. of the Rev. Ollivier Etough; and has issue 1e to 3e.

1e. Welby Atty, b. 1 Ap. 1872; m. Aug. 1902, Freda, da. of William Brown; and has issue 1f to 2f.

1f. William James Welby Atty, b. Mar. 1905.

2f. Daphne Freda Atty, b. 8 Feb. 1904.

2e. *Gertrude Atty*, d. 6 Ap. 1909; m. 22 May 1902, *Archibald Vaughan Campbell-Lambert* (*Foxearth Hall, and Lyston Hall, Essex*); *and had issue* 1f to 2f.

1f. John Vaughan Campbell-Lambert, b. Nov. 1905.

2f. Gertrude Eleanor Kathleen Campbell-Lambert, b. 18 Sept. 1903.

3e. Eleanor Atty.

3d. Adeline Atty (*Cavendish Hall, Suffolk*), m. 1st, *as 2nd wife*, 1 Feb. 1860, James Malcolm of Freelands, co. Oxford [Bt. (1665) Coll.], d. 16 July 1878; 2ndly, *as 2nd wife*, 19 Nov. 1885, John Ramsey L'Amy of Dunkenny, d. 26 Mar. 1892; and has issue 1e to 2e.

1e. Sir James William Malcolm of Innertiel, 9th Bt. [S. 1665], J.P., *formerly* Capt. Royal Pembroke Artillery Mil. (*Tostock Place, Suffolk*), b. 29 Mar. 1862; m. 14 Nov. 1885, Evelyn Alberta, da. of Albert George Sandeman of Presdales, co. Herts [by his wife, Donna Maria Carlota Perpetua, da. of Pedro Jose (de Moraes-Sarmento), 2nd Viscount da Torre de Moncorvo [Portugal, 1835], Ambassador to the Court of St. James']; and has issue 1f to 4f.

1f. Michael Albert James Malcolm, b. 9 May 1898.

2f. Alexander Ernest William Malcolm, b. 4 Oct. 1900.

3f. Elspeth Mary Isabel Malcolm, b. 12 June 1899.

4f. Griselda Helen Adeline Malcolm, b. 10 July 1903.

2e. Charles Edward Malcolm, *late* Lieut. Scots Guards (*White's*), b. 2 Dec. 1865; m. 28 Dec. 1894, the Hon. Beatrix Mary Leslie, previously wife of Charles Lindsay Orr Ewing, M.P., da. of William James (Hove-Ruthven), 8th Lord Ruthven [S.]; and has issue 1f to 3f.

1f. Arthur William Alexander Malcolm, b. 1 June 1903.

2f. Honoria Adeline Malcolm.

3f. Beltine Violet Malcolm.

4d. Harriet Atty, m. 4 Jan. 1860, Capt. William Alexander Kerr, V.C., Mahratta Horse, *s.p.*

5d. Georgina Atty.

4b. Caroline Whichcote, d. 1844; m. 4 May 1814, *Francis Willes of Row Green, co. Herts*; *and had issue* (with a son, *Francis, who* d.s.p.) 1c.

1c. Margaret Sophia Willes, m. 27 Ap. 1846, William Alexander Mackinnon of Acryse Park, and Belvedere, co. Kent., Chief of his Clan, F.R.S., D.L., High Sheriff for that co. 1885, and M.P. Ryde 1852-3 and Lymington 1857-68, d. 14 Sept. 1903; and has issue 1d to 4d.

[Nos. 16670 to 16695

of The Blood Royal

1d. Francis Alexander Mackinnon of Acryse, Chief of his Clan, J.P., D.L., *late* Capt. and Hon. Major East Kent Yeo. (*Acryse Park, near Folkestone; Belvedere, near Broadstairs*), b. 9 Ap. 1848; m. 19 Ap. 1888, the Hon. Emily Isabel, da. and co-h. of Arthur William Acland (Hood), 1st and only Baron Hood of Avalon [U.K.], G.C.B.; and has issue 1e to 3e.

    1e. Alexander Hood Mackinnon, Younger of Mackinnon, b. 8 Jan. 1892.

    2e. Arthur Avalon Mackinnon, b. 8 Nov. 1893.

    3e. Aline Emily Hood Mackinnon.

2d. Sir William Henry Mackinnon, K.C.B., C.V.O., Lieut.-Gen. and Director-Gen. of Territorial Army at Headquarters, Vice-Chairman of Territorial Force Advisory Council, *formerly* Comdg. Imp. Yeo. at Aldershot 1901-4, in South Africa 1899-1900, &c. &c. (15 *Ovington Square, S.W.; Guards', &c.*), b. 15 Dec. 1852; m. 14 Dec. 1881, Madeleine Frances, da. of Lt.-Col. Villiers La Touche Hatton of Clonard, *late* Grenadier Guards; and has issue 1e.

    1e. Nora Fynvola Mackinnon, m. 9 Jan. 1905, Capt. Arthur George Edward Egerton, Coldstream Guards [descended from King Henry VII., &c.], s.p.

3d. Caroline Emma Mackinnon.

4d. Sophia Louisa Mackinnon.

5b. *Catherine Whichcote*, d. 27 *June* 1860; m. 19 *Sept.* 1816, *the Rev. John Hanmer* [*Baronet* (1774) *Coll.*], d. 4 *Oct.* 1850; *and had issue* 1c *to* 5c.

1c. Francis Henry Hanmer, Col. Indian Army, b. 20 Oct. 1825; d. 2 Feb. 1876; m. 16 Oct. 1860, *Mary Ann Catharine, da. of Charles Gordon of Edintore, co. Banff, and Greshop, co. Moray*, d. 9 *June* 1879; *and had issue* 1d *to* 2d.

1d. Norman Gordon Whichcote Hanmer (*Fendalton, Christ Church, N.Z.*), b. 3 Aug. 1863; *unm.*

2d. Flora Emmeline Mary Hanmer, m. 23 Aug. 1887, Charles Thomas Gordon of Cairness (*Cairness, Aberdeen*); and has issue 1e to 4e.

    1e. John Charles Hanmer Gordon, b. 28 Nov. 1893.

    2e. Francis Walden Gordon, b. 10 Oct. 1895.

    3e. Stella Mary Gordon.

    4e. Marjorie Violet Gordon.

2c. *Humphrey Hanmer*, b. 20 *July* 1827; d. 24 *Dec.* 1892; m. 21 *Oct.* 1856, *Harriet, da. of George Battarbee of Chorlton Hall, co. Cheshire; and had issue* 1d *to* 2d.

1d. George Hanmer (*Tilford Ferry Road, Christchurch, New Zealand*), b. 11 Jan. 1859; m. 12 May 1885, Ruth, da. of C. Percy Cox; and has issue 1e to 6e

    1e. Humphrey George Hanmer, b. 6 Ap. 1886.

    2e. John Percy Hanmer, b. 7 July 1889.

    3e. Anthony Hugh Hanmer, b. 18 Sept. 1890.

    4e. Dorothy Harriet Hanmer, b. 28 Jan. 1888.

    5e. Madeline Ruth Hanmer, b. 18 Sept. 1890.

    6e. Municent Clara Hanmer, b. 22 Dec. 1891.

2d. Catherine Hanmer (96 *Castle Road, Bedford*), m. 19 Nov. 1885, Edward Wingfield Hanmer, d. 28 Feb. 1901; and has issue 1e to 4e.

    1e. Edward Henry John Hanmer, b. 27 Nov. 1888.

    2e. Humphrey Richard Hanmer, b. 24 Nov. 1890.

    3e. Evelyn Mary Harriet Hanmer, b. 7 Feb. 1887.

    4e. Florence Catherine Alicia Hanmer, b. 9 Dec. 1895.

3c. *George Hanmer*, b. 4 *Sept.* 1833; d. 16 *Feb.* 1906; m. 13 *July* 1871, *Margaret Eliza* (*Stone Cross House, Crowborough, Sussex*), *da. of the Rev. William Spencer Edwards of Lewes; and had issue* 1d.

1d. Thomas Anthony Hanmer, Resident Magistrate (*Mombasa*), b. 17 Ap. 1872.

4c. *Sophia Hanmer*, d. 1 *Ap.* 1882; m. 1839, *John Lees Ainsworth of Barkside, co. Lanc.; and had issue* (2 *sons and* 3 *das., of whom only* 2 *das. now survive*).

[Nos. 16696 to 16722.

The Plantagenet Roll

5c. *Catherine Hanmer*, d. 1845; m. *James Holmes;* and had issue (a son).
6b. *Louisa Whichcote*, d. 28 Aug. 1889; m. 30 Ap. 1829, *the Rev. C. C. Wheat;* and had issue.
2a. *Frances Whichcote*, d. (–); m. *William Manners.*

75. Descendants of FRANCES WHICHCOT (Table IX.), *bapt.* at Scotton 23 May 1733; *d.* 25 Ap. 1811; *m.* at Harpswell 23 June 1761, WILLIAM HILDYARD of Grimsby, *d.* 2 Dec. 1781; and had issue 1*a* to 4*a*.

1a. *Rev. William Hildyard, Rector of Winestead, co. Yorks,* b. 6 July 1762; d. 25 Feb. 1842; m. 12 Dec. 1793, *Catharine, da. of Isle Grant of Ruckland, co. Linc.,* d. 6 May 1855; *and had issue* 1b *to* 4b.
1b. *Rev. Frederic Hildyard, Rector of Swanington, co. Norfolk,* b. 8 May 1803; d. 4 Nov. 1891; m. 9 July 1840, *Letitia, da. of John Shore of Guildford Street, London,* d. 8 Oct. 1896; *and had issue* 1c *to* 3c.
1c. *Rev. William Hildyard, Rector of St. Patrick Elenthera, Bahamas,* b. *at Swanington, Norfolk,* 19 Jan. 1844; d. *at Nassau, Bahamas,* 19 June 1873; m. c. 1870, *Harriet, da. of* (—) *Wade,* d. Oct. 1896; *and had issue* 1d.
1d. Mary Hildyard, *m.* 26 July 1905, the Rev. Aubrey Rothwell Hay Johnson, Rector of North Wootton (*North Wootton Rectory, King's Lynn*); and has issue 1e to 3e.
1e. Christopher Hildyard Johnson, *b.* 10 July 1910.
2e. Mary Hildyard Johnson, *b.* 19 May 1907.
3e. Elizabeth Dorothea Johnson, *b.* 18 Jan. 1909:
2c. Jessie Ellen Hildyard, *m.* 27 Nov. 1862, the Hon. Robert Henley Shaw Eden, J.P. [B. Auckland Coll.] (*Tyddynllan, Llandrillo, Merioneth*); *and has issue.* See the Essex Volume, p. 361, Nos. 35503–35519.
3c. Kate Hildyard, *m.* 5 Mar. 1867, Robert Arthur Barkley, *d.* 22 Ap. 1910 (*Palgrave Priory, Diss*); and has issue 1d to 4d.
1d. George Hildyard Barkley, *b.* 29 Mar. 1873.
2d. Frederic Hildyard Barkley, *b.* 30 Aug. 1879.
3d. Lettice Kate Barkley, *unm.*
4d. Hilda Barkley, *m.* 16 Oct. 1899, Ernest Barkley Raikes, Bar.-at-Law (*Bombay*); and has issue 1e to 4e.
1e. Thomas Barkley Raikes, *b.* 16 Dec. 1902.
2e. Robert Barkley Raikes, *b.* 2 Mar. 1904.
3e. Ruth Martha Barkley Raikes, *b.* 26 Aug. 1900.
4e. Elizabeth Barkley Raikes, *b.* 17 Jan. 1907.
2b. *Rev. Horatio Samuel Hildyard, Rector of Lofthouse, in Cleveland,* b. 17 Oct. 1805; d. 10 Ap. 1886; m. 12 June 1861, *Octavia* (55 *Upperton Gardens, Eastbourne*), *da. of William Richardson of York; and had issue* 1c *to* 5c.
1c. Horatio Nelson Hildyard, *b.* 11 May 1862; *d.* 30 July 1900; *m.* 21 Aug. 1890, *Maud Lewis, da. of Major Jackson; and had issue* 1d.
1d. Katharine Hildyard, *b.* 16 July 1891.
2c. Henry Hildyard (*Hebron, Yarmouth, Nova Scotia*), *b.* 27 Feb. 1868; *m.* 4 Oct. 1889, Maggie, da. of (—) Davis; and has issue 1d to 5d.
1d. Robert Hildyard, *b.* 16 July 1900.
2d. Christopher George Hildyard, *b.* 12 July 1902.
3d. Frances Hildyard, *b.* 15 Sept. 1891.
4d. Pearl Hildyard, *b.* 25 Ap. 1898.
5d. Joan Hildyard, *b.* 13 Dec. 1904.
3c. Mary Louisa Hildyard, *unm.*
4c. Octavia Hildyard, *unm.*
5c. Elizabeth Frances Hildyard, *unm.*

[Nos. 16723 to 16763.

of The Blood Royal

3b. Rev. James Hildyard, B.D., Rector of Ingoldsby, co. Linc., b. 11 Ap. 1809; d. 27 Aug. 1887; m. 19 Aug. 1847, Elizabeth Matilda, da. of George Kinderley, d. 18 Ap. 1894; and had issue 1c to 2c.

 1c. Nora Catherine Hildyard, m. 11 Oct. 1877, Col. William Henry Vallack-Tom (Cawsand, Cornwall), s.p.

 2c. Evelyn Matilda Hildyard, unm.

4b. Rev. Alexander Grant Hildyard, Vicar of Madingley, co. Camb., b. 27 Aug. 1812; d. 5 Ap. 1885; m. 12 June 1851, Mary Ann (see p. 156), da. of George Hildyard of Hale End, co. Essex, d. 2 Dec. 1903; and had issue 1c to 3c.

 1c. George Grant Hildyard (Market Deeping, Lincoln), b. 4 Mar. 1853; unm.

 2c. Robert Loxham Hildyard (27 Avenue Macmahon, Paris), b. 26 May 1855; m. 1st, 30 Ap. 1890, Mary Dalrymple, da. of the Rev. George Shand, Rector of Heydon, d. 25 Sept. 1891; 2ndly, in Paris 17 Aug. 1907, Marie Alexandrine, da. of Eugene Loth of Reims; and has issue 1d to 2d.

  1d. Peter Georges D'Eyncourt Hildyard, b. 4 Mar. 1910.

  2d. Catharine Cecilia Hildyard, b. 3 Ap. 1891.

 3c. Frederic William Hildyard (77A Lexham Gardens, South Kensington), b. 6 Oct. 1863; m. 5 July 1898, Elizabeth Cecilia, da. of Hugh Wade-Gery, s.p.

2a. Rev. John Hildyard, Vicar of Bonby, co. Lincoln, b. 7 July 1763; d. 13 Nov. 1827; m. 25 Sept. 1787, Mary, da. of Isle Grant of Ruckland, co. Lincoln, d. 17 Ap. 1849; and had issue 1b to 3b.

1b. Rev. William Hildyard, Rector of Hameringham-cum-Scrayfield, co. Linc., b. 26 Dec. 1790; d. 17 Mar. 1872; m. 8 Jan. 1818, Mary, da. of the Rev. William Hett, Canon of Lincoln, d. 28 Jan. 1853; and had issue 1c to 2c.

 1c. Rev. Charles Frederic Hildyard of Bury, co. Lancs., b. 16 July 1823; d. 13 Jan. 1906; m. 23 June 1857, Louisa Eliza, da. of J. W. Hamilton, d. 11 Dec. 1886; and had issue 1d to 7d.

  1d. Rev. William Hildyard (Wickmere Rectory, Norwich), b. 9 May 1858; m. 17 Ap. 1894, Ida Jane, da. of Henry Lemon; and has issue 1e to 3e.

   1e. Brian Rider Hildyard, b. 17 Feb. 1895.

   2e. Denis Leslie Hildyard, b. 24 Jan. 1901.

   3e. Jean Hyacinth Hildyard, b. 17 Feb. 1895.

  2d. Francis Edward Hildyard (York Place, Ashton-under-Lyne), b. 31 Aug. 1859.

  3d. Rev. Lyonel D'Arcy Hildyard (Rowley Rectory, Little Weighton, Hull), b. 5 Feb. 1861; m. 8 Aug. 1895, Dora Annie Florence Thoroton (see p. 309), da. of Capt. Robert Charles Thoroton Hildyard, R.E.; and has issue 1e to 2e.

   1e. Christopher Hildyard, b. 28 Ap. 1901.

   2e. Noel Florence Dora Hildyard, b. 22 Dec. 1896.

  4d. Cecil George Ormerod Hildyard, b. 7 Ap. 1865.

  5d. Lucy Viola Margaret Hildyard (7 Hill House Road, Norwich), b. 3 Ap. 1867.

  6d. Louisa Rosalind Hildyard, b. 29 Mar. 1869.

  7d. Lilias Mary Hildyard, b. 29 Mar. 1869.

 2c. Sophia Elizabeth Rose Hildyard, d. 19 Mar. 1910; m. as 2nd wife, 15 June 1865, the Rev. Charles Richmond Tate, Vicar of Send and Ripley, co. Surrey, afterwards Rector of Trent, co. Som., Fellow of Corpus Christi Coll., Oxon., d. 1 Aug. 1895; and had issue 1d to 4d.

  1d. Harry Russell Tate (Kyambu, Nairobi, B. East Africa), b. 1 Sept. 1870; m. 28 Dec. 1907, Eveline Syndercombe, da. of Henry Syndercombe Bower of Fontmell Parva, co. Dorset, J.P.

  2d. Joseph George Tate (West Marton, Skipton, Yorks), b. 19 Ap. 1875; unm.

  3d. Sophia Hildyard Tate, m. 30 Aug. 1894, Evelyn Arthur Hellicar [son of the Rev. Arthur Gresley Hellicar, Rector of Bromley, Kent] (Hildegarde, Bickley, Kent); and has issue 1e.

   1e. Mary Gresley Hellicar, b. 31 Dec. 1896. [Nos. 16764 to 16786.

The Plantagenet Roll

4d. Lucy Hett Tate (*Detroit, Michigan*), m. 2 Aug. 1889, James Talboys Barratt, d. Sept. 1901 ; and has issue 1e to 3e.

1e. Charles Frederick Talboys Barratt, b. 2 Nov. 1892.
2e. Nina Catharine Barratt, b. 25 May 1890.
3e. Lucy Barratt, b. 7 July 1894.

2b. *George Hildyard of Hale End, co. Essex*, b. 4 *June* 1798 ; d. 28 *May* 1872 ; m. *at Walthamstow Parish Church*, 13 *Sept.* 1823, *Jane, da. and event. sole h. of Robert Loxham of Hale End*, d. 10 *Sept.* 1871 ; *and had issue* 1c.

1c. Mary Ann Hildyard, b. 29 Mar. 1826 ; d. 2 Dec. 1893 ; m. 12 June 1851, the Rev. Alexander Grant Hildyard, Curate of Easton, near Stamford, d. 5 Ap. 1885 ; and had issue.

See p. 155, Nos. 16765–16769.

3b. *Mary Ann Hildyard*, b. 30 *Mar.* 1803 ; d. *June* 1884 ; m. 19 *Oct.* 1832, *George Murray of Rosemount, co. Ross ; and had issue* 1c *to* 4c.

1c. *William John Murray, afterwards* (R.L. 30 *May* 1882) *Bankes, of Rosemount*, b. 19 *May* 1835 ; d. 17 *July* 1884 ; m. 19 *Dec.* 1861, *Eleanor Slarkie Letterewe* [*descended from George, Duke of Clarence, K.G.* (see Clarence Volume, p. 163)] (*Winstanley Hall, Wigan*), *da. of Meyrick Bankes of Winstanley ; and had issue.*

See the Clarence Volume, p. 164, Nos. 2600–2608.

2c. *Hugh Hildyard Murray*, b. 24 *June* 1838 ; d. 13 *Sept.* 1896 ; m. 16 *Feb.* 1866, *Frances Jane, da. of Herbert Park Marshall ; and had issue* 1d *to* 3d.

1d. Jessie Margaret Murray, M.B., *unm.* (14 *Endsleigh Street, Tavistock Square, W.C.*).

2d. Mary Ethel Murray, *unm.*

3d. Edith May Murray, *unm.*

3c. Caroline Georgiana Murray, m. 1st, Robert Blair of Blacksales, co. Ayr, d. (−) ; 2ndly, Frederick Torquato Portal-Turner, *d.s.p.* Jan. 1910 ; and has issue 1d to 5d.

1d. George Blair.
2d. Frederick Blair.
3d. Alice Maud Mary Blair (*Lismore, Letchworth, Hitchin*), *unm.*
4d. Frances Blair, *unm.*
5d. Hilda Caroline Hildyard Blair, m. 26 Oct. 1891, Frederick Thomas Verschoyle of Castle Troy, J.P., Capt. *late* 2nd Brig. South Irish Div. R.A. (*Castle Troy, co. Limerick*); and has issue 1e to 3e.

1e. Frederick Hildyard Hawkins Stuart Verschoyle, b. 21 Nov. 1894.
2e. Hilda Caroline Gwendoline Verschoyle.
3e. Moira Hamilton Verschoyle.

4c. *Frances Isabella Murray*, b. 1 *Ap.* 1841 ; d. *at Government House, Bermuda*, 14 *May* 1900 ; m. *as* 1st *wife*, 11 *June* 1862, *Gen. Sir George Digby Barker, K.C.B., J.P.* [*descended from George* (*Plantagenet*), *Duke of Clarence, K.G.*] (*Clare Priory, Clare, R.S.O., Suffolk*); *and has issue.*

See the Essex Volume, Clarence Supplement, p. 553, Nos. 21679/53–62.

3a. *Frances Hildyard*, b. 8 *Dec.* 1764 ; d. (−) ; m. *the Rev. William Thorold of Weelsby House, co. Lincoln*, d. (−) ; *and had issue* 1b *to* 4b.

1b. *Frances Charlotte Thorold*, d. (−) ; m. 29 *May* 1803, *Robert Mansel, Adm. R.N. ; and had* (*with other*) *issue* 1c.

1c. *Maria Antonia Mansel*, d. (−) ; m. *Henry Thorold of Cuxwold, co. Linc.*, d. 1871 ; *and had issue* (*with a son, Henry, killed in the Crimea*) 1d *to* 4d.

1d. William Thorold of Cuxwold Hall, Lord of the Manor and Patron of the Living, d.s.p.

2d. Richard Thorold of Cuxwold Hall, Lord of the Manor and Patron of the Living, sometime 10th Hussars, b. 1843 ; d.s.p. 1905 ; m. 1885, Alice Hamilton

[Nos. 16787 to 16826.

# of The Blood Royal

(18 *John Street, Berkeley Square, W.*), *widow of Edward S. Potter of Fullwood, co. Glos., da. of the Rev. E. Creek, Vicar of Swanmore, co. Hants.*

3d. Frederick Henry Thorold.

4d. *Mary Sophia Thorold,* b. May 1836; d. 2 Feb. 1889; m. *as 2nd wife,* 6 Ap. 1856, *Richard Christopher Naylor of Hooton Hall, co. Cheshire,* d. 30 Nov. 1899; *and had issue* 1e *to* 2e.

1e. Mittie Naylor, *m.* 14 June 1882, Derrick Warner William (Westenra), 5th [I.] and 4th [U.K.] Baron Rossmore (*Rossmore Park, Camla Vale, co. Monaghan*); and has issue 1f to 3f.

1f. Hon. William Westenra, b. 12 July 1892.

2f. Hon. Richard Westenra, b. 15 Oct. 1893.

3f. Hon. Mary Westenra, b. 1 Dec. 1890.

2e. Mary Naylor.

2b. *Sophia Thorold,* d. (–); m. *Edward Barker of Blackrook, co. Monmouth.*

3b. *Helen Thorold,* d. 1865; m. *Alexander Grant, Solicitor for Scottish Appeals,* d. 1852; *and had issue* 1c *to* 4c.

1c. *Alexander William Thorold Grant, now* (R.L. 8 Nov. 1864) *Grant-Thorold, of Weelsby House, co. Lincoln, J.P., D.L., High Sheriff co. Lincoln* 1870, b. 29 Feb. 1820; d. 1 Feb. 1908; m. 23 *July* 1863, *Anna Hamilton, da. of Adm. Sir James Stirling,* d. 13 Oct. 1899; *and had issue* 1d *to* 3d.

1d. *Richard Stirling Grant-Thorold (Craigallochie, B.C.; 3 Grosvenor Gardens, W.),* b. 9 Aug. 1868.

2d. Hilda Grant-Thorold, *m.* 12 Oct. 1886, Lieut.-Col. Augustus Campbell Spencer, *late* 5th Lancers and 1st Dragoon Guards [D. of Marlborough [E.] and B. Churchill [U.K.] Coll., and a descendant of King Henry VII. (see the Tudor Roll, p. 338)] (*Lascombe, Puttenham, Surrey*); and has issue 1e to 2e.

1e. Richard Augustus Spencer, Lieut. R.F.A., b. 14 Dec. 1888.

2e. Edward Almeric Spencer, b. 26 Dec. 1892.

3d. Constance Mary Grant-Thorold, *m.* 17 Dec. 1904, Richard Joshua Cooper, C.V.O., Lieut.-Col. Irish Guards (3 *Grosvenor Gardens, S.W*).

2c. Frederick Augustus Grant, b. (—); *m.* Katharine Arabella, da. of (—) Clay; and has (with other) issue 1d.

1d. James Erskine Grant.

3c. Helen Grant, *m.* Charles Ridley Hinds.

4c. Katharine Grant, *m.* Frederick Edward Hillersdon.

4b. *Harriet Thorold,* d. (–); m. *the Rev. Joseph Gedge, Rector of Bilderton, co. Suffolk.*

4a. *Jane Hildyard,* b. 27 Feb. 1767; d. (–); m. *as 2nd wife at Louth,* 27 Feb. 1792, *Thomas Marris of Barton-on-Humber, Banker,* d. *at Leicester* 1843; *and had issue* (*with* 2 *sons and a da.* d. *young*) 1b *to* 8b.

1b. Thomas Marris, b. 3 Ap. 1793; d. *unm.*

2b. *John Marris,* b. 12 Sept. 1795; d. *at Plymouth.*

3b. *William Marris, Physician in London,* b. 26 Aug. 1797.

4b. *Henry Marris,* b. 5 Dec. 1801; d. *in '80s*; m. *and had issue* 1c.

1c. *William Henry Marris of Leicester, Auctioneer,* d. *after* 1890; m. *and had issue* 1d.

1d. W. H. Marris, *formerly* of Kibworth, co. Leicester, M.D.

5b. *Robert Marris,* b. 27 *June* 1805; d. *c.* 1880; m. *and had issue* 1c *to* 3c.

1c. *Samuel Arthur Marris,* b. 5 Sept. 1842; d. 10 Ap. 1906; m. 29 *May* 1865, *Emma, da. of Charles Bream of Leicester,* d. 30 Oct. 1908; *and had issue* 1d *to* 3d.

1d. Edward Hildyard Marris (1 *Douglas House, Maida Hill, W.*), b. 10 Dec. 1873; *m.* 18 Dec. 1897, Ethel Mary, da. of James Ward of Dublin; and has issue 1e to 2e.

1e. Edward Hildyard Marris, b. 24 Jan. 1906.

2e. Marjory Iris Marris, b. 21 May 1899.   [Nos. 16827 to 16845.

The Plantagenet Roll

2d. Reginald Willows Marris (*Rangoon, Burmah*), b. 12 June 1887; *unm.*

3d. Ethel Elfie Marris, m. 29 Aug. 1908, Percy Alexander Shelley (63 *Magdalen Road, Wandsworth Common, S.W.*).

2c. William Charles Marris, Accountant and Auditor (18 *New Street, Leicester*), b. (—); m. (—), da. of (—); and has issue 1d to 7d.

1d. Robert William Marris, b. 7 Jan. 1876; m. 17 Ap. 1909, Hilda, da. of John Cheater; and has issue 1e.

1e. Horace William Marris, b. (—).

2d. Lionel Percy Marris, b. 24 Dec. 1877; m. 14 Dec. 1902, Edith Emily, da. of John Loach; and has issue 1e to 3e.

1e. Nellie Loach Marris, b. 28 July 1903.

2e. Dorothy Selina Marris, b. 21 May 1906.

3e. Edith Loach Marris, b. 26 May 1909.

3d. Henry Edward Marris, Grocer and Confectioner (27 *Jermyn Street, Leicester*), b. 1 Dec. 1879; m. 25 Ap. 1905, Jeannie Steven, da. of James Agnew; and has issue 1e to 3e.

1e. William James Marris, b. 6 Nov. 1905.

2e. Henry Edward Marris, b. 13 Nov. 1906.

3e. Jenny Agnes Marris, b. 22 May 1908.

4d. Edith Wright Marris, m. 29 Sept. 1898, Percy Haslehurst Adams; and has issue (with a da. d. young) 1e.

1e. Francis William Adams, b. 24 Mar. 1901.

5d. Harriet Agnes Marris, *unm.*

6d. Fanny Helen Marris, m. 4 June 1908, George Stonson Slater; *s p*

7d. Dorothy Margaret Marris, *unm.*

3c. *Fanny Helen Marris*, d. (? *unm.*) 1898.

6b. George Hildyard Marris, Farmer in Lincoln, b. 16 Mar. 1808; d. (—); m. and had large family.

7b. *Jane Marris*, b. 26 Nov. 1799.

8b. *Helen Marris*, b. 29 Sept. 1806.   [Nos. 16846 to 16863.

76. Descendants of FRANCES WHICHCOTE (Table IX.), d. 31 Mar. 1720; m. JAMES NELTHORPE of Little Grimsby, co. Lincoln, *bapt.* 14 Mar. 1670; d. (will dated 23 May 1755, proved 29 Ap.) 1756; and had issue 1a to 3a.

1a. Rev. Charles Nelthorpe, Rector of Broughton, d. (—); m. *Eleanor, da. of Nathaniel Maddison of Alvingham*, bapt. 12 Feb. 1691; bur. 26 Oct. 1770; and had issue 1b.

1b. Eleanor Nelthorpe, d. (—); m. *William Hollingworth*.

2a. Richard Nelthorpe, living 1740.[1]

3a. Griffith Nelthorpe of Little Grimsby, d. (will dated 10 Sept. 1740, *proved* 10 Oct.) 1755; m. *Mary, da. and co-h. of John Nelthorpe of Bigby,* d. (—); and had issue 1b to 2b.

1b. John Nelthorpe of Little Grimsby Hall, co. Linc., d. (—); m. *Mary, da. of Robert Cracroft of Hackthorn,* d. (—); *and had issue* 1c.

1c. *Mary Jonetta Nelthorpe*, d. 17 Jan. 1822; m. as 2nd *wife*, 4 Mar. 1799, William (Beauclerk), 8th Duke of St. Albans [E.] [*a descendant of the Lady Isabel Plantagenet*], d. 17 July 1825; *and had issue.*

See the Essex Volume, pp. 175–179, Nos. 23663–23795.

[Nos. 16864 to 16996.

---

[1] Maddison's "Lincolnshire Pedigrees," ii. 620; Harl. Soc. Pub.

# of The Blood Royal

2b. *Elizabeth Nelthorpe*, b. c. 1748; bur. 23 *July* 1801; m. 10 *May* 1768, *John Maddison of Alvingham, co. Linc., and Gainsborough, High Sheriff co. Linc.* 1779, bapt. 25 *Oct.* 1718; bur. 13 *July* 1785; *and had issue*[1] 1c *to* 3c.

1c. *John Maddison of Gainsborough and Alvingham*, bapt. 4 *Feb.* 1770; d. 4 *Jan.* 1838; m. 25 *Mar.* 1795, *Elizabeth, da. of John Andrews of Alford*, d. (−); *and had issue* 1d *to* 3d.

1d. *John Maddison*, bapt. 25 *Mar.* 1802; d. *at Ackworth, co. York* ; m. 25 *Aug.* 1824, *Georgiana, da. of Thomas Curtis of Bath*, d. *Mar.* 1871 ; *and had issue* 1e.

1e. *Katharine Mary Maddison*, b. 14 *May* 1827 ; d. 26 *Mar.* 1902; m. 19 *Ap.* 1855, *the Rev. Edmund Hall, Rector of Myland, co. Essex*, d. 7 *Feb.* 1903 ; *and had issue* 1f *to* 3f.

1f. Rev. George Clement Maddison Hall, Rector of Southery (*Southery Rectory, Downham Market*), b. 24 Ap. 1856 ; *m.* 7 Aug. 1894, Katharine, da. of the Rev. Arthur Charles Copeman ; and has issue (with a son, Henry Clement, who d. young) 1g to 3g.

1g. Basil Arthur Edmund Maddison Hall, b. 9 Ap. 1897.

2g. Mary Doris Maddison Hall, b. 31 May 1895.

3g. Katharine Joyce Maddison Hall, b. 28 Dec. 1902.

2f. Mary Helen Constance Hall.

3f. Anna Mildred Elizabeth Hall, m. 7 Aug. 1888, the Rev. James Henry Browne, Vicar of Roehampton (*The Vicarage, Roehampton, S.W.*); and has issue 1g to 3g.

1g. Richard Maddison Browne, b. 9 Mar. 1891.

2g. Maurice Edmund Browne, b. 4 Sept. 1892.

3g. Margaret Dorothea Browne, b. 23 Dec. 1895.

2d. *Richard Thomas Maddison*, afterwards (*R.L.* 18 *Dec.* 1849) *Combe, of Earnshill, co. Som.*, bapt. 10 *Oct.* 1813 ; d. 1880 ; m. 1850, *Elizabeth Delicia, da. of Gen. Sir John Mitchell, K.C.B.* ; *and had issue* 1e *to* 2e.

1e. Richard Thomas Combe, J.P. (*Earnshill, Curry Rivell, Somerset*), b. 30 Nov. 1854 ; *m.* June 1903, Evelyn, da. of Lieut.-Col. Francis Henry of Elmstree House, co. Gloucester ; and has issue 1f.

1f. Evelyn Delicia Combe.

2e. Constance Delicia Combe.

3d. *Mary Combe Maddison*, b. 1 *May* 1810; d. 16 *Sept.* 1879 ; m. 18 *June* 1835, *Richard Hare, Comm. R.N.*, d. 27 *May* 1876 ; *and had issue* 1e *to* 2e.

1e. Richard Thomas Hare, Lieut.-Col. Indian Army, B.C.C. (6 *Somerset Place, Bath*), b. 6 June 1836 ; *m.* Gertrude Adeline, da. of the Rev. John Joseph Spear, M.A.; and has issue 1f to 2f.

1f. Ethel Gertrude Hare.

2f. Mabel Maddison Hare.

2e. Robert Powell Hare, Lieut.-Col. *late* R.H.A., *b.* 27 July 1842 ; *m.* 27 July 1880, Christine Sarah, da. of Donald Maclaine of Lochbuie, "The Maclaine," Chief of his Clan, J.P., D.L. ; and has issue 1f to 5f.

1f. Richard Hare.

2f. Stuart Hare.

3f–5f. 3 das.

2c. *Rev. George Maddison, Vicar of North Reston*, bapt. 18 *Sept.* 1775 ; d. 26 *Oct.* 1827 ; m. *Elizabeth, da. of the Rev. Kingsman Baskett of Pocklington, co. York*, d. 1849 ; *and had issue* 1d *to* 2d.

1d. *Ven. George Maddison, Vicar of Grantham, Archdeacon of Ludlow, &c.*, b. 9 *June* 1809; d. 30 *Jan.* 1895 ; m. 12 *Oct.* 1839, *Jane, da. of Richard Philpott of Chichester*, d. 5 *Mar.* 1891 ; *and had issue* 1e. [Nos. 16997 to 17014.

---

[1] Maddison's "Lincolnshire Pedigrees," ii. 620.

The Plantagenet Roll

1e. Rev. *George Henry Maddison, Vicar of Tuckhill, co. Salop,* b. 9 *Mar.* 1853; d. 9 *Mar.* 1898; m. 16 *June* 1885, *Mary, da. of the Rev. John Temple, Rector of Bothenhampton, co. Dorset;* and had issue 1*f* to 3*f*.

1*f*. George Lionel Temple Maddison, *b.* 26 Oct. 1888.

2*f*. Elvira Mary Maddison, *b.* 6 Mar. 1886.

3*f*. Gladys Mabel Maddison, *b.* 15 Mar. 1887.

2d. *Elizabeth Maddison,* b. 20 *Aug.* 1804; d. 27 *Jan.* 1878; m. 4 *Sept.* 1832, *the Rev. Charles Green, Rector of Burgh Castle, co. Suffolk;* d. 9 *Aug.* 1857; and had issue 1*e*.

1e. Rev. Charles Edward Maddison Green, *formerly* Rector of Ledbury, Prebendary of Hereford, &c. (*St. Katharine's, Ledbury*), *b.* 24 July 1836; *m.* 20 July 1869, Ella Doveton, da. of William Meybohm Rider Haggard of Bradenham Hall, co. Norfolk; and has 1*f* to 3*f*.

1*f*. Charles Arthur Maddison Green, *b.* 17 June 1877, *m.* 8 Ap. 1907, Christian Margaret, da. of the Rev. George Lucas, Rector of Mulbarton, co. Norfolk; and has issue 1*g*.

1*g*. Hester Christian Maddison Green, *b.* 8 Feb. 1908.

2*f*. Edward Roland Maddison Green, *b.* 5 Mar. 1887.

3*f*. Ella Frances Maddison Green, *m.* 15 Sept. 1884, Harry Spencer Horsfal Bickham (*The Hilltop, near Ledbury*); and has issue 1*g*.

1*g*. Richard Harry Spencer Bickham, *b.* 28 July 1908.

3c. *Ann Maddison,* bapt. *at Gainsborough* 25 Sept. 1772.

[Nos. 17015 to 17023.

77. Descendants of GEORGE MADDISON of Stainton Vale, co. Linc., and *afterwards* (1799) of Dunstable Priory, co. Beds, Lieut.-Col. 4th Regt., &c. (Table IX.), *bapt.* 20 Aug. 1729; *d.* 10 Jan. 1807; *m.* 11 Oct. 1857, MARY, da. and event. h. of Capt. Launcelot BAUGH, 41st Regt., *bur.* 24 Jan. 1791; and had issue 1*a* to 4*a*.

1a. *John Thomas Maddison of Norton, co. Durham, Col. 4th Regt. of Foot,* b. 9 *Ap.* 1759; d. *Jan.* 1837; m. 1781, *Matilda, da. of* (—) *MacNeill of Gallichoilly, co. Argyll,* d. (–); *and had issue* 1*b* to 2*b*.

1b. *Ann Theodosia Maddison,* d. (–); m. 1 *Ap.* 1809, *Aubone Altham Surtees of Newcastle;* and had issue 1*c*.

1c. *Matilda Sarah Surtees,* d. (–); m. (—) *Pyke;* and had issue (*with several das.* m. *with issue in New Zealand*) 1*d*.

1d. Eldon Pyke.

2b. *Jane Maddison,* b. 14 *Feb.* 1795; d. 28 *Feb.* 1829; m. 30 *Oct.* 1821, *John Dent of Thirsk, co. Yorks,* d. 30 *July* 1839; *and had issue* 1*c* to 2*c*.

1c. Matilda Mary Dent, *b.* 3 Feb. 1825; living *unm.* 1910.

2c. Emma Dent, *b.* 28 Aug. 1826; *m.* 1 May 1851, Thomas Vaisey of Stratton, co. Glouc., *b.* 22 May 1825; *d.* 10 May 1903; and has issue 1*d* to 4*d*.

1d. Arthur William Vaisey (*Holly Field, Tring, Herts*), *b.* 8 Feb. 1852; *m.* 7 Sept. 1876, Esther, da. of William Lawrence Bevir of Cirencester; and has issue 1*e* to 9*e*.

1e. Harry Bevir Vaisey (*Lincoln's Inn*), *b.* 22 June 1877; *m.* 20 Aug. 1903, Eleonora Mary, da. of the Rev. William Quennell, Rector of Shenfield, co. Essex; and has issue 1*f* to 2*f*.

1*f*. Arthur William Vaisey, *b.* 20 Oct. 1905.

2*f*. Juliana Margaret Vaisey, *b.* 7 Sept. 1904.

2e. Roland Maddison Vaisey, *b.* 31 Dec. 1886.

3e. Margaret Vaisey, *b.* 4 June 1878.

[Nos. 17024 to 17032.

# of The Blood Royal

4e. Violet Vaisey, m. 7 Nov. 1907, John Brooke Scrivenor (*Batu Gajah, Malay States*); and has issue 1f to 2f.

1f. Thomas Vaisey Scrivenor, b. at Batu Gajah 28 Aug. 1908.

2f. Phebe Scrivenor, b. at Batu Gajah 9 Ap. 1910.

5e. Lilian Vaisey, b. 31 Aug. 1881.

6e. Veronica Vaisey, b. 24 June 1883.

7e. May Vaisey, b. 27 May 1885.

8e. Olive Vaisey, b. 13 Ap. 1889.

9e. Iris Vaisey, b. 5 June 1892.

2d. John Ernest Dent Vaisey (*Lexden, Whyteleafe, Surrey*), b. 28 Ap. 1853; m. 20 Ap. 1880, Judith, da. of William Lawrence Bevir of Cirencester; and has issue 1e to 4e.

1e. John Clere Vaisey, b. 24 Dec. 1880.

2e. Thomas Lionel Vaisey, b. 14 Dec. 1883.

3e. Francis Dent Vaisey, b. 3 Dec. 1885.

4e. Maud Vaisey, b. 27 June 1882.

3d. *Charles Thomas St. Clere Vaisey*, b. 28 *Jan.* 1857; d. 5 *June* 1905; m. 1 *Sept.* 1888, *Emily Jessie, da. of John Guyse Sparke, Major Bengal S.C.; and had issue 1e to 2e.*

1e. Guy Maddison Vaisey, b. 15 July 1889.

2e. Monica Vaisey, b. 3 May 1891.

4d. Edith Agnes Vaisey, *unm.*

2a. *George Maddison*, Lieut.-Col. 65th Regt., b. 24 Nov. 1762; d. 5 *Aug.* 1816; m. *Sept.* 1793, *Mary, da. of the Rev. Henry Alington of Swinhope, co. Lincoln,* d. 14 *June* 1850; *and had issue* 1b.

1b. *George Wilson Maddison of Partney Hall, co. Linc., J.P.,* b. 29 *Ap.* 1797; d. 10 *June* 1888; m. 1 *Mar.* 1825, *Frances Elizabeth, da. of Sir Alan Bellingham,* 2nd Bt. [*G.B.*], d. 29 *Ap.* 1886; *and had issue* 1c *to* 4c.

1c. *Henry Maddison of Partney Hall,* b. 16 *Ap.* 1829; d. 11 *Feb.* 1906; m. 28 *Nov.* 1867, *Clare, da. of Francis Slater of Christchurch, New Zealand; and had issue* 1d *to* 4d.

1d. Henry George Maddison (*Partney Hall, Spilsby, co. Lincoln*), b. 23 Aug. 1868.

2d. Humphrey Maddison, Lieut. 1st Batt. Derbyshire Regt., b. 23 Sept. 1876.

3d. Frances Emily Theodosia Maddison.

4d. Clara Cornelia Maddison.

2c. *Sidney Maddison of Horncastle, co. Lincoln,* b. 27 *Feb.* 1832; d. 12 *Feb.* 1909; m. 3 *Nov.* 1869, *Elizabeth, da. of Samuel Mann; and has issue* 1d *to* 2d.

1d. Edward Maddison (*Orlando, Florida*), b. 2 Oct. 1871.

2d. Isabel Emilia Lucy Maddison, m. 21 Ap. 1896, Nicholas Caesar Corsellis Lawton of Wyvenhoe Hall, co. Essex (2 *Mount Pleasant Crescent, Hastings*); and has issue 1e to 2e.

1e. Sydney Corsellis Lawton, b. 6 Dec. 1896.

2e. John Corsellis Lawton, b. Aug. 1868.

3c. Rev. Arthur Roland Maddison, F.S.A., Priest Vicar and Prebendary of Lincoln Cathedral (*Vicar's Court, Lincoln*), b. 26 July 1843.

4c. Frances Theodosia Maddison.

3a. *Charles Maddison, Capt. Bengal Cavalry,* b. 5 *Sept.* 1770; d. 1845; m. 1791, *Mary, da. of the Rev. John Harrington, D.D., Rector of Thruxton, and Prebendary of Salisbury,* d. (–); *and had issue* 1b.

1b. *Rev. John George Maddison,* d. 1856; m. 1815, *Thomas Anne, da. of Alexander Macrae of Jamaica,* d. 1864; *and had issue* 1c *to* 7c.

1c. *Rev. Charles John Maddison of Douglas, Isle of Man,* b. 1817; d. (–); m.

[Nos. 17033 to 17057a.

The Plantagenet Roll

1844, *Julia*, da. of the Rev. *Benjamin Cracknell* of *Bath*, d. (–); and had issue 1d to 5d.
    1d. Julia Sophia Maddison.
    2d. Mary Thomasine Maddison.
    3d. Agnes Rowley Maddison.
    4d. Minna Isabel Maddison.
    5d. Theodosia Ellen Maddison.

    2c. *Alexander Macrae Maddison of Agivey, co. Derry*, b. 24 Dec. 1820; d. 1861; m. 1856, *Eliza*, da. of *Capt. Stephen Shairp, R.N.*, d. (–); and had issue 1d to 4d.
        1d. Roland John George Maddison.
        2d. Ida Agnes Maddison.
        3d. Maud Mary Maddison.
        4d. Hilda Frances Maddison.

    3c. *George Latham Maddison of Toronto*, b. 2 Jan. 1823; d. 24 Dec. 1881; m. 14 *Sept.* 1848, *Mary Catharine*, da. of the Rev. *Charles Winstanley*; and had issue 1d to 3d.
        1d. Alfred John George Maddison (*Richmond, Virginia, U.S.A.*), b. 24 June 1849.
        2d. *Charles Edmund Maddison*, b. 25 Sept. 1852; d. 21 Jan. 1895; m. *Esther Ann*, da. of *William Warwick* of *Toronto* ; and had issue 1e to 4e.
            1e. William Warwick Maddison.
            2e. Muriel Maddison.
            3e. Grace Ina Maddison.
            4e. Alice Winstanley Maddison.
        3d. George Ernest Maddison, b. 8 Feb. 1854.

    4c. *Thomasine Maddison*, d. 20 Jan. 1893; m. 1844, *Charles Sidney Hawkins* of *Over Norton House, co. Oxon*.
    5c. *Sophia Maddison*, d. (? s.p.); m. 1847, *John Ettrick* [4th son of *William Ettrick* of *High Barnes, co. Durham*].
    6c. *Theodosia Maddison*, d. (? s.p.); m. *Col. Conolly Dysart*.
    7c. *Agnes Halford Maddison*, d. (? s.p.); m. *John Smythe* [son of *John Smythe* of *Ardmore, co. Derry*].

  4a. *Katharine Maddison*, b. Dec. 1769; d. Aug. 1823; m. 21 May 1796, *Latham Blacker* of *Newent, co. Glouc.*, Major 65th Regt.; and had issue 1b to 3b.
    1b. *Martha Blacker*, d. 17 Feb. 1878; m. 29 Dec. 1823, the Rev. *John Fendall* of *Meserdine, co. Glouc.*, d. 18 June 1862; and had issue 1c to 2c.
        1c. Catharine Jane Fendall (*Milbrooke, Albert Road, Malvern*).
        2c. *Harriet Fendall*, b. 28 July 1826; m. 22 June 1848, *John Fendall Newton* [only son of the Rev. *John Farmer Newton*, Vicar of Kirby in Cleveland, co. Yorks] (*Ardmillan, Oswestry*); and has issue 1d to 10d.
            1d. *Benjamin Newton* (*Yarm-on-Tees, York*), b. 12 May 1860; m. 19 May 1886, *Selina*, da. of the Rev. *Alleyne FitzHerbert* of *Tissington, co. Derby*; and has issue 1e to 3e.
                1e. Robert Newton, b. 23 Jan. 1893.
                2e. May Gladys Newton, b. 3 May 1887.
                3e. Daisy Frances Newton, b. 5 June 1890.
            2d. *William Latham Newton* (*Holtby House, York*), b. 12 Jan 1862; m. 17 Feb. 1886, *Violet*, da. of (—) *Harrison*; and has issue 1e to 2e.
                1e. Giles Fendall Newton, b. 27 May 1891.
                2e. Blanche Emily Newton, b. 20 June 1887.   [Nos. 17058 to 17081.

of The Blood Royal

3d. Mary Catharine Newton, m. 27 Aug. 1885, Leonard Apsley Smith (Newent); and has issue 1e.

    1e. John Leonard Apsley Smith, b. 25 Oct. 1886.

4d. Elizabeth Martha Newton, unm.

5d. Laura Harriet Newton, unm.

6d. Anne Eva Newton, unm.

7d. Frances Judith Newton, unm.

8d. Caroline Newton, m. 21 Ap. 1881, the Rev. Arthur Garmondsway Waldy, M.A. (Oxon.), Rector of Yarm (Yarm Rectory, N.R. Yorks); and has issue 1e to 5e.

    1e. John Newton Waldy, b. 25 Feb. 1884; m. 2 Sept. 1908, Mabel, da. of John Robson of Newton Bellingham.

    2e. Rowland Gray Waldy, b. 20 June 1890.

    3e. Cuthbert Temple Waldy, b. 31 Aug. 1891.

    4e. Violet Mary Waldy, b. 9 Dec. 1887.

    5e. Dorothy Elizabeth Waldy, b. 6 Feb. 1897.

9d. Rose Newton, unm.

10d. Mabel Theodosia Newton, unm.

2b. Catharine Blacker, d. 13 Aug. 1865; m. 5 July 1826, Richard Foley Onslow of Slardene, co. Glouc., d. 12 Mar. 1879; and had issue.

See the Essex Volume, pp. 320–321, Nos. 33255–33266.

3b. [da.] Blacker ?   [Nos. 17082 to 17108.

78. Descendants, if any, of KATHARINE MADDISON (Table IX.), bapt. 26 May 1724; d. (–); m. JOHN LAWRENCE of Putney [grandson of Sir John Lawrence, Lord Mayor of London during the Plague].[1]

79. Descendants of THEODOSIA MADDISON [Table IX.), b. at Ketton 15 June 1725; d. 20 Feb. 1821; m. 23 June 1752, JOHN (MONSON), 2nd BARON MONSON [G.B.], d. 23 July 1774; and had issue.

See the Exeter Volume, Table XIII., pp. 243–252, Nos. 9109–9497.

[Nos. 17109 to 17497.

80. Descendants of ANNE MADDISON (Table IX.), b. c. 1728; d. at Lea 31 Aug. 1783; m. at Little Grimsby 7 Aug. 1747, the Rev. Sir WILLIAM ANDERSON of Broughton, 6th Baronet [E.], d. 9 Mar. 1785; and had issue 1a to 6a.

1a. Sir Edmund Anderson, 7th Bt. [E.], b. 11 Sept. 1758; d.s.p. 30 May 1799.

2a. Rev. Sir Charles Anderson of Broughton and Lea Hall, 8th Bt. [E.], Prebendary of Lincoln and Rector of Lea, b. 5 Oct. 1767; d. 24 Mar. 1846; m. 13 Dec. 1802, Frances Mary, da. of Sir John Nelthorpe of Scawby, co. Lincoln, 6th Bt. [E.], d. 18 Aug. 1836; and had issue 1b.

1b. Sir Charles Henry John Anderson, 9th and last Bt. [E.], b. 25 Nov. 1804; d. 8 Oct. 1891; m. 11 Sept. 1832, Emma, da. of John Savile Foljambe of Osberton, co. Notts, d. 8 Aug. 1870; and had issue.

See the Clarence Volume, p. 608, Nos. 26758–26762.   [Nos. 17498 to 17502.

---

[1] See Crisp's "Visitation Notes," vi. p. 55.

The Plantagenet Roll

3a. *Anne Anderson*, b. 28 *May* 1753; d. 12 *July* 1830; m. 1*st*, 30 *Aug*. 1771, Samuel Thorold *of Harmston Hall, co. Linc.*, d. 19 *Jan.* 1820; 2*ndly*, (—) *Rosser* (or *Roys*); *and had issue* 1b *to* 2b.

1b. Louise Thorold, d. (–); m. 28 Feb. 1796, *Capt. Simpson, 2nd Regt.*

2b. Theodosia Thorold, d. 1806; m. *Sept.* 1800, *Lieut. Gibbons, 37th Regt.*

4a. *Catharine Maria Anderson*, b. 16 *Mar.* 1756; d. *Nov.* 1788; m. *as* 1*st wife*, 31 *July* 1777, *Arthur Lemuel Shuldham of Dunmanway, co. Cork, and Pallas Green, co. Limerick*, d. *Aug.* 1839; *and had issue* 1b *to* 4b.

1b. *Edmund William Shuldham of Dunmanway*, Lieut.-Gen. H.E.I.C.S., Quartermaster-Gen. at Bombay, b. 1 Dec. 1778; d. 17 Nov. 1852; m. 3 *Dec.* 1817, *Harriet Eliza Bonar, da. of Thomas Rundell, M.D., of Bath*, d. 31 *July* 1847; *and had issue* 1c.

1c. *Harriet Maria Catharine Shuldham, da. and* (31 *July* 1904) *in her issue h.,* d. 15 *Aug.* 1884; m. 5 *Aug.* 1852, *George Patrick Pery* (*Evans-Freke*), *7th Baron Carbery* [I.], d. 25 *Nov.* 1889; *and had issue* 1d.

1d. Hon. Georgiana Dorothea Harriet Evans-Freke, *m.* 22 June 1876, James Francis (Bernard), 4th Earl of Bandon [I.] (*Castle Bernard, Bandon, co. Cork*).

2b. *Molyneux Shuldham*, Comm. R.N., b. 27 Ap. 1781; d. 25 Feb. 1866; m. 3 Dec. 1820, *Frances, da. of the Rev. Thomas Naunton Orgil Leman* (see p. 170) *of Brampton Hall, co. Suffolk*, d. 22 *Jan.* 1866; *and had issue* 1c *to* 4c.

1c. *Arthur James Shuldham*, Col. late 2nd Batt. Inniskillen Fusiliers, b. 13 Sept. 1823; d. 17 Oct. 1905; m. 1*st*, 8 *Jan.* 1857, *Katharine Dora, da. and co-h. of the Rev. C. E. Dukinfield, Vicar of Edenhall, co. Cumb.*, d. 19 *Aug.* 1865; 2*ndly*, 14 *Sept.* 1869, *Lucy Elizabeth, da. of Sir William Sidney Thomas, 3rd Bt.* [G.B.]; *and had issue* 1d *to* 10d.

1d. Edmund Dukinfield Shuldham, b. 29 Nov. 1857.

2d. Molyneux Charles Dukinfield Shuldham, b. 13 Aug. 1861.

3d. Herbert Leman Dukinfield Shuldham, b. 13 Feb. 1863.

4d. Sidney Arthur Naunton Shuldham, b. 27 June 1870; *m.* 27 Oct. 1900, Florence Kate, da. of A. Perkins of Cape Town.

5d. Victor Lemuel Shuldham, b. 23 Oct. 1872; *m.* 1 Jan. 1906, Violet, da. of (—) Pedingham of East London, Cape Colony; and has issue.

6d.[1] *Margaret Evelyn Shuldham*, d. 26 *Aug.* 1893; *m. the Rev. A. E. Sewart; and had issue.*

7d.[1] Geraldine Maud Shuldham, *m.* 19 Jan. 1901, Henry Walker; and has issue.

8d.[1] Eleanor Maria Shuldham, *m.* 9 Sept. 1888, the Rev. Theodore Edward Fortescue Cole (*Nagpur, Central Provinces, India*); and has issue 1e to 2e.

1e. Lancelot Arthur Shuldham Cole, b. 11 Ap. 1891.

2e. Humfrey Theodore Shuldham Cole, b. 5 Dec. 1896.

9d.[1] Dora Frances Mary Blanche Shuldham, *unm.*

10d.[2] Violet Lucy Hester Shuldham, *m.* 11 June 1901, Henry Manby Colegrave; and has issue.

2c. *Rev. Naunton Lemuel Shuldham*, b. 24 Sept. 1831; d. 24 *July* 1874; m. 8 *Aug.* 1866, *Sophia Frances, da. of John Mathew Quantock of Norton Manor, co. Som.*, d. 17 *Ap.* 1874; *and had issue* 1d.

1d. Frank Naunton Quantock Shuldham (*Norton Manor, Ilminster*), b. 25 Mar. 1868; *m.* 9 Ap. 1890, Emily, da. of William Macalpine-Leny of Dalswinton and Glencoe; and has issue 1e.

1e. Walter Frank Quantock Shuldham, b. 17 June 1892.

3c. Catharine Leman Shuldham, *m.* 5 July 1849, the Rev. William Wrighte Gilbert-Cooper, Vicar of Burwash Weald, co. Sussex; and has issue 1d to 6d.

1d. Arthur Edward Gilbert-Cooper, b. 4 Oct. 1853.

2d. William Naunton Roger Gilbert-Cooper, b. 14 Sept. 1867; *m.* Mabel Evelyn, da. of Surg.-Gen. H. T. Rose.

3d. Mary Frances Gilbert-Cooper. [Nos. 17503 to 17520.

of The Blood Royal

4d. Fanny Catharine Alice Gilbert-Cooper, m. 27 Dec. 1876, Ralph Sillery Benson, Madras Civil Service.

5d. Edith Shuldham Gilbert-Cooper, m. 9 Ap. 1885, Alfred Holland (see p. 170).

6d. Amy Dora Gilbert-Cooper.

4c. *Frances Molyneux Shuldham*, d. 27 Aug. 1854 ; m. 1853, *Lieut.-Col. Henry Lye*, 13*th Bombay Native Infantry*, d. 1872 ; *and had issue* 1d.

1d. Harry Shuldham Lye, now (21 Oct. 1909) Shuldham-Lye, Capt. Royal Irish Regt., b. 15 July 1854.

3b. *Arthur Shuldham, Lieut.-Col. H.E.I.C.S.*, b. 1790 ; d. 23 *Feb.* 1835 ; m. 1*st*, (—), *da. of* (—) *Sibley*, d.s.p. (-) ; 2*ndly*, 20 *Jan.* 1823, *Charlotte, da. of Innis Delamaine, Major H.E.I.C.S.*, d. 23 *Jan.* 1867 ; *and had issue* 1c *to* 3c.

1c. Arthur Innis Shuldham, *late* Lieut.-Col. Indian Army, b. 30 Ap. 1830 ; m. 5 Nov. 1871, Julia, da. of Thomas Barnes.

2c. Charlotte Katharine Shuldham, m. 4 Ap. 1843, Major-Gen. Robert Unwin ; and has issue 1d to 2d.

1d. Emily Constance Unwin, m. 31 Dec. 1874, Augustus Lawrence Francis, Headmaster of Blundell's School, Tiverton (*Tiverton*) ; and has issue 1e to 4e.

1e. Augustus Claude Francis, b. 22 Feb. 1878.

2e. Harold Vansittart Francis, b. 25 Sept. 1883.

3e. Constance Amy Francis, m. 4 Jan. 1905, Richard John Bayntun Hippisley of Ston Easton, J.P., Major N. Somerset Imp. Yeo. (*Ston Easton Park, near Bath ; Junior Carlton*) ; and has issue 1f.

1f. John Preston Hippisley, b. 1905.

4e. Hilda Francis.

2d. Mabel Unwin.

3c. Amelia Ward Shuldham, m. 28 Feb. 1854, Fitz-Edward Hall, C.E., D.C.L. ; and has issue 1d to 2d.

1d. Richard Daniel Hall, b. 18 Feb. 1863.

2d. Katharine Frances Hall.

4b. *Maria Lucy Eliza Shuldham*, d. 26 *Oct.* 1817 ; m. 3 *Sept.* 1801, *the Rev. Joseph Guerin, Rector of Bagborough and Norton Fitzwarren*, d. 12 *Nov.* 1863 ; *and had issue* 1c.

1c. *Edmund Arthur Guerin, Col. Indian Army*, b. 22 *Ap.* 1804 ; d. (-) ; m. 20 *Sept.* 1836, *Louisa, da. of Joseph Gilbert ; and has issue* 1d *to* 2d.

1d. Joseph Arthur Guerin, H.E.I.C.S., b. 12 July 1837 ; m. July 1871, Elizabeth Walker, da. of the Rev. Dudley Oland Crosse, Vicar of Pawlett, co. Som. ; and has issue 1e to 2e.

1e. Joseph Guerin, b. 25 Jan. 1875.

2e. Emily Maud Guerin.

2d. *Emily Louisa Guerin*, d. 9 *May* 1865 ; m. 10 *Sept.* 1856, *Charles Frederic Keays, Major-Gen. Bombay Army ; and had issue* 1e *to* 5e.

1e. Frederic Edmund Keays, b. 25 Oct. 1857.

2e. Henry Guerin Keays, b. 9 Ap. 1862 ; m. 17 Aug. 1884, Edith, da. of George Jinman, M.R.C.S.

3e. Arthur Maitland Keays, b. 14 Ap. 1865.

4e. Evelyn Louisa Frances Keays, m. 16 Feb. 1878, Newton Plomer Fowell, Capt. R.H.A.

5e. Maud Emily Keays.

5a. *Theodosia Dorothy Anderson*, b. 4 *Ap.* 1757 ; d. 5 *May* 1831 ; m. 1 *Jan.* 1778, *the Rev. Richard Vevers, Rector of Saxby, co. Leicester, of Stoke Albany and of Kettering, co. Northants*, d. 17 *Jan.* 1838 ; *and had issue* (*with* 5 *sons and* 6 *das.* d.s.p.) 1b. [Nos. 17521 to 17544.

The Plantagenet Roll

1b. *Theodosia Anne Vevers, da. and event. h.*, b. 21 Nov. 1779; d. 28 *June* 1852; m. 18 *Oct.* 1804, *Thomas* (Denman), 1st *Baron Denman* [U.K.], *Lord Chief-Justice of England*, d. 22 *Sept.* 1854; *and had issue* 1c *to* 10c.

1c. *Thomas (Denman, afterwards (R.L.* 20 Dec. 1876) *Aitchison), 2nd Baron Denman* [U.K.], b. 30 *July* 1805; d.s.p. 9 *Aug.* 1894.

2c. *Hon. Richard Denman*, b. 13 *Jan.* 1814; d. 19 *Mar.* 1887; m. 28 *Oct.* 1840, *Emma* [*herself a descendant of Edward III. through Mortimer-Percy*], *da. of Hugh Jones of Larkhill, co. Lanc.*, d. 2 *Jan.* 1904; *and had issue.*

See pp. 60–61, Nos. 566–610.

3c. *Right Hon. George Denman, P.C., Q.C., M.P., a Judge of the High Court, &c.*, b. 23 *Dec.* 1819; d. 21 *Sept.* 1896; m. 19 Feb. 1852, *Charlotte, da. of Samuel Hope of Liverpool*, d. 19 *Dec.* 1905; *and had issue* 1d *to* 5d.

1d. George Lewis Denman, Metropolitan Police Magistrate (36 *Evelyn Gardens, S.W.*), *b.* 5 May 1854.

2d. Arthur Denman, F.S.A., Clerk of Assize, S.E. Circuit 1887 (29 *Cranley Gardens, S. Kensington*), b. 1 May 1857; m. 17 Dec. 1884, Katharine Agnes [descended from George, Duke of Clarence, K.G.], da. of Edward Nathaniel Conant of Lyndon Hall, co. Rutland; and has issue.

See the Clarence Volume, p. 613, Nos. 26863–26865.

3d. Lancelot Baillie Denman, *late* Comm. R.N., *b.* 15 Jan. 1861; *m.* 27 Ap. 1892, Blanche Isabella Pauline, da. of William Ernest de Veulle of Jersey.

4d. *Charlotte Edith Denman*, b. 15 *May* 1855; d. 29 *Dec.* 1884; m. 19 *June* 1883, *the Rev. William Henry Draper, Rector of Adel, formerly* (1883–1889) *Vicar of Alfreton, and* (1889–1899) *of The Abbey, Shrewsbury (Adel Rectory, Leeds); and had issue* 1e.

1e. Mark Denman Draper, *b.* 15 Dec. 1884.

5d. Grace Denman, *m.* 6 Nov. 1890, Sidney Gambier Parry (*Downham House, near Billericay, Essex*); and has issue 1e to 3e.

1e. Michael Denman Gambier Parry, *b.* 1891.

2e. Richard Gambier Parry, *b.* 1894.

3e. Edith Joan Gambier Parry, *b.* 1892.

4c. *Rev. the Hon. Lewis William Denman, Rector of Willian, co. Herts*, b. 23 *Mar.* 1821; d. 6 *May* 1907; m. 1st, 18 *June* 1850, *Frances Marianne* (see p. 280), *da. of Thomas Eden of The Bryn, Swansea*, d. 25 *Ap.* 1862; 2ndly, 22 *Aug.* 1865, *Frances Starkie Mary, da. of Col. Henry Armytage, Coldstream Guards*, d.s.p. 24 *Dec.* 1893; *and had issue* 1d *to* 4d.

1d. Lewis William Eden Denman (*Church Norton, Selsey, Chichester*), b. 9 May 1857; *m.* 5 Aug. 1889, Emma, da. of Charles Rainbow; and has issue 1e to 2e.

1e. Joseph Alban Denman, *b.* 17 June 1890.

2e. Theodosia Victoria Denman.

2d. Frances Emily Denman
3d. Theodosia Louisa Denman } (*May Bank, Horeham Road, Sussex*).
4d. Caroline Annie Denman

5c. *Hon. Theodosia Denman*, b. 16 *Sept.* 1806; d. 20 *May* 1895; m. 21 *Nov.* 1825, *Ichabod Charles Wright of Mapperley Hall, co. Notts*, d. 14 *Oct.* 1871; *and had issue* 1d *to* 6d.

1d. *Charles Ichabod Wright of Stapleford Hall, co. Notts, and Watcombe Park, co. Devon, M.P. co. Nottingham*, b. 19 *Sept.* 1828; d. 9 *May* 1905; m. 9 *June* 1852, *Blanche Louisa, da. of Henry Corles Bingham of Wartnaby Hall, co. Leic.; and had issue* 1e *to* 5e.

1e. Charles Bingham Wright of Mapperley, *late* Capt. S. Notts Yeo. Cav., *b.* 19 Nov. 1854.

2e. Nevill Wright, *b.* 26 Nov. 1857.

3e. Blanche Theodosia Wright.

[Nos. 17545 to 17609.

# of The Blood Royal

4e. Rosamond Frances Wright, m. 15 Aug. 1883, Elias John Webb of Tiddington, Major 4th Batt. Worcester Regt. (*Tiddington, Stratford-on-Avon ; The Brownsend, co. Glouc.*).

5e. Grace Henrietta Wright, m. 7 Nov. 1885, Richard Campbell-Davys of Neuadd-faur, co. Carmarthen, and Askomel, co. Argyll, J.P., D.L., d. 15 Nov. 1905; and has issue 1f to 4f.

1f. Ivor Elystan Campbell-Davys of Neuadd-fawr and Askomel (*Neuadd-fawr, Llandovery*), b. 4 Aug. 1890.
2f. Eva Gwladys Campbell-Davys.
3f. Grace Edith Campbell-Davys.
4f. Lilian Elan Campbell-Davys.

2d. Henry Smith Wright (*Oaklands Park, Chichester*), b. 27 June 1839 ; m. 1st, 17 Oct. 1865, Mary Jane, da. of William Cartledge of Woodthorpe, co. Notts, d. 4 Dec. 1866 ; 2ndly, 6 Feb. 1869, Josephine Henrietta, da. of the Rev. John Adolphus Wright, Rector of Ickham, co. Kent ; and has issue 1e to 6e.

1e. Henry Adolphus Smith Wright, Capt. *late* Royal Fusiliers (*Nutbourne Place, Pulborough, Sussex*), b. 13 Dec. 1869 ; m. 8 June 1904, Dorothy Cécile Renton, da. of Col. E. de Barry Barnett; and has issue (2 children).

2e. George Lewis Smith Wright, b. 30 Jan. 1872 ; m. 30 July 1902, Ismay, da. of C. C. Hopkinson.

3e. Edward Henry Smith Wright, British South Africa Company (3 *Upton Park, Slough*), b. 4 Sept. 1875 ; m. 23 July 1902, Isie Margaret, da. of Gerald Young ; and has issue 1f to 4f.

1f. Edward Gerald Smith Wright, b. 7 Dec. 1903.
2f. John Evelyn Smith Wright, b. 19 July 1907.
3f. Henry Gordon Smith Wright, b. 23 June 1908.
4f. Josephine Margaret Smith Wright.

4e. John Harold Smith Wright, Lieut. R.N., b. 18 Aug. 1882.

5e.[1] Edith Mary Wright, m. Donald Campbell (*Templeton, Hungerford, Berks*).

6e.[2] Alice Dorothea Smith Wright, m. Richard Manders (*Stonehurst, Killiney, co. Dublin*).

3d. Frederick Wright (*Lenton Hall, co. Notts*), b. 12 Aug. 1840 ; m. 12 Feb. 1863, Ada Joyce, da. of the Rev. John Bateman of East and West Leake, co. Notts ; and had issue 1e to 7e.

1e. Frederick Denman Wright, b. 17 Dec. 1872.
2e. Emily Theodosia Wright.
3e. Mary Neville Wright.
4e. Florence Ada Wright.
5e. Margaret Joyce Wright.
6e. Hilda Dorothy Wright.
7e. Maud Frances Bateman Wright.

4d. Rev. George Howard Wright, Chaplain at Naples, *formerly* Assist. Chap. at Rome (1902–1903) and San Remo (1903–1904), &c. (*Whitehill House, near West Liss, Hants*), b. 1 June 1845 ; m. 12 July 1870, Anne Frances, da. of the Rev. Edmund Roberts Larken ; and has issue 1e to 3e.

1e. George Denman Larken Wright, b. 31 Aug. 1872.
2e. Eric James Wright, b. 12 Nov. 1880.
3e. Theodosia Anne Emily Wright.

5d. Theodosia Harriet Wright, m. 8 Sept. 1863, William Houston Sinclair (*Morton Manor, Brading, I.W.*) ; and has issue 1e to 4e.

1e. Charles George Sinclair, b. 5 Jan. 1865.
2e. William Frederick Sinclair, b. 26 Ap. 1867.
3c. John Houston Sinclair, b. 6 Dec. 1869.
4e. Theodosia Agnes Sinclair.

6d. Frances Wright, m. 30 May 1861, Edward William Cropper of Great Crosby, co. Lanc., J.P., b. 7 July 1833 ; d. 29 Jan. 1906; and has issue 1e to 8e.

[Nos. 17610 to 17644.

The Plantagenet Roll

1*e.* Rev. James Cropper, M.A. (Camb.), Vicar of Penrith (*St. Andrew's Vicarage, Penrith*), *b.* 2 May 1862; *m.* 8 Mar. 1888, Ethel Frances, da. of G. Perceval Smith; and has issue 1*f* to 5*f.*
  1*f.* Paul Cropper, *b.* 29 Jan. 1889.
  2*f.* Edward Perceval Cropper, *b.* 15 July 1896.
  3*f.* Richard Alfred Cropper, *b.* 2 Dec. 1899.
  4*f.* Frances Alice Cropper.
  5*f.* Martha Phyllis Cropper.

2*e.* John Cropper, *b.* 17 Sept. 1864; *m.* 6 Feb. 1895, Ann Ellen, da. of T. A. Walker; and has issue 1*f* to 3*f.*
  1*f.* Thomas Andrew Cropper, *b.* 14 May 1898.
  2*f.* Dorothea Alice Denman Cropper.
  3*f.* Eleanor Grace Cropper.

3*e.* Charles Henry Edward Cropper, *b.* 25 Jan. 1866; *m.* 30 Ap. 1891, Ethel Mary, da. of the Rev. Conrad Green; and has issue 1*f* to 3*f.*
  1*f.* Charles Leonard Cropper, *b.* 26 Jan. 1894.
  2*f.* Alexander Cropper, *b.* 8 Dec. 1896.
  3*f.* Madge Ethel Cropper.

4*e.* Rev. Frederick William Cropper, M.A. (Camb.) (8 *Montpellier Terrace, Cheltenham*), *b.* 1 Feb. 1871; *m.* 30 Dec. 1897, Florence Barton, da. of the Rev. Thomas Davis Jones, Vicar of Caerwent; and has issue 1*f* to 2*f.*
  1*f.* Charles Frederick John Cropper, *b.* 6 June 1901.
  2*f.* Violet Gwenllian Cropper.

5*e.* Frances Mildred Theodosia Cropper, *m.* 17 Jan. 1889, Conrad Theodore Green; and has issue.

6*e.* Anne Wakefield Cropper.

7*e.* Emily Mabel Cropper, *m.* 28 Ap. 1894, the Rev. Hubert Edmund Hamilton Probyn (*Abbenhall Lodge, Mitcheldean, Glouc.*) [descended from the Lady Anne, sister of King Edward IV. (see Exeter Volume, p. 198)]; and has issue 1*f* to 3*f.*
  1*f.* Edward Hamilton Probyn, *b.* 17 Sept. 1908.
  2*f.* Emily Araminta Probyn.
  3*f.* Margaret Eleanor Probyn.

8*e.* Eveline Wright Cropper.

6*c.* Hon. Elizabeth Denman, *b.* 21 *Nov.* 1807; *d.* 5 *Aug.* 1880; *m.* 3 *May* 1838, the Ven. Francis Hodgson, *Provost of Eton and Archdeacon of Derby*, *d.* 29 *Dec.* 1852; *and had issue* 1*d* to 4*d.*

  1*d.* James Thornton Hodgson, *b.* 4 *May* 1845; *d.* 1880; *m.* 15 *June* 1872, Maria Blanche, sister of Harry William Verelst of Aston Hall, co. York; *and had issue* 1*e* to 5*e.*
    1*e.* Francis Coke Denman Hodgson, *b.* 10 Dec. 1874.
    2*e.* James Vaughan Hodgson, *b.* 3 July 1878.
    3*e.* Maud Vevers Hodgson.
    4*e.* Sybil Blanche Hodgson.
    5*e.* Lilian Verelst Hodgson.
  2*d.* Elizabeth Denman Hodgson, *m.* 17 Ap. 1882, Herbert Charles MacCarthy.
  3*d.* Matilda Frances Hodgson.
  4*d.* Jane Theodosia Hodgson.

7*c.* Hon. Frances Denman, *b.* 17 *Sept.* 1812; *d.* 29 *Ap.* 1890; *m.* 8 *July* 1846, Admiral Sir Robert Lambert Baynes, *K.C.B.*, *d.* 7 *Sept.* 1869; *and had issue* 1*d.*
  1*d.* Henry Compton Anderson Baynes, *late* Capt. R.N., *b.* 13 Oct. 1852; *m.* 21 Aug. 1884, Isabel, da. of Admiral Sir Joseph Nias, K.C.B.

8*c.* Hon. Margaret Denman, *b.* 8 *Aug.* 1815; *d.* 11 *June* 1899; *m.* 1*st*, 23 *Nov.* 1841, Henry William Macaulay [*brother of Lord Macaulay*], *d.* 24 *Sept.* 1846;

[Nos. 17645 to 17677.

# of The Blood Royal

2ndly, as 2nd wife, 10 Aug. 1848, Edward Cropper of Swaylands, co. Kent, J.P., d. 23 May 1877; 3rdly, 22 Ap. 1879, Col. John Owen, d.s.p. 1890; and had issue 1d to 6d.

1d. Henry Denman Macaulay, late Lieut. R.N., b. 10 Aug. 1843; m. 18 Feb. 1868, Selina, da. of Sir Joseph Needham, Chief-Justice of Trinidad; and has issue 1e to 3e.

    1e. William Edward Babington Macaulay, b. 2 Feb. 1869.

    2e. Arthur James Denman Macaulay, R.N., b. 14 May 1870.

    3e. Thomas Cary Elwes Cropper Macaulay (*Alexandria*), b. 15 Aug. 1871.

2d. Joseph Babington Macaulay, b. 17 Oct. 1846; m. 8 July 1869, Eleanor, da. of Henry Studdy of Waddeton Court, co. Devon, J.P., D.L.; and had issue 1e to 5e.

    1e. Aulay Babington Macaulay, R.M.S., R.N.R., b. Nov. 1876; *unm*.

    2e. Edward Macaulay, b. 3 Nov. 1877; *unm*.

    3e. Eleanor Josephine Macaulay, *unm*.

    4e. Maud Olive Macaulay, m. 19 Aug. 1903, Robert Perry Bruce (*Villa Arco, Via Soffiano, Florence*); and has issue 1f to 4f.

        1f. Michael Macaulay Bruce, b. 4 Sept. 1904.

        2f. Robert Macaulay Bruce,
        3f. Nigel Macaulay Bruce, } b. (twins) 6 Feb. 1906.

        4f. Edward Macaulay Bruce, b. 9 Feb. 1908.

    5e. Lois Macaulay, *unm*.

3d. Edward Denman Cropper, now (R.L. 14 Nov. 1874) Thornburgh-Cropper (*Dingle Bank, Lancashire; Swaylands, Kent*), b. 23 May 1854; m. 4 July 1874, Minnie Virginia, da. and h. of William Butler Thornburgh of San Francisco.

4d. Amelia Margaret Elizabeth Cropper, m. 1st, 4 June 1867, Henry Studdy of Waddeton Court, co. Devon, Comm. R.N., d.v.p. 13 Sept. 1880; 2ndly, 1881, William Thomas Summers of Milton, co. Pembroke (*Esthlon, Newmarket; Torcross, S. Devon*); and has issue 1e to 3e.

    1e. Henry Edward Macaulay Studdy, Capt. (ret.) *late* Rough Riders, served in S. Africa (10 *Souldern Road, West Kensington*), b. 19 Mar. 1868; m. 12 Jan. 1893, Mary, da. of John Grigg of Colebrook, Plympton, co. Devon; and has issue 1f to 5f.

        1f. Henry Studdy, b. 20 Ap. 1894.

        2f. Edward Studdy, b. 22 Sept. 1895.

        3f. John Studdy, b. 25 Oct. 1901.

        4f. Arthur Redmond Studdy, b. 11 Ap. 1905.

        5f. Mary Studdy.

    2e. Eleanor Margaret Studdy, m. as 2nd wife, 30 Jan. 1892, Sir Harald George Hewett, 4th Bt. [U.K.], Capt. and Hon. Major R.G.A. (*The Red House, Chilworth, Hants*); and has issue 1f to 4f.

        1f. Harald Hewett, b. 22 Oct. 1892.

        2f. John George Hewett, b. 23 Oct. 1895.

        3f. George Nele Hewett, b. 30 Aug. 1901.

        4f. Margaret Hewett.

    3e. Anita Georgina Edith Studdy, m. 1st, 9 Jan. 1899, Capt. David Longfield Beatty, *late* 4th Hussars, d. 3 Ap. 1904; 2ndly, 27 Ap. 1909, Harold Lett (*Kilgibbon, co. Wexford*); and has issue 1f.

        1f. Henry Longfield Beatty, b. 4 Mar. 1901.

5d. Florence Anne Cropper, m. 1 July 1873, Arthur Frederick Holdsworth of Widdicombe, J.P., *late* Capt. South Devon and North Lincoln Militia, *previously* R.N. (*Widdicombe House, Kingsbridge, Devon*); and has issue 1e to 4e.

    1e. Arthur Mervyn Holdsworth, 1st Royal Berkshire Regt., b. 5 Nov. 1875.

    2e. Frederick John Cropper Holdsworth, 2nd Devonshire Regt., b. 7 Nov. 1886.

    3e. Florence Evelyn Holdsworth.

    4e. Joan Holdsworth.   [Nos. 17678 to 17711.

The Plantagenet Roll

6d. Marion Eliza Blanche Cropper, m. 5 Mar. 1878, Lieut.-Col. Rowley Richard Conway Hill, late 31st Regt. (Hamble House, Hamble, Hants); and has issue 1e to 9e.
  1e. Rowley Arthur Edward Hill, R.H.A., b. 3 Jan. 1879.
  2e. Hugh Rowley Hill, R.F.A., b. 18 Feb. 1880.
  3e. Conway Rowley Hill, R.F.A., b. 16 Sept. 1881.
  4e. Oliver Charles Rowley Hill, R.F.A., b. 22 Nov. 1883.
  5e. Leslie Rowley Hill, R.F.A., b. 28 Dec. 1884.
  6e. Blanch Edith Hill.
  7e. Margaret Hill.
  8e. Janet Dorothy Hill.
  9e. Helen Irene Susan Hill.

9c. Hon. Anne Denman, b. 26 June 1822; d. (-); m. 18 Aug. 1846, Frederick Holland, Comm. R.N., d. 21 July 1860; and had issue 1d to 7d.
  1d. Edward Holland, b. 30 Aug. 1850.
  2d. Frederick Arthur Holland, b. 17 Oct. 1853.
  3d. Richard Lancelot Holland, b. 24 Ap. 1858.
  4d. Alfred Holland, b. 14 Aug. 1859; m. 9 Ap. 1885, Edith Shuldham (see p. 165), da. of the Rev. William Wrighte Gilbert-Cooper.
  5d. Annie Susan Holland.
  6d. Charlotte Holland ⎫ (twins).
  7d. Theodosia Caroline Holland ⎭

10c. Hon. Caroline Amelia Denman, b. 26 Aug. 1823; d. (-); m. 3 Feb. 1846, the Rev. John George Beresford, Vicar of St. Andrew's, Whittlesea, and Rector of Bedale, d. 17 July 1899; and had issue.
See the Exeter Volume, p. 245, Nos. 9156-9207.

6a. Henrietta Jane Anderson, b. 20 May 1761; d. 9 Mar. 1843; m. 3 Dec. 1783, the Rev. Naunton Thomas Orgill Leman of Brampton Hall, co. Suff., d. 31 Jan. 1837; and had issue 1b to 2b.
  1b. Rev. Robert Orgill Leman of Brampton Hall, b. 12 Ap. 1799; d. 24 Feb. 1869; m. 1st, 25 Mar. 1824, Isabella Camilla, da. of Sir William Jervis Twysden, 7th Bt. [E.], d. 7 Mar. 1850; 2ndly, 29 Mar. 1859, Ellen Maria, da. of the Rev. John Alexander Ross, Vicar of Westwell, co. Kent; and had issue 1c to 5c.
    1c. Naunton Robert Twysden Orgill Leman of Brampton Hall, b. 12 Sept. 1825; m. 11 Aug. 1869, Rose Elizabeth, da. of the Rev. John Alexander Ross, Vicar of Westwell; and has issue 1d.
      1d. Robert Naunton Orgill Leman, b. 2 Oct. 1870.
    2c. Anderson Thomas John Orgill Leman, b. 31 Jan. 1862.
    3c.[1] Frances Henrietta Eliza Flora Leman.
    4c.[2] Beatrice Amelia Ellen Leman.
    5c.[2] Ethel Helena Mary Leman.
  2b. Frances Leman, d. 22 Jan. 1866; m. 3 Dec. 1820, Molyneux Shuldham, Comm. R.N., d. 25 Feb. 1866; and had issue.
See pp. 164-165, Nos. 17504-17524. [Nos. 17712 to 17807.

81. Descendants of ELIZABETH WHICHCOT (Table IX.), bapt. at Harpswell 20 Mar. 1706; bur. at Glentworth 19 Feb. 1774; m. 19 Feb. 1730, the Ven. WILLIAM BASSETT, Archdeacon of Stow, b. 7 June 1703; bur. at Glentworth 13 July 1765; and had issue (with a son who d.s.p. and 2 other das. known to have d. in infancy) 1a to 10a.

1a. William Bassett, d. 18 Nov. 1738.
2a. Richard Bassett of Glentworth, b. 15 Sept. 1744; d. 12 July 1805; m. 1 July 1774, Martha, da. of Joseph Armitage of High Royd, Huddersfield, d. (-); and had issue 1b to 2b.

# of The Blood Royal

1*b*. Rev. Henry Bassett, Rector of *North Thoresby*, b. 12 *Ap*. 1778; d. 1 *May* 1852; m. 1 *Oct*. 1811, Catharine, da. of John Fardell of Lincoln, d. 6 *June* 1859; and had issue 1*c* to 2*c*.

    1*c*. Henry Basselt of Ingham, co. Linc., b. 18 *Jan*. 1817; d. 18 *July* 1888; m. 3 *Jan*. 1856, Emily Mary, da. of Henry Wood of London, d. 23 *Feb*. 1897; *and had issue* 1*d* to 3*d*.

        1*d*. Rev. Henry John Bassett, B.A. (Oxon.), Vicar of Hagnaby and East Kirkby (*East Kirkby Vicarage, Spilsby*), b. 17 Jan. 1859; m. 21 June 1894, Gertrude Mary, da. of Periera Brown of Glentworth Hall, co. Linc.; and has issue 1*e*.

            1*e*. Ralph Periera Henry Bassett, b. 16 Feb. 1896.

        2*d*. Isabel Emily Bassett, *unm*.

        3*d*. Katharine Phœbe Bassett, *unm*.

    2*c*. Catharine Mary Bassett, b. 5 Oct. 1823; d. 31 *Jan*. 1902; m. 4 *June* 1850, *the Rev. John Gilbert Day of Pitsford, co. Northants*, d. 19 *Nov*. 1903; *and had issue* 1*d* to 2*d*.

        1*d*. Julia Catherine Day (*The Limes, Plestbury Road, Cheltenham*), m. 25 Ap. 1878, Frederick Charles Fardell, d. 3 Aug. 1899.

        2*d*. Blanche Mary Day, *unm*.

  2*b*. Martha Bassett, b. 27 Sept. 1776; d. 18 Feb. 1869; m. 17 Oct. 1798, *John Wilson of Seacroft Hall and Cliffe Hall, co. Yorks*, d. 12 Nov. 1836; *and had issue* 1*c* to 2*c*.

    1*c*. Richard Bassett Wilson of *Cliffe Hall, co. Yorks*, b. 3 *Ap*. 1806; d. 23 *Mar*. 1867; m. 5 Dec. 1839, Anne, da. and co-h. of *William FitzGerald of Adelphi, co. Clare*, d. 11 *July* 1877; *and had issue* 1*d* to 7*d*.

        1*d*. John Gerald Wilson, C.B., b. 29 Dec. 1841; d. 8 *Mar*. 1902; m. 4 *June* 1873, Angelina Rosa Geraldine, da. of Rev. the Hon. Henry O'Brien; *and had issue* 1*e* to 6*e*.

            1*e*. Murrough John Wilson (*Cliffe Hall, Darlington*), b. 14 Sept. 1875; m. 16 Feb. 1904, Sybil May, da. of Sir Powlett Charles John Milbank, 2nd Bt. [U.K.]; and has issue 1*f* to 2*f*.

                1*f*. Geraldine Edith Mary Wilson, b. 19 Dec. 1905.

                2*f*. Kathleen May Wilson, b. 16 Aug. 1909.

            2*e*. Denis Daly Wilson, Capt. 17th Bengal Cavalry, b. 22 Oct. 1878.

            3*e*. Frank O'Brien Wilson, Lieut. R.N., b. 30 Ap. 1883.

            4*e*. Harriet Anne Dorothy Wilson, *m*. 12 July 1904, Frederick Richard Charles Milbank, J.P. [son and h.-app. of Sir Powlett Charles John Milbank, 2nd Bt. [U.K.], J.P., D.L.] (*Abbey House, Ludlow*); and has issue 1*f* to 2*f*.

                1*f*. Mark Vane Milbank, b. 11 Jan. 1907.

                2*f*. John Gerald Frederick Milbank, b. 17 Ap. 1909.

            5*e*. Gladys Mary Wilson, *m*. 15 Aug. 1905, John Beaumont Hotham, B.A. (Camb.), a Clerk in the House of Lords [B. Hotham Coll.] (*70 Warwick Square, S.W.*); and has issue 1*f* to 2*f*.

                1*f*. Dorothy Jean Hotham, b. 12 Aug. 1907.

                2*f*. Margaret Hotham, b. 14 Aug. 1909.

            6*e*. Geraldine Wilson.

        2*d*. William Henry Wilson, *now* (R.L. 20 July 1872) FitzGerald-Wilson (*Adelphi, Corofin, co. Clare*), b. 22 Ap. 1844; *m*. 21 Nov. 1885, Olave, da. of Russell C. Stanhope of Parsonstown Manor, co. Meath; and has issue 1*e* to 2*e*.

            1*e*. Francis William Wilson-FitzGerald, 1st Royal Dragoons, b. 8 Dec. 1886.

            2*e*. Olave Clare Wilson-FitzGerald, b. 11 Feb. 1888.

        3*d*. Maurice FitzGerald Wilson (*Ashburn Gardens, London, W.*), b. 4 Feb. 1858; *m*. 2 Aug. 1884, Florence May, da. of the Ven. Hopkins Badnall, D.D., Archdeacon of the Cape of Good Hope; and has issue 1*e* to 2*e*.

            1*e*. Maurice Fiennes FitzGerald Wilson, b. 22 June 1886.

            2*e*. Bassett FitzGerald Wilson, b. 1 Sept. 1888.   [Nos. 17808 to 17831.

The Plantagenet Roll

4d. *Juliana Cecilia Wilson*, d. 15 Nov. 1898; m. 14 Sept. 1865, Thomas Charles Johnson Sowerby of Snow Hall, Darlington; and had issue 1e to 8e.

1e. Charles Fitzgerald Sowerby, Capt. R.N., b. 31 July 1866.

2e. William Bassett Sowerby (*Newcastle-on-Tyne*), b. 13 Ap. 1870; m. 14 Sept. 1900, Lena, da. of William Hunter; and has issue 1f.

1f. Guy Spencer Sowerby, b. 5 Aug. 1905.

3e. Edward Chaytor Sowerby (*Sudborough, Northants*), b. 2 Sept. 1872; m. 4 July 1907, Muriel, d. of J. Gardiner Muir of Farming Woods, co. Northants; and has issue 1f.

1f. Thomas Muir Sowerby, b. 6 Sept. 1908.

4e. Maurice Eden Sowerby, Capt. R.E., b. 5 Dec. 1874.

5e. Gerald Sowerby, Lieut. R.N. (*Myrtle, Newcastle, co. Down*), b. 31 July 1878; m. 14 Jan. 1904, Lady Mabel Marguerite, da. of Hugh (Annesley), 5th Earl of Annesley [I.]; and has issue 1f.

1f. Gerald Francis Annesley Sowerby, b. 5 Nov. 1904.

6e. Mabel Frances Sowerby.

7e. Edith Mary Sowerby, m. 12 Nov. 1903, Sir Henry Spencer Moreton Havelock-Allan, 2nd Bt. [U.K.] (*Blackwell Grange and Blackwell Hall, Darlington*).

8e. Mary Gertrude Sowerby.

5d. Mary Lucia Wilson.

6d. Augusta Jane Wilson, m. 30 June 1870, Thomas Robins Bolitho of Trengwainton (*Trengwainton, Hea Moor, R.S.O., Cornwall*), s.p.

7d. Emily Gertrude Wilson, m. 17 Dec. 1878, James FitzGerald Bannatyne of Summerville, co. Limerick (*Haldon, Exeter*); and has issue 1e to 3e.

1e. James FitzGerald Bannatyne, b. 25 Nov. 1883.

2e. Mary Stuart Bannatyne, b. 1 May 1881.

3e. Victoria Vera Bannatyne, b. 11 Sept. 1887.

2c. *John Wilson of Seacroft Hall*, co. Yorks, b. 1 Jan. 1808; d. 29 Jan. 1891; m. 13 Ap. 1846, Anna Maria Isabella, da. of Roderick Macleod of Cadboll, co. Ross, M.P., d. 26 Dec. 1903; and had issue 1d to 4d.

1d. Darcy Bruce Wilson (*Seacroft Hall, near Leeds*), b. 17 June 1851.

2d. Arthur Henry Wilson (*Sandridge Park, Totnes*), b. 24 Ap. 1853; m. 12 Nov. 1885, Alice Louisa, da. of George Drake Wainwright; and has issue 1e.

1e. Gladys Sabine Fyers Wilson, b. 6 Oct. 1886.

3d. Constance Wilson, m. 6 Jan. 1887, the Rev. Charles John Aylmer Eade, M.A. (Camb.), Vicar of Aycliffe (*Aycliffe Vicarage, Darlington*); and has issue 1e to 3e.

1e. John Eade, b. 18 Dec. 1887.

2e. Charles Eade, b. 19 July 1900.

3e. Aylmer Eade, b. 29 Jan. 1902.

4d. Louisa Wilson.

3a. *Thomas Bassett*, b. 22 Jan. 1747.

4a. *John Bassett*, b. 22 Feb. 1748.

5a. *Charles Bassett*, b. 21 July 1749, was married and had a wife living at Glentworth in 1811.[1]

6a. *Frances Bassett*, b. 22 Feb. 1731.

7a. *Katherine Bassett*, b. 14 Jan. 1732.

8a. *Anne Bassett*.

9a. *Lydia Bassett*, b. 17 Feb. 1742.

10a. *Charlotte Bassett*, b. 20 Sept. 1743.   [Nos. 17832 to 17856.

---

[1] Maddison's "Lincolnshire Pedigrees," i. 107.

of The Blood Royal

82. Descendants of ELIZABETH TEMPEST (Table IX.), d. (-); m. JOHN SOUTH of Kelstern, co. Lincoln, who was nominated a Knight of the Royal Oak in 1660; and had issue.

See p. 150.

83. Descendants, if any surviving, of ANNE CLIFTON (Table IX.), d. (-); m. Sir FRANCIS RODES, 2nd Bt. [E.], d. 1651; and had issue 1a to 2a.

1a. *Sir Francis Rodes, 3rd Bt. [E.], b. c. 1647; d. 14 Mar. 1675; m. (licence dated 1 May) 1665, Martha, da. of William Thornton of Grantham, co. Linc., d. 25 Oct. 1719; and had issue 1b to 3b.*
  1b. *Sir John Rodes, 4th Bt. [E.], b. 1670; d. unm. Oct. 1743.*
  2b. *Frances Rodes, da. and co-h., d. (-); m. Gilbert Heathcote of Calthorp or Cuthorp, co. Derby, M.D.; and had issue 1c to 3c.*
    1c. *Cornelius Heathcote, M.D., d. (-); m. Elizabeth, da. of (—) Middlebrooke; and had issue 1d.*
    1d. *John Heathcote, d. (-); m. Millicent, da. of (—) Saterthwaite; and had issue (with others whose issue is known to be extinct) 1e.*
    1e. *Mary Heathcote, m. 1st, (—) Miers; 2ndly, Capt. Massey.*
    2c. *Martha Heathcote, d. (-); m. 1744, Benjamin Bartlett of Bradford.*
    3c. *Elizabeth Heathcote, d. (-); m. 1746, Peter Acklom of Hornsey, co. Yorks.*
  3b. *Anne Rodes, da. and co-h., d. (-); m. William Thornton of Bloxham.*
2a. *Jane Rodes, d. (-); m. Capt. William Hossay of London.*

84. Descendants of Lady MARGARET CLIFFORD (Table VIII.), b. c. 1540; d. 19 Sept. 1596; m. 7 Feb. 1555, HENRY (STANLEY), 4th EARL OF DERBY [E.], K.G., d. 25 Sept. 1593; and had issue.

See the Tudor Roll, Table LXXXII., and pp. 358-563, Nos. 27543-36735.

Nos. 17857 to 27049.

85. Descendants of PEREGRINE (BERTIE), 3rd DUKE OF ANCASTER AND KESTEVEN [G.B.] and MARQUIS OF LINDSEY, and 18th BARON WILLOUGHBY DE ERESBY [E.], Hereditary Lord Great Chamberlain of England, P.C. (Table X.), b. 1714; d. 12 Aug. 1778; m. 2ndly, 27 Nov. 1750, MARY, sometime Mistress of the Robes to Queen Charlotte, da. of Thomas PANTON of Newmarket, co. Cambridge, d. at Naples Oct. 1793; and had issue 1a to 3a.

1a. *Robert (Bertie), 4th Duke of Ancaster and Kesteven [G.B.], &c., b. 17 Oct. 1736; d. unm. 8 July 1779.*
2a. *Priscilla Barbara Elizabeth (née Bertie), 20th Baroness Willoughby de Eresby [E.], Joint Hereditary Great Chamberlain of England, b. 16 Feb. 1761; d. 29 Dec. 1828; m. 23 Feb. 1779, Peter (Burrell), 1st Baron Gwydyr [G.B.], b. 16 June 1754; d. 29 June 1820; and had issue 1b to 2b.*
  1b. *Peter Robert (Burrell, sometime (R.L. 5 Nov. 1807) Burrell-Drummond, and finally (R.L. 26 June 1829) Drummond-Willoughby), 21st Baron Willoughby de*

The Plantagenet Roll

Eresby [E.] *and 2nd Baron Gwydyr* [G.B.], *P.C., &c.,* b. 19 *Mar.* 1782; d. 22 *Feb.* 1865; m. 19 *Oct.* 1807, *Lady Clementina, da. and h. of James* (*Drummond*), 11*th Earl of Perth* [S.] *and* 1*st Baron Perth* [G.B.], d. 26 *Jan.* 1865; *and had issue* 1c *to* 3c.

1c. *Alberic* (*Burrell*), 22*nd Baron Willoughby de Eresby* [E.], 3*rd Baron Gwydyr* [G.B.], b. 25 Dec. 1821; d. *unm.* 26 *Aug.* 1870.

2c. *Clementina Elizabeth,* suo jure 23*rd Baroness Willoughby de Eresby* [E.], *&c., Joint Hereditary Great Chamberlain of England, da. and* (1870) *co-h.,* b. 2 *Sept.* 1809; d. 13 *Nov.* 1888; m. 8 *Oct.* 1827, *Sir Gilbert John Heathcote,* 5*th Bt.* [G.B.], *afterwards* (26 *Feb.* 1856) 1*st Baron Aveland* [U.K.] [*descended from King Henry* VII.], d. 6 *Sept.* 1867; *and had issue.*

See the Tudor Roll, pp. 206–207, Nos. 21514–21530.

3c. *Hon. Charlotte Augusta Annabella Drummond-Willoughby, Joint Hereditary Great Chamberlain of England, da. and* (1870) *co-h.,* b. 3 *Nov.* 1815; d. 26 *July* 1879; m. *as 2nd wife,* 10 *Aug.* 1840, *Robert John* (*Smith, afterwards* (*R.L.* 26 *Aug.* 1839) *Carrington*), 2*nd Baron Carrington* [G.B. *and* I.], b. 16 *June* 1796; d. 17 *Mar.* 1868; *and had issue* 1d *to* 5d.

1d. Charles Robert (Carrington, now (R.L. 24 Ap. 1896) Wynn-Carrington), 1st Earl Carrington [U.K.], 3rd Baron Carrington [G.B. and I.], Joint Hereditary Lord Great Chamberlain of England, K.G., P.C., G.C.M.G., President of the Board of Agriculture, *formerly* Lord Chamberlain of the Household to Queen Victoria 1892-1895, Gov. and Comm.-in-Chief of New South Wales 1885–1890, &c. &c. (*Gwydyr Castle, Llanrwst, Wales; Daw's Hill, High Wycombe;* 53 *Prince's Gate, S.W.*), b. 16 May 1843; m. 15 July 1878, the Hon. Cecilia Margaret [a descendant of the Lady Isabel Plantagenet (see Essex Volume, p. 46)], da. of Charles (Harbord), 5th Baron Suffield [G.B.]; and has issue 1e to 6e.

1e. Albert Edward Samuel Charles Robert Wynn-Carrington, Viscount Wendover, for whom H.M. the King stood Sponsor, b. 24 Ap. 1895.

2e. Lady Marjorie Cecilia Wynn-Carrington, m. 12 Feb. 1901, Charles Henry Wellesley (Wilson), 2nd Baron Nunburnholme [U.K.], D.S.O., &c. (*Ferriby Hall, North Ferriby, East Yorks*): and has issue 1f to 2f.

1f. Hon. Charles John Wilson, b. 25 Ap. 1904.

2f. Hon. Cecilia Monica Wilson.

3e. Lady Alexandra Augusta Wynn-Carrington, for whom H.M. Queen Alexandra was Sponsor.

4e. Lady Ruperta Wynn-Carrington, m. 7 Dec. 1905, William Legge, Viscount Lewisham [s. and h. of the 6th Earl of Dartmouth and a descendant of King Henry VII. (see Tudor Roll, p. 199)] (*Patshull House, Wolverhampton*); and has issue 1f to 2f.

1f. Hon. Mary Cecilia Legge.

2f. Hon. Elizabeth Legge.

5e. Lady Judith Sydney Mee Wynn-Carrington.

6e. Lady Victoria Alexandrina Wynn-Carrington, for whom H.M. Queen Victoria was Sponsor.

2d. Hon. Sir William Henry Peregrine Carington (R.L. 21 Aug. 1880), *previously* Carrington, K.C.V.O., C.B., Extra Equerry to H.M. the King, *formerly* Equerry to H.M. the King and to Queen Victoria 1882–1902, Capt. and Lieut.-Col. Grenadier Guards, M.P. for Wycombe 1868–1883, &c. (*Burfield, Old Windsor;* 6 *Cadogan Square, S.W.*), b. 28 July 1845; m. 28 Sept. 1871, Juliet, da. of Francis Warden.

3d. Hon. Rupert Clement George Carington (R.L. 21 Aug. 1880), *previously* Carrington, C.V.O., D.S.O., Lieut.-Col. Comdg. 68th Australian Light Horse, *formerly* Col. Comdg. 3rd Regt. New South Wales Imperial Bushmen in South Africa 1899–1902, M.P. co. Bucks 1880–1885, &c. (*Momalong, N.S. Wales*), b. 17 Dec. 1852; m. Ap. 1891, Edith, da. of John Horsfall of Widgiewa, N.S. Wales; and has issue 1e.

1e. Rupert Victor John Carington, b. 1891.   [Nos. 27050 to 27080.

# of The Blood Royal

4d. Hon. Augusta Clementina Carrington (11 *Hobart Place, S.W.; Dunalley Lodge, Halliford-on-Thames*), *m.* 7 July 1864, Archibald Campbell (Campbell), 1st Baron Blythswood [U.K.], *d.s.p.* 8 July 1908.

5d. Hon. Eva Elizabeth Carrington, *m.* 5 July 1869, Charles Augustus (Stanhope), 8th Earl of Harrington [G.B.] [descended from George (Plantagenet), Duke of Clarence, K.G. (see Clarence Volume, p. 348)] (*Elvaston Castle, near Derby; Harrington House, Craig's Court, Charing Cross, W.C., &c.*), *s.p.*

2b. Hon. Lindsey Merrik Peter Burrell, b. 20 *June* 1786; d. 1 *Jan.* 1848; m. 13 *July* 1807, Frances, da. of James Daniell, d. 25 *Aug.* 1846; *and had issue* 1c to 5c.

1c. Peter Robert (Burrell), 4th Baron Gwydyr and 5th Baronet [G.B.], &c., b. 27 *Ap.* 1810; d. 3 *Ap.* 1909; m. 1st, 10 *Dec.* 1840, Sophia, da. and h. of Frederick William Campbell of Barbreck, d. 14 *Mar.* 1843; 2ndly, 8 *May* 1856, Georgina, da. of George Peter Holford of Westonbirt, co. *Glouc.*, d. 20 Nov. 1892; *and had issue* 1d to 2d.

1d. Willoughby Merrik Campbell (Burrell), 5th Baron Gwydyr and 6th Baronet [G.B.], F.R.G.S., J.P., D.L., Hon. Col. 4th Batt. Suffolk Regt., *formerly Capt.* Rifle Brig. (*Stoke Park, Ipswich; 60 Pont Street, S.W.; Carlton*), b. 26 Oct. 1841; *m.* 1st, 4 Sept. 1873, Mary, da. and h. of Sir John Banks, K.C.B., M.D., Physician-in-Ordinary to Queen Victoria, *d.* 26 June 1898; 2ndly, 4 June 1901, Anne, da. of John Ord of Overwhitton, co. Roxburgh; and has issue 1e.

1e. Hon. Catharine Mary Sermonda Burrell, *m.* 16 July 1902, John Henniker Heaton (94 *Cromwell Road, S.W.*); and has issue 1f to 3f.

1f. John Victor Peregrine Henniker Heaton, *b.* 10 Feb. 1903.

2f. Peter Joseph Henniker Heaton, *b.* 9 May 1907.

3f. Mary Araluen Henniker Heaton.

2d.[2] Hon. Cicely Burrell.

2c. Georgiana Charlotte Burrell, b. 1811; d. 21 *Sept.* 1843; m. *as 1st wife*, 6 *Dec.* 1838, *James Hamilton Lloyd-Anstruther of Hintlesham Hall, co. Suffolk*, J.P., D.L. [*Baronet of Balcaskie Coll.*], d. 23 Dec. 1882; *and had issue* 1d.

1d. Robert Hamilton Lloyd-Anstruther of Hintlesham, J.P., D.L., Major and Hon. Lieut.-Col. *late* Rifle Brig., *formerly* M.P. for S.E. Suffolk 1886–1892 (*Hintlesham Hall, Ipswich; 37 Eccleston Square, S.W.*), *b.* 21 Ap. 1841; *m.* 5 July 1871, Gertrude Louisa Georgiana [descended from King Henry VII. (see Tudor Roll, p. 337)], da. of Francis Horatio FitzRoy of Frogmore, co. Hants [D. of Grafton Coll.]; and has issue 1e.

1e. Fitz Roy Hamilton Lloyd-Anstruther, Lieut. Army Motor Reserve (12 *Chapel Street, Belgrave Square, S.W.*), *b.* 5 July 1872; *m.* 11 Oct. 1898, the Hon. Rachel [descended from King Henry VII. (see Tudor Roll, p. 216)], da. of Augustus Cholmondeley (Gough-Calthorpe), 6th Baron Calthorpe [G.B.]; and has issue 1f.

1f. Richard Hamilton Lloyd-Anstruther, *b.* 28 Mar. 1908.

3c. Susan Anne Burrell, b. 1816; d. 16 *Aug.* 1850; m. 29 *July* 1839, *William Crosbie, afterwards (R.L.* 11 Nov. 1880) *Talbot-Crosbie of Ardfert Abbey, co. Kerry,* d. 4 *Sept.* 1899; *and had issue.*

See the Exeter Volume, p. 395, Nos. 33269–33303.

4c. Hon. Marcia Sarah Elizabeth Burrell, had *R.W. as da. of a Baron* 17 Dec. 1870, b. 1821; d. 22 Oct. 1889; m. 1st, 24 *Ap.* 1851, *the Rev. Charles Cameron*, d. 1 *Dec.* 1861; 2ndly, 14 *Ap.* 1868, *Walter Whittington; and had issue* 1d to 5d.

1d. Charles Hamilton Hone Cameron, L.R.C.P., M.R.C.S., D.P.H. (*Gildredge House*, 21 *The Goffs, Eastbourne*), *b.* 30 Sept. 1852; *m.* 30 Ap. 1878, Mary Louise Savile, da. of Robert Walter Mexborough Shepherd; and has issue 1e to 4e.

1e. Charles Peter Gwydyr Cameron, Lieut. R.G.A., *b.* 18 Jan. 1885.

2e. Ewen Paul Burrell Cameron, *b.* 27 Sept. 1897.

3e. Stella Willoughby Savile Cameron, *m.* 1 Oct. 1903, Clement Cobbold, Bar.-at-Law (*Hyntle Place, Hintlesham, Suffolk; Belstead Lodge, Ipswich*); and has issue 1f to 2f. [Nos. 27081 to 27130.

The Plantagenet Roll

1*f*. Cameron Fromanteel Cobbold, *b*. 14 Sept. 1904.
2*f*. Marcia Ruth Jean Cameron Cobbold.

2*d*. Marcia Frances Lyttleton Cameron, *m*. 18 Ap. 1888, the Rev. Henry Kilburn Law; and has issue 1*e* to 4*e*.
1*e*. Henry Merrik Burrell Law, *b*. 11 Dec. 1890.
2*e*. Charles Lindsey Gwydyr Law, *b*. 3 Aug. 1893.
3*e*. Marcia Georgina Cameron Law.
4*e*. Margaret Frances Willoughby Law.

3*d*. Emma Georgina Cameron, *m*. 22 Dec. 1885, the Rev. Thomas Kirkpatrick, *d*. 30 May 1888; and has issue 1*e*.
1*e*. Charles Edward Cameron Kirkpatrick, *b*. 2 Dec. 1886.

4*d*. Clare Charlotte Cameron, *m*. 17 July 1883, the Rev. William John Margetts, Vicar of Baildon (*Baildon Vicarage, near Shipley, Yorks*); and has issue 1*e* to 6*e*.
1*e*. John Theodore Cameron Margetts, *b*. 16 Feb. 1892.
2*e*. Grace Cameron Margetts.
3*e*. Winifred Willoughby Margetts, *m*. Jan. 1910, Lacy Francis Taverner (*Kobe, Japan*).
4*e*. Dorothy Lucy Clare Margetts.
5*e*. Marcia Georgina Lyttleton Margetts.
6*e*. Mary Cicely Burrell Margetts.

5*d*. Lucy Amelia Cameron, *m*. 24 July 1884, Edward Hill Dobson; and has issue 1*e*.
1*e*. Stephanie Cicely Clare Dobson.

5*c*. Hon. Charlotte Anne Burrell, had R.W. *as da. of a Baron* 17 Dec. 1870, *b*. 1822; *d*. 8 Dec. 1907; *m*. 9 Oct. 1851, Charles Wilmot Smith of Ballynanty House, co. Liverpool, J.P.; *and had issue* 1*d* to 5*d*.

1*d*. John Wilmot Crosbie Smith of Ballynanty (*Ballynanty House, Bruff, co. Limerick; Killuran Abbey, co. Clare*), *b*. 9 Feb. 1853; *m*. 1 Oct. 1874, Jane Grant, da. of Andrew Sherlock Lawson of Aldborough, co. York; and has issue 1*e* to 6*e*.
1*e*. Charles Wilmot Smith, *b*. 4 Sept. 1880.
2*e*. Andrew Wilmot Smith, Lieut. R.N., *b*. 21 May 1885.
3*e*. Charlotte Isabella Smith.
4*e*. [da.] Smith.
5*e*. [da.] Smith.
6*e*. [da.] Smith.

2*d*. Willoughby Lloyd Smith, *b*. 24 July 1859.
3*d*. George Charles Bertie Smith, *b*. 4 Mar. 1861.
4*d*. Emma Georgina Smith.
5*d*. Charlotte Mary Smith.

3*a*. Lady Georgiana Charlotte Bertie, *b*. 7 Aug. 1764; *d*. 23 *June* 1838; *m*. 25 Ap. 1791, *George James (Cholmondeley), 1st Marquis [U.K.], 4th Earl [E.], and 6th Viscount [I.] Cholmondeley, K.G.*, *d*. 10 Ap. 1827; *and had issue*.
See the Clarence Volume, pp. 127-128, Nos. 1503-1544. [Nos. 27131 to 27201.

86. Descendants of Lady MARY BERTIE (Table X.), *d*. 23 May 1774; *m*. 21 Feb. 1747, SAMUEL GREATHEED of Guy's Cliffe, co. Warwick; and had (with possibly other) issue 1*a*.

1*a*. Bertie Greatheed, *afterwards* (R.L. 20 May 1819) Bertie-Greatheed *of Guy's Cliffe*, *d*. (–); *m*. (—); *and had (with possibly other) issue* 1*b*.
1*b*. (—) Bertie-Greatheed *of Guy's Cliffe*, *d*. (–); *m*. (—); *and had issue* 1*c*.
1*c*. Anne Caroline Bertie-Greatheed *of Guy's Cliffe*, *b*. c. 1805; *d*. 8 *June* 1882; *m*. 20 *Mar*. 1822, *the Hon. Charles Percy, afterwards* (R.L. 10 Ap. 1826) Greatheed-Percy, *d*. 11 Oct. 1870, leaving issue a da. who d. unm. 15 Feb. 1891.

# of The Blood Royal

87. Descendants of Lady JANE BERTIE (Table X.), d. 1793 ; m. 1743, Gen. EDWARD MATHEW, Equerry to King George III., Gen. Comdg. the Guards Brigade in North America, and *afterwards* Governor of Grenada 1784-1789, b. c. 1727 ; d. 25 Dec. 1805 ; and had issue 1a to 5a.

1a. *Brownlow Mathew, afterwards (R.L. 5 May 1819) Bertie-Mathew,* b. (-) ; d. 29 *Ap.* (? *Sep.*) 1826 ; m. 2 *Ap.* 1807, *Harriet Anne, da. of North Naylor, H.E.I.C.S. [by his wife (—), sister of Sir Albemarle Bertie, Bt.]*, d. (-) ; *and had issue (with 2 other sons and 3 das. known to have d.s.p)* 1b *to* 3b.
    1b. Edward Bertie-Mathew.
    2b. *Jane Bertie-Mathew,* d. (-) ; m. *Alphonso (Ferrero), Marquis of La Marmora (Marchese della Marmora) [Italy], K.A.I., K.C.B., G.C.L.H., Field-Marshal, Premier and Minister of Foreign Affairs to King Victor Emmanuel II.* 1864-1866, &c., b. 1804 ; d.s.p. *at Florence* 5 *Jan.* 1878.
    3b. *Elizabeth Bertie-Mathew.*

2a. *Jane Mathew, twin with* 3a, d. 5 *June* 1830 ; m. 2 *Sept.* 1766, *Thomas Maitland,* d. 2 *Dec.* 1797 ; *and had issue (with 3 sons and a da., d.s.p.)* 1b *to* 4b.
    1b. Sir Peregrine Maitland, G.C.B., *General, commanded Guards at Waterloo, afterwards Governor and Com.-in-Chief at the Cape of Good Hope* 1843-1846, &c., b. 6 *July* 1777 ; d. 30 *May* 1854 ; m. 1st, 8 *June* 1803, *the Hon. Louisa, da. of Sir Edward Crofton,* 2nd *Bt.* [I.] ; 2ndly, 9 Oct. 1815, Lady Sarah [*descended from King Henry VII.* (see Tudor Volume, p. 468)], *da. of Charles (Lennox),* 4th *Duke of Richmond* [E.], *Lennox* [S.]*, and Aubigny* [F.]*, K.G.,* d. 8 *Sept.* 1873 ; *and had issue (with a son by* 1st *wife, who* d. unm.) 1c *to* 7c.
    1c. *Charles Lennox Brownlow Maitland, C.B., K.L.H., Col.* 1st *Batt. Duke of Edinburgh's Regt., Lieut.-Gov. Chelsea Hospital* 1869-1870, b. 27 *Sept.* 1823 ; d. (? unm.).
    2c. Horatio Arthur Lennox Maitland, Admiral R.N., b. 13 Mar. 1834.
    3c. *Sarah Maitland,* d. (-) ; m. 14 *Jan.* 1837, *Gen. Thomas Bowes Forster* [*son of Lieut.-Col. John Randall Forster*], d. 21 *Mar.* 1870 ; *and had issue (with a son* d. unm.) 1d *to* 6d.
        1d. Bowes Lennox Forster, Lieut.-Gen., *formerly Col. Comdg. R.A.,* b. 9 Oct. 1837 ; m. 18 Jan. 1868, Jessie Kate, da. of William Mackenzie, C.B., C.S.I., Inspector-Gen. of Hospitals, India, and Hon. Physician to Queen Victoria ; and has issue 1e to 5e.
            1e. William Anson Maitland Prendegast Forster, b. 21 Ap. 1869.
            2e. Stuart Boscawen Erode Desbrisay Forster, b. 5 Oct. 1870.
            3e. George Norman Bowes Forster, b. 26 Oct. 1872.
            4e. Lenox Weston Glendower Forster, b. 28 Sept. 1874.
            5e. Isabella Gertrude Forster.
        2d. Peregrine Henry Forster, b. 2 July 1848.
        3d. Susan Charlotte Forster, m. 28 Ap. 1874, the Rev. Charles Garbett, M.A. (Oxon.), Vicar of Tongham, d. (-) ; and had issue 1e to 5e.
            1e. Rev. Cyril Forster Garbett, M.A. (Oxon.), Vicar of Portsea (*The Vicarage, Portsea*), b. 6 Feb. 1875.
            2e. Basil Maitland Garbett, b. 13 July 1876.
            3e. Clement Steuart Garbett, b. 21 July 1877.
            4e. Leonard Gillilan Garbett, b. 1 Mar. 1879.
            5e. Elsie Mary Katherine Garbett.
        4d. Sarah Caroline Forster, m. 20 Oct. 1869, Edward Howorth Greenly, Lord of the Manor of Titley, M.A. (Oxon.), J.P., D.L., High Sheriff co. Hereford 1881, &c. (*Titley Court, R.S.O., Hereford*) ; and has issue 1e to 5e.

[Nos. 27202 to 27216.

The Plantagenet Roll

1e. Walter Howorth Greenly, J.P., D.S.O., Major 12th Lancers and Cavalry Staff Officer to the Inspector-Gen. of the Forces (*Cavalry Club*), b. 2 Jan. 1875.

2e. John Henry Maitland Greenly, b. 25 July 1885.

3e. Alice Maud Greenly, m. 9 Jan. 1907, Robert Napier Greathed, Capt. R.A. ; and has issue 1f.

1f. Elisabeth Sarah Greathed.

4e. Ethel Mary Greenly.

5e. Lucy Margaret Greenly, m. 2 July 1902, the Hon. Antony Schomberg Byng [3rd son of the 5th Earl of Strafford and a descendant of King Henry VII. (see Tudor Roll, p. 169)] (6 *Mansion Place, Queen's Gate, S.W.*) ; and has issue 1f to 2f.

1f. William Humphrey Schomberg Byng, b. 31 May 1906.

2f. Gillian Sarah Byng.

5d. Emily Berlinga Forster.

6d. Louisa Margaret Jane Forster.

4c. *Caroline Charlotte Maitland*, d. 8 *Jan.* 1897 ; m. 17 *July* 1837, *John George Turnbull, Accountant-Gen. at Madras*, d. 2 *Jan.* 1872 ; *and had issue (with others d.s.p.)* 1d *to* 3d.

1d. Charles Frederic Alexander Turnbull of Whiteways, co. Surrey, Col. (ret.), formerly Comdg. Duke of Cornwall's L.I., Extra A.D.C. to the Com.-in-Chief at Aldershot 1881-1883, b. 26 June 1847 ; m. 7 Jan. 1890, Evelyn Selina, da. of John Lambart Broughton of Tunstall, co. Salop ; and has issue 1e to 2e.

1e. Dudley Ralph Turnbull, b. 15 Oct. 1891.

2e. Sylvia Nora Evelyn Turnbull.

2d. *Caroline Maria Turnbull*, d. 1878 ; m. 5 *June* 1860, *Alexander William Adair of Heatherton Park, co. Som., and Colhays, co. Devon, J.P., Lieut.-Col. Comdg. 2nd Somerset L.I., previously 52nd Foot*, b. 28 *Jan.* 1829 ; d. 1864 ; *and had issue (with a son and 2 das. d. young)* 1e *to* 2e.

1e. Gerald Adair, b. 7 Nov. 1865 ; d. (–).

2e. Evelyn Adair, m. 29 Ap. 1883, Joseph E. Wood [son of Joseph Carter Wood of Felcourt, co. Surrey].

3d. Georgiana Sarah Turnbull (*Whiteways, Farnham, co. Surrey*), m. 5 Jan. 1864, Allan Shafto Adair, J.P., Major 13th L.I. ; b. 20 Dec. 1836 ; d. 26 Dec. 1902 ; and has issue 1e.

1e. Desmond Adair, Lieut. Gordon Highlanders, b. 20 Dec. 1865.

5c. *Georgina Louisa Maitland*, d. 5 *Jan.* 1852 ; m. *as 1st wife*, 2 *Jan.* 1844, *the Rev. Sir Thomas Eardley Wilmot Blomefield, 3rd Bt.* [U.K.], d. 21 *Nov.* 1878 ; *and had issue*.

See the Tudor Roll, pp. 468–469, Nos. 32924–32941.

6c. *Emily Sophia Maitland*, d. 16 *Dec.* 1891 ; m. 13 *Jan.* 1846, *Admiral Lord Frederic Herbert Kerr, R.N.* [*M. of Lothian Coll.*], d. 15 *Jan.* 1896 ; *and had issue*.

See the Tudor Roll, p. 469, Nos. 32942–32963.

7c. *Eliza Mary Maitland*, b. 1832 ; d. (–) ; m. 14 *July* 1857, *Major-Gen. John Desborough, R.A., C.B.* (*Gross House, Northam, Bideford*) ; *and had issue*.

See the Tudor Roll, p. 469, Nos. 32964–32973.

2b. *Rev. Charles David Maitland, Incumbent of St. James', Brighton, formerly Capt. R.A.*, b. 3 *Sept.* 1785 ; d. 12 *Oct.* 1865 ; m. 15 *Ap.* 1814, *Elizabeth Adye, da. of John Miller*, d. 18 *Aug.* 1874 ; *and had issue* 1c *to* 5c.

1c. *Rev. Charles Maitland, M.A., M.D., Author of* " *The Church in the Catacombs,*" b. 6 *Jan.* 1815 ; d. 31 *July* 1866 ; m. 5 *Nov.* 1842, *Julia Charlotte, widow of James Thomas, da. of Henry Barrett*, d. 29 *Jan.* 1864 ; *and had issue* 1d.

1d. Julia Caroline Maitland, d. 27 Feb. 1890 ; m. 18 July 1861, the Rev. David Wauchope, M.A. (Oxon.), formerly Rector of Church Lawford [Bt. of Edmonstone (S. 1667) Coll.] (*Banister Gate, Southampton*) ; and had issue 1c to 3e.

[Nos. 27217 to 27282.

# of The Blood Royal

1e. Rev. David Maitland Don-Wauchope, M.A. (Oxon.), *late* Rector of Elstead (*Elstead, Godalming*), b. 4 Mar. 1864; m. 17 July 1888, Ethel Sarah, da. of Lewis Maxey Stewart; and has issue 1f to 2f.

    1f. Andrew Maxey Wauchope, b. 13 Dec. 1890.

    2f. Oswald Stewart Wauchope, b. 2 July 1897.

2e. Anne Julia Wauchope

3e. Caroline Wauchope.

2c. Rev. *Brownlow Maitland*, M.A. (*Camb.*), *Minister of Brunswick Chapel, Marylebone* 1849–1870, *and Sec. and Chaplain to his uncle, Gen. Sir Peregrine, Maitland, while Gov. of the Cape of Good Hope*, b. 12 *June* 1816; d. 27 *Oct.* 1902; m. 1*st*, 19 *July* 1848, *Josephine, da. of Alexander Erskine* "*of Dun*," d. 8 Dec. 1870; 2*ndly*, 4 *June* 1872, *Emily* (41 *Montagu Square*, W.), *da. of Samuel Warren, Q.C., D.C.L., F.R.S., M.P., a Master in Lunacy aud Author of* "*Ten Thousand a Year*"; *and had issue* (*with* 3 *sons and* 2 *das. by* 1*st wife, who* d.s.p.) 1d.

    1d.² Mary Eleanor Maitland.

3c. *Edward Maitland, Novelist and Essayist*, b. 27 *Oct.* 1824; d. (-); m. 3 *May* 1855, *Esther Charlotte, da. of William Bradley of Sydney, N.S.W.; and had issue* 1d.

    1d. Charles Bradley Maitland, Army Surgeon, Indian M.S., b. 5 Jan. 1856.

4c. *John Thomas Maitland*, R.N., b. 4 *Aug.* 1826; d. 11 *Mar.* 1855; m. 1848, *Mary Jane, da. of the Rev. Francis Pym, Rector of Willian*, co. *Bed.* [*who* m. 2*ndly, in Canada, c.* 1856/7, (—) *Wainwright*]; *and had issue* 1d.

    1d. Lionel Maitland, d. (?s.p.) *Sept.* 1873.

5c. Eardley Maitland, C.B., Col. R.A., Superintendent Royal Gun Factory, Woolwich, served in Indian Mutiny, Relief of Lucknow, &c., has medal with 3 clasps (6 *Westbourne Mansions, Westbourne Terrace*, W.), b. 10 Nov. 1833; m. 1st, 29 May 1855, Elizabeth Odell, da. of Thomas Baillie, d. 6 Aug. 1877; 2ndly, 15 Mar. 1883, Caroline Helen, da. of Thomas Metcalfe of Highgate, Hastings; and has issue (with 3 sons and a da. who *d.s.p.*) 1d to 4d.

    1d.² Eardly Thomas Maitland, b. 1888.

    2d.¹ Ella Laura Katherine Maitland, m. and has issue (3 das.).

    3d.¹ Emily Maitland, m. and has issue (a son and da., the latter of whom is m. with issue).

    4d.² Helena Victoria Augusta Maitland, Novelist.

3b. *Jane Maitland*, d. 18 *May* 1816; m. *Lieut.-Col. Richard Warren, Scots Fusiliers*, d. 1819; *and had issue* (*with* 5 *sons and* 3 *das. who* d.s.p.) 1c *to* 2c.

1c. *Mary Jane Warren*, d. 28 *Aug.* 1875; m. 1*st*, 15 *July* 1825, *the Rev. Cecil Smith of Lydeard House*, co. *Som.*, d. 12 *May* 1861; 2*ndly*, 1867/8, *the Rev. John Clare Pigot of Thrumpton Lodge, Weston-super-Mare*, d. 2 Dec. 1880; *and had issue* 1d.

    1d. *Cecil Smith of Lydeard House*, J.P., Bar.-at-Law I.T., b. 31 *May* 1826; d. 23 *Sept.* 1891; m. 28 *Sept.* 1858, *Amelia* (see p. 180), *da. of Sir Peter Stafford Carey*, d. 18 *Dec.* 1880; *and had issue* 1e *to* 7e.

        1e. Cecil Smith of the Croft, Botley, co. Hants (6 *Ladbroke Square*, W.), b. 5 Jan. 1860; m. 7 Sept. 1889, Elizabeth Emily, da. of Philip John Hammond; and has issue 1f to 2f.

            1f. Robert Philip Cecil Smith, b. 16 Ap. 1899.

            2f. Mary Cecil Smith.

        2e. Janet Charlotte Smith.

        3e. Caroline Ellen Smith.

        4e. Amy Smith.

        5e. Grace Smith.

        6e. Mabel Smith.

        7e. Susan Constance Smith. [Nos. 27283 to 27303.

The Plantagenet Roll

2c. Emily Aubrey Warren, d. 2 Feb. 1881; m. 16 Feb. 1835, *Sir Peter Stafford Carey, M.A. (Oxon.), Bar.-at-Law M.T., Prof. of English Law at Univ. Coll., London, 1838-1845, Bailiff of Guernsey 1845-1883, &c.,* d. (-); *and had issue (with a son and da. who d.s.p.)* 1d to 6d.

1d. Frances Carey, m. 7 Aug. 1861, Col. Ernest le Pelley, Seigneur of Sark, *formerly* 5th Foot; and has issue 1e to 5e.

 1e. Ernest Brownlow le Pelley, b. 1 June 1862.
 2e. Edward Carey le Pelley, b. 2 Nov. 1870.
 3e. Caroline Mary le Pelley.
 4e. Fanny Ernestine le Pelley.
 5e. Amelia Maitland le Pelley.

2d. *Amelia Carey*, d. 18 Dec. 1880; m. 28 Sept. 1858, *Cecil Smith of Lydeard House, co. Som.,* d. 23 Sept. 1891; *and had issue.*
See p. 179, Nos. 27295-27303.

3d. *Caroline Carey*, d. 6 Feb. 1883; m. 5 Dec. 1860, *Lieut.-Col. Julius Alphonso Carey, formerly Belgian Consul at Alicante, A.D.C. to Lieut.-Gov. of Guernsey; and had issue (with a son who* d. young) 1e to 4e.

 1e. Harold Stafford Carey, b. 28 Sept. 1861.
 2e. Wilfred Sausmarez Carey, b. 22 May 1863.
 3e. Mervyn Dobree Carey.
 4e. Elaine Biddulph Carey.

4d. Beatrice Carey, m. 26 Dec. 1867, Thomas Brooksbank, Bar.-at-Law I.T.; and has issue 1e.

 1e. Thomas Brooksbank, b. 12 July 1878.

5d. Emily Jane Carey.

6d. *Sophia Stafford Carey,* d. 19 Aug. 1871; m. 19 Aug. 1863, *the Rev. William John Mellish, M.A. (Camb.), Rector of Winestead, Hull,* d. (-); *and had issue (with a son* d. young) 1e to 4e.

 1e. John Stafford Mellish, b. 5 Aug. 1864.
 2e. Peter Bertie Mellish, b. 25 Nov. 1866.
 3e. Elizabeth Aubrey Mellish.
 4e. Dorothea Katherine Mellish.

4b. *Caroline Maitland,* d. 25 Nov. 1830; m. *Col. William Roberts, R.A.,* d. 9 July 1851; *and had issue (with* 4 sons d. unm.) 1c to 2c.

1c. *Henry Charles Roberts, Major Bengal Army,* b. 29 Nov. 1817; d. 24 Feb. 1880; m. 12 May 1864, *Jane, da. of John Beckley of Paignton, co. Devon; and had issue* 1d to 3d.

 1d. Henry Maitland Roberts, b. 14 June 1868; *unm.*

 2d. Laura Maria Roberts, m. 8 Ap. 1902, the Rev. Lonsdale Ragg, Preb. of Buckden, in Lincoln Cathedral, Author of "Dante and his Italy," "The Mohammedan Gospel of Barnabas," "The Church of the Apostles," and other works (*Westminster Club, Whitehall Court, S.W.; Tickencote Rectory, Stamford*); and has issue 1e.

  1e. Beatrice Laura Victoria Ragg, b. 6 Mar. 1907.

 3d. Edith Douglas Roberts (8 *Ferndale, Tunbridge Wells*).

2c. *Bertie Mathew Roberts, Major 26th Cameronians, D.L. co. Lanc.,* b. 11 Nov. 1822; d. 27 Oct. 1894; m. 1st, 1 July 1852, *Frances Jane Lennard, da. of Gen. Sir William Cator, K.C.B.,* d. 21 Sept. 1867; 2ndly, 1872, *Laura, widow of Alexander Forteall of Newton, N.B., and da. of Gen. Henry Tufnell Roberts, Bengal Cav.; and had issue* 1d to 2d.

 1d. Rev. Harry Bertie Roberts, M.A. (Oxon.), Rector of West Wickham (*West Wickham Rectory, Kent*), b. 28 Mar. 1855; *unm.*

 2d. *William Bertie Roberts, Lieut. Royal Welsh Fusiliers,* b. 29 June 1856; d. 5 Dec. 1899; m. 12 Oct. 1882, *Camille, da. of John Corbett of Inpney, Droit-*
               [Nos. 27304 to 27334.

# of The Blood Royal

wich, and *Ynys-y-Maengwyn, co. Merioneth ; and had issue (with a da., Sylvia, who* d. *young,* 14 *Jan.* 1907) 1e *to* 2e.

 1e. Rev. Roger Harry Bertie-Roberts, B.A. (Oxon.), Assist. Curate at Lillington, near Leamington, *b.* 5 Oct. 1883 ; *unm.*

 2e. Cicely Bertie-Roberts, *unm.*

 3a. *Mary Mathew,*[1] d. (-) ; m. *Lieut.-Col. Warren, Coldstream Guards.*

 4a. *Anne Mathew,* d. (-) ; m. *as* 1st *wife, James Austen of Alton [elder brother of Adm. Sir Francis William Austen, G.C.B., R.N.*], d. (-) ; *and had issue* 1b.

 1b. *Jane Anna Elizabeth Austen,* d. (-) ; m. 1814, *the Rev. Benjamin Langlois Lefroy, Rector of Ashe [descended from King Henry VII., &c.*], d.   1829 ; *and had issue.*

See the Tudor Roll, pp. 401–402, Nos. 29804–29823.

 5a. *Penelope Susannah Mathew,* b. c. 1764 ; d. 27 *Aug.* 1828, *aged* 64 ; m. 1st, 1787, *David Dewar of St. Christopher's, W.I., and of Enham House and Doles, co. Hants,* d. 20 *Nov.* 1794 ; 2ndly, 23 *Oct.* 1799, *Capt. Charles Cumberland, Royal Horse Guards Blue* [3rd *son of Richard Cumberland " the dramatist"*], b. 21 *May* 1764 ; d. 12 *May* 1835 ; *and had issue* 1b *to* 5b.

 1b. *David Albemarle Bertie Dewar of Doles, co. Hants, and Great Cumberland Place, London,* d. 25 *Nov.* 1859 ; m. 19 *May* 1821, *Anne Louise, da. of Col. Richard Magenis [by his wife, Lady Elizabeth Anne,* née *Cole, a descendant of the Lady Anne Plantagenet*], d. *Nov.* 1855 ; *and had no issue.*

See the Exeter Volume, p. 139, Nos. 1975–1980.

 2b. *Richard Edward Cumberland of Middlecave House, co. York, Comm. R.N.,* b. 23 *Sept.* 1800 ; d. 2 *Ap.* 1882 ; m. 1st, 19 *Jan.* 1828, *Penelope Mary, da. of* (—) *Bankhead, M.D.,* d. 15 *Ap.* 1836 ; *and had issue (with* 2 *other sons and a da. who* d. *unm.)* 1c *to* 4c.

 1c. Charles Edward Cumberland, C.B., J.P., Major-Gen. (*ret.*) R.E. (*Manor House, Maidstone*), *b.* 27 Jan. 1830 ; *m.* 1st, 12 June 1883, Elizabeth Anne, widow of the Right Rev. Addington Venables, Lord Bishop of Nassau, da. of the Rev. William Moss King, *d.* 1891 ; 2ndly, 18 Ap. 1907, Adelaide Annabella Mary McLeod [descended from George, Duke of Clarence, K.G., brother of Kings Edward IV. and Richard III. (see Essex Volume, Clarence Supplement, p. 561)], da. of Philip Henry Crampton of Fassaro, co. Wicklow.

 2c. William Bentinck Cumberland, Hon. Major-Gen. and Col. (*ret.*) R.A. (21 *Bramham Gardens, South Kensington*), *b.* 21 July 1833 ; *m.* 5 Sept. 1865, Louisa Anna, da. of Brig.-Gen. Manson, C.B., R.A. ; and has issue 1d to 3d.

  1d. Louis Bertie Cumberland, Capt. (*ret.*) King's Royal Rifle Corps, *b.* 1 July 1870.

  2d. Adela Mary Cumberland.

  3d. Norah Harriet Cumberland.

 3c. Penelope Maria Elizabeth Cumberland, *unm.*

 4c. Emma Anne Cumberland.

 3b. *Charles Brownlow Cumberland, Major-Gen. and Col. Comdg.* 96th *Regt.* 1842–1856, b. 21 *Nov.* 1801 ; d. 27 *Nov.* 1882 ; m. 2 *Aug.* 1825, *Russell, nat. da. of the Hon. Archibald Gloucester of Mount Joshua, Antigua,* d. 28 *June* 1870 ; *and had issue* 1c *to* 7c.

 1c. *Richard Felix Wilson Cumberland, Capt.* 96th *Regt.,* b. 21 *May* 1826 ; d. 28 *June* 1871 ; m. 1855, *Jessie, da. of* (—) *Landale ; and had issue (with a son who* d. *young)* 1d *to* 9d.

  1d. Charles Thomas Cumberland, *b.* 16 Dec. 1850.

  2d. George Landale Cumberland, *b.* 4 June 1853.

  3d. Richard Landale Cumberland, *b.* 21 June 1855. [Nos. 27335 to 27372.

---

[1] Burke's " Landed Gentry," 1871, p. 903. No such da. is, however, mentioned in the pedigree in Foster's " Noble and Gentle Families."

The Plantagenet Roll

4d. Bentinck Landale Cumberland, b. 3 Jan. 1864.
5d. Mary Gertrude Gordon Landale Cumberland.
6d. Jessie Landale Cumberland.
7d. Maud Landale Cumberland.
8d. Florence Landale Cumberland.
9d. Rose Landale Cumberland.

2c. Charles Burrell Cumberland, General Surveyor, India, b. 21 Feb. 1828; d. at Bareilly, India, 17 Dec. 1875; m. 9 Oct. 1865, Marianne, da. of David Cowan of New Scone, co. Perth, d. 23 May 1869; and had issue 1d.
   1d. Charles Russell Cumberland, b. 12 Aug. 1866.

3c. George Bentinck Cumberland, Capt. 96th Foot, b. 16 Ap. 1829; d. (–); m. 1st, Georgina Anne, da. of James Barlow; 2ndly, Mary, da. of Walter Stocker; and had issue 1d to 6d.
   1d.[1] James Bentinck Cumberland, b. 1 June 1863.
   2d.[1] Archibald Roland Cumberland, b. 3 June 1867.
   3d.[2] Walter Bertie Cumberland, b. 15 Jan. 1881.
   4d.[1] Dora Russel Cumberland, b. 7 July 1866.
   5d. Adela Georgina Cumberland, b. 22 Sept. 1869.
   6d. Marie Cumberland.

4c. Peregrine Bertie Cumberland of Melbourne, b. 26 Jan. 1834; m. Lillie, da. of (—); and has issue 1d to 5d.
   1d. Charles Bertie Cumberland, b. 1871 (? 19 Darling Street, S. Yarra, Melbourne).
   2d. Reginald Gloucester Cumberland.
   3d. Cecil George Cumberland.
   4d. Vivian Bentinck Cumberland.
   5d. Adela Muriel Cumberland.

5c. Bentinck Laporte Cumberland, Lieut. 82nd Foot, b. 3 Dec. 1839; d. (? unm.)

6c. Georgiana Penelope Cumberland, d. 7 July 1877; m. 29 Ap. 1856, Capt. William Archibald Eyton of Barford House, co. Warwick, 96th Regt [3rd son of Thomas Eyton of Eyton, co. Salop], d. 11 Sept. 1869; and had issue (with a da. who d. unm.) 1d to 7d.
   1d. William Charles Campbell Eyton (Yeator House, Baschurch, near Shrewsbury), b. 2 Nov. 1859.
   2d. Archibald Cumberland Eyton, b. 29 Aug. 1866.
   3d. Violet Elizabeth Eyton, m. 9 Aug. 1878, the Rev. Francis Robert Dayrell, B.A. (Camb.) [descended from King Henry VII., &c. (see Tudor Roll, p. 324, and Essex Volume Supplement, p. 470)] (Tyn Lôn, Rhydyfelin, Aberystwyth; Lew Grange, Shrewsbury); and has issue 1e to 2e.
      1e. Francis William Dayrell, b. 8 June 1882.
      2e. Violet Elizabeth Mildred Dayrell, b. 24 Dec. 1879.
   4d. Rose Adela Russel Eyton, b. 10 June 1860.
   5d. Lilias Agnes Charlotte Eyton, b. 30 July 1861.
   6d. Isabel Georgina Eyton, b. 25 Aug. 1862.
   7d. Evelyn Margaret Eyton, b. 6 Sept. 1863.

7c. Adela Russell Cumberland.

4b. George Burrell Cumberland, Lieut.-Col., formerly Major 42nd Highlanders, b. 10 Mar. 1804; d. 22 May 1865; m. 9 Sept. 1845, Margaret Delicia, da. of Gen. Sir John Macleod, K.C.B., C.B., Col. 77th Regt., d. Dec. 1902; and had issue (with a son who d. young) 1c to 5c.

1c. George Bentinck Macleod Cumberland, Lieut.-Col., formerly Major the Black Watch, served in Ashantee (1874) and Egyptian (1882) Campaigns (107 Eaton Square, S.W.), b. 22 June 1846.

2c. Charles Sperling Cumberland, Major formerly East Lancashire Regt. (10 Duke Street, St. James', S.W.), b. 5 Dec. 1847.   [Nos. 27373 to 27403.

# of The Blood Royal

3c. Elizabeth Penelope Cumberland, m. 24 Nov. 1875, Alexander Dick-Cunyngham [2nd son of Sir William Hanmer Dick-Cunyngham, 6th and 8th Bt. [S.]] (15 Eccleston Square, S.W.; St. James'; Ranelagh; New, Edinburgh); and has issue 1d to 4d.

1d. George Alastair Dick-Cunyngham, Capt. 2nd Batt. Rifle Brig., served in South Africa 1900-1902, 2 medals and 5 clasps, b. 11 May 1881; m. Aug. 1908, Sybil Vera Elise, da. of Edward Stisted Mostyn Price of Gunley Hall, Chirbury, co. Salop.

2d. Katharine Mary Delicia Dick-Cunyngham.

3d. Evelyn Dick-Cunyngham, m. July 1907, Reginald Everitt Lambert [son of Edward Tiley Lambert of Telham Court, Battle, co. Sussex]; and has issue 1e.

1e. Audrey Elizabeth Lambert.

4d. Mary Isabel Annie Dick-Cunyngham.

4c. Maud Fraser Cumberland.

5c. Amabel Mary Cumberland.

5b. *Georgina Cumberland*, d. (–); m. *at Broadwater, Sussex*, 12 *Sept.* 1831, *the Rev. Henry William Stuart, Chaplain H.E.I.C.S.*, d. 5 *Oct.* 1856; *and had issue* 1c *to* 6c.

1c. Rev. Henry Cumberland Stuart, M.A. (Camb.), Incumbent of Wragby, b. 31 *Jan.* 1833; d. (? s.p.); m. 7 *Aug.* 1858, *Eleanor Caroline, da. of Lieut.-Col. Charles Bevan*, d.s.p. 18 *May* 1880.

2c. Charles Bentinck George Stuart, b. 9 July 1843.

3c. Arthur Edward Stuart, b. 21 Dec. 1850; m. June 1880, Mary Halton, da. of William Jephson of Sutton, co. Notts.

4c. Georgina Adela Anna Stuart.

5c. Mary Emily Eliza Stuart.

6c. Alice Rosalind Bertie Stuart. [Nos. 27404 to 27416.

88. Descendants of Lord VERE BERTIE, M.P. (Table X.), d. 13 Sept. 1768; m. 1736, ANNE, da. of (—) CASEY of Braunston, near Lincoln, d. (–); and had issue.

See the Clarence Volume, Table LXXIV., and pp. 590-599, Nos. 25396-26281.
[Nos. 27417 to 28302.

89. Descendants of Lord MONTAGU BERTIE, Capt. R.N. (Table X.), d. 12 Aug. 1753; m. ELIZABETH, da. of William PIERS, M.P. for Wells, d. (–); and had issue.

See the Clarence Volume, Table LXXIV., and pp. 599-603, Nos. 26282-26530.
[Nos. 28303 to 28551.

90. Descendants, if any, of Lady LOUISA BERTIE (Table X.), d. (–); m. 1736, THOMAS BLUDWORTH, Groom of the Bedchamber to the Prince of Orange.

91. Descendants, if any, of the Hon. ANNE WHARTON (Table X.), d. (–); m. WILLIAM CARR; and of the Hon. MARGARET WHARTON, d. (–); m. 1st, Major DUNCH of Pusey, d. 1679 (by whom she had issue now extinct); 2ndly, c. 1690, Sir THOMAS SEYLIARD or SULYARD, 2nd Bt. [E.], d.s.p. 1692; 3rdly, WILLIAM ROSS.

The Plantagenet Roll

92. Descendants of JANE TYNTE, da., and in her issue (25 Aug. 1785) h. of Sir John Tynte, 2nd Bt. [E.], M.P. (Table X.), d. 1741; m. as 1st wife, at Gray's Inn Chapel, 23 Ap. 1737, Major RUISSHE HASSELL, R.H.G.; and had issue 1a.

1a. *Jane Hassell of Halswell, co. Somerset, and Cefn-Mably, co. Glamorgan*, da. and h., d. 1825; m. 1765, Col. *John Johnston, afterwards (R.L. 29 Oct. 1785) Kemeys-Tynte*, 1st Foot Guards, Groom of the Bedchamber and Comptroller to the Household to H.R.H. George, Prince of Wales, afterwards King George IV., d. 1807; and had issue 1b.

1b. *Charles Kemeys Kemeys-Tynte of Halswell and Cefn-Mably, M.P., Col. W. Somerset Yeo.*, was declared by a Committee for Privileges of the House of Lords, in 1845, senior co-h. to the Barony of Wharton [E.], b. 29 May 1778; d. 23 Nov. 1860; m. 1798, Ann, widow of Thomas Lewis of St. Pierre, da. of the Rev. Thomas Leyson of Bossaleg, d. Ap. 1835; and had issue 1c to 3c.

1c. *Charles John Kemeys-Tynte of Halswell and Cefn-Mably, and of Burleigh Hall, co. Leic., M.P., Col. Royal Glamorgan Light Infantry Militia*, senior co-h. to the Baronies of Wharton and Grey de Wilton [E.], b. 9 Ap. 1800; d. 16 Sept. 1882; m. 1st, 1821, Elizabeth, da. and co-h. of Thomas Swinnerton of Butterton Hall, co. Stafford [by Mary, da. of Charles Milborne of The Priory, Abergavenny, and his wife Lady Martha, née Harley], d. 10 May 1838; 2ndly, 15 Ap. 1841, Vincentia, da. of Wallop Brabazon of Rath House, co. Louth, d. 14 Oct. 1894; and had issue 1d to 10d.

1d. *Charles Kemeys Kemeys-Tynte of Halswell, &c., J.P., D.L., Capt. 11th Hussars and Grenadier Guards, and Col. 1st Somerset Militia*, senior co-h. to the Baronies of Wharton and Grey de Wilton [E.], b. 16 Mar. 1822; d. 10 Jan. 1891; m. 1st, 1848, Mary, da. of the Rev. George Frome of Punchnoll, co. Dorset, d. 14 May 1864; 2ndly, 1873, Hannah, widow of Thomas Lewis, da. of (—), d. 17 Feb. 1875; and had issue 1e to 3e.

1e. *Halswell Milborne Kemeys-Tynte of Halswell, &c., J.P., D.L., Capt. 1st Somerset Militia*, senior co-h. to the Baronies of Wharton and Grey de Wilton [E.], b. 5 June 1852; d. 18 Feb. 1899; m. 1875, Rosabella Clare, da. of Theobald Walsh of Tyrrelston, co. Kildare [re-m. 2ndly, 2 June 1900, Lieut.-Col. Henry de Courcy Rawlins of Stoke Courcy]; and had issue 1f to 3f.

1f. Charles Theodore Halswell Kemeys-Tynte of Halswell and Cefn-Mably, J.P., *late* Lieut. Royal Monmouthshire Engineers (Mil.) (*Halswell Park, Goathurst, Bridgwater; Cefn-Mably, Cardiff*), b. 18 Sept. 1876; m. 10 Aug. 1899, Dorothy (see p. 393), da. of Major-Gen. Sir Arthur Edward Augustus Ellis, G.C.V.O, &c.; and has issue 1g to 2g.

1g. Charles John Halswell Kemeys-Tynte, b. 12 Jan. 1908.

2g. Elizabeth Dorothy Kemeys-Tynte.

2f. Eustace Kemeys-Tynte of Burleigh Hall (*Burleigh Hall, Loughborough, co. Leicester*), b. 10 Ap. 1878; m. 13 Aug. 1902, Annie, da. of John Emerson; and has issue 1g to 2g.

1g. Nicholas Halswell Kemeys-Tynte, b. 4 Aug. 1903.

2g. Eleanor Vanessa Rosabella Kemeys-Tynte.

3f. Mary Arabella Swinnerton Kemeys-Tynte, m. 21 Ap. 1909, Guy Colin Campbell, Lieut. King's Royal Rifle Corps (son and h.-app. of Lieut.-Col. Sir Guy Theophilus Campbell, 3rd Bt. [U.K.]].

2e.[1] Rachel Elizabeth Henrietta Kemeys-Tynte.

3e.[2] Grace Kemeys-Tynte.

2d. John Brabazon Kemeys-Tynte, *late* Lieut. 5th Fusiliers, *previously* R.N., Baltic (1854) Medal, b. 24 June 1842.

3d. St. David Morgan Kemeys-Tynte, *late* Lieut. West Somerset Yeo. Cav. (*10 Royal Crescent, Bath*), b. 1 Mar. 1846; m. 21 Ap. 1897, Alice, widow of Anthony Hammond, J.P., da. of the Rev. Thomas J. Lee.   [Nos. 28552 to 28562.

of The Blood Royal

4*d*. Arthur Marcus Philipps Kemeys-Tynte, *late* Capt. Royal Glamorgan Mil., Zulu (1879) and Canada (1885) Medals (*Ottawa, Canada*), *b.* 22 Mar. 1850; *m.* Dec. 1889, Ruby, da. of R. Clark of Ottawa.

5*d*. Fortescue Tracy Freke Kemeys-Tynte (*Lake Mills, Wisconsin, U.S.A.*), *b.* 31 Jan. 1856; *m.* 17 Aug. 1899, Gertrude, da. of J. D. Waterbury of Oztalan, Wisconsin.

6*d*. Edward Plantagenet Kemeys-Tynte, *late* Capt. 3rd Welsh Regt., Zulu (1879) Medal and Clasp (*Highleigh, Teignmouth*), *b.* 13 Sept. 1858; *m.* 21 Feb. 1889, Beatrice Mary, da. of Lansdowne Daubeny of Norton Malreward; and has issue 1*e* to 2*e*.

1*e*. Mary Vincentia Blanche Edwardrina Kemeys-Tynte.

2*e*. Beatrice Margaret Gwladys Clare Kemeys-Tynte.

7*d*. Vincentia Margaret Anne Kemeys-Tynte.

8*d*. Mabel Louisa Frances Kemeys-Tynte.

9*d*. Maud Maria Kemeys-Tynte, *m.* 23 July 1885, Amherst Henry Gage Morris of Netherby (*Nunburnholme Rectory, York*).

10*d*. Blanche Elizabeth Plantagenet Kemeys-Tynte, *m.* 22 Oct. 1909, the Hon. Edgar Dawdney, *formerly* Lieut.-Gov. of British Columbia.

2*c*. Louisa Kemeys-Tynte, d. 31 Aug. 1872; m. 1834, *Simon Fraser Campbell*, d. 28 *Mar.* 1872.

3*c*. Henrietta Anne Kemeys-Tynte, d. 24 Mar. 1880; m. 14 Sept. 1833, *Thomas Arthur Kemmis of Croham Hurst, Croydon, M.P., J.P., Capt. Grenadier Guards,* b. 16 *Mar.* 1806; d. 25 *Dec.* 1858; *and had issue* 1*d*.

1*d*. Arthur Henry Nicholas Kemmis, J.P., D.L., *late* Capt. 1st Somerset Militia, High Sheriff King's Co. 1862 (*Croham Hurst, Croydon*), *b.* 13 July 1834; *m.* 11 July 1862, Emma Jane, da. of E. Collins. [Nos. 28563 to 28572.

93. Descendants of GEORGE LOCKHART of Carnwath (Table XI.), *b.* 1700; *d.* Oct. 1764; *m.* 15 Mar. 1727, FERGUSIA, da. and co-h. of Sir George WISHART of Clifton Hall, co. Edinburgh, *d.* (–); and had issue 1*a* to 3*a*.

1*a*. *James* (*Lockhart, afterwards Lockhart-Wishart*), 1st *Count of Lockhart* (*Graf von Lockhart*) [*H.R.E.*] *of Carnwath and Lee, K.M.T., a General in the Imperial Service and a Lord of the Bedchamber to the Emperor,* d. 6 *Feb.* 1790; m. 1*st, Matilda, da. of* (—) *Lockhart of Castle Hill,* d. (–); 2*ndly,* 18 *June* 1770, *Marianne, da. and h. of Adam Murray of Belredding,* d. (–); *and had issue* 1*b to* 3*b*.

1*b*. *Charles* (*Lockhart-Wishart*), 2*nd Count of Lockhart* (*Graf von Lockhart*), [*H.R.E.*], d.s.p. 4 *Aug.* 1802.

2*b*.[1] *Countess Matilda Theresa Lockhart-Wishart,* d. 1 *Feb.* 1791; m. *as* 1*st wife,* 1788, *Lieut.-Gen. Sir Charles Lockhart-Ross of Balnagowan, 7th Bt.* [*S.*], *M.P.,* d. 8 *Feb.* 1814; *and had issue* 1*c*.

1*c*. *Matilda Lockhart-Ross of Oldliston,* d. 4 *Sept.* 1819; m. 6 *Jan.* 1812, *Adm. Sir Thomas John Cochrane, G.C.B.* [*E. Dundonald Coll.*], d. 19 *Oct.* 1872; *and had issue.*

See the Exeter Volume, pp. 625–626, Nos. 53022–53062.

3*b*.[2] *Countess Matilda Lockhart-Wishart,* d. 14 *Sept.* 1850; m. 19 *Feb.* 1791, *Anthony Aufrère of Hoveton and Foulsham Old Hall, co. Norfolk; and had issue.*

2*a*. *Charles Lockhart, afterwards Macdonald of Largie, co. Argyll,* b. 28 *Feb.* 1740; d. (–); m. 16 *Aug.* 1762, *Elizabeth, da. and h. of John Macdonald of Largie; and had issue* 1*b to* 6*b*.

1*b*. *Sir Alexander Macdonald, afterwards* (1802) *Lockhart of Lee and Carnwath,* 1*st Bt.* [*U.K.*], *so cr.* 24 *May* 1806; *suc. as head of the family on the death*
[Nos. 28573 to 28613.

The Plantagenet Roll

of his cousin, the 2nd Count of Lockhart, 1802, d. 22 June 1816; m. Jane, da. of Daniel M'Neill of Gallichoilly, co. Argyll (re-m. 2ndly, John McNeill, Provost of Inveraray and) d. 4 Sept. 1857; and had issue 1c to 2c.

1c. Sir Charles Macdonald Lockhart of Lee and Carnwath, 2nd Bt. [U.K.], b. 8 Feb. 1799; d. 8 Dec. 1832; m. 29 Feb. 1819, Emilia Olivia [descended from the Lady Ann, sister of King Edward IV. (see Exeter Volume, p. 469)], da. of Lieut.-Gen. Sir Charles Lockhart-Ross, 7th Bt. [S.], d. 24 June 1866; and had issue 1d.

1d. Mary Macdonald Lockhart, d. 10 Dec. 1851; m. 15 Sept. 1837, the Hon. Augustus Henry Reynolds-Moreton, afterwards Moreton-Macdonald of Largie, M.P. [E. Ducie Coll., and a descendant of King Henry VII., &c.], d. 14 Feb. 1862; and had issue.

See the Tudor Roll, pp. 268–269, Nos. 24520–24544.

2c. Sir Norman Macdonald Lockhart of Lee and Carnwath, 3rd Bt. [U.K.], b. 10 Dec. 1802; d. 9 May 1849; m. 23 Feb. 1836, Margaret, da. of John M'Lean of Campbelltown, co. Argyll, d. 21 Jan. 1895; and had issue 1d to 6d.

1d. Sir Norman Macdonald Lockhart of Lee and Carnwath, 4th Bt. [U.K.], b. 1845; d. unm. 20 May 1870.

2d. Sir Simon Macdonald Lockhart of Lee and Carnwath, 5th Bt. [U.K.], M.V.O., Col. late Comdg. 1st Life Guards, formerly Brig.-Gen. Comdg. Cavalry Brigade at the Curragh 1900–1901, and A.D.C. to Com.-in-Chief 1899–1900, &c. (The Ley, Lanark; Carnwath House, Lanark; Carlton, &c.), b. 13 Mar. 1849; m. 14 Dec. 1898, Hilda Maud, da. of Col. Augustus Henry Moreton-Macdonald [younger son of the Hon. Augustus Henry Reynolds-Moreton and his wife Mary, née Macdonald-Lockhart, named above].

3d. Jane Margaret Maria Lockhart, d. 16 May 1901; m. 23 Sept. 1862, Sir (William) Gerald Seymour Vesey FitzGerald, K.C.I.E., C.S.I., J.P., formerly Political A.D.C. to Sec. of State for India 1874–1901 (Carlton); and had issue 1e.

1e. Geraldine Tryphena Margaret FitzGerald.

4d. Maria Theresa Lockhart.

5d. Cordelia Euphemia Lockhart, d. 20 June 1872; m. 8 June 1867, John Stanley Mott of Barningham Hall, J.P., late Major P.W.O Norfolk Art. Mil. [descended from King Henry VII.] (Barningham Hall, Hanworth); and had issue 1e.

1e. Theresa Caroline Mott, m. 20 July 1898, Major Charles Edward Radclyffe, D.S.O. (Little Park, Wickham, Hants).

6d. Esther Elizabeth Lockhart.

2b. John Macdonald, alias Lockhart, d. (? s.p.).

3b. James Macdonald, alias Lockhart, d. (? s.p.).

4b. Norman Macdonald, alias Lockhart of Tabrax, co. Lanark, d. (–); m. Philadelphia, da. of John M'Murdo of Dumfries; and had (with other) issue 1c.

1c. Elizabeth Macdonald, d. 13 Oct. 1888; m. 1838, Eaglesfield Bradshaw Smith of Eyam, co. Derby, and Blackwood House, co. Dumfries.

5b. Elizabeth Macdonald, d. (–); m. 1st, Capt. McNeill, d. (–); 2ndly, 1801, William Putman McCabe.

6b. Matilda Macdonald, d. (–); m. John Campbell of Glensaddel.

3a. Clementina Lockhart, d. 31 Mar. 1803; m. 1761, the Hon. John Gordon (see p. 188), Lieut.-Col. 81st Regt. [E. of Aboyne Coll.], d. 30 Oct. 1778; and had issue 1b to 2b.

1b. John Gordon, Major-Gen. and Col. Comdt. 2nd Brigade Bengal Cav., b. 8 July 1765; d. (? s.p.) 1832; m. Nov. 1810, Eliza, da. of Robert Morris, M.P. for Gloucester.

2b. Grace Margaret Gordon, b. 27 Sept. 1766; d. 1832; m. 13 Ap. 1794, William Graham of Mossknow, co. Dumfries, d. 1832; and had issue 1c to 3c.

1c. William Graham of Mossknow, J.P., D.L., Col. 12th, 16th, and 17th Lancers, b. 22 Jan. 1797; d. 2 Mar. 1882; m. 25 Feb. 1830, Anne, da. and h. of Hugh Mair of Redhall and Wyseby, d. 8 Jan. 1887; and had issue 1d to 6d.

[Nos. 28614 to 28643.

# of The Blood Royal

1*d*. William Mair Graham of Mossknow, b. 21 May 1832; d. *unm.* 27 Feb. 1899.

2*d*. John Gordon Graham of Mossknow and Wyseby, J.P., D.L., Major-Gen. *late* 1st Royal Dragoons (*Mossknow, near Ecclefechan*), b. 11 July 1833; *m.* 11 Oct. 1871, Susana Elizabeth Touchet [descended from George (Plantagenet), Duke of Clarence, K.G. (see Clarence Volume, p. 470)], da. of Sir John Hay of Park, 7th Bt. [S.]; and has issue 1*e* to 7*e*.

    1*e*. William Fergus Graham, *late* Lieut. King's Own Scottish Borderers, b. 13 Sept. 1874.

    2*e*. Malcolm Hay Graham, twin, b. 26 Sept. 1877.

    3*e*. Claude Graham, Lieut. Northants Regt., b. 4 Sept. 1881.

    4*e*. Cecil Erskin Graham, Lieut. Border Regt., b. 9 June 1883.

    5*e*. Violet Graham.

    6*e*. Alice Graham.

    7*e*. Mary Theresa Graham.

3*d*. Charles Steuart Gordon of Gladstone, Queensland, b. 15 Mar. 1835; d. at Gladstone, 5 Dec. 1883; m. 1862, Sarah, da. of G. White; *and had issue* (3 sons and 4 das.).

4*d*. Rosina Anne Graham.

5*d*. Grace Harriet Graham, *m.* 6 Dec. 1864, John Murray of Murraythwaite, co. Dumfries, J.P., Com. R.N., *d.* 2 Aug. 1872; and has issue 1*e* to 5*e*.

    1*e*. William Murray of Murraythwaite, J.P. (*Murraythwaite, Ecclefechan*), b. 31 Oct. 1865; *m.* 12 Ap. 1892, Evelyn, da. of John Bruce; and has issue 1*f* to 3*f*.

        1*f*. Margaret Elizabeth Murray.

        2*f*. Vivian Murray.

        3*f*. Eleanor Justina Murray.

    2*e*. Marion Gertrude Murray.

    3*e*. Flora Murray.

    4*e*. Edith Murray.

    5*e*. Helen Murray.

6*d*. Clementina Mary Graham, *m.* 6 Aug. 1880, H. Fowle Smith, Surgeon-Gen. A.M.D. (*Gretna Hall, Gretna Green*); and has issue 1*e*.

    1*e*. Meliora Clementina Smith.

2*c*. Clementina Graham, d. (?) *unm.*

3*c*. Johanna Grace Graham, d. (-); m. 2 Ap. 1829, Erskine Douglas Sandford, Advocate, Sheriff of Galloway [*son of the Lord Bishop of Edinburgh*], d. (-); *and had issue* 1*d* to 2*d*.

1*d*. William Graham Sandford, Diplo. Service, one of the Royal Body Guard for Scotland, *formerly* Capt. Royal Peeblesshire Rifles, b. 30 Nov. 1834.

2*d*. Frances Grace Margaret Sandford. [Nos. 28644 to 28665.

94. Descendants of ALEXANDER LOCKHART of Craighouse, a Lord of Session under the designation of Lord COVINGTON (Table XI.), *d*. (-); *m*. 1725, MARGARET, da. of Robert PRINGLE of Edgefield, a Lord of Session;[1] and had (with possibly other) issue 1*a*.

1*a*. William Lockhart, Capt. R.N., son and h., served heir to father 15 May 1783.

---

[1] *Ex inform.* Sir James Balfour Paul, Lord Lyon King.

The Plantagenet Roll

95. Descendants, if any, of MARGARET LOCKHART (Table XI.), *d.* at Bath 24 Nov. 1762; *m.* 1st, as 3rd wife, JOHN (FLEMING), 6th EARL OF WIGTOUN [S.], *d. (s.p.* by her) 10 Feb. 1744; 2ndly, PETER MACELLIGOT, a Major-Gen. in the Austrian Service.

96. Descendants of GRACE LOCKHART (Table XI.), *d.* 17 Nov. 1738; *m.* 1st, 20 June 1724, JOHN (GORDON), 3rd EARL OF ABOYNE [S.], *d.* 7 Ap. 1732; 2ndly, as 1st wife, Dec. 1734, JAMES (STUART), LORD DOUN, *afterwards* (1739), 8th EARL OF MORAY [S.], K.T., *d.* 5 July 1767; and had issue 1*a* to 4*a*.

1*a*. Charles *(Gordon)*, *4th Earl of Aboyne* [S.], b. *c.* 1728; d. 28 *Dec.* 1795; m. 1*st*, 22 *Ap.* 1759, *Lady Margaret*, da. *of Alexander (Stewart)*, 6*th Earl of Galloway* [S.], d. 2 *Aug.* 1762; *and had issue.*
See the Tudor Roll, Table CXXII., and pp. 527–531, Nos. 35196–35336.

2*a*. Hon. *John Gordon, Lieut.-Col. 81st Regt.*, b. 19 *June* 1728; d. 30 *Oct.* 1778; m. 1761, *Clementina*, da. *of George Lockhart of Carnwath*, d. 31 *Mar.* 1803; *and had issue.*
See p. 187, Nos. 28644–28665.

3*a*. Hon. *Lockhart Gordon, Judge-Advocate-Gen. of Bengal*, b. 1732; d. at Calcutta 24 *Mar.* 1788; m. 3 *Oct.* 1770, *the Hon. Catherine* (see Essex Volume, p. 240), da. *of John Wallop, styled Viscount Lymington*, d. *May* 1813; *and had issue* 1*b* to 3*b*.

1*b*. *Rev. Lockhart Gordon*, b. 28 *July* 1775; d. (–); m.
2*b*. *Loudoun Harcourt Gordon, in the Army*, b. 9 *May* 1780.
3*b*. *Katherine Gordon.*

4*a*. Francis *(Stuart)*, *9th Earl of Moray* [S.], *and 1st Baron Stuart of Castle-Stuart* [G.B.], *a Rep. Peer*, b. 11 *Jan.* 1737; d. 28 *Aug.* 1810; m. 28 *June* 1763, *the Hon. Jean*, da. *and in her issue* (26 *May* 1878) *h. of John (Gray)*, 11*th Lord Gray* [S.], d. 19 *Feb.* 1786; *and had issue* 1*b* to 3*b*.

1*b*. Francis *(Stuart)*, *10th Earl of Moray* [S.], *and 2nd Baron Stuart* [G.B.], K.T., b. *(twin)* 2 *Feb.* 1771; d. 12 *Jan.* 1848; m. 1*st*, 26 *Feb.* 1795, *Lucy*, da. *of Gen. John Scott of Balcomie*, d. 3 *Aug.* 1798; 2*ndly*, 7 *Jan*, 1801, *Margaret Jane*, da. *of Sir Philip Ainslie of Pilton*, d. 3 *Ap.* 1837; *and had issue* 1*c* to 5*c*.

2*b*. Francis *(Stuart)*, *11th Earl of Moray* [S.], *and 3rd Baron Stuart* [G.B.], b. 7 *Nov.* 1795; d. *unm.* 6 *May* 1859.

2*c*. John *(Stuart)*, *12th Earl of Moray* [S.], *and 4th Baron Stuart* [G.B.], b. 25 *Jan.* 1797; d. *unm.* 8 *Nov.* 1867.

3*c*. Archibald George *(Stuart)*, *13th Earl of Moray* [S.], *and 5th Baron Stuart* [G.B.], b. 3 *Mar.* 1810; d. *unm.* 12 *Feb.* 1872.

4*c*. George Philip *(Stuart)*, *14th Earl of Moray* [S.], *and 6th Baron Stuart* [G.B.], *and* (1878) 18*th Lord Gray* [S.], b. 14 *Aug.* 1816; d. *unm.* 16 *Mar.* 1895.

5*c*. *Lady Jane Stuart*, b. 30 *Nov.* 1802; d. 14 *Mar.* 1880; m. 1*st*, 25 *Jan.* 1832, *Sir John Archibald Drummond Stewart*, 6*th Bt.* [S.], d.s.p. 20 *May* 1838; 2*ndly*, 25 *Aug.* 1838, *Jeremiah Lonsdale Pounden of Brownswood, co. Wexford*, d. 3 *Mar.* 1887; *and had issue* 1*d*.

1*d*. Eveleen *(Pounden)*, 19*th Lady Gray* [S.] *(Brownswood, co. Wexford;* 14 *The Boltons, S.W.)*, b. 3 *May* 1841; *m.* 9 Sept. 1863, James Maclaren Smith, *afterwards* (R.L. 7 May 1897) Smith-Gray, *d.* 26 Feb. 1900; and had issue 1*e* to 4*e*.

1*e*. James Maclaren Stuart Smith, now (R.L. 7 May 1897) Gray, Master of Gray, M.A. (Camb.), *late* Capt. Rifle Brigade (*Cum-Irfon, Llanwrtyd Wells, Brecon*), *b.* 4 June 1864. [Nos. 28666 to 28830.

188

# of The Blood Royal

2e. Hon. Ethel Eveleen Smith, m. 23 July 1888, Henry Tufnell Campbell [son of John Thomas Campbell by his wife Lady Anne Katharine, née Bethune] (7 *Collingham Gardens, S.W.*).

3e. Hon. Thora Zelma Grace Gray.

4e. Hon. Kathleen Eileen Moray Gray.

2b. Hon. *Archibald Stuart*, b. (*twin*) 2 Feb. 1771; d. 30 Oct. 1832; m. 17 Mar. 1793, *Cornelia, da. of Edmund Morton Pleydell of Milbourne St. Andrew, Dorset*, d. 1 Mar. 1830; *and had issue* 1c.

1c. Rev. *Edmund Luttrell Stuart, Rector of Winterborne Houghton, Dorset*, b. 21 Feb. 1798; d. 5 Nov. 1869; m. 2 Sept. 1834, *Elizabeth, da. of the Rev. J. L. Jackson, Rector of Swanage*, d. 28 Mar. 1885; *and had issue* 1d to 4d.

1d. **Edmund Archibald** (Stuart, *sometime* (1878-1895) *Gray*), 15th *Earl of Moray* [S.], 7th *Baron Stuart* [G.B.], b. 5 Nov. 1840; d.s.p. 11 June 1901; m. 6 Sept. 1877, *Anna Mary* (*Tarbat House, Kildary, Ross-shire; 7 Ainslie Place, Edinburgh*), da. of the Rev. George J. Collinson.

2d. **Francis James** (Stuart, *sometime* (1895-1901) *Stuart-Gray*), 16th *Earl of Moray* [S.], 8th *Baron Stuart of Castle Stuart* [G.B.], *J.P., formerly Major and Lieut.-Col. 1st Batt. King's Liverpool Regt.*, b. 24 Nov. 1842; d.s.p. 20 Nov. 1909; m. 24 June 1879, *Gertrude Floyer, da. of the Rev. Francis Smith, Rector of Tarrant Rushton, Dorset*.

3d. **Morton Gray** (Stuart, *sometime* (1901-1909) *Stuart-Gray*), 17th *Earl of Moray* [S.], 9th *Baron Stuart of Castle Stuart* [G.B.] (*Darnaway Castle, Forres, Elgin; Castle Stuart, Inverness; Donibristle Park, Aberdour, Fife; Doune Lodge, Perth*), b. 16 Ap. 1855; m. 17 Dec. 1890, Edith Douglas (see p. 190), da. of Rear-Adm. George Palmer; and has issue 1e to 4e.

1e. Hon. Francis Douglas Stuart-Gray, b. 10 July 1892.

2e. Hon. Archibald John Morton Stuart-Gray, b. 14 Nov. 1894.

3e. Hon. James Gray Stuart-Gray, b. 9 Feb. 1897.

4e. Lady Hermione Moray Stuart-Gray.

4d. Lady *Cornelia Stuart*, had Royal Warrant as da. of an Earl 10 Ap. 1897; m. 29 July 1873, the Rev. William Henry Augustus Truell of Clonmannon, *formerly Vicar of Wall* (*Clonmannon, co Wicklow*); and has issue 1e to 8e.

1e. Robert Holt Stuart Truell, b. 6 Dec. 1875.

2e. Edmund Gray Stuart Truell, b. 14 Aug. 1878.

3e. William Henry Stuart Truell, b. 28 Feb. 1890.

4e. Mary Louisa Truell, m. 3 Sept. 1903, John Milne, M.B. (68 *Manchester Old Road, Middleton, Manchester*); and has issue 1f to 2f.

1f. Richard Henry John Milne, b. 1907.

2f. Elizabeth Marjorie Milne.

5e. Cornelia Isabel Truell, m. 14 June 1900, Frank Mortimer Rowland, M.D. (26 *St. John Street, Lichfield*); and has issue 1f to 5f.

1f. William George Stuart Rowland, b. 22 Oct. 1902.

2f. Ernest Mortimer Rowland, b. 4 Mar. 1904.

3f. Frank Edward Rowland, b. 30 Sept. 1905.

4f. Helen Isabel Rowland.

5f. Grace Elizabeth Rowland.

6e. Kathleen Augusta Truell.

7e. Gertrude Margaret Truell.

8e. Constance Elizabeth Truell.

3b. *Lady Grace Stuart*, d. 23 Mar. 1846; m. 10 July 1789, *George Douglas of Cavers*, d. 14 Nov. 1814; *and had (with possibly other) issue* 1c.

1c. *James Douglas of Cavers*, b. 9 Oct. 1790; d. 17 Aug. 1861; m. 7 Sept. 1820, *Emma, da. of Sir David Carnegie, 4th Bt.* [S.] [*E. of Southesk Coll.*], b. 29 May 1794; d. 25 Sept. 1882; *and had* (*with* 1 *other son and* 2 *das.* d.s.p.) *issue* 1d to 4d. [Nos. 28831 to 28854.

The Plantagenet Roll

1d. James Douglas of Cavers, b. 24 May 1822; d.s.p. 29 July 1878.

2d. Mary Douglas, da. and in her issue (1878) co-h., d. 12 May 1859; m. 15 Ap. 1857, William Elphinstone Malcolm of Burnfoot, co. Dumfries, d. 30 Dec. 1908; and had issue 1e.

1e. Mary Malcolm of Cavers, m. 12 Nov. 1879, Edward Palmer, now Palmer-Douglas, J.P., D.L., Capt. late Rifle Brigade (Cavers, near Hawick); and has issue (with a son, Malcolm, b. 29 Mar. 1882; d. unm. 12 Mar. 1902) 1f.

1f. Archibald Palmer-Douglas, B.A. (Camb.), b. 21 Aug. 1880.

3d. Emma Douglas, da. and in her issue (1878) co-h., b. 10 Jan. 1829; d. 11 Jan. 1870; m. 3 July 1860, Capt. Robert Erskine Anderson, 107th Regt., d. 25 Sept. 1903; and had issue 1e to 5e.

1e. Robert Douglas Anderson, Major (ret.) R.A., b. 11 Nov. 1862; unm.

2e. James Douglas Anderson, Major (ret.) R.A., b. 27 Nov. 1863.

3e. John Hamilton Anderson, Major 2nd E. Lancashire Regt., b. 13 June 1865.

4e. Emma Anderson.

5e. Wilhelmina Christian Anderson, m. 19 Dec. 1906, Francis Edward Roberts, J.P. (3 Sandown Terrace, Chester).

4d. Ellen Douglas, da. and (1878) co-h., m. 21 Oct. 1859, Rear-Adm. George Palmer, R.N. (36 Eversley Road, Bexhill-on-Sea); and has issue 1e to 4e.

1e. George Douglas Palmer, b. 1 June 1865.

2e. Harry Douglas Palmer, Major R.M.L.I., now attached to the Egyptian Army, Financial Sec. Egyptian Army, formerly comdg. 11th Soudanese, has 3rd Class Medjidie, b. 22 Aug. 1866; m. 20 Jan. 1909, Ethel Maud, da. of J. Borwick of 77 Prince's Gate, S.W.

3e. Ellen Douglas Palmer, m. 12 Aug. 1885, the Rev. George Fossick Wilson (Devonia, Heath Road, Weybridge); and has issue 1f.

1f. Stuart Douglas Wilson, R.N., b. 24 Mar. 1890.

4e. Edith Douglas Palmer, m. 17 Dec. 1890, Morton Gray (Stuart-Gray), 17th Earl of Moray [S.], 9th Baron Stuart of Castle Stuart [G.B.], &c. (Kinfauns Castle, co. Perth; Gray House, co. Forfar); and has issue.

See p. 189, Nos. 28835–28838. [Nos. 28855 to 28871.

97. Descendants, if any surviving, of MARY LOCKHART (Table XI.), d. (–); m. as 2nd wife, JOHN RATTRAY of Edinburgh, M.D., cadet of Craighall; and had issue 1a.[1]

1a. Mary Rattray.

98. Descendants, if any surviving, of BARBARA LOCKHART (Table XI.), b. 16 Dec. 1677; d. (–); m. 2ndly, the Hon. DANIEL CARMICHAEL of Mauldsley, d. Oct. 1708; and had issue 1a.

1a. Daniel Carmichael of Mauldsley, d. 25 Oct. 1765; m. 24 Jan. 1842, Emilia, da. of the Rev. John Hepburn, Minister of Old Greyfriars, Edinburgh, d. 9 Jan. 1769; and had issue 1b to 3b.

1b. Thomas (Carmichael), 5th Earl of Hyndford [S.], d. unm. 14 Feb. 1811.

2b. Andrew (Carmichael), 6th Earl of Hyndford [S.], b. 1758; d. unm. 18 Ap. 1817.

3b. Grizel Carmichael, d. (–); m. Archibald Nisbet of Carfin, d. 20 Oct. 1807; and had issue 1c to 2c.

1c. Archibald Nisbet of Carfin, and, on the death of his uncle (1817), of Mauldsley.

2c. Jean Nisbet, d. (–); m. Thomas Gordon of Harperfield.

---

[1] Douglas' "Baronetage of Scotland," i. 278.

# of The Blood Royal

99. Descendants of JANE WHARTON, da. and in her issue co-h. of the Hon. Sir THOMAS WHARTON, K.B. (Table X.), *d.* (−); *m.* JOHN DIGBY of Mansfield Woodhouse; and had issue (with 3 other das. *d.s.p.*) 1*a* to 4*a*.

1*a*. *Frances Digby,* bur. 4 *May* 1736; m. 1727, *Sir Thomas Legard,* 4*th Bt.* [*E.*], d. 1735; *and had issue* 1*b* to 2*b*.

1*b*. *Sir Digby Legard,* 5*th Bt.* [*E.*], d. 4 *Feb.* 1773; m. *Aug.* 1755, *Jane* (see p. 196), *da. and event. co-h. of George Cartwright,* d. 15 *Sept.* 1811; *and had issue* 1*c* to 7*c*.

1*c*. *Sir John Legard,* 6*th Bt.* [*E.*], d.s.p. 16 *July* 1807.

2*c*. *Sir Thomas Legard,* 7*th Bt.* [*E.*], bapt. 5 *Dec.* 1762; d. 5 *July* 1830; m. 26 *Dec.* 1802, *Sarah, da. of* (—) *Bishop,* d. 26 *Jan.* 1814; *and had issue* 1*d* to 3*d*.

1*d*. *Sir Thomas Digby Legard,* 8*th Bt.* [*E.*], b. 30 *May* 1803; d. 10 *Dec.* 1860; m. 31 *May* 1832, *the Hon. Frances* [*a descendant of the Lady Anne, sister of King Edward IV., &c.*], *da. of Charles* (*Duncombe*), 1*st Baron Feversham* [*U.K.*], d. 15 *June* 1881; *and had issue.*

See the Exeter Volume, p. 648, Nos. 55763–55769.

2*d*. *Henry Willoughby Legard,* 9*th Lancers,* b. 1805; d. 21 *Nov.* 1845; m. 26 *Oct.* 1839, *Charlotte Henrietta* [*a descendant of the Lady Anne, sister of King Edward IV., &c.*], *da. of Henry Willoughby of Birdsall, co. York* [*B. Middleton Coll.*], d. 25 *Jan.* 1844; *and had issue* 1*e* to 2*e*.

1*e*. *Sir Algernon Willoughby Legard,* 12*th Bt.* [*E.*] (*Ganton Hall, Yorks*), b. 14 *Oct.* 1842; *m.* 27 *July* 1872, *Alicia Egerton,* da. of the Rev. George Brooks, M.A.

2*e*. *Rev. Cecil Henry Legard,* M.A. (Camb.), LL.M., Rector of Cottesbrooke (*Cottesbrooke Rectory, Northampton*), b. 28 *Nov.* 1843; *m.* 29 *Ap.* 1873, Emily Mary, d. of James Hall of Scorborough Hall, Beverley; and has issue 1*f* to 2*f*.

1*f*. Digby Algernon Hall Legard, B.A. (Camb.) (*Headon Lodge, Brompton S.O., Yorks*), b. 7 *Dec.* 1876; *m.* 2 *June* 1904, Georgiana Blanche Elaine, da. of William Joseph Starkey Barber-Starkey; and has issue 1*g* to 2*g*.

1*g*. Thomas Digby Legard, *b.* 16 *Oct.* 1905.

2*g*. John D'Arcy Legard, *b.* May 1908.

2*f*. Gertrude Cassandra Legard, *unm.*

3*d*. *Harriet Legard,* d. *at Halifax* 19 *July* 1851; m. 14 *Aug.* 1820, *Edward Nelson Alexander of Heathfield, Halifax* [2*nd son of Lewis Alexander of Hopwood Hall, Halifax, Solicitor, by his wife Elizabeth, da. of the Rev. Edward Nelson of Halifax, M.A.*], b. 16 *May* 1797; d. *at Windermere* 20 *Sept.* 1859; *and had issue* 1*e* to 4*e*.

1*e*. *Rev. Disney Legard Alexander, M.A.* (*Oxon.*), *Vicar of Ganton,* b. 29 *June* 1821; d. 25 *Feb.* 1868; m. 13 *June* 1849, *Juana Maria, da. of John Barrow of Ringwood Hall, co. Derby,* d. 6 *Aug.* 1866; *and had issue* (*with a son who* d. *unm.*) 1*f* to 5*f*.

1*f*. Rev. John Barrow Alexander, M.A. (Camb.), *formerly* H.B.M.'s Vice-Consul at Tacoma, Wash., U.S.A., 1884–1897, *previously* Rector of Port Townsend, Wash. (4 *Warwick Gardens, Kensington, W.*), *b.* 12 *Mar.* 1850; *unm.*

2*f*. *Edward Disney Alexander of Milton, co. Northants,* b. 27 *July* 1857; d. 30 *Mar.* 1907; m. 5 *Aug.* 1886, *Amy Frances Jane* (see p. 193), *da. of Francis William Montgomery of Kettering,* d. 1902; *and had issue* (*with a da., Amy Juana,* b. *Aug.* 1887; d. *young*) 1*g* to 2*g*.

1*g*. Edward Montgomery Alexander of Milton House (*Milton House, Northants; Borobridge, Yorks*), *b.* 22 *Dec.* 1888.

2*g*. Noel Legard Alexander, *b.* 24 *Dec.* 1894.

3*f*. Henry Alexander (*Bryn Mawr, Seattle, Wash., U.S.A.*), *b.* 24 *Nov.* 1860; *m.* at Raton, New Mexico, 2 *June* 1886, Katharine, da. of William H. Adams of Raton afsd.; and has issue 1*g* to 4*g*. [Nos. 28872 to 28888.

The Plantagenet Roll

1g. Robert Disney Alexander, b. 15 Aug. 1887.
2g. Winifred Alexander.
3g. Beatrice Alexander.
4g. Phyllis Alexander.

4f. Matilda Alexander (4 *Warwick Gardens, Kensington, W.*), m. 17 Sept. 1868, Walter Hudson of York, Capt. 100th Royal Canadian Regt., *afterwards* in Holy Orders and Rector of Carlton in Lindrick, d. 24 Nov. 1885 ; and has issue 1g to 9g.

1g. Walter Alexander Hudson (*Riverside, California*), b. 21 Feb. 1872; m. 24 July 1909, Anna Lena, widow of Joseph Gooding, da. of (—) Viberg.

2g. Francis Disney Hudson (*Riverside, California*), b. 6 Aug. 1873 ; *unm.*

3g. Charles Louis Hudson (*Northallerton*), b. 11 June 1875 ; m. 20 Oct. 1906, Ethel May, da of Marmaduke Proudlock ; and has issue 1h.

1h. Richard Disney Hudson, b. 30 May 1909.

4g. Emily Margarette Hudson, m. 18 Aug. 1906, Philip Karl Beisiegel (*Uppingham, Rutland*) ; and has issue 1h to 2h.

1h. Walter Karl Beisiegel, b. 13 July 1907.
2h. Lilian Margarette Beisiegel, b. 16 Ap. 1909.

5g. Grace Ellen Hudson.
6g. Ethel Maud Hudson.
7g. Mabel Juana Hudson.
8g. Nora Blanche Hudson.
9g. Nona Muriel Hudson.

5f. Ellen Alexander, m. 19 Mar. 1891, Robert Piper Loy (*Hunteville, Ontario, Canada*) ; and has issue 1g to 3g.

1g. Walter Alexander Loy, b. 9 Jan. 1895.
2g. Zoë Gwendolyn Alexander Loy, b. 8 May 1893.
3g. Mary Irene Alexander Loy, b. 4 Feb. 1896.

2e. *Charlotte Matilda Alexander*, b. 3 Oct. 1822 ; d. 5 *May* 1876 ; m. *at Halifax* 21 Oct. 1847, the Rev. Thomas Andrew Walker, M.A. (Oxon.), Rector of Kilham, d. 14 *Ap.* 1905 ; *and had issue 1f to 4f*.

1f. Rev. Onebye Robert Walker, b. 25 *Sept.* 1849 ; d. 4 *June* 1908 ; m. 4 *June* 1878, Fanny Hyndman, da. of the Rev. John Blair, Vicar of Brompton ; and had issue (*with 3 others d. young*) 1g to 3g.

1g. Robert Andrew Walker, in U.S. Navy, b. 3 Nov. 1883.
2g. Fanny Walker, b. 26 Ap. 1879.
3g. Hilda Blair Walker, b. 29 Sept. 1882.

2f. Minnie Paula Walker, m. at Ilford 3 Oct. 1876, the Rev. Arthur Ingleby, M.A. (*St. Clement's, Heene, Worthing*) ; and has issue 1g to 3g.

1g. Richard Arthur Oakes Ingleby, Solicitor (87 *Chester Terrace, Eaton Square, S.W.*), b. 27 Jan. 1879.

2g. Charles Herbert Evelyn Ingleby (*Melbourne, Victoria*), b. 2 May 1881.

3g. Ethel Mary Rose Ingleby, b. 6 July 1877.

3f. Harriet Caroline Walker (*Worthing*), *unm.*
4f. Nina Walker (*Hove*), *unm.*

3e. *Eliza Alexander*, b. 1825 ; d. 18 Dec. 1867 ; m. *Aug.* 1848, *Richard Bowser, Bishop Auckland, Durham, Solicitor*, d. 13 Feb. 1882 ; *and had issue* (*with a son and da. d. young*) 1f to 2f.

1f. Harry Moreland Bowser (*Bishop Auckland*), b. 8 Dec. 1863 ; m. June 1895, Annie, da. of (—) Lavender of Sydney, Australia.

2f. Caroline Bowser, m. 9 July 1879, Thomas Alexander McCullagh, M.D. (*Bishop Auckland, Durham*) ; and has issue 1g to 4g.   [Nos. 28889 to 28920.

# of The Blood Royal

1*g*. Alexander McCullagh, Lieut. R.N., *b*. 23 Ap. 1880.

2*g*. Herbert Rochfort McCullagh, Durham L.I., *b*. 15 June 1881.

3*g*. Arthur Cecil Hays McCullagh, M.B., *b*. 20 Nov. 1882.

4*g*. Florence Danvers McCullagh, *b*. 1 June 1885.

4*e*. Frances Catherine Alexander, d. 5 Mar. 1892; m. 1st, *Francis William Montgomery of Kettering*, d. 28 Aug. 1870; 2ndly, *John Brown Izon of Walsgrave Hall*, d. (-); *and had issue* 1*f* to 2*f*.

1*f*. Amy Frances Jane Montgomery, b. 3 *Aug*. 1860; d. 1902; m. 5 *Aug*. 1886, *Edward Disney Alexander of Milton, co. Northants*, d. 30 *Mar*. 1907; *and had issue*.

See p. 191, Nos. 28886–28887.

2*f*. Florence Montgomery, *m*. 30 July 1890, the Rev. Ernest Lembert Daniels, Rector of Holcott (*Holcott Rectory, Northants*), *s.p.*

3*c*. Rev. William Legard, Vicar of Ganton, d. 19 Feb. 1826; m. 7 Feb. 1803, *Cecilia Elizabeth, da. of James Oldershaw of Stamford, M.D.*, d. 31 Dec. 1854; *and had issue* 1*d* to 3*d*.

1*d*. James Anlaby Legard, Capt. R.N., K.T.S., b. 13 Oct. 1805; d. 25 *June* 1869; m. 6 *May* 1845, *Catherine [a descendant of the Lady Anne, sister of King Edward IV.], widow of Henry Ralph Beaumont, da. of Sir George Cayley, 6th Bt.* [E.], d. 11 *Mar*. 1887; *and had issue*.

See the Exeter Volume, p. 697, Nos. 57863–57876 and Nos. 57894–57897.

2*d*. William Barnabas Legard, Col. Bengal Army, b. 27 Dec. 1810; d. 27 *Jan*. 1890; m. 11 Dec. 1845, *Ann Maria, da. of Richard Onebye Walker of London*, d. *and had issue* 1*e*.

1*e*. Evelyn Mary Legard, *m*. 1886, William J. Gillett (*Ashley House, Shalford, Surrey*).

3*d*. Rev. Frederick Legard, *settled in Australia*, d. 26 *June* 1897; m. *and had issue*.[1]

4*c*. Digby Legard of Watton Abbey, co. *Yorks*, b. 1766; d. (-); m. 11 *Dec*. 1797, *Frances [a descendant of the Lady Anne, sister of King Edward IV., &c.], da. of Ralph Creyke of Marton; and had issue*.

See the Exeter Volume, p. 689, Nos. 57567–57600.

5*c*. Jane Legard, bapt. 8 *July* 1756; d. (-); m. 29 Oct. 1785, (—) *Smith of Sunderlandwick, co. York*.

6*c*. Frances Legard, b. 3 *July* 1757; d. 6 *Ap*. 1827; m. 19 Feb. 1780, *Thomas Grimston* (see p. 196) *of Grimston Garth and Kilnwick, co. York*, b. 29 Dec. 1753; d. 2 May 1821; *and had issue* 1*d* to 2*d*.

1*d*. Charles Grimston of Grimston Garth and Kilnwick, J.P., D.L., Col. East York Militia, b. 2 *July* 1791; d. 21 *Mar*. 1859; m. 10 Nov. 1823, *Jane, da. of the Very Rev. Thomas Trench, Dean of Kildare [neice of 1st Baron Ashtown]*, d. 26 *Jan*. 1873; *and had issue* 1*e* to 13*e*.

1*e*. Marmaduke Jerard Grimston of Grimston Garth and Kilnwick, J.P., D.L., Col. East York Art. Mil., b. 27 Nov. 1826; d. 14 Nov. 1879; m. 3 *July* 1856, *Florence Victoria, da. of Col. Hardress Robert Saunderson [by his wife Lady Maria, née Luttrell*] [m. 2ndly, 2 Jan. 1883, *Col. Sir Edmund Frederick Du Cane, K.C.B.*, *and*], d. 7 *June* 1903; *and had issue* 1*f* to 2*f*.

1*f*. Florence Maria Grimston, dau. and co-h., *m*. as 2nd wife 10 Oct. 1882, Edward Byrom of Culver and Kersall Cell, D.L., High Sheriff co. Devon 1888 (*Culver, near Exeter; Kersall Cell, co. Lancaster; Grimston Garth, co. York*); and has issue 1*g* to 2*g*.

1*g*. Edward Luttrell Grimston Byrom, *b*. 25 June 1885.

2*g*. Rose Effie Jerardine Byrom. [Nos. 28921 to 28983.

---

[1] Foster's " Baronetage," 1880, p. 355.

The Plantagenet Roll

2f. Rose Armatrude Frances Grimston, da. and co-h. (*Grimston Garth, near Hull*), m. 19 June 1889, Col. George Bertie Benjamin Hobart, J.P., D.L., *late* R.A. [E. of Buckinghamshire Coll. and a descendant of George, Duke of Clarence, K.G. (see Clarence Volume, p. 544)], d. 27 Oct. 1907; and has issue 1g.

    1g. Armatrude Bertie Sophia Effie Hobart, b. 20 May 1890.

  2e. *Walter John Grimston of Bracken, co. York, Major R.A.*, b. 9 Feb. 1828; d. 18 Oct. 1899; m. 2ndly, 3 June 1865, Josephine, da. of Thomas Green Wilkinson; and had issue 1f to 6f.

    1f. Ernest Walter Grimston, heir male of the Grimstons of Grimston Garth, b. 13 Sept. 1876.

    2f. Charlotte Josephine Grimston.

    3f. Evelyn Maude Cecilia Grimston.

    4f. Helena Winifred Grimston.

    5f. Beatrice Letitia Grimston.

    6f. Violet Adele Grimston.

  3e. William Henry Grimston, J.P., Hon. Col. 3rd Batt. East Yorkshire Regt. (*High Hall, Etton, Yorks*), b. 1 Nov. 1830; m. 1st, 11 Ap. 1860, Anna, da. of George Harrison of Hailsham, co. Sussex, d. 1878; 2ndly, 27 July 1882, Catharine Sarah, da. of John Charlesworth Dodgson-Charlesworth of Chapelthorpe Hall, co. York.

  4e. *Daniel Thomas Grimston, LL.B. (Camb.)*, b. 8 July 1832; d. 3 Mar. 1872; m. 1 Aug. 1860, Jane Malvina Williamza [a descendant of the Lady Isabel Plantagenet (see Essex Volume, p. 44)], da. of George Morant, J.P. [re-m. 2ndly, 3 Feb. 1883, John Hugh Dillon, who d. 30 Aug. 1894]; and had issue 1f to 5f.

    1f. Sylvester George Grimston (*Montreal*), b. 22 Oct. 1863; m. 21 Jan. 1898, Mary Elizabeth, da. of James Penfold, Manager of the Bank of British North America at Montreal.

    2f. Charles Digby Grimston (*Montreal*), b. 14 July 1867; m. 14 Aug. 1906, Olive, da. of (—) Mills of Bracebridge, Ontario.

    3f. Lydia Maude Grimston.

    4f. Jane Malvina Williamza Grimston.

    5f. Geraldine Mary Grimston.

  5e. Rev. Alexander Grimston, Canon of York and Vicar of Stillingfleet (*Stillingfleet Vicarage, Yorks*), b. 27 Nov. 1835; m. 29 Oct. 1863, Una Kate [descended from the Lady Isabel Plantagenet (see Essex Volume, p. 255)], da. of Capt. Rowland William Taylor Money; and has issue (with a son, Charles Rowland, who d. unm. 9 Sept. 1889) 1f to 6f.

    1f. Edith Maud Grimston.

    2f. Constance Eleanor Grimston.

    3f. Alice Mabel Grimston.

    4f. Hilda Grimston.

    5f. Florence Brenda Grimston.

    6f. Cicely Mildred Grimston.

  6e. *Maria Emma Grimston*, b. 23 Oct. 1824; d. 6 Mar./19 Ap. 1907; m. 8 July 1858, *Major William Forbes, 77th Regt.* [youngest son of James Forbes of Kingairlock, co. Ayr], d. 29 Nov. 1882; and had issue 1f to 5f.

    1f. Katharine Annie Forbes (*Chelsea*), m. 2 Oct. 1893, Charles Blackwell Moneypenny, d. 2 Aug. 1894.

    2f. Magdalena Gertrude Forbes, m. 20 Oct. 1890, Charles Irwin Clark Williams.

    3f. Cecil Forbes.

    4f. Alice Forbes.

    5f. Marion Forbes.

  7e. Frances Dorothy Grimston (*Ardmore, Chislehurst*), m. 24 Nov. 1853, the Rev. John Frewen Moor, M.A., Vicar of Ampfield, near Romsey [descended from the Lady Anne, sister to Kings Edward IV. and Richard III.] (see Exeter Volume, p. 424), d. 5 Jan. 1906; and has issue 1f to 2f. [Nos. 28984 to 29010.

# of The Blood Royal

1ƒ. Rev. Charles Moor, D.D., *late* Vicar of Gainsborough and Canon of Lincoln (*Apley Rise, Westgate-on-Sea*), b. 10 May 1857 ; m. 10 July 1889, Constance Mary, da. of Robert Moon, M.A., Bar.-at-Law ; and has issue 1g to 5g.

    1g. Christopher Moor, b. 2 Feb. 1892.

    2g. Frewen Moor, b. 28 Ap. 1893.

    3g. Oswald Moor, b. 26 July 1901.

    4g. Rosalie Moor.

    5g. Veronica Moor.

2ƒ. Selina Mary Moor.

8e. Jane Grimston.

9e. Catherine Grimston, b. 27 Jan. 1829 ; d. 8 Feb. 1869 ; m. 22 Sept. 1856, the Rev. *Edward Gordon*, Vicar of Kildale and afterwards of Atwick, both co. York (*Mundesley, Norfolk*) ; and had issue 1ƒ to 6ƒ.

    1ƒ. Rev. Edward Cyril Gordon, Rector of Carrington (*Carrington Rectory, Wirksworth, Derby*), b. 23 Oct. 1858 ; m. 12 Aug. 1898, Ellen, da. of R. Y. Bazett, H.E.I.C.C.S., Bombay, s.p.

    2ƒ. Charles Grimston Gordon (*Southrepps, Norwich, Norfolk*), b. 7 Mar. 1860 ; m. 4 Nov. 1890, Florence, da. of Harrison Hodgson, d. 15 Sept. 1892 ; and has issue 1g.

        1g. Florence Gordon, b. 25 Aug. 1892.

    3ƒ. Francis Gordon, b. 2 Feb. 1869 ; *unm.*

    4ƒ. Helen Elizabeth Mary Gordon, *unm.*

    5ƒ. Blanche Theodora Gordon, m. Dec. 1895, Edward Tisdall, Paymaster of the Forces, R.N., s.p.

    6ƒ. Lucy Beatrice Gordon, *unm.*

10e. Elizabeth Grimston (*Cheltenham*), m. 4 May 1870, James King of Clara, co. Fermanagh, and Langfield, co. Tyrone, d. c. 1882 ; and has issue 1ƒ to 4ƒ.

    1ƒ. Rev. Marmaduke James Gilbert King, Perpetual Curate of St. Gabriel's, Bishop Wearmouth (*Bishop Wearmouth*), b. 3 Aug. 1871 ; m. 14 Nov. 1906, Catherine Primrose, da. of the Rev. J. C. P. Aldous, Vicar and Rural Dean of Duffield ; and has issue 1g.

        1g. Elinor Catherine King.

    2ƒ. Henry Charles King (*St. Marnock's Farm, Salisbury, Rhodesia*), b. 1 Ap. 1873.

    3ƒ. Alice Cicell King.

    4ƒ. Florence Maude King.

11e. Maude Grimston (*The Ridgeway, Wimbledon*), m. 24 June 1889, the Rev. George Constantine, D.D., d.s.p. 6 Oct. 1891.

12e. Cicell Grimston, m. 29 Aug. 1871, Capt. Francis Loftus Tottenham (*The Garden House, Mildmay Park, N.*) ; and has issue 1ƒ to 6ƒ.

    1ƒ. Percy Marmaduke Tottenham, Egyptian Irrigation Dept., b. 17 Aug. 1873 ; m. 31 Aug. 1909, Angel, da. of Edward Mervyn Archdale of Riverside, co. Fermanagh.

    2ƒ. Francis Loftus Tottenham, R.N., b. 17 Aug. 1880.

    3ƒ. Anna Maude Tottenham, m. 2 July 1907, Major-Gen. Henry Wylie (*Hill Top Cottage, Farnham Common*), s.p.

    4ƒ. Mabel Gertrude Tottenham, m. 5 Oct. 1907, Dudley Carmalt Jones, M.D. (*Eastcote*) ; and has issue 1g.

        1g. Evelyn Carmalt Jones, b. 20 July 1908.

    5ƒ. Edith Leonora Tottenham, *unm.*

    6ƒ. Grace Marguerite Tottenham, *unm.*

13e. Octavia Grimston (*Kingswood, Weybridge*), m. 10 Jan. 1867, Herbert Clifford Saunders, Q.C., Bar.-at-Law, d. 25 Aug. 1893 ; and has issue 1ƒ to 9ƒ.

[Nos. 29011 to 29041.

The Plantagenet Roll

1*f*. Herbert Stewart Saunders, M.A., *b.* 18 May 1872.
2*f*. Una Mary Josephine Saunders, *b.* 5 Sept. 1869.
3*f*. Maude Irene Saunders, *b.* 23 Feb. 1871.
4*f*. Rose Pellipar Saunders, *b.* 9 Aug. 1873.
5*f*. Grace Helena Saunders, *b.* 30 Oct. 1874.
6*f*. Violet Constance Saunders, *b.* 19 Feb. 1876.
7*f*. Florence Muriel Saunders, *b.* 19 Nov. 1878.
8*f*. Cicell Ione Saunders, *b.* 22 Ap. 1881.
9*f*. Octavia Elfrida Saunders, *b.* 13 Oct. 1885.

2*d*. *Oswald Grimston of Mersham Bitterne, co. Hants*, b. 22 *Oct.* 1794 ; d. 31 *July* 1872 ; m. 16 *Sept.* 1830, *Mary Ernle* [*descended from the Lady Isabel Plantagenet* (see Essex Volume, p. 255)], *da. of the Rev. Kyrle Ernle Money, M.A., Preb. of Hereford*, d. 8 *Jan.* 1892 ; *and had issue* 1*e* to 2*e*.

1*e*. Oswald James Augustus Grimston, J.P., D.L., *late* Col. Comdg. 3rd Batt. Royal Warwickshire Regt. (*The Lodge, Itchen, co. Hants*), *b.* 27 Aug. 1831 ; *m.* 1st, 15 Ap. 1856, Frances Eliza, da. of Lieut.-Col. Henry Dundas Campbell, *d.* 6 July 1869 ; 2ndly, 21 Aug. 1876, Louisa Mary, widow of John William Sanders, da. of Capt. Rowland Money, 41st Madras N.I. ; and has issue (with a son who *d.s.p.*) 1*f* to 6*f*.

1*f*. Rollo Estouteville Grimston, C.I.E., Lieut.-Col. Indian Army, *b.* 26 Oct. 1861.

2*f*. Sylvester Bertram Grimston, Major Indian Army, *b.* 27 Nov. 1864 ; *m.* 16 May 1904, Nina, da. of Lieut.-Col. George William Macaulay ; and has issue 1*g* to 2*g*.

1*g*. George Sylvester Grimston, *b.* 2 Ap. 1905.
2*g*. Frances Nina Grimston, *b.* 16 July 1907.
3*f*. Lionel Augustus Grimston, *b.* 18 Ap. 1868.
4*f*. Horace Legard Grimston, *b.* 30 Jan. 1880.
5*f*.[1] Brenda Grimston, *m.* 4 July 1882, the Rev. Owen Tudor, Vicar of Willingdon (*Willingdon Vicarage, Sussex*).
6*f*.[2] Pauline Grimston, *b.* 28 June 1877.

2*e*. Mary Adelaide Emma Grimston (*Fir Bank, Ascot, Berks*), *m.* 19 Sept 1867, Gen. James Michael, C.S.I., C.F.J., Knt. of Grace of St. John of Jerusalem, &c., J.P., *late* Madras Staff Corps, *d.* 17 Feb. 1907 ; and has issue 1*f*.

1*f*. Mildred Douglas Michael.

7*c*. *Henrietta Charlotte Legard*, d. (-) ; m. (—) *Smith of Yorkshire*.

2*b*. *Jane Legard*, d. 11 *Nov.* 1758 ; m. 12 *Mar.* 1753, *John Grimston of Grimston Garth and Kilnwick, co. York*, b. 17 *Feb.* 1725 ; d. 21 *June* 1780 ; *and had issue* 1*c*.

1*c*. *Thomas Grimston of Grimston Garth and Kilnwick*, b. 29 *Dec.* 1753 ; d. 2 *May* 1821 ; m. 19 *Feb.* 1780, *Frances, da. of Sir Digby Legard, 5th Bt.* [E.], d. 1827 ; *and had issue*.

See p. 193, Nos. 28981–29061.

2*a*. *Jane Digby*, d. (-) ; m. *Francis Fycher of Grantham Grange*.[1]

3*a*. *Mary Digby*, d. (-) ; m. *George Cartwright of Ossington, co. Notts ;* and *had issue* (*with a son and* 3 *other das. all* d.s.p.) 1*b* to 4*b*.

1*b*. *Mary Cartwright, da. and event. co-h.*, d.s.p. 21 *July* 1764 ; m. 10 *Ap.* 1758, *Sir Charles Louis Buck, 4th Bt.* [E.], d.s.p. 7 *June* 1782.

2*b*. *Dorothy Cartwright*,[2] *da. and event. co-h.*

3*b*. *Jane Cartwright, da. and event. co-h.*, d. 15 *Sept.* 1811 ; m. *Aug.* 1755, *Sir Digby Legard, 5th Bt.* [E.], d. 4 *Feb.* 1773 ; *and had issue*.

See p. 191, Nos. 28872–29061. [Nos. 29042 to 29332.

---

[1] Thoroton's "Notts," i. 317.   [2] See note on p. 197.

of The Blood Royal

4b. Anne Cartwright,[1] da. and event. co-h.

4a. Philadelphia Digby, da. and co-h., d. 14 Jan. 1765; m. 1730, Sir George Cayley, 4th Bt. [E.], d. Sept. 1791; and had issue.
See the Exeter Volume, pp. 696–698, Nos. 57769–57955.

[Nos. 29333 to 29519.

100. Descendants, if any, of ELIZABETH WHARTON (Table X.), m. (—) BENNETT; and of the Hon. ELEANOR WHARTON, d. (−); m. WILLIAM THWAYTES of Long Marston.

101. Descendants, if any, of MARY MUSGRAVE (Table XII.), d. (−); m. THOMAS DAVISON of Blakiston, co. Durham.

102. Descendants of Sir PHILIP MUSGRAVE, 6th Bt. [E.], M.P. (Table XII.), b. c. 1711; d. 5 or 25 July 1795; m. 24 June 1742, JANE, da. of John TURTON of Orgreave, co. Stafford, d. (will proved) 1802; and had issue 1a to 5a.

    1a. Sir John Charden Musgrave, 7th Bt. [E.], b. 15 Jan. 1757; d. 24 July 1806; m. 13 July 1791, Mary, da. of the Rev. Sir Edmund Filmer, 6th Bt. [E.], d. 9 Jan. 1838; and had issue 1b to 3b.
    1b. Sir Philip Christopher Musgrave, 8th Bt. [E.], M.P., b. 12 July 1794; d.s.p.s. 16 July 1827.
    2b. Rev. Sir Christopher John Musgrave, 9th Bt. [E.], b. 1798; d. 11 May 1834; m. Sept. 1825, Mary Anne, da. (see p. 206) of Edward Hasell of Dalemain, d. shortly before Oct. 1835; and had issue 1c to 3c.
    1c. Georgiana Musgrave, da. and co-h., d. 11 Ap. 1868; m. 29 July 1847, the Hon. Frederick Petre [B. Petre Coll.], d. 18 July 1906; and had issue.
See the Clarence Volume, p. 372, Nos. 12725–12739.
    2c. Augusta Musgrave, b. 10 Feb. 1830; d. 11 Oct. 1901; m. 1st, 27 Aug. 1850, Col. Henry Frederick Bonham, 10th Hussars, d. 16 Feb. 1856; 2ndly, 26 May 1857, John Edward Cornwallis (Rous), 2nd Earl of Stradbroke [U.K.], and Baron Rous [G.B.], and 7th Bt. [E.], d. 27 Jan. 1886; and had issue 1d to 8d.
    1d. Henry Walter Musgrave Bonham, Col. formerly Grenadier Guards (Arthur's), b. 11 Nov. 1852; m. 26 Aug. 1875, Georgiana, da. of Thomas Sheriffe of Henstead Hall, Suffolk.
    2d. George Edward John Mowbray (Rous), 3rd Earl of Stradbroke [U.K.], and Baron Rous [G.B.], 8th Bt. [E.], C.V.O., C.B., Vice-Adm. of Suffolk, and Chairman Suffolk Territorial Force, &c. (Henham Hall, Wangford, Suffolk), b. 19 Nov. 1862; m. 23 July 1898, Helena Violet Alice, da. of Lieut.-Gen. James Keith Fraser, C.M.G. [Bt. Coll.]; and has issue 1e to 5e.
    1e. John Anthony Alexander Rous, Viscount Dunwich, H.M. Queen Alexandra Sponsor, b. 1 Ap. 1903.
    2e. Hon. William Keith Rous, b. 10 Mar. 1907.
    3e. Lady Pleasance Elizabeth Rous.
    4e. Lady Catherine Charlotte Rous.
    5e. Lady Betty Helena Joanna Rous.
    3d. Edith Charlotte Musgrave Bonham, b. 30 May 1851; d. at Johannesburg 17 Feb. 1903; m. 21 July 1870, the Rev. William Belcher, formerly Vicar of Walberswick and Blythburgh, and Rector of Heveningham (Ipswich); and had issue (with a son who d. young) 1e to 4e.

[Nos. 29520 to 29541.

---

[1] One of these is said to have m. a Sir (—) Middleton.

The Plantagenet Roll

1*e*. Reginald George Holland Belcher, Lieut. Lincolnshire Regt., twin, *b*. 22 Ap. 1878.
2*e*. Frederick Harry Bonham Belcher, twin, *b*. 22 Ap. 1878.
3*e*. Musgrave Vanneck Gordon Belcher, *b*. 30 July 1881.
4*e*. Edith Augusta Anna Bonham Belcher, *m*. 25 Mar. 1899, George Lipscombe, R.N. (*Melrose, The Grange, Beccles*); and has issue 1*f* to 7*f*.
1*f*. George Lipscombe, *b*. 13 Dec. 1899.
2*f*. William Henry Lipscombe, *b*. 30 May 1901.
3*f*. Frederick Edmund Lipscombe, *b*. 20 Nov. 1904.
4*f*. Edith Mary Lipscombe, *b*. 5 Sept. 1903.
5*f*. Elizabeth Catherine Lipscombe, *b*. 3 May 1906.
6*f*. Margaret Mary Lipscombe, *b*. 28 July 1907.
7*f*. Agnes Lipscombe, *b*. 17 Ap. 1909.

4*d*. Lady Augusta Fanny Rous, *m*. 8 May 1880, Cecil Francis William Fane [E. of Westmorland Coll.], whom she divorced 1904; and has issue 1*e* to 2*e*.
1*e*. Charles George Cecil Fane, *b*. 8 Ap. 1881.
2*e*. John Lionel Richards Fane, *b*. 2 Jan. 1884.

5*d*. Lady Sophia Evelyn Rous (*Boscombe Cottage, I.W.*), *m*. 20 Ap. 1888, Capt. George Hamilton Heaviside, 6th Dragoons, *d*. 27 Nov. 1906.
6*d*. Lady Adela Charlotte Rous, *m*. 19 Feb. 1887, Thomas Belhaven Henry Cochrane, M.V.O., J.P., D.L., Dept.-Gov., Steward and Sheriff of the Isle of Wight, and Capt. of Carisbrooke Castle [E. of Dundonald Coll., and a descendant of the Lady Anne, sister to King Edward IV., &c. (see Exeter Volume, p. 626)] (*Carisbrooke Castle, I.W.; Quarr Abbey, Ryde, I.W.*).
7*d*. Lady Hilda Maud Rous, *b*. 3 Feb. 1867; d. 15 Aug. 1904; *m*. 31 Jan. 1901, Charles Fitzroy Ponsonby M'Neill [*descended from George (Plantagenet), Duke of Clarence, K.G.* (see Clarence Volume, p. 336)] (*Carlton Curlieu Manor House, near Leicester; Kilsant House, Broadway, Worcester*); and had issue 1*e* to 2*e*.
1*e*. Ronald Frank Rous M'Neill, *b*. 15 Jan. 1894.
2*e*. Brenda Mary Adela M'Neill, *b*. 8 Nov. 1897.

8*d*. Lady Gwendoline Audrey Adeline Brudenell Rous, *m*. 26 June 1895, Lieut.-Col. Richard Beale Colvin, C.B. (*Monkhams, Waltham Abbey*); and has issue 1*e* to 2*e*.
1*e*. Richard Beale Rous Colvin, *b*. 12 Feb. 1900.
2*e*. Audrey Mary Maude Colvin.

3*c*. Harriet Musgrave, da. and co-h., d. 29 July 1863; *m*. as 1st *wife*, 28 Ap. 1851, *the Right Hon. Sir Walter Barttelot Barttelot of Stopham*, 1st Bt. [U.K. 9 June 1875], P.C., M.P., C.B., &c., Col. 2nd Sussex R.V., *b*. 10 Oct. 1820; *d*. 2 Feb. 1893; and had issue 1*d* to 4*d*.
1*d*. *Sir Walter George Barttelot of Stopham*, 2nd Bt. [U.K.], J.P., D.L., Major 2nd V.B. Royal Sussex Regt., *previously* 5th Dragoon Guards, b. 11 Ap. 1855; d. (*being killed in Boer War*) 23 July 1900; m. 3 June 1879, Georgiana Mary, da. of George Edmond Balfour of Sidmouth Manor [*re-m*. 2*ndly*, 22 Oct. 1902, Beville Molesworth St. Aubyn]; *and had issue* 1*e* to 3*e*.
1*e*. Sir Walter Balfour Barttelot of Stopham, 3rd Bt. [U.K.], Lieut. 1st Batt. Coldstream Guards, served in South Africa 1900–1902 (*Stopham House, Pulborough; 10 Berkeley Square, W.*), *b*. 22 Mar. 1880; *m*. 17 Nov. 1903, Gladys St. Aubyn, da. of William Collier Angove of 83 Onslow Gardens, S.W.; and has issue 1*f* to 2*f*.
1*f*. Walter de Stopham Barttelot, *b*. 27 Oct. 1904.
2*f*. William Frederick Geoffrey Nelson Barttelot, *b*. 21 Oct. 1905.
2*e*. Nigel Kenneth Walter Barttelot, Lieut. R.N., and Com. Instructor Royal

[Nos. 29542 to 29566.

of The Blood Royal

Naval Vol. Reserve, b. 9 Ap. 1883; m. 10 Jan. 1906, Dorothy Maud, da. of Frederick Aldcroft Kay of Manchester.

3e. Irene Margaret Mary Barttelot.

2d. Edith Harriet Barttelot, m. 12 June 1884, Major-Gen. Henry Crichton Sclater, R.A., C.B., now Comdg. 4th (Quetta) Div., *formerly* Q.M.G. in India (*Flagstaff House, Quetta*).

3d. Evelyn Fanny Barttelot (13 *Egerton Place, S.W.*), m. 29 Mar. 1883, Charles Munro Sandham of Rowdell, co. Sussex, d. 1892; and has issue 1e to 3e.

1e. Charles Barttelot Sandham, b. 1887.

2e. Edith Mary Georgina Sandham, m. 1907, Hamilton Hugh Berners, Lieut Irish Guards.

3e. Ada Margaret Sandham.

4d. Ada Mary Barttelot, m. 17 Oct. 1882, Col. William Frederick Cavaye, Comdg. Middlesex Brig., E. Command (40 *Egerton Crescent, S.W.; Birchenbridge, Horsham*)

3b. Sir George Musgrave of Edenhall, 10th Bt. [E.], b. 14 *June* 1799; d. 29 Dec. 1872; m. 26 *June* 1828, Charlotte, da. of Sir *James Graham of Netherby*, 1st Bt. [G.B.], d. 26 *June* 1873; *and had issue* 1c *to* 4c.

1c. Sir Richard Courtenay Musgrave of Edenhall, 11th Bt. [E.], M.P., Lord-Lieut. co. Westmorland, b. 21 *Aug.* 1838; d. 13 Feb. 1881; m. 17 *Jan.* 1867, Adora Frances Olga, da. of Peter Wells [re-m. 2ndly, 18 Ap. 1882, Henry Charles (Brougham), 3rd Lord Brougham and Vaux [U.K.], K.C.V.O.]; *and had issue* 1d *to* 5d.

1d. Sir Richard George Musgrave of Edenhall, 12th Bt. [E.], D.L., *late* Argyll and Sutherland Highlanders (*Edenhall, Langwathby, R.S.O.; 17 Charles Street, Berkeley Square, W.*), b. 11 Oct. 1872; m. 9 Feb. 1895, the Hon. Eleanor [descended from the Lady Isabel Plantagenet (see the Essex Volume, p. 46)], da. of Charles (Harbord), 5th Baron Suffield [G.B.]; and has issue 1e to 2e.

1e. Nigel Courtenay Musgrave, b. 11 Feb. 1896.

2e. Christopher Musgrave, b. 4 May 1899.

2d. Philip Richard Musgrave, *late* Lieut. 3rd Batt. Royal Sussex Regt. (*Bachelors'*), b. 26 Nov. 1873; m. (—).

3d. Thomas Charles Musgrave (*Union*), b. 28 Nov. 1875.

4d. Dorothy Anne Musgrave, m. 12 June 1895, Henry Francis Compton (see p. 467) of Minstead, J.P., D.L., *formerly* M.P., &c. (*Minstead Manor, Lyndhurst; Mapperton House, Beaminster, Dorset*); and has issue 1e to 3e.

1e. Henry Richard Compton, b. 12 Oct. 1899.

2e. Phyllis Dorothy Compton, b. 17 Mar. 1896.

3e. Daphne Compton, b. 24 Feb. 1897.

5d. Zoe Caroline Musgrave, m. 16 Jan. 1893, Alexander Farquharson of Invercauld, Lieut.-Col. Comdg. 7th Batt. Gordon Highlanders [descended from King Henry VII. (see Tudor Roll, p. 462)] (*Invercauld, Ballater; 40 Park Street, Grosvenor Square, W.*); and has issue 1e to 2e.

1e. Myrtle Farquharson.

2e. Sylvia Farquharson.

2c. Caroline Musgrave, m. 8 Mar. 1859, William Stanley of Dalegarth and Ponsonby, co. Cumberland, J.P., D.L., b. 14 Sept. 1829; d. 18 Dec. 1881; and had issue 1d to 8d.

1d. Edward Stanley of Ponsonby Hall, J.P., D.L., b. 20 Nov. 1859; d. *unm.* 26 Feb. 1894.

2d. William Stanley of Ponsonby Hall, J.P., D.L., *late* Capt. Westmorland and Cumberland Yeo. Cav. (*Southwaite Hill, Carlisle*), b. 10 Ap. 1861.

3d. Philip Stanley (21 *Palliser Road, West Kensington*), b. 2 Mar. 1870; m. 3 Aug. 1907, Norah, da. of Edmund Stamp Mackrell of Craven House, Warminster; and has issue 1e to 2e.

1e. Nicholas Austhwaite Stanley } (twins), b. 28 Feb. 1909.
2e. Elizabeth Norah Stanley

[Nos. 29567 to 29590.

The Plantagenet Roll

4d. *Charlotte Stanley*, d. 18 June 1895; m. 10 Dec. 1890, *John Henry Lowry*; and had issue 1e.

   1e. Caroline Lowry.

5d. *Margaret Stanley*, m. 21 Ap. 1897, the Rev. Hildebrand Thomas Giles Alington, M.A. (Oxon.), Rector of Newnham Courteney [Cadet of Alington of Swinhope] (*Newnham Courteney Rectory, Oxford*); and has issue 1e to 2e.

   1e. Noel Stanley Alington, b. 4 Jan. 1899.

   2e. Ursula Margaret Alington, b. 9 Nov. 1904.

6d. Lucy Mildred Stanley.

7d. Constance Madeline Stanley.

8d. *Constance Augusta Stanley*, m. 17 July 1900, Alfred Russell Fordham of Melbourn Bury, J.P., M.A. (Camb.), Bar.-at-Law (*Melbourn Bury, Royston*); and has issue 1e to 2e.

   1e. Alfred Stanley Fordham, b. 2 Sept. 1897.

   2e. Joyce Madeline Fordham.

3c. *Agnes Musgrave*, d. 12 Mar. 1901; m. 19 *June* 1862, *the Rev. Malise Reginald Graham*, M.A., Rector of Arthuret [Bt. of Netherby Coll.], b. 15 Feb. 1833; d. 18 Nov. 1895; *and had issue* 1d *to* 5d.

   1d. Arthur Malise Graham, b. 1865.

   2d. *Reginald Graham*, b. 22 May 1867; d. 15 Feb. 1908; m. 21 Jan. 1897, *Helen Dacia* (2 Park Mansions, Albert Gate, S.W.), *da. of G. S. Herck of St. Petersburg*; *and had issue* 1e.

   1e. Ernest Reginald Graham, b. 7 Feb. 1898.

   3d. Rev. Ivor Charles Graham, Rector of Arthuret (*Arthuret Rectory, Longtown, Cumberland*), b. 1868.

   4d. Sophia Augusta Graham.

   5d. Maud Agnes Graham.

4c. *Sophia Musgrave*, m. 3 Aug. 1869, Samuel Steuart Gladstone of Capenoch (*Capenoch, Dumfries*; 40 Lennox Gardens, S.W.); and has issue 1d to 2d.

   1d. Hugh Steuart Gladstone of Capenoch, J.P., M.A. (Camb.), F.Z.S., F.R.S.E., formerly Lieut. 3rd Batt. K.O.S.B., served in South Africa 1900-1902, has Queen's Medal with 3 Clasps and King's Medal with 2 Clasps (*Capenoch, Thornhill, Dumfries*), b. 30 Ap. 1877; m. 24 Jan. 1906, Cecil Emily, da. of Gustavus Arthur Talbot [E. of Shrewsbury Coll.]; and has issue 1e.

   1e. John Gladstone, b. 17 Jan. 1907.

   2d. *Winifred Steuart Gladstone*, m. 14 July 1896, Sydney Roden Fothergill of Lowbridge, J.P., D.L., Major Westmorland and Cumberland Hussars, served in S. Africa as Capt. 34th Imp. Yeo. 1902 (*Lowbridge House, Kendal, Westmorland*); and has issue 1e to 3e.

   1e. Richard Fothergill, b. 3 Jan. 1901.

   2e. Christopher Francis Fothergill, b. 21 Ap. 1906.

   3e. Mildred Helen Sophia Fothergill.

2a. *Christopher Musgrave of Kempton Park, co. Midx.*, d. 11 Aug. 1833; m. the Hon. Elizabeth Anne [descended from the Lady Isabel Plantagenet], da. of Andrew (Archer), 2nd Baron Archer [G.B.], d. 8 Aug. 1847; *and had issue*.

See the Essex Volume, p. 145, Nos. 16461–16490.

3a. *Jane Musgrave*, d. (–); m. *Joseph Musgrave of Kypier* (see p. 216).

4a. *Charlotte Musgrave*, d. (–); m. 1774, *the Rev. Charles Mordaunt* (see p. 411), Rector of Massingham [2nd son of Sir Charles Mordaunt, 6th Bt. [E.]], d. 22 Jan. 1820; *and had issue* 1b.

   1b. *Rev. Charles Mordaunt*, Rector of Badgworth, d. (–); m. 1812, *Frances Harriet*, da. of James Sparrow of Flax Bourton, d. 1866; *and had issue* 1c *to* 2c.

   1c. *John Mordaunt*, 17th Lancers, d. 15 Nov. 1881; m. 1st, 1843, Harriet

[Nos. 29591 to 29641.

# of The Blood Royal

Maria, da. of Capt. Cumberledge, R.N., d. 1849 ; 2ndly, *Isabel*, da. of Major Fletcher Norton Balmain, Madras Cavalry; *and had issue* 1d *to* 9d.

1d.¹ James Sparrow Mordaunt, Lieut.-Col., *formerly* Major Leinster Regt., b. 14 Nov. 1843 ; m. (—), da. of (—); and has issue 1e.

    1e. [son] Mordaunt, b. 4 June 1886.

2d.¹ Francis Lionel Mordaunt.

3d.¹ John Mordaunt.

4d.² Harry Mordaunt.

5d.² Charles Mordaunt.

6d.² Philip Musgrave Mordaunt.

7d.¹ Mildred Mordaunt.

8d.² Harriet Isabel Mordaunt.

9d.² Katherine Mordaunt.

2c. *Charlotte Mordaunt*, d. (-) ; m. *the Rev. John Matthew, Rector of Chelvey ; and had issue*.

5a. *Henrietta Musgrave*, d. 16 *June* 1812 ; m. 26 *May* 1774, *Sir John Morris of Clasemont*, 1st Bt. [U.K.], so cr. 12 *May* 1806 ; b. 15 *July* 1745 ; d. 25 *June* 1819 ; *and had issue* 1b *to* 3b.

1b. Sir *John Morris*, 2nd Bt. [U.K.], b. 14 *July* 1775 ; d. 24 *Feb*. 1855; m. 5 *Oct*. 1809, *the Hon. Lucy Juliana, da. of John (Byng),* 5th *Viscount Torrington* [G.B.], d. 27 Nov. 1881 ; *and had issue* 1c *to* 7c.

1c. Sir *John Armine Morris*, 3rd Bt. [U.K.], D.L., b. 13 *July* 1813 ; d. 8 *Feb*. 1893; m. 21 *Dec*. 1847, *Catherine*, da. of Ronald MacDonald, d. 16 *Mar*. 1890 ; *and had issue* 1d *to* 7d.

1d. Sir Robert Armine Morris of Clasemont, 4th Bt. [U.K.], J.P., D.L., High Sheriff co. Glamorgan 1900, *late* Major Welsh Regt. (*Sketty Park, Swansea ; Westcross, near Swansea*), b. 27 July 1848 ; m. 12 Feb. 1885, Lucy Augusta, da. of Thomas Cory of Nevill Court, Tunbridge Wells, d. 15 Nov. 1902 ; and has issue 1e to 6e.

    1e. Tankerville Robert Armine Morris, b. 9 June 1892.

    2e. John Torrington Morris, b. 6 June 1896.

    3e. Lucy Gwladys Morris.

    4e. Valerie Ermyntrude Morris.

    5e. Dulcie Elaine Morris.

    6e. Sibyl Rowena Morris.

2d. John Morris, *late* Hon. Lieut.-Col. Welsh Div. R.A. (*Castle House, Broadstairs*), b. 9 Sept. 1850 ; m. 25 July 1881, Jessie, da. of William Fowler ; and has issue (with a son, John Armine Robert, b. 3 Oct. 1882, d. unm. 16 May 1908, and a da. d. young) 1e.

    1e. Jessie Harriet Amy Blanch Morris.

3d. George Cecil Morris, b. 10 Ap. 1852.

4d. Arthur Ronald Morris, b. 18 Nov. 1855.

5d. Herbert Morris, b. 17 June 1858 ; m. 25 July 1880, Marjory Rachel, da. of John Barron ; and has issue 1e to 3e.

    1e. John Barron Morris, b. 5 Mar. 1882.

    2e. Herbert Morris.

    3e. Katherine Daisy Morris.

6d. Henrietta Ellen Morris (*Havod, Sketty S.O., Glamorganshire*), m. as 2nd wife, 10 Oct. 1876, Felix Hussey Webber, a Clerk in the House of Commons (see p. 280), d. 19 Ap. 1905 ; and has issue 1e to 2e.

    1e. Horace Armine William Webber, Lieut. R.F.A., b. 28 Nov. 1880.

    2e. Laura Gwendolen Webber, m. 8 Sept. 1899, Edmund Ussher David (*Yscallog, Llandaff*); and has issue 1f to 2f.

        1f. Humphrey Edmund David, b. 6 Sept. 1900.

        2f. Rodney Felix Armine David, b. 19 June 1907.

The Plantagenet Roll

7d. Amy Blanche Caroline Morris, d. 14 Aug. 1907; m. 1885, Major Robert Bowen Robertson, 2nd Brig. Welsh Div. R.A. (*Fairlawn, Chandlers, Hants*); and had issue 1e to 6e.

    1e. Charles Armine Bowen Robertson, b. 1886.
    2e. Percy Robert Musgrave Robertson, b. 1892.
    3e. Tudor Peregrine Morris Robertson, b. 1896.
    4e. Amy Kate Alice Robertson.
    5e. Nellie Maude Robertson.
    6e. Rosamond Lucy Robertson.

2c. George Byng Morris, *J.P., D.L.*, b. 25 Mar. 1816; d. 3 Dec. 1899; m. 23 Oct. 1852, *Emily Matilda* (*Danygraig, Bridgend*), da. of Charles H. Smith of Derwen Fawr, co. Glamorgan; and had issue 1d to 10d.

    1d. Robert Townsend Morris, b. 9 July 1853.
    2d. Charles Smith Morris, b. 12 Dec. 1854; *m.* 1888, Maud Mary, da. of the Rev. George Alston, Rector of Studland ; and has issue 1e to 4e.

        1e. Charles Alan Smith Morris, b. 15 May 1895.
        2e. Mabel Travers Morris.
        3e. Daisy Emily Smith Morris.
        4e. Lucy Maud Morris.

    3d. George Lockwood Morris, *formerly* Lieut. Royal Monmouthshire Engineers Militia, b. 29 Jan. 1859; *m.* 1889, Wilhelmina, da. of Thomas Cory; and has issue 1e to 3e.

        1e. Cedrick Lockwood Morris, b. 1889.
        2e. Muriel Emily Morris.
        3e. Nancy Morris.

    4d. Musgrave Morris, b. 18 Nov. 1864; *m.* 1892, Edith, da. of K. Lockhart of Minnedosa, Manitoba.

    5d. Thomas Byng Morris, b. 24 July 1866; *m.* 24 Aug. 1898, Edith Amy, da. of F. S. Bishop of Benrick, Dee Hills Park, Chester; and has issue 1e.

        1e. Rosamund Byng Morris.

    6d. Frank Hall Morris, b. 16 July 1869.

    7d. Edith Charlotte Morris, *m.* 1887, Francis Montagu Lloyd, J.P., Bar.-at-Law (*The Grange, Newnham-on-Severn*); and has issue 1e.

        1e. Leslie Skipp Lloyd, b. 1891.

    8d. Fanny Matilda Morris, m. 16 Sept. 1882, Henry Bathurst Christie, C.E., *formerly* Ceylon P.W.D.

    9d. Lucy Emily Morris, *m.* 1887, Lieut.-Col. Henry Selwyn Goodlake, *late* 4th Batt. Gloucestershire Regt., *formerly* Lancashire Fusiliers.

    10d. Rose Herbert Morris.

3c. Frederick Morris, *Comm. R.N.*, b. 25 *Jan.* 1819; d. 23 *Jan.* 1903; m. 28 *Jan.* 1854, *Agnes* (*Denmead, Cosham, Hants*), da. and h. of Charles Brandford Lane of Castle Grant and Clermont, Barbados; and had issue 1d to 3d.

    1d. Frederick Morris, Major *late* Royal Welsh Fusiliers, Burmah (1885–1887), Hazara (1891), and China (1900) Medals and Clasps, is Sec. Club of Western India, Poona (*Poona, Bombay*), b. 20 Dec. 1854; *m.* 1884, Sybil, da. of John Rowland, B.C.S.

    2d. Charles Lane Morris, *formerly* Lieut. 1st Warwickshire Mil., *b.* 1857; *m.* 1903, Mabel Emily, da. of the Rev. Augustus Cooper of Upper Norwood, and Syleham Hall, co. Suffolk.

    3d. Percy Byng Morris (*Denmead, Cosham, Hants*), b. 1871.

4c. Charles Henry Morris, *C.B., O.L.H., a Gen. in the Army*, b. 27 Feb. 1824; d. 12 Oct. 1887; m. 16 *Sept.* 1869, *Lady Blanche* [*descended from George (Plantagenet), Duke of Clarence, K.G.* (see Clarence Volume, p. 628)] (*Holly Mount, Lyndhurst, Hants*), da. of George Godolphin (Osborne), 8th *Duke of Leeds* [E.], &c.; and had issue 1d to 2d.

[Nos. 29672 to 29699.

# of The Blood Royal

1*d*. Ethel Harriet Morris, *m*. 2 Dec. 1905, Gerald Cloete, a Resident Magistrate, Orangia (*Frankfort, O.R.C.*).

2*d*. Lilla Guendolen Morris.

5*c*. *Henrietta Juliana Morris*, d. 7 *Oct.* 1871 ; m. 2 *Mar.* 1838, *Albert Lascelles Jenner, 5th son of Robert Jenner of Wenvoe Castle, co. Glamorgan,* d. *Oct.* 1864 ; *and had issue* 1*d* to 2*d*.

1*d*. George Francis Birt Jenner, C.M.G., *formerly* Minister Resident for Guatemala 1897–1902, at Bogota 1892–1897, &c. (*Villa les Alouettes, Cannes ; St. James'*), *b*. 26 May 1840 ; *m*. 1867, Stephanie, da. of Alexis Emilianoff of Ragatova, Orel Govt., Russia.

2*d*. Cecil Armine Jenner, *Major Turkish Service*, d. 1896 ; m. *and had issue* 1*e*.

1*e*. Georgina Jenner.

6*c*. *Beatrice Charlotte Morris*, d. (–) ; m. *the Rev. Thomas Charles Hyde Leaver, M.A., Rector of Rockhampton* 1848–1859 ; d. 1871 ; *and had issue* (*a son and da*.).

7*c*. *Matilda Anne Cecilia Morris*, d. 29 *June* 1906 ; m. 26 *May* 1851, *Jasper Hall Livingstone of* 12 *The Strand, Ryde, I.W.* ; d. 1900 ; *and had issue* 1*d* to 3*d*.

1*d*. Hubert Armine Anson Livingstone, C.M.G., R. E., served in South Africa, as Assist.-Director of Railways, *b*. 19 Aug. 1865.

2*d*. Guy Livingstone, *b*. 8 June 1868.

3*d*. Lucy Byng Livingstone, *m*. 2 Oct. 1875, Herman William Tinne, J.P. co. Kent (*Union Club, S.W.*).

2*b*. *Matilda Morris*, d. (? s.p.) 5 *July* 1850 ; m. 13 *Nov.* 1807, *Edward Jesse of West Bromwich, co. Stafford*.

3*b*. *Caroline Morris*, d. (? s.p.) 26 *Jan.* 1883 ; m. 6 *Sept.* 1824, *the Rev. George Lillie Wodehouse Fauquier*. [Nos. 29700 to 29706.

103. Descendants, if any, of the Rev. CHRISTOPHER MUSGRAVE, Rector of Barking and Fellow of All Souls Coll., Oxon., *d*. (–) ; *m*. 1757, (—), widow of (—) PERFECT of Hatton Garden ; and of Lieut.-Col. HANS MUSGRAVE (Table XII.).

104. Descendants of the Rev. CHARDIN MUSGRAVE, M.A., D.D., Provost of Oriel Coll., Oxon., 1757–1768 (Table XII.), *b. c*. 1724, matric. 3 Mar. 1740, aged 16 ; *d*. 8 Jan. 1768 ; *m*. CATHERINE, sister and h. of Bartholomew Tipping of Woolley Park, co. Berks (who *d.s.p*. 13 Dec. 1798), da. of Bartholomew TIPPING, *d*. 21 Feb. 1795 ; and had issue 1*a*.

1*a*. *Mary Anne Musgrave of Woolley Park and Ibstone House, co. Bucks,* da. and h., b. *c*. 1767 ; d. 28 *Dec*. 1841 ; m. 1788, *her cousin, the Rev. Philip Wroughton* (see p. 210), d. 6 *June* 1812 ; *and had issue* 1*b* to 2*b*.

1*b*. *Bartholomew Wroughton of Woolley Park, co. Berks, J.P., D.L.*, b. 18 *Jan*. 1791 ; d.s.p. 21 *May* 1858.

2*b*. *Philip Wroughton of Ibstone House and Woolley Park, J.P., High Sheriff co. Bucks* 1857, b. 24 *Dec*. 1805 ; d. 28 *Dec*. 1862 ; m. 2*ndly*, 22 *Ap*. 1841, *Blanche*, da. *of John Norris of Hughenden House, co. Bucks*, d. 8 *Jan*. 1903 ; *and had issue* 1*c* to 6*c*.

1*c*. *Philip Wroughton of Woolley Park, J.P., D.L., formerly M.P. for Berks* 1876–1885, *and for the Abingdon Div*. 1885–1895, b. 6 *Ap*. 1846 ; d. *June* 1910 ; m. 4 *Feb*. 1875, *Evelyn Mary*, da. *of Sir John Neeld*, 1*st Bt*. [*U.K.*] ; *and had issue* 1*d* to 7*d*.

The Plantagenet Roll

1d. Philip Musgrave Neeld Wroughton of Woolley Park, Lieut. Berks Yeo. (*Woolley Park, Wantage*), b. 30 Aug. 1887.

2d. Dorothy Florence Mary Wroughton, m. 6 Aug. 1908, the Rev. Herbert Boyne Lavallin Puxley, Rector of Westonbirt (*Westonbirt Rectory, Glos.*).

3d. Muriel Evelyn Mary Wroughton.

4d. Florence Mary Wroughton, m. 2 Feb. 1904, Capt. George Arthur Patrick Rennie, D.S.O., King's Royal Rifle Corps.

5d. Winifred Mary Wroughton, m. 27 Ap. 1901, Capt. Sir Frederick Henry Walter Carden, 3rd Bt. [U.K.], 1st Life Guards (11 *Sloane Court, S.W.; Stargroves, Newbury*); and has issue 1e to 2e.

1e. Henry Christopher Carden, b. 16 Oct. 1908.
2e. Enid Evelyn Carden.

6d. Violet Blanche Mary Wroughton.
7d. Mary St. Quintin Mary Wroughton.

2c. Edward Norris Wroughton, b. 19 July 1847; d. 11 Oct. 1902; m. 1872, Florence, da. of Henry Farren, d. 29 Mar. 1878; *and had issue* 1d to 3d.

1d. John Bartholomew Wroughton, Capt. Royal Sussex Regt., b. 14 Feb. 1874; m. 7 Dec. 1904, Alma May, da. of Willoughby Oakes of Holmbrook, Farnborough.

2d. Edward Henry Wroughton (3 *Hare Court, Temple*), b. 29 Oct. 1875.

3d. Arthur Charles Wroughton, Lieut. South Lancashire Regt., b. 4 July 1877.

3c. William Musgrave Wroughton, Master of the Pytchley Hounds 1894-1902, and of the Woodland and Pytchley Hounds 1903-1908 (*Creation Lodge, Northampton; 77 Chester Square, S.W.*), b. 24 Sept. 1850; m. 24 June 1880, Edith Constance, da. of Henry Cazenove of Lilies, Aylesbury; and has issue 1d to 3d.

1d. Musgrave Cazenove Wroughton, b. 1 Oct. 1891.
2d. Cicely Musgrave Wroughton.
3d. Dulce Wroughton.

4c. Emma Louisa Wroughton, m. 13 July 1861, Henry Joseph Toulmin of The Pré, *formerly* of Childwickbury, co. Herts, J.P., D.L., Capt. Herts Yeo. Cav., late 13th Light Dragoons (*The Pré, near St. Albans*); and has issue 1d to 10d.

1d. Henry Wroughton Toulmin, b. 2 Mar. 1871.
2d. Philip Musgrave Toulmin, b. 1 Feb. 1887.

3d. Mary Toulmin, m. 1st, 26 Nov. 1890, Algernon William George (Evans-Freke), 9th Baron Carbery [I.] [descended from George (Plantagenet), Duke of Clarence, K.G. (see the Clarence Volume, p. 262)], d. 12 June 1898; 2ndly, 11 Feb. 1902, Arthur Wellesley Sandford, M.D. (*Frankfield House, co. Cork*); and has issue 1e to 4e.

1e. John (Evans-Freke), 10th Baron Carbery [I.] (*Castle Freke, co. Cork*), b. 10 May 1892.
2e. Hon. Ralfe Evans-Freke, b. 23 July 1897.
3e. Christopher Sandford, b. 5 Dec. 1902.
4e. Anthony Sandford, b. 14 Aug. 1905.

4d. Evelyn Toulmin, m. 16 July 1901, Edward MacGregor Duncan (*Fernhill Cottage, Windsor Forest*).

5d. Florence Josephine Toulmin, m. 11 Feb. 1897, Herbert Legard Fife, J.P. (see p. 191) [also a descendant of Edward III. through Mortimer-Percy] (*Staindrop House, near Darlington*); and has issue 1e to 2e.

1e. Dorothy Florence Fife.
2e. Marjorie Agnes Fife.

6d. Edith Mabel Toulmin, m. 19 June 1906, the Rev. Alan Chaplin, M.A. (Camb.), Rector of Chesterton [son of Clifford Chaplin of Broughton Astley Hall] (*Chesterton Rectory, Peterborough*); and has issue 1e to 2e.

1e. Stephen Chaplin, b. 30 Mar 1907.
2e. Beryl Chaplin, b. 28 Oct. 1909.

7d. Lilian Toulmin, *unm*. [Nos. 29707 to 29738.

# of The Blood Royal

    8d. Constance Mary Toulmin, *unm.*
    9d. Gladys May Toulmin, *unm.*
    10d. Isobel Marguerite Toulmin, *unm.*

    5c. *Mary Anne Wroughton*, d. 14 *July* 1891; m. 24 *May* 1870, *Col. John Bonham of Ballintaggart, R.H.A., J.P. cos. Kildare and Wicklow, and High Sheriff co. Carlow* 1900 (*Ballintaggart, Colbinstown, co. Kildare*); *and had issue* 1d *to* 5d.
        1d. Francis Warren Bonham, *b.* 1871.
        2d. John Wroughton Bonham, *b.* 1875.
        3d. Georgina Maye Bonham.
        4d. Mary Alice Bonham.
        5d. Margaret Leslie Bonham.

    6c. Blanche Caroline Wroughton.   [Nos. 29739 to 29747.

105. Descendants, if any, of MARY MUSGRAVE, *m.* 1st, HUGH LUMLEY; 2ndly, JOHN PIGOTT (Table XII.).

106. Descendants of JULIA MUSGRAVE (Table XII.), *d.* 1778; *m.* WILLIAM HASELL of Dalemain, co. Cumberland, *b.* 1716; *d.* 1778; and had issue 1a to 4a.

    1a. *Christopher Hasell*, 3rd *son, but in his issue* (6 *Ap.* 1794) *h.*, d. (–); m. (–), *da. of* (–) *Goade*, d. (–); *and had issue* 1b *to* 2b.
    1b. *Edward Hasell of Dalemain*, b. 1765; d. 24 *Dec.* 1825; m. 1*st*, 1792, *Elizabeth, da. of William Carus of Kirkby Lonsdale*, d. 1810; 2*ndly*, 1812, *Jane, da. of the Rev. Robert Whitehead, Rector of Cronside*, d. *Nov.* 1816; *and had issue* 1c *to* 7c.
    1c. *Edward Williams Hasell of Dalemain, J.P., D.L., Lieut.-Col. Comdg. Westmorland and Cumberland Yeo. Cav. and Chairman of Quarter Sessions*, b. 10 *July* 1796; d. 7 *Ap.* 1872; m. 12 *July* 1826, *Dorothea, da. of Edward King of Hungerhill, co. York*, d. 15 *June* 1885; *and had issue* 1d *to* 8d.
        1d. John Edward Hasell of Dalemain, J.P., D.L., High Sheriff co. Cumberland 1887, B.A. (Oxon.), *late* Capt. Westmorland and Cumberland Yeo. Cav. (*Dalemain, Penrith*), *b.* 19 Sept. 1839; *m.* 4 July 1877, Frances Maud, da. of Henry Flood of View Mount, co. Kilkenny; and has issue 1e to 2e.
            1e. Dorothy Julia Hasell.
            2e. Eva Frances Hatton Hasell.
        2d. Rev. George Edmund Hasell, Rector of Aikton and Hon. Canon of Carlisle (*Aikton Hall, Wigton, Cumberland*), *b.* 26 Sept. 1847; *m.* 27 Oct. 1880, Helen, da. of the Rev. William Sinclair [and grandda. of Sir John Sinclair, 1st Bt. [G.B.], P.C., M.P., F.R.S.]; and has issue 1e to 2e.
            1e. Edward William Hasell, Thomas Exhibitioner, Queen's Coll., Oxon., 1906, *b.* 16 Jan. 1888.
            2e. Godfrey Sinclair Hasell, *b.* 2 Nov. 1889.
        3d. Dorothea Hasell.
        4d. Elizabeth Julia Hasell.
        5d. Alice Jane Hasell, *m.* 5 Sept. 1861, J. M. Formby.
        6d. Mary Hasell, *m.* 28 Sept. 1854, W. Parker.
        7d. Henrietta Maria Hasell, *m.* June 1876, H. W. Verey, Official Referee.
        8d. Frances Anne Hasell.
    2c. *Christopher Hasell, Capt. Bengal Army*, b. 1814; d (? s.p.) *May* 1861.
    3c. *William Lowther Hasell, Capt. Bengal Army*, d. (? s.p.) *June* 1849.
                                               [Nos. 29748 to 29759.

The Plantagenet Roll

4c.¹ *Mary Anne Hasell*, d. *shortly before Oct.* 1835; m. *Sept.* 1825, *the Rev. Sir Christopher John Musgrave, 9th Bt.* [E.], d. 11 *May* 1834; *and had issue.*
See p. 197, Nos. 29520-29573.

5c.¹ *Julia Hasell,* d. *(? unm).*

6c.¹ *Jane Hasell,* d. *(? unm.).*

7c.² *Maria Hasell,* d. *Dec.* 1855; m. 11 *Ap.* 1836, *Major George Graham, Registrar-Gen. of Births, Marriages, and Deaths* 1839-1879 [*Bt. of Netherby Coll.*], d. 20 *May* 1888; *and had issue.*
See the Tudor Roll, p. 507, Nos. 34307-34310; and Essex Volume, Tudor Supplement, pp. 494-495, Nos. 34307-34310/3.

2b. *Eliza Hasell,* d. (-); m. *Richard Haughton* (see below).

2a. *John Hasell,* d. (?).

3a. *Julia Hasell,* d. (-); m. *Richard Haughton of Liverpool; and had* (with possibly other) *issue* 1b.

1b. *Richard Haughton,* d. (-); m. *Eliza* (see above), *da. of Christopher Hasell.*

4a. *Jane Hasell,* b. 22 *Ap.* 1745; d. 11 *Aug.* 1820; m. *as 2nd wife,* 3 *Oct.* 1765, *William Salmond,* b. 4 *Aug.* 1737; d. 4 *Aug.* 1779; *and had issue* 1b *to* 2b.

1b. *James Hanson Salmond of Waterfoot, co. Cumberland, Major-General H.E.I.C.S., a distinguished Indian officer, was offered but declined a Baronetcy,* b. 17 *Aug.* 1766; d. 1 *Nov.* 1837; m. 1*st,* 2 *July* 1798, *Louisa, da. of David Scott of Dunninald, M.P.,* d. *June* 1805; *and had issue* 1c.

1c. *James Salmond of Waterfoot, J.P., Lieut.-Col. Westmorland and Cumberland Yeo. Cav., previously 2nd Dragoon Guards, &c.,* b. 15 *June* 1805; d. 24 *Nov.* 1880; m. 16 *Aug.* 1832, *Emma Isabella* [*descended from George, Duke of Clarence,* K.G.], *da. of D'Ewes Coke of Brookhill Hall, co. Derby, J.P., D.L.,* d. 8 *Mar.* 1886; *and had issue.*
See the Clarence Volume, pp. 186-187, Nos. 3131-3176.

2b. *Francis Salmond, Capt. H.E.I.C.S., and Master Attendant, Fort Marlbro', Sumatra,* b. 28 *Nov.* 1770; d. 23 *Nov.* 1823; m. 21 *Dec.* 1805, *Anne, da. of Charles Salmond,* d. 22 *Aug.* 1812; *and had issue* 1c *to* 3c.

1c. *James William Salmond, Resident Councillor at Penang and Malacca,* b. 16 *Aug.* 1807; d. 12 *Mar.* 1848; m. 3 *Oct.* 1839, *Fenella Cullen, da. of William Alexander Mackenzie of Seatwell and Strathgarve, co. Ross,* d. (-); *and had issue* 1d *to* 3d.

1d. *Francis Mackenzie Salmond, Lieut.-Col. Royal Scots Fusiliers,* b. 11 *Mar.* 1841; d. 1 *Nov.* 1900; m. 22 *July* 1868, *Isabel Clara, sister of Sir R. C. Hart, V.C., da. of Lieut.-Gen. Henry George Hart of Netherby, co. Dorset; and had issue* 1e *to* 4e.

1e. Francis Mackenzie Salmond, b. 15 Oct. 1872.

2e. Hubert Mackenzie Salmond, b. 18 Dec. 1874.

3e. Henry Bertram Salmond, b. 8 Jan. 1878.

4e. Isabel Frank Fenella Salmond.

2d. Fenella Salmond.

3d. *Julia Maria Salmond,* m. 27 *Aug.* 1879, *the Rev. Theodore Crane Dupuis,* Preb. of Wells and Vicar of Burnham (*Burnham Vicarage, S.O., Somerset*).

2c. *Louisa Jane Salmond,* d. (-); m. 1843, *Andrew Grieve of Edinburgh, J.P.; and had issue.*

3c. *Emily Parker Salmond,* b. 9 *June* 1812; d. 9 *May* 1863; m. 1850, *the Rev. Charles Adam John Smith, Vicar of Macclesfield; and had issue.*

[Nos. 29760 to 29872.

107. Descendants, if any, of BARBARA MUSGRAVE (Table XII.), d. (-); m. 1st, JOHN HOGG of Scotland; 2ndly, CHIEF BARON IDLE.

of The Blood Royal

108. Descendants of ANNE MUSGRAVE (Table XII.) *d.* 1780; *m.* HENRY AGLIONBY of Nunnery, co. Cumberland, High Sheriff for that co. 1763, &c., *b.* 1715; *d.* 1770; and had issue 1*a* to 4*a*.

1*a*. *Christopher Aglionby of Nunnery*, d.s.p. 1785, *last male of his family.*
2*a*. *Elizabeth Aglionby, da. and co-h. in* 1785, d. (? s.p.) 1822; m. (—) *Bamber.*
3*a*. *Anne Aglionby, da. and co-h. in* 1785, d. (–); m. *the Rev. Samuel Bateman of Newbiggin Hall, co. Cumberland ; and had issue (apparently an only son)* 1*b*.
1*b*. *Henry Aglionby Bateman, afterwards Aglionby of Newbiggin Hall and Nunnery, M.P.*, b. 28 *Dec.* 1790; d. (? s.p.) 1854.
4*a*. *Mary Aglionby, da. and co-h. in* 1785, d. 8 *Sept.* 1816; m. *John Orfeur Yates of Skirwith Abbey, co. Cumberland ; and had issue* 1*b* to 2*b*.
1*b*. *Francis Yates, afterwards Aglionby of Nunnery, M.P.*, b. 1780; d. 1 *July* 1840; m. 8 *Feb.* 1814, *Mary, da. of John Matthews of Wigton Hall, co. Cumberland*, d. 20 *Aug.* 1854; *and had issue (with an elder da. who* d. *unm.)* 1*c* to 2*c*.
1*c*. *Mary Aglionby, da. and co-h.*, d. 7 *Aug.* 1882; m. *Ap.* 1845, *the Rev. Beilby Porteus, Canon of Carlisle*, d. (–); *and had issue* 1*d* to 4*d*.
1*d*. July Mary Porteus, da. and co-h., *m.* 27 Oct. 1869, Capt. James Mortimer Webster, 18th Royal Irish, *s.p.*
2*d*. Mary Aglionby Porteus, da. and co-h., *m.* 28 Sept. 1880, Comm. the Hon. Henry Noel Shore, R.N. [3rd son of Charles John, 2nd Baron Teignmouth [I.]] (*Mount Elton, Clevedon*); and has issue 1*e* to 3*e*.
1*e*. Hugh Aglionby Shore, in Public Works Dept., India, *b.* 12 July 1881.
2*e*. Lionel Henry Porteus Shore, Lieut. R.N., *b.* 18 Nov. 1882.
3*e*. Noel Beilby Porteus Shore, Indian Police, *b.* 6 July 1887.
3*d*. Emma Porteus, da. and co-h., *m.* 1st, 20 Jan. 1880, Arthur Morres Hill, d. (–); 2ndly, (—) Platt, *s.p.*
4*d*. Henrietta Porteus, da. and co-h., *m* Major-Gen. Robert Cole, Indian Army ; and has issue 1*e* to 4*e*.
1*e*. Alan Aglionby Cole, *b.* 1886.
2*e*. Humphrey Porteus Cole, *b.* 1894.
3*e*. Ursula Cole.
4*e*. Doris Grace Cole.

2*c*. *Jane Aglionby, da. and co-h.*, d. 21 *May* 1874; m. *Ap.* 1847, *Charles Fetherstonhaugh of Staffield Hall, Penrith*, d. (–); *and had issue* 1*d*.
1*d*. *Elizabeth Aglionby Fetherstonhaugh, da. and h.*, d. 1885; m. 18 *Oct.* 1871, *Col. Arthur Cooper, now (R.L.* 11 *Aug.* 1885) *Aglionby, of Staffield Hall and Drawdykes, C.B., J.P.* (*Staffield Hall, Carlisle*); *and had issue* 1*e* to 2*e*.
1*e*. Arthur Charles Aglionby, Bar.-at-Law, Capt. 3rd Batt. Connaught Rangers, *b.* 1872.
2*e*. Constance Muriel Aglionby.

2*b*. *John Yates of Virginia, U.S.*, b. *at Skirwith Abbey, Cumberland*, 3 *Ap.* 1779 ; d. *at Nunnery* 6 *July* 1851 ; m. 7 *Ap.* 1803, *Julia, da. of Robert W. Lovell of Fredericksburg, Virginia*, d. 8 *June* 1866; *and had issue (with* 2 *other sons and a da., Mrs. Keyes, who* d.s.p.) 1*c* to 5*c*.
1*c*. *Charles Yates, afterwards* (1854) *Aglionby, of Nunnery*, b. *at Germanna, Virginia,* 4 *June* 1807; d. 30 *Jan.* 1891; m. 28 *May* 1844, *Fanny, da. of Col. James W. Walker of Madison Co., Virginia,* d. 29 *Jan.* 1902; *and had issue* 1*d* to 3*d*.
1*d*. Rev. Francis Keyes Aglionby, M.A., D.D., Vicar of Christ Church, Westminster, *formerly* Rector of Hampton Poyle, *late* of Nunnery, which he sold 1892
[Nos. 29873 to 29886.

The Plantagenet Roll

(*Christ Church Vicarage, Victoria Street, Westminster, S.W.; Mount Pleasant, West Virginia, U.S.*), b. 22 Nov. 1848; m. 9 Aug. 1876, Amy, da. of the Right Rev Edward Henry Bickersteth, Lord Bishop of Exeter; and has issue 1e to 7e.

1e. Francis Basil Aglionby, B.C.L., Solicitor, b. 25 July 1878.
2e. Charles Edward Aglionby, Lieut. R.N., b. 26 June 1882.
3e. John Orfeur Aglionby, b. 16 Mar. 1884.
4e. Arthur Hugh Aglionby, B.A. (Oxon.), b. 4 Nov. 1885.
5e. Wilfred Henry Aglionby, b. 16 Ap. 1890.
6e. Rosa Frances Aglionby.
7e. Alice Mary Aglionby.

2d. John Orfeur Aglionby, b. 1 Mar. 1851; *unm.*
3d. Jeanette Elizabeth Aglionby.

2c. *Francis Yates of Flowing Springs, Jefferson Co., W. Va., Col. Virginia State Milita and a Member of the Virginian Senate*, b. *at Walnut Grove, Jefferson Co., W. Va.*, 24 Sept. 1811; d. *at Flowing Springs* 1 *Jan.* 1892; m. 1*st*, 1840, Ann Elizabeth, da. of *Bacon Burwell of Jefferson Co.*, d. *at Flowing Springs* 28 *June* 1862; 2*ndly, at Charlestown*, 25 *June* 1863, Sydney Virginia, da. *of Jabez Berry Rooker of co. Stafford*, d. 22 *Ap.* 1899; *and had issue* 1d *to* 5d.

1d. John Orfeur Yates, *Confederate States Army*, b. *at Flowing Springs* 22 *Ap.* 1845; d. *at Gap View, in that co., Sept.* 1899; m. *at Wytheville* 31 *Oct.* 1878, Emma (Roanoke, Virginia), da. *of Col. Joseph Kent of Wythe Co., Va.; and had issue* 1e to 6e.

1e. Francis Yates, b. at Wytheville.
2e. Joseph Kent Yates, b. at Wytheville.
3e. Lewis Cochran Yates, b. at Wytheville.

4e. Frances Stuart Yates, m. 2 Jan. 1907, Wayte Bell Timberlake, Merchant (*Staunton, Va.*); and has issue 1f.

1f. Wayte Bell Timberlake, b. 23 Nov. 1908.

5e. Marie Harrison Yates, *unm.*
6e. Bettie Montgomery Yates, *unm.*

2d. Arthur Bacon Yates (*Fredericksburg, Virginia*), b. at Flowing Springs 28 July 1848; m. at Fredericksburg 23 Ap. 1872, Susan, da. of James Hord Bradley of Fredericksburg, Va.; and has issue 1e to 4e.

1e. Lucilla Bradley Yates, *unm.*

2e. Ann Burwell Yates, m. at Washington, D.C., 2 June 1898, Alpheus Wilson Embrey of Fredericksburg; and has issue 1f to 4f.

1f. Alpheus Wilson Embrey, b. in Fredericksburg 13 Feb. 1901.
2f. Wilford Smith Embrey, b. there 24 Aug. 1907.
3f. Anne Elizabeth Embrey.
4f. Susan Julia Embrey.

3e. Mary Louise Yates, m. Louis Albert van Ericksen; and has issue 1f.

1f. Mary Louisa van Ericksen, b. in Birmingham, Alabama, 18 Jan. 1900.

4e. Susan Mallory Yates, *unm.*

3d.[1] Janet Burwell Yates, b. in Jefferson Co. afsd., m. at Flowing Springs 1 Nov. 1870, Charles Valentine Wagner of Baltimore, Maryland, Cotton Broker, *formerly* Confederate States Army, served four years and six weeks under Generals Robert E. Lee and Stonewall Jackson (1649 *Amsterdam Avenue,*141*st Street, New York*), s.p.

4d.[1] Octavia Latane Yates (*Woodville, Rappahannock Co., Virginia*), b. at Flowing Springs afsd.; m. 29 Oct. 1868, William Stephenson Mason of Charlestown, Jefferson Co., Stock Raiser, *formerly* Confederate States Army; and has issue 1e to 3e.

1e. Anne Isabelle Mason, b. in Charlestown afsd.; *unm.*
2e. Margaret Duncan Mason, b. in Charlestown afsd.; *unm.*
3e. Virginia Stephenson Mason, b. in Glen Ayre, Rapp. Co., Va.; *unm.*

[Nos. 29887 to 29917.]

# of The Blood Royal

5d.² Mary Brooke Yates, b. at Flowing Springs afsd. 8 Jan. 1866; m. there 14 Oct. 1891, Adrian Garrett Wynkoop, Attorney-at-Law (306 *South Samuel Street, Charlestown, W. Va.*); and has issue 1e to 5e.
 1e. Adrian Garrett Wynkoop, b. 20 Nov. 1893.
 2e. Francis Yates Wynkoop, b. 28 July 1899.
 3e. Brooke Lovell Wynkoop, b. 3 Aug. 1902.
 4e. Sydney Virginia Wynkoop.
 5e. Julia Yates Wynkoop.

 3c. *Janet Yates, b. at Fox Neck, Culpepper Co., Va.,* 12 Jan. 1804; d. 25 Feb. 1875; m. *in Jefferson Co.., W. Va.,* 19 *Oct.* 1826, *George Brooke Beall of Walnut Grove, Jefferson Co., W. Va.,* b. 1802; d. 20 Aug. 1855; *and had issue (with* 2 *other sons and* 2 *das.* d. *unm.)* 1d to 5d.
 1d. Hezekiah Beall *(Wortham, Texas),* b. 17 Aug. 1830; m. 1st, 4 May 1869, Nancy Jane, da. of William O. Alexander of Freestone Co., Texas, *d.s.p.s.* 1870; 2ndly, 9 Aug. 1870, Arthurilla Wilmoth, da. of Thomas Petigrew Groves of Freestone Co., afsd.; and has issue (with a son and da. d. young) 1e to 7e.
 1e. George Brooke Beall *(Armarillo, Texas),* b. 21 Feb. 1872; *unm.*
 2e. William Willis Beall, b. 15 June 1879; *unm.*
 3e. John Yates Beall, b. 2 July 1882; m. at Wortham, Texas, 20 July 1902, Eva Alice, da. of (—) Evans of Wortham; and has issue 1f to 3f.
 1f. George William Beall, b. 19 May 1908.
 2f. Ruth Elizabeth Beall, b. 29 May 1903.
 3f. Lillian Adina Beall, b. 15 Aug. 1905.
 4e. Mary Yates Beall, *unm.*
 5e. Emma Webb Beall, m. at Wortham afsd. 16 Oct. 1898, John Thomas Bounds *(Wortham, Texas);* and has issue 1f to 3f.
 1f. Kenneth Bounds, b. 22 Aug. 1902.
 2f. Thomas Allen Bounds, b. 27 July 1904.
 3f. Charles Hezekiah Bounds, b. 29 Ap. 1908.
 6e. Annie Elizabeth Beall, *unm.*
 7e. Julia Lovell Beall, *unm.*

 2d. *John Yates Beall, Confederate States Navy,* b. 1 *Jan.* 1835; d. *unm. (being taken prisoner at Suspension Bridge, N.Y., and shot in Governor's Island)* 24 *Feb.* 1865.
 3d. Mary Yates Keyes Beall *(Charlestown, W. Virginia),* b. 2 Jan. 1829; *unm.*
 4d. Anne Orfeur Beall, b. 24 June 1839; m. 1 Dec. 1870, David E. Henderson, *formerly* Confederate States Army *(Charlestown, W. Virginia);* and has issue.
 5d. Elizabeth Beall *(Charlestown, W. Virginia),* b. 6 Mar. 1842; m. 26 Ap. 1881, Richard Henderson, Confederate States Army, d. 22 June 1905.

 4c. *Anne Yates,* b. *at Walnut Grove, Jefferson Co., Virginia,* 15 *July* 1815; d. *at Sunny Side, Madison Co., Virginia,* 13 Ap. 1857; m. 18 Nov. 1847, *the Rev. William Thomas Leavell,* d. *at Hedgesville, Berkeley Co., W. Va.,* 25 *Aug.* 1899; *and had issue* 1d to 5d.
 1d. *William Thomas Leavell, B.L., M.A., and Medalist, of Washington and Lee University, Lexington, Va.,* d. 4 Feb. 1900; m. 14 Ap. 1898, Lucy Nelson, da. of Robert Nelson Pendleton ; *and had issue* 1e.
 1e. William Thomas Leavell (a da.), b. posthumous.
 2d. *Rev. Francis Keyes Leavell, in Holy Orders of the American Episcopal Church, M.A., Medalist Washington and Lee University,* d. 19 Dec. 1886; m. *Elizabeth Hunter,* da. *of Charles Thurston ; and had issue* 1e.
 1e. Elizabeth Hunter Leavell.
 3d. Julia Yates Leavell *(Charlestown, W. Virginia),* m. at Media, Jefferson Co., W. Virginia, 12 Oct. 1869, Major Edward H. McDonald, *late* 11th Virginian Cavalry, Confederate States Army; and has issue 1e to 10e. [Nos. 29918 to 29943.

The Plantagenet Roll

1e. Edward Leavell McDonald, b. 3 Sept. 1870.
2e. William Thomas McDonald, b. 6 Aug. 1875.
3e. Angus William McDonald, b. 2 May 1877.
4e. Peerce Naylor McDonald, b. 5 July 1879.
5e. Marshall Woodrow McDonald (*Louisville, Kentucky*), b. 24 Aug. 1884.
6e. John Yates McDonald, b. 10 Jan. 1887.
7e. Francis Leavell McDonald, b. 28 May 1891.
8e. Annie Yates McDonald.
9e. Julia Terrill McDonald.
10e. Mary Aglionby McDonald.

4d. Anne Elizabeth Leavell, m. 30 Oct. 1874, John Moncure Daniel, Clerk of Circuit Court, Jefferson Co., W. Va., *formerly* Confederate States Army (*Charlestown, West Virginia*); and has issue 1e to 6e.

1e. William Aglionby Daniel, b. in Jefferson Co. 11 July 1878.
2e. John Moncure Daniel, b. 26 May 1883; m. 15 Dec. 1908, Margaret, da. of the Rev. Richard Wilde Micou, D.D., Professor at Episcopal Theological Seminary, Fairfax Co., W. Va.
3e. Francis Warwick Daniel, b. 4 July 1886.
4e. Anne Leavell Daniel.
5e. Elizabeth Julia Daniel.
6e. Mary Mildred Daniel.

5d. Mary Aglionby Leavell, d. 10 Mar. 1900; m. at Zion Church, Charlestown, W. Virginia, 31 Oct. 1884, Capt. William R. Johnson, *formerly* Confederate States Army (*The Crescent, West Virginia*); and had issue 1e to 4e.

1e. William Ransom Johnson.
2e. John Pegram Johnson.
3e. Francis Leavell Johnson.
4e. Mary Aglionby Johnson.

5c. *Julia Yates*, b. at Walnut Grove afsd. 25 *July* 1819; d. *there* 3 *June* 1895; m. *there* 1 Oct. 1839, William Lovell Terrill, b. at Fredericksburg, Va., 9 *Mar.* 1815; d. 15 Feb. 1890; and had issue (*with a son, John Uriel, d. unm. 15 Nov. 1878, and a da., Anne Elizabeth, d. unm.* 10 Feb. 1900) 1d.

1d. Julia Lovell Terrill (*Charles Town, West Virginia, U.S.A.*).

[Nos. 29944 to 29965.

109. Descendants, if any, of ELIZABETH MUSGRAVE (Table XII.), d. (–); m. 1st, EDWARD SPRAGGE of Greenwich; 2ndly, JOHN JOHNSTONE of London.

110. Descendants of DOROTHY MUSGRAVE (Table XII.), b. c. 1727; d. 31 Oct. 1799; bur. at St. Thomas' Church, Salisbury, M.I.; m. the Rev. WILLIAM WROUGHTON, Rector of Welbourn, co. Lincoln [son of the Rev. Charles Wroughton, Rector of Codford St. Peter, co. Wilts, 1681–1729], b. 1716; d. 3 Aug. 1770; and had issue 1a to 5a.

1a. Rev. *Philip Wroughton*, b. 1758; d. 6 *June* 1812; m. 1788, *Mary Anne* (see p. 203), *da. of the Rev. Chardin Musgrave, D.D.*, d. 28 Dec. 1841; *and had issue.* See p. 203, Nos. 29707–29749.

2a. *George Wroughton of Adwick-le-Street, near Doncaster, Col. 3rd West York Militia*, b. *at West Wycombe* c. 1759; d. *at Newington* 24 Oct. 1816; m. *in India* 17 Ap. 1787, *Diana Elizabeth*, da. *of the Rev. Thomas Denton, M.A., Rector of Ashtead, Surrey*, d. 5 *June* 1849; *and had issue* (*with* 4 *sons and* 2 *das.* d.s.p.) 1b to 6b. [Nos. 29966 to 30006.

of The Blood Royal

1b. Robert Wroughton, Major 69th Bengal Infantry, and Dep. Surveyor-Gen. of India, b. at Adwick 2 Aug. 1797; d. at Futteghur, Bengal, 14 Feb. 1850; m. Sophia, da. of Capt. Wright; and had issue (with 2 sons who d.s.p.) 1c to 6c.

    1c. Frederic Turner Wroughton, C.B., Col. in the Army, b. 20 Mar. 1821; d. 17 Sept. 1878; m. Sarah Cecilia Ann, da. of (—) Fassell, d. in Christchurch, N.Z., 1908; and had issue 1d to 4d.

        1d. Cecil Frederick Maurice Wroughton, Manager Union Bank, Ashburton (Ashburton, N.Z.), b. 2 May 1859; m. Ap. 1891, Fanny Theresa, da. of the Hon. Alfred de Bathe Brandon of Wellington, N.Z.; and has issue 1e to 2e.

            1e Frederick Brandon Wroughton, b. 21 Nov. 1897.
            2e. Lucy Cecilia Wroughton, b. 24 Mar. 1892.

        2d. Eva Hannah Wroughton, m. George Callender of Christchurch, N.Z.

        3d. Mabel Fanny Wroughton, m. James Callender of Invercargill, N.Z.; and has issue.

        4d. Lilian Emma Wroughton, m. (—) Addley of Christchurch, N.Z.

    2c. Robert Chardin Wroughton, Gen. in the Army, b. 3 Sept. 1822; d. Nov. 1871, m. Sarah, da. of Col. R. L. Stacy, C.B., A.D.C.; and had issue 1d to 4d.

        1d. Robert Charles Wroughton, Indian Forest Service (16 Spencer Mansions, Queen's Club Gardens, W.), m.s.p.

        2d. Henry Bruce Wroughton, Capt. R.N. (Ireland), m.s.p.

        3d. Lewis Wroughton, Secretary to Basutoland Govt. (Maseru, Basutoland), b. (—); m. 25 Ap. 1902, Frances Charlotte, da. of (—) Lloyd; and has issue 1e to 2e.

            1e. Robert Lewis Wroughton.
            2e. Henry Banastre Wroughton.

        4d. Edith Isabella Wroughton, m. Edward Turner (Willbrook, Estcourt, Natal); and has issue (9 children).

    3c. Charles Nesbitt Wroughton, R.N., b. 4 Sept. 1835, went to New Zealand, and has not since been heard of.

    4c. Sophia Isabella Wroughton, b. at Goruckpur, India, 26 July 1826; d. 22 Dec. 1879; m. at Allyghur, India, 15 Feb. 1848, Capt. George William Wright Fulton, Bengal Engineers, b. 23 Nov. 1825; d. (being killed at the siege of Lucknow) 14 Sept. 1857; and had issue 1d to 5d.

        1d. Frederick Fulton (Napier, New Zealand), b. 1 June 1850; unm.

        2d. Robert Fulton, Col. Indian Army (Mitcham Lodge, Kimbolton Avenue, Bedford), b. 12 July 1852; m. 7 July 1894, Blanche Eleanor Moffatt, da. of Col. D. W. Martin, 75th Regt.; and has issue 1e to 2e.

            1e. John Oswald Fulton, b. 16 July 1897.
            2e. Gwendoline Fulton, b. 19 Jan. 1896.

        3d. William Wright Fulton (Taitimu, Mangaweka, Rangitiki, New Zealand), b. 30 May 1854; m. 1879, Helen, da. of R. Bett of Marton, N.Z.; and has issue 1e to 4e.

            1e. Heward Fulton, b. 9 June 1880.
            2e. Norman Fulton, b. 23 Mar. 1883.
            3e. Frederick Robert Fulton, b. 2 June 1890.
            4e. George William Wright Fulton, b. 7 Mar. 1901.

        4d. George Sibley Fulton (Marton, Wanganui, New Zealand), b. 27 Sept. 1857; unm.

        5d. Ellen Charlotte Fulton, m. 1881, Charles William Wallace of Messrs. R. G. Shaw & Co., of 88 Bishopsgate Street Within (6 Langford Place, St. John's Wood, N.W.); and has issue 1e to 5e.

            1e. Charles William Wallace.
            2e. Robert Wallace.
            3e. Helen Charlotte Wallace.
            4e. Tara Wallace.
            5e. Jessie Helen Wallace.

[Nos. 30007 to 30034.

The Plantagenet Roll

5c. Ellen Wroughton, b. 29 Oct. 1837; d. at Dunedin, N.Z., 20 Nov. 1887; m. at Mecan Meer, Punjaub, 13 Jan. 1858, Lieut.-Gen. John Fulton, B.A., b. 4 Oct. 1827; d. at Christchurch, N.Z., 14 July 1899; and had issue (with a son and da. d.s.p.) 1d to 8d.

1d. Sydney Wroughton Fulton, Stockbroker (369 Collins Street, Melbourne, Victoria), b. 30 Jan. 1859; m. at St. Columba's, Hawthorne, Victoria, 3 Jan. 1894, Elizabeth Maude, da. of John Simpson Armstrong, Q.C., Bar.-at-Law; and has issue 1e to 3e.

1e. Sheelah Alice Wroughton Fulton, b. at Brighton, Victoria, 20 Jan. 1895.

2e. Eileen Maude Wroughton Fulton, b. at Heidelberg, Victoria, 16 Oct. 1896.

3e. Lorna Hope Wroughton Fulton, b. at Melbourne 23 Nov. 1899.

2d. Perceval James Fulton (Warrnambool, Victoria), b. at Amritsur, India, 26 Mar. 1860; unm.

3d. Walter Menzies Fulton (Box 5465, Johannesburg), b. at Amritsur afsd. 30 Oct. 1866; m. in St. John's Cathedral, Napier, N.Z., 21 Nov. 1896, Adèle, Gwendoline (see p. 103), da. of Horace William Baker, s.p.

4d. Onslow Henry Crofton Fulton (Wallsend, New South Wales), b. at Amritsur afsd. 21 Mar. 1868; unm.

5d. Harry Townsend Fulton, D.S.O., Major 2nd Batt. 2nd Gurkhas, b. at Dalhousie, India, 15 Mar. 1869; m. at St. Thomas' Cathedral, Bombay, 1905, Ada Hermina, da. of John Dixon of Auckland, N.Z.

6d. Bertram Sproule Fulton, National Bank of South Africa (Pretoria), b. at Lee, co. Kent, 12 June 1871; m. at Wellington, N.Z., 1902, Lillian, da. of (—) Loveday; and has issue 1e.

1e. Hylma Adèle Fulton, b. 1906.

7d. Ethel Ann Fulton.

8d. Hilda Caroline Fulton, m. 15 Sept. 1908, Richard Bohm of the New Zealand and Union S.S.C. Service (Wellington, N.Z.); and has issue 1e.

1e. John Richard Fulton Bohm, b. at Auckland, N.Z., 24 June 1909.

6c. Fanny Wroughton, b. 8 Jan. 1844; d. at Ealing 11 Nov. 1897; m. at Amritsur, Punjaub, 7 Nov. 1863, Col. Oswald Menzies, Indian Army (32 Mount Park Road, Ealing); and had issue 1d to 3d.

1d. Georgina Fanny Menzies, m. 7 Nov. 1889, Robert Loraine Ker; and has issue 1e to 8e.

1e. Thomas Menzies Ker, b. 12 July 1899.

2e. Margaret Ker, b. 31 May 1891.

3e. Joan Ker, b. 19 Sept. 1892.

4e. Elsie Ker, b. 28 Mar. 1894.

5e. Phyllis Ker, b. 25 Mar. 1897.

6e. Helen Ker, b. 7 Ap. 1901.

7e. Doris Ker, b. 15 Oct. 1903.

8e. Ruth Ker, b. 15 May 1905.

2d. Eliza Marion Menzies, m. 4 Dec. 1894, Capt. Julian Stuart Dallas, Indian Army; and has issue 1e to 2e.

1e. Juliet Dallas.

2e. Eileen Dallas.

3d. Alice Norah Menzies, unm.

2b. John Chardin Wroughton, H.E.I.C.S., b. at Adwick 19 May 1799; d. at Paris 30 Nov. 1854; m. 2ndly, 1835, Georgina Grace, da. of the Hon. Henry Chamier, Member of Council, Madras, d. at Coimbatore 6 Dec. 1847; and had issue (with 2 sons who d.s.p.) 1c to 4c.

1c. William Nesbitt Wroughton, Col. Indian Army (1 Lansdowne Road, Bedford), b. at Ootacamund 6 Feb. 1840; m. 1 Oct. 1859, Morgiana C., da. of Col. J. Bird; and has issue (with a son d.s.p.) 1d to 7d.   [Nos. 30035 to 30061.]

of The Blood Royal

1*d*. Henry William Frank Wroughton, in Salt Revenue Dept. (*Bellary, India*), *b*. 8 Aug. 1860; *m*. at Coonoor, Nilgiris, S. India, 1 June 1887, Edith Amy, da. of James Tavenor Nash; and has issue 1*e* to 3*e*.

    1*e*. Eric Nisbitt Macleod Wroughton, *b*. 10 Mar. 1888.
    2*e*. John Henry Theodore Wroughton, *b*. 22 Aug. 1892.
    3*e*. Edith Margaret Grace Wroughton,

2*d*. Theodore Ambrose Wroughton, Canadian Rifles, *b*. 1862; *m.s.p*.

3*d*. William Haultain Wroughton. M.D. (*Witheral, Carlisle*), *b*. 1871; *m*. Edith, da. of (—) Havers; and has issue 1*e* to 3*e*.

    1*e*. John Wroughton.
    2*e*. William Edward Wroughton.
    3*e*. Dorothy Wroughton.

4*d*. Arthur Oliver Bird Wroughton, Capt. R.A.M.C. (*Osborne*), *b*. 29 Oct. 1872; *m*. 23 Aug. 1905, Roberta, da. of Major-Gen. William Stenhouse, *s.p*.

5*d*. Morgiana Lilian Wroughton, *b*. 1864; *m*. at Bangalore 25 July 1882, [Sir] Bannatyne Macleod, I.C.S., M.A. (Camb.), Bar.-at-Law, a District Magistrate, and by descent 6th Bt. [S. 1723][1] (*Madras*); and has issue 1*e* to 7*e*.

    1*e*. William Bannatyne Macleod, Lieut. Indian Army, *b*. at Bangalore 1883.
    2*e*. Roland Theodore Wroughton Macleod, *b*. 1900.
    3*e*. Nesbitt Bannatyne Wroughton Macleod, *b*. in India.
    4*e*. Alan James Macleod, *b*. in England.
    5*e*. Alexander Macleod, *b*. in England.
    6*e*. Marguerita Lilian Chamier Macleod.
    7*e*. Meriel Clare Wroughton Macleod.

6*d*. Grace Augusta Wroughton, *m*. 1st, July 1891, Arthur Augustus Hewer, M.D., d. 1 July 1894; 2ndly, 5 May 1906, Ernest Leonard Mahon, Tea Planter (*Coorg, S. India*); and has issue 1*e*.

    1*e*. John Arthur Langton Wroughton Hewer, *b*. 21 Ap. 1892.

7*d*. Frances Meriel Wroughton, *m*. 1893/4, Major Leslie Warner Yale Campbell, Indian Army [son of Major-Gen. Alexander Campbell]; and has issue (with 2 das. *d*. young) 1*e* to 4*e*.

    1*e*. Kenneth Leslie Campbell.
    2*e*. Duncan Francis Lisle Campbell.
    3*e*. Joan Leslie Campbell, *b*. in India.
    4*e*. Helen Patricia Campbell, *b*. Aug. 1909.

2*c*. *Francis John Wroughton, Col. Comdg. 9th Madras N.I., b. at Coimbatore* 16 *Aug*. 1841; d. *at Rangoon* 12 *June* 1887; m. *at Tonghoo* 28 *Sept*. 1875, *Margaret Georgina, da. of John Algie of Lisduff, co. Galway; and had issue 7 children, now dispersed in Cape Town, Basutoland, and the West Coast of Africa.*

3*c*. *Arthur Frederic Wroughton*, b. *at Coimbatore* 24 *May* 1844; d. *at South Norwood* 12 *Ap*. 1907/8; m. 1st, *Donata C. S., da. of N. Armstrong, 30th Regt.;* 2ndly, *Clara, da. of* (—) *Wildgoose; and had issue* 1*d to* 3*d*.

    1*d*.[1] Stuart Abercrombie Wroughton, *b*. in Canada 16 May 1875.
    2*d*.[1] Charles Wetherall Wroughton, *b*. in Canada 17 May 1877.
    3*d*.[2] Chardin Wroughton, *b*. 7 Dec. 1899.

4*c*. *Grace Matilda Wroughton*, b. *at Coimbatore* 17 *Aug*. 1845; d. *at Brighton* 13 *Oct*. 1893/4; m. 1863, *Capt. Charles Mayvore Smith*, d. (—); *and had issue* (1 *son and* 4 *das.*) 1*d to* 5*d*.

    1*d*. Charles Wroughton Smith.
    2*d*. Alice Smith.
    3*d*. Minnie Smith.
    4*d*. Mabel Smith.
    5*d*. Rosalind Zeima Smith.   [Nos. 30062 to 30094.

---

[1] Ruvigny's "Jacobite Peerage," p. 110.

The Plantagenet Roll

3b. *Nesbitt Wroughton, Capt. 5th Madras Light Cavalry*, b. *at Adwick* 11 Feb. 1811; d. *in London* 16 Aug. 1855; m. *at Sholapore, India*, 18 *Jan.* 1844, *Jane, da. of Edward Armstrong of the Hook, Applegirth, co. Dumfries, Advocate, and Sheriff for that afsd. co.*, d. *at Jaulnah, India*, 23 *Nov.* 1853; *and had issue* (with 2 sons, Nevill Nesbitt Armstrong, Forest Ranger (1st Grade) in Punjaub, b. *at Sholapore* 10 *June* 1845; d.s.p. *at Jhelum, N.W.P.*, 12 Aug. 1871; *and George Chardin Murray*, b. 1848; d. *at Jaulnah, Madras, Nov.* 1853) 1c.

1c. Meriel Matilda Catherine Wroughton *(Adwick Villa, Harrow Road, Sudbury)*, *m.* at the British Legation, Brussels, 19 July 1888, Major Crommelin Henry Ricketts, Madras S.C., *d.s.p.* 11 Ap. 1892.

4b. *Barbara Charlotte Wroughton*, b. *at Adwick* 8 Ap. 1796; d. *at Guernsey* 16 Ap. 1872; m. 24 *July* 1823, *the Rev. James Steuart Murray Anderson of Brighton, M.A.*, d. *at Bonn* 22 *Sept.* 1869; *and had issue* (with 2 *elder sons* d.s.p.) 1c to 3c.

1c. *Rev. Fortescue Lennox Macdonald Anderson, Rector of St. Baldred's, North Berwick*, b. 15 *June* 1832; d. 17 *June* 1899; m. 1st, 23 May 1865, Charlotte Frances, *da. of William Fisher*, d. 31 *July* 1872; 2ndly, 6 Oct. 1882, Emma, *da. of John Sidley;* and had issue (with a 2nd da. d. unm.) 1d to 8d.

1d.¹ Lennox Stuart Anderson, Sec. Royal Portrush Golf Club *(Portrush, Ireland)*, b. 3 Sept. 1870; *m.* 1895, Mary Louisa, da. of William Black Ferguson; and has issue 1e to 2e.

1e. Bernard Stuart Anderson, *b.* 22 Mar. 1896.

2e. James Fortescue Stuart Anderson, *b.* 19 Sept. 1906.

2d.² Fortescue Wroughton Anderson (76 *Pearl Street, Toronto, Canada*), b. 3 Aug. 1883; *m.* 23 Oct. 1909, Elizabeth Florence, da. of John Cobourg McKendry of Ontario.

3d.¹ Helen Charlotte Maud Anderson, *m.* 6 Jan. 1891, George Gordon Robertson, Chartered Accountant *(St. Baldred's, Mitcham, Surrey)*; and has issue 1e to 2e.

1e. Lennox Gordon Robertson, *b.* 15 Nov. 1894.

2e. Maud Marian Schoedde Gordon Robertson, *b.* 17 Dec. 1891.

4d.¹ Meriel Anderson, *m.* 6 Oct. 1885, the Rev. Cecil William Nash, Rector of Kincardine O'Neil *(Kincardine O'Neil Rectory, Aberdeenshire)*; and has issue 1e to 3e.

1e. Thomas Stuart Nash, *b.* 27 Mar. 1889.

2e. George Cecil Nash, *b.* 31 Dec. 1897.

3e. Meriel Eileen Ella Vere Nash, *b.* 5 Aug. 1886.

5d.¹ Florence Wroughton Anderson, *m.* Aug. 1893, Major Charles Edward Sawyer *(Grancy Villa, Lausanne)*; and has issue 1e to 3e.

1e. Edward Sawyer, *b.* 1896.

2e. Dagmar Morwena Alice Sawyer, *b.* Sept. 1894.

3e. Brenda Hildegarde Sawyer, *b.* 1899.

6d.¹ Blanch Anderson *(Salthorpe House, Wroughton, near Swindon)*, *unm.*

7d.² Barbara Wroughton Anderson, *m.* 5 Jan. 1907, Allen Wynard Gardener *(Columbia, Isle of Pines, West Indies)*; and has issue 1e to 2e.

1e. Violet Allen Gardener, *b.* 7 Jan. 1908.

2e. Barbara Allen Gardener, *b.* 26 Aug. 1909.

8d.² Diana Wroughton Anderson, *unm.*

2c. *Musgrave Wroughton Anderson of Studley Park, Melbourne*, b. 1837; d. 1870; m. *in Australia* 1860, *Charlotte, da. of the Hon. Henry Miller of Melbourne* [*who* m. 2ndly, 17 Dec. 1872, *the Hon. Sir Henry John Wrixon, K.C.M.G., President Legislative Council of Victoria*]; *and had issue* (with a son d. young) 1d to 2d.

1d. Lilian Charlotte Anderson, *m.* 13 Feb. 1889, Alan Sidney Wentworth

[Nos. 30095 to 30116.

of The Blood Royal

Stanley, J.P., Capt. and Hon. Major 4th Batt. Suffolk Regt. (*Chesterfield House, Great Chesterfield, Essex; Wellington*); and has issue (with a son *d.* young) 1*e*.

1*e*. Alan Wroughton Wentworth Stanley, *b.* 3 Jan. 1891.

2*d.* Helen Maud Anderson, *m.* 18 Dec. 1890, Charles Wentworth Stanley, *formerly* of Longstowe Hall, co. Camb., J.P., D.L., M.A. (Camb.), Capt. and Hon. Major 4th Batt. Suffolk Regt. (*Merton Grange, Gamlingay, co. Camb.; Wellington*); and has issue 1*e* to 2*e*.

    1*e*. Charles Sidney Bowen Wentworth Stanley, *b.* 20 Jan. 1892.

    2*e*. Barbara Charlotte Wentworth Stanley, *b.* 31 Jan. 1901.

3*c*. Diana Matilda Anderson, *m.* 3 May 1854, Randolph Robinson (*Waldeck House, 19 South Parade, Southsea*); and has issue 1*d*.

    1*d*. Maud Robinson, *m.* 15 Nov. 1881, John Ross Divett (43 *St. Ronan's Road, Southsea*); and has issue 1*e*.

        1*e*. Randolph Divett, R.N., *b.* 17 May 1883.

5*b*. *Diana Denton Turner Wroughton*, b. at Doncaster 5 *Feb.* 1801; d. 27 *May* 1819; m. *as 1st wife,* 1818, *Lieut.-Gen. James Eckford, C.B.,* d. 2 *June* 1867; *and had issue* 1*c*.

1*c*. *George Henry Eckford, Indian C.S., b.* 24 *Aug.* 1818; d. 18 *Oct.* 1877; m. *June* 1837, *Catherine, da. of James Haldane,* d. 31 *May* 1897; *and had issue* 1*d*.

1*d*. Emily Jane Eckford (*Rosario*, 30 *St. Ronan's Road, Southsea*), *m.* at Patna, Bengal, 24 Nov. 1864, Col. Andrew David Geddes, Col. Comdg. 83rd Regimental District, Belfast, *formerly* 27th Inniskillings, *d.* at Belfast 23 Dec. 1888; and has issue (with a son, Cosmo Gordon, and 2 das. Marion Margaret and Caroline Gordon, *d. unm.*) 1*e* to 8*e*.

    1*e*. Ernest David Eckford Geddes, Capt. and Brevet-Major R.M.A., *b.* 15 Nov. 1869.

    2*e*. Malcolm Henry Burdett Geddes, Capt. 64th Pioneers, Indian Army, *b.* 20 Feb. 1874; *m.* 21 Oct. 1905, Annie Vera Eleanor, da. of Col. James Christie, Indian Army; and has issue 1*f* to 2*f*.

        1*f*. Andrew James Wray Geddes, *b.* 31 July 1906.

        2*f*. Eleanor Lilian Lorna Geddes.

    3*e*. Emily Ethel Geddes, *m.* 8 Oct. 1902, Capt. Edward Augustus Alfred de Salis, D.S.O., 4th Batt. Worcestershire Regt. (*Imperial Service Club*), *s.p.*

    4*e*. Diana Catherine Geddes, *unm.*

    5*e*. Violet Alice Geddes, *m.* 30 June 1903, Capt. Frederick Lewis Dibblee, R.M.A.; and has issue 1*f* to 2*f*.

        1*f*. David Lewis Dibblee, *b.* 10 Sept. 1909.

        2*f*. Margaret Emily Dibblee.

    6*e*. *Lilian Maud Geddes,* d. 4 *July* 1907; m. 20 *Nov.* 1901, *Lieut. Lionel Berkeley Holt Haworth, Indian Army, attached to Political Dept. Indian Govt.; and had issue* 1*f* to 2*f*.

        1*f*. Cyril Francis Rafe Haworth, *b.* 3 Sept. 1902.

        2*f*. Radclyffe Lionel Geddes Haworth, *b.* 7 Aug. 1904.

    7*e*. Mabel Ada Geddes, *m.* 11 Ap. 1908, Lieut. Cyril Charles Johnson Barrett, Indian Army, attached to Political Dept. Indian Govt. (*Bombay*): and has issue 1*f*.

        1*f*. Edwin Cyril Geddes Barrett, *b.* 15 Feb. 1909.

    8*e*. Gwendoline Olivia Geddes, *unm.*

6*b*. *Mary Frances Matilda Wroughton,* b. *at Adwick* 15 *Sept.* 1806; d. *at Brighton Ap.* 1872; m. *her cousin, the Rev. Robert Abercrombie Denton,* d. 25 *Feb.* 1857; *and had issue* (*with two sons* d. *young*) 1*c* to 2*c*.

1*c*. Sir George Chardin Denton, K.C.M.G., Governor of the Gambia, *formerly* Capt. 57th Regt. (*Government House, Bathurst, Gambia*), *b.* 22 June 1851; *m.* July

[Nos. 30117 to 30139.

The Plantagenet Roll

1879, Jean Margaret Alan, da. of Alan Stevenson, d. 19 July 1900; and had issue 1d to 2d.

1d. George Clarke Denton, b. 22 Ap. 1881.

2d. Julia Maud Mary Denton.

2c. Julia Sibella Denton (*Hilltop, Headington Hill, Oxford*), m. 1886, Fitzjames E. Watt, Commissary Gen., d.s.p. Mar. 1902.

3a. Francis Wroughton, H.E.I.C.S., d. (? s.p.) in India.

4a. Catherine Wroughton, d. (–); m. as 1st *wife*, 1786, the Rev. Robert Price, LL.D., Preb. of Durham [*descended from George, Duke of Clarence, K.G.*], d. 7 Ap. 1823; and had issue.

See the Clarence Volume, pp. 361-362, Nos. 12329-12372.

5a. (—) Wroughton, d. (–); m. Capt. Mainwaring.[1] [Nos. 30140 to 30186.

111. Descendants of BARBARA MUSGRAVE (Table XIII.), d. (–); m. as 2nd wife, 1720, THOMAS HOWARD of Corby Castle, co. Cumberland [D. of Norfolk Coll.] (see p. 402), d. 1740; and had issue 1a.

1a. *Philip Howard of Corby Castle*, b. 1730; d. 8 *Jan.* 1810; m. 11 *Nov.* 1754, *Anne* [*descended from the Lady Ann, sister of King Edward IV., &c.*], da. of *Henry Witham of Cliffe; and had issue.*

See the Exeter Volume, pp. 558-559, Nos. 49774-49891.

[Nos. 30187 to 30304.

112. Descendants of GEORGE MUSGRAVE, Storekeeper of the Ordnance at Chatham (Table XIII.), d. (–); m. SARAH, widow of Lieut. Young, da. of Benjamin ROSELL; and has issue 1a to 3a.

1a. *Joseph Musgrave of Kypier*, d. (–); m. *Jane* (see p. 200), da. of Sir Philip Musgrave, 6th Bt. [E.].

2a. Thomas Musgrave.

3a. George Musgrave, M.P. for Carlisle 23 Mar. 1768 to 30 Sept. 1774; d. (–); m. (—), da. of (—); and had issue 1b.

1b. George Musgrave of Marylebone and Shillington Manor, co. Bedford, J.P., and High Sheriff 1828, b. 8 Sept. 1769; d. 27 June 1861; m. 19 Aug. 1790, Margaret, da. of Edmund Kennedy of Grafton, d. 19 Sept. 1859; and had issue 1c to 5c.

1c. Rev. George Musgrave of Shillington Manor and Borden Hall, co. Kent, M.A. (Oxon.), Translator of Homer's "Oyyssey," &c., b. 1 July 1798; d. 26 Dec. 1883; m. 1st, 4 July 1827, Charlotte Emily, da. of Thomas Oakes, Senior Member of Council and President of the Board of Revenue, Madras; and had issue 1d.

1d. Edward Musgrave of Shillington Manor, b. 26 Ap. 1835; d. (–); m. July 1860, Henrietta Maria, da. of John Teschemaker of Aunsfert, British Guiana, D.C.L., d. (–); and had issue 1e to 3e.

1e. Horace Edgar Musgrave of Shillington Manor, co. Beds, and Borden Hall, co. Kent, Painter, New Brighton, Christchurch (*Orari, South Canterbury, New*

[No. 30305.

---

[1] These particulars are taken from a MS. pedigree lent by Philip Wroughton of Woolley and endorsed: "This pedigree was drawn out by and is in the handwriting of my late brother, Charles Jackson, Esq., of Doncaster, from original information supplied by John White, Esq., of Doncaster, brother-in-law of Col. George Wroughton of Adwicke-le-Street. Mr. White's notes are in my possession. —J. E. Jackson, Leigh Delamere, Wilts, October 28, 1883," and now amplified and brought down as far as possible.

of The Blood Royal

Zealand), b. 3 Sept. 1861 ; *m.* 8 Ap. 1891, Cecilia Elizabeth, da. of George Arthur Emilius Ross of Stoney Croft, Riccarton, Christchurch, N.Z. ; and has issue 1*f* to 2*f*.

    1*f*. Christopher Musgrave, *b.* 1 Feb. 1893.
    2*f*. Ethel Marion Musgrave.
    2*e*. Philip Cranstoun Musgrave, Lieut. R.N., *b.* 6 Aug. 1863.
    3*e*. Ethel Henrietta Musgrave.

   2*c. Henry Musgrave, J.P., D.L., Bar.-at-Law,* b. 8 *July* 1800; d. (-); m. *Sarah Popplewell, da. of Richard Pullan of Harewood, co. York,* d. *Sept.* 1861 ; *and had issue* 1*d*.

    1*d*. George Arthur Musgrave of Horton, co. Glouc., *b.* 1843 ; *m.* Aug. 1867, Theresa, da. and h. of Jacques Jones of Hill House, co. Glouc.; and has issue 1*e* to 4*e*.

       1*e*. Henry Arthur Fitzherbert Musgrave, *b.* 1869.
       2*e*. Richard Rosewell Musgrave, *b.* 1872.
       3*e*. Arthur Franklyn Musgrave, *b.* 1877.
       4*e*. Christopher Brooke Musgrave, *b.* 1880.

   3*c. Thomas Musgrave,* d. (? s.p.).
   4*c. Georgiana Musgrave,* d. (-); m. 22 *Aug.* 1822, *C. Berners Plestow of Watlington Hall, co. Norfolk,* d. *May* 1849 ; *and had issue* 1*d to* 2*d*.

    1*d*. Charles John Berners Plestow, *late* 7th Dragoon Guards, *b.* July 1823.
    2*d*. Henry Berners Plestow, *b.* 1825 ; d. (? s.p.) *before* 1880.

   5*c. Emma Musgrave,* d. (-); m. *June* 1831, *James Higham* [*son of Samuel Higham, Comptroller of the National Debt Office*], d. (-); *and had issue* 1*d to* 3*d*.

    1*d*. George Lascelles Higham, *b.* 1834; *m.* 1861, Eliza, da. of (—) Gilbertson.
    2*d*. Henrietta Higham.
    3*d*. Emily Higham, *m.* 1863, William Harrison Briscoe ; and has issue.

                                                           [Nos. 30306 to 30318.

113. Descendants, if any, of ELIZABETH MUSGRAVE, *d.* (-); *m.* JOHN WYNEVE of Brettenham, co. Suffolk ; and of DOROTHY MUSGRAVE, *d.* (-); *m.* JAMES HAWLEY of Brentford, co. Midx. (Table XII.).

114. Descendants of MARGARET MUSGRAVE (Table XII.), *d.* (-); *m.* RALPH SHIPPERDSON of Murton and Pidding Hall Garth, co. Durham, Major Durham Militia 1712, *d.* 16 June 1719 ; and had issue [1] 1*a*.

   1*a. Edward Shipperdson of Pidding Hall Garth,* d. (-) ; m. *Margaret, da. of George Baker of Elemore ; and had issue* 1*b*.

   1*b. Ralph Shipperdson of Pidding Hall Garth,* d. 8 *Nov.* 1793; m.1779,*Frances, da. and event. h. of the Rev. Samuel Kirkshaw, D.D., Vicar of Leeds ; and had issue* 1*c to* 3*c*.

    1*c. Edward Shipperdson of Pidding Hall Garth, J.P., D.L.,* b. 20 *Sept.* 1780 ; d. *unm.*

    2*c. Frances Shipperdson,* d. (-); m. *William Appletree of Goldings, near Basingstoke,* d. (-); *and had issue (at least)* 1*d*.

      1*d*. Francis Russell Appletree or Apletre of Goldings.   [No. 30319.

---

[1] Burke's "Pedigrees of Founders' Kin," liv. ; "Commoners," i. 108 ; and "Landed Gentry," 1–6.

The Plantagenet Roll

3c. *Margaret Shipperdson,* d. (−); m. 9 *Aug.* 1803, *Walter Charles Hopper of Belmont, co. Durham,* b. 25 *July* 1772; d. 15 *Jan.* 1853; *and had issue* 1d *to* 6d.

1d. *Rev. Edmund Hector Hopper, afterwards (R.L.* 25 *Mar.* 1856) *Shipperdson of Pittington Hall Garth, and Murton-in-the-Whins and The Hermitage, co. Durham, J.P., M.A., and Fellow of Christ's College, Camb.,* b. 25 *Sept.* 1806; d. (−); m. 1 Nov. 1838, *Adeline,* da. *of John Kerrich of Harleston, co. Norfolk; and had issue* 1e to 3e.

1e. Thomas Henry Shipperdson, b. 26 Aug. 1839.

2e. *Mary Adeline Shipperdson,* d. 2 *June* 1866; m. 10 *Dec.* 1863, *Sir Henry Pottinger,* 3rd *Bt.* [U.K.], *J.P., D.L., &c. (The Pines, Queen's Road, Richmond, Surrey); and had issue* 1f.

1f. Ethel Adeline Pottinger, m. 21 Ap. 1885, Henry Meysey (Meysey-Thompson), 1st Baron Knaresborough [U.K.], &c. &c. [also descended from Edward III. through Mortimer-Percy] *(Kirby Hall, near York);* and has issue.

See p. 114, Nos. 10645–10649.

3e. Isabella Henrietta Shipperdson.

2d. *Ven. Augustus Macdonald Hopper, M.A., J.P., Archdeacon of Norwich,* b. 11 *Aug.* 1816; d. (−); m. 15 *Ap.* 1847, *Charlotte,* da. *of the Rev. John Holmes of Gawdy Hall, co. Norfolk; and had issue* 1e to 4e.

1e. Edmund Charles Hopper, b. 23 June 1856.

2e. Anthony Shipperdson Hopper, b. 17 June 1858.

3e. Annie Margaret Hopper.

4e. Constance Hopper.

3d. *Mary Anne Frances Hopper,* d. 20 *Jan.* 1868; m. *John Smith of Burley House, Leeds.*

4d. *Caroline Elizabeth Hopper,* d. (−); m. *the Rev. James Boucher [nephew ex sorore of Richard Pigott,* 7th *Viscount Molesworth* [I.].

5d. *Isabella Margaret Hopper,* d. (−); m. *Francis Russell Apletre of Goldings, co. Hants.*

6d. *Frances Hopper.* [Nos. 30320 to 30331.

115. Descendants of FRANCES MUSGRAVE (Table XII.), d. (−); m. EDWARD HUTCHINSON of Wickham, co. York, aged 21, 1665; *living* 1690; and had issue 1a to 2a.[1]

1a. Richard Hutchinson *of Wickham, living* 1706.

2a. William Hutchinson *of York, Merchant,* living 1714; m. *Elizabeth,* da. *of Richard Washington of Ardwick, co. York; and had issue* 1b.

1b. Thomas Hutchinson *of York, and afterwards of Newsham in that co., Merchant, living* 1738; m. *Elizabeth,* da. *of Jonathan Johnson of Earby Hall, in Newsham; and had issue* 1c.

1c. *Francis Hutchinson of Newsham and Earby Hall,* d. 1812; m. *Anne,* da. *of Thomas Newby of Barningham; and had issue* 1d *to* 5d.

1d. *William Hutchinson,* d. 1830; m. *and had (with possibly other) issue* 1e.

1e. *Anne Johnson Hutchinson,* d. 19 *Nov.* 1861; m. *George Sowerby of Putteridge Park, co. Herts, and Dalton Hall, co. Yorks, J.P., D.L.,* d. 9 *May* 1868; *and had (with other) issue* 1f.

1f. George Sowerby *of Putteridge and Dalton afsd., and of Dalston Hall, co. Cumberland, J.P., Col. Durham Militia,* b. 17 *Feb.* 1832; d. 2 *Aug.* 1888; m. 29 *Oct.* 1863, *Emily Isabella Jane,* da. *of Robert Airey of Jesmond, Newcastle-on-Tyne; and had issue (with a son, Francis Hubert Airey,* d. *unm. in S. Africa* 21 *Ap.* 1901) 1g *to* 5g.

---

[1] Plantagenet-Harrison's "Yorkshire," p. 183.

of The Blood Royal

1*g*. Thomas George Sowerby of Putteridge, &c., J.P., Lord of the Manor of Lilley, co. Herts, Major and Hon. Lieut.-Col. 3rd Batt. Durham L.I., served in S. Africa 1900–1901 (*Putteridge Park, Luton, Herts ; Dalston Hall, Carlisle ; Dalton Hall, Richmond, Yorks*), *b.* 8 Ap. 1866 ; *m.* 8 July 1897, Ellen Catherine, da. of Marlborough Robert Pryor of Weston Park, co. Herts ; and has issue 1*h* to 2*h*.

    1*h*. Richard Thomas Reynolds Sowerby, *b.* 5 May 1898.

    2*h*. Hubert Dennison Sowerby, *b.* 21 Jan. 1902.

2*g*. Harry John Sowerby, J.P., D.S.O., Lieut.-Col. and Hon. Col. Comdg. 4th Batt. Durham L.I., served in S. Africa 1900–1901 (*Dalton Hall, Richmond, Yorks*), *b.* 28 Nov. 1867.

3*g*. Emily Frances Annie Sowerby, *m.* 12 June 1894, Frederick William Fellowes [descended from George, Duke of Clarence, K.G., brother of Edward IV. (see the Clarence Volume, p. 87)] (*The Lane House, King's Walden, Hitchin*) ; and has issue 1*h*.

    1*h*. Reginald William Lyon Fellowes, *b.* 6 Aug. 1895.

    4*g*. Lilian Mary Sowerby.

    5*g*. Violet Florence Sowerby.

2*d*. Thomas Hutchinson, b. 1780 ; d. (? s.p.) 1873.

3*d*. Elizabeth Hutchinson, m. 1*st*, *William Johnson of Earby Hall ;* 2*ndly*, *Joseph Glover of Dalton Fields ; and had issue.*

4*d*. Anne Hutchinson, m. *Michael Glover of Aldburgh ; and had issue.*

5*d*. Margaret Hutchinson, b. 23 Ap. 1787 ; d. *at Newsham* 31 *Dec.* 1864 ; m. 13 *Sept.* 1808, *Marley Harrison of Washton, co. York* [*himself a descendant of the Plantagenets*], b. *at Stubb House, co. Durham,* 22 *Feb.* 1772 ; d. 14 *July* 1822 ; *and had issue (with* 6 *other children, all of whom* d.s.p.s. ; *the last survivor, Penelope,* d. 23 *Jan.* 1902) 1*e.*

1*e*. George Henry de Strabolgie Neville Plantagenet-Harrison, *a Marshal-Gen. in the Armies of various South American States, and afterwards a Gen. in the Danish Service, and later in that of the German Confederation, Author of a "History of Yorkshire," &c.,* b. 14 *July* 1817 ; d. 2 *July* 1890 ; m. *and had issue* 1*f.*

1*f*. Blanche Plantagenet Plantagenet-Harrison, *m.* 27 Ap. 1892, John Christopher Cain Routh (*Clints House, Gayle, near Hawes, Yorks ; Baxterley, Rusthall, Tunbridge Wells*), s.p.   [Nos. 30332 to 30340.

116. Descendants of MARY (*née* EURE), *suo jure de jure* 16th BARONESS SCROPE of Bolton [E.][1] (Table XIII.), *b. c.* 1651, being aged 15 in 1666 ; *d.* (–), when the right of the Barony fell into abeyance ; *m.* after 1687, MICHAEL JOHNSTON of Twyzell Hall, co. Durham ; *d.* 12 Ap. 1714 ; and had issue 1*a*.

1*a*. Mary Johnson, *eldest da. and in her issue* (12 *Ap.* 1814), *sole h., a co-h. to the Barony of Scrope,*[2] b. 1689 ; d. 8 *June* 1730 ; m. 1*st, c. Oct.* 1716, *John Brockholes of Claughton Hall, co. Lanc.,* d. 6 *Mar.* 1719 ; 2*ndly,* 2 *Jan.* 1724, *Richard Jones of Caton, co. Lancaster,* d. 23 *Nov.* 1732 ; *and had issue* 1*b* to 2*b.*

1*b*. Michael Jones *of Caton, co. Lancaster,* b. 23 *Nov.* 1729 ; d. 24 *July* 1801 ; m. 23 *Oct.* 1773, *Mary, widow of Edward Cosney, da. of Matthew Smith,* d. 1814 ; *and had issue* 1*c* to 7*c*.[2]

1*c*. Charles Jones, *Capt. 1st Dragoon Guards, who on the extinction of all the issue of the sisters of his grandmother by the death of Mary Bryer,* 12 *Ap.* 1814, *became* de jure 17*th Baron Scrope of Bolton* [E. 1371]; *living May* 1825.

2*c*. Michael Jones *of Lincoln's Inn, Bar.-at-Law, F.S.A., living May* 1825 ; m. *Ann, da. of Robert Etherington of Gainsborough, co. Linc.,* d.s.p. 4 *Ap.* 1804.

---

[1] G. E. C.'s " Complete Peerage," vii. 88.

[2] See pedigree in Nicolas' "Synopses of the Peerage of England," i., Addenda, p. 22.

The Plantagenet Roll

3c. *Edward Jones, Capt.* 29*th Foot, living unm. May* 1825.
4c. *James Jones, Major in the Army, K.C.S., &c., living* s.p. *May* 1825; m. *Louisa Dacre, da. of Peter Moore, M.P.*
5c. *Mary Jones, living* s.p. *May* 1825; m. *at St. Omer's, Ap.* 1818, " *Le Comte Pierre de Sandelin, Seigneur D'Halines, near St. Omer's, in France.*"
6c. *Constantia Jones, living unm. May* 1825.
7c. *Katherine Jones, d. unm.* 1799.

2b. *Katherine Brockholes,* b. 30 *Ap.* 1718; d. 21 *Nov.* 1784; m. 8 *Nov.* 1739, *Charles (Howard), 9th Duke of Norfolk* [E.], *&c.,* d. 31 *Aug.* 1786, *leaving an only son, who* d.s.p.s. 23 *Dec.* 1815.

117. Descendants of Sir HENRY CHOLMLEY of Whitby and Roxby (Table XIII.), *bur.* at St. John's, York, 13 Jan. 1616; *m.* MARGARET [descended from the Lady ANNE, sister to Kings Edward IV. and Richard III.], da. of Sir William BABTHORPE, *b.* 15 Ap. 1628; and had issue.

See the Exeter Volume, Table LVIII., and pp. 607–679, Nos. 51968–57332.
[Nos. 30341 to 35705.

118. Descendants, if any surviving, of JOHN (CONSTABLE), 2nd VISCOUNT DUNBAR [S.], (Table XIII.), *b. c.* 1615; *d. c.* 1667; will dated 15 Dec. that year; *m.* before 1649, MARY, da. of Thomas (BRUDENELL), 1st Earl of Cardigan [E.]; and had issue 1*a* to 4*a*.

1a. *Robert (Constable), 3rd Viscount Dunbar* [S.], b. *c.* 1651; d. 23 *Nov.* 1714.
2a. *William (Constable), 4th Viscount Dunbar* [S.], b. *c.* 1654; d.s.p.l. 15 *Aug.* 1718.
3a. *Hon. Cecily Constable,* d. (–); m. 5 *Sept.* 1665, *Francis Tunstall of Scargill and Wycliffe, co. York; and had issue, which apparently became extinct on the death of Francis Sheldon,* alias *Constable, of Burton Constable,* 12 *Feb.* 1821.[1]
4a. *Hon. Catherine Constable,* d. (–); m. *after* 5 *Sept.* 1665, *John More of Kirklington, co. Notts; and had issue* 1b *to* 2b.
1b. *John More,* } *both living* 30 *Aug.* 1717, *when they are named in the*
2b. *Winifred More,* } *will of the 4th Lord Dunbar.*[2]

119. Descendants of the Hon. CATHERINE CONSTABLE (Table XIII.), *living* 1653; *d.* (–); *m.* WILLIAM MIDDLETON of Stockheld, co. York, *d.* 1658; and had issue.

See the Exeter Volume, Table XXII., and pp. 333–336, Nos. 24284–24535.
[Nos. 35706 to 35957.

120. Descendants of the Hon. ALATHEA FAIRFAX (XIV.), *d.* (–); *m. c.* Jan. 1677, WILLIAM (WIDDRINGTON), 3rd LORD WIDDRINGTON [E.], *d.* 10 Feb. 1695; and had issue 1*a* to 4*a*.

1a. *William (Widdrington), 4th Lord Widdrington* [E.], d. 17 *Ap.* 1743, *having been attainted* 7 *July* 1716 *for his share in the* "'15"; m. 1*st* (*marriage bond dated*

---

[1] Foster's "Yorkshire Pedigrees."
[2] Balfour Paul's "Scots Peerage," iii. 298.

of The Blood Royal

13 *Ap.*) 1700, *Jane, da. and event.* (1698) *h. of Sir Thomas Tempest of Stella, 4th Bt.* [*E.*], d. 9 *Sept.* 1714; *and had issue which became extinct* 26 *Mar.* 1792.

2*a.* Hon. Charles Widdrington, *attainted* 31 *May*–7 *July* 1716; *and said to have* d.s.p. *at St. Omers* 1756.

3*a.* Hon. Mary Widdrington, d. *July* 1731; m. Richard Towneley *of Towneley* [*descended from George, Duke of Clarence, K.G.*], b. 1687; d. *Aug.* 1735; *and had issue.*

See the Clarence Volume, Table XXXIV. and pp. 314–318, Nos. 9083–9214.

4*a.* Hon. Elizabeth Widdrington, d. 7 *Jan.* 1765; m. Marmaduke (Langdale), 4*th Lord Langdale* [*E.*] [*descended from the Lady Anne, sister to King Edward IV., &c.*], d. 8 *Jan.* 1771; *and had issue.*

See the Exeter Volume, pp. 460–461, Nos. 36724–37038.

[Nos. 35958 to 36304/100.

121. Descendants, if any, of ALATHEA FAIRFAX (Table XIV.), *d.* (–); *m.* JOHN FORCER.

122. Descendants, if any, of the Hon. PHILIP FAIRFAX, of the Hon. MARY FAIRFAX, and of the Hon. CATHERINE FAIRFAX, *d.* 1715; *m.* GEORGE METHAM of Metham, co. York [1] (Table XIV.).

123. Descendants of the Hon. DAVID ERSKINE of Armondell, King's Advocate (Table XIV.), *b.* 1 Nov. 1746; *d.* 8 Oct. 1817; *m.* 1st, 30 Mar. 1772, CHRISTIAN, da. and h. of George FULLERTON of Broughton Hall, *d.* 1804; *and had issue* 1α to 3*a.*

1*a.* Henry David (Erskine), *12th Earl of Buchan* [S.], b. *July* 1783; d. 13 *Sept.* 1857; m. 1*st*, 28 *Sept.* 1809, *Elizabeth Cole, da. and co-h. of Major-Gen. Sir Charles Shipley, Gov. of Grenada,* d. 5 *Oct.* 1828; 2*ndly*, 26 *June* 1830, *Elizabeth, da. of John Harvey of Castle Semple, co. Renfrew,* d. 17 *Dec.* 1838; *and had issue* 1*b to* 5*b.*

1*b.* Henry Erskine, Lord Cardross, b. 22 *Oct.* 1812; d.v.p. 21 *Dec.* 1836; m. 15 *May* 1832, *Jean Halliday, da. of Archibald Torry of Edinburgh,* d. 11 *Sept.* 1886; *and had issue* 1*c.*

1*c.* Hon. John Berry Erskine of Dryburgh and Holmes, da. and h. of entail, b. 16 *Feb.* 1833; d. 16 *Mar.* 1870; m. 8 *Ap.* 1856, *the Rev. George Eden Biber, afterwards* (1856) *Biber-Erskine, B.A.*, d. 25 *July* 1866; *and had issue* 1*d to* 2*d.*

1*d.* George Oswald Harry Erskine Biber-Erskine of Dryburgh and Newmains, J.P., heir-general of the Erskines, Earls of Buchan (*Dryburgh Abbey, co. Berwick; Newmains, Dryburgh*), b. 24 *May* 1857; m. 15 *Aug.* 1893, Lucy, da. of T. A. Urwick of Corfe Mullen, co. Dorset.

2*d.* Henry Erskine Biber-Erskine, b. 17 *July* 1858.

2*b.* David Stuart (Erskine), *13th Earl of Buchan* [S.], b. 6 *Nov.* 1815; d. 3 *Dec.* 1898; m. 1*st*, 27 *Ap.* 1849, *Agnes Graham, da. of James Smith of Craigend, co. Stirling,* d. 2 *Sept.* 1875; *and had issue* 1*c to* 2*c.*

1*c.* Shipley Gordon Stuart (Erskine), *14th Earl of Buchan, &c.* [S.] (*Almondwell House, Linlithgow; 6 Aldford Street, Park Lane, W.; Carlton*), b. 27 *Feb.* 1850; m. 9 *Nov.* 1876, Rosalie Louisa, da. of Capt. Jules Alexander Sartoris of Hopsford Hall, Coventry; and has issue 1*d to* 4*d.*

1*d.* Ronald Douglas Stuart Mar Erskine, Lord Cardross, *late* Lieut. Scots Guards, b. 6 *Ap.* 1878. [Nos. 36305 to 36308.

---

[1] In Burke's "Extinct Peerage," p. 194, she is confused with her aunt (see p. 292), and is made to marry 2ndly Sir Arthur Ingram.

The Plantagenet Roll

2*d*. Lady Muriel Agnes Stuart Erskine, *m*. 7 Jan. 1903, Major the Hon. Charles Strathavon Heathcote-Drummond-Willoughby, *late* Scots Guards [2nd son of Gilbert Henry, 1st Earl of of Ancaster [U.K.], P.C., and a descendant of King Henry VII., &c.] (19 *Cheyne Walk, S.W.*); and has issue 1*e* to 2*e*.

    1*e*. Charles Peregrine Heathcote-Drummond-Willoughby, *b*. 13 Sept. 1905.
    2*e*. Rosalie Heathcote-Drummond-Willoughby, *b*. 10 July 1908.

3*d*. Lady Marjorie Gladys Stuart Erskine.

4*d*. Lady Evelyn Hilda Stuart Erskine, *m*. 24 June 1903, Major the Hon. Walter Edward Guinness, M.P. [3rd son of Edward Cecil, 1st Viscount Iveagh [U.K.], K.P.] (*Knockmaroon, Castleknock, co. Dublin; The Manor House, Bury St. Edmunds;* 11 *Grosvenor Place, S.W.*); and has issue 1*e*.

    1*e*. Bryan Walter Guinness, *b*. 27 Oct. 1905.

2*c*. Hon. Albany Mar Stuart Erskine, Capt. 3rd Batt. Duke of Wellington's Regt., *b*. 24 Feb. 1852; *m*. 16 May 1878, Alice Ellen, da. of Alfred Keyser of Cross Oak, Berkhampstead, *d*. 19 Sept. 1902.

3*b*. *Lady Christian Isabella Erskine*, b. Oct. 1820; d. 3 *July* 1886; m. 4 *June* 1840, *John Gordon of Aikenhead, co. Lanark, J.P., D.L.*, d. 6 *Aug*. 1897; *and had issue* 1*c to* 4*c*.

    1*c*. John Henry Gordon of Aikenhead, *b*. 21 Oct. 1842; d.s.p. 7 Feb. 1902.

    2*c*. Henry Erskine Gordon of Aikenhead, J.P., D.L., Major and Hon. Lieut.-Col. Lanark Imp. Yeo. (*Aikenhead House, Cathcart*), *b*. 11 Sept. 1849; *m*. 1 Oct. 1895, Bertha Agnes, da. of Major J. Finlay of Castle Toward, co. Argyll; and has issue 1*d* to 5*d*.

        1*d*. Joan Victoria Christian Erskine Gordon.
        2*d*. Nancy Althea Gordon.
        3*d*. Dorothy Bertha Gordon.
        4*d*. Violet Erskine Gordon.
        5*d*. Barbara Isobel Gordon.

    3*c*. Charles Shipley Gordon (*Ronerdenan, Merton Park, Surrey*), *b*. 12 Oct. 1851; *m* 2 Aug. 1875, Mary, da. of Capt. James Stirling Crawfurd-Stirling-Stuart [Bt. of Pollok (1682) Coll.]; and has issue 1*d* to 4*d*.

        1*d*. John Stuart Gordon, *b*. 13 Feb. 1881.
        2*d*. Hamilton William Fortescue Gordon, *b*. 1883.
        3*d*. Muriel Isabella Erskine Gordon.
        4*d*. Gwendoline Mary Harriet Gordon.

    4*c*. Hamilton Gordon (*The Wildernesse, Hayward's Heath, Sussex*), *b*. 13 Feb. 1856; *m*. 3 Oct. 1898, Alice Jane Erroll (see below), da. of John Young of Westridge.

4*b*. *Lady Alicia Diana Erskine*, b. Feb. 1822; d. 31 *Oct*. 1891; m. 1st, 6 *June* 1843, *Rev. the Hon. Somerville Hay* [*E. of Erroll Coll. and a descendant of the Lady Anne, sister of King Edward IV*. (see Exeter Volume, p. 682), d. 25 *Sept*. 1853; 2ndly, 5 *July* 1858, *Capt. James Young of Westridge, I.W.*, d. 1877; *and had issue* 1*c to* 3*c*.

    1*c*. Somerville Hay, *b*. (posthumous) 19 Nov. 1853.
    2*c*. John Harry Erskine Young, *b*. 19 Aug. 1859.
    3*c*. Alicia Jane Erroll Young, *m*. 1898, Hamilton Gordon (see above).

5*b*. *Lady Margaret Erskine*, b. 15 *Nov*. 1834; d. 22 *Nov*. 1872; m. *as* 1*st wife*, 24 *Ap*. 1860, *Sir William Vincent of Stoke D'Abernon*, 12*th Bt*. [*E*.], *J.P., D.L., C.A., Vice-Chairman Surrey C.C. and Deputy Chairman Surrey Quarter Sessions* (*Stoke D'Abernon Chase, Leatherhead, Surrey*); *and had issue* 1*c*.

    1*c*. Francis Erskine Vincent, *late* Lieut. 1st Life Guards (*Ormesby, Great Yarmouth*), *b*. 24 May 1869; *m*. 4 July 1893, Margaret Louisa, da. of John Holmes of Brooke Hall, co. Norfolk; and has issue 1*d* to 3*d*.

        1*d*. Anthony Francis Vincent, *b*. 30 June 1894.
        2*d*. Victor Norman Erskine Vincent, *b*. 9 Feb. 1897.
        3*d*. Evelyn Joseph Vincent, *b*. 25 Sept. 1900.

[Nos. 36309 to 36334.

# of The Blood Royal

2a. Elizabeth Compton Erskine, d. (-) ; m. 21 Oct. 1801, Col. George Callander of Craigforth, co. Stirling, Lieut.-Col. Rifle Brigade, b. Mar. 1770; d.v.p. 18 Feb. 1824; and had issue 1b to 5b.

1b. James Henry Callander of Craigforth and Ardkinglas, M.P., b. 18 Aug. 1803; d. 31 Jan. 1851; m. 1st, 29 Aug. 1877, the Hon. Jane Plumer (see p. 227), da. of David Montague (Erskine), 2nd Lord Erskine [U.K.], d. 30 Mar. 1846; 2ndly, 1 July 1847, Charlotte Edith Eleanora [descended from George, Duke of Clarence, K.G. (see Clarence Volume, p. 479)], da. of John George Campbell, Cadet of Islay; and had issue 1c to 5c.

1c. George Frederick William Callander of Craigforth and Ardkinglas, J.P., D.L. (Craigforth House, Stirling; Ardkinglas Lodge, Inveraray, Argyll), b. 28 July 1848; m. 20 Jan. 1876, Alice, da. of John Cornelius Craigie-Halkett of Cramond.

2c. Henry Barrington Callander (Stone Hill Cottage, Ardkinglas, Argyll), b. 19 July 1849; m. 9 Nov. 1875, Sophia Leonora, da. of Edward Clough Taylor of Kirkham Abbey.

3c.[1] Frances Jane Callander, 3rd Abbess of Cleever since 1892.

4c.[1] Mary Hermione Callander, m. 1st, 16 Sept. 1862, Charles Sartoris of Wilcote, co. Oxon., J.P., and High Sheriff for that co. 1872; d. 22 Sept. 1884; 2ndly, 1886, George Henry Dawkins, J.P. [descended from George, Duke of Clarence, K.G. (see Clarence Volume, p. 177)] (Wilcote, Charlbury S.O., Oxon.).

5c.[1] Jane Sevilla Callander, m. 12 Jan. 1869, Lord Archibald Campbell, J.P., D.L. [descended from Kings Henry VII. and Edward IV. (see Tudor Roll, p. 230), George, Duke of Clarence, K.G., &c. &c.] (Coombe Hill Farm, Norbiton, Kingston-on-Thames); and has issue 1d to 2d.

1d. Niall Diarmid Campbell (28 Clarges Street, W.), b. 16 Feb. 1872.

2d. Elspeth Angela Campbell.

2b. John Alexander Callander, b. 19 Sept. 1809; d. (-) ; m. Aug. 1837, Emma, da. of John Young of Westridge, I.W.; and had issue (2 sons and 5 das.).

3b. Elizabeth Anne Callander, d. 13 Ap. 1839; m. 11 Aug. 1831, Henry William Vincent of Lily Hill, co. Berks [Bt. of Stoke D'Abernon E. 1620 Coll.], b. 5 Sept. 1796; d. 14 Feb. 1865; and had issue 1c to 2c.

1c. Susan Anne Vincent, d. 1 Oct. 1899; m. 28 Jan. 1864, John Henry Bagot Lane of King's Bromley, J.P., Lieut.-Col. Coldstream Guards [descended from King Henry VII., &c.], d. 22 Mar. 1886; and had issue.

See the Tudor Roll, p. 308, Nos. 25856–25866, and the Exeter Volume, p. 434, Nos. 34998–35014.

2c. Harriet Maria Vincent, m. 12 Ap. 1860, James Carter Campbell of Ardpatrick, J.P., D.L., Capt. (ret.) R.N. (Ardpatrick, Tarbert, co. Argyll; The Hall, Filkins, co. Oxford); and has issue 1d to 3d.

1d. Henry Hervey Campbell, M.V.O., Capt. R.N., b. 27 Feb. 1865.

2d. Susan Eleanor Campbell, m. 11 Jan. 1888, Arthur Frederick Churchill Tollemache of Ballincor, King's Co., Heir to Baronetcy [G.B. 1793], J.P. [descended from King Henry VII., &c. (see Tudor Roll, p. 202)] (The Red House, Westgate-on-Sea); and has issue 1e to 3e.

1e. Arthur Henry William Tollemache, b. 5 Ap. 1894.

2e. Eleanor Louisa Cornelia Tollemache.

3e. Hermione Edith Agnes Tollemache.

3d. Edith Elizabeth Campbell, m. 26 Ap. 1887, Capt. Eustace Maudslay, late 16th Lancers (Blaston Manor, Uppingham); and has issue 1e to 5e.

1e. Colin Eustace Maudslay, b. 3 Ap. 1888.

2e. Ronald Vincent Maudslay, b. 27 June 1889.

3e. Marjorie Edith Maudslay.

4e. Irene Isabel Maudslay.

5e. Vere Sybil Maudslay.

[Nos. 36335 to 36370.

The Plantagenet Roll

4b. *Caroline Frances Callander*, d. (-); m. 17 *Jan*. 1832, *Robert Dunmore Napier of Ballykinrain, co. Stirling*, d. 1846.

5b. *Agnes Callander*, d. 1837; m. 1836, *William Dunmore, H.E.I.C.S.*

3a. *Henrietta Erskine*, d. (-); m. 11 *May* 1812, *Peter Smith, M.D.*

124. Descendants of THOMAS (ERSKINE), 1st BARON ERSKINE [U.K.], Lord Chancellor of Great Britain (Table XIV.), b. 21 Jan. 1750; d. 17 Nov. 1823; m. 1st, 29 May 1770, FRANCES, da. of Daniel MOORE, M.P., d. 22 Dec. 1805; 2ndly, 12 Oct. 1818, SARAH [da. of ——] BUCK, d. 25 Oct. 1825; and had issue 1a to 7a.

1a. *David Montagu (Erskine), 2nd Baron Erskine [U.K.]*, b. 1777; d. 19 *Mar.* 1855; m. 1st, 16 *Dec.* 1799, *Frances, da. of Gen. George Cadwalader of Philadelphia*, d. 25 *Mar.* 1843; *and had issue* 1b *to* 12b.

1b. *Thomas Americus (Erskine), 3rd Baron Erskine [U.K.]*, b. 3 *May* 1802; d.s.p. 10 *May* 1877.

2b. *John Cadwalader (Erskine), 4th Baron Erskine [U.K.]*, b. 1804; d. 28 *Mar.* 1882; m. 1*st*, 30 *Ap.* 1829, *Margaret, da. of John Martyn*, d. 21 *June* 1862; *and had issue* 1c *to* 3c.

1c. William Macnaghten (Erskine), 5th Baron Erskine [U.K.], J.P., D.L. (*Spratton Hall, Northampton; Carlton*), b. 7 Jan. 1841; m. 2 July 1864, Caroline Alice Martha, da. of William Grimble; and has issue 1d to 4d.

1d. Hon. Montagu Erskine (*Westwood Lodge, Windlesham, Surrey; Carlton*), b. 13 Ap. 1865; m. 16 Jan. 1895, Florence, da. of Edgar Flower of The Hill, Stratford-on-Avon, and Middlehall Park, co. Worcester; and has issue 1e to 3e.

1e. Donald Flower Cardross Erskine, b. 3 Jan. 1899.

2e. Richard Alistair Erskine, b. 8 Jan. 1901.

3e. Victoria Esme Erskine, b. 3 Jan 1897

2d. Hon. (Stuart Joseph) Ruaidhri Erskine (*Taigh an Fhraoich, Banchory-Dwenich, Aberdeenshire*), b. 15 Jan. 1869; m. 1st, 18 July 1891, Muriel Lilias Colquhoun, da. of Major-Gen. George Farquhar Irving Graham, d. 27 Ap. 1895; 2ndly, 6 Aug. 1902, Dona Maria Guadalupe Zaara Cecilia, da. of Joseph Robert Heaven of the Forest of Birse, Aberdeenshire [by his wife, Mary Guadalupe Ignacia Antoinette, *suo jure* 1st Marchioness of Braceras [P.S.]], *s.p.s.*

3d. Hon. Esmé Standish Erskine, b. 5 Mar. 1873.

4d. Hon. Margaret Erskine, m. 23 Oct. 1890, Capt. Henry Edmund Lacon, J.P., *late* 71st Highlanders (*Blythmore, Claydon, Ipswich*).

2c. Hon. Frances Macnaghten Erskine, b. 29 *May* 1839; d. 5 *May* 1872; m. 12 *Jan.* 1861, *Standish Grady Rowley of Sylvan Park, co. Meath*, LL.D., D.L., M.R.I.A., d. 1 *May* 1882; *and had issue (with a son and da. d. unm.)* 1d *to* 2d.

1d. Clotworthy Rowley, b. 12 Feb. 1872; *m.s.p.*

2d. Georgie Alice Rowley, m. 9 Nov. 1892, Fanshawe Tower Tufnell (*Mariskalls, Felstead, Essex*); and has issue 1e to 2e.

1e. Rowley Erskine Tufnell, b. 30 Nov. 1902.

2e. Fanshawe Edward Standish Tufnell, b. 27 Ap. 1904.

3c. Hon. Margaret Catherine Erskine, m. 1st, 30 Ap. 1872, the Rev. Evelyn Henry Villebois Burnaby, Rector of Burrough-on-the-Hill [marriage dissolved 1886]; 2ndly, 7 June 1887, Sydney Beaumont Willoughby [B. Middleton Coll., [Nos. 36371 to 36383.

# of The Blood Royal

and a descendant of the Lady Anne, sister to King Edward IV., &c. (see Exeter Volume, p. 615)] (63 *Goldington Road, Bedford*); and has issue 1*d* to 2*d*.

1*d*. Christopher John Willoughby, *b*. 1889.

2*d*. Kathleen Riette Winifred Burnaby.

3*b*. Hon. *David Erskine, Major 21st and 51st Regts., and Lieut.-Col. Comdg. Natal Carabineers, Colonial Sec., Natal*, b. 1816 ; d. 21 *June* 1903 ; m. 1*st*, 12 *Nov*. 1839, *Anne Maria, da. of Josiah Spode of Tasmania*, d. at *Pietermaritzburg* 3 *Nov*. 1860; 2*ndly,* 26 *Sept.* 1870, *Emma Florence* (*Sissinghurst, Kent*), *da. of Capt. Charles J. Harford, 12th Lancers ; and had issue* 1c *to* 8c.

1*c*. Stuart Townsend Erskine, *b*. 23 Nov. 1844; *m*. 17 Jan. 1864/6, Jessie Smith, da. of David Dale Buchanan of Natal, Advocate.

2*c*. St. Vincent Whitshed Erskine, *b*. 22 Feb. 1846; *m*. 1870, Alice, da. of David Dale Buchanan of Natal, Advocate.

3*c*. Herman Harford Erskine, Cape Colony Civil Service, *b*. 21 Sept. 1871 ; *m*. 3 May 1899, Adela Eva, da. of Richard Feilding Nevins ; and has issue 1*d*.

1*d*. Angela Augusta Erskine.

4*c*. Robert Henry Erskine, H.B.M.'s Vice-Consul at Fredericia (*Fredericia, Denmark*), *b*. 31 Dec. 1873.

5*c*.¹ Fanny Cadwalader Erskine, *m*. 22 Aug. 1862, the Hon. Sir Michael Henry Gallwey, K.C.M.G., *formerly* Chief-Justice of Natal (*Pietermaritzburg*).

6*c*.¹ Annie Barton Erskine, *m*. 14 Aug. 1872, Major Arthur Henry Pain, *formerly* 1st Batt. Gordon Highlanders.

7*c*. Sevilla Florence Erskine, *m*. 1 Aug. 1908, George Glass Hooper, C.E. (30 *Palace Court, Bayswater Hill, W*.) ; and has issue 1*d*.

1*d*. Mary Erskine Glass Hooper, *b*. 24 May 1909.

8*c*. Gladys Kathleen Erskine, *m*. 1903, Percy John Ling, Paymaster R.N. ; and has issue 1*d*.

1*d*. David Erskine Ling, *b*. 5 Sept. 1908.

4*b*. Hon. *Edward Morris Erskine, C.B., Envoy Extra. and Min. Plen. to Athens* 1864–72, *and to Stockholm* 1872-81, b. 28 *Mar*. 1817 ; d. 19 *Ap*. 1883 ; m. 24 *July* 1847, *Caroline, widow of Andrew Loughnan, da. of Robert Hamilton Vaughan*, d. 23 *Oct*. 1877 ; *and had issue* 1c *to* 4c.

1*c. Mary Maud Erskine*, b. 19 *Ap*. 1848; d. 1892; m. 1*st*, 16 *Ap*. 1872, *William John Percy Lawton of Lawton Hall, co. Chester,* d. 8 *Nov*. 1883 ; 2*ndly,* 8 *Sept*. 1885, *the Rev. George William Charles Skene, M.A., Rector of Barthomley ; and had issue* 1d *to* 4d.

1*d*. John William Edward Lawton of Lawton (*Lawton Hall, Cheshire*), *b*. 24 June 1873.

2*d*. Ralph Lupus Erskine Lawton, *b*. 26 June 1878.

3*d*. Gwendolen Maud Lawton, *m*. 21 Nov. 1905, Edward Charles Crewe-Read (see below).

4*d*. Mary Emily Lawton.

2*c. Elizabeth Steuarta Erskine*, b. 3 Feb. 1850 ; d. 9 *Aug*. 1905 ; m. 2 *Mar*. 1875, *Offley John Crewe-Read of Llandinam Hall, co. Montgomery, J.P., Lieut.-Col. South Wales Borderers*, b. 3 *Dec*. 1848; *and had issue* 1d *to* 2d.

1*d*. Randolph Offley Crewe-Read, *late* of Llandinam, *b*. 12 Ap. 1876.

2*d*. Edward Charles Crewe-Read, *b*. 15 June 1877 ; *m*. 21 Nov. 1905, Gwendolen Maud (see above), da. of William John Percy Lawton of Lawton.

3*c*. Evelyn Constance Erskine, *m*. 1 June 1876, Francis William White, F.R.G.S., *late* Comr. of Customs at Hankow, China, *d*. (-) ; and has issue.

4*c*. Christina Edith Eleanor Erskine, *unm*.

5*b*. *James* (*Erskine*), 1*st Baron Erskine* (*Freiherr von Erskine*) [*Bavaria*], so cr. 18 *Jan*. 1872, b. 4 *Sept*. 1819/21 ; d. 4 *Jan*. 1904 ; m. 27 *Feb*. 1849, *the Countess Wilhelmina* (*Countess Lerchenfeld*), *da. of Anthony Joseph Clements, Count Toerring Minucci of Munich ; and had issue* 1c *to* 2c.   [Nos. 36384 to 36404.

The Plantagenet Roll

1c. Herman David Montagu (Erskine), 2nd Baron Erskine (Freiherr von Erskine) [Bavaria], an Officer in the Bavarian Army, b. 12 Feb. 1854.

2c. Baroness Hermine Maria Erskine.

6b. Hon. *Frances Erskine*, b. 1801; d. (? s.p.) 7 *June* 1876; m. *Nov.* 1824, *Gabriel Shawe*, d. 11 *Feb.* 1851.

7b. Hon. *Mary Erskine*, b. 28 *Feb.* 1806; d. 15 *Mar.* 1874; m. 16 *June* 1832, *Herrman, Count of Baumgarten (Graf von Baumgarten) [Bavaria]*, d. 11 *Jan.* 1846.

8b. Hon. *Sevilla Erskine*, d. 12 *Mar.* 1835; m. *as 1st wife*, 23 *Dec.* 1830, *Sir Henry Francis Howard, G.C.B.* [*D. of Norfolk Coll.* (see Exeter Volume, p. 559)], d. 28 *Jan.* 1898; *and had issue* 1c.

1c. Adela Howard, a Benedictine nun.

9b. Hon. *Steuarta Erskine*, b. *Oct.* 1810; d. at Genoa 17 *Sept.* 1863; m. 6 *Oct.* 1828, *Yeats Brown of Stuppington, co. Kent, H.B.M.'s Consul at Genoa*, d. *before* 1863.

10b. Hon. *Elizabeth Erskine*, b. *Ap.* 1812; d. 19 *July* 1886; m. 1 *Ap.* 1832, *Sir St. Vincent Keene Hawkins-Whitshed of Killincarrick, 2nd Bt.* [*U.K.* 1834], d. 1870; *and had issue* 1c *to* 3c.

1c. *Sir St. Vincent Bentinck Hawkins-Whitshed, 3rd and last Bt.* [*U.K.*], b. 12 *Feb.* 1837; d. 9 *Mar.* 1871; m. 8 *Dec.* 1858, *Anne Alice, da. of Rev. the Hon. John Gustavus Handcock* [*B. Castlemaine* [*I.*] *Coll.*] [*who re-m. 2ndly*, 17 *Dec.* 1885, *James Percival Hughes and*] d. 1871; *and had issue* 1d.

1d. Elizabeth Alice Frances Hawkins-Whitshed, *m.* 1st, June 1879, Col. Frederick Augustus Burnaby, *d.* Feb. 1885; 2ndly, Mar. 1886, John Frederick Main, *d.* Ap. 1892; 3rdly, June 1900, Francis Bernard Aubrey Le Blond of Roughetts, Hildenborough, co. Kent (*Killincarrick House, Greystones, co. Wicklow*); and has issue 1e.

1e. Harry Arthur Gustavus St. Vincent Burnaby of Killincarrick (*Carlton*), b. May 1880.

2c. *Elizabeth Sophia Hawkins-Whitshed*, d. 4 *Jan.* 1858; m. *as 1st wife*, 18 *Feb.* 1857, *Lieut.-Gen. Arthur Cavendish-Bentinck* [*D. of Portland* [*E.*] *Coll.*], d. 11 *Dec.* 1877; *and had issue* 1d.

1d. William John Arthur Charles (Cavendish-Bentinck), 6th Duke [G.B.] and 7th Earl [E.] of Portland, 2nd Baron Bolsover [U.K.], &c., K.G., P.C., G.C.V.O., &c. &c., Master of the Horse to H.M. the King 1886–1892 and 1895–1905 (*Welbeck Abbey, Worksop; Fullarton House, Troon, co. Ayr; 3 Grosvenor Square, W., &c. &c.*), b. 28 Dec. 1857; *m.* 11 June 1889, Winifred, a Lady of Grace of St. John of Jerusalem, da. of Thomas Yorke Dallas-Yorke of Walmsgate, Louth; and has issue 1e to 3e.

1e. William Arthur Henry Cavendish-Bentinck, Marquis of Titchfield, b. 16 Mar. 1893.

2e. Lord Francis Morven Dallas Cavendish-Bentinck, b. 27 July 1900.

3e. Lady Victoria Alexandrina Violet Cavendish-Bentinck.

3c. *Renira Hawkins-Whitshed*, d. 30 *Aug.* 1894; m. 18 *Nov.* 1862, *Rear-Adm. Edwin John Pollard of Haynford Hall, R.N., J.P., D.L.*, d. 15 *Sept.* 1909; *and had issue* 1d *to* 6d.

1d. James Hawkins Whitshed Pollard, Major Royal Scots Fusiliers (*Haynford Hall, Norwich*), b. 13 May 1866; *m.* 18 Oct. 1899, Clare Evelyn, da. of G. Hamilton Low, Royal Canadian Rifles; and has issue 1e to 2e.

1e. Hamilton Hawkins Whitshed Pollard, b. 13 Ap. 1903.

2e. Arthur Rodney Erskine Pollard, b. 22 Aug. 1906.

2d. Arthur Erskine St. Vincent Pollard, Capt. Border Regt., b. 30 July 1869.

3d. Renira Elizabeth Pollard.

4d. Lucy Clara Pollard.

5d. Sevilla Florence Pollard.

6d. Grace Emily Pollard.

[Nos. 36405 to 36421.

of The Blood Royal

11b. Hon. Harriet Erskine, b. Ap. 1814; d. 19 Nov. 1855; m. 29 Aug. 1833, Charles Woodmass of Alveston, co. Warwick.

12b. Hon. Jane Plumer Erskine, b. 9 May 1818; d. 30 Mar. 1846; m. as 1st wife, 29 Aug. 1837, James Henry Callander of Craigforth, M.P., d. 31 Jan. 1851; and had issue.

See p. 223, Nos. 36337–36341.

2a. Very Rev. the Hon. Henry David Erskine, Dean of Ripon, b. 1786; d. 27 July 1859; m. 4 May 1813, Lady Harriet [descended from the Lady Anne, sister of Kings Edward IV. and Richard III., &c.], da. of John (Dawson), 1st Earl of Portarlington [I.], d. 16 Dec. 1827; and had issue.

See the Exeter Volume, p. 301, Nos. 15216–15243.

3a. Right Hon. the Hon. Thomas Erskine, one of the Judges of the Court of Common Pleas, b. 12 Mar. 1788; d. 9 Nov. 1864; m. 10 Dec. 1814, Henrietta Eliza, da. of Henry Traill, d. 21 Aug. 1865; and had issue 1b.

1b. Rev. Thomas Erskine, Rector of Alderley, co. Chester, b. 12 Nov. 1828; d. 22 Feb. 1878; m. 8 Ap. 1856, Emmeline Augusta (Cowley Street, Westminster, S.W.), da. of Henry John Adeane of Babraham; and had issue 1c to 5c.

1c. Henry Adeane Erskine, Lieut.-Col. 3rd Northumberland Transport Supply Column, and Agent for Bank of England in Newcastle (Newcastle-on-Tyne), b. 1 Mar. 1857; m. 8 July 1891, Florence Eliza Palmer, da. of the Ven. Frank Robert Chapman, Archdeacon of Sudbury; and has issue 1d to 4d.

1d. Henry David Erskine, b. 17 Oct. 1897.

2d. Margaret Helen Erskine, b. 6 Oct. 1892.

3d. Christian Mary Erskine, b. 7 Mar. 1894.

4d. Griselda Beatrice Erskine, b. 2 Jan. 1900.

2c. Thomas Edward Erskine, H.B.M. Consul at St. Louis (British Consulate, St. Louis, U.S.A.), b. 24 June 1859; m. 17 Nov. 1888, Amy Gertrude, da. of Lieut.-Gen. Robert Bruce; and has issue 1d to 5d.

1d. Thomas Erskine, b. 20 Feb. 1897.

2d. John Steuart Erskine, b. 8 Nov. 1900.

3d. Marjory Rachel Helen Erskine.

4d. Diana Isobel Erskine.

5d. Violet Amy Erskine.

3c. Robert Steuart Erskine (10 Ovington Gardens, S.W.), b. 15 Dec. 1860; m. 7 Mar. 1899, Beatrice Caroline [descended from the Lady Anne, sister of Kings Edward IV. and Richard III. (see Exeter Volume, p. 301), and also from Lady Elizabeth Percy, née Mortimer], da. of Henry Linwood Strong, Bar.-at-Law.

4c. Edward John Erskine, b. 18 Ap. 1864; m. 1888, Gertrude, da. of H. or J. Harding of Sydney, N.S.W.; and has issue 1d to 3d.

1d. Steuart Edward Erskine, b. 1902.

2d. Sybil Gertrude Erskine.

3d. Dona Maud Erskine.

5c. David Erskine, b. 5 Ap. 1873.

4a. Hon. Hampden Erskine, b. 5 Dec. 1821.

5a. Hon. Frances Erskine, d. 25 Mar. 1859; m. 20 Jan. 1802, the Rev. Samuel Holland, D.D., Prebendary and Precentor of Chichester and Rector of Poynings, Hurst Pierpoint, d. 16 Ap. 1857.

6a. Hon. Elizabeth Erskine, d. 2 Aug. 1800; m. 17 Nov. 1798, Sir David Erskine [illegitimate son of the 11th Earl of Buchan].

7a. Hon. Mary Erskine, d. 1864; m. 29 Jan. 1805, Edward Morris, a Master in Chancery, d. 13 Ap. 1815. [Nos. 36422 to 36472.

The Plantagenet Roll

125. Descendants of WILLIAM FRASER of Fraserfield [Lord Saltoun [S.], Coll.] (Table XIV.), b. 28 Sept. 1725 ; d. 31 Oct. 1788 ; m. 5 Jan. 1752, RACHEL, da. of the Rev. Hugh KENNEDY of Rotterdam, d. 3 June 1800 ; and had issue 1a to 4a.

1a. *Alexander Fraser, of Fraserfield, on his elder brother's death, previously H.E.I.C.S.*, b. 8 *Jan.* 1761 ; d. 18 *July* 1807 ; m. 20 *Ap.* 1795, *Mary Christina, da. of George Moir*, d. 12 *Sept.* 1813 ; *and had issue (with another da. who d. unm.) 1b to 3b.*

1b. *Margaret Fraser of Fraserfield*, d. 19 *Aug.* 1839 ; m. 27 *May* 1816, *Henry David Forbes-Mitchell of Balgownie, J.P., D.L.* [*Bt. of Craigievar* [S.] *Coll.* (see p. 232)], d. 24 *July* 1869 ; *and had issue 1c to 5c.*

1c. *Henry Erskine Forbes-Mitchell of Kinmundy, co. Aberdeen, J.P., Lieut.-Col. and Major 21st Hussars*, b. 14 *July* 1821 ; d. 1891 ; m. 12 *Ap.* 1855, *Letitia Angelina, da. of Gen. George St. Patrick Lawrence, K.C.S.I., C.B.*, d. 29 *Oct.* 1857 ; *and had issue 1d to 2d.*

1d. Margaret Isabella Forbes-Mitchell.

2d. Louisa Letitia Forbes-Mitchell, m. 7 Oct. 1879, Capt. Christian Ernest Arp von Düring, *formerly* Prussian Army ; and has issue 1e to 3e.

1e. Arp Henry George Louis Charles John von Düring, b. 1880.

2e. Letitia Charlotte Helen von Düring, } twins.
3e. Isabelle Uda Catherine von Düring, }

2c. *Margaret Moir Forbes-Mitchell*, d. 1 *Nov.* 1904 ; m. 25 *Mar.* 1846, *Alexander Kinloch Forbes, Judge of the High Court, Bombay* (see p. 230), d. *at Poonah* 30 *Aug.* 1865 ; *and had issue 1d to 5d.*

1d. *Rev. John Fraser Forbes, M.A. (Oxon.), Chaplain, Bombay*, b. 17 *June* 1847 ; d. 1887 ; m. 13 *June* 1878, *Edith Palin, da. of Henry Wenden of Barnes, Surrey ; and had issue 1e to 4e.*

1e. Alistair Esme Buchan Forbes, an Engineer, b. 1881.

2e. Agnes Dorothy Mary Forbes.

3e. Emmeline Brita Cahusac Forbes.

4e. Edith Margaret Lyndhurst Forbes.

2d. Henry David Erskine Forbes, *formerly* Assist. Sup. in Revenue Dept., Bombay, b. 19 Ap. 1849 ; m. 1884, Alice Georgina, da. of Henry Ingle.

3d. *Rev. Edward Esme Forbes, Vicar of Roffey, formerly Capt. I.S.C. (Roffey Vicarage, Horsham)*, b. 1 Sept. 1855 ; *m.* 1st, 10 July 1880, Frederica Maude, da. of Brig.-Gen. George Frederick De Berry, d. (–) ; 2ndly, 8 Ap. 1902, Florence Emily Louise, da. of Capt. W. Pemberton Hesketh, 42nd Highlanders.

4d. Margaret Theodora Lawrence Forbes.

5d. Emmeline Maria Elizabeth Forbes, *m.* 1899, Charles Scott Chisholme.

3c. *Rachel Louisa Forbes-Mitchell*, b. *at Balgownie* 5 *Ap.* 1826 ; d. *at Paris* 6 *Dec.* 1896 ; m. *at Balgownie* 29 *Mar.* 1846, *Major-Gen. Francis Gregor Urquhart, C.B.* [*Cadet of Craigston*], b. *at Aberdeen* 28 *Nov.* 1813 ; d. *at Bernay, Eure*, 19 *Sept.* 1889 ; *and had issue (with a da., Margaret Isabella Mary, d. unm.* 1 *Sept.* 1891) 1d.

1d. Emily Henrietta Agnes Urquhart, b. at Cork 28 Sept. 1852 ; *m.* at Paris 24 Nov. 1885, Charles Koenig, sometime Artillery Instructor at the St. Cyr Military School (*Château de St. Aubin de Scellon, par Thiberville, Eure*) ; and has issue (with a da. d. young) 1e.

1e. Paul Francis Louis Joseph George Koenig, now serving with the Artillery at Versailles, b. at Plélan-le-Petit, Côtes du Nord, 12 Sept. 1888.

4c. *Emmeline Forbes-Mitchell*, d. 4 *Ap.* 1881 ; m. 29 *Ap.* 1851, *the Rev. John Gabriel Ryde, M.A. (Oxon.), Incumbent of Trinity Church, Melrose*, d. *there* 7 *Dec.* 1868 ; *and had issue 1d to 9d.*

1d. William Erskine Curteis Ryde, b. 3 May 1855.

2d. Arthur John Ryde, b. 14 Feb. 1857.   [Nos. 36473 to 36489.

228

of The Blood Royal

3d. Rev. Lewis Forbes Ryde, M.A. (Oxon.) (89 *St. Helen's Gardens, North Kensington*), b. 10 Mar. 1859.

4d. Francis Edward Ryde, Major *late* West Indian Regt., b. 15 Nov. 1862.

5d. Herbert George Ryde, b. 16 Aug. 1864.

6d. Cyril Alexander Ryde, b. 21 May 1866.

7d. Henrietta Fraser Ryde.

8d. Caroline Elizabeth Ryde.

9d. Ada Margaret Ryde.

5c. *Georgina Mary Agnew Forbes*, d. 2 *May* 1905; m. 24 *Dec.* 1857, *Robert Spottiswood Farquhar-Spottiswood of Muiresk, co. Aberdeen*, d. 2 *Ap.* 1873; *and had issue* 1d *to* 3d.

1d. Henry Alexander Farquhar-Spottiswood of Muiresk, J.P. (*Muiresk, Turriff, co. Aberdeen*), b. 18 Aug. 1859; *m.* 1 June 1882, Elizabeth Agnes, da. of Sir George Samuel Abercromby, 6th Bt. [S.]; and has issue 1*e* to 2*e*.

1e. Alistair Robert Farquhar-Spottiswood, Lieut. R.N., b. 10 Aug. 1885.

2e. Violet Douglas Farquhar-Spottiswood.

2d. Thomas William Farquhar-Spottiswood, b. 13 May 1871.

3d. Mary Georgina Farquhar-Spottiswood (*Mount St. Ternan, Banchory, Kincardineshire*).

2b. *Rachael Fraser, da. and co-h.*, b. 2 *May* 1798; d. 13 *Feb.* 1867; m. 15 *July* 1828, *William Maxwell*, b. 26 *Aug.* 1791; d. 17 *Nov.* 1869; *and had issue (with* 4 *sons and a da.* d. *unm.*) 1c *to* 2c.

1c. *Wellwood Maxwell*, b. 14 *July* 1830; d. 6 *Jan.* 1909; m. 14 *Ap.* 1864, *Isabella, da. of William Moir of Park, co. Aberdeen*, d. 4 *June* 1898; *and had issue* 1d *to* 6d.

1d. William George Maxwell, Solicitor, b. 7 Mar. 1870; *unm.*

2d. Wellwood James Maxwell, Chartered Accountant (*Holmfield, Aigburth, Liverpool*), b. 31 Mar. 1872; *unm.*

3d. Mary Elizabeth Maxwell, *unm.*

4d. Rachael Maxwell, *unm.*

5d. Isabella Margaret Maxwell, *unm.*

6d. Catherine Louisa Maxwell, *unm.*

2c. Katharine Isabella Maxwell, *unm.*

3b. *Mary Fraser, da. and co-h.*, d. 23 *Feb.* 1873; m. 10 *Feb.* 1825, *William Urquhart of Craigston, co. Aberdeen, J.P., D.L.*, d. *Mar.* 1847; *and had issue* 1c.

1c. *Mary Isabella Urquhart of Craigston*, d. 12 *Dec.* 1873; m. 20 *Aug.* 1846, *William Pollard, afterwards* (R.L. 11/24 *June* 1847) *Pollard-Urquhart of Castle Pollard, co. Westmeath, M.P., J.P., D.L.*, d. 1 *June* 1871; *and had issue* 1d *to* 8d.

1d. Walter William Dutton Pollard-Urquhart of Castle Pollard, J.P., D.L., b. 10 *July* 1847; d.s.p. 29 *Dec.* 1892.

2d. Francis Edward Romulus Pollard-Urquhart of Craigston and Castle Pollard, Lieut.-Col. (ret.) R.A., J.P., D.L., High Sheriff co. Westmeath 1901 (*Castle Pollard, co. Westmeath ; Craigston Castle, Turriff, co. Aberdeen*), b. 8 Sept. 1848; *m.* 28 Nov. 1888, Louisa Henrietta, da. of Garden Duff of Hatton Castle, d. 1 Oct. 1908.

3d. Rev. Arthur de Capel Broke Pollard-Urquhart, b. 1 Ap. 1850.

4d. Michael Bruce Pollard-Urquhart, b. 25 Dec. 1851; d. 29 Ap. 1879; m. *June* 1875, *Florence Adeline, da. of* (—) *Billings ; and had issue* 1e.

1e. Michael Bruce Pollard-Urquhart, Lieut. Scottish Rifles, b. 15 Aug. 1879.

5d. Montagu Alexis Pollard Urquhart, C.E., b. 9 May 1859; *m.* July 1882, Honora Elizabeth, da. of the Rev. L. A. Buckley of Alderford; and has issue 1e to 3e.

1e. William Edward Pollard-Urquhart.

2e. Arthur Lewis Pollard-Urquhart.

The Plantagenet Roll

3e. *Nora Mary Pollard-Urquhart*, d. Aug. 1909; m. !16 *Jan.* 1906, *Arthur Harold Loughborough, R.A.*

6d. Adah Mary Louisa Pollard-Urquhart, *m.* Oct. 1882, Dudley Billings.

7d. Leonora Anna Maria Helen Pollard-Urquhart.

8d. Octavia Harriet Pollard-Urquhart, *m.* July 1888, Charles Humphreys, M.D. (2 *Avenue Crescent, Mill Hill Park, Acton, W.*); and has issue 1e to 2e.

1e. Frances Styles Humphreys, *b.* 15 Jan. 1896.

2e. Mildred Humphreys, *b.* 7 June 1889.

2a. *Henry David Fraser, an Officer in the British Army and a Brig.-Gen. in the Portuguese,* b. 27 *Ap.* 1762; d. 4 Aug. 1810; m. 6 *Oct.* 1800, *Mary Christina, da. of John Forbes of Skellater, G.C.B.A., G.C.C.S., Field-Marshal and Gov. of Rio de Janeiro, &c.,* d. *at Lisbon ; and had issue* (with 2 sons and a da. who d.s.p.) 1b to 2b.

1b. *Sophia Maria Jane Fraser,* d. (-); m. 1827, *Count Henry Francis de Bombelles,* d. 1850; *and had issue.*

2b. *Margaret Alexia Fraser,* d. (-); m. *the Marquis of Gargallo.*

3a. *Erskine Fraser of Woodhill, co. Aberdeen, Col. 109th Regt.,* b. 23 *June* 1766; d. 21 *Jan.* 1804; m. 3 *May* 1794, *Elizabeth, da. of Thomas Forbes of Ballogie,* d. 18 *Aug.* 1813; *and had issue* 1b.

1b. *William Fraser of Woodhill, Lieut.-Col. in the Army,* b. 21 Nov. 1796; d. 13 *July* 1872; m. 20 Aug. 1833, *Mary Elizabeth, da. of Thomas Starkie Shuttleworth of Ashton, co. Lanc.; and had issue* 1c.

1c. Elizabeth Fraser.

4a. *Katherine Anne Fraser,* d. 27 Dec. 1836; m. 27 Mar. 1777, *Duncan Forbes, afterwards* (1772) *Forbes-Mitchell of Thainstone, co. Aberdeen* [3rd *son of Sir Arthur Forbes of Craigievar, 4th Bt.* [S. 1629]], b. 26 *Mar.* 1757; d. 6 *Oct.* 1796; *and had issue* (with 3 elder sons, *&c.,* who d.s.p.) 1b to 3b.

1b. *John Forbes-Mitchell of Thainstone,* b. 21 *Mar.* 1786; d. *in France* 9 *July* 1822; m. 8 Feb. 1809, *Ann, da. of Lieut.-Col. George Powell, H.E.I.C. Art.,* d. Sept. 1861; *and had issue* 1c *to* 3c.

1c. *Duncan Forbes-Mitchell of Thainstone, J.P., D.L.,* b. 30 Oct. 1812; d. 13 Aug. 1870; m. 18 Feb. 1824, *Maria, da. of Lieut.-Col. Robert Anthony Bromley, H.E.I.C.S.,* d. 1892; *and had issue* 1d *to* 3d.

1d. *John Forbes-Mitchell of Thainstone, J.P., D.L., F.S.A.,* b. 25 *June* 1843; d.s.p. 25 *Ap.* 1882; m. 28 *July* 1870, *Jane Maria* (*Thainstone, Kintore ; Queen's Cross, Aberdeen*), *da. of Thomas James Rawson of Farrowville, co. Carlow.*

2d. Maria Forbes-Mitchell, *m.* 20 July 1878, John Alexander Stuart, *late* of the Admiralty and of the Office of the Secretary of State for War.

3d. Elizabeth Erskine Forbes-Mitchell (*Dacca House, Colchester*), *m.* 20 Sept. 1870, Lieut.-Col. John Nathaniel Gower, 78th Regt., *d.* Sept. 1905 ; and has issue 1e to 3e.

1e. John Forbes Gower, *b.* 1877.

2e. Hugh Duncan Gower, *b.* 1882.

3e. Alice Lilian Gower.

2c. *John George Forbes, Major H.E.I.C.S.,* b. 4 *Mar.* 1814; d. 29 *Ap.* 1860; m. 17 *June* 1837, *Eliza Maria, da. of John Leckie,* d. 10 *July* 1857; *and had issue* 1d.

1d. Charles Pulteney Forbes, Major-Gen., *formerly* Col. and Lieut.-Col. Comdg. 2nd Batt. Leinster Regt. (*Fairlawn, Bath Road, Reading*), *b.* 29 Nov. 1840; *m.* 13 Jan. 1864, Hannah, da. of John Sims.

3c. *Alexander Kinloch Forbes, Judge of the High Court of Bombay,* b. 7 *July* 1821; d. *at Poonah* 31 *Aug.* 1865; m. 25 *Mar.* 1846, *Margaret Moir, da. of Henry David Forbes-Mitchell of Balgownie,* d. 1 Nov. 1904; *and had issue.*

See p. 228, Nos. 36478–36485. [Nos. 36515 to 36534.

# of The Blood Royal

2b. Alexander Forbes, Brazilian Merchant, b. 13 Oct. 1788; d. 3 Feb. 1843; m. 11 Sept. 1811, Janet, da. of Sir William Forbes of Craigievar, 5th Bt. [S.], d. 15 Feb. 1846; and had issue 1c to 4c.

1c. Duncan Forbes of Ernan Lodge, co. Aberdeen, b. 7 Nov. 1815; d. 1894; m. 14 Ap. 1852, Sarah, da. of Sir John Forbes of Craigievar, 7th Bt. [S.], d. 6 Oct. 1891; and had issue 1d to 5d.

1d. John Forbes, b. 24 Mar. 1855.

2d. Alexander Mansfield Forbes, b. 28 Ap. 1858; m. 1887, Mary Antoinette, da. of Alexander Forbes of Galliris, co. Aberdeen; and has issue 1e to 3e.

1e. Duncan Alexander Forbes, b. 1888.

2e. Mansfield Duval Forbes, b. 1889.

3e. Mhari Margaret Forbes.

3d. William Henry Forbes, b. 26 Aug. 1860.

4d. Charlotte Jessie Forbes.

5d. Katherine Elizabeth Forbes.

2c. William Forbes, Major-Gen. H.E.I.C.S., b. 29 May 1820; d. 6 May 1877; m. 1st, Sophia Adams, da. of (—) Fell, d. (–); 2ndly, Frances Helen, da. of R. S. M. Spry, d. 1896; and had issue 1d to 5d.

1d.[1] John Forbes, b. at Agra 1853; d. (?s.p.).

2d.[2] William Alexander Forbes, formerly Capt. 4th Batt. Devonshire Regt., b. 1861; m. 1902, Katherina Fanny, da. of the Rev. E. Royds of Brereton.

3d.[2] Duncan James Forbes, b. 1864.

4d.[2] Henrietta Jessie Forbes.

5d.[2] Rachel Helen Forbes.

3c. Sarah Forbes, d. 4 Ap. 1851; m. 20 Feb. 1844, Alexander Gordon of Newton, co. Aberdeen, d. 8 Aug. 1868; and had issue 1d to 4d.

1d. Alexander Morison Gordon, b. 14 July 1846; m. 26 July 1870, Margaret, da. of Capt. James Crawford, Bombay Engineers; and has issue 1e.

1e. Margaret Helena Gordon.

2d. Duncan Forbes Gordon, Capt. 92nd Gordon Highlanders, b. 30 May 1849.

3d. Janet Forbes Gordon, m. 10 June 1869, Frederick de Lemare Morison, Col. 1st Royal Scots; and has issue 1e to 2e.

1e. Alexander Edward Forbes Morison.

2e. Isabel Gordon Morison.

4d. Jane Margaret Gordon.

4c. Katharine Anne Forbes, d. 3 Aug. 1903; m. 1 Dec. 1840, John Angus, J.P., Advocate, Town Clerk of Aberdeen and Sheriff-Substitute for that co., d. 6 Nov. 1878; and had issue 1d to 5d.

1d. Alexander Forbes Angus, J.P. (Sydney, N.S.W.; Junior Carlton), b. 25 Ap. 1844; m. 14 Mar. 1883, Miriam Adelaide, da. of the Hon. Samuel Aaron Joseph of Sydney, M.L.A., s.p.s.

2d. John Angus, Lieut.-Col. Army Pay Dept., formerly York and Lancaster Regt. (Grosvenor Club), b. 9 Nov. 1845; m. 5 Sept. 1870, Edith Mary, da. of Edward Ronald Douglas, C.I.E., Dep. Director-Gen. Post Office of India; and has issue 1e.

1e. Ella Ernan Forbes Douglas Angus.

3d. William James Angus, formerly Lieutenant Highland L.I. Militia (United Empire), b. 11 Jan. 1856.

4d. Margaret Forbes Angus, m. as 2nd wife, 17 July 1873, William John Renny of Danevale Park, Kirkcudbright, D.L., d. 25 Jan. 1879; and had issue 1e to 3e. [Nos. 36535 to 36558.

The Plantagenet Roll

1e. Percy Cyril Forbes Napier Renny (*Bath Club*), b. 1 Sept. 1875.
2e. Angus Gordon Lyle Renny, } b. (twins) 9 July 1876.
3e. Stanley Alexander Renny,

5d. Janet Christian Angus, *m.* 3 Aug. 1880, James Alexander Beattie, C.E. (*Dalbeattie, Murtle, co. Aberdeen ; Scottish Conservative*); and has issue 1e to 2e.
1e. Rev. Walter Roland Jardine Beattie, b. 31 Dec. 1883.
2e. Lilias Berkeley Beattie.

3b. *Henry David Forbes-Mitchell of Balgownie, J.P., D.L.*, b. 12 Nov. 1790; d. 24 July 1869; m. 27 May 1816, *Margaret, da. and co-h. of Alexander Fraser of Fraserfield*, d. 19 Aug. 1839; *and had issue.*
See p. 228, Nos. 36473–36501. [Nos. 36559 to 36593.

126. Descendants of Lady FRANCES ERSKINE (Table XIV.), *b.* 1700; *d.* 1774; *m.* 11 July 1726, Col. JAMES GARDINER of Bankton, *d.* (being killed at the battle of Prestonpans), 22 Sept. 1745; and had issue (with 9 others *d.* young) 1*a* to 4*a*.

1a. *David Gardiner, Cornet in Sir John Cope's Dragoons July 1747*, b. 1727.
2a. *James Gardiner, an Officer in the Army*, b. 1728.
3a. *Frances Gardiner*, d. 7 Dec. 1811; m. 1750, *Sir William Baird of Saughton, 5th Bt.* [S.], *Capt. R.N.*, d. 17 Aug. 1771; *and had (with possibly other) issue* 1b.
1b. *Sir James Gardiner Baird, 6th Bt.* [S.], *Lieut.-Col. 28th Light Dragoons*, d. 23 June 1836; m. 1st, 1781, *Henrietta, da. of Wynne Johnston of Hilltown ; and had issue* 1c to 5c.
1c. *William Baird, Capt. in the Army,* d.v.p.; m. 28 Mar. 1809, *Lucy, da. of Thomas Dickson of Prospect House, co. Hants ; and had issue* 1d to 6d.
1d. *Sir James Gardiner Baird, 7th Bt.* [S.], *D.L., Capt. 10th Hussars*, b. 20 Aug. 1813; d. 6 Jan. 1896; m. 13 Mar. 1845, *Henrietta Mary, da. of John Wauchope of Edmonstone, co. Edin.* [Bt. Coll. (see p. 233)], d. 3 Nov. 1896; *and had issue* 1e.
1e. Sir William James Gardiner Baird of Saughton, 8th Bt. [S.], J.P., *late Lieut.-Col. and Hon. Col. Lothians and Berwickshire Imp. Yeo., formerly 7th Hussars* (*The Knoll, North Berwick ; Carlton ; New* (*Edinburgh*)), b. 23 Feb. 1854; *m.* 3 Ap. 1879, the Hon. Arabella Rose, da. of William Wallace (Hozier), 1st Baron Newlands [U.K.]; and has issue 1f to 3f.
1f. James Hozier Gardiner Baird, Capt. 4th Batt. Argyll and Sutherland Highlanders, b. 25 Nov. 1883.
2f. William Frank Gardiner Baird, *formerly* Lieut. 7th Dragoon Guards, &c., b. 18 Ap. 1885.
3f. Frances Harriet Baird.

2d. *David Baird*, b. 28 *Ap.* 1815; d. (? *unm.* s.p.).
3d. *Mackenzie William Baird*, b. 8 Dec. 1816 (? s.p.).
4d. *Henrietta Jemima Baird*, b. 14 *Jan.* 1810; d. 7 Feb. 1889; m. 4 *Feb.* 1836, *John Hoskins of South Perrot, co. Som.*
5d. *Mary Alicia Baird*, b. 18 *Ap.* 1811; d. (? *unm.*).
6d. *Frances Baird*, b. 26 *Ap.* 1819; d. (? *unm.*).

2c. *Richard Frederick Baird.*
3c. *Margaret Mary Baird.*
4c. *Henrietta Warrander Cecilia Baird*, d. 8 Nov. 1826; m. Sept. 1815, *John Wauchope of Edmonstone*, d. 27 June 1837; *and had issue* 1d to 2d.

[Nos. 36594 to 36597.

of The Blood Royal

1*d.* Sir John Wauchope, *afterwards* (1862) *Don-Wauchope*, 8*th Bt.* [*S.*] 1667, *Chairman of the Board of Education for Scotland, &c.,* b. 10 *July* 1816; d. 12 *Dec.* 1893; m. 26 *Ap.* 1853, *Bethia Hamilton, da. of Andrew Buchanan of Greenfield, co. Lanark; and had issue* 1*e to* 6*e.*

1*e.* Sir John Douglas Don-Wauchope, 9th Bt. [S.] (*Edmonstone, Gilmerton, Midlothian; Newton House, Millerhill, Dalkeith*), b. 15 *Sept.* 1859.

2*e.* Andrew Ramsay Don-Wauchope (5 *Neville Street, Onslow Square, S.W.*), *b.* 29 Ap. 1861; *m.* 28 Oct. 1903, Maizie, da. of Major-Gen. Sir William Salmond, K.C.B.

3*e.* Patrick Hamilton Don-Wauchope, W.S. (13 *Saxe-Coburg Place, Edinburgh; New Club*), *b.* 1 May 1863; *m.* 10 June 1897, Georgiana Renira, da. of George Fitzjohn; and has issue 1*f.*

1*f.* Patrick George Don-Wauchope, *b.* 7 May 1898.

4*e.* Bethia Hamilton Don-Wauchope.

5*e.* Henrietta Cecilia Don-Wauchope, *m.* 29 Nov. 1882, Major Ernest Digby Mansel, *formerly* Highland L.I. [Bt. of Muddlescombe [E. 1621] Coll.] (*Naval and Military*).

6*e.* Clotilde Georgina Don-Wauchope (16 *Cheyne Court, Chelsea*), *m.* 29 Jan. 1886, the Hon. Arthur Henry Browne [4th son of John Cavendish, 3rd Lord Kilmaine [I.], and a descendant of Lady Anne, sister of King Edward IV. (see Exeter Volume, p. 432), *d.* 3 May 1908; and has issue 1*f* to 3*f.*

1*f.* Clotilde Mary Hamilton Browne.
2*f.* Clementina Bethia Evelyn Browne.
3*f.* Gertrude Cicely Juliet Browne.

2*d. Henrietta Mary Wauchope,* d. 3 Nov. 1896; m. 13 *Mar.* 1845, *Sir James Gardiner Baird of Saughton, 7th Bt.* [*S.*], d. 3 Nov. 1896; *and had issue.* See p. 232, Nos. 36594–36597.

5*c. Alicia Sophia Baird,* d. (?*unm.*).

4*a. Richenora Gardiner,* m. *Lawrence Inglis; and had issue.*[1]

[Nos. 36598 to 36611.

127. Descendants of ALATHEA FAIRFAX (Table XIV.), *d.* (–) ; *m.* RALPH PIGOTT of Whitton; and had issue[2] 1*a.*

1*a. Nathaniel Pigott,* d. 1804; m. *Anna Mathurina, da. of* (—) *de Beriol, Grand Baillie of the Lordship of Aigemont Tavinque in the Austrian Netherlands,* d. 1792; *and had issue* (*with others*) 1*b.*

1*b. Charles Gregory Pigott, afterwards* (*Act Parl.* 1793) *Fairfax of Gilling Castle, co. York, to which estate he suc. on the death of his cousin, the Hon. Anne Fairfax,* 8 *May* 1793; *second son,* b. *c.* 1768; d. 29 *Dec.* 1845; m. 9 *June* 1794, *Mary, da. of Henry Goodricke* [*eldest son and h.-app. of Sir John Goodricke, 5th Bt.* [*E.* 1641]], d. 28 *Jan.* 1845; *and had issue* 1*c* to 4*c.*

1*c. Charles Gregory Fairfax of Gilling,* bapt. 14 *June* 1796; d.s.p. 21 *Ap.* 1871.

2*c. Mary Ann Fairfax,* b. 16 *Ap.* 1795; d. (? *unm.*).

3*c. Harriet Fairfax,* bapt. 15 *Dec.* 1804; d.s.p.; m. 22 *Feb.* 1838, *Francis Cholmley of Bransby Hall, co. York,* d.s.p. 3 *Aug.* 1855.

4*c. Lavinia Fairfax,* bapt. 24 *Oct.* 1802; d. (–); m. *the Rev. James Alexander Barnes, Rector of Gilling, living* 1874.

---

[1] Paul's "Scots Peerage," ii. 276.
[2] Foster's "Yorkshire Pedigrees"; Burke's "Commoners," ii. 113.

The Plantagenet Roll

128. Descendants, if any surviving, of Sir ROBERT LATON of East Laton and Sexhow, co. Yorks, who granted a lease of East Laton for 99 years to James Brook, 4 Sept. 1669, and afterwards sold the said place to his brother Bryan, 21 Sept. 1671 [1] (Table XV.), d. (–); m. ANNE, da. of (———); and had issue (with 3 elder sons, Thomas, Alexander, and John, who all d.s.p.) 1a to 5a.

   1a. *Robert Laton or Layton of Norwich, who was living* 31 *Jan.* 1703, *when he filed a Bill in Chancery claiming the Manor of East Laton against Sir James Brook, Bt.*
   2a. *Charles Laton.*
   3a. *Elizabeth Laton, living* 1691; m. *Anthony Danby of Leek, co. York.*
   4a. *Mary Laton, living* 1691; m. *Thomas Brasse of Flasse, co. Durham.*
   5a. *Catherine Laton, living a widow* 1691; m. (—) *Leeke.*

129. Descendants, if any, of BRYAN LATON of East Laton, co. York, which Manor he bought from his elder brother Robert for £3000, 21 Sept. 1671, and afterwards, 28 Mar. 1678, sold to Sir James Brook, Bt. (Table XV.), d. (–); m. and had issue 1a.

   1a. *Charles Laton, son and h., living* 31 *Jan.* 1703, *when he was one of the defendants in a suit in Chancery on the complaint of his cousin Robert Laton.*

130. Descendants of Sir WILLIAM FOULIS of Ingleby, co. York, 5th Bt. [E.] (Table XV.), b. c. 1680; bur. 11 Dec. 1756; m. 1721, MILDRED, da. of Henry (DAWNAY), 2nd Viscount Downe [I.], bur. 6 Feb. 1780; and had issue 1a.

   1a. *Sir William Foulis, 6th Bt.* [E.], b. 1729; bur. 17 *June* 1780; m. 1758, *Hannah, da. and h. of John Robinson of Buckton, co. York,* d. (a. *June*) 1812; *and had issue* 1b *to* 2b.
   1b. *Sir William Foulis, 7th Bt.* [E.], bapt. 30 *Ap.* 1759; d. 5 *Sept.* 1802; m. 1789, *Mary Anne* [also descended from Edward III. through Mortimer-Percy, (see p. 397)], *da. of Edmund Turnor of Panton House, co. Linc.,* d. 18 *Oct.* 1831; *and had issue* 1c *to* 5c.
   1c. *Sir William Foulis, 8th Bt.* [E.], bapt. 29 *May* 1790; d. 7 *Nov.* 1845; m. 11 *May* 1825, *Mary Jane, da. of Gen. Sir Charles Ross, 6th Bt.* [S.] [by his wife, Lady Mary, née FitzGerald], d. 11 *June* 1852; *and had issue* 1d.
   1d. *Mary Foulis, da. and h.,* d. 14 *June* 1891; m. *as* 1*st wife*, 23 *Ap.* 1850, *Philip* (Sidney), 2*nd Baron de L'Isle and Dudley* [U.K.] [senior representative and heir of line of the Lady Anne Plantagenet, sister of Kings Edward IV. and Richard III. (see Exeter Volume, p. 77)], d. 17 *Feb.* 1898; *and had issue* 1e *to* 3e.
   1e. *Philip* (Sidney), 3*rd Baron de L'Isle and Dudley* [U.K.] [present senior representative and heir of line of the Lady Anne Plantagenet, &c.] (*Penhurst Place, Tonbridge, Kent; Ingleby Manor, Middlesbrough; Carlton*), b. 14 *May* 1853; m. 12 *July* 1902, *the Hon. Elizabeth Maria,* widow *of William Harvey Astell, J.P., D.L., da. of Standish Prendergast* (Vereker), 4*th Viscount Gort* [I.].

[No. 36612.]

---

[1] Plantagenet Harrison's "History of York," p. 530.

# of The Blood Royal

2e. Hon. Algernon Sidney, Lieut.-Col. and Brevet-Col. R.A. (*Marlborough*), b. 11 June 1854.

3e. Hon. William Sidney, Bar. Inner Temple (107 *Sloane Street, S.W.*), b. 19 Aug. 1859; m. 5 Dec. 1905, Winifred, da. of Roland Yorke Bevan; and has issue 1f to 2f.

    1f. William Philip Sidney, b. 23 May 1909.

    2f. Mary Olivia Sidney, b. 20 Nov. 1906.

2c. Rev. Sir Henry Foulis of Ingleby, 8th and last[1] Bt. [E.], bapt. 15 *Sept.* 1800; d.s.p. 7 Oct. 1876.

3c. Hannah Foulis, d. 1869; m. 28 *Nov.* 1815, *the Rev. Danson Richardson Roundell, sometime* (1806-51) *Currer, and finally* (*R.L.* 21 Oct. 1851) *Roundell of Gledstone, J.P., D.L.*, b. 3 Ap. 1784; d. 10 *Mar.* 1873; *and had issue* 1d to 3d.

    1d. William Roundell of Gledstone, High Sheriff co. York 1881, b. 17 July 1817; d. 21 Oct. 1881; m. 20 Ap. 1864, *Harriet Jane, da. of Francis Benyon Hackett of Moor Hall*, d. 30 Sept. 1895; *and had issue* 1e.

    1e. Richard Foulis Roundell of Gledstone, J.P., Capt. 5th Batt. Northumberland Fusiliers (*Gledstone, Skipton-in-Craven*), b. 4 Nov. 1872; m. 29 Nov. 1898, Beatrice Maud, da. of Sir Matthew Amcotts Wilson of Eshton Hall, 3rd Bt. [U.K.], J.P.; and has issue 1f to 3f.

        1f. Richard Henry Selborne Roundell, b. 27 Sept. 1901.

        2f. Diana Georgina Amcotts Roundell, b. 2 Jan. 1900.

        3f. Nancy Lea Roundell, b. 25 Dec. 1902.

    2d. Charles Savile Roundell, J.P., D.L., M.P. 1880-95, *Private Sec. to Earl Spencer while Lord-Lieut. of Ireland*, b. 19 July 1827; d. 3 Mar. 1906; m. 10 *May* 1873, *Julia Anne Elizabeth* [*descended from King Henry VII.* (see Tudor Roll, p. 208)]; *and had issue* 1e.

        1e. Christopher Foulis Roundell (*Dorfold Hall, Cheshire*), b. 11 July 1876.

    3d. Mary Anne Roundell, d. 20 *June* 1898; m. *as 2nd wife*, 11 Jan. 1855, *Capt. John Hotham of Scraftwood, co. Notts* [Bt. *Coll.*], d. 1881; *and had issue* 1e to 3e.

        1e. George Hotham, b. 4 Ap. 1856.

        2e. Mary Hotham, *unm.*

        3e. Lucy Hotham, *unm.*

4c. Mary Ann Foulis, d. 1 Feb. 1860; m. 19 *Jan.* 1822, *Sir Tatton Sykes of Sledmere*, 4th Bt. [G.B.] [*descended from King Henry VII.*], d. 21 Mar. 1863; *and had issue.*

See the Tudor Roll, pp. 389-390, Nos. 29382-29406.

5c. Sophia Frances Foulis, d. (–); m. 21 *Aug.* 1873, *Philip D. Pauncefort Duncombe of Great Brickhill, co. Bucks.*

2b. John Robinson Foulis of Buckton, j.u. d. 29 Ap. 1826; m. 16 Nov. 1795, *Decima Hester Beatrix* [*descended from King Henry VII.* (see Tudor Roll, p. 391)]. da. of Sir Christopher Sykes, 2nd Bt. [G.B.], b. 15 Dec. 1775; d. Ap. 1843; *and had issue* (*with others who* d.s.p.) 1c to 2c.

    1c. Elizabeth Foulis, da. and co-h., d. (–); m. *Vice-Adm. George Edward Watts, C.B.*, d. 2 Jan. 1860; *and had issue.*[2]

    2c. Lucy Dorothea Foulis, d. 1886; m. 26 Ap. 1827, *the Rev. Charles Wasteneys Eyre of Rampton, co. Notts*, d. 30 Oct. 1862; *and had issue.*

See the Exeter Volume, pp. 612-613, Nos. 52175-52180.

[Nos. 36613 to 36655.

---

[1] See G. E. C.'s "Complete Baronetage," i. 136.

[2] Foster's "Yorkshire Pedigrees."

The Plantagenet Roll

131. Descendants of WILLIAM CHALONER of Guisboro', co. York (Table XV.), *bur.* (? at St. Maurice's, York) 14 July 1756 ; *m.* MARY, da. of James FINNY of Finnyham, co. Stafford ; and had issue 1a to 4a.

1a. *William Chaloner of Guisboro', J.P., D.L.,* b. 14 *Aug.* 1745; d. 8 *May* 1793; m. 8 *Aug.* 1771, *Emma, sister of Adm. Sir Eliab Harvey, G.C.B., da. of William Harvey of Chigwell ; and had issue* 1b *to* 3b.

1b. *Robert Chaloner of Guisboro', J.P., D.L., M.P., and Lord Mayor of York* 1817, b. 23 *Sept.* 1776 ; d. 7 *Oct.* 1842 ; m. 24 *Jan.* 1805, *the Hon. Frances Laura [descended from the Lady Anne of Exeter, sister of King Edward IV., &c.], da. of Thomas (Dundas), 1st Baron Dundas [G.B.],* d. 27 *Nov.* 1843 ; *and had issue.*
See the Exeter Volume, p. 260, Nos. 9779-9798.

2b. *Charlotte Chaloner,* b. *(twin)* 12 *Ap.* 1787 ; d. (-) ; m. *Thomas Barton Bowen, Bar.-at-Law, and one of the Commissioners of the Court of Insolvency.*

3b. *Williamina Chaloner,* b. *(posthumous)* 6 *Nov.* 1793 ; d. (-) ; m. *Col. Alexander Wynch [2nd son of Alexander Wynch, Governor of Madras* 2 *Feb.* 1773-*Dec.* 1775 (see Supp.)], b. *at Cuddalore, Madras,* 10 *Aug.* 1751 ; d. (-) ; *and had issue* (2 *das., of whom one was* b. *at Tunbridge Wells,* 3 *Mar.* 1818).

2a. *Edward James Chaloner of Lincoln, Surgeon,* d. (-) ; m. *Theophania, da. of* (—) *Burridge of Lincoln ; and had issue* 1b *to* 3b.

1b. *Edward Chaloner, Capt. in the Army,* d. (? s.p.) *of wounds received at the storming of Morne Fortune, St. Lucia, bur. at St. Martin's, York,* 4 *July* 1807 ; m. (—).[1]

2b. *Theophania Chaloner,* b. 23 *Jan.* 1779 ; d. 9 *June* 1857 ; m. 12 *Aug.* 1798, *Thomas Lodington Fairfax of Steeton and Newton Kyme, co. York,* d. 1 *July* 1840 ; *and had issue.*
See the Exeter Volume, pp. 535-536, Nos. 48976-49015.

3b. *Louisa Chaloner,* d. (-) ; m. *the Rev. Edmund Edmonson, Vicar of Cokingham.*

3a. *Anne Chaloner,* d. 22 *Feb.* 1805 ; m. 12 *May* 1761, *Edward (Lascelles), 1st Baron Harewood [G.B.],* so *cr.* 16 *June* 1796, *and Earl of Harewood [U.K.],* so *cr.* 7 *Sept.* 1812, d. 3 *Ap.* 1820 ; *and had issue* 1b *to* 3b.

1b. *Henry (Lascelles), 2nd Earl of Harewood [U.K.], &c.,* b. 25 *Dec.* 1767 ; d. 24 *Nov.* 1841 ; m. 3 *Sept.* 1794, *Henrietta [descended from the Lady Isabel Plantagenet], da. of Lieut.-Gen. Sir John Sebright,* 6*th Bt.* [E.], d. 15 *Feb.* 1840 ; *and had issue.*
See the Essex Volume, p. 324, Nos. 33493-33589.

2b. *Lady Frances Lascelles,* b. 11 *June* 1762 ; d. 31 *Mar.* 1817 ; m. 4 *Oct.* 1784, *the Hon. John Douglas,* b. 1 *July* 1756 ; d. 1 *May* 1818; *and had issue* 1c *to* 7c.

1c. *George Sholto (Douglas), 19th Earl of Morton* [S.], b. 23 *Dec.* 1789 ; d. 31 *Mar.* 1858 ; m. 3 *July* 1817, *Frances Theodora [descended from the Lady Anne, sister to King Edward IV., &c.], da. of the Right Hon. Sir George Henry Rose, G.C.H., P.C., M.P.,* d. 12 *July* 1879 ; *and had issue.*
See the Exeter Volume, pp. 645-646, Nos. 55598-55673.

2c. *Rev. the Hon. Charles Douglas of Earlsgift, co. Tyrone, who had a Royal Warrant of Precedency as son of an Earl* 23 *Aug.* 1835, b. 10 *Mar.* 1796 ; d. 28 *Jan.* 1857 ; m. 1st, 2 *Mar.* 1816, *Lady Isabella, da. of Arthur (Gore), 2nd Earl of Arran* [I.], d. 30 *Nov.* 1838 ; 2*ndly,* 28 *Dec.* 1852, *Agnes Julia, da. of Capt. John S. Rich of Woodlands, Castle Connell [who re-m.* 2*ndly, Oct.* 1862, *Lieut.-Col. Wills Croft Gason*] ; *and had issue* 1d *to* 7d.

1d. *William Grant Douglas, Comm. R.N.,* b. 25 *Feb.* 1824 ; d. 16 *Dec.* 1898 ; m. 1st, 16 *Dec.* 1851, *Elizabeth, da. of William Inglis,* d. *May* 1865 ; 2*ndly,* 6 *June* [Nos. 36656 to 36888.

---
[1] Foster's " Yorkshire Pedigrees."

# of The Blood Royal

1867, *Elizabeth Frances* (37 *South Parade, Southsea*), *da. of Thomas Agmondesham Vesey of Caledon, co. Tyrone ; and had issue 1e to 6e.*

1e. Sholto Osborne Gordon Douglas, B.A. (Oxon.), *b.* 14 Sept. 1873.

2e.[1] Bessie Henrietta Douglas, *m.* 1st, 1 Feb. 1875, Claud William Leslie Ogilby of Altnachree Castle, co. Tyrone (see below), *d.* 1894 ; 2ndly, 1895, Hugo Bartels.

3e.[1] Ada Charlotte Douglas, *m.* 1st, 1886, Harris St. John Dick, *d.* 1886 ; 2ndly, 1892, Frederick Gray Maturin.

4e.[1] Mary Louisa Douglas, *m.* 17 Jan. 1877, Colin Bent Phillip.

5e.[1] Margaret Caroline Douglas, *m.* as 2nd wife, 1883, the Rev. Edward Douglas Prothero (see below).

6e.[2] Maude Isabel Gore Douglas, *m.* 23 Ap. 1895, Capt. Cuthbert Edward Hunter, R.N.

2d. *Gordon James Douglas of Poppleton House, York,* b. 27 *Aug.* 1835 ; d. 1904; m. 12 *Aug.* 1858, *Louisa, da. of James Turbett of Owenstoun, co. Dublin ; and had issue* 1e.

1e. Isabella Sophia Frances Douglas, *m.* 20 Sept. 1883, Belford Randolph Wilson, Capt. 4th Royal Irish Dragoons, *d.* 1897.

3d. *Augusta Frederica Douglas,* b. 22 *Nov.* 1819 ; d. (–) ; m. 15 *Dec.* 1842, *Henry Poore Cox, d.* 8 *May* 1876 ; *and had issue* 1e *to* 6e.

1e. *William Douglas Cox,* b. 1 *June* 1844 ; d. 1905; m. 2 *Ap.* 1865, *Mary Anne Amelia Catherine (Tokio, Japan), da. of the Rev. Edward Pole* [*Bt.* (*E.* 1628) *Coll.*] ; *and had issue* 1f *to* 2f.

1f. Edward Pole Cox, *b.* 28 Jan. 1866.

2f. Henry Augustus Cox, *b.* 13 Nov. 1876.

2e. Henry Poore Cox, *b.* 10 Dec. 1846 ; *m.* 4 Dec. 1875, Augusta Anne, da. of Surgeon-Major William Walter Weld ; and has issue 1f.

1f. Alice Frederica Cox, *b.* 21 Nov. 1878.

3e. Charles Louis Hamilton Cox, *b.* 27 Nov. 1850.

4e. George Nelson Cox, *b.* 3 Feb. 1861.

5e. Caroline Marianne Cox.

6e. Annie Elizabeth Georgiana Cox.

4d. *Julia Mary Douglas,* b. 18 *Aug.* 1822 ; d. (–) ; m. 20 *July* 1848, *Lieut.-Col. George James Montgomery, G.C.S., d. at Agra* 20 *Sept.* 1860 ; *and had issue* 1e *to* 3e.

1e. *Isabella Montgomery,* d. 15 *May* 1877 ; m. *Charles Edward Macnamara ; and had issue* (*a son and* 2 *das.*).

2e. Elizabeth Charlotte Montgomery.

3e. Georgiana Louisa Jane Montgomery.

5d. Caroline Douglas, *b.* 7 Dec. 1826 ; *m.* 17 Dec. 1844, Lieut.-Col. Edward Prothero, 3rd West York L.I. Mil., *d.* 1887 ; and has issue 1e.

1e. *Rev. Edward Douglas Prothero, Rector of Turweston,* d. (–) ; m. 1*st,* 2 *June* 1877, *Annie, widow of Charles Church, da. of John Cunningham of Grahamslaw,* d. (–) ; 2*ndly,* 1883, *Margaret Caroline* (see above), *da. of Capt. William Grant Douglas, R.N.*

6d. *Adelaide Charlotte Douglas,* b. 16 *June* 1830; d. (–) ; m. 30 *Jan.* 1851, *William Ogilby of Altnachree Castle, co. Tyrone,* d. 1 *Sept.* 1873 ; *and had issue* 1e *to* 7e.

1e. *Claud William Leslie Ogilby of Altnachree Castle, Lieut.* 31*st Regt.,* b. 1851 ; d. 1894 ; m. 17 *Feb.* 1875, *Bessie Henrietta* (see above), *da. of Capt. William Grant Douglas, R.N.* [*who rem.* 2*ndly,* 1895, *Hugo Bartels*].

2e. James Douglas Ogilby, *b.* 1853.

3e. Adelaide Charlotte Ogilby.

4e. Isabella Caroline Ogilby.

5e. Beatrice Emma Elizabeth Ogilby.

6e. Louisa Ogilby.

7e. Edith Sophia Ogilby.

[Nos. 36889 to 36912.

The Plantagenet Roll

7d. Louisa Emma Douglas, b. 19 Nov. 1831; d. (-); m. 29 Sept. 1857, Charles Burton Fox; and had issue 1e to 6e.
    1e. Charles Douglas Fox, b. 21 Jan. 1867.
    2e. Constance Douglas Fox.
    3e. Alice Louisa Fox.
    4e. Beatrice Elizabeth Fox.
    5e. Maude Cecilia Fox.
    6e. Katherine Fox.

3c. Edward Gordon (Douglas, afterwards (R.L. 25 Jan. 1841) Douglas-Pennant), 1st Baron Penrhyn [U.K.], so cr. 3 Aug. 1866, b. 20 June 1800; d. 31 Mar. 1886; m. 1st, 6 Aug. 1833, Juliana Isabella Mary [descended from the Lady Anne, sister of King Edward IV., &c.], da. and co-h. of George Hay Dawkins Pennant of Penrhyn Castle, co. Carnarvon, d. 25 Ap. 1842; 2ndly, 26 Jan. 1846, Lady Maria Louisa [descended from George, Duke of Clarence], da. of Henry (FitzRoy), 5th Duke of Grafton [E.]; and had issue.

See the Exeter Volume, pp. 457-458, Nos. 36503-36558; and the Clarence Volume, p. 339, Nos. 10873-10881.

4c. Lady Frances Douglas, b. 10 Jan. 1786; d. Aug. 1833; m. 21 Ap. 1804, Lieut.-Gen. the Hon. Sir William Stewart, G.C.B. [E. of Galloway Coll.], d. 7 Jan. 1827; and had issue.

See the Tudor Roll, pp. 502-503, Nos. 34122-34143.

5c. Lady Harriet Douglas, b. 8 June 1792; d. 26 Aug. 1833; m. 1st, 25 Nov. 1809, James Hamilton, Viscount Hamilton [son and h.-app. of John James, 1st Marquis of Abercorn [G.B.], K.G.], d.v.p. 27 May 1814; 2ndly, 8 July 1815, George (Gordon), 4th Earl of Aberdeen [S.], K.G., d. 14 Dec. 1860; and had issue 1d to 7d.

    1d. James (Hamilton), 1st Duke [I.], 7th Marquis [G.B.], and 10th Earl [S.] of Abercorn, 14th Duke of Châtellerault [F.], &c., K.G., P.C., &c., b. 21 Jan. 1811; d. 31 Oct. 1885; m. 25 Oct. 1832, Lady Louisa Jane [descended from King Henry VII.], da. of John (Russell), 6th Duke of Bedford [E.], K.G., d. 31 Mar. 1905; and had issue.

    See the Tudor Roll, pp. 481-484, Nos. 33416-33558.

    2d. Right Hon. Lord Claud Hamilton, P.C., M.P., b. 27 July 1813; d. 3 June 1884; m. 7 Aug. 1844, Lady Emma Elizabeth [descended from Lady Anne, sister of King Edward IV.], da. of Granville Leveson (Proby), 3rd Earl of Carysfort [I.], d. 24 June 1900; and had issue.

    See the Exeter Volume, p. 185, Nos. 6638-6645.

    3d-6d. (Sons by 2nd husband.) See the Tudor Roll, pp. 463-465, Nos. 32741-32797.

    7d. Lady Harriet Hamilton, b. 21 Mar. 1812; d. 19 Mar. 1884; m. 15 May 1836, Admiral William Alexander Baillie-Hamilton, R.N. [E. of Haddington Coll.], d. 1 Oct. 1881; and had issue 1e to 5e.

        1e. Sir William Alexander Baillie-Hamilton, K.C.M.G., C.B., late Chief Clerk of the Colonial Office, and Officer of Arms of the Order of St. Michael and St. George, formerly Col. Comdg. Lothians and Berwickshire Yeo., &c. &c. (55 Sloane Street, S.W.; Carlton), b. 6 Sept. 1844; m. 21 June 1871, Mary Aynscombe, da. of the Rev. John Mossop, Rector of Hothfield; and has issue 1f to 2f.

            1f. George Douglas Baillie-Hamilton, Capt. 2nd Batt. Royal Scots, b. 26 Sept. 1875.

            2f. Walter Stuart Baillie-Hamilton, Private Sec. to the Gov. of S. Australia (Adm. Sir Day H. Bosanquet, G.C.V.O., K.C.B.), b. 9 Aug. 1880.

        2e. Charles Robert Baillie-Hamilton, late Clerk to the Treasury, b. 24 Sept. 1848.

        3e. James Baillie-Hamilton, b. 24 Ap. 1851; m. 10 Aug. 1886, Lady Evelyn, da. of John (Campbell), 8th Duke of Argyll [S.], K.G., K.T.

[Nos. 36913 to 37218.

# of The Blood Royal

4e. Harriet Eleanor Baillie-Hamilton (37 *Bedford Square, W.C.*), *m.* 22 Sept. 1863, Henry Samuel King of the Manor House, Chigwell, co. Essex, J.P., *d.* 17 Nov. 1878; and has issue 1*f* to 6*f*.

1*f*. Arthur Hamilton King (42 *Cambridge Street, Hyde Park, W.*), *b.* 24 Jan. 1866; *m.* 26 Oct. 1897, Charlotte Elizabeth, da. of the Rev. Charles Christopher Ellison of the Manse, Bracebridge, co. Linc.

2*f*. Violet Mary King, *m.* 9 Feb. 1898, Algernon Christian Baily (*Woodford Green, Essex*); and has issue 1*g* to 2*g*.

    1*g*. Michael Henry Hamilton Baily, *b.* 6 Dec. 1901.
    2*g*. Blanche Emma Violet Baily, *b.* 1 Oct. 1899.

3*f*. Harriet Frances Margaret King.

4*f*. *Katharine Douglas King*, *d.* 26 *Mar.* 1901; *m.* 26 *June* 1900, *the Rev. Edmund Godfrey Burr, M.A.* (*Oxon.*), *Rector of Chatham* (*The Rectory, Chatham*); *and had issue* 1*g* *to* 2*g*.

    1*g*. Katherine Veronica Mary Burr, } *b.* (twins) 25 Mar. 1901.
    2*g*. Filumena Mary Douglas Burr,

5*f*. Honora Lilian King.
6*f*. Laura Beatrice King.

5e. Laura Frances Baillie-Hamilton, *m.* as 2nd wife, 19 Oct. 1901, Ralph Gooding, B.A., M.D., J.P., D.L. (13 *Church Terrace, Blackheath, S.E.*).

6c. *Lady Elizabeth Emma Douglas*, *b.* 8 Oct. 1794; *d.* 2 *Feb.* 1857; *m.* 10 *July* 1827, *William Hamilton-Ash of Ashbrook, co. Londonderry, D.L., d.* 30 *Nov.* 1866; *and had issue* 1*d*.

1*d*. *Caroline Hamilton-Ash*, *d.* 13 *Jan.* 1901; *m.* as 2nd wife, 7 *July* 1853, *John Barre Beresford of Learmount, co. Londonderry* [*E. of Tyrone Coll.*], *d.* 30 *Aug.* 1895; *and had issue* 1*e* *to* 6*e*.

1e. William Randall Hamilton Beresford, now (R.L. 26 June 1901) Beresford-Ash of Ashbrook, D.L., Major Royal Welsh Fusiliers (*Ashbrook, Londonderry*), *b.* 19 June 1859; *m.* 23 Oct. 1886, Florence Marion [descended from King Henry VII. (see the Tudor Roll, p. 412)], da. of Lord Henry Ulick Browne [M. of Sligo Coll.]; and has issue 1*f*.

    1*f*. Douglas Beresford-Ash, *b.* 3 Sept. 1887.

2e. Marcus John Barre Beresford, Major South Wales Borderers, South African Medals and Clasps (*Sports*), *b.* 10 Ap. 1868.

3e. Emma Clara Beresford, *m.* 20 Dec. 1881, Francis Coffin Macky of Belmont, J.P., D.L., Capt. *late* 3rd Dragoon Guards (*Belmont, Londonderry*); and has issue 1*f* to 4*f*.

    1*f*. John Barre Beresford Macky, 2nd Lieut. Royal Warwickshire Regt., *b.* 5 Aug. 1889.
    2*f*. Eleanora Caroline Lucia Macky, *m.* 28 Feb. 1907, His Honour Judge (John Fitzpatrick) Cooke, Judge of Donegal County Court (*Glengollan, Fahan, co. Donegal*), *s.p.*
    3*f*. Gladys Kathleen Macky.
    4*f*. Emily Clara Macky.

4e. Barbara Caroline Beresford.

5e. Mary Elizabeth Beresford, *m.* 6 Feb. 1899, Henry John Cooke (*Boom Hall, co. Londonderry*); and has issue 1*f* to 3*f*.

    1*f*. John Sholto Fitzpatrick Cooke, *b.* 1906.
    2*f*. Frances Caroline Cooke.
    3*f*. Clara Elizabeth Douglas Cooke.

6e. Louisa Gertrude Douglas Beresford, *m.* 22 Aug. 1894, Major John Edward Pine-Coffin of Portledge, D.S.O., Royal N. Lancashire Regt. (*Portledge, near Bideford, Devon*); and has issue 1*f* to 4*f*. [Nos. 37219 to 37244.

The Plantagenet Roll

1*f*. Edward Claude Pine-Coffin, *b*. 25 May 1895.
2*f*. Richard Geoffrey Pine-Coffin, *b*. 1 Dec. 1908.
3*f*. Gertrude Beresford Pine-Coffin.
4*f*. Gwendolyn Mary Pine-Coffin.

7*c*. *Lady Caroline Douglas*, b. 17 Dec. 1797 ; d. 7 *Nov*. 1873 ; m. 31 *Dec*. 1817, *William Augustus Pitt Lane-Fox*, d. 1832 ; *and had issue*.
See the Exeter Volume, p. 450, Nos. 35653–35677.

3*b*. *Lady Mary Anne Lascelles*, b. 22 *Nov*. 1775 ; d. 10 *June* 1831 ; m. 20 *Ap*. 1801, *Richard York of Wighill Park, D.L., Lieut.-Col. West Riding Yorkshire Hussar Yeomanry, High Sheriff co. York* 1832, d. 27 *Jan*. 1843 ; *and had issue* 1*c*.

1*c*. *Edward York of Wighill Park*, *J.P., D.L.*, b. 6 *Jan*. 1802 ; d. 26 *Jan*. 1861 ; m. 25 *Nov*. 1835, *Penelope Beatrix* [*descended from King Henry VII*. (see Tudor Roll, p. 390)], *da. of the Rev. Christopher Sykes, Rector of Roos*, d. *June* 1873 ; *and had issue* 1*d* to 5*d*.

1*d*. *Edward Christopher York of Hutton Hall, J.P.*, b. 14 *Oct*. 1842 ; d. 14 *Dec*. 1885 ; m. 1st, 27 *Jan*. 1870, *Isabel Augusta* [*descended from Lady Anne, sister of King Edward and Richard III*. (see Exeter Volume, p. 536)], *da. of Thomas Fairfax of Steeton, co. York, J.P., D.L.*, d. 21 *Ap*. 1875 ; 2ndly, 1876, *Celina Rose, da. of the Rev. Charles Marsden, Vicar of Gargrave ; and had issue* 1*e* to 7*e*.

1*e*. Edward York of Hutton, J.P., *late* Capt. 1st Royal Dragoons (*Hutton Hall, Long Marston, Yorks*), b. 16 Jan. 1872 ; *m*. 10 May 1906, Violet Helen [descended maternally from Kings Henry VII. and Edward IV. (see Tudor Roll, p. 502), and paternally from the latter's brother George, Duke of Clarence, K.G. (see Clarence Volume, p. 270)], da. of the Right Hon. Sir Frederick George Milner, 7th Bt. [G.B.], P.C., M.P. ; and has issue 1*f* to 2*f*.

1*f*. Christopher York, *b*. 27 July 1909.
2*f*. Louise Violet Diana York.

2*e*. Richard Lister York, *b*. 29 Mar. 1880.
3*e*. Francis Stafford York, *b*. 18 Sept. 1883.
4*e*. Edwin Arthur York, *b*. 27 Feb. 1885.
5*e*. Beatrix Penelope Lucy York.
6*e*. Mabel Rose York.
7*e*. Sibell Marguerite York, *m*. 1908, Leslie Reid, *late* 8th Hussars.

2*d*. *Lucy Mary York*, d. 21 *Feb*. 1893 ; m. *as 1st wife*, 16 *Ap*. 1857, *Edward Brooksbank of Healaugh, Lord of the Manor and Patron of that place, LL.B*. (*Camb*.), *J.P.* (*Healaugh Manor, Tadcaster ; Newton House, Whitby*) ; *and had issue* 1*e* to 4*e*.

1*e*. Edward Clitherow Brooksbank, B.A. (Camb.), J.P., Major *late* York Art., *b*. 24 Nov. 1858 ; *m*. 8 Ap. 1885, Katharine Graham, da. of Hugh Morris Lang of Broadmeadows, Selkirk ; and has issue 1*f* to 4*f*.

1*f*. Stamp Brooksbank, *b*. 17 Jan. 1887.
2*f*. Edward York Brooksbank, *b*. 16 Dec. 1889.
3*f*. Hugh Godfrey Brooksbank, *b*. 24 Dec. 1893.
4*f*. Margaret Graham Brooksbank.

2*e*. Philip Brooksbank (*Nelson, British Columbia*), *b*. 5 Jan. 1869.

3*e*. *Laura Sophia Brooksbank*, b. 14 *Nov*. 1861 ; d. 29 *June* 1887 ; m. 18 *June* 1885, *Frederick William Slingsby* (*Red House Moor, Monkton, York*) ; *and had issue* 1*f* to 2*f*.

1*f*. Thomas Slingsby, Lancashire Fusiliers, *b*. 18 Mar. 1886.
2*f*. Henry Slingsby, *b*. 13 June 1887.

4*e*. Lucy Hilda Brooksbank.

3*d*. Caroline Penelope York, *m*. 28 Sept. 1864, the Rev. John Morland Rice, Rector of Bramber, Sussex, *d.s.p*. 1894.

4*d*. *Laura Marianne York*, *m*. 22 Sept. 1870, Adm. Ernest Rice, R.N. (*Siberts-wold Place, Kent*) ; and has issue 1*e* to 3*e*.

1*e*. Arthur Rice, Lieut. R.N.

of The Blood Royal

2e. Laura Gwenllian Rice, m. 4 Oct. 1894, the Hon. Walter John James, J.P. [son and h.-app. of Walter Henry, 2nd Baron Northbourne [U.K.], and a descendant maternally of King Henry VII., &c. (see the Tudor Roll, p. 308)] (1 *Courtfield Road, S.W. ; Travellers' ; Athenæum*); and has issue 1f to 4f.

1f. Walter Ernest Christopher James, b. 18 Jan. 1896.
2f. Dorothea Gwenllian James.
3f. Mary Beatrix James.
4f. Jane Margaret James.

3e. Beatrice Lucy Rice, m. 1 June 1901, Major Eric Pearce-Serocold, King's Royal Rifles; and has issue 1f.

1f. Elizabeth Laura Pearce-Serocold, b. 20 May 1903.

5d. Harriet York, m. 3 Feb. 1880, Richard Hewetson of York; and has issue 1e to 3e.

1e. Richard Stafford Hewetson.
2e. Mary Hewetson.
3e. Dorothy Hewetson.

4a. *Mary Chaloner*, b. 22 Dec. 1743; d. 2 Oct. 1803; bur. *in Guisboro' Church with husband*; m. 11 *June* 1763, *Gen. John Hale of Plantation, near Guisboro', co. York, Col. 17th Light Dragoons and Gov. of Londonderry* [4th son of Sir Bernard Hale, Chief Baron of the Exchequer [I.]], b. 1728; d. 20 *Mar.* 1806; *and had issue* (*with* 6 *other sons and* 5 *das who* d.s.p.) 1b *to* 10b.

1b. *Hon. John Hale of Lower Canada, Paymaster-Gen. to the Forces in Canada, Receiver-Gen. of that Province, formerly Mil. Sec. to H.R.H. the Duke of Kent*, b. 27 *Mar.* 1764; d. 24 *Dec.* 1838; m. 3 *Ap.* 1799, *Elizabeth Frances, sister to William Pitt*, 1st *Earl Amherst* [*U.K.*], *da. of Lieut.-Gen. William Amherst*, b. 2 *Ap.* 1774; d. *at Quebec* 18 *June* 1826; *and had issue* (*with* 3 *sons and a da. who* d.s.p.) 1c *to* 4c.

1c. *Edward Hale, Member of the Quebec Legislative Council, a godson of H.R.H. the Duke of Kent*, b. *in Quebec* 6 *Dec.* 1801; d. *there* 26 *Ap.* 1875; m. *there* 10 *Mar.* 1831, *Elizabeth Cecilia, da. of the Hon. Mr. Justice Bowen of Quebec*, b. 20 *Feb.* 1813; d. 19 *Feb.* 1850; *and had issue* 1d *to* 6d.

1d. Edward John Hale (50 *Des Carrières Street, Quebec*), b. in Quebec 14 Jan. 1833; m. there 17 Oct. 1866, Justine Elise, da. of James Sewell of Quebec, M.D.; and has issue 1e.

1e. Edward Russell Hale, Capt. Army Service Corps (*Kingston, Ontario*), b. in Quebec 10 Feb. 1870; m. 15 Aug. 1893, Ethel, da. of Frederick Montizambert, M.D.; and has issue 1f to 3f.

1f. Frederick Amherst Hale, b. 26 Mar. 1895.
2f. Jeffery John Hale, b. 28 Ap. 1897.
3f. Helen Justine Hale, b. 19 Sept. 1898.

2d. *Edward Chaloner Hale, Attorney-at-Law*, b. 9 *May* 1844; d. 9 *Mar.* 1909; m. 12 *Mar.* 1873, *Sarah Ellen, da. of John Chillas*; *and had issue* 1e *to* 2e.

1e. Edward Chaloner Hale (*Plantation, Lennoxville, Quebec, Canada*), b. at Lennoxville 6 June 1884; m. in Montreal 11 Mar. 1909, Rae Blanch, da. of Ambrose Hines Müdgett of Plymouth, New Hampshire, U.S.A.

2e. Frances Eliza Cecilia Hale, m. at Lennoxville Ap. 1905, Richard Trevor Buchanan (*Woodlands, Quebec*); and has issue 1f to 2f.

1f. Edward Trevor Buchanan, b. 13 Ap. 1906.
2f. John Hale Buchanan, b. 23 Nov. 1907.

3d. William Amherst Hale (*Sleepy Hollow, Sherbrooke, Quebec*), b. at Sherbrooke 23 Feb. 1847; m. at Rivère du Loup, Quebec, 2 Aug. 1884, Ellen, da. of Stewart Derbishire, Private Sec. to Lord Durham; and has issue 1e to 6e.

1e. Edward Amherst Forbes Hale, b. 21 June 1894.
2e. Martha Gladys Forbes Hale.
3e. Mary Stewart Hale.
4e. Vera Derbishire Amherst Hale.
5e. Cecilia Montagu Hale.
6e. Elizabeth Alicia Amherst Hale.

[Nos. 37295 to 37321.

The Plantagenet Roll

4d. Ellen Frances Hale (*Sherbrooke, Quebec*), b. in Quebec; *unm.*
5d. Mary Hale (*Sherbrooke, Quebec*), b. in Sherbrooke; *unm.*
6d. Lucy Anne Hale, b. in Sherbrooke; *m.* there 16 Sept. 1863, Henry Turner Machin, Assist. Treasurer of the Province of Quebec (*Quebec*); *s.p.*

2c. William Amherst Hale, Capt. 52nd Regt., b. 25 *Jan.* 1809; d. 25 *Sept.* 1844; m. *Nov.* 1839, *Caroline, da. of Capt. J. Jenkins of New Brunswick* [who m. 2ndly, *T. S. Stayner and*] d. 14 *May* 1876; *and had issue* 1d *to* 2d.

1d. Mary Louisa Hale (30 *Hereford Square, S.W.*), *m.* 24 Jan. 1865, Robert Bethune of Nydie, co. Fife, J.P., Major 92nd Highlanders [2nd son of Lieut.-Gen. Alexander Bethune, *formerly* Sharp, of Blebo], b. 29 July 1827; d. 27 July 1904; and has issue 1e to 5e.

1e. Henry Alexander Bethune of Nydie and Mountquhanie, J.P., Major 6th Vol. Batt. Black Watch, *formerly* Gordon Highlanders (*Nydie, co. Fife; Naval and Military*), b. 12 July 1866; *m.* 2 Sept. 1902, Elinor Mary, da. of John Brown Watt of Sydney, N.S.W.; and has issue 1f.

1f. Mary Sharp Bethune.

2e. Eleanor Mary Bethune, *m.* as 2nd wife, 23 Sept. 1901, Capt. Frederick Campbell Maconchy, D.S.O., *late* East Yorks Regt. (86 *Brook Street, S.W. ; Naval and Military*).

3e. Louisa Cecilia Bethune, *m.* as 2nd wife 1903, Lieut.-Col. William Crawfurd Middleton, *late* Royal Scots Greys; and has issue 1f to 2f.

1f. Robert Campbell Middleton, b. 3 July 1907.
2f. Doris Mary Middleton.

4e. Jane Millicent Bethune.

5e. Margaret Bethune, *m.* 10 Nov. 1900, the Rev. Francis Walter Boyd, M.A.; and has issue 1f.

1f. Mary Cecilia Boyd.

2d. Caroline Henrietta Hale (14 *Eaton Square, S.W.*), *m.* 19 Feb. 1861, the Hon. Pascoe Charles Glyn, M.P., D.L. [6th son of George Carr, 1st Baron Wolverton [U.K.]], d. 3 Nov. 1904; and has issue 1e to 4e.

1e. Geoffrey Carr Glyn, D.S.O., Major N. Somerset Yeo., and *late* Mil. Sec. to Governor of Madras (Sir Arthur Lawley, K.C.M.G.) (*White's ; Marlborough*), b. 19 Ap. 1864; *m.* 20 July 1889, the Hon. Winifred [descended from the Lady Isabel Plantagenet (see Essex Volume, p. 46)], da. of Charles (Harbord), 5th Baron Suffield [G.B.]; and has issue 1f.

1f. Louise Gwendoline Glyn, b. 21 Sept. 1891.

2e. Maurice George Carr Glyn, *late* Lieut. Dorset Yeo. Cav. (21 *Bryanston Square, W.; Albury Hall, Little Hadham*), b. 12 Mar. 1872; *m.* 6 Oct. 1897, the Hon. Maud, da. of Robert Wellesley (Grosvenor), 2nd Baron Ebury [U.K.]; and has issue 1f to 3f.

1f. Christopher Pascoe Robert Glyn, b. 8 Oct. 1899.
2f. Francis Maurice Grosvenor Glyn, b. 9 Aug. 1901.
3f. Martin St. Leger Glyn, b. 5 Dec. 1902.

3e. Maud Louisa Glyn, *m.* 12 Oct. 1887, Henry Percy St. John, a Clerk in the House of Lords [V. Bolingbroke Coll., a descendant of George, Duke of Clarence, K.G. (see Clarence Volume, p. 489)] (64 *Eccleston Square, S.W.*); and has issue 1f to 3f.

1f. Geoffrey Robert St. John, b. 4 Jan. 1889.
2f. Margaret Olivia St. John.
3f. Ursula Mary St. John.

4e. Agnes Mary Glyn, *m.* 23 Feb. 1884, Col. Francis Onslow Barrington Foote, R.A., *formerly* Comdt. Royal Mil. School of Music (*Manor House, Barnes, Surrey*); and has issue 1f to 4f. [Nos. 37322 to 37346.

of The Blood Royal

1*f*. Alan Wortley Barrington Foote, *formerly* Lieut. 4th Hussars, *b.* 1885.
2*f*. Philip Ward Barrington Foote, Lieut. Royal Fusiliers, *b.* 1889.
3*f*. Randle Charles Barrington Foote, *b.* 1890.
4*f*. Sibell Mary Barrington Foote.

3*c*. George Carleton Hale, *b*. 30 Oct. 1812; *d*. 22 *May* 1892; m. 1*st*, 1840, Henrietta, *da*. *of Capt*. Thomas Trigge, *Barrack-Master-Gen.*, *Quebec*, d.s.p. *Sept*. 1842; 2*ndly*, 6 *June* 1847, *Ellen*, *da*. *of James Sampson of Kingston, Ont., M.D.*, *d.* 28 Feb. 1854; *and had issue* 1*d to* 4*d*.

1*d*. Jeffery Hale (*London, Canada*), *b*. 20 May 1850; *m*. 8 Sept. 1881, Louisa Galt, da. of Duncan Campbell of Simcoe, Ont.; and has issue 1*e* to 2*e*.

1*e*. George Carleton Hale, *b*. 30 June 1885.

2*e*. Jessie Campbell Hale, *m*. 19 June 1909, George Stephen Hensley of the Bank of Montreal, Canada.

2*d*. Henrietta Hale } (*Forest House, Coleman's Hatch, Sussex*).
3*d*. Frances Alicia Hale

4*d*. Mary Caroline Percy Hale, *m*. 28 July 1886, the Rev. Robert Percy Trevor Tennent, Vicar of Acomb (*Acomb Vicarage, Yorks*); and has issue 1*e* to 7*e*.

1*e*. Jeffery Bernard Hale Tennent, *b*. 6 Aug. 1889.
2*e*. Oswald Moncrieff Tennent, *b*. 16 June 1894.
3*e*. Mary Percy Clare Tennent.
4*e*. Frances Maud Tennent.
5*e*. Constance Hilda Madeline Tennent.
6*e*. Stephanie Millicent Tennent.
7*e*. Marjorie Augusta Tennent.

4*c*. Elizabeth Harriet Hale, *d*. 31 *May* 1897; *m. at Quebec* 5 Feb. 1838, Rear-Adm. John Orlebar, R.N. [3rd son *of John Orlebar of Hinwich*], *b*. 18 Oct. 1810; *d*. 11 *May* 1901; *and had issue* 1*d to* 6*d*.

1*d*. Rev. Henry Amherst Orlebar, Rector of King's Cliffe (*King's Cliffe Rectory, Wansford, R.S.O.*), *b*. 19 Nov. 1844; *m*. 9 Aug. 1894, Constance, da. of the Rev. Richard Bryans, M.A.; and has issue 1*e* to 3*e*.

1*e*. Ralph Chaloner Orlebar, *b*. 6 Dec. 1895.
2*e*. Constance Muriel Orlebar, *b*. 5 Sept. 1885.
3*e*. Dorothy Eleanor Orlebar, *b*. 7 Oct. 1889.

2*d*. *John Hale Orlebar, Lieut. R.N.,* *b*. 28 *Sept.* 1846; *d.* (? *unm.*) 1892.

3*d*. Rev. Jeffrey Edward Orlebar, Vicar of Southsea (*Southsea Vicarage, Camb.*), *b*. 25 Nov. 1857; *m*. 16 Jan. 1877, Clara Albinia, da. of Alexander Duff; and has issue 1*e* to 3*e*.

1*e*. Jeffrey Alexander Amherst Orlebar, *b*. 3 Mar. 1879.
2*e*. Marie Elspeth Maud Orlebar.
3*e*. Clarice Knightley Orlebar.

4*d*. *Hotham George Orlebar*, *b*. 9 *Nov*. 1853; *d*. (? *unm.*) 1 *Nov*. 1883.
5*d*. Harriot Orlebar.
6*d*. Frances Hale Orlebar.

2*b*. Henry Hale, *H.E.I.C. Maritime Service*, *b*. 30 Oct. 1765; *d*. 16 *May* 1818; m. 27 *June* 1809, *Elizabeth*, *da. and co-h., and in her issue* (24 *June* 1873) *h. of the Rev. Henry Hildyard of Stokesley, co. York*, *d*. 20 Feb. 1856; *and had issue* (*with* 2 *sons who* d.s.p.) 1*c to* 4*c*.

1*c*. Bernard Hale of Doncaster, *Bar.-at-Law*, *b*. 6 *Ap*. 1812; *d*. 13 *May* 1875; m. 5 Aug. 1858, *Elizabeth, da. of William Gurley of Petershope, St. Vincent, W.I.*, *d*. 11 *May* 1891; *and had issue* 1*d*.

1*d*. Rev. Bernard George Richard Hale, Vicar of Edenhall (*Edenhall Vicarage, Langwathby, R.S.O., Cumberland*), *b*. 26 Oct. 1859; *m*. 2 Aug. 1893, Charlotte Sarah, da. of John Bush of Beauthorn, Ullswater; and has issue 1*e*.

1*e*. John Bernard Windham Hale, *b*. 4 Ap. 1905. [Nos. 37347 to 37375.

The Plantagenet Roll

2c. *John Richard Westgarth Hale, afterwards* (R.L. 19 *June* 1855) *Hildyard of Horsley House and Unthank, J.P., D.L., High Sheriff* (1883) *co. Durham, and Chairman of Quarter Sessions, N.R. York,* b. 17 *June* 1813; d. 24 *Oct.* 1888; m. 24 Aug. 1860, Mary Blanche [*descended from George, Duke of Clarence, K.G.* (see Clarence Volume, p. 463)], da. *of Sir Richard Digby Neave, 3rd Bt.* [G.B.]; *and had issue* 1d *to* 8d.

1d. John Arundell Hildyard of Horsley and Hutton-Bonville, J.P., D.L., High Sheriff co. Durham 1900 (*Horsley House, near Stanhope; Hutton-Bonville Hall, Northallerton; Carlton*), b. 24 Aug. 1861.

2d. Edward Digby Hildyard, b. 20 Aug. 1864.

3d. Blanche Hildyard, m. 19 Nov. 1889, Charles Edward Leake Ringrose, Bar.-at-Law, Registrar of Deeds for N.R. York (*The Registrar House, Northallerton*); and has issue 1e to 2e.

1e. Christopher Hildyard Ringrose, R.N., b. 30 Nov. 1890.

2e. Euphemia Blanche Ringrose.

4d. Phillis Mary Hildyard, m. 5 Mar. 1904, Capt. Henry Grenville Bryant, D.S.O., King's Shropshire L.I.

5d. Elizabeth Muriel Hildyard.

6d. Venetia Dorothy Hildyard.

7d. Gertrude Isabel Hildyard.

8d. Cicely Frances Hildyard.

3c. *George Charles Hale, Agent to the Earl of Derby,* b. 10 *Jan.* 1818; d. *Nov.* 1902; m. 1 *Aug.* 1862, Bessie Armit [*descended from the Lady Isabel Plantagenet* (see Essex Volume, p. 72)] (*Knowsley*), da. *of John Eyre of Eyre Court Castle; and had issue* 1d *to* 6d.

1d. Windham Edward Hale, Agent for the Earl of Derby's Lancashire Estates (*Mowbreck Hall, Kirkham*), b. 25 Oct. 1864; m. 12 July 1894, Kezia, da. of Major Cunliffe, 1st Bengal Fusiliers.

2d. George Duckworth Hale, b. 3 June 1868.

3d. Robert Eyre Hale, b. 2 July 1871; m. 7 Dec. 1909, Elsie Emma, da. of Sir Lindsay Wood, 1st Bt. [U.K.].

4d. Lionel Hugh Hale, b. 4 July 1875; m. 25 June 1899, Kathleen, da. of (—) Kincaird of W. Virginia.

5d. John Hale, b. 8 Aug. 1880; m. 14 Oct. 1906, Mary Maud, da. of John Hughes; and has issue 1e.

1e. Ida Mary Armit Hale, b. 29 July 1907.

6d. Muriel Alice Mary Hale.

4c. *Elizabeth Anne Hale,* b. 13 *Ap.* 1816; d. 26 *May* 1878; m. *Feb.* 1846/7, *the Rev. John Burdon of Castle Eden, co. Durham, Rector of English Bicknor, co. Glos,* b. 14 *Oct.* 1811; d. 12 *Nov.* 1893; *and had issue* 1d *to* 3d.

1d. Rowland Burdon of Castle Eden, J.P., Lieut.-Col. and Hon. Col. 1st Vol. Batt. Durham L.I. (*The Castle, Castle Eden, co. Durham*), b. 19 June 1857; m. 17 Feb. 1887, Mary Arundell, da. of Wyndham Slade of Montys Court, co. Somerset; and has issue 1e to 4e.

1e. Rowland Burdon, b. 6 Feb. 1893

2e. Frances Mary Burdon.

3e. Joan Burdon.

4e. Lettice Burdon.

2d. John George Burdon (*Benwell Hall, Newcastle-on-Tyne*), b. 27 July 1859; m. Feb. 1892, Blanche Louisa [descended from George, Duke of Clarence, K.G. (see Clarence Volume, p. 331)], da. of Gen. Edward Arthur Somerset, C.B. [D. of Beaufort Coll.]; and has issue 1e to 3e.

1e. Noel Edward Burdon, b. 25 Dec. 1893.

2e. John Burdon, b. 10 Nov. 1896.

3e. Elizabeth Alyson Blanche Burdon, b. 20 Ap. 1895. [Nos. 37376 to 37401.

# of The Blood Royal

3*d*. Elizabeth Anne Burdon (*Munstone House, Hereford*).

3*b*. William Hale of Acomb, co. York, Col. N. Yorkshire Mil., b. 17 *July* 1771; d. 23 Nov. 1856; m. 18 Nov. 1802, *Frances, da. of Rowland Webster of Stockton-on-Tees*, d. 25 *Mar.* 1841; *and had issue* (*with a son and* 4 *das. who d.s.p.*) 1*c* to 3*c*.

1*c*. *Mary Emily Hale*, b. 28 *Oct.* 1803; m. 31 *Aug.* 1824, H. *Charles Elsley of Patrick Brompton and Mt. St. John*; *and had issue* (*with* 1 *son and* 5 *das., of whom only one, Eliza, is living*).

2*c*. *Frances Hale*, b. 16 *Mar.* 1805; d. 18 *Oct.* 1842; m. *as* 1*st wife*, 8 *July* 1834, *Lamplugh Wickham Hird, afterwards* (1843) *Wickham, of Chestnut Grove, co. York*, d. 2 *Jan.* 1863; *and had issue* 1*d*.

1*d*. William Wickham Wickham of Chestnut Grove, J.P., *late* Capt. Yorkshire Hussars (*Chestnut Grove, near Boston Spa, Yorks*), b. 16 Sept. 1835; m. 27 Oct. 1868, Katherine Louisa [descended from the Lady Anne, sister of King Edward IV.], da. of Thomas Fairfax of Newton-Kyme, d. 4 July 1892; and has issue.

See the Exeter Volume, p. 535, Nos. 48994–49004.

3*c*. *Harriot Emma Hale*, b. 30 *May* 1814; d. 30 *Ap.* 1844; m. 15 *Aug.* 1838, *the Rev. H. Hawkins*; *and had issue* (*with a son and da. d. young*) 1*d*.

1*d*. Rev. William Webster Hawkins (*Acomb, Yorks*), b. 1842; *m.* 1877, Kate L., da. of P. Leyburn, *d.* 1902; and has issue 1*e* to 5*e*.

1*e*. Charles Francis Hawkins, Capt. R.A., *b.* 30 Jan. 1880.

2*e*. Rose Mary Hawkins.

3*e*. Beatrice Hawkins.

4*e*. Harriet Emma Hawkins, *m.* 12 Dec. 1907, Thomas Bowman Henry Whytehead, Merchant Service (see p. 314); and has issue 1*f*.

1*f*. Nancy Bowman Whytehead.

5*e*. Olive Hawkins.

4*b*. *Vicissimus Hale*, H.E.I.C.S., b. 6 *Mar.* 1788; d. *in Bombay Jan.* 1826; m. 17 *Mar.* 1808, *Amelia S., da. of* (—) *Dundas of co. Stirling*, d. (–); *and had issue* (*with* 2 *sons who d.s.p.*) 1*c* to 4*c*.

1*c*. *William Dundas Hale*, b. 25 *July* 1817; d. 1879; m. 13 *Ap.* 1845, *Sarah, da. of John Chisholm of Hamilton, Ont.*; *and had issue* (*with* 2 *das. who d.s.p.*) 1*d* to 3*d*.

1*d*. John Hale.

2*d*. Alice Hale, *m.* Joseph Cull (*Mitchell, Ont.*); and has issue 1*e* to 2*e*.

1*e*. Henry Cull.

2*e*. Edith Cull.

3*d*. Florence Hale (6 *Classic Avenue, Toronto*), *m.* Arthur Murton of Guelph, Ontario; *d.* (–); and has issue 1*e* to 2*e*.

1*e*. Norman Murton.

2*e*. Edith Murton.

2*c*. *Elizabeth Jane Hale*, b. 12 *May* 1814; d. 15 Jan. 1865; m. 22 *Mar.* 1834, *the Hon. John Wetenhall, M.P.P., Canada*; *and had issue* (*with* 3 *sons d. unm.*) 1*d* to 2*d*.

1*d*. William Wetenhall, *b*. 1836; *m*. 1856, (—), da. of Major Burrows; *s.p.*

2*d*. *Frances Emilia Wetenhall*, b. 12 *Dec.* 1834; *d*. 24 *May* 1887; m. 1857, *Henry Seton Strathy* (71 *Queen's Park, Toronto, Canada*); *and had issue* (*with* 1 *son d. unm.*) 1*e* to 6*e*.

1*e*. *Philip John Neesham Strathy*, b. 12 *Dec.* 1861; *d*. 2 *Jan.* 1908; m. *Frances, da. of* (—) *Alley*; *and had issue* 1*f* to 3*f*.

1*f*. Hugh Strathy, *b*. 15 Sept. 1884.

2*f*. Donald Strathy, *b*. 1903.

3*f*. Phyllis Strathy, *b*. 1898.

The Plantagenet Roll

2e. *Emilius William Wetenhall Strathy*, b. 24 July 1867; d. 23 Ap. 1898; m. 1892, Birdie (c/o Mrs. Tempest, Port Hope, Ont.), da. of W. S. Tempest; and had issue 1f to 2f.

    1f. Edgar Strathy, b. 3 July 1894.
    2f. Harry Strathy, b. 18 Sept. 1898.

3e. Henry Edmund Brekenridge Strathy, M.D., L.R.C.P., F.R.C.S. (Edin.) (171 *Bolton Road, Bury, Lancs.*), b. 23 July 1869; m. 25 Ap. 1908, Louie, da. of John Edwards; s.p.

4e. Frances Elizabeth Strathy, m. 31 Jan. 1888, the Rev. Duncan Macalister Donald, M.A., B.D., Minister of Moulin (*Moulin Manse, Pitlochry, co. Perth*); and has issue 1f to 3f.

    1f. Douglas Alan Donald, b. 29 Dec. 1888.
    2f. Ian Strathy Donald, b. 21 Mar. 1896.
    3f. Mary Theodora Donald, b. 31 Oct. 1891.

5e. Mary Theodora Strathy, m. 22 Sept. 1884, Augustus Henry Frazer Lefroy, K.C., M.A. (Oxon.), Professor of Roman Law and Jurisprudence, &c., at the University of Toronto [descended from King Henry VII., &c. (see the Tudor Roll, p. 401)] (171 *Balmoral Avenue, Toronto*); and has issue 1f to 3f.

    1f. Henry Cicherley Lefroy, b. 23 July 1890.
    2f. Langlois Dundas Lefroy, b. 16 June 1892.
    3f. Frazer Keith Lefroy, b. 1 Feb. 1895.

6e. Lilian Mabel Strathy, m. 17 Oct. 1894, Frederick Broughall (1 *Elmsley Place, Toronto*); and has issue 1f to 4f.

    1f. Deric Broughall, b. 26 Oct. 1896.
    2f. Seton Broughall, b. 6 Oct. 1897.
    3f. Jack Broughall, b. 30 Nov. 1899.
    4f. Gwyneth Broughall, b. 16 Ap. 1904.

3c. *Emily Hale*, b. 22 Dec. 1815; d. *at London, Ont.*, 19 Nov. 1891; m. 1842, William James Imlach, H.E.I.C.S., d. *at London, Ont.*, 20 Feb. 1902; *and had issue* (with 3 other children who d.s.p.) 1d to 4d.

1d. William Dundas Imlach of London, Ont., b. 1845; d. 1888; m. Louise, da. of Charles Smith of New York; *and had issue* (with a 3rd child, d. young) 1e to 2e.

    1e. Bertram Dundas Imlach.
    2e. Grace Imlach, m. (—) Ware of New York.

2d. Eliza Imlach, d. 2 Aug. 1907; m. 29 May 1866, the Rev. Edward Edmund Newman, Canon of Huron; and had issue 1e to 2e.

    1e. Edward Newman, b. 7 Nov. 1867; m. Matilda, da. of (—) Carter of Simcoe, Ont.; s.p.

    2e. Charlotte Dundas Newman, m. 15 Nov. 1899, William George Hinds (14 *The Ramparts, Quebec; Kingston, Ont.*); and has issue 1f.

        1f. Newman Hinds, b. 3 July 1901.

3d. Emily Catherine Imlach
4d. Gertrude Harriet Imlach } (222 *Piccadilly Street, London, Ont.*), *unm.*

4c. *Harriet Margaret Hale*, b. 21 June 1819; d. *at Tenby, co. Pemb.*, 26 Sept. 1855; m. 21 June 1838, Robert Anstruther Maingy of Guernsey, C.E., d. *at the siege of Fredericksburg during the American War*, 18 Nov. 1862; *and had issue* 1d.

1d. Emilia Sophia Dundas Maingy (11 *Hirkmur Street, Hamilton, Ont.*), m. at Stratford, Ont., 4 Sept. 1862, James Edwin O'Reilly, B.A. (Toronto Univ.), Bar.-at-Law, and afterwards Judge of the Supreme Court in Hamilton, Ont., d. there 27 Feb. 1907; *and had issue* (with a son, Robert Miles, d. young, and a da., Jane Alice, d. *unm.* 27 July 1907) 1e to 6e.

1e. Edwin Patrick O'Reilly, B.A. (Toronto Univ.), M.D. (M'Gill Univ., Montreal), d. *unm.* on service in South Africa 17 May 1901. [Nos. 37433 to 37457.

# of The Blood Royal

2e. Lily Harriet O'Reilly, *unm.*

3e. Helen Brephne O'Reilly, *m.* Ap. 1895, Harry Webb (*Winnipeg*).

4e. Ethel Dundas O'Reilly, *m.* Ap. 1905, Philip Alexander (*Hamilton, Ontario*); and has issue 1*f*.

1*f*. Patricia Jane Alexander.

5e. Jessie Ford O'Reilly, *m.* Nov. 1908, Douglas Harington Chisholm (*Winnipeg*).

6e. Anne Louise B. O'Reilly, *m.* Capt. Duncan Frederick Campbell, D.S.O., Black Watch, *formerly* Lancashire Fusiliers, served in South Africa 1899–1901, including relief of Ladysmith, &c. (despatches) (*Woodlands, Elderslie, Renfrewshire*); and has issue 1*f* to 2*f*.

1*f*. Archibald Patrick Campbell.

2*f*. John Dundas Campbell.

5*b*. Mary Hale, twin, b. 10 May 1768; d. 20 Nov. 1837; m. 2 Feb. 1784, Thomas Lewin *of Redgeway Castle and The Hollies, Eltham, co. Kent*, b. 19 Ap. 1753; d. 1843; *and had issue (with* 3 *sons and* 2 *das. who d.s.p.)* 1*c* to 7*c*.

1*c*. Frederick Mortimer Lewin *of the Hollies, co. Kent*, b. 30 Aug. 1798; d. 17 June 1877; m. 9 Ap. 1839, Augusta Diana, *da. of* Thomas Gisborne Babington *of Rothley Temple, co. Leic., J.P.*, d. 25 Mar. 1856; *and had issue (with* 2 *sons and* 2 *das. who d.s.p.)* 1*d* to 4*d*.

1*d*. Mortimer Lewin (*Little Bedwyn, Hungerford, Wilts*), *b.* 13 Oct. 1847; *m.* Oct. 1881, Louisa Mary, da. of Major George Thompson; and has issue 1*e* to 2*e*.

1*e*. Winifred Mary Lewin, *unm.*

2*e*. Dorothy Babington Lewin, *unm.*

2*d*. Mary Hale Lewin, *m.* 10 June 1865, Col. Henry Masterman Thompson [son of Major George Thompson] (9 *Clarence Parade, Southsea*); and has issue 1*e* to 4*e*.

1*e*. Arthur Hale Thompson, Major 1st Goorkas, *b.* 25 Ap. 1866; *m.* 21 Sept. 1899, Eleanor, da. of Dr. Temple, D.S.O.; *s.p.*

2*e*. William Maxwell Thompson, Capt. R.E., *b.* 18 Nov. 1870; *m.* 18 July 1900, Helen, da. of (—) Bull; and has issue 1*f* to 2*f*.

1*f*. Oliver Thompson, *b.* 12 Jan. 1906.

2*f*. Margaret Helen Thompson, *b.* July 1901.

3*e*. Noel Gilliatt Thompson, in the Army, *b.* 13 July 1872.

4*e*. Millicent Babington Thompson, *m.* 18 Nov. 1901, Capt. Robert William Harling; and has issue 1*f* to 2*f*.

1*f*. Katherine Elizabeth Harling, *b.* 17 Jan. 1905.

2*f*. Helen Marjorie Harling, *b.* 22 Mar. 1908.

3*d*. Diana Spencer Lewin, b. 15 July 1843; d. 14 Nov. 1903; m. 10 Mar. 1867, Colonel Edward Spread Beamish, *Bombay Artillery*; *and had issue* 1*e* to 6*e*.

1*e*. Frederick Chaloner Beamish, has settled in Orangia, South Africa, *b.* 24 Nov. 1870; *m.* 17 Jan. 1905, Elizabeth, da. of John Campbell Dick; and has issue 1*f*.

1*f*. Lisette Beamish, *b.* 11 July 1906.

2*e*. Edward Percy FitzRoy Beamish (*Myburghsfontein, Orangia*), *b.* 20 Dec. 1873.

3*e*. Rev. Charles Noel Bernard Beamish, Diocesan Missioner (*Wolvesey Palace, Winchester*), *b.* 12 Feb. 1877.

4*e*. Augusta Diana Beamish, *unm.* ⎫
5*e*. Olive Mary Beamish, *unm.* ⎬ (*Myburghsfontein, Orangia*).
6*e*. Cecilia Hamilton Beamish, *unm.* ⎭

4*d*. Julia Babington Lewin (66 *Church Road, St. Leonards-on-Sea*).

2*c*. William Charles James Lewin, *H.E.I.C. Bengal Art.*, b. 15 June 1805; d.
[Nos. 37458 to 37485.

The Plantagenet Roll

4 *Dec.* 1846; m. 18 *June* 1827, *Jane Elizabeth, da. of Stephen Laprimaudaye*, b. 11 *May* 1803; d. 15 *Aug.* 1877; *and had issue (with 6 other children who* d. *unm.)* 1*d* to 5*d.*

1*d. Edward Powney Lewin,* b. 31 *Aug.* 1833; d. (*being killed at Lucknow*) 1857; m. *Eliza, da. of John Prior; and had issue* 1*e.*

1*e.* Ada Henrietta Lewin, *m.* 3 Dec. 1879, Alpin F. Thompson; and has issue (with 3 others *d.* young) 1*f* to 3*f.*

1*f.* Alpin Erroll Thompson, *b.* 14 May 1893.
2*f.* Dorothea Bethune Thompson, *b.* 3 Feb. 1882.
3*f.* Vivian Irene Thompson, *b.* 10 Jan. 1891.

2*d.* Frederick Dealtry Lewin (14 *Kidbrook Park Road, Blackheath, S.E.*), *b.* 9 Nov. 1835; *m.* 15 Oct. 1879, Christina, da. of Major-Gen. Charles Scrope Hutchinson, R.E., C.B.; and has issue (with a da., Christabel Harriet, who *d.* young) 1*e* to 3*e.*

1*e.* Francis Hutchinson Laprimaudaye Lewin, Lieut. R.N., *b.* 29 Oct. 1880.
2*e.* Edward Hale Lewin, Capt. 46th Punjabis, Indian Army, *b.* 27 Dec. 1881.
3*e.* Rev. William George Lewin, Curate of St. John's, Bethnal Green, *b.* 6 Jan. 1883.

3*d.* William Henry Lewin, Comm. (ret.) R.N. (*Down House, Frant, Tunbridge Wells*), *b.* 11 Nov. 1843; *m.* 5 Ap. 1870, Caroline, da. of Comm. Edward George Elliott, R.N.; and has issue (with a da., Adelaide Laprimaudaye, who *d. unm.* 16 Feb. 1893) 1*e* to 3*e.*

1*e.* Henry Frederick Elliott Lewin, Capt. R.F.A., *b.* 26 Dec. 1872.
2*e.* Charles Laprimaudaye Lewin, Comm. R.N., *b.* 23 Aug. 1875.
3*e.* Honoria Caroline Lewin, *m.* 21 Feb. 1900, Comm. Henry Cyril Royds Brocklebank, R.N.,; and has issue 1*f* to 3*f.*

1*f.* Thomas Anthony Brocklebank, *b.* 5 June 1908.
2*f.* Margaret Petrina Brocklebank, *b.* 1 Feb. 1901.
3*f.* Elinor Joan Ida Brocklebank, *b.* 10 Dec. 1901.

4*d.* Jane Elizabeth Lewin (*Haddenham Hall, Bucks*).

5*d.* Frances Gisborne Lewin (*Haddenham Hall, Bucks*), *m.* 30 Ap. 1861, Henry Green, *d.* 7 June 1900; and has issue 1*e* to 10*e.*

1*e.* Richard Henry Green, *b.* 17 June 1865; *m.* 24 July 1894, Mary, da. of Henry Mackeson of Hythe, Brewer; and has issue 1*f* to 4*f.*

1*f.* George Richard Green, *b.* 4 Dec. 1897.
2*f.* Margaret Mackeson Green, *b.* 14 July 1895.
3*f.* Nancy Lawrie Green, *b.* 23 Jan. 1899.
4*f.* Rachel Mary Green, *b.* 2 July 1903.

2*e.* John Frederick Ernest Green, Capt. R.N., *b.* 8 Aug. 1866; *m.* 22 May 1901, Maud, da. of Col. Charles McInroy of The Burn, Edzell; and has issue 1*f* to 2*f.*

1*f.* Henry Green, *b.* 14 Nov. 1906.
2*f.* Joan Green, *b.* 30 June 1904.

3*e.* Walter Laprimaudaye Green, *b.* 13 Aug. 1872; *m.* 26 Mar. 1901, Christine, da. of (—) Conybere; *s.p.*
4*e.* Arthur Dowson Green, *b.* 13 Ap. 1874.
5*e.* Edward Cecil Green, *b.* 29 Ap. 1877.
6*e.* George Pritzler Green, *b.* 12 Nov. 1881.

7*e.* Alice Mary Green, *m.* 27 July 1889, Capt. Charles Cooke, Merchant Service (ret.), *formerly* Green's Blackwall Ships (*Duclair, Seine Inf., France*); and has issue 1*f* to 3*f.*

1*f.* Charles Henry Joseph Cooke, *b.* 8 Dec. 1898.
2*f.* Lavinia Mary Elizabeth Cooke, *b.* 6 July 1890.
3*f.* Catherine Ella Laprimaudye Cooke, *b.* 23 Dec. 1892.

[Nos. 37486 to 37518.

# of The Blood Royal

8e. Frances Elizabeth Green, *unm.*

9e. Mabel Lucy Green, *unm.*

10e. Margaret Helen Green, m. 24 July 1900, George Henry Woolley, Solicitor (*Cossington, Leicester*); and has issue 1f to 6f.

1f. Stephen Woolley, b. 9 Feb. 1904.
2f. Philip Woolley, b. 23 Oct. 1906.
3f. Margaret Frances Woolley, b. 3 Dec. 1901.
4f. Honor Woolley, b. 4 Mar. 1903.
5f. Lucy Sophia Woolley, b. 10 May 1905.
6f. Helen Mary Woolley, b. 8 May 1906.

3c. *George Herbert Lewin, Attorney-at-Law*, b. 1808; d. 1857; m. 1837, *Mary*, da. *of John Friend of Birchington, Isle of Thanet*, d. 1890; *and had issue* (*with a son d. unm.*) 1d to 4d.

1d. Thomas Herbert Lewin, Col. Bengal Staff Corps, *late* 104th Regt. (*Parkhurst, Abinger Common, Dorking*), b. 1 Ap. 1839; m. 24 July 1876, Margaret, da. of John Robinson McLean, F.R.S., M.P.; and has issue 1e to 3e.

1e. Charles McLean Lewin, Capt. 4th Queen's Own Hussars, b. 11 Ap. 1880; m. Sept. 1908, Beatrice Emma, da. of Henry Barlow Webb of Holmdale, Holmbury, co. Surrey; and has issue 1f.

1f. [da.] Lewin, b. 26 July 1909.

2e. Everest Hannah Grote Lewin, m. 24 July 1901, Thomas Martin Macdonald [2nd son of Neil Macdonald of Dunach, Argyllshire] (*Bargvillean, Taynuilt, Argyllshire*); *s.p.*

3e. Audrey Hale Lewin, m. 1902, Nicholas Edwin Waterhouse (*Feldemore, Holmbury, Surrey*).

2d. *William C. J. Lewin*, b. 1847; d. 1879; m. *J.*, da. *of* (—) *Lewis; and had issue* (2 sons and 1 da.).

3d. Harriet Lewin (17 *St. Mildred's Road, Ramsgate*), m. 1862, Bankes Tomlin of Dumpton Park, Thanet, Capt. Dragoon Guards [2nd son of Robert Sackett Tomlin of Dane Court, co. Kent, and Westgate House, co. Northants, J.P., D.L.], *d.*1908; and has issue 1e to 2e.

1e. Herbert Gore Tomlin, b. 1873.
2e. Latham Julian Tomlin, b. 1886.

4d. Isabella Charlotte Lewin, m. 25 Sept. 1872, Gen. Nathaniel Stevenson, *late* Col. Royal Inniskilling Fusiliers and Gov. of Guernsey [2nd son of Nathaniel Stevenson of Braidwood, co. Lanark, J.P.] (24 *Rutland Court, W.; United Service*); and has issue 1e to 3e.

1e. Natalie Marguerite Stevenson, m. 20 Jan. 1896, Major Herbert Gordon, 93rd Highlanders (*Westhorpe, Marlow, Bucks*); and has issue 1f to 2f.

1f. Charles Gilbert Skerrow Gordon.
2f. Joan Violet Gordon.

2e. Harriet Mary Stevenson.
3e. Edwina Katherine Isabel Stevenson.

4c. *Edward Bernard Hale Lewin of the G.P.O., London*, b. *at Bexley, Kent*, 1 *July* 1810; d. *at Blackheath* 3 *Mar.* 1878; m. 10 Oct. 1850, *Maria Matilda* [*also a descendant of King Edward III.* (*see the Mortimer-Percy Volume, Part II.*)], da. *of Francis Rivaz, d. at Shortlands, Kent*, 12 *Jan.* 1905; *and had issue* 1d to 5d.

1d. Arthur Hale Lewin (23 *Farnaby Road, Bromley, Kent*), b. 14 June 1854; m. 7 Oct. 1884, Catherine Ann, da. of James Chapman; *d.s.p.s.* 24 Nov. 1885.

2d. Wilfred Hale Lewin, Col. (ret.) Indian Army (*Dorunda, Bromley, Kent*), b. 18 May 1856; m. 1st, at Poona, India, 31 Oct. 1885, Kate, da. of Thomas Weston Baggallay, *d.* at Jalna, Deccan, 14 Dec. 1888; 2ndly, at Shortlands, 10 Ap. 1890, Isabella Marion, da. of James Brown Alston; and has issue 1e to 3e.

[Nos. 37519 to 37543.]

The Plantagenet Roll

1*e*. Richard Alston Hale Lewin, Durand Scholar at Wellington College, *b.* at Jalna 10 Dec. 1891.

2*e*. Phyllis Margaret Lewin, *b.* at Hingoli, Deccan, 3 Jan. 1887.

3*e*. Mary Dorothea Lewin, *b.* at Hingoli 24 Sept. 1893.

3*d*. Harold Chaloner Lewin, Solicitor (*Birchdale, Bromley, Kent*), *b.* 19 July 1859; *m.* 21 July 1892, Frances Elizabeth, da. of James Brown Alston; and has issue (with a son, Kenneth Alston, *b.* 26 Mar. 1896, *d. unm.* 22 Feb. 1908) 1*e* to 4*e*.

    1*e*. Edward Chaloner Lewin, now at Marlborough College, *b.* 25 Sept. 1893.

    2*e*. Francis Harold Lewin, now at Marlborough College, *b.* 16 Mar. 1895.

    3*e*. Mary Hope Lewin, *b.* 10 Sept. 1900.

    4*e*. Margery Theodora Lewin, *b.* 12 Sept. 1908.

4*d*. Marion Amy Lewin, *m.* 9 Aug. 1873, His Honour Judge Henry Tindal Atkinson [son of Henry Tindal Atkinson, Sergeant-at-Law] (3 *Clanricarde Gardens, Notting Hill Gate, W.*); and has issue (with a da., Violet Mary, *d.* young) 1*e* to 5*e*.

    1*e*. Edward Hale Tindal Atkinson, *b.* 19 Sept. 1878.

    2*e*. Ethel Marion Atkinson.

    3*e*. Amy Maud Atkinson.

    4*e*. Enid Katherine Atkinson.

    5*e*. Doris Mary Atkinson.

5*d*. Edith Gertrude Agnes Lewin (23 *Farnaby Road, Bromley, Kent*), *unm.*

5*c*. *Mary H. Lewin*, b. 1785; d. 1825; m. *Hippesley Marsh; and had issue of whom* 1*d*.

    1*d*. Hippesley Cunliffe Marsh, Col. *formerly* Bengal S.C. (*Tunbridge Wells*).

6*c*. *Harriet Lewin*, b. 1 *July* 1792; d.s.p. 29 *Dec.* 1878; m. 5 *Mar.* 1820, *George Grote, Banker, D.C.L., LL.D., M.P. for London, the Historian of Greece*, b. 17 *Nov.* 1794; d.s.p. 18 *June* 1871.

7*c*. *Frances Eliza Lewin*, b. 16 *Feb.* 1804; d. 21 *Aug.* 1888; m. 1832, *Nils Samuel von Koch, a Noble of Sweden* [1815, No. 2244], *Attorney-General* (*Justitickanster*) *of Sweden*, b. 10 *Mar.* 1801; d. *at Augerum* 13 *June* 1881; *and had issue* 1*d to* 4*d*.

1*d*. Nils Thomas Grote von Koch, a Noble of Sweden [1815, No. 2244], Chamberlain (Kammarherren) to H.M. the King of Sweden, and Secretary of Legation, a Landed Proprietor (*Senäte, Lidköping, Sweden*), *b.* 30 July 1833; *m.* 28 June 1861, Hedvig Alida Isabella, da. of Martin Vilhelm Rhedin; and has issue 1*e* to 2*e*.

    1*e*. Noble Nils Thomas Vilhelm von Koch, a Gentleman-in-Waiting to H.M. the King of Sweden (*Rönö, Sweden*), *b.* 22 Feb. 1864; *m.* 5 Aug. 1896, the Countess Jacquette Marie Anna, da. of Gen. Count Malcolm Walter Hamilton [Ct. Hamilton [Sweden 1751] Coll.]; and has issue 1*f* to 6*f*.

        1*f*. Noble Nils Thomas Malcolm von Koch, *b.* 11 Aug. 1897.

        2*f*. Noble Jacques Bo Nils von Koch, *b.* 9 Nov. 1907.

        3*f*. Noble Hedvig Anna von Koch, *b.* 13 June 1899.

        4*f*. Noble Maria Margareta von Koch, *b.* 13 Nov. 1900.

        5*f*. Noble Lilian Isabella von Koch, *b.* 2 Dec. 1901.

        6*f*. Noble Signe Jacquette von Koch, *b.* 27 Jan. 1903.

    2*e*. Noble Isabella Hedvig Frances Wilhelmina von Koch, an Artist, *unm.*

2*d*. Noble Fabian Wilhelm von Koch, *formerly* a Judge (*Hälla, Falun, Sweden*), *b.* 10 June 1837; *m.* 17 Ap. 1873, the Baroness Hedda Johanna, da. of Major Baron Bengt Carl Fredrik Leijonhufvud [B. Leijonhufvud [Sweden 1651] Coll.], by his wife, Countess Anna Elisabeth Johanna, *née* Hamilton; and has issue 1*e* to 5*e*.

    1*e*. Noble Carl Fabian Richert von Koch, Civil Engineer and Dr. of Elec. (*Stockholm*), *b.* 29 July 1879; *m.* 22 Oct. 1906, Elisabeth, da. of George W. Carpenter of Philadelphia; and has issue 1*f* to 2*f*.

        1*f*. Noble Sigfrid Fabian Richert von Koch, *b.* 7 June 1909.

        2*f*. Noble Hedda Soldis Elisabeth von Koch, *b.* 27 Oct. 1907.

[Nos. 37544 to 37572.

# of The Blood Royal

2e. Noble Carl Wathier Gordon von Koch, Student, b. 13 Aug. 1887.

3e. Noble Nanny Frances Hedda von Koch, m. 17 Aug. 1905, Adolf August Emanuel Johansson, teol o filo. Kand (teacher) (*Gefle*).

4e. Noble Jane Marie Mathilda von Koch, m. as 2nd wife, 11 Sept. 1899, Baron Joseph Hermelin, Member of the Swedish Diet [B. Hermelin [Sweden 1766] Coll.] (*Motala, Sweden*); and has issue 1f to 5f.

1f. Baron Peter Fabian Samuel Axel Hermelin, b. at Ulfosa 2 Sept. 1909.

2f. Baroness Barbro Hedda Eugenia Hermelin, b. 27 June 1900.

3f. Baroness Karin Ebba Sofia Hermelin, b. 9 Ap. 1902.

4f. Baroness Nanny Jane Ingeborg Hermelin, b. 7 Feb. 1904.

5f. Baroness Birgitta Hermelin, b. 17 Aug. 1906.

5e. Noble Anna Mary Elvine von Koch, m. 14 Ap. 1909, Frithiof F^{son} Holmgren, Engineer (*Zürich*).

3d. Noble Richert Vogt von Koch, Lieut.-Col., *formerly* Royal (Swedish) Horse Guards (12 *Riddargatin, Stockholm*), b. 22 Dec. 1838; m. 4 July 1865, the Baroness Agathe Henriette, da. of Gen. Baron Fabian Jakob Wrede af Elimä [B. Wrede af Elimä [Sweden 1653] Coll.]; and has issue 1e to 7e.

1e. Noble Nils Fabian Helge von Koch, Professor of Mathematics (*Djursholm, Sweden*), b. 25 Jan. 1870; m. 23 Sept. 1893, Signe Sofia Charlotte, da. of Magnus Neijber; and has issue 1f to 4f.

1f. Noble Fabian Magnus von Koch, b. 22 Oct. 1894.

2f. Noble Gunnar Magnus Richert von Koch, b. 11 July 1897.

3f. Noble Agnes Lisa Augusta Agathe von Koch, b. 13 Oct. 1899.

4f. Noble Signe Maj. von Koch, b. 1 May 1908.

2e. Noble Richert Gerard Halfred von Koch, Editor of the *Social Tidskrift* (*Stockholm*), b. 13 Jan. 1872; m. 11 July 1906, Carola Maria Euphrosyne, da. of Dr. Carl Sahl.

3e. Noble Nils Arne von Koch, Filos Kand (teacher) (*Västerås, Sweden*), b. 14 Jan. 1875; m. 6 Ap. 1909, Ella, da. of Isaac Neuendorff, Chief Pay Dept. Swedish Admiralty.

4e. Noble Richert Sigurd Valdemar von Koch, Composer (*Ornö, Sweden*), b. 28 June 1879; m. 8 Nov. 1904, Karin Maria, da. of Capt. Carl Magnell.

5e. Noble Nils Ragnar von Koch, Jur. Kand (Solicitor) (*Stockholm*), b. 29 Ap. 1881.

6e. Noble Harriet Ebba von Koch, Artist (*Stockholm*).

7e. Noble Frances Aurore von Koch, m. 26 Sept. 1891, Count Hugo Hansson Wachtmeister af Johannishus [C. Wachtmeister af Johannishus [Sweden 1687] Coll.] (*Gullbärna, Sweden*); and has issue 1f to 3f.

1f. Countess Ebba Frances Agathe Wachtmeister af Johannishus, b. 26 Mar. 1897.

2f. Countess Signe Aurore Wachtmeister af Johannishus, b. 3 June 1898.

3f. Countess Sigrid Richissa Wachtmeister af Johannishus, b. 27 June 1899.

4d. Noble Oscar Francis von Koch, Solicitor (*Stockholm*), b. 7 Mar. 1845; m. 27 Nov. 1876, Hanna, da. of (——) Lundhquist.

6b. *Ann Hale* (twin), b. 10 Mar. 1768; d. 5 Dec. 1853; m. 1*st, as* 2*nd wife,* 1785/7, *Lieut.-Col. Henry Walker Yeoman of Woodlands, near Whitby, J.P.*, b. 1749; d. 1801; 2*ndly,* 1801, *Col. Leon Smelt, Governor of the Isle of Man; and had issue* 1c *to* 6c.

1c. *Henry Walker Yeoman of Woodlands, J.P., D.L.*, b. 13 *July* 1789; d. 14 *Sept.* 1875; m. 5 *Feb.* 1816, *Lady Margaret Bruce* [*descended from Lady Anne, sister to King Edward IV.*, &c.], *da. of Lawrence* (*Dundas*), 1*st Earl of Zetland* [*U.K.*], &c., d. 13 *Sept.* 1860; *and had issue.*

See the Exeter Volume, pp. 257-258, Nos. 9731-9740.

[Nos. 37573 to 37607.

The Plantagenet Roll

2c. *Constantine Yeoman, Major in the Army* (twin), b. 1791; d. *July* 1852; m. 28 *Mar.* 1842, *Mary Smelt, da. of the Rev. Alexander Crigan, D.D.* [who m. 2ndly, *Sheffield Cox of St. Leonards*]; *and had issue* (with 2 sons and a da. who d. young) 1d.

1d. Mary Janette Hale Yeoman, m. 23 June 1864, the Rev. Richard Edward Warner, Rector of Stoke and Canon of Lincoln (*Stoke Rectory, Grantham*); and has issue 1e to 7e.

    1e. Leonard Ottley Warner, b. (—); m. (—), da. of (—); and has issue 1f to 4f.

    1f. Ashton Christopher Fenwick Warner.

    2f. John Warner.

    3f. Audrey Elizabeth Cromwell Warner.

    4f. Joyce Trevor Warner.

    2e. Basel Hale Warner, b. (—); m. (—), da. of (—); and has issue 1f.

    1f. Joan Warner.

    3e. Richard Cromwell Warner, b. (—); m. (—), da. of (—); and has issue 1f to 2f.

    1f. Oliver Martin Wilson Warner.

    2f. Grace Elinor Mary Warner.

    4e. Lawrence Dundas Warner.

    5e. Wynyard Alexander Warner.

    6e. Marmaduke Warner.

    7e. Constance Emma Cromwell Warner, m. (—) Weigall; and has issue 1f to 3f.

    1f. Richard Edward Cromwell Weigall.

    2f. Geoffrey Stephen Cormac Weigall.

    3f. Dulce Helen Weigall.

3c. *Bernard Yeoman, Capt. R.N.* (twin), b. 1791; d. 23 *Ap.* 1836; m. 1823, *Charlotte, da. of Sir Everard Home, 1st Bt.* [U.K.], d. 21 *Jan.* 1878; *and had issue.*

See p. 116, Nos. 10700–10723.

4c. *Robert Smelt*, d. 1817.

5c. *Frances Smelt*, m. (—) *Bacon.*

6c. *Jessica Smelt*, m. (—) *Cresnell.*

7b. *Harriot Hale*, b. 16 *June* 1769; d. 10 *Ap.* 1834; m. 21 *Ap.* 1794, *Lawrence (Dundas), 1st Earl of Zetland* [U.K.], *2nd Baron Dundas* [G.B.] [*descended from the Lady Anne, sister of King Edward IV., &c.*], d. 19 *Feb.* 1839; *and had issue.*

See the Exeter Volume, pp. 256–260, Nos. 9689–9885.

8b. *Emma Hale*, b. 16 *June* 1782; d. *May* 1861; m. *Oct.* 1808, *Major Charles Lloyd, 66th Regt.*, d. (*being drowned in Ireland*) 5 *Feb.* 1809; *and had issue* 1c.

1c. Rev. Charles Lloyd, Canon and Rector of Chalfont St. Giles, co. Bucks, d. 29 Ap. 1883; m. 20 Ap. 1841, Caroline Alicia, da. of the Rev. Charles Sheffield, M.A. [2nd son of Sir Robert Sheffield, 3rd Bt.], d. 29 June 1893; and had issue (with 2 elder sons d. unm.) 1d to 10d.

1d. Francis Aylmer Lloyd (*Hurstbury, Witley, Surrey; St. Stephen's*), b. 6 Sept. 1845; m. 2 Aug, 1883, Eugenie Alphonsene, widow of William Milner, da. of Charles Gaudin; and has issue 1e to 3e.

    1e. Francis Charles Aylmer Lloyd, b. 19 Aug. 1884.

    2e. Florence Eugenie Aylmer Lloyd, b. 2 Mar. 1887.

    3e. Gerald Aylmer Lloyd, Welsh Regt., b 17 Ap. 1888.

2d. Robert Oliver Lloyd, Col. R.E., Chairman, County of Pembroke Territorial Force Association (*Treffgarne Hall, S.O., Pembrokeshire*), b. 20 Mar. 1849; m. 7 June 1877, Mary Isabella, da. of Major-Gen. Dillon Gustavus Pollard [also a descendant of King Edward III. (see the Mortimer-Percy Volume, Part II.)]; and has issue 1e to 3e. [Nos. 37608 to 37851.

# of The Blood Royal

1e. Charles Whitworth Robert Lloyd, b. 28 June 1879.

2e. Francis Oswald Lloyd, b. 26 Ap. 1883.

3e. Ursula Mary Vere Lloyd, b. 16 Mar. 1891.

3d. Leonard Sheffield Lloyd (*Holmcroft, Hampton Hill, Midx.*), b. 17 Jan. 1851; m. 11 June 1885, Mary Dora, da. of Capt. Charles Grigan; and has issue 1e.

1e. Dorothy Mary Vere Lloyd, b. 3 May 1887.

4d. Cyril Hope Lloyd (*Morden, Manitoba, Canada*), b. 28 Feb. 1853; m. 2 Mar. 1878, Alice Augusta, da. of Hartley Dunsford of Lindsay, Ontario; and has issue 1e to 7e.

1e. Digby Sheffield Lloyd, B.A., b. 31 July 1883.

2e. Cyril Geoffrey Lloyd, b. 27 May 1887.

3e. Hartley Dunsford Lloyd, b. 12 Nov. 1889.

4e. Muriel Hope Lloyd, m. 27 Dec. 1904, Robert Ernest Turnbull (2175 *Rae Street, Regina, Sask.*); and has issue 1f to 3f.

1f. Alice Elizabeth Turnbull.

2f. Muriel Helen Turnbull.

3f. Mona Ruth Turnbull.

5e. Ruth Lloyd.

6e. Alice Marjorie Lloyd, m. 20 Oct. 1909, Arthur Hutchinson (*Morden, Manitoba*).

7e. Kate Rubidge Lloyd.

5d. Marmaduke Bernard Lloyd (1016 *Pandora Avenue, Victoria, British Columbia*), b. 11 July 1857; m. 1882, Henrietta, da. of Hartley Dunsford of Lindsay, afsd.; and has issue 1e to 2e.

1e. Leonard Rubidge Lloyd, b. 1890.

2e. Violet Alicia Lloyd, b. 1886.

6d. Giles William Lloyd, b. 1 Dec. 1860.

7d. Perceval Allen Lloyd, F.R.C.S., (Eng.), L.R.C.P. (Lond.), Dep. Coroner S. Div. Pembrokeshire (*Chalfont House, Haverfordwest*), b. 25 May 1863; m. Feb. 1906, Alice Auder Cecile, da. of Arthur Say; and has issue 1e to 2e.

1e. John Perceval Auder Lloyd, b. 10 May 1909.

2e. Marjorie Elizabeth Vere Lloyd, b. 14 Dec. 1906.

8d. Lucy Emma Julia Lloyd, *unm.*

9d. Caroline Octavia Mary Vere Lloyd, m. 16 July 1874, the Rev. Francis Amcotts Jarvis, M.A. (Camb.), Vicar of Burton (*Burton Vicarage, Doncaster*); and has issue 1e.

1e. Charles Francis Cracroft Jarvis, Capt. Yorks Regt. (*Boodle's*), b. 3 May 1875, m. 9 June 1906, Helen Constance, widow of Capt. Stair Hathorn Johnston Stewart of Physgill, da. of Sir Edward Hunter-Blair, 4th Bt. [G.B.]; and has issue 1f.

1f. Ralph George Edward Jarvis, b. 1907.

10d. Margaret Alice Lloyd.

9b. *Elizabeth Hale (twin)*, b. 12 Feb. 1784; d. 19 *Mar.* 1845; m. *at Kensington* 2 *Mar.* 1819, *the Rev. Benjamin Puckle, Rector of Grafham, co. Hunts*, d. *at Bagnierre de Bigorres, in the Pyrenees*, 1853; *and had issue (with 2 das. who d.s.p.)* 1c to 3c.

1c. *Rev. Benjamin Hale Puckle, Rector of Grafham*, b. 1822; d. 1892; m. 1*st, Maria, da. of* (—) *Nunn*; 2*ndly*, 20 *July* 1853, *Eleanor, da. of the Right Hon. Sir Maziere Brady*, 1*st Bt.* [*U.K.*], *P.C., Lord Chancellor* [*I.*], d.s.p. 18 *Feb.* 1891.

2c. *Frederic Hale Puckle, settled in Australia*, b. 24 *Sept.* 1823; d. 7 *May* 1909; m. 4 *May* 1858, *Fanny, da. of the Rev. Edward Selwyn, Rector of Hemingford Abbots*, d. 30 *Jan.* 1896; *and had issue (with a da. d. unm.)* 1d to 3d.

The Plantagenet Roll

1*d*. Selwyn Hale Puckle, M.B., C.M. (*Bishop's Castle, Salop*), *b*. at Hamilton, Victoria, 9 June 1859; *m*. 4 Sept. 1888, Annie, da. of B. A. Bremner of Morningside, Edinburgh, M.D.; and has issue (with a da. *d*. young) 1*e* to 5*e*.

1*e*. Frederick Hale Puckle, *b*. 8 June 1889.
2*e*. Bruce Hale Puckle, *b*. 10 Nov. 1891.
3*e*. George Hale Puckle, *b*. 21 Dec. 1892.
4*e*. Phyllis Hale Puckle.
5*e*. Mary Hale Puckle.

2*d*. Louisa Hale Puckle } (*Dapdune, Guildford*).
3*d*. Eleanor Hale Puckle }

3*c*. George Hale Puckle (*Nine Oaks, Windermere*), *b*. 20 Dec. 1825.

10*b*. *Jane Hale* (twin), *b*. 12 Feb. 1784; *d*. 20 Aug. 1821; *m. as 2nd wife, at Kensington, 25 May 1815, the Rev. Henry Budd, Rector of White Roothing, co. Essex, d. 27 June 1850; and had issue (with another son and 2 das. d.s.p.) 1c.*

1*c*. Richard Hale Budd *of New Brighton, Melbourne, Australia, Inspector-General of Schools*, *b*. 6 Mar. 1816; *d*. 27 Mar. 1909; *m*. 13 June 1843, *Elizabeth*, da. *of Liddle Purves; and had issue (with 4 sons and 2 das. who d.s.p.) 1d to 2d.*

1*d*. Mary Elizabeth Budd } (*Roothing, Brighton, Victoria*).
2*d*. Emma Eliza Budd }

[Nos. 37880 to 37890.]

132. Descendants of the Rev. WILLIAM CHALONER, M.A., Queen's College, Cambridge (Table XV.), *b*. 17 May 1687; *d*. (–); *m*. 5 May 1724, ANNE, da. of J. HODGSON of Bishop Auckland, co. Durham; and had issue (with 2 sons who *d.s.p.*)[1] 1*a* to 2*a*.

1*a*. *Edward James Chaloner of Lincoln* (2nd son), d. (–); m. (–); *and had (with possibly other) issue* 1*b*.
1*b*. Theophania Chaloner, *b*. 23 Jan. 1779; *d*. 9 June 1857; *m*. 12 Aug 1799, *Thomas Lodington Fairfax of Steeton, co. York*, *d*. 1 July 1840; *and had issue*.[2] See the Exeter Volume, p. 535, Nos. 48976–49015.

2*a*. *Robert Chaloner of Bishop Auckland*, *b*. 1 Feb. 1729; *d*. (–); *m*. 12 Sept. 1763, *Dorothy*, da. *of Sir John Lister-Kaye, 4th Bt.* [*E*.], *b*. 27 Feb. 1741; *and had issue* 1*b* to 3*b*.

1*b*. Rev. John Chaloner, M.A. (*Oxon*.), *Rector of Newton Kyme* 1815–1830, *b*. 3 June 1765; *d*. 4 Nov. 1830; *m*. 12 Nov. 1798, *Augusta Anne*, da. *of Robert Sutton of Scofton, co. Notts*, *d*. 3 Feb. 1850; *and had issue* 1*c* to 2*c*.

1*c*. Rev. John William Chaloner, M.A. (*Camb*.), *Rector of Newton Kyme*, *b*. 1 Sept. 1811; *d*. 12 Mar. 1894; m. 1st, *Marcella Louisa*, da. *of Charles Legh of Adlington, co. Chester*, *d*. 22 Nov. 1866; 2ndly, *Arabella*, da. *of Joseph Harrison of Orgrave, co. York; and had issue* (with a 3rd son *d*. *unm*.) 1*d* to 3*d*.

1*d*. Charles William Chaloner (*Grove End, Albion Crescent, Scarborough*), *b*. 15 Oct. 1840; *m*. 26 Ap. 1894, Florence, da. of Capt. John Rhind; *s.p.s.*
2*d*. John Erskine Chaloner, settled in America, *b*. 12 Feb. 1842.
3*d*. Henry Edward Chaloner (*Box 193, Johannesburg, Transvaal*), *b*. 18 Sept. 1845; *m*. 23 July 1868, Louisa, da. of W. H. Hodding of 84 Gloucester Place, Portman Square, London, W., M.D.; and has issue 1*e* to 3*e*.

[Nos. 37891 to 37933.]

---

[1] Foster's "Yorkshire Pedigrees," where, however, Edward, the 2nd son, is also said to have *d.s.p.*

[2] Burke's "Landed Gentry," 1906, p. 555, and Foster's "Yorkshire Pedigrees," Fairfax Pedigree.

of The Blood Royal

1*e*. Cecil Erskine Sweet Chaloner, *b*. at Lydenburg, Transvaal, 7 June 1880.

2*e*. Constance Marcella Chaloner, *m*. at Doornfontein, Johannesburg, 22 Feb. 1895, Edward Richard Headly Hutt, Mining Engineer, Manager, Dundee Coal Coy. (*Talana, Dundee, Natal*); and has issue 1*f* to 2*f*.

    1*f*. Joyce Chaloner Hutt, *b*. at Johannesburg 15 Aug. 1897.

    2*f*. Myrtle Gwendoline Hutt, *b*. at Wilbank, near Middelburg, 7 Aug. 1905.

3*e*. Ada Gwendoline Chaloner, *m*. at St. Mary's Church, Johannesburg, 5 Feb. 1902, Thomas Alexander Glenny, Land Agent and Accountant (*Rand Club, Johannesburg*); and has issue 1*f* to 2*f*.

    1*f*. Harry Wallis Glenny, *b*. at Crown Mine, Mayfair, Johannesburg, 15 Aug. 1904.

    2*f*. Alexander Hennen Glenny, *b*. at Clifton Hill, London, 26 May 1906.

2*c*. Augusta Maria Chaloner, b. 23 May 1809; d. 19 July 1859; m. 26 Nov. 1831, *William Bennett Martin of Worsboro' Hall, co. Yorks, and Thurgarton Priory, co. Notts, J.P., D.L.*, b. 7 Oct. 1796; d. 6 Ap. 1847; *and had issue* (with an elder son and 2 das. who d. unm.) 1*d* to 4*d*.

1*d*. *William Henry Michael Aloysius Martin-Edmunds of Worsboro' Hall, D.L.*, b. 8 May 1847; d. 6 Oct. 1899; m. 3 Aug. 1870, Emily Frances [*descended from the Lady Anne, sister to King Edward IV*. (see Exeter Volume, p. 277)], *da. of John Hubert Washington Hibbert of Bilton Grange* [*by his wife Julia, da. of Sir Henry Joseph Tichborne, 8th Bt*. [*E*.]]; *and had issue* 1*e* to 3*e*.

    1*e*. Cecilia Elizabeth Mary Agnes Martin-Edmunds of Worsboro' (*Worsboro' Hall, Barnsley, York*).

    2*e*. Magdalen Mary Josephine Martin-Edmunds, *m*. 11 Oct. 1905, Ronald Charles Scott-Murray [3rd son of Charles Aloysius Scott-Murray of Hambleden].

    3*e*. Olyve Mary Evelyn Martin-Edmunds, *m*. 9 Ap. 1902, Eustace Theodore Heaven, Capt. *late* Lancashire Art. [2nd son of Joseph Robert Heaven of Forest of Birse by his wife Maria, 1st Marchioness of Braceras [Papal States]]; and has issue (with an elder da. *d*. young) 1*f* to 5*f*.

        1*f*. Eustace Joseph Benedict Heaven, *b*. 16 Ap. 1903.

        2*f*. Mark Joseph Robert Severius Heaven, *b*. 10 May 1904.

        3*f*. Edgar Joseph Heaven, *b*. 25 Sept. 1908.

        4*f*. Barbara Mary Josephine Heaven, *b*. 2 May 1907.

        5*f*. Merial Mary Teresa Tichborne Heaven, *b*. 5 Dec. 1909.

2*d*. *Maria Elizabeth Martin*, d. 26 *Sept*. 1891; m. 28 Aug. 1855, *the Hon. Francis Dudley Montagu-Stuart-Wortley* [2nd *son of John*, 2nd *Baron Wharncliffe* [*U.K*.] *and a descendant of King Henry VII*.], d. 21 Oct. 1893; *and had issue.*
See the Tudor Roll, p. 525, Nos. 35120–35139.

3*d*. *Amelia Mary Martin*, b. 21 July 1835; d. 9 Oct. 1895; m. 29 Ap. 1858, *Edward Chivers Bower of Broxholme, co. York, J.P., D.L., Capt. West Yorkshire Mil.*, b. 22 Aug. 1826; d. 18 Ap. 1896; *and had issue* 1*e* to 9*e*.

    1*e*. Edward Thomas Chivers Bowers, *b*. 9 Feb. 1859.

    2*e*. George Chivers Bower, *b*. 19 June 1860.

    3*e*. Francis Chivers Bower, *b*. 23 July 1861.

    4*e*. Arthur Wentworth Chivers Bower, *b*. 8 Nov. 1866.

    5*e*. Augusta Mary Chivers Bower.

    6*e*. Amy Elizabeth Chivers Bower.

    7*e*. Ethel Alice Chivers Bower.

    8*e*. Cicely Maria Chivers Bower.

    9*e*. Beatrice Lilian Chivers Bower.

4*d*. *Julia Constance Martin*, b. 11 *Sept*. 1837; d. (–); m. 9 *Aug*. 1863, *Stephen Soames, Bar.-at-Law; and had issue.*

2*b*. *Charles Chaloner*, d. (? s.p.) *at Snaith*. [Nos. 37934 to 37977.

The Plantagenet Roll

3b. *Dorothy Chaloner,* b. 25 *May* 1766 ; d. (-) ; m. *the Rev. Robert Greville, Rector of Bonsall and Winstone, co. Dorset; and had (with possibly other) issue* 1c.

1c. *Robert Kaye Greville of George Square, Edinburgh, LL.D., a Botanist of note,* b. 13 *Dec.* 1794; d. 4 *June* 1866 ; m. 1816, *Charlotte* (see p. 270), *da. and co-h. of Sir John Eden,* 4th *Bt.* [*E.*], *M.P.; and had issue* 1d *to* 5d.

1d. Robert Greville, d. (?) *unm.*
2d. Chaloner Greville.
3d. Charlotte Greville, *m.* the Rev. (—) Hogarth.
4d. Emmeline Greville, *m.* (—) Drummond.
5d. [da.] Greville.   [Nos. 37978 to 37981.

133. Descendants, if any, of CATHERINE CHALONER (Table XV.), d. (-) ; *m.* G. MELTHORP of York.

134. Descendants of KATHERINE LAMPLUGH, eldest sister and co-h. of Thomas Lamplugh of Lamplugh (Table XV.), *d.* 1804 ; *m.* in Belfray's Church, York, 1754, the Rev. GODFREY WOLLEY, Rector of Thurnscoe and Warmsworth, co. York, *b.* 1722 ; *d.* 1 May 1788 ; and had issue 1a to 7a.

1a. *Edward Wolley, afterwards* (R.L. 19 *May* 1810) *Copley of Fulford Grange, co. York, eldest son,* d. (-) ; m. *and had issue (with a da. who* d. *unm.)* 1b.

1b. *Edward Thomas Copley of Nether Hall, co. York,* b. *c.* 1800; d. 8 Oct. 1849 ; m. 3 *Aug.* 1826, *Emily Mary, da. of Sir John Pemistone Milbanke,* 7*th Bt.* [*E.*], d. 1 *June* 1844; *and had issue (with another son, John Milbanke, who* d. *unm.)* 1c *to* 2c.

1c. *George Edward Copley,* b. *Ap.* 1834 ; d. 27 *Dec.* 1878 ; m. *Annie, da. of Oswald Smithson of York ; and had issue (a da.).*

2c. Arthur White Copley (*Casa Copley, Mentone, France*), b. 8 Aug. 1836 ; *unm.*

2a. *Thomas Wolley, Admiral R.N.,* d. (-) ; m. *Frances Edith, da. of Gilbert Francklyn of Aspeden Hall, co. Herts, and had issue (with a da. who* d.s.p.) 1b *to* 3b.

1b. *Rev. Thomas Lamplugh Wolley, Rector of Portishead, co. Som.,* d. (-) ; m. *Emily, da. of James Willis ; and had issue (with a da., Rhoda Florence,* d. *unm.* 1909) 1c.

1c. Arthur Lamplugh Wolley (5 *Kildare Terrace, Bayswater ; Orotava, Teneriffe*), b. (—); *m.* Annie, da. of (—) Bernard ; *s.p.*

2b. *Henry Wolley, R.N.,* b. 6 *May* 1810; d. 3 *Dec.* 1898 ; m. 1st, 12 *July* 1838, *Charlotte Elizabeth, da. of Joseph Seymour Biscoe of Hempstead, co. Glouc.* [*and grandda. of Vincent Biscoe of Austin Friars, London, by his wife Lady Mary, da. of Edward* (*Seymour*), 8*th Duke of Somerset* [*E.*]], d. 28 *Feb.* 1851; *and had issue* 1c *to* 4c.

1c. Rev. Henry Francklyn Wolley, Hon. Canon of Canterbury, Vicar of St. Mary's, Shortlands (*St. Mary's Vicarage, Shortlands, Kent*), b. 1 July 1839 ; *m.* 5 July 1871, Emily, da. of the Rev. Frederick Brown, Rector of Nailsea, co. Somerset ; and has issue 1d to 4d.

1d. Hugh Seymour Lamplugh Wolley, Lieut. 56th Punjabi Rifles, Indian Army, b. 1882.

2d. Margaret Katharine Wolley.
3d. Mary Lilian Wolley.
4d. Mabel Stephana Wolley.

2c. Edith Emma Wolley, *unm.*   [Nos. 37982 to 37989.

# of The Blood Royal

3c. Charlotte Louisa Wolley, b. 12 June 1842; m. 1863, James Palladio Basevi, R.E. [son of George Basevi, the well-known Architect], d. 17 July 1871; and has issue 1d to 2d.

1d. William Henry Basevi, Major A. P. Dept. (*Hill Lodge, Milverton Terrace, Leamington*), b. 24 May 1865; m. 20 Oct. 1889, Ethel Wina, da. of William Gill of Plymouth; and has issue 1e to 2e.

1e. James Basevi, b. 21 Sept. 1890.

2e. Doris Frances Basevi, b. 27 May 1893.

2d. Rev. Charles Lionel Basevi (*The Oratory, Brompton, S.W.*), b. 30 Aug. 1867.

4c. Alice Portia Wolley, m. 3 Oct. 1867, Thomas Monck-Mason, Bombay C.S. [descended from the Lady Isabel Plantagenet (see Essex Volume, p. 97)], b. 1 Sept. 1837; d. 17 Feb. 1874; and has issue (with a da. who d. young) 1d to 4d.

1d. Roger Henry Monck Mason, Capt. Royal Munster Fusiliers, b. 19 Feb. 1871; m. 7 June 1901 (dissolved Aug. 1909), Ethel Beatrice, da. of Capt. Cecil Strickland; s.p.

2d. Thomas George Monck Mason (*Masonbrook, Cranbrook, Western Australia*), b. 30 Sept. 1872; m. Sept. 1902, Jane, da. of (—) Climie of Ballochmyle, W. Australia; and has issue 1e.

1e. Eileen Alice Portia Monck Mason, b. Sept. 1903.

3d. Edith Mary Monck Mason.

4d. Winifred Alice Monck Mason (*93 Oakley Street, Chelsea, S.W.*).

3b. Frances Louisa Wolley, d. 14 *July* 1874; m. 9 *Sept.* 1844, the Rev. Robert Craufurd, afterwards (1812) *Gregan Craufurd of Paris* [*Bt. of Kilbirney* [*G.B.* 1781] *Coll.*], d. 1868; *and had issue* 1c *to* 3c.

1c. Henry Robert Gregan Craufurd, J.P., late R.A. (*Brightwood, Aldbury, Tring*), b. 13 Aug. 1845; m. 1st, 18 July 1872, Fanny, da. of the Rev. James Williams of Tring Park, d.s.p. 16 Dec. 1876; 2ndly, 30 July 1878, Alice, da. of the Rev. Richard Mountford Wood, Rector of Aldbury; and has issue 1d to 4d.

1d. Robert Quentin Gregan Craufurd, Capt. Royal Scots Fusiliers, b. 9 Mar. 1880; m. Oct. 1909, Mildred, da. of the Right Hon. William Kenny, P.C., Judge of the King's Bench Div., High Court of Justice [I.].

2d. Archibald Gregan Craufurd, Capt. Gordon Highlanders, b. 2 Aug. 1881.

3d. James Gregan Craufurd, b. 23 Feb. 1886.

4d. Emma Katherine Gregan Craufurd.

2c. Charles Quentin Craufurd, Capt. R.N. (*Army and Navy*), b. 2 Dec. 1847; m. 1 June 1878, Esmeralda Calligary, da. of Count Valsamachi of Corfu; and has issue 1d to 2d.

1d. Quentin Gregan Craufurd, b. 1879; m.

2d. Maud Gregan Craufurd, m. (—) Dashwood (*12 Tite Street, Chelsea*).

3c. Emma Katherine Gregan-Craufurd, m. 26 Sept. 1874, Edward Broughton Pillans of Milan, d. 1889; and has issue (with a son, Brian, who d.s.p.) 1d to 4d.

1d. Robert Pillans.

2d. David Craufurd Pillans, R.N.

3d. Mary Pillans, m. 1908, Henri Chevallier (*Paris*).

4d. Esmé Katherine Pillans.

3a. Isaac Wolley, Adm. R.N., d.s.p.

4a. Rev. Godfrey Wolley, M.A., J.P., *Rector of Hawnby and Vicar of Hutton Bushel*, co. York, b. 4 Mar. 1760; d. 20 Nov. 1822; m. 1st. 28 Ap. 1791, *Ellice, da. of Richard Cass of Snainton*, co. *York* [*by his wife Ellice, da. of William Stockdale of Scarborough*], d. 13 Mar. 1800; 2ndly, *Frances, widow of* (—) *Spencer, da. of* (—) *Barker ; and had issue* (*with* 4 *other sons and* 6 *das. by 2nd wife, who d.s.p.*) 1b *to* 6b. [37990 to 38013.

The Plantagenet Roll

1b.[1] *Godfrey Wolley, Adm. R.N.*, b. 15 *June* 1799; d. 15 *Oct.* 1870; m. 17 *May* [? 1830], *Mary, da. of Bryan Taylor of Bridlington*, d. 25 *July* 1863; *and had issue* (*with a da., Selina Louisa,* d. *unm.*) 1c *to* 2c.

1c. Mary Charlotte Ellice Wolley, b. 5 *Nov.* 1832; d. 13 *Sept.* 1861; m. 30 *June* 1857, *Frederic Smith,* d. 16 *Ap.* 1882; *and had issue* 1d *to* 2d.

1d. Godfrey Smith (*Llanellen Court, Abergavenny*), b. 28 Jan. 1859; *m.* 27 Nov. 1884, Eliza, da. of George Young of Longton, co. Staff., Solicitor; *s.p.*

2d. Agnes Smith, *unm.*

2c. Katharine Emily Wolley, *m.* 30 July 1864, the Rev. Sackett Hope, M.A. (Oxon.), Vicar of Chedworth 1879–1898, &c. (*Chedworth, The Leas, Folkestone*); and has issue (with 4 others d. young) 1d to 9d.

1d. John Lamplugh Allen Hope, M.R.C.S. (Eng.), L.R.C.P. (Lond.) (*Devonshire House, Addlestone*), b. 14 Oct. 1866; *m.* 13 Ap. 1896, Rose, da. of Thomas Herring; and has issue 1e to 2e.

1e. Constance Katharine Mary Hope.

2e. Ruth Olga Margaret Hope.

2d. Godfrey Dawson Taylor Hope, M.A. (Oxon.) (*Turleigh, Bradford-on-Avon*), b. 31 Mar. 1868; *m.* 21 Dec. 1899, Ethel Jessie, da. of William Dwyer Way; and has issue 1e to 2e.

1e. John Godfrey Adrian Hope, b. 1 May 1907.

2e. Dorothea Katharine Esther Hope.

3d. Reginald Henry Walton Hope (*Greenmount, Cornwall Road, Uxbridge*), b. 19 Jan. 1872; *m.* 29 Aug. 1905, Mabel Constance, da. of Edwin Beard; and has issue 1e.

1e. Monica Constance Alice Hope.

4d. Cyril Edward Wolley Hope, b. 22 Ap. 1876; *unm.*

5d. Rev. Alban Sackett Hope, M.A. (Oxon.) (*St. Bartholomew's, Dover*), b. 22 June 1877; *unm.*

6d. Noel Eustace Hope, B.A. (Oxon.), A.R.C.M., b. 25 Mar. 1880; *unm.*

7d. Mary Katharine Sackett Hope, *unm.*

8d. Beatrice Sarah Louisa Hope, *unm.*

9d. Isabel Ruth Duodecima Hope, *unm.*

2b.[2] *Thomas Wolley, C.B., Chief Clerk in the Admiralty,* d. (–); m. *Matilda Frances, da. of the Rev.* (—) *Hatch, Rector of Kingston-on-Thames; and had issue* (*with an elder son who* d.s.p.) 1c.

1c. Godfrey Lamplugh Isaac Wolley, "Godfrey Lamplugh," an Actor.

3b.[1] *Honor Wolley,* b. 11 *Feb.* 1792; d. 28 *Oct.* 1827; m. *in the Abbey Church, St. Albans,* 28 *Jan.* 1812, *the Rev. William Stockdale of Mears Ashby Hall, co. Northants, J.P., M.A., and Fellow of Jesus Coll., Camb.,* b. 5 *Ap.* 1767; d. 17 *Feb.* 1858; *and had issue* (*with 3 other sons and 2 das. who* d. *unm.*) 1c *to* 4c.

1c. Rev. William Walter Stockdale, Rector of Wychling, co. Kent, b. 6 *Mar.* 1814; d. 19 *Feb.* 1893; m. 1st, Mary Martha Margaret, da. of James Douglas of Rhydyfran, co. Cardigan, d. *Oct.* 1853; 2ndly, 16 *Ap.* 1857, Emma, da. of James Ashenden, d. 15 *Feb.* 1886; *and had issue* (*with a da.* d. *young*) 1d *to* 2d.

1d.[1] Reginald Walter Stockdale, b. 9 *Jan.* 1852; d. (–); m. Adela, da. of the Rev. James John Douglas, Prebendary of Perth; and had issue (with 3 other children) 1e to 2e.

1e. Reginald Walter Douglas Stockdale, b. 11 Ap. 1892.

2e. Mary Louisa Stockdale, b. 11 Dec. 1893.

2d.[2] Godfrey Henry Wolley Stockdale, Col. R.E., b. 1 Aug. 1858; *m.* 15 Nov. 1884, Ida Eliza, da. of Gen. Horatio Scott; and has issue 1e to 2e.

1e. Godfrey Eric le Scot Stockdale, b. 1 June 1888.

2e. Dorothy Honor Stockdale, b. 5 May 1893. [Nos. 38014 to 38036.

of The Blood Royal

2c. Henry Minshull Stockdale of Mears Ashby Hall, M.A. (Camb.), Bar.-at-Law of Lincoln's Inn, J.P., D.L., and *late* Chairman Northants Quarter Sessions and Capt. Northants Militia *(Mears Ashby Hall, Northampton)*, b. 30 Sept. 1822; m. 12 Aug. 1858, Sarah Emily, da. of the Rev. Robert Hervey Knight, Rector of Weston Favell, d. 15 May 1896; and has issue (with a son and da. who d. unm.) 1d to 5d.

1d. Henry Minshull Stockdale, J.P., M.A. (Camb.), Bar.-at-Law of the Inner Temple, *late* Major 3rd Batt. Northants Regt. *(Mears Ashby Hall, Northants)*, b. 8 Feb. 1861; m. 7 July 1896, Florence Margaret Rose [descended from the Lady Isabel Plantagenet (see Essex Volume, p. 269)], da. of the Rev. Charles Villiers, Rector of Croft, co. York; and has issue 1e to 2e.

1e. Henry Charles Minshull Stockdale, b. 5 Ap. 1902.
2e. Edmund Villiers Minshull Stockdale, b. 16 Ap. 1903.

2d. Rev. Robert William Stockdale, M.A. (Camb.), Vicar of St. Silas, Hunslet *(St. Silas's Vicarage, Hunslet, Yorks)*, b. 31 Oct. 1862; m. 1 Mar. 1905, Emily, da. of Israel Fozard; and has issue 1e to 2e.

1e. Honor Stockdale.
2e. Katherine Fozard Stockdale.

3d. Herbert Edward Stockdale, Major R.H.A., b. 22 June 1867; m. 4 Feb. 1909, Margaret Frances, da. of the Rev. James Tufton Bartlet, Canon of Lincoln.

4d. Emily Honor Stockdale, *unm.*
5d. Mabel Katharine Mary Stockdale, *unm.*

3c. *Catherine Frances Stockdale*, b. 22 *Jan.* 1816; d. 27 *Sept.* 1860; m. 23 *Mar.* 1841, *the Rev. Thomas Bury Wells, M.A (Camb.), Rector of Portlemouth, co. Devon, formerly Lieut. R.N.*, b. *Jan.* 1795; d. 23 *May* 1879; *and had issue (with a son and da. who* d.s.p.) *1d to 6d.*

1d. Lionel Bury Wells, M.I.C.E. *(Horsecombe, Salcombe, Devon)*, b. 12 Feb. 1843; m. 11 Oct. 1871, Mary Eliza, da. of the Rev. T. P. Kirkman, Rector of Croft, co. Lanc., F.R.S.; and has issue (with a da. d. young) 1e to 6e.

1e. Lionel Fortescue Wells, C.E., b. 20 Oct. 1877.
2e. Katharine Elmina Wells, m. 16 Aug. 1901, Harry Augustus Whittall [son of Sir (James) William Whittall, Founder and President of the British Chamber of Commerce of Turkey] *(Broussa, Hale, Altringham)*; and has issue 1f to 2f.

1f. Lionel Harry Whittall, b. 8 May 1907.
2f. Katharine Marion Whittall, b. 21 Feb. 1906.

3e. Mary Dorothea Wells.
4e. Elizabeth Rose Wells.
5e. Elinor Kirkman Wells.
6e. Muriel Bury Wells.

2d. Henry Lake Wells, C.I.E., Lieut.-Col. R.E., b. 8 *Mar.* 1850; d. 1898; m. *Alice Bertha, da. of the Rev. Hugh Bacon of Baxterley, co. Warwick; and had issue* 1e to 5e.

1e. *Lionel Salisbury Wells, Lieut. Queen's Own Corps of Guides*, b. 1885; d. 1908.
2e. Victor Horace Wells, b. 1897.
3e. Bessie Margaret Fortescue Wells.
4e. Honor Lake Wells.
5e. Kathleen Esther Wells.

3d. Thomas Bury Wells, b. Oct. 1856; m. Bertha, da. of William Palmer of Montreal; *s.p.*
4d. Katherine Alicia Wells, m. Robert Sterne, Comm. R.N.; *s.p.*
5d. Elizabeth Ellen Wells, *unm.*
6d. Caroline Emily Wells, *unm.* [Nos. 38037 to 38063.

The Plantagenet Roll

4c. *Ellen Stockdale*, b. 7 *Jan.* 1826; d. 9 *Nov.* 1901; m. 14 *Ap.* 1860, *James Pain of Aspley Guise, co. Beds*, d. 4 *Jan.* 1878; *and had issue (with a son and* 4 *das.* d. *unm.*) 1d to 3d.

1d. *John Athill James Pain*, b. 2 *Oct.* 1864; d. 22 *Dec.* 1899; m. 29 *Ap.* 1893, *Edith Jane, da. of William Stagg*, d. 13 *Jan.* 1901; *and had issue* 1e *to* 3e.
    1e. James Crichton Pain, b. 10 Sept. 1895.
    2e. Catherine Mary Pain, b. 13 Mar. 1894.
    3e. Mary Henrietta Pain, b. 8 Sept. 1897.

2d. Henrietta Mary Pain
3d. Amabel Barbara Pain } (*Woodlands, Woburn Sands*), *unm.*

4b.[1] *Catherine Wolley*, b. 16 *Mar.* 1793; d. (–); m. 15 *Nov.* 1810, *the Rev. Stephen Allen*, d. (–); *and had issue* 1c *to* 4c.
    1c. Rev. Stephen Allen, D.D.
    2c. *Thomas Allen*, m. *and had several children*.
    3c. *Godfrey Allen, emigrated to New Zealand*.
    4c. *Katharine Allen*, d. (–); m. *in New Zealand*, (—) *Wray or Ray; and had issue (a da.)*.

5b.[2] *Isabella Wolley*.
6b.[2] *Caroline Wolley*.

5a. *Honor Wolley*, d. 1845; m. *as 2nd wife, the Rev. Anthony Fountaine Eyre of Baronburgh, co. York*, d. 14 *Feb.* 1794; *and had issue (with a son and* 3 *das.* d. *unm.*) 1b.

1b. *Rev. Anthony William Eyre, Rector of Hornsea*, b. 20 *Nov.* 1783; d. 1848; m. *Sarah, da. of David Mapleton of Bath, M.D.*, d. (–); *and had issue (with* 2 *sons and* 2 *das.* d. *unm.*) 1c *to* 3c.

1c. *Edward John Eyre of the Grange, Staple Aston, co. Oxon., sometime Governor of Jamaica*, b. 5 *Aug.* 1815; d. 3 *Nov.* 1901; m. 3 *Ap.* 1850, *Adelaide Fanny, da. of Capt. F. Ormond, R.N.*, d. 15 *May* 1905; *and had issue* 1d *to* 7d.

1d. *Gervas Selwyn Eyre*, Bar.-at-Law, Lieut.-Col. Indian Army, *formerly Commissioner of Division, Burmah* (*The Hudnalls, St. Briavel's, S.O., Glos*), b. 25 July 1851; m. 29 Jan. 1874, Lucy Dorothea, da. of the Rev. E. J. Baines, Vicar of Golding, co. Kent; and has issue 1e.
    1e. Lucy Marguerite Eyre, b. 9 Dec. 1874.

2d. Edward Broughton Eyre, Lieut. (ret.) R.N., b. 23 Mar. 1853; *unm.*
3d. *Charles Ormond Eyre* (*Fiji*), b. 5 Dec. 1856; m. and has issue.
4d. Harry Eyre, *late* Colonial Service, Gold Coast, b. 13 Feb. 1861; *unm.*
5d. Sydney Frederick Eyre, b. 30 Oct. 1871; *unm.*
6d. *Ada Austin Eyre* (*Delamont, Killyleigh, co. Devon*), m. 15 Sept. 1881, Alexander Hamilton Miller Haven Gordon of Florida Manor, and Delamont, co. Devon, J.P., D.L., d. 5 July 1910; and has issue 1e to 10e.
    1e. Alexander Robert Gisborne Gordon, Capt., Roy. Irish Reg., b. 28 July 1882.
    2e. Eyre Gordon, Scholar Queen's College, Oxford, Indian C.S., b. 28 Feb. 1884.
    3e. John de la Hay Gordon, 67th Punjabis, Indian Army, b. 30 Mar. 1887.
    4e. Edward Ormond Gordon, b. 1 Mar. 1888.
    5e. Henry Gisborne Gordon, b. 29 Aug. 1889.
    6e. Eldred Pottinger Gordon, b. 24 May 1891.
    7e. Ivy Dorothy Catherine Gordon,
    8e. Marjorie Frances Gordon,
    9e. Honor Gordon, } *unm.*
    10e. Marion Alice Gordon,

7d. May Lilian Eyre, *unm.*

2c. *Caroline Eyre*, d. 23 *May* 1863; m. *as* 1st *wife*, 10 *June* 1839, *the Rev. James Hare Wake, Vicar of Sutton in Forest, co. Yorks* [*Bt.* (*E.* 1621) *Coll.*], b. 19 *Feb.* 1805; d. 5 *Dec.* 1874; *and had issue* 1d *to* 7d.   [Nos. 38064 to 38086.

of The Blood Royal

1*d*. Rev. Baldwin Eyre Wake, M.A. (Oxon.), Vicar of Ruswarp (*Ruswarp Vicarage, Whitby, Yorks*), b. 20 Mar. 1840; *m.* 16 June 1868, Adelaide Bowles, da. of the Rev. Henry Cleveland, Rector of Romald Kirk, Darlington; and has issue 1*e* to 3*e*.

1*e*. Rev. Hereward Eyre Wake, M.A. (Oxon.), Vicar of Castle Cary (*Castle Cary Vicarage, Somerset*), b. 8 June 1869; *m.* 18 Ap. 1899, Mary Frances, da. of James Sealy Lawrence of 5 Upper Addison Gardens, W.; and has issue 1*f* to 2*f*.

1*f*. Hereward Baldwyn Lawrence Wake, b. 26 Aug. 1900.
2*f*. Torfrida Marjory Wake, b. 11 May 1902.

2*e*. Torfrida Mary Wake.
3*e*. Margaret Gladys Hermione Wake.

2*d*. Gervas Fountayne Wake (*Victoria, British Columbia*), b. 15 Ap. 1853; *m.* 9 June 1881, his cousin, Amy Rosamond, da. of Capt. Baldwin Arden Wake, R.N.; and has issue 1*e* to 3*e*.

1*e*. Hereward Eyre Wake, b. 16 July 1888.
2*e*. Rosamond Adelaide Alice Wake, *m.* 14 Aug. 1907, Frederick Paget Norbury (*The Norrest, Malvern*); and has issue 1*f*.

1*f*. Christopher Paget Norbury, b. 8 Oct. 1908.

3*e*. Gladys Maude Mary Wake.

3*d*. Emily Honor Wake, *m.* 15 Sept. 1868, Arthur Charles Cleveland (23 *Eversley Road, Bexhill*); and has issue 1*e* to 4*e*.

1*e*. Hereward Wake Cleveland, b. 1880.
2*e*. Ethel Mary Wake Cleveland.
3*e*. Blanche Seton Cleveland.
4*e*. Evelyn Eyre Cleveland.

4*d*. Lucy Joan Wake.

5*d*. Edith Caroline Wake, *m.* 29 Nov. 1864, Capt. Martin Budd Lewin, *formerly* 51st Regt. (78 *Elliscombe Road, Old Charlton, Kent*); and has issue 1*e* to 8*e*.

1*e*. *Robert Hutchinson Wake Lewin*, b. 8 Jan. 1869; d. (? s.p.).
2*e*. Arthur Wyndham Wake Lewin, b. 3 Mar. 1871.
3*e*. Francis Ashby Wake Lewin, b. 17 May 1873.
4*e*. Fenton Gervas Martin Lewin, b. 20 Nov. 1875,
5*e*. George Edward de Montfleury Lewin, b. 23 Dec. 1876.
6*e*. Caroline Edith Constance Lewin.
7*e*. Gladys Bertha Joan Lewin.
8*e*. Torfrida Dorothy Wilhelmina Lewin.

6*d*. Bertha Charlotte Wake.
7*d*. Gertrude Maud Wake.

3*c*. *Fanny Eyre*, b. 1820; d. (–); m. *Joshua Mashill of Pudsey, co. York, Surgeon*; and had issue 1*d*.

1*d*. Clara Ruth Mashill, *m.* H. A. Wickers, M.D.; and has issue (a da.).

6*a*. *Cordelia Wolley*, d. (–); m. *John Bower*; and had issue.

7*a*. *Katherine Wolley*, d. (–); m. *at Fulford 16 Oct. 1789, John Raper of Abberford and Lotherton, co. York, and Lamplugh, co. Cumberland* (see p. 262), d. 3 *July* 1824; *and had issue* 1*b* to 3*b*.

1*b*. *John Lamplugh Raper, afterwards* (R.L. 10 *Mar.* 1825) *Lamplugh-Raper of Lamplugh*, b. 19 *July* 1790; d.s.p. 13 *Ap.* 1867.

2*b*. *Henry Raper of Lamplugh*, b. 12 *Feb.* 1795; d.s.p. 16 *May* 1867.

3*b*. *Anne Raper*, da. and in her issue (16 *May* 1867) *sole h.*, d. 19 *Dec.* 1857; m. 19 *July* 1815, *James Brooksbank of The Bailey, Durham, J.P.* [2nd son of *Benjamin Brooksbank of Healaugh, co. York, J.P.*], b. 21 *Sept.* 1786; d. 27 *Feb.* 1870; *and had issue* 1*c* to 2*c*.

1*c*. *James Brooksbank, Bar.-at-Law*, b. 27 *Sept.* 1816; d.v.p. 27 *Mar.* 1863; m. 4 *Feb.* 1824, *Marianne, da. of Thomas Edmonds of London*, d. 11 *Oct.* 1852; *and had issue* 1*d* to 2*d*. [Nos. 38087 to 38114.]

The Plantagenet Roll

1*d*. Walter Lamplugh Brooksbank, Lord of the Manor of Lamplugh and Patron of the Living, J.P. (*Lamplugh Hall, Cockermouth ; Fir Bank, Penrith, Cumberland*), *b.* 4 Nov. 1850 ; *m.* 8 Aug. 1877, Mary Anne Madeleine, da. of Francis Greenwell of Durham, J.P. ; and has issue 1*e* to 5*e*.

    1*e*. James Lamplugh Brooksbank, *b.* 21 Feb. 1889.
    2*e*. Katherine Dorothy Aurora Brooksbank.
    3*e*. Honor Elizabeth Brooksbank.
    4*e*. Myrtle Philippa Brooksbank.
    5*e*. Una Frances Honora Brooksbank.

2*d*. Marianne Elizabeth Annie Brooksbank, *m.* 26 Jan. 1875, William Delisle Powles (40 *Sussex Gardens, Hyde Park, W.*) ; and has issue 1*e* to 3*e*.

    1*e*. John Copley Powles, Lieut. (*ret.*) R.N., *b.* 22 Nov. 1875.
    2*e*. Rev. Robert Cowley Powles, M.A. (Oxon.), *b.* 22 June 1877.
    3*e*. Francis Brooksbank Powles, B.A. (Oxon.), *b.* 27 Ap. 1882.

2*c*. Rev. *Walter Brooksbank, M.A., Rector of Lamplugh*, b. 5 *Aug.* 1830 ; d. 20 *Oct.* 1908 ; m. 29 *May* 1855, *Elizabeth Jane, da. of Stephen Poyntz Denning ; and has issue* 1*d to* 6*d*.

    1*d*. Stephen Poyntz Brooksbank, C.E., *b.* 11 May 1856 ; *m.* and has issue (a da.).
    2*d*. Hugh Lamplugh Brooksbank, B.A. (Camb.), *b.* 25 Feb. 1867 ; *m.* 27 Dec. 1900, Sybil Lavallin, da. of the Rev. Herbert Boyne Lavallin Puxley of Lavallin House, Tenby, Rector of Caton.
    3*d*. Ethel Brooksbank, *m.* 13 June 1882, the Rev. Ernest Edward Stock, Vicar of Rocliffe (*Rocliffe Rectory, Carlisle*) ; and has issue 1*e* to 8*e*.

        1*e*. Hugh Russell Stock, *b.* 19 July 1883.
        2*e*. Reginald Walter Stock, *b.* 4 Aug. 1886.
        3*e*. Christopher Herbert Stock, *b.* 5 July 1888.
        4*e*. Cecil Ernest Stock, *b.* 23 Dec. 1892.
        5*e*. Ethel Marjory Stock, *b.* 5 May 1885.
        6*e*. Beatrice Mildred Stock, *b.* 31 July 1889.
        7*e*. Gertrude Mary Stock
        8*e*. Katharine Maud Stock } (twins), *b.* 11 May 1899.

    4*d*. Gertrude Brooksbank (twin), *m.* 29 Nov. 1883, Samuel Taylor of Eccleston Hall and Birkdault, co. Lancaster, J.P., B.A., Bar.-at-Law, *late* Lieut. 3rd Batt. South Lancashire Regt. (*Birkdault, Haverthwaite, near Ulverston*) ; and has issue 1*e* to 4*e*.

        1*e*. Rev. Samuel Taylor, B.A. (Camb.), *b.* 6 Oct. 1884.
        2*e*. Richard Brooksbank Taylor, Lieut. Border Regt., *b.* 8 Dec. 1885.
        3*e*. Geoffrey Fell Taylor, *b.* 8 Nov. 1890.
        4*e*. Nancy Taylor.

    5*d*. Katherine Brooksbank (twin).
    6*d*. Philippa Beatrice Brooksbank, *m.* 28 July 1892, Anthony Gerard Salvin of Hawksfold, co. Sussex, Capt. Yorkshire R.G.A. Militia (*Woodfold, Fernhurst*) ; and has issue 1*e*.

        1*e*. Philippa Malorie Salvin.   [Nos. 38115 to 38143.

135. Descendants of ANNE LAMPLUGH, sister and co-h. of the Rev. Thomas Lamplugh of Lamplugh (Table XV.), *d.* (–) ; *m.* 8 Oct. 1750, JOHN RAPER of Lotherton, co. York ; and had issue 1*a* to 4*a*.

1*a*. *John Raper of Abberford and Lotherton, co. York, and Lamplugh, co. Cumberland*, d. 3 *July* 1824 ; m. 16 *Oct.* 1789, *Katherine, da. of the Rev. Godfrey Wolley ; and had issue.*

See p. 261, Nos. 38115–38143.   [Nos. 38144 to 38172.

of The Blood Royal

2a. *Anne Raper*, d. aged 84, bur. *in Church of St. Martin's, Coney Street, York, M.I.*; m. *George Townend*; *and had issue* 1b.

1b. *Anne Townend, only da. and apparently only child,*[1] b. c. 1762; d. *at Clapham Rise,* 29 *Dec.* 1858, *aged* 86; m. 1st, *John Moore, Capt.* 3rd *Dragoon Guards,* d. (-) ; 2ndly, *Edmund Lally, Capt.* 4th *Dragoon Guards* [*descended from George Plantagenet, Duke of Clarence* (see Essex Volume, Clarence Supp., p. 528)]; *and had issue* (*with a son, Edmund Lally, who* d. *at Eton*) 1c to 6c.

1c. *Ann Moore, da. and co-h.,* d. (-) ; m. *the Rev. Jocelyn Wiley of Heworth, co. York.*

2c. *Frances Moore, da. and co-h.*

3c. *Georgiana Moore,* 3rd *da.*[2] *and co-h.,* d. 1845; m. 16 *Dec.* 1824, *her cousin, Henry Raper of Lamplugh* (see p. 261), d.s.p. 16 *May* 1867.

4c. (—) *Moore, da. and co-h.,* d. (-) ; m. *Wynn Aubrey.*

5c. *Anna Katherine Lally, da. and co-h.,* d. 2 *May* 1900 ; m. *the Rev. Edward John Speck, Sec. Church Pastoral Aid Society,* d. (-) ; *and had issue* 1d.

1d. Rev. *Jocelyn Henry Speck* (*St. Martin's Vicarage, Bedford*), b. 1857 ; m. Rosalie, da. of Alexander Dalrymple; and has issue 1e to 3e.

1e. John Speck, b. 1888.

2e. Gwendolen Lally Speck.

3e. Stella Speck.

6c. *Augusta Lally,* d. 10 *Sept.* 1898; m. 11 *Oct.* 1843, *the Rev. Henry Roxby Roxby, Rector of St. Olave, Old Jewry,* d. 14 *Jan.* 1860; *and had issue* 1d *to* 3d.

1d. Rev. Edmund Lally Roxby, M.A. (Camb.), Hon. Canon of Gloucester, Rector of Cheltenham (*The Rectory, Cheltenham*), b. 21 Aug. 1844.

2d. Carus Wilson Roxby, b. 26 Dec. 1845.

3d. Herbert Roxby, Capt. R.N., b. 9 Feb. 1848.

3a. *Honor Raper,* d. (-) ; bur. *in the Church of St. Martin, Coney Street, York,* m. *John Kendall of Hatfield, co. York,* d. (-) ; bur. *in the Church of St. Martin afsd.* ; *and had issue* (*with an eldest son John, lost at sea*) 1b to 5b.

1b. *Henry Edward Kendall of London, an eminent Architect,* d. (-) ; m. *Anna Maria, da. of* (—) *Lyon* ; *and had issue* 1c *to* 6c.

1c. *Henry Edward Kendall of Brunswick Square, London, Architect,* d. (-); m. *Mary, da. and h. of Thomas Amery Cobham of Uckfield, co. Sussex* ; *and had issue* 1d *to* 6d.

1d. *Henry Robert John Edmunds Kendall,* d. (-).

2d. Thomas Cobham John Kendall.

3d. Edward Herne Kendall.

4d. Arthur James Kendall.

5d. Anna Maria Mardow Kendall.

6d. Mary Leonora Kendall.

2c. *George Kendall.*

3c. *John Kendall, Lieut.* 28th *Bengal Native Infantry,* d. (? s.p.) 17 *Ap.* 1852.

4c. *Charles Kendall.*

5c. *Emma Kendall,* d. (-) ; m. *William Covey of Wilton Street, Belgrave Square,* d. (-) ; *and had issue* (*with a son, Charles, Major Durham L.I.,* d. *unm.*) 1d *to* 3d.

1d. Emma Covey, *unm.* [Nos. 38173 to 38185.

---

[1] "Outlines of the Genealogy of the Hassards and their Connections, York" (H. Sotheran, Bookseller, Coney Street, 1858).

[2] Burke's "Landed Gentry," 1906, under Brooksbank of Lamplugh, p. 206. This da. is not mentioned in "Outlines of the Genealogy of the Hassards," &c., from which particulars of the other das. are taken, unless, indeed, she is identical with the da. (there called 3rd) who *m.* Wynn Aubrey, in which case Henry Raper must have been her second husband.

The Plantagenet Roll

2d. Fanny Shelley Covey, d. 11 Jan. 1908; m. Quintin William Francis Twiss of H.M. Treasury, d. 7 Aug. 1900; and had issue 1e to 5e.

1e. Horace William Twiss, Solicitor (*Schiffbauerdamm* 15, *Berlin, N.W.*), b. 24 Mar. 1865; m. in New York 8 Oct. 1892, Lilian Beatrice, da. of Henry Simms.

2e. Arthur Quintin Twiss, b. 16 Nov. 1867; unm.

3e. Effie Fanny Twiss, unm.

4e. Annie Constance Twiss, m. 6 Feb. 1893, Ernest Blechynden Waggett, M.A. (Camb.), M.R.C.S., L.R.C.P., Surgeon, Nose, Throat, and Ear Dept., Charing Cross Hospital, and Consulting Surgeon, London Throat Hospital (39 *Wimpole Street, W.*); and has issue 1f.

1f. Judith Blechynden Waggett, b. 4 May 1897.

5e. Mildred Caroline Twiss, unm.

3d. Myra Jane Covey, unm.

6c. Sophia Kendall, b. 31 Aug. 1811; d. 17 Feb. 1879; m. 23 Jan. 1830, Lewis Cubitt [uncle of George (Cubitt), 1st Lord Ashcombe [U.K.] P.C.], b. 29 Sept. 1799; d. 9 June 1883; and had issue 1d to 4d.

1d. Lewis Cubitt of Orr House, Hastings, Capt. 26th Cameronians, b. 5 Dec. 1834; d. 20 Nov. 1872; m. 31 Mar. 1869, Charlotte Anne, da. of Robert William Kennard of Theobalds, co. Herts, M.P., J.P., D.L.; and had issue 1e.

1e. Thomas (Cubitt, now (R.L. 10 Dec. 1904) Riccardi-Cubitt), 1st Count Riccardi-Cubitt [Italy, 27 May 1904], which title he had Royal Licence to use in the United Kingdom 16 Dec. 1905 (*Eden Hall, Edenbridge, Kent*), b. 8 May 1870; m. 23 Nov. 1893, Fede Maria, *suo jure* Countess Riccardi [Italy, 3 May 1904], da. and h. of Adolfo, 3rd Count Riccardi [Sardinia, 2 Ap. 1833], K.M.L., K.C.I., Col. Italian R.A., and Equerry to King Victor Emmanuel III.; and has issue 1f to 4f.

1f. Charles Cyril Riccardi-Cubitt, heir to mother's title, b. 28 Jan. 1896.

2f. Vera Alicia Maria Riccardi-Cubitt.

3f. Theodora Fede Maria Riccardi-Cubitt.

4f. Monica Yolanda Riccardi-Cubitt.

2d. Ellen Cubitt, m. as 2nd wife, 7 Dec. 1858, Edgar Alfred Bowring, C.B., formerly Librarian and Registrar to Board of Trade, and M.P. for Exeter 1868–1874 [son of Sir John Bowring, LL.D., Min. Plen. to China] (30 *Eaton Place, S.W.*); and has issue 1e to 2e.

1e. Algernon Cunliffe Bowring (30 *Eaton Place, S.W.*), b. 27 Sept. 1859; unm.

2e. Victor Bowring, now (D.P.) Bowring Hanbury (5 *Belgrave Square, S.W.; Ilam Hall, Ashbourne*), b. 26 Mar. 1867; m. 16 Feb. 1904, Ellen, widow of the Right Hon. Robert William Hanbury of Ilam, P.C., M.P., President of the Board of Agriculture, da. and h. of Col. Knott Hamilton.

3d. Agnes Cubitt, m. 31 Oct. 1855, Lieut.-Col. Henry Charles Cunliffe-Owen, R.E., C.B., V.C., d. 7 Mar. 1867; and has issue 1e.

1e. Edward Cunliffe-Owen, C.M.G., Bar.-at-Law, was Sec. to the Fisheries, Health, and Inventions Exhibition, and Assist.-Sec to Royal Commissioners of Colonial and Indian Exhibition 1886 (69 *Oxford Terrace, Hyde Park, W.*), b. 1 Jan. 1857; m. 18 Ap. 1882, Emma Pauline, da. of Sir (Francis) Philip Cunliffe-Owen, K.C.B., K.C.M.G., C.I.E.; and has issue 1f to 4f.

1f. Francis Edward Cunliffe-Owen, b. 22 Dec. 1884.

2f. Alexander Robert Cunliffe-Owen, b. 25 Aug. 1898.

3f. Dorothy Mary Cunliffe-Owen.

4f. Sybil Cunliffe-Owen.

4d. Ada Cubitt, unm.

2b. George Kendall, Capt. R.M., served under Nelson at the Nile, Copenhagen, and Trafalgar, upon which last occasion he commanded the Marines on board the Neptune, b. c. 1783; d. (? s.p.) 8 Mar. 1840.

3b. Richard Kendall, Major R.A., b. c. 1808; d. (? s.p.) in Barbados 3 Sept. 1843.

[Nos. 38186 to 38207.

of The Blood Royal

4b. Honor Kendall, d. 3 June 1814; m. 23 Ap. 1805, Thomas Shann of Tadcaster, b. 13 Mar. 1768; d. 9 Feb. 1852; and had issue (with 2 sons who d. unm.) 1c.

1c. George Shann of York, M.D., b. 18 May 1809; d. 3 Oct. 1882; m. 16 Ap. 1845, Jane, da. of the Rev. William Gray, Canon of Ripon and Vicar of Brafferton, d. at York 6 Sept. 1899; and had issue (with 2 other sons who d.s.p.) 1d to 9d.

    1d. George Shann, M.A. (Camb.), b. 22 July 1846.

    2d. Frederick Shann, B.A. (Camb.), M.R.C.S., L.R.C.P., J.P., V.D. (Farnham, Knaresborough), b. 22 Ap. 1849.

    3d. Alfred Shann, b. 1 July 1850.

    4d. Henry Charles Shann, Surgeon (Michlegate Hill House, York), b. 21 Feb. 1852; m. 23 July 1885, Caroline Mary, da. of Sir William Henry Flower, K.C.B., F.R.S.; and has issue 1e to 5e.

        1e. Edward Warington Shann, B.Sc. (St. Andrews), b. 6 Sept. 1886.

        2e. Gerald Davenant Shann, b. 23 Dec. 1888.

        3e. Charles Douglas Shann, b. 4 Mar. 1907.

        4e. Vera Flower Shann.

        5e. Rosetta Mary Shann.

    5d. Rev. Reginald Shann, M.A. (Trin. Coll., Camb.), Rector of Chenies (Chenies Rectory, Rickmansworth, Bucks), b. 18 July 1854; m. 11 Sept. 1879, Elizabeth, da. of the Rev. Edward Hoare, M.A., Vicar of Holy Trinity, Tunbridge Wells, Canon of Canterbury [by his wife Maria Eliza, da. of Sir Benjamin Collins Brodie, 1st Bt. [U.K.], M.D., F.R.S., D.C.L.]; and has issue 1e to 4e.

        1e. Rev. Charles Brodie Shann, M.A. (Camb.), b. 8 Dec. 1884.

        2e. Reginald Arthur Shann, b. 26 June 1891.

        3e. Lettice Mary Shann, B.Sc. (London).

        4e. Ethel Katharine Shann, M.B. (Camb.).

    6d. William Arthur Shann, formerly of St. Anne's, Lowestoft (Camberley, Surrey), b. 10 June 1857; m. 25 Ap. 1900, Clara, widow of Capt. V. R. Rae, West York Regt., da. of Thomas Moss, s.p.

    7d. Thomas Lawrence Shann, M.A. (Camb.) (The Quarry Cottage, Farnham, near Knaresborough), b. 21 Sept. 1858; m. 4 Aug. 1892, Lucy Fenwick, da. of Joseph Watson of Gateshead; and has issue 1e to 4e.

        1e. Kenneth Shann, b. 22 Ap. 1895.

        2e. Honor Shann.

        3e. Mary Grace Shann.

        4e. Faith Shann.

    8d. Lucy Honor Shann, unm.

    9d. Laura Jane Shann, unm.

5b. Mary Ann Kendall, d. 19 Oct. 1851; m. 26 Jan. 1808, Richard Samuel Hassard, afterwards (R.L. 7 Aug. 1807) Short, Lord of the Manors of Edlington, East Keal, and part of Clerkenwell, b. 20 Ap. 1754; d. 24 Oct. 1826; and had issue (with an elder son and a da., Mrs. Maitland, who d.s.p.) 1c to 7c.

1c. John Hassard Short of Edlington Grove, co. Lincoln, J.P., D.L., b. 18 Nov. 1810; d. 4 Dec. 1893; m. 24 Nov. 1831, Margaret, da. of Lieut.-Col. Richard Elmhirst of Ashby Grove, co. Linc., d. 2 Feb. 1881; and had issue 1d to 6d.

    1d. Edward Hassard Short, now (D.P. 1 Jan. 1899) Hassard, J.P., co. Lincoln (Edlington Manor, Horncastle, co. Lincoln), b. 22 Aug. 1848; m. 11 Mar. 1873, Geraldine Rachel, da. of John Henry Blagrave of Calcot Park, co. Bucks, and Barrow Court, co. Somerset; and has issue 1e to 2e.

        1e. Hubert Edward Hassard, b. 15 Oct. 1877.

        2e. Digby Valentine Hassard, b. 14 Feb. 1879.

    2d. Algernon Lawson Hassard Short, late Lieut. Royal North Gloucestershire Militia, settled in North Carolina (350 West 115th Street, New York), b. 20 Feb. 1852; m. 13 Jan. 1875, Routh Elizabeth, da. of Col. John Luther Bridgers of

[Nos. 38208 to 38233.

The Plantagenet Roll

Taboro, N. Carolina, U.S.A.; and has issue (with a son, Reginald Elmhirst Hassard Short, b. 17 Mar. 1878; d. 30 Nov. 1895) 1e.

1e. Katharine Routh Bridgers Hassard Short.

3d. Caroline Mary Short, m. 23 July 1868, Charles Godfrey Bolam, late 7th Royal Fusiliers (*Dunchurch, near Rugby*); and has issue 1e to 5e.

1e. Rev. Cecil Edward Bolam, Rector of St. Mary Magdalene, Lincoln (*Lincoln*), b. 7 Mar. 1875; m. 18 Nov. 1902, Beatrice Helen, da. of James Rhodes of Rotherham, co. York; and has issue 1f.

1f. Joyce Helen Bolam.

2e. Mabel Marian Bolam, m. 26 June 1901, John Edmonds, Land Agent (*The Manor House, Islip, Thrapston*); and has issue 1f.

1f. Winifred Mary Edmonds.

3e. Katharine Mary Bolam, *unm.*

4e. Muriel Agnes Bolam, m. 6 Ap. 1899, the Rev. Sydney Sparks Herington, M.A., Rector of Heydour (*Heydour Rectory, near Grantham*).

5e. Beatrice Margaret Bolam, m. 24 Jan. 1907, the Rev. Robert Harvey Baldwin Crosthwaite, M.A., Rector of Calthorpe (*Calthorpe Rectory, near Rugby*).

4d. Frances Adela Short, m. Dec. 1879, Gen. Thomas Augustus Carey, Bengal Staff Corps, *d.s.p.* 23 May 1892.

5d. *Katharine Jane Hassard Short*, b. 26 Dec. 184—; d. 16 *Feb.* 1902; m. 22 Oct. 1877, *the Rev. Edwin Thomas James Marriner, BA. (Camb.) (The Pollards, Thurlow Hill, Torquay); and had issue* 1e.

1e. Gwendolyn Marian Monlas Marriner.

6d. Gertrude Elmhirst Short, now (D.P. 1 Jan. 1899) Hassard.

2c. *Rev. Henry Short, afterwards Hassard,* b. 21 *Mar.* 1812; d. 30 *Jan.* 1885; m. 1842, *Lucy, da. of the Rev. John Martin Butt, M.A., d.* 17 *May* 1898; *and had issue* 1d *to* 4d.

1d. Henry Hassard Hassard, b. 21 Feb. 1844; m. 6 Nov. 1872, Elizabeth Anna, da. of Felix McKinnan; and has issue.

2d. Rev. Richard Samuel Hassard, M.A. (Oxon.), Sub-Dean and Canon of Truro Cathedral (*Truro*), b. 9 May 1848; m. 7 Ap. 1874, Edith, da. of John Costeker.

3d. Lucy Alice Hassard, m. 1871, the Rev. William Mason, D.D., d. (—); and has issue.

4d. Emily Constance Hassard, m. 5 Nov. 1885, the Rev. Robert Thomas Shea, M.A. (Camb.), Vicar of Little Wakering (*Little Wakering Vicarage, Southend*).

3c. *William Short of Harrogate, M.D.,* b. 28 *May* 1813; d. 1 *Nov.* 1879; m. 6 *Aug.* 1837, *Isabella, da. of James Dixon of Cottingham Hall, co. York [and great-niece of the Rev. William Mason the Poet]; and had issue (with* 2 *sons d.s.p.)* 1d *to* 8d.

1d. William James Short, b. 27 Aug. 1840; m. Emma, da. of (—) Petley, *d.s.p.* 13 Oct. 1868.

2d. Frederick Hugh Short, Chief Clerk of the Crown Office, Royal Courts of Justice, late Capt. 3rd V.B. Royal West Kent Regt., b. 19 Mar. 1843; m. 8 Oct. 1872, Maud Eliza, da. of John Downes of the City of London, Merchant, twice Master of the Salters' Company; and has issue (with a son killed in action in South Africa 25 June 1900) 1e to 2e.

1e. Rev. Frederick Winning Hassard-Short, M.A. (Ch. Coll., Camb.), Vicar of St. Albans, Dartford (99 *East Hill, Dartford, Kent*), b. 5 Aug. 1873.

2e. Adrian Hugh Short, late Midshipman R.N., Associate King's Bench Div. 1900–1908, now Court of Criminal Appeal, Royal Courts of Justice, b. 3 Aug. 1879; m. 21 Sept. 1908, Millicent Eliza, da. of Capt. Thomas Renouf of Jersey.

3d. Charles Mason Short, settled in South America, b. 6 Mar. 1848; m. Mary, da. of (—) Irwin.

4d. John Locke Broadbent Short, Crown Office, b. 8 Oct. 1853; m. 5 July 1881,

[Nos. 38234 to 38255.

of The Blood Royal

Edith Constance, da. of John James Harrison, J.P., D.L., Col. 3rd West Yorkshire Militia, now 5th Batt. West Yorkshire Regt., a Col. 1st West Yorkshire Rifle Vol.; and has issue 1e to 6e.
    1e. William Hassard Short, b. 18 May 1886.
    2e. James Hassard Short, b. 2 June 1887.
    3e. John Hassard Short, b. 23 Feb. 1889.
    4e. May Short.
    5e. Violet Short.
    6e. Daisy Blanche Short.

  5d. Frances Marion Short, m. George Moncrieff Govan, M.D., Brigade Surgeon (ret.) Indian Medical Service; and has issue (with a da. d.s.p.) 1e to 6e.
    1e. Rev. George William Govan, Rector of Wittycombe (*Wittycombe Rectory, Carhampton, Taunton*), b. 9 Aug. 1861; m. 14 June 1892, Annie, da. of John Rowland Howells of Cardiff; and has issue 1f.
      1f. Eileen Frances Govan, b. 18 Oct. 1897.

    2e. Henry Maitland Govan.
    3e. Douglas Moncrieff Govan, Lieut. Indian Army, b. 5 Oct. 1875.
    4e. Ethel Mary Govan, m. Major John Lampen, Indian Army.
    5e. Anne Maud Govan.
    6e. Frances Eleanor Govan, m. Major Lewis Gordon Fisher, Indian Medical Service [son of William Lewis Ferdinand Fisher, Professor of Natural Philosophy and Mathematics, St. Andrews]; and has issue 1f to 5f.
      1f. Edith Fischer.
      2f. Nora Margaret Fischer.
      3f. Effie Govan Fischer.
      4f. Dorothy Tweedie Fischer.
      5f. Mary Eleanor Fischer.

  6d. Louisa Anne Short, m. 29 Mar. 1864, William Williams, M.R.C.S., L.S.A., of Redcar, Yorks, d. 2 May 1872; and has issue 1e to 6e.
    1e. Edward Frederick Maitland Williams, b. 26 Feb. 1865; m. in Canada, Ada, da. of (—) Hancock; and has issue 1f to 4f.
      1f. Guy Williams, b. 1 Feb. 1899.
      2f. Francis William Williams.
      3f. Gwendoline Williams.
      4f. Violet Louise Williams.

    2e. Isabella Williams.
    3e. Louisa Williams.
    4e. Juliana Katherine Williams.
    5e. Gwladys Williams.
    6e. Gwendoline Williams.

  7d. Annie Harriette Short, d. (–); m. Capt. Frederick Mills Harris, Indian Staff Corps; and had issue 1e to 2e.
    1e. Maud Harris, m. Henry Swayne.
    2e. Anne Harris, m. Capt. Rooke, R.E.

  8d. Eleanor Theresa Short, m. 10 May 1879, Capt. Charles German Alison, late 91st Argyll and Sutherland Highlanders, late Chief Constable of Somerset; and has issue (with 3 das. d. young) 1e to 5e.
    1e. Charles Hugh Alison, b. 5 Mar. 1883.
    2e. Roger Vincent Alison, Lieut. R.N., b. 22 Jan. 1885.
    3e. Geoffrey Richard Alison, b. 14 Ap. 1886.
    4e. Laughton Hassard Alison, b. 19 Ap. 1890.
    5e. Eleanor Isabella Joan Alison.

[Nos. 38256 to 38293.

The Plantagenet Roll

4c. *Mary Anne Short*, d. (-); m. 20 *Nov.* 1832, *William Blanshard, M.A., Bar.-at-Law, Recorder of Doncaster, Chairman of Quarter Sessions,* d. *Nov.* 1872; *and had issue* 1d *to* 4d.

    1d. Henry Edward Blanshard, b. 12 May 1846.
    2d. Caroline Margarette Blanshard, m. William Crawford, Bar.-at-Law.
    3d. Edith Blanshard.
    4d. Florence Jane Blanshard.

    5c. *Lucy Short,* d. (-); m. *Frederick Richard Lucas of Louth, co. Lincoln.*

    6c. *Jane Hassard Short,* d. 9 *Feb.* 1852; m. *Dec.* 1839, *William Garfit of Boston, co. Linc.,* b. *Feb.* 1810; d. 2 *Sept.* 1875; *and had issue* 1d *to* 4d.

    1d. William Garfit of West Skirbeck House, J.P., D.L., High Sheriff co. Lincoln 1892, M.P. for Boston 1895–1906, and *formerly* Capt. 2nd Batt. Lincolnshire R.V. (*West Skirbeck House, Boston; 7 Chesham Place, S.W.; Carlton, &c.*), b. 9 Nov. 1840; m. 28 May 1868, Mary Krause, da. of Conolly Norman of Fahan House, co. Donegal; and has issue 1e.

    1e. Frances Mary Garfit, m. 9 Feb. 1892, Graham Lionel John Wilson of The Grove, M.A. (Oxon.), Bar.-at-Law, Capt. 4th Batt. North Staffordshire Regt. (*The Grove, Market Drayton*); and has issue 1f.

    1f. Lionel Garfit Wilson, b. 6 Nov. 1896.

    2d. Arthur Garfit, b. 23 Sept. 1847; m. 7 Aug. 1883, Frances, da. of E. Downe; and has issue 1e.

    1e. Stella Frances Garfit, b. 16 Mar. 1890.

    3d. Marianne Garfit.

    4d. Mary Louisa Garfit.

    7c. *Maria Louisa Short,* d. (-); m. 5 *Aug.* 1856, *Edgar John Meynell of Kilvington Hall, co. York, J.P., Judge of Durham County Court and Recorder of Doncaster* [*descended from Anne, Duchess of Exeter*], d. 15 *Jan.* 1901; *and had issue.*

    See the Exeter Volume, p. 337, Nos. 24536–24543.

    4a. *Margaret Raper,* d. (-); m. (-) *Franks of Misterton, co. Leic.*

[Nos. 38294 to 38312.]

136. Descendants, if any, of JANE LAMPLUGH (Table XV.), d. (-); m. SAMUEL PAWSON of York, Merchant.

137. Descendants, if any, of CORDELIA CHALONER (Table XV.), d. (-); m. at St. Olave's, York, 4 May 1732, RICHARD GRAHAM of Whitewell, co. York [3rd son of Sir Reginald Graham of Norton Conyers, 2nd Bt. [E. 1662]].

138. Descendants, if any, of MARY FOULIS (Table XV.), d. (-); m. WILLIAM TURNER of Stainsby.

139. Descendants of MARY FOULIS (Table XV.), bur. (apparently) 19 Aug. 1694; m. as 2nd wife (contract dated July) 1660, ROBERT SHAFTO of Benwell Tower, Northumberland, bapt. 30 May 1626; d.v.p. 8 Nov. 1668; and had issue 1a to 4a.[1]

    1a. *Robert Shafto of Benwell Tower, High Sheriff co. Northbd.* 1696, bapt. 10 *Mar.* 1664; d. 1714, *shortly after* 14 *Mar.*; m. *Dorothy,* da. *and* (1700) *co-h. of Sir Thomas Heselrigge,* 3rd Bt. [E.], d. *after* 1715; *and had issue* 1b *to* 2b.

---

[1] Surtees' "Durham," 1823, iii. 296.

of The Blood Royal

1b. *Robert Shafto of Benwell Tower, High Sheriff* 1718; d. 3 *Nov.* 1735; m. 1715, *Mary, da. and event. sole h. of Ralph Jenison of Elswick; and had issue (with a 2nd son, Jenison, who* d.s.p. 1771) 1c to 2c.

    1c. *Robert Shafto of Benwell, co. Northbd., and Wratting Park, co. Camb., High Sheriff co. Northbd.* 1754, d. 18 *June* 1780; m. 14 *Ap.* 1752, *Camilla, da. and co-h. of Thomas Allan of the Flatts, Chester-le-Street,* bur. 19 *June* 1782; *and had issue (with 2 sons who* d.s.p.) 1d.

    1d. *Camilla Shafto of Benwell, da. and* (30 *Aug.* 1781) *h.,* bapt. 14 *Feb.* 1756; liv. 1822; m. 23 *Sept.* 1784, *Hugh, otherwise William, Adair, Capt. 25th Regt.,* liv. 1822; *and had issue then* 1e to 3e.

        1e. *Robert Shafto Adair,* b. 26 *June* 1786.

        2e. *William Adair.*

        3e. *Alexander Adair.*

    2c. *Thomas Shafto,* 3rd *son.*

    2b. *Dorothy Shafto, mentioned in father's will* 14 *Mar.* 1714.

    2a. *Henry Shafto, Bar.-at-Law,* bapt. 13 *Mar.* 1666; bur. (? s.p.) 3 *Feb.* 1711.

    3a. *Jane Shafto,* bapt. 5 *Feb.* 1663; *executcr to will of her uncle, Mark Shafto,* 19 *Oct.* 1700, *and then wife of James Sanderson of Durham, Clerk.*

    4a. *Mary Shafto, mentioned in father's will* 2 *Nov.* 1668.

140. Descendants of Sir JOHN EDEN of West Auckland, 4th Bt. [E.], M.P. (Table XVI.), b. 16 Sept. 1740; d. 23 Aug. 1812; m. 2ndly, 9 Ap. 1767, DOROTHEA, da. and h. of Peter JOHNSON, Recorder of Durham, d. 21 June 1792; and had issue 1a to 7a.

    1a. *Sir Robert Eden, afterwards (R.L.* 15 *Feb.* 1811) *Johnson-Eden,* 5*th Bt.* [*E.*], b. 25 *Oct.* 1774; d. *unm.* 4 *Sept.* 1844.

    2a. *Morton John Eden, afterwards (R.L.* 26 *Oct.* 1812) *Davidson-Eden, of Beamish Park,* b. 30 *June* 1778; d. *unm.* 28 *June* 1841.

    3a. *Dorothea Eden, da. and in her issue* (1844) *co-h.,* d. 1830; m. 1st, 22 *June* 1790, *Henry Methold, Capt. Durham Fencible Cav.* 1798, d. *May* 1799; 2ndly, *Gen. Daniel Seddon; and had issue (with* 3 *other sons who also* d.s.p. *and a da. who presumably did the same)* 1b.

        1b. *John Methold, afterwards (R.L.* 25 *Sept.* 1844) *Eden, of Beamish Park, co. Durham,* d. *unm.* 1885.

    4a. *Catherine Eden, da. and co-h.,* b. c. 1770; d. 19 *Mar.* 1872 *in her* 102*nd year;* m. *Nov.* 1803, *Robert Eden Duncombe Shafto of Whitworth Park, co. Durham, M.P.,* b. 23 *Mar.* 1776; d. 17 *Jan.* 1848; *and had issue.*

    See the Exeter Volume, pp. 308-310, Nos. 19416-19495.

    5a. *Emmeline Eden, da. and co-h.,* d. 21 *July* 1850; m. *as* 2*nd wife,* 9 *Nov.* 1809, *Thomas Northmore of Cleve, M.A., F.R.S.* (see p. 52), d. *May* 1851; *and had issue* 1b *to* 7b.

        1b. *Emmeline Eden Northmore,* d. (? *unm.*).

        2b. *Charlotte Osgood Northmore,* d. (-); m. 4 *Aug.* 1835, *Capt. John Whitlock, Madras Army,* d. 27 *May* 1849; *and had issue.*

        3b. *Cornelia Risdon Northmore,* d. 21 *Aug.* 1870; m. 8 *May* 1857, *Benjamin Jones of Llanelly; and had issue.*

        4b. *Adelina Johnson Northmore,* d. (? *unm.*).

        5b. *Caroline Amelia Brunswick Northmore, for whom Queen Caroline was Sponsor,* d. (-); m. 17 *Mar.* 1847, *Capt. George Longworth Dames, 66th Regt.,* d. 20 *Mar.* 1860; *and had issue.*

        6b. *Elfrida St. Aubyn Northmore.*

        7b. *Gertrude Johnes Northmore.*

[Nos. 38313 to 38392.

The Plantagenet Roll

6a. *Eleanor Eden, da. and co-h.*, d. *at Bruges* 22 *Nov.* 1864; m. 1813, *the Rev. Thomas Furness Wilson of Burley Hall, co. York; and had issue.*
7a. *Charlotte Eden, da. and co-h.*, d. (-); m. 1816, *Robert Kaye Greville of Wyaston and Edinburgh, LL.D.*, d. 4 *June* 1866; *and had issue.*
See p. 220, Nos. 37978–37981. [Nos. 38393 to 38396.

141. Descendants of Sir ROBERT EDEN, 1st Bt. [G.B.], so cr. 19 Oct. 1776, Governor of Maryland (Table XVI.), b. c. 1741; d. 2 Sept. 1784; m. 26 Ap. 1763, the Hon. CAROLINE, sister and h. of Frederick (CALVERT), 7th Baron Baltimore [I.], da. of Charles, 6th Baron Baltimore [I.], d. c. 1803; and had issue 1a to 3a.

1a. *Sir Robert Morton Eden, 2nd Bt.* [G.B.], b. c. 1767; d. 14 *Nov.* 1909; m. 10 *Jan.* 1792, *Anne, da. and h. of James Paul Smith, of New Bond Street*, d. 14 *July* 1808; *and had issue* 1b *to* 7b.
1b. *Sir Frederick Eden, 3rd Bt.* [G.B.], *killed, unm., at New Orleans*, 24 *Dec.* 1814.
2b. *Sir William Eden, 4th Bt., of Maryland* [G.B.], *and* (1844) 6th Bt. *of West Auckland* [E.], b. 31 *Jan.* 1803; d. 20 *Oct.* 1873; m. 23 *Ap.* 1844, *Elfrida Susanna Harriet, da. of Col. William Iremonger of Wherwell Priory, co. Hants*, d. 8 *July* 1882; *and had issue* 1c *to* 4c.
1c. Sir William Eden, 7th Bt. [E.], and 4th Bt. [G.B.], J.P., D.L., Hon. Col. 6th Batt. Durham L.I. (*Windlestone, Ferryhill, co. Durham;* 12B *Waterloo Place, S.W.*), b. 4 Ap. 1849; m. 20 July 1886, Sybil Frances, da. of Sir William Grey, K.C.S.I. [E. Grey Coll.]; and has issue 1d to 5d.
1d. John Eden, b. 9 Oct. 1888.
2d. Timothy Calvert Eden, b. 3 May 1893.
3d. Robert Anthony Eden, b. 12 June 1897.
4d. William Nicholas Eden, b. 14 Mar. 1900.
5d. Elfrida Marjorie Eden, b. 5 June 1887; m. 29 Ap. 1909, Leopold Guy Francis Maynard Greville, Lord Brooke, M.V.O. [son and h.-app. of Francis Richard Charles Guy, 5th Earl of Warwick [G.B.], and a descendant of King Henry VII. (see the Tudor Roll, pp. 196–335)] (*Warwick Castle, Warwick*).

2c. *Morton Eden*, b. 25 *June* 1859; d. 31 *Mar.* 1909; m. 1894, (—), *whom he divorced* 1896.
3c. *Helen Eden*, d. 26 *May* 1878; m. *as* 1st *wife*, 12 *Aug.* 1871, *Capt. William St. Lo Malet, 8th Hussars* [*Bt. of Wilbury* [G.B. 1791] *Coll., also a descendant of King Edward III. through the Mortimer-Percy marriage* (see Part II.)], b. 20 *Nov.* 1843; d. 26 *Aug.* 1885; *and had issue* 1d *to* 5d.
1d. Sir Edward St. Lo Malet, 5th Bt. [G.B.], &c. (34 *Corso d'Italia, Rome*), b. 14 Sept. 1872; m. 12 Nov. 1901, Louise Michelle, da. of Phillibert Dubois; and has issue 1e.
1e. Charles St. Lo Malet, b. at Rome 1 Nov. 1906.
2d. Henry Charles Malet, Capt. 8th Hussars, *formerly* Cape Mounted Rifles, served in South Africa 1899–1902, Queen's Medal and 4 Clasps, King's Medal and 2 Clasps, b. 21 Sept. 1873; m. 1 Feb. 1906, Mildred Laura Lambert, da. of Capt. H. Stephen Swiney of Gensing House, St. Leonard's-on-Sea; and has issue 1e to 2e.
1e. Edward William St. Lo Malet, b. 28 Nov. 1908.
2e. Ermyntrude Virginia St. Lo Malet.
3d. Elfrida St. Lo Malet, m. 1898, Capt. Richard John Carey Oakes, Royal Garrison Regt.; and has issue 1e to 2e.
1e. Elfrida Avice May Oakes.
2e. Marguerite Julia Oakes. [Nos. 38397 to 38410.

# of The Blood Royal

4d. Helen Avice Harriet Malet (Braham, Ray Park Avenue, Maidenhead).

5d. Hilda Mary Jeanne Malet, m. 3 Ap. 1900, Farquhar Celynin Lloyd [a descendant of Joan of Acre, da. of King Edward I.[1]] (Marelands Court, Southwater, near Horsham; Yewlands, Crofton, Vancouver Island); and has issue 1e to 2e.

1e. Richard Llewellyn Lloyd, b. 1 Jan. 1901.

2e. Stella Hilda Emily Lloyd, b. 26 Mar. 1908.

4c. Edith Eden, m. 1st, as 3rd wife, 20 July 1875, William George (Eden), 4th Baron Auckland [I. and G.B.], d. 27 Feb. 1890; 2ndly, 10 June 1897, Philip Symons (Stonepitt Grange, Seal, Sevenoaks).

3b. Right Rev. Robert Eden, D.D., Lord Bishop of Moray and Ross, Primus of Scotland, b. 2 Sept. 1804; d. 26 Aug. 1886; m. 17 Sept. 1827, Emma, da. of Sir James Allan Park, a Justice of the Common Pleas, d. 24 Nov. 1880; and had issue 1c to 9c.

1c. Frederick Morton Eden, Bar. Lincoln's Inn, formerly Fellow of All Souls Coll., Oxford, and Capt. Oxford Militia (63 Warwick Road, S.W.), b. 1 Nov. 1829; m. 1st, 23 May 1857, Louisa Ann (see p. 274), da. of Vice-Adm. Hyde Parker, C.B., d. 9 Mar. 1868; 2ndly, 4 Oct. 1870, Fanny Helen, da. of Edward Pomeroy Barrett-Lennard [Bt. Coll.]; and has issue 1d to 6d.

1d. Morton Eden, b. 8 Sept. 1859.

2d. Frederick Charles Eden, b. 6 Mar. 1864.

3d. Rowland Frederick Eden (18 Abingdon Villas, Kensington, W.), b. 17 Aug. 1874; m. 1899, Marie Bernadette Anita, da. of Col. Henry George Saunders, Indian Army; and has issue 1e.

1e. Frederick Augustus Morton Eden, b. 1 May 1904.

4d. Algernon Graham Eden, served in South Africa (Medals) 1901-02, b. 1877.

5d.[1] Alice Eden, unm.

6d.[2] Dorothy Ione Helen Eden, m. 1 Jan. 1902, Arthur Dalrymple Forbes-Gordon, late 20th Hussars [B. Sempill Coll.] (Langlea, co. Roxburgh).

2c. Henley Eden (Woodstock, Ascot), b. 8 Mar. 1838; m. 15 Ap. 1871, Amy Frances [descended from King Henry VII. (see Tudor Roll, p. 169)], da. of Lord Charles Lennox Kerr [M. of Lothian Coll.]; and has issue 1d to 2d.

1d. Schomberg Henley Eden, Capt. 1st Batt. Black Watch, served in South Africa, Queen's Medal and 4 Clasps, b. 18 Mar. 1873.

2d. Charles William Guy Eden, Colonial C.S., b. 20 June 1874.

3c. Rev. Robert Allan Eden, M.A. (Oxon.), Vicar of Old St. Pancras (58 Oakley Square, N.W.), b. 27 Dec. 1839; unm.

4c. William Alexander Eden, Col. R.A. (ret.) (Ower Cottage, Fawley, Hants), b. 16 June 1843; m. 18 July 1885, Giovanna Anna Malvina, widow of Col. Macbean of Tomatin, da. of (—), s.p.

5c. Lucy Eden, d. (-); m. 12 June 1849, the Rev. Herbert Samuel Hawkins, Rector of Beyton, d. 1893; and had issue 1d to 6d.

1d. Edward Robert Hawkins, b. 6 May 1850; m. 1888, Katie Clyde, da. of Capt. Edward Barkley, R.N.

2d. Herbert Eden Hawkins, b. 15 May 1852.

3d. Charles Henley Hawkins, b. 21 Aug. 1854.

4d. Mabel Ellen Hawkins.

5d. Margaret Mary Hawkins.

6d. Gertrude Lucy Hawkins.

6c. Caroline Eden (87 Great King Street, Edinburgh), m. 11 Sept. 1851, Col. Arthur A'Court Fisher, C.B., R.E., d. 2 Nov. 1879; and has issue 1d to 6d.

1d. Arthur William Fisher, b. 23 Sept. 1852.

2d. Charles Sidney Dalton Fisher, Capt. formerly 2nd Batt. Midx. Regt., served in South Africa, Queen's and King's Medals and 8 Clasps, mentioned in Despatches, b. 20 Mar. 1866. [Nos. 38411 to 38437.

---

[1] See Foster's "Noble and Gentle Families, &c.," p. 146.

The Plantagenet Roll

3d. Frederick A'Court Fisher, b. 1 Dec. 1873; m. 1902, Emma Lucy Athela, da. of the Rev. John Edward Alexander Inge, M.A., Rector of Gayton.

4d. Alice Elizabeth Fisher (15 *Walker Street, Edinburgh*), m. 19 Aug. 1879, James Allan Park, 42nd (Black Watch) Royal Highlanders, b. 20 Aug. 1853; d. from wounds received at Tel-el-Kebir 1882; and has issue (with a da. d. young) 1e.

1e. Florence Ida Allan Park.

5d. Annie Caroline Ann Fisher, m. 17 Nov. 1887, William Macbean; and has issue 1e to 4e.

1e. Ronald Eden Macbean, b. 19 July 1890.

2e. Ian Gordon Macbean, b. 24 Feb. 1892.

3e. Aileen Clelia Macbean.

4e. Muriel Jean Macbean.

6d. Ethel Mary Fisher.

7c. Alice Eden, d. 24 Nov. 1894; m. 5 Dec. 1857, *the Right Hon. George Ward Hunt, P.C., M.P. [descended from the Lady Isabel Plantagenet]*, d. 29 *July* 1877; and had issue.

See the Essex Volume, p. 123, Nos. 15690-15702.

8c. Emma Selina Eden, d. (-); m. 8 *June* 1861, *the Rev. Dacres Olivier, Rector of Wilton and Canon of Salisbury*, d. 12 *Sept*. 1908; *and had issue* 1d *to* 10d.

1d. George Herbert Olivier, b. 1863; d. (? s.p.) Nov. 1893.

2d. Rev. Henry Eden Olivier, M.A. (Oxon.), Vicar of St. James', Croydon (*St. James' Vicarage, Croydon*), b. 1866; m. 2 July 1895, Gertrude Isabella [descended from the Lady Anne, sister to King Edward IV., &c. (see Exeter Volume, p. 173), da. of the Rev. Canon Edward Capel Cure, M.A., Rector of St. George's, Hanover Square; and has issue 1e to 3e.

1e. Jasper George Olivier, b. 20 Ap. 1896.

2e. Arthur Eden Olivier, b. 6 July 1898.

3e. Martin John Olivier, b. 20 Feb. 1900.

3d. Alfred C. S: Olivier, b. 1867; m. 1900, Fanny Mary (Mrs. Bernard Beere), widow of Capt. Edward Cholmeley Dering [s. and h. app. of Sir Edward Cholmeley Dering, 8th Bt.], da. of Francis Welby Whitehead.

4d. Arthur Frank Olivier, b. 1868.

5d. Sidney Richard Olivier, Comm. R.N., b. 1870; m. 1897, Etheldred Mary, da. of Capt. Henry John Hodgson, R.N.; and has issue 1e to 5e.

1e. Reginald Henry Dacres Olivier, b. 1899.

2e. Sidney John Olivier (twin), b. 1905.

3e. Joan Etheldred Olivier.

4e. Lilian Rosemary Olivier.

5e. Gillian Emma Olivier (twin).

6d. Reginald Ernest Olivier, b. 1871.

7d. Robert Harold Olivier, Capt. 2nd Batt. Duke of Cornwall's L.I., served in South Africa 1899-1902, 2 Medals and 6 Clasps, b. 1879.

8d. Mary Olivier, m. Jan. 1895, Comm. Charles James Collins, R.N., d. 12 Aug. 1908.

9d. Edith Maud Olivier.

10d. Emma Mildred Olivier.

9c. Mary Eden.

4b. *George Morton Eden, Lieut.-Gen. in the Army*, b. 10 *May* 1806; d. *at Berne* 11 *Nov*. 1862; m. 18 *Jan*. 1834, *Louisa Anne, da. of George Robert Eyres*, d. 5 *Nov*. 1878; *and had issue* 1c *to* 3c.

1c. *Morton Parker Eden, Lieut.-Col. R.A.*, b. 11 *Mar*. 1835; d. 18 *Sept*. 1880; m. 4 *Ap*. 1861, *Georgina Louisa Helen, da. of Gen. H. Pester, R.A.*, d. 22 *Ap*. 1890; *and had issue* 1d *to* 4d. [Nos. 38438 to 38477.

# of The Blood Royal

1d. Frederick Schomberg Eden, b. 7 Mar. 1872.

2d. Beatrice Caroline Eden, m. 5 Oct. 1889, Charles Cockburn Talbot; and has issue 1e to 3e.

1e. Robert Charles Talbot, b. 2 Dec. 1891.

2e. John Angelo Talbot, b. 12 May 1893.

3e. Cecile Ione Talbot.

3d. Georgina Clarice Eden, m. 25 Sept. 1895, the Rev. William Henry Paine, M.A. (37 *Westminster Palace Gardens, S.W.*).

4d. Lilian Eden, m. 16 May 1895, Capt. William Nicolas McGachen, R.N. (ret.) (see p. 417); and has issue 1e.

1e. Armine Nicolas Eden McGachen.

2c. *Charles Calvert Eden of Kingston Grange, H.B.M. Diplo. Ser.*, b. 5 Nov. 1837; d. 10 *Mar.* 1878; m. 16 Dec. 1862, *the Baroness Cecile (The Grange, Kingston, Somerset), da. of* (—) *Baron de Senner, of Merchligen, Switzerland; and had issue* 1d to 3d.

1d. Morton Frederic Eden, b. 16 June 1865.

2d. Evelyn Louisa Cecile Eden.

3d. Violet Cecile Eden, m. 30 Aug. 1899, Capt. Arthur Street, A.S.C.; and has issue 1e.

1e. John Noel Eden Street, b. 1902.

3c. Fanny Evelyn Mary Eden (*Hillside, Kingston, Taunton*).

5b. *Sir Charles Eden, K.C.B., Vice-Adm. R.N.*, b. 3 *July* 1808; d.s.p. 7 *Mar.* 1878.

6b. *Marianne Eden*, d. 13 *May* 1859; m. Nov. 1812, *Francis Mallet Sponge*, d. (? s.p.) *Ap.* 1857.

7b. *Caroline Eden*, d. 10 *Nov.* 1854; m. 11 *July* 1821, *Vice-Adm. Hyde Parker, C.B., Senior Naval Lord of the Admiralty* [Bt. (1681) *Coll.*], d. 26 *May* 1854; *and had issue* 1c *to* 4c.

1c. *Sir William Parker, 9th Bt.* [E.], *Capt. 44th Regt., D.L.*, b. 2 *Sept.* 1826; d. 24 *May* 1891; m. 22 *Nov.* 1855, *Sophia Mary, da. of Nathaniel Clarke Barnardiston of The Ryes, Sudbury*, d. 16 *May* 1903; *and had issue* 1d *to* 10d.

1d. Rev. Sir William Hyde Parker, 10th Bt. [E.], Lord of the Manor of Long Melford, M.A. (Camb.), J.P., C.A., *formerly* Chaplain to the Bishop of Barbados (*Melford Hall, Long Melford, Suffolk*), b. 8 Ap. 1863; *m.* 18 Nov. 1890, Ethel, da. of John Leech of Gorse Hall, Dukinfield; and has issue 1e to 3e.

1e. William Stephen Hyde Parker, b. 23 Jan. 1892.

2e. Harry Hyde Parker, b. 17 Feb. 1905.

3e. Mary Stephanie Hyde Parker.

2d. Edmond Hyde Parker, Capt. R.N., Flag Capt. at Portsmouth, b. 30 Jan. 1868; *m.* 1908, Helen Margaret, da. of the Rev. George Raymond Portal, M.A., Canon of Winchester.

3d. Laurence Hyde Parker (*Smeatham Hall, Bulmer, Sudbury, Suffolk*), b. 23 Oct. 1870; *m.* 19 Ap. 1906, Ada Letitia Moor, da. of Joseph Alphonsus Horsford of Long Melford, M.R.C.S.; and has issue 1e to 2e.

1e. Mary Hyde Parker, b. 19 Mar. 1908.

2e. Dorothy Bridget Hyde Parker, b. 6 Mar. 1909.

4d. John Barnardiston Parker, 4th Class Medjidie, b. 7 Ap. 1879; *m.* 31 Jan. 1906, Dora Katherine, da. of Canon Bromley of Newcastle-on-Tyne.

5d. Anne Hyde Parker, *m.* 29 Ap. 1886, Col. Arthur Staniforth Hext, *formerly* Suffolk Regt. (*Trenarren, St. Austell, Cornwall*); and has issue 1e to 4e.

1e. Rhoda Marjorie Hext.

2e. Sybil Mary Hext.

3e. Margaret Hext } (twins).
4e. Amy Hext

[Nos. 38478 to 38504.

The Plantagenet Roll

6d. Margaret Hyde Parker, m. (her cousin) 15 Feb. 1881, George Eden Hunt of Wadenhoe House, co. Northants [son of the Right Hon. George Ward Hunt (see above)], d. 1892 ; and had issue.
See p. 272, Nos. 38447–38449.

7d. Sophia Hyde Parker.

8d. Amy Hyde Parker.

9d. Mary Hyde Parker, m. 25 Ap. 1889, Charles Arthur Abraham [son of Canon Abraham] (*Spire Hollin House, Glossop, Derby*) ; and has issue 1e to 3e.

1e. Christopher Charles Abraham, b. 1 June 1893.

2e. Geoffrey Austen Abraham, b. 13 Feb. 1899.

3e. Doris Mary Abraham.

10d. Dorothy Hyde Parker, m. 30 Dec. 1903, Hugh Wilfrid Sherlock [son of the Rev. Harry Sherlock of Bildeston] (56 *West Park, Eltham, Kent*) ; and has issue 1e.

1e. Hugh Sherlock, b..1905.

2c. Louisa Ann Parker, d. 9 Mar. 1868 ; m. 3 May 1857, *Capt. Frederick Morton Eden ; and had issue*.
See p. 271, Nos. 38417–38418, and 38422.

3c. Caroline Maria Parker, d. 11 Nov. 1890 ; m. 12 Ap. 1849, *Col. John Home Purves, Equerry and Comptroller of the Household to H.R.H. the Duchess of Cambridge* [Bt. (1665) Coll.], d. 2 July 1867 ; *and had issue* 1d to 3d.

1d. Charles Hyde Home Purves, D.L., b. 1850 ; d. 19 Feb. 1887 ; m. 26 June 1877, Frances Mabel (*Purves, Greenlaw, R.S.O.*), da. of Clement Archer of Hill House, Midx. ; *and had issue* 1e to 2e.

1e. Sir John Home-Purves, now (1894) Home-Purves-Hume-Campbell, of Marchmont, 8th Bt. [S.], Capt. Lothians and Berwickshire Imp. Yeo., *formerly* Lieut. 2nd Life Guards (*Marchmont, Greenlaw, S.O.*), b. 9 Aug. 1879 ; m. 1 Oct. 1901, Emily Jane [descended from King Henry VII. (see the Tudor Roll, p. 166)], da. of the Rev. Robert Digby Ram, Preb. of St. Paul's ; and has issue 1f to 2f.

1f. Mabel Jane Home-Purves-Hume-Campbell.

2f. Elsie Barbara Home-Purves-Hume-Campbell.

2e. Alice Home Purves, m. 6 July 1904, Major St. John Louis Hyde du Plat Taylor, D.S.O., Brig.-Major of a Territorial Force Inf. Brigade, *formerly* R.A. (*Purves, Greenlaw*) ; and has issue 1f.

1f. Frederica Mabel Joan du Plat Taylor.

2d. Augusta Louisa Helen Purves }
3d. Alexandra Mary Caroline Purves } (39 *Cheyne Walk, S.W.*).

4c. Fanny Letitia Parker (*Meaford, Ventnor, I.W.*).

2a. William Eden, *Gen. in the Army*, d.s.p.l.[1]

3a. [da.] Eden.[2] [Nos. 38505 to 38527.

142. Descendants of WILLIAM (EDEN), 1st BARON AUCKLAND [I., 18 Nov. 1789] and 1st BARON AUCKLAND of West Auckland [G.B., 22 May 1793], P.C. (Table XVI.), d. 28 May 1814 ; m. 26 Sept. 1776, ELEANOR, sister of Gilbert, 1st Earl of Minto [U.K.], da. of the Right Hon. Sir Gilbert ELLIOTT, 3rd Bt. [S.], P.C., b. 1758 ; d. 18 May 1818 ; and had issue 1a to 6a.

1a. George (Eden), 2nd Baron [G.B. and I.] *and* (21 Dec. 1839) 1*st Earl of Auckland* [U.K.], G.C.B., b. 25 Aug. 1784 ; d. *unm.* 1 Jan. 1849.

---

[1] Foster's " Baronetage," 1880, p. 186.   [2] Burke's " Peerage," 1907, p. 574.

of The Blood Royal

2a. Robert John (Eden), 3rd Baron Auckland [G.B. and I.], Lord Bishop of Bath and Wells, D.L., b. 10 July 1799; d. 25 Ap. 1870; m. 15 Sept. 1825, Mary [descended from the Lady Isabel Plantagenet], da. of Francis Edward Hurt of Alderwasley, d. 25 Nov. 1872; and had issue.
See the Essex Volume, pp. 360-361, Nos. 35486-35531.

3a. Hon. Elizabeth Charlotte Eden, b. 21 Mar. 1780; d. 17 Ap. 1847; m. 31 Mar. 1800, Francis Godolphin (Osborne), 1st Baron Osborne [U.K.] [2nd son of the 5th Duke of Leeds [E.], &c., descended from George, Duke of Clarence, K.G.], d. 15 Feb. 1850; and had issue.
See the Clarence Volume, pp. 627-629, Nos. 28054-28117.

4a. Hon. Caroline Eden, b. July 1781; d. 2 Mar. 1851; m. 17 June 1806, Arthur Vansittart of Shottesbrooke and Clewer, co. Berks, J.P., D.L., M.P. for Windsor 1804, Col. Berks Militia [of the old Dutch family of Van Sittart, who settled in England under Charles II.], bapt. 28 Dec. 1775; d. 31 May 1829; and had issue (with 2 sons and a da. who d. unm.) 1b to 10b.

1b. Arthur Vansittart of Shottesbrooke and Foot's Cray, J.P., Cornet 2nd Life Guards, b. 2 May 1807; d. 22 Ap. 1859; m. 26 May 1831, Diana Sara, da. of Gen. Sir John Gustavus Crosbie, G.C.H., d. Sept. 1881; and had issue (with 2 sons who d.s.p.) 1c.

1c. Rose Sophia Vansittart of Shottesbrooke, d. 8 Jan. 1892; m. 27 Nov. 1856, Oswald Augustus Smith of Hammerwood, co. Sussex, D.L., b. 21 Oct. 1826; d. 24 Aug. 1902; and had issue 1d to 3d.

1d. Basil Guy Oswald Smith of Shottesbrooke (Shottesbrooke Park, Berks; 33 Grosvenor Street, W.), b. 28 Sept. 1861; m. 15 Nov. 1893, Rose Marguerite, da. of Charles Bruce Henry Somerset [D. of Beaufort Coll., and descended from George, Duke of Clarence, K.G. (see Clarence Volume, p. 332)]; and has issue 1e.

1e. Nancy Oswald Smith, b. 19 May 1896.

2d. Rupert Oswald Smith, b. 29 Jan. 1864.

3d. Maurice Oswald Smith, b. 3 Ap. 1866.

2b. Robert Vansittart of Driffield, co. Berks, J.P., Lieut.-Col. Coldstream Guards and a Page of Honour to H.R.H. the Duchess of Gloucester and Edinburgh, b. 24 Jan. 1811; d. 2 May 1872; m. 4 Nov. 1845, Elizabeth Harriet, da. of John Willes Fleming of Stoneham Park, M.P., d. 3 Ap. 1906; and had issue 1c to 9c.

1c. Robert Arnold Vansittart of Foot's Cray, J.P., D.L., Lord of the Manors of Ruxley and North Cray, late Capt. 7th Dragoon Guards (Foot's Cray Place, Sidcup, Kent), b. 21 Oct. 1851; m. 30 July 1878, Alice, da. of Gilbert James Blane of Foliejon Park, co. Berks; and has issue 1d to 6d.

1d. Robert Gilbert Vansittart, M.V.O., 3rd Sec. Diplo. Service, b. 20 June 1881.

2d. Arnold Bexley Vansittart, b. 24 Sept. 1889.

3d. Guy Nicholas Vansittart, b. 8 Sept. 1893.

4d. Sibell Alice Vansittart.

5d. Honoria Edith Vansittart.

6d. Marjorie Marie Vansittart.

2c. Catherine Caroline Vansittart, m. as 2nd wife, 14 Jan. 1869, Thomas Campbell, Cadet of Golgrain; and has issue.

3c. Fanny Vansittart, m. 26 Ap. 1866, Walter Long of Preshaw and The Holt, co. Hants, and Muchelney, co. Som., J.P., late 11th Regt. (The Holt, Bishop's Waltham, Hants); and has issue (with a son and 2 das. who d. young) 1d to 6d.

1d. Walter Vansittart Long, b. 27 Nov. 1868; m. 25 Ap. 1894, Mary Lilian, da. of Col. Philip Arthur Pleydell-Bouverie-Campbell-Wyndham of Dunoon [E. of Radnor Coll.].

2d. Ethel Fanny Long, m. 19 July 1892, Arthur Hildyard Robinson (The Mill House, Bishop's Waltham); and has issue.   [Nos. 38528 to 38652.

The Plantagenet Roll

3d. Katharine Teresa Long, *m.* 5 June 1895, Robert Eden Richardson, B.A. (Camb.) [3rd son of John Crow Richardson of Glanbrydan Park (see p. 278)] (*Morestead House, Hants*); and has issue 1e to 3e.

1e. Douglas Courtenay Richardson, *b.* 28 Dec. 1905.
2e. Katharine Doris Richardson, *b.* 6 Jan. 1900.
3e. Maude Eden Richardson, *b.* 3 Oct. 1901.

4d. Mildred Bertha Long, *m.* 1 May 1900, Charles Hugh Finch (*Costessy House, Norwich*).

5d. Moena Louisa Long, *unm.*

6d. Evelyn Alice Long, *m.* 12 July 1904, Henri Ernst Armand Delille.

4c. Bertha Vansittart.

5c. Edith Vansittart, *m.* 25 Aug. 1870, Robert Peel Wethered [5th son of Owen Wethered of Remmantz, J.P.], *d.* 2 Nov. 1873 ; *s.p.s.*

6c. Mary Emily Vansittart, *m.* 19 Jan. 1876, Henry Corry Fitzherbert, J.P. [4th son of Thomas Fitzherbert of Black Castle, J.P., D.L.] (*Milbrook, Queen's Co.*); and has issue 1d to 2d.

1d. Arnold Vesey Fitzherbert, *b.* 18 Mar. 1878.

2d. Edith Clare Fitzherbert, *m.* 8 July 1897, Arthur Mildmay Hall-Dare, 3rd son of Robert Westley Hall-Dare of Newtonberry, J.P., D.L.; and has issue 1e to 2e.

1e. Derrick Arthur Hall-Dare, *b.* 4 Dec. 1900.
2e. Irene Clare Hall-Dare.

7c. Louisa Vansittart, *m.* the Rev. Alfred Cox.

8c. Constance Mary Vansittart, *m.* Lieut.-Col. Charles Wigram Long, R.A., M.P. for Evesham 1906 [2nd son of the Ven. Archdeacon Charles Maitland Long] (*Severn Bank, Severn Stoke, Worc.; Carlton*).

9c. Evelyn Jane Vansittart, *m.* 4 Nov. 1882, Edward Strangways Neave [Bt. (1795) Coll.] (*5 Warwick Road, Ealing*); and has issue 1d to 7d.

1d. Edward Arthur Neave, *b.* 2 Aug. 1883.
2d. Gerald Vansittart Neave, *b.* 2 Oct. 1884.
3d. Guy Morier Neave, *b.* 21 Oct. 1886.
4d. Digby Frank Neave, *b.* 25 May 1892.
5d. Hugh Alexander Neave, *b.* 1 June 1893.
6d. Eric Lloyd Strangways Neave, *b.* 1898.
7d. Evelyn Henrica Neave.

3b. *William Vansittart of Brunswick Square, Brighton, H.E.I.C.S., D.L., M.P., Windsor*, b. 2 *May* 1813; d. 15 *Jan.* 1876; m. 1st, 1 *July* 1839, *Emily* [*descended from the Lady Anne, sister of King Edward IV., &c.* (see Exeter Volume, p. 583)], *da. of Gen. Robert Leslie-Anstruther*, d. *on her passage home from India* 25 *May* 1844; 2ndly, 2 Dec. 1847, *Henrietta, da. and co-h. of John Humphreys*, d. 19 *May* 1852; 3rdly, 6 Feb. 1866, *Melanie* [*also descended from the Lady Anne* (see Exeter Volume, p. 235)], *da. of Sir Richard Jenkins, G.C.B., M.P., &c.* (re-m. *Henry Pepys and*), d. 1891; *and had issue* 1c *to* 4c.

1c. William Henry Vansittart, *b.* 25 May 1844.

2c. Charles Edward Bexley Vansittart, *late* Capt. Antrim Rifles, *b.* Dec. 1867; *m.* 28 July 1888, Constance Frances (who obtained a divorce 1904), da. of Sir Thomas Macdonald Miller, 4th Bt. [G.B.]; and has issue 1d to 2d.

1d. Constance Hilda Maude Bexley Vansittart.
2d. Melanie Bexley Vansittart.

3c.[1] *Emily Eden Vansittart*, d. 27 *May* 1905; m. 1 Oct. 1861, *George Palmer of Nazing Park, co. Essex, J.P., Bengal C.S.*, b. 12 Nov. 1828; d. 13 *Sept.* 1902; *and had issue* 1d.

1d. *Emily Charlotte Palmer*, d. 1891; m. 1889, *Robert Francis Crawley* [*descended from George, Duke of Clarence* (see Clarence Volume, p. 155)]; *and had issue.* [Nos. 38653 to 38680.

# of The Blood Royal

4c.² Caroline Betha Vansittart, m. 1st, 21 Nov. 1869, Reginald Wyniatt of Dymock, co. Gloucester, d. (-) ; 2ndly, 13 Sept. 1882, Horace Drummond Dean.

4b. George Nicholas Vansittart, b. June 1814; d. 12 May 1889; m. 1 June 1852, Elizabeth Ann, da. and co-h. of James Mansfield of Midmar Castle, co. Aberdeen, d. 19 Nov. 1875; and had issue 1c to 3c.

 1c. Arthur George Vansittart, H.B.M.'s Consul-Gen. at Port-au-Prince, formerly Diplo. Ser. (British Consulate, Port-au-Prince, Hayti), b. 22 Nov. 1854.

 2c. Coleraine Nicholas Vansittart, late Lieut. Berks Militia, b. 3 Dec. 1860; m. 1886, Marie (who obtained a divorce 1896), da. of Gustave Vincent; and has issue 1d to 2d.

  1d. Francis de Mansfield Vansittart, b. 10 Feb. 1891.

  2d. Violet Vansittart, b. 15 Aug. 1887.

 3c. Emily Christina Vansittart (36 Via Palestro, Rome).

5b. Henry Vansittart, Civil and Session Judge, H.E.I.C.S., b. 3 Nov. 1816; d. 13 Jan. 1896; m. Mary Amelia, da. of Capt. William Hugh Dobbie, R.N., d. 18 June 1886; and had issue 1c to 7c.

 1c. Henry Vansittart, Bar.-at-Law, late Lieut. R.M.A. (Saharanpur, India), b. 4 Aug. 1849; m. 1st, 19 Oct. 1878, Mary Virginia, da. of Francis Johnson Jessop of Derby, d. 1886; 2ndly, 1888, Ellen, da. of (—) Dianopolis; and has issue 1d to 2d.

  1d.¹ Amelia Mary Vansittart.

  2d.² Ellen Vansittart.

 2c. Charles Vansittart, late a Clerk in the Finance Dept., India, b. 1 Jan. 1853; m. 24 Feb. 1881, Katherine Frances (see Part II.), da. of Lieut.-Gen. Charles Pollard; and has issue (with a son and da. who d. young) 1d.

  1d. Dorothy Mary Vansittart.

 3c. Herbert Vansittart (9 Portland Avenue, Exmouth), b. 13 Ap. 1854; m. 12 Dec. 1893, Mary Agatha, da. of Adm. William Dobbie, R.N.; and has issue (with a son d. young) 1d to 2d.

  1d. Agatha Mary Vansittart, b. 10 Oct. 1895.

  2d. Hilda Florence Vansittart, b. 23 May 1908.

 4c. Eden Vansittart, Col. Indian Army (The Chalet, Bournemouth), b. 19 Ap. 1856; m. 16 Dec. 1889, Ethel, da. of R. D. Spedding, I.C.S.; and has issue 1d.

  1d. Vera Mary Eden Vansittart.

 5c. Edith Vansittart, m. 26 Dec. 1868, Major-Gen. Newton Barton, Bengal Staff Corps (ret.) (5 Onslow House, South Kensington).

 6c. Florence Mary Vansittart, m. 24 Oct. 1871, Lieut.-Gen. John Mackie Stewart, Bengal Army [Cadet of Cairnsmore] (Carruchan, Dumfries; Naval and Military); and has issue 1d to 4d.

  1d. John Henry Keith Stewart, Capt. Indian Army, and D.A.A.G. India (Naval and Military), b. 31 Aug. 1872; m. 30 Sept. 1898, Frances Jane [descended from George, Duke of Clarence, K.G., brother of King Edward IV., &c. (see Clarence Volume, p. 592)], da. of the Hon. George Augustus Hobart-Hampden [E. of Buckinghamshire Coll.]; and has issue 1e to 2e.

   1e. Florence Edith Keith Stewart, b. 3 Sept. 1899.

   2e. Julia Constance Keith-Stewart, b. 24 Sept. 1903.

  2d. Patrick Alexander Vansittart Stewart, Capt. K.O. Scottish Borderers (Naval and Military), b. 29 June 1875.

  3d. James Montgomery Vansittart Stewart, Capt. 10th Gurkha Rifles, b. 12 July 1877.

  4d. Herbert William Vansittart Stewart, Lieut. Royal Scots Fusiliers, b. 15 Aug. 1886.

 7c. Rosamond Vansittart, unm.

6b. Rev. Charles Vansittart, M.A., Rector of Shottesbrooke, b. 8 Mar. 1820; d.

[Nos. 38681 to 38705.

The Plantagenet Roll

14 *July* 1878; m. 27 *May* 1845, *Frances Rosalie, da. and co-h. of Hans Busk of Glenalder, co. Radnor, D.L.*, d. 10 *May* 1899; *and had issue (with a da. who* d. *unm.)* 1c *to* 3c.

1c. Sidney Nicholas Vansittart, *b.* 10 Jan. 1847.

2c. Arthur Vansittart, in the Pontifical Zouaves, has Medal and Mentana Cross, *b.* 3 Nov. 1849.

3c. *Cyril Bexley Vansittart, Chamberlain of the Cape and Sword to Popes Pius IX. and Leo XIII.*, b. 28 *Aug.* 1851; d. *unm. at Rome* 22 *Jan.* 1887.

7b. *Caroline Vansittart,* d. 30 *Sept.* 1883; m. 9 *July* 1828, *George Charles (Mostyn), 6th Baron Vaux of Harrowden* [*E.* 1523], *who had that Barony called out of abeyance in his favour* 12 *Mar.* 1838 [*descended from George, Duke of Clarence, K.G. (see Clarence Volume, p. 421)*], d. 28 *Jan.* 1883; *and had issue.*
See the Clarence Volume, pp. 421–422, Nos. 16289–16303.

8b. *Charlotte Eleanor Vansittart,* d. (–); m. *as 2nd wife,* 4 *Aug.* 1842, *the Rev. Edward Serocold Pearce-Serocold (R.L.* 30 *July* 1842), *previously Pearce, of Cherryhinton, co. Camb., J.P.,* d. (–); *and had issue* 1c *to* 2c.

1c. Charlotte Pearce-Serocold, da. and co-h. of mother, *m.* 1866, the Ven. Hemming Robeson, Archdeacon of North Wilts.

2c. Teresa Eden Pearce Serocold, da. and co-h. of mother, *m.* 1866, John Crow Richardson of Glanbrydan Park, co. Carmarthen, and Pant-y-Gwydir, co. Glamorgan, J.P., D.L., Col. Comdg. 3rd Glamorgan Rifle Vol., *d.* 16 Nov. 1903; and has issue 1*d* to 2*d*.

1d. *Ernald Edward Richardson of Glanbrydan, &c., J.P., Capt. Royal Carmarthen Art. Mil., M.A. (Oxon.),* b. 31 *July* 1869; d. 7 *July* 1909; m. 9 *Feb.* 1898, *Irene Caroline, da. of Col. Ynyr Henry Burges of Parkanaur, co. Tyrone; and had issue* 1e *to* 4e.

1e. Ernald Wilbraham Richardson (*Glanbrydan Park, Manordilo, Carmarthen; Pant-y-Gwydir, Swansea*), *b.* 21 July 1900.

2e. Llewellyn George Richardson, *b.* 1902.

3e. John Crow Richardson, *b.* 4 Nov. 1905.

4e. Rose Eirene Ynyr Stella Richardson.

2d. Robert Eden Richard Richardson, B.A. (Camb.) (*Morestead House, Hants*), *b.* 18 Dec. 1872; *m.* 5 June 1895, Katharine Teresa, da. of Walter Long of Preshaw; and has issue.
See p. 276, Nos. 38654–38656.

9b. *Martha Louisa Vansittart,* d. 1877; m. 4 *Aug.* 1841, *William Chapman of South Hill, co. Westmeath, D.L.* [*3rd son of Sir Thomas Chapman, 2nd Bt.* [*I.*]], d. 25 *Jan.* 1889; *and had issue* 1c *to* 3c.

1c. Thomas Robert Tighe Chapman of South Hill, J.P., heir-presumptive to the Baronetcy, *b.* 6 Nov. 1846; *m.* 24 July 1873, Edith Sarah Hamilton, da. of George Augustus Rochfort-Boyd of Middleton Park, co. Westmeath, D.L.; and has issue 1*d* to 4*d*.

1d. Eva Jane Louisa Chapman.

2d. Rose Isabel Chapman.

3d. Florence Lina Chapman.

4d. Mabel Cecile Chapman.

2c. Francis Vansittart Chapman, J.P. (*South Hill, Delvin, co. Westmeath*), *b.* 9 Sept. 1849.

3c. Caroline Margaret Chapman (*Killua Castle, Clonmellon, co. Westmeath*), *m.* 9 Jan. 1894, her cousin, Sir Montagu Richard Chapman, 5th Bt. [I.], *d.s.p.* 22 Jan. 1907.

10b. *Sophia Vansittart,* d. (–); m. 7 *Jan.* 1841, *Thomas Andrew Anstruther, Madras C.S.* [*Bt. of Balcaskie* [*S.* 1694] *Coll.*], d. 14 *Ap.* 1876; *and had issue (with* 3 *sons who* d.s.p.) 1c. [Nos. 38706 to 38739.

# of The Blood Royal

1c. Philip Robert Anstruther, Lieut.-Col. 94th Regt., b. 30 Jan. 1841; d. 26 Dec. 1880; m. 12 Jan. 1875, Zaida Mary (Balchrystie, Colinsburgh, Fife), da. of Sir Thomas Erskine of Cambo, 2nd Bt. [U.K.]; and had issue 1d to 3d.

1d. Philip George Anstruther of Thirdpart, Capt. 2nd Batt. Seaforth Highlanders, served in South Africa, has Queen's and King's Medals and 4 Clasps, b. 25 Oct. 1875.

2d. Robert Abercrombie Anstruther, Capt. R.F.A., served in South Africa, has Queen's Medal with Clasps, b. 3 Aug. 1879.

3d. Mary Rosamond Anstruther, m. 21 Nov. 1900, Edward Windsor Hussey of Scotney Castle, J.P., D.L., Bar.-at-Law (Scotney Castle, Lamberhurst).

5a. Hon. Mary Louisa Eden, b. 14 Sept. 1788; d. 2 Dec. 1858; m. 26 June 1806, Andrew Wedderburn, afterwards (R.L. 24 June 1814) Colville, d. (? s.p.) 3 Feb. 1856.

6a. Hon. Mary Dulcibella Eden, b. 1 Sept. 1793; d. 20 Mar. 1862; m. 15 July 1819, Charles Drummond [V. Strathallan [S.] Coll., and a descendant of King Henry VII., &c.], d. 28 Aug. 1858; and had issue.

See the Tudor Roll, pp. 534–535, Nos. 35706–35742. [Nos. 38740 to 38779.

143. Descendants of THOMAS EDEN of Wimbledon, Deputy-Auditor of Greenwich Hospital (Table XVI.), d. 1 May 1805; m. 7 July 1783, MARIANA, da. of Arthur JONES of Reigate Priory, co. Surrey; and had issue 1a to 6a.

1a. Thomas Eden of The Bryn, co. Glamorgan, Sec. to Gov. of Ceylon, b. 29 Nov. 1787; d. 4 Nov. 1845; m. 4 Jan. 1810, Frances Eliza, da. of the Hon. John Rodney [B. Rodney Coll.], d. 5 Jan. 1879; and had issue 1b to 8b.

1b. Rev. John Patrick Eden, Hon. Canon of Durham, b. 6 July 1813; d. 6 May 1885; m. 3 May 1850, Catherine Frances, da. of Col. Henry Stobart, d. 11 Sept. 1898; and had issue 1c to 9c.

1c. John Henry Eden, Lieut.-Col. (ret.) H.M.'s Inspector of Constabulary, N. Dist., &c. (Bishopton Grange, Ripon; United Service), b. 10 May 1851; m. 12 Oct. 1893, Lady Florence [descended from King Henry VII., &c. (see Tudor Roll, p. 259)], da. of Somerset Richard (Lowry-Corry), 4th Earl of Belmore [I.]; and has issue 1d to 4d.

1d. Robert John Patrick Eden, b. 26 Ap. 1896.

2d. George Wilfrid Eden, b. 13 Aug. 1903.

3d. Christian Florence Eden.

4d. Norah Madeline Eden.

2c. Arthur Francis Eden (Penlan, Swansea), b. 3 June 1852; m. 5 July 1882, Frances, da. of the Rev. Robert Springett, Vicar of Brafferton.

3c. Right Rev. George Rodney Eden, D.D., 2nd Lord Bishop of Wakefield, formerly Bishop of Dover 1890–1897 (Bishopgarth, Wakefield), b. 9 Sept. 1853; m. 4 July 1889, Constance Margaret, da. of the Rev. Henry John Ellison, Hon. Canon of Canterbury and Chaplain-in-Ordinary to Queen Victoria; and has issue 1d to 5d.

1d. John Rodney Eden, b. 4 July 1892.

2d. Gerald Balfour Eden, b. 12 Aug. 1896.

3d. Margaret Agnes Eden.

4d. Dorothy Frances Eden.

5d. Mary Catharine Eden.

4c. Charles Hamilton Eden (Glyndderwen, Black Pyl, S.O., Glamorgan), b. 2 Ap. 1855; m. 27 Jan. 1885, Caroline Sophia, da. of the Rev. Charles Henry Ford, Vicar of Bishopston; and has issue 1d to 3d.

1d. Charles Henry Hamilton Eden, Royal Mil. Acad., Woolwich, b. 12 Mar. 1889.

2d. Frances Catherine Eden.

3d. Dulcibella Eden. [Nos. 38780 to 38795.

The Plantagenet Roll

5c. Rev. Frederick Nugent Eden, M.A. (Camb.), Vicar of Rusthall (*Rusthall Vicarage, Tunbridge Wells*), b. 3 Sept. 1857; *unm.*

6c. Rev. Henry Culley Eden, M.A. (Camb.), Vicar of Holy Innocents', Hammersmith (205 *Goldhawk Road, W.*), b. 4 Nov. 1858; *unm.*

7c. Robert Gerald Rodney Eden (*Rhyd-yr-Helyg, Sketty, Glamorgan*), b. 7 Jan. 1860; *m.* 11 Ap. 1901, Elizabeth Anne, da. of the Right Rev. Thomas Bunbury, D.D., Lord Bishop of Limerick, Ardfort, and Aghadoe.

8c. Frances Margaret Eden (*Selwyn Croft, Cambridge*), *m.* 27 June 1893, the Rev. Richard Appleton, Fellow of Trin. Coll. and 4th Master of Selwyn Coll., Camb., Hon. Canon of Durham, *d.* 1 Mar. 1909.

9c. Mary Dulcibella Eden (*Rusthall Vicarage, Tunbridge Wells*).

2b. *William Frederick Eden*, Col. in the Army, b. 31 Aug. 1814; d. 14 Nov. 1867; m. 1 Jan. 1838, *Marie Sidonie*, da. *of Jean Isidor Delaselle*, d. 1894; *and had issue* (with 2 elder sons who d.s.p.) 1c.

1c. Henry Hamilton Forbes Eden, Major Army Motor Reserve, *formerly* Hon. Lieut.-Col. 3rd Batt. Norfolk Regt., served in South Africa, has Queen's Medal and 3 Clasps (*Eden Lodge, Cromer; Junior United Service, &c.*), b. 28 Oct. 1856; *m.* 11 Dec. 1878, Emily Clara Charlotte, widow of S. Bedford Edwards, da. of (—).

3b. *Louisa Frances Catherine Eden*, d. 26 Nov. 1898; m. 26 *May* 1859, *the Rev. John Robert Hall, Hon. Canon of Canterbury, Rector of Hunton*, d. 1892; *and had issue* 1c.

1c. Frances Caroline Hall.

4b. *Frances Marianne Eden*, d. 25 *Ap.* 1862; m. *as 1st wife*, 18 *June* 1850, *Rev. the Hon. Lewis William Denman*, d. 6 *May* 1907; *and had issue.*
See p. 166, Nos. 17601–17606.

5b. *Sarah Frederica Eden, d.* 4 Nov. 1903; m. *Aug.* 1841, *Montagu Wilmot of Norton House, co. Glamorgan* [*Bt. of Osmaston* [*G.B.*] *Coll.*], d. 8 *Dec.* 1880; *and had issue.*
See the Essex Volume, pp. 135–136, Nos. 16037–16055.

6b. *Caroline Elizabeth Eden*, d. 11 *Nov.* 1872; m. *as 1st wife*, 28 *Ap.* 1859, *Felix Hussey Webber* (see p. 201), *a Clerk in the House of Commons*, d. 19 *Ap.* 1905; *and had issue* 1c *to* 4c.

1c. Gerald Rodney Webber, *b.* 23 Feb. 1863; *m.* 24 Oct. 1889, Eiteuse, da. of Augustus Baylis, and has issue 1d to 2d.

1d. Arthur Rodney Webber, *b.* 7 Sept. 1890.
2d. Gladys Janthe Webber, *b.* 20 Sept. 1892.

2c. *Felix Arthur Webber*, *M.A.*, *R.N.*, b. 15 *Ap.* 1866; d. *unm.* 17 *July* 1885.
3c. Helen Kate Webber, *unm.*

4c. Caroline Grace Webber, *m.* 14 Jan. 1901, Henry Fenwick Haszard, Comm. R.N., *d.* 31 Mar. 1898; and has issue 1d to 2d.

1d. Gerald Fenwick Haszard, *b.* 22 Oct. 1894.
2d. Gladys Grace Haszard, *b.* 19 Feb. 1892.

7b. Emily Georgiana Eden (*The Bryn, Swansea*).

8b. *Mary Dulcibella Eden*, d. 9 *Ap.* 1909; m. *as 2nd wife*, 17 *July* 1867, *Captain Iltid Thomas of Glanmor*, d. 2 *Sept.* 1889; *and had issue* 1c *to* 4c.

1c. Iltid Edward Thomas (*Glanmor, Swansea*), *b.* 1 July 1873.

2c. Isabel de Winton Thomas, *m.* 24 Ap. 1896, Francis William Gilbertson (*Glyn Teg, Pontardawe, Swansea*); and has issue 1d.

1d. Mary Dulcibella Frances Gilbertson.

3c. Dulcibel Iltuta Thomas.

4c. Amabel Charlotte Thomas, *m.* 23 Sept. 1902, Maurice Walter Henty; and has issue 1d.

1d. Richard Iltid Henty, *b.* 25 June 1903. [Nos. 38796 to 38841.

of The Blood Royal

2a. John Eden, C.B., Gen. in the Army, b. 25 Mar. 1789; d. 6 Oct. 1874; m. 1st, at Quebec, Aug. 1829, Anne, da. and in her issue (13 Oct. 1858) co-h. of Sir John Caldwell of Castle Caldwell, 5th Bt. [I.], d. at Montreal Nov. 1841; 2ndly, 4 July 1843, Charlotte Carse, da. of Edmund Saul Prentice of Armagh, d. (–); and had issue 1b to 5b.

1b. William Thomas Eden, Col. late Bombay S.C., b. 23 Ap. 1838.

2b. Frederick Morton Eden, Major late R.M.L.I., Egyptian Medal with Clasps and Bronze Star (Ivybridge, Devon), b. 28 Dec. 1847; m. 6 July 1881, Minnie Pitts, da. of Edward Allen of Stowford Lodge, Devon, J.P., s.p.s.

3b. George Henry Eden, Lieut. R.N. (ret.) (The Gull, Boundary Road, West Worthing), b. 7 Oct. 1849; m. 1901, Miriam Sophia, da. of W. Farnham; and has issue 1c.

1c. Hugh Morton Eden, b. 1903.

4b. Frances Charlotte Eden, m. 18 Sept. 1872, Montagu St. John Maule, B.A., S.C.L., Solicitor (Chapel House, Park Street, Bath); and has issue 1c to 3c.

1c. Henry Noel St. John Maule, b. 1873.

2c. Walter John Maule, b. 1878.

3c. Ethel Mary St. John Maule.

5b. Emily Elizabeth Eden, m. 3 Sept. 1874, Ernest Wallace Rooke, Solicitor (Stratton House, Bath).

3a. Arthur Eden, Assist. Comptroller of the Exchequer, b. 9 Aug. 1793; d. 1874; m. 1824, Frances, widow of William Baring [Bt. Coll.], sister of Charles, 1st Baron Sydenham [U.K.], and da. of John Buncombe-Poulett-Thomson of Waverley Abbey, co. Surrey, d. 25 Mar. 1877; and had issue 1c to 4c.

1c. Arthur John Eden (19 Bedford Square, W.C.), b. 1827; unm.

2c. Frederick Eden (Palazzo Barbarigo, Venice), b. 1828; m. 28 Feb. 1865, Caroline, da. of E. Joseph L. Jeykill of Wargrave Hill; s.p.

3c. Mabel Eden, b. 20 Jan. 1837; d. 20 Ap. 1889; m. 3 Ap. 1861, Frederick Cox, Banker and Army Agent (Stanswood Cottage, Fawley, Southampton); and had issue (with an elder son, Horace Frederick, d.s.p. July 1899) 1d to 5d.

1d. Reginald Henry Cox, Banker (26 Pont Street, S.W.), b. 30 Dec. 1865; m. 3 May 1890, Sybil Mary, da. of Thomas M. Wequelin.

2d. Hubert Arthur Cox, Banker (3 Grosvenor Crescent, S.W.), b. 16 Feb. 1871; unm.

3d. Algernon Charles Cox, Banker (57 Sloane Street, S.W.), b. 23 Aug. 1876; m. 6 Nov. 1901, Lilian Gertrude, da. of William Grazebrook; and has issue 1e to 2e.

1e. Frederick Cox, b. 21 Nov. 1902.

2e. Isabel Valentine Cox, b. 14 Feb. 1906.

4d. Lilian Cox, m. 8 Mar. 1888, Henry Vaughan Rudstow-Read [descended from the Lady Anne, sister of King Edward IV. (see Exeter Volume, p. 532)].

5d. Mabel Horatia Cox.

4c. Dulcibella Eden, d. 25 Oct. 1903; m. 23 Jan. 1856, Hugh Hammersley of Sun House, Chelsea, Army Agent, d. Sept. 1882; and had issue 1d to 9d.

1d. Arthur Charles Hammersley, Banker (56 Prince's Gate, S.W.), b. 22 Dec. 1856; m. 1st, 2 Sept. 1882, Mary Louisa [descended from the Lady Anne, sister of Edward IV. (see the Exeter Volume, p. 294)], da. of George Herbert Frederick Campbell, Cadet of Cawdor, J.P., D.L., d. 12 Nov. 1899; 2ndly, 15 Ap. 1902, Violet Mary (see p. 82), da. of William Peere Williams-Freeman of Clapton, co. Northants; and has issue 1e to 7e.

1e.[1] Hugh Charles Hammersley, b. 23 Feb. 1892.

2e.[2] Christopher Ralph Hammersley, b. 4 Jan. 1903.

3e.[2] David Frederick Hammersley, b. 15 July 1904.

[Nos. 38842 to 38863.

The Plantagenet Roll

4e.¹ Gwendolen Mary Hammersley, m. Jan. 1908, George Henry Draper Post [son of Frederick A. Post of 58 Eccleston Square]; and has issue 1f to 2f.
  1f. Pauline Post, b. Dec. 1908.
  2f. Cynthia Alma Post, b. 22 Dec. 1909.
5e.¹ Cynthia Edith Hammersley, unm.
6e.¹ Doris Hammersley, unm.
7e.² Monica Violet Hammersley, unm.

2d. Hugh Greenwood Hammersley, Banker (*The Grove, Hampstead;* 16 *Sackville Street, W.*), b. 4 July 1858; m. 30 Aug. 1889, Mary Frances [descended from the Lady Isabel Plantagenet (see the Essex Volume, p. 289)], da. of Owen Grant; and has issue 1e.
  1e. Eve Mary Hammersley, d. unm.

3d. Guy Frederick Hammersley, b. 27 Jan. 1871.

4d. Margaret Dulcibella Hammersley (51 *Elm Park Gardens, S.W.*), m. 13 Jan. 1883, Sidney Francis Godolphin Osborne [son of the Rev. Lord Sidney Godolphin Osborne, and a descendant of George, Duke of Clarence, K.G. (see Clarence Volume, p. 628)], d. 22 Oct. 1903; and has issue 1e to 3e.
  1e. Francis D'Arcy Godolphin Osborne, Attaché Diplo. Ser., b. 16 Sept. 1884.
  2e. Sidney Hugh Godolphin Osborne, b. 28 Dec. 1887.
  3e. Maurice Godolphin Osborne, b. 1 July 1889.

5d. Dora Edith Hammersley, m. 1880, Sir Francis Alexander Campbell of the Foreign Office and 7 Onslow Crescent, W., K.C.M.G., C.B. [descended from the Lady Anne, sister of King Edward IV., &c. (see Exeter Volume, p. 294)].
  1e. Ronald Hugh Campbell, a Clerk in the Foreign Office (33 *South Street, Brompton, S.W.*), b. 1883; m. Helen, da. of (—) Graham; and has issue 1f.
    1f. Mary Campbell, b. 1908.
  2e. Ivan Campbell, b. 1887.
  3e. Mabel Verena Campbell.

6d. Mabel Barbara Hammersley, m. 27 Oct. 1887, Walter Nassau Senior [son of Nassau John Senior (12 *Chichester Terrace, Brighton*); and has issue 1e.
  1e. Oliver Nassau Senior, b. 28 Nov. 1901.

7d. Maud Emily Hammersley, m. 26 Oct. 1891, Henry William Duff-Gordon [descended from George, Duke of Clarence, K.G. (see the Clarence Volume, p. 246)] (*Avott Green, Welwyn, Herts*); and has issue (with a da. d. young) 1e to 3e.
  1e. Douglas Frederick Duff-Gordon, b. 12 Sept. 1892.
  2e. Cosmo Lewis Duff-Gordon, b. 3 Mar. 1897.
  3e. Anne Maud Duff-Gordon, b. 3 Jan. 1903.

8d. Beatrice Hammersley, m. 20 July 1898, Philip Apsley Treherne [son of Goring Apsley Treherne] (*The Corner, Thursley, Surrey*).
9d. Sylvia Hammersley, unm.

4a. Robert Eden, H.E.I.C.S., *Magistrate at Tinnevelly*, b. 13 May 1800; d. 23 Ap. 1879; m. 21 Ap. 1829, Frances Mary [*descended from the Lady Anne, sister of King Edward IV.*], da. of the Rev. Rowland Egerton-Warburton, d. 11 Jan. 1898; and had issue.
See the Exeter Volume, p. 516, Nos. 44910–44914.

5a. Marianne Eden, d. 12 Jan. 1865; m. 1st, 19 Dec. 1807, *John Spalding of Holme, co. Kirkcudbright, M.P.*, d. 26 Aug. 1815; 2ndly, 1 Ap. 1819, Henry (Brougham), 1st Baron Brougham and Vaux [U.K.], Lord Chancellor of the United Kingdom 1830–34, d. at Cannes 7 May 1868; *and had issue 1b to 2b.*
  1b. *John Eden Spalding of Holme, J.P.*, b. 4 Oct. 1808; d. 29 Mar. 1869; m. 18 Aug. 1831, the Hon. Mary Wilhelmina, da. of John Henry (Upton), 1st Viscount Templetown [I.], d. 20 Mar. 1876; *and had issue* (with a son and da. who d.s.p.) 1c.
  [Nos. 38864 to 38893.

# of The Blood Royal

1c. Augustus Frederick Montagu Spalding of Holme and Shirmers, J.P., D.L. (*The Holme, New Galloway;* 11 *Ashley Place, S.W.; Carlton, &c.*), b. 23 Oct. 1838; *unm.*

2b. Marianne Dora Spalding, d. 2 *Jan.* 1891; m. 22 *Dec.* 1834, *Sir Alexander Malet, 2nd Bt.* [G.B.], K.C.B., d. 28 *Nov.* 1886; *and had issue* 1c *to* 2c.

1c. Sir Henry Charles Eden Malet, 3rd Bt. [G.B.], J.P., Lieut.-Col. Gren. Guards, b. 25 *Sept.* 1835; d. 12 *Jan.* 1904; m. 18 *Feb.* 1873, *Laura Jane Campbell, da. of John Hamilton of Hilston Park, co. Mon.; and had issue* 1d.

1d. Vera Jean Hamilton Malet, *m.* 21 Jan. 1903, Dorotheos Antoniadi [son of Michael Antoniadi of Constantinople]; and has issue 1e.

1e. Henry Edward Roger Fortuné Amédée Malet Antoniadi, b. 1904.

2c. Right Hon. Sir Edward Baldwin Malet, 4th Bt. [G.B.], P.C., G.C.B., G.C.M.G., b. 10 *Oct.* 1837; d.s.p. 30 *June* 1908.

6a. Dora Eden, d. (–); m. Adm. Sir Graham Moore, G.C.B., R.N. [*brother of Sir John Moore, the hero of Corunna*]. [Nos. 38894 to 38896.

144. Descendants of FREDERICK MORTON (EDEN), 1st Lord HENLEY [I.], so cr. 9 Nov. 1799, having been Ambassador to the Courts of Vienna and Madrid (Table XVI.), b. 8 July 1752; d. 6 Dec. 1830; m. 7 Aug. 1783, Lady ELIZABETH, sister and h. of Robert, 2nd and last Earl, and da. of Robert (HENLEY), 1st Earl of Northington [G.B.], d. 20 Aug. 1821; and had issue 1a to 2a.

1a. Robert Henley (*Eden, afterwards (R.L. 31 Mar. 1831) Henley*), 2nd Baron Henley [I.], b. 3 *Sept.* 1789; d. 3 *Feb.* 1841; m. 11 *Mar.* 1823, *Harriet Eleanor, da. of Sir Robert Peel, 1st Bt.* [G.B.], d. 7 *May* 1869; *and had issue* 1b *to* 2b.

1b. Anthony Henley (Henley), 3rd Baron Henley [I.], M.P., b. 12 *Ap.* 1825; d, 27 *Nov.* 1898; m. 1st, 30 *July* 1846, *Julia Augusta, da. of the Very Rev. John Peel. D.D., Dean of Worcester*, d. 15 *Feb.* 1862; 2ndly, 30 *June* 1870, *Clara Campbell Lucy* (9 *Beaufort Gardens, S.W.*), *da. of Joseph Henry Storie Jekyll; and had issue* 1c *to* 6c.

1c. Frederick (Henley), 4th Baron Henley [I.], J.P. (*Watford Court, near Rugby*), b. 17 *Ap.* 1849; *m.* 20 Oct. 1900, Augusta Frederica, da. of Herbert Langham of Cottesbrooke Park [Bt. Coll.], *d.s.p.* 27 July 1905.

2c. Hon. Anthony Ernest Henley, heir-presumptive, C.E., b. 3 July 1858; *m.* 1st, 17 Aug. 1882, Georgiana Caroline Mary, da. of Lieut.-Col. Richard Michael Williams [Bt. Coll.], *d.s.p.* 26 Aug. 1888; 2ndly, 12 Sept. 1889, Emmeline Stuart, da. of George Gammie Maitland; and has issue 1d.

1d. Joan Beryl Henley, b. 1 Aug. 1893.

3c. Hon. Anthony Morton Henley, Capt. 5th Lancers, served in South Africa 1900–02, Bar.-at-Law, &c. (*Wellington; Cavalry*), b. 4 Aug. 1873; *m.* 24 Ap. 1906, the Hon. Sylvia Laura [descended from George, Duke of Clarence, K.G. (see Clarence Volume, p. 442)], da. of Edward Lyulph (Stanley), 4th Baron Stanley of Alderley [U.K.].

4c. Hon. Francis Robert Henley, M.A. (Oxon.) (*9 Beaufort Gardens, S.W.; Wellington*), b. 11 Ap. 1877.

5c.[1] Hon. Gertrude Augusta Henley, *unm.*

6c.[2] Hon. Evelyn Henley, *m.* 9 Aug. 1881, John Langham Reed (*Thornby, Northants*); and has issue 1d to 3d.

1d. Herbert Langham Reed, b. 1882.

2d. Cecil Langham Reed, b. 1884.

3d. Evelyn Langham Reed. [Nos. 38897 to 38906.

The Plantagenet Roll

2*b*. Rev. the Hon. Robert Henley, M.A. (Oxon.), *formerly* Vicar of Putney (*Eden Lodge, Putney*), *b.* 7 Mar. 1831; *m.* 1 June 1852, Emily Louisa, da. of Robert Aldridge of New Lodge, Horsham, *d.* 20 Aug. 1893; and has issue 1*c* to 7*c*.

1*c*. Rev. Robert Eden Henley, M.A. (Oxon.), Vicar of Wharton (*Wharton Vicarage, near Winsford*), *b.* 10 Sept. 1861.

2*c*. Charles Beauclerk Henley, *b.* 7 Feb. 1869.

3*c*. Constance Laura Henley, *m.* 16 Ap. 1890, the Rev. Robert Stewart Gregory, M.A., Rector of Much Hadham (*Much Hadham Rectory, Herts*); and has issue 1*d* to 5*d*.

1*d*. Robert Henley Gregory, *b.* 3 Mar. 1891.
2*d*. Francis Stewart Gregory, *b.* 3 Mar. 1893.
3*d*. John Stephen Gregory, *b.* 26 June 1898.
4*d*. Violet Emily Gregory.
5*d*. Mary Noel Gregory.

4*c*. Beatrice Mary Henley.
5*c*. Ethel Maud Henley.
6*c*. Mildred Caroline Henley.
7*c*. Mabel Augusta Henley.

2*a*. Rev. the Hon. William Eden, Rector of Bishopsbourne, and Senior Preacher in Canterbury Cathedral, *b.* 9 Nov. 1792; *d.* 4 May 1859; m 19 *Jan.* 1820, Anna Maria, Dowager Baroness Grey de Ruthvyn [E.], da. of William Kelham, d. 23 Oct. 1875; *and had issue* 1*b* to 5*b*.

1*b*. Rev. Arthur Eden, *Vicar of Ticehurst, b.* 3 *Jan*. 1825; *d. 17 Nov.* 1908; *m*. 24 Aug. 1848, *Alice Julia, da. of Thomas Annesley Whitney of Merton, co. Wexford, d.* 18 *Dec.* 1897; *and had issue* 1*c* to 8*c*.

1*c*. William Gaven Eden, *late Lieut. R.N. (Tannygraiy, near Portmalre, N. Wales), b.* 26 July 1849; *m.* 4 Jan. 1876, Augusta Rose, da. of Matthew Bell of Bourne Park, co. Kent; and has issue 1*d* to 6*d*.

1*d*. Cecil Eden, *b.* 3 Oct. 1876.
2*d*. Morton Eden, *b.* 9 Dec. 1881.
3*d*. Constance Eden.
4*d*. Nora Eden.
5*d*. Hilda Eden.
6*d*. Alice Nesta Eden.

2*c*. Arthur Yelverton Eden, J.P. (*Granville House, Arundel*), *b.* 19 Mar. 1856; *m*. 22 Nov. 1888, Fanny Spencer, da. and h. of John Theodore Louis Le Blanch, of Beechfield, co. Chester; and has issue 1*d* to 3*d*.

1*d*. Barbara Yelverton Eden.
2*d*. Lelgarde Edith Eleanor Eden.
3*d*. Dulcie Flora Eden.

3*c*. Alice Lizzie Eden, *m.* 27 Sept. 1883, William Sherrard (*Pro Bank House, Fermoy, co. Cork*); and has issue 1*d*.

1*d*. Arthur William Eden Sherrard, *b.* 17 Aug. 1884.

4*c*. *Mary Constance Eden*, b. 11 *May* 1852; *d.* 29 *Mar.* 1884; m. 30 *Ap.* 1878, *Augustus Hills Cobbold (Brownhill, Nurseling, Southampton); and has issue* 1*d* to 2*d*.

1*d*. Neville Eden Cobbold, *b.* 15 Ap. 1882.
2*d*. Alice Mary Cobbold, *m.* 12 Dec. 1905, Comm. Duncan Tatton Brown, R.N.

5*c*. *Eleanor Agnes Eden*, b. 29 *July* 1853; *d.* 4 *Feb.* 1897; m. 18 *Dec.* 1879, *Vice-Adm. Henry Bedford Woollcombe, R.N.*, b. 25 *Ap.* 1831; *d.* 14 *Feb.* 1904; *and had issue* 1*d*.

1*d*. Eleanor Mary Woollcombe.

6*c*. Edith Amelia Eden, *m*. 1st, 26 Oct. 1876, Charles Davers Eden, R.N.,

[Nos. 38907 to 38936.

of The Blood Royal

d.s.p.s. 25 Feb. 1895; 2ndly, 1 June 1901, Col. Arthur Fred Eden-Perkins (*Dodwith, Bursledon, Hants*).

7c. Flora Colclough Eden.

8c. Julia Augusta Maria Eden.

2b. Robert Charles Eden, Lieut.-Col. U.S. Army, b. 31 Aug. 1836; m. 26 Jan. 1865, Annie Gardner, da. of Andrew Bain of Bonhill, co. Dumbarton; and has issue 1c to 6c.

1c. Morton Edward Eden, b. 17 Sept 1867; m. 1894, Marie Elizabeth, da. of James Stewart of Dansville, New York; and has issue 1d.

1d. Robert Henley Stewart Eden, b. 1896.

2c. Reginald Yelverton Eden, b. 15 Dec. 1871; m. 18—, Sophia, da. of T. Hart of Warren, U.S.A.; and has issue.

3c. Mabel Wenonah Eden.

4c. Ethel Elizabeth Eden.

5c. Sybil Constance Eden.

6c. Charlotte Annie Maude Eden.

3b. Mary Yelverton Eden, m. 4 July 1848, Samuel Lucas Lancaster-Lucas of Wateringbury Place, co. Kent, d. 1894; and has issue 1c to 5c.

1c. *William Matthias Lancaster-Lucas*, b. 27 *Ap.* 1849; d. (? s.p.).

2c. *Charles Eden Lancaster Lancaster-Lucas*, b. 16 *June* 1854; d. (? s.p.).

3c. Mary Helewise Ursula Lancaster-Lucas.

4c. Flora Lancaster-Lucas.

5c. Katharine Elizabeth Lancaster-Lucas, m. 1888, Col. Ralph Basnett Rastell Williamson, *formerly* 43rd L.I.; and has issue 1d to 3d.

1d. Ralph W. B. R. Williamson, b. 1890.

2d. Katherine Elizabeth Williamson.

3d. Ruth Mary Florence Williamson.

4b. Charlotte Maria Eden (*Glemham Hall, Wickham Market*), m. 1st, 17 Oct. 1850, Dudley, Lord North [son and h. app. of Francis, 6th Earl of Guilford [G.B.]], *d.v.p.* 28 Jan. 1860; 2ndly, 10 July 1861, Major Alexander George Dickson, 3rd Hussars, M.P., d. 3 July 1889; and has issue 1c to 3c.

1c. *Dudley Francis (North), 7th Earl of Guilford [G.B.] and 9th Baron Guilford [E.]*, b. 14 *July* 1851; d. 19 *Dec.* 1885; m. 4 *May* 1874, *Georgiana* (4 *Lennox Gardens, S.W.*) [*descended from the Lady Anne, sister of King Edward IV.* (see the Exeter Volume, p. 322)], da. of Sir George Chetwynd, 3rd Bt. [G.B.]; and had issue 1d to 2d.

1d. *Frederick George (North), 8th Earl of [G.B.] and 10th Baron Guilford [E.]* (*Waldershare Park, Dover; Glemham Hall, Wickham Market*), b. 19 Nov. 1876; m. 25 June 1901, Mary Violet, da. of William Hargrave Pawson of Shawdon; and has issue 1e to 2e.

1e. Francis George North, Lord North, b. 15 June 1902.

2e. Hon. John Montagu North, b. 28 Feb. 1905.

2d. Lady Muriel Emily North.

2c. Hon. *Morton William North*, b. 31 *Oct.* 1852; d. 26 *Ap.* 1895; m. 3 *Ap.* 1879, *Hilda Hylton* [*descended from George, Duke of Clarence, K.G.* (see Clarence Volume, p. 189), da. and co-h. of Capt. Hylton Joliffe [son and h.-app. of 1st Lord Hylton [U.K.]],, d. 19 Feb. 1902; and had issue 1d to 3d.

1d. Dudley John North, *formerly* Lieut. 3rd Batt. Norfolk Regt., b. 9 Jan. 1880.

2d. Hylton George Morton North, b. 13 Sept. 1885.

3d. Roger North, b. 24 Sept. 1888.

3c. *Lady Flora Mildred North*, b. 25 *Ap.* 1855; d. 1 *Mar.* 1886; m. *as 1st wife*, 28 Dec. 1880, Sir Robert Rodney Wilmot of Osmaston, 6th Bt. [G.B.] [*himself*

[Nos. 38937 to 38961.]

The Plantagenet Roll

a descendant of Edward III. through the Mortimer-Percy marriage] (*Binfield Grove, Bracknell, Berks*); *and had issue.*
See p. 280, Nos. 38811–38814 (also Essex Volume, p. 135).

5b. Flora Jane Eden (*Brokenhurst Park, Hants*), m. as 2nd wife, 2 Ap. 1866, John Morant of Brokenhurst, J.P., D.L., High Sheriff co. Hants 18— [descended from the Lady Anne, sister of King Edward IV., &c. (see the Exeter Volume, p. 685)], *d.* 30 May 1899; and had issue 1c to 3c.

1c. Edward John Harry Eden Morant of Brokenhurst, J.P., Hon. Attaché Diplo. Ser. (*Brokenhurst Park, near Lymington*), b. 1868.

2c. Francis George Morant, b. 1869.

3c. Mabel Caroline Flora Morant, m. 1889, Herbert George Alexander; and has issue. [Nos. 38962 to 38969.

145. Descendants of DULCIBELLA EDEN (Table XVI.), *d.* (–); *m.* 1767, MATTHEW BELL of Woolsington, Col. Northumberland Militia, *d.* 1811; and had issue 1a to 7a.

1a. *Matthew Bell of Woolsington, M.P., High Sheriff co. Northbd.* 1797, d. 18—; m. 9 *June* 1792, *Sarah Frances*, da. of *Charles Brandling of Gorforth House, co. Northbd.; and had issue* (with 4 elder sons and 2 das. who all d.s.p.) 1b to 3b.

1b. *Rev. John Bell, Vicar of Rothwell, Hon. Canon of Ripon and Rural Dean*, b. 29 *June* 1805; d. 24 Oct. 1869; m. 20 Nov. 1828, *Isabella Elizabeth, da. of Sir Charles Loraine, 5th Bt.* [E.], d. 15 *Mar.* 1881; *and had issue* (with 5 *other sons and a da. who* d. *young*) 1c to 7c.

1c. Charles Loraine Bell of Woolsington, J.P., D.L., High Sheriff co. Northbd. 1895 (*Woolsington, Newcastle-on-Tyne*), b. 3 July 1836; m. 13 Ap. 1871, Anna Roberta, da. of Charles Bernard, 24th Regt.; and has issue 1d to 4d.

1d. Walter Loraine Bell (*Woolsington, Newcastle-on-Tyne*), b. 30 May 1877; m. 30 Nov. 1890, Winifred Margaret, widow of John Loxley Firth of Hope, co. Derby, da. of Henry William Watson of Burnopfield, co. Durham.

2d. Margaret Ellen Bell, m. 12 June 1901, her cousin, Claude Henry Watson (see p. 287) (*Sunnyside, Woolsington, Newcastle-on-Tyne*); and has issue 1e to 2e.

1e. Godfrey Charles Watson, b. 9 Ap. 1907.

2e. Dorothy Helen Watson, b. 6 May 1902.

3d. Isabel Gertrude Bell (*Houndless Water, Haslemere, Surrey*), m. 14 July 1898, Lieut.-Col. Eustace Guinness of Burton Hall, co. Dublin, R.A., *d.* (being killed in the Boer War) 30 Oct. 1901; and has issue 1e to 2e.

1e. Eustace Francis Guinness, b. Jan. 1900.

2e. Humphrey Patrick Guinness, b. Mar. 1902.

4d. Dulcibella Mildreda Bell.

2c. William Bell, b. 24 Mar. 1839.

3c. Frank Bell, b. 21 May 1842.

4c. Isabella Elizabeth Bell (*Palazzo Consiglio, Rione Amadeo, Naples*).

5c. *Frances Sarah Bell,* b. *Ap.* 1835; d. 23 *Ap.* 1905; m. 23 *Ap.* 1863, *the Rev. Shepley Watson Hemmingway, afterwards Watson, Rector of Bootle, Cumberland,* b. 11 *Jan.* 1827; d. 23 *Ap.* 1899; *and had issue* 1d *to* 4d.

1d. Rev. Arthur Herbert Watson, Vicar of Long Preston (*Long Preston Vicarage, Leeds*), b. May 1864; m. Feb. 1900, Louisa Caroline [descended from the Lady Anne, sister of King Edward IV., &c. (see the Exeter Volume, p. 568)], da. of Thomas Edward Yorke of Beverley Hall, co. York, J.P.; and has issue 1e to 5e.

1e. Edward Shepley Watson, b. Feb. 1901.

2e. Oliver Arthur Watson, b. Sept. 1902.

3e. Martin Yorke Watson, b. Nov. 1905.

4e. Beatrice Helen Frances Watson, b. May 1907.

5e. Joan Margaret Louisa Watson, b. June 1909. [Nos. 38970 to 38987.

of The Blood Royal

2*d*. Cyril Francis Watson, Land Agent (*Greysouthen, Cockermouth, Cumberland?*), *b*. 23 Oct. 1866 ; *m*. 3 Jan. 1900, Katharine Anna Keatinge, da. of the Rev. Canon Jeremy Taylor Pollock [a descendant of Bishop Jeremy Taylor] ; and has issue 1*e* to 3*e*.

    1*e*. George Loraine Pollock Watson, *b*. 8 June 1902.
    2*e*. Cyril Jeremy Taylor Watson, *b*. 28 Dec. 1904.
    3*e*. Eileen Frances Katharine Watson, *b*. 13 Mar. 1901.

3*d*. Claude Henry Watson (*Sunnyside, Woolsington, Newcastle-on-Tyne*), *b*. 4 Jan. 1869 ; *m*. 12 June 1901, his cousin, Margaret Ellen (see above), da. of Charles Loraine Bell of Woolsington ; and has issue.
See p. 286, Nos. 38973–38974.

4*d*. Loraine John Watson (1 *St. George's Crescent, Stanwix, Carlisle*), *b*. 23 Oct. 1871 ; *m*. Ap. 1901, his cousin, Ethel Gertrude (see below), da. of Richard Harrison ; *s.p.*

6*c*. Emma Rachel Bell, *m*. 10 June 1869, Capt. Albert Adams, 24th Regt. (*Clyde House, Dawlish, South Devon*) ; and has issue (with 2 others, sons, who *d*. young) 1*d* to 6*d*.

    1*d*. Algernon Frank Adams, *b*. 8 Ap. 1870 ; *d. unm.* in South Africa during the War, Sept. 1901.
    2*d*. Reginald Shute Adams, farming in Canada, *b*. 15 Sept. 1872 ; *m*. (—), da. of (—) ; and has issue 1*e* to 3*e*.
        1*e*. Reginald Adams.
        2*e*. Walter Adams.
        3*e*. Una Adams.
    3*d*. Arthur Cecil Paget Adams, farming in the United States, *b*. 21 Feb. 1875 ; *unm*.
    4*d*. Gerald Colman Surtees Adams, *b*. 21 July 1877 ; *d. unm.* (being killed in action at Magersfontein) 11 Dec. 1899.
    5*d*. George Rorke Adams, farming in the United States, *b*. 30 Ap. 1880 ; *unm*.
    6*d*. Mildred Gertrude Adams.

7*c*. Gertrude Mary Bell, *b. c*. 1849 ; *d*. 25 Oct. 1878 ; m. 1 Aug. 1872, Richard Harrison, *d*. June 1906 ; *and had issue* 1*d* to 6*d*.

    1*d*. John Harrison } (twins), *b*. Oct. 1878 ; *unm*.
    2*d*. Henry Harrison
    3*d*. Ethel Gertrude Harrison, *m*. Ap. 1901, her cousin, Loraine John Watson (see above) (1 *St. George's Crescent, Stanwix, Carlisle*) ; *s.p.*
    4*d*. Evelyn Harrison.
    5*d*. Elsie Harrison.
    6*d*. Beatrice Harrison.

2*b*. William Bell, *d*. (-) ; *m*. Jane, da. of William Ridley of Park End, co. Northbd., *d*. (-) ; *and had issue* 1*c*.

    1*c*. Sara Bell (*Castlehill, Middleham, S.O., Bedale*), *m*. Gen. Ingilby ; *s.p.*

3*b*. Sarah Frances Bell, *d*. 10 or 19 Aug. 1874 ; m. 25 *May* 1826, *Sir John James Walsham of Knill Court, co. Hereford*, 1st Bt. [*U.K.*], so cr. 30 *Sept*. 1831, *D.L. and High Sheriff co. Radnor* 1870, *b*. 6 *June* 1805 ; *d*. 10 *Aug*. 1874 ; *and had issue* 1*c* to 4*c*.

    1*c*. Sir John Walsham, 2nd Bt. [*U.K.*], K.C.M.G., M.A. (*Camb.*), J.P., D.L., H.B.M.'s Envoy Extra. and Min. Plen. to the Courts of Pekin 1885–1892 and Bucharest 1892–1894, *b*. 29 *Oct*. 1830 ; *d*. 10 Dec. 1895 ; *m*. 5 *Mar*. 1867, *Florence, da. of the Hon. Peter Campbell Scarlett, C.B.* [*B. Abinger Coll.*] ; *and had issue* 1*d* to 2*d*.

        1*d*. Sir John Scarlett Walsham, 3rd Bt. [*U.K.*], an Inspector of Chinese Labour to Transvaal Govt. (*Knill Court, Kington, Hereford ; Germiston, Transvaal*), *b*.

[Nos. 38988 to 39011.

The Plantagenet Roll

15 Oct. 1869; *m.* 20 Nov. 1906, Bessie Geraldine Gundreda (see pp. 363 and 492), da. of Vice-Adm. John Borlase Warren, R.N. [Bt. Coll.]; and has issue 1*e*.

1*e*. Barbara Walsham.

2*d*. Percy Romilly Walsham, in Chinese Maritime Customs, *b*. 1871; *m*. 1899, Charlotte Cunninghame, da. of William Wykeham Myers of Formosa, M.B., C.M.; and has issue 1*e* to 3*e*.

1*e*. Percy Robert Stewart Walsham, *b*. 6 Ap. 1904.
2*e*. Florence Mary Walsham.
3*e*. Gladys Newell Walsham.

2*c*. Rev. Francis Walsham, M.A. (*Durham*), *Rector of Knill*, b. 9 *Ap.* 1832; d. (-); m. 20 *June* 1865, *Marianne*, da. of *Charles James Barnett of Bays Lawn, co. Glouc., M.P.*; *and had issue* 1*d to* 3*d*.

1*d*. John Charles Walsham (*Holmwood, Pannal Ash, Harrogate*), *b*. 11 Sept. 1866; *m*. 22 May 1902, Alice Maude, widow of John Alfred Pike, Surgeon, da. of John Headland.

2*d*. Florence Augusta Walsham, *m*. 14 Sept. 1892, John Cecil Thornhill of Castle Bellingham, co. Louth (*Rathmullen House, Drogheda*); and has issue 1*e* to 4*e*.

1*e*. Humphrey Thornhill, *b*. 1894.
2*e*. Kathleen Thornhill.
3*e*. Phyllis Thornhill.
4*e*. Sheila Thornhill.

3*d*. Mary Caroline Walsham, *m*. 1897, Algernon Estcourt Keys-Wells (28 *Church Street, Walsham*); and has issue 1*e*.

1*e*. William Yorke Keys-Wells, *b*. 10 May 1908.

3*c*. Anna Walsham, d. 18 *Aug.* 1905; m. 20 *May* 1855, *Major-Gen. O'Bryen Bellingham Woolsey of Milestown and Priorland, late R.A., J.P., D.L., High Sheriff co. Louth* 1889 (*Milestown Castle, Bellingham*); *and had issue* 1*d*.

1*d*. Alice Woolsey, *m*. 21 Ap. 1887, Cecil Butler, Bar.-at-Law [B. Dunboyne Coll.], *d*. 6 Dec. 1901; and has issue 1*e*.

1*e*. Cecilia Frances Butler.

4*c*. Fanny Walsham, *m*. as 2nd wife, 30 Oct. 1883, Thomas Edward Yorke of Bewerley and Halton Place, J.P., High Sheriff co. York [descended from the Lady Anne, sister of King Edward IV. (see the Exeter Volume, p. 568)] (*Bewerley Hall, Pateley Bridge, Leeds*).

2*a*. Stephen Bell, d. (? s.p.).

3*a*. Robert Bell *of Fenham Hall, co. Northbd., Mayor of Newcastle* 1822, d. 1850; m. *Anna Mildreda*, da. of *Childers Walbanke-Childers of Cantley, co. York*, d. (-); *and had issue* 1*b*.

1*b*. Mildreda Eliza Bell, d. 17 *Mar.* 1850; m. *as* 1*st wife*, 21 *Sept.* 1848, *Matthew Robert Bigge, J.P.* [8*th son of Col. Charles William Bigge of Linden, co. Northbd., J.P., D.L.*], d. 17 *July* 1906; *and had issue* 1*c*.

1*c*. Anna Mildreda Bigge, *m*. 7 Jan. 1875, Albert George Legard, *late* H.M. Chief Inspector of Schools for Wales [Bt. Coll., and himself a descendant of King Edward III. through Mortimer-Percy (see p. 193)] (*BrowHill, Batheaston, Somerset*).

4*a*. Henry Bell *of Newbiggen House, co. Northbd.*, d. 1830; m. 2 *June* 1807, *Susannah Jane*, da. of *Major Rowland Mainwaring of Four Oaks, co. Warwick* [who with her brother, Rear-Adm. Rowland Mainwaring of Whitmore Hall, was 19*th in descent from King Henry III.*], d. 11 Aug. 1871, aged 83; *and had issue* 1*b to* 4*b*.

1*b*. Matthew Bell, *b*. 29 May 1814.
2*b*. Rowland Mainwaring Bell, *b*. 8 Dec. 1821.
3*b*. Susanna Maria Bell, b. 13 *Aug.* 1816; d. 22 *Jan.* 1904; m. 26 *Nov.* 1835,

[Nos. 39012 to 39030.

of The Blood Royal

Samuel Goodin Barrett, d. 20 June 1876; and had issue (with 3 sons and a da. d. unm.) 1c to 7c.

1c. Henry Barrett, b. 5 Aug. 1838; d. 27 Oct. 1895; m. 25 July 1878, Julia Blanche (18 Inverna Gardens, London), da. of Thomas Brace; and had issue 1d to 3d.

    1d. Arthur Barrett, b. 30 Nov. 1880.
    2d. Charles Barrett, b. 29 July 1886.
    3d. Evelyn Barrett.

2c. Charles Rollo Barrett, J.P. (*Whitehill Hall, Pelton Fell, S.O., co. Durham*), b. 26 May 1854; m. 6 July 1882, Mary Delmar, da. of Alfred Barry of Newland Lodge, Sevenoaks; and has issue 1d to 5d.

    1d. Rollo Samuel Barrett, b. 28 Ap. 1883.
    2d. Kenneth Delmar Barrett, b. 6 Nov. 1886.
    3d. Lindsay Alfred Barrett, b. 8 July 1891.
    4d. Dulcibella Mary Barrett.
    5d. Brenda de Courcy Barrett.

3c. Robert Bell Barrett, J.P. (*Skipton Castle, Yorks*), b. 29 Mar. 1856; m. 12 Jan. 1893, Frances Madeline, da. of William Robinson of Reedley Hall, Burnley, J.P.; and has issue 1d to 4d.

    1d. Robin Coventry Barrett, b. 17 Feb. 1895.
    2d. Harry Eden Barrett, b. 20 Sept. 1903.
    3d. Monica Dulcibella Barrett.
    4d. Vera Doris Madeline Barrett.

4c. Maria Margaret Barrett, b. 5 June 1840; d. 5 Aug. 1903; m. 4 June 1868, Adam Gillies-Smith of Agsacre, North Berwick, d. 8 Jan. 1900; and had issue (with 2 sons who d.s.p.) 1d to 3d.

    1d. Margaret Gillies-Smith
    2d. Coventry Barrett Gillies-Smith } (*Agsacre, North Berwick*), unm.
    3d. Adelaide Cathcart Gillies-Smith

5c. Jeannette Susanna Barrett, m. 21 Dec. 1865, Charles Tennant Couper (*Woodstone, Row, Dumbarton*); and has issue 1d to 7d.

    1d. John Charles Couper, W.S. (*15 Rutland Street, Edinburgh*), b. 10 Oct. 1867; m. 17 Nov. 1899, Elsie Winifred, da. of Benjamin Hall Blyth of Edinburgh, C.E.; and has issue 1e to 3e.

        1e. Ian Charles Blyth Couper, b. 11 May 1901.
        2e. Millicent Jeanette Couper.
        3e. Annabel Elsie Couper.

    2d. Samuel Barrett Couper, M.D., M.R.C.S. (*Blaby, Leicester*), b. 20 July 1876; m. 12 June 1899, Marjorie, da. of J. H. W. Davies of Minden, St. John's Park, Blackheath.

    3d. Charlotte Maria Couper, m. 26 May 1900, the Rev. Charles Inglebert Baldwin, Vicar of Belper (*Christchurch Vicarage, Belper, Derby*); s.p.

    4d. Edith Jeannette Couper, m. 23 Dec. 1901, George Edward Herne [son of Col. George Edward Herne, 103rd Bombay Fusiliers] (*Balgarvie, St. John's, near Woking*); and has issue 1e to 3e.

        1e. George Charles Barrett Herne, b. 15 Aug. 1895.
        2e. Dulcibella Jeannette Herne.
        3e. Edith Dorothea Margaret Herne.

    5d. Dulcibella Margaret Couper, unm.

    6d. May Coventry Couper, m. 17 Oct. 1905, Com. Francis St. George Brooker, R.N.; sp.

    7d. Maud Barrett Couper, m. 3 Nov. 1906, Henry John Bell Edge [son of

[Nos. 39031 to 39061.

The Plantagenet Roll

Adm. William Henry Edge, R.N.] (*South Binns, Heathfield*); and has issue 1*e* to 2*e*.
 1*e*. Archibald Edge, *b.* Jan. 1907.
 2*e*. Elsie Edge.

 6*c*. *Dulcibella Barrett*, b. 11 Nov. 1846; d. 3 Dec. 1879; m. 14 *July* 1870, *Collingwood Lindsay Wood of Freeland, Forgandenny, co. Perth*, d. 10 *July* 1906; and had issue (with a son d. young) 1*d* to 4*d*.
 1*d*. Dulcibella M. Wood.
 2*d*. Ethel Wood.
 3*d*. Jeannette Wood.
 4*d*. Muriel Wood.

 7*c*. *Emma Bassett Barrett*, b. 20 Oct. 1848; d. 4 *May* 1891; m. 25 *Sept.* 1873, *Sir Lindsay Wood*, 1st *Bt*. [U.K. 27 Sept. 1897] (*The Hermitage, Chester-le-Street; Carlton*); and had issue 1*d* to 6*d*.
 1*d*. Arthur Nicholas Lindsay Wood, *b*. 29 Mar. 1875.
 2*d*. Henry Lindsay Wood, *b*. 28 Oct. 1878.
 3*d*. Collingwood Lindsay Wood, *b*. 19 Nov. 1881; *m*. 30 Ap. 1907, Lilian, da. of William Sopper of 3 Upper Belgrave Street, S.W., and Drummaglass, co. Inverness; and has issue 1*e* to 2*e*.
  1*e*. Ian Lindsay Wood, *b*. Mar. 1909.
  2*e*. Heather Wood.
 4*d*. Robert Lindsay Wood, *b*. 28 Feb. 1884.
 5*d*. Maria Lindsay Wood, *m*. 11 Ap. 1899, the Hon. Claud Eustace Hamilton-Russell, D.L. [son of Gustavus, 8th Viscount Boyne] (*Cleobury Court, Bridgnorth*) and has issue 1*e* to 3*e*.
  1*e*. Arthur Gustavus Lindsay Hamilton-Russell, *b*. 30 Ap. 1900.
  2*e*. Edric Claude Hamilton-Russell, *b*. 24 Nov. 1904.
  3*e*. Jean Katherine Hamilton-Russell.
 6*d*. Elsie Emma Lindsay Wood, *unm*.

 4*b*. Janette Charlotte Bell, *b*. 14 Nov. 1818; *m*. 22 Sept. 1841, Robert M'Alpine, *d*. 25 Dec. 1866; and has issue 1*c* to 5*c*.
 1*c*. Cunyngham Martyn M'Alpine, *b*. 24 Dec. 1842; *s.p.*
 2*c*. Henry Charles M'Alpine, *b*. 6 May 1849; *d. unm.* 18 Oct. 1894.
 3*c*. Robert Kyle M'Alpine, Adm. R.N. (*Brighton*), *b*. 20 Jan. 1851; *m*. 5 Jan. 1899, Louisa Jane, da. of James Leith-Hay, Younger of Rannes and Leith Hall, co. Aberdeen.; *s.p.s.*
 4*c*. Kenneth M'Alpine (*Loose, near Maidstone*), *b*. 11 Ap. 1858; *unm*.
 5*c*. Maria Louisa M'Alpine, *unm*.

 5*a*. *Jane Bell*, d. 14 *Ap*. 1793; m. as 1st *wife*, 7 *Jan*. 1792, *William* (Hay), 17*th Earl of Erroll* [S.], *&c*. [*descended from the Lady Anne, sister of King Edward IV., &c.*], d. 26 *Jan*. 1819; *and had issue*.
 See the Exeter Volume, p. 682, Nos. 57387–57391.

 6*a*. *Dulcibella Bell*, d. *c*. 1857; m. *the Rev. Robert Moore, Preb. and Canon of Canterbury* (see *p*. 291), d. *Sept*. 1865; *and had issue* (with 3 sons and 2 other das. who d.s.p.) 1*b*.
 1*b*. *Catherine Moore*, b. *c*. 1813; d. 14 *July* 1888; m. *the Rev. John Duncombe Shafto* [*descended from the Lady Anne, sister of King Edward IV*. (see Exeter Volume, p. 308)], d. 6 *Aug*. 1863; *and had issue* 1*c* to 2*c*.
 1*c*. Catherine Mary Fitzwilliam Duncombe Shafto, *unm*.
 2*c*. Dulcibella Maria Duncombe Shafto (*St. Martin's, Sevenoaks*), *m*. 11 Sept. 1866, the Rev. Arthur Majendie, Rector of Bladon, *d*. 15 Jan. 1895; and has issue.
 See the Exeter Volume, p. 309, Nos. 19440–19444.

 7*a*. *Maria Bell*, d. (? *unm*.).   [Nos. 39062 to 39096.

# of The Blood Royal

146. Descendants of CATHERINE EDEN (Table XVI.), *d.* (-) ; *m.* as 2nd wife, 23 Jan. 1770, the Most Rev. JOHN MOORE, Lord Archbishop of Canterbury, *bapt.* 13 Jan. 1730 ; *d.* 18 Jan. 1805 ; and had issue 1*a* to 4*a*.

 1*a*. *Rev. George Moore, M.A., Preb. of Canterbury and Rector of Wrotham*, d. (-) ; m. 1*st*, 19 *June* 1795, *Lady Maria Elizabeth* [*descended from the Lady Anne, sister to Kings Edward IV. and Richard III.* (see the Exeter Volume, p. 687)], *da. of James* (*Hay, previously Boyd*), 15*th Earl of Erroll* [*S.*], *&c.*, d. 3 *June* 1804 ; 2*ndly*, 1806, *Harriet Mary, da. of Sir Brook Bridges*, 3*rd Bt.* [*G.B.*], *M.P.* [*by his wife Fanny*, née *Fowler, a co-h. of the Barons FitzWalter* [*E.* 1295]]; *and had* (*with possibly other issue by 2nd wife*) 1*b to 2b*.

 1*b*. *Rev. Edward Moore of Frittenden House, co. Kent, M.A., Hon. Canon of Canterbury and Rural Dean*, b. 1814 ; d. 1889 ; m. 29 *Mar.* 1842, *Lady Harriet Janet Sarah Montagu* [*descended from Kings Henry VII. and Edward IV., &c.*], *da. of Charles William Henry* (*Douglas-Scott*), 4*th Duke of Buccleuch and 6th Duke of Queensberry* [*S.*], *K.T.*, d. 16 *Feb.* 1870 ; *and had issue.*

See the Tudor Roll, pp. 161–162, Nos. 19862–19899.

 2*b*. Caroline Mary Moore.

 2*a*. *Charles Moore, M.P. for Woodstock.*

 3*a*. *Robert Moore, M.A., Preb. of Canterbury*, b. c. 1778 ; d. *Sept.* 1865; m. *Dulcibella, da. of Matthew Bell of Woolsington*, d. c. 1857; *and had issue.*

See p. 290, Nos. 39090–39096.

 4*a*. John Moore.   [Nos. 39097 to 39142.

147. Descendants, if any, of ELIZABETH EDEN (Table XVI.), *d.* (-) ; *m.* MATTHEW WHITFIELD of Whitfield, co. Northumberland.

148. Descendants, if any, of HANNAH EDEN (Table XVI.), *d.* (-) ; *m.* JAMES MICKLETON of Durham.

149. Descendants of JOHN EDEN of Newcastle, Merchant (Table XVI.), *d.* (-) ; *m.* ELIZABETH, da. of (—) HENDMARSH of Little Bentley, *d.* (-) ; and had issue (a son and 2 das.).[1]

150. Descendants of the Rev. LATON EDEN, Rector of Hartborne, co. Northumberland (Table XVI.), *d.* (-) ; *m.* (—), da. of the Rev. (—) JOHNSON ; and had issue (several sons and das.).[1]

151. Descendants, if any surviving, of MARGARET LATON (Table XV.), *d.* after 1664 ; *m.* WILLIAM LATON or LAYTON of Dalemayne, co. Cumberland, *b.* c. 1624 ; living and aged 40 in 1664 ; and had issue 1*a* to 8*a*.[2]

 1*a*. *Thomas Laton*, b. c. 1656 ; *aged* 8 *in* 1664.
 2*a*. *William Laton*, b. 1663.

---

[1] Brydges' "Collins," viii. 288.
[2] Foster's "Visitations of Cumberland and Westmorland."

The Plantagenet Roll

3a. Mary Laton.
5a. Ann Laton.
7a. Katharine Laton.
4a. Isabel Laton.
6a. Margaret Laton.
8a. Elizabeth Laton.

152. Descendants of the Hon. CATHERINE FAIRFAX (Table XIV.), d. 23 Feb. 1666; m. 1st, ROBERT STAPYLTON of Wighill, M.P., d. 12 Mar. 1634; 2ndly, as 2nd wife, Sir MATTHEW BOYNTON, 1st Bt. [E.], d. (s.p. by her) Mar. 1647; 3rdly, as 2nd wife, Sir ARTHUR INGRAM of Temple Newsham, d. 4 July 1655; 4thly, 1657, WILLIAM WICKHAM of Roxby [grandson of William, Bishop of Winchester, by his wife Antonia, one of the five das. of John Barlow, Bishop of Chichester, who all married Bishops]; and had issue (with others whose lines all failed, two das. by 1st husband).

See Exeter Volume, Table XLIX., pp. 535-536, Nos. 48976-49015.

[Nos. 39143-39182.

153. Descendants, if any, of the Hon. JANE FAIRFAX (Table XIV.), m. CUTHBERT MORLEY.

154. Descendants of Sir THOMAS NORCLIFFE of Langton (Table XVII.), bapt. 24 Feb. 1641; d. in France after 16 Sept. 1684; m. (settl. dated 1/2 Jan.) 1670, FRANCES (Table VII.), da. and h. of Sir WILLIAM VAVASOUR of Copmanthorpe, 1st Bt. [E.], b. in Drury Lane 26 Oct. 1654; d. at Chelsea 12 Dec. 1731; and had issue.

See p. 119, Nos. 10775-10977.

[Nos. 39183-39385.

155. Descendants of JOHN GRIMSTON of Grimston Garth, co. York (Table XVII.), b. 17 Feb. 1725; d. 21 June 1780; m. 12 Mar. 1753, JANE, da. of Sir Thomas LEGARD, 4th Bt. [E.], d. 11 Nov. 1758; and had issue.

See p. 196, Nos. 29062-29142.

[Nos. 39386 to 39466.

156. Descendants, if any, of DOROTHY GRIMSTON (Table XVII.), b. 9 July 1663; bur. 24 July 1700; m. 4 Nov. 1684, NATHANIEL GOOCH of Hull, bur. 17 June 1705; and of ANNE GRIMSTON, b. 18 Ap. 1669; m. THOMAS RYDER.

of The Blood Royal

157. Descendants, if any surviving, of JOHN HATFEILD of Laughton, co. York (Table XVI.), *bapt.* 24 Sept. 1676 ; *d.* Nov. 1751 ; *m.* 17 Mar. 1698, MARY, da. and event. h. of Elkana RICHE of Bullhouse, near Penistone, *bur.* 30 July 1742 ; and had issue 1*a* to 2*a*.

> 1*a*. *Aurengzebe Hatfeild of Laughton*, bapt. 4 *June* 1710; d. *Aug*. 1752; m. Dec. 1746, *Susanna, da. of John Hatfeild of Hatfeild (who* m. 2*ndly*, 24 *June* 1760, *Capt. William Marshall of Newton Kyme* (see below) *and*), d. 18 *Nov*. 1793 ; *and had issue which became extinct* 11 *Jan.* 1791.
>
> 2*a*. *Rosamond Hatfeild, da. and in her issue* (1791) *h.*, d. (-) ; m. (—) *Barker of Mansfield ; and had issue* (2 *das.*).¹

158. Descendants, if any, of ANTONIA HATFEILD (Table XVII.), *d.* (-) ; *m.* E. WILMOT of Duffield ; or of DOROTHY HATFEILD, wife of WILLIAM WOODHOUSE of Reresby, co. Leic.

159. Descendants of WILLIAM MARSHALL of Newton Kyme, co. York, Capt. Heavy Dragoons (Table XVIII.), *b.* 1718 ; *d.* 12 June 1775 ; *m.* 24 June 1760, SUSANNA, widow of Aurengzebe HATFEILD of Laughton (see above), da. of John HATFEILD of Hatfeild, *d.* 18 Nov. 1793 ; and had issue 1*a*.

> 1*a*. *William Marshall of Newton Kyme and Laughton, Lieut.-Col. West Yorkshire Militia*, b. 17 *July* 1764 ; d. 17 *Jan.* 1815 ; m. 1793, *Christiana, da. and event. h. of Godfrey Higgins of Skellow Grange and Wadworth, near Doncaster*, d. 2 Oct. 1832 ; *and had issue* 1*b to* 2*b*.
>
> 1*b*. *William Marshall, afterwards* (R.L. 26 Dec. 1833) *Hatfeild of Newton Kyme and Laughton*, b. 17 *June* 1799 ; d. *unm*. 7 *Sept*. 1844.
>
> 2*b*. *Christiana Marshall of Laughton, Skellow Grange and Wadworth*, d. (-) ; m. 9 *Sept.* 1825, *Randall Gossip, afterwards* (R.L. 16 Oct. 1844) *Hatfeild of Thorp Arch, co. Yorks*, b. 28 *May* 1800 ; d. 1853 ; *and had issue* (*with* 3 *sons and* 4 *das. who d.s.p. or whose issue is extinct*) 1*c to* 2*c*.
>
> 1*c*. *John Hatfeild of Thorp Arch and Laughton, J.P.*, b. 15 *June* 1846 ; d. 5 *July* 1889 ; m. 10 *June* 1869, *Mariana Frances, da. of Adolphe Davide*, d. 14 Oct. 1894 ; *and had issue* 1*d*.
>
> 1*d*. John Randall Hatfeild of Thorp Arch and Laughton (*Edlington Hall, Horncastle, co. Lincoln ; Thorp Arch Hall, Tadcaster ; Skellow Grange, Doncaster*), b. 21 Sept. 1873 ; *m.* 23 Oct. 1901, Nest, da. of W. Hyde of Market Stainton Grange, co. Linc. ; and has issue 1*e*.
>
> 1*e*. Christine Joyce Hatfeild.
>
> 2*c*. Lucy Hatfeild, *unm.* [Nos. 39467 to 39469.

160. Descendants of FRANCES NORCLIFFE (Table XVII.), Executor to her mother in 1686, *m.* after that year NICHOLAS RICHARDS of Westminster.

---

¹ Foster's "Yorkshire Pedigrees."

The Plantagenet Roll

161. Descendants of Sir JOHN SWINBURNE, 3rd Bt. [E. 1660] (Table XVIII.), b. 8 July 1698; d. Jan. 1745; m. 1721, MARY, da. of Edward BEDINGFELD of Gray's Inn, Counsellor-at-Law [son of Sir Henry Bedingfeld, 1st Bt. [E.]], d. 7 Feb. 1761; and had issue 1a to 6a.

1a. Sir John Swinburne, 4th Bt. [E.], b. 2 July 1724; d. unm. 1 Feb. 1763.

2a. Sir Edward Swinburne, 5th Bt. [E.], b. 24 Jan. 1733; d. 2 Nov. 1786; m. 1761, Christiana, da. and h. of Robert Dillon, d. 13 Aug. 1768; and had issue 1b to 2b.

1b. Sir John Edward Swinburne, 6th Bt. [E.], M.P., F.R.S., b. 6 Mar. 1762; d. 26 Sept. 1860; m. 8/13 July 1787, Emilia Elizabeth. da. of Richard Henry Alexander Bennet of Beckenham, d. 28 Mar. 1839; and had issue 1c to 4c.

1c. Edward Swinburne of Calgarth Park, Windermere, b. 24 June 1788; d.v.p. 14 Nov. 1850; m. 1st, 13 Dec. 1819, Anna Antonia, da. of Capt. Robert Nassau Sutton, 58th Regt., d. 1844; and had issue 1d to 5d.

1d. Sir John Swinburne, 7th Bt. [E.], Capt. R.N. (ret.), J.P., High Sheriff co. Northbd. 1866, M.P. for Lichfield 1885–92 (Capheaton, Newcastle-on-Tyne), b. 1831; m. 1st, 1 Jan. 1863, Emily Elisabeth, da. of Rear-Adm. Henry Broadhead, R.N., d. 23 July 1881; 2ndly, 10 Sept. 1895, Mary Eleanor, da. and h. of John Corbett, d.s.p. 16 May 1900; 3rdly, 7 June 1905, Florence Caroline, da. of James Moffat of Windsor, D.L.; and has issue 1e to 5e.

1e. Hubert Swinburne, LL.B. (Camb.), Capt. Northumberland Imp. Yeo. (Wellington; Brooks'), b. 23 Jan. 1867; m. 20 Sept. 1905, Alice Pauline (see p. 43), da. of Nathaniel George Clayton of Chesters, co. Northbd.; and has issue 1f.

1f. Joan Swinburne, b. 7 Aug. 1906.

2e. Umfreville Percy Swinburne (Arthurs'; Bachelors'), b. 24 Nov. 1868; m. 31 July 1905, Arnoldine Georgiana, widow of (—) Peacocke, da. of Thomas Arnold Marten of Oystermouth, co. Glam.

3e. Robert Swinburne, b. 10 Feb. 1871.

4e. Marguerite Swinburne, unm.

5e. Rameh Theodora Swinburne (24 Wilton Street, S.W.; Lacie, Abingdon, Berks), m. 19 July 1887, Richard Chamberlain of Oak Mount, Birmingham, d. 2 Ap. 1899; and has issue 1f.

1f. Richard Chamberlain, b. 28 May 1888; drowned 26 May 1906.

2d. Mary Swinburne, m. 11 Nov. 1862, Capt. William Ross, Gentleman Usher to Queen Victoria, d. 1874.

3d. Ruth Swinburne, m. 27 Oct. 1858, William Edward Maude of Blawith, co. Lancaster, d. 1904.

4d. Jane Swinburne, m. 1860, Professor Paul Thumann, d. 1908; and had issue.

5d. Katherine Swinburne, d. 16 July 1896; m. 1863, Ferdinand Breymann; and had issue.

2c. Charles Henry Swinburne, Adm. R.N., b. 2 Ap. 1797; d. 4 Mar. 1877; m. 19 May 1836, Lady Jane Henrietta [descended from King Henry VII. (see the Tudor Roll, p. 193)], da. of George (Ashburnham), 3rd Earl of Ashburnham [G.B.], d. 26 Nov. 1896; and had issue (with others who d.s.p.) 1d to 2d.

1d. Algernon Charles Swinburne, the Poet, b. 5 Ap. 1837; d. unm. 10 Ap. 1909.

2d. Isabel Swinburne (61 Onslow Square, S.W.).

3c. Emily Elizabeth Swinburne, d. 19 Dec. 1882; m. 8 Ap. 1824, Sir Henry George Ward, G.C.M.G., Governor of Madras, d. there 2 Aug. 1860.

4c. Elizabeth Swinburne, d. 1896; m. 7 June 1828, John William Bowden, d. 15 Sept. 1844.

[Nos. 39470 to 39480.

of The Blood Royal

2b. *Robert (Swinburne)*, 1st Baron Swinburne (*Freiherr von Swinburne*) [*Austria*], so cr. 12/28 May 1863, a Gen. in the Imperial Service and Gov. of Milan, b. 12 July 1763; d. (-); m. (—); and had issue which became extinct 25 June 1907.

3a. *Henry Swinburne of Hamsterley*, co. Durham, Vendre Master at Trinidad, Author of "Travels through Spain," "Travels in the Two Sicilies," &c., b. 19 July 1743; d. at Trinidad Ap. 1803; m. 24 Mar. 1767, Martha, da. of John Baker of Chichester, Solicitor-Gen. of the Leeward Islands; and had issue (*with 4 sons and 2 other das. who all d. unm.*) 1b to 4b.

1b. *Mary Frances Swinburne*, d. 1828; m. 1793, Paul Benfield of Woodhall Park, co. Herts, and of Grosvenor Square, London, M.P.

2b. *Carolina Mariana Swinburne*, d. 1856; m. Richard Walker of Michel Grove, co. Sussex.

3b. *Harriet Swinburne*, d. 1861; m. 1814, John Walker of Purbrook Park, co. Hants.

4b. *Maria Antonia Swinburne*, d. 3 Sept. 1869; m. as 2nd wife, 20 Feb. 1811, Major-Gen. Oliver Robert Jones, 18th Hussars, 2nd son of Robert Jones of Fonman Castle, b. 8 Sept. 1776; and had issue 1c to 3c.

1c. *Robert Oliver Jones of Fonman Castle*, J.P., D.L., High Sheriff co. Glamorgan 1838, and Chairman of the Quarter Sessions for that co., b. 16 Dec. 1811; d. 13 Nov. 1886; m. 1st, 13 Sept. 1843, Alicia, 2nd da. of Evan Thomas of Llwynmadoc, co. Brecon, &c., d. 1 Ap. 1851; and had issue 1d to 2d.

1d. Oliver Henry Jones of Fonmon Castle, Bar.-at-Law, I.T., B.A. (Oxon.), J.P., D.L., and Vice-Chairman Glamorgan Quarter Sessions (*Fonman Castle, Cardiff; 39 Ashley Gardens, S.W.*), b. 7 Jan. 1846; m. 1900, Frances Beatrice, da. of George Lyall of Hedley, co. Surrey, J.P., M.P., Governor of the Bank of England.

2d. Edith Alicia Jones, m. 14 Jan. 1874, Robert Arthur Valpy of the Inner Temple, Bar.-at-Law [eldest son of Robert Harris Valpy of Enborne Lodge, Newbury, J.P., D.L.]; and has issue.

2c. *Oliver John Jones*, Rear-Adm. R.N., b. 15 Mar. 1813; d. 11 Jan. 1878; m. 23 July 1872, Annie Maria Louisa, widow of N. E. Vaughan, da. of Edward Warnster Strangeways of Alne, co. York.

3c. *Rosa Antonia Jones*, d. (-); m. 9 Aug. 1838, the Rev. John Montague Cholmeley, M.A. (Oxon.), Vicar of Standen, co. Herts, b. 2 Dec. 1812; d. 31 Jan. 1860; and had issue 1d to 3d.

1d. Henry John Cholmeley, Capt. 16th Regt., b. 10 May 1842.

2d. Antonia Cholmeley, m. 4 Ap. 1872, the Ven. William Conybeare Bruce, M.A. (Oxon.), Canon of Llandaff and Vicar of St. Woolas [nephew of the 1st Lord Aberdare] (*St. Woolas' Vicarage, Newport, Monmouth*); and has issue 1e to 2e.

1e. Montague William John Bruce, b. 19 Jan. 1873.

2e. Mary Rosa Bruce.

3d. Laura Selina Cholmeley.

4a. *Teresa Swinburne*, d. Oct. 1786; m. 1746, Edward Charlton of Hesleyside and East Appleton, co. Northbd., d. 1767; and had issue 1b.

1b. *William Charlton of Hesleyside*, d. 19 Feb. 1797; m. 1778, Margaret, da. of John Fenwick of Morpeth, M.D., d. 12 Mar. 1833; and had issue 1c.

1c. *William John Charlton of Hesleyside, &c.*, High Sheriff co. Northbd. 1837, b. 6 May 1784; d. 25 Sept. 1846; m. 21 Oct. 1809, Katherine Henrietta, da. of Francis Cholmeley of Brandsby, co. York, d. 31 July 1849; and had issue 1d to 3d.

1d. *William Henry Charlton of Hesleyside*, J.P., D.L., High Sheriff co. Northbd. 1857, b. 22 Oct. 1810; d. 15 June 1880; m. 20 June 1839, Barbara Anne [descended from George, Duke of Clarence, K.G.], da. of Michael Tasburgh (R.L. 20 June 1810), previously Anne, of Burghwallis, d. 30 Jan. 1898; and had issue.

See the Clarence Volume, p. 385, Nos. 14629–14643.

2d. Edward Charlton, D.C.L., M.D., b. 23 July 1814; d. 14 May 1874; m. [Nos. 39481 to 39502.

295

The Plantagenet Roll

2*ndly*, 5 *Ap.* 1864, *Margaret, da. of Mr. Serjeant Bellasis; and had issue* 1*e to* 6*e.*

1*e.* Edward Francis Benedict Charlton, R.N., *b.* 21 Mar. 1865.
2*e.* William Lancelot Stanislaus Charlton, *b.* 7 May 1867 ; *m.* Theresa Mary, da. of Thomas Walmesley of Lilystone, co. Essex ; and has issue.
3*e.* Oswin John Charlton, *b.* 15 Aug. 1871.
4*e.* George Victor Bellasis Charlton, *b.* 16 Ap. 1873.
5*e.* Francis James Louis Charlton, *b.* 1 Aug. 1874.
6*e.* Elsie Janet Charlton, *m.* 30 Jan. 1899, Edward Doran Webb (*Gaston House, Wardour, Tisbury, S.O.*).

3*d. Mary Charlton, d.* 2 *Aug.* 1854 ; m. 12 *June* 1850, *the Marquis Giuseppe Pasqualino of Palermo ; and had issue.*

5*a. Mary Swinburne, d.* (-) ; m. 1754, *Edward Bedingfeld* [2*nd son of Sir Henry Arundell Bedingfeld*, 3*rd Bt.* [E.], *descended from King Henry VII., &c.*] ; *and had issue.*
See the Tudor Roll, Table XLIV.

6*a. Isabel Swinburne, d.* (-) ; m. *at Hovingham* 1755, *Thomas Crathorne of Ness, co. York ; bur.* 2 *Feb.* 1764 ; *and had issue* (*with* 3 *elder sons and* 1 *da. who all apparently* d.s.p.) 1*b.*
1*b. George Crathorne, afterwards Tasburgh of Crathorne, b.* 23 *Ap.* 1761 ; *bur.* 9 *Sept.* 1825 ; m. *Barbara, widow of George Tasburgh of Bodney, da. of Thomas Fitzherbert of Swinnerton, co. Staff., d. July* 1808 ; *and had issue.*
See the Clarence Volume, pp. 384–385, Nos. 14618–14643.

[Nos. 39503 to 39534.

162. Descendants of THOMAS SWINBURNE (Table XVIII.), *b.* 2 May 1705 ; *d.* (-) ; *m.* MARY, widow of Thomas Thornton, da. and co-h. of Anthony MEABURNE of Pontop Hall, co. Durham, *d.* 1 Feb. 1772 ; and had issue 1*a.*

1*a. Thomas Swinburne of Pontop Hall, co. Durham, d. Oct.* 1825 ; m. 1781, *Charlotte, da. and co-h. of Robert Spearman ; and had* (*with possibly others*) *issue* 1*b.*
1*b. Thomas Robert Swinburne of Pontop Hall, J.P., D.L., Lieut.-Gen. in the Army, b. Mar.* 1794 ; *d.* 28 *Feb.* 1864 ; m. 1*st,* 8 *Dec.* 1818, *Maria, da. of the Rev. Anthony Coates, d.* 21 *July* 1820 ; 2*ndly, Oct.* 1826, *Helen, da. of James Aspinall, d.* 10 *Mar.* 1860 ; *and had issue* 1*c to* 2*c.*
1*c. Thomas Anthony Swinburne of Pontop Hall, and of Eilean Shona, co. Inverness, Capt. R.N., b.* 13 *July* 1820 ; *d.* 7 *Dec.* 1893 ; m. 21 *July* 1852, *Mary Anne, da. of Capt. Edward Fraser, d.* 21 *Mar.* 1894 ; *and had issue* 1*d to* 4*d.*
1*d.* Thomas Robert Swinburne, Major *late* R.M.A., Egyptian Medal and Bronze Star 1882 and Soudan Clasp 1884–1885 (*Reeds, Liss, Hants ; United Service*), *b.* 4 Oct. 1853 ; *m.* 9 Mar. 1886, Louisa Gertrude, da. of Robert Stewart of Kinlochmoidart ; and has issue 1*e* to 2*e.*
1*e.* Thomas Anthony Stewart Swinburne, Lieut. R.E., *b.* 6 Dec. 1886.
2*e.* Margaret Frances Troth Swinburne.

2*l.* James Swinburne, F.R.S., an Engineer (*Woodhurst, Oxted, Surrey ;* 82 *Victoria Street, S.W.*), *b.* 28 Feb. 1858 ; *m.* 1st, 28 Dec. 1886, Ellen, da. of R. H. Wilson of Gateshead-on-Tyne, M.D., *d.* 14 Jan. 1893 ; 2ndly, 25 May 1898, Lilian Gilchrist, da. of Sir (Thomas) Godfrey Carey, Bailiff of Guernsey ; and has issue 1*e* to 4*e.*
1*e.* Anthony Swinburne, *b.* 27 Dec. 1887.
2*e.* Spearman Charles Swinburne, *b.* 8 Jan. 1893.
3*e.* Ida Swinburne, *b.* 2 Dec. 1899.
4*e.* Marjorie Swinburne, *b.* 19 Ap. 1904.

3*d.* John Swinburne, *formerly* Lieut. 3rd Batt. Black Watch (*Hanaertsburg, Transvaal*), *b.* 18 Aug. 1861 [Nos. 39535 to 39543.

# of The Blood Royal

4d. *Henry Swinburne,* b. 9 *Oct.* 1866; d. 28 *Jan.* 1900; m. 21 *Aug.* 1895, *Annie, da. of Major Berkeley ; and had issue* 1e.

1e. Troath Swinburne.

2c. *James Swinburne of Marcus, co. Forfar, D.L., Lieut.-Col. late* 4th *Hussars,* b. 29 *July* 1830; d. 1881; m. 20 *Ap.* 1870, *Constance Mary [descended from the Lady Anne, sister of Kings Edward IV., &c.]; and had issue.*

See the Exeter Volume, p. 548, Nos. 49562–49564. [Nos. 39544 to 39547.

163. Descendants of ANNE SWINBURNE (Table XVIII.), living 1708; m. (Settlement dated 2 Sept.) 1687, NICHOLAS THORNTON of Netherwitton, co. Northbd., *bur.* 13 Mar. 1700; and had issue 1a to 8a.

1a. *John Thornton of Netherwitton, took part in the '15, for which he was convicted of high treason* 7 *July* 1716, *but reprieved* 12 *July following;* bur. 16 *Ap.* 1742; m. *(Settlement dated* 22 *May)* 1708, *Margaret, da. of Rowland Eyre ; and had issue* 1b *to* 7b.

1b. *Thomas Thornton of Netherwitton,* d. 26 *Oct.* 1740; m. *(Settlement dated* 20 *Ap.)* 1733, *Mary, da. and co-h. of Anthony Meaburn of Pontop, co. Durham (re-m.* 2ndly*, Thomas Swinburne,* 3rd *son of Sir William Swinburne,* 3rd *Bt.],* b. 4 *Feb,* 1713; bur. 28 *Ap.* 1786; *and had issue* 1c *to* 2c.

1c. *Anne Thornton of Netherwitton,* d. a. 1761.

2c. *Catharine Thornton of Netherwitton,* m. *as* 2nd *wife,* 1758, *William Salvin of Croxdale,* d. 21 *Jan.* 1800; *and had issue.*

See the Exeter Volume, p. 529, Nos. 48740–48777, and 48821–48835.

2b. *Nicholas Thornton,* 2nd *son, living* 20 *Ap.* 1733.

3b. *James Thornton, will dated* 27 *May* 1761; m. *Elizabeth, da. of Roger Meynell,* d. 17 *Sept.* 1762; *and had issue.*

See the Exeter Volume, pp. 337–338, Nos. 24570–24614.

4b. *Rowland Thornton, living (and mentioned in father's will)* 1 *Dec.* 1741.

5b. *Margaret Thornton,* d. *unm.* 179-.

6b. *Anne Thornton, living* 1740.

7b. *Mary Thornton,* d. *at Morpeth* 9 *Nov.* 1773; m. *John Fenwick of Morpeth, M.D.; and had issue* 1c *to* 2c.

1c. *James Fenwick of Netherwitton.*

2c. *(—) Fenwick of Durham, M.D.*

2a. Nicholas Thornton, \
3a. William Thornton, \
4a. Henry Thornton, } *living* 25 *Dec.* 1688. \
5a. Arthur Thornton, \
6a. Anne Thornton, \

7a. *Catharine Thornton,* bur. 3 *Oct.* 1695.

8a. *Isabella Thornton, will dated* 1711.[1] [Nos. 39548 to 39645.

164. Descendants of Sir HENRY LAWSON of Brough, 2nd Bt. [E.] (Table XVIII.), *b. c.* 1663; *d.* 9 May 1726; *m. c.* 1688, ELIZABETH, da. of Robert KNIGHTLEY of Offchurch, co. Warwick, *d.* 1735; and had issue 1a to 3a.

1a. *Sir John Lawson,* 3rd *Bt.* [E.], b. *c.* 1689; d. 19 *Oct.* 1739; m. *c.* 1712, *Mary, da. of Sir John Shelley of Michelgrove,* 3rd *Bt.* [E.], d. (-); *and had issue* 1b *to* 2b.

---

[1] Hodgson's "Northumberland," I. ii. 318–319.

The Plantagenet Roll

1b. *Sir Henry Lawson*, 4th Bt. [E.], b. c. 1712; d. Oct. 1781; m. *Anastasia, da. of Thomas Maire of Lartington Hall, co. York*, d. 5 Nov. 1764; *and had issue.*
See the Clarence Volume, Table XXXIV, and pp. 318–320, Nos. 9215–9266, and Essex Volume Supp., p. 540, Nos. 9240/1–5.

2b. *John Lawson of Bath*, d. 23 Jan. 1791; m. *Elizabeth, da. of Thomas William Selby of Biddleston, co. Northumberland*; *and had issue* 1c to 2c.

1c. *John Lawson of York, M.D.*, d. (–); m. *Clarina, widow of William Birmingham, da. of John Fallon of Cloona, co. Roscommon*; *and had issue* 1d.

1d. *Clarinda Lawson, da. and h.*, d. 10 Jan. 1861; m. 2 Oct. 1825, *Sir William Lawson (formerly Wright) of Brough, 1st Bt.* [U.K.], d. 22 June 1865; *and had issue.*
See above, Nos. 39657–39672; also Clarence Vol., pp. 318–319, Nos. 9225–9240.

2c. *Elizabeth Lawson*, d. 6 Aug. 1791; m. as 1st wife, *John Webbe, afterwards (1782) Webbe-Weston, of Sutton Place, co. Surrey*; *and apparently had issue.*
See the Exeter Volume, p. 704, Note 2, Nos. 58308–58327.

2a. *Anne Lawson*, d. (–); m. 20 Sept. 1707, *William Witham of Cliffe, co. York, will dated 8 July* 1723; *and had issue.*
See the Exeter Volume, pp. 558–560, Nos. 49748–49913.

3a. *Elizabeth Lawson*, bur. 21 Dec. 1732; m. 1714, *Stephen Tempest of Broughton*, d. 11 Ap. 1744; *and had issue.*
See the Clarence Volume, pp. 320–327, Nos. 9267–9505.

[Nos. 39646 to 40143.

165. Descendants of RALPH BLAKISTON of Chester-le-Street (Table XVIII.), d. (will dated 17 Mar. 1700, proved) 1704; m. MARY, da. of (—) SAMPSON of Chester-le-Street; and had issue 1a to 6a.[1]

1a. *William Blakiston, son and h.* 1700; bur. 19 Feb. 1710.

2a. *Ralph Blakiston, 2nd son*, 1700; bur. 6 Feb. 1718.

3a. *Michael Blakiston, 3rd son*, 1700; bur. at Chester-le-Street 6 June 1758; m. (–); *and had issue* 1b to 2b.

1b. *Anne Blakiston*, bapt. at Chester afsd. 28 Feb. 1739.

2b. *Mary Blakiston*, bapt. there 9 Feb. 1743.

4a. *Anthony Blakiston of Lowford, Bishop Wearmouth, 4th son* 1700; b. c. 1696; *living* 1732 aged 36.

5a. *Jane Blakiston*, bur. at Chester 23 Nov. 1774; m. c. 1726, *Sir Ralph Conyers of Horden, co. Durham, 5th Bt.* [E. 1628], *a Glazier in Chester-le-Street*, bapt. there 20 June 1697; d. 22 Nov. 1767; *and had issue* 1b to 4b.

1b. *Sir Blakiston Conyers, 6th Bt.* [E.], *Capt. R.M.*, bapt. at Chester 7 Dec. 1721; bur. there unm. 4 Nov. 1791.

2b. *Sir Nicholas Conyers, 7th Bt.* [E.], bapt. 27 July 1729; d. 1796; m. (—) [*said to have been a niece of Lord Cathcart*], d. at Greenock; *and had issue* 1c:

1c. *Sir George Conyers, 8th Bt.* [E.], d.s.p.

3b. *Sir Thomas Conyers, 9th Bt.* [E.], bapt. 12 Sept. 1731; d.s.p.m.s. *in the Workhouse at Chester-le-Street* 15 Ap. 1810; m. 24 Jan. 1754, *Isabel, da. of James Lambton of Whitehall, co. Durham*, bur. 10 Nov. 1779; *and had issue* 1c to 3c.

1c. *Jane Conyers*, b. 24 Jan. 1758; d. *in* 1813; m. at *St. Margaret's, Crossgate, Durham*, 19 Sept. 1778, *William Hardy of Chester-le-Street, a working man.*[2]

2c. *Elizabeth Conyers*, b. 21 Nov. 1758; *living* 1813; m. at Chester-le-Street 4 July 1785, *Joseph Hutchinson of Chester-le-Street, a working man.*[2]

---

[1] Surtees' "Durham," ii. 231.
[2] Burke's "Vicissitudes of Families," 2nd Series, p. 29.

# of The Blood Royal

    3c. *Dorothy Conyers,* b. 5 *Ap.* 1762; *living at Sedgefield, co. Durham,* 1813; m. *at Richmond* 30 *Nov.* 1795, *Joseph Barker, a working man.*[1]

    4b. *William Conyers, Major Chatham Div. R.M.,* bapt. *at Chester* 14 *July* 1735; d. *at Rochester c.* 1800; m. (—); *and had issue* 1c.

    1c. *Jane Conyers, living near London, and then aged about* 13, 1800.[2]

    6a. *Elizabeth Blakiston, living unm.* 1732; m. *John Dunn of Tudhow, co. Durham; and had issue* 1b *to* 2b.[3]

    1b. *John Dunn.*
    2b. *Margaret Dunn.*

166. Descendants, if any surviving, of JAMES LAWSON (Table XVIII.), d. (-); m. (—); and had issue 1a to 4a.

    1a. *Ralph Lawson.*
    2a. *Henry Lawson.*
    3a. *Mary Lawson,* m. (—) *Paston of co. Norfolk.*
    4a. *Elizabeth Lawson.*

167. Descendants, if any, of ANNE LAWSON (Table XVIII.), d. (-); m. HENRY WIDDRINGTON of Bentland, co. Northumberland.

168. Descendants, if any, of MARGARET CONSTABLE (Table XIII.), d. 1663; m. Sir EDWARD STANHOPE of Edlington and Grimston, co. York.

169. Descendants of MARY CONSTABLE (Table XIII.), will dated 17 Ap. 1669, proved at York; m. c. 1610, Sir THOMAS BLAKISTON of Blakiston, 1st Bt. [E.] (see footnote, p. 98), so cr. 27 May 1615; d. 1630; and had issue 1a to 2a.

    1a. *Margaret Blakiston,* b. 1614.
    2a. *Mary Blakiston,* m. *Sir Thomas Smith of Broxton, co. Notts; and had issue.*[4]

170. Descendants, if any surviving, of JOSEPH CONSTABLE of Upsall, co. York (Table XIII.), d. (-); m. MARY, da. of Thomas CRATHORNE of Crathorne, d. (-); and had issue.

See the Essex Volume, Exeter Supplement, p. 677.

171. Descendants of JANE PUDSEY (Table XIX.), bapt. 14 Nov. 1683; bur. 17 July 1708; m. as 1st wife, 7 Aug. 1705, WILLIAM DAWSON of Langcliffe, J.P., Major Yorks Militia, d. June 1762; and had issue 1a.

    1a. *Ambrose Dawson of Langcliffe Hall and Bolton,* F.R.C.P., b. Nov. 1707; d. 17 Dec. 1794; m. 1742, *Mary, sister of Sir Willoughby Aston,* 5th Bt. [E.], *da. of Richard Aston; and had issue* 1b *to* 5b.

---

    [1] Burke's "Vicissitudes of Families," 2nd Series, p. 29.
    [2] Surtees' "Durham," i. 29.   [3] *Ibid.* ii. 231.
    [4] Burke's "Extinct Baronetage," p. 65.

The Plantagenet Roll

1b. *Pudsey Dawson of Langcliffe Hall, Major of Liverpool and Col. Comdg. Royal Liverpool Vol.*, b. 16/27 *Feb.* 1752; d. 19 *Ap.* 1816; m. 1774, *Elizabeth Anne, da. of James Scott of Amsterdam*, d. 2 *Feb.* 1837; *and had issue (with 6 sons and 2 das. who d. unm.)* 1c *to* 4c.

1c. *Richard Dawson of Liverpool*, b. 14 *Oct.* 1783; d. 18 *Feb.* 1850; m. 2 *June* 1812, *Mary Anne, da. of William Perkin of Cartmell, co. Cumberland; and had issue* 1d *to* 2d.

1d. *Richard Pudsey Dawson of Delbury Hall, co. Salop, and Hornby Castle, co. York, &c., J.P., D.L.*, b. 10 *Jan.* 1821; d. (-); m *Louisa Elizabeth, da. of Thomas Starkie Shuttleworth of Preston; and had issue* 1e *to* 7e.

1e. Richard Pudsey Dawson, *b.* 30 Nov. 1859.
2e. Willoughby Pudsey Dawson, *b.* 30 Jan. 1862.
3e. Charles Pudsey Dawson, *b.* 14 Aug. 1863.
4e. Ambrose Pudsey Dawson, *b.* 4 July 1865.
5e. Thomas Starkie Pudsey Dawson, *b.* 13 May 1867.
6e. Mary Louisa Pudsey Dawson.
7e. Lucy Margaret Pudsey Dawson.

2d. *Mary Seamand Dawson*, b. 15 *May* 1814; d. (-); m. 7 *Feb.* 1843, *Henry Ribton Hoskins; and had issue* 1e.
1e. Alexander Hoskins.

2c. *Edward Dawson*, b. 1797; d. *in Bermuda Jan.* 1843; m. *Eliza, da. of* (—) *Liot*, d. (-); *and had issue* 1d.
1d. Elizabeth Anne Pudsey Dawson, m. *the Rev. R. Burrowes.*

3c. *Mary Dawson*, b. 16 *May* (? *Nov.*) 1779; d. (-); m. 1809, *Anthony Littledale of Liverpool*, b. 2 *Oct.* 1777; d. 20 *Jan.* 1820; *and had issue.*

4c. *Jane Dawson*, b. 1795; d. *in childbirth* 183-; m. 1832, *the Rev. John Jennings, Canon of Westminster; and had issue* 1d-.
1d. Ambrose Dawson Jennings, b. 183-.

2b. *William Dawson of Caius Coll., Camb.*, 1771, b. 5 *Sept.* 1753; d. (-); m. 1st, (—), *da. of* (—) *O'Kill;* 2ndly, *at New York, Eleanor, da. of* (—) *Lee; and had issue (with* 2 *other sons and* 2 *das. who all d. unm.)* 1c *to* 3c.

1c.¹ *Rev. Richard Dawson of Halton Gill, Rector of Bolton by Bolland*, d. (-); m. 11 *Aug.* 1774, (—), *da. of the Rev. William Hutton Long of Maids Moreton; and had issue* 2 *das. who both d.s.p.*

2c.² *William Dawson of New York*, d. (-); m. (—), *da. of* (—) *Jay; and had issue* 1d.

1d. Mary Jay Dawson, *m.* 22 Sept. 1870, Col. Colville Frankland, *late* 2nd Batt. Royal Dublin Fusiliers [5th son of Sir Frederick William Frankland, 8th Bt. [E.]] (67 *Brunswick Place, Hove; Junior United Service*); and has issue 1e to 6e.

1e. Robert Cecil Colville Frankland, Transvaal C.S., *formerly* Lieut. S. Staffs Regt., *b.* 7 July 1877.
2e. Thomas Hugh Colville Frankland, Lieut. 2nd Batt. Royal Dublin Fusiliers, *b.* 17 Oct. 1879.
3e. Katherine Marian Colville Frankland.
4e. Eleanor Colville Frankland, *m.* 6 Ap. 1905, Thomas Maberley Cobbe (*Newbridge House, Donabate, co. Dublin*).
5e. Beatrice Colville Frankland.
6e. Mary Olive Elsie Frankland.

3c.² *Frances Laura Dawson*, b. 4 *July* 1814; d. 25 *July* 1904; m. 20 *July* 1847, *the Ven. William Macdonald, M.A., Archdeacon of Wilts and Canon Residentiary of Salisbury, Vicar of Bishops Canning*, b. 10 *Aug.* 1783; d. 24 *June* 1862; *and had issue* 1d *to* 5d.   [Nos. 40144 to 40159.

of The Blood Royal,

1*d.* Rev. Frederick William Macdonald, Rector of Wishford and Rural Dean (*Wishford Rectory, Salisbury*), b. 3 Ap. 1848; *m.* 6 Jan. 1874, Frances Lucy, da. of John Matthews of Pimperne, Dorset; *s.p.*

2*d.* Robert Estcourt Macdonald, *b.* 15 Aug. 1854; *m.* 1st, 10 Aug. 1891, Agnes Gwyn, da. of G. Gwyn Elger, *d.* 23 Aug. 1895; 2ndly, 17 Ap. 1909, Dorothy Horatia, da. of Col. Edmund Bacon Hulton; *s.p.*

3*d.* Eleanor Frances Macdonald, *unm.*

4*d.* Flora Georgiana Macdonald, *m.* 10 Ap. 1879, the Rev. Herbert William Sneyd Kynnersley, *d.s.p.* 1 Nov. 1886.

5*d.* Marion Kinneir Macdonald, *unm.*

3*b.* Richard *Dawson*, b. 21 A*p.* 1755; d. (-); m. *Elizabeth*, da. of *William Crosbie*; and had issue 1*c* to 3*c*.

1*c.* Richard Crosbie *Dawson*, b. 7 *Jan.* 1799; d. 1 *June* 1880; m*:* 10 A*p.* 1828, *Annie*, da. of *George Ashby Pritt*, d. 7 Feb. 1858; *and had issue* 1*d* to 5*d.*

1*d.* Rev. *Richard Dawson*, *Vicar of Sutton Benger, co. Wilts*, b. 1 *July* 1829; d. 19 *July* 1903; m. 21 *July* 1863, *Alice*, da. of *John Simmons of Moseley Heath, near Birmingham*, d. 2 *July* 1879; *and had issue* (*with* 3 *das. who* d. *unm.*) 1*e* to 3*e.*

1*e.* Richard Crosbie Dawson (*Sutton Benger, Chippenham*), *b.* 21 May 1871; *m.* 27 July 1908, Frances Sarah, da. of John Coller of Draycott Cerne, co. Wilts; and has issue 1*f.*

1*f.* Richard Pudsey Dawson, *b.* 22 June 1909.

2*e.* Cyril John Dawson, *b.* 16 Ap. 1873; *m.* 26 Sept. 1904, Elizabeth, da. of Peter Pockett; and has issue 1*f.*

1*f.* Richard Cyril Dawson, *b.* 14 Aug. 1905.

3*e.* Willoughby Crosbie Dawson (*Meadow Leigh, Fitton Road, Bristol*), *b.* 25 Mar. 1875; *m.* 25 Ap. 1905, Alice Mary, da. of Sydney Herbert of Bristol; and has issue 1*f.*

1*f.* Alice Doreen Maud Dawson, *b.* 17 Nov. 1905.

2*d.* George James Crosbie Dawson of May Place (*May Place, Newcastle, Staffordshire*), *b.* 30 Ap. 1841; *m.* 7 Aug. 1872, Catherine Webber, da. of the Rev. George Mackie, D.D.; and has issue 1*e* to 2*e.*

1*e.* George Crosbie Dawson, *b.* 3 May 1873; *unm.*

2*e.* Constance Ethel Crosbie Dawson, *unm.*

3*d.* Rev. Ambrose Pudsey Dawson, Rector of Harston (*Harston Rectory, Grantham*), *b.* 30 Mar. 1843; *m.* Mary, da. of the Rev. J. P. Middleton; and has issue 1*e* to 7*c.*

1*e.* Ambrose Middleton Dawson.

2*e.* Hugh Pudsey Dawson.

3*e.* Helen Mary Dawson.

4*e.* Annie Ruth Dawson.

5*e.* Margaret Pudsey Dawson.

6*e.* Elizabeth Pudsey Dawson.

7*e.* Rachel Irene Dawson.

4*d.* Annie Mary Dawson (12 *Warwick Crescent, London*).

5*d.* Harriet Dawson, *m.* 14 Sept. 1873, Joseph Wagstaff Blundell; and has issue 1*e.*

1*e.* Benson Dawson Blundell, *b.* (—); *m.* and has issue.

2*c.* William *Ambrose Dawson*, b. 21 *Jan.* 1800; d. *Dec.* 1860, m. *June* 1830, *Charlotte Jemima*, da. of (—) *Clay*; *and had issue* (*with* 2 *sons who* d. *unm.*) 1*d.*

[Nos. 40160 to 40184.

The Plantagenet Roll

1*d*. Catherine Charlotte Dawson (18 *Pembroke Road, Kensington, W.*), *m*. as 2nd wife, Oct. 1870 or 1874, Sylvester Frank Richmond [descended from the Lady Isabel Plantagenet (see Essex Volume, p. 128)], *d.s.p.* 4 Sept. 1894.

3*c*. Elizabeth Dawson, b. 1794; d. 1867; m. 1823, *Castel William Clay of Liverpool*, b. 1795; d. 1845; *and had issue (with a youngest son, Benjamin Sherard, d. unm.)* 1*d* to 2*d*.

1*d*. Castel Pelham Clay, b. 1825; d. 1863; m. 1854, *Eva Emily, da. of Charles Paul Berkeley; and had issue (with a da. d. young)* 1*e* to 2*e*.

1*e*. Evelyn Emily Clay, *b*. Sept. 1855.

2*e*. Charlotte Elizabeth Clay, *b*. Oct. 1857; *m*. 1894, the Rev. William Erskine.

2*d*. Charlotte Elizabeth Clay, b. 12 *Aug*. 1828; d. 28 *May* 1904; m. 19 *Oct*. 1848, *the Rev. Arthur Rawson of Bromley* [3rd son of *William Henry Rawson of Haugh End, co. York*], b. 17 *Sept*. 1818; d. 18 *May* 1882; *and had issue (with a son d. unm.)* 1*e* to 9*e*.

1*e*. Herbert Evelyn Rawson (*Comyn Hill, Ilfracombe*), *b*. 12 June 1852; *unm*.

2*e*. Henry Ernest Rawson, *b*. 13 Ap. 1854; *m*. Ap. 1894, Minna Alice, da. of (—) Schwartz; and has issue 1*f* to 2*f*.

1*f*. Arthur Ernest George Rawson, *b*. 8 Oct. 1896.

2*f*. John Sherard Rawson, *b*. Jan. 1900.

3*e*. Charles Selwyn Rawson, *b*. 28 June 1855; *m*. 18 Ap. 1894, Alice Anne, da. of (—) Cruickshank; and has issue 1*f* to 3*f*.

1*f*. Arthur John Selwyn Rawson, *b*. 8 July 1896.

2*f*. Castel Duff Rawson, *b*. 30 Mar. 1906.

3*f*. Dorothea Alice Jennetta Rawson, *b*. 30 Oct. 1907.

4*e*. Sherard Rawson, *b*. 19 Nov. 1868; *m*. 1904, Althea, da. of (—) Turpie.

5*e*. Mary Sibella Rawson, *unm*.

6*e*. Emily Frances Rawson, *unm*.

7*e*. Charlotte Arabella Rawson, *m*. 7 Feb. 1905, Martin Chichester Harris [descended from the Lady Anne, sister of King Edward IV. (see Essex Volume Supplement, p. 630)] (43 *Cathcart Road, S.W.*).

8*e*. Ellen Beatrice Rawson, *unm*.

9*e*. Ethel Rawson, *m*. 24 Sept. 1896, Capt. Archibald Thomas Carter, R.N., *d*. 30 Nov. 1899; and has issue 1*f*.

1*f*. Sybil Carter, *b*. 17 June 1897.

4*b*. *Mary Dawson*, b. 29 *Ap*. 1747; d. (–); m. 15 *Dec*. 1778, *William Crosbie of Liverpool*.

5*b*. *Elizabeth Dawson*, b. 18 *Jan*. 1750; d. (–); m. 17 *Oct*. 1776, *Col. Charles Rooke; and had issue*. [Nos. 40185 to 40202.

172. Descendants, if any surviving, of ELIZABETH PUDSEY, wife of JOHN WEBB (? WELD); of her aunt, ELIZABETH PUDSEY, wife of ROGER [son and h. of John] TALBOT of Thornton; and of her great-uncles and aunts: STEPHEN, *bapt*. at Bolton 11 Nov. 1610; WILLIAM, *bapt*. 1 Oct. 1615; RALPH, *bapt*. 19 Jan. 1616; VALENTINE, *bapt*. 18 Feb. 1618; MARY, living 1620; ISABEL, *bapt*. 9 Nov. 1592, living 1620; TROTHE, *bapt*. 9 May 1594, living 1620; ELIZABETH, living 1620; ANNE, *bapt*. 11 Nov. 1610; and JANE, *bapt*. 25 Jan. 1612 (Table XIX.).

of The Blood Royal

173. Descendants, if any, of MARY PUDSEY (Table XIX.), b. 24 May 1690; d. (-); m. at Houghton-le-Skerne 24 May 1708. WILLIAM HULLOCK of Barnard Castle, Merchant, d. (-); and was father or grandfather of 1a.[1]

1a. *Timothy Hullock of Barnard Castle, a Master Weaver and proprietor of a timber yard there*, b. c. 1732; d. 1805, aged 73;[2] m. (—); *and had issue at least* 1b.

1b. *Sir John Hullock, Baron of the Exchequer*, 16 Ap. 1823; b. 3 Ap. 1767; d. (? s.p.) 31 *July* 1829; m. *Mary, da. of* (—), d. 18 *Nov.* 1852.[3]

174. Descendants, if any, of CATHERINE PUDSEY (Table XIX.), m. ROBERT PLACE of Picton, co. York [2nd son of Christopher Place of Dinsdale, co. Durham], living 20 May 1696.[4]

175. Descendants of THOMAS PUDSEY of Hackfort, co. York (Table XIX.), b. 17 Aug. 1567; d. between 20 Feb./31 May 1620; m. (—); and had issue (at least) 1a.

1a. *Philippa Pudsey, living* 1623, *and a legatee under the will of her uncle, Ambrose Pudsey.*

176. Descendants of CATHERINE TROTTER of Skelton Castle, co. York (Table XIX.), d. (-); m. JOSEPH HALL of Durham, d. 1733; and had issue 1a to 4a.

1a. *John Hall, afterwards Stevenson, of Skelton Castle, the " Eugenius " of Sterne*, b. c. 1718; d. 1785; m. *Anne, da. and h. of Ambrose Stevenson of Manor House, co. Durham* [*by his wife Anne, da. and event. h. of Anthony Wharton of Gilling Wood, co. York*], d. 1790; *and had issue* 1b.

1b. *Joseph William Hall Stevenson of Skelton Castle*, b. c. 1741; d. 1786; m. *Anne, da. and h. of James Foster of Drumgoon, co. Fermanagh ; and had issue* 1c to 5c.

1c. *John Hall, afterwards* (R.L. 20 Nov. 1807) *Wharton of Skelton Castle, M.P.*, b. c. 1766; d. 2 *June* 1843; m. *Susan Mary Anne, da. of Gen. John Lambton of Lambton*, d. 19 *Aug.* 1854; *and had issue* 1d to 2d.[5]

1d. *Susan Stevenson.*

2d. *Margaret Stevenson.*

2c. *James Hall, Major-Gen. 21st Light Dragoons,* d.s.p. 1841.

3c. *Rev. William Hall or Stevenson, afterwards Wharton, M.A., Vicar of Gilling*, b. c. 1768; d. 26 *May* 1842; m. 19 *Ap.* 1808, *the Hon. Charlotte* [*descended from the Lady Anne, sister of King Edward IV.*], *da. of Thomas* (*Dundas*), *1st Lord Dundas* [G.B.], d. 5 *Jan.* 1855; *and had issue.*

See the Exeter Volume, pp. 259-260, Nos. 9764-9778.

4c. *Margaret Hall.* [Nos. 40203 to 40217.

---

[1] Foster's " Yorkshire Families," Pudsey Pedigree.
[2] *Gentleman's Magazine*, 1829, ii. 275.
[3] D. N. B., *Notes and Queries*, 7th Series, viii. 48, 197.
[4] Surtees' " Durham," iii. 236; Hutchinson's " Durham," iii. 147.
[5] Graves' " Cleveland," p. 354.

The Plantagenet Roll

5c. *Francis Hall*, d. (? s.p.) ; m. 30 *Oct*. 1792, *the Hon. John Theophilus Rawdon* [2nd son of John, 1st Earl of Moira [I.]], b. 19 *Nov*. 1757 ; d. *May* 1808 ; *and, according to some accounts, had issue*.

2a. *George Hall, a Col. in the Army*, d. (-) ; m. (—), *natural da. of Lord William Manners, M.P.* [2nd son of John, 2nd Duke of Rutland [E.], K.G.]; *and had issue (a da.)*.[1]

3a. *Thomas Hall, a Gen. in the Army*, d. (-) ; m. (—), *da. of* (—) *Carter of co. Cambridge; and had issue* 1b *to* 2b.[1]

   1b. *John Hall*.
   2b. *Elizabeth Hall*.

4a. *Frances Elizabeth Hall*, d. (-) ; m. *Walter Ramsden, afterwards Hawksworth, of Hawksworth, co. York*, d. 12 *Oct*. 1760 ; *and had issue* 1b *to* 2b.

   1b. *Walter Ramsden Beaumont Hawksworth, afterwards* (R.L. 2 *Sept*. 1786, *Fawkes, of Hawksworth and Farnley, High Sheriff co.* York 1789, b. 11 *Aug*. 1746 ; d. 17 *Oct*. 1792 ; m. 28 *Dec*. 1768, *Amelia, da. of James Farrer; and had issue* 1c *to* 6c.

      1c. *Walter Ramsden Hawksworth, afterwards* (R.L. 1 *Dec*. 1792) *Fawkes, of Farnley, co. York, M.P., and High Sheriff* 1823, b. 2 *Mar*. 1769 ; d. 1825 ; m. 1st, 28 *Aug*. 1794, *Maria, descended from the Lady Anne, sister of King Edward IV., &c.*], *da. of Robert Grimston of Neswick*, d. 10 *Dec*. 1813 ; *and had issue*.

      See the Exeter Volume, pp. 676–678, Nos. 57242–57295.

      2c. *Francis Ramsden Hawksworth, otherwise Fawkes, of Brambro Grange, Doncaster*, b. 12 *Oct*. 1774 ; d. (-) ; m. *Eliza Ann Mary* [*descended from the Lady Anne, sister of King Edward IV., &c.*], *da. of Robert Grimston of Neswick*, d. (-) ; *and had issue*.

      See the Exeter Volume, pp. 678–679, Nos. 57296–57321.

      3c. *Rev. Ayscough Hawksworth, otherwise Fawkes, Rector of Leathley*.

      4c. *Rev. Richard Hawksworth, otherwise Fawkes*, b. 17 *Mar*. 1780 ; d. (-) ; m. *Isabella, da. of Sir Michael Pilkington, 6th Bt.* [E.]; *and had issue* 1d *to* 3d.

         1d. *Isabella Frances Hawksworth, da. and co-h.*, d. (-) ; m. *Mar*. 1824, *James Pickering Ord of Langton Hall, co. Leicester; and had issue* (*a da. who* d. ? *unm*.).

         2d. *Amelia Hawksworth, da. and co-h.*, b. 24 *Sept*. 1807 ; d. 17 *June* 1862 ; m. 13 *Sept*. 1827, *the Rev. Charles Vanden Bempde Johnstone, M.A., Canon of York, Vicar of Felixkirk* [2nd son of Sir Richard, 1st Bt. [G.B.]], b. 24 *Aug*. 1800 ; d. 15 *May* 1882 ; *and had issue* 1e *to* 4e.

            1e. *Rev. Charles Vanden Bempde Johnstone, M.A.* (Durham), *Vicar of Hackness* (*Hackness Vicarage, Scarborough*), b. 17 June 1828.

            2e. *Laura Georgiana Vanden Bempde Johnstone* (*Bayard's Lodge, Knaresborough*).

            3e. *Charlotte Frances Vanden Bempde Johnstone*, d. 14 *Mar*. 1888 ; m. 8 *Feb*. 1866, *Edmund Walker of Mount St. John, Thirsk*, d. 17 *May* 1873 ; *and had issue* 1f *to* 2f.

               1f. *Arthur John Walker* (*Mount St. John, Thirsk*), b. 23 *Dec*. 1869.
               2f. *Frederick Edmund Walker* (*Ravensthorpe Manor, Thirsk*), b. 29 *Mar*. 1871.

            4e. *Caroline Vanden Bempde Johnstone* (*Bayard's Lodge, Knaresborough*).

         3d. *Maria Hawksworth, da. and co-h.*, d. (-) ; m. 9 *June* 1828, *the Rev. Thomas Dayrell of Shudy Camps, co. Camb., M.A., J.P., D.L., Rector of Long Marston*, b. 28 *May* 1802 ; d. 18 *May* 1866 ; *and had issue* 1e *to* 7e.

            1e. *Marmaduke Frances Dayrell of Shudy Camp*, b. 4 *Jan*. 1834 ; d. *unm*. 1877.

            2e. *Thomas Dayrell of Shudy Camps, Lieut.-Col. Bengal S.C.*, b. 1 *May* 1838 ; d.s.p. 1890.

[Nos. 40218 to 40302.

---

[1] Graves' "Cleveland," p. 354.

# of The Blood Royal

3e. Rev. Richard Dayrell of Shudy Camps, Rector of Lillingstone Dayrell, b. 8 June 1841; d.s.p.; m. 27 July 1871, Evangeline Elizabeth Adelaide (Shudy Camps Park, Linton), da. of Samuel Orr of Innishannon, co. Cork, M.D.

4e. Isabel Jane Dayrell, m. 20 July 1869, Gerald Henry Baird Young, late 43rd Light Infantry (Fairlight House, Fawcett Street, S.W.); and has issue 1f to 5f.

1f. Isabel Mary Young, unm.
2f. Edith Gertrude Young, unm.
3f. Geraldine Frances Young, unm.
4f. Isie Margaret Young, m. 23 July 1902, Edward Henry Smith-Wright; and has issue 1g to 4g.

1g. Edward Gerald Smith-Wright.
2g. John Evelyn Smith-Wright.
3g. Henry Gordon Smith-Wright.
4g. Josephine Margaret Smith-Wright.

5f. Gwendolen Mary Young, m. 5 Nov. 1902, Capt. Julian Mayne Young, A.S.C.; and has issue 1g.

1g. Dayrell Francis Mayne Young.

5e. Mary Anne Dayrell (Leslie House, Spa Place, Cheltenham), unm.
6e. Caroline Charlotte Dayrell, m. 25 Ap. 1876, the Rev. Henry West (103 Cheriton Road, Folkestone).
7e. Emily Elizabeth Dayrell, m. 25 Ap. 1878, Richard Samuel Bagnell (Ryall Hill, Upton-on-Severn, Worcester); and has issue 1f to 2f.

1f. Richard Dayrell Bagnell, b. 23 Ap. 1879.
2f. Myrtle Dayrell Bagnell, b. 10 Aug. 1887.

5c. Amelia Hawksworth, d. 25 June 1834; m. 12 May 1794, Godfrey Wentworth Wentworth (R.L. 10 Mar. 1789), formerly Armytage, of Wooley, M.P., J.P., D.L., High Sheriff co. York 1796 [3rd son of Sir George Armytage, 3rd Bt. [S.], M.P.], b. 9 May 1773; d. 14 Sept. 1834; and had issue 1d to 3d.

1d. Godfrey Wentworth of Woolley Park, co. York, J.P., D.L., &c., b. 14 Sept. 1797; d. 22 Sept. 1865; m. 20 June 1822, Anne, da. of Walter Fawkes of Farnley Hall, co. York, d. 9 June 1842.

See p. 304, Nos. 40261–40268 (Exeter Volume, p. 677, Nos. 57285–57292).

2d. Catherine Frances Wentworth, d. 1838; m. 27 July 1822, John Marcus Clements of Glenboy, co. Leitrim, M.P., Lieut.-Col. 18th Hussars [descended from the Lady Isabel Plantagenet], d. 1833; and had issue.

See the Essex Volume, p. 295, Nos. 32334–32338.

3d. Dorothy Harriet Wentworth, d. (–); m. 2 July 1831, Sir Samuel Hancock, Senior Exon. of the Yeomen of the Guard.

6c. Frances Elizabeth Hawksworth, d. (–); m. Charles John Brandling of Gosforth.

2b. Frances Hawksworth, d. Dec. 1815; m. Le Gendre Starkie of Huntroyde, co. Lancaster, d. 20 Sept. 1791; and had (with possibly other) issue 1c.

1c. Le Gendre Pierce Starkie of Huntroyde, J.P., Vice-Lieut. co. Lancaster and High Sheriff 1806, b. 1770; d. 25 Oct. 1807; m. Charlotte, da. of the Rev. Benjamin Preedy, D.D., Rector of Brington, d. 30 Ap. 1801; and had issue (with 2 elder sons and a da. who d.s.p.) 1d to 2d.

1d. Le Gendre Nicholas Starkie of Huntroyde, J.P., D.L., M.P. for Pontefract 1826–1830, b. 1 Dec. 1799; d. 15 May 1865; m. Feb. 1827, Anne, da. of Ambrose Chamberlain of Rylston-in-Craven, co. York, d. 27 Dec. 1888; and had issue 1e to 4e.

1e. Le Gendre Nicholas Starkie of Huntroyde, J.P., D.L., and High Sheriff co. Lancaster 1868, M.P. for Clitheroe 1853–1856, Col. Comdg. 3rd Batt. E. Lancashire Regt., b. 10 Jan. 1828; d. 13 Ap. 1899; m. 15 Oct. 1867, Jemima Monica Mildred [descended from George, Duke of Clarence, K.G., brother of King Edward IV. (see Clarence Volume, p. 321)] (Ribbleton Hall, Preston), da. of Henry Tempest of Lostock Hall, co. Lanc.; and had issue 1f to 2f. [Nos. 40303 to 40330.

The Plantagenet Roll

1*f*. Edmund Arthur Le Gendre Starkie of Huntroyde, J.P., Capt. 4th Batt. E. Lancashire Regt. (*Huntroyde, Burnley; Lovely Hall, Blackburn*), b. 10 Feb. 1871; m. 19 July 1898, Maud Margaret Dolores Anne [descended from the Lady Anne, sister of King Edward IV. (see the Exeter Volume, p. 465)], da. of Major William Michael Ince Anderton of Euxton Hall, co. Lanc.; *s.p.s.*

2*f*. Pierce Cecil Le Gendre Starkie, Lieut. Lancashire Hussars, b. 14 Sept. 1882.

2*e*. *John Pierce Chamberlain Starkie of Ashton Hall, co. Lanc., LL.D., J.P., M.P. for N.E. Lancashire 1868-1880*, b. 28 *June* 1830; d. 12 *June* 1888; m. 27 *June* 1861, *Anne Charlotte Amelia* (*Scarthwaite, near Lancaster*), da. *of Harrington George Frederic Hudson of Bessingby, co. York; and had issue* 1*f to* 3*f*.

1*f*. Francis Chamberlain Le Gendre Starkie (*Ashton Hall, Lancaster*), b. 30 Mar. 1863; m. Ellen, da. of (—) Cooper.

2*f*. Charlotte Le Gendre Starkie, m. as 2nd wife, 28 July 1885, James Edward Platt, J.P. (*Bruntwood, Cheshire*).

3*f*. Susan Katherine Le Gendre Starkie, *unm.*

3*e*. Rev. Henry Arthur Starkie, M.A. (Camb.), *formerly* Rector of Radcliffe, Manchester, b. 1 Jan. 1838.

4*e*. *Anne Elizabeth Starkie*, d. 24 *Jan.* 1869; m. 19 Aug. 1858, *the Rev. George William Horton, M.A., Vicar of Wellow, cadet of Horton of Howroyde, co. York* [*and a descendant of King Henry VII.* (see the Tudor Roll, p. 465)], d. 6 *May* 1886; *and had issue* 1*f to* 2*f*.

1*f*. Rev. Le Gendre George Horton, M.A. (Camb.), Vicar of Wellow (*Wellow Vicarage, Bath*), b. 12 July 1859; m. 3 Sept. 1891, his cousin Mabel Augusta Hawksworth [descended from Edward III. both through Lady Anne, sister of King Edward IV., and through Mortimer-Percy], da. of the Rev. Frederick Fawkes; and has issue 1*g* to 3*g*.

1*g*. Le Gendre George William Horton, b. 14 June 1892.

2*g*. Frederick Henry Le Gendre Horton, b. 8 Aug. 1894.

3*g*. Dorothy Mary Horton.

2*f*. Anne Frances Horton, m. 16 Aug. 1888, the Rev. Atherton Gwillym Rawstorne, Suffragan Bishop of Whalley 1909 and Rector of Croston (*Croston Rectory, Preston*); and has issue 1*g* to 6*g*.

1*g*. Richard Atherton Rawstorne, b. 13 Mar. 1893.

2*g*. George Streynsham Rawstorne, b. 22 Jan. 1895.

3*g*. Robert Gwyllim Rawstorne, b. 16 Nov. 1907.

4*g*. Frances Marion Rawstorne.

5*g*. Jennett Rawstorne.

6*g*. Marjory Ella Rawstorne.

2*d*. *Charlotte Le Gendre Starkie*, d. 13 *Dec.* 1848; m. *as* 1*st wife,* 12 *June* 1819, *Col. Henry Armytage, Coldstream Guards* [3rd *son of Sir George Armytage,* 4*th Bt.* [E.]], b. 29 *Oct.* 1796; d. 30 *Oct.* 1861; *and had issue* 1*e* to 3*e*.

1*e*. Henry Armytage, Col. Coldstream Guards, b. 1 Feb. 1828; d. 18 *Ap.* 1901; m. 12 Feb. 1851, the Hon. Fenella [*descended from King Henry VII.*], da. *of Maurice Frederick (FitzHardinge Berkeley),* 1st *Baron FitzHardinge* [U.K.], *G.C.B.,* d. 20 *Nov.* 1903; *and had issue.*

See the Tudor Roll, p. 472, Nos. 33061–33065.

2*e*. *Harriette Elizabeth Armytage*, d. *Ap.* 1901; m. 15 *June* 1858, *Richard John Streatfeild* [4th *son of Henry Streatfeild of Chiddingstone, co. Kent, J.P., D.L.*], b. 7 *Nov.* 1833; d. 22 *Mar.* 1877; *and had issue* 1*f* to 2*f*.

1*f*. Mervyn Armytage Streatfeild.

2*f*. Roland Henry Armytage Streatfeild.

3*e*. *Emma Armytage*, d. 27 *Dec.* 1881; m. *as* 1*st wife,* 14 *Oct.* 1858, *Rev. the Hon. Henry Bligh* [3rd *son of Edward,* 5*th Earl of Darnley* [I.], *and a descendant of George, Duke of Clarence, K.G.*], d. 4 *Mar.* 1905; *and had issue.*

See the Clarence Volume, p. 288, Nos. 7788–7799.   [Nos. 40331 to 40366.

# of The Blood Royal

177. Descendants, if any surviving, of CATHERINE TROTTER (Table XIX.), d. (-); m. as 2nd wife, WILLIAM BOWER of Bridlington, co. York, b. 1654; d. (-); and had issue 1a to 4a.[1]

    1a. *Henry Bower of York, and afterwards of Killerby Hall, near Scarborough*, d. *unm*. 1770.

    2a. *George Bower of Bridlington*, d. (-); m.; *and had issue* 1b.

    1b. *Freeman Bower of Killerby Hall and Bawtry, co. York, J.P., D.L.*

    3a. *Robert Bower of Sleights, near Whitby and Welham*, d.s.p. 1777.

    4a. *Mary Bower*, d. (-); m. 1st, 1727, *Peter Whitton, Lord Mayor of York* 1728, d. (-); 2ndly, 1742, *George Perrott, Baron of the Exchequer*.

178. Descendants, if any, of MARGARET TROTTER, wife of GEORGE LAWSON; and of HANNAH TROTTER, wife of CHARLES PERROTT; of HUGH TROTTER, GEORGE TROTTER, and their sister MARY, wife of JOHN FULTHORPE of Tunstall, co. Durham; and of ELIZABETH TROTTER, wife of GEORGE NEVILL (Table XIX.).

179. Descendants of ANTHONY MEYNELL of Kilvington, co. York (Table XIX.), b. 1592; d. 1669; m. MARY, da. of James TWAITES of Long Marston, co. York, d. 1669; and had issue 1a to 6a.

    1a. *Thomas Meynell of Kilvington*, b. 1615; d. (-); m. 1637, *Gerard, da. of William Ireland of Nostel Abbey, co. York* [m. 2ndly, *Capt. Edward Saltmarshe*]; *and had issue* 1b *to* 5b.

    1b. *Roger Meynell of Kilvington*, b. 1639/40; bur. 9 Nov. 1683; m. *Mary* [descended from the Lady Anne, sister of King Edward IV.], *da. and h. of Sir John Middleton of Thurntofte*, bur. 30 Ap. 1685; *and had issue*.

    See the Exeter Volume, Table XXII., and pp. 336-338, Nos. 24536-24614.

    2b. *John Meynell*.

    3b. *William Meynell*.

    4b. *Mary Meynell*, bur. at Goodraingate, co. York, 9 Feb. 1686; m. *John Brigham of Wyton*.

    5b. *Elizabeth Meynell*.

    2a. *Winifred Meynell*, m. 1st, *Thomas Killingbeck of Allerton Grange, co. York;* 2ndly, *Thomas Barlow of Barlow, co. Lanc*.

    3a. *Clare Meynell*, d. (-); m. c. 1658, *Sir Richard Foster, 2nd Bt.* [E.], d. c. (?) 1680; *and had issue* 1b *to* 2b.

    1b. *Sir Richard Foster, 3rd Bt.* [E.], b. c. 1653; d.s.p. a. 1714.

    2b. *Mary Foster*, d. (-); m. (—) *Collingwood of Hetton in the Hole, co. Durham*.

    4a. *Collett Meynell*.

    5a. *Catharine Meynell*.

    6a. *Frances Meynell*.   [Nos. 40367 to 40445.

180. Descendants, if any, of MARY MEYNELL, wife of GEORGE POLE of Spinkhill; and of ANNE MEYNELL, wife of THOMAS GRANGE of Harlsey, co. York (Table XIX.).

---

[1] Burke's "Landed Gentry."

The Plantagenet Roll

181. Descendants, if any, of CATHERINE CHOLMLEY (Table XIII.), d. (-); m. RICHARD DUTTON of Whitby.

182. Descendants of CONYERS (DARCY), 1st EARL OF HOLDERNESS (1682), 5th Lord CONYERS (1509), and 2nd Lord DARCY and CONYERS (1641) [E.] (Table XX.), bapt. 24 Jan. 1599; d. 14 June 1689; m. a. June 1619, GRACE, da. and h. of Thomas ROKEBY of Skiers, co. York, bur. 4 Jan. 1658; and had issue 1a to 4a.

 1a. *Conyers (Darcy), 2nd Earl of Holderness, &c.* [E.], b. c. 1620; d. 13 Dec. 1692; m. 2ndly, 6 Feb. 1650, Lady Frances, da. of Thomas (Howard), 1st Earl of Berkshire [E.], bur. 10 Ap. 1670; and had issue.
 See the Clarence Volume, Table LXXVIII., and pp. 626-637, Nos. 28040-28849.

 2a. *Lady Ursula Darcy*, d. (-); m. *Sir Christopher Wyvill, 3rd Bt.* [E.], *M.P.*, bur. 8 Feb. 1681; and had issue.
 See the Exeter Volume, Table LII., and pp. 549-553, Nos. 49588-49656.

 3a. *Lady Elizabeth Darcy*, bapt. 8 Dec. 1624; d. (-); m. 18 Oct. 1650, Sir Henry Stapylton of Myton, 1st Bt. [E.], so cr. 22 June 1660, M.P., d. 1679; and had issue.
 See pp. 99-117, Nos. 10149-10723.

 4a. *Lady Grace Darcy*, d.s.p.m. a. 1658; m. as 1st wife, 18 Oct. 1655, Sir John Legard of Ganton, 1st Bart. [E.], so cr. 29 Dec. 1660; d. 1678; and had issue 1b.

  1b. *Grace Legard*, aged 18, 31 Aug. 1665; m. *John Hill of Thornton, co. York.*
                 [Nos. 40446 to 41899.

183. Descendants, if any surviving, of the Hon. Sir WILLIAM DARCY (Table XX.), d. (-); m. DOROTHY, da. of Sir George SELBY of Newcastle; and had issue.[1]

184. Descendants of MARIA CATHERINE DARCY (Table XX.), d. 21 Aug. 1747; m. May 1738, Sir ROBERT HILDYARD of Winestead, 3rd Bt. [E.], M.P., d. 1 Feb. 1781; and had issue 1a to 2a.

 1a. *Sir Robert Darcy Hildyard, 4th Bt.* [E.], b. 1743; d.s.p.s. 6 Nov. 1814.
 2a. *Catherine Hildyard*, d. (-); m. as 2nd wife, James Whyte of Denbies, co. Surrey, d. (-); and had issue 1b.
  1b. *Anne Catherine Whyte*, da. and event. sole h., d. (-); m. May 1815, Col. Thomas Blackborne Thoroton, afterwards (R.L. 23 May 1815) *Hildyard of Flintham*, co. Notts, d. July 1830; and had issue 1c to 8c.
   1c. *Thomas Blackborne Thoroton Hildyard of Flintham Hall, M.P., J.P., D.L., High Sheriff co. Notts* 1862, and *Chairman Quarter Sessions*, b. 8 Ap. 1821; d. 19 Mar. 1888; m. 3 May 1842, Anne Margaret, da. of Col. John Staunton Rochfort of Clogrenane, co. Carlow; and had issue 1d to 4d.
    1d. Thomas Blackborne Thoroton Hildyard of Flintham, J.P., late Lieut. Rifle Brigade (*Flintham Hall, near Newark*), b. 10 Mar. 1843; m. 18 July 1871, Eleanor, da. of the Right Hon. Henry Herbert of Muckross, co. Kerry, P.C.; s.p.
                    [No. 41900.

---

[1] Plantagenet Harrison's "History of Yorkshire," p. 119.

# of The Blood Royal

2d. Robert Charles Thoroton Hildyard, Capt. R.E., b. 3 Nov. 1844; d. (? s.p.) 25 Jan. 1885; m. 31 Aug. 1871, Anne Catharine (see below), da. of Robert D'Arcy Hildyard of Colburn, d. 1906; and had issue (with an elder son, Robert, who d. unm. 1908) 1e to 3e.

1e. Cecil Thoroton Hildyard (Canada).

2e. Dorothy Anne Florence Thoroton Hildyard, m. 8 Aug. 1895, the Rev. Lyonel D'Arcy Hildyard, Rector of Rowley [himself descended from King Edward III. through Mortimer-Percy (Rowley Rectory, Hull); and has issue.
See p. 155, Nos. 16776-16777.

3e. Kathleen Hildyard, unm.

3d. Sir Henry John Thoroton Hildyard, K.C.B., Col. H.L.I., formerly Gen. Comdg. Troops in South Africa 1904-1908, Director-Gen. of Mil. Education and Training at Headquarters 1903-1904, &c., served in S. Africa 1899-1902 in command of 2nd Brigade and subsequently of 2nd Division, Egypt (Medal with Clasp and Bronze Star) 1882, &c. (United Service), b. 5 July 1846; m. 20 May 1871, Annette, da. of Adm. James Prevost; and has issue 1e to 3e.

1e. Harold Charles Thoroton Hildyard, Major R.F.A., b. 16 July 1872; m. 18 Aug. 1909, Selina, da. of the Rev. Savile L'Estrange Malone.

2e. Gerard Moresby Thoroton Hildyard, Bar.-at-Law, b. 3 June 1874.

3e. Reginald John Thoroton Hildyard, Capt. Royal West Kent Regt., b. 11 Dec. 1876.

4d. Edith Mary Thoroton Hildyard, m. 28 Mar. 1895, Edward Bromley, Clerk of Assize (12 Eccleston Square).

2c. Robert D'Arcy Hildyard of Coburn Manor, co. York, b. Sept. 1823; d. 23 Oct. 1882; m. 21 Sept. 1842, Anna F. J., da. of Capt. Lauford Burne, 3rd Dragoon Guards, d. 4 Mar. 1896; and had issue 1d to 5d.

1d. Robert Maxwell Thoroton D'Arcy Hildyard of Coburn, Capt. 68th Durham L.I., b. 4 Oct. 1867; d. 11 Mar. 1907; m. Gertrude Mary (Coburn Manor, near Richmond, Yorks), da. of Edward Burdon; and had issue 1e to 2e.

1e. Robert Vernon Saville D'Arcy Hildyard of Coburn Manor, b. 2 Ap. 1904.

2e. Christopher John Ross Thoroton D'Arcy Hildyard, b. 27 Jan. 1907.

2d. Wilhelmina Catharine Hildyard, d. 1898; m. Charles Irwin, Royal Irish Fusiliers, d. (-); and has issue 1e to 4e.

1e. Charles Irwin.

2e. Frederick Irwin.

3e. Annie Irwin.

4e. Marie Elsie Irwin, m. 1 Oct. 1901, William Ashford, M.D. (Riversmeet, Topsham, R.S.O., Devon); and has issue 1f.

1f. Christopher Lee Ashford, b. 4 Aug. 1908.

3d. Anne Catharine Hildyard, d. 1906; m. 31 Aug. 1871, Robert Charles Thoroton Hildyard (see above), d. 25 Jan. 1885; and had issue.
See above, Nos. 41901-41905.

4d. Mary Hildyard, m. Major Charles Urquhart, late 87th Regt., d. Nov. 1909; and has issue 1e to 2e.

1e. Charles Frederick Urquhart, b. (—); m. Sybil, da. of (—) Betherton.

2e. Florence Urquhart, m. Col. Henry Denne Robson, formerly Col. Comdg. Queen's Regt.

5d. Florence Sophia Ann Hildyard (Varnes, Lympstone, Devon); m. 16 Nov. 1886, Col. William Robert Purchas, R.E., d. 23 Oct. 1909; and has issue 1e to 2e.

1e. Annie Florence Emily Purchas.

2e. Dorothy Marian Purchas.

3c. Henry Charles Hildyard, d. (? s.p.).

4c. John George Bowes Hildyard of Winestead, J.P. (Cherry Burton House,
[Nos. 41901 to 41929.

The Plantagenet Roll

Hull), b. 8 June 1828; m. 12 Feb. 1857, Caroline, da. of Robert Dennison of Wapling-ton Manor, co. York, d. 5 Jan. 1894; and has issue (with 2 sons who d.s.p.) 1d to 2d.
    1d. Mabel Hildyard.
    2d. Evelyn Caroline Hildyard.
    5c. Anne Catharine Hildyard, d. (? unm.).
    6c. Mary Anne Hildyard.
    7c. Elizabeth Frances Hildyard, d. 3 Ap. 1894; m. 17 Mar. 1741, Sir John Charles Thorold, 11th Bt. [E.], b. 26 June 1816; d. 26 Ap. 1866; and had issue (with a 4th son and da. who d.s.p.) 1d to 4d.
        1d. Sir John Henry Thorold, 12th Bt. [E.], Hon. LL.D. (Camb.), J.P., D.L., High Sheriff co. Linc. 1876 and M.P. for Grantham 1865–1868 (Syston Park, near Grantham; Carlton), b. 9 Mar. 1842; m. 3 Feb. 1869, the Hon. Alexandrina Henrietta Matilda [descended from the Lady Anne, sister of King Edward IV., &c.], da. of Henry (Willoughby), 8th Baron Middleton [G.B.]; and has issue.
        See the Exeter Volume, p. 613, Nos. 52198–52203.
        2d. Montague George Thorold, formerly Mid. R.N. (Honington Hall, Grantham; 1 Abbot's Court, Kensington Square, W.), b. 23 Aug. 1845; m. 2 July 1881, Emmeline Laura, Dowager Lady Rivers [U.K.], da. of Capt. John Pownell Bastard (see p. 73).
        3d. Cecil Thorold of Boothby, co. Linc., J.P., D.L., Capt. 1st Life Guards, b. 5 Oct. 1847; d. 26 Feb. 1895; m. 2 Sept. 1875, Annie Charlotte, da. of Gen. Edward Stopford Claremont, C.B. [who m. 2ndly, 25 Sept. 1902, Ralph Henry Seymour Hall, d. 29 Jan. 1903]; and had issue 1e.
            1e. Marguerite Thorold, m. 21 Sept. 1897, the Hon. Maurice Raymond Gifford, C.M.G. [4th son of Robert Francis, 2nd Baron Gifford [U.K.], and descended maternally from King Henry VII. (see the Tudor Roll, p. 470)] (Boothby Hall, Grantham); and has issue 1f to 4f.
                1f. Charles Maurice Elton Gifford, b. 4 Mar. 1899.
                2f. Diana Frederica Gifford.
                3f. Joan Gifford.
                4f. Vera Mary Gifford.
        4d. Edith Mary Thorold (9 Wilbraham Place, S.W.).
    8c. Esther Sophia Hildyard.   [Nos. 41930 to 41947.

185. Descendants of JAMES DARCY of Sedbury Park, co. York, M.P. (Table XX.), b. c. 1621; d. (–); m. ISABEL, da. of Sir Marmaduke WYVILL, 2nd Bt. [E.]; and had issue.

See the Exeter Volume, Table LII., and pp. 554–558, Nos. 49657–49747.
[Nos. 41948 to 42038.

186. Descendants of the Hon. BARBARA DARCY (Table XX.), b. 3 May 1600; bur. 31 Mar. 1696; m. 22 Ap. 1617, MATTHEW HUTTON of Marske, co. York, a well-known Royalist, b. 20 Oct. 1597; d. (–); and had issue 1a to 7a.

    1a. John Hutton of Marske, b. 6 Oct. 1625; d. 21 Mar. 1664; m. (Articles dated 13 Sept.) 1651, Frances, da. of Bryan Stapylton of Myton, co. York, bur. 5 May 1684; and had issue.
    See p. 120, Nos. 10978–11168.
    2a. Dorothy Hutton, b. 22 July 1620; bur. (?) 6 Aug. 1644; m. as 1st wife, Sir Philip Warwick.
    3a. Elizabeth Hutton, b. at Richmond 4 Mar. 1630.
    4a. Barbara Hutton, b. at Richmond 23 Oct. (? Nov.) 1630; m. at Marske 16/25 Ap. 1655, Thomas Lister of Bawtry and of the Inner Temple, d. at Bawtry 4 May 1670   [Nos. 42039 to 42229.

of The Blood Royal

5a. Mary Hutton, b. at Marske 4 Feb. 1637; m. at Richmond a. 1662 (not 12 June 1663), Richard Peirse of Hutton Bonville; and had issue 1b to 4b.

1b. John Peirse of Lasenby Hall, co. York, b. 1662; d.v.p. 5 Oct. 1694; m. Elizabeth, da. of Sir Henry Marwood, Bt., d. 26 Mar. 1726; and had issue 1c to 3c.

1c. Henry Peirse of Bedale, M.P., b. 1692; d. 1759; m. Anne, da. of (—) Johnson; and had issue 1d to 2d.

1d. Henry Peirse of Bedale and Hutton Bonville, M.P., b. 1754; d. 1824; m. 16 Aug. 1777, the Hon. Charlotte Grace, da. of John (Monson), 2nd Baron Monson [G.B.], d. 19 July 1793; and had issue.

See the Exeter Volume, pp. 244-246, Nos. 9156-9244.

2d. Anne Peirse, d. 6 Ap. 1809; m. John Sawrey Morritt of Rokeby Park, co. York, d. 3 Aug. 1791; and had issue 1e to 2e.

1e. John Bacon Sawrey Morritt of Rokeby Park, M.P., the well-known classical scholar and traveller, b. 1771; d.s.p. 12 July 1843.

2e. Rev. Henry Morritt, d. (—); m. Alice Margaret, da. of the Rev. F. Cookson, Vicar of Leeds; and had issue (with a da., Mrs. Hely Hutchinson, d.s.p.) 1f to 2f.

1f. William John Sawrey Morritt of Rokeby Park, M.P., b. 12 Sept. 1813; d.s.p. 13 Ap. 1874.

2f. Robert Ambrose Morritt of Rokeby Park, J.P., D.L., b. 9 May 1816; d. 1890; m. 11 Ap. 1872, Mary Blanche Mitchell [a descendant of King Henry VII. (see the Tudor Roll, p. 550)], da. of Alexander Mitchell Innes of Ayton Castle [by his wife Charlotte, da. of Sir Thomas Dick Lauder, 7th Bt. [S. 1690]; and had issue (with 2 sons d.s.p.) 1g to 5g.

1g. Henry Edward Morritt of Rokeby Park, Lieut. Royal Warwickshire Regt. (Rokeby Park, Barnard Castle; Colton Lodge, Tadcaster; 17 Southwell Gardens, S.W.), b. 3 Mar. 1880; m. 1903, Grace Lillia, da. of (—) Chapman of Highland Park, Illinois.

2g. Charlotte Greta Morritt.

3g. Florence Catherine Morritt.

4g. Hilda Mary Morritt.

5g. Linda Beatrice Morritt.

2c. Mary Peirse, b. 1686.[1]

3c. Dorothy Peirse, b. 1693.[1]

2b. Thomas Peirse of Hutton Bonville and Thimbleby, will dated 9 Sept. 1720; prov. 9 June 1725; m. 2 Ap. 1700, Anne [descended from the Lady Anne, sister of King Edward IV. (see the Exeter Volume, Table XVII.)], da. and co-h. of Sir William Hustler of Acklam, d. Dec. 1753; and had issue (with others known to have d.s.p.) 1c to 7c.

1c. William Peirse of Hutton Bonville and Thimbleby, bur. 29 Jan. 1753; m. 1726, Dorothy [sister of Joseph, and] da. of (—) Stillington of Kelfield, co. York; and had issue 1d.

1d. Mary Peirse, da. and event. h., m. the Rev. Edward Stillingfleet of West Bromwich, co. Stafford.

2c. Richard Peirse of Hutton Bonville and Thimbleby, d. 26 June 1759; m. Rachel [sister of William, and] da. of (—) Bayne, d. 24 Jan. 1771; and had issue 1d to 2d.

1d. Richard William Peirse of Hutton Bonville, &c., b. 20 Jan. 1753; d. 25 Nov. 1798; m. 1780, Elizabeth, da of Christopher Fawcett of Newcastle-on-Tyne, d. 3 Sept. 1791; and had issue 1e to 3e.

1e. Richard William Christopher Peirse of Thimbleby Lodge, b. 28 June 1781; d. 18 Dec. 1844; m. 29 Aug. 1803, Maroa, da. of the Rev. Richard Clarke of Bedale, d. 20 Aug. 1859; and had issue 1f to 4f. [Nos. 42230 to 42323.

---

[1] Foster's "Yorkshire Families."

The Plantagenet Roll

1*f*. Richard William Peirse *of Northallerton, Capt. 3rd Dragoon Guards and afterwards Registrar of Deeds for the North Riding*, b. 14 *Aug*. 1804; d. 24 *July* 1872; m. 23 *Oct*. 1831, *Mary Anne Eliza, widow of* J. S. *Highatt of Lower Cheve, near Exeter, da. of John Tharp of Chippenham Park, co. Camb.; and had issue* 1*g*.

1*g*. Arabella Georgiana Peirse, da. and h., *m*. 27 July 1853, George Thomas Duncombe, now (R.L. 12 July 1887) Peirse-Duncombe of Winthorpe Hall, *formerly* Capt. 11th Hussars, &c. [nephew of Charles, 1st Lord Feversham, and a descendant of the Lady Anne, sister of King Edward IV. (see the Exeter Volume, p. 650)] (*Winthorpe Hall, Newark; 25 Queen's Gate, S.W.*); and has issue (with a son and 2 das. *d*. unm.) 1*h* to 8*h*.

1*h*. Charles Slingsby Peirse-Duncombe, *b*. 18 May 1870.

2*h*. Richard Slingsby Peirse-Duncombe, *b*. 25 Aug. 1872; *m*. 1898, Josephine, da. of (—) Foster.

3*h*. Elizabeth Slingsby Peirse-Duncombe.

4*h*. Georgiana Slingsby Peirse-Duncombe.

5*h*. Edith Slingsby Peirse-Duncombe.

6*h*. Ruth Slingsby Peirse-Duncombe, *m*. 5 May 1892, Comm. Richard Nigel Gresley, R.N. [Bt. Coll.] (*Ivy House, Barton-under-Needwood, Burton-on-Trent*); and has issue 1*i* to 2*i*.

1*i*. Roger Gresley, *b*. 26 Feb. 1895.

2*i*. Dorothy Gresley.

7*h*. Mildred Slingsby Peirse-Duncombe, *m*. 30 July 1888, Thomas Herbert Bindley; and has issue 1*i* to 2*i*.

1*i*. Herbert Duncombe Bindley, *b*. 8 Feb. 1891.

2*i*. Mildred Duncombe Bindley.

8*h*. Winifred Slingsby Peirse-Duncombe, *unm*.

2*f*. Charles Milbank *Peirse*, b. 27 *Aug*. 1811; d. (—); m. 1844, (—), da. *of John George of co. Kent*.

3*f*. Ayshford George Peir e, b. 6 Nov. 1814; d. 6 *June* 1873; m. c. 1842, *Marianna Emma, da. of Major Brooke of Littlethorp, near Ripon; and had issue* (a da.[1]).

4*f*. Harriet Jane *Peirse*, d. (—); m. 28 Feb. 1832, *Henry Claridge of Jervaulx Abbey, co. York; and had issue*.

2*e*. James *Peirse, Lieut*. 23rd *Foot*, b. 12 *Nov*. 1782; d. *abroad Mar*. 1843; m. 9 *July* 1807, *Sophia, da. of the Rev. Richard Clarke of Bedale, d. abroad; and had issue*.

3*e*. Elizabeth *Peirse*, d. (—); m. 12 *Oct*. 1812, *the Rev. George Ford Clarke of Thornton Watlass, co. York*.

2*d*. Anne *Peirse*, b. 15 *Oct*. 1751; m. *Joseph Williamson of Melton Hall, co. York*.

3*c*. Thomas *Peirse, afterwards* (R.L. 8 May 1784) *Hustler, of Acklom, co. York*, d. 1784; m. 3rdly *at York*, 10 Feb. 1769, *Constance, da. of Ralph Hutton of Knapton* [*by his wife, Constance, da. of Sir Francis Boynton*, 4th Bt. [E. 1618], *M.P.*]; *and had issue*.

See the Exeter Volume, pp. 702–703, Nos. 58067–58078.

4*c*. Anne *Peirse*, m. *Richard Hodson of Witton-le-Wear, co. Durham*.

5*c*. Mary *Peirse*, m. 6 Feb. 1728, *Joseph Stillington of Kelfield, co. York*.

6*c*. Dorothy *Peirse*.

7*c*. Elizabeth *Peirse*.

3*b*. Barbara[2] *Peirse*, bur. *at Bolton-on-Swale* 8 *Oct*. 1690; m. *as* 1*st wife at* [Nos. 42324 to 42348.

---

[1] Foster's "Yorkshire Families."
[2] Not Katherine, as in Foster.

# of The Blood Royal

Danby Wiske, 13 June 1682, John Wastell of Bolton-on-Swale and Ainderby Steeple [son of Leonard Wastell of Scorton, co. York], b. 23 Jan. 1660; bur. 25 Oct. 1738; and had issue (with 3 sons, whose issue is extinct) 1c to 3c.

1c. John Wastell of London, Merchant, b. 21 June 1686; d. *in Jamaica* 1717; m. Annabella, da. of Thomas Williams; and had issue (with a son, Philip, d.s.p.) 1d to 5d.

1d. Elizabeth Wastell, d. 1774; m. *at the Chapel Royal, Whitehall*, 6 Dec. 1748, Gen. Sir Philip Honeywood, K.C.B., Governor of Hull, d. 17 June 1752.

2d. Barbara Wastell, m. (—) O'Brien.

3d. Audrey Wastell.

4d. Mary Wastell.

5d. Catherine Wastell, m. (—) Cotton.

2c. Rev. Henry Wastell, M.A. (Camb.), Rector of Simonburn, co. Northbd., b. 19 Feb. 1689; d. 1771; m. 1734, Frances, da. of William Bacon of Steward Peel, co. Northbd., d. 1748; and had issue (with an elder son d. unm.) 1d to 3d.

1d. John Wastell of Ainderby, co. York, and Risby, co. Suffolk, J.P., D.L., Winner of the Oakes 1802, b. 1736; d. 1 Dec. 1811; m. Hannah, da. of (—) Chicken, d. Oct. 1831; and had issue (with 3 das. of whom no issue survives) 1e.

1e. Rev. John Daniel Wastell of Risby, b. 20 July 1782; bur. 20 July 1874; m. Frances (see p. 316), da. of Bacon William Wastell, d. 26 Aug. 1851; and had issue (with 3 sons d. unm.) 1f to 3f.

1f. Eleanora Wastell, da. and co-h., b. c. 1812; d. 24 Dec. 1838; m. *as 1st wife*, Thomas Siubbs Walker of Maunby, co. York; and had issue 1g to 2g.

1g. Thomas Stubbs Walker of Maunby Hall, b. c. 1840; d. 11 Jan. 1878; m. 1st, 9 Ap. 1861, Jane, da. of J. G. Lamb of Ryton, co. Durham, d. 6 July 1865; 2ndly, 15 Oct. 1867, Mariann, da. of Lawrence Oliphant of Condie and Newton, co. Perth, M.P., J.P., D.L., d. 5 Nov. 1903; and had issue (with 2 sons by 2nd wife, Thomas Gerald, d. unm. at Cape Town during the S. African War 12 May 1901, and Harry Grenville, d. unm. in British Columbia 20 Mar. 1898) 1h to 4h.

1h.[1] Violet Eleanor Walker, "Sister Violet" (*St. Hilda's Home, Paddington*).

2h.[1] Constance Helen Walker, unm.

3h.[1] Florence Jane Walker, m. 20 July 1897, the Rev. Percy Wonnacott, Vicar of Waltham Cross (*Waltham Cross Vicarage, Herts*); s.p.

4h.[2] Muriel Lilias Walker, m. 12 Ap. 1902, her cousin, Major Alan Hill Walker, V.C. (see below) (*Maunby Hall, Thirsk*); and has issue 1i to 2i.

1i. Gerald Alan Hill-Walker, b. 4 Jan. 1903.

2i. Thomas Harry Hill-Walker, b. 29 Aug. 1904.

2g. Frances Miriam Walker, b. 25 July 1835; d. 30 Ap. 1904; m. 18 Aug. 1858, Capt. Thomas Hill, Chief Constable of the North Riding 1859–1898 [son of Richard Hill of the Hall, Thornton, Pickering], b. 8 Sept. 1822; d. 5 Nov. 1899; and had issue (with a da. d. young) 1h to 3h.

1h. Alan Hill, now (D.P. 10 May 1902) Hill-Walker of Maunby Hall, V.C., Major *late* Northants Regt., served at Lang's Neck, &c. (*Maunby Hall, Thirsk*), b. 12 July 1859; m. 12 Ap. 1902, his cousin, Muriel Lilias, da. and co-h. of Thomas Stubbs Walker of Maunby Hall; and has issue.

See above, Nos. 42353–42354.

2h. Cecil Hill, Col. R.E. (*Wood Hill, Cork*), b. 25 Oct. 1861; m. 30 Nov. 1893, Edith, da. of Charles Lambert; and has issue 1i.

1i. Cecil Vivian Hill, b. 3 Nov. 1908.

3h. Maude Hill, "Sister Maude" (*St. Mary's Home, Wantage*).

2f. Frances Wastell, da. and co-h., b. 13 Feb. 1813; d. 26 Dec. 1858; m. *as 1st wife*, 19 July 1836, William Whytehead of York, d. 20 Jan. 1888; and had issue (with 2 sons and 3 das. d.s.p.) 1g to 7g.

1g. Thomas Bowman Whytehead, b. 16 Mar. 1840; d. 5 Sept. 1907; m. at

[Nos. 42349 to 42360.

The Plantagenet Roll

Auckland, N.Z., 15 Sept. 1870, Caroline Forster (24 Gondar Gardens, West Hampstead), da. of the Rev. Thomas Drought of Punketstown House, co. Kildare; and had issue (with an eldest son, William Wastell Drought, who fell in action in S. Africa, 20 Ap. 1900) 1h to 8h.

1h. Thomas Bowman Henry Whytehead, Merchant Service, British India Coy., Bombay, b. 22 Oct. 1872; m. 12 Dec. 1907, Harriet Emma (see p. 245), da. of the Rev. William Webster Hawkins of Acomb; and has issue 1i.

1i. Nancy Bowman Whytehead.

2h. Hugh Richard Augustine Whytehead, Indian Army, b. 17 May 1881; unm.

3h. Christopher John Wastell Whytehead, b. 26 Aug. 1887.

4h. Lionel Wanley Wastell Whytehead, b. 3 Sept. 1892.

5h. Eleanora Frances Drought Whytehead.

6h. Mary Alice Bayly Whytehead.

7h. Isabella Margaretta Eliza Wastell Whytehead, m. 3 Sept. 1902, Herbert John Watson [eldest son of H. E. Watson of Petworth] (St. Helen's, Cockermouth); and has issue 1i.

1i. John Alexander Watson, b. 29 May 1903.

8h. Caroline Louisa Hinemoa Drought Whytehead.

2g. William Wastell Whytehead, b. 6 Feb. 1848; m. 14 Aug. 1889, Jessie, da. of William Whytehead Boulton of Highgate House, Beverley; s.p.

3g. Rev. Henry Robert Whytehead, M.A. (Camb.), Vicar of Warminster (The Vicarage, Warminster), b. 10 Oct. 1849; m. 6 Sept. 1876, Sarah May Louise [also descended from Edward III. through Mortimer-Percy (see p. 474)], da. of the Rev. Charles Clement Layard; and has issue (with an elder son, the Rev. Wastell Layard, who d. unm. 1903) 1h to 3h.

1h. Henry Layard Whytehead, b. 31 May 1879.

2h. John Layard Whytehead, b. 19 Oct. 1880.

3h. Rev. Ralph Layard Whytehead, St. John's Coll., Oxon. (Church Road, Ilfracombe), b. 3 Oct. 1883.

4g. Hugh Edward Whytehead, b. 30 Mar. 1853; d. 11 June 1901; m. 20 Jan. 1886, Maud, da. of (—) Holtom, M.D.; and had issue 1h to 3h.

1h. Hugh Holtom Whytehead, b. 11 Aug. 1895.

2h. Gladys Holtom Whytehead.

3h. Doris Holtom Whytehead.

5g. Alice Whytehead, m. 6 June 1872, Arthur Horatio Poyser, M.A. (Oxon.), Bar.-at-Law (Burniston, Sydenham, Kent); and has issue 1h to 5h.

1h. Arthur Hampden Ronald Wastell Poyser, B.A. (Oxon.), Bar.-at-Law, b. 30 Sept. 1884.

2h. Alice Ianthe Poyser.

3h. Ina Frances Poyser, m. 6 June 1900, Gerald Edgell Mills, Bar.-at-Law [2nd son of Sir Richard Mills, K.C.B., K.C.V.O.] (Risby, Sanderstead, Surrey); and has issue 1i to 3i.

1i. Gerald Hilary Mytton Mills, b. 7 Jan. 1904.

2i. David Richard Poyser Mills, b. 1 Mar. 1907.

3i. Ina Iris Mills.

4h. Irene Grace Poyser, unm.

5h. Gwladys Isabelle Poyser, m. 6 June 1901, Henry Clendon Daukes [2nd son of the Rev. S. Whitfield Daukes] (Summer Hill, Norbury).

6g. Louisa Frances Whytehead, m. 6 June 1872, the Rev. Canon Benjamin Lamb, Vicar of Clapham (Clapham Vicarage, Lancaster); and has issue (with 2 das. d. unm.) 1h to 8h.

1h. Rev. Gilbert Henry Lamb, B.A. (Camb.) (Tuticorin, South India), b. 14 Sept. 1875; unm. [Nos. 42361 to 42389.

# of The Blood Royal

2h. Charles Edward Lamb, Solicitor (*Vincent House, Kettering*), b. 1 July 1878; m. 19 Nov. 1902, Alice, da. of Samuel Hey, J.P., F.R.C.S.; and has issue 1i.

1i. Florence Mary Lamb, b. 15 Sept. 1904.

3h. Percy Hutchinson Lamb, Acting Govt. Super. of Cotton Culture, Uganda, b. 6 May 1883; *unm.*

4h. Harold Victor Lamb, b. 6 May 1883; *unm.*

5h. Jesse Lamb, Physician and Surgeon (*Tarn Taran, India*), *unm.*

6h. Louisa Whytehead Lamb,⎫
7h. Maud Lamb,   ⎬ *unm.*
8h. Alice Margaret Lamb,   ⎭

7g. Emmeline Fanny Whytehead, m. 12 Aug. 1880, Marcus Valentine English (*Orton Longueville, Peterborough*); and has issue 1h to 6h.

1h. Marcus Claude English, B.A. (Camb.), b. 8 May 1886.
2h. Guy Whytehead English, b. 28 July 1888.
3h. Reginald Wastell English, b. 12 Ap. 1894.
4h. Margaret English.
5h. Olave English.
6h. Phyllis English.

3f. *Mary Wastell*, b. 18 *May* 1815; d. 24 *July* 1863; m. 24 *Aug.* 1843, *John Worlledge, M.A. (Camb.), County Court Judge for Suffolk and Chancellor of the Diocese of Norwich*, b. 2 *June* 1809; d. 19 *July* 1881; *and had issue (with 2 sons and a da. d.s.p.) 1g to 3g.*

1g. Rev. Arthur John Worlledge, M.A. (Camb.), Canon and Chancellor of Truro Cathedral (*Truro*), b. 29 May 1848; *unm.*

2g. Edward William Worlledge, M.A. (Camb.), Solicitor and Registrar of Yarmouth County Court (10 *Albert Square, Great Yarmouth*), b. 27 Jan. 1850; m. 1 June 1876, Edith Georgiana, da. of the Rev. William Wigston, Vicar of Rushmere St. Andrew, Ipswich; and had issue (with 2 sons, Cyril Edward, b. 15 July 1877; d. 5 Feb. 1893, and Noel Arthur, Lieut. 75th Carnatic Inf., b. 23 May 1883; d. unm. 7 Ap. 1908) 1h to 3h.

1h. Audrey Mary Worlledge.
2h. Edith Cicely Worlledge.
3h. Olive Margaret Worlledge.

3g. *Alfred Cranworth Worlledge*, Major A.P.D., b. 15 Nov. 1857; d. 24 Dec. 1903; m. 18 *June* 1885, *Annabella Mary Garnons, da. of the Rev. Preb. Garnons Williams*, d. 18 *Feb.* 1908; *and had issue* 1h.

1h. John Penry Garnons Worlledge, Lieut. R.E., b. 22 Sept. 1887.

2d. *Henry Wastell of Newburgh*, d. (-); m. *Anne, widow of Middleton Teasdale, da. and co-h. of John Bacon [by his wife Jane, da. and h. of John Marshall of Walltown]*; *and had issue* 1e.

1e. *Rev. Henry Wastell of Walltown and Newburgh, co. Northbd., Fellow of Clare Hall, Oxon*, d. (-); m. *Anne, da. of (—) Henderson*, d. (-); *and had issue* 1f.

1f. *Anne Lindsay Wastell of Newburgh Hall, da. and h.*, d. 12 *May* 1884; m. 19 *Dec.* 1843, *Gustavus Hamilton Coulson of Stonehouse, co. Cumb., Capt. R.N., J.P., D.L.*, d. 23 *Nov.* 1868; *and had issue* 1g to 7g.

1g. Henry John Wastell Coulson of Walltown, J.P., Bar.-at-Law (*Langton Lodge, Blandford*), b. 13 Nov. 1848; m. 14 July 1875, Caroline Stewart, da. of Henry Unwin of the Bengal C.S.; and has issue (with a son, Gustavus Hamilton Blenkinsopp, V.C., D.S.O., Lieut. King's Own Scottish Borderers, killed *unm.* in action at Lambrechfontein 19 May 1901) 1h to 3h.

1h. Florence Lindsay Coulson.
2h. Isabel Forbes Coulson, m. 24 July 1902, Lisle March Philipps, *formerly* Capt. Remington's Guides.
3h. Inez Lisle Coulson, m. 24 Ap. 1906, Lieut. Edward Tyrrell Inman, R.N.

[Nos. 42390 to 42414.

The Plantagenet Roll

2g. Anne Alicia Coulson.

3g. Mary Arabella Coulson.

4g. Frances Jane Wastell Coulson, m. 10 Oct. 1876, Arthur Hamilton Unwin, B.C.S.; and has issue.

5g. Theodosia Hamilton Coulson.

6g. Maud Maria Lisle Coulson.

7g. Margaret Lindsay Coulson.

3d. Bacon William Wastell, b. 1740; d. Nov. 1821; m. Eleanor, da. of William Fetherstonhaugh, d. 6 Mar. 1818; and had issue 1e to 3e.

1e. Mary Wastell, m. John Forster.

2e. Eleanor Wastell, m. William Hodgson.

3e. Frances Wastell, b. 1781; d. 26 Aug. 1851; m. the Rev. John Daniel Wastell; and had issue.

See p. 313, Nos. 42349–42410.

3c. Elizabeth Wastell, bapt. 22 Sept. 1690; d. a. 1731; m. at York Minster, 30 Dec. 1712, Christopher Bayles of Laxton, Chamberlain (1714) and Sheriff (1717) of Hull, d. 1744; and had issue 1d.

1d. Deborah Bayles, da. and event. sole h., b. 1724; d. 1782; m. at Drypool, co. York, 12 Aug. 1746, Michael Inman of Beverley, Nidderdale, d. 1784; and had issue 1e to 2e.

1e. Christopher Inman, afterwards Inman Whaley Bayles, bapt. 30 Nov. 1748; d. 8 Oct. 1801; m. at St. Saviour's, Jersey, 12 May 1786, Marie, da. of Noe Gautier of St. Helier, Jersey, d. 11 Nov. 1843; and had issue (with 4 other sons who d. unm.) 1f to 2f.

1f. Wastell Edwin Bayles, b. 25 July 1787; d. 19 Sept. 1868; m. Ann Luard, da. of (—) Robert, d. 15 Sept. 1865; and had issue (with 2 sons and 2 das. who d.s.p.) 1g.

1g. Martha Bayles, unm.

2f. Gascoigne Noe Edwin Bayles of Guernsey, b. 1793; d. 3 July 1860; m. at St. Peter Port, 11 Feb. 1826, Charlotte, da. of John Grut of Guernsey, d. 18 Oct. 1882; and had issue (with a son d.s.p.) 1g to 3g.

1g. Mary Gautier Bayles, b. 23 Mar. 1836; d. 26 Mar. 1896; m. 17 Aug. 1860, the Rev. Alfred John French, B.A. (Lond.) (Grangewood, Princes Avenue, West Kirby); and had issue (with a da. d. young) 1h to 9h.

1h. Alfred Stead French, b. 13 Oct. 1868.

2h. Herbert Noel French, b. 28 Feb. 1871.

3h. Reginald Ernest French, b. 17 Feb. 1874.

4h. Rosa Maria French.

5h. Marian Algeo French.

6h. Eliza Pulsford French, b. 6 June 1864; d. 24 Nov. 1903; m. 5 June 1894, John Howe Bourne (Montarina, Sea Bank Road, Liscard, Cheshire); and had issue 1i to 2i.

1i. John Pulsford Bourne, b. 12 Nov. 1898.

2i. Hilda Caroline Bourne.

7h. Emily Birchenall French.

8h. Eleanor Elizabeth French.

9h. Maud Mary French.

2g. Louise Charlotte Bayles, m. John Fisher Le Page of Manchester and Cheadle, M.D. [son of William Le Page of Guernsey] (The Poplars, Cheadle, Manchester); and has issue 1h to 4h.

1h. John Herbert Perceval De Jersey Le Page, d. young, ⎫
2h. Florence Bertha Louise De Wilton Le Page, M.A., ⎬ unm.
3h. Ethel Mabel Beatrice De Jersey Le Page, ⎪
4h. Winifred Maud Mary d'Estelle Le Page, ⎭

[Nos. 42415 to 42497.

of The Blood Royal

3g. *Rose Algeo Bayles*, b. 8 *May* 1839; d. 21 *Ap.* 1886; m. 14 *Nov.* 1865, *the Rev. Edwin Webster*, d. 1892; *and had issue (with a son d.s.p. and 2 das.* d. *in infancy*) 1h *to* 7h.

1h. Walter Pulsford Webster, b. 10 Oct. 1870; *unm.*
2h. Howard Birchenall Webster, b. 5 Mar. 1875; *unm.*
3h. Charles Frederick Smythe Webster, b. 21 Dec. 1880; *unm.*
4h. Mary Gautier Webster, *unm.*
5h. Elizabeth Overton Webster, *unm.*
6h. Laura Inman Webster, *m.* 28 Ap. 1900, James MacKenzie, Engineer, H.M. Postal Telegraph Dept. (67 *Langholm Crescent, Darlington*); and has issue 1i.

1i. James Walter MacKenzie, b. 14 July 1906.

7h. Mabel Gwendoline Allen Webster.

2e. *Whaley Charles Inman*, b. at *Kingston-on-Hull* 6 *Aug.* 1754; d. 1826; m. 5 *Sept./*19 *Dec.* 1783, *Mary, da. of* (—) *Oliver,* d. 1807; *and had issue (with* 4 *sons and a da.* d. *unm.*) 1f *to* 2f.

1f. *Deborah Inman,* bapt. *at Bedale* 25 *Mar.* 1785; d. 1826; m. *at Bedale* 21 *Dec.* 1808, *the Rev. Richard Inman, Rector of Todwick, near Sheffield, for fifty years,* bur. 1826; *and had issue (with* 4 *sons and* 5 *das. who* d.s.p.) 1g *to* 5g.

1g. *Rev. Thomas Inman, B.A.*, b. 11 *Nov.* 1818; d. 12 *Jan.* 1894; m. *Dec.* 1850, *Lavinia Louisa, da. of Col. Burton,* d. 24 *May* 1856; *and had issue (with a da.* drowned at sea) 1h *to* 2h.

1h. Lavinia Wyat Inman (*Lanark Street, Balclutha, Otago, New Zealand*), b. 4 Nov. 1851; *m.* 16 Nov. 1880, Andrew Purves of Kirkcaldy, co. Fife, b. 7 Dec. 1841; *d.* 12 Dec. 1907; and has issue 1i to 3i.

1i. Andrew Hope Purves, Watchmaker's Assistant, b. 21 June 1883.
2i. Thomas Burton Purves, University Student, Dunedin, *formerly* Headmaster of Kelso School, N.Z., b. 14 July 1885; *m.* 27 Jan. 1908, Margaret, da. of John Faddes; and has issue 1j.

1j. Eva Mary Purves, b. 16 Mar. 1909.

3i. Charles Evans Purves, Cycle Mechanic, b. 30 June 1887; *unm.*

2h. Mary Charlotte Inman (*The Wilderness, Mitcheldean, Glos.*), *unm.*

2g. *Richard Inman of Manitoba,* d. (–); m. *Mary Ann, da. of* (—); *and had issue (a son and da.)* 1h *to* 2h.

1h. Herbert Inman *of Hamilton, Manitoba,* b. 30 *Mar.* 1848; d. 1903; m. (—) (*Hamilton, Manitoba*), *da. of* (—); *and had issue* (3 *sons and* 1 *da.*).
2h. Marion Inman, d. (–); m. (—) *Way of Australia, M.D.; and had issue* (2 *sons and* 2 *das.*).

3g. *Mary Inman,* b. 15 *Dec.* 1810; d. 1 *Mar.* 1892; m. 5 *Ap.* 1839, *the Rev. Henry Austin Oram,* b. 17 *Mar.* 1813; d. 19 *Feb.* 1880; *and had issue (with a son and* 3 *das.* d. *unm.*) 1h *to* 4h.

1h. Rev. Reginald Austin Oram, M.A. (Camb.), Rector of Weeting (*Weeting Rectory, Brandon, Suffolk*), b. 3 Jan. 1846; *m.* 14 July 1881, Fanny Forbes Becher, da. of Major-Gen. Saxton; and has issue 1i to 2i.

1i. Gladys Mary Oram.
2i. Eileen Margaret Oram.

2h. *Catharine Inman Oram,* b. 9 *Jan.* 1840; d. 12 *Ap.* 1909; m. 28 *Feb.* 1867, *Mander John Smyth* (*Bowles Lodge, Colchester*); *and had issue* 1i *to* 9i.

1i. Reginald Mander Smyth, M.D. (*Linford Sanatorium*), b. (—); *m.* June 1906, Gladys, da. of (—) Black-Hawkins, *d.s.p.* Feb. 1910.
2i. Charles Inman Smyth (*Highfield, Compton, Wolverhampton*), b. 12 Dec. 1868; *m.* Jessie, da. of (—); and has issue 1j to 2j.

1j. Kenneth Bowes Inman Smyth, b. 31 Jan. 1907.
2j. Beatrice Lesbia Smyth, b. 17 Aug. 1908.   [Nos. 42498 to 42518.

The Plantagenet Roll

3*i*. Sydney Fairfax Smyth (*Livingstone Road, Hounslow*), *b*. 13 Ap. 1877; *m*. 6 Jan. 1898, Mary, da. of (—) M'Carthy; and has issue 1*j* to 2*j*.
  1*j*. John Fairfax Smyth, *b*. 28 Oct. 1898.
  2*j*. Christine May Smyth, *b*. 28 May 1900.
4*i*. Sophia Smyth, *unm*.
5*i*. Christine Smyth, *unm*.
6*i*. Rachel Smyth, *unm*.
7*i*. Janet Smyth, *unm*.
8*i*. Dora Smyth, *unm*.
9*i*. Gertrude Smyth, *m*. Vincent Cook; and has issue 1*j*.
  1*j*. Phyllis Cook.

3*h*. Frances Lucy Oram, *m*. 16 Jan. 1873, the Rev. Benjamin Hunter, B.A. (London), Vicar of Aukborough, *formerly* (1864–1870) a Solicitor (*Aukborough Vicarage, Doncaster*); and has issue 1*i* to 9*i*.
  1*i*. Herbert Austin Hunter (*West Hartlepool, Durham*), *b*. 18 Jan. 1875; *m*. 27 Aug. 1904, Annie, da. of Robert Brown of Scarborough; and has issue 1*j* to 3*j*.
    1*j*. Oram Hunter, *b*. 11 Mar. 1907.
    2*j*. Marjory Eileen Hunter, *b*. 9 Oct. 1905.
    3*j*. Lucy Mabel Hunter, *b*. 31 Oct. 1908.
  2*i*. Edward William Baptist Hunter, *b*. 24 June 1878; *unm*.
  3*i*. Marcus Charles Inman Hunter (*The Firs, Station Road, Bedford*), *b*. 23 May 1882; *m*. 27 July 1909, Edith Emily, da. of (—) Cornelius.
  4*i*. Benjamin D'Arcy Hunter, *b*. 26 June 1885; *unm*.
  5*i*. Helen Mary Hunter (*Papakaio, Oamaru, Otago, N.Z.*), *unm*.
  6*i*. Kate Angela Hunter, *unm*.
  7*i*. Annie Christabel Hunter, *unm*.
  8*i*. Lily Lucy Hunter, *unm*.
  9*i*. Dorothy Hunter, *unm*.

4*h*. Annie Elizabeth Oram (*Margaret Lodge, West Lyss, Hants*), *m*. 20 Oct. 1880, the Rev. Charles Somes Saxton, M.A., Rector of Beechamwell [eldest son of Major-Gen. Saxton], *d*. 14 Jan. 1893; and has issue 1*i*.
  1*i*. Walter Theodore Saxton, M.A., F.L.S. (South African College, Cape Town), *b*. 16 Oct. 1882; *m*. 19 Dec. 1906, Dorothy, da. of the Rev. E. Apthorpe; and has issue 1*j*.
    1*j*. Dorothy Joyce Saxton, *b*. 20 Sept. 1908.

4*g*. Barbara Inman (*Oxford Parade, Cheltenham*), *b*. 27 Oct. 1816; living aged 94; *unm*.

5*g*. Annie Inman, *b*. 6 Oct. 1823; *d*. 29 Dec. 1905; *m*. 7 Sept. 1854, the Rev. Anthony Edwards, Vicar of All Saints, Leeds, *d*. 29 Mar. 1874; *and had issue* 1*h* to 3*h*.
  1*h*. Ambrose Cadwallader Edwards, *b*. 27 June 1858 ⎱ (21 *Prince of Wales*
  2*h*. Annie Orah Edwards, *unm*. ⎰ *Terrace, Scarborough*).
  3*h*. Kathleen Edwards, *unm*.

2*f*. Barbara Inman, bapt. at Bedale 22 Feb. 1789; *d*. Nov. 1877; *m*. at Bedale 23 July 1808, James Orton, M.D., President of the Bombay Medical Board [son of the Rev. James Orton of Hawkeswell, co. York], *b*. 20 Ap. 1784; *d*. Feb. 1856; *and had issue* 1*g* to 4*g*.
  1*g*. Reginald Orton of Sunderland, Surgeon, *b*. 27 Jan. 1810; *d*. 1 Sept. 1862; *m*. 1st, 4 Oct. 1836, Caroline Agnes, da. of Orton Bradley-Bradley, *d*. (—); 2ndly, 25 Mar. 1841, Mary Isabella, da. of Turner Thompson; *and had issue* (*with others who d.s.p.*) 1*h* to 4*h*.
    1*h*.[1] Reginald Orton, *settled in New Zealand*, *b*. 22 Mar. 1839; *d*. 9 July 1895; *m*. 2 Dec. 1865, Jeannie (*The Bungalow, Pleasant Point, Timaru, Canterbury, N.Z.*), da. of S. Manson; *and had issue* 1*i* to 11*i*.
      1*i*. Reginald Orton (*Geraldine, N.Z.*), *b*. 11 Sept. 1866; *m*. 17 June 1889, Rachel, da. of W. Ashby; and has issue 1*j*.
        1*j*. Isabella Jean Orton, *b*. 13 Oct. 1890.

[Nos. 42519 to 42550.

# of The Blood Royal

2*i*. Malcolm Orton, Huntsman (*Claremont, Canterbury, N.Z.*), *b.* 21 July 1871; *m.* 1891, Louisa, da. of W. Cookson; and has issue 1*j* to 6*j*.[1]

1*j*. Reginald Hunter Orton, *b.* 29 Dec. 1900.
2*j*. Malcolm Manson Orton, *b.* 21 June 1902.
3*j*. Kenneth Orton, *b.* 21 Aug. 1904.
4*j*. Stella Orton, *b.* 28 Aug. 1891.
5*j*. Korita Orton, *b.* 16 Sept. 1897.
6*j*. Erica Linda Orton, *b.* 15 Feb. 1899.

3*i*. *Bruce Orton*, b. 10 *Jan*. 1877; d. 1906; m. 1896, (—), *da. of J. Brosnahaw; and had issue* (*with a da.* d. *young*) 1*j* to 2*j*.

1*j*. Hilda Orton, *b.* 13 July 1897.
2*j*. Beatrice Orton, *b.* 3 Jan. 1906.

4*i*. Allan Orton (*Cook Street, Heathcote Valley, Christchurch, N.Z.*), *b.* 17 Jan. 1884; *m.* 11 Sept. 1905, Robina, da. of J. Reid; and has issue (3 children).[1]

5*i*. Caroline Agnes Orton, *m.* 27 Dec. 1893, T. Mee (*Claremont, Timaru, N.Z.*); and has issue (with 2 others[1]) 1*j* to 2*j*.

1*j*. Wellesley Thomas Mee, *b.* 13 Aug. 1894.
2*j*. Alexander Reginald Mee, *b.* 2 Oct. 1896.

6*i*. Marion Jeanne Orton, *m.* 28 Dec. 1892, Farquhar Macdonald (*Ashburton, N.Z.*); and has issue 1*j* to 3*j*.

1*j*. Allan Farquhar Macdonald, *b.* 19 Oct. 1893.
2*j*. Reginald Orton Macdonald, *b.* 5 July 1895.
3*j*. John William Macdonald, *b.* 8 Nov. 1898.

7*i*. Bessie Anne Orton, *m.* W. White (*Kaikoura, N.Z.*); and has issue 1*j* to 3*j*.

1*j*. Leo Orton White, *b.* 20 Mar. 1898.
2*j*. Una Katherine White, *b.* 30 Dec. 1900.
3*j*. Zeta Marion White, *b.* 5 June 1905.

8*i*. Mabel Ada Orton, *m.* 9 Ap. 1902, Holford Whittaker (*Hamilton, North Island, N.Z.*); and has issue 1*j*.

1*j*. Orton Whittaker, *b.* 6 Dec. 1906.

9*i*. Jeannette Mary Orton, *m.* 1907, Francis Edwin Lamb, Architect (78 *Church Street, Masterton, North Island, N.Z.*).

10*i*. Linda Ethel Orton, *m.* 2 Oct. 1905, John Nixon (*Waitomo Caves, North Island, N.Z.*); and has issue (2 children).[1]

11*i*. Cora Evelina Modlin Orton, *m.* 19 Dec. 1906, Alfred Andrew Sutherland Hintz (*Nelson, N.Z.*); and has issue (1 child).[1]

2*h*.[1] Caroline Anne Orton, *m.* 28 Sept. 1858, Robert Modlin of Sunderland, M.R.C.S., *formerly* 17th Lancers; and has issue 1*i*.

1*i*. Barbara Bessie Orton Modlin, *m.* 29 Mar. 1897, Percy Bayley of Beacon Hill, Brede, co. Sussex; and has issue 1*j*.

1*j*. Cicely Conyers Bayley, *b.* 20 Feb. 1898.

3*h*.[2] Emma Catherine Orton, *m.* 14 Nov. 1877, Edward Sawer (*Isleworth*); and has issue 1*i* to 3*i*.

1*i*. Edward Reginald Sawer, Civil Service (*Buluwayo*).
2*i*. Katharine Mary Sawer.
3*i*. Rose Hilda Sawer.

4*h*.[2] *Ada Orton*, b. 21 *Nov.* 1853; d. 28 *Oct.* 1896; m. *Ernest Reynolds* (*Marere,* 12 *Wanganui Avenue, Ponsonby, Auckland, New Zealand*); *and had issue* 1*i* to 3*i*.

1*i*. Ernest Orton Reynolds (*Chicago*), *b.* 6 Oct. 1886.
2*i*. Reginald Hugh Reynolds, *b.* 13 Nov. 1890.
3*i*. Violet Mary Reynolds, *m.* 10 Mar. 1910, Leslie Radmall of Chingford, co. Essex (*Canada*). [Nos. 42551 to 42586.

---

[1] See Appendix.

The Plantagenet Roll

2g. *Annie Inman Orton*, b. 27 Oct. 1816; d. 11 Nov. 1898; m. *in Bombay 6 Dec.* 1837, *Col. Samuel Hennell, H.E.I.C.S., sometime H.B.M.'s Resident, Persian Gulf*, b. 6 *July* 1799; d. 13 *Sept.* 1880; *and had issue (with others* d.s.p.) 1h.

1h. Arthur Reginald Hennell, Lieut.-Col. (ret.) *formerly* 1st Batt. Hants Regt. (*Jenniscombe, Tiverton, S. Devon*), b. at Bushire 27 Mar. 1849; *m.* 27 Mar. 1879, Frances Elizabeth, da. of John Phillips of Winsley Hall, co. Salop; and has issue (with a son *d.* young) 1*i* to 8*i*.

1*i*. Arthur Samuel Hennell, b. 29 Oct. 1884.
2*i*. Frederick John Hennell, b. 12 May 1888.
3*i*. James Reginald Hennell, b. 5 Jan. 1891.
4*i*. Edward Biscoe Hennell, b. 21 Nov. 1893.
5*i*. Frances Annie Emily Hennell.
6*i*. Kathleen Rosa Hennell.
7*i*. Lucy Ada Hennell.
8*i*. Mary Edith Hennell.

3g. *Emma Orton*, d. 25 *Sept.* 1889; m. *as 2nd wife,* 11 *Ap.* 1839, *Col. Bruce Seton, H.E.I.C.S.* [*3rd son of Sir Alexander Seton of Abercorn,* 5*th Bt.* [S. 1663]], d. 27 Nov. 1876; *and had issue* 1h *to* 5h.

1h. *Alexander Reginald Seton, Lieut.-Col. R.E.*, b. 25 *May* 1840; d. 12 Nov. 1887; m. 18 *Sept.* 1862, *Emma Elizabeth* (see p. 321) (156 *Croydon Road, Anerley, S.E.*), *da. of Major William Loch,* 1*st Bombay Lancers; and had issue* 1*i to* 6*i*.

1*i*. Bruce Gordon Seton, Heir-presumptive to the Baronetcy [S. 1663], Major Indian Med. Ser. and Sec. to the Director-Gen. Indian Med. Ser., has Medal for the Waziristan Exp. 1894/5 (severely wounded) and Tochi Field Force (1897) (*East India United Service*), b. 13 Oct. 1868; *m.* 16 Mar. 1895, Ellen Mary, da. of Lieut.-Col. Frank Armstrong; and has issue 1*j* to 4*j*.

1*j*. Alexander Hay Seton, b. 14 Aug. 1904.
2*j*. Bruce Lovat Seton, b. 22 May 1909.
3*j*. Jean Gordon Seton.
4*j*. Marie de Seton Seton.

2*i*. Charles Monteath Seton, Admiralty Victualling Dept., Sydney (*Royal Naval Yard, Sydney, N.S.W.*), b. 30 Mar. 1880.

3*i*. Walter Warren Seton, M.A. (Lond.), is Sec. Univ. College, Gower Street, W.C. (*University College Hall, Ealing*), b. 4 Oct. 1882.

4*i*. Katharine Marion Seton (*Glenrose, Croydon Road, Anerley, S.E.*).

5*i*. Elsie Madeleine Seton, *m.* 8 May 1901, Algernon James Pollock (*Brackley, Charlton Road, Weston-super-Mare*); and has issue 1*j* to 3*j*.

1*j*. Erskine Reginald Seton Pollock, b. 1 Jan. 1905.
2*j*. Alan Winton Seton Pollock, b. 30 June 1907.
3*j*. Aileen Marion Seton Pollock.

6*i*. Aileen Mary Seton, *m.* 22 Sept. 1899, Frank Binford Hole (*The Mount, Edgefield, Melton Constable, Norfolk*); and has issue 1*j*.

1*j*. Bruce Binford Hole, b. 24 Jan. 1901.

2h. *Bruce Outram Seton, Lieut.-Col. R.E.*, b. 7 *May* 1841; d. 29 *July* 1901; m. 21 *July* 1880, *Louisa Harriet Manderson, da. of Dep. Surg.-Gen. Charles Thomas Paske*, d. 31 *Mar.* 1886; *and had issue* 1*i to* 3*i*.

1*i*. Evelyn Seton, *m.* 1 Oct. 1902, Major Percy Molesworth Sykes, C.M.G., Indian Army, *formerly* 2nd Dragoon Guards (*British Consulate-Gen., Meshed, Persia*); and has issue 1*j* to 3*j*.

1*j*. Arthur Frank Seton Sykes, b. 1903.
2*j*. Charles Mortimer Sykes, b. 1907.
3*j*. Edward Molesworth Sykes, b. 10 Jan. 1910.

2*i*. Ruth Mary Seton, *m.* 15 Feb. 1905, Marmaduke Brian Sunderland, son of Lieut.-Col. Sunderland of Ravensden Grange, Beds; and has issue 1*j* to 2*j*.

1*j*. Bridget Mary Sunderland.
2*j*. Phyllis Joan Sunderland. [Nos. 42587 to 42616.

of The Blood Royal

3*i*. Violet Adela Seton, *m*. 18 May 1904, Charles Henry Seton (see below) (*Heath House, Aston-on-Clun, Salop*); and has issue 1*j* to 2*j*.

1*j*. Christopher Bruce Seton, *b*. 3 Oct. 1909.

2*j*. Joyce Phœbe Seton.

3*h*. Charles Compton Seton, *formerly* Lieut. R.E. (*Heath House, Hopton Heath, Salop*), *b*. 24 July 1846; *m*. 30 July 1868, Phœbe Elizabeth, da. of Sir Henry William Ripley, 1st Bt. [U.K.]; and has issue 1*i* to 2*i*.

1*i*. Charles Henry Seton (*Heath House, Aston-on-Clun, Salop*), *b*. 28 Ap. 1869; *m*. 18 May 1904, Violet Adela (see above), da. of Lieut.-Col. Bruce Seton; and has issue.

See above, Nos. 42618–42619.

2*i*. Margaret Annie Phœbe Seton, *m*. 12 Oct. 1898, Capt. Arthur Pelham Frankland, D.S.O. [2nd son of Lieut.-Col. Sir William Adolphus Frankland, 9th Bt. [E. 1660], R.E.] (*Culford House, Felixstowe*); and has issue 1*j* to 2*j*.

1*j*. Marion Annie Margaret Frankland.

2*j*. Rosalind Lucy Seton Frankland.

4*h*. Henry James Seton, Major *formerly* 2nd Batt. Royal Irish Rifles, served in S. Africa 1899 (Medal with 2 Clasps) (*Crutchfield, Walton-on-Thames*), *b*. 27 Aug. 1854; *m*. 1st, 6 Dec. 1888, Elizabeth, da. of Henry James Byron [B. Byron Coll.], *d*. 2 Sept. 1897; 2ndly, 3 May 1899, Marie Bowles, da. of Percy Hale Wallace of Belfast; and has issue 1*i*.

1*i*. Marie Seton, *b*. 20 Mar. 1910.

5*h*. Emma Alice Seton, *d*. 10 Jan. 1884; *m. as 1st wife*, 18 July 1876, Henry Ripley, J.P. [4th son of Sir Henry William Ripley, 1st Bt. [U.K.], M.P.] (*Ashley Manor, Cheltenham*); and had issue 1*i* to 3*i*.

1*i*. Henry Edward Ripley, *b*. 6 Jan. 1884.

2*i*. Dorothy Alice Seton Ripley.

3*i*. Marian Janet Ripley, *m*. 14 Jan. 1899, Thomas Herbert Littlejohn of Hampstead, F.R.C.S., Edin. [son of Sir Henry Littlejohn of Edinburgh]. *d*. 4 Sept. 1905.

4*g*. Catherine Orton, *b*. 30 Ap. 1821; *d*. 11 June 1904; m. 31 Aug. 1841, m. Col. William Loch, 1st Lancers, Indian Army, d. 19 Nov. 1860; *and had issue* 1*h* to 4*h*.

1*h*. William Loch, Col. *in the Army and Political Resident at Khakmandu*, *b*. 8 Nov. 1846; *d*. 8 Aug. 1901; *m*. 1st *at Calcutta*, 6 Mar. 1876, *Edith Mary, da. of the Hon. James Gibbs, I.C.S., Member of the Viceregal Council*, d. 12 May 1898; 2ndly, 8 Nov. 1899, Grace, da. of Major Sir George Wingate, K.C.S.I., R.E.; *and had issue* 1*i* to 2*i*.

1*i*. Percy Gordon Loch, in the Foreign Office at Baghdad, *b*. 14 Jan. 1887; *unm*.

2*i*. Kenneth Morley Loch, Cadet at Woolwich, *b*. 16 Sept. 1891.

2*h*. Frederick Phayre Loch (*Harker Lodge, Carlisle*), *b*. 21 July 1857; *m*. Feb. 1886, Georgina, da. of Charles Burn, C.E.; and has issue 1*i* to 3*i*.

1*i*. Charles William Loch, M.E. (*Lawless, West Australia*), *b*. 12 Feb. 1887; *m*. 16 June 1908, Mary Elizabeth, da. of the Rev. Canon Deed, D.D.

2*i*. Frederick Sydney Loch (*Kirndeem, Culcairn, N.S.W.*), *b*. 24 Jan. 1889.

3*i*. Eric Erskine Loch, Cadet at Sandhurst, *b*. 1901.

3*h*. Emma Elizabeth Loch (156 *Croydon Road, Annerly, S.E.*), *m*. 18 Sept. 1862, her cousin, Lieut.-Col. Alexander Reginald Seton, R.E., *d*. 12 Nov. 1887; and has issue.

See p. 320, Nos. 42596–42609.

4*h*. Katharine Annie Louise Loch, *m*. 5 Oct. 1868, the Hon. Sir George Edward Knox, a Judge of the High Court of Judicature of the United Provinces of India and formerly a Member of Bengal Council (*River View, Allahabad*); and has issue 1*i* to 7*i*. [Nos. 42617 to 42653.

The Plantagenet Roll

1*i*. Stuart George Knox, Major Indian Army, now Political Agent at Koweit on the Persian Gulf, *b.* 7 Oct. 1869; *m.* 15 Mar. 1893, Ethel, da. of the Right Hon. Sir John Edge, P.C.; and has issue 1*j* to 2*j*.

1*j*. Stuart George Edge Inman Knox, *b.* 27 Nov. 1896.

2*j*. John Knox, *b.* 26 Sept. 1904.

2*i*. Ernest Francis Knox, Major Indian Army, *b.* 27 July 1871.

3*i*. Robert Welland Knox, I.M.S., *b.* 6 Sept. 1873; *m.* 31 Dec. 1900, Lilian, da. of Col. John Loch, Bengal Cavalry; and has issue 1*j*.

1*j*. Esme Margaret Knox.

4*i*. Kenneth Nevill Knox, I.C.S., *b.* 21 July 1878.

5*i*. Gordon Daniell Knox, Assist. Editor *Times of India* (*Bombay*), *b.* 10 July 1880.

6*i*. Katharine Margaret Knox, *m.* 16 Nov. 1898, the Rev. Percy Hugh Chapman, M.A., LL.D., Chaplain at Bareilly (*Bareilly, U.P., India*); and has issue (with a son, Kenneth Hugh, *d.* young) 1*j* to 2*j*.

1*j*. Winifred Margaret Chapman.

2*j*. Janet Marion Chapman.

7*i*. Angel Dorothy Knox, *m.* 17 Nov. 1908, Spencer Pelham Flowerdew, A.M.I.C.E., Indian State Railways; and has issue 1*j*.

1*j*. George Douglas Hugh Flowerdew, *b.* 12 Jan. 1910.

4*b*. Dorothy Peirse, m. *Thomas Stillington of Kelfield, co. York.*

6*a*. Elizabeth Hutton, *b.* at Richmond 14 Mar. 1638.

7*a*. Othy Hutton, bapt. 8 Nov. 1642.   [Nos. 42654 to 42666.

187. Descendants, if any surviving, of the Hon. URSULA DARCY (Table XX.), *d.* (–); *m.* JOHN STILLINGTON of Kelfield, co. York, *d.* 1658; and had issue (with 3 elder sons and a da. who *d. unm.*) 1*a* to 5*a*.[1]

1*a*. *Thomas Stillington of Kelfield, aged 36, 22 Mar.* 1665; m. *Dorothy, da. of Joseph Micklethwayte of York, M.D,; and had issue* 1*b* to 2*b*.

1*b*. *Thomas Stillington, aged 6 months, 22 Mar.* 1665.

2*b*. *Ursula Stillington.*

2*a*. *Margaret Stillington,* m. *the Rev. John Shaw of Rotheram, co. York.*

3*a*. *Mary Stillington,* m. *William Drake of Barnoldswicke-Cotes, co. York.*

4*a*. *Olive Stillington.*

5*a*. *Ursula Stillington,* m. *George Tolson of Stakes, co. York.*

188. Descendants, if any, of the Hon. MARGARET DARCY (Table XX.), *d.* (–); *m.* Sir THOMAS HARRISON.

189. Descendants of the Hon. DOROTHY DARCY (Table XX.) *d.* (–); *m.* JOHN DALTON of Hawkswell, co. York, *bapt.* 17 Sept. 1603; *d.* of wounds received while conducting the Queen from Burlington to Oxford, *bur.* in York Minster 26 July 1644; and had issue 1*a* to 6*a*.

1*a*. *Sir William Dalton of Hawkswell,* d. 23 *Mar.* 1675; m. *Elizabeth, da. of Sir Marmaduke Wyvill, 2nd Bt.* [*E.*]; *and had issue.*

See Exeter Volume, pp. 563-564, Nos. 50255-50274.   [Nos. 42667 to 42686.

---

[1] Foster's "Visitation of York."

# of The Blood Royal

2a. *Thomas Dalton of York, and afterwards of Bedale, admon.* 10 *July* 1710; m. (*Lic. dated* 16 *Mar.*) 1665, *Anne, da. of Sir Marmaduke Wyvill*, 2nd *Bt.* [*E.*], bur. 28 *Nov.* 1675; *and had issue.*
See the Exeter Volume, p. 564, Nos. 50275–50680.

3a. *Mary Dalton,* d. 1674; m. *as* 2nd *wife, John Beverley of Great Smeaton, co. York,* d. 7 *Oct.* 1680; *and had issue* [1] 1b *to* 6b.

    1b. *John Beverley, aged* 9, 19 *Aug.* 1665.
    2b. *Thomas Beverley.*
    3b. *Dorothy Beverley, aged* 11, 19 *Aug.* 1665.
    4b. *Elizabeth Beverley.*
    5b. *Mary Beverley.*
    6b. *Anne Beverley.*

4a. *Barbara Dalton,* d. (-); m. *Charles Tancred of Arden, co. York, High Sheriff for that co.* 1694; *and had issue* (24 *children of whom* [2]) 1b *to* 18b.

    1b. *Henry Tancred.*

    2b. *William Tancred of Arden,* d. (-); m. *Elizabeth, da. and co-h. of Thomas Carter, Lord Mayor of York; and had issue* 1c *to* 5c.

        1c. *Charles Tancred of Arden,* d. (-); m. *about* 28 *June* 1734, *Barbara, da. of the Rev. Darcy Dalton, Rector of Aston; and had issue.*
        2c. *Thomas Tancred.*
        3c. *William Tancred,* bapt. (?) *at Belfrey's, York,* 25 *Nov.* 1694.
        4c. *Henry Tancred.*
        5c. *Barbara Tancred,* m. *William Stables of Pontefract.*

    3b. *Charles Tancred.*
    4b. *Jordan Tancred,* m. (—), *da. of* (—) *Holland.*
    5b. *John Tancred.*
    6b. *Charles Tancred.*
    7b. *James Tancred,* m. *Catherine, da. of* (—) *Sutherland.*
    8b. *Francis Tancred,* m. *Catherine, da. of* (—) *Blitheman.*
    9b. *Christopher Tancred.*
    10b. *Richard Tancred.*
    11b. *Thomas Tancred.*
    12b. *Nicholas Tancred.*
    13b. *Dorothy Tancred.*
    14b. *Elizabeth Tancred.*
    15b. *Dorothy Tancred.*
    16b. *Barbara Tancred,* m. *the Rev. William Ellesley, Rector of Ryther.*
    17b. *Jane Tancred,* m. *John Warcop of Gatenby.*
    18b. *Dorothy Tancred,* m. *William Warwick of Aiscough.*

5a. *Dorothy Dalton.*
6a. *Ursula Dalton.* [Nos. 42687 to 43092.

190. Descendants of KATHERINE BEST (Table XX.), m. before Oct. 1683, EDWARD GODDARD of Leatherhead, co. Surrey; and had issue 1a to 2a.

1a. *Edward Goddard,* m. 27 *Nov.* 1705, *Elizabeth, widow of* (—) *Place of Richmond, da. of* (—); *and had issue.* [3]

2a. *Katherine Goddard,* d. (-); m. *at Gilling,* 31 *Jan.* 1705, *Henry Darcy of Coburn Manor, and afterwards of Sedbury, co. York; and had issue.*
See pp. 308–310, Nos. 41900–41947. [Nos. 43093 to 43140.

---

[1] "Visitation of York," by Sir William Dugdale, 1665, Surtees Soc. Pub. xxxvi. 35.
[2] Foster's "Yorkshire Pedigrees."   [3] Foster's "Yorkshire Families."

The Plantagenet Roll

191. Descendants of WILLIAM MOLINEUX, Mayor of Doncaster 1721 [Bt. of Teversal Coll.] (Table XX.), b. 1681; d. 1756; m. KATHERINE, widow of William Squire of Doncaster, da. of Richard SHEPHERD of the same place; and had issue 1a to 2a.

1a. Darcy Molineux of Leeds, Merchant, d. 1789; m. and had issue 1b to 4b.
1b. Sir Darcy Molineux, 8th Bt. [E. 1611] on the death of his remote kinsman, 9 June 1812; d.s.p. 1816.
2b. William Molineux, d.s.p. 1813.
3b. Elizabeth Molineux, m. Edward Gray.
4b. Isabella Molineux, m. John Holgate.
2a. Elizabeth Molineux, b. 1714.

192. Descendants of JOHN MOLINEUX of Mansfield, co. Notts, and Wolverhampton, co. Stafford [Baronet of Teversal Coll.] (Table XX.), d. 1754; m. MARY, da. of Richard BIRCH of Wolverhampton, d. 1735; and had issue (with a son, William, who d. young, 1726) 1a to 8a.

1a. Thomas Molineux of Wolverhampton, b. 17 Mar. 1704; d. about 25 Aug. 1791; m. at St. Paul's Cathedral, London, Margaret, da. of (—) Gisborne, d. 25 Aug. 1791; and had issue 1b to 3b.
1b. John Molineux of Wolverhampton, b. 14 May 1736; d. 28 Ap. 1785; m. Margaret, widow of (—) Walker of Wolverhampton, da. of (—); and had issue 1c to 2c.
1c. Sarah Gisborne Molineux, d. Oct. 1831; m. Isaac Scott of Wolverhampton; and had issue a da., Margaretta, who d. unm. 9 June 1852.
2c. Mary Anne Molineux, m. John Lingard of Wolverhampton; and had issue (with a younger da. d. unm.) 1d to 2d.
1d. John Lingard.
2d. Sarah Gisborne Lingard, m. Charles S. Stokes of Murrell's End, Newent, co. Gloucester; and had issue.[1]
2b. Richard Molineux, d. 1784; m. Mary (see p. 328), da. of Benjamin Molineux of Wolverhampton; and had issue 1c to 3c.
1c. Mary Ann Molineux, d. (–); m. James Clutterbuck of Hyde House, co. Gloucester, J.P., D.L. [younger brother of Lewis Clutterbuck of Ford House, Wolverhampton].
2c. Caroline Molineux, d. (–); m. Robert Hodgson [son of Brian Hodgson of Swinscoe, co. Stafford]; and had issue 1d to 3d.
1d. Robert Molineux Hodgson of Paris, d. at Versailles 26 July 1876.
2d. Caroline Hodgson.
3d. Ellen Hodgson.
3c. Elizabeth Molineux, m. Thomas Brooke.

3b. Thomas Gisborne Molineux of London, Merchant, d. 13 May 1807; m. Mary, da. of (—) Brice; and had issue 1c to 2c.
1c. Francis Molineux of London, Merchant, Lieut. London Vol. 1803; b. 14 Sept. 1785; d. 15 Mar. 1852; m. 13 Oct. 1819, Sarah, d. of Joseph Molineux of Lewes, Banker (see p. 326); and had issue 1d to 3d.

---

[1] One of their granddaughters, Ada, m. 23 Feb. 1881, William Joshua, eldest son of William Goulding of Summer Hill, Cork, M.P. for that city 1877.

of The Blood Royal

1*d.* Gisborne Molineux, Hon. Sec. of the Canada Coy., and one of the founders and Fellow and Member of Council of the Royal Colonial Institute, author of "Memoir of the Molineux Family," 1882, d.s.p.
  2*d.* Francis Molineux, d. unm. 1850.
  3*d.* Mary Elizabeth Molineux.
 2*c.* Anne Molineux, m. 13 Nov. 1803, *Josiah Rhodes of London, Merchant, Capt. London Vol.;* and had issue 1*d.*
  1*d.* Mary Anne Rhodes, m. *William Fawcett of Yarm-on-Tees, co. York, Solicitor;* and had issue.[1]
 2*a.* Richard Molineux of Cateaton (now Gresham) Street, London, a Common Councilman for the Cripplegate Ward, d. 1762; m. *Sarah, da. of Zachary Gisborne,* d. 1770; and had issue 1*b.*
  1*b.* Mary Molineux, d. (–); m. 24 *June* 1750, *Capt. George Barber of Somerford Hall, Brewood, co. Stafford,* d.s.p.
 3*a.* John Molineux of Gainsborough, co. Linc., m. *Elizabeth, da. of (—) Wass;* and had issue 2 das. whose issue is extinct.
 4*a.* Joseph Molineux of Lewes, co. Sussex, Receiver-Gen. of Stamps and Taxes 1745-1764, b. 1713; d. 1771; m. *Ann, da. of William Brett of Lewes, M.D.,* d. 1782; and had issue (with 2 sons and 2 das. who d.s.p.) 1*b* to 2*b.*
  1*b.* Joseph Molineux of Lewes, Banker, b. 7 *Mar.* 1754; d. 1813; m. 2· *Dec.* 1777, *Elizabeth, da. of Thomas West of Southover, Lewes,* d. 20 *July* 1815; and had issue (with 2 sons and 2 das. who d. young) 1*c* to 7*c.*
   1*c.* George Molineux of Isfield and Lewes, Banker, J.P., b. 17 *Mar.* 1791; d. 27 *Jan.* 1855; m. 1815, *Frances Ann, da. of Thomas Ramsay of London;* and had issue (with 3 sons and a da.) 1*d* to 5*d.*
    1*d.* George Molineux of Isfield, J.P., b. 6 *Aug.* 1816; d. 20 *Jan.* 1893; m. 1st, 2 Oct. 1840, *Maria Ann, da. and h. of the Rev. Joseph Hurlock, M.A.,* d. 11 *Mar.* 1875; and had issue 1*e* to 6*e.*
     1*e.* George Fitzherbert Molineux, b. 27 Aug. 1841; *unm.*
     2*e.* Rev. Charles Hurlock Molineux, Vicar of Staveley and Canon of Southwell (*Staveley Vicarage, Chesterfield, Derby*), b. 28 Oct. 1842; *unm.*
     3*e.* Philip Horace Molineux (*Malling House, Lewes*), b. 12 Aug. 1844; *unm.*
     4*e.* Rev. Arthur Ellison Molineux, M.A., Vicar of Minster (*Minster Vicarage, Ramsgate*), b. 5 Feb. 1846; m. 16 July 1874, Eleanor Margaret, da. of Matthew Bell of Bourne Park, co. Kent, J.P.; and has issue 1*f* to 2*f.*
      1*f.* Agnes Irene Molineux.
      2*f.* Evelyn Margaret Molineux.
     5*e.* Harold Parminter Molineux of Isfield, J.P., Major *formerly* Essex Regt. (*The Cottage, Isfield, Sussex; Mornington, Eastbourne*), b. 16 Ap. 1850; m. 4 Jan. 1881, Rosa Eugenie Katharine, da. of Henry King of Isfield Place, J.P.; and has issue 1*f* to 5*f.*
      1*f.* George King Molineux, 2nd Lieut. 5th Fusiliers, b. 15 Ap. 1887.
      2*f.* Henry Gisborne King Molineux, b. 9 May 1891.
      3*f.* Dorothy Eugénie Molineux.
      4*f.* Katharine Augusta Molineux, m 7 Ap. 1910, Lieut.-Com. Harold Ernest Sulivan, R.N.
      5*f.* Annie Rosa Molineux.
     6*e.* Mildred Constance Molineux.
    2*d.* Joseph Molineux, b. 3 *June* 1818; d. 1876; m. 20 *Oct.* 1857, *Caroline, da. of the Rev. E. Symons, Rector of Ringmer;* and had issue several das.
    3*d.* Henry Molineux, b. 23 July 1830.   [Nos. 43141 to 43154.

---
[1] William Rhodes, the eldest son, of The Grange, Stainton in Cleveland, m. Rosalie, da. of Claude de Queiros of Calcutta. Marianne, the second da., m. Anthony Temple of Kington, co. Hereford, son of the Rev. W. S. Temple of Daisdale, co. Durham.—"Memoirs of the Molineux Family," p. 67.

The Plantagenet Roll

4d. *Frances Molineux*, b. 11 *May* 1821; d. 16 *Nov*. 1868; m. 22 *July* 1840, her cousin, *Job Smallpeice of Field Place, Compton, co. Surrey*, d. 21 *May* 1875; *and had issue* (see Appendix).

5d. *Cordelia Molineux*, b. 28 *Jan*. 1827; d. 20 *July* 1895; m. *Jan*. 1853, *Joseph Ewart of Manchester, Merchant [Cadet of Craigcleuch]*, b. 1807; d. 1861; *and had issue* (with a son, Russell, d. unm. 19 Nov. 1900) 1e to 3e.

    1e. Ernest Molineaux Ewart, b. 6 Nov. 1853; *unm*.
    2e. Emily Frances Ewart (*India*), *unm*.
    3e. *Marianne Ramsay Ewart*, b. 20 *Dec*. 1856; d. 5 *April* 1901; m. 6 *Dec*. 1888, *Henry James Richardson*; *and has issue* 1f.
        1f. Gulielma Ewart Richardson, b. 20 Nov. 1890.

2c. *Elizabeth Molineux*, b. 1779; d. (–); m. *C. Chitty of Lewes*.

3c. *Cordelia Molineux*, b. 1780; d. 1859; m. *Job Smallpeice of Northbrook, co. Surrey*, d. 1842; *and had issue* (with 2 sons and 3 das. d. unm.) 1d to 4d.

1d. *Job Smallpeice of Field Place, Compton, co. Surrey*, b. c. 1808; d. 21 May 1875; m. 22 *July* 1840, *Frances, da. of George Molineux of Isfield and Lewis*, d. 16 *Nov*. 1868; *and had issue* (see above).

2d. *Mark Smallpeice of Guildford*, b. 29 *Dec*. 1812; d. 29 *Sept*. 1901; m. 1839, *Alicia, da. of Heathfield Young of Dorking*, d. 15 *June* 1903; *and had issue* (with 2 sons and 2 das. d. unm.) 1e to 6e.

    1e. *Ferdinand Smallpeice* (*Cross Lanes, Guildford*), b. 14 July 1843; *m*. 13 May 1875, Mary Jane, da. of William Haydon Smallpeice of Guildford; *and has issue* 1f.
        1f. *Ferdinand William Smallpeice* (*Browning's Down, Guildford*), b. 27 May 1877; *m*. 7 June 1904, Cecilia Mary Delves [descended from the Lady Anne, sister of King Edward IV. (see Exeter Volume, p. 224)], da. of Col. John Delves Broughton [Bt. Coll.]; and has issue 1g to 2g.
            1g. Cecilia Lucy Smallpeice, b. 29 June 1905.
            2g. Rosemary Anstice Smallpeice, b. 18 Aug. 1909.
    2e. Humphry Smallpeice (*Guildford*), b. 5 Dec. 1848; *unm*.
    3e. Stanley Smallpeice (*Haslemere*), b. Feb. 1852; *m*. and has issue (1 da.).
    4e. James Smallpeice (*Guildford*), b. July 1854; *m*. and has issue (4 das.).
    5e. Alice Smallpeice, *unm*.
    6e. Grace Smallpeice, *unm*.

3d. *Frederick Smallpeice*, d. *April* 1855; m. *Maria, da. of* (—) *Keen;* *and had issue* (4 das.).

4d. *Emma Smallpeice*, d. (–); m. 1852, *James Ward;* *and had issue* (with a da. d. unm.) 2 sons (both m., one having a son and 2 das., the other a da.) and 3 das., of whom one is m. and has 2 sons.

4c. *Sarah Molineux*, b. 1783; d. 16 *Ap*. 1854; m. 13 *Oct*. 1819, *Francis Molineux of London, Merchant*, d. 15 *Mar*. 1852; *and had issue*. See p. 324.

5c. *Jane Molineux*, b. 1786; d. (–); m. *Joseph Browne of Holcombe House, co. Glouc*.

6c. *Maria Molineux*, b. 1789; d. (–); m. *Henry Sparkes of Shalford and Summerberry, co. Surrey; and had issue* 1d.

1d. *Maria Sparkes*, d.s.p. 4 *Sept*. 1863; m. *as 1st wife*, 19 *June* 1860, *Sir John Charles Kenward Shaw, 7th Bt.* [E.], d.s.p.

7c. *Grace Molineux*, b. 1793; d. (–); m. *William Browne of Minchinhampton, co. Gloucester*.

2b. *Elizabeth Molineux*, d. (–); m. *A. Verrall of Lewes*.

5a. *Benjamin Molineux of Molineux House, Wolverhampton, Banker*, d. 1772; m. *Elizabeth, da. of George Fieldhouse*, d. (–); *and had issue* 1b to 3b.

1b. *George Molineux of Wolverhampton, Banker and Iron Merchant, J.P. and High Sheriff co. Stafford* 1791, d. 22 *Sept*. 1820; m. *Jane, da. of* (—) *Robinson*, d. (–); *and had issue* (with 5 younger sons and 3 das. who all d.s.p.) 1c.

[Nos. 43155 to 43167.

# of The Blood Royal

1c. Rev. George Fieldhouse Molineux, M.A., Rector of Ryton and Preb. of St. Peter's, Wolverhampton, J.P., d. 30 Sept. 1840; m. Maria, da. of William Hardman of Manchester, d. 1858; and had issue (with 4 sons and 4 das. who d.s.p.) 1d to 4d.

1d. Rev. William Hardman Molineux, Rector of Elmsett, co. Suffolk, b. 1801; d. 11 May 1864; m. 12 Oct. 1852, Elizabeth, da. of Edward Pemberton of Plas Isas, co. Flint, J.P.; and had issue 1e to 2e.

1e. William Pemberton Molineux (Ashby Hall, Great Yarmouth), b. 23 Oct. 1853; m. Anna, da. of Robert Kidman; and has issue 1f.

1f. William Francis Pemberton Molineux, b. 24 Jan. 1899.

2e. Rev. George Edward Francis Molineux, M.A. (Trinity Coll., Dublin), Vicar of Colyton (Colyton Vicarage, Devon), b. 15 Ap. 1855; m. 23 Sept. 1890, Ada Louisa, da. of the Rev. Sackville Hamilton Berkeley; and has issue 1f to 6f.

1f. George Berkeley Molineux, b. 16 Mar. 1903.
2f. Laurence Peile Molineux, b. 10 Aug. 1908.
3f. Constance Hamilton Molineux.
4f. Mabel Elizabeth Sackville Molineux.
5f. Frances Mary Pemberton Molineux.
6f. Muriel Berkeley Molineux.

2d. Charles Edward Molineux of Oakley Penkridge, co. Stafford, J.P., b. 1810; d. 3 Nov. 1880; m. 17 Mar. 1845, Jane, da. of Orson Bidwell of Albrighton, co. Salop, d. 5 Ap. 1902; and had issue 1e.

1e. Mary Jane Molineux, m. 25 Ap. 1867, Frederick John Staples-Browne of Brashfield House, J.P., Bar.-at-Law (Brashfield House, Bicester; The Elms, Bampton, Oxford); and has issue 1f to 2f.

1f. Richard Charles Staples-Browne, M.A. (Camb.), b. 29 June 1881; m. 17 Feb. 1909, Sylvia Maud, da. of Sir Charles Philip Huntington, 1st Bt. [U.K.], M.P. (14 Harrington Gardens, S.W.).

2f. Mary Frederica Staples-Browne.

3d. Thomas Molineux of Beechfield, Bowden, co. Chester, Silk Spinner, b. 16 May 1807; d. 3 June 1855; m. 24 Jan. 1839, Mary, da. of William Lomas of Manchester, d. 30 Jan. 1851; and had issue (with 2 sons and a da. who d. unm.) 1e to 4e.

1e. George William Molineux (Betchworth House, Chideock, Bridport, Dorset), b. 25 Dec. 1848; m. 29 Sept. 1883, Edith, da. of John Eddowes Bowman, d. 8 Aug. 1909.

2e. Emily Molineux, b. 15 Oct. 1840; d. 7 June 1901; m. 3 Feb. 1874, the Rev. John Barratt Fawssett, M.A., Rector of Laughton (Glebe Avenue, Enfield); and had issue 1f to 3f.

1f. Richard Maurice Fawssett (Pinewoods, Ash, Surrey), b. 11 May 1875; m. 30 Aug. 1904, Sybil Wentworth, da. of the Rev. Henry Allen Steel; s.p.

2f. John Leonard Fawssett, b. 1 Mar. 1877; unm.

3f. Francis William Fawssett, M.B. (London) (260 Fore Street, Upper Edmonton, N.), b. 14 Oct. 1878; m. 21 Ap. 1904, Mildred Evelyne, da. of the Rev. Edward Pole Williams; and has issue 1g.

1g. Evelyne Mary Helen Fawssett, b. 23 Mar. 1905.

3e. Alice Mary Molineux, m. 29 July 1869, the Rev. John Trew, B.A. (Trinity Coll., Dublin), Vicar of Drighlington (Drighlington Vicarage, near Bradford); and has issue (with a son who d. young) 1f to 4f.

1f. John M'Cammon Trew, b. 1 Ap. 1870.
2f. Basil Molineux Trew, b. 18 Aug. 1885.
3f. Laura Mary Trew, m. 30 Jan. 1897, William Towler (Gildersome, Yorks); and has issue (with a da. d. young) 1g to 2g.

1g. Eric William Towler, b. 28 Ap. 1900.
2g. Cyril John Towler, b. 20 Feb. 1907.
4f. Mary Trew, unm.
4e. Fanny Molineux, unm.

[Nos. 43168 to 43192.

The Plantagenet Roll

4*d*. *Harriet Molineux*, b. 18 *Aug*. 1811; d. *Ap*. 1880; m. 12 *Sept*. 1844, *Thomas Lomas of Manchester*, b. 20 *Oct*. 1798; d. *Oct*. 1870; *and had issue* 1*e*.

1*e*. *George Henry Lomas*, b. 24 *Aug*. 1848; d. 24 *Oct*. 1906; m. 14 *Aug*. 1873, *Margaret Elizabeth*, da. *of John Courtney Bluett of Gray's Inn, Bar.-at-Law; and had issue* 1*f* to 3*f*.

1*f*. Alfred Lomas, M.D. (*Ashfield House, Castleton, near Manchester*), b. 21 May 1874; m. 2 Oct. 1902, Alice Winifred, da. of Frederick Price of Highfield, Sale, co. Chester, Solicitor; *s.p.*

2*f*. Harold Lomas, b. 14 Sept. 1875; m. 25 Aug. 1901, Virginia Washington, da. of Gen. Wager Swayne of New York, and Shinnecock, Long Island; and has issue 1*g* to 2*g*.

1*g*. Virginia Washington Lomas, b. at Washington 7 Mar. 1904.

2*g*. Elaine Margaret Lomas, b. at Baltimore 15 Ap. 1906.

3*f*. Ethel Mary Lomas, m. 28 Oct. 1905, Henry Cort Harold Carpenter, M.A. (Oxon.), Ph.D. (Leipzig); *s.p.*

2*b*. *Sarah Molineux*, d. (–); m. *Lewis Clutterbuck of Ford House*.

3*b*. *Mary Molineux*, d. (–); m. *Richard Molineux of Wolverhampton, Banker*, d. 1784; *and had issue*.
See p. 324.

6*a*. *Anne Molineux*.
7*a*. *Mary Molineux*.
8*a*. *Elizabeth Molineux*. [Nos. 43193 to 43197.

193. Descendants of LUCIUS CHARLES (CARY), 7th VISCOUNT FALKLAND [S.] (Table XX.), *d*. 27 Feb. 1785; *m*. 1st, 6 Ap. 1734, JANE, widow of James Fitzgerald, Lord Villiers, da. of Richard BUTLER of London, Conveyancer, *d*. in France 20 Dec. 1751; and had issue 1*a* to 5*a*.

1*a*. *Lucius Ferdinand Cary, Master of Falkland, Commander of the British Forces in Tobago*, d. there v.p. 20 *Aug*. 1780; m. *Mar*. 1760, *Anne*, da. *of Col. Charles Leith; and had issue* 1*b* to 6*b*.

1*b*. *Henry Thomas (Cary), 8th Viscount Falkland* [S.], b. 27 Feb. 1766; d. *unm*. 22 May 1796.

2*b*. *Charles John (Cary), 9th Viscount Falkland* [S.], *Capt. R.N.*, b. Nov. 1768; d. *of wounds received in a duel* 2 *Mar*. 1809; m. 25 *Aug*. 1802, *Christiana*, da. *of* (—) *Anton*, d. 25 *July* 1822; *and had issue* 1*c* to 3*c*.

1*c*. *Lucius Bentinck (Cary), 10th Viscount Falkland* [S.], 1st *Baron Hunsdon* [U.K.], P.C., b. 5 Nov. 1803; d.s.p.s. 12 *Mar*. 1884.

2*c*. *Plantagenet Pierrepoint (Cary), 11th Viscount Falkland* [S.], *Adm. R.N.*, b. 8 *Sept*. 1806; d.s.p. 1 *Feb*. 1886.

3*c*. *Hon. Byron Charles Ferdinand Plantagenet Cary, Capt. R.N.*, b. 5 Oct. 1808; d. 21 Feb. 1874; m. 19 Feb. 1844, *Selina Mary*, da. *of the Rev. Francis Fox of Fox Hall, co. Longford*, d. 10 Aug. 1868; *and had issue* 1*d* to 4*d*.

1*d*. Byron Plantagenet (Cary), 12th Viscount Falkland and a Rep. Peer [S.], J.P., D.L., Lieut.-Col. and Hon. Col. (ret.) 4th Batt. Yorkshire Regt., *formerly* Royal Sussex Regt. (26 *Upper Grosvenor Street, S.W.; Carlton, Marlborough, &c.*), b. 3 Ap. 1845; m. 25 Sept. 1879, Mary, a Lady of Grace of St. John of Jerusalem in England, da. of Robert Reade of New York; and has issue 1*e* to 6*e*.

1*e*. Lucius Plantagenet Cary, Master of Falkland, Capt. Grenadier Guards, served in South Africa 1900–1902 (139 *St. James' Court, Buckingham Gate, S.W.*), b. 23 Sept. 1880; m. 6 Ap. 1904, Ella Louise, da. of E. W. Catford; and has issue 1*f* to 2*f*.

1*f*. Lucius Henry Charles Plantagenet Cary, b. 25 Jan. 1905.

2*f*. Byron Plantagenet Cary, b. 28 June 1908. [Nos. 43198 to 43201.

# of The Blood Royal

2e. Hon. Byron Plantagenet Cary, Lieut. R.N., b. 25 Jan. 1887.
3e. Hon. Philip Plantagenet Cary, b. 24 Sept. 1895.
4e. Hon. Catherine Mary Cary.
5e. Hon. Mary Selina Cary.
6e. Hon. Letice Cary.

2d. Hon. Emma Amelia Cary, had Royal Warrant as a Viscount's da. 29 Sept. 1886, m. 8 Mar. 1869, Thomas Benyon Ferguson, Bar.-at-Law, d. 12 Nov. 1875; and has issue 1e to 2e.

1e. Annie Selina Emma Ferguson, m. 1898, Hugh Wyndham Montgomery, *formerly* 17th Lancers.
2e. Edith Nora Ferguson.

3d. Hon. Selina Catherine Cary, had Royal Warrant as a Viscount's da. 29 Sept. 1886, m. 27 Sept. 1877, Charles Edward Fox, Bar.-at-Law, Master of Equity, High Court of Bombay, d. 6 Nov. 1897; and had issue 1e to 3e.

1e. Agnes Selina Fox.
2e. Dorothy Fox.
3e. Catherine Mary Fox, m. 16 July 1908, Capt. Alexander Adams, *late* R.E. (*Kingston, Canada*).

4d. Hon. Annie Christina Cary, had Royal Warrant as a Viscount's da. 29 Sept. 1886; m. June 1898, Capt. Servante Morland, 7th Batt. Rifle Brig. (*Hextle House, near Tonbridge, Kent*).

3b. *Charlotte Maria Cary*, b. Nov. 1764; d. (-); m. *Samuel Charters; and had issue.*
4b. *Lucia Cary*, d. (? s.p.); m. *at Calcutta* 10 *Jan.* 1783, *Major John Grattan, 100th Regt., Adj.-Gen. to the Forces in India.*
5b. *Lavinia Matilda Cary.*
6b. *Hon. Emelia Sophia Cary, had Royal Warrant as a Viscount's da.* 1834; m. 1798, *Major Charles Thomas Grant of Grant.*

2a. Hon. *Mary Elizabeth Cary*, b. 1738; d. 1 *Oct.* 1783; m. *the Ven. John Law, D.D., Archdeacon of Rochester,* d. 5 *Feb.* 1827, *aged* 88.
3a. Hon. *Frances Cary.*
4a. Hon. *Mary Cary.*
5a. Hon. *Charlotte Cary*, m. *June* 1799, *Anthony Chapman.*

[Nos. 43202 to 43214.

194. Descendants, if any, of DOROTHY MOLINEUX (Table XX.), d. (-); m. TOBET HODGSON of Bishop Burton, co. York.

195. Descendants, if any surviving, of the Hon. MARY DARCY (Table XX.), m. ACTON BURNELL of Winkburn Hall, co. Notts; and had issue. Their apparently last surviving descendant 1a.

1a. *D'Arcy Burnell of Winkburn Hall*, d.s.p. *leaving his estates to his widow, who* d. 1874, *when they passed to his distant relative, Peter Pegge, afterwards Pegge-Burnell of Beauchief Abbey, co. Derby.*[1]

196. Descendants of Lady ELIZABETH CLIFFORD (Table VIII.), d. (-); m. 1533, Sir CHRISTOPHER METCALFE of Nappa, co. York, J.P., b. c. 1513; d. 1574; and had issue 1a to 2a.

1a. *James Metcalfe of Nappa*, b. c. 1554; d. 1580; m. *Joan, da. of John Savile of Stanley, co. York; and had issue* 1b.

---
[1] Burke's " Landed Gentry."

The Plantagenet Roll

1b. *Sir Thomas Metcalfe of Nappa*, b. c. 1579 ; d. 26 July 1650/5 ; m. *Elizabeth*, da. of *Sir Henry Slingsby of Scriven ;* and had issue.
See pp. 72-74, Nos. 9115-9381.

2a. *Margaret Metcalfe*, m. *as 2nd wife, George Middleton of Leighton*, co. Lanc., b. 1522 ; d. (-) ; *and had issue (with 2 other sons and 3 das.)* 1b.

1b. *Thomas Middleton of Leighton Hall*, d. (-) ; m. *Katharine*, sister of *Sir Richard Hoghton*, 1st Bt. [E.], da. of *Thomas Hoghton of Hoghton Tower*, co. Lanc. ; *and had issue (with 8 das.)* 1c to 2c.

1c. *Sir George Middleton of Leighton*, 1st Bt. [E.], so cr. 24 June 1642, b. 1600 ; d. 27 Feb. 1673 ; m. 1st, *Frances*, da. and h. of *Richard Rigg of Little Strickland ;* and had issue 1d.

1d. *Mary Middleton of Leighton*, da. and h., d. (-) ; m. *Somerford Oldfield of Somerford*, co. Chester, aged 35, 14 Sept. 1663 ;[1] *and had issue* 1e to 6e.

1e. *George Somerford (Middleton] Oldfield of Leighton and Somerford, which latter he sold*, b. 1660, *being aged* 3, 14 *Sept.* 1663 ; d. (-) ; m. (?) *Lady Clarke ;* and had issue 1f.

1f. [da.] *Oldfield of Leighton*, da. and event. sole h., m. *Albert Hodgson*, j.u. of *Leighton*, attainted for his share in the '15, *living* 1740 ;[2] *and had issue* 1g to 2g.

1g. *Anne Hodgson of Leighton*, d.s.p. ; m. *Charles Townley of Townley*.

2g. *Mary Hodgson*, d.s.p. ; m. 1737, *Ralph Standish of Standish*.

2e. *Anne Oldfield*.
3e. *Mary Oldfield*.
4e. *Elizabeth Oldfield*.
5e. *Catherine Oldfield*.
6e. *Frances Oldfield*.

2c. *Robert Middleton*, d. (-) ; m. *Jane*, da. and co-h. of *Thomas Kitson of Warton ;* and had issue (who resided until recently at Warton in very reduced circumstances.[3] *One of his sons)* 1d.

1d. (—) *Middleton*, m. *and had (with possibly other) issue* 1e *to* 2e.

1e. *Robert Middleton, Mariner*, d. 1699, *leaving issue a large family*.

2e. *Margaret Middleton*, m. *Thomas Booker, Gent. ;* and had (with possibly other) issue 1f.

1f. *Robert Booker of Broughton*, m. *and had issue* 1g.

1g. *Margaret Booker*, da. and h., m. *Robert Preston* [son of *Richard Preston of Cockerham*]. [Nos. 43215 to 43481.

197. Descendants, if any surviving, of the Hon. JOSCELINE PERCY (Table II.), *d.* 8 Sept. 1532 ; *m.* MARGARET, da. of Walter FROST of Fetherstone, co. York, *d.* 15 Nov. 1530 ; and had issue 1*a*.

1a. *Edward Percy of Beverley*, b. c. 1524 ; d. 22 Sept. 1590 ; bur. at *St. Mary's Church, Beverley ;* m. *Elizabeth*, da. of *Sir Thomas Waterton of Walton*, J.P., bur. at *St. Mary's afsd.* 14 *Dec.* 1607, *aged* 89 ; *and had (with other) issue*[4] 1b *to* 4b.

1b. *Alan Percy of Beverley*, M.P. 1603 ; b. 1560 ; d. 1632 ; m. 1589, *Mary*, da. of *Ralph Moore of Beswick in Holderness ;* and had issue (with 4 sons, *Henry* (son and h., d. c. 1590-1), *Jasper, Alan*, and *Francis*, known to have d.s.p.) 1c to 3c.

1c. *Josceline Percy of Beverley*, d. 1653 ; m. *Elizabeth*, da. of *William Fitzwilliam of Maplethorpe*, co. Linc. ; *and had issue* 1d to 4d.

1d. *Alan (Percy)*, de jure 12*th Earl of Northumberland* [E.] *on the death of his remote kinsman the* 11*th Earl*, 21 *May* 1670, d.s.p. 1688 ; *will dated* 1687.

2d. *John Percy*.
3d. *Charles Percy, living* 1652, *fate unknown*.

---

[1] Ormerod's " Cheshire," iii. 60. [2] Burke's " Extinct Baronetcies," p. 354.
[3] Ibid. [4] See Appendix.

# of The Blood Royal

4d. *Eleanor Percy*, m. *William Farrand of West Hall, near Addingham, co. Yorks.*[1]

2c. *Edward Percy*, b. 1594; d. 27 Aug. 1630; bur. *at Petworth.*

3c. *Frances Percy*, m. *Ralph Elleker of Risby Park, co. York; and had issue now extinct.*[2]

2b. *Thomas Percy, Constable of Alnwick and Auditor to the 9th Earl of Northumberland, one of the Conspirators in the Gunpowder Plot, killed at Holbeach 1605; m. Martha, da. of Robert Wright of Holderness, co. York; and had issue (with a da., Elizabeth, d. young at Alnwick 1602) 1c to 2c.*

1c. *Robert Percy.*

2c. [*da.*] *Percy*, m. *Robert Catesby of Ashley Legers, co. Northants, son of the Conspirator.*[3]

3b. *Ellen Percy*, m. *Ralph Moore of Beswicke in Holderness; and had issue.*[4]

4b. [*da.*] *Percy*, m. *John Berney of Dale Bank, co. York.*[5]

198. Descendants of HENRY (STAFFORD), 1st Lord Stafford [E.] (Table XXI.), b. 18 Sept. 1501; d. 30 Ap. 1563; m. 1518, the Lady URSULA, da. of Sir Richard POLE, K.G. [by his wife Margaret (Plantagenet), *suo jure* Countess of Salisbury [E.]], d. 12 Aug. 1570; and had issue.

See the Clarence Volume, Table LXVII. *et seq.*, and pp. 537-646, Nos. 22808-31936. [Nos. 43482 to 52610.

199. Descendants of THOMAS (HOWARD), 21st or 14th EARL OF ARUNDEL, EARL OF SURREY, and EARL MARSHAL [E.], K.G. (Table XXI.), b. 7 July 1585; d. at Padua 26 Sept. 1646; m. 1606, Lady ALŒTHEA, *suo jure* (1681) Lady FURNIVAL (1295), STRANGE of Blackmere (1309) and Talbot (1331) [E.], da. and event. sole h. of Gilbert (TALBOT), 7th Earl of Shrewsbury [E.], &c., d. 24 May 1654; and had issue.

See the Exeter Volume, Table XVIII. and pp. 291-292, Nos. 11740-14581. [Nos. 52611 to 55452.

200. Descendants of FREDERICK AUGUSTUS (HERVEY), 4th EARL OF BRISTOL [G.B.], and Lord Hervey (1799), 5th Lord Howard de Walden [E.], Bishop of Derry [I.] (Table XXI.), b. 1 Aug. 1730; d. at Albano, near Rome, 8 July 1803; m. 10 Aug. 1752, ELIZABETH, da. and event. h. of Sir James DAVERS, 3rd Bt. [E.], d. 15 Dec. 1800; and had issue 1a to 3a.

1a. *John Augustus Hervey, Lord Hervey*, b. 1 Jan. 1757; d.v.p. 10 Jan. 1796; m. 4 Oct. 1779, *Elizabeth, da. of Colin Drummond of Quebec*, d. 4 Sept. 1818; *and had issue* 1b.

1b. Hon. *Elizabeth Catherine Caroline Hervey*, b. 1 Aug. 1780; d. 21 Jan. 1803; m. 2 Aug. 1798, *Charles Rose (Ellis), 1st Baron Seaford* [U.K.], so cr. 15 July 1826; b. 19 Dec. 1771; d. 1 July 1845; *and had issue 1c to 2c.*

---

[1] Brydge's "Collins," ii. 303.
[2] Brenan's "House of Percy." Collins says James, 2nd son of Ralph Elleker.
[3] Ibid.   [4] Ibid. Omitted by Collins.
[5] Brydge's "Collins," ii. 303. Omitted by Brenan.

The Plantagenet Roll

1c. Charles Augustus (Ellis), 6th Baron Howard de Walden [E.] in suc. to his great-grandfather, and 2nd Baron Seaford [U.K.], G.C.B., K.T.S., b. 5 June 1799; d. 29 Aug. 1868; m. 8 Nov. 1828, Lady Lucy [descended from King Henry VII. (see Tudor Roll, p. 245)], da. and event. co-h. of William Henry (Cavendish-Bentinck), 4th Duke of Portland [G.B.], &c., d. 29 July 1899; and had issue 1d to 3d.

1d. Frederick George (Ellis), 7th Baron Howard de Walden [E] and 3rd Baron Seaford [U.K.], b. 9 Aug. 1830; d. 3 Nov. 1899; m. 27 Ap. 1876, Blanche, da. and co-h. of William Holden of Palace House, co. Lanc. [re-m. 2ndly, 25 Mar. 1903, Henry Ladlow (Lopes), 2nd Baron Ludlow [U.K.]; and had issue 1e.

1e. Thomas Evelyn (Ellis), 8th Baron Howard de Walden [E.] and 4th Baron Seaford [U.K.], and a co-h. to the Barony of Ogle [E. 1461], Capt. 2nd County of London Yeo., formerly 10th Hussars (Kilmarnock; Audley End, Saffron Walden; Seaford House, 37 Belgrave Square, S.W.), b. 9 May 1880.

2d. Rev. the Hon. William Charles Ellis, M.A. (Oxon.), Rector of Bothal-with-Hebburn (Bothalhaugh, Morpeth), b. 22 July 1835; m. 16 Dec. 1873, Henrietta Elizabeth, da. of Henry Metcalfe Ames of Linden; and has issue 1e to 6e.

1e. Henry Guysulf Bertram Ellis, b. 7 Mar. 1875.

2e. Humphrey Cadogan Ellis, b. 21 Jan. 1879.

3e. Francis Bevis Ellis, b. 17 Ap. 1883.

4e. Roland Arthur Ellis, b. 7 June 1884.

5e. Lucy Henrietta Katharine Ellis, m. 28 July 1908, William Brabazon Lindesay (Graham-Toler), 4th Earl of Norbury [I.] (Carlton Park, Market Harborough).

6e. Henrietta Christobel Ellis.

3d. Hon. Evelyn Henry Ellis, late R.N. (Rosenau, near Datchet; 35 Portland Place, W.), b. 9 Aug. 1843; m. 9 Mar. 1882, Albertha Mary (p. 333), da. of Gen. the Hon. Sir Arthur Edward Hardinge, K.C.B., C.I.E.; and has issue 1e to 2e.

1e. Arthur Evelyn Paul Ellis, b. 27 Ap. 1894.

2e. Mary Ellis.

2c. Hon. Augustus Frederick Ellis, Lieut.-Col. 60th Rifles, M.P., b. 17 Sept. 1800; d. 16 Aug. 1841; m. 25 June 1828, Mary Frances Thurlow, da. of Sir David Cunynghame, 5th Bt. [S.] [re-m. 2ndly, William, Baron von Munster and] d. 12 Sept. 1851; and had issue 1d to 5d.

1d. Charles David Cunynghame Ellis, Major 60th Rifles, b. 25 July 1833; d. 5 Dec. 1906; m. 17 Nov. 1859, Emily (Pebbles Court, Holyport, Maidenhead), da. of Major-Gen. Sir Guy Campbell, 1st Bt. [U.K.], C.B.; and had issue 1e to 4e.

1e. Augustus Frederick Guy Ellis (Fort George Penn, Annotta Bay, Jamaica; Stanford Wood, Bradfield, Berks), b. 10 Dec. 1868; m. 10 Jan. 1899, Mary Agnes, widow of the Hon. E. G. Levy, da. of the Hon. Henry Westmorland, both of Jamaica.

2e. Mary Pamela Ellis (Larkfield, Holyport Road, Maidenhead), m. as 2nd wife, 2 July 1889, Col. David Milne-Home of Wedderburn, D.L., late R.H.G., d. 19 Nov. 1901; and has issue 1f.

1f. Charles Alexander Milne-Home, b. 25 Ap. 1891.

3e. Helen Louisa Georgina Ellis, m. 16 Ap. 1885, James Grahame Stewart (Stonewall, Edenbridge, Kent); and has issue 1f to 2f.

1f. John Cecil Graham Stewart, b. 1897.

2f. Felicia Louise Marie Stewart.

4e. Lucy Emily Madeline Ellis (Pebbles Court, Holyport, Maidenhead).

2d. Sir Arthur Edward Augustus Ellis, G.C.V.O., C.S.I., G.C.D., Major-Gen. Grenadier Guards, Equerry to H.M. the King and Comptroller in Lord Steward's Dept. 1901-1907, b. 13 Dec. 1837; d. 11 June 1907; m. 2 May 1864, the Hon. Mina Frances (29 Portland Place, W.), da. and co-h. of Henry (Labouchere), 1st Baron Taunton [U.K.]; and had issue 1e to 7e.

1e. Henry Arthur Augustus Ellis, a Clerk in the House of Commons, b. 13 Feb. 1866. [Nos. 55453 to 55471.

# of The Blood Royal

2c. Gerald Montagu Augustus Ellis, Capt. (ret.) Rifle Brigade, *formerly* a Page of Honour to Queen Victoria, served in India 1897-1898 (Medal with Clasps) and in S. Africa 1899-1901 (Medal with 5 Clasps), b. 13 Sept. 1872.

3c. Mary Evelyn Ellis, m. 17 Dec. 1885, Ralph Sneyd of Keele [descended from King Henry VII. (see Supplement to Essex Volume, p. 476] (*Keele Hall, Newcastle-under-Lyme*).

4c. Albertha Lilian Magdalen Ellis, for whom H.M. King Edward was Sponsor.

5c. Alexandra Mina Ellis, for whom H.M. Queen Alexandra was Sponsor, m. 4 Nov. 1899, Sir Arthur Hardinge, K.C.B., K.C.M.G., H.B.M.'s Minister at Brussels (see below) (*British Legation, Brussels; Bencombe, Dursley, Glouc.*); and has issue 1f.

1f. Henry Arthur Mina Hardinge, b. 1 Oct. 1904.

6c. Evelyn Mary Ellis, m. 22 June 1898, Walter William Kerr [M. of Lothian Coll. and a descendant of King Henry VII. (see Tudor Roll, p. 168)].

7c. Dorothy Ellis, m. 10 Aug. 1899, Charles Theodore Halswell Kemeys-Tynte of Cefn Mably and Halswell (*Cefn Mably, Cardiff, &c.*); and has issue 1f.

1f. Elizabeth Dorothy Kemeys-Tynte (same as Nos. 28553-28554, p. 184).

3d. Mary Georgiana Frances Ellis, a Woman of the Bedchamber to H.M. Queen Alexandra when Princess of Wales, 1865-1901, m. 30 Dec. 1858, Gen. the Hon. Sir Arthur Edward Hardinge, K.C.B., C.I.E., G.C.D. [Vt. Hardinge Coll.], d. 15 July 1892; and has issue 1e to 3e.

1e. Sir Arthur Henry Hardinge, K.C.B., K.C.M.G., H.B.M.'s Minister to the Court of Brussels, *formerly* at Teheran (*British Legation, Brussels; Bencombe, Dursley, Glouc.*), b. 12 Oct. 1859; m. 4 Nov. 1899, Alexandra Mina (see above), da. of Sir Arthur Edward Augustus Ellis, G.C.V.O., &c. ; and has issue 1f.

1f. Henry Arthur Mina Hardinge, b. 1 Oct. 1904 (same as No. 55476, above).

2e. Albertha Mary Hardinge, m. 9 Mar. 1882, the Hon. Evelyn Henry Ellis (*Rosenau, near Datchet, &c.*); and has issue.

See p. 332, Nos. 55462-55463.

3e. Hon. Mary Ellis, *formerly* Maid of Honour to Queen Victoria, m. 17 July 1894, Major Ivone Kirkpatrick, S. Staffordshire Regt., and an A.D.G. in India.

4d. Annie Eliza Margaret Ellis (5 *Piazza Madonna degli Aldobrandini, Florence*), m. 13 June 1859, Col. Sir Charles Edward Mansfield, K.C.M.G., *formerly* H.B.M.'s Minister and Consul-Gen. at Lima [younger brother of William Rose, 1st Baron Sandhurst [U.K.], G.C.B.], d. 1 Aug. 1907; and has issue 1e to 3e.

1e. John Charles Ellis Mansfield, a Pasha and Major-Gen. in the Egyptian Army (*Cairo*), b. 8 Aug. 1860; m. 20 Oct. 1889, Lina Marie Eugenie, da. of Alexander Lulistoff; and has issue 1f.

1f. John Charles Mansfield, b. 21 Sept. 1890.

2e. Frederick Henry Edward Mansfield (*Rhodesia, S. Africa*), b. 4 Nov. 1864; m. 1904, Kate, da. of Stephen Dorey of Wool, co. Dorset.

3e. Mildred Mary Blanche Mansfield.

5d. Augusta Louisa Caroline Ellis, a Lady-in-Waiting to H.I. and R.H. the Dow.-Duchess of Saxe-Coburg-Gotha (Duchess of Edinburgh) (*The King's Cottage, Kew*), m. 25 Dec. 1861, Debonnaire John (Monson), 8th Baron Monson [G.B.], C.V.O. [descended from Anne, Duchess of Exeter], d. 18 June 1900; and has issue.

See the Exeter Volume, p. 243, Nos. 9109-9115.

2a. *Frederick William* (*Hervey*), 5th Earl [G.B.] *and* (30 *June* 1826) 1*st Marquis of Bristol* [U.K.], 5*th Lord Hervey* [E.], *&c., F.R.S.*, b. 2 Oct. 1769; d. 15 Feb. 1859; m. 20 Feb. 1798, *the Hon. Elizabeth Albana, da. of Clotworthy* (*Upton*), 1*st Baron Templetown* [I.], d. 25 May 1844; *and had issue* 1b *to* 8b.

1b. *Frederick William* (*Hervey*), 2*nd Marquis* [U.K.] *and* 6*th Earl* [G.B.] *of Bristol, and* 6*th Baron Hervey* [E.], b. 15 *July* 1800; d. 30 *Oct.* 1864; m. 9 *Oct.*
[Nos. 55472 to 55500.

The Plantagenet Roll

1830, Lady Katherine Isabella [*descended from King Henry VII.*], da. of John (Manners), 5*th Duke of Rutland* [E.], K.G., d. 20 *Ap.* 1848; *and had issue.*
See the Tudor Roll, pp. 296-297, Nos. 25460-25479.

2*b*. Lord William Hervey, C.B., b. 27 *Sept.* 1805; d. 6 *May* 1850; m. 8 *Sept* 1844, *Cecilia Mary*, da. *of Vice-Adm. Sir Thomas Fremantle*, G.C.B., d. 24 *Nov.* 1871; *and had issue* 1c *to* 3c.

1*c*. Sir George William Hervey, K.C.B., Sec. and Comptroller-Gen. of the National Debt (*Finchley House, Finchley; Carlton, &c.*), b. 16 June 1845; m. 9 Feb. 1881, Emily Dora [descended from George, Duke of Clarence, K.G. (see the Clarence Volume, p. 176)], da. of Lord Charles Pelham Clinton [D. of Newcastle Coll.]; and has issue 1*d* to 4*d*.

1*d*. Gerald Edward William Hervey, *formerly* Lieut. Suffolk Regt., b. 5 Dec. 1881.

2*d*. Philip Henry Charles Hervey, b. 13 Jan. 1883.

3*d*. Eric George Hervey, b. 6 Dec. 1884.

4*d*. Claude Arthur Hervey, b. 16 Mar. 1891.

2*c*. Francis Arthur Hervey, b. 11 *Mar.* 1849; d. 13 *Jan.* 1905; m. 1 *June* 1876, *Louisa Maude* (*Hedgerley, Esher*), *da. of Richard Rice Clayton of Hedgerley Park, co. Bucks; and had issue* 1*d to* 3*d.*

1*d*. Richard George Hervey, Lieut. R.N., b. 17 July 1879.

2*d*. Alec Francis Hervey, b. 8 Oct. 1885.

3*d*. Lionel Arthur Hervey, b. 24 June 1889.

3*c*. Augusta Elizabeth Hervey (12 *Moore Street, Cadogan Square, S.W.*).

3*b*. Right Rev. Lord Arthur Charles Hervey, Lord Bishop *of Bath and Wells* 1869-1894, b. 20 *Aug.* 1808; d. 9 *June* 1894; m. 30 *July* 1839, *Patience*, da. *of John Singleton*, d. 14 *Dec.* 1904; *and had issue* 1c *to* 8c.

1*c*. Rev. John Frederick Arthur Hervey, M.A. (Camb.), Rector of Shotley and a C.A. Suffolk (*Shotley Rectory, Ipswich*), b. 11 Nov. 1840; m. 22 Ap. 1885, Emily, da. of Thomas Ely; and has issue 1*d* to 4*d*.

1*d*. Arthur Charles Constantine Hervey, b. 18 Dec. 1886.

2*d*. Margaret Caroline Hervey.

3*d*. Mary Edith Emily Hervey.

4*d*. Patience Gertrude Hervey.

2*c*. George Henry William Hervey (*Church House, Tendring, Essex*), b. 17 Feb. 1843; m. 1st, 13 July 1876, Emma, da. of William Arkwright of Sutton Scarsdale, co. Derby, d. 29 Ap. 1877; 2ndly, 3 July 1879, Mary, da. of William Wells Cole, d. 21 Aug. 1900; and has issue 1*d* to 5*d*.

1*d*. Douglas George Hervey, b. 3 Ap. 1880.

2*d*. Gerald Arthur Hervey, B.A. (Camb.), b. 3 Oct. 1881.

3*d*.[1] Gwendolen Emma Hervey.

4*d*.[2] Geraldine Mary Hervey.

5*d*.[2] Eveline Victoria Hervey.

3*c*. Rev. Sydenham Henry Augustus Hervey, *formerly* Vicar of Wedmore (*Angel Hill, Bury St. Edmunds*), b. 20 Dec. 1846; *unm.*

4*c*. Constantine Rodney William Hervey, *late* Col. R.A. (*Thurston Cottage, Bury St. Edmunds*), b. 6 Dec. 1850; m. 12 Aug. 1886, Mary Frances, da. of William Hanford Flood of Flood Hall and Farmley, co. Kilkenny; and has issue 1*d*.

1*d*. Alice Lucy Patience Hervey.

5*c*. Rev. James Arthur Hervey, Rector of Chipstead (*Chipstead Rectory, Surrey*), b. 26 Sept. 1854; m. 15 July 1886, Margaret Augusta, da. of Sir Robert Percy Douglas, 4th Bt. [G.B.]; and has issue 1*d*.

1*d*. Thomas Arthur Percy Hervey, b. 23 July 1887.

6*c*. Katherine Patience Georgiana Hervey (*Purbrook Park, Cosham, Hants*),

[Nos. 55501 to 55546.

of The Blood Royal

m. 9 Ap. 1872, Charles Hoare [descended from King Henry VII. (see the Tudor Roll, p. 273)], *d.* 30 Mar. 1898; and had issue 1*d* to 7*d*.

1*d*. Charles Hervey Hoare, Capt. Glamorgan Imp. Yeo. (*Hockridge, Cranbrook, Kent*), *b.* 16 Dec. 1875; *m.* 1909, Marie, widow of Sir Lepel Henry Griffin, K.C.S.I., da. of Ludwig Leupold of La Coronato, Genoa.

2*d*. Arthur Hervey Hoare, *b.* 25 July 1877.

3*d*. Guy Hervey Hoare, *b.* 16 Oct. 1879.

4*d*. Reginald Hervey Hoare, 3rd Sec. Dip. Ser., *b.* 1882.

5*d*. Patience Mary Hoare.

6*d*. Constance Sarah Hoare.

7*d*. Katherine Angela Adeleza Hoare.

7*c*. Patience Mary Hervey, *m.* 17 July 1873, Charles Rowland Palmer Morewood of Alfreton, J.P., D.L., High Sheriff co. Warwick 18— (*Alfreton Park, Derby; Ladbroke Hall, Southam; 66 Queen's Gate, S.W.*); and has issue 1*d* to 2*d*.

1*d*. Rowland Charles Arthur Palmer-Morewood, J.P. (*Ladbroke Hall, Southam, co. Warwick*), *b.* 9 Jan. 1879.

2*d*. Clara Winifred Sarah Palmer, *m.* 27 Ap. 1905, Alwyne Mason [eldest son of Robert Harvey Mason of Necton Hall] (*Necton Hall, Norfolk*).

8*c*. Caroline Augusta Hervey (*The Grove, Alfreton*).

4*b*. *Rev. Lord Charles Amelius Hervey*, D.D., *b.* 1 Nov. 1814; *d.* 11 *Ap.* 1880; *m.* 15 *Aug.* 1839, *Lady Harriet Charlotte Sophia* [*descended from King Henry VII.*], *da. of Dudley* (*Ryder*), *1st Earl of Harrowby* [*U.K.*], *d.* 25 *Sept.* 1899; *and had issue.*

See the Tudor Roll, p. 526, Nos. 35149–35173.

5*b*. *Lord Alfred Hervey*, M.P., *and a Lord of the Treasury, &c.*, *b.* 25 *June* 1816; *d.* 15 *Ap.* 1875; *m.* 5 *Aug.* 1845, *Sophia Elizabeth* (see p. 451), *da. of Lieut.-Gen. John Chester Bagot* [*Bt. Coll.*], *d.* 20 *Sept.* 1892; *and had issue* 1*c to* 3*c*.

1*c*. Rev. Frederick Alfred John Hervey, C.V.O., M.A. (Camb.), Canon of Norwich and Domestic Chaplain and Chaplain-in-Ordinary to H.M. King Edward, &c., *formerly* Rector of Sandringham and Chaplain to Queen Victoria (*The Close, Norwich*), *b.* 18 May 1846; *m.* 13 Oct. 1881, Mabel Elizabeth [descended from King Henry VII. (see the Tudor Roll, p. 466)], da. of Major-Gen. Augustus Frederick Francis Lennox [D. of Richmond and Lennox Coll.]; and has issue 1*d*.

1*d*. Alexandra Leila Hervey, for whom H.M. Queen Alexandra stood Sponsor.

2*c*. Algernon Charles George Hervey (*Church Walk House, Hunstanton*), *b.* 28 Sept. 1851; *unm.*

3*c*. Mary Frederica Sophia Hervey (22 *Morpeth Mansions, S.W.*).

6*b*. *Lady Augusta Hervey*, *b.* 29 Dec. 1798; *d.* 17 *Mar.* 1880; m. *as 2nd wife*, 18 *Sept.* 1832, *Frederick Charles William Seymour* [*M. of Hertford Coll.*], *d.* 7 *Dec.* 1856; *and had issue.*

See the Clarence Volume, p. 137, Nos. 1810–1807 and 1810–1814.

7*b*. *Lady Georgiana Elizabeth Hervey*, *d.* 16 *Jan.* 1869; *m. as 1st wife*, 12 *July* 1836, *Rev. the Hon. John Grey* [*E. Grey Coll.*], *d.* 11 *Nov.* 1895; *and had issue.*

See the Essex Volume, p. 183, Nos. 24013–24014.

8*b*. *Lady Sophia Elizabeth Caroline Hervey*, *b.* 26 *Ap.* 1811; *d.* 30 *Sept.* 1863; *m.* 1st, 18 *July* 1835, *William Howe Windham of Felbrigg Hall, co. Norfolk*, *d.* 22 *Dec.* 1855; 2ndly, 10 *May* 1858, (—) *Giubilio.*

3*a*. *Lady Mary Caroline Hervey*, *d.* 10 *Jan.* 1842; *m. as 2nd wife*, 22 *Feb.* 1776, *John* (*Creichton*), *1st Earl of Erne* [*I.*], P.C., *d.* 15 *Sept.* 1828; *and had issue* 1*b*.

1*b*. *Lady Caroline Elizabeth Mary Creichton*, *b.* 1778; *d.* 23 *Ap.* 1856; *m.* 30 *Mar.* 1799, *James Archibald* (*Stuart-Wortley-Mackenzie*), *1st Baron Wharncliffe* [*U.K.*], *d.* 19 *Dec.* 1845; *and had issue.*

See the Exeter Volume, pp. 297–298, Nos. 14808–14882.

[Nos. 55547 to 55675.

The Plantagenet Roll

201. Descendants of the Hon. LEPEL HERVEY (Table XXI.), b. Jan. 1723; d. 11 Mar. 1780; m. 26 Feb. 1743, CONSTANTINE (PHIPPS), 1st BARON MULGRAVE [I.], bapt. 22 Aug. 1722; d. 13 Sept. 1775; and had issue.

See the Exeter Volume, Table XII., and pp. 236-237, Nos. 8448-8702.
[Nos. 55676 to 55930.

202. Descendants of the Hon. MARY HERVEY (Table XXI.), b. 1726; d. 9 Ap. 1815; m. 31 Oct. 1745, GEORGE FITZGERALD of Turlough, co. Mayo, Capt. in the Austrian Service, d. 23 June 1782; and had issue 1a to 2a.

1a. George Robert FitzGerald of Turlough, d. (-); m. 1st (settl. dated 10 Feb.), 1770, Jane, da. of the Right Hon. William Conolly of Castletown, co. Kildare [by his wife Lady Anne, née Wentworth], d. 1780; and had issue 1b.

1b. Mary Anne FitzGerald.

2a. Charles Lionel FitzGerald of Turlough, Lieut.-Col. N. Mayo Militia, d. 29 Ap. 1805; m. 1777, Dorothea, da. of Sir Thomas Butler, 6th Bt. [I.], M.P., d. 11 Ap. 1829; and had issue 1b to 4b.

1b. Thomas George FitzGerald of Turlough Park, co. Mayo, and Maperton House, co. Som., Lieut.-Col. in the Army, D.L., b. 5 June 1778; d. (-); m. 1st, 6 Sept. 1806, Delia, da. of Joshua Field of Heaton, co. York, d. (-); 2ndly, 29 Ap. 1819, Elizabeth, da. of James Crowther of Bolshay Hall, co. York, d. 15 Sept. 1838; and had issue 1c to 4c.

1c.¹ Charles Lionel William FitzGerald of Turlough Park, d. 9 Nov. 1834; m. Dorothea Julia (see p. 340), da. of Patrick Kirwan of Dalgin, d. (-); and had (with possibly other) issue 1d.

1d. Charles Lionel FitzGerald of Turlough, J.P., D.L., b. 24 Aug. 1833; d.s.p. 28 Dec. 1902.

2c. Henry Thomas George FitzGerald of Maperton House, co. Som., J.P., Major sometime 1st Life Guards, b. 5 Mar. 1820; d. 25 May 1890; m. 23 May 1839, Elizabeth Harriott, da. of the Rev. Samuel Wildman Yates, Vicar of St. Mary's, Reading, d. 26 Nov. 1884; and had issue 1d to 4d.

1d. George Wildman Yates FitzGerald, b. 29 Mar. 1840; d.v.p. at sea 29 June 1873; m. at Christ Church, Sydney, N.S.W., 13 Oct. 1869, Frances Isabella, da. of Sprott Boyd, M.D., d. 23 Mar. 1900; and had issue 1e.

1e. Elizabeth Harriot FitzGerald, m. 8 June 1898, Freeman Roper, J.P. (Forde Abbey, Chard, Somerset); and has issue 1f to 3f.

1f. George FitzGerald Roper, b. 19 Ap. 1899.
2f. Geoffrey Desmond Roper, b. 26 Feb. 1901.
3f. Isobel Katharine Roper, b. 23 May 1904.

2d. Charles Lionel Wingfield FitzGerald of Turlough, b. 26 Dec. 1841; d.s.p. 7 Jan. 1909; m. 1893, Adolphine Caroline Annie Helena Marie (Turlough Park, Castlebar, co. Mayo; Winterton Hall, Hythe, Southampton), da. of Capt. Schmitz, Imperial German Army.

3d. Charlotte Elizabeth Harriott FitzGerald, m. 14 Nov. 1867, Major-Gen. John Talbot Coke, J.P. [descended from George, Duke of Clarence, K.G.] (Trusley, co. Derby; Debdale Hall, Mansfield); and has issue.

See the Clarence Volume, pp. 183-184, Nos. 3043-3058.

4d. Frances Geraldine FitzGerald, m. 30 Ap. 1868, Sir Richard George Glyn, 3rd Bt. [G.B.], late Capt. 1st Dragoons, J.P., D.L., C.C., and High Sheriff co. Dorset 1869 (Gaunt's House, Wimborne); and has issue 1e to 2e.

[Nos. 55931 to 55952.

# of The Blood Royal

1*e*. Richard FitzGerald Glyn, Lieut. Army Motor Reserve, *formerly* 1st Dragoons, served in S. Africa 1900 (*Fontmell Magna, Shaftesbury*), *b*. 13 May 1875; *m*. Dec. 1906, Edith Hilda, da. of Douglas George Hamilton Gordon [E. of Aberdeen Coll.]; and has issue 1*f* to 2*f*.

    1*f*. Richard Hamilton Glyn, *b*. 12 Oct. 1907.

    2*f*. Gerald Glyn, *b*. Jan. 1909.

    2*e*. Geraldine Mary Glyn, *m*. 30 Nov. 1898, Ralph Paget [M. of Anglesey Coll. and a descendant of the Lady Isabel Plantagenet (see Essex Volume, p. 110)] (*St. Mary's Grange, Salisbury*).

    3*c*.[2] Elizabeth Geraldine FitzGerald, *m*. Ap. 1840, John Eveleigh Wyndham of Stock Dennes, co. Som., M.A., J.P., *b*. 25 May 1814; *d*. 9 Nov. 1887; and has issue (with an eldest da., Mary Geraldine, *d*. young 1851) 1*d* to 10*d*.

    1*d*. Thomas Heathcote Gerald Wyndham, *M.A., Fellow of Merton College*, b. 1842; *d*. (? *unm*.) 11 Nov. 1876.

    2*d*. Edward John Eveleigh Wyndham, *b*. 1846; *m*. 1886, Amy, da. of J. K. Huntley of West Hall, co. Flints.

    3*d*. Charles Hugh Wyndham, *late* 21st Fusiliers, *b*. 1848.

    4*d*. Francis Wadham Wyndham, *b*. 1851.

    5*d*. Jane Florence Wyndham.

    6*d*. Alice Wyndham.

    7*d*. Blanche Wyndham.

    8*d*. Eva Wyndham.

    9*d*. Isabel Wyndham.

    10*d*. Geraldine Wyndham.

    4*c*.[2] Mary Dorothea FitzGerald, *m*. the Rev. Edward Newton Dickenson; and has issue 1*d* to 4*d*.[1]

    1*d*. Edward Newton Dickenson.

    2*d*. Clara Dickenson.

    3*d*. Cecil Dickenson.

    4*d*. Lily Dickenson.

    2*b*. *Edward Thomas FitzGerald, Lieut.-Col. in the Army and A.Q.M.G. with the Guards at Waterloo*, b. 22 Dec. 1784; *d*. 19 *Sept*. 1845; m. 20 *Nov*. 1811, *Emma, da. of Edmond Green of Medham, I.W*., d. 1862 ; *and had issue* 1*c to* 6*c*.

    1*c*. *Lionel Charles Henry William FitzGerald, K.T.S., 2nd W.I. Regt., served with Doña Maria's Forces in Portugal* 1832–1834, b. 9 *Sept*. 1812; *d*. 21 Dec. 1894; m. 31 *Jan*. 1839, *Sarah Caroline, da. of the Hon. Patrick Brown of Nassau, N.P*., d. 19 *Nov*. 1856 ; *and had issue* 1*d to* 2*d*.

    1*d*. Desmond FitzGerald, C.E. (*Brookline, Boston, Mass., U.S.A*.), *b*. 20 May 1846; *m*. 21 June 1870, Elizabeth Parker Clarke, da. of Stephen Salisbury of Brookline afsd., M.D.; and has issue 1*e* to 4*e*.

    1*e*. Harold FitzGerald (127 *East 56th Street, New York*), *b*. 19 May 1877; *m*. 3 Oct. 1903, Eleanor, da. of Gen. Lewis FitzGerald of New York; and has issue 1*f*.

    1*f*. Eleanora FitzGerald.

    2*e*. Stephen Salisbury FitzGerald, *b*. 19 Sept. 1878; *m*. 9 Sept. 1906, Agnes, da. of Francis Blake of Weston, Mass.

    3*e*. Caroline Elizabeth FitzGerald, *m*. 12 Dec. 1899, Charles Augustus van Rensselaer (130 *East 56th Street, New York*); and has issue 1*f* to 2*f*.

    1*f*. Charles Augustus van Rensselaer, *b*. 28 Sept. 1902.

    2*f*. Stephen van Rensselaer, *b*. 29 Nov. 1905.

    4*e*. Harriot FitzGerald, *m*. 18 Nov. 1897, Robert Jones Clark (*Dedham, Mass*.); and has issue 1*f* to 2*f*.   [Nos. 55953 to 55979.

---

[1] Burke's " Landed Gentry of Ireland," 1899, p. 144.

The Plantagenet Roll

1*f.* Robert FitzGerald Clark, *b.* 13 Sept. 1898.
2*f.* Geraldine Clark.
2*d.* Ormond Edward FitzGerald, *b.* 6 July 1849; *unm.*
2*c.* Edward Thomas FitzGerald, *b.* 19 Sept. 1817; d. (–); m. 1856, *Annie Ffarington, da. of Leonard S. Cox; and had issue* 1*d* to 2*d.*
1*d.* Edward Leonard FitzGerald, *b.* 17 *June* 1859; d. 1896; m. 3 *Aug.* 1882, *Florence Elizabeth Sophia, da. of Robert J. Hunter; and had issue* 1*e* to 6*e.*
1*e.* Edward Walter FitzGerald, *b.* 19 Jan. 1885; *unm.*
2*e.* Desmond FitzGerald, *b.* 1 Sept. 1893.
3*e.* Florence FitzGerald, ⎫
4*e.* Marjorie FitzGerald, ⎪
5*e.* Dorothy FitzGerald, ⎬ *unm.*
6*e.* Audrey FitzGerald, ⎪
2*d.* Anne FitzGerald, ⎭

3*c.* Desmond Gerald FitzGerald, *b.* 28 Dec. 1834; d. 5 *Jan.* 1908; m. 20 *May* 1862, *Louisa, da. of Matthew Crawford of Crumlin, co. Westmeath*, d. 30 *Nov.* 1906; *and had issue* 1*d* to 5*d.*
1*d.* Desmond Gerald FitzGerald of Turlough, High Sheriff co. Mayo 1909 (*Turlough Park, Castlebar, co. Mayo*), *b.* 25 May 1863.
2*d.* Ormonde Edward FitzGerald (*Charleville, Turlough, co. Mayo*), *b.* 1 Mar. 1865; *m.* 16 June 1900, Rebecca Susanna, da. of Becher Lionel Fleming of Newcourt, co. Cork; and has issue 1*e* to 2*e.*
1*e.* Gerald FitzGerald, *b.* Ap. 1904.
2*e.* Elizabeth Cicely FitzGerald.

3*d.* Cecil Henry FitzGerald, C.E., *b.* 5 Jan. 1871; *m.* May 1904, Mary, da. of (—) Rinter of Lydenburg, Transvaal; and has issue 1*e* to 2*e.*
1*e.* Cecil FitzGerald, *b.* Ap. 1905.
2*e.* Sheelah Nesta FitzGerald.

4*d.* Emma Louisa Hope FitzGerald, *m.* Oct. 1902, Duncan A. MacLeod [2nd, son of the Rev. John MacLeod, D.D., Rector of Govan], *d.* 11 Dec. 1907; and has issue 1*e* to 2*e.*
1*e.* Duncan Crawford MacLeod, *b.* 24 Ap. 1907
2*e.* Deirdre Hope Gwendolen MacLeod.

5*d.* Ruby Gwendoline FitzGerald.

4*c.* Louisa FitzGerald, d. (–); m. 1841, *the Rev. Edward Powell*, d. (–); *and had issue* (with a da., Mrs. Thompson, d.s.p.)[1] 1*d* to 4*d.*
1*d.* Robert Powell, *b.* 1842; d. 1904; m. 1863, *Julia, da. of Joshua F. Whittell of Helmsley Lodge, co. York; and had issue* 1*e* to 5*e.*
1*e.* Joshua Edward Powell, *b.* (—); *m.* 1908, (—), da. of (—); and has issue 1*f.*
1*f.* [da.] Powell.
2*e.* Robert Powell, *b.* (—); *m.* 1909, Kathleen, da. of W. J. Shannon of Killine, co. Dublin.
3*e.* Louisa Powell, *unm.*
4*e.* Annie Florence Powell, *unm.*
5*e.* Henrietta Powell, *unm.*

2*d.* Edward FitzGerald Powell, *b.* (—); d. 1878; m. *Frances, da. of* (—) *Darley of co. York; and had issue* 1*e* to 2*e.*
1*e.* Edward Darley Powell, C.E., *b.* 1877; *m.* 1909, (—), da. of (—).
2*e.* Marian Powell, *unm.* [Nos. 55980 to 56008.

---

[1] *Ex inform.* D. G. FitzGerald of Turlough.

of The Blood Royal

3d. Henry Powell, b. (—); m. Frances, da. of Winter Irving of Australia; and has issue 1e.
    1e. Henry Irving FitzGerald Powell, b.
  4d. *Louisa Powell*, d. (-); m. *Henley J. Edwards, Lieut. Indian Navy*, d. (-); and had issue 1e to 5e.
    1e. Arthur Edwards, b. (—); m. and has issue.
    2e. [son] Edwards.
    3e. [son] Edwards.
    4e. Gerald Edwards, *unm*.
    5e. Geraldine Spencer Edwards, m. 6 Jan. 1891, Mountifort Longfield, J.P. (see p. 498) (*Sea Court, Timoleague, co. Cork*).
  5c. *Catherine Dorothea FitzGerald*, d. 1878; m. 1848, *Frederick Barry*, d. (-); and had issue [1] 1d to 2d.
    1d. Mary Barry, *unm*.
    2d. Amy Barry, m. Horatio Francis Hoskins; and has issue 1e to 2e.
      1e. Noel Hoskins.
      2e. Francis Desmond Hoskins.
  6c. *Dorothea Frances FitzGerald*, d. (-); m. 1847, *Peter Bourke*, d. (-); and had issue (with other sons and 2 das. who both m. and left issue) 1d to 3d.
    1d. *John Bourke*, d. (-); m. *and had issue.*
    2d. Peter Bourke, b. (—).
    3d. Desmond Bourke, b. (—).
 3b. *Charles Lionel FitzGerald, Lieut.-Col. and Hon. Brig.-Gen. in Peninsular War*, d. (-); m. *Marianne, da. of Lieut.-Col. Breedon, R.M.*; and had issue (all settled in the Colonies [1]) 1c to 6c.
  1c. *Charles Lionel FitzGerald, Lieut.-Col. R.A.*, d. (-); m. (—), *da. of Lieut.-Col. Pettey, R.A.*; and had issue (with other sons) 1d to 3d.
    1d. Charles Lionel FitzGerald,
    2d. Ormonde FitzGerald,   all resident in Canada.
    3d. Olive FitzGerald,
  2c. *Hervey FitzGerald*, d. (-); m. *and had issue* 1d.
    1d. Hervey FitzGerald.
  3c. *Alfred John FitzGerald, Lieut.-Col. 60th Rifles*, b. 8 Nov. 1842; d.s.p.
  4c. *Ormonde FitzGerald*, d. (-); m. *and had issue (with other sons)* 1d to 3d.
    1d. Henry FitzGerald, Indian Frontier Police.
    2d. Ormonde FitzGerald.
    3d. Augusta FitzGerald, m.
  5c. *Henry FitzGerald*, d. (-); m. (—), *da. of* (—) *Knott*; and had issue (several sons and das.).
  6c. *Augustus FitzGerald*, d. (-); m. *and had issue* 1d to 4d.
    1d. Hervey FitzGerald, b. (—); m. (—).
    2d. Desmond FitzGerald, b. (—).
    3d. Florence FitzGerald.
    4d. Gertrude FitzGerald.
 4b. *Dorothea Mary FitzGerald*, d. (-); m. 1806/8, *Patrick Kirwan of Dalgin Park, co. Mayo*, d. 1854; *and had issue* 1c to 6c.
  1c. *Charles Lionel Kirwan, afterwards Maitland-Kirwan, of Dalgin, J.P., D.L., High Sheriff co. Mayo* 1846, b. July 1811; d. 1862; m. 25 Oct. 1842, *Matilda Elizabeth, da. of William Maitland of Auchlane and Gelston*; and had issue 1d to 9d.
    1d. Charles Lionel Maitland-Kirwan of Gelston Castle, b. 9 July 1843; d.s.p. 11 Nov. 1889.   [Nos. 56009 to 56032.

---

[1] *Ex inform.* D. G. FitzGerald of Turlough.

The Plantagenet Roll

2d. William Francis Maitland-Kirwan of Gelston Castle, J.P., D.L., Lord of the Barony of Gelston, *late* Capt. 78th Highlanders (*Gelston Castle, Castle Douglas, Kircudbright*), b. 1845; m. 20 Nov. 1879, Mary Alice, da. of James Tyrrell of Auchangreagh, co. Longford; s.p.

3d. Lionel Maitland-Kirwan, b. Ap. 1849; m. 29 Aug. 1878, Agnes, da. of Wellwood Herries Maxwell of Munches, J.P., D.L., M.P.; and has issue 1e to 3e.

   1e. Lionel FitzGerald Maitland-Kirwan, Lieut. R.N., b. 1879.
   2e. Matilda Rowe Maitland-Kirwan.
   3e. A. Marguerite Maitland-Kirwan.

4d. *James Maitland Maitland-Kirwan*, b. 1853; d. 1907; m. *2 June 1876, Edith Mary O'Sullivan, da. of J. Bateman; and had issue 1e to 3e.*

   1e. James Douglas Maitland-Kirwan, b. 1889.
   2e. Mary Douglas Maitland-Kirwan.
   3e. Edith Valerie Maitland-Kirwan.

5d. Gerald Maitland-Kirwan, b. 1862; m. (—); and has issue 1e.

   1e. Gerald Maitland-Kirwan, b. 1897.

6d. Mary Agnes Maitland-Kirwan, m. 25 June 1868, Lieut.-Col. Hamilton Campbell; and has issue 1e.

   1e. Charles Lionel Kirwan Campbell, Major 16th Lancers, b. 1 Nov. 1873.

7d. Dorothea FitzGerald Maitland-Kirwan, m. 29 Mar. 1877, William Jardine Herries Maxwell of Munches, M.A. (Oxon.), J.P., D.L., M.P. for co. Dumfries 1892-1895 and 1900-1906, Convener of the Stewartry of Kircudbright (*Munches, near Dalbeattie; Terraughty, near Dumfries*); and has issue 1e to 7e.

   1e. William Jardine Herries Maxwell, Lieut. Cameron Highlanders, b. 8 June 1882.
   2e. Charles Lionel Maxwell, b. Aug. 1883.
   3e. Desmond Maxwell, Lieut. R.N., b. Oct. 1886.
   4e. John Maxwell, b. June 1889.
   5e. Matilda Elizabeth Maxwell.
   6e. Jean Helen Maxwell.
   7e. Victoria Maxwell.

8d. Matilda Douglas Maitland-Kirwan, m. Major-Gen. Oldfield; and has issue 1e.

   1e. Henry Oldfield, b. 1880.

9d. Eva Maitland-Kirwan, m. 24 July 1895, Major the Hon. Percy Cecil Evans-Freke, D.L. [2nd son of Algernon William George, 9th Baron Carbery [I.], and a descendant of George, Duke of Clarence, K.G. (see Clarence Volume, p. 262)] (*Bisbrook Hall, Uppingham*); and has issue 1e.

   1e. Maida Cecil-Evans-Freke.

2c. Martin Frances Kirwan.
3c. Caroline Kirwan.
4c. *Dorothea Julia Kirwan*, d. (—); m. *Charles Lionel William FitzGerald of Turlough, d. 9 Nov. 1834; and had issue.*
See p. 336.
5c. *Mary Kirwan.*
6c. *Julia Emma Kirwan.*   [Nos. 56033 to 56058.]

203. Descendants of the Hon. THOMAS HERVEY, M.P. (Table XXI.), b. 20 Jan. 1699; d. 10 Jan. 1775; m. 1744, ANNE, da. and co-h. of FRANCIS COGHLAN, Councillor of Law, Ireland, d. 27 Dec. 1761; and had issue 1a.

   1a. William Thomas Hervey, Col. in the Guards, d. (—); m. *Elizabeth, da. and h. of Francis Marsh.*

of The Blood Royal

204. Descendants of Rev. the Hon. HENRY HERVEY, *afterwards* (Act Parl. 22 Mar. 1744) ASTON, D.D. (Table XXI.), *b.* 5 Jan. 1700; *d.* (–); *m.* 2 Mar. 1730, CATHERINE, sister and h. of Sir Thomas Aston of Aston, 4th Bt. [E.], da. of Sir Thomas ASTON, 3rd Bt. [E.], *d.* (–); and had issue 1*a*.

1*a. Henry Hervey Aston of Aston, co. Chester,* d. (–); m. (—), *da. of* (—) *Dickinson; and had issue* 1*b to* 2*b.*
1*b. Henry Hervey Aston of Aston, Col. in the Army,* d. 23 *Dec.* 1798; m. 16 *Sept.* 1789, *the Hon. Harriet, da. of Charles* (*Ingram-Shepherd*), 9*th Viscount Irvine* [S.]; *and had issue.*
See the Essex Volume, p. 150, Nos. 17211–17243.
2*b. Anna Sophia Aston,* d. (–); m. 1782, *Anthony Hodges.*
[Nos. 56059 to 56091.

205. Descendants of the Hon. FELTON HERVEY, M.P. (Table XXI.), *b.* 12 Feb. 1712; *d.* 18 Aug. 1773; *m.* DOROTHY, widow of Charles PITFIELD, da. of Solomon ASHLEY, *d.* 8 Nov. 1761; and had issue 1*a* to 4*a*.

1*a. Felton Lionel Hervey, Lieut. R.H.G.,* d. 9 *Sept.* 1785; m. 2 *Mar.* 1779, *Selina Mary, da. and h. of Sir John Elwill,* 4*th Bt.* [G.B.] [m. 2*ndly,* 21 *Sept.* 1797, *the Right Hon. Sir William Henry Fremantle, G.C.H., P.C., and*] d. 23 *Nov.* 1841; *and had issue.*
See the Essex Volume, pp. 56–59, Nos. 5620–5713.
2*a. Emily Hervey,* ⎫
3*a. Caroline Hervey,* ⎬ d. (? *unm.*).
4*a. Elizabeth Hervey,* ⎭
[Nos. 56092 to 56185.

206. Descendants, if any surviving, of Lady LOUISA CAROLINE ISABELLA HERVEY (Table XXI.), *b.* 1715; *d.* 11 May 1770; *m.* 23 Sept. 1731, Sir ROBERT SMYTH of Smith Street, Westminster, 2nd Bt. [G.B. 1714], *d.* 10 Dec. 1783; *bur.* at West Ham Church; and had issue 1*a* to 2*a*.

1*a. Sir Hervey Smyth,* 3*rd Bt.* [G.B.], *Col. Foot Guards, A.D.C. to Gen. Wolfe,* b. 1734; d. *unm.* 2 *Oct.* 1811.
2*a. Anna Mirabella Henrietta Smyth,* b. 1738; d. (–); m. 1761, *William Beale Brand of Polsted Hall, co. Suffolk.*

207. Descendants, if any surviving, of GEORGE (HOWARD), 4th EARL OF SUFFOLK [E.] (Table XXI.), *b. c.* 1625; *d.* 21 Ap. 1691; *m.* 1st, CATHERINE, da. of John ALLEYNE of Northanger in Blenham, co. Beds, *d. a.* July 1683; and had issue 1*a* to 2*a*.

1*a. Lady Mary Howard, da. and co-h.,* d. 1712; m. *Lieut.-Gen. Percy Kirke, Col. of "Kirke's Lambs," Keeper of Whitehall Palace, Governor of Tangiers* 1682–1684, d. *at Brussels* 31 *Oct.* 1691; *and had* (*with other*) *issue* 1*b to* 2*b.*[1]

---

[1] Jewitt's "Reliquary," vi. p. 217. D.N.B.

The Plantagenet Roll

1b. *Percy Kirke, Lieut.-Gen. and Col. of " Kirke's Lambs," Keeper of Whitehall Palace*, b. 1684; d.s.p. 1 *Jan.* 1741; *eldest surv. son.*
2b. *Diana Kirke*, m. *John Dormer of Rousham, co. Oxford; and had issue* 1c.
1c. *Diana Dormer, sole h. to uncle*, d. *unm.* 22 *Feb.* 1743; *bur. in Westminster Abbey with uncle and grandfather.*
2a. *Lady Anne Howard, da. and co-h.*, m. *William Jephson, M.P., Marlow.*

208. Descendants, if any, of Lady DIANA HOWARD (Table XXI.), *d.* June 1710; *bur.* at Walden; *m.* Col. JOHN PITT.

209. Descendants of Lady CATHERINE HOWARD (Table XXI.), *d.* at the Hague 1650; *m.* 1st, GEORGE (STUART), 8th Lord d'Aubigny [F.] [2nd surviving son of Esmé, Duke of Lennox [S.]], *d.* (being slain *ex parte Regis* at the Battle of Edgehill) 23 Oct. 1642; 2ndly, as 1st wife, *c.* 1649, JAMES (LIVINGSTON), 1st EARL OF NEWBURGH [S.], *d.* 26 Dec. 1670; and had issue 1*a* to 2*a*.

1a. *Charles (Stuart), 6th Duke of Lennox* [S.] *and 3rd Duke of Richmond and 6th Baron Clifton of Leighton Bromswold* [E.], b. 7 *Mar.* 1640; d.s.p.s. 12 *Dec.* 1872.
2a. *Katherine (Stuart), suo jure 7th Baroness Clifton of Leighton Bromswold* [E.], *sister and h.*, bapt. 5 *Dec.* 1640; bur. 11 *Nov.* 1702; m. 1*st, c.* 1661, *Henry O'Brien, Viscount Ibrackan* [*son and h.-app. of Henry (O'Brien), 7th Earl of Thomond* [I.]], d.v.p. *Sept.* 1678; *and had issue* 1*b*.
1b. *Katherine (O'Brien), suo jure 8th Baroness Clifton, &c.* [E.], b. 29 *Jan.* 1673; d. *in New York* 11 *Aug.* 1706; m. 10 *July* 1688, *Edward (Hyde), 3rd Earl of Clarendon* [E.], d. 31 *Mar.* 1723; *and had issue.*
See the Exeter Volume, Table XXVII., and pp. 387-396, Nos. 32552-33533.
[Nos. 56186 to 57167.

210. Descendants of Lady ELIZABETH HOWARD (Table XXI.), *d.* 11 Mar. 1705; *m.* as 2nd wife, 1 Oct. 1642, ALGERNON (PERCY), 10th EARL OF NORTHUMBERLAND [E]., K.G., K.B., *bapt.* 13 Oct. 1602; *d.* 13 Oct. 1668; and had issue.
See pp. 66-71, Nos. 749-1999. [Nos. 57168 to 58418.

211. Descendants of ROGER (BOYLE), 2nd EARL OF ORRERY [I.] (Table XXI.), *bapt.* 24 Aug. 1646; *d.* 29 Mar. 1682; *m.* 6 Feb. 1665, Lady MARY (see p. 431), da. of Richard (SACKVILLE), 5th Earl of Dorset [E.], *d.* 4 Nov. 1710; and had issue 1*a* to 2*a*.

1a. *Lionel (Boyle), 3rd Earl of Orrery* [I.], b. 1670; d.s.p.s. 31 *Aug.* 1703.
2a. *Charles (Boyle), 4th Earl of Orrery* [I.] *and 1st Baron Boyle of Marston* [G.B.], *so cr.* 5 *Sept.* 1711, b. 28 *July* 1674; d. 28 *Aug.* 1731; m. 30 *Mar.* 1706, *Lady Elizabeth, da. of John (Cecil), 5th Earl of Exeter* [E.], d. 12 *June* 1708; *and had issue.*
See the Tudor Roll, Table XCVII. and pp. 418-428, Nos. 30324-30994.
[Nos. 58418 to 59088.

of The Blood Royal

212. Descendants of HENRY (BOYLE), 1st EARL OF SHANNON [I.] (Table XXI.), d. 28 Dec. 1764; m. 2ndly, Sept. 1726, Lady HARRIET, da. of Charles (BOYLE), 3rd Earl of Cork [I.] and 2nd Earl of Burlington [E.], d. 13 Dec. 1746; and had issue.

See the Tudor Roll, Table XLV., pp. 252-263, Nos. 23255-23604.

[Nos. 59089 to 59438.

213. Descendants of Capt. WILLIAM BOYLE, Commissioner of Appeals [I.] (Table XXI.), d. 1725; m. 1711, MARTHA BEAUFOY, da. of Sir Samuel GARTH, Physician to the Forces in Ireland; and had issue (with 2 sons who d.s.p.) 1a to 3a.

1a. *Beaufoy Boyle*, b. c. 1714; d. 17 *May* 1765; m. 11 *June* 1736, *John Wilder of Nunhide, co. Berks, and Shiplake, co. Oxford, J.P., D.L.*, bur. 13 *July* 1772; *and had issue* 1b *to* 4b.

1b. *Rev. Henry Wilder of Purley Hall, co. Berks, Rector of Sulham, D.C.L. and Fellow of St. John's Coll., Camb.*, b. Sept. 1744; d. 22 *Jan.* 1814; m. *Joan, da. of William Thoyts of Sulhamstead*, d. 1837; *and had issue* 1c *to* 8c.

1c. *John Wilder of Purley and Sulham, J.P., D.L.*, bapt. 30 *Oct.* 1769; d. 22 Feb. 1834; m. 22 Nov. 1797, *Harriet, da. of the Rev. Edward Beadon, Rector of North Stoneham*, d. 4 *Oct.* 1825; *and had issue* 1d.

1d. *Rev. Henry Watson Wilder of Purley, Rector of Sulham*, b. 3 *Nov.* 1798; d. *(being drowned off Yarmouth), I.W.*, 2 *July* 1836; m. 8 *Ap.* 1828, *Augusta, sister of Sir Charles Joshua Smith, 2nd Bt.* [*U.K.*], *da. of Charles Smith of Suttons, M.P.*, d. *(being drowned with her husband)* 2 *July* 1836; *and had issue* 1e *to* 2e.

1e. *Frederick Wilder of Purley and Sulham, J.P.*, b. 2 *July* 1832; d.s.p. 13 *May* 1899.

2e. *Rev. Henry Beaufoy Wilder of Purley and Sulham, M.A., L.S.A., M.R.C.S. (Eng.), Rector of Sulham*, b. 25 *Oct.* 1834; d. 25 *Ap.* 1908; m. 1 *July* 1858, *Augusta, da. of Langham Christie of Preston Deanery, co. Northants*, d. 17 *Nov.* 1892; *and had issue* 1f *to* 5f.

1f. Rev. Henry Charles Wilder, M.A., Rector of Sulham (*Purley Hall, Berks; Sulham House, Reading; Athenæum*), b. 7 July 1860; m. 20 Ap. 1893, Cicely Helen [descended from the Lady Anne, sister of King Edward IV., &c. (see Exeter Volume, p. 133)], da. of the Rev. Arthur Bourchier Wrey, M.A. [Bt. Coll.]; and has issue 1g to 4g.

1g. Henry Arthur John Wilder, b. 26 Mar. 1894.
2g. Frederick Wrey Wilder, b. 23 Sept. 1899.
3g. Augusta Helen Mary Wilder, b. 29 Aug. 1895.
4g. Alice Victoria Wilder, b. 20 Mar. 1897.

2f. Francis Langham Wilder (*Underwood, Whitchurch, Oxon*), b. 26 July 1863; m. 28 Oct. 1903, Beatrice [descended from George, Duke of Clarence, K.G., brother of King Edward IV. (see Clarence Volume, p. 497)], da. of Lieut.-Col. Frederick Drummond Hibbert; and has issue 1g to 3g.

1g. John Charles Wilder, b. 18 Oct. 1904.
2g. Frances Elizabeth Wilder.
3g. Augusta Beaufoy Wilder.

3f. Augusta Mary Wilder.
4f. Helen Margaret Wilder.
5f. Eveline Irene Wilder.

2c. *William Wilder, living* unm. 1837. [Nos. 59439 to 59450.

The Plantagenet Roll

3c. *George Lodowick Wilder*, d. (-); m. *Augusta Ivy Mary*, da. of *Edmund Walcot of Winckton*, co. Hants, d. (-); and had issue 1d to 2d.
    1d. Edmund Wilder.
    2d. George Wilder.

4c. *Francis Boyle Shannon Wilder* of Busbridge Hall, co. Surrey, b. 18 Dec. 1785; d. (? sp.) (-); m. 4 Sept. 1834, *Augusta*, da. of *John Cornwall* of Hendon [by his wife the Hon. Susannah Hall, née Gardner].

5c. *Mary Anne Wilder*, d. (-); m. the Rev. *Frederick Beadon*, Rector of North Stoneham, co. Hants; and had issue (1 son and 2 das.).

6c. *Harriet Wilder*, d. (? s.p.); m. *Charles Dixon* of Stanstead, co. Sussex.

7c. *Lucy Wilder*, d. (-); m. the Rev. *John Pannel* of Aldsworth, co. Sussex; and had issue (1 son and 1 da.).

8c. *Charlotte Beaufoy Wilder*, d. (-); m. *William Blackwood* of London; and had issue (1 da.).

2b. *Harryot Anne Wilder*,⎫
3b. *Mary Wilder*,   ⎬ b. at Shiplake; living unm. 1766.
4b. *Lucy Wilder*,   ⎭

2a. *Henrietta Boyle*, d. (? s.p.); m. 9 Dec. 1736, *William Nichols* of Froyle, co. Bucks.

3a. *Elizabeth Boyle*, b. 1715; d. (-); m. 9 Oct. 1736, *Matthew Graves* of Chiswick; and had issue 1b.

1b. *Elizabeth Graves*, living at Huglescote 18 Oct. 1802; m. as 3rd wife, *William Bainbridge* of Palsgrave, Head Street, Southampton Buildings, Chiswick, and Newark, co. Leic., b. 7 Jan. 1720; d. 22 Ap. 1780; and had issue (with a son, Henry, d. young) 1c.

1c. *Matthew Bainbridge* of Huglescote Grange, co. Leic., b. 14 Ap. 1763; d. 6 June 1802; m. *Elizabeth*, da. of *Isaac Dawson* of Huglescote, d. (-); and had issue (with a son, Matthew, d. young 1792) 1d to 3d.
    1d. Henry Bainbridge ⎱ (twins).
    2d. Isaac Bainbridge ⎰
    3d. Mary Elizabeth Bainbridge.
                                                                                   [Nos. 59451 to 59452.

214. Descendants of the Right Hon. and Most Rev. JOSEPH DEANE (BOURKE), 3rd EARL OF MAYO [I.], Lord Archbishop of Tuam (Table XXI.), d. 20 Aug. 1794; m. 1760, ELIZABETH, sister of John, 1st Earl of Clanwilliam [I.], da. of Sir Richard MEADE, 2nd Bt. [I.], d. 13 Mar. 1807; and had issue 1a to 7a.

1a. *John (Bourke)*, 4th Earl of Mayo [I.], P.C., G.C.H., b. 18 June 1766; d.s.p. 23 May 1849.

2a. Right Rev. the Hon. *Richard Bourke*, Lord Bishop of Waterford and Lismore, b. 22 Ap. 1767; d. 15 Nov. 1832; m. 20 Mar. 1795, *Frances*, da. of the Most Rev. *Robert Fowler*, Lord Archbishop of Dublin, d. 10 Jan. 1827; and had issue 1b to 3b.

1b. *Robert (Bourke)*, 5th Earl of Mayo [I.], b. 12 Jan. 1797; d. 12 Aug. 1867; m. 3 Aug. 1820, *Anne Charlotte*, da. and h. of the Hon. *John Jocelyn* [E. of Roden Coll.], d. 26 Jan. 1867; and had issue.
See the Clarence Volume, pp. 299-300, Nos. 8366-8393.

2b. Lady *Mildred Bourke*, had Royal Warrant as an Earl's da. 19 Oct. 1849, b. 18 Dec. 1795; d. 29 July 1869; m. 2 Aug. 1821, *Robert John Uniacke* of Woodhouse, co. Waterford, J.P., D.L., d. 29 Mar. 1851; and had issue.
See the Essex Volume, p. 295, Nos. 32358-32365.

                                                                                   [Nos. 59453 to 59488.

# of The Blood Royal

3b. Lady Catherine Bourke, b. 19 *July* 1804; d. 12 *Sept.* 1876; m. 8 *June* 1830, the *Rev. Henry Prittie Perry, Rector of Newcastle, co. Limerick* [2nd son of *Samuel Perry of Woodrooff, co. Tipperary*]; and had issue 1c to 8c.

1c. *Samuel William Perry*, b. 1831; d. (? s.p.) 14 *Aug.* 1898; m. *Elizabeth Jane, da. of Hastings Otway, Recorder of Belfast.*

2c. *Henry Robert Pritttie Perry*, d. (? s.p.) 24 *Aug.* 1903.

3c–8c. 6 das.

3a. Very *Rev. the Hon. Joseph Bourke, Dean of Ossory*, b. 24 *Dec.* 1771; d. 3 *May* 1843; m. 23 *Ap.* 1799, *Mary, da. and co-h. of Sackville Gardiner* [uncle of the 1st Viscount Mountjoy [I.]], d. (–); and had issue 1b.

1b. *Rev. Sackville Gardiner Bourke, Rector of Hathcrop, co. Glouc.*, b. 1 *May* 1805; d 30 *Jan.* 1860; m. 6 *June* 1839, *Lady Georgiana Sarah* [descended from *King Henry VII.* (see Tudor Roll, p. 237)], *da. of John William (Ponsonby), 4th Earl of Bessborough* [I.], d. 25 *June* 1861; and had issue 1c to 2c.

1c. Ven. Cecil Frederick Joseph Bourke, Archdeacon of Buckingham (*Hill House, Taplow*), b. 1 Sept. 1841.

2c. Lucy Josepha Maria Bourke.

4a. *Rev. the Hon. George Theobald Bourke*, b. 15 *Ap.* 1770; d. 22 *Dec.* 1847; m. 1808, *Augusta Georgiana, da. of Thomas Webster*, d. 7 *Oct.* 1863; and had issue 1b to 3b.

1b. *Richard Bourke, Bar.-at-Law*, b. 22 *Feb.* 1811; d. 21 *May* 1856; m. 26 *June* 1849, *Gertrude, da. of Robert Borrowes of Gilltown, co. Kildare* [re-m. 2ndly, 12 *Aug.* 1858, *Anthony North Peat*]; and had issue 1c to 3c.

1c. Southwell George Theobald Bourke, Bar.-at-Law, M.T., *formerly* Lieut. R.N., J.P., and Acting Police Magistrate, Georgetown (*Georgetown, British Guiana ; Junior United Service*), b. 23 July 1851; m. 27 July 1881, Catherine Jane, da. of William Cameron of Tudor House, Lee, co. Kent.

2c. Hubert Edward Madden Bourke, Lieut. (ret.) R.N. (*Naval and Military*), b. 7 Dec. 1853; m. 4 Aug. 1881, Rose, da. of Henry Blackett; and has issue 1d to 3d.

1d. Dermot Southwell Richard Bourke, b. 14 Ap. 1884.

2d. Cecil Hugh Bourke, b. 24 Jan. 1892.

3d. Vivian Margaret Nellie Bourke.

3c. *Augusta Georgiana Clara Bourke*, b. 1850; d. 29 *Feb.* 1870; m. 6 *Dec.* 1867, *Charles de Gannes of Pierrefonds ;* and had issue 1d.

1d. Charlotte de Gannes, *m.* 1889, Paul Revoil, French Ambassador to the Court of Madrid (*French Embassy, Madrid*).

2b. *Rev. John Bourke, Rector of Kilmeaden, co. Waterford*, b. 15 *Aug.* 1812; d. 15 *Mar.* 1891; m. 8 *Feb.* 1842, *Louisa Maria, da. of James David Potts*, d. 14 *Nov.* 1870; and had issue 1c to 5c.

1c. Arthur Edward Desborough Bourke, B.A. (T.C.D.), Bar.-at-Law, Inspector Local Govt. Board, Ireland, b. 3 Dec. 1852; d. 31 *Jan.* 1903; m. 2 *Ap.* 1888, *Maude Margaret* (21 *Lincoln Place, Dublin*), *da. of Henry Blake Mahon of Belleville, co. Galway ;* and had issue 1d to 2d.

1d. Arthur John Henry Bourke, b. 9 May 1897.

2d. Eleanor Louise Bourke.

2c. Henry Beresford Bourke, D.S.O., Lieut.-Col. *formerly* 3rd West India Regt. (*United Service*), b. 2 June 1855.

3c. Elizabeth Margaret Bourke.

4c. Louisa Mary Josephine Bourke.

5c. Alice Mildred Bourke.

3b. *Thomas Joseph Deane Bourke, Lieut.-Col. 34th Regt.*, b. 7 *Mar.* 1815; d. 25 *Feb.* 1875; m. *Jan.* 1849, *Mary, da. of the Ven. Robert Wallis, Archdeacon of Nova Scotia*, d. 1895; *and had issue* 1c *to* 5c. [Nos. 59489 to 59502.

The Plantagenet Roll

1c. George Deane Bourke, C.B., Col. R.A.M.C., L.R.C.S.I., Principal Med. Officer, Irish Command, has Nile (1884-1885) and Burmah (1888-1889) Medals with Clasps, &c. (*Dublin*), b. 15 Oct. 1852; m. 24 Jan. 1883, Mary Morrow, da. of John Stairs of Fairfield, Halifax, N.S., J.P.; and has issue 1d.

1d. Ulick John Deane Bourke, Lieut. 2nd Batt. Oxfordshire and Bucks L.I., b. 13 Ap. 1884.

2c. Robert John Bourke (*Boodle's*), b. 18 Ap. 1854.

3c. Frederick Arthur Deane Bourke (*Battleford, Saskatchewan, Canada*), b. 6 July 1856; m. 1887, Anne Caird, da. of Col. Hutchinson of Cheltenham.

4c. Margaret Augusta Deane Bourke.

5c. Mary Josephine Deane Bourke.

5a. *Lady Mary Anne Bourke*, d. 24 Mar. 1830; m. *as 2nd wife*, 1806, *Admiral Thomas Sotheby*, d. 1832; *and had issue (with a younger da. who d.s.p.)* 1b to 4b.

1b. Rev. Thomas Hans Sotheby, Vicar of Milverton, b. 1809; d. 1888; m. 27 Dec. 1838, *Jane, da. of the Ven. Anthony Hamilton, Archdeacon of Colchester* [*B. Belhaven Coll.*], d. 1842; *and had issue* 1c.

1c. Rev. Walter Edward Hamilton Sotheby, Vicar of Gillingham and Rural Dean (*Gillingham Rectory, Dorset*), b. 23 Feb. 1842; m. 24 Oct. 1893, the Hon. Frederica Spring [descended from George, Duke of Clarence, K.G., brother of King Edward IV. (see the Clarence Volume, p. 562)], sister of Thomas, 2nd Baron Monteagle [U.K.], da. of the Hon. Stephen Edmond Spring Rice.

2b. *Sir Edward Southwell Sotheby, K.C.B., Admiral R.N.*, b. 14 *May* 1813; d. 6 *Jan.* 1902; m. 24 *June* 1864, *Lucy Elizabeth, da. of Henry John Adeane of Babraham, co. Camb.*, d. 6 *Jan.* 1904; *and had issue* 1c *to* 3c.

1c. William Edward Sotheby (*Parcian, Llanengrad, Menai Bridge, Anglesey*), b. 18 Dec. 1865; m. 24 Oct. 1894, Margaret, da. of William Williams of Parcian, co. Anglesey; and has issue 1d to 2d.

1d. Lionel Frederick Southwell Sotheby, b. 16 Aug. 1895.

2d. Nigel Walter Adeane Sotheby, b. 19 Sept. 1896.

2c. Herbert George Sotheby, of H.M. Privy Purse Office, Buckingham Palace (26 *Green Street, Park Lane, W.*), b. 9 Nov. 1871; m. 23 Sept. 1909, Catharine Barbara, da. of Sir Baldwyn Leighton, 8th Bt. [E.].

3c. Alfred Frederick Sotheby, of H.M. Probate Office, Somerset House (26 *Green Street, Park Lane, W.*), b. 22 Nov. 1874; unm.

3b. *Mary Anne Sotheby*, d. 19 Aug. 1881; m. *as 2nd wife, her cousin*, 1830, *Charles Sotheby of Sewardstone, Rear-Admiral of the Blue*, d. 26 *Jan.* 1854; *and had issue (with a son, Major-Gen. Frederick Edward Sotheby, and a da. d. unm.)* 1c to 3c.

1c. Eleanor Catherine Sotheby (*The Grange, Weston Park, Bath*).

2c. Jane Louisa Sotheby, m. 18 Nov. 1873, Lieut.-Col. Thomas William Cator [descended from the Lady Anne, sister of King Edward IV. (see Exeter Volume, p. 633)], d.s.p. 14 Jan. 1900.

3c. Cecilia Elizabeth Sotheby (*The Grange, Weston Park, Bath*).

4b. *Charlotte Sotheby*, d. 15 *Jan.* 1845; m. *as 1st wife*, 9 *Mar.* 1837, *the Rev. Robert Boothby Heathcote, J.P.* [*descended from the Lady Anne, sister of King Edward IV.*], d. 19 *Sept.* 1865; *and had issue.*

See the Essex Volume, p. 675, Nos. 57679/11-12.

6a. *Lady Charlotte Bourke*, d. 15 *June* 1806; m. *as 1st wife*, 27 *July* 1793, *William Browne of Browne's Hill, M.P., J.P., and Custos Rotulorum, co. Carlow*, b. *Jan.* 1793; d. 1 *Ap.* 1840; *and had issue* 1b to 4b.

1b. Robert Clayton Browne of Browne's Hill, J.P., D.L., High Sheriff co. Carlow 1831, b. 28 *Jan.* 1799; d. 22 *July* 1888; m. 28 Oct. 1834, *Harriette Augusta, da. of Hans Hamilton of Dublin, M.P.*, d. *Jan.* 1908; *and had issue* 1c to 3c. [Nos. 59503 to 59519.

346

# of The Blood Royal

1c. *William Clayton Browne (afterwards R.L. 2 Mar. 1889) Browne-Clayton, of Browne's Hill, J.P., D.L., and High Sheriff co. Carlow* 1859, b. 20 Nov. 1835; d. 13 Jan. 1907; m. 10 Jan. 1867, Caroline, da. of John Watson Barton of Stapleton Park, co. York; *and had issue* 1d *to* 12d.

1d. Robert Clayton Browne-Clayton, *late* Major 5th Lancers (*Browne's Hill, co. Carlow*), b. 24 Feb. 1870; m. 16 Nov. 1905, Mary Magdalene, da. of Edward Wienholt of Jondaryan, Queensland; and has issue 1e to 2e.

1e. William Patrick Browne-Clayton, b. 27 Sept. 1906.

2e. Annette Mary Browne-Clayton, b. 28 Ap. 1908.

2d. *William Clayton Browne-Clayton, 2nd Lieut. Royal West Kent Regt.*, b. 29 July 1873; d. *unm. (being killed in action at Agrah Malakan)* 30 Sept. 1897.

3d. Lionel Denis Browne-Clayton, b. 10 Aug. 1874.

4d. Mary Caroline Browne-Clayton, m. as 2nd wife, 6 Oct. 1898, Thomas Henry Bruen Ruttledge of Bloomfield, J.P., D.L., High Sheriff co. Mayo 1902 (*42 North Great George Street, Dublin; Bloomfield, Hollymount, co. Mayo*); and has issue 1e to 2e.

1e. Robert Francis Ruttledge, b. 11 Sept. 1899.

2e. William Ruttledge, b. 29 July 1901.

5d. Annette Constance Browne-Clayton.

6d. Margaret Frances Browne-Clayton.

7d. Florence Hope Brown-Clayton, m. 28 Ap. 1904, Col. Horace James Johnston, D.S.O., 3rd Batt. West Riding Regt. (*Watch Hill House, Canonbie, Dumfries*); and has issue 1e to 2e.

1e. Francis William Johnston, b. 19 Aug. 1905.

2e. Patrick James Johnston, b. 7 Jan. 1908.

8d. Kathleen Octavia Louisa Browne-Clayton.

9d. Madeline Emma Browne-Clayton.

10d. Lucy Victoria Browne-Clayton, m. 12 Dec. 1901, Claud Edward Pease (*Cliff House, Marske-by-the Sea, Yorks*); and has issue 1e to 3e.

1e. Diana Vere Pease, b. 4 Oct. 1902.

2e. Lucy Margaret Pease, b. 3 Feb. 1904.

3e. Olive Mary Caroline Pease, b. 16 May 1906.

11d. Juliet Harriet Vere Browne-Clayton.

12d. Caroline Zoë Browne-Clayton, m. 14 Dec. 1905, Capt. Herbert Chase Hall, Northumberland Fusiliers; s.p.

2c. Robert Clayton Browne, b. 3 May 1839.

3c. *Annette Caroline Browne*, d. 16 Feb. 1892; m. 12 Feb. 1863, *Denis William Pack-Beresford of Fenagh Lodge, M.P.* [*descended from the Lady Isabel Plantagenet* (see Essex Volume, p. 159), d. 28 Dec. 1881; *and had issue* 1d *to* 7d.

1d. Denis Robert Pack-Beresford of Fenagh, J.P., D.L., High Sheriff co. Carlow 1890 (*Fenagh House Lodge, Bagnalstoun, co. Carlow*), b. 23 Mar. 1864; m. 11 Aug. 1891, Alice Harriet Cromie [descended from George, Duke of Clarence, K.G. (see Clarence Volume, p. 280)], da. of James Acheson Lyle of Portstewart.

2d. Charles George Pack-Beresford, Major Royal West Kent Regt., b. 21 Nov. 1869.

3d. Henry John Pack-Beresford, Capt. Highland L.I., b. 22 Aug. 1871; m. 28 July 1904, Sybil Maud, da. of John Bell of Rushpool Hall, co. York; and has issue 1e to 2e.

1e. Denis John Pack-Beresford, b. 27 Oct. 1905.

2e. Tristram Anthony Pack-Beresford, b. 8 May 1907.

4d. Reynell James Pack-Beresford, b. 21 Dec. 1872; m. 17 June 1899, Florence, da. of Frederick Leith of Walmer, co. Kent.; and has issue 1e to 2e.

1e. Arthur Reynell Pack-Beresford, b. 28 Ap. 1906.

2e. Joyce Annett Pack-Beresford, b. 27 July 1900. [Nos. 59520 to 59548.

The Plantagenet Roll

5d. Hugh de la Poer Pack-Beresford, b. 11 July 1874.
6d. Elizabeth Harriet Pack-Beresford.
7d. Annette Louisa Pack-Beresford.

2b. *Joseph Deane Browne, Capt. Carabineers*, d. 1 Jan. 1878; m. *Georgina, da. of (—) Thursby*.

3b. *Elizabeth Browne*, d. 15 Jan. 1871; m. 31 Jan. 1814, *Sir Jonah Denny Wheeler-Cuffe of Leyrath, 1st Bt.* [I.], d. 9 May 1853; *and had issue* 1c to 5c.

1c. Sir Charles Frederick Denny Wheeler-Cuffe, 2nd Bt. [I.], D.L., *formerly* Major 66th Regt., served as A.A.G. during Indian Mutiny 1858–1859, &c. (*Leyrath, co. Kilkenny; United Service*), b. 1 Sept. 1832; m. 2 July 1861, the Hon. Pauline, da. of Henry (Villiers-Stuart), 1st Baron Stuart de Decies [U.K.], *d.s.p.* 5 July 1895.

2c. *Otway Wheeler-Cuffe, formerly Capt. R.M. Artillery and Hon. Major Waterford Art.*, b. 1 Mar. 1836; d. 30 Dec. 1908; m. 14 Sept. 1865, *Louisa Frances Florence* (*Woodlands, Waterford*), da. *of the Rev. Luke Fowler, Preb. of Aghour*; d. 22 Dec. 1906; *and has issue* 1d to 2d.

1d. Otway Fortescue Luke Wheeler-Cuffe, Lieut. Indian Army Reserve, M.I.C.E., P.W.D., Burmah (*Rangoon*), b. 9 Dec. 1866; *m.* 3 June 1897, Charlotte Isabel, da. of William Williams; *s.p.*

2d. Pauline Florence Elizabeth Wheeler-Cuffe, m. 29 Ap. 1897, Frederick Richard Cowper Reed, Trin. Coll., Camb. (*Gaultier, Madingley Road, Cambridge*); *s.p.*

3c. *Rosetta Wheeler-Cuffe*, d. 27 May 1901; m. *as 2nd wife*, 8 Jan. 1853, *Admiral of the Fleet Sir Thomas John Cochrane, G.C.B.* [*E. of Dundonald Coll.*], d. 19 Oct. 1872; *and had issue*.

See the Exeter Volume, p. 626, Nos. 53041–53043.

4c. *Elinor Mildred Wheeler-Cuffe*, d. 14 Oct. 1884; m. 5 Dec. 1840, *her cousin, Richard Wheeler of the Rocks, co. Kilkenny, J.P.*, d. 9 Ap. 1861; *and had issue* 1d to 3d.

1d. Edward Wheeler, Lieut.-Col. (ret.) R. M. Art. (*The Rocks, Kilkenny*), b. 18 Aug. 1850; m. 3 July 1888, Isabel Charlotte, da. of Major James Palliser Costobadie, 70th Regt.; and has issue 1e to 2e.

1e. Charles Palliser Wheeler, Royal Military College, Sandhurst, b. 10 July 1889.

2e. Pauline Gladys Laura Wheeler.

2d. John William Wheeler (6 *Gardiner's Row, Dublin*), b. 23 May 1859; *unm.*

3d. Minnie Wheeler (6 *Gardiner's Row, Dublin*), *unm.*

5c. *Frances Letitia Wheeler-Cuffe*, d. 29 Dec. 1908; m. 20 Aug. 1846, *Capt. Charles William Tupper, late 7th Fusiliers; and had issue* 1d to 2d.

1d. Sir (Charles) Lewis Tupper, K.C.I.E., C.S.I., Pres. Indian Telegraph Committee since 1906, and *formerly* an additional member of Gov.-Gen.'s Council 1900–1903, and temporary member Executive Council 1905–1906, Vice-Chancellor Punjab Univ., &c. (*Glenlyn, East Molesey*), b. 16 May 1848; *m.* 2 Oct. 1875, Jessie, da. of Major-Gen. Henry Campbell Johnstone, C.B.; and has issue 1e to 3e.

1e. Geoffrey Tupper, b. 11 Dec. 1878.

2e. Frank Gaspard Tupper, b. 11 Aug. 1886.

3e. Ruth Tupper, *m.* 16 Feb. 1905, Lewis French, M.A. (Oxon.), I.C.S., Assist. Commr., Punjab; and has issue 1f.

1f. Dorothy Margaret French, b. 14 Nov. 1905.

2d. Reginald Godfrey Otway Tupper, Capt. R.N., H.M.S. *Excellent*, an A.D.C. to H.M. the King, &c., b. 16 Oct. 1859; *m.* 1888, Emily Charlotte, da. of Lieut.-Gen. H. Greer, C.B.

4b. *Charlotte Browne*, d. (—); m. 1835, *William Brownlow of Knapton House, Queen's Co., and Loughderry, co. Monaghan, J.P., D.L.* [*descended from the Lady Anne, sister of King Edward IV.* (see Exeter Volume, p. 206)], b. 1802; d. 18 July 1881; *and had issue* (*with a da.*) 1c to 2c.   [Nos. 59549 to 59568.

of The Blood Royal

1c. Francis Brownlow, C.B., Lieut.-Col. 72nd Highlanders, served in Crimean and Afghan Wars, b. 19 July 1836; d. (being killed in action at Kandahar) 31 Aug. 1880; m. 1878, Effie Constance, da. of Col. Robert Christopher Tytler [m. 2ndly, 1 Aug. 1885, Alfred (Porcelli), Baron Porcelli di Sant Andrea [Sicily], Col. (ret.) R.E.]; and had issue 1d.

1d. Norman Francis Brownlow, b. 31 Oct. 1879.

2c. William Vesey Brownlow, Major-Gen. and Col. 1st Dragoon Guards, C.B., J.P., High Sheriff co. Monaghan 1907, served in Zulu (1879) and Boer (1880–1881) Wars, formerly Col. Comdg. 22nd Regt. Dist. 1889–1894 (Eveley Liphook, Hants), b. 12 June 1841; m. 1st, 19 Nov. 1881, Lady Anne Henrietta, da. of John Hamilton (Dalrymple), 10th Earl of Stair [S.], d. 18 Feb. 1898; 2ndly, 1 June 1904, Lady Kathleen Susan Emma, da. of John Stuart (Bligh), 6th Earl of Darnley [I.].

7a. Lady Theodosia Eleanor Bourke, b. a. 1781; d. 23 Aug. 1845; m. 1807, Robert Hale Blagden Hale of Alderley, co. Glouc., d. 20 Dec. 1855; and had issue 1b to 4b.

1b. Robert Blagden Hale of Alderley, M.P., J.P., High Sheriff co. Glouc. 1870, b. 29 Sept. 1807; d. 22 July 1883; m. 17 Aug. 1832, Anne Jane, da. of George Peter Holford of Westonbirt, co. Glouc., d. 18 Ap. 1879; and had issue 1c to 5c.

1c. Robert Hale of Alderley, J.P., Major-Gen., formerly Col. 7th Hussars, A.D.C. to H.R.H. the Duke of Cambridge 1879–1886, b. 9 July 1834; d. unm. 12 May 1907.

2c. Mathew Holford Hale (Alderley, near Wooton-under-Edge), Col. formerly 26th Cameronians, b. 26 July 1835; unm.

3c. Anne Hale (Dunachton House, Inverness), m. 24 Nov. 1859, Thomas Henry Sherwood, Lieut. 21st Fusiliers, b. 2 May 1832; d. 7 May 1895; and has issue 1d to 5d.

1d. Thomas Edward Sherwood (Makarika, Waipiro Bay, New Zealand), b. 28 Feb. 1861; m. 9 Sept. 1893, Mary Sophia, da. of Frederick Addington Goodenough of Calcutta; and has issue 1e to 2e.

1e. Robert Goodenough Sherwood, b. 21 June 1894.

2e. Frederick Hale Sherwood, b. 15 Ap. 1900.

2d. Arthur Robert Sherwood (Victoria, British Columbia), b. 4 Aug. 1862; m. 14 Sept. 1895, Elizabeth Lucy, da. of W. Crickmay of Vancouver; and has issue 1e to 2e.

1e. Thomas Mathew Sherwood, b. 20 May 1902.

2e. Agnes Anne Florence Sherwood, b. 6 Jan. 1901.

3d. Harold Joseph Sherwood, Major R.E., b. 22 June 1865; d. at Roorkee, India, 24 Jan. 1907; m. 10 May 1906, Margaret Emily, da. of the Rev. W. Millar Nicolson, D.Sc.; and had issue 1e.

1e. Anne Josephine Hale Sherwood, b. 29 Ap. 1907.

4d. Eveline Anna Sherwood, m. 6 June 1899, Robert Rist Hedley (Nelson, British Columbia); and has issue 1e to 3e.

1e. Robert Hale Hedley, b. 29 Ap. 1900.

2e. Mathew Sherwood Hedley, b. 2 May 1905.

3e. Anne Hedley, b. 6 Aug. 1901.

5d. Ethel Georgina Theodosia Sherwood, m. 1 Aug. 1895, the Very Rev. Vernon Staley, Provost of St. Andrew's Cathedral, Inverness, Author of " Plain Words on the Holy Catholic Church," " The Catholic Religion," " The Natural Religion," " The Practical Religion," and many works on liturgiology (Dunachton House, Inverness); and has issue 1e.

1e. Edward Vernon Staley, b. 6 Jan. 1899.

4c. Theodosia Hale } (Alderley, near Wooton-under-Edge).
5c. Georgina Hale

2b. John Richard Blagden Hale of Bradley Court, co. Glouc., Col. 1st Life
[Nos. 59569 to 59587.

The Plantagenet Roll

Guards and 3rd King's Own Light Dragoons, b. 5 June 1810; d. 13 Oct. 1864; m. 27 Ap. 1848, Jane, da. of the Rev. Thomas George Clare, Vicar of Walmer, co. Kent, and Rector of St. Andrew's, Holborn, d. 4 Mar. 1861; and had issue 1c to 3c.

1c. Jane Clare Hale of Bradley Court (*Bexley House, Melrose Road, Southfields, S.W.*), m. 1st, 11 Feb. 1873, Col. Alfred Cook, 40th Regt.; d.s.p.s. 20 June 1885; 2ndly, 27 Ap. 1887, the Rev. John Gregory, M.A., Vicar of St. Mary's, Far Cotton, co. Northants, d.s.p. 2 July 1905.

2c. Edith Harriet Blagden Hale (*Waverley, Albemarle Road, Beckenham*), m. 23 Jan. 1877, Col. Hugh Halse Ley of Penzance, co. Cornwall, 3rd Batt. Duke of Cornwall's L.I., b. 1 Aug. 1851; d. 5 Dec. 1906; and has issue 1d to 4d.

1d. Arthur Edwin Hale Ley, Capt. 20th Deccan Horse, Indian Army, b. 18 June 1879; m. 15 Feb. 1909, Ena Doris, da. of Capt. Gwynne Harrison, niece of Sir Frederick Gwynne-Harrison.

2d. Lindsay Hugh Ley, Tea Planter (*Travancore, S. India*), b. (twin) 1 Sept. 1881.

3d. Richard Halse Ley, Mining Engineer (*Nelson, Victoria, B.C.*), b. (twin) 1 Sept. 1881; m. 3 July 1907, Jessie, da. of William Blakemore, d. at Nelson afsd. 15 Mar. 1909; and has issue 1e.

1e. Margaret Jessie Ley, b. 3 Mar. 1909.

4d. Victoria Eleanor Joan Ley, m. 22 Ap. 1909, Carlos Bovill, Lieut. R.A.

3c. Constance Eleanor Blagden Hale, *unm.*

3b. Right Rev. Mathew Blagden Hale, D.D., M.A. (Camb.), *Lord Bishop of Brisbane 1875–1885, previously 1st Lord Bishop of Perth, W.A., 1857–1875, and Archdeacon of Adelaide 1847–1857*, b. 18 June 1811; d. 3 Mar. 1895; m. 1st, 25 Feb. 1840, Sophia, da. of George Clode of London, Merchant, b. 20 Jan. 1813; d. 27 Mar. 1845; 2ndly, in W. Australia 1848, Sabina Dunlop, da. of Col. John Molloy, Rifle Brigade (*Waterloo Medal*), b. at Augusta, W.A., 7 Nov. 1831; d. in Tasmania Aug. 1905; and had issue 1c to 8c.

1c.[2] Robert Dalton Hale, Assayer (*Broken Hill Silver Mine, Australia*), b. at Poonindei, Port Lincoln, South Australia, 11 Ap. 1853; *unm.*

2c.[2] Edward Mathew Hale, Comm. R.N. (*Leonard Stanley, Glouc.*), b. 11 May 1865; m. 21 Nov. 1905, Helen Ethel, da. of William Denis-Browne of Leamington; and has issue 1d to 2d.

1d. Mathew Blagden Hale, b. 9 Sept. 1906.

2d. Theodosia Hale.

3c.[2] Harold Hale (*Cotswold, New Norfolk, Tasmania*), b. Mar. 1869; m. 1901, Georgina, da. of Gen. Officer of Melbourne, Vic.; and has issue 1d to 4d.

1d. Harold Mathew Officer Hale, b. 28 Sept. 1902.

2d. Robert Blagden Hale.

3d. Margaret Georgiana Hale.

4d. Muriel Constance Hale.

4c.[2] Ernest Nathaniel Hale, B.A. (Camb.) and Assistant Master Uppingham School (*Uppingham School*), b. 11 July 1871.

5c.[2] Arthur Frederick Hale (*Glandore, Eidsvold, Queensland*), b. 25 Sept. 1873; *unm.*

6c.[1] Amy Hale, m. 15 June 1869, the Rev. Willoughby Balfour Wilkinson, Vicar of Bishop's Itchington, *formerly of St. Paul's, Stonehouse, and St. Luke's, Birmingham* (*The Vicarage, Bishop's Itchington, near Leamington*); and has issue (with 2 sons d. in infancy) 1d to 4d.

1d. Mathew Hale Wilkinson (*Glandore, Eidsvold, Queensland*), b. 12 Aug. 1879; *unm.*

2d. George Jerrard Wilkinson, B.A. (Camb.), b. 16 Aug. 1885; *unm.*

3d. Amy Hale Wilkinson, m. 10 Aug. 1901, Arthur Joseph Burder Rankin of

[Nos. 59588 to 59610.

of The Blood Royal

Birmingham, Solicitor (*Harborough House, Kingswood, Warwickshire*); and has issue 1e to 2e.
    1e. Arthur Christian Rankin, b. 9 May 1902.
    2e. Janice Mary Rankin.
  4d. Clementina Wilkinson, *unm.*
  7c.[1] Mary Hale, m. 15 Ap. 1868, the Rev. George Christian, Vicar of Billesdon (*Billesdon Vicarage, Leicestershire*) ; *s.p.*
  8c.[2] Georgiana Theodosia Hale, m. 1904, Capt. John Hutton Bisdee, V.C. (*Hutton Park, Tasmania*); *s.p.*
    4b. *Theodosia Eleanor Hale,* d. 23 *Aug.* 1857; m. 27 *Sept.* 1842, *Thomas George Wills-Sandford* (see p. 374) *of Willsgrove and Castlerea, co. Roscommon, J.P., D.L.,* b. 15 *Aug.* 1817; d. 13 *Ap.* 1887; *and had issue 1c to 6c.*
    1c. *William Robert Wills-Sandford of Willsgrove and Castlerea, J.P., Capt. 2nd Dragoons and Royal Scots Greys,* b. 12 *Ap.* 1844; d. 3 *Ap.* 1889; m. 26 *Mar.* 1874, *Adelaide Elizabeth, da. of Henry Jephson of Glenbrook, co. Wicklow, by his wife Adelaide, da. of Sir Philip Crampton,* 1st *Bt.* [*U.K.*], *M.D., F.R.S.,* d. 29 *June* 1880; *and had issue 1d to 3d.*
      1d. Thomas George Wills-Sandford of Willsgrove and Castlerea (*Willsgrove; Castlerea; both co. Roscommon*), b. 9 Nov. 1879; m. 12 Feb. 1907, Kathleen Fanny, da. of Robert Burrowes of Stradone, co. Cavan; and has issue 1e.
        1e. William Robert Wills-Sandford, b. 3 Feb. 1909.

      2d. Charlotte Georgina Wills-Sandford, m. 17 Mar. 1898, Charles Wood, Fellow of Gonville and Caius Coll., Camb. (17 *Cranmer Road, Cambridge*); and has issue 1e to 4e.
        1e. Patrick Bryan Sandford Wood, b. 18 Feb. 1899.
        2e. Edward Mathew Sandford Wood, b. 19 Ap. 1900.
        3e. Catherine Elizabeth Sandford Wood, b. 8 Dec. 1902.
        4e. Joan Kathleen Sandford Wood, b. 13 Feb. 1907.
      3d. Mary Adelaide Wills Sandford, *unm.*
    2c. Edward Wills-Sandford, now (R.L. 12 Jan. 1889) Sandford-Wills, J.P. (*Cashlieve, Ballinlough, co. Roscommon; Kildare Street*), b. 20 Feb. 1851; m. 28 May 1889, Amy Henrietta, da. of Henry Guinness of Burton Hall, Stillorgan, co. Dublin; and has issue 1d to 2d.
      1d. Lucy Eleanor Sandford-Wills.
      2d. Mary Grace Sandford-Wills.
    3c. Godfrey Robert Wills-Sandford, b. 5 Oct. 1852.
    4c. Theodosia Eleanor Wills-Sandford.
    5c. Alice Mary Wills-Sandford.
    6c. Evelyn Louisa Wills-Sandford, m. 20 July 1881, William Frederick Hammersly Smith Hamilton (*Dromahaere, co. Leitrim*); and has issue 1d.
      1d. Evelyn Eleanor Smith, m. 16 Feb. 1904, George H. Mercer, R.I.C. (*The Barracks, Galway*); and has issue 1e to 2e.
        1e. Evelyn Alice Violet Mercer, b. 7 Feb. 1905.
        2e. Olive Mary Nora Mercer, b. 13 Mar. 1906.   [Nos. 59611 to 59633.

215. Descendants of CATHERINE DEANE (Table XXI.), d. 5 July 1743; m. as 1st wife, 17 Dec. 1735, JOHN (LYSAGHT), 1st BARON LISLE [I.], so cr. 18 Sept. 1758; d. 15 July 1781; and had issue 1a to 2a.

  1a. *John* (*Lysaght*), *2nd Baron Lisle* [*I.*], d. 8 *Jan.* 1798; m. 1778, *Marianne, da. of George Connor of Ballybricken, co. Cork,* d. 19 *Oct.* 1815; *and had issue* 1b *to* 4b.

The Plantagenet Roll

1*b.* John (Lysaght), 3rd Baron Lisle [*I.*], b. 6 *Aug.* 1781; d.s.p. 26 *Nov.* 1834.

2*b.* George (Lysaght), 4th Baron Lisle [*I.*], b. 6 *June* 1783; d. 7 *July* 1868; m. 1*st,* 11 *Oct.* 1810, *Elizabeth, da. of Samuel Knight,* d. 12 *Ap.* 1815; 2*ndly,* 14 *Oct.* 1816, *Elizabeth Anne, da. of John Davy Foulkes,* d. 1 *Nov.* 1825; *and had issue* 1*c to* 2*c.*

1*c.* John Arthur (Lysaght), 5th Baron Lisle [*I.*], b. 12 *Oct.* 1811; d. 18 *Ap.* 1898; m. 6 *Mar.* 1837, *Henrietta, da. of John Charch,* d. *Ap.* 1860; *and had issue* 1*d to* 4*d.*

1*d.* George William James (Lysaght), 6th Baron Lisle [*I.*], *formerly* Lieut. Devon Mil. Art. and Jackson Forest Rangers, Waikato Militia, served during Maori War 1864–1865 (*Annabella Terrace, co. Cork*), b. 29 Jan. 1840; *m.* 31 Oct. 1868, Amy Emily, da. of Ayliffe Langford of Ventnor and St. Heliers, Jersey; and has issue 1*e* to 2*e.*

1*e.* Hon. Horace George Lysaght, J.P. (*Newmarket Cottage, co. Cork*), b. 16. Feb. 1873; *m.* 28 June 1899, Alice Elizabeth, da. of Sir John Wrixon-Becher, 3rd Bt. [U.K.]; and has issue 1*f* to 3*f.*

1*f.* John Nicholas Horace Lysaght, b. 10 Aug. 1903.

2*f.* Horace James William Lysaght, b. 22 Sept. 1908.

3*f.* Alice Amy Lysaght.

2*e.* Hon. Kathleen Eily Lysaght.

2*d.* Hon. Frederick Lysaght, *formerly* Lieut. Devon Art. Mil., b. 27 May 1841; *m.* 1st, 31 Dec. 1867, Annie Elizabeth, da. of Ayliffe Langford of Ventnor afsd., d. 24 May 1868; 2ndly, 10 Nov. 1868, Elizabeth Lavinia, da. of D. Le Couteur of St. Peter's, Jersey; and has issue 1*e.*

1*e.* Frederick Edward John Lysaght, b. 1868.

3*d.* Rev. the Hon. Henry Lysaght, *late* Vicar of St. Mary's, Middleton (53 *Banbury Road, Oxford*), b. 10 Mar. 1847; *m.* 14 Jan. 1875, Susan Isabelle, da. of Philip Scott of Hill House, Queenstown; and has issue 1*e.*

1*e.* Rev. John Arthur Constantine Lysaght, B.A., Vicar of Carham (*The Elms, Kennington, Oxford*), b. 13 Sept. 1876; *m.* 8 Ap. 1902, Mary Nicholl, da. of Adam Feltiplace Blandy of The Warren, Abingdon; and has issue 1*f* to 3*f.*

1*f.* Winifred Joyce Lysaght.

2*f.* Kathleen Mary Lalage Lysaght.

3*f.* Renee Primrose Lysaght.

4*d.* Hon. Philippa Charlotte Lysaght, *m.* 1884, Arthur Octavius Marwood (25 *Westbourne Gardens, Folkestone*); and has issue 1*e* to 3*e.*

1*e.* Arthur Henry Lysaght Marwood, Lieut. 1st Batt. York and Lancaster Regt., b. 1885.

2*e.* Charles Philip Lysaght Marwood, Lieut. Royal Warwickshire Regt., b. 1888.

3*e.* Edith Marion Lysaght Marwood.

2*c.* Hon. Catherine Charlotte Lysaght, b. 25 *Sept.* 1822; d. 22 *Dec.* 1905; m. 19 *Dec.* 1844, *the Rev. John Eyre Yonge, M.A., Rector of Hempstead,* d. 11 *June* 1890; *and had issue.*

See the Clarence Volume, p. 159, Nos. 2469–2487.

3*b.* Hon. Elizabeth Lysaght, d. 1813; m. *James Hall.*

4*b.* Hon. Catharine Lysaght, d. (–); m. 1803, *Thomas Delany Hale.*

2*a.* Hon. Mary Lysaght, d. (–); m. *Kingsmill Pennefather, M.P. for Cashel* 1753, 1761, 1771, d.v.p. *May* 1771; *and had issue* 1*b to* 6*b.*

1*b.* Richard Pennefather of New Park, M.P., Lieut.-Col. Tipperary Militia, d. *May* 1831; m. 1*st,* 1782, *Anna, da. and h. of Matthew Jacob of St. Johnstown, co. Tipperary; and had issue* 1*c to* 7*c.*

1*c.* **Kingsmill Pennefather,** *Lieut.-Col. Tipperary Militia,* d.v.p. 1819; m. 1*st, Maria, da. of Burton Persse of co. Galway,* d. (–); 2*ndly, Grace, da. of Thomas Burton of Grove,* d. (–); *and had issue* 1*d to* 2*d.* [Nos. 59634 to 59669.]

# of The Blood Royal

1*d*.¹ Anna Pennefather, d. 31 Dec. 1887; m. 25 May 1833, *Stephen Charles Moore of Barne, co. Tipperary, J.P., D.L., High Sheriff for that co.* 1867, b. 12 Mar. 1808; d. 10 Ap. 1873; *and had issue* 1e to 6e.

1*e*. *Stephen Moore of Barne, J.P., D.L., M.P. co. Tipperary* 1875–1880, *and High Sheriff for that co.* 1885, *formerly Capt.* 63rd Regt., b. 23 Aug. 1836; d. 9 July 1897; m. 1st, 1 Oct. 1867, *Anna Maria, da. and h. of Wilmer Wilmer of* 24 *Wilton Crescent, London*, d. 22 Dec. 1886; 2ndly, 11 July 1888, *Martha Mary, da. of the late John Morgan of Brampton Park, co. Hunts*; *and had issue* 1f to 6f.

1*f*. Randal Kingsmill Moore of Barne, J.P., D.L., *formerly* Lieut. 3rd Batt. Leinster Regt. (*Barne, near Clonmel*), b. 12 Feb. 1873.

2*f*. Stephen Thomas Moore, now (R.L. 6 Feb. 1903) Wilmer, Lieut. 16th Lancers, b. 7 Feb. 1881.

3*f*. Anna Eleanor Isabel Moore, *m*. 11 Mar. 1895, Francis Simon Low, *formerly* 2nd Life Guards [only son and h. of Francis Wise Low of Kilshane, J.P.] (37 *Cadogan Square, S.W.*); and has issue 1g.

1*g*. [da.] Low.

4*f*. Geraldine Elena Moore.

5*f*. Mary Augusta Moore, *m*. 11 Mar. 1903, Capt. Noel Arbuthnot Thomson, Seaforth Highlanders.

6*f*. Stephanie Hilda Grace Moore, *m*. 21 Nov. 1901, the Rev. John Carleton Steward, Rector of Mulbarton (*Mulbarton Rectory, Norfolk*).

2*e*. Richard Albert Moore (*Queensland*), b. 19 May 1848; *m*.

3*e*. Charles Henry Algernon Moore, b. 8 Aug. 1851; *m*. Mary, da. of Gen. Foster.

4*e*. Anna Maria Moore, *m*. Dec. 1866, Col. Charles Thornhill, R.A.; and has issue 1f.

1*f*. Charles Thornhill.

5*e*. Katherine Grace Moore, *m*. 25 Aug. 1870, Sir Francis John Milman of Levaton, 4th Bt. [G.B.], *formerly* Hon. Major and Adj. 2nd Brig. Welsh Div. R.A. (*Woodlands, Bexley Road, Erith*); and has issue 1f to 7f.

1*f*. Francis Milman, b. 27 Oct. 1872.

2*f*. William Ernest Milman, b. 11 Aug. 1875.

3*f*. Lionel Charles Patrick Milman, Lieut. R.A., b. 23 Feb. 1877.

4*f*. Stephen Walter Milman, b. 15 Nov. 1879.

5*f*. Henry Augustus Milman, b. 1882.

6*f*. Hugh Milman, b. 1884.

7*f*. Violet Grace Milman.

6*e*. Elmina Constance Moore, *m*. 5 Jan. 1875, Henry Burroughs (*Boston, Mass., U.S.A.*); and has issue.

2*d*. *Catherine Pennefather*, d. 1 Jan. 1843; m. 17 Aug. 1840, *the Hon. Henry Alexander Savile* [2nd *son of John,* 3rd *Earl of Mexborough* [*I.*]], d. 1 Mar. 1850; *and had issue* 1e.

1*e*. *William Savile, Capt.* 9*th Lancers, D.L.*, b. 8 Oct. 1841; d. 4 Ap. 1903; m. 12 June 1865, *Emily* [*descended from George, Duke of Clarence, K.G.* (see the Clarence Volume, p. 131)] (20A *St. James' Place, S.W.*), *da. of Capt. Delmé Seymour Davies of Penlan*; *and had issue* 1f to 2f.

1*f*. John Herbert Drax Savile, Capt. *late* Rifle Brigade.

2*f*. Beatrice Anne Louisa Savile.

2*c*. *Matthew Pennefather of New Park, M.P., J.P., D.L., High Sheriff co. Tipperary* 1826, b. 1784; d. (-); m. 1814, *Anna, da. of Daniel Connor of Ballybricken, co. Cork*; *and had issue* 1d to 4d.

1*d*. Daniel Francis Pennefather, b. 1816.

2*d*. Richard Pennefather.

3*d*. Mary Pennefather.

4*d*. Anna Pennefather. [Nos. 59670 to 59695.

The Plantagenet Roll

3c. *William Pennefather of Lakefield*, d. 4 Feb. 1872; m. 1819, Charity Maria, da. of Richard Long of Longfield, co. Tipperary ; and had issue 1d to 4d.

1d. *Richard Pennefather of Lakefield, J.P.*, b. 19 Jan. 1826; d. 1876; m. 24 Feb. 1857, Emma Elizabeth, da. of Robert Darwin Vaughton of Ashfurlong House, co. Warwick ; and had issue 1e to 5e.

1e. William Vaughton Pennefather of Lakefield (*Stoke Lodge, Milborough ; Lakefield*), b. 14 Jan. 1862; m. 17 Nov. 1891, Louisa Mary [descended from George, Duke of Clarence, K.G. (see Clarence Volume, p. 164)], da. of William John Bankes, *formerly* Murray, of Winstanley ; and has (with other) issue 1f.

1f. Richard Pennefather, b. 1893.

2e. Richard Dymoke Pennefather, b. 1865.

3e. Maria Emma Pennefather.

4e. Harriet Lavinia Pennefather.

5e. Anna Louisa Pennefather.

2d. William Pennefather.

3d. *Matthew Pennefather*, d. 1859.

4d. *William John Copley Lyndhurst Pennefather*, d. 1865.

4c. *Dorothea Pennefather*. d. (? s.p.) 1845 ; m. 1st, *Richard Lockwood of Cashel*, d. (-) ; 2ndly, as 2nd wife, 1 Oct. 1827, Capt. Thomas Sadleir of Castletown, co. Tipperary, 99th Regt., d. (s.p. by her) 22 Oct. 1842.

5c. *Catherine Pennefather*, d. (-) ; m. 31 Dec. 1801, *Lieut.-Col. Owen Lloyd of Rockville, co. Roscommon*, d. 12 Ap. 1840 ; *and had (with other) issue* 1d *to* 2d.

1d. *William Lloyd of Rockville* (eldest son), b. 28 Feb. 1803 ; d. 7 Jan. 1870 ; m. 22 Sept. 1829, Anne (see p. 356), da. of Major Acheson Montgomery Moore, d. (-) ; *and had issue* 1e *to* 2e.

1e. *Owen Richard Nathaniel Lloyd of Rockville, Major in the Army*, b. 7 July 1830 ; d. 17 Nov. 1863 ; m. 20 Sept. 1855, Frances Maria, da. of William Hutchinson of Carrick-on-Shannon, M.D., d. 2 Oct. 1885 ; *and had issue* 1f *to* 3f.

1f. William Lloyd of Rockville, J.P., D.L., High Sheriff co. Roscommon 1889, *formerly* Capt. and Hon. Major 5th Batt. Connaught Rangers (*Rockville, Drumsna, Roscommon ; Kildare Street*), b. 8 July 1858 ; m. 28 Jan. 1884, Mary Brodribb, da. of Major William Lancelot Hutchinson ; and has issue 1g to 3g.

1g. William Hutchinson Lloyd, b. 2 Ap. 1885.

2g. Coote Richard FitzGerald Lloyd, b. 2 July 1887.

3g. Gwendoline Elizabeth May Lloyd.

2f. John Charles Lloyd, b. (—) ; *m.* Margaret, da. of (—) Waldron; and has issue 1g to 2g.

1g. Owen John Montgomery Lloyd.

2g. Frances Maria Lloyd.

3f. *Anna Montgomery Lloyd*, d. 190- ; m. *the Rev. William Kennedy Brodribb, B.A., Rector of Putley, co. Herts*, d. (-); *and had issue* 1g *to* 2g.

1g. Owen Adams Kennedy Brodribb.

2g. *Eanswith Alice Kennedy Brodribb*, d. (-)

2e. Acheson Montgomery Lloyd, b. 26 Oct. 1831 ; *m.* 18 Jan. 1865, Catherine (see p. 355), da. of the Rev. James Wentworth Mansergh ; and has issue 1f.

1f. William Owen Lloyd, b. 29 July 1866.

2d. *Catherine Lloyd* (3rd da.), d. 27 Sept. 1891 ; m. 31 Oct. 1835, *the Rev. James Wentworth Mansergh* (see p. 361), *Rector of Kilmore* [*Cadet of Grenane*], d. 1845 ; *and had issue (with 2 other sons who d.s.p.)* 1e *to* 2e.

1e. *Daniel James Mansergh of Grallagh Castle, co. Tipperary, J.P., Col. Comdg. South Tipperary Art. Mil., formerly 19th Regt.*, b. 3 Nov. 1836 ; d. (-) ; m. 3 July 1866, Margaret, da. of Austin Cooper of Camas.

[Nos. 59696 to 59712.]

# of The Blood Royal

2e. Catherine Mansergh, m. 18 Jan. 1865, Acheson Montgomery Lloyd (see p. 354); and has issue.
See p. 354, No. 59712.

6c. *Margaret Pennefather*, d. 1874; m. Feb. 1811, *Ambrose Going of Ballyphilip, co. Tipperary*, b. Oct. 1785; d. Aug. 1857; *and had issue 1d to 7d*.

1d. *William Going of Ballyphilip, J.P., D.L.*, b. *June* 1815; d. 1878; m. Oct. 1841, *Jane Eliza, da. of Benjamin Frend of Rocklow, co. Tipperary*, d. 2 Oct. 1892; *and had issue (with a son and da.* d.s.p.*) 1e to 3e*.

1e. *Benjamin Frend Going of Ballyphilip, J.P., D.L., High Sheriff co. Tipperary* 1883, b. 17 Ap. 1852; d. 7 Mar. 1883; m. 16 Jan. 1879, *Florence Isabella Anna, da. of Richard Fitzroy Creagh of Millbrooke and Athassel, co. Tipperary*; *and had issue 1f to 3f*.

1f. *William Ambrose Going of Ballyphilip*, b. 31 Oct. 1881; d.s.p. 7 Mar. 1897.

2f. Mabel Anna Going of Ballyphilip, m. 25 Jan. 1908, Capt. Charles Morris Threlfell, *late* 8th Hussars (*Nun Monkton, York*); and has issue 1g.

1g. Charles Reginald Morris Threlfell, b. 15 Oct. 1908.

3f. Bena Going of Ballyphilip (*Ballyphilip, Killenaule, Tipperary*).

2e. Eliza Going, m. 5 Nov. 1873, Major Alexander W. Bailey, Fermanagh L.I., s.p.

3e. Arabella Jane Going, *unm.*

2d. *Richard Pennefather Going, J.P.*, b. 1821; d.s.p. 1872; m. 1862, *Letitia Elizabeth, da. of the Rev. Robert Bury of Killora, co. Cork*.

3d. *John Going of Wilford, co. Tipperary*, b. Aug. 1822; d.s.p. 1873.

4d. *Anna Going*, d. 1865; m. 1835, *the Rev. Anthony Armstrong, Rector of Killorskully*; *and had issue a da., Meta*, d. 1908.

5d. *Margaret Isabella Going*, d. 12 *June* 1858; m. 1841, *Christopher F. Tuthill of Dublin, M.D.*; *and had issue, George and Ambrose, both dead (? s.p.)*.

6d. *Elizabeth Frances Going*, d. 25 *July* 1867; m. *as 1st wife*, 30 *Ap*. 1846, *John Hervey Adams of Northlands, co. Cavan, Bar.-at-Law, J.P., High Sheriff for that co. and Monaghan* 1854, b. 28 *Ap*. 1818; d. 8 *May* 1871; *and had issue 1e to 4e*.

1e. Samuel Allen Adams of Northlands, J.P., *formerly* Lieut. Tipperary Art. Mil. (*Northlands, Carrickmacross*), b. 1 Mar. 1847; *m*. 13 June 1871, Frances Dorothea [descended from the Lady Anne, sister of Kings Edward IV. and Richard III. (see Exeter Volume, p. 542)], da. of the Rev. Decimus William Preston, M.A., Rector of Killinkere [and grandda. of William Preston, a Judge of the Court of Appeal, by his wife the Hon. Frances Dorothea, da. and co-h. of John (Evans), 5th Baron Carbery [I.]]; and has issue (with 3 das. *d.* young) 1f to 6f.

1f. John Hervey Stuart Adams, b. 30 Dec. 1875.

2f. Samuel Allen Adams, b. 11 Ap. 1882.

3f. Ambrose Douglas Adams, b. 9 May 1889.

4f. Olive Mildred Adams.

5f. Mary Henrietta Mabel Adams.

6f. Hazel Gertrude Adams.

2e. *Ambrose Going Adams, J.P.*, b. 22 *Mar*. 1850; d. 11 *Jan*. 1888; m. 3 Oct. 1872, *Anne Jane Foster, da. of the Rev. William Watkyns Deering, M.A.*; *and had issue 1f to 2f*.

1f. Clara Elizabeth Charlotte Adams, *m*. 1 June 1894, Frederick Foster McClintock.

2f. Ethel Annie Adams.

3e. Margaret Anna Adams, *m*. 4 Ap. 1871, Ormsby Colville McClintock Jones of Mount Edward, co. Sligo, J.P. (*Mount Edward; Drangan, Foxrock, co. Dublin*); and has issue (with 2 sons *d.s.p.*) 1f to 5f.

1f. Percy James Colville Jones, b. 22 Nov. 1872.

2f. John Henry Colville Jones, b. 28 Aug. 1874. [Nos. 59713 to 59731.

The Plantagenet Roll

3*f*. William Ambrose Colville Jones, *b*. 16 Sept. 1886.
4*f*. Digby Colville Jones, *b*. 1892.
5*f*. Dorothy Colville Jones.

4*e*. Elizabeth Frances Adams, *m*. 3 Sept. 1872, Robert Edward Follett Jones [son of Major James Jones of Mount Edward] (*Alverstoke, Foxrock, co. Dublin*); and has issue (with 3 sons *d*. young) 1*f* to 2*f*.
   1*f*. Sidney Follett Jones, *b*. 20 June 1879.
   2*f*. Elsie Noel Jones.

7*d*. *Dorothea Going*, *d*. 1873; *m*. *May* 1848, *Samuel Murray Going of Liskaveen House, co. Tipperary; and had issue, John*, d. (-), *and Margaret and Mary, one of whom* m. *as 2nd wife, Nov.* 1883, *Owen Lloyd Mansergh, afterwards Going, J.P.*, d.s.p. 3 Oct. 1892.

7*c*. *Eliza Pennefather*, d. 26 *Ap*. 1835; m. 1st, 1813, *Major Acheson Montgomery-Moore* [*Cadet of Garvah, co. Tyrone*], b. 17 *Oct.* 1788; d. (-); 2ndly, *as* 1st *wife*, 10 Aug. 1816, *Sir John Judkin-FitzGerald of Lisheen*, 2nd *Bt.* [U.K.], b. 27 Aug. 1787; d. 28 Feb. 1860; *and had issue* 1*d to* 2*d*.
   1*d*. Sir Thomas Judkin FitzGerald, 3rd Bt. [U.K.], b. 20 July 1820; d. 27 Ap. 1864; m. 25 Jan. 1845, *Emma Louisa Maunsell, da. of Henry White of Golden Hills, co. Tipperary; and had issue* 1*e to* 5*e*.
      1*e*. Sir Joseph Capel Judkin-FitzGerald of Lisheen, 4th Bt. [U.K.], *b*. 9 Aug. 1853; *m*. 5 June 1872, Constance Sarah, da. of Capt. William Augustus Hyder, 10th Hussars; and has issue 1*f* to 2*f*.
         1*f*. Thomas Judkin Judkin-FitzGerald, *b*. 1873.
         2*f*. Evelyn Constance Hyder Judkin-FitzGerald.
      2*e*. Robert Uniacke Judkin-FitzGerald, *b*. 1855.
      3*e*. Eliza Anna Judkin-FitzGerald, *m*. 1872, John E. Roberts of Clifton, Bristol.
      4*e*. Emma Augusta Judkin-FitzGerald, *m*. 1872, Edmund T. Hale, *formerly* of The Grange, co. Somerset.
      5*e*. Henrietta Mary De la Poer Judkin-FitzGerald, *m*. 1874, William Powell Keale, *formerly* of Nelson Lodge, Bristol, d. (-).

   2*d*. *Anne Montgomery-Moore*, d. (-); m. 22 *Sept.* 1829, *William Lloyd of Rockville*, d. 7 *Jan.* 1870; *and had issue.*
   See p. 354, Nos. 59703–59712.

2*b*. *Rev. John Pennefather, D.D., Rector of St. John's, Newport, co. Tipperary*, d. (-); m. *Elizabeth, da. of Major Perceval*, d. (-); *and had issue* 1*c to* 9*c*.
   1*c*. *Kingsmill Pennefather, Major Limerick Militia*, d. 1860; m. 1*st, Frances, da. of Major Townsend of Monckton Hall*, d. (-); 2ndly, 1842, *Jane Catherine Patricia* [*descended from George, Duke of Clarence, K.G.* (see the Essex Volume Supplement, p. 558)], *da. of Thomas de Grenier de Fonblanque, K.H.*, d. 6 May 1886; *and had issue* 1*d to* 8*d*.
      1*d*.¹ John Pennefather.
      2*d*.² Charles Edward de Fonblanque Pennefather, *b*. 23 June 1848; *m*. Maizie, da. of C. Seward of Melbourne; and has issue 1*e* to 3*e*.
         1*e*. John Pennefather.
         2*e*. Charles Pennefather.
         3*e*. Edward Pennefather.

      3*d*.² De Fonblanque Pennefather, J.P. (*Kinnersley Castle, co. Hereford*), *b*. 29 Mar. 1856; *m*. 28 Ap. 1886, Madeline, da. of Sir Robert Prescott Stewart; *s.p.*
      4*d*.¹ Elizabeth Pennefather.
      5*d*.¹ Fanny Pennefather.
      6*d*.¹ Caroline Pennefather.
      7*d*.¹ Clare Pennefather.   [Nos. 59732 to 59764.

of The Blood Royal

8*d.*² *Ruth Pennefather,* d. *Sept.* 1906; m. *William Nimo (Oakhill Park, near Liverpool)*; *and had issue* 1*e to* 4*e.*
  1*e.* William Pennefather Nimo, *b.* 6 Sept. 1881.
  2*e.* Charles Nimo, b. 4 *Aug.* 1883; d. 20 *Ap.* 1909.
  3*e.* Kingsmill Nimo, *b.* 23 June 1885.
  4*e.* Dorothea Nimo.

2*c. William Westby Pennefather, Lieut. R.N.,* d. (? s.p.); m. *Elizabeth, da. of William Harding.*
3*c. Sir John Lysaght Pennefather, K.C.B., G.C.L.H., K.C.M.L., Gen. and Col.* 22*nd Foot,* d. 1872; m. 1830, *Margaret, da. of John Carr of Mountrath.*
4*c. Joseph Lysaght Pennefather, Bar.-at-Law,* d. (-); m. *Elizabeth, da. of* (—) *Rea of Barnwood, co. Glouc.; and had issue* 1*d.*
  1*d.* Julia Pennefather.

5*c. Robert Percival Pennefather, Lieut. and Adj.* 3*rd Bengal Cav.,* d. (-); m. *Elizabeth, da. of* (—) *Benson,* d. 28 *Mar.* 1887; *and had issue* 1*d to* 2*d.*
  1*d. Henry Vansittart Pennefather, Capt.* 41*st Foot,* b. 1791; d. *in Natal* 9 *Aug.* 1888; m. 23 *Oct.* 1860, *Margaretta Luchesa Jane Maria, widow of Col. John Temple West, da. and h. of Sir John George Reeve De la Pole,* 8*th Bt.* [*E.*], d. (-).
  2*d. Laura Pennefather,* d. (-); m. *George Rae, M.D., Bengal Med. Estab.*

6*c. Anne Pennefather,* d. *Dec.* 1863; m. *Sept.* 1814, *William Ryan of Ballymackeogh, co. Tipperary,* d. 27 *Nov.* 1835; *and had issue* 1*d to* 8*d.*
  — 1*d. William Ryan of Ballymackeogh, J.P.,* b. 1 *Dec.* 1815; d. 13 *Feb.* 1890; m. 29 *Nov.* 1842, *Jane, sister of Sir Edward Grogan,* 1*st Bt.* [*U.K.*], *M.P., da. of John Grogan, Bar.-at-Law,* d. 17 *Nov.* 1895; *and had issue* 1*e to* 3*e.*
  1*e.* Charles Arthur Ryan of Ballymackeogh, J.P. (*Ballymackeogh, Newport, Tipperary*), *b.* 7 Nov. 1853; *m.* 24 Feb. 1903, Mary, da. of Henry Ormsby Rose of Ballyculleen, co. Limerick.
  2*e.* Anne Alicia Susanna Ryan, *m.* 8 Jan. 1881, Ringrose Drew [Cadet of Drewscourt], *d.* 23 Dec. 1895; and has issue 1*f* to 4*f*.
  1*f.* Francis William Massy Drew.
  2*f.* Ringrose Charles Wellington Drew.
  3*f.* Alicia Jeannette Drew.
  4*f.* Anna Everina Margaret Drew.

  3*e.* Jeannette Ryan, *m.* 10 Aug. 1886, Edward Herbert Maunsell (*Macleod, Alberta, Canada*); and has issue.
  2*d. John Ryan,* d. *Sept.* 1873; m. 1843, *Louisa Ricarda, da. of Major Kingsmill Pennefather of Knockinglass, co. Tipperary; and had issue* 1*e to* 4*e.*
  1*e. Rev. William Ewer Ryan, M.A.,* d. (-).
  2*e. John Pennefather Ryan, M.D.,* d. (-).
  3*e. Frances Elizabeth Ryan,* d. (? unm.).
  4*e. Louisa Mary Ryan,* d. (? s.p.); m. 1885, *Townsend Hall of Pilton, co. Devon.*
  3*d. George Henry Ryan, M.D., Surg. R.N.,* d.s.p.
  4*d. Robert Perceval Ryan,* d. (? s.p.).
  5*d. Edward Ryan,* d. (? s.p.).
  6*d. Elizabeth Ryan,* d. (? s.p.).
  7*d. Clara Ryan,* d. (? s.p.).
  8*d. Laura Ryan,* d. (? s.p.).

7*c. Mary Charity Pennefather,* d. 2 *July* 1834; m. *as* 1*st wife,* 15 *May* 1809, *Henry Vansittart of Eastwood, Woodstock, Canada, Vice-Adm. R.N.* [5*th son of George Vansittart of Bisham Abbey, co. Berks, M.P., J.P., D.L.* (see p. 455)], d. 14 *Mar.* 1842; *and had issue* 1*d to* 4*d.*
  1*d. John George Vansittart of Woodstock and Ottawa, Canada,* b. 15 *Ap.* 1813;
[Nos. 59765 to 59775.

The Plantagenet Roll

d. 13 Oct. 1869; m. 11 Aug. 1835, *Isabella Carrick*, da. *of James Royse Yelding of Tralee, co. Kerry*, d. 7 Feb. 1903; *and had issue 1e to 3e*.

1e. John Pennefather Vansittart, P.W.D., India, bapt. 22 Oct. 1837; d. 1887; m. 1 Oct. 1879, *Isabella Maud (Toronto, Canada)*, da. *of the Hon. John Alexander, a Canadian Senator; and had issue 1f to 2f*.

 1f. George Edward Vansittart, b. 1884.

 2f. Cecil Isabella Vansittart, b. at Mussooree, N.W.P., India, 12 June 1880.

2e. James Graham Vansittart of Osgood Hall, Bar, Medal, and Clasps for Fenian Raid of 1866, b. 18 June 1839; d. 22 June 1901; m. 1868, *Letitia*, da. *of Henry Prittie Bayly of Ballykeefe, Limerick*; *and had issue 1f*.

 1f. Frances Isabella Linda Vansittart, *m.* 6 June 1900, Lorne Bruce Chadwicke Livingstone, Bar.-at-Law [son of William Livingstone of Musselburgh, Scotland] (*Osgood Hall, Tilsonburg, Ontario*); and has issue 1g to 3g.

  1g. John Pennefather Livingstone, b. 6 June 1902.

  2g. Margaret Vansittart Livingstone, b. 7 Mar. 1901.

  3g. Isobel Kingsforth Livingstone, b. 4 Jan. 1910.

3e. *Charles Edward Vansittart, Lieut.-Col. Army Ordnance Dept.*, b. 3 Mar. 1847; d. 16 Aug. 1898; m. 12 May 1894, *Teresa, widow of the Rev. Joseph Wolstenholme*, da. *of* (—), d. 15 May 1905; *and had issue 1f*.

 1f. Mignon Vansittart.

2d. Henry Vansittart of Canada, b. 26 May 1815; d. 1 Nov. 1868; m. 4 Oct. 1848, *Emily Louisa*, da. *of Edward Huggins of The Old Manor Estate, Nevis, W.I.*, d. 1 July 1869; *and had issue (with 2 sons and 2 das. d.s.p.) 1e*.

1e. Fanny Georgina Vansittart, *m.* as 2nd wife, 18 Oct. 1883, the Rev. John Wynn Werninck (see p. 359), Rector of Weston Bampfylde, *formerly* Vicar of Stanton Drew (*Weston Bampfylde Rectory, Sparkford, Som.*); and has issue 1f to 5f.

 1f. Pelham Vansittart Wynn Werninck, b. 20 Sept. 1884.

 2f. Henry Vansittart Wynn Werninck, b. 12 Mar. 1877.

 3f. Kathleen Marjorie Wynn Werninck.

 4f. Fanny Gladys Wynn Werninck.

 5f. Alice Maude Wynn Werninck.

3d. *Elizabeth Vansittart*, d. 8 Aug. 1873; m. 4 Ap. 1836, *Robert Riddell [Bt. [S. 1628] Coll.]*, d. 18 Nov. 1864; *and had issue 1e to 6e*.

1e. Robert Vansittart Riddell, Col. *late* R.E., sometime Master of H.M.'s Mint, Bombay (*Essex Lodge, Liverpool Gardens, Worthing*), b. 12 Mar. 1840; *m.* 27 Ap. 1870, *Louisa Flora Steel*, da. *of Gen. Alexander Dick*; and has issue 1f to 4f.

 1f. Robert Buchanan Riddell, Capt. and Brevet-Major R.A., served in S. Africa 1899-1900, Medal and 5 Clasps, b. 1 Ap. 1872.

 2f. Edward Vansittart Dick Riddell, Capt. and Brevet-Major R.A., served in S. Africa 1899-1900, b. 30 Mar. 1873; *m.* 20 Feb. 1902, Edith Mary, da. of Major-Gen. E. P. Bingham Turner, R.A.; and has issue 1g.

  1g. Edward Alexander Buchanan Riddell, b. 8 Feb. 1903.

 3f. John Balfour Riddell, Capt. R.F.A., b. 2 May 1880; *m.* 5 Aug. 1908, Margaret Alice, da. of John William Smith of The Rectory, Oundle.

 4f. Ethel Riddell, *m.* 27 July 1901, Charles Dingwall Williams; and has issue 1g.

  1g. Charles Dingwall Williams, b. 1902.

2e. Henry Vansittart Riddell, Col. Bengal N.I., b. 9 Oct. 1841; d. 14 Jan. 1888; m. 1st, 1 Nov. 1864, *Alice*, da. *of Richard Attwood*, d. 1884; 2ndly, 1886, *Annie*, da. *of Stephen Francis Shairp of St. Maur* (see Supp.); *and had issue 1f to 3f*.

 1f.[1] Laurie Archibald Riddell, b. 1877.

 2f.[1] Mary Alice Riddell, *m.* 1st, 17 Feb. 1885, Capt. John Hawley Burke, W. Yorks Regt., d. 24 Oct. 1887; 2ndly 1890, John Burke; and has issue 1g to 4g.

[Nos. 59776 to 59797.

# of The Blood Royal

1g. Noel Hawley Michael Burke, b. 1885.

2g. Arthur Laurie Burke, b. 1887.

3g. John Lawrence Burke, b. 1891.

4g. Yvonne Lilian Gervaise Burke.

3f. Clara Edith Riddell.

3e. *Walter Riddell, Lieut.-Col. R.A.*, b. 27 Ap. 1845; d. 15 Oct. 1895; m. 27 Sept. 1877, *Charlotte Margaret, da. of Brig.-Gen. James George Neill, C.B.*; and had issue 1f.

1f. Florence Agnes Isabel Riddell.

4e. Mary Clare Riddell (*St. Cuthberga, Rushton Crescent, Bournemouth*), m. 1883, John Broughton, d.s.p. 5 Mar. 1906.

5e. Elizabeth Janet Riddell, *unm.*

6e. Caroline Edith Westby Riddell, d.s.p. 28 Nov. 1881; m. as 1st wife, 2 Sept. 1880, the Rev. John Wynn Werninck (see p. 358).

4d. *Mary Charity Vansittart*, d. 3 Sept. 1866; m. 11 June 1838, *Spencer Mackay of Blandford, Canada*, d. 1860; and had issue 1e to 6e.

1e. *Spencer Henry Mackay, Major 101st Royal Munster Fusiliers*, b. 21 Jan. 1842; d. 20 Ap. 1905; m. *Mary Horan, da. of J. Thompson*; and had issue 1f to 3f.

1f. Spencer Edward Mackay, b. Aug. 1878; m. 19 Sept. 1910, May, da. of Col. Penton.

2f. William Mackay, b. Nov. 1879.

3f. Ethel Maud Mackay.

2e. Edward Vansittart Mackay, *late* Indian Police (10 *College Road, Clifton*), b. 11 July 1849; m. 1886, Nina, da. of J. C. Whitty; and has issue 1f to 3f.

1f. Eric Vansittart Mackay, b. Sept. 1891.

2f. Claude Lysaght Mackay, b. Oct. 1894.

3f. Verna Maude Vansittart Mackay.

3e. Louisa Mary Mackay, *unm.*

4e. Elizabeth L. Mackay, m. 1892, the Rev. John Watson Gordon Bishop, *formerly* Chaplain at Grasse 1883-1886 (*Dudley House, Sandown, I.W.*); s.p.

5e. Rosa M. Mackay (26 *St. James' Road, Tunbridge Wells*), m. C. Stanley of Roughan Park, Dungannon, d.s.p.

6e. Gertrude Mackay, m. 14 Aug. 1873, Arthur H. Bowles (*Temple Court, near Guildford*); and has issue (with a da., Florence Maud Ethel, d. unm.) 1f to 6f.

1f. *Arthur Frederick Vansittart Bowles*, b. 10 Nov. 1875; d. 1 Dec. 1908; m. 1903, *Edith, da. of W. C. Prangley*; and had issue (a da., Edith).

2f. Charles Edward Bowles, M.E. (*South Africa*), b. 27 Nov. 1876.

3f. Rosa Gertrude Eleanor Bowles, m. 1902, Henry Clutton Broock (*Lake View, Northwood, Midx.*); and has issue (2 sons).

4f. Mary Edith Bowles, m. 1905, Guy Fleming (*Mexico*).

5f. Lilian Maude Bowles, m. 1908, Hugh Merriman (*Hall Dene, Marrow, near Guildford*).

6f. Margaret Irene Bowles, *unm.*

8c. *Clare Pennefather*, d. (-); m. *Thomas Evans of Ashore, co. Tipperary, Lieut. R.N.*

9c. *Laura Pennefather*, d. (-); m. (—) *Philips of Mount Philips.*

3b. *William Pennefather, M.P. for Cashel 1783-1797, Surveyor-Gen. in Ireland, &c.*, d. (-); m. *Frances, da. of Francis Nisbett of Derrycarne, co. Leitrim*; and had issue 1c to 5c.

1c. *William Pennefather, H.E.I.C.S.*, d. *unm* 1826.

2c. *Richard Daniel Pennefather of Kilbracken, co. Leitrim, J.P., D.L., Col. E. Kent Militia*, b. 13 Aug. 1818; d. 7 Sept. 1881; m. 7 Oct. 1868, the Hon. *Sarah Anna, da. of Hervey (de Montmorency), 4th Viscount Mountmorres* [I.], *LL.D., Dean of Achonry*; and had issue 1d to 3d.   [Nos. 59798 to 59821.

The Plantagenet Roll

1*d*. Rev. William de Montmorency Pennefather, M.A. (Oxon.) (*Lincoln College, Oxford*), *b*. 27 Aug. 1869 ; *unm*.

2*d*. Anna de Montmorency Pennefather, *m*. 1st, as 3rd wife, 26 Sept. 1900, Col. George Fleming of Higher Leigh, co. Devon, C.B., LL.D., *d*. 13 Ap. 1901 ; 2ndly, 11 Sept. 1905, Alfred Moore, *otherwise* More, now (D.P. 24 Ap. 1906) Alfred Thomas More, B.Sc. (*Morecot, Abingdon*) ; and has issue (with Daniel de Montmorency Thomas More, *b*. 24 Nov. 1907 ; *d*. 29 Jan. 1908) 1*e*.

1*e*. David Pennefather Thomas More, *b*. 24 June 1906.

3*d*. Mary Eva de Montmorency Pennefather.

3*c*. Margaret Pennefather, d. Dec. 1873 ; m. 1824, *Richard Warren of Lisgoold*, M.D. [Bt. Coll. (see p. 363)], d. Dec. 1870 ; *and had issue 1d to 2d*.

1*d*. Frances Warren, d. (-) ; m. 1st, *Capt. Oldham, 2nd Regt.*, d. (*being killed in Kaffir War*) 18—; 2ndly, 1859, *William Connor of Milton, co. Cork*.

2*d*. Augusta Warren, d. 1 Dec. 1873 ; m. *as 1st wife*, 22 *Aug.* 1854, *her kinsman Richard Lane Warren, 35th Regt.*, b. 29 *Jan*. 1828 ; d. (-) ; *and had issue 1e to 6e*.

1*e*. William Pennefather Warren, *b*. 16 Ap. 1860.

2*e*. Richard Warren, *b*. 5 Dec. 1861.

3*e*. Ethel Warren, *m*. Henry Daunt of Kinsale [4th son of Achilles Daunt of Tracton Abbey, co. Cork].

4*e*. Augusta Julia Warren.

5*e*. Cherry Frances Warren.

6*e*. Violet Laura Warren.

4*c*. Elizabeth Pennefather, d. (-) ; m. *as 2nd wife*, *Phineas Bury of Little Island, co. Cork*, J.P., Capt. 7th Dragoons, d. 1853 ; *and had issue 1d to 3d*.

1*d*. Phineas Bury of Little Island, J.P., Capt. 15th Hussars, b. 7 Mar. 1841 ; d.s.p. 9 May 1895.

2*d*. William Phineas Bury of Curraghbridge, co. Limerick, b. 27 Nov. 1842 ; d. (-) ; m. *Harriet, da. of Arthur Forbes of Newstone, co. Meath* ; *and had issue 1e*.

1*e*. William Phineas Bury of Curraghbridge and Little Island (*Carrigrenane, Little Island, co. Cork ; Curraghbridge, Adare, co. Limerick*).

3*d*. Frances Jane Bury, *m*. Major C. T. Tuckey, 41st Regt.

5*c*. Frances Mary Pennefather, d. (? s.p.) 1848 ; m. *Col. Arthur St. George Herbert Stepney, C.B., Coldstream Guards*.

4*b*. Mary Pennefather, d. (-) ; m. *Daniel Conner of Ballybricken, co. Cork ;* *and had* (*with possibly other*) *issue* 1*c*.

1*c*. Daniel Conner of Ballybricken, J.P., d. (-) ; m. *his cousin Anna, da. of William Pennefather ; and had* (*with possibly other*) *issue* 1*d*.

1*d*. Richard Conner of Ballybricken, d. 1862 ; m. 1833, *Elizabeth, da. of* (—) *Perrott*, d. 1853 ; *and had issue 1e to 4e*.

1*e*. Daniel Conner of Ballybricken, J.P., b. 27 Sept. 1835 ; d. 31 Dec. 1899 ; m. 14 *June* 1866, *Emily, da. of Henry Steigen Berger of 30 Cleveland Square, Hyde Park, W*. *; and had issue 1f to 6f*.

1*f*. Daniel Henry Conner of Ballybricken (*Ballybricken, co. Cork*), b. 5 Ap. 1867 ; m. 14 Jan. 1902, Florence Jane, da. of Capt. Horace Townshend, 99th Regt.

2*f*. Richard Conner, Major Gloucester Regt., b. 29 Dec. 1868.

3*f*. Henry Conner } (twins), b. 17 Sept. 1872.
4*f*. Samuel Conner, Staff Surgeon, R.N.

5*f*. Emily Conner.

6*f*. Kathleen Louisa Conner.

2*e*. William Conner, M.D., *m*. 6 June 1872, Ellen Lawrence, da. of William Colbourne of Monkstown, co. Cork.

3*e*. George Conner, Col. 28th Regt., d. (-).

4*e*. Elizabeth Mary Conner, *m*. 28 Ap. 1870, Samuel Willy Perrott.

[Nos. 59822 to 59841.

# of The Blood Royal

5b. *Catherine Pennefather*, d. 17 Nov. 1834; m. *June* 1788, *Daniel Mansergh of Cashel, High Sheriff co. Tipperary* 1789 [*Cadet of Grinane*], b. c. 1773; d. 10 *June* 1823; *and had issue* 1c *to* 5c.

1c. *Nicholas Mansergh of Macrony Castle, co. Cork, J.P., M.A., last Recorder of Cashel* 1836, b. 20 *May* 1789; d. (? s.p.) *Oct.* 1865.

2c. *Daniel Mansergh of Ballyshean, Cashel, Capt. in the Army*, d. (–); m. 1st, 22 *Aug.* 1836, (—), da. of (—) *Budd of Kilkenny*, d. (-); 2ndly, *Eleanor Jane*, da. *of George Riall of Parsonstown*, d. 21 *Aug.* 1893; *and had issue* 1d *to* 5d.

1d.¹ Henry Mansergh, d. 1889.
2d.¹ [son] Mansergh.
3d.¹ [da.] Mansergh.
4d.¹ [da.] Mansergh.
5d.² Helen Elizabeth Frances Mansergh.

3c. *Rev. James Wentworth Mansergh, Rector of Kilmore*, d. 1845; m. 31 *Oct.* 1835, *Catherine*, da. *of Col. Owen Lloyd of Rockville*, d. 27 *Sept.* 1891; *and had issue.*
See p. 354, Nos. 59713–59714.

4c. *Mary Mansergh*, d. (–); m. *Edward Pennefather of Marlow, near Cashel; and had issue* 5 *sons, of whom one was father of Richard Lloyd Pennefather of Marlow, Goold's Cross, co. Tipperary.*

5c. *Catherine Mansergh*, b. 5 *Ap.* 1805; d. 25 *Sept.* 1898; m. 10 *July* 1840, *Richard Martin of Castle Jane, co. Cork*, b. 15 *Dec.* 1786; d. 16 *Ap.* 1870; *and had issue* 1d *to* 3d.

1d. Richard Mansergh Martin of Castle Jane (*Castle Jane, Glanmire, co. Cork*), b. 22 Mar. 1843; *m.* 3 Oct. 1905, Leonarda, da. of Capt. John Crawford Langford of Kingstown, co. Dublin; *s.p.*

2d. Daniel Nicholas Martin, M.D., Lieut.-Col. (ret.) Indian M.S. (*Churston, co. Devon*), b. 4 Aug. 1844; *m.* 15 Jan. 1895, Etheldreda, da. of the Rev. J. W. Hardman of Cadbury House, Yatton, LL.D.; and has issue 1e.

1e. Viola Martin, b. 25 Mar. 1896.

3d. James Wentworth Martin, *formerly* Madras P.W. Dept. (*Banisters, Finchampstead, Berks*), b. 24 Jan. 1847; *m.* 13 Dec. 1900, Violet, da. of the Rev. Canon Joseph Hammond of New Beckingham; and has issue 1e to 2e.

1e. James Mansergh Wentworth Martin, b. 5 Aug. 1902.
2e. [son] Wentworth Martin, b. 10 Feb. 1906.

6b. *Margaret Pennefather*, d. 1833; m. *the Rev. Robert Warren of Crookstown House, co. Cork* [5th *son of Sir Robert Warren of Warren's Court*, 1st *Bt.* [*I.* 1784]], d. 1830; *and had issue* 1c *to* 3c.

1c. *Rev. Robert Warren, Rector of Cannoway, co. Cork*, b. 7 *Mar.* 1794; d. 7 *May* 1879; m. 26 *May* 1824, *Mary*, da. *of David Crawford of Ballyshannon, J.P., R.N.; and had issue* 1d *to* 4d.

1d. *Robert Warren of Crookstown*, b. 8 Oct. 1826; d. 6 *May* 1903; m. 6 *Sept.* 1859, *Sophia* (*Crookstown, co. Cork*), da. *of Henry Braddell of Mallow; and had issue* 1e *to* 5e.

1e. Robert Warren of Crookstown (*Crookstown House, co. Cork*), b. 22 May 1870; *m.* 1 Jan. 1904, Maria Frances Lumley, da. of William Lumley Perrier of Maryborough, Douglas, co. Cork; and has issue 1f to 2f.

1f. Augustus John Warren, b. 9 Sept. 1909.
2f. Gladys Irene Warren, b. 20 May 1908.

2e. Mary Frances Warren, *unm.*

3e. Sophia Louise Clowser Warren, *m.* 17 June 1891, Jasper Drury, *formerly* of the Bush, Youghal, co. Cork (*Douglas, Isle of Man*); and has issue 1f to 2f.

1f. Jasper Drury, b. 17 Feb. 1893.
2f. Robert Warren Drury, b. 27 Oct. 1894. [Nos. 59842 to 59860.

The Plantagenet Roll

4e. Alice Sarah Warren, m. 1893, Major Arthur Phelps, Army Ser. Corps, *formerly* Dept. Assist. Dir. of Quartering H.Q. 1904–1908, and D.A.A.G. South Africa 1901–1902 (*Modern Imperial Hotel, Lliema, Malta*).

5e. Maude Warren.

2d. Richard Warren, Major-Gen. (ret.) R.E. (12 *Portland Terrace, Southsea; Junior United Service*), b. 31 May 1828; m. 1st, 24 Feb. 1852, Emily, da. of William Lauder of Dominica, d. 7 Aug. 1891; 2ndly, 27 Dec. 1893, Martha Elizabeth, widow of Robert Pitcairn of Sydney, Bar.-at-Law, da. of Stephen Hawley Dunstall of Wolverhampton; and has issue (with others who d.s.p.) 1e to 7e.

1e. Herbert Lauder Warren, Staff Paymaster R.N., b. 1 Ap. 1855; d. 9 Jan. 1897; m. 7 Nov. 1885, *Ella Christian* (*Vectis Lodge, Victoria Road South, Southsea*), da. of Christian Hoyer Millar of *Blair Castle, co. Perth*; and had issue 1f to 2f.

1f. Ella Christian Louise Lauder Warren.
2f. Kathleen Pelham Lauder Warren.

2e. Albert Edward Warren, b. 29 May 1856; d. 27 Feb. 1899; m. 1884, *Emily*, da. of Talbot Palmer of *Waterloo Ville, co. Hants*; and had issue 1f to 6f.

1f. Edward Richard Warren, b. 28 Oct. 1888.
2f. Henry Charles Herbert Warren, b. 3 Nov. 1898.
3f. Emily Ruth Warren, m. 1907, (—) Hardy (*Cape Town*).
4f. Dorothy Talbot Warren, m. 1907, Bernard Twedale.
5f. Winifred Mary Warren, m. the Rev. E. W. Watt.
6f. Marjorie Anne Warren.

3e. Henry Herrick Warren, b. 22 Dec. 1857; m. 1908, Elizabeth, da. of John Leader of *Keale, co. Cork*.

4e. Richard Augustus Warren, H.M.'s Customs, Natal (*Durban, Natal*), b. 31 Mar. 1862; m. 12 Ap. 1898, Marie Charlotte Alice, da. of Attwell Hayes Allen of *Sea View, Queenstown, co. Cork*; s.p.

5e. Percy Bliss Warren, Lieut.-Col. Indian Army, has Medal and Clasp for Chin-Lushai Exped. 1889–1890 (*Junior United Service*), b. 23 Ap. 1864; m. 11 Jan. 1892, Margaret Ellen, da. of William Langdon Martin of *Windsor Villas, Plymouth*; and has issue 1f to 4f.

1f. Richard Crawford Warren, b. 25 Sept. 1898.
2f. Wallis Langden Warren, b. 13 Feb. 1900.
3f. Geoffrey Martin Warren, b. 3 Mar. 1908.
4f. Margaret Joan Warren.

6e. William Waldegrave Warren, Lieut. R.N.R., b. 5 Sept. 1867; m. 4 Sept. 1901, Alice Matilda, da. of the Rev. Joseph Barton of *East Leigh, Havant*; and has issue 1f.

1f. Arthur Lionel Waldegrave Warren, b. 15 July 1902.

7e. Emily Margaret Warren, m. 21 Jan. 1891, Major Arthur Gambier Norris, R.G.A.

3d. Sarah Warren, d. (—); m. 15 July 1852, *her cousin*, John Warren Payne-Sheares, d. 14 Jan. 1902; and had issue 1e to 2e.

1e. Somers Henry Payne, J.P., D.L. (*Carrigmahon, Monkstown*), b. 27 June 1853; m. 23 May 1878, Edith Anne, da. of James Leslie of *Lecaron, co. Cork*; and has issue 1f to 4f.

1f. Robert Leslie Payne, Capt. Connaught Rangers, b. 7 May 1880.
2f. James Cecil Warren Payne, b. 9 Oct. 1882.
3f. Edith Elizabeth Payne.
4f. Margery Warren Payne.

2e. Mary Helen Payne, m. 1889, the Very Rev. William Joseph Wilson, M.A. (T.C.D.), Dean of Cloyne and Canon of Kilbrogan in Cork Cathedral (*The Deanery, Cloyne, co. Cork*). [Nos. 59861 to 59887.

# of The Blood Royal

4d. Margaretta Warren (*Bellmount, Crookstown, co. Cork*), m. 19 Jan. 1858, Capt. Edward Herrick of Bellmount, co. Cork, J.P., 12th Regt., d. 28 May 1879; and has issue 1e to 2e.

1e. John Edward Henry Herrick of Bellmount, *formerly* Capt. 3rd Batt. Royal Munster Regt. (*Bellmount, Crookstown, co. Cork*), b. 28 Jan. 1862; m. 12 Dec. 1883, Emily Frances, da. of James Low Holmes of Carrigmore, co. Cork.

2e. Robert Warren Herrick, M.D. (30 *Regent Street, Nottingham*), b. 23 Jan. 1864; m. 25 June 1891, Edith, da. of Joseph Whitaker of Ramsdale, Notts; and has issue 1f to 2f.

1f. John Riversdale Warren Herrick, b. 22 May 1893.

2f. Robert Lysle Warren Herrick, b. 26 May 1895.

2c. *Richard Warren of Lisgoold, M.D.*, b. Feb. 1795; d. Dec. 1870; m. 1824, *Margaret, da. of William Pennefather, M.P., Surveyor-Gen. of Ireland*, d. Dec. 1873; *and had issue.*

See p. 360, Nos. 59826–59831.

3c. *Mary Warren*, d. (–); m. 23 Nov. 1823, *Sir John Borlase Warren of Warren's Court, 4th Bt.* [*I.*], d. 4 Dec. 1863; *and had issue 1d to 8d.*

1d. Sir Augustus Riversdale Warren, 5th Bt. [I.], J.P., D.L., High Sheriff co. Cork, Hon. Col. 4th Batt. Royal Munster Fusiliers, *formerly* 20th Regt., Crimea and Indian Mutiny Medals and Clasps (*Army and Navy ; Hurlingham*), b. 24 Aug. 1833; m. 1st, 28 Ap. 1864, Georgina, da. of the Rev. John Blennerhassett, M.A., d. 10 Nov. 1893; 2ndly, 5 Feb. 1898, Ella Rosa [descended from the Lady Anne, sister of Kings Edward IV. and Richard III. (see Essex Volume, p. 636)], *formerly* wife of Col. Frederick William Clarkson (whom she divorced 1887), da. of Major-Gen. John Octavius Chichester; and has issue 1e.

1e. Augustus Riversdale John Blennerhassett Warren, J.P., *formerly* Lieut. 3rd Batt. Royal Munster Fusiliers (*Warren's Court, Lisarda, co. Cork*), b. 11 Mar. 1865; m. 12 Jan. 1898, Agnes Georgina, da. of George Maurice Ievers of Inchera, Glanmire, co. Cork; and has issue 1f.

1f. Augustus George Digby Warren, b. 23 Oct 1898.

2d. John Borlase Warren, Vice-Adm. R.N., Crimea and Chinese Medals (*United Service*), b. 27 Mar. 1838; m. 12 Sept. 1874, Mary Elizabeth St. Leger, da. of Major Robert St. Leger Atkins of Water Park, co. Cork; and has issue 1e to 3e.

1e. Bessie Geraldine Gundreda Warren, m. 20 Nov. 1906, Sir John Scarlett Walsham, 3rd Bt. [U.K.] (see p. 287) (*Knill Court, Kington, co. Hereford ; Germiston, Transvaal*); and has issue 1f.

1f. Barbara Walsham.

2e. Mary Detta St. Leger Warren.

3e. Louisa Ursula Warren.

3d. Mary Warren (*Archburn, Knock, Belfast*), m. 10 May 1859, the Rev. Thomas Robert Hamilton, Chaplain R.N., and Rector of St. Mark's, Dundela, d. 1905; and has issue 1e to 4e.

1e. *Hugh Cecil Waldegrave Hamilton, Lieut. Queensland Permanent Forces, formerly 2nd Brig. N. Irish Div. R.A.*, b. 17 Nov. 1864; d. (?).

2e. Augustus Warren Hamilton, a Partner in the Firm of Hamilton & McMaster of Belfast (*Canadian Villa, Knock, Belfast*), b. 12 Aug. 1866; m. 1897, Annie Sergeant, da. of William Harley of Newcastle, Mirramichie, New Brunswick; and has issue 1f to 3f.

1f. John Borlase Warren Hamilton, b. 1905.

2f. Ruth Sergeant Hamilton.

3f. Annie Harley Hamilton.

3e. Lilian Frances Hamilton, m. 1882, William Sufferin, LL.D. (*Gundreda Cottage, Cockenzie, Prestonpans*).

4e. Florence Augusta Hamilton. [Nos. 59888 to 59913.

The Plantagenet Roll

4d. *Margaret Warren*, d. 1881; m. 14 *Aug.* 1851, *Charles Bosworth Martin, J.P. co. Cork, Leic. Yeo. Cav. (Clonmoyle House, Aghabullogue, Cork); and had issue* 1e *to* 3e.

  1e. Charles Augustus Martin, b. 29 Oct. 1855.
  2e. William John Borlase Martin, b. 11 Feb. 185-.
  3e. Anne Margaretta Martin.

5d. *Charlotte Warren*, d. 22 *Ap.* 1886; m. 8 *Feb.* 1848, *Robert Heard of Kinsale and Pallastown, co. Cork, High Sheriff for that co.* 1870, *Capt. S. Cork Mil.,* d. 12 *Sept.* 1896; *and had issue* 1e *to* 5e.

  1e. *Robert Wilkes Heard of Kinsale and Pallastown*, b. 17 *July* 1852; d. 17 *Ap.* 1897; m. 20 *June* 1888, *Charlotte Amyand Powys* [*descended from the Lady Isabel Plantagenet* (see the Essex Volume, p. 382)] (10 *Fisher Street, Kinsale, co. Cork), da. of Henry Atherton Adams of Wynters, co. Essex, J.P.* [*who re-m.* 16 *Aug.* 1898, *Richard Charles Pratt*]; *and had issue* 1f *to* 5f.

    1f. Robert Henry Warren Heard of Kinsale and Pallastown (*Pallastown and Ballydaly, Kinsale; The Lodge, Lackamore, co. Tipperary*), b. 6 Mar. 1895.
    2f. Margaret Marion Atherton Heard.
    3f. Evelyn Mary Warren Heard.
    4f. Kathleen Vittoria Fiorenza Servatt Heard.
    5f. Amyand Dorothy Heard.

  2e. Augustus Riversdale Heard.
  3e. Mary Warren Heard, m. 23 May 1876, Sir William Quartus Ewart, 2nd Bt. [U.K.], J.P., D.L., High Sheriff co. Antrim 1907 (*Glenmachan, Strandtown, Belfast; Junior Carlton*); and has issue 1f to 5f.

    1f. Robert Heard Ewart, b. 5 Nov. 1879.
    2f. Charles Gordon Ewart, b. 1885.
    3f. Charlotte Hope Ewart.
    4f. Isabella Kelso Ewart.
    5f. Margaret Gundreda Ewart.

  4e. *Charlotte Heard*, d. 18 *Feb.* 1892; m. *as* 1st *wife*, 6 *Dec.* 1888 (*Gilbert King, who afterwards* (1895) *suc. his father as) Sir Gilbert King,* 4th *Bt.* [*U.K.*], *M.A., High Sheriff cos. Roscommon* 1892 *and Leitrim* 1894 *and* 1904, *&c.* [*a descendant of King Edward I.*] (*Charlestown, Drumsna, Roscommon;* 21 *Fitzwilliam Square South, Dublin); and has issue* 1f.

    1f. Mary Rowley King.

  5e. Catherine Jane Heard, m. Sept. 1887, Major Herbert Eyre Robbins, R.M. (*Winkleigh, Queen's Road, Tunbridge Wells*); and has issue.

6d. *Esther Warren*, d. 12 *Mar.* 1877; m. 1867, *Ralph Fuller of Kilkondy House, Lisardu, co. Cork; and had issue* 1f.

  1f. George Robert Fuller, b. 1867.

7d. *Elizabeth Warren*, d. 1899, *William Massy Hutchinson Massy of Mount Massy, J.P.* (*Mount Massy, Macroom); and had issue* 1e *to* 4e.

  1e. Hugh Hutchinson Massy, b. 1869.
  2e. John Warren Massy, b. 1870.
  3e. Rose Catherine Massy.
  4e. Alice Massy.

8d. *Frances Augusta Warren*, m. 10 Ap. 1867, Capt. Charles Henry Chauncy, *formerly* 22nd and 41st Regts. (44 *Lee Park, Blackheath, S.E.*); and has issue 1e to 7e.

  1e. Augustus Charles Chauncy, Dist. Agent G.E.R.C., Major 20th Batt. co. of London Div. (19 *Henry Road, West Bridgford, Nottingham*), b. 11 Dec. 1867; m. 1897, Rebecca Mary St. Clair, da. of Major W. R. Isles, 19th Regt.; and has issue 1f.

    1f. Francis Charles Martin Chauncy.   [Nos. 59914 to 59938.

of The Blood Royal

2e. John Borlase Warren Chauncy (16 *Craigerne Road, Blackheath*), b. 22 Jan. 1869 ; m. 20 Ap. 1899, Emily, da. of Col. Bayley, R.A. ; and has issue 1f to 3f.
    1f. Charles Frederick Chauncy, b. 6 May 1900.
    2f. Robert Augustus Chauncy, b. 6 July 1906.
    3f. Anna Frances Chauncy.

3e. Charles Henry Kemble Chauncy, Capt. Indian Army, 124th Infantry, b. 21 Dec. 1873 ; m. 3 Jan. 1902, Constance Margaret, da. of G. W. Sealy ; and has issue 1f to 2f.
    1f. Leslie Chauncy.
    2f. Helen Chauncy.

4e. James Hornidge Chauncy, M.R.C.S. (Eng.), L.R.C.P. (Lond.) (*St. Mary's, near Sidney ; Delegate, New South Wales*), b. 1880 ; m. 1907, Adela, da. of (—) Newton.

5e. Edith Julia Frances Rose Chauncy, m. 1901, Major Arthur Gosset Crawford, 84th Punjabis, Indian Army ; and has issue 1f to 2f.
    1f. George Oswald Crawford, b. 1902.
    2f. Dick Crawford, b. 1909.

6e. Eleanor Aufride Mary Chauncy.

7e. Kate Isabel Chauncy.   [Nos. 59939 to 59951.

216. Descendants of MARGARET DEANE (Table XXI.), d. (-) ; m. JOHN FITZGERALD of Innishmore, co. Kerry, 15th Knight of Kerry, M.P., d. June 1741 ; and had issue (with 3 other children : Maurice, 16th Knight, b. 1733, Joseph, and Margaret, who all d.s.p.) 1a.

1a. *Elizabeth FitzGerald, da. and event. h.,* d. (-) ; m. Oct. 1752, *Richard Townsend, otherwise Townshend, of Castle Townsend, co. Cork, M.P., and High Sheriff for that co.* 1753, *Col. Cork Militia,* d. Dec. 1783 ; *and had issue* 1b.

1b. *Right Hon. Richard Boyle Townsend, otherwise Townshend, of Castle Townsend, P.C., M.P., High Sheriff co. Cork* 1785, b. 1756 ; d. 26 Nov. 1826 ; m. 16 May 1784, *Henrietta, da. of John Newenham of Maryborough, co. Cork,* d. Dec. 1848 ; *and had issue (with 4 other sons and a da. who d.s.p.)* 1c *to* 2c.

1c. *Rev. Maurice FitzGerald Stephens Townsend, afterwards* (1870) *Townshend of Castle Townshend, J.P., D.L., Vicar of Thornbury, co. Glouc.,* b. 7 May 1791 ; d. 21 Mar. 1872 ; m. 16 May 1826, *Alice Elizabeth, da. and h. of Richmond Shute of Iron Acton, co. Glouc.* [*by his wife Harriet, sister and h. of Henry Hankes Willis Stephens of Eastington and Chavenage House, co. Glouc.*], d. 21 Mar. 1872 ; *and had issue* 1d *to* 3d.

1d. *Henry John Townshend, J.P., 2nd Life Guards,* b. 1 Nov. 1827 ; d.v.p. 7 Sept. 1869 ; m. 29 Sept. 1864, *Jane Adeliza Clementina, da. of John Hamilton Hussey de Burgh of Kilfinnan Castle, co. Cork, J.P. ; and had issue* 1e *to* 2e.

1e. Maurice FitzGerald Stephens Townshend of Shana Court, *formerly* of Castle Townshend (*Riviere Lodge, Glandore, Cork*), b. 4 Nov. 1865 ; *unm.*

2e. Hubert de Burgh FitzGerald Stephens Townshend, J.P., *late* Capt. 4th Batt. Essex Regt., has South African Medal with 2 Clasps (*Shepperton Park, Leap, co. Cork*), b. 4 Ap. 1867 ; *unm.*

2d. Geraldine Henrietta Townshend (*Thornbury House, Thornbury, R.S.O., co. Glouc.*), m. as 2nd wife, 30 Ap. 1870, Major-Gen. Pierrepont Henry Mundy of Thornbury House, co. Glouc., J.P., R.H.A. [6th son of Gen. Godfrey Basil Mundy (2nd son of Edward Miller Mundy of Shipley, M.P.), by the Hon. Sarah Brydges, da. of George Brydges (Rodney), 1st Baron Rodney [G.B.], Adm. R.N.], d.s.p. 16 Feb. 1889.

3d. Alice Gertrude Townshend (*Compton, Guildford*), m. 25 'Mar. 1856, Rev.
    [Nos. 59952 to 59955.

The Plantagenet Roll

the Hon. Courtenay John Vernon [3rd son of Robert, 1st Baron Lyveden [U.K.]], d. 2 July 1892; and had issue 1e to 3e.

1e. Courtenay Robert Percy (Vernon), 3rd Baron Lyveden [U.K.], *formerly* Capt. 3rd Batt. Highland L.I., is President of the British Committee for the Study of Foreign Municipal Institutions (3 *Earl's Avenue, Folkestone*), b. 29 Dec. 1857; m. 12 Feb. 1890, Fanny Zelie, da. of Major Hill of Wollaston Hall, co. Northants; and has issue 1f to 2f.

1f. Hon. Robert FitzPatrick Courtenay Vernon, b. 1 Feb. 1892.

2f. Hon. Victoria Wyndham Dorothy Vernon.

2e. Hon. Sydney Charles FitzPatrick Vernon (*High Wycombe, Bucks*), b. 14 July 1862; m. 7 Jan. 1897, Emilie Louise, da. of Charles Lorkin of Hockley, co. Essex.

3e. Hon. Evelyn Mary Geraldine Vernon, m. 7 Aug. 1877, the Rev. Hugh Hodgson Gillett, M.A., Rector of Compton and Canon of Peterborough (*Compton Rectory, Guildford*); and has issue 1f to 5f.

1f. Hugh Vernon Gillett, b. 12 June 1878.

2f. Charles Richard Gillett, Lieut. R.A. and Instructor in Gunnery at Malta, b. 24 Aug. 1880; m. 8 Feb. 1906, Gwynne, da. of Robert Keate of 14 Rosary Gardens, S.W.

3f. George Maurice Gerald Gillett, b. 17 Nov. 1882.

4f. Sybil Evelyn Gillett.

5f. Gertrude Mary Gillett.

2c. *Henrietta Augusta Townsend*, d. Dec. 1869; m. 12 Oct. 1822, Thomas Somerville of Drishane, co. Cork, J.P., D.L., and High Sheriff for that co. 1863, d. 19 May 1882; and had issue 1d to 2d.

1d. *Thomas Henry Somerville of Drishane, J.P., D.L., and High Sheriff co. Cork* 1888, *Lieut.-Col.* 3rd Buffs, b. 29 Oct. 1824; d. 15 Mar. 1898; m. 29 June 1857, Adelaide Eliza, da. of Adm. Sir Josiah Coghill, 3rd Bt. [G.B.], d. 3 Dec. 1895; and had issue 1e to 7e.

1e. Thomas Cameron FitzGerald Somerville of Drishane, Col. Comdg. King's Own Royal Lancaster Regt. (*Drishane, Skibbereen, co. Cork*), b. 30 Mar. 1860.

2e. Henry Boyle Townsend Somerville, Capt. R.N. (*Maxwelton, The Hale, Edgware*), b. 7 Sept. 1863; m. 7 Ap. 1896, Helen Mabel, da. of Sir George Wigram Allen of Toxteth, Sydney, K.C.M.G.; and has issue 1f to 4f.

1f. Raymond Thomas Somerville, b. 14 Mar. 1897.

2f. Brian Aylmer Somerville, b. 27 Jan. 1900.

3f. Michael Fitzgerald Somerville, b. 13 Sept. 1908.

4f. Diana Marian Somerville.

3e. Aylmer Coghill Somerville, J.P., Capt. S. of Ireland Imp. Yeo. (*Penleigh House, Westbury, Wilts; Castle Townshend, co. Cork*), b. 23 Sept. 1865; m. 1st, 1 Oct.1888, Emmeline Sophia, da. of Daniel Sykes of Oaklands, co. Glouc., d. 13 Feb. 1900; 2ndly, 3 July 1901, Nathalie Adah, da. of William Barrow Turner of Ponsonby Hall, co. Cumberland; and has issue 1f to 4f.

1f.[1] Desmond Henry Sykes Somerville, b. 6 Aug. 1889.

2f.[2] Thomas Henry Gilbert Somerville, b. 29 Ap. 1907.

3f.[1] Gillian Margaret Hope Somerville.

4f.[2] Elizabeth Geraldine Aylmer Somerville.

4e. John Arthur Coghill Somerville, Major Royal Sussex Regt. (*Junior Naval and Military*), b. 26 Mar. 1872.

5e. Hugh Gualtier Coghill Somerville, Capt. R.N. (*Junior Naval and Military*), b. 10 July 1873; m. 1900, Mary, da. of W. Hancock of Patras.

6e. Edith Anna Ænone Somerville.

7e. Elizabeth Hildegarde Augusta Somerville, m. 11 July 1893, Sir Egerton Bushe Coghill, 5th Bt. [G.B.], J.P. (*Glen Barrahane, Castle Townshend, co. Cork*); and has issue 1f to 4f. [Nos. 59956 to 59980.

of The Blood Royal

1f. Marmaduke Nevill Patrick Somerville Coghill, b. 17 Mar. 1896.
2f. Nevill Henry Kendal Aylmer Coghill, b. 19 Ap. 1899.
3f. Joscelyn Ambrose Cramer Coghill, b. 30 Sept. 1902.
4f. Katherine Adelaide Hildegarde Coghill.
2d. Henrietta Somerville. [Nos. 59981 to 59985.

217. Descendants of WILLIAM (O'BRIEN), 4th EARL OF INCHIQUIN (Table XXI.), d. 18 July 1777; m. 1st, 28 Mar. 1720, ANNE (HAMILTON) suo jure 2nd COUNTESS OF ORKNEY [S.], d. 7 Dec. 1756; and had issue 1a.

1a. Mary (O'Brien), suo jure 3rd Countess of Orkney [S.], b. a. 1721; d. 10 May 1791; m. 5 Mar. 1753, Murrough (O'Brien), 1st Marquis of Thomond [I.] (see below), d. 10 Feb. 1808; and had issue 1b.

1b. Mary (O'Brien), suo jure 4th Countess of Orkney [S.], b. 1755; d. 20 Dec. 1831; m. 21 Dec. 1771, the Hon. Thomas Fitzmaurice of Llewenny, co. Denbigh [2nd son of John, 1st Earl of Shelburne [I.]], d. 28 Oct. 1793; and had issue 1c.

1c. John Fitzmaurice, Viscount Kirkwall, b. 9 Oct. 1778; d.v.p. 23 Nov. 1820; m. 11 Aug. 1802, the Hon. Anna Maria, da. of John (de Blaquiere), 1st Baron de Blaquiere [I.]; d. 31 Jan. 1843; and had issue 1d to 2d.

1d. Thomas John Hamilton (Fitzmaurice), 5th Earl of Orkney [S.], b. 8 Aug. 1803; d. 16 May 1877; m. 14 Mar. 1826, the Hon. Charlotte Isabella, da. of George (Irby), 3rd Baron Boston [G.B.], d. 7 Sept. 1883; and had issue.
See the Essex Volume, pp. 116-118, Nos. 15509-15556.

2d. Hon. William Edward Fitzmaurice, M.P., co. Bucks, Major 2nd Life Guards, b. 21 Mar. 1805; d. 18 June 1889; m. 1st, 3 Aug. 1837, Hester, da. of Henry Harford of Down Place, co. Berks, d. 24 Aug. 1859; and had issue 1e to 3e.

1e. Cecil Henry Fitzmaurice, late R.N., b. 25 Aug. 1844; m. 1870, Elizabeth Maria, da. of (—) Hatton, d. 1902; and has issue 1f.

1f. Cecil Edward Fitzmaurice, b. 27 July 1871.

2e. Agnes Isabella Fitzmaurice, d. 5 Dec. 1863; m. 27 Nov. 1860, William Reginald Hesketh of Gwrych Castle, co. Denbigh.

3e. Flora Louisa Fitzmaurice, m. 4 Nov. 1869, Arthur William Baker, formerly 60th Regt.; and has issue. [Nos. 59986 to 60036.

218. Descendants of the Hon. JAMES O'BRIEN, M.P. (Table XXI.), d. (-); m. MARY, da. of the Very Rev. William JEPHSON, Dean of Kilmore, d. (-); and had issue 1a to 5a.

1a. Murrough (O'Brien), 5th Earl of Inchiquin [I.] and 1st Marquis of Thomond [I. 29 Dec. 1800] and 1st Baron Thomond of Taplow [U.K. 2 Oct. 1801], d. 9 Feb. 1808; m. 1st, 5 Mar. 1753, Mary (O'Brien), suo jure 3rd Countess of Orkney [S.], d. 10 May 1791; and had issue.
See above, Nos. 59986-60036.

2a. Edward O'Brien, d. Mar. 1801; m. Mary, da. of (—) Carrick; and had issue 1b to 5b.

1b. William (O'Brien), 2nd Marquis of Thomond and 6th Earl of Inchiquin [I.], 1st Baron Tadcaster [U.K. 3 July 1826], d. 21 Aug. 1846; m. 16 Sept. 1899, Elizabeth, da. and h. of Thomas Trotter of Duleck, d. 3 Mar. 1852; and had issue 1c to 3c.

1c. Lady Susan Maria O'Brien, d. 25 Mar. 1857; m. 12 Aug. 1824, Rear-Adm. the Hon. George Frederick Hotham, R.N. (p. 522), d. 19 Oct. 1856; and had issue 1d to 3d. [Nos. 60037 to 60087.

The Plantagenet Roll

1*d*. Charles (*Hotham*), 4th Baron Hotham [*I.*] and 14th Bt. [*E.*], d. unm. 29 May 1872.
2*d*. John (*Hotham*), 5th Baron Hotham [*I.*] and 15th Bt. [*E.*], b. 13 May 1838; d. unm. 13 Dec. 1907.
3*d*. Hon. Susan Frances Hotham (46 *Belgrave Road, S.W.*), m. 6 June 1877, the Rev. Alexander Cosby Jackson, d. 23 Feb. 1907; and has issue 1*e*.
  1*e*. Augusta Frances Cyrilla Jackson.

2*c*. Lady Sarah O'Bryen, d. 9 Feb. 1859; m. 3 Ap. 1830, Major *William Stanhope Taylor* [son of Thomas Taylor of Sevenoaks by his wife Lady Lucy Rachel, née Stanhope], d. (–); and had (with possibly other) issue 1*d*.
  1*d*. O'Bryen Taylor, *Major and Standard-Bearer H.M.'s Body-Guard of Gentlemen-at-Arms*, d. (–); m. (—); and had (with possibly other) issue 1*e*.
    1*e*. Mabel O'Bryen Taylor, m. 16 June 1896, Sir Sydney James O'Bryen Hoare, 6th Bt. [I.]; and has issue.
    See p. 369, Nos. 60108–60109.

3*c*. Lady Elizabeth O'Brien, d. 9 May 1870; m. as 1st wife, Sir *George Stucley Stucley* (*R.L.* 27 July 1858), previously *Buck*, 1st Bt. [U.K. 26 Ap. 1859], M.P., J.P., D.L., Col. Comdg. Devonshire Art., b. 17 Aug. 1812; d. 13 Mar. 1900; and had issue.
See p. 483, Nos. 103413–103414.

2*b*. James (*O'Brien*), 3rd and last Marquis of Thomond and 7th Earl of Inchiquin [*I.*], &c., Adm. R.N.; d.s.p. 3 July 1855.
3*b*. Lord Edward O'Bryen, *Capt. R.N.*, d. 9 Mar. 1824; 2ndly, 11 Ap. 1815, Gertrude Grace, sister of *Paul, 1st Baron Methuen* [*U.K.*], da. of Paul Cobb Methuen of Corsham, d. 1 May 1817; and had issue 1*c* to 2*c*.
  1*c*. Gertrude Matilda O'Bryen, d. 17 Dec. 1869; m. 17 June 1840, the Rev. Thomas Plumptre Methuen, *M.A.* [nephew of *Paul, 1st Baron Methuen*], b. 14 Aug. 1814; d. 17 Dec. 1869; and had issue 1*d* to 2*d*.
    1*d*. Rev. Paul Edward O'Bryen Methuen (*Bicknoller, Mount Beacon, Bath*), b. 15 May 1841.
    2*d*. Charles Lucas Methuen, *Lieut. 79th Highlanders*, b. 25 Sept. 1842; d. 17 Aug. 1905; m. 25 June 1872, Eleanor Mary, da. of the Rev. Alfred Harford of Locking, co. Som.
  2*c*. Mary Catherine O'Bryen, d. 10 May 1885; m. 20 Jan. 1842, the Rev. John Hamilton Forsyth, d. 25 June 1848; and had issue (with another son who d.s.p.) 1*d*.
    1*d*. Thomas Hamilton Forsyth, *Col. late 62nd Regt.* (*Northwold, Bournemouth*), b. 29 Dec. 1843; m. 5 Aug. 1873, Anne Noel [descended from Lady Anne, sister of King Edward IV., &c. (see Exeter Volume, p. 194)], da. of Edward Andrew Noel, J.P., D.L. [E. of Gainsborough Coll.]; and has issue 1*e* to 3*e*.
      1*e*. Ronald Graham Hamilton Forsyth, b. 1 Dec. 1875; m. 30 Dec. 1904, Helen Crosbie, da. of Crosby Stewart Sawyer of St. Barbara, California; and had issue 1*f*.
        1*f*. Thomas Hamilton Forsyth, b. 1 Sept. 1905.
      2*e*. Annie Cecilia Noel Forsyth.
      3*e*. Mary Beatrice Gertrude Forsyth.
    2*d*. Douglas Methuen Forsyth, *Comm. (ret.) R.N.* (*Leavington House, Ryde, I.W.*), b. 19 Ap. 1847; m. 1 Oct. 1874, Kate, da. of Capt. William O'Brien, 53rd Regt.; and has issue 1*e* to 3*e*.
      1*e*. Douglas William O'Bryen Forsyth, b. 6 Oct. 1880.
      2*e*. Archibald Hamilton O'Bryen Forsyth, b. 16 May 1884.
      3*e*. Katharine Mary O'Bryen Forsyth.

4*b*. Lady Mary O'Bryen, d. 28 June 1840; m. 1st, 2 Feb. 1780, Sir Richard

[Nos. 60088 to 60104.

of The Blood Royal

Cox, 4th Bt. [*I.*], d. 6 *Sept.* 1784 (*by whom she had an only da., Maria, who apparently* d. *young*); 2ndly, *Jan.* 1786, *the Right. Hon. William Saurin, P.C., Attorney-General* [*I.*], d. (-) ; *and had issue* 1c *to* 3c.

 1c. *Edward Saurin, Adm. R.N.*, d. 28 *Feb.* 1878 ; m. 15 *July* 1828, *Lady Mary* [*descended from King Henry VII.* (see Tudor Roll, p. 524)], *da. of Dudley* (*Ryder*), 1st *Earl of Harrowby* [*U.K.*] ; *and had* (*with other*) *issue* 1d.

  1d. *William Granville Saurin, eldest son*, d. 1893 ; m. 2 *Aug.* 1865, *Madine Nicolaievora, da. of* (—) *de Smirnoff, P.C. and a Senator of Russia ; and had* (*with other*) *issue* (*an eldest da., Susan Marcia, who* d. *unm.* 3 *Ap.* 1878).

   2c. James Saurin,   } both living May 1819.
   3c. Mark Anthony Saurin,}

 5b. *Lady Harriet O'Bryen*, d. 1 *May* 1851 ; m. 17 *Ap.* 1800, *Sir Joseph Wallis Hoare of Annabella, 3rd Bt.* [*I.*], d. 26 *Nov.* 1852 ; *and had issue* 1c *to* 7c.

  1c. *Sir Edward Hoare, 4th Bt.* [*I.*], b. 23 *Dec.* 1801 ; d. 15 *Nov.* 1882 ; m. 24 *Ap.* 1824, *Harriet, da. and co-h. of Thomas Hercy Barritt of Garbrand Hall, co. Surrey*, d. 25 *Jan.* 1880 ; *and had issue* 1d *to* 2d.

   1d. *Sir Joseph Wallis O'Bryen Hoare, 5th Bt.* [*I.*], *J.P., D.L.*, b. 11 *Nov.* 1828 ; d. 30 *Ap.* 1904 ; m. 6 *Aug.* 1857, *Cecilia Eleanor Selina, da. of James Ede of Ridgeway Castle, co. Hants*, d. 7 *Jan.* 1888 ; *and had issue* 1e *to* 3e.

    1e. Sir Sydney James O'Bryen Hoare, 6th Bt. [I.], *formerly* Lieut. Midx. Regt. (16 *The Grange, Wimbledon*), *b.* 2 July 1860 ; *m.* 16 June 1896, Mabel O'Bryen, da. of Major O'Bryen Taylor, Standard-Bearer to H.M.'s Body-Guard of Gentlemen-at-Arms ; and has issue 1f to 2f.

     1f. Edward O'Bryen Hoare, *b.* 29 Ap. 1898.
     2f. Terence O'Bryen Hoare, *b.* 21 Jan. 1904.

    2e. Kathleen Henrietta Hoare.

    3e. Norah Cecile Helen Hoare (*Rostellan, Pear Tree Avenue, Itchen, Hants*).

   2d. *Anne Hoare*, d. 24 *Feb.* 1910 ; m. 4 *June* 1856, *Thomas Leslie, M.A., Bar.-at-Law* [*son of the Right Rev. John Leslie, D.D., Lord Bishop of Kilmore*], d. 15 *Feb.* 1880 ; *and had issue* 1e *to* 5e.

    1e. Rev Edward Charles Leslie, M.A. (Oxon.), Rector of Winterborne-Came, (*Winterborne-Came, Dorset*), *b.* 15 July 1858 ; *m.* 6 Nov. 1906, Margaret Elizabeth, da. of Henry Joseph Moule of Dorchester.

    2e. Arthur Trevor O'Bryen Leslie, Capt. *formerly* 3rd Vol. Batt. E. Surrey Regt. (46 *Comeragh Road, West Kensington, W.*), *b.* 23 May 1868 ; *m.* 7 Oct. 1896, Guendolen Amy, da. of Sir Charles Rugge-Price, 6th Bt. [U.K.] ; *s.p.s.*

    3e. Harriet Eleanor Josephine Leslie.

    4e. Annie Isabella Leslie.

    5e. Frances Emily Clotilda Leslie.

  2c. *William O'Bryen Hoare, Capt. R.N.*, b. 23 *Mar.* 1807 ; d. 26 *Mar.* 1886 ; m. 2 *May* 1834, *Caroline, da. of John Hornby of The Hook, co. Hants*, d. 9 *Jan.* 1891 ; *and had issue* 1d.

   1d. Elizabeth Clotilda Hoare (1 *Liverpool Gardens, Worthing*).

  3c. *Joseph James Parish Hoare*, b. 22 *Mar.* 1811 ; d. 17 *Dec.* 1889 ; m. 17 *Ap.* 1834, *Helen Moritz Dillon, da. of Henry Arthur Hardman of Mount Hardman, Grenada ; and had issue* 1d *to* 7d.

   1d. Rev. James O'Bryen Dott Richard Hoare, M.A. (Camb.), Vicar of Papanui (*Christchurch, New Zealand*), *b.* 12 Mar. 1835 ; *m.* 23 Feb. 1865, Frances Eleanor, da. of the Rev. Thomas Henderson ; and has issue 1e to 7e.

    1e. Arthur Hoare, Electrical and Mechanical Engineer (*Bombay*), *b.* 30 Nov. 1866.

    2e. Philip Hoare, Public Accountant (*New South Wales*), *b.* 28 Nov. 1871 ; *m.* 1897, Florence, da. of F. Evans ; and has issue 1f.

     1f. Donovan O'Bryen Hoare. [Nos. 60105 to 60121.

The Plantagenet Roll

3e. John Hoare, Mechanical Engineer (*Queensland*), b. 23 Dec. 1873; m. 1904, Margaret Jane, da. of E. S. Leversedge; and has issue 1f to 2f.
   1f. James O'Bryen Hoare.
   2f. Joan Mary Hoare.

4e. Denys Hoare, Accountant and Coy. Manager (*Brownlow, 21 Mansfield Avenue, Christchurch, N.Z.*), b. 30 Nov. 1875; m. 17 Jan. 1906, Frances, da. of Thomas York; and has issue 1f.
   1f. Norah Frances O'Bryen Hoare.

5e. Mary Hoare, *unm.*

6e. Janet Hoare, m. 1899, Geoffrey John Phillips, C.E. (*Cape Town*); and has issue 1f to 2f.
   1f. Geoffrey O'Bryen Phillips.
   2f. Marjory O'Bryen Phillips.

7e. Helen Hoare, m. Ap. 1910, Hugh Mostyn Trevor.

2d. *Joseph George Wallis Hoare, R.N.*, b. 26 *July* 1838; d. 14 *May* 1883; m. 1st, 1 *June* 1865, *Susan Mary, da. of Capt. F. W. Paul, R.N.*, d. 13 *Sept.* 1874; 2ndly, 9 *Ap.* 1878, *Mary Martha, da. of H. White England of Kingsbury, co. Som.; and had issue* 1e *to* 5e.

1e. Helen Susan Kathleen Hoare (*La Floresta, Barranquilla, Colombia*), m. in Barranquilla 2 Ap. 1894, John Meek of Liverpool and Barranquilla, Jr., d. 6 Oct. 1907; and has issue 1f to 2f.
   1f. John Wallace Meek, b. 22 Dec. 1902.
   2f. Francis Forwood O'Bryen Meek, b. 2 July 1905.

2e. Lily Hoare (8A *Nevern Road, Earl's Court, S.W.*), *unm.*

3e. Edith Mary Hoare, m. in Barranquilla 25 May 1897, Fritz Rudolf Fuhrhop; and has issue (see Appendix).

4e. Marie Violet Hoare, *unm.*

5e. Olive Buchanan Hoare, m. 21 June 1904, William Gerald Morris, M.I.C.E. (*Muchelney, Broxbourne, Herts*); and has issue 1f to 3f.
   1f. William Arabi Morris ⎫
   2f. Wallace Gerald Morris ⎭ (twins), b. 3 Ap. 1905.
   3f. Mary Daphne Morris, b. 15 Nov. 1907.

3d. *Arthur Calvert Hoare*, b. 24 *Mar.* 1840; d. 4 *Ap.* 1898; m. 29 *Jan.* 1869, *Charlotte Rosina, da. of Joseph Robinson, otherwise Robertson, of co. Banff; and had issue* 1e *to* 4e.

1e. Arthur Carrick Dickson Hoare (*Isthmian*), b. 23 Oct. 1874.

2e. Helen Brownlow Hoare, m. 21 Sept. 1904, Wilhelm Ernst Harald Solger, Lieut. 7th E. Prussian Inf.

3e. Brenda Marie Hoare, m. 18 Oct. 1905, Charles Henry Dorward Moberly, Agent, Bank of Bengal (*Hyderabad, Deccan, India*); and has issue 1f.
   1f. Brenda Winifred Moberly.

4e. Sidney Josephine Fitzmaurice Hoare, m. 29 May 1909, Walter Granville Warburton of Bombay and Karachi, East India Merchant (*Sind Club, Karachi*).

4d. Charles Campbell William Hoare, *formerly* one of H.M.'s Inspectors of Factories (*Gulistan, 65 Laurie Park Road, Sydenham, S.E.*), b. 31 Dec. 1841; m. 25 July 1867, Blanche, da. of Frederick Richard Phayre of Killoughram, co. Wexford; and had issue 1e to 3e.

1e. Carl Frederick Hoare, b. 21 Sept. 1869.

2e. Mary Annesley Hoare, m. 1890, Charles Frederick Edwards, C.E.

3e. Blanche Evelyn Hoare.

5d. *Oliver William Simpson Hoare, Capt. Lanark Militia*, b. 3 *Oct.* 1843; d. Oct. 1902; m. 27 *Oct.* 1864, *Anne, da. of George James of Ridgeway, co. Hants*, d. 1881; *and had issue* 1e *to* 7e.   [Nos. 60122 to 60150.

# of The Blood Royal

1e. Oliver George St. Clair Hoare (*Santa Rosa, S. America*), b. 18 Sept. 1866; m. 1892, Helen, da. of Robert Lloyd Peel.

2e. Basil O'Bryen Hoare, b. 1 Mar. 1870.

3e. Walter James Hoare, b. 4 Oct. 1871.

4e. Gerald Robbin O'Bryen Hoare, b. 11 Nov. 1879.

5e. Isabella Hoare, m. 1897, Isaac Benjamin Oyles.

6e. Constance Helen Hoare, m. 1901, Major Philip L. Stevenson, *late* 5th Lancers.

7e. Geraldine Erin Hoare, m. 26 Sept. 1893, Edmund Beverly Blair McKean (*New Park, co. Herts*).

6d. Edward Senior Hoare, b. 15 *July* 1851; d. 24 Aug. 1895; m. 16 *Aug.* 1870, *Sophia Elizabeth, da. of the Rev. J. S. Hird of Sunningdale ; and had issue* 1e.

1e. Cyril Bertie Edward Hoare (*Bleak House, Dyke Road, Brighton*), b. 29 Sept. 1882; m. 24 Oct. 1907, Isabel Mary, da. of Edward Fielder of Anerley, S.E.; and has issue 1f.

1f. Hermione Sophia O'Bryen Hoare, b. 27 Feb. 1910.

7d. *Marion Maria Dorothea Hoare*, d. 14 Oct. 1896; m. 20 Feb. 1855, *John Turner-Turner, formerly Phillipson, of Avon, co. Hants*, d. 8 Feb. 1874; *and had issue* 1e *to* 2e.

1e. John Edmund Unett Phillipson Turner (*Avon Castle, Ringwood, Hants*), b. 19 Feb. 1856.

2e. Gwendoline Evelyn Fitzmaurice Turner, m. 28 Oct. 1878, John Aitken of Mount Aitken (*Wyke Hall, Gillingham, Dorset*).

4c. *John Lynam Parish Hoare, Major 13th Bombay N.I.*, d. (? s.p.) 12 *June* 1882; m. 4 *May* 1840, *Jane Ellis, da. of Lieut.-Col. Charles Payne.*

5c. *Harriet Hoare*, d. 8 *Oct.* 1827; m. 17 *Oct.* 1826, *Francis Hurt Sitwell of Ferney Hall, co. Salop*, d. 22 Aug. 1835; *and had issue* 1d.

1d. William Willoughby George Hurt Sitwell of Ferney Hall, J.P., High Sheriff co. Salop 1855 (*Ferney Hall, Craven Arms, Salop*), b. 2 Oct. 1827; m. 1st, 29 Sept. 1853, Harriet Margaret, da. of William Henry Harford of Barley Wood, d. 18 May 1855; 2ndly, 8 July 1858, Eliza Harriet, da. of Richard Burton Phillipson of Dunston Hall, Stafford, d. 21 June 1888; and has issue 1e to 2e.

1e. Willoughby Harford Sitwell, J.P., Lieut. 6th Dragoons, b. 18 May 1855; m. 7 Sept. 1880, Rose Augusta Cecil, da. of James Henry Brabazon of Mornington [E. of Meath [I.] Coll.]; and has issue 1f.

1f. Willoughby Hurt Sitwell, b. 30 Ap. 1881.

2e. Francis Hurt Sitwell, J.P., Lieut.-Col. *late* Shropshire I.Y., b. 14 Jan. 1860.

6c. *Mary Hoare*, d. (? s.p.) 11 *Dec.* 1836; m. 1832, *Capt. Matthew Charles Forster, R.N.*, d. 1 Feb. 1897.

7c. *Elizabeth Hoare*, d. 21 *Sept.* 1872; m. 1838, *the Rev. James Payne Horsford, Colonial Chaplain, Ceylon Ecclesiastical Estab. ; and had issue.*

3a. Mary O'Bryen.

4a. Anne O'Bryen, d. 19 *Jan.* 1745; m. *as 2nd wife*, 23 Mar. 1744, *the Most Rev. Michael Cox, D.D., Lord Archbishop of Cashel* 1754–1779 [*Bt.* [*I.* 1706] *Coll.*], b. 2 Nov. 1691; d. 28 *May* 1779; *and had issue* 1b.

1b. *Richard Cox of Castletown*, b. 15 *Jan.* 1745; d. *July* 1790; m. 25 *Jan.* 1766, *Mary, da. of Francis Burton* [*Bt. of Pollerton Coll.*], d. (–); *and had issue* 1c *to* 6c.

1c. *Michael Cox of Castletown*, b. 14 *Ap.* 1768; d. 1836; m. *the Hon. Mary, da. of Henry* (*Prittie*), *1st Baron Dunalley* [*I.*], d. 12 Feb. 1859; *and had issue* 1d *to* 2d.

1d. *Sir Richard Cox, 8th Bt.* [*I.*], d. 7 *May* 1846.

2d. *Catherine Cox*, d. 14 *Sept.* 1879; m. 1st, *June* 1833, *Capt. William Villiers-Stuart, M.P.* [*M. of Bute Coll.*], d. 7 Nov. 1873; *and had issue.*

See the Clarence Volume, pp. 146–147, Nos. 2097–2105.

[Nos. 60151 to 60174.

The Plantagenet Roll

2c. Sir Francis Cox, 9th Bt. [I.], b. 23 July 1769; d.s.p. 6 Mar. 1856.
3c. Rev. Richard Cox, Rector of Cahirconlish, co. Limerick, b. 20 Sept. 1771; d. 1834; m. Sarah, da. of the Rev. Ralph Hawtrey, d. (-); and had (with other) issue 1d to 5d.
    1d. Sir Ralph Hawtrey Cox, 10th Bt. [I.], b. 1808; d.s.p. 12 Ap. 1872.
    2d. Sir Michael Cox, 11th Bt. [I.], b. 1810; d. unm., 15 June 1872.
    3d. Sir Francis Hawtrey Cox, 12th Bt. [I.], b. c. 1816; d.s.p. 17 Oct. 1873.
    4d. William Saurin Cox, sometimes said to have succ. as 13th Bt., d.s.p.s.
    5d. Anne Cox, m. the Rev. Thomas Lyon.
4c. William Cox, b. 6 Jan. 1773, } d.s.p.m. and presumably s.p.
5c. Benjamin Cox, b. 20 Jan. 1775, }
6c. Rachel Cox, b. 9 Nov. 1770; d. (-); m. Ponsonby Hore of Harperstown, co. Wexford [son of Walter Hore of the same by his wife Lady Anne, née Stopford].

5a. Lady Henrietta O'Brien, d. 17 Nov. 1797; m. 1st, Terence O'Loghlin, d. (-); 2ndly, 5 Oct. 1769, Sir William Vigors Burdett of Dunmore, 2nd Bt. [I.], d. 17 Dec. 1798; and had issue (with a younger son d. unm.) 1b to 2b.
    1b. Sir William Bagenal Burdett, 3rd Bt. [I.], bapt. 16 July 1770; d. 14 Dec. 1840, leaving issue an only da., who d.s.p.
    2b. Mary Orkney Burdett, d. at Radipole, co. Dorset, 17 Dec. 1857; m. 1800, Burton Newenham [son of Sir Edward Newenham, Cadet of Coolmore, co. Cork], d. (-); and had issue (with 6 children, of whom no issue survives) 1c to 3c.
        1c. William Burton Newenham of Fitzwilliam Square, Dublin, b. 2 June 1806; d. May 1877; m. 15 Oct. 1853, Frances Louisa, da. and h. of Francis Wortham of Swaversy, co. Camb.; and had issue 1d.
            1d. Francesca Louise Newenham, m. 19 Dec. 1882, George Reginald Trappes [Cadet of Nidd (see Essex Volume, p. 673)] (The Hawthornes, Hanley Swan, Worcestershire); s.p.
        2c. Rev. Bagenal Burdett Newenham, Vicar of Bilton, co. York, b. in Dublin 3 Mar. 1816; d. 19 Oct. 1901; m. in London 19 Feb. 1857, Helen Louisa, da. of Hambly Knapp; and had issue 1d to 3d.
            1d. Edward Burdett Newenham, B.A. (Oxon.) (Provincerssingel 20, Rotterdam), b. 29 Sept. 1858; m. Dec. 1891, Susan Frances, da. of William Joy of London; and has issue 1e to 4e.
                1e. William Edward Burdett Newenham, b. Feb. 1899.
                2e. Frederick Alfred Joy Newenham, b. Jan. 1902.
                3e. Robert O'Brien Newenham, b. June 1903.
                4e. Emily Frances Newenham, b. 31 Dec. 1892.
            2d. Frederick George Newenham (New Zealand), b. 29 June 1860; unm.
            3d. Rev. Arthur O'Brien Newenham, M.A. (Oxon.), Rector of Cowthorpe (Cowthorpe Rectory, Wetherby), b. 15 Feb. 1862; m. 13 June 1889, Eliza Ada, da. of William Thompson; and has issue 1e to 2e.
                1e. Gerald Arthur Burdett Newenham, b. 25 Jan. 1898.
                2e. Irene Ada Newenham, b. 29 June 1893.
        3c. Grace Anna Newenham, b. 4 Feb. 1805; d. Mar. 1887; m. 3 Mar. 1827, James Stuart Brownrigg [nephew of Lieut.-Gen. Sir Robert Brownrigg, 1st Bt. [U.K. 1816], G.C.B.], d. in Paris Nov. 1879; and had issue (with a son and a da., Mrs. Dillon-Trant, who d.s.p.) 1d to 3d.
            1d. Grace Anna Maria Brownrigg, da. and co-h., b. 1 Feb. 1831; d. 1 Ap. 1890; m. 12 July 1849, Henry Alexander Leishman of the Mauritius, b. 16 Sept. 1821; d. 19 Mar. 1881; and had issue (with 2 sons d. young) 1e to 6e.
                1e. Henry James Charles Leishman (Nanarup, Western Australia), b. 12 July 1850; m. 12 July 1880, Alice, da. of Judge Bunny of Melbourne; and has issue 1f to 3f. [Nos. 60175 to 60185.

# of The Blood Royal

1*f*. Hugh Arthur Leishman, *b.* Aug. 1886.
2*f*. Lilian Leishman ⎫
3*f*. Grace Leishman ⎬ (twins), *b.* 8 May 1882.

2*e*. Stuart Brownrigg Leishman (*Queensland*), *b.* 12 Sept. 1862; *m.* 1st at Melbourne, June 1888, Augusta Nicola, da. of Dr. G. A. Mein, *d.* 1897; 2ndly, at Brisbane, 8 July 1904, Gertrude Isobel, da. of (—) Blakeney; and has issue 1*f*.
    1*f*. George Alexander Burdett Leishman, *b.* 11 Nov. 1892.

3*e*. Grace Augusta Matilda Leishman, *m.* 21 Feb. 1878, the Rev. Alfred Edward Beavan, M.A. (Oxon.), Chaplain of Normanfield, Hampton Wick (*The Grange, King Charles Road, Surbiton Hill, Surrey*); *s.p.*

4*e*. Eliza Mary Leishman, *m.* 26 Ap. 1883, the Rev. Arthur Adair Farnell, *d.s.p.* 22 Sept. 1902.

5*e*. Lilian Louisa Leishman, *m.* 15 June 1886, Harry Frank Dibben; and has issue 1*f* to 3*f*.
    1*f*. Arthur Douglas Harry Dibben, *b.* 15 May 1887.
    2*f*. Eric Dibben, *b.* 7 Dec. 1894.
    3*f*. Muriel Dibben, *b.* 22 Oct. 1892.

6*e*. Rose Elmyra Alexandrina Leishman, *unm.*

2*d*. *Augusta Henrietta Anne Brownrigg*, da. and co-h., b. 24 *May* 1833; d. *at Trouville* 10 *July* 1900; m. 12 *July* 1849, *Hambly Knapp of Upton Park, Slough*, d. (–); *and had issue* (*with a son and 2 das.* d. *unm.*) 1*e* *to* 5*e*.

1*e*. Charles Cornwallis Knapp (*St. Helen's Cottage, Byfleet, Surrey*), *b.* 25 Aug. 1852; *m.* 30 Oct. 1882, Georgiana Harriet, da. of George Augustus Pollard of Rostrevor, co. Devon, J.P.; and has issue (with a son, Cedric Jerome, *b.* 7 Ap. 1890; *d.* 11 June 1896) 1*f*.
    1*f*. Florence Helen Knapp.

2*e*. Rev. Ashley Henry Arthur Knapp, in Holy Orders of the Roman Catholic Church, *b.* 16 Sept. 1866.

3*e*. Augusta Emma Grace Knapp, *m.* 6 Feb. 1873, Frederic Shenstone (*Sutton Hall, Barcombe, Sussex*); and has issue (with a son, Frederick Wyattville Smith, *b.* 17 June 1876, *d.* young) 1*f*.
    1*f*. Adela Shenstone.

4*e*. Georgina Annie Ashley Knapp, *unm.*

5*e*. Rosalie Violet Olympe Knapp, *unm.*

3*d*. *Caroline Malcy Matilda Brownrigg*, da. and co-h., b. *at the Cape* 12 *May* 1839; d. 1 *Jan*. 1900; m. 15 *July* 1865, *George Harvey Jay of Sherlocks Hall, co. Kent, and* 16 *Westbourne Street, London, W*., d. 5 Nov. 1881; *and had issue* 1*e* *to* 3*e*.

1*e*. Harvey Brownrigg Jay, late D.C.L.I. (*The White Lodge, Purton, Wilts*), *b.* 13 Mar. 1868; *m.* 22 July 1893, Kate Bellville, da. of Francis John Bucelle; and has issue 1*f* to 5*f*.
    1*f*. George Harvey Brownrigg Jay, *b.* 3 Aug. 1894.
    2*f*. Judith Malcé Brownrigg Jay.
    3*f*. Marjorie Grace Brownrigg Jay.
    4*f*. Gwyneth Mary Brownrigg Jay.
    5*f*. Myra Kathleen Brownrigg Jay.

2*e*. *Grace Isabel Brownrigg Jay*, b. 30 *Nov*. 1866; d. 13 *June* 1897; m. 18 *July* 1887, *the Rev. Henry John Claude Torry, M.A.* (*Camb.*), *Rector of Streat* (*Streat Rectory, Hassocks*); *and had issue* 1*f*.
    1*f*. John Shirley Archibald Torry, *b.* 17 July 1889.

3*e*. Ethel Rose Brownrigg Jay, *m.* 1 Feb. 1897, Major Walter Dougall, *formerly* "The Carabineers," 6th Dragoon Guards (*Silton Hall, Nether Silton, Northallerton*); and has issue 1*f* to 2*f*.
    1*f*. Ferrers Mackintosh Dougall, *b.* 1 Nov. 1897.
    2*f*. Eustace Melville Dougall, *b.* 7 Feb. 1903.

[Nos. 60186 to 60214.

The Plantagenet Roll

219. Descendants of Lady HENRIETTA O'BRIEN (Table XXI.), d. 1730; m. 1717, ROBERT SANDFORD of Castlerea, M.P. co. Roscommon; and had issue 1a to 5a.

1a. Henry Sandford of Castlerea, d. 12 Feb. 1797; m. 21 Sept. 1750, the Hon. Sarah, da. of Stephen (Moore), 1st Viscount Mountcashell [I.], d. 3 Oct. 1764; and had issue 1b to 2b.

1b. Henry Moore (Sandford), 1st Baron Mount Sandford [I.], d.s.p. 14 June 1814.

2b. Rev. William Sandford, b. 1752; d. 17 Aug. 1809; m. 1789, Jane, da. of the Right Hon. Silver Oliver of Castle Oliver, co. Limerick, d. (-); and had issue 1c to 3c.

1c. Henry (Sandford), 2nd Baron Mount Sandford [I.], d.s.p.; m. 14 June 1828.

2c. Mary Grey Sandford, da. and event. (1828) co-h., b. 1791; d. 1851; m. as 2nd wife, 11 Oct. 1816, William Robert Wills, afterwards (R.L. 13 Sept. 1847) Wills-Sandford of Willsgrove, co. Roscommon, J.P., D.L., d. 11 Aug. 1859; and had issue (with 2 das. unm.) 1d to 4d.

1d. Thomas George Wills-Sandford of Willsgrove and Castlerea, J.P., D.L., b. 15 Aug. 1817; d. 13 Ap. 1887; m. 29 Sept. 1841, Theodosia Eleanor Blagden, da. of Robert Blagden Hale of Alderley, co. Glouc., d. 23 Aug. 1857; and had issue. See p. 351, Nos. 59616–59633.

2d. William Sandford Wills-Sandford of Garryglass, Queen's Co., and Compton Castle, co. Somerset, J.P., 83rd Regt., b. 26 Mar. 1822; d. 8 Feb. 1882; m. 30 May 1849, Julia, da. of William Fosier of Stourton Court, co. Worc., d. May 1883; and had issue 1e to 5e.

1e. Arthur Pakenham Wills-Sandford of Garryglass, &c. (The Priory House, Sherborne, Dorset), b. 7 Jan. 1856.

2e. Reginald Wills-Sandford (2802 Garber Street, Berkeley, California, U.S.A.), b. 3 May 1862; m. 9 Mar. 1892, Mary Woods, da. of Chauncey Hatch Phillips; and has issue 1f.

1f. Georgina Maude Wills-Sandford.

3e. Florence Mary Wills-Sandford, m. 8 Feb. 1872, John Graham Carrick Moore, Lieut. R.H.G.; s.p.

4e. Geraldine Wills-Sandford, m. 1st, 19 Oct. 1899, Arthur Dendy, d. Jan. 1900; 2ndly, Nov. 1908, Loftus Moller le Champion (Wickenthorp, Templecombe); s.p.

5e. Maude Wills-Sandford, m. 14 June 1890, John Hunter-Blair [7th son of Sir Edward Hunter-Blair, 4th Bt. [G.B.], J.P., D.L.] (Elmbank, Halliford-on-Thames); and has issue 1f.

1f. Colin Edward Hunter-Blair, b. 13 Feb. 1898.

3d. Elizabeth Sydney Wills-Sandford, d. 21 Feb. 1873; m. 18 July 1844, Godfrey Wills, d. Sept. 1866; and had issue (with a son, Ormond Kingsley, d.s.p.) 1e.

1e. Aline Mary Wills, b. Nov. 1861; d. 7 Mar. 1897; m. 17 Oct. 1882, Charles Edward Wynne Eyton [Cadet of Leeswood] (The Tower, Mold, N. Wales); and had issue 1f to 5f.

1f. Robert Mainwaring Eyton (South Africa), b. Jan. 1886.

2f. Charles Sandford Wynne Eyton (South Africa), b. Oct. 1888.

3f. Dorothy Elizabeth Eyton.

4f. Joan Katherine Eyton.

5f. Aline Margaret Eyton.

4d. Caroline Julia Wills-Sandford (2 St. Paul's Place, St. Leonards-on-Sea).

3c. Eliza Catherine Sandford, da. and (1828) co-h., b. 1796; d. 1867; m. 15 Jan. 1822, Very Rev. the Hon. Henry Pakenham, Dean of St. Patrick's [5th son of the 2nd Baron Longford [I.], d. 26 Dec. 1863; and had issue 1d to 2d.

[Nos. 60215 to 60245.]

# of The Blood Royal

1d. *Henry Sandford Pakenham*, now (R.L. 26 May 1847) *Pakenham-Mahon of Strokestown, J.P., D.L., 8th Hussars,* b. 6 Feb. 1823; d. 28 Mar. 1893; m. 11 Mar. 1847, *Grace Catherine [descended from the Lady Isabel Plantagenet (Westbrook, Ryde, I.W.), da. and h. of Major Denis Mahon of Strokestown, co. Roscommon:* and had issue.
See the Essex Volume, p. 82, Nos. 6483–6489.

2d. *William Sandford Pakenham*, b. 10 Jan. 1826; d. 26 Nov. 1886; m. 15 Jan. 1857, *Constantia Henrietta Frances, da. of Sir William Verner, 1st Bt.* [U.K.]; and had issue 1e to 6e.

1e. William Wingfield Verner Pakenham, *formerly* Lieut.-Col. Indian Army, b. 14 Nov. 1857; m. 1 Jan. 1883, *Frances Josephine, da. of Dep. Surg.-Gen. Joseph Marcus Joseph, M.D., Madras Med. Ser.*; and has issue 1f to 2f.

1f. William Henry Verner Pakenham, b. 2 June 1885.
2f. Ida Constance Pakenham.

2e. Frederick Edward Sandford Pakenham, b. 15 Ap. 1859; m. 1898, *Margarita Louisa, da. of Maurice Ceely Maude* [V. Hawarden Coll.]; and has issue 1f.

1f. Michael Ceely Sandford Pakenham, b. 26 Ap. 1903.

3e. Francis Henry Godfrey Pakenham, b. 21 Jan. 1865; m. 1890, (—), da. of (—) Russell.
4e. Robert Sandford Pakenham, b. 1 May 1866.
5e. Hamilton Richard Pakenham, b. 25 Nov. 1867; m. 18—, (—), da. of (—) Strickland.
6e. Constance Selena Pakenham.

2a. *Robert Sandford, Gen. in the Army,* d. (? s.p.) 1793.
3a. *Mary Sandford,* d. (? s.p.); m. *Robert Cooke.*
4a. *Anne Sandford,* d. (? s.p.); m. *John Bourne.*
5a. *Henrietta Sandford,* d. (? s.p.); m. *Edward Nicholson.*

[Nos. 60246 to 60261.

220. **Descendants of Lady MARY O'BRIEN** (Table XXI.), b. in London 12 Feb. 1692; d. Feb. 1780; m. 7 Mar. 1709, ROBERT (FITZGERALD), 19th EARL OF KILDARE [I.], P.C., b. 4 May 1675; d. 20 Feb. 1744; and had issue 1a to 2a.

1a. *James (FitzGerald), 20th Earl of Kildare and* (26 Nov. 1766) *1st Duke of Leinster* [I.], *1st Viscount Leinster* [G.B. 21 Feb. 1747], b. 29 May 1722; d. 19 Nov. 1773; m. 7 Feb. 1747, *Lady Emilia Mary, da. of Charles (Lennox), 2nd Duke of Richmond* [E.] *and Lennox* [S.] [rem. 2ndly, 1774, *William Ogilvy and*] d. 27 Mar. 1814; *and had issue.*
See the Exeter Volume, pp. 468–477, Nos. 41433–41780, and Supplement, 41759/1–19.

2a. *Lady Margaretta FitzGerald*, b. 2 July 1729; d. *at Naples* 19 Jan. 1766; m. *as 1st wife,* 1 Mar. 1748, *Wills (Hill), 1st Earl of Hillsborough* [I.], *and afterwards* (20 Aug. 1789) *1st Marquis of Downshire* [I.] *and* (28 Aug. 1772) *Earl of Hillsborough* [G.B.], *P.C.,* d. 7 Oct. 1793; *and had issue* 1b to 3b.

1b. *Arthur (Hill), 2nd Marquis of Downshire, &c.* [I.], *and Earl of Hillsborough* [G.B.], b. 3 Mar. 1753; d. 7 Sept. 1801; m. 29 June 1786, *Mary, afterwards* (29 June 1802) *suo jure 1st Baroness Sandys* [U.K.], *da. of the Hon. Martin Sandys,* d. 1 Aug. 1836; *and had issue.*
See the Essex Volume, pp. 142–144, Nos. 16212–16318.

2b. *Lady Mary Amelia Hill,* b. 16 Aug. 1750; d. (*being burnt to death at Hatfield House,* 28 Nov. 1835; m. 2 Dec. 1773, *James (Cecil), 1st Marquis* [G.B.] *and 7th Earl* [E.] *of Salisbury, K.G.,* d. 13 June 1823; *and had issue.*
See the Exeter Volume, pp. 216–219, Nos. 7652–7738.   [Nos. 60262 to 60822.

The Plantagenet Roll

3b. *Lady Charlotte Hill*, b. 18 *Mar.* 1754; d. 17 *Jan.* 1804; m. 7 *May* 1776, *John Chetwynd* (*Talbot, afterwards* (R.L. 19 *Ap.* 1786) *Chetwynd-Talbot*), 1st *Earl and* 3rd *Baron Talbot* [G.B.], d. 19 *May* 1793; *and had issue* 1c.

1c. *Charles* (*Chetwynd-Talbot*), 2nd *Earl Talbot, &c.* [G.B.], K.G., b. 25 *Ap.* 1777; d. 10 *Jan.* 1849; m. 28 *Aug.* 1800, *Frances Thomasina*, da. *of Charles Lambart of Beau Parc, co. Meath*, d. 30 *Dec.* 1819; *and had issue*.

See the Essex Volume, pp. 220-223, Nos. 29531-29713.

[Nos. 60823 to 61005.

221. Descendants, if any, of Lady CATHERINE BOYLE (Table XXI.), b. c. 1653; d. 3 Sept. 1681, aged 28, bur. at Richmond, co. Surrey; m. RICHARD BRETT of co. Somerset.

222. Descendants of Lady ANNE HOWARD (Table XXI.), d. (-); m. a. 1646, THOMAS WALSINGHAM of Scadbury, co. Kent (sold about 1619), and of Little Chesterford, co. Essex, d. 22 Nov. 1691; and had issue (with another da., Lady Osborne, who d.s.p.) 1a to 3a.[1]

1a. *James Walsingham of Little Chesterford*, d.s.p. 28 *Oct.* 1728, *aged* 82.

2a. *Barbara Walsingham*, d. 23 *Nov.* 1723; m. a. 1685, *Henry* (*Browne*), 5th *Viscount Montagu* [E.], d. 25 *June* 1717; *and had issue*.
See the Clarence Volume, pp. 394-396, Nos. 15001-15122.

3a. *Frances Walsingham*, d. a. 1728; m. *John Rossiter of Somersby, co. Linc.*; *and had issue* 1b.

1b. *Arabella Rossiter*, da. and h., m. as 1st *wife, Henry Villiers* (see p. 377), d. 1753.

[Nos. 61006 to 61127.

223. Descendants of Lady FRANCES HOWARD (Table XXI.), bur. in Westminster Abbey 27 Nov. 1677; m. as 1st wife, Sir EDWARD VILLIERS, Knight-Marshal of the Royal Household and Governor of Tynemouth Castle [V. Grandison [I.] Coll.], bur. with wife, 2 July 1689; and had issue 1a to 7a.

1a. *Edward* (*Villiers*), 1st *Earl of Jersey* [E.], b. 1656; d. 25 *Aug.* 1711; m. 17 *Dec.* 1781, *Barbara* (*who was cr. by King James III. in exile, Ap.* 1716)[2] *Countess of Jersey* [E.], da. *of William Chiffinch of Febbers, co. Berks*, d. *in Paris* 22 *July* 1735; *and had issue* 1b *to* 2b.

1b. *William* (*Villiers*), 2nd *Earl of Jersey* [E.], b. c. 1682; d. 13 *July* 1721; m. 22 *Mar.* 1705, *Judith*, da. and h. *of Frederick Herne*, bur. 31 *July* 1735; *and had issue* 1c *to* 2c.

1c. *William* (*Villiers*), 3rd *Earl of Jersey* [E.] *and* (1766) 6th *Viscount Grandison* [I.], d. 28 *Aug.* 1769; m. 23 *June* 1733, *Anne, Dowager-Duchess of Bedford* [E.], da. *and in her issue* (1803) *co-h. of Scroop* (*Egerton*), 1st *Duke of Bridgewater* [G.B.], d. 16 *June* 1762; *and had issue*.
See the Tudor Roll, pp. 358-371, Nos. 27543-28029.

2c. *Thomas* (*Villiers*), 1st *Earl of Clarendon* [G.B. 14 *June* 1776], b. 1709; d. 11 *Dec.* 1786; m. 30 *Mar.* 1752, *Lady Charlotte*, da. *of William* (*Capel*), 3rd *Earl of Essex* [E.], d. 3 *Sept.* 1790; *and had issue*.
See the Exeter Volume, pp. 379-384, Nos. 26875-27057.

[Nos. 61128 to 61797.

---

[1] Manning and Bray's "Surrey," ii. 540.
[2] Ruvigny's "Jacobite Peerage," p. 63.

of The Blood Royal

2b. *Lady Mary Villiers*, d. 17 *Jan.* 1735; m. 1st, 1709, *Thomas Thynne of Old Windsor* (see p. 435), d. 24 *Ap.* 1710; 2ndly, 1711, *George (Granville), 1st Baron Lansdowne* [*G.B.*] *and 1st Duke of Albemarle* [*E.*], so cr. *by King James III. in exile* 3 *Nov.* 1721[1] (see p. 465), d. 30 *Jan.* 1735; *and had issue* 1c *to* 3c.

1c. *Thomas (Thynne), 2nd Viscount Weymouth* [*E.*], b. *posthumous* 21 *Mar.* 1710; d. 13 *Jan.* 1751; m. 2ndly, 3 *July* 1733, *Lady Louisa, da. of John (Carteret), 1st Earl Granville* [*G.B.*], *K.G.*, d. 26 *Dec.* 1736; *and had issue.*

See the Tudor Roll, Table XXXVI., pp. 212–222, Nos. 21654–22022.

2c. *Lady Mary Granville*, d. *Nov.* 1735; m. 1730, *William Graham of Platten, near Drogheda.*

3c. *Lady Grace Granville*, d. 1 *Nov.* 1769; m. 28 *Mar.* 1740, *Thomas (Foley), 1st Baron Foley* [*G.B.*], d. 14 or 18 *Nov.* 1777; *and had issue.*

See the Essex Volume, pp. 320–322, Nos. 33109–33411.

2a. *Henry Villiers, Col. in the Army and* (8 *July* 1702) *Governor of Tynemouth Castle*, d. 18 *Aug.* 1707; m. (—), da. *of* (—); *and had issue* 1b.

1b. *Henry Villiers, Governor of Tynemouth Castle*, d. (? s.p.) 29 *May* 1753; m. 1st, *Arabella* (see p. 376), da. *and h. of John Rossiter of Somersby, co. Linc.*; 2ndly, *Mary, sister of Lieut.-Gen. Thomas Fowke, da. of* (—) *Fowke.*

3a. *Elizabeth Villiers*, d. 19 *Ap.* 1733; m. 25 *Nov.* 1695, *George (Hamilton), 1st Earl of Orkney* [*S.*], *K.T.*, d. 29 *Jan.* 1737; *and had issue* 1b *to* 3b.

1b. *Anne (Hamilton), suo jure 2nd Countess of Orkney* [*S.*], d. 7 *Dec.* 1756; m. 29 *Mar.* 1720, *William (O'Brien), 4th Earl of Inchiquin* [*I.*], d. 18 *July* 1777; *and had issue.*

See p. 367, Nos. 59986–60036.

2b. *Lady Frances Hamilton*, d. 27 *Dec.* 1772; m. 27 *June* 1724, *Thomas (Lumley), 3rd Earl of Scarbrough* [*E.*] *and 4th Viscount Lumley* [*I.*], *K.B.* (see p. 431), d. 15 *Mar.* 1752; *and had issue.*

See the Exeter Volume, pp. 632–635, Nos. 53563–53667.

3b. *Lady Henrietta Hamilton*, d. 22 *Aug.* 1732; m. as 1st *wife*, 9 *May* 1728, *John (Boyle), 5th Earl of Cork and Orrery* [*I.*], d. 23 *Nov.* 1762; *and had issue.*

See p. 342, Nos. 58509–58552.

4a. *Catherine Villiers, living* 1702; m. 1st, 20 *July* 1685, *James Louis (Le Vasseur-Cougnée), 1st Marquis of Puissar* [*F.*], *Col.* 24*th Regt.* 1695, d. app. s.p. 1701;[2] 2ndly, 1702, *Col. William Villiers.*

5a. *Barbara Villiers*, d. 19 *Sept.* 1708; m. *John (Berkeley), 4th Viscount Fitzhardinge* [*I.*], d. 19 *Dec.* 1712; *and had issue which became extinct on the death of Sir Thomas Clarges, 4th Bt.*, 1834.

6a. *Frances or Anne Villiers*, d. *Nov.* 1688; m. as 1st *wife*, *Feb.* 1678, *Hans William (Bentinck), 1st Earl of Portland* [*E.*], *K.G.*, d. 23 *Nov.* 1709; *and had issue* 1b *to* 4b.

1b. *Henry (Bentinck), 2nd Earl* [*E.*] *and* (6 *July* 1716) *1st Duke of Portland* [*G.B.*], b. 17 *Mar.* 1682; d. 4 *July* 1726; m. 9 *June* 1704, *Lady Elizabeth, da. of Wriothesley (Noel), 3rd Earl of Gainsborough* [*E.*], d. *Mar.* 1733; *and had issue.*

See the Essex Volume, pp. 156–160, Nos. 18189–19078.

2b. *Lady Mary Bentinck*, b. 1679; d. 20 *Aug.* 1726; m. 1st, 28 *Feb.* 1698, *Algernon (Capel), 2nd Earl of Essex* [*E.*], d. 10 *Jan.* 1710; *and had issue.*

See the Exeter Volume, pp. 374–385, Nos. 26747–27271.

3b. *Lady Anna Margaretha Bentinck*, b. *at the Hague and bapt. there* 19 *Mar.* 1683; d. *there* 3 *May* 1763; m. 1701, *Arent, Baron van Wassenaer, Lord of Duvenvoirde, Voorschoten, Veur, T'Woud, Rosande, and Harsselo, Ambassador Extraordinary for the States-General to the Court of St. James*, bapt. *at the Hague* 1 *Dec.* 1669; d. *there* 15 *Dec.* 1721; *and had issue* 1c *to* 2c. [Nos. 61798 to 64084.

---

[1] Ruvigny's "Jacobite Peerage," p. 3.
[2] Ruvigny's "Nobilities of Europe," p. 108.

The Plantagenet Roll

1c. Baroness Jacoba Maria van Wassenaer, Lady of Duvenvoirde, &c., b. at the Hague 4 Oct. 1709; d. at Duvenvoorde Castle, Voorschoten, 1 Oct. 1771; m. at the Hague 20 Oct. 1732, Frederik Willem (Torck), Baron Torck, Lord of Heerjansdam and Petkum and heir of Rosendael, b. 6 Sept. 1691; d. at Arnhem 1 Nov. 1761; and had issue 1d.

1d. Assueer Jan (Torck), Baron Torck, Lord of Rosendael, &c., b. at the Hague 11 July 1733; d. at Wageningen 21 Feb. 1793; m. at Rosendael Castle 8 June 1758, Baroness Eusebia Jacoba, da. of Baron (—) de Rode van Heeckeren tot Overlaer, b. at Overlaer Castle, Laren, 16 Mar. 1740; d. at Wageningen 3 Dec. 1793; and had issue 1e to 2e.

1e. Reinhard Jan Christiaan (Torck), Baron Torck, Lord of Rosendael, &c., b. at Rosendael Castle 2 Aug. 1775; d. there 2 Jan. 1810; m. at Eck en Wiel 9 Sept. 1800, Baroness Gooswina Geurdina, da. of Baron (—) van Neukirchen genaamd van Nyvenheim [H.R.E.], b. at Arnhem 25 Mar. 1781; d. at Utrecht 6 Dec. 1830; and had issue 1f to 2f.

1f. Assueer Lubbert Adolf (Torck), Baron Torck van Rosendael, b. at Roesendael Castle 23 Nov. 1806; d. there 18 Aug. 1842; m. at the Hague 29 Aug. 1834, Jkvr Louise Catharina Wilhelmina, da. of Johan Willem (Huyssen), 1st Baron Huyssen van Kattendijke [Netherlands, 16 Oct. 1827], b. at Brunswick 20 July 1812; d. at the Hague 5 Mar. 1843; and had issue 1g.

1g. Baroness Ada Catharina Torck van Rosendael, b. at Rosendael Castle 26 Oct. 1835; d. there 13 Jan. 1902; m. at the Hague 14 Dec. 1854, Reinhard Jan Christiaan (van Pallandt), 7th [H.R.E. 1675] and 4th [Neth. 1814] Baron van Pallandt, Burgomaster of Rosendael (see p. 379), b. there 7 July 1826; d. there 24 Dec. 1899; and had issue 1h to 3h.

1h. Reinhard Adolf (van Pallandt), 8th [H.R.E.] and 5th [Neth.] Baron Torck van Pallandt (Rosendael Castle), b. 24 Dec. 1857; unm.

2h. Baron Frederik Jacob Willem van Pallandt (Rosendael), b. at Rosendael Castle 11 Sept. 1860; m. there 20 May 1886, Constantia Alexine Loudon, da. of Hugh Hope [by his wife Baroness Jacoba Cornelia Wilhelmina, née van Pallandt]; and has issue 1i to 5i.

1i. Baron Reinhard Jan Christiaan van Pallandt, b. 24 Jan. 1888.

2i. Baron Hugh Hope Alexander van Pallandt, b. 30 May 1891.

3i. Baron Willem Frederick Torck van Pallandt, b. 4 Sept 1892.

4i. Baroness Helena Susanna Cornelia van Pallandt, b. 20 Jan. 1895.

5i. Baroness Cecilia Emelie Louisa van Pallandt, b. 3 Nov. 1899.

3h. Baron Werner Karel van Pallandt, Lord of (Heer van) Petkum (Rosenheuvel te Rosendael), b. 26 Dec. 1863; m. at the Hague 17 May 1888, Baroness Adolphine Wilhelmine Charlotte, Lady van Nyenhuis and Ammerfelde (see p. 379), da. of Hendrik Antoni Zwier (van Knobelsdorff), 2nd Baron van Knobelsdorff [Neth. 18 Ap. 1837]; and has issue 1i to 5i.

1i. Baron Assueer Lubbert Adolf van Pallandt, b. 11 July 1889.

2i. Baron Emilius Johan van Pallandt, b. 17 May 1893.

3i. Baron Karel Werner van Pallandt, b. 23 Aug. 1900.

4i. Baroness Henriette Jeanne Adelaide van Pallandt, b. 25 Aug. 1890.

5i. Baroness Adolphine Wernardine Charlotte Wilhelmine van Pallandt, b. 13 June 1902.

2f. Baroness Henriette Jeanne Adelaide Torck, b. at Rosendael 14 Aug. 1802; d. at Keppel Castle 30 Nov. 1877; m. at Rosendael 19 Aug. 1824, Adolph Werner Carel Willem (van Pallandt), 5th Baron van Pallandt, H.R.E. [12 July 1675], and 2nd Baron van Pallandt [Neth. 28 Aug. 1814], Lord of (Heer van) Keppel, Barlham, &c., b. at the Hague 25 June 1802; d. at Keppel Castle 22 Jan. 1874; and had issue 1g to 6g.

1g. Frederik Jacob Willem (van Pallandt), 6th [H.R.E.] and 3rd [Neth.] Baron van Pallandt, b. 3 June 1825; d.s.p. 17 May 1888.

2g. Reinhard Jan Christiaan (van Pallandt), 7th [H.R.E.] and 4th [Neth.]

[Nos. 64085 to 64097.

# of The Blood Royal

Baron van Pallandt, b. at Rosendael Castle 7 July 1826; d. there 24 Dec. 1899; m. at the Hague 14 Dec. 1854, Baroness Ada Catherine, da. and h. of Assueer Lubbert Adolph (Torck), Baron Torck van Rosendael, d. at Rosendael Castle 13 Jan. 1902; and had issue.

See p. 378, Nos. 64085-64097.

3g. Baron Emilius Joan van Pallandt (*Keppel Castle*), b. at Rosendael Castle 18 Sept. 1829; *unm*.

4g. Baron Floris van Pallandt, Lord of (Heer van) Hagen, b. at the Hague 25 Feb. 1835; d. 29 Dec. 1902; m. at the Hague 15 May 1863, Johanna Wilhelmina, da. of Mr. Pieter François van Hoogstraten, d. at Almen 18 Aug. 1901; *and had issue 1h to 2h*.

1h. Baron François Johan van Pallandt (*Hastière, Belgium*), b. 3 Feb. 1866; m. at Brussels 25 Ap. 1908, Marie Louise Ghislaine, da. of (—) Defays.

2h. Baroness Henriette Jeanne van Pallandt, m. at the Hague 9 Oct. 1884, Jonkheer Vincent Johan Gerard Beelaerts van Blokland [Jhr. Neth. 15 Ap. 1815 Coll.] (*The Hague*); and has issue 1i.

1i. Jkr. Vincent Pieter Adriaan Beelaerts van Blokland, b. at the Hague 7 June 1889.

5g. Baroness Adelaide Jeanne Henriette van Pallandt, Lady of the Palace to H.M. the Queen (*Nyenhuis onder Heine en s'Gravenhage*), m. at Keppel 10 Oct. 1863, Hendrik Antoni Zwier (van Knobelsdorff, 2nd Baron van Knobelsdorff (Neth. 18 Ap. 1837], Heer van de Gelder, Nyenhuis, &c., b. at Gelder Castle 28 June 1840; d. at the Hague 24 Feb. 1905; and has issue 1h to 2h.

1h. Frederik Willem Adriaan Karel (van Knobelsdorff), 3rd Baron van Knobelsdorff van de Gelder [Neth.] (*The Hague*), b. at Keppel 2 Sept. 1865.

2h. Baroness Adolphine Wilhelmine Charlotte van Knobelsdorff, Lady van Nyenhuis, &c., m. 17 May 1888, Baron Werner Karel van Pallandt, Lord of Petkum [B. (H.R.E.) Coll.] (*Rosenheuvel te Roosendaal*); and has issue.

See p. 378, Nos. 64093-64097.

6g. Baroness Catharine Louise Wilhelmine van Pallandt (*The Hague*), m. 15 May 1863, Baron Henri van Pallandt, Lord of (Heer van) Wolfswaard [B. van Pallandt (H.R.E. 12 July 1675) Coll.], b. at Arnhem 14 Jan. 1841; d. at the Hague 1 Nov. 1901; and had issue 1h to 2h.

1h. Baroness Everdine Susette van Pallandt, m. at the Hague 14 July 1887, Guillaume Charles, Baron Snouckaert van Schauburg [Neth. 24 Nov. 1816], Chamberlain and Treasurer of the Household to H.M. the Queen, *formerly* to King William III. (*The Hague*); and has issue 1i.

1i. Baron Willem Carel Snouckaert van Schauburg, b. at the Hague 24 Aug. 1888.

2h. Baroness Adolphine Wernardine van Pallandt (*The Hague*), *unm*.

2e. *Baroness Henriette Christine Alexandrine Torck, Lady of (Vrouwe van) Duvenvoorde, Voorschoten, Veur, and Heerjansdam*, b. at the Hague 31 Mar. 1764; d. 11 Aug. 1792; m. at Rosendael Castle 5 Oct. 1788, *Adolph Hendrik, Count van Rechteren* [H.R.E.], *Heer van Collendoorn*, b. at the Hague 26 Oct. 1738; d. there 3 Dec. 1805; *and had issue 1f*.

1f. Countess Maria van Rechteren, Vrouwe van Pettkum, Duvenvoirde, &c., b. at Zutphen 27 July 1789; d. at s'Gravenhage 30 Ap. 1808; m. *as 1st wife* 5 Oct. 1806, *Jan Gijsbert Ludolf Adriaan (van Neukirchen), 1st Baron van Neukirchen gen. Nyvenheim* [Neth. 25 Mar. 1822], *Heer van Eck en Wiel*, b. at Arnhem 12 Dec. 1783; d. at Paris 21 Dec. 1818; *and had issue 1g*.

1g. *Baroness Henriette Jeanne Christine van Neukirchen, Vrouwe van Duvenvoorde, Voorschoten, &c.*, b. at Eck 19 Sept. 1807; d. at Hyères 16 Nov. 1849; m. *at Roosendaal* 8 July 1830 (3rd) *Jhr Nicolaas Johan Steengracht* [Neth. 1 July 1816], *Heer van Moyland, Till, &c.*, b. 13 Jan. 1806; d. at Moyland, near Cleves, 4 Oct. 1866; *and had issue 1h to 3h*. [Nos. 64098 to 64126.

The Plantagenet Roll

1h. *Nicolaas Adriaan (Steengracht),* 1st *Baron Steengracht van Moyland* [*Neth.* 19 *Dec.* 1888], *Heer van Moyland en Till, Chamberlain of the Household to King William III.,* b. 29 *Mar.* 1834 ; d. *at Moyland Castle* 29 *June* 1906 ; m. 1st, 3 *Dec.* 1868, *Jkvr Maria Theodora, da. of Willem Frans (van Herzeele),* 2nd *Baron vån Herzeele* [*Neth.* 30 *Mar.* 1829], d. 29 *Oct.* 1895 ; 2ndly, 3 *Aug.* 1901, *Irene Theresia Lidvina Christine Paule Clara, da. of Edler Hugo Heinrich Raphael Jacob von Kremer-Auenrode ; and had issue* 1i *to* 2i.

1i. Hendrik (Steengracht), 2nd Baron Steengracht van Moyland [Neth.] (*Moyland bij Cleve*), b. 1 Dec. 1869 ; m. 24 Nov. 1897, Helene, da. of Charles de Struve ; 2ndly, in London 1905, Olga Louisa Charlotta, da. of Jacob Pieter van Braam ; and has issue 1j.

1j. Jhr. Henry Adolf Adriaan Gustav Steengracht, b. at Cleves 28 July 1905.

2i. Jhr. Gustav Adolph von Steengracht-Moyland, b. 15 Nov. 1902.

2h. *Jkvr. Cornelia Maria Steengracht, Lady of the Palace to the Queen Mother,* b. 24 *May* 1831 ; d. *at Duivenvoorde Castle* 7 *Sept.* 1906 ; m. *at Voorschoten* 19 *Dec.* 1855, *William Assueer Jacob (Schimmelpennick),* 2nd *Baron Schimmelpennick van der Oye* [*Neth.* 22 *Aug.* 1820], LL.D., b. *at Karlsruhe* 26 *July* 1834 ; d. *at Cadenabbia* 2 *June* 1886 ; *and had issue* 1i *to* 5i.

1i. Alexander Willem (Schimmelpennick), 3rd Baron Schimmelpennick van der Oye [Neth.], LL.D. (*Oud-Clingendaal te Wassenaer*), b. 10 July 1859 ; m. 1st, 24 Aug. 1888, Baroness Cornelia Elizabeth, da. of Gen. Baron Gijsbert Jan Anne Adolph van Heematra [B. v. Heematra [Neth. 2 Ap. 1826] Coll.], d. at Nordrach, Baden, 29 Dec. 1901 ; 2ndly, 19 Ap. 1905, Jeanne Françoise, da. of Leon Chassagnard ; and has issue 1j to 3j.

1j. Baron Willem Anne Assuerus Jacob Schimmelpennick van der Oye, b. at Rome 5 Oct. 1889.

2j. Baron Leon Frans Carel Schimmelpennick van der Oye, b. at Wassenaer 26 Oct. 1905.

3j. Baroness Ludolphine Henriette Schimmelpennick van der Oye, b. at St. Petersburg 20 July 1891.

2i. Baron Hendrik Nicolaas Schimmelpennick van der Oye (*Amersfoort*), b. 4 Ap. 1862 ; m. 10 Feb. 1887, the Countess Cecile Eugénie Marie Desirée, da. of Count du Monceau ; and has issue 1j to 8j.

1j. Baron René Henri Schimmelpennick van der Oye, b. at Kloetinge 7 Feb. 1893.

2j. Baron Felix Cornelius Schimmelpennick van der Oye, b. there 14 May 1901.

3j. Baron Henri Felix Marie Schimmelpennick van der Oye, b. at Goes 16 Jan. 1903.

4j. Baroness Marie Cornelie Aimee Schimmelpennick van der Oye, b. at Goes 29 Nov. 1887.

5j. Baroness Felicia Maria Schimmelpennick van der Oye, b. at Kloetinge 6 July 1889.

6j. Baroness Cornelie Marie Henriette Antonia Gustavine Schimmelpennick van der Oye, b. there 24 Oct. 1895.

7j. Baroness Cécile Emelie Alexandrine Schimmelpennick van der Oye, b. there 25 May 1899.

8j. Baroness Ida Henriette Schimmelpennick van der Oye, b. at Amersfoort 19 Nov. 1904.

3i. Baroness Henriette Marie Sophie Schimmelpennick van der Oye, m. 21 July 1881, Jhr. Mr. Dirk Arnold Willem van Tets [Neth. 26 Aug. 1837], Heer van Goudriaan, &c. (*s'Gravenhage*) ; and has issue 1j to 3j.

1j. Jhr. George Catharinus Willem van Tets, b. 31 Aug. 1882 ; m. at Noordwykerhout 6 May 1909, Jkvr. Pauline Johanna, da. of Jhr. Mr. Abraham Daniel Theodore Gevers [Neth. 27 Oct. 1842].

2j. Jkvr. Henriette van Tets, b. in Constantinople 31 Mar. 1888.

3j. Jkvr. Digna Hendrika van Tets, b. in Constantinople 31 Mar. 1889.

[Nos. 64127 to 64146.

of The Blood Royal

4i. Baroness Maria Cornelia Schimmelpennick van der Oye, b. at s'Gravenhage 30 Oct. 1857; d. there 11 Dec. 1897; m. there as 1st wife 14 Mar. 1878, Jhr. Mr. Sir Jacob Willem Gustaaf Boreel van Hogelanden, 10th Bt. [E. 21 Mar. 1645], Burgomaster of Haarlem, Chamberlain to H.M. Queen Wilhelmina and formerly a Gentleman of the Privy Chamber to King William III. (Waterland, Velsen, en Haarlem); and had issue 1j to 2j.

 1j. Jkvr. Cornelia Maria Boreel, m. 27 Nov. 1902, Baron Frederik Willem van Tuyll van Serooskerken [B. van Tuyll van Serooskerken [Neth. 21 Mar. 1822] Coll.] (*Villa Edison te Aerdenhout-Bloemendaal*); and has issue 1k to 3k.

  1k. Baron Jacob Willem Gustaaf van Tuyll van Serooskerken, b. 4 Aug. 1906.

  2k. Baroness Marie Cornelie van Tuyll van Serooskerken, b. 5 Oct. 1903.

  3k. Baroness Alicia Thecla Ann van Tuyll van Serooskerken, b. 28 Feb. 1905.

 2j. Jkvr. Agnes Boreel, m. at Velsen 17 Oct. 1907, Ernest Cremers (*Villa la Canetta te Noordwijk aan Zee*).

5i. Baroness Cornelia Schimmelpennick van der Oye, m. 1st, 9 July 1889, Jhr. Ernst Hendrik van Loon [Neth. 2 June 1822, Coll.] (*s'Gravenhage*); and has issue 1j to 2j.

 1j. Jhr. Louis Charles van Loon (*Noordhey, Voorschoten*), b. 15 Feb. 1891.

 2j. Jkvr. Antoinette Cornelie van Loon, b. 5 June 1893.

3h. Jhr. Mr. Hendricus Adolphus Steengracht, Heer van Duivenvoorde Voorschoten en Veur, Gentleman of the Chamber and afterwards Special Chamberlain to King William III. and ex-Member of the States for South Holland (*K. Duivenvoorde te Voorschoten, s'Gravenhage ; Nice*), b. 25 Ap. 1836.

 2c. Baroness Louise Isabella Hermeline van Wassenaer, da. and co-h., bapt. at the Hague 19 Feb. 1719; d. at Amerongen 23 Ap. 1756; m. at Voorschoten 2 May 1742, Frederik Willem (van Reede), 4th Earl of Athlone [I.], 5th Baron van Reede [Denmark 1671], b. 1 Apr. 1717; d. at Arnhem 1 Dec. 1747; and had issue 1d.

  1d. Frederik Christiaan Reynhard (van Reede), 5th Earl of Athlone [I.], 6th Baron [Denmark] and 1st Count [H.R.E. 25 Sept. 1790] van Reede, Lord of Amerongen, Middacht Elst, Ginkell, &c., in Utrecht, Ranger of that Province, b. at the Hague 31 Jan. 1743; d. at Teddington, co. Midx., 13 Dec. 1808; m. at the Hague 29 Dec. 1765, Baroness Anna Elizabeth Christina, da. of Jan (van Tuyell), Baron van Tuyll van Serooskerken [Neth.], Heer van Zuylen en Westbroek, b. at Zuylen Castle 9 Sept. 1745; d. at the Hague 16 Jan. 1819; and had issue 1e to 4e.

   1e. Frederick William (van Reede), 6th Earl of Athlone [I.], &c., b. at Utrecht 22 Oct. 1766; d.s.p. at Greenwich 5 Dec. 1810.

   2e. Reynoud Diederik Jacob (van Reede), 7th Earl of Athlone [I.], &c., b. at Utrecht 2 July 1773; d. at the Hague 31 Oct. 1823; m. at Paris 19 Mar. 1818, Henrietta Dorothea Maria, da. and event. h. of John Williams Hope of Amsterdam, d. 30 Sept. 1830; and had issue 1f.

    1f. George Godard Henry (van Reede), 9th Earl of Athlone [I.], &c., b. at Utrecht 21 Nov. 1820; d. unm. at Bath 2 Mar. 1843.

   3e. William Gustaf Frederik (van Reede), 9th and last Earl of Athlone [I.], &c., 5th Count [H.R.E.] and 10th Baron [Denmark] van Reede, Lord of Ginkell, Amerongen, &c., in the Netherlands, b. at Utrecht 21 July 1780; d.s.p. at the Hague 4 May 1844.

   4e. Lady (Countess) Jacoba Helena van Reede-Ginkell, da. and in her issue (21 May 1844) sole h., b. 21 Dec. 1767; d. 6 Sept. 1839; m. 20 Mar. 1785, Count John Charles Bentinck, Major-Gen. British Army [E. of Portland [E. 1689] and C. Bentinck [H.R.E. 1732] Coll.], d. 22 Nov. 1833; and had issue 1f to 2f.

    1f. William Christian Frederick (Bentinck), 4th Count Bentinck [H.R.E.], &c., K.C. Teutonic Order, Chamberlain to King William I., &c., b. 15 Nov. 1787; d. 8 June 1855; m. 16 Ap. 1841, the Countess Pauline Albertine, da. of Friedrich Franz, Count of Münnich, d. 12 Oct. 1898; and had issue 1g.

     1g. Countess Jacqueline Christine Anne Adelaide Bentinck, m. at s'Gravenhage [Nos. 64147 to 64156.

The Plantagenet Roll

6 Nov. 1874, Frederick Magnus, Sovereign Count of Solms-Wildenfels, Knight of Malta, Hereditary Member of the Upper House of the Saxon Diet, &c., &c. (*Castle of Wildenfels, near Dresden*); and has issue 1h to 5h.

   1h. Frederick Magnus, Hereditary Count, b. 1 Nov. 1886.

   2h. Countess Sophie von Solms-Wildenfels, b. 9 Feb. 1877.

   3h. Countess Magna Marie Augustine Adele van Solms-Wildenfels, b. 31 Aug. 1883.

   4h. Countess Anne von Solms-Wildenfels, b. 14 June 1890.

   5h. Countess Gesele Clementina Christophera Carola von Solms-Wildenfels, b. 30 Dec. 1891.

  2f. *Charles Anthony Ferdinand (Bentinck), 5th Count Bentinck* [H.R.E.], *Lord of Middachten*, K.C. Teutonic Order, Lieut.-Gen. in the British Service, b. 4 Mar. 1792; d. 28 Oct. 1864; m. 30 *Jan.* 1846, *the Countess Caroline Mechtild Emma Charlotte Christine Louisa, da. of Charles, Reigning Count of Waldeck and Pyrmont*, d. 28 Feb. 1899; *and had issue* 1g to 5g.

   1g. *Henry Charles Adolphus Frederick William (Bentinck), 6th Count Bentinck* [H.R.E.], *which title he resigned to his next brother* 1874, K.C. Teutonic Order, Lieut.-Col. Coldstream Guards, b. 30 Dec. 1846; d. 18 *June* 1903; m. 8 Dec. 1874, *Henrietta Eliza Cathcart* (53 Green Street, Park Lane, W.), *da. of Robert McKerrell of Hillhouse*; *and had issue* 1h to 7h.

     1h. Count Robert Charles Bentinck, Lieut. Derbyshire Imp. Yeo. (*Bath Club*), b. 5 Dec. 1875.

     2h. Count Charles Henry Bentinck, 2nd Sec. Diplo. Ser. (*H.B.M.'s Legation, The Hague; St. James'; National*), b. 23 Ap. 1879.

     3h. Count Henry Duncan Bentinck, B.A. (Camb.), Lieut. Coldstream Guards (*Guards*), b. 24 June 1881.

     4h. Count Arthur William Douglas Bentinck, B.A. (Camb.), 2nd Lieut. Coldstream Guards (*Guards*), b. 24 July 1887.

     5h. Countess Renira Christine Bentinck, *m.* 6 Dec. 1898, Baron Alexander van Heeckeren van Kell [B. van Heeckeren [Neth. 28 Mar. 1815] Coll.], LL.D., Burgomaster of Ede, Gelderland (*Wielbergen, onder Angerlo*); and has issue 1i to 6i.

       1i. Baron Alexander William Henry Walraven van Heeckeren van Kell, b. (twin) 19 Mar. 1906.

       2i. Baron Henry Robert van Heeckeren van Kell, b. 9 Dec. 1907.

       3i. Baroness Albertine Renira Alexandra Henrietta Mechtild Ottoline van Heeckeren van Kell, b. 29 Sept. 1899.

       4i. Baroness Renira Sophia Louise Rudolphine van Heeckeren van Kell, b. 6 Aug. 1901.

       5i. Baroness Henrietta van Heeckeren van Kell, b. 12 July 1903.

       6i. Baroness Lilian Guinevere Justine May van Heeckeren van Kell, b. (twin) 19 Mar. 1906.

     6h. Countess Ursula Victoria Henrietta Bentinck.

     7h. Countess Naomi Mechtild Henrietta Bentinck.

  2g. *William Charles Philip (Bentinck), 7th Count Bentinck* [H.R.E.] *on his brother's resignation, Count and Baron of Aldenburg and Count of Waldeck-Limpurg, which latter title he assumed by letters patent* 1889; *obtained Royal Licence for himself and the other descendants of his father to assume and use their foreign honours in the United Kingdom* 22 Mar. 1886; *is a* K.M., K.C.T.O., *and a Hereditary Member of the Würtemberg Upper House*, 3rd Sec. H.B.M.'s Diplo. Service (*Middachten Castle, near Arnhem; and 13 Voorhout, The Hague, Holland; Gaildorf, Würtemberg; St. James' Club, London, &c. &c.*), b. 28 Nov. 1848; *m.* 8 Mar. 1877, *the Baroness Mary Cornelia, Vrouwe* (Lady) *van Obdam*, &c., *da. of Baron Jacob Derk Carel van Heeckeren*, LL.D., Grand Master of the Horse to King William III. [B. van Heeckeren [Neth. 28 Mar. 1815] Coll.]; *and has issue* 1h to 4h. [Nos. 64157 to 64175.

# of The Blood Royal

1*h*. William Frederick Charles Henry, Hereditary Count, K.C.T.O., Lieut. Prussian Gardes du Corps (28 *Burggrafenstrasse, Potsdam*), b. 22 June 1880.

2*h*. Count Frederick George Unico William Bentinck, b. 21 June 1888.

3*h*. Countess Mechtild Corisande Renira Mary Bentinck, m. 1 Sept. 1905, Casimir Frederick, Hereditary Count of Castell, Capt. 5th Prussian Lancers [son and h.-app. of H.S.H. the Reigning Prince of Castell-Rudenhausen] (*Rudenhausen, Upper Franconia, Bavaria*); and has issue 1*i*.

1*i*. Countess Marie Emma Agnes Victoria Elizabeth Caroline Mechtilde of Castell, b. at Dusseldorf 8 Mar. 1907.

4*h*. Countess Isabella Antoinette Mary Clementina Bentinck.

3*g*. Count Charles Reginald Adelbert Bentinck, K.C.T.O., *late* Capt. 2nd Prussian Dragoon Guards (*Zuylestein, Utrecht*), b. 9 Feb. 1853; m. 28 Sept. 1878 (dissolved 1885), Countess Helena Agnes Alexandrina Amelia Caroline, da. of Count Charles of Waldeck-Pyrmont; and has issue 1*h*.

1*h*. Countess Mary Amelia Mechtild Agnes Bentinck, b. 16 Sept. 1879.

4*g*. Count Godard John George Charles Bentinck, Lord of Amerongen, Ginkel, Elst, Zuylestein, &c., K.C.T.O. (*Amerongen Castle, Utrecht*), b. 3 Aug. 1857; m. 12 June 1884, the Countess Augustine Wilhelmina Louise Adrienne, da. of Count Jules Auguste von Bylandt [C. of Bylandt [H.R.E. 19 May 1678] Coll.], &c.; and has issue 1*h* to 5*h*.

1*h*. Count Charles Arthur Renaud William Godard Augustus Bentinck, b. 16 Aug. 1885.

2*h*. Count Godard Adrian Henry Jules Bentinck, b. 21 Feb. 1887.

3*h*. Count John Victor Richard Rudolph Bentinck, b. 5 Feb. 1895.

4*h*. Count William Henry Ferdinand Godard Bentinck, b. 20 Dec. 1900.

5*h*. Countess Elizabeth Mechtild Marie Sophia Louise Bentinck.

5*g*. Countess Victoria Mary Frederica Mechtild Bentinck (*Zuylestein, Utrecht*).

4*b*. Lady *Isabella Bentinck*, b. 4 *May* 1688; d. *at Paris* 23 *Feb.* 1728; m. *as 2nd wife*, 2 *Aug.* 1714, *Evelyn* (*Pierrepont*), 1*st Duke of Kingston* [*G.B.*], K.G., d. 5 *Mar.* 1726; *and had issue* 1*c*.

1*c*. Lady *Caroline Pierrepont*, m. 1712, *Thomas Brand*.

7*a*. *Mary Villiers*, d. 17 *Ap.* 1753; m. *as 2nd or 3rd wife, Ap.* 1691, *William* (*O'Brien*), 3*rd Earl of Inchiquin* [*I.*], d. 24 *Dec.* 1719; *and had issue*.

See pp. 367–376, Nos. 59986–61005. [Nos. 64176 to 65209.

224. Descendants of THOMAS (HOWARD), 1st EARL OF BERKSHIRE [E.], K.G., K.B. (Table XXI.), *b. c.* 1590; *d.* 16 July 1669; *m.* 26 May 1614, Lady ELIZABETH, da. and co-h. of William (CECIL), 2nd Earl of Exeter [E.], *bur.* 24 Aug. 1672; and had issue.

See the Clarence Volume, Table LXXVII., and pp. 624–637, Nos. 27996–28849. [Nos. 65210 to 66063.

225. Descendants, if any surviving, of the Hon. Sir CHARLES HOWARD (Table XXI.), *d.* (–); *m.* MARY, widow of the Hon. THOMAS DARCY [son and h. of Thomas, 1st Earl of Rivers [E.]], and previously of Sir ALAN PERCY, K.B., da. and h. of Sir John FITZ of Fitzford and Cavistock, co. Devon; and had issue 1*a*.

1*a*. *Elizabeth Howard, da. and h.*

The Plantagenet Roll

226. Descendants of EDWARD (HOWARD), 1st BARON HOWARD of Escrick [E. 12 Ap. 1628], K.B. (Table XXI.), d. 24 Ap. 1675; m. 30 Nov. 1623, the Hon. MARY, da. and co-h. of John (BOTELER), 1st Baron Boteler of Bramfield [E.], bur. 30 Jan. 1634; and had issue 1a to 3a.

1a. Thomas (Howard), 2nd Baron Howard of Escrick [E.], d.s.p.s. at Bruges 24 Aug. 1678.
2a. William (Howard), 3rd Baron Howard of Escrick [E.], bur. 24 Ap. 1694; m. Frances, da. of Sir James Bridgman of Castle Bromwich, co. Warwick, d. 19 Dec. 1716; and had issue 1b.
1b. Charles (Howard), 4th and last Baron Howard of Escrick [E.], d.s.p. 29 Ap. 1715.
3a. Hon. Anne Howard, da. and in her issue (29 Ap. 1715) sole h., bur. 4 Sept. 1703; m. Charles (Howard) 1st Earl of Carlisle [E.], P.C. (see p. 398), d. 24 Feb. 1685; and had issue 1b.
1b. Edward (Howard), 2nd Earl of Carlisle [E.], b. c. 1646; d. 23 Ap. 1692; m. (lic. dated 27 Ap. 1668), Elizabeth, widow of Sir William Berkeley, da. and co-h. of Sir William Uvedale of Wickham, co. Hants, bur. there 30 Dec. 1696; and had issue 1c.
1c. Charles (Howard), 3rd Earl of Carlisle [E.], b. 1669; d. 1 May 1738; m. 25 July 1683, Lady Anne, da. of Arthur (Capell), 1st Earl of Essex [E.], d. 14 Oct. 1752; and had issue.
See the Exeter Volume, Table XXVII., and pp. 385-386, Nos. 27272-28169.

[Nos. 66064 to 66961.

227. Descendants of Lady ELIZABETH HOWARD (Table XXI.), bapt. 11 Aug. 1586; d. 17 Ap. 1658; m. 1st, as 2nd wife (settl. dated 23 Dec. 1605), WILLIAM (KNOLLYS), 1st EARL OF BANBURY [E.], K.G., b. c. 1547; d. 25 May 1632; 2ndly, before 2 July 1632, EDWARD (VAUX), 4th BARON VAUX of Harrowden [E.], d.s.p. 8 Ap. 1661; and had issue (whose legitimacy is disputed).

228. Descendants of Lady FRANCES HOWARD (Table XXI.), b. 30 Sept. 1589; d. 23 Aug. 1632; m. 1st, 5 Jan. 1606, ROBERT (DEVEREUX), 3rd EARL OF ESSEX [E.] (from whom she was divorced Oct. 1613), d.s.p.s. 14 Sept. 1646; 2ndly, 26 Dec. 1613, ROBERT (KERR, alias CARR), 1st EARL OF SOMERSET [E.], K.G., d. 17 July 1645; and had issue 1a.

1a. Lady Anne Carr, da. and h., b. 9 Dec. 1615; d. 10 May 1684; m. 11 July 1637, William (Russell), 5th Earl and (11 May 1694) 1st Duke of Bedford [E.], K.G., K.B., d. 7 Sept. 1700; and had issue 1b to 2b.
1b. William Russell, Lord Russell, M.P., b. 29 Sept. 1639; d.v.p. (being executed for high treason) 21 July 1683; m. (lic. dated 31 July) 1669, Lady Rachel, widow of Francis Vaughan, Lord Vaughan, da. and co-h. of Thomas (Wriothesley), 4th Earl of Southampton [E.], K.G. [by his wife Rachel, sister of Henry (de Massue), 1st Marquis of Ruvigny and Raineval [F.], P.C.], d. 29 Sept. 1723; and had issue.
See the Essex Volume, Table XIII., and pp. 173-190, Nos. 21135-25217.

[Nos. 66962 to 71044.

# of The Blood Royal

2b. *Lord James Russell*, d.[1] 22 *June* 1712; m. *Elizabeth, da. of* (—) *Lloyd* [re-m. 2ndly, 14 Ap. 1721, Sir Henry Houghton, 5th Bt. [E.] and] d. 1 Dec. 1736; *and had issue* 1c.

1c. *Tryphena Russell of Maidwell, co. Northants, da. and h.*, d. (–); m. 1725, *Thomas Scawen of Carshalton Park, co. Surrey, M.P.*, d. 11 *Feb.* 1774; *and had issue* 1d *to* 2d.

1d. *James Scawen of Carshalton Park, M.P*

2d. *Tryphena Scawen*, b. 31 *Dec.* 1730; d. 2 *Dec.* 1807; m. *as 2nd wife*, 14 *June* 1759, *Henry (Bathurst), 2nd Earl Bathurst* [G.B.] *and Lord High Chancellor* [G.B.], d. 6 *Aug.* 1794; *and had issue* 1e.

1e. *Henry (Bathurst), 3rd Earl Bathurst* [G.B.], K.G., P.C., b. 22 *May* 1762; d. 27 *July* 1834; m. 1 *Ap.* 1789, *Lady Georgina, da. of Lord George Henry Lennox*, d. 20 *Jan.* 1841; *and had issue*.

See the Clarence Volume, pp. 636–637, Nos. 28837–28849.

[Nos. 71045 to 71057.

229. Descendants of JAMES (CECIL), 3rd EARL OF SALISBURY [E.], K.G. (Table XXII.), b. 1648; d. June 1683; m. 1665, Lady MARGARET, da. of John (MANNERS), 8th Earl of Rutland [E.], d. at Paris 30 Aug. 1682; and had issue.

See the Exeter Volume, Table XI., and pp. 216–236, Nos. 7652–8318; Essex Volume, p. 378, Nos. 36474–36480. [Nos. 71058 to 71731.

230. Descendants of the Hon. FRANCES CECIL (Table XXII.), d. 15 June 1723; m. (lic. dated 24 Dec. 1679) Sir WILLIAM BOWYER, 2nd Bt. [E.], M.P., d. 13 Feb. 1722; and had issue 1a to 3a.

1a. *Cecil Bowyer*, b. 1 *June* 1684; d.v.p. 5 *Dec.* 1720; m. 22 *July* 1707, *Juliana, da. of Richard Parker of Hedsor* [Bt. Coll.]; *and had issue* (*with another son and da. known to have d. young*) 1b *to* 4b.

1b. *Sir William Bowyer, 3rd Bt.* [E.], b. c. 1710; d. 12 *July* 1768; m. 21 *Aug.* 1733, *Anne, da. of the Right Hon. Sir John Stonhouse, 7th Bt.* (1628) *and 4th Bt.* (1670) [E.], P.C., M.P., d. 22 *May* 1785; *and had issue* 1c *to* 4c.

1c. *Sir William Bowyer, 4th Bt.* [E.], b. c. 1736; d.s.p. *Ap.* 1799.

2c. *Sir George Bowyer, 5th Bt. of Denham* [E.] *and* (8 *Sept.* 1794) *1st Bt. of Radley* [G.B.], *Admiral of the Blue, M.P.*, b. 1739; d. 6 *Dec.* 1799; m. 2ndly, 4 *June* 1782, *Henrietta, da. and h. of Sir Piercy Brett, M.P., Admiral of the White*, d. *Nov.* 1845; *and had issue* 1d *to* 2d.

1d. *Sir George Bowyer, 6th* [E.] *and 2nd* [G.B.] *Bt., M.P.*, b. 3 *Mar.* 1783; d. 1 *July* 1860; m. 19 *Nov.* 1808, *Anne Hammond, da. of Capt. Sir Andrew Snape Douglas, R.N.*, d. 1844; *and had issue* 1e *to* 3e.

1e. *Sir George Bowyer, 7th* [E.] *and 3rd* [G.B.] *Bt., K.M., G.C.S.G., M.P.*, b. 8 *Oct.* 1811; d. *unm.* 7 *June* 1883.

2e. *Sir William Bowyer, 8th* [E.] *and 4th* [G.B.] *Bt.*, b. *Oct.* 1812; d.s.p. 30 *May* 1893.

3e. *Henry George Bowyer, one of H.M.'s Inspectors of Schools*, b. 3 *Jan.* 1813; d. 25 *Sept.* 1883; m. 20 *Feb.* 1855, *Katherine Emma* (1 *Clarendon Crescent, Leamington*), *da. and h. of the Rev. George Sandby*; *and had issue* 1f *to* 3f.

1f. Sir George Henry Bowyer, 9th Bt. of Denham [E.] and 5th Bt. of Radley [G.B.] (1 *Clarendon Crescent, Leamington*), b. 9 Sept. 1870; m. 4 May 1899, Ethel, da. of Francis Hawkins (which m. was dissolved 7 Nov. 1900).

[No. 71732.

---

[1] Burke's "Peerage" has s.p.

The Plantagenet Roll

2*f*. Beatrice Mary Bowyer, *m.* 1890, James Frederick Shaw; and has ssue 1*g.*
1*g*. Charles Henry Shaw, *b.* 1893.

3*f*. Helen Gertrude Bowyer, a Nun of the Order of the Assumption.

2*d*. Henrietta Bowyer, d. 1864; m. 10 Oct. 1812, *Charles Sawyer of Heywood Lodge, co. Berks, J.P., D.L.*, d. 2 *June* 1876; *and had issue (with others who all d.s.p.)* 1*e* to 3*e*.

1*e*. Rev. George Herbert Sawyer, LL.B., B.C.L. (152 *Caversham Road, Reading*), *b.* 29 Mar. 1826; *unm.*

2*e*. Rev. William George Sawyer, M.A. (Camb.), Rector of Taplow 1890–1897, &c. (*Stanlow, Maidenhead*), *b.* 24 Nov. 1829; *m.* 29 Ap. 1862, Margaret, da. of the Rev. C. A. Sheppard of Great Milton, co. Oxon.; and has issue 1*f* to 7*f*.

1*f*. Edmund Charles Sawyer of Heywood (*Heywood Lodge, Maidenhead*), b. 2 Mar. 1871.

2*f*. Herbert William Sawyer, *b.* 1 Ap. 1874.
3*f*. William Ellis Sawyer, *b.* 4 May 1878.
4*f*. Guy Henry Sawyer, *b.* 18 May 1882.
5*f*. Agnes Elizabeth Sawyer.
6*f*. Margaret Henrietta Sawyer.
7*f*. Dorothy Alice Sawyer.

3*e*. Charlotte Sawyer.

3*c*. *Richard Bowyer, afterwards Atkins-Bowyer, of Clapham,* d. 21 Nov. 1820; m. 1773, *Elizabeth, da. of* (——) *Brady; and had issue* 1*d* to 3*d*.

1*d*. *William Bowyer, afterwards* (R.L. 16 Nov. 1835) *Atkins-Bowyer of Braywick Grove, co. Berks, and Clapham, co. Surrey, Brigade-Major to the Forces at Halifax, N.S.,* b. 1779; d. 9 *Feb.* 1844; m. 1803, *Frances, da. of the Hon. Behning Wentworth, Colonial Secretary for Nova Scotia,* d. 24 *Jan.* 1856; *and had issue* 1*e* to 7*e*.

1*e*. *Henry Atkins-Bowyer of Steeple Aston and Clapham, D.L., Lieut-Col. 1st Oxford Univ. Rifle Vols., previously 14th Hussars,* b. 1805; d. 29 *July* 1871; m. 15 *Jan.* 1833, *Isabella Duncan, da. of James H. Byles of Bowden Hall, co. Glouc.,* d. 12 Nov. 1841; *and had issue (with 3 sons who d.s.p.)* 1*f*.

1*f*. Isabel Caroline Eliza Atkins-Bowyer, *m.* 23 June 1873, Bertie Wentworth Vernon of Harefield and Stoke Bruerne Park, J.P., High Sheriff co. Northants 1892 (*Stoke Bruerne Park, Towcester; Harefield Park, near Uxbridge*); s.p.s.

2*e*. Rev. *William Henry Wentworth Atkins-Bowyer, Rector of Clapham,* b. 3 Feb. 1807; d. 25 Feb. 1872; m. 1st, 1831, *Emily, da. of Henry Harford of Downe Place, Maidenhead,* d. 1839; 2*ndly*, 1844, *Charlotte* [*descended from King Henry VII.* (see Essex Volume Supplement, p. 469)], *da. of Capt. William Wells, R.N.* [*by his wife, Lady Elizabeth, née Proby*], d. 3 *May* 1862; *and had issue* 1*f* to 7*f*.

1*f*. Wentworth Grenville Bowyer, Lieut.-Col. R.E., heir-presumptive to the Baronetcies (1660 [E.] and 1794 [G.B.]) (*Weston Manor, Olney, Bucks*), b. 10 Nov. 1850; *m.* 29 Oct. 1883, Eva Mary [a descendant of the Lady Anne, sister of Kings Edward IV. and Richard III.], da. of Major-Gen. Charles Stuart Lane, C.B., Cadet of King's Bromley; and has issue 1*g* to 5*g*.

1*g*. George Edward Wentworth Bowyer, *b.* 16 Jan. 1886.
2*g*. Richard Grenville Bowyer, R.N., *b.* 18 May 1890.
3*g*. John Francis Bowyer, *b.* 11 Jan. 1893.
4*g*. Hilda Mary Bowyer, *b.* 2 Ap. 1887.
5*g*. Mildred Elizabeth Bowyer, *b.* 16 Ap. 1898.

2*f*. Edward Wentworth Bowyer (*The Manor House, Wellington, Salop*), b. 25 June 1862; *m.* 8 Jan. 1895, the Hon. Georgiana Harriet, da. of Richard Assheton (Cross), 1st Viscount Cross [U.K.], G.C.B.; and has issue 1*g* to 2*g*.

1*g*. Richard Wentworth Bowyer, *b.* 27 Dec. 1895.
2*g*. Helen Georgiana Bowyer, *unm.*   [Nos. 71733 to 71755.

# of The Blood Royal

3*f*.¹ Frances Emily Atkins-Bowyer, d. (-); m. 26 Aug. 1865, *Edward Till of Clapham Common, co. Surrey*; and had issue 1g to 2g.

    1*g*. Violet Beatrice Tell.

    2*g*. Ruth Felicity Tell, *m*. Herbert Jackson; and has issue (3 sons).

4*f*. Beatrice Ann Bowyer, d. Oct. 1907; m. 16 Nov. 1878, *the Rev. Henry Ley Greaves*, d. 27 Dec. 1899; *and had issue* 1g to 3g.

    1*g*. Humphrey Grenville Ley Greaves, *b*. 22 Mar. 1887.

    2*g*. Dorothy Charlotte Ley Greaves, *m*. 1905, Francis Quarles Harrison.

    3*g*. Marjorie Beatrice Millicent Ley Greaves, *m*. 20 July 1904, William Arthur Newcombe (*Wooton Court, Canterbury*); and has issue 1h to 2h.

        1*h*. Arthur Peter Ley Newcombe, *b*. 31 July 1909.

        2*h*. Hilda Violet Marjorie Lockhart Newcombe, *b*. 20 Dec. 1906.

5*f*. Marion Frances Bowyer (*Weston Underwood, Olney, Bucks*).

6*f*. Cecil Bowyer.

7*f*. Lilian Bowyer, *m*. 11 July 1876, Henry Charles Zerffi (47 *Warrington Crescent, W.*); and has issue 1g.

    1*g*. Henry Gustavus Wentworth Zerffi, *b*. 12 July 1881.

3*e*. Frances Augusta Atkins-Bowyer, b. at Halifax, Nova Scotia, 1804; d. 16 Nov. 1869; m. 1*st*, 20 Aug. 1825, *the Rev. George Augustus Legge* [*E. of Dartmouth Coll.*], d.s.p. 16 *June* 1826; 2*ndly*, 28 Oct. 1828, *the Rev. Samuel Wyatt Cobb, M.A.* (Oxon.), Rector of Ightham, co. Kent [*son of the Rev. Thomas Cobb, Rector of the same*], d. 22 Dec. 1856; *and had issue* (*with 4 sons d. young*) 1*f* to 4*f*.

1*f*. Augusta Louisa Cobb, b. 8 Oct. 1829; d. 31 *Jan*. 1897; m. 26 Oct. 1858, *the Rev. David Payne Williams, Senior Chaplain, Bengal* [*son of the Rev. David Williams, Rector of Bleadon and Kingston Seymour, co. Som.*]; *and had issue* (*with a son and da. d. young*) 1g to 3g.

    1*g*. Henry Llewellyn Williams, Indian Police, *b*. at Delhi 14 Aug. 1862; *m*. Ap. 1884, Mary Elizabeth, da. of Cecil Burton, Cantonment Magistrate, Jullunder; and has issue 1*h* to 5*h*.

        1*h*. Cecil Walter Hackett Williams, *b*. at Saharanpur, 11 June 1885.

        2*h*. Edward Williams, *b*. in India, 17 Feb. 1895.

        3*h*. David Williams, *b*. at Murree, Sept. 1898.

        4*h*. Evelyn Amy Williams, *b*. in India, 22 Feb. 1888.

        5*h*. Phyllis Williams, *b*. 29 June 1893.

    2*g*. Lilian Augusta Williams, *b*. at Delhi; *m*. at Simla, 4 June 1904, William George Goldney, Indian Police [*son of Samuel Alfred Goldney of Langley Furse, co. Bucks*].

    3*g*. Evelyn Helen Catherine Williams, *b*. at Murree; *m*. Nov. 1902, Robert Donald Spencer, Indian Police [*son of Robert Spencer of Lahore*]; and has had issue, Helen Monica, *d*. in infancy.

2*f*. Katharine Mary Cobb, b. 11 Sept. 1832; d. 4 Nov. 1905; m. 26 Oct. 1858, *Henry Walmesley Hammond, Bengal C.S.* [*son of the Rev. John Hammond, Rector of Priston, co. Som.*]; *and had issue* (*with a son, William John*, d. *unm*. 24 Aug. 1901) 1g to 5g.

    1*g*. Rev. Anthony Hammond, M.A. (Oxon.), Rector of St. Anthony's, Stepney (*St. Anthony Rectory, Stepney, E.*), *b*. 29 Nov. 1864; *m*. 27 Aug 1891, Isabel Sarah Catherine Mary, da. of the Rev. H. Martin, Vicar of Thatcham; and has issue (with a son *d*. young) 1*h* to 3*h*.

        1*h*. Anthony Hammond, *b*. 5 June 1893.

        2*h*. Cicely Margaret Hammond, *b*. 19 Apr. 1896.

        3*h*. Evelyn Dorothea Hammond, *b*. 25 Oct. 1905.

    2*g*. Henry Edward Denison Hammond, M.A. (Oxon.), *b*. 26 Nov. 1866; *unm*.

    3*g*. Robert Francis Frederick Hammond, *b*. 15 Oct. 1868; *unm*.

    4*g*. Mary Katharine Hammond ⎫
    5*g*. Isabel Bowyer Hammond ⎬ (1 *St. Stephen's Road, Bayswater*).

[Nos. 71756 to 71782.

The Plantagenet Roll

3f. Alice Cobb, a Sister of Mercy (*St. Wilfrid's, Exeter*).

4f. Margaret Katharine Cobb, m. 22 June 1880, Ivan Vernon Watson [son of Dr. J. I. Watson, F.R.G.S., K.C. Charles III. of Spain]; and has issue 1g to 2g.

  1g. George Ivan Augustine Watson, b. 25 July 1887.

  2g. Laura Cicely Watson.

4e. *Henrietta Elizabeth Atkins-Bowyer*, d. 1849; m. *Charles Vincent Eyre of Calais; and had issue (at least)* 1f.

  1f. [da.] Eyre, m. (—) Perret; and had issue.

5e. *Penelope Maria Atkins-Bowyer*, d. 1859; m. *the Rev. William Francklin, Rector of Thursley, co. Surrey*, d. (–); *and had issue (with 3 sons d. unm.)* 1f.

  1f. Emily Wentworth Francklin, b. 4 Aug. 1845; d. 23 Feb. 1889; m. 13 Feb. 1866, *Florance Wyndham of Great Marlow, co. Bucks* [youngest son of Wadham Wyndham of Great Marlow], d. 27 Dec. 1897; *and had issue* 1g to 3g.

    1g. Emily Wentworth Wyndham (175 *Clive Road, West Dulwich*), unm.

    2g. Alice Mary Wyndham, b. 19 May 1871; d. 18 Dec. 1906; m. 16 June 1881, *Arthur Edmund Little of Ireland; and had issue* 1h to 2h.

      1h. Kathleen Mary Little.

      2h. Dorothy Little.

    3g. Edith Constance Wyndham, m. 24 Sept. 1887, Charles Crouch, Cashier, London & County Bank (*East Finchley*); and has issue 1h to 2h.

      1h. Harold Wyndham Crouch, b. 4 June 1900.

      2h. Dora Edith Crouch.

6e. *Anne Elizabeth Atkins-Bowyer*, b. 27 Oct. 1818; d. 13 Nov. 1890; m. 13 Feb. 1850, *the Rev. Henry William Hodgson, Rector of Ashwell, co. Herts*, b. 22 Jan. 1821; d. 23 Ap. 1898; *and had issue* 1f to 2f.

  1f. Rev. Hugh Alexander Hodgson, M.A. (Camb.), Rector of Beddington since 1891 (*Beddington Rectory, Croydon*), b. 17 Mar. 1856; m. 19 Oct. 1880, Kate Alice, da. of Thomas Hill Barrows of the Grange, Great Malvern; and has issue 1g to 6g.

    1g. Douglas Bowyer Hodgson, b. 4 Jan. 1882.

    2g. Christopher Michael Hodgson, b. 29 Sept. 1883.

    3g. Grenville Henry Hodgson, b. 27 Aug. 1885.

    4g. Ruth Christabel Hodgson, b. 26 Sept. 1887.

    5g. Winifred Mary Hodgson, b. 7 July 1889.

    6g. Noel Wentworth Hodgson, b. 24 Dec. 1898.

  2f. Margaret Annie Hodgson, m. 1st, 8 July 1879, Henry Dent Hinrich-Dent of Hallaton Manor, Uppingham, d. 31 May 1883; 2ndly, 27 June 1888, Richard Cotton Rowley (*The Wrekin, Milton Road, Harpenden*); and has issue 1g.

    1g. Dalbiac Thomas Cotton Rowley, b. 7 Ap. 1889.

7e. *Eleanor Catherine Atkins-Bowyer*, b. 27 Nov. 1822; d. 7 Oct. 1892; m. 2 May 1846, *Beaumont Hankey of 15 Southwell Gardens, S.W., and 71 St. James' Street, S.W.*, d. 18 Feb. 1909; *and had (with a son, the Rev. Wentworth Beaumont Hankey, d. unm. 16 June 1905) issue* 1f to 4f.

  1f. Douglas Hankey, b. 6 Mar. 1856; unm.

  2f. Evelyn Mary Hankey (43 *Lexham Gardens, W.*).

  3f. Helen Frances Hankey, b. 18 Sept. 1857; d. 9 Mar. 1906; m. 1st, 1879, *William Roderick Hallett Edwards, Lieut. R.N.*, d. 10 Dec. 1885; 2ndly, 1888, *Major Henry Wyndham Davidson, 103rd Regt.*, d. 21 July 1899; *and had issue* 1g.

    1g. Lilian Helen Davidson, b. 22 Aug. 1890.

  4f. Mabel Hankey, m. 4 July 1878, Martin Fletcher Luther, Lieut. (ret.) R.N. (*Adelaide Crescent, Brighton*); and has issue 1g to 3g.

    1g. Guy Fletcher Luther, Capt. Sherwood Foresters, b. 13 Aug. 1879.

    2g. Alan Charles Grenville Luther, Capt. K.O. Yorkshire Light Infantry, b. 17 Sept. 1880.

    3g. John Wentworth Luther, b. 16 July 1886.   [Nos. 71783 to 71809.

# of The Blood Royal

2d. Cornelius Atkins-Bowyer, C.B., Col. in the Army, d. (-) ; m. Sophia, da. of (—) Hopkinson, Comm. R.N. ; and had issue 1e to 3e.

1e. William Atkins-Bowyer, d. (? s.p.).

2e. Henry Atkins-Bowyer, d. (? s.p.) in India.

3e. Augusta Atkins-Bowyer, d. (? unm.).

3d. Frances Penelope Atkins-Bowyer, d. 1836; m. as 1st wife, 24 Aug. 1807, Lieut.-Col. James Forest Fulton, K.H. 92nd Foot, A.D.C. to Sir George Prevost, Gov.-Gen. of Canada, b. 30 Sept. 1780; d. Dec. 1854; and had issue (with 3 elder sons and a da. who all d.s.p.) 1e.

1e. Richard Robert Fulton, formerly 44th Regt. and afterwards R.I.C. (Parsonstown, King's Co.), b. 7 May 1823 ; m. 10 Nov. 1857, Margaret Ormsby, da. of Robert Twiss of Parteen, co. Tipperary; and has issue 1f to 2f.

1f. Elizabeth Frances Fulton, m. 10 Jan. 1883, Capt. John Edward Maxwell Pilkington, 28th Regt., d. 12 July 1898 ; and had issue 1g to 2g.

1g. Ulick Wetherall Pilkington, b. 7 May 1898.

2g. Eileen Mary Pilkington, b. 7 Nov. 1883.

2f. Mary Ormsby Fulton, m. 21 June 1888, Lieut.-Col. Alfred Ruttledge, 14th Regt.; and has issue 1g to 3g.

1g. John Forrest Ruttledge, b. 1 Aug. 1894.

2g. Richard Theodore Ruttledge, b. 14 Dec. 1897.

3g. Eric Peter Knox Ruttledge, b. 24 Aug. 1899.

4c. Penelope Bowyer, d. 9 June 1820 ; m. 1st, 5 Aug. 1765, George John Cooke of Harefield Park, co. Midx., M.P. ; 2ndly, Major-Gen. Edward Smith [uncle of Adm. Sir Sydney Smith, G.C.B.] ; and had issue 1d to 5d.

1d. Sir George Cooke, K.C.B., K.S.G., K.T.S., &c., Lieut.-Gen. and Col. 77th Regt., d. unm. 3 Feb. 1837.

2d. Sir Henry Frederick Cooke, K.C.H., C.B., K.M.M., K.S.G., M.P., Major-Gen., d.s.p. 10 Mar. 1837.

3d. Kitty Cooke, d. (-) ; m. 1st, George Bond, Sergeant-at-Law ; 2ndly, James Trebeck ; and had issue 1e.

1e. Elinor Bond, da. and h., d. 7 Dec. 1862 ; m. at St. George's, Hanover Square, 1826, Capt. Richard Kirwan, 94th Regt. [3rd son of Hyacinth Kirwan of Cregg Castle], d. 6 Jan. 1853; and had issue (with a 3rd son and a da., Mrs. Cooch, d.s.p.) 1f to 2f.

1f. Rev. Richard Kirwan, b. 11 Dec. 1828 ; d. 2 Sept. 1872 ; m. 29 Oct. 1859, Rose Helen, da. of the Rev. Barrett Lampet of Great Bardfield ; and had issue 1g to 6g.

1g. Rev. Robert Mansel Kirwan, M.A. (Oxon.), Chaplain Bengal Eccles. Estab., b. 13 Mar. 1861 ; m. 29 Oct. 1902, Marguerite Theodora, da. of Henry Trenton Wadley ; s.p.

2g. Rev. Ernest Cecil Kirwan, M.A. (Oxon.), Rector of Holy Trinity, Guildford (Holy Trinity Rectory, Guildford), b. 10 Sept. 1867 ; unm.

3g. Lionel Edward Kirwan (Madras), b. 12 Feb. 1869 ; m. 3 Feb. 1903, Evelyn Waller, da. of Edward W. Stoney of Madras, C.I.E.; and has issue 1h to 3h.

1h. Patrick Lionel Kirwan, b. 19 Dec. 1905.

2h. Ralph Bertram Kirwan, b. 17 Dec. 1908.

3h. Hyacinth Ethel Kirwan, b. 22 Oct. 1903.

4g. Bertram Richard Kirwan, Major R.A. (12 York Mansions, Battersea Park, S.W.), b. 17 May 1871 ; m. 20 Oct. 1897, Helen, da. of Col. Hogg, Indian Army ; and has issue 1h to 2h.

1h. Rudolph Charles Hogg Kirwan, b. 22 May 1903.

2h. Kathleen Helen Kirwan, b. 2 Jan. 1899.

5g. Gerald William Claude Kirwan, b. 3 Aug. 1872 ; unm.

6g. Eleanor Augusta Mary Kirwan, m. 9 Feb. 1897, Reginald Barlow Plumer, Mysore C.S.; s.p.

[Nos. 71810 to 71828.

The Plantagenet Roll

2*f*. *George Kirwan, Capt. 25th Regt.*, b. 1830; d. 1899; m. *Ellen Ewbank, da. of Lieut.-Col. R. G. Chambers, 5th Bengal Cavalry*, d. 1 May 1897; *and had issue (with 5 others d.s.p.) 1g to 6g.*

1*g*. George Brudenell Kirwan (*Texas, U.S.A.*), *m.* (—).

2*g*. Francis Vernon Brudenell Kirwan, Lieut. A.S.C. (*Portsmouth*), b. 15 May 1878; *unm.*

3*g*. Noel Gerald Brudenell Kirwan (*Santaveri, Mysore*), b. 25 Dec. 1880.

4*g*. Ella D'Arcy Kirwan, *m.* 1896, the Rev. Christopher Frederic Wellesley Hatchell, M.A. (Camb.), Chaplain Madras Eccles. Estab. (*Vepery, Madras*); and has issue 1*h* to 2*h*.

1*h*. Eric Wellesley Hatchell, b. Oct. 1898.

2*h*. Sheila D'Arcy Hatchell.

5*g*. Katherine Brudenell Kirwan, *m.* Charles Ievers Lopdell, A.M.I.C.E.; and has issue 1*h* to 2*h*.

1*h*. Eileen Lopdell.

2*h*. Hyacinthe Lopdell.

6*g*. Florence Sydney Brudenell Kirwan, *unm.*

4*d*. *Penelope Anne Cooke*, b. c. 1760; d. 2 Feb. 1826; m. 8 Mar. 1794, *Robert (Brudenell), 6th Earl of Cardigan [E.]*, d. 14 Aug. 1837; *and had issue.* See the Tudor Roll, Table XXI. and pp. 171-178, Nos. 20337-20447.

5*d*. *Maria Cooke*, d. at Geneva 3 Oct. 1827; m. 28 Feb. 1804, *Major-Gen. Henry Charles Edward Vernon of Hilton Park, co. Stafford, C.B.*, d. 22 Mar. 1861; *and had issue 1e to 3e.*

1*e*. *Henry Charles Vernon of Hilton Park, J.P., D.L., High Sheriff co. Stafford 1867*, b. 9 Jun. 1805; d. 26 Feb. 1886; m. 15 Mar. 1828, *Catherine, da. of Richard Rice Williams of Hendredenny, co. Glam.*, d. 29 Mar. 1884; *and had issue (with 2 sons and 2 das. d. unm.) 1f to 4f.*

1*f*. *Augustus Leveson Vernon of Hilton, J.P., D.L., High Sheriff co. Staff. 1899 (Hilton Park, Wolverhampton; Carlton, &c.)*, b. 30 Sept. 1836; *m.* 17 Nov. 1864, Selina Anne [descended from George, Duke of Clarence, K.G. (see the Clarence Volume, p. 395)], da. of Walter Peter Giffard of Chillington; and has issue 1*g* to 4*g*.

1*g*. *Henry Arthur Leveson Vernon of Culmleigh, Stoke Canon, Exeter, D.L.*, b. 3 Sept. 1868; d.v.p. 28 Dec. 1899; *m.* 2 June 1896, *Georgiana Frances D'Anyers, da. of Henry Rodolph d'Anyers Willis of Halsnead, J.P., D.L.; and had issue 1h.*

1*h*. Dorothy Vernon, b. 28 Jan. 1898.

2*g*. Walter Bertie William Vernon, b. 18 Oct. 1871; *m.* 15 Sept. 1897, Esther Hodgson, widow of Francis Robinson Hartland Atcherley of Marton Hall, da. of John Mills; and has issue 1*h*.

1*h*. Richard Leveson Vernon, b. 26 Nov. 1900.

3*g*. Henrietta Catherine Vernon.

4*g*. Selina Mary Vernon.

2*f*. *Rev. Frederick Wentworth Vernon, Vicar of Rangeworthy*, b. 8 Jan. 1839; d. 20 May 1906; m. 1st, 6 June 1867, Ellen Mary Woodhouse, da. of Hugh Woodhouse Acland, d. June 1883; 2ndly, 13 Aug. 1885, Edith Serena Hill (*Cleveden*), da. of the Rev. William Henry Boothby, Vicar of Hawkesbury [Bt. Coll.]; and has issue (with 2 sons and 5 das., d. young) 1*g* to 7*g*.

1*g*. Hugh Woodhouse Vernon, b. 9 Oct. 1872.

2*g*. Charles Percy Vernon (*The Highlands, Symonds, Yat, co. Hereford*), b. 22 Sept. 1873.

3*g*. Richard Francis Vernon (*26 Banbury Road, Oxford*), b. 13 Sept. 1874.

4*g*. Evelyn Vernon, b. 31 May 1889.

5*g*. Roger Vernon, b. 27 Oct. 1893.

6*g*. Peter Wentworth Vernon, b. 12 Ap. 1895.

7*g*. Millicent Eleanor Vernon, b. 8 Ap. 1887. [Nos. 71829 to 71962.

# of The Blood Royal

3*f*. Rev. William George Vernon, M.A. (Camb.), *formerly* Vicar of St. John's, Kenilworth (*The Croft, Avenue Road, Malvern*), *b*. 8 Ap. 1840; *m*. 8 Feb. 1866, Alexandrina Adelaide, da. of William Davey Sole of Devonport; and has issue 1*g*.

    1*g*. Cecil Charles William Vernon (*The Firs, Llandrinis, Llanymyneck, S.O.*), *b*. 24 July 1868; *m*. 29 Oct. 1893, Charlotte Isabel Leane, da. of R. W. Flick of Banbury; and has issue 1*h* to 4*h*.

        1*h*. Eric Cecil Wentworth Vernon, *b*. 1896.
        2*h*. Leveson George Vernon, *b*. 1898.
        3*h*. Sidney Richard Wentworth Vernon, *b*. 1909.
        4*h*. Isabel Adelaide Vernon, *b*. 1907.

4*f*. Rev. Edward Hamilton Vernon, Rector of Burnett (*Burnett Rectory, Clifton, Bristol*), *b*. 16 Jan. 1844; *m*. 1st, Fanny, da. of (—) Ibbotson of Sunderland; 2ndly, Miriam, da. of the Rev. Henry Fisher of Leamington; 3rdly, (—); and has issue (2 sons and 2 das.).

2*e*. William Frederick Vernon of Harefield Park, co. Midx., J.P., D.L., *b*. 7 Nov. 1807; d.s.p. *Sept*. 1889.

3*e*. George Augustus Vernon of Harefield Park, J.P., D.L., Lieut.-Col. Coldstream Guards, *b*. 31 May 1811; d. 25 Nov. 1896; *m*. 1 June 1842, Louisa Jane Frances, da. of Admiral Bertie Cornelius Cator, R.N., d. 20 Dec. 1880; *and had issue (with an elder son* d. *young) 1f to 7f*.

1*f*. Bertie Wentworth Vernon of Harefield and Stoke Bruerne, J.P. and High Sheriff co. Northants 1892, *formerly* R.N. (*Harefield Park, near Uxbridge; Stoke Bruerne Park, Towcester*), *b*. 26 Oct. 1846; *m*. 23 June 1873, Isabel Caroline Eliza (see p. 386), da. of Lieut.-Col. Henry Atkyns-Bowyer of the Grange, Steeple Aston; s.p.s.

2*f*. Herbert Charles Erskine Vernon, I.C.S., *b*. 28 Sept. 1851; d. 15 Feb. 1893; *m*. Helen Mayne, da. of Gen. Liptrott; *and had issue* 1*g* to 3*g*.

    1*g*. Henry Albemarle Vernon, *b*. 5 Dec. 1879.
    2*g*. Grenville Bertie Vernon, *b*. Sept. 1884.
    3*g*. Louisa Muriel Vernon, *m*. 20 Oct. 1906, Edward Harington, J.P., B.A. (Oxon.), Bar.-at-Law, County Court Judge, Circuit No. 45 [3rd son of Sir Richard Harington, 11th Bt. [E. 1611] (20 *Ovington Square, S.W.*); and has issue 1*h*.

        1*h*. Edward Henry Vernon Harington, *b*. 13 Sept. 1907.

3*f*. Mary Vernon, *m*. Charles Pringle; s.p.s.
4*f*. Edith Henrietta Sophia Vernon.

5*f*. Louisa Jane Vernon, *m*. 1st, 26 July 1870, Gen. Edward Westby Donovan, K.L.H., East Yorkshire Regt. [2nd son of Richard Donovan of Ballymore, co. Wexford], *d*. Jan. 1897; 2ndly, 16 Mar. 1898, Com. Frederick E. Thomas, R.N.; and has issue 1*g*.

    1*g*. Edward Herbert Donovan, Lieut. R.N., *b*. 8 Oct. 1874.

6*f*. Lizzie Vernon, *m*. 1st, 22 Ap. 1873, Capt. Henry Bowyer of the Grange, Steeple Aston [Bt. Coll.], d.s.p. 6 May 1882; 2ndly, 1882, William Frederick Gore-Langton (*Padbury Lodge, Bucks*); and has issue 1*g* to 3*g*.

    1*g*. Francis Wilfrid Gore-Langton, Lieut. Coldstream Guards, *b*. 14 Ap. 1884.
    2*g*. Gerald Wentworth Gore-Langton, Lieut. 18th Hussars, *b*. 23 Aug. 1885.
    3*g*. Montagu Vernon Gore-Langton, Lieut. Irish Guards, *b*. 28 Aug. 1887.

7*f*. Muriel Isabel Vernon.

2*b*. Richard Bowyer, d. (? *unm*.).
3*b*. Thomas Bowyer, d. (? *unm*.).
4*b*. Charlotte Bowyer, d. (? *unm*.).

2*a*. William Bowyer, *b*. 14 July 1688; d. (-); *m*. Elizabeth, da. of Richard Parker of Hedsor afsd.; *and had issue* 1*b* to 3*b*.

    1*b*. Richard Bowyer, bapt. at Woburn 4 Ap. 1718.
    2*b*. William Bowyer.

[Nos. 71963 to 71983.

The Plantagenet Roll

3b. *Juliana Bowyer*, m. *the Rev. George Burville of Bexley, co. Kent; and had issue*.[1]

3a. *Diana Bowyer*, bapt. 7 Oct. 1680; d. (-); m. *Philip Jennings of Duddleston, co. Salop; and had issue*[2] 1b.

1b. *Edward Jennings*, b. 23 Oct. 1706.

231. Descendants, if any, of the Hon. ROBERT CECIL, d. (-); m. (—), da. of (—) HOPTON; of the Hon. PHILIP CECIL, d. (-); m. (—), da. of (—) ALLEN; and of the Hon. WILLIAM CECIL, d. (-); m. ELIZABETH, da. of Sir Thomas LAWLEY of Spoonhill, 1st Bt. [E.], M.P.[3] (Table XXII.).

232. Descendants of EDMUND TURNOR of Stoke Rochford and Panton, co. Lincoln (Table XXII.), b. c. 1708; d. 5 Jan. 1769; m. ELIZABETH, da. and event. co-h. of Henry FERNE of Snitterton, co. Derby, d. 4 Dec. 1765; and had issue 1a to 5a.

1a. *Edmund Turnor of Stoke Rochford, &c.*, d. 1805; m. *Mary, da. of John Disney of Lincoln; and had issue* 1b to 8b.

1b. *Edmund Turnor of Stoke Rochford, &c., F.R.S., F.S.A., M.P. for Midhurst, Author of a History of Grantham, and an eminent Antiquary*, b. 1755; d. 19 Mar. 1829; m. 1st, 7 May 1795, *Elizabeth, da. of Philip Broke*, d. 1801; 2ndly, *Dorothea, da. of Lieut.-Col. Tucker*, d. *May* 1854; *and had issue* (with another son and 2 das., of whom no issue survives) 1c to 5c.

1c. *Christopher Turnor of Stoke Rochford, J.P., D.L., and High Sheriff co. Lincoln* 1833, *M.P. for S. Lincoln* 1841–47, b. 4 Ap. 1809; d. 7 Mar. 1886; m. 2 Feb. 1837, *Lady Caroline* [herself a descendant of Edward III. through Mortimer-Percy], *da. of George William (Finch-Hatton), 9th Earl of Winchilsea* [E.], d. 13 Mar. 1888; *and had issue*.

See p. 130, Nos. 12182–12211.

2c. *Cecil Turnor*, d. (? s.p.).

3c. *Rev. Algernon Turnor*, d. *Aug.* 1842; m. 9 *Jan.* 1840, *Sophia* (see p. 151), *da. of Sir Thomas Whichcote, 6th Bt.* [E.].

4c. *Henry Marten Turnor, Capt. King's Dragoon Guards*, d. (-); m. 28 *July* 1840, *the Hon. Marianne* [descended from the Lady Anne, sister of King Edward IV.], *da. of Godfrey (Macdonald), 3rd Baron Macdonald* [I.], d. 12 *July* 1876; *and had issue* 1d to 4d.

1d. *Reginald Charles Turnor, late Major 1st Life Guards* (*Tidmarsh, Berks*), b. 26 *Sept.* 1850; d. 14 *June* 1910; m. 1st, *Gabrielle, da. of the Marquis Sampieri*; 2ndly, *Laura, da. of J. Lucas; and had issue* 1e to 3e.

1e.[2] Christopher Turnor.

2e.[1] Renée Turnor.

3e.[2] Joan Turnor.

2d. Harriet Mina Turnor, m. 1 July 1869, John (Scott), 3rd Earl of Eldon
[Nos. 71984 to 72018.

---

[1] Lipscombe's "Bucks," iv. 446.

[2] Ibid. According to Burke's "Royal Descents" (ii. xcv.) and "Landed Gentry" (1906, p. 1718) she had also a da. Jane, who m. Thomas ap John Vaughan of Plas Thomas, co. Salop, whose alleged *great grandson* by her, Philip Vaughan of Burlton, ancestor of the present family, was *bapt.* 10 *Oct.* 1690. As the said Jane's mother was *bapt.* 7 Oct. 1680, this descent is impossible.

[3] Brydges' "Collins," ii. 491. Wotton's "Baronetage," ii. 262.

# of The Blood Royal

[U.K.] (*Stowell Park, Northleach, co. Glouc.;* 43 *Portman Square, W.*); and has issue.

See the Exeter Volume, p. 591, Nos. 51408–51415.

3*d.* Florence Turnor, *m.* (—) Neville of (—); and has issue 1*e.*
1*e.* [da.] Neville, *m.* (—) Wheeler.
4*d.* Mabel Turnor, *m.* (—) Morgan; *s.p.*
5*c.* Elizabeth Edmund Turnor, d. 1868; m. *Frederick Manning.*
2*b.* George Turnor, d. (-); m. *Eleanor, da. of (——) Hanmer; and had issue.*[1]
3*b.* John Turnor.
4*b.* Charles Turnor.
5*b.* Elizabeth Frances Turnor, d. 27 *Ap.* 1835; m. 2 Dec. 1783, *Samuel Smith of Woodhall Park, co. Herts* [*next younger brother of Robert, 1st Baron Carrington [I. and G.B.*], b. 14 *Ap.* 1754; d. 12 *Mar.* 1834; *and had issue* 1*c* to 9*c.*
1*c.* Abel Smith of Woodhall, *J.P., M.P. co. Herts* 1835–47, b. 17 *July* 1788; d. 23 Feb. 1859; m. 2nd*ly*, 12 *July* 1826, *Frances Anne* [*descended from the Lady Isabel Plantagenet, da. of Gen. Sir Harry Calvert, 1st Bt. [U.K.], G.C.B.*, d. 18 *Nov.* 1885; *and had issue.*

See the Essex Volume, pp. 303–306, Nos. 32716–32817.

2*c.* Samuel George Smith *of Sacombe Park, co. Herts, M.P.*, b. 19 *July* 1789; d. 4 *Oct.* 1863; m 4 *July* 1821, *Eugenia* [*descended from the Lady Isabel Plantagenet*], *da. of the Rev. Robert Chatfield, D.C.L.*, d. 5 *Jan.* 1838; *and had issue.*

See the Essex Volume, pp. 264–266, Nos. 30974–31025.

3*c.* Henry Smith *of Wilford House, co. Notts,* b. 1·2 *Dec.* 1794; d. 7 Feb. 1874; m. 14 *July* 1824, *Lady Lucy* [*descended from George, Duke of Clarence, K.G.*], *da. of Alexander* (*Leslie-Melville*), 10*th Earl of Leven and* 7*th Earl of Melville* [*S.*], d. 23 Dec. 1865; *and had issue.*

See the Essex Volume, Clarence Supplement, p. 525, Nos. 1324/291–308.

4*c.* Sophia Smith, d. 2 *Ap.* 1844; m. 19 *July* 1803, *William Dickinson of Kingweston, co. Som., M.P. for that co. in seven successive Parliaments,* b. 1 *Nov.* 1771; d. *at Naples* 19 *Jan.* 1837; *and had issue* 1*d* to 4*d.*
1*d.* Francis Henry Dickinson *of Kingweston, J.P., D.L., High Sheriff co. Som.* 1853, *M.P. West Som.* 1841–1847, b. 6 *Jan.* 1813; d. 17 *July* 1890; m. 8 *Sept.* 1835, *his cousin* (see p. 397) *Caroline, da. of Major-Gen. Thomas Cary*, d. 19 *Ap.* 1897; *and had issue* (*with others who* d.s.p.) 1*e* to 8*e.*
1*e.* William Dickinson of Kingweston, *late* Somerset Militia (*Kingweston, Somerton, Somerset*), b. 20 Aug. 1839; *m.* 1st, 31 Mar. 1875, Helen Isabella, da. of George Bairnsfather, H.E.I.C.S., d. 19 Ap. 1888; 2ndly, 1 Jan. 1896, Isabel Frances, da. of Col. Evanson Harison, R.A.; and has issue 1*f* to 4*f.*
1*f.* William Francis Dickinson, b. 20 Mar. 1877.
2*f.* John McLennan Dickinson, b. 20 Mar. 1881.
3*f.* Hugh Cary Dickinson, b. 19 Oct. 1884.
4*f.* George Bairnsfather Dickinson, b. 4 Jan. 1886.
2*e.* Reginald Dickinson (121 *St. George's Square, London, S.W.*), b. 27 Jan. 1841.
3*e.* Arthur Dickinson (*Somerton, Somerset*), b. 18 Jan. 1847; *m.* 16 Ap. 1873, Alice Berkeley, widow of the Rev. George Goodden, da. of Augustus Woodforde of Ansford, co. Som.; and has issue 1*f* to 2*f.*
1*f.* Francis Arthur Dickinson, Capt. Duke of Cornwall's L.I., and attached to Egyptian Army, b. 6 Feb. 1874.
2*f.* Stephen Carey Dickinson, b. 9 Aug. 1875; *m.* 1 Feb. 1905, Hilda Grace, da. of Arthur Leckconby Phipps.
4*e.* Sophia Caroline Dickinson.
5*e.* Frances Dickinson. [Nos. 72019 to 72212.

---

[1] Burke's "Commoners," i. 301.

The Plantagenet Roll

6e. Lucy Dickinson, m. 1st, 5 Ap. 1866, William Henry Dorrien-Magens, d. 4 Ap. 1875; 2ndly, 16 May 1888, the Rev. Iltyd Jenkin Rosser, Vicar of Austrey (*Austrey Vicarage, Atherstone*); and has issue 1f.

1f. Constance Lucy Dorrien-Magens, m. 6 Sept. 1892, the Rev. Francis Henry Greville Knight, M.A. (Oxon.), Rector of Leadenham (*Leadenham Rectory, Lincoln*); and has issue 1g to 2g.

1g. Ruth Constance Dorrien Knight.
2g. Katharine Lucy Knight.

7e. Mary Dickinson, m. 24 Ap. 1878, Thomas Charles (Agar-Robartes), 6th Viscount Clifden [I.], 6th Baron Mendip [G.B.] and 2nd Baron Robartes [U.K.], J.P., D.L. [descended from George, Duke of Clarence, K.G., brother of Edward IV.] (*Lanhydrock House, Bodmin*; 1 *Great Stanhope Street, W.*); and has issue.
See the Clarence Volume, p. 640, Nos. 30079-30087.

8e. Edith Dickinson.

2d. Edmund Henry Dickinson *of Chapmanslade, co. Wilts, J.P.*, b. 30 June 1821; d. 22 Ap. 1897; m. 14 May 1861, Emily Dulcibella [*descended from Edward III. through Lady Isabella Plantagenet* (see Essex Volume, p. 361), *and also through Mortimer-Percy* (see this Volume, p. 275)], *da. of Robert John (Eden), 3rd Baron Auckland [G.B. and I.], Lord Bishop of Bath and Wells*, d. 27 Jan. 1893; and had issue 1e to 4e.

1e. Robert Edmund Dickinson, M.P. for Wells 1899-1906, b. 1 Aug. 1862; unm.
2e. Philip Francis Dickinson, b. 2 Aug. 1863; unm.
3e. Oswald Eden Dickinson, b. 17 Nov. 1869; unm.
4e. Violet Mary Dickinson (21 *Manchester Street, W.*), unm.

3d. *Sophia Gertrude Dickinson*, b. 13 Nov. 1814; d. 20 June 1902; m. 22 Sept. 1840, the Rev. John Stuart Hippisley Horner *of Mells Park, co. Som., Preb. of Wells and Rector of Mells*, b. 9 Oct. 1810; d. 9 Ap. 1874; *and had issue* 1e to 8e.

1e. Sir John Francis Fortescue Horner of Mells, K.C.V.O., M.A., J.P., D.L., and High Sheriff 1885 co. Som., Bar.-at.Law, *formerly* (1895-1907) 'Commissioner of Woods and Forests (*Mells Park, Frome;* 9 *Buckingham Gate, S.W.*), b. 28 Dec. 1842; m. 18 Jan. 1883, Frances, da. of William Graham, *formerly* M.P. for Glasgow; and has issue (with a younger son d. young) 1f to 3f.

1f. Edward William Horner, b. 3 May 1888.
2f. Cicely Margaret Horner, m. 7 Dec. 1908, Hon. George Lambton, 5th son of George Frederick, 2nd Earl of Durham [U.K.] (*Mesnil Warren, Newmarket*); and has issue 1g.

1g. John Lambton, b. 31 July 1909.

3f. Katharine Frances Horner, m. 25 July 1907, Raymond Asquith, Bar.-at-Law [son of the Right Hon. Herbert Asquith, P.C., M.P.] (49 *Bedford Square, W.C.*); and has issue 1g.

1g. Helen Frances Asquith, b. 22 Oct. 1909.

2e. Rev. George William Horner, Editor of the Coptic New Testament (12 *St. Helen's Place, E.C.*), b. (twin) 10 June 1849.

3e. Maurice Horner, J.P. co. Som. (12 *St. Helen's Place, E.C.*), b. (twin) 10 June 1849.

4e. John Stuart Horner (*Caverleigh, Surbiton*), b. 30 Aug. 1855; m. 26 July 1887, Emily Green, da. of Col. James Francis Birch, 3rd West India Regt.; and has issue 1f to 4f.

1f. Bernard Stuart Horner, b. 5 Dec. 1889.
2f. Maurice Stuart Horner, b. 18 Dec. 1893.
3f. David Stuart Horner, b. 29 July 1900.
4f. Olivia Stuart Horner.
5e. Elizabeth Gertrude Horner.
6e. Margaret Maria Horner.
7e. Caroline Sophia Horner.
8e. Alice Muriel Horner.

[Nos. 72213 to 72248.

# of The Blood Royal

4d. Caroline Dickinson, b. 7 July 1817; d. 18 July 188(?); m. 6 July 1843, *William Bence-Jones of Lisselan, co. Cork, M.A., J.P., Bar.-at-Law,* b. 5 *Oct.* 1812; d. 22 *June* 1882; *and had issue* 1e *to* 5e.

1e. William Francis Bence-Jones of Lisselan, b. 9 *Mar.* 1856; d. *unm.* 20 *Nov.* 1883.

2e. Reginald Bence-Jones of Lisselan, J.P., D.L., High Sheriff co. Cork 1894 (*Lisselan, Clonakilty, co. Cork*), b. 4 Nov. 1865; *m.* 9 Oct. 1890, Ethel Annie, da. of D. C. da Costa of Barbados, W.I.; and has issue 1*f* to 2*f*.

1*f.* Campbell William Winthrop Bence-Jones, b. 21 Ap. 1894.

2*f.* Philip Reginald Bence-Jones, b. 12 Jan. 1897.

3e. Caroline Sophia Jones, *m.* 16 Aug. 1877, Francis Henry Blackburne Daniell [only son of Capt. George Daniell, R.N., by his wife Alice Catherine, da. of the Right Hon. Francis Blackburne, Lord Chancellor of Ireland] (19 *Nevern Place, Earl's Court Road, S.W.*); and has issue (with a son, Francis Reginald, b. 23 Sept. 1882; *d.* unm. 21 Sept. 1903) 1*f* to 4*f*.

1*f.* George Francis Blackburne Daniell, b. 8 June 1878.

2*f.* William Arthur Blackburne Daniell, Capt. Royal Fusiliers, b. 26 Jan. 1881.

3*f.* Henry Edmund Blackburne Daniell, b. 11 Feb. 1885.

4*f.* Alice Caroline Blackburne Daniell, *m.* 20 June 1906, Edward Granville Browne, Sir Thomas Adams' Professor of Arabic in the University of Cambridge and Fellow of Pembroke College, Author of " A Literary History of Persia," " A Year among the Persians," and other works and papers on Oriental subjects [son of Sir Benjamin Chapman Browne, D.C.L.] (*Cambridge*); and has issue 1*g*.

1*g.* Patrick Reginald Evelyn Browne, b. 28 May 1907.

4e. Mary Lilias Jones, *m.* 1 Feb. 1886, the Rev. Robert Henry Charles, D.D., M.A., Professor of Biblical Greek at T.C.D. 1898-1906, Fellow of the British Academy, Grinfield Lecturer, Oxford University, 1905-1910, Author of many well-known works (24 *Bardwell Road, Oxford*).

5e. Philippa Frances Jones, *m.* as 2nd wife, 12 Aug. 1885, Sir Frederick Albert Bosanquet, K.C., J.P., Common Serjeant of the City of London since 1900, formerly Recorder of Worcester 1879-1891 and of Wolverhampton 1891-1900, &c. (12 *Grenville Place, S.W.; Cobbe Place, Lewes*); and has issue 1*f* to 2*f*.

1*f.* William Sidney Bence Bosanquet, b. 9 May 1893.

2*f.* Edith Madeline Bosanquet.

5c. *Frances Anne Smith,* d. 20 *Feb.* 1862; m. 18 *Ap.* 1806, *Claude George Thornton of Marden Hill, co. Herts, High Sheriff for that co.* 1838, b. 20 *Jan.* 1776; d. 4 *Aug.* 1866; *and had issue* 1d *to* 2d.

1d. George Smith Thornton *of Marden Hill, J.P.*, b. 20 *Nov.* 1808; d. *May* 1867; m. 16 *Oct.* 1839, *Agnes, da. of the Rev. Henry Pole of Altham Place, co. Berks* [who m. 2ndly, 1869, *John Henry Blagrave of Calcot Park and*] d. 27 *Jan.* 1895; *and had issue* 1e.

1e. Godfrey Henry Thornton, b. 16 Aug. 1856.

2d. Rev. Spencer Thornton, M.A., *Vicar of Wendover*, b. 12 *Oct.* 1813; d. 12 *Jan.* 1850; m. 7 *Sept.* 1839, *Caroline Adelaide, da. of James Du Pré of Wilton Park, co. Bucks,* d. 17 *Feb.* 1898; *and had issue (with an elder son* d.s.p.) 1e *to* 6e.

1e. Henry Edward Thornton (58 *The Ropewalk, Nottingham*), b. 31 Aug. 1842; *m.* 1st, 15 Feb. 1871, Katherine Charlotte, sister to Field-Marshal the 1st Baron Grenfell [U.K.], P.C., G.C.B., da. of Pascoe St. Leger Grenfell of Maesteg, co. Glamorgan, *d.* 16 Jan. 1906; 2ndly, 19—, Isabel Mary [descended from the Lady Isabel Plantagenet (see the Essex Volume, p. 304)], da. of Robert Smith of Goldings, co. Herts, J.P., D.L.; and has issue 1*f* to 9*f*.

1*f.* Henry Grenfell Thornton, b. 9 Feb. 1873.

2*f.* Pascoe Spencer Thornton, b. 3 Mar. 1877.

3*f.* Rev. Claude Cyprian Thornton, M.A. (Camb.), Vicar of Greasley (*Greasley* [Nos. 72249 to 72266.

The Plantagenet Roll

Vicarage, Notts), b. 2 July 1878 ; m. 12 Sept. 1905, Alice Mary, da. of Frederick Sillery Bishop of Northwood, co. Midx. ; and has issue 1g.

  1g. Pascoe Cyprian Thornton, b. 20 Jan. 1907.

 4f. Godfrey St. Leger Thornton, Capt. R.F.A., b. 21 Mar. 1881.

 5f. Rev. John Gordon Thornton, B.A., Curate of St. Andrews, Auckland (Castle Lodge, Bishop Auckland), b. 23 Dec. 1884.

 6f. Robert Henry Thornton, b. 6 Oct. 1909.

 7f. Nina Katherine Thornton, m. 15 June 1898, the Rev. Frank Theodore Woods, M.A. (Camb.), Vicar of Bishop Auckland (The Vicarage, Bishop Auckland).

 8f. Susan Theresa Thornton, m. 31 July 1895, the Rev. John Bernard Barton, M.A. (Camb.), Rector of St. Pancras (St. Pancras Rectory, Rousdon, Devon); and has issue 1g to 4g.

  1g. Bernard Cecil Leslie Barton.
  2g. Arthur Grenfell Barton.
  3g. Raymond Henry Barton.
  4g. Nina Joyce Katherine Barton.

 9f. Gertrude Fanny Thornton, m. as 2nd wife, 2 Oct. 1907, Frank Evelyn Seely, J.P., Major and Hon. Lieut.-Col. S. Notts Hussars T.D. Yeo. [2nd son of Sir Charles Seely, 1st Bt. [U.K.]] (Calverton Hall, Nottingham); and has issue 1g.

  1g. Sheila Katherine Seely.

2e. Rev. Claude Cecil Thornton, M.A. (Camb.), Rector of Northwold (Northwold Rectory, Norfolk), b. 21 Jan. 1844 ; m. 1st, 10 July 1866, Fanny, da. of John Barton of East Leigh, Havant, d. 28 Dec. 1878 ; 2ndly, 19 Sept. 1882, Alice Henrietta, da. of Christopher William Giles Puller of Youngsbury Ware, co. Herts, M.P., J.P. ; and has issue (with a son d. unm.) 1f to 12f.

 1f. Claude Du Pré Thornton, b. 27 Sept. 1867 ; m. 9 Sept. 1909, Fanny Theodosia Savignac, da. of (—) Stedman.

 2f. Douglas Montagu Thornton, b. 18 Mar. 1873 ; d. 8 Sept. 1907 ; m. 7 Nov. 1899, Elaine, da. of Sir William Anderson, K.C.B. ; and had issue 1g.

  1g. Cecil Anderson Montagu Thornton, b. 11 May 1901.

 3f. Reginald Christopher Thornton, b. 18 July 1883.

 4f. Rev. Lionel Spencer Thornton, B.A. (Camb.), Curate of Lingfield, Surrey, b. 27 June 1884.

 5f. Bernard Giles Thornton, b. 22 Sept. 1885.
 6f.[1] Adelaide Frances Thornton,
 7f.[1] Evelyn Maude Thornton,
 8f.[1] Katharine Emily Cecilia Thornton,   } unm.
 9f.[2] Winifred Mary Thornton,
 10f.[2] Elsie Caroline Thornton,
 11f.[2] Alice Nora Thornton,
 12f.[2] Christabel Monica Thornton,

3e. Rev. George Ruthven Thornton, Vicar of St. Barnabas, Kensington, b. 23 Mar. 1845 ; d. 19 June 1895; m. 12 Oct. 1869, Theresa (18 Craven Hill, Hyde Park, W.), da. of John Labouchere of Broom Hall, co. Surrey ; and had issue (with a da., Theresa, d. unm.) 1f to 8f.

 1f. Edward Labouchere Ruthven Thornton, I.C.S., District and Session Judge (Madras), b. 10 July 1870 ; m. 13 Nov. 1893, Mabel, da. of (—) Higgenbotham, d. (-) ; and has issue 1g.

  1g. Dorothy Mabel Thornton, b. 25 Ap. 1896.

 2f. Spencer Ruthven Thornton, b. 10 Aug. 1871; unm.

 3f. Arthur Ruthven Thornton, served in Lumsden's Horse, S. Africa, b. 10 Sept. 1876.

 4f. Maxwell Ruthven Thornton, Solicitor (Penang), b. 11 July 1878 ; m. Nov. 1909, Kathleen, da. of (—) Yates of co. York.   [Nos. 72267 to 72296.

# of The Blood Royal

5*f*. Rev. George Ruthven Thornton, M.A., Org. Sec. S. Amer. M.S. for S.E. Dist. (33 *Melville Road, Barnes*), *b*. 30 Sept. 1882; *m*. 22 Ap. 1908, Frances Penelope [descended from the Lady Isabel Plantagenet (see the Essex Volume, p. 346)], da. of Jacob Phillipps of 21 Addison Gardens, W.

6*f*. Francis Ruthven Thornton, *b*. 5 Aug. 1884; *unm*.

7*f*. Cicely Ruthven Thornton, *m*. 4 Sept. 1903, the Rev. Charles Rainsford, Vicar of All Saints, Hertford.

8*f*. Mary Louisa Ruthven Thornton, *unm*.

4*e*. *Julia Frances Thornton*, d. (–); m. 1868, *the Rev. William Thomas Henry Wilson, formerly Rector of Burlingham* (4 *Holmesdale Gardens, Hastings*); *and had issue* 1*f* to 4*f*.

  1*f*. William Thornton Pender Wilson, Lieut. R.N.
  2*f*. John Wilson.
  3*f*. [da.] Wilson, *m*. A. F. (?) Ives.
  4*f*. [da.] Wilson, *m*. M. (?) Webster.

5*e*. Caroline Sophia Thornton, *unm*.

6*e*. Emily Montagu Thornton, *unm*.

6*c*. *Mary Smith*, d. (–); m. 25 *Jan*. 1811, *Thomas Daniel of Aldridge Lodge, co. Stafford*.

7*c*. *Caroline Smith*, d. 17 Feb. 1816; m. 1814, *Major-Gen. Thomas Cary*, d. 9 *Nov*. 1824; *and had issue* 1*d*.

  1*d*. *Caroline Cary*, b. *at Eltham Palace, co. Kent*, 29 *Jan*. 1816; d. *at Kingweston* 19 *Ap*. 1897; m. 8 Sept. 1835, *Francis Henry Dickinson of Kingweston, J.P., D.L., M.P.*, d. 17 *July* 1890; *and had issue*.
  See p. 393, Nos. 72202–72227.

8*c*. *Barbara Smith*, d. 9 *Jan*. 1861; m. 25 *Oct*. 1836, *Lieut. James John Gordon of Hadlow House, co. Kent, R.N*.

9*c*. *Charlotte Smith*, d. 26 *Ap*. 1879; m. 19 *Oct*. 1825, *the Hon. Alexander Leslie-Melville [E. of Leven and Melville Coll.*], d. 19 *Nov*. 1881; *and had issue*.
See the Essex Volume, Clarence Supplement, pp. 523–524, Nos. 1324/209–291.

6*b*. *Mary Turnor*, d. 18 *Oct*. 1831; m. 1789, *Sir William Foulis of Ingleby*, 7th Bt. [E.], d. 5 Sept. 1802; *and had issue*.
See p. 234, Nos. 36612–36649.

7*b*. *Diana Turnor*, b. *c*. 1763; d. 4 *Feb*. 1824; m. 24 *June* 1785, *Sir Thomas Whichcote, 5th Bt*. [E.], d. 22 Sept. or 4 Oct. 1828; *and had issue*.
See p. 150, Nos. 16642–16722.

8*b*. *Frances Turnor*, d. (? *um*.).

2*a*. *John Turnor, Capt. of Dragoons*, d. (? s.p.) 1752.

3*a*. *Diana Turnor*, b. *c*. 1712; d. 1793; m. *Bennet Langton of Langton, co. Linc*., d. 1769; *and had issue*.
See the Clarence Volume, Table LXIX., and pp. 545–550, Nos. 23355–23486.

4*a*. *Elizabeth Turnor*, d. (? s.p.); m. *Edward Andrewes of Brockhill House, co. Glouc*.

5*a*. *Isabella Turnor*, d. (? s.p.); m. *Lieut.-Gen. Alexander Drewry*.

[Nos. 72297 to 72666.

233. Descendants of Lady ANNE CECIL (Table XXII.), *b*. 1612; *d*. 6 Dec. 1637; *m*. as 1st wife *a*. 1630, ALGERNON (PERCY), 10th EARL OF NORTHUMBERLAND [E.], K.G., K.B., *bapt*. 13 Oct. 1602; *d*. 13 Oct. 1668; and had issue.

See p. 71, Nos. 2000–3422.   [Nos. 72667 to 74089.

The Plantagenet Roll

234. Descendants of Lady ELIZABETH CECIL (Table XXII.), d. 19 Nov. 1689; m. (lic. 4 Mar.) 1639, WILLIAM (CAVENDISH), 3rd EARL OF DEVONSHIRE [E.], b. 10 Oct. 1617; d. 23 Nov. 1684; and had issue 1a to 2a.

1a. William (Cavendish), 4th Earl and (12 May 1694) 1st Duke of Devonshire [E.], K.G., b. 25 Jan. 1641; d. 18 Aug. 1707; m. 26 Oct. 1662, Lady Mary, da. of James (Butler), 1st Duke of Ormonde [E. and I.], K.G., d. 31 July 1710; and had issue 1b to 2b.

1b. William (Cavendish), 2nd Duke of Devonshire, &c. [E.], K.G., b. c. 1672; d. 4 June 1729; m. 21 June 1688, Lady Rachel, da. of William Russell, Lord Russell, d. 28 Dec. 1725; and had issue.
See the Essex Volume, Table XIII., and pp. 174–190, Nos. 22908–24381.

2b. Lord James Cavendish of Stayley Park, co. Devon, M.P., d. 14 Dec. 1751; m. Anne, da. of Elihu Yale, Governor of Fort St. George, in the East Indies, d. 27 June 1734; and had issue 1c.

1c. Elizabeth Cavendish, da. and after the death (30 June 1751) of her brother William, sole h., d. 4 Aug. 1779; m. Feb. 1732, Richard Chandler, afterwards (Act Parl. 26 Mar. 1752) Cavendish, M.P. [son and h. of the Right Rev. Edward Chandler, Lord Bishop of Durham], d. (apparently s.p.) 22 Nov. 1769.[1]

2a. Lady Anne Cavendish, b. c. 1649; d. 18 June 1703; m. 2ndly (lic. 4 May), 1670, John (Cecil), 5th Earl of Exeter [E.], d. at Issy, near Paris, 29 Aug. 1700; and had issue.
See the Tudor Roll, Table XCVII., and pp. 414–428, Nos. 30220–30994.

[Nos. 74090 to 76338.

235. Descendants of Lady CATHERINE CECIL (Table XXII.), d. 18 Aug. 1652; m. 9 May 1645, PHILIP (SYDNEY), 3rd EARL OF LEICESTER [E.], d. 6 Mar. 1698; and had issue.

See the Essex Volume, p. 88, Nos. 9363–9375.   [Nos. 76339 to 76351.

236. Descendants of CHARLES (HOWARD), 1st EARL OF CARLISLE [E.] (Table XXIII.), b. 1629; d. 24 Feb. 1685; m. the Hon. ANNE, da. of Edward (HOWARD), 1st Baron Howard of Escrick [E.], bur. 4 Sept. 1703; and had issue.

See p. 384, Nos. 66064–66961.   [Nos. 76352 to 77249.

237. Descendants of MARY HOWARD (Table XXIII.), d. (–); m. Sir JONATHAN ATKINS, Governor of [Jersey and afterwards] of Barbados, d. there 1702, aged 99; and had issue (with apparently other das.)[2] 1a.

1a. Frances Atkins, styled co-h. to brother, b. 20 Mar. 1659; d. (–); m. 1st, Sir Robert Hackett, d. 31 Mar. 1679; 2ndly, Col. Thomas Walrond [a younger son of Humphrey (Walrond), 1st Marquis of Vallado [Sp. 1653], Governor of Barbados], d. 1694; and had (with other) issue 1b.

1b. Frances Walrond, elder da. and co-h., b. in Barbados 1680; d. in London 1716; m. 1st, George Græme of Barbados; 2ndly, William Adams of the same Island; and had (with possibly other) issue 1c.

---

[1] Gentleman's Magazine, 1793, pp. 974, 1000, 1131.
[2] Burke's "Royal Families," ii. cciii., from which all these particulars are taken.

# of The Blood Royal

1c. *Thomas Adams, a Master in Chancery at Barbados*, b. 1699; d. 1764; m. *Margaret, da. of Lieut.-Gen. Thomas Maxwell; and had (with possibly other) issue* 1d.

1d. *William Adams of Barbados*, d. *in Jamaica* 1781; m. *Elizabeth Ann, da. of the Rev. Thomas Coxeter; and had (with possibly other) issue* 1e.

1e. *Edward Hamilton Adams of Middleton Hall, co. Carmarthen, M.P. and High Sheriff for that co.*, d. 2 *June* 1842; m. *Amelia Sophia, da. of Capt. John Macpherson; and had issue* 1f *to* 6f.

1f. Edward Adams of Middleton Hall.
2f. William Adams.
3f. Mary Adams.
4f. Sophia Adams.
5f. Caroline Adams.
6f. Matilda Adams.   [Nos. 77250 to 77255.

238. Descendants of CATHERINE HOWARD (Table XXIII.), d. 4 July 1668; m. c. 1660, Sir JOHN LAWSON of Brough, 1st Bt. [E.], d. 26 Oct. 1698; and had issue.

See pp. 297–298, Nos. 39646–40143.   [Nos. 77256 to 77753.

239. Descendants of FRANCES DOWNING (Table XXIII.), d. (–); m. JOHN COTTON, son and h. of Sir John Cotton, 1st Bt. [E.], M.P., b. c. 1650; d.v.p. 1681; and had issue 1a to 3a.

1a. *Sir John Cotton, 3rd Bt.* [E.], *M.P.*; d.s.p. 5 *Feb.* 1731.

2a. *Thomas Cotton*, d. (–); m. *Frances, da. and h. of William Langton of Peterborough; and had issue a da., Mary, who must have* d. *unm.*

3a. *Frances Cotton, da. and event. h., having the privilege of appointing successive Cottonian Family Trustees to the British Museum, vested in her and the male issue of her four das. in succession, according to their seniority, by Act of Parliament,* 1752, b. 1675/7; d. 21 *Nov.* 1756; m. *William Hanbury of Little Marcle, co. Hereford* [*son of Sir Thomas Hanbury*], d. 19 *Oct.* 1737; *and had issue (with 2 other das. who* d.s.p.) 1b *to* 2b.

1b. *Mary Hanbury, da. and co-h.*, b. 1708; d. 20 *Dec.* 1796; m. 12 *Dec.* 1732, *the Rev. Martin Annesley, D.D., Preb. of Sarum* [*V. Valentia Coll.*], b. 5 *Oct.* 1701; d. 4 *June* 1749; *and had issue (with* 4 *other sons and* 1 *da. who* d.s.p.) 1c *to* 3c.

1c. *Rev. Arthur Henry Annesley, D.D., Vicar of Chewton Mendip*, b. 8 *May* 1735; bur. 12 *July* 1792; m. 7 *Nov.* 1761, *Alice, da. and h. of Francis Keyte Dighton of Clifford Chambers, co. Glouc.*, d. 29 *Nov.* 1790; *and had issue (with a da. who* d.s.p.) 1d.

1d. *Rev. Arthur Annesley, Rector and Lord of the Manor of Clifford Chambers, a Cottonian Family Trustee of the British Museum*, b. 30 *Oct.* 1768; d. 9 *Feb.* 1845; m. 14 *Jan.* 1800, *Elizabeth Vere, da. of George Booth Tyndale of Bathford* [*descended from George, Duke of Clarence, K.G.*], d. 15 *June* 1865; *and had issue.*

See the Clarence Volume, pp. 542–544, Nos. 23283–23354.

2c. *Katherine Annesley*, b. 20 *Mar.* 1738; d. 22 *Ap.* 1826; m. *as 2nd wife,* 1 *Jan.* 1761, *the Rev. John Trollope, D.D.* [*Bt.* (E. 1641) *Coll.*], d. 10 *July* 1794; *and had issue* 1d *to* 2d.

1d. *Arthur William Trollope, Capt. 40th Regt.*, b. 15 *Dec.* 1771; d. 20 *Sept.* 1799; m. 26 *Dec.* 1797, *Mary, da. of Barnard Foord of Beverley, M.D.*, d. 19 *July* 1822; *and had issue* 1e *to* 2e.

1e. *Barnard Trollope, afterwards* (R.L. 30 *Oct.* 1861) *Foord-Bowes, of Cowlam, co. Yorks,* b. 25 *Oct.* 1798; d. 10 *June* 1870; m. 27 *July* 1818, *Mary, da. of Samuel Greathed*, d. 7 *Jan.* 1861; *and had issue a da. who* d.s.p.   [Nos. 77754 to 77825.

The Plantagenet Roll

2e. *William Henry Trollope, Capt. H.E.I.C.S.*, b. 4 *Ap.* 1800; d. 24 *Sept.* 1873: m. 30 *July* 1834, *Mary Arthur, da. of John Arthur Worsop of Landford House, co. Wilts*, d. 1891; *and had issue* 1*f to* 3*f.*

1*f. Edward Charles Trollope, Major R.A.*, b. 20 *Aug.* 1849; d. 23 *Feb.* 1904; m. 1*st*, 5 Oct. 1871, *Louisa Sarah, da. of Robert Pipon of Beaumont, Jersey*, d. 19 *Aug.* 1882; 2*ndly*, 27 *May* 1886, *Eva Annie Noel* (45 *Lower Belgrave Street, S.W.*), *da. of Capt. Frederick Dampier Rich, R.N.* [*Bt. Coll.*]; *and had issue* 1*g to* 2*g.*

1*g.*[1] Mary Emily Arthur Trollope.

2*g.*[2] Constance Zara Trollope.

2*f. Mary Anne Trollope*, d. 15 *Sept.* 1897; m. 19 *Aug.* 1862, *Frederick Ashe Bradburne of Lyburne, co. Hants* (*Bramshaw Lodge, Lyndhurst, Hants*); *and had issue* 1*g to* 4*g.*

1*g.* Frederick Arthur Bradburne, b. 1863.

2*g.* Henry Humphrey Brucker Bradburne, b. 1869.

3*g.* John Edward Bradburne, b. 1875.

4*g.* Charles Wyndham Bradburne, b. 1879.

3*f.* Eliza Maria Trollope (19 *Montague Road, Richmond Hill, Surrey*), m. 19 Aug. 1862, the Rev. George Goodwin Pownall Glossop, Rector of West Dean, co. Hants, d. 23 Ap. 1874; *and had issue* 1*g* to 9*g.*

1*g.* Rev. Charles Henry James Glossop, M.A. (Camb.), Rector of Brympton (*Brympton Rectory, Yeovil*), b. 25 July 1864; m. 27 June 1894, Ada, da. of the Rev. Richard George Watson; *and has issue* 1*h.*

1*h.* George Charles William Glossop, b. 26 Mar. 1906.

2*g.* Francis Edward Glossop, Major 1st Batt. Leicestershire Regt., b. 25 Aug. 1866; m. 1 Oct. 1902, Ellen Sabine, da. of Capt. Thomas Malcolm Sabine Pasley, R.N. [Bt. Coll.].

3*g.* Rev. Arthur George Barnard Glossop, M.A. (Oxon.), a Missionary of the Universities Mission to Brit. Central Africa (*Likoma, Nyassaland; 19 Montague Road, Richmond Hill, S.W.*), b. 9 Nov. 1867.

4*g.* William Richard Newland Glossop, b. 26 Nov. 1868.

5*g.* John Collings Taswell Glossop, Comm. R.N., b. 23 Oct. 1871.

6*g.* Harry Anthony Pownall Glossop, Lieut. R.N., b. 14 Jan. 1873.

7*g.* Mary Eliza Glossop, m. 20 May 1886, Campbell Fortescue Stapleton Sanctuary (*Mangerton, Melplash, R.S.O., Dorset*); *and has issue* 1*h* to 5*h.*

1*h.* Campbell Thomas Sanctuary, b. 31 July 1889.

2*h.* Arthur George Everard Sanctuary, b. 8 Nov. 1892.

3*h.* Harry Nicholson Sanctuary, b. 11 June 1898.

4*h.* Mary Frances Alice Sanctuary.

5*h.* Isabel Gemma Sanctuary.

8*g.* Ellen Maria Glossop.

9*g.* Alice Emma Harriet Glossop.

2*d. George Barne Trollope, Rear-Adm. R.N., C.B.*, b. 17 *Ap.* 1779; d. 31 *May* 1850; m. 18 *Mar.* 1813, *Barbara, da. of Joseph Goble*, d. 11 *July* 1874; *and had issue* 1*e to* 3*e.*

1*e.* Rev. John Joseph Trollope, M.A. (Oxon.), Preb. of Hereford, b. 15 Nov. 1817; d. 8 *Jan.* 1893; m. 7 Dec. 1850, Anne Mary Theresa, widow of Capt. Henry Frederic Alston, 99th Regt., da. of John Walsh of Anne Mount, co. Kilkenny, d. 22 Nov. 1905; *and had issue* 1*f* to 2*f.*

1*f.* Helen Lucy Trollope.

2*f.* Catherine Annesley Trollope (*Montpelier Grove, Cheltenham*), m. 1902, the Rev. James Albert Owen, d. 16 July 1907.

2*e. Rev. Charles Trollope, Rector of Stibbington, Hon. Canon of Ely*, b. 4 *Feb.* 1819; d. 8 *Sept.* 1907; m. 30 *Oct.* 1872, *Eleanor, da. of the Rev. William Hiley Bathurst of Lydney Park, co. Glouc.*; *and had issue* 1*f to* 2*f.* [Nos. 77826 to 77849.

# of The Blood Royal

1*f*. Rev. Charles Henry Bathurst Trollope, M.A. (Camb.), Rector of Escrick (*Escrick Rectory, York*), b. 27 Ap. 1876.

2*f*. Eleanor Mary Trollope.

3*e. Frederick Trollope, Capt. Bengal S.C.*, b. 20 *July* 1820; d. 11 *Sept.* 1857; m. 24 *Oct.* 1844, *Mary Victoria, da. of Charles Francis; and had issue* 1*f* to 2*f*.

1*f. George Frederick Trollope*, b. 31 *July* 1845; d. 21 *June* 1871; m. 18 *June* 1870, *Clara Sophia, da. of* (—) *Hudswell; and had issue* 1*g*.

1*g*. Frederick William Trollope, *b*. 14 Feb. 1871.

2*f*. Charles William Annesley Trollope, a Clerk in the Exchequer and Audit Dept. (*Morningside, Marryat Road, Wimbledon*), b. 20 Jan. 1850; *m*. 23 Aug. 1877, Marian Eirene, da. of the Rev. William Watson; and has issue 1g to 3g.

1*g*. George Henry Annesley Trollope, *b*. 12 Dec. 1879.

2*g*. Leonard Edward Annesley Trollope, *b*. 13 Mar. 1892.

3*g*. Dorothy Marion Annesley Trollope.

3*c. Elizabeth Annesley*, bapt. 5 *Oct.* 1745; d. 21 *July* 1816; m. 20 *June* 1771, *George Booth Tyndale of Bathford, co. Som.*, d. 28 *Dec.* 1779; *and had issue.*

See the Clarence Volume, pp. 538–544, Nos. 23152–23354.

2*b. Catherine Hanbury, da. and co-h.*, b. 1711; d. 1779; m. *as 3rd wife*, 2 *Ap.* 1737, *Velters Cornewall of Moccas Court, co. Hereford, M.P.*, d. 3 *Ap.* 1768; *and had issue* 1*c*.

1*c. Catherine Cornewall of Moccas Court, da. and h.*, b. 15 *Mar.* 1752; d. 17 *Mar.* 1835; m. 15 *July* 1771, *Sir George Armyard, afterwards* (1771) *Cornewall, 2nd Bt.* [G.B.], *M.P.*, b. 8 *Nov.* 1748; d. 26 *Sept.* 1819; *and had issue* 1*d* to 4*d*.

1*d. Sir George Cornewall, 3rd Bt.* [G.B.], b. 16 *Jan.* 1774; d. 27 *Dec.* 1835; m. 26 *Sept.* 1816, *Jane, niece of James, 1st Baron Sherborne* [G.B.], *da. of William Naper of Loughcrew, co. Meath*, d. 13 *Feb.* 1853; *and had issue* 1*e* to 4*e*.

1*e. Sir Velters Cornewall, 4th Bt.* [G.B.], b. 20 *Feb.* 1824; d. *unm*. 14 *Oct.* 1868.

2*e. Rev. Sir George Henry Cornewall, 5th Bt.* [G.B.], J.P., D.L., *Rector of Moccas*, b. 13 *Aug.* 1833; d. 25 *Sept.* 1908; m. 4 *June* 1867, *Louisa Frances, da. of Francis Bayley, Judge of the Westminster County Court*, d. 2 *Feb.* 1900; *and had issue* 1*f* to 3*f*.

1*f*. Sir Geoffrey Cornewall, 6th Bt. [G.B.], J.P., D.L., Barrister I.T., &c. (*Moccas Court, Hereford*), b. 7 May 1869; *unm.*

2*f*. William Francis Cornewall, Barrister I.T. (1 *Hare Caurt, Temple, E.C.*), *b*. 16 Nov. 1871.

3*f*. Mary Louisa Cornewall.

3*e. Catherine Elizabeth Cornewall*, d. 1896; m. 7 *Ap.* 1840, *Thomas William Chester Master of Knole Park and The Abbey, Cirencester, M.P.*, d. 30 *Jan.* 1899; *and had issue.*

See the Tudor Roll, p. 385, Nos. 29174–29190.

4*e. Henrietta Cornewall*, d. 25 *June* 1900; m. 29 *July* 1858, *the Rev. Augustus Chester Master*, d. 10 *Dec.* 1887; *and had issue.*

See the Tudor Roll, p. 386, Nos. 29199–29203.

2*d. Frances Elizabeth Cornewall*, d. 20 *Feb.* 1864; m. 12 *Dec.* 1805, *Henry* (*Devereux*), *14th Viscount Hereford* [E.], d. 31 *May* 1843; *and had issue.*

See the Essex Volume, pp. 363–364, Nos. 35574–35605.

3*d. Harriet Cornewall*, d. 11 *Aug.* 1838; m. *as 1st wife*, 11 *Mar.* 1805, *the Right Hon. Sir Thomas Frankland Lewis, 1st Bt.* [U.K.], P.C., M.P., b. 14 *May* 1780; d. 22 *Jan.* 1855; *and had issue* 1*e* to 2*e*.

1*e. Right Hon. Sir George Cornewall Lewis, 2nd Bt.* [U.K.], P.C., M.P., *the eminent Statesman and Author*, b. 21 *Oct.* 1806; d.s.p. 13 *Ap.* 1863.

2*e. Rev. Sir Gilbert Frankland Lewis, 3rd Bt.* [U.K.], M.A., *Canon of Wor-*

[Nos. 77850 to 78116.

The Plantagenet Roll

cester, b. 21 July 1808; d. 18 Dec. 1883; m. 3 Aug. 1843, Jane [descended from George, Duke of Clarence, K.G. (see Clarence Volume, p. 247)], da. of Sir Edmund Antrobus, 2nd Bt. [U.K.], d. 20 Oct. 1899; and had issue 1f to 3f.

1f. Sir Herbert Edmund Frankland Lewis, 4th Bt. [U.K.], J.P., D.L. (*Harpton Court, near Kington, co. Radnor*), b. 31 Mar. 1846; m. 4 Mar. 1889, Maria Louisa, widow of Col. George Frederick Dallas, K.L.H. [Bt. Coll.], da. of James Arthur Taylor of Strensham Court.

2f. Mary Anna Lewis.

3f. Elinor Lewis, m. as 2nd wife, 7 Jan. 1890, Col. Sir St. Vincent Alexander Hammick, 3rd Bt. [U.K.] (*Little Stodham, Liss, Hants*).

4d. Caroline Cornewall, d. 23 Ap. 1875; m. 15 Feb. 1810, Sir William Duff Gordon, 2nd Bt. [U.K.], d. 8 Mar. 1823; and had issue.

See the Clarence Volume, p. 246, Nos. 5867-5886.   [Nos. 78117 to 78139.

240. Descendants, if any surviving, of MARY DOWNING (Table XXIII.), d. (–); m. 28 June 1705, THOMAS BARNARDISTON of Bury and Wyverstone, co. Suffolk; and had issue 1a to 3a.[1]

1a. Thomas Barnardiston, Sergeant-at-Law, b. 1706; d. unm. 1752.

2a. Mary Barnardiston, m. Edward Goate of Brenteleigh, co. Suffolk.

3a. Elizabeth Barnardiston, d. after 1774; m. 14 Sept. 1743, the Right Rev. John Ewer, D.D., Lord Bishop of Landaff 1761-1768 and Bangor 1768-1774; d. 28 Oct. 1774, leaving issue 1b.

1b. Margaret Frances Ewer.

241. Descendants of ALATHEA HOWARD (Table XXIII.), d. 3 Sept. 1677; m. THOMAS (FAIRFAX), 2nd VISCOUNT FAIRFAX [I.], d. 24 Sept. 1641; and had issue.

See pp. 220-221, Nos. 35958-36304/100.   [Nos. 78140 to 78586.

242. Descendants of Sir FRANCIS HOWARD of Corby Castle, co. Cumberland (Table XXIII.), b. 29 Aug. 1588; d. 11 Ap. 1660; m. 1st, MARGARET, da. of John PRESTON of Furness, co. Lancaster, d. 7 Sept. 1625; 2ndly, MARY, da. of Sir Henry WIDDRINGTON of Widdrington, d. 22 July 1672; and had issue 1a to 4a.

1a.[2] Francis Howard of Corby Castle, Gov. of Carlisle, b. 29 June 1635; d. 1702; m. 1st, Ann, da. of William Gerard of Bryn, d. 1679; 2ndly, Mary Ann Dorothy, da. of Richard Towneley of Towneley; and had issue (with two elder das. by 1st wife, whose issue failed in 1711, and a younger da. who d. unm.) 1b.

1b. Anne Howard, da. and in her issue (if any) sole-h., m. Marmaduke Langdale of Houghton.

2a.[2] William Howard of Corby Castle, d. 1708; m. Jane, da. of John Dalston of Acornbank, co. Westmorland; and had issue 1b to 4b.

1b. Thomas Howard of Corby Castle, d. (–); m. 2ndly, 1724, Barbara, da. of Philip Musgrave; and had issue.

See p. 216 (Sec. 111), Nos. 30187-30304.

2b. William Howard.

3b. John Howard.   [Nos. 78587 to 78704.

---

[1] "Proceedings of the Suffolk Institute of Archæology," iv. 155.

# of The Blood Royal

4b. *Elizabeth Howard*, m. *William Sanderson of Armathwaite*.

3a.¹ *Elizabeth Howard*, d. (-) ; m. 11 *Nov.* 1632, *Edward Standish of Standish, co. Lancaster*, aged 47, 22 *Sept.* 1664; d. (-) ; *and had issue* 1b *to* 3b.

1b. *William Standish of Standish*, b. c. 1638 ; d. 8 *June* 1705 ; m. *Cecilia, da. and h. of Sir Robert Bindlosoe*, 1st Bt. [E], d. 19 *Jan.* 1730 ; *and had issue* 1c.

1c. *Ralph Standish of Standish, forfeited for his share in the '15*, d. (-) ; m. *Lady Philippa, da. of Henry* (Howard), *6th Duke of Norfolk* [E.], d. 5 *Ap.* 1731 ; *and had issue.*

See the Exeter Volume, p. 291, Nos. 13756-13799.

2b. *Mary Standish*, d. (-) ; m. (—) *Daniel of Heton Place, Sudbury, co. Suffolk.*

3b. *Elizabeth Standish*, d. (-) ; m. *as* 1st *wife (cont. dated* 18 *Jan.)* 1678, *John Witham of Cliffe, co. York; and had issue.*

See the Exeter Volume, pp. 558-560, Nos. 49748-49913.

4a.² *Margaret Howard*, d. (-) ; m. *as* 1st *wife, Sir Thomas Haggerston of Haggerston*, 2nd Bt. [E.], d. c. 1710 ; *and had issue (9 sons and a da. of whom only one left issue, viz.)* 1b.

1b. *William Haggerston*, d.v.p. (-) ; m. *Anne, da. and event h. of Sir Philip Constable*, 3rd Bt. [E.] ; *and had issue.*

See the Exeter Volume, pp. 529-530, Nos. 48488-48835.

[Nos. 78705 to 79262.

243. Descendants of Sir CHARLES HOWARD (Table XXIII.), d. (-) ; m. DOROTHY, da. of Sir Henry WIDDRINGTON ; and had issue.[1]

244. Descendants of THOMAS HOWARD (Table XXIII.), d. (-) ; m. ELIZABETH, da. of Sir William EURE; and had issue (with a son, Thomas, who d. unm.) 1a to 2a.

1a. *Frances Howard,*
2a. *Mary Howard,* } *one of whom* m. (—) *Fetherston.*[2]

245. Descendants, if any, of MARY HOWARD (Table XXIII.), d. (-) ; m. Sir JOHN WINTOUR of Lydney, co. Glouc.

246. Descendants of Sir JOHN COTTON, 3rd Bt. [E.], M.P. (Table XXIII.), b. 1621; d. 12 Sept. 1702; m. 1st, DOROTHY, da. and h. of Edmund ANDERSON of Stratton and Egworth, co. Bedford ; 2ndly, 20 Oct. 1658, ELIZABETH, da. and h. of Sir Thomas HONYWOOD, d. 3 Ap. 1702 ; and had issue 1a to 4a.

1a.¹ *John Cotton, son and h.*, b. 1650 ; d.v.p. 1681 ; m. *Frances, da. and in her issue* (6 *Feb.* 1764) *co-h. of Sir George Downing*, 1st Bt. [E.], M.P. ; *and had issue.*
See pp. 399-402, Nos. 77754-78139.

2a.² *Sir Robert Cotton*, 5th Bt. [E.], b. c. 1679 ; d. 12 *July* 1749; m. 1st, *Elizabeth, da. of* (—) *Wigston ; and had issue* 1b. [Nos. 79263 to 79648.

---

[1] A son, William, is mentioned in Brydges' "Collins," iii. 502 ; and a 4th son is supposed to have been the Henry Howard who settled at Conway in the middle of the seventeenth century, and was ancestor of the Howards of Wygfair, co. Denbigh. See Burke's "Landed Gentry," 1906, p. 863.

[2] Brydges' "Collins," iii. 502.

The Plantagenet Roll

1b. *Sir John Cotton, 6th Bt.* [E.], d. 27 *Mar.* 1752; m. *Jane, da. of Sir Robert Burdett, 3rd Bt.* [E.], d. 1769; *and had issue* 1c *to* 4c.
1c. *Jane Cotton,* m. *Oct.* 1741, *Thomas Hurt of Warfield, co. Berks.*
2c. *Elizabeth Cotton.*
3c. *Frances Cotton.*
4c. *Mary Cotton.*

3a.[1] *Dorothy Cotton,* d. (−); m. *William Dennis of co. Glouc.*
4a.[2] *Elizabeth Cotton,* d. (−); m. 1*st, Lyonel Walden of Huntingdon;* 2*ndly,* (—) *Smith of Westminster; and had issue (with a son who* d. unm. *and possibly other children by* 2*nd husband)* 1b *to* 2b.
1b. *Elizabeth Walden,* d. (−); m. 1*st, Charles Pitfield;* 2*ndly, Talbot Touchet; and had issue (with possibly others by* 2*nd husband, a son Charles and da. Elizabeth,* 1*st wife of Edward Bigland of Long Whatton, co. Leic., who both* d.s.p.).
2b. *Hester Walden,* d. (−); m. *Humphrey Orme of Peterborough, Capt.* R.N.; *and had (with possibly other) issue* 1c.[1]
1c. *Walden Orme of Peterborough, son and h.,* d. (−); m. *Sarah, da. of Adland Squire Stukeley of Holbeach, co. Linc.; and had (with possibly other issue)* 1d.
1d. *Walden Orme of Peterborough, son and h.,* d. 1809; m. (—), *da. of Robert Tomlin of Edith Weston, co. Rutland; and had (with possibly other) issue* 1e.
1e. *Humphrey Orme of Peterborough, Capt.* 11*th Light Drag., served at Waterloo.*

247. Descendants of Sir ARMINE WODEHOUSE, 5th Bt. [E.], M.P. for Norfolk 1737–68 (Table XXIII.), b. 1714; d. 21 May 1777; m. 3 Oct. 1738, LETITIA, da. and co-h. of Sir Edmund BACON, 6th and Premier Bt. [E.], bur. 7 Ap. 1758; and had issue 1a to 3a.

1a. *John (Wodehouse),* 1*st Baron Wodehouse* [G.B.], *so* cr. 26 *Oct.* 1797; b. 4 *Ap.* 1741; d. 29 *May* 1834; m. 30 *Mar.* 1769, *Sophia, da. and h. of the Hon. Charles Berkeley of Bruton Abbey, co. Som.* [*B. Berkeley of Stratton Coll.*], d. 16 *Ap.* 1825; *and had issue* 1b *to* 3b.
1b. *John (Wodehouse),* 2*nd Baron Wodehouse* [G.B.], b. 11 *Jan.* 1771; d. 29 *May* 1846; m. 17 *Nov.* 1796, *Charlotte Laura, da. and h. of John Norris of Witton Park and Witchingham, co. Norfolk,* d. *June* 1845; *and had issue* 1c *to* 5c.
1c. Hon. *Henry Wodehouse,* b. 19 *Mar.* 1799; d.v.p. 29 *Ap.* 1834; m. 7 *Ap.* 1825, *Anne, da. of Theophilus Thornhaugh Gurdon of Letton, co. Norfolk,* d. 29 *Ap.* 1834; *and had issue* 1d.
1d. *John (Wodehouse),* 3*rd Baron Wodehouse* [G.B.] *and* (1 *June* 1866) 1*st Earl of Kimberley* [U.K.], K.G., P.C., *Lord President of the Council* 1892–1894, *Secretary of State for India* 1882–1885, 1886, *and* 1892–1894, *and for Foreign Affairs* 1894–1895, *Lord-Lieutenant of Ireland* 1864–1866, *Ambassador at St. Petersburg* 1856–1858, &c., *a distinguished Statesman,* b. 7 *Jan.* 1826; d. 8 *Ap.* 1902; m. 16 *Aug.* 1847, *Lady Florence, C.I., da. and co-h. of Richard (FitzGibbon),* 3*rd Earl of Clare* [I.], d. 4 *May* 1895; *and had issue* 1e *to* 4e.
1e. John (Wodehouse), 2nd *Earl of Kimberley* [U.K.], 4th Baron Wodehouse [G.B.] *and* 9th Bt. [E.], &c. (*Kimberley House, Wymondham, Norfolk; Witton Park, North Walsham, &c.*), b. 10 Dec. 1848; m. 22 June 1875, Isabel Geraldine, da. of Sir Henry Josias Stracey, 5th Bt. [U.K.]; *and has issue* 1f *to* 4f.
1f. John Wodehouse, Lord Wodehouse, M.P. (*Witton Park, North Walsham*), b. 11 Nov. 1883.
2f. Hon. Philip Wodehouse, b. 1 Oct. 1886.
3f. Hon. Edward Wodehouse, b. 12 Ap. 1898.
4f. Lady Isabel Wodehouse.   [Nos. 79649 to 79653.

---

[1] Burke's "Royal Families," i. LIX.

# of The Blood Royal

2e. Hon. Armine Wodehouse, C.B., M.P., b. 24 Sept. 1860; d. 1 May 1901; m. 6 June 1889, Eleanor Mary Caroline (21 Sloane Gardens, S.W.), da. of Matthew Arnold; and had issue 1f.

1f. Roger Wodehouse, b. 24 Sept. 1890.

3e. Lady Alice Wodehouse (41 Charles Street, Berkeley Square, W.), m. 14 Aug. 1872, Hussey Packe of Prestwold Hall, J.P., D.L., Chairman Leicester County Council [descended from the Lady Anne, sister of King Edward IV. (see Essex Volume Supplement, p. 676)], d. 8 Oct. 1908; and has issue 1f to 3f.

1f. Edward Hussey Packe of Prestwold Hall, J.P., D.L. (Prestwold Hall, Loughborough; Caythorpe Hall, Grantham), b. 6 Jan. 1878; m. 11 Dec. 1909, the Hon. Mary Sydney, da. of Edward Arthur (Colebrooke), 1st Baron Colebrooke [U.K.], C.V.O.

2f. Florence Marion Packe, m. 10 Aug. 1905, Capt. the Hon. Cuthbert James [2nd son of Walter Henry, 2nd Lord Northbourne [U.K.]] (Junior United Service; Garrick); and has issue 1g to 2g.

1g. Thomas James, b. 10 July 1906.

2g. Olivia Mary James, b. 11 Dec. 1909.

3f. Sybil Alice Packe.

4e. Lady Constance Wodehouse (Beechey Grange, Parkstone, Dorset).

2c. Hon. Edward Wodehouse, afterwards (R.L. 21 Sept. 1838) Thornton-Wodehouse, Vice-Adm. R.N., b. 5 June 1802; d. 17 Mar. 1874; m. 10 Nov. 1838, Diana, da. of Col. Thornton of Falconer's Hall, co. Yorks, d. 13 Mar. 1884; and had issue 1d to 3d.

1d. Albert Wodehouse, Col. R.A. (ret.) (United Service), b. 5 Feb. 1840; m. 1 July 1874, Elizabeth Katherine, da. of the Hon. George Edgcumbe.

2d. Cecilia Wodehouse, m. 24 July 1879, Baron Ferdinand von Liliencron [Baron Liliencron [H.R.E. 5 June 1673] Coll.] (Florence).

3d. Mary Diana Wodehouse (17 Montpelier Square, S.W.), m. 4 Ap. 1878, Charles Conway Thornton of the Diplo. Service, d. 17 May 1902; and has issue 1e.

1e. Charles Edward Conway Thornton, b. 25 Mar. 1879.

3c. Hon. Berkeley Wodehouse, C.M.G., Col. E. Norfolk Mil., H.B.M.'s Consul at Dunkirk, b. 14 May 1806; d. 13 Sept. 1877; m. 5 June 1837, Fanny, da. of Alexander Holmes of Curragh, co. Kildare, d. 2 Ap. 1871; and had issue 1d to 2d.

1d. Killegrew Reginald Berkeley Wodehouse, Col. late 1st Batt. Highland L.I. (Lexden House, Colchester; Wellington, &c.), b. 9 Sept. 1843; m. 22 Feb. 1881, Katharine Elizabeth, da. of James Marke Wood of Liverpool; and has issue 1e to 3e.

1e. Reginald Berkeley Wodehouse, b. 13 Ap. 1886.

2e. Philip Edward Berkeley Wodehouse, b. 20 Nov. 1887.

3e. Laura Mary Katherine Wodehouse.

2d. Charles Francis Berkeley Wodehouse, a Dist. Commr. of Cyprus, formerly Lieut. 77th Regt. (Papho, Cyprus; Llwynbedw, Boncat, R.S.O., South Wales), b. 1 Aug. 1855; m. 21 July 1881, Francie, da. of Arthur H. Sanders Davies of Pentre, co. Pemb.; and has issue 1e to 4e.

1e. Clarence John D'Everton Berkeley Wodehouse, Inspector Cyprus Mil. Police, Acting A.D.C. to High Commr. of Cyprus, and Lieut. 3rd (Reserve) Batt. Norfolk Regt. (Government House, Nicosia; Auxiliary Forces Club, &c.), b. 31 May 1882.

2e. Mary Jessie Gwyn Berkeley Wodehouse.

3e. Kitty Dagmar Berkeley Wodehouse.

4e. Armine Frances Berkeley Wodehouse.

4c. Rev. the Hon. Alfred Wodehouse, b. 10 June 1814; d. 6 Sept. 1848; m. 21 Ap. 1840, Emma Hamilla, da. of Reginald George Macdonald of Clanranald, M.P. [by his wife Lady Caroline, née Edgcumbe, descended from the Lady Anne, sister of King Edward IV. (see the Exeter Volume, p. 664)], d. 5 Ap. 1852; and had issue (with a da., Mrs. Wyndham, d.s.p.) 1d to 4d. [Nos. 79654 to 79674.

The Plantagenet Roll

1*d*. Hobart Wodehouse, *b*. 23 Ap. 1842.

2*d*. Henry Wodehouse, *b*. 2 Jan. 1849.

3*d*. Hamilla Caroline Wodehouse, *b. Jan*. 1841; d. 1879; m. 8 *Nov*. 1876, *Edward Taylor, H.B.M.'s Vice-Consul at Dunkirk*, d. (-); *and had issue* 1*e to* 2*e*.

1*e*. Laura Taylor, *m*. (—) Lawford of Shanghai.

2*e*. Mary Taylor, *m*. (—) Hornby.

4*d*. Ernestine Emma Wodehouse (*The Island, Derwentwater, Keswick*), *m*. 17 May 1866, John Marshall, *d*. 1894; and has issue (3 sons).

5*c. Hon. Laura Sophia Wodehouse*, b. 13 *Jan*. 1801; d. 17 *Feb*. 1869; m. 28 *June* 1825, *Raikes Currie of Bush Hall, co. Midx., and Minley Manor, co. Hants, M.P., J.P., D.L*., b. 15 *Ap*. 1801; d. 16 *Oct*. 1881; *and had issue* (*with* 2 *sons and* 2 *das. who* d.s.p.) 1*d to* 2*d*.

1*d*. *Bertram Wodehouse Currie of Minley Manor, J.P., High Sheriff for London* 1892, b. 25 *Nov*. 1827; d. 29 *Dec*. 1896; m. 30 *Oct*. 1860, *Caroline, da. of Sir William Lawrence Young, 4th Bt*. [*G.B*.], *M.P*., d. 16 *Ap*. 1902; *and had issue* 1*e*.

1*e*. Laurence Currie of Minley and Coombe Warren, J.P. (*Minley Manor, Farnboro'; Coombe Warren, Kingston-on-Thames;* 1 *Richmond Terrace, Whitehall S.W.*), *b*. 7 Nov. 1867; *m*. 23 Feb. 1895, Edith Sibyl Mary [descended from King Henry VII. (see Tudor Roll, p. 522)], da. of the Right Hon. George Henry Finch, P.C., M.P.; and has issue 1*f* to 3*f*.

1*f*. Bertram Francis George Currie, *b*. 18 June 1899.

2*f*. Edith Catherine Currie.

3*f*. Daphne Mary Currie.

2*d*. *Philip Henry Wodehouse* (*Currie*), 1*st Baron Currie* [*U.K*.], *so cr*. 25 *Jan*. 1899, *P.C., G.C.B., H.B.M.'s Ambassador at Rome*, 1898–1903, *&c.,* b. 13 *Oct*. 1834; d.s.p. 13 *May* 1906.

2*b. Hon. Philip Wodehouse, Vice-Adm. of the White*, b. 16 *July* 1773; d. 21 *Jan*. 1838; m. 7 *May* 1814, *Mary Hay* [*descended from the Lady Anne, sister of King Edward IV*.], *da. of Charles Cameron*, d. 1 *Oct*. 1854; *and had issue*.
See the Essex Volume, pp. 664-665, Nos. 57522/1-5.

3*b*. *Rev. the Hon. William Wodehouse, M.A.,* b. 4 *Aug*. 1782; d. 3 *Ap*. 1870; m. 11 *Feb*. 1807, *Mary, da. of Thomas Hussey of Galtrim, co. Meath* [*by his wife, Lady Mary, née Walpole, descended from the Lady Isabel Plantagenet* (see Essex Volume, p. 190)], d. 29 *Nov*. 1865; *and had issue* 1*c to* 3*c*.

1*c*. *George Wodehouse, Vice-Adm. R.N*., b. 8 *July* 1810; d. 15 *Feb*. 1900; m. 20 *July* 1848, *Eleanor Charlotte, da. of Andrew Mortimer Drummond* [*E. of Perth Coll*.] *by his wife, Lady Emily, née Percy* [*a descendant of King Henry VII*. (see Tudor Roll, p. 194)], d. 27 *Mar*. 1888; *and had issue* 1*d to* 2*d*.

1*d*. Sir Josceline Heneage Wodehouse, K.C.B., C.M.G., Lieut.-Gen. R.A., Comdg. N. Army India 1908, *formerly* Gov. and Com.-in-Chief of Bermuda, a Major-Gen. in the Egyptian Army and Gov. of Egyptian Frontier Provinces 1889–1893, &c., &c. (*Murree, Punjab*), *b*. 17 July 1852; *m*. 1st, 1 Oct. 1885, Constance, da. of Sir Charles D'Aguilar, K.C.B., *d.s.p*. 21 Aug. 1886; 2ndly, 15 May 1901, Mary Joyce, da. of Robert Sacheverell Wilmot Sitwell of Stainsby House, co. Derby; and has issue 1*e*.

1*e*. Armine George Wodehouse, *b*. 25 May 1904.

2*d*. Evelyn Georgiana Susan Wodehouse (10 *Palace Mansions, Addison Bridge, Kensington, W*.).

2*c*. *Arthur Wodehouse of Saltville, Toronto*, b. 17 *Jan*. 1813; d. *Feb*. 1893.

3*c*. *Rev. Algernon Wodehouse, M.A*., b. 13 *May* 1814; d. 2 *May* 1882; m. 26 *Nov*. 1844, *Lady Eleanor, da. of George* (*Ashburnham*), 3*rd Earl of Ashburnham* [*G.B*.], *K.G*., d. 6 *Mar*. 1895; *and had issue*.
See the Tudor Roll, p. 193, Nos. 21169–21176.

2*a. Rev. the Hon. Philip Wodehouse, M.A., Preb. of Norwich*, b. 1 *May* 1745; [Nos. 79675 to 79703.

of The Blood Royal

d. 14 Feb. 1811; m. 29 *July* 1775, *Apollonia, da. and co-h. of John Nourse of Woodeaton, co. Oxon.*, d. 21 *Mar.* 1817; *and had issue* 1b *to* 4b.

1b. Philip Wodehouse, Col. in the Army, b. 6 Aug. 1788; d. 15 Dec. 1846; m. 13 *June* 1832, *Lydia, da. of Joseph Lea*, d. 8 *May* 1892; *and had issue* 1c *to* 8c.

1c. Rev. Philip John Wodehouse, M.A. (8th Wrangler 1859, and Fellow Caius Coll.) (Camb.), Preb. of Exeter and Rector of Bratton Fleming (*Bratton Fleming Rectory, N. Devon*), b. 6 Oct. 1836; m. 1st, 20 Jan. 1876, Constance Helen, da. of Wade Browne of Monkton Farleigh, d.s.p. 23 Feb. 1877; 2ndly, 25 Sept. 1879, Marion Bryan, da. of the Rev. Gilbert J. Wallas of Shobrooke; and has issue 1d to 4d.

    1d. Philip George Wodehouse, Lieut. R.N., b. 26 Nov. 1883.
    2d. Charles Gilbert Wodehouse, b. 28 Dec. 1885.
    3d. Helen Marian Wodehouse.
    4d. Christine Lucy Wodehouse.

2c. *Charles Wodehouse, C.I.E., Col. I.S.C.*, b. 8 *May* 1838; d. 18 *Aug.* 1893; m. 3 *Dec.* 1862, *Jemima, da. of George Forbes*, d. 11 *Aug.* 1886; *and had issue* 1d *to* 3d.

    1d. Frederick William Wodehouse, Major Indian Army, now attached to Bombay Political Dept., has Chin-Lushai (1889–1890) and Delhi Durbar Medals (*The Residency, Kolhapur*), b. 7 Ap. 1867; m. 5 Ap. 1893, Mary Helen, da. of George Nugent Lambert, Sup. Engineer, Sind; and has issue 1e to 3e.

        1e. Constance Mary Wodehouse.
        2e. Kathleen Doris Letitia Wodehouse.
        3e. Sybil Margaret Wodehouse.

    2d. Ernest Charles Forbes Wodehouse, D.S.O., Major Worcestershire Regt., served in S. Africa 1900–1902, has Queen's Medal with 3 clasps and King's Medal with 2 clasps (*United Service*), b. 5 Aug. 1871; m. 18 Ap. 1906, Amy Violet, da. of Swinton Isaac of Boughton Park, co. Worc.

    3d. Amabel Lucy Wodehouse (42 *Courtfield Gardens, W.*), m. as 2nd wife, 13 Ap. 1898, Gen. John Augustus Fuller, C.I.E., R.E.

3c. Rev. Frederick Armine Wodehouse, B.A. (Camb.), Rector of Gotham and Vicar of Ratcliff-on-Soar (*Gotham Rectory, near Derby*), b. 1 July 1842; m. 7 Sept. 1880, Alice Elizabeth Juliana [descended from King Henry VII. (see Tudor Roll, p. 300)], da. of Rev. the Hon. Atherton Legh Powys [B. Lilford Coll.]; and has issue 1d to 4d.

    1d. Arthur Powys Wodehouse, Lieut. Indian Army, b. 2 June 1881.
    2d. Frederic Armine Wodehouse, b. 23 June 1884.
    3d. Norman Atherton Wodehouse, Lieut. R.N., b. 18 May 1887.
    4d. Mabel Evelyn Wodehouse.

4c. Henry Ernest Wodehouse, C.M.G., *formerly* Hong-Kong C.S. and a Member of Executive Council, and Pol. Magistrate there (1 *Royal Crescent, Cheltenham*), b. 14 July 1845; m. 3 Feb. 1877, Eleanor, da. of the Rev. J. Bathurst Deane, M.A.; and has issue 1d to 4d.

    1d. Philip Peveril John Wodehouse, Assist. Sup. of Police, Hong-Kong, b. 26 Sept. 1877.
    2d. Ernest Armine Wodehouse, Prof. Eng. Lit. Elphinstone College, Bombay, b. 11 May 1879.
    3d. Pelham Grenville Wodehouse, Author and Journalist, b. 15 Oct. 1881.
    4d. Richard Launcelot Deane Wodehouse, b. 30 May 1892.

5c. Albert Philip Wodehouse, Col. late Royal Inniskilling Fusiliers, b. 9 Nov. 1846; m. 1881, Amy, da. of Henry Villiers.

6c. Lydia Josephine Wodehouse.

7c. Lucy Apollonia Wodehouse, m. 18 June 1867, the Rev. Edward Whitmore Isaac (*Hanley Castle Vicarage, Worcester*); and has issue 1d to 4d.

[Nos. 79704 to 79727.

The Plantagenet Roll

1*d*. Edward Swinton Wodehouse Isaac, *b*. 1871.
2*d*. Gwendoline Lucy Isaac.
3*d*. Gertrude Harriet Isaac.
4*d*. Mary Charlotte Lydia Isaac.

8*c*. Harriet Elizabeth Wodehouse (*Burfield, Christchurch, New Zealand*), *m*. 25 July 1861, the Rev. Henry Bromley Cocks, Vicar of Sydenham, N.Z. [B. Somers Coll.], *d*. 1894 ; and has issue 1*d* to 10*d*.

1*d*. Reginald Wodehouse Cocks, *b*. 31 Aug. 1863 ; *m*. 1883, Mary Myra, da. of (—) Thompson of Alabama, U.S.A.

2*d*. Henry Somers Cocks, *b*. 16 *June* 1865 ; d. (? s.p.) 1897.

3*d*. Rev. Philip John Cocks, Vicar of Sydenham, N.Z. (*Sydenham Vicarage, Canterbury, N.Z.*), *b*. 31 Oct. 1866 ; *m*. 20 June 1895, Mary, da. of John Gebbie ; and has issue 1*e* to 5*e*.

1*e*. Henry Bromley Cocks, *b*. 15 Ap. 1896.
2*e*. John Reginald Cocks, *b*. 19 May 1898.
3*e*. Edgar Basil Cocks, *b*. 22 June 1899.
4*e*. Hubert Maurice Cocks, *b*. 6 Aug. 1901.
5*e*. Edith May Somers Cocks, *b*. 2 Dec. 1905.

4*d*. Frederick Armine Cocks (*Lytt Street, Spreydon, Christchurch*), *b*. 27 Jan. 1871 ; *m*. 1899, Mary Louisa, da. of Capt. Parsons of Rangoria, N.Z. ; and has issue 1*e* to 4*e*.

1*e*. Douglas Edgar West Cocks, *b*. 1899.
2*e*. Armine Christopher Somers Cocks, *b*. 1903.
3*e*. Charles John Somers Cocks, *b*. Ap. 1904.
4*e*. Patrick Somers Cocks, *b*. Sept. 1905.

5*d*. Charles Richard Cocks, *b*. 31 Dec. 1877.
6*d*. Arthur Eustace Cocks, *b*. 23 Dec. 1882.
7*d*. Frances Mercy Cocks, *m*. 1894, Walter Septimus Fisher, Official Assig. N.Z. (*Forbury Road, Cav., Dunedin, N.Z.*) ; and has issue 1*e* to 2*e*.

1*e*. Harriet Mercy Fisher.
2*e*. Margaret Agatha Fisher.

8*d*. Harriet Lydia Muriel Cocks.
9*d*. Katharine Agatha Cocks.
10*d*. Monica Cocks.

2*b*. Ven. Charles Nourse Wodehouse, *Archdeacon of Norwich*, b. 8 *Sept*. 1790 ; d. *Mar*. 1870 ; m. 19 *Dec*. 1821, Lady Dulcibella Jane, da. of William (Hay), 17*th Earl of Erroll* [S.], d. 10 *Jan*. 1885 ; *and had issue*.

See the Exeter Volume, pp. 682-684, Nos. 57387-57428.

3*b*. Letitia Wodehouse, d. 1864 ; m. 9 *June* 1804, George Boulton Mainwaring.

4*b*. Lucy Wodehouse, d. 21 *June* 1829 ; m. 26 *June* 1809, Edmund Wodehouse *of Sennow Lodge, M.P.* (see p. 409), d. 21 *Aug*. 1855 ; *and had issue* (*with 6 other sons and* 2 *das. who d.s.p.*) 1*c*.

1*c*. Sir Philip Edmond Wodehouse, *K.C.B., G.C.S.I., Governor of the Cape of Good Hope* 1861-1871, *&c., &c.*, b. 26 *Feb*. 1811 ; d. 25 *Oct*. 1887 ; m. 19 *Dec*. 1833, Katherine Mary, da. *of Francis James Templer, Treasurer of Ceylon*, d. 6 *Oct*. 1866 ; *and had issue* 1*d*.

1*d*. Right Hon. Edmond Robert Wodehouse, P.C., M.A. (Oxon.), Bar-at-Law, M.P. for Bath 1880-1906, &c. (56 *Chester Square, S.W.; Minley Grange, Farnborough*), *b*. 3 June 1835 ; *m*. 1 June 1876, Adela Harriett Sophia [descended from King Henry VII. (see Tudor Roll, p. 369)], da. of the Rev. Charles Walter Bagot [B. Bagot Coll.].

3*a*. Hon. Thomas Wodehouse *of Sennow, co. Norfolk, Bar.-at-Law*, b. Feb.

[Nos. 79728 to 79795.

# of The Blood Royal

1747; d. c. 1803; m. 12 Sept. 1782, Sarah, sister of John, 1st Baron Cawdor [G.B.], da. of Pryce Campbell of Stackpole Court, co. Pemb., d. (-); and had issue 1b to 4b.

1b. Edmond Wodehouse of Sennow, M.P. E. Norfolk, b. 26 June 1784; d. 21 Aug. 1855; m. 26 June 1809, Lucy, da. of the Rev. Philip Wodehouse, d. 21 June 1829; and had issue.
See p. 408, No. 79795.

2b. Rev. Thomas Wodehouse, Canon of Wells and Rector of Norton, Kent, b. 13 Oct. 1788; d. 22 Mar. 1840; m. 3 June 18—, Anne, da. of the Right Rev. Walker King, D.D., Lord Bishop of Rochester, d. 6 Mar. 1854; and had issue 1c to 5c.

1c. Francis Arthur Wodehouse, b. 18 June 1831; m. 1879, Frances (see below), da. of the Rev. Nathaniel Wodehouse, d.s.p. 30 Dec. 1891.

2c. Edmond Henry Wodehouse, C.B., M.A. (Oxon.), Bar.-at-Law and sometime a Commr. of Inland Revenue (Oxford and Cambridge), b. 17 Feb. 1837; m. 26 May 1864, Louisa Clara (see below), da. of the Rev. Nathaniel Wodehouse.

3c. Sarah Frances Wodehouse, m. 15 May 1850, William Spencer Dawson of Cobham, co. Kent.

4c. Anne Wodehouse, m. 13 Ap. 1852, the Rev. James Carleton King.

5c. Agnes Wodehouse, d. (-); m. 11 Feb. 1865, George Sandes Williams, Ceylon C.S.; and has issue 1d.

1d. John Wodehouse Williams.

3b. Rev. Nathaniel Wodehouse, Vicar of Dulverton, b. 2 Nov. 1802; d. 23 Oct. 1870; m. 27 Sept. 1829, Georgiana [descended from the Lady Anne, sister of King Edward IV.], da. of Rev. the Hon. William Capell, d. 1892; and had issue.
See the Exeter Volume, pp. 378-379, Nos. 26853-26874.

4b. Susan Wodehouse, d. 2 Nov. 1834; m. 13 June 1822, Thomas John Dashwood, Senior Merchant on the Bengal Establishment [Bt. of Kirtlington Coll.], d. 17 June 1836; and had issue 1c to 3c.

1c. Thomas Alexander Dashwood, J.P., B.A. (Oxon.), Bar.-at-Law, b. 22 Feb. 1826; d. 9 Jan. 1909; m. 3 Oct. 1866, Charlotte Eliza (Everton House, Shanklin, I.W.), da. of the Rev. Charles Knyvett; and had issue 1d to 6d.

1d. Thomas Henry Knyvett Dashwood, b. 3 Jan. 1876; m. 5 Ap. 1910, Florence Kathleen, da. of J. F. Hugh Smith, F.R.C.S.

2d. Mary Susan Dashwood, m. 19 Jan. 1892, Arthur Geoffry Robins, d. (-); and has issue 1e to 4e.

1e. Henry Daryll Geoffry Dashwood Robins, b. 1892.

2e. Arthur Prichard Townsend Robins, b. 1902.

3e. Audrey Maud Mary Robins.

4e. Stella Rose Robins.

3d. Maud Dashwood.

4d. Florence Dashwood.

5d. Rose Dashwood.

6d. Alice Katherine Dashwood.

2c. Ellen Catherine Dashwood }
3c. Louisa Blanch Dashwood } (Sonning, Reading). [Nos. 79796 to 79835.

248. Descendants of Sophia Wodehouse (Table XXIII.), d. Ap. 1738; m. 2ndly, as 2nd wife, 7 July 1730, Sir Charles Mordaunt, 6th Bt. [E. 1611], d. 11 Mar. 1778; and had issue 1a to 2a.

1a. Sir John Mordaunt, 7th Bt. [E.], M.P., LL.D, b. c. 1735; d. 18 Nov. 1806; m. 3 Jan. 1769, Elizabeth, da. and co-h. of Thomas Prowse of Axbridge, co. Somerset, d. 5 Oct. 1826; and had issue 1b to 8b.

The Plantagenet Roll

1b. Sir Charles Mordaunt, 8th Bt. [E.], M.P., b. c. 1771; d. 30 May 1823; m. 1807, Marianne, da. of William Holbech of Farnborough, co. Warwick, d. 1842; and had issue 1c to 2c.

1c. Sir John Mordaunt, 9th Bt. [E.], b. 24 Aug. 1808; d. 27 Sept. 1845; m. 7 Aug. 1834, Caroline Sophia'[descended from King Henry VII., da. of the Right Rev. George Murray, D.D., Lord Bishop of Rochester]; and had issue.

See the Tudor Roll, pp. 449-450, Nos. 31677-31702.

2c. Mary Mordaunt, d. 11 June 1851; m. as 1st wife, 14 Mar. 1841, the Right Hon. Sir Thomas Dyke Acland, 11th Bt. [E.], P.C., M.P., D.C.L., d. 29 May 1898; and had issue 1d to 4d.

1d. Sir (Charles) Thomas Dyke Acland, 12th Baronet [E.], J.P., D.L., M.A. (Oxon.), M.P. for E. Cornwall 1882-1885 and for N.E. Cornwall 1885-1892, Parl. Sec. to the Board of Trade and Church Estate Commr. 1886, &c. (*Killerton, Exeter ; Holnicote, Taunton*), b. 16 July 1842; m. 1 Nov. 1879, Gertrude, sister to William, 1st Lord Waleran [U.K.], P.C., da. of Sir John Walrond Walrond, 1st Bt. [U.K.].

2d. Right Hon. Arthur Herbert Dyke Acland, P.C., Hon. Fellow of Balliol Coll., Oxon., Vice-President of the Committee of Council on Education 1892-1895, M.P. for Rotheram 1885-1892, offered but declined a Peerage 1908, &c., &c. (*Dunkerry House, Felixstowe ;* 29 *St. James' Court, Buckingham Gate, S.W.*), b. 13 Oct. 1847; m. 14 June 1873, Alice Sophia, da. of the Rev. Francis Macaulay Cunningham, M.A., Rector of Brightwell; and has issue 1e to 2e.

1e. Francis Dyke Acland, M.P., Financial Sec. to War Dept., and a Member of the Army Council, &c. (*Colby Hall, Askrigg, Yorks ;* 118 *Grosvenor Road, S.W.*), b. 7 Mar. 1874; m. 31 Aug. 1905, Eleanor Margaret, da. of Charles James Cropper of Ellergreen, co. Westmorland [by his wife the Hon. Edith Emily, *née* Holland].

2e. Mabel Alice Acland.

3d. Mary Lydia Acland, m. 30 Oct. 1872, the Rev. Richard Hart Hart-Davis, *formerly* Vicar of All Saints, Dunsden (*The Ridgefield, Caversham, Reading*); and has issue 1e to 8e.

1e. Hugh Vaughan Hart-Davis (twin), b. 25 July 1883.

2e. Katharine Lucy Hart-Davis.

3e. Mary Hart-Davis.

4e. Dorothy Hart-Davis.

5e. Agnes Cecily Hart-Davis.

6e. Stella Frances Hart-Davis.

7e. Helen Verena Hart-Davis (twin).

8e. Sylvia Charity Hart-Davis.

4d. Agnes Henrietta Acland, m. 11 Aug. 1885, Frederick Henry Anson [descended from the Lady Anne, sister of King Edward IV. (see Exeter Volume, p. 91), and also through Mortimer-Percy] (72 *St. George's Square, S.W.*); and has issue 1e to 2e.

1e. Mary Acland Anson.

2e. Frances Gertrude Anson.

2b. Rev. John Mordaunt, Rector of Wickham, co. Bucks, d. 1806.

3b. Elizabeth Mordaunt.

4b. Sophia Mordaunt.

5b. Mary Mordaunt, d. 17 July 1821; m. 1802, John Erskine, Comptroller of Army Accounts [younger brother of James, 2nd Earl of Rosslyn [U.K.]], d. 10 Feb. 1817; and had issue (a da., Lady Acland, who d.s.p. 14 May 1892).

6b. Catherine Mordaunt, d. 7 May 1852; m. 26 Oct. 1811, the Rev. Francis Mills of Pillerton, M.A. (Oxon.), Rector of Barford, co. Warwick [younger brother of William Mills of Bisterne, M.P.], b. 29 June 1759; d. 23 Ap. 1851; and had issue.

See p. 146, Nos. 16540-16555.

7b. Charlotte Mordaunt, d. May 1848; m. 15 Ap. 1800, Richard Hippisley Tuckfield of Fulford, co. Devon.   [Nos. 79836 to 79893.

of The Blood Royal

8b. *Susan Mordaunt*, d.s.p. 5 Feb. 1830; m. *as 4th wife*, 30 Aug. 1814, *William (Eliot), 2nd Earl of St. Germans [U.K.]*, d. 19 Jan. 1845.

2a. *Rev. Charles Mordaunt, Rector of Massingham*, d. 22 Jan. 1820; m. 1774, *Charlotte, da. of Sir Philip Musgrave, 6th Bt. [E.]; and had issue.*

See p. 200, Nos. 29642-29651. [Nos. 79894 to 79903.

249. Descendants of ARMINE L'ESTRANGE of Hunstanton, co. Norfolk, da. and event. co-h. of Sir Nicholas L'ESTRANGE, otherwise LE STRANGE, 4th Bt. [E.], M.P., a co-h. to the Baronies of Hastings and Camois [E. 1383] (Table XXIII.), d. 29 May 1768; m. NICHOLAS STYLEMAN of Snettisham, co. Norfolk, d. 6 Jan. 1746; and had issue 1a to 2a.

    1a. *Nicholas Styleman of Hunstanton and Snettisham, D.L.*, d.s.p. 9 Jan. 1788.

    2a. *Rev. Armine Styleman, M.A., (Camb.), Rector of Ringstead*, d. 3 Ap. 1803; m. *Anne, da. of Capt. James Blakeway, R.N.; and had issue 1b to 4b.*

    1b. *Henry Styleman of Hunstanton, &c., High Sheriff co. Norfolk* 1804; d. 25 Mar. 1819; m. 2ndly, 5 Dec. 1809, *Emilia, da. of Benjamin Preedy of St. Albans*, d. 20 Feb. 1873; *and had issue 1c to 3c.*

    1c. *Henry L'Estrange Styleman, afterwards (R.L. 23 July 1839) Styleman-le Strange of Hunstanton, J.P., D.L., Capt. 1st W. Norfolk Militia*, b. 25 Jan 1815; d. 27 July 1862; m. 25 July 1839, *Jamesina Joyce Ellen, da. and event. co-h. of John Stewart of Belladrum, co. Inverness. M.P.* [*who* m. 2ndly, 7 Sept. 1863, *Charles Wynne Finch of Voelas and*], d. 6 July 1892; *and had issue (with a son and da. who d.s.p.) 1d to 4d.*

    1d. Hamon Styleman-le Strange, now (D.P. 1 May 1874) le Strange of Hunstanton, M.A., F.S.A., J.P., D.L., C.A., a Chairman of the Norfolk Quarter Sessions and High Sheriff for that co. 1880, *formerly* Sec. Diplo. Ser. (*Hunstanton Hall, Norfolk;* 1 *Eaton Place, S.W.*), b. 25 Nov. 1840; m. at Boston, 20 Dec. 1866, Emmeline, da. of William Austin of Boston, Mass., U.S.A.; and has issue 1e to 6e.

    1e. Roland le Strange, J.P., D.L., Lieut. P.W.O. Norfolk Art. (*Hunstanton Hall, Norfolk*), b. 5 Mar. 1869; m. 22 Oct. 1891, the Hon. Agneta Frances Delaval (see p. 422), da. of Delaval Loftus (Astley), 10th Baron Hastings [E.]; and has issue 1f to 2f.

    1f. Charles Alfred le Strange, for whom H.R.H. Alfred, Duke of Saxe-Coburg-Gotha (Duke of Edinburgh), was Sponsor, b. 9 Dec. 1892.

    2f. Bernard le Strange, b. 23 Aug. 1900.

    2e. Rev. Austin le Strange, M.A. (Oxon.), Rector of Great Ringstead (*Ringstead Rectory, King's Lynn*), b. 22 May 1874; m. 16 Ap. 1903, Katharine Ellen Grey, da. of Rev. the Hon. Hugh Wynne Lloyd-Mostyn [B. Mostyn Coll.]; and has issue 1f to 3f.

    1f. Hamon le Strange, b. 5 June 1904.
    2f. Viola le Strange, b. 30 Sept. 1905.
    3f. Dorothy le Strange, b. 1 Nov. 1907.

    3e. Eric le Strange (*Eaton, Sedgeford, King's Lynn*), b. 20 Jan. 1878; m. 17 Oct. 1906, Nita Florence, da. of Francis Frederick Gordon [M. of Huntly Coll.]; and has issue 1f.

    1f. Gordon le Strange, b. 4 Oct. 1907.

    4e. Emmeline le Strange, m. 22 Jan. 1898, Capt. Charles Harcourt Gam Wood, *late* 15th Hussars (*Caerberis Builth, S. Wales*); and has issue 1f to 3f.

    1f. Eric Harcourt Wood.
    2f. David Sam Wood.
    3f. Beris Harcourt Wood.
    5e. Maud le Strange, } twins.
    6e. Sybil le Strange, }

[Nos. 79904 to 79919.

The Plantagenet Roll

2d. Guy Styleman-le Strange, now (D.P. 1875) le Strange (*Athenæum*), b. 24 July 1854 ; *m.* 4 Aug. 1887, Wanda Irene, da. of William Cornwallis Cartwright Aynhoe, M.P., *d.s.p.* 3 Feb. 1907.

3d. Jamesina Styleman le Strange (*Hunstanton, Norfolk*), *m.* 19 July 1866, the Rev. Adolphus Waller, M.A. [younger son of Sir Thomas Wathen Waller, 2nd Bt. [U.K.] (see p. 536)], *d.* 16 July 1890 ; and has issue 1*e*.

1*e*. Rev. Wathen Henry Waller, M.A. (Camb.), Town Chaplain, St. Mary's, Mandalay, *formerly* R.N., has Egyptian (1882) Medal with Bronze Star (*Civil Lines, Mandalay, Burma*), *b.* 4 June 1867 ; *unm*.

4d. Ada Styleman-Le Strange, b. 17 Sept. 1848 ; d. 28 Sept. 1873 ; m. as 1st *wife*, 9 *June* 1870, *Edward Heneage Wynne Finch of Stokesley*, J.P. (*Stokesley, co. Yorks*); *and had issue* 1*e*.

1*e*. Heneage Wynne-Finch, B.A. (Oxon.), *b.* 30 Ap. 1871.

2c. Emilia L'Estrange Styleman, d. 5 Ap. 1901 ; m. 29 May 1834, *the Rev. Frederick Thomas William Coke Fitzroy, M.A.* [*B. Southampton Coll.*], *d.* 20 *Feb.* 1862 ; *and had issue*.

See the Clarence Volume, pp. 345–346, Nos. 11286–11289.

3c. Armine L'Estrange Styleman, b. 3 Oct. 1819 ; m. 28 *July* 1840, *Capt. William Charles James Campbell, 3rd Dragoon Guards, 3rd son of Col. William Campbell of Ensay Island, Harris, d. at Hastings, 18 Ap.* 1880 ; *and had issue* (*with a son d. young*) 1*d to* 3*d*.

1d. Rev. William Fraser Campbell, Rector of Kintbury, co. Berks, b. 14 Jan. 1843 ; d. 29 Jan. 1886 ; m. 9 Sept. 1869, Georgina Jane, *da. of Lionel Oliver of Heacham, co. Norfolk* ; *and had issue* (*with a da. d. young*) 1*e to* 5*e*.

1*e*. James Fraser Campbell (*Penticton, British Columbia*), *b.* 30 Nov. 1870 ; *m.* 23 Nov. 1909, Dora Whaites, da. of Arthur Brown of Norwich.

2*e*. William McLeod Campbell, Suffolk Regt., *b.* 30 May 1879.

3*e*. Donald Fraser Campbell, *b.* 21 Dec. 1881.

4*e*. Armine le Strange Campbell,
5*e*. Katharine Grant Campbell, } *unm*.

2d. Archibald Campbell (*The Limes, Shrewsbury*), *b.* 21 July 1853 ; *m.* 28 July 1904, Katharine, da. of Samuel Poultney Smith.

3d. Flora Campbell, *m.* 30 Ap. 1873, John Windsor Stuart, Col. Argyle and Bute Vol. Art. [M. of Bute Coll., and a descendant of the Lady Anne, sister of Kings Edward IV. and Richard III. (see the Exeter Volume, p. 295)] ; and has issue 1*e* to 3*e*.

1*e*. Henry Campbell Stuart (*West Glen, Kyles of Bute*), *b.* 2 Mar. 1874 ; *m.* 20 Ap. 1904, Eileen Barbara, da. of Major H. G. Fenton-Newall ; and has issue 1*f* to 3*f*.

1*f*. Mary Barbara Stuart, *b.* 13 Jan. 1905.

2*f*. Margaret Windsor Stuart, *b.* 15 Oct. 1908.

3*f*. Flora Emily Windsor Stuart, *b.* 26 Feb. 1910.

2*e*. John Dudley Stuart (*Pontcanna House, Cardiff*), *b.* 1 Sept. 1875 ; *m.* 30 Ap. 1902, Florence Emily, da. of Charles Hunter, Ch. Eng. Bute Docks, Cardiff.

3*e*. Elizabeth Ada Mary Stuart, *b.* 20 Oct. 1908, Francis Gerald Cradock-Hartopp [Bt. Coll.] (*Edensor, Bakewell*) ; and has issue 1*f*.

1*f*. Gwendolen Mary Cradock-Hartopp, *b.* 29 Dec. 1909.

2b. Catherine Styleman, b. c. 1759 ; d. 29 Ap. 1825 ; m. 1st, *the Rev. Edward Rogers North, Vicar of Harlow, co. Essex, and Rector of Ringstead, co. Norfolk,* d. (? s.p.) ; 2ndly, *as* 2*nd wife,* 4 *Aug.* 1808, *Sir Mordaunt Martin,* 4*th Bt.* [*E.*], d. (s.p. *by her*) 24 *Sept.* 1815.

3b. Anne Styleman, b. at Ringstead 20 Dec. 1760 ; d. 20 Oct. 1823 ; m. 1st, *as* 2*nd wife,* 16 *Mar.* 1789, *Tomkyns Dew of Lincoln's Inn Fields and of Portland*

[Nos 79920 to 79941.

412

of The Blood Royal

Place, London, and of Whitney Court, co. Hereford, Lord of the Manors of Clifford and Whitney and High Sheriff co. Hereford, b. 1720; bur. at Marylebone 6 Nov. 1799; 2ndly, 29 Mar. 1806, Lieut.-Col. Thomas Powell, 14th Regt., d. 20 Mar. 1856; and had issue 1c to 3c.

1c. Tomkyns Dew of Whitney Court, High Sheriff co. Hereford, b. 9 July 1791; d. 1 Feb. 1853; m. 29 Ap. 1813, Margaret Beatrice, da. of the Rev. Timothy Napleton, Rector of Powderham, d. 11 July 1877; and had issue (with 3 sons and 4 das. who d.s.p.) 1d to 7d.

1d. Tomkyns Dew of Whitney Court, J.P., D.L., High Sheriff co. Hereford 1868, Bar.-at-Law I.T., &c., b. 10 Sept. 1816; d. 26 Jan. 1891; m. 13 May 1879, Ada Isabella, da. of Capt. Edward Rudston Read, 9th Lancers (who m. 2ndly, 4 Feb. 1892, Charles Joseph Brown); and had issue 1e.

1e. Rosamond Clifford Dew, b. 11 Sept. 1887.

2d. Rev. Henry Dew, B.A. (Camb.), J.P., Rector of Whitney, b. 18 Mar. 1819; d. 16 Nov. 1901; m. 16 Sept. 1845, Mary Elizabeth, da. of Thomas Monkhouse of London, d. 30 Jan. 1900; and had issue 1e to 10e.

1e. Henry Monkhouse Dew (1 Wilbury Villas, Nelson Street, Hereford), b. 14 Jan. 1850; m. 1st, 3 Nov. 1881, Minnie Phœbe, widow of Arthur Stenning, da. of (—) Jackson of Whittlesea, co. Camb., d.s.p. 14 May 1899; 2ndly, 5 Feb. 1902, Lena Mary Meta, da. of Rev. T. J. Bewsher, Rector of Cley-next-the-Sea; s.p.

2e. Arthur Tomkyns Dew, formerly R.M. for Matang, Perak (Monkerton Manor, Pinhoe, Devon), b. 5 Mar. 1853; m. at the English Church, Taiping, Straits Settlements, 31 Dec. 1891, Lucy Elizabeth (see p. 417), da. of the Rev. Charles Amphlett of Four Ashes Hall, Bridgnorth, co. Salop; s.p.

3e. Rev. Edward Napleton Dew, M.A., B.D. (Oxon.), Vicar of St. Michael and All Angels, Gallywood (Gallywood Vicarage, Chelmsford), b. 30 Mar. 1859; m. 3 Jan. 1888, Caroline, da. of Lieut.-Gen. Edward William Boudier, Madras S.C.; and has issue 1f.

1f. Harry Edward le Strange Dew, b. 27 Ap. 1889.

4e. Walter Frederick Dew, Tea Planter (Ceylon), b. 3 Jan. 1863/4; m. 1st, 28 Feb. 1895, Ethel Grace, da. of the Rev. Charles Down, d. 31 May 1898; 2ndly, 2 Oct. 1907, Nancy, da. of the Rev. Edward Smith; and has issue 1f.

1f. Sylvia Grace Alice Temple Dew, b. 6 Nov. 1896.

5e. Emily Mary Dew, b. 2 Sept. 1846; unm.
6e. Jane Beatrice Dew, b. 30 Ap. 1848; unm.

7e. Armine Dew, b. 12 Sept. 1854; m. 30 June 1874, Col. George William Furlonge (see p. 417), late 21st Royal Scots (formerly North British) Fusiliers (Seaton, Devonshire); and has issue 1f to 2f.

1f. George Henry Stuart Furlonge, P. & O. Coy. Service, Lieut. R.N.R., served in China 1900 (Medal), b. 29 Mar. 1875.

2f. Charles le Strange Furlonge, C.E., Lieut. R.N.R., served throughout South African War (2 Medals and Clasps), b. 7 Oct. 1878.

8e. Helen Frances Dew, unm.
9e. Alice Horrocks Dew, unm.

10e. Louisa Margaret Dew, m. 1st, 28 Feb. 1889, Edward Ayton Safford of London, Solicitor; 2ndly, (—); s.p.

3d. Frederick Napleton Dew, Major 88th Connaught Rangers, served in Crimea 1855–1856 and Indian Mutiny 1857–1858, Medals and Clasps, J.P., D.L., co. Hereford, b. 29 Mar. 1836; d. Aug. 1908; m. 24 Ap. 1861, Henrietta Lucy, da. of the Rev. Charles David Brereton of Little Massingham; and had issue 1e to 7e.

1e. Armine Brereton Dew, Major I.S.C., Political Agent at Gilgit, Kashmir, served in Black Mountain Expedition 1891 (Medal with Clasp), b. 27 Sept. 1867; m. 15 Sept. 1900, Esmé Mary Dorothea [descended from the Lady Anne, sister of Edward IV. (see Exeter Volume, p. 221)], da. of Sir Adalbert Talbot; and has issue 1f.

1f. Armine Roderick Dew, b. 20 Mar. 1906.   [Nos. 79942 to 79958.

The Plantagenet Roll

2e. Rev. Roderick Dew, M.A. (Oxon.), Rector of Kilkhampton (*Kilkhampton Rectory, Cornwall*), b. 21 Oct. 1872; m. 26 Sept. 1905, Gladys Mary, da. of Col. Gerveys Richard Grylls; and has issue 1ƒ to 3ƒ.

1ƒ. Gerveys Roderick Dew, b. 20 Dec. 1909.
2ƒ. Mary Lucy Agnes Dew, b. 5 Oct. 1906.
3ƒ. Frances Evelyn Margaret Mary Dew, b. 2 Feb. 1908.

3e. Gertrude Frances Dew, b. at Futtyghur, N.W.P. (*28 Bramham Gardens, S.W.*), m. Arthur Clegg Stratten, d.s.p. 18 June 1907.

4e. Isabel Mary Dew, m. 6 Feb. 1890, John Cockburn (*The Abbey, North Berwick*); and has issue 1ƒ to 3ƒ.

1ƒ. Archibald Frederick Cockburn, b. 21 Nov. 1890.
2ƒ. Isabel Stella Cockburn, b. 15 Jan. 1892.
3ƒ. Laelia Armine Cockburn, b. 23 Mar. 1894.

5e. Annette Beatrice Dew, m. 5 Ap. 1899, Moncreiff Cockburn (*2 Ashburn Gardens, S.W.*); and has issue 1ƒ to 3ƒ.

1ƒ. Archibald Moncreiff Cockburn, b. 3 May 1900.
2ƒ. Frederick Armine Cockburn, b. 19 June 1902.
3ƒ. Elizabeth Lucy Mary Cockburn, b. 11 June 1908.

6e. Alice Henrietta Dew, m. 23 Jan. 1908, Col. Richard Prescott Decie (*Pontrilas Court, Hereford*); s.p.

7e. Margaret Louise Dew, m. 18 Nov. 1902, Capt. Philip James Stopford, R.N. [E. of Courtown Coll.]; s.p.

4d. *Elizabeth Sophia Dew*, b. 17 *Jan.* 1815; d. 8 *Oct.* 1898; m. 23 *Aug.* 1841, *Arthur Pryor of Hylands, co. Essex, J.P., D.L., and High Sheriff for that co.* 1866, b. 7 *Jan.* 1816; d. 25 *Sept.* 1904; *and had issue (with a da.* d.s.p.) le *to* 8e.

1e. Arthur Vickris Pryor of Hylands, co. Essex, J.P., D.L., B.A. (Oxon.) (*Egerton Lodge, Melton Mowbray; Carlton; Travellers', &c.*), b. 3 Aug. 1846; m. 14 Sept. 1886, Elizabeth Charlotte Louisa, Dow.-Countess of Wilton [U.K.], da. of William (Craven), 2nd Earl of Craven [U.K.]; s.p.

2e. Roderick Pryor (*Weston Lodge, Stevenage, Berks*), b. 1 Mar. 1854; m. 11 Sept. 1906, Caroline [descended from King Henry VII. (see Tudor Roll, p. 450)], da. of the Rev. Osbert Mordaunt [Bt. Coll.]; and has issue 1ƒ.

1ƒ. Peter Pryor, b. 25 Sept. 1907.

3e. Edmund Pryor, b. 4 *Oct.* 1850; d. *Feb.* 1888; m. 28 *Feb.* 1876, *Evelyn Horatia* (*Chagford, S.O.*), *da. of Rev. the Hon. Francis Sylvester Grimston* [*E. of Verulam Coll.*]; *and had issue (with a son, Guy Francis,* b. 5 *Nov.* 1876; d. *unm.* 28 *July* 1902) 1ƒ *to* 3ƒ.

1ƒ. John Arthur Pryor, b. 5 Nov. 1884; m. Blanche Marion, da. of Major Burrell; and has issue 1g.

1g. Blanche Evelyn Marion Pryor, b. 27 Feb. 1908.
2ƒ. Katharine Pryor, m. E. Scott James; and has issue 1g to 2g.
1g. Edward John James, b. 4 Oct. 1906.
2g. Angela Horatia Emma James, b. 28 Sept. 1902.
3ƒ. Elizabeth Pryor, unm.

4e. *Robert Pryor*, b. 17 *Mar.* 1852; d. 5 *July* 1905; m. 8 *Jan.* 1884, *Matilda, da. of Vincent Eyre; and had issue* 1ƒ.

1ƒ. Phyllis Olive Barbara Pryor, m. 25 Sept. 1909, Capt. Evelyn George Harcourt Powell, Grenadier Guards.

5e. Lucy Elizabeth Pryor, b. 3 *Mar.* 1845; d. 21 *Nov.* 1902; m. *July* 1867, *David Powell, Governor of the Bank of England* 1892-1895, b. 16 *Ap.* 1840; d. 2 *Sept.* 1897; *and had issue (with a son d. young)* 1ƒ *to* 4ƒ.

1ƒ. David Powell, M.A. (Camb.), a Director of the New River Coy. (*Overstrand, Grove Park Road, Chiswick, W.; Travellers'*), b. 13 June 1868.

[Nos. 79959 to 79984.]

# of The Blood Royal

2*f*. Albert Laurence Powell, Major 19th Hussars, *b*. 29 Nov. 1869; *m*. 10 Mar. 1897, Ella Eugenie Elizabeth, da. of Charles Augustus T. Breul; and has issue (with a da. *d*. young) 1*g* to 2*g*.

1*g*. John Augustus Laurence Powell, *b*. 24 Jan. 1898.

2*g*. Elizabeth Evelyn Powell, *b*. 25 Dec. 1906.

3*f*. Felix Edmund Powell, Chief Inspector of Cleansing Service, Egyptian Public Health Dept. (*Cairo*), b. 24 July 1873.

4*f*. Robert Montagu Powell, Capt. R.A., *b*. 19 May 1881; *m*. 18 Nov. 1905, Kathleen Mary Douglas, da. of Frederic de Pledge.

6*e*. Edith Louisa Pryor, *m*. 1881, Francis Richard Sutton [descended from the Lady Anne, sister of King Edward IV. (see the Exeter Volume, p. 160)] (*The Canons, Thetford, Norfolk*); and has issue 1*f* to 4*f*.

1*f*. Richard Coningsby Sutton, *b*. 12 *Mar*. 1882; d. 12 *Sept*. 1905; m. 9 *Mar*. 1904, *Frances Olive* (? *Katherine Helen*), *da. of Francis Foljambe Anderson of Lea, co. Lincoln; and had issue* 1*g to* 3*g*.

1*g*. Francis Richard Heywood Sutton, *b*. 10 Feb. 1905.

2*g*. Olinda Margaret Sutton } (twins), *b*. 4 Mar. 1906.
3*g*. Olivia Katherine Sutton }

2*f*. Francis Arthur Sutton, *b*. 15 Feb. 1884.

3*f*. Olinda Emily Sutton, *m*. July 1909, Arthur Campbell Watson, Lieut. 7th Hussars.

4*f*. Sylvia Katherine Sutton, *m*. Ap. 1909, John St. Vigor Fox.

7*e*. *Emily Pryor*, d. 1 *Feb*. 1884; m. 19 *June* 1872, *Walter Edward Grimston of Bures, co. Essex* [*E. of Verulam* [*U.K.*] *Coll., and a descendant of George, Duke of Clarence* (see the Clarence Volume, p. 157)] (*Earls Colne, Essex*); *and had issue* 1*f* to 4*f*.

1*f*. Susan Edith Grimston, *m*. 14 June 1899, Major Arthur Faulconer Poulton, *late* Suffolk Regt., Chief Constable of Berkshire (*Highgrove, Reading*).

2*f*. Cecilia Grimston, *m*. 11 June 1904, Capt. Forrester Colvin Watson, 7th Dragoon Guards and Adj. Essex. Yeo.

3*f*. Mary Noel Grimston, *m*. 11 Jan. 1905, Henry Hamilton Gepp, Lieut. Essex Yeo. (*Hill House, Hatfield Peverel, Essex*); and has issue 1*g*.

1*g*. Miriam Helen Gepp, *b*. 5 Feb. 1906.

4*f*. Eleanor Vera Grimston, *m*. 1908, Arthur Mervyn Toulmin.

8*e*. Katherine Pryor.

5*d*. *Louisa Dew*, b. 15 *Nov*. 1820; d. 23 *Nov*. 1909; m. 19 *June* 1849, *the Rev. William Latham Bevan, M.A., Vicar of Hay, Canon of St. David's and Archdeacon of Brecon* [*elder son of William Hibbs Bevan of Crickhowell, J.P., High Sheriff co. Brecon* 1841], b. 1 *May* 1821; d. 24 *Aug*. 1908; *and had issue* 1*e* to 6*e*.

1*e*. William Armine Bevan (11 *The Boltons, South Kensington*), *b*. 20 June 1855; *m*. 22 Aug. 1885, Amy, da. of the Rev. F. Wayet, *d.s.p* 16 Mar. 1909.

2*e*. Ven. Edward Latham Bevan, Vicar and Archdeacon of Brecon (*Brecon*), *b*. 1861; *unm*.

3*e*. Mary Louisa Bevan, *m*. 16 Nov. 1886, Henry Philip Dawson of Hartlington Hall, Capt. R.A. [eldest son of Capt. Henry Dawson by his wife, Harriet Emma, da. of Sir Philip Baingridge, K.C.B. [also a descendant of Edward III. (see the Mortimer-Percy Volume, Pt. II.)] (*Hartlington Hall, Skipton*); and has issue 1*f* to 2*f*.

1*f*. Henry Christopher Dawson, *b*. 12 Oct. 1889.

2*f*. Gwendoline Mary Dawson.

4*e*. Alice Catherine Bevan, *m*. 14 Aug. 1883, Capt. Thomas Llewellyn Morgan, R.H.A. [son of Col. Morgan of St. Helens, Swansea] (*The Poole, Hereford*); and has issue 1*f* to 2*f*.

1*f*. Jeffrey Morgan, *b*. 14 Ap. 1890.

2*f*. Sibell Morgan, *b*. 18 Dec. 1891.

[Nos. 79985 to 80010.

The Plantagenet Roll

5e. Frances Emily Bevan, m. 1 June 1897, the Rev. Lewis Davies, Vicar of Talgarth [son of J. M. Davies of Antaron, co. Cardigan, J.P., D.L.] (*Talgarth Vicarage, Brecon*).

6e. Ellen Bevan, *unm*.

6d. *Emily Dew*, b. 21 May 1825; d. 17 Dec. 1889; m. *at Whitney*, 16 Aug. 1849, *Andrew Amédée Miéville of London [of an old Swiss family, formerly of Yverdon]*, d. 23 Mar. 1873; *and had issue 1e to 5e.*

1e. Edward Amédée Miéville, b. 25 Sept. 1851; m. at Oswego, U.S.A., 22 May 1873, Helena Maude, da. of Charles C. Mattoon, d. 1902; and has issue 1f.

1f. Charles Amédée Miéville, b. in New York 8 July 1876; m. Maybelle Louise, da. of (—) Thomas; and has issue 1g.

1g. Olive Vivian Miéville, b. 16 June 1901.

2e. Sir Walter Frederick Miéville, K.C.M.G., F.R.G.S., late President of the Egyptian Maritime and Quarantine Board of Health (68 *Wilbury Road, Hove, Sussex*), b. 17 July 1855; m. 28 Mar. 1882, Theodora Johanna, da. of Henry Frederick Taylor of Alexandria; *s.p.*

3e. Charles Ernest Miéville, Hon. Sec. Professional Golfers' Association (1 *Freeland Road, Ealing Common*), b. 7 May 1858; m. 16 Nov. 1882, Alice Huleatt Garcia, da. of Major William John Bampfield; and has issue 1f to 4f.

1f. Ernest Frederick Miéville, b. 25 Feb. 1891.

2f. Eric Charles Miéville, b. 31 Jan. 1896.

3f. Alice Daisie Miéville.

4f. Gladys Miéville.

4e. Herbert Le Strange Miéville, served through Boer War with 1st City (Grahamstown) Vols., Medals and 2 Clasps (*Johannesburg*), b. 31 Mar. 1866; m. 6 Aug. 1902, Edith Ellen Goddard, da. of (—) Watson; *s.p.s.*

5e. Emily Frances Miéville, m. 28 July 1874, Edward Stone, F.S.A., Solicitor (3 *Lansdowne Place, Blackheath, S.E.*); and has issue 1f to 10f.

1f. Edward Stone, Lieut. 2nd Dragoon Guards, served in S. Africa with W. Australian Imperial Bushmen's Corps (Medal with 3 Clasps), b. 14 Mar. 1876.

2f. Arthur Stone, M.A. (Camb.), b. 27 June 1877.

3f. Reginald Guy Stone, Lieut. R.N., b. 9 Feb. 1880.

4f. Francis le Strange Stone, Solicitor, b. 14 June 1886.

5f. Walter Napleton Stone, b. 7 Dec. 1891.

6f. Edith Emily Stone, m. 1 Jan. 1908, Cyril Arthur Priday (23 *Langlands Road, Sidcup*); and has issue 1g.

1g. Joan Priday, b. 27 Sept. 1908.

7f. Dorothy Stone.

8f. Marjorie Armine Stone.

9f. Phyllis Louisa Stone, m. 14 Ap. 1910, William Henry Strickland Ball, Lieut. R.N.

10f. Eleanor Whitney Stone.

7d. *Lucy Beatrice Dew*, b. 8 Ap. 1829; d. 9 Mar. 1907; m. 10 Ap. 1855, *the Rev. Charles Amphlett (R.L. 19 Mar. 1855), formerly Dunne of Four Ashes Hall, Bridgnorth, co. Salop, Lord of the Manor of Earl's Croome, co. Worc., M.A. (Oxon.), &c. [2nd son of Thomas Dunne of Gatley Park, co. Hereford, J.P., D.L.]*, b. 25 Ap. 1818; d. 5 Mar. 1891; *and had issue (with a son and da. d. young) 1e to 4e.*

1e. Charles Grove Amphlett, D.S.O., Major (ret.) South Staffordshire Regt., served in S. Africa in command of 1st Batt. Mounted Inf. (*Four Ashes Hall, near Stourbridge*), b. 8 Mar. 1862; *unm*.

2e. Rev. George Le Strange Amphlett, Rector of Earl's Croome and Hill Croome (*Earl's Croome Rectory, Worcestershire*), b. 3 Sept. 1868; m. 6 Jan. 1904, Blanche Katherine Adine, da. of the Rev. Canon Henry William Coventry, J.P. [E. of Coventry Coll.]; and has issue 1f to 3f.

1f. Leila Blanche Amphlett, b. 19 Oct. 1905.

[Nos. 80011 to 80037.]

# of The Blood Royal

2f. Ann Elizabeth Amphlett, b. 29 Jan. 1907.
3f. Justina Alice Amphlett, b. 22 Sept. 1908.
3e. Lucy Elizabeth Amphlett, m. 31 Dec. 1891, Arthur Tomkyns Dew, R.M. (see p. 413); s.p.
4e. Mabel Amphlett, m. 19 Nov. 1895, Arthur Edward Lloyd Oswell, A.R.I.B.A. (*Coton Hill Cottage, Berwick Road, Shrewsbury*); s.p.

2c. Ann Dew, b. 10 Jan. 1790; d. *at Cheltenham* 18 Ap. 1873; m. *at Paris* c. 1820, *John McGachen, Capt. 72nd (Seaforth) Highlanders*, d. (-); *and had issue* (with 4 other sons) 1d.

1d. Rev. Nicolas Howard McGachen, B.A. (Oxon.), *formerly* (1881–1899) Vicar of Littlebourne (12 *Marine Parade, Dover*), b. (—); m. (—), da. of (—); and has issue (with 4 other children) 1e to 2e.

1e. William Nicolas McGachen, Comm. (ret.) R.N., b. (—); m. 16 May 1895, Lilian, da. of Lieut.-Col. Morton Parker Eden, R.A.; and has issue. See p. 273, No. 38485.

2e. Anne McGachen, m. the Rev. J. Bowen, *formerly* an Army Chaplain.

3c. *Armine Dew*, b. 14 Oct. 1794; d. *at Bath* 2 *Sept.* 1856; m. *as* 1st *wife, at the British Embassy, Paris*, 29 Dec. 1819, *Lieut.-Col. Charles John Furlonge, 21st Royal North British Fusiliers*, b. 9 Jan. 1793; d. 27 Dec. 1872; *and had issue* (*with* 3 *das. who* d. *unm.*) 1d *to* 3d.

1d. Charles George Henry Furlonge, J.P. and Coroner, *formerly* a Chief Clerk W.O. (*Lisle, Tasmania*), b. 17 June 1829; m. 10 Dec. 1868, Laura, da. of Capt. Herbert Ryves, R.N.; and has issue (with a son, Charles, b. Aug. 1869, d. (?) unm.) 1e to 9e.

1e. Charles George Herbert de Lisle Furlonge, b. 29 Dec. 1879; *unm.*
2e. George Le Strange Furlonge (*Hunstanton, Lisle Road Station, Tasmania*), b. 1 Ap. 1883; *unm.*
3e. Laura Eliza Armine Furlonge,
4e. Armine Furlonge,
5e. Marian Elizabeth Furlonge,
6e. Annie Styleman Furlonge, } *unm.*
7e. Elizabeth Adelaide Furlonge,
8e. Caroline Grace Ryves Furlonge,
9e. Isabel Arundel Rosaline Furlonge,

2d. George William Furlonge, Col. (ret.) *formerly* 21st Royal Scots Fusiliers, served in the Crimea, has Medal and Clasps (*Lynwood, Seaton, Devonshire*), b. 31 July 1834; m. 30 June 1874, Armine, da. of the Rev. Henry Dew of Whitney; and has issue. See p. 413, Nos. 79952–79953.

3d. *Caroline Warner Furlonge*, m. 3 July 1851, Nelson Girdlestone of the Admiralty [great-nephew of Admiral Lord Nelson] (24 *Church Road, St. Leonards-on-Sea*); and has issue (with 2 sons and a da. d.s.p.) 1e to 8e.

1e. *Nelson Styleman Girdlestone, late* R.N. (*Port Elizabeth, Cape Colony*), b. 5 May 1852; m. 1876, Maria, da. of John Thornhill, d. 1909; s.p.

2e. *Charles Henry Girdlestone*, b. 13 *June* 1857; d. 1884; m. 18—, Alice (7 *Cora Terrace, Grahamstown, Cape Colony*), da. *of Benjamin Roberts of Grahamstown; and had issue* 1f *to* 2f.

1f. L'Estrange Girdlestone.
2f. Hugh Bertie Girdlestone.

3e. Francis Crawford Girdlestone (*Port Elizabeth, Cape Colony*), twin, b. 15 May 1861; m. 1882, Norah, da. of Colonel Richard Athol Nesbitt, C.B.; and has issue 1f to 4f.

1f. Cedric Girdlestone, b. 1897.
2f. Hilary Girdlestone, b. 1898.
3f. Ronald Girdlestone, b. 1904.
4f. Violet Girdlestone.

[Nos. 80038 to 80067.

The Plantagenet Roll

4e. Armine Horatia Josephine Girdlestone (*Grahamstown, Cape Colony*), b. 30 Oct. 1853; m. Feb. 1876, Edwin Atherstone of Grahamstown, S. Africa, M.D., d. (-); and has issue (with 2 sons d.s.p.) 1f to 2f.
    1f. Roderic Atherstone.
    2f. Alice Armine Atherstone.

5e. Marian Adelaide Frances Girdlestone, b. 4 Aug. 1855; m. Herbert Rees, S. African Civil Ser., Clerk to the Mines Office (*Barkly West, Cape Colony*); s.p.

6e. Grace Geraldine Girdlestone, b. 4 Mar. 1860; m. William (? A. H.) Holland (*Upper Bell Street, Grahamstown, Cape Colony*); and has issue 1f to 4f.
    1f. Frederic Holland.
    2f. Lionel Holland.
    3f. Doris Holland.
    4f. Cecile Holland.

7e. Florence Nelson Girdlestone, m. 6 Feb. 1890, Edward John Bishop Gardner, Attorney-at-Law (*Barkly West, Cape Colony*); and has issue 1f to 4f.
    1f. Reginald (Rex) Llewellyn Gardner, b. 5 Oct. 1891.
    2f. Nelson Percy Edward Gardner, b. 2 Feb. 1895.
    3f. Dorothy Florence Gardner.
    4f. Grace Maud Gardner.

8e. Lilian Rose Madelaine Girdlestone, b. 28 Oct. 1868; m. Llewellyn Powys Jones, *formerly* Resident Magistrate at Buluwayo (*Fife Street, Buluwayo, Rhodesia*); and has issue 1f.
    1f. Lionel Powys Jones, b. 1894.

4b. Lucy Styleman, b. 1 July 1766; d. (-); m. *William Herring of St. Faith's House, Norwich*, J.P. [elder son of the Rev. J. Herring, D.D., Dean of St. Asaph, and great-nephew of Thomas Herring, Archbishop of Canterbury 1747-1757], d. 1827; and had issue (with a da., Lucy, d. unm.) 1e to 2e.

1e. William Herring of St. Faith's House, J.P., b. 1798; d. 1853; m. *Maria Elizabeth*, sister of Sir Henry Robinson, C.B., J.P., D.L., da. of George Robinson of Knapton House, co. Norfolk, J.P., d. 29 Feb. 1896; *and had issue* (with a son and da. d. young) 1f to 4f.

    1f. William Herring, J.P., Lieut.-Col. *late* 27th Inniskillings (*Narborough House, Norfolk*), b. 20 Mar. 1839; m. Nov. 1876, Jessie, da. of Col. William Welsby, J.P., *formerly* 3rd Batt. Liverpool Regt.; and has issue (with 2 other sons who d. unm.) 1g to 3g.
        1g. William Henry Armine Herring, B.A. (Camb.), Lieut. R.F.A., b. Feb. 1882; d. unm. 10 Sept. 1909.
        2g. Margaret Styleman Herring.
        3g. Elsie le Strange Herring.

    2f. *Maria Elizabeth Herring*, b. c. 1834; d. 14 Jan. 1871; m. 1852, Capt. Joseph Edwin Day of Swardestone, co. Norfolk, West Norfolk Mil. [son and h. of James Day of Horsford, co. Norfolk], b. 16 July 1830; d. 16 Sept. 1864; *and had issue* (with a son and da. d. unm.) 1g to 2g.
        1g. James L'Estrange Day, b. 20 Aug. 1855; unm.
        2g. Augusta Maud Mary Day (*Tanglewood, Brownshill, Glos.*), unm.

    3f. Frances Henrietta Herring (*31 Cambridge Road, Southend-on-Sea*), m. 10 Jan. 1861, the Rev. George Metcalfe, Rector of Christ Church, Upwell, d. 10 Oct. 1888; 2ndly, 23 Ap. 1898, John Major, d. 1910; and has issue 1g to 6g.

        1g. Herbert Charles Metcalfe, Capt. 2nd Batt. Northants Regt., Chief Constable of Somerset (*Rowford Lodge, Cheddon, Fitzpaine, Taunton*), b. 9 May 1864; m. 3 Jan. 1899, Dorothea Maud, da. of Capt. Brodnex Knight, Queen's Bays [and grand-da. of Edward Knight of Chawton House, co. Hants, by his 1st wife, Mary Dorothea, da. of the Right Hon. Sir Edward Knatchbull, 9th Bt. [E.], P.C.]; and has issue 1h to 3h.   [Nos. 80068 to 80090.

# of The Blood Royal

1*h*. Christopher Le Strange Metcalfe, *b*. 23 May 1907.
2*h*. Violet Beatrice Armine Metcalfe.
3*h*. Daphne Geraldine Dorothea Metcalfe.

2*g*. Rev. Armine George Metcalfe, B.A. (Camb.), Rector of Norbury (*Norbury Rectory, Ashbourne, Derbyshire*), *b*. 2 Aug. 1868; *m*. 23 Jan. 1901, Mary Bernina, da. of Frederick Charles Millar, Q.C., Bencher of the Inner Temple; and has issue 1*h* to 2*h*.

1*h*. Armine Ernest George Metcalfe, *b*. 7 Oct. 1901.
2*h*. Harold Guy Metcalfe, *b*. 28 Sept. 1905.

3*g*. Harold William Metcalfe, Partner, Messrs Osborne & Chappel, Mining and Consulting Engineers (*Ipoh, Perak, Federated Malay States*), *b*. 11 Aug. 1876; *m*. 30 Sept. 1908, Edith, da. of J. Cresswell, M.D.; and has issue 1*h*.

1*h*. Nigel William Metcalfe, *b*. 25 Sept. 1909.

4*g*. Edith Augusta Metcalfe, *m*. 12 Ap. 1882, the Rev. Henry Teasdale Hutchinson, Vicar of Sancton (*Sancton Vicarage, R.S.O., York*); and has issue 1*h* to 3*h*.

1*h*. Charles Hilton Hutchinson, *b*. 28 Aug. 1885.
2*h*. Henrietta Styleman Hutchinson.
3*h*. Beatrice Lilian Mary Hutchinson.

5*g*. Anna Georgina Metcalfe, } *unm*.
6*g*. Katherine Alice Mary Metcalfe, }

4*f*. Lucy Styleman Herring (*Stanhoe, Bitterne Park, Southampton*), *m*. as 2nd wife, Major-Gen. Henry Vincent Mathias, B.S.C. (see p. 420), *d*. 3 Feb. 1901; and has had issue (2 children *d*. in infancy in India).

2*e*. Rev. Armine Herring, Patron and Rector of Thorpe Episcopi, Norwich, *b*. 28 Ap. 1801; *d*. 21 Jan. 1867; *m*. June 1830, Mary Elizabeth, da. of George Robinson of *Knapton House, co. Norfolk*, *d*. 17 Dec. 1850; *and had issue (with a son, the Rev. Armine Styleman Herring, Vicar of St. Paul's, Clerkenwell, d.s.p. 5 June 1896) 1f to 2f*.

1*f*. Henry Le Strange Herring, *late* Capt. 87th Royal Irish Rifles, served in the Crimea with 30th Regt. (*The Old Rectory, Thorpe, Norwich*), *b*. 5 Dec. 1832; *m*. 1st, 21 June 1865, Mary Elizabeth, da. of John Bell of Toronto, Q.C., *d*. 21 Jan. 1871; 2ndly, 27 Ap. 1881, Emma, da. of Col. William Welsby of Southport, J.P.; and has issue 1*g* to 5*g*.

1*g*.[1] Armine Bell Le Strange Herring (*Canada*), *b*. 11 Aug. 1866; *m*. in Ontario 1903, Maud Olive, da. of (—) Farrol; *s.p*

2*g*.[1] Styleman Percy Bell Le Strange Herring, Solicitor (*Croft House, Belaugher, Wroxham, Norfolk*), *b*. 28 Aug. 1868; *m*. 24 May 1897, Frederica Sydney, da. of Capt. Herbert, R.N.; *s.p*.

3*g*.[2] Henry William Herring, Lieut. R.E., *b*. 29 July 1882; *unm*.

4*g*.[1] Alice Henrietta Le Strange Herring, *unm*.

5*g*.[2] Coela Elizabeth Le Strange Herring, *m*. 18 Sept. 1907, Capt. Arthur Howarth Pryce Harrison, 33rd Punjabis, Indian Army; and has issue 1*h*.

1*h*. Hugh Devereux Harrison, *b*. 24 June 1908.

2*f*. Alice Elizabeth Herring, *m*. 4 June 1872, Capt. Charles Sumner Pinwill, 27th Inniskillings Regt., *d*. 30 Aug. 1889; and has issue 1*g*.

1*g*. Alice Stackhouse Pinwill, *m*. 4 Aug. 1897, the Rev. Raymond Williams, M.A. (Oxon.), Vicar of Fisherton-Delamere (*Fisherton-Delamere Vicarage, Wylye, S.O., Wilts*).

3*e*. Henrietta Herring, *d*. Oct. 1832; *m*. as 1st *wife*, 1825, *Capt. George Mathias, 79th Highlanders, afterwards in Holy Orders and one of the Chaplains to Queen Victoria, d. 10 Mar. 1884; and had issue (with das. who d.s.p.) 1f to 2f*.

1*f*. Henry Vincent Mathias, Major-Gen. B.S.C., previously 5th Bengal N.I.,

[Nos. 80091 to 80114.

The Plantagenet Roll

b. 20 Nov. 1830; d. 3 Feb. 1901; m. 1st at Dinapore, India, 8 Mar. 1854, Eleanor Matilda, da. of Capt. Edward Mathias, 44th Regt., d. 19 June 1867; 2ndly, 22 June 1869, Lucy Styleman, da. of William Herring of St. Faith's House, J.P. (see p. 419); and had issue (with 4 sons and a da. who d. young or s.p.) 1g to 5g.

1g. Leonard John Mathias, Lieut.-Col. Indian S.C., b. 26 Nov. 1860; m. at Calcutta, 29 Jan. 1890, Sarah, da. of J. Swinhoe; and has issue 1h to 3h.

1h. Leonard William Henry Mathias, b. 31 Oct. 1890.
2h. George Edwin Mathias, b. 29 Ap. 1895.
3h. Pearl Glory Mathias.

2g. Hubert Mathias, Duke of Cornwall's L.I., served in Boer War, b. 1863.

3g. Eleanor Marion Mathias, m. 4 Oct. 1878, George Waddington, Bombay C.I.; and has issue 1h.

1h. George O'Neill Waddington, b. 17 Oct. 1879.

4g. Susan Constance Mathias, m. Dec. 1876, Robert Logan, Bengal C.S.; and has issue 1h to 3h.

1h. Robert Hector Logan, b. 1877.
2h. Guy L'Estrange Logan, b. 1882.
3h. Constance Ruby Logan.

5g. Lilla Maie Mathias, m. Nov. 1885, Col. Robert Drury, R.A.M.C.; and has had issue (two das. d. young).

2f. Rev. George Henry Duncan Mathias, Fellow of King's Coll., Camb., b. 5 Oct. 1832; d. 7 June 1869; m. 21 Ap. 1857, Fanny, da. of William Brown Lockwood of Bury St. Edmunds, d. (–); and had issue 1g to 8g.

1g. Duncan L'Estrange Mathias, in Coutts' Bank (440 Strand), b. 31 Mar. 1860; unm.

2g. George Mathias (South America), b. 26 June 1864; m. 25 May 1890, Caroline, da. of (—) Evans; and has issue (with a son d. young) 1h to 2h.

1h. George Harold Duncan Mathias, b. 15 Jan. 1901.
2h. Geraldine Mathias, b. 28 Mar. 1903.

3g. Marian Ella Mathias, unm.

4g. Ida Mathias, m. 23 Ap. 1879, Gustav Lahusen of Bremen, Merchant (Breitenweg 8, Bremen); and has issue 1h to 7h.

1h. Christian Heinrich Lahusen, 13th Dragoons, German Army, b. in Buenos Ayres 31 May 1881; m. 16 Ap. 1907, Ida, da. of Oscar Caro; and has issue 1i to 2i.

1i. Johann Gustav Leberecht Lahusen, b. in Metz 18 Ap. 1908.
2i. Ida Leonore Lahusen, b. in Bremen 16 Jan. 1907.

2h. Friedrich George Henry Duncan Lahusen, b. in Bremen 15 Aug. 1888.
3h. Diedrich Henry Fritz Gerald Lahusen, b. in Uruguay 6 Mar. 1894; unm.
4h. Violet Fanny Anna Lahusen, m. 23 Jan. 1903, Friedrich Wilhelm Vincenz Meyer, now Meyer-Lahusen, Merchant (Bremen); and has issue 1i to 2i.

1i. Hans Gustav Reinhold Meyer-Lahusen, b. in Bremen 12 Feb. 1908.
2i. Ida Marie Helene Meyer-Lahusen.

5h. Marie Lahusen, m. 22 June 1906, Reinhold Kulenkampff-Pauli.
6h. Charlotte Lucy Anne Lahusen, m. 22 June 1906, Reginald Calvert Booth (Estancia San Juan, Conchillas, Uruguay); and has issue 1i.

1i. Violet Ida Maria Booth, b. 7 Feb. 1908.

7h. Armine Therese Margaret Lahusen, unm.

5g. Lucy Angela Mathias, m. 21 May 1901, Francis Thackeray Green, of the Bank of England (21 Putney Common South, S.W.).

6g. Amy Mathias, m. 27 Ap. 1897, Hugh Henry Mathias [son of Archdeacon Mathias of Christchurch, New Zealand]; and has issue (with a da. d. young) 1h to 2h.

1h. Lionel Armine Mathias, b. 23 Jan. 1907.
2h. Judith Amy Duncan Mathias.   [Nos. 80115 to 80148.

of The Blood Royal

7g. Geraldine Mathias, m. 21 Nov. 1897, Eduard Seemann; and has issue 1h to 5h.

1h. Eduard Duncan Christian Franz Seeman, b. June 1909.
2h. Julia Angela H. A. Seemann, b. 8 Jan. 1899.
3h. Mary A. Ida Seemann, b. 3 May 1900.
4h. Margaret Olga Gladys Seemann, b. 21 July 1901.
5h. Inez Geraldine Constance Seemann, b. 2 Ap. 1903.

8g. Armine Mathias, m. 5 Oct. 1887, Johann Carl Lahusen of Bremen, Merchant (*Delmenhorst, Germany*); and has issue (with a son, Carl Wilhelm, d. young) 1h to 8h.

1h. (Christian Friedrich Georg) Carl Lahusen, b. Delmenhorst 17 July 1888.
2h. Diedrich (Duncan) Lahusen, b. at Delmenhorst 1 Sept. 1889.
3h. (Johann Heinrich) Gustav Lahusen, b. in Bremen 5 Dec. 1890.
4h. Johannes (Christian) Lahusen, b. in Bremen 21 Feb. 1892.
5h. Heinrich (Ludwig) Lahusen, b. at Delmenhorst 14 Sept. 1894.
6h. Friedrich (Johannes) Lahusen, b. at Delmenhorst 2 June 1900.
7h. (Fanny Marie) Armine Lahusen, b. at Delmenhorst 26 Nov. 1898.
8h. Anna Agnes Clara Lahusen, b. at Delmenhorst 11 Mar. 1905.

[Nos. 80149 to 80163.]

250. Descendants of LUCY L'ESTRANGE, otherwise LE STRANGE, da. and event. co-h. of Sir Nicholas L'Estrange, otherwise Le Strange, 4th Bt. [E.], M.P., co-h. to the Baronies of Hastings (1290) and Camoys (1383) [E.] (Table XXIII.), *bapt.* 23 Jan. 1699; *d.* 25 July 1739; *m.* as 1st wife, 1721, Sir JACOB ASTLEY, 3rd Bt. [E.] (see p. 428), *b.* 3 Jan. 1692; *d.* 5 Jan. 1760; and had issue 1a to 3a.

1a. *Sir Edward Astley, 4th Bt. [E.], M.P.,* bapt. 26 *Dec.* 1729; d. 27 *Mar.* 1802; m. 1st, 1751, *Rhoda, da. of Francis Blake Delaval of Seaton Delaval, co. Northbd.,* d. *Oct.* 1757; *2ndly, 24th Feb.* 1759, *Anne, da. of Christopher Milles of Nackington, co. Kent,* d. 11 *July* 1792; *3rdly, Elizabeth, da. of* (———) *Bullen,* d.s.p.m. 1810; *and had issue (with apparently a da. or das. by 3rd wife)* 1b *to* 2b.

1b. *Sir Jacob Henry Astley, 5th Bt. [E.], M.P.,* b. 12 *Sept.* 1756; d. 28 *Ap.* 1817; m. 14 *Jan.* 1789, *Hester, da. and co-h. of Samuel Browne of King's Lynn,* d. 13 *Jan.* 1855; *and had issue* 1c *to* 5c.

1c. *Jacob (Astley), 16th Baron Hastings [E.* 1290], *having the abeyance of that Barony terminated in his favour* 18 *May* 1841, b. 13 *Nov.* 1797; d. 27 *Dec.* 1859; m. 22 *Mar.* 1819, *Georgiana Carolina, da. of Sir Henry Watkin Dashwood, 3rd Bt. [E.],* d. 28 *June* 1835; *and had issue* 1d *to* 2d.

1d. *Jacob Henry Delaval (Astley), 17th Baron Hastings and 7th Bt. [E.],* b. 21 *May* 1822; d.s.p. 8 *Mar.* 1871.

2d. *Delaval Loftus (Astley), 18th Baron Hastings and 8th Bt. [E.], Rector of East Barsham,* b. 24 *Mar.* 1825; d. 28 *Sept.* 1872; m. 8 *Aug.* 1848, *the Hon. Frances Diana [descended from the Lady Anne, sister of King Edward IV.* (see Exeter Volume, p. 163)], *da. of Charles (Manners-Sutton), 1st Viscount Canterbury [U.K.], G.C.B.; and had issue* 1e *to* 3e.

1e. *Bernard Edward Delaval (Astley), 19th Baron Hastings, &c. [E.],* b. 9 *Sept.* 1855; d. unm. 22 *Dec.* 1875.

2e. *George Manners (Astley), 20th Baron Hastings and 10th Bt. [E.],* b. 4 *Ap.* 1857; d. 18 *Sept.* 1904; m. 17 *Ap.* 1880, *the Hon. Elizabeth Evelyn (Melton Constable, Norfolk; Delaval, Newcastle-on-Tyne; 9 Seymour Street, Portman Square, W.), da. of Charles (Harbord), 5th Baron Suffield [E.]; and had issue* 1f *to* 5f.

The Plantagenet Roll

1*f*. Albert Edward Delaval (Astley), 21st Baron Hastings and 11th Bt. [E.] (*Melton Constable, Norfolk ; Seaton Delaval, Newcastle-on-Tyne*), *b.* 24 Nov. 1882 (King Edward sponsor), *m.* 11 Feb. 1907, Marguerite Helen, da. of Lord Henry Gilbert Ralph Nevil [M. of Abergavenny Coll.]; and has issue 1*g*.

1*g*. Hon. Helen Elizabeth Delaval Astley, *b.* 12 Nov. 1907.

2*f*. Hon. Jacob John Astley, Lieut. 16th Lancers, *b.* 5 Mar. 1884.
3*f*. Hon. Charles Melton Astley, *b.* 5 May 1885.
4*f*. Hon. Alexandra Rhoda Astley (Queen Alexandra sponsor), *b.* 28 Sept. 1886.
5*f*. Hon. Hester Astley, *b.* 17 May 1899.

3*e*. Hon. Agneta Frances Delaval Astley, *m.* 22 Oct. 1891, Roland le Strange, J.P., D.L. (*Hunstanton Hall, Norfolk*); and has issue.
See p. 411, Nos. 79906-79907.

2*c*. Francis L'Estrange Astley, *Lieut.-Col. in the Army*, b. 27 Feb. 1801; d. 9 *Ap.* 1866; m. 1*st*, 28 *July* 1836, *Charlotte, da. of Nathaniel Micklethwaite of Taverham, co. Norfolk*, d. 29 *July* 1848; 2*ndly*, 7 *Sept.* 1854, *Rosalind Alicia* [*descended from King Henry VII.* (see Tudor Roll, p. 455)], *da. of Sir Robert Frankland Russell, 7th Bt.* [*É.*], d. 27 *Aug.* 1900; *and had issue* 1*d* to 6*d*.

1*d*. Francis Nathaniel Astley, *Capt. Carabineers*, b. 26 *May* 1837; d. 1868; m. 25 Mar. 1863, *Jane, da. of W.H. Binney; and had issue* 1*e* to 3*e*.

1*e*. Francis Jacob L'Estrange Astley, *b.* 17 Ap. 1866.
2*e*. Edward Henry Nathaniel Astley, *b.* 25 Nov. 1868.
3*e*. Charlotte Mabel Astley.

2*d*. Frederic Bernard Astley, b. 18 *Aug.* 1843; d. 19 *Aug.* 1876; m. 4 *Oct.* 1866, *Emma Augusta, da of Charles Schreiber of Roundway Park, Suffolk* [*who* m. 2*ndly*, 25 *Jan.* 1879, *Major Ludovic Montefiore Carmichael and*] d. 1883; *and had issue* 1*e* to 4*e*.

1*e*. Delaval Graham L'Estrange Astley, *formerly* Major N. Somerset Yeo. Cav. (*Plumstead Hall, Norwich*), *b.* 7 Dec. 1868; *m.* 1 July 1897, Kate, da. of J. K. Clark of Ghoolendaadi, N.S.W., and Beaumont, Bath; and has issue 1*f* to 2*f*.

1*f*. Joan Doreen Astley, *b.* 19 Jan. 1901.
2*f*. Betty L'Estrange Astley, *b.* 8 Oct. 1902.

2*e*. Bernard Armine Frederick Astley, *b.* 4 Aug. 1873.
3*e*. Lilian Augusta Muriel Astley.

4*e*. Blanche Rhoda Delaval Astley, *m.* 2 Dec. 1897, Thomas John Green (*Watford*).

3*d*. Bertram Frankland Astley, *afterwards* (R.L. 1901) *Frankland-Russell-Astley* of *Chequers Court, co. Bucks*, J.P., D.L., b. 27 Feb. 1857; d. 11 Feb. 1904; m. 30 *Ap.* 1887, *Lady Florence* [*descended from King Henry VII.* (see Tudor Roll, p. 365)] (21 *Eaton Place, S.W.*), *da. of George* (*Conyngham*), *3rd Marquis Conyngham* [*I.*] [*who* m. 2*ndly*, 17 *June* 1905, *Capt. the Hon. Claud Heathcote-Drummond-Willoughby*]; *and had issue* 1*e* to 2*e*.

1*e*. Henry Jacob Delaval Astley of Chequers Court (*Chequers Court, Bucks*), *b.* 3 Mar. 1888; *m.*
2*e*. Olive Joan Astley.

4*d*. Rev. Hubert Delaval Astley, M.A. (Oxon.), *formerly* Rector of Ellesborough (*Benham Valence, Newbury, Bucks*), *b.* 14 July 1860; *m.* 30 July 1895, Constance Edith, widow of Sir Richard Francis Sutton, 5th Bt. [G.B.], da. of Sir Vincent Rowland Corbet, 3rd Bt. [U.K.]; and has issue 1*e* to 2*e*.

1*e*. Philip Reginald Astley, *b.* 9 June 1896.
2*e*. Ruth Constance Astley.

5*d*. Reginald Basil Astley (*Bachelor's*), *b.* 8 Jan. 1862.

6*d*.[1] *Charlotte Laura Astley*, d. 18 *Nov.* 1905; m. 12 *Feb.* 1867, *the Hon. Graham Edward Henry Manners Sutton* [*V. Canterbury Coll.*], d. 30 *May* 1888; *and had issue.*

See the Exeter Volume, p. 162, Nos. 2901-2903.   [Nos. 80164 to 80190.

# of The Blood Royal

3c. *Anne Astley*, d. 1833; m. 1820, *Thomas Potter Macqueen of Ridgemount, co. Bedford; and had issue.*

4c. *Editha Astley*, d. 27 Mar. 1871; m. 23 Mar. 1825, *Warden Sergison of Cuckfield Park, co. Sussex, J.P., D.L.,* d. 22 May 1868; *and had issue* 1d *to* 2d.

1d. *Warden Sergison of Cuckfield Park, J.P., D.L., Capt. 4th Hussars*, b. 13 July 1835; d. 16 July 1888; m. 8 Jan. 1867, *Emilia, da. of Sir William Gordon Gordon-Cumming, 2nd Bt.* [U.K.] [who m. 2ndly, 12 Sept. 1891, *the Rev. Seymour Edgell*]; *and had* 1e *to* 2e.

1e. Charles Warden Sergison of Cuckfield Park, J.P., D.L., *formerly* Capt. Scots Guards, served in South Africa 1899–1900 (*Cuckfield Park, Sussex; Slaugham Place, Sussex*), b. 25 Nov. 1867; m. 24 June 1891, the Hon. Florence Emma Louisa [descended from King Henry VII. (see Tudor Roll, p. 204)], da. of Charles (Hanbury-Tracy), 4th Baron Sudeley [U.K.]; and had issue 1f to 2f.

1f. Prudence Ida Evelyn Sergison, b. 2 Sept. 1892.

2f. Cynthia Mary Sergison, b. 10 May 1897.

2e. Editha Elma Sergison, m. 6 Aug. 1890, Joseph Henry Russell (Bailey), 2nd Baron Glanusk [U.K.], D.S.O., Lord-Lieut. co. Brecon, and Pres. co. Brecon Territorial Force, and Hon. Col. and Lieut.-Col. Comdg. 3rd Batt. S. Wales Borderers, *formerly* Gren. Guards (*Glanusk Park, near Crickhowell; Peterstone Park, Brecon; Hay Castle and Llangoed Castle, Brecon*); and has issue 1f to 4f.

1f. Hon. Wilfred Russell Bailey, b. 27 June 1891.

2f. Hon. Gerald Sergison Bailey, b. 1893.

3f. Hon. Bernard Michael Bailey, b. 1899.

4f. Hon. Dulcie Editha Bailey.

2d. *Editha Agnes Sergison* (*Rendcomb Park, Cirencester*), m. as 2nd wife, 5 May 1888, James Taylor of Rendcomb, J.P., *d.s.p.* 1 Nov. 1896.

5c. *Agnes Astley*, d. 30 July 1871; m. Sept. 1825, *the Rev. John Henry Sparke of Gunthorpe Hall, M.A., Canon of Ely and Chancellor of the Diocese,* d. 8 Feb. 1870; *and had issue* (*with an elder son, Henry Astley, killed in the charge of the Light Brigade at Balaclava*) 1d *to* 3d.

1d. *Edward Bowyer Sparke of Gunthorpe, M.A., J.P., D.L., High Sheriff co. Norfolk* 1877, b. 28 July 1832; d. 1 June 1910; m. 4 July 1872, *Annie (Gunthorpe Hall, Briningham, Norfolk; 66 Eaton Square, S.W.) [descended from the Lady Anne, sister of King Edward IV.* (see Supp.)], *da. of Lieut.-Col. John Marcon of Wallington Hall, co. Norfolk; and had issue* 1e *to* 2e.

1e. Henry Bowyer Sparke of Gunthorpe, J.P., *formerly* Scots Guards, served in South Africa 1900–1902 (*Gunthorpe Hall, Briningham, Norfolk; Carlton; Bachelors'*), b. 10 Feb. 1875; m. 12 Oct. 1904, Eileen, da. of the Right Hon. Sir Charles Stewart Scott, P.C., G.C.B., G.C.M.G.; and has issue 1f to 2f.

1f. Michael Edward Bowyer Sparke, b. 5 Aug. 1905.

2f. Reginald Charles Bowyer Sparke, b. 22 Feb. 1908.

2e. Ethel Agnes Sparke, *unm.*

2d. *John Frances Sparke, Major 68th and 84th Regts.,* b. 25 July 1835; d. 27 Feb. 1888; m. 2ndly, *Mary Adela, da. of George Edwin Taunton of The Marfords, co. Chester* (*marriage dissolved*); *and had issue* 1e.

1e. Agnes Violet L'Estrange Astley Sparke, *unm.*

3d. *Agnes Sparke*, b. 4 June 1834; d. 18 June 1892; m. 20 Jan. 1870, *the Rev. Robert Arbuthnot Law, Rector of Gunthorpe-cum-Bale,* d. 11 Dec. 1889; *and had issue* 1e *to* 3e.

1e. Arbuthnot Patrick Astley Law, b. 5 July 1872.

2e. Herbert Henry Bingham Law, b. 23 Oct. 1873.

3e. Alexander Delaval Hamilton Law, b. 18 Oct. 1874.

2b. *Rev. Henry Nicholas Astley*, b. 5 Jan. 1767; d. 14 Aug. 1854; m. 20 Feb. 1798, *Sarah, da. of the Rev. J. Pitman; and had issue* 1c *to* 3c.

[Nos. 80191 to 80207.

The Plantagenet Roll

1c. Rev. Henry L'Estrange Milles Astley, Rector of Foulsham, b. 27 Dec. 1804; d. (—); m. 1841, *Dulcibella, da. of Col. William Gooch of Carleton, co. York; and had issue 1d to 3d.*

1d. William Henry L'Estrange Milles Astley, *bapt.* 2 Ap. 1838 [1] (*sic.*).

2d. Evelyn Astley, *m.* (—).

3d. Dulcibella Louisa Astley, *m.* (—) [3rd son of the Viscount of Kersebrique].

2c. *Jane Mary Astley,* d. 16 *Aug.* 1903; m. 1 *Oct.* 1833, *the Rev. William Frank Cubitt, M.A., Rector of Fritton, co. Suffolk,* d. 22 *June* 1882; *and had issue* 1d *to* 6d.

1d. Frank Astley Cubitt of Thorpe Hall, &c., J.P., *formerly* Capt. 5th Fusiliers (*Thorpe Hall, Norwich; Frittcn House, Great Yarmouth*), b. 20 Nov. 1834; *m.* 16 Oct. 1861, Bertha Harriott, da. of Capt. Thomas Blakiston, R.N. [Bt. Coll.]; and has issue 1e to 4e.

1e. Bertram Blakiston Cubitt, a Principal Clerk in the War Office (*Hillstead, Brentwood, Essex*), b. 20 Aug. 1862; *m.* 21 Ap. 1897, Leila, da. of Capt. W. Norman Leslie, Gordon Highlanders; and has issue 1f to 2f.

1f. Frank Leslie Cubitt, b. 19 Jan. 1898.

2f. Alan Blakiston Cubitt, b. 24 Feb. 1903.

2e. Julian Francis Cubitt, b. 16 Aug. 1869.

3e. Thomas Astley Cubitt, D.S.O., Major R.F.A., b. 9 Ap. 1871.

4e. Theresa Helen Cubitt, *m.* 7 Sept. 1905, Dr. Moritz Julius Born, a Professor at Munich University (*Munich*).

2d. Rev. Spencer Henry Cubitt, Rector of Scarning, b. 7 Nov. 1839; d. 1879; m. *Catherine, da. of William Garforth of Steeton, co. Yorks,* d. 1879; *and had issue* 1e *to* 3e.

1e. Rev. Spencer Henry Cubitt, M.A. (Camb.), Rector of Fritton (*Fritton Rectory, Great Yarmouth*), b. 7 Nov. 1869; *m.* 9 Nov. 1904, Jeanie Blythe, da. of E. W. Bacon of Oldbury Grange, Bridgnorth.

2e. Ida Cubitt, *m.* John R. Pearson (*Ripon, Yorks*); and has issue.

3e. Mabel Cubitt, *m.* 10 Feb. 1892, Major William Thwaites, R.F.A.

3d. Lucy Cubitt.

4d. Emily Jane Cubitt.

5d. Sophia Anne Cubitt (*Wistow Lodge, Huntingdon*), *m.* 1869, Charles de La Pryme, M.A., J.P., Bar.-at-Law; and has issue 1e to 5e.

1e. Alexander George de La Pryme, M.A., Universities Mission, Central Africa, b. Nov. 1870.

2e. Percy Christopher de La Pryme, Capt. A.S.C., b. 24 Sept. 1875.

3e. William Henry Astley de La Pryme, Lieut. P.W.O. Yorkshire Regt., b. 20 Feb. 1880.

4e. Louis de La Pryme.

5e. Helen de La Pryme.

6d. Georgiana Helen Cubitt, *m.* 14 Sept. 1876, John Rochfort Blakiston [Bt. Coll.] (*The Wilderness, Westend, Southampton*); and has issue 1e to 4e.

1e. John Francis Blakiston, b. 21 Nov. 1882.

2e. Margaret Blakiston.

3e. Catherine Blakiston.

4e. Mary Helen Blakiston.

3c. *Anne Astley,* b. 14 *Jan.* 1808; d. 26 *May* 1878; m. 15 *Oct.* 1835, *the Rev. Henry James Lee-Warner of Thorpland Hall, co. Norfolk, Hon. Canon of Norwich,* d. 10 *July* 1885; *and had issue* 1d *to* 9d.

1d. Rev. James Lee-Warner of Thorpland Hall, M.A. (Oxon.), *formerly* Rector
[Nos. 80208 to 80234.

---

[1] Lodge's "Peerage," 1909, p. 943.

# of The Blood Royal

of Beckley (*Thorpland Hall, Norfolk*), b. 13 Aug. 1836; m. 7 May 1874, Agnes Louisa, da. of the Rev. Henry Philip Marsham of Rippon Hall; and has issue 1e to 4e.

 1e. George Lee-Warner (*Innerfail, Spruce Coutee, Alberta, Canada*), b. 8 Feb. 1875; m. 6 Nov. 1905, Margaret, da. of Grant Ogilvie; and has issue 1f to 2f.

  1f. George Lee-Warner, b. 16 July 1906.
  2f. Edgar Lee-Warner, b. 10 June 1909.

 2e. Rev. Alfred Lee-Warner, M.A. (Oxon.) (47 *Gordon Road, Alverstoke*), b. 6 Oct. 1877.

 3e. James Lee-Warner, b. 29 Ap. 1889.
 4e. Caroline Lee-Warner.

2d. Henry Lee-Warner, J.P. (*The Paddocks, Swaffham*), b. 3 Jan. 1842; m. 29 Dec. 1868, Eleanor, da. of Robert Blake-Humfrey of Wroxham, J.P., D.L.

3d. John Lee-Warner (25 *Courtfield Road, S.W.*), b. 27 Jan. 1843; m. 17 Nov. 1880, Blanche, da. of Henry Hall Dare; and has issue 1e to 5e.

 1e. Harry Granville Lee-Warner, Lieut. R.F.A., b. 1 Jan. 1883.

 2e. Anne Agatha Lee-Warner, m. 27 Jan. 1904, Eustace Gurney of Sprowston Hall, J.P., M.A. (Oxon.) (*Sprowston Hall, Norwich*); and has issue 1f to 4f.

  1f. John Gurney, b. 3 July 1905.
  2f. Jocelyn Eustace Gurney, b. 24 Feb. 1910.
  3f. Catherine Gurney.
  4f. Rosamond Agatha Gurney.

 3e. Ruth Veronica Lee-Warner.
 4e. Gilian Cicely Lee-Warner.
 5e. Blanche Maud Lee-Warner.

4d. Edward Lee-Warner (67 *St. George's Square, S.W.*), b. 10 Jan. 1845; m. 12 Feb. 1884, Maria Harvey, da. of Onley Savill-Onley of Stisted Hall, co. Essex, J.P., D.L.; and has issue 1e to 2e.

 1e. Edward Henry Lee-Warner, b. 22 Jan. 1887.
 2e. Maria Gladys Lee-Warner, b. 20 Feb. 1885.

5d. Sir William Lee-Warner, K.C.S.I., J.P., M.A., and a Member of Council of India, *formerly* Sec. in Political and Secret Departs. of India Office 1895-1902, &c., &c. (*Eaton Tower, Caterham, Surrey*), b. 18 Ap. 1846; m. 2 Aug. 1876, Ellen Paulina, da. of Gen. Henry William Holland, C.B.; and has issue 1e to 3e.

 1e. Philip Henry Lee-Warner, b. 5 June 1877; m. 24 June 1907, Mary King, da. of Gen. Thomas Sherwin of Boston, Mass.; and has issue 1f.

  1f. Isabel Ellen Lee-Warner.

 2e. William Hamilton Lee-Warner, Assist. Resident, Brunei, b. 14 Oct. 1880.
 3e. Roland Paul Lee-Warner, b. 4 Jan. 1892.

6d. Lucy Lee-Warner.
7d. Anne Lee-Warner.

8d. Maria Lee-Warner (*Bolwick Hall, Marsham, near Aylsham*), m. 3 July 1873, Charles Louis Buxton, J.P., C.C. [6th son of Sir Edward North Buxton, 2nd Bt. [U.K.], M.P.], d. 23 Ap. 1906; and has issue 1e to 4e.

 1e. Walter Louis Buxton, B.A. (Camb.), J.P., *formerly* Capt. King's Own Norfolk Imp. Yeo. (*Brooks'*), b. 6 May 1875.

 2e. *Norah Louis Buxton*, b. 14 Ap. 1874; d. 17 Ap. 1907; m. 22 Nov. 1904, *William Done Bushell; and had issue* 1f.

  1f. Maurice Done Bushell, b. 6 Ap. 1907.

 3e. Amy Louis Buxton.
 4e. Millicent Louis Buxton, m. 16 Nov. 1909, Gerard Anstruther Wathen.

9d. Emma Lee-Warner, *unm.*   [Nos. 80235 to 80267.

The Plantagenet Roll

2*a.* Rev. John Astley, b. 1734; d. 1803; m. 1762, Catherine, da. of Philip Bell of Wallington, co. Norfolk; and had issue 1b to 2b.[1]
   1*b.* Catherine Astley.
   2*b.* Lucy Astley.

3*a.* Blanch Astley, b. 1726; d. 3 *May* 1805; m. 1751, *Edward Pratt of Ryston*, co. Norfolk, d. 18 *June* 1784; and had issue 1b to 3b.
   1*b.* Edward Roger Pratt of Ryston, High Sheriff co. Norfolk 1798; b. 24 Oct. 1756; d. 5 *Mar.* 1838; m. 3 Dec. 1788, *Pleasance, da. and co-h. of Samuel Browne of King's Lynn*, d. 3 Oct. 1807; and had issue (with 4 other sons and 2 das. who d.s.p.) 1c to 4c.
      1*c.* Rev. Jermyn Pratt of Ryston, b. 6 Feb. 1798; d. 15 *May* 1867; m. 4 *May* 1847, *Mary Louisa [descended from King Henry VII.* (see the Tudor Roll, p. 450)], da. of the Right Rev. Lord George Murray, Bishop of Rochester [younger son of the 3rd Duke of Atholl [S.]], d. 5 *May* 1878; and had issue (with 2 other das. d.s.p.) 1d to 6d.
         1*d.* Edward Roger Murray Pratt of Ryston, J.P., C.C., Col. *formerly* Norfolk Art. *(Ryston Hall, near Downham, Norfolk),* b. 3 Dec. 1847; *m.* 12 July 1881, the Hon. Louisa Frances, da. of John (Mulholland), 1st Baron Dunleath [U.K.]; and has issue 1e to 5e.
            1*e.* Edward Roger Pratt, b. 2 June 1882.
            2*e.* Jermyn Harold Pratt, b. 12 July 1883.
            3*e.* Lionel Henry Pratt, b. 17 Dec. 1889.
            4*e.* Dorothy Louisa Pratt.
            5*e.* Ursula Frances Pratt.
         2*d.* Walter Jermyn Murray Pratt *(Wallington Lodge, Baldock, Herts),* b. 6 Feb. 1853; *m.* 1878, Elizabeth, da. of the Rev. Henry George.
         3*d.* Reginald Henry Murray Pratt *(Portagela Prairie, Canada),* b. 29 May 1854; *m.* 1887, Maria, da. of the Rev. Henry George; and has issue 1e to 5e.
            1*e.* Horace Reginald Pratt, b. 26 Jan. 1888.
            2*e.* Cecil Arden Pratt, b. 29 Nov. 1889.
            3*e.* Alwyn Murray Pratt, b. 7 Sept. 1892.
            4*e.* Gerald Henry Pratt, b. 20 May 1895.
            5*e.* Bernard Edward Pratt, b. 1 Mar. 1904.
         4*d.* Blanche Eleanor Murray Pratt, *m.* 30 Ap. 1891, Capt. James Boyle, M.V.O., H.B.M. Consul for Madeira 1907, *formerly* at Copenhagen, &c. [E. of Glasgow Coll.] *(British Consulate, Funchal, Madeira).*
         5*d.* Henrietta Mary Murray Pratt, *m.* 24 Jan. 1895, Cecil Henry Spencer Perceval [E. of Egmont Coll. and a descendant of George, Duke of Clarence, K.G. (see the Clarence Volume, p. 209] *(Longwitton Hall, co. Northumberland).*
         6*d.* Alice Rosalind Murray Pratt, *m.* 14 July 1885, the Rev. Charles Francis Townley of Fulbourne, co. Camb., Rector of Christchurch, Wisbech [descended from King Henry VII. (see the Tudor Roll, p. 393)] *(Christchurch Rectory, Wisbech);* and has issue 1e to 4e.
            1*e.* Charles Evelyn Townley, b. 22 Jan. 1888.
            2*e.* Gladys Mary Townley.
            3*e.* Rosalinde Cecil Townley.
            4*e.* Selina Georgiana Townley.
      2*c.* Rev. William Pratt, Rector of *Harpley-cum-Bircham*, b. 2 Nov. 1803; d. 2 Nov. 1874; m. 1835, *Louisa, da. of William Coxhead Marsh of Gaynes Park, co. Essex*, d. 7 *June* 1877; and had issue (with 2 other sons who d.s.p.) 1d to 9d.
         1*d.* William Roger Pratt, Indian C.S. (ret.) *(41 Hill St., Berkeley Square),* b. 27 Ap. 1837. [Nos. 80268 to 80288.

---

[1] Betham's "Baronetage," 1802, ii. 76.

# of The Blood Royal

2*d*. Henry Marsh Pratt, C.B., Col. (ret.) Indian Army (43 *Courtfield Gardens, S.W.*), *b.* 24 Oct. 1838; *m.* 7 Mar. 1891, Evelyn Margaret, da. of Clayton William Freake Glyn of Durrington House, Harlow [Bt. Coll.]; and has issue 1*e* to 2*e*.

1*e*. Pleasance Millicent Mary Pratt.
2*e*. Evelyn Lucy Pratt.

3*d*. William Dering Pratt, *formerly* Dep. Inspector-Gen. of Police, Bengal (36 *West Cromwell Road, S.W.*), *b.* 5 Sept. 1842; *m.* 30 Nov. 1867, Louisa Constance, da. of Henry Steel, H.E.I.C.S.; and has issue 1*e* to 2*e*.

1*e*. Henry Roger Evelyn Pratt, D.S.O., Capt. 36th Sikhs, Indian Army, *b.* 8 Dec. 1875; *m.* 20 Dec. 1909, Yolande, da. of Edmund Tower.
2*e*. Amy Pratt.

4*d*. Rev. Dashwood Pratt, B.A. (Camb.), Vicar of Barney (*Barney Vicarage, East Dereham, Norfolk*), *b.* 5 Oct. 1845; *unm.*

5*d*. Emily Blanche Pratt, *b.* 19 Ap. 1847; *d.* 24 *June* 1874; m. 1870, Henry John Denis Dugmore of Bagthorpe Hall, co. Norfolk, d. 1883; *and had issue* 1*e*.

1*e*. Henry Norris Pratt Dugmore of Bagthorpe (*Bagthorpe Hall, King's Lynn*), *b.* (—); *unm.*

6*d*. Hester Sophia Astley Pratt, *unm.*

7*d*. Harriett Pratt, *unm.*

8*d*. Laura Louisa Pratt, *m.* 19 May 1886, Arthur Hussey of 11 Stone Buildings, Lincoln's Inn, Solicitor (15 *Grange Road, Ealing*); and has issue 1*e* to 2*e*.

1*e*. William Jermyn Hussey, *b.* 2 Ap. 1887.
2*e*. Emily Blanche Hussey.

9*d*. Eveline Pratt, *m.* 14 May 1885, Major-Gen. Charles Grant Mansell Fasken, C.B., Indian Army, now Comdg. Bannoo Brigade, India (*Bannoo, Punjab, India*); and has issue 1*e* to 3*e*.

1*e*. Douglas Fasken, *b.* 16 Sept. 1896.
2*e*. Grace Evelyn Fasken.
3*e*. Myrtle Annie Fasken.

3*c*. Maria Pratt, *d.* 14 *Jan.* 1856; m. 1834, Henry W. Coldham of Anmer Hall, co. Norfolk, D.L., *d.* Nov. 1871; *and had issue* 1*d* to 3*d*.

1*d*. Henry James Coldham of Anmer Hall, d. 13 *July* 1887; m. Agatha Geraldine de Courcy (Essenden, near Hatfield, Herts), da. of (—) Hamilton; *and had issue* (2 sons and 5 das.).

2*d*. Maria Elizabeth Coldham, *m.* Capt. James Mason, 94th Regt.; *d.* July 1901.
3*d*. Lucy Coldham (*Preston Cottage, near Uppingham*), *m.* Rev. H. Lucas.

4*c*. Lucy Pratt, d.s.p. 12 *May* 1854; m. 1st, 10 *Jan.* 1826, William (*Thellusson*), 3rd Baron Rendlesham [U.K.], d.s.p. 13 *Sept.* 1839; 2*ndly*, 2 Feb. 1841, Stewart Marjoribanks of Bushey, co. Herts, *M.P., J.P.*, d. *Sept.* 1863.

2*b*. Sarah Maria Pratt, d. (—); m. *the Rev. Charles Collyer of Gunthorpe Hall*, co. Norfolk, d. (—); *and had issue (with possibly others)* 1*c*.

1*c*. Harriet Collyer, d. (—); m. *her cousin-german,* Lieut.-Col. William Collyer of Gimingham, co. Norfolk, *J.P.. H.E.I.C.S.*, d. 1861.

3*b*. Lucy Pratt, d. (—); m. *Hadmond Alpe of Hardingham*.

[Nos. 80289 to 80307.

251. Descendants of EDMOND WODEHOUSE of East Lexham, co. Norfolk (Table XXIII.), *d.* (—); *m.* 1st, MARY, widow of WILLIAM GUYBON, da. of Sir Philip PARKER; and had issue (with a son and 2 das. who *d.s.p.*) 1*a*.

1*a*. Lucy Wodehouse, d. (—); m. *Lewis Monnoux of Sandy*.

The Plantagenet Roll

252. Descendants of JOHN WODEHOUSE of Fettwell (Table XXIII.), d. (-); m. ANNE, widow of WILLIAM SAMWELL, da. of Sir Denner STRUTT, 1st Bt. [E. 1642], d. (-); and had issue 1a.

1a. Elizabeth Wodehouse.

253. Descendants of BLANCHE WODEHOUSE (Table XXIII.), d. (-); m. 6 Feb. 1661, Sir JACOB ASTLEY, 1st Bt. [E. 25 Jan. 1660], M.P., co. Norfolk 1685–1722, d. 17 Aug. 1729; and had issue 1a.

1a. Sir Jacob Astley, 2nd Bt. [E.], b. 20 July 1667; d. 7 July 1739; m. 2 Dec. 1690, Elizabeth, da. and h. of Thomas Bransby of Caistor, co. Norfolk, d. 30 Mar. 1738; and had issue 1b to 3b.

1b. Sir Jacob Astley, 3rd Bt. [E.], b. 3rd Jan. 1692; d. 5 Jan. 1760; m. 1st, 1721, Lucy, da. and event. co-h. of Sir Nicholas L'Estrange, 4th Bt. [E.], d. 25 July 1739; and had issue.

See pp. 421–427, Nos. 80164–80307.

2b. Elizabeth Astley, d. (-); m. Caleb Elwin of Thirning.

3b. Jemima Astley, d. (-); m. 1st, 1731, Roger Metcalfe of St. Giles-in-the-Fields, co. Midx., M.D., b. 8 Mar. 1680; d. (-); 2ndly, Henry Groom, of the City of London; and had issue (with 2 sons d.s.p.) 1c.

1c. Christopher Metcalfe of Hawstead, a literary friend of the poet Dryden, b. 1 Ap. 1732; d. 24 June 1794; m. 19 May 1753, Ellen, da. and h. of Christopher Barton of Bromley, co. Midx., and Hawstead, co. Suffolk, d. 6 Mar. 1775; and had issue (with a son and 6 das. d. unm.) 1d to 2d.

1d. Christopher Barton Metcalfe of Hawstead, b. 28 Aug. 1759; d. 15 Aug. 1881; m. Sophia, da. of Robert Andrews of Auberies, co. Essex, d. 27 Feb. 1815; and had issue 1e to 4e.

1e. Henry Metcalfe of Hawstead, b. 10 Ap. 1791; d. 1849; m. 1820, Frances Jane, da. of Martin Whish, Commr. of Excise, d. 29 Ap. 1830; and had issue (with a da. d. young) 1f to 3f.

1f. Henry Christopher Metcalfe of Hawstead, 91st Regt., b. 4 Sept. 1822; d. 16 Ap. 1881; m. 5 Dec. 1845, Mary, da. of George Price of Grahamstown, South Africa, 21st Light Dragoons; and had issue (with a da. d. unm.) 1g to 4g.

1g. Henry George Price Metcalfe of Hawstead, b. 16 Sept. 1846; d. (-); m. (—), da. of (—); and had issue 1h to 6h.

1h. Henry Christopher Metcalfe, b. 1875.
2h. George Harry Price Metcalfe.
3h. John Joseph Metcalfe.
4h. Frederica Sophia Metcalfe.
5h. Daisy Emma Whish Metcalfe.
6h. Alice Georgina Metcalfe.

2g. Christopher Barton Metcalfe, b. 6 Jan. 1860.

3g. Frances Jane Whish Metcalfe, m. 25 Feb. 1873, Col. Thomas George Booth of Hawstead House, A.P.D., late 10th Regt. (Hawstead House, Bury St. Edmunds); s.p.

4g. Ellen Marie Metcalfe, d. 22 Mar. 1877; m. Edward Beall; and had issue 1h to 2h.

1h. Edward Beall, b. Feb. 1877.
2h. Lucy Beall.

2f. Philip Roger Colville Metcalfe of Erith, co. Kent., b. 12 May 1827; d. (-); m. 14 Aug. 1860, Martha, da. of William James Mostnan of Bury St. Edmunds; and had issue (with 2 das. d. unm.) 1g to 4g. [Nos. 80308 to 80461.

# of The Blood Royal

1g. Harry Philip Metcalfe, b. 22 Aug. 1865.
2g. Clarissa Kate Metcalfe.
3g. Anne Florence Metcalfe.
4g. Frances Martha Metcalfe.

3f. *Walter Charles Metcalfe of Epping, co. Essex*, b. 26 May 1828; d. (-); m. 1850, *Mary*, da. *of Richard B. Andrews of Epping; and had issue* 1g *to* 2g.
    1g. Gilbert Metcalfe, b. 1851.
    2g. Clara Metcalfe.

2e. *Ellen Metcalfe*,
3e. *Frances Sophia Metcalfe*, } d. (?) *unm.*

4e. *Emma Metcalfe*, d. 14 Feb. 1840; m. *as* 1st *wife, the Rev. Nathaniel Colvile, M.A., Rector of Little Livermere, co. Suffolk; and had issue* 1f *to* 2f.
    1f. Augusta Letitia Colvile.
    2f. Clara Harriet Emma Colvile.

2d. *Frederica Sophia Metcalfe*, b. 3 Nov. 1763; d. 5 Ap. 1834; m. *James Mure of Cecil Lodge, co. Herts* [2nd *son of William Mure of Caldwell, M.P., a Baron of the Exchequer*]; *and had issue (with an elder son* d.s.p.[1]*)* 1e *to* 6e.
    1e. *James Mure*, d. (-); m. *Harriet*, da. *of Brice Pearce of Munkham, co. Essex.*
    2e. *Philip William Mure*, d. (-); m. *Louisa*, da. *of Sir Thomas Andrew Strange, Chief Justice of Madras.*
    3e. *Frederica Mure*, d. (-); m. *Col. Horatio George Broke* [3rd *son of Philip Bower Broke of Nacton, co. Suffolk*]; *and had issue* 1f.
        1f. Horace Broke, b. 26 Sept. 1827.
    4e. *Catherine Mure*,
    5e. *Ellen Mure*, } d. (? *unm.*).
    6e. *Harriet Mure*,

[Nos. 80462 to 80470.

254. Descendants, if any surviving, of MARGARET WODEHOUSE (Table XXIII.), d. (-); m. THOMAS SAVAGE of Elmley Castle, co. Worcester;[2] and had issue 1a to 4a.

1a. *Thomas Savage of Elmley Castle*, bur. 22 Ap. 1694; m. *and had issue* 1b.
1b. *Thomas Savage of Elmley Castle*, d. 7 May 1742; m. *May* 1700, *Elizabeth, widow of Thomas (Coventry),* 1st *Earl of Coventry* [E.], da. *of Richard Graham or Grimes*, bur. 10 Ap. 1724; *and had issue* 1c *to* 3c.
    1c. *Elizabeth Savage*, da. *and co-h.*, m. *William Byrche of Leacroft, co. Staff., LL.D., Chancellor of Worcester; and had issue* 1d *to* 3d.
        1d. *Thomas Byrche*, afterwards *Savage of Elmley*, d.s.p. 1776.
        2d. *Elizabeth Byrche*, m. *John Perrot; and had issue (with app. other) issue* 1e *to* 2e.
            1e. Thomas Perrot.
            2e. Mary Perrot.
        3d. *Jane Byrche*, m. *Richard Clavering of co. Northbd.; and had (with app. other) issue* 1e *to* 2e.
            1e. *Robert Clavering*, afterwards (R.L. 21 Oct. 1797) *Savage.*
            2e. Jane Clavering.
    2c. *Margaret Savage*, d. (-); m. *Thomas Coventry, Bar.-at-Law, M.P. for Bridport* 1762, 1768, *and* 1774 [*nephew of William,* 5th *Earl of Coventry*], d. *app.* s.p.

---

[1] Gage's "Suffolk," p. 446.   [2] Nash's "Worcester," i. 383.

The Plantagenet Roll

3c. *Mary Savage*, d. (–); m. *Humphrey Monnoux* of *Sandy*, co. *Beds*, a Bencher of Gray's Inn; and had issue 1d.

1d. *Sir Philip Monnoux*, 5th Bt. [*E.* 4 Dec. 1660], b. c. 1739; d. 17 Ap. 1805; m. 22 June 1762, *Elizabeth*, da. of *Ambrose Riddell* of *Eversholt*, co. *Beds*, d. 12 Sept. 1770; and had issue (with 2 other das.[1]) 1e to 3e.

1e. *Sir Philip Monnoux*, 6th Bt. [*E.*], d. unm. 27 Feb. 1809.

2e. [da.] *Monnoux*, m. 1st, Sir *John Payne*; 2ndly, Col. *Buckworth*.

3e. *Frances Monnoux*, m. 3 Oct. 1809, the Hon. *Samuel Henry Ongley* [2nd son of *Robert*, 1st Baron *Ongley* [*I.* 1776], d. certainly s.p.m. and app. s.p. 1822.

2a. *Anne Savage*, m. *Samuel Bracebridge* of *Lindley*, co. *Leic.* [2nd son of *Abraham Bracebridge* of *Atherston*, co. *Warwick*]; and had issue (with *Abraham*, *Thomas*, and *Elizabeth*, d.v.) 1b to 6b.

1b. *Samuel Bracebridge*. M.P. for *Tamworth*, b. c. 1716; aged 14, 1730;[2] d. in the Isle of Scio 1786.[3]

2b. *Robert Bracebridge*, b. c. 1723; aged 7, 1730.[2]

3b. *Rev. Philip Bracebridge*, b. c. 1724; aged 6, 1730;[2] d. 1762; and had issue 1c to 2c.

1c. *Anne Bracebridge* of *Lindley Hall*, m. *Robert Abney* of *Lindley Hall*, High Sheriff (?) co. *Leic.*; and had issue 1d.

1d. [da.] *Abney*, m. the Rev. *Samuel B. Heming*.

2c. *Amicia Bracebridge*, m. *George Heming*; and apparently had issue at least one son (see above).

4b. *James Bracebridge*, b. c. 1725; aged 5, 1730.[2]

5b. *Maria Bracebridge*, b. c. 1710; aged 20, 1730.[2]

6b. *Mary Ann Gratia Bracebridge*, b. c. 1719; aged 11, 1730.[2]

3a. *Lucy Savage*, d. 21 May 1721; m. *Thomas Adderly* of *Woddington*, co. *Warwick*; and had issue[4] (with a son, *Gilbert*, d. young) 1b to 2b.

1b. *Thomas Adderly*.

2b. *Elizabeth Adderly*.

4a. [da.] *Savage*, m. (—) *Reed* of *Luggardine*.

255. Descendants of Lady MARGARET HOWARD (Table XXI.), d. 4 Sept. 1591; m. as 1st wife (lic. 4 Feb.) 1580, ROBERT (SACKVILLE), 2nd EARL OF DORSET [*E.*], d. 27 Feb. 1609; and had issue 1a to 4a.

1a. *Richard (Sackville)*, 3rd Earl of *Dorset* [*E.*], b. 28 Mar. 1589; d. 28 Mar. 1624; m. 25 Feb. 1609, *Anne*, suo jure 14th Baroness de *Clifford* [*E.*], d. 22 Mar. 1676; and had issue 1b.

1b. Lady *Margaret Sackville*, da. and event. sole h., b. c. 1614; d. 14 Aug. 1676; m. 21 Ap. 1629, *John (Tufton)*, 2nd Earl of *Thanet* [*E.*], d. 6 May 1664; and had issue.

See pp. 128-131, Nos. 11638-13475.

2a. *Edward (Sackville)*, 4th Earl of *Dorset* [*E.*], K.G., b. 1590; d. 17 July 1652; m. a. 12 Mar. 1612, *Mary*, da. and h. of Sir *George Curzon* of *Croxall*, co. *Derby*, bur. 3 Sept. 1645; and had issue 1b.

1b. *Richard (Sackville)*, 5th Earl of *Dorset* [*E.*], b. 16 Sept. 1622; d. 27 Aug. 1677; m. a. 1638, Lady *Frances*, da. and event. h. of *Lionel (Cranfield)*, 1st Earl of *Middlesex* [*E.*]; and had issue 1c to 2c.   [Nos. 80471 to 82308.

---

[1] Burke's "Extinct Baronetcies."
[2] Dugdale's "Worcester," 1730, p. 1057.
[3] Burke's "Commoners," i. 273.
[4] Nash's "Worcester," p. 1096.

of The Blood Royal

1c. *Richard (Sackville), 6th Earl of Dorset* [E.], K.G., b. 24 Jan. 1638; d. 29 Jan. 1706; m. 2ndly, 7 Mar. 1685, *Lady Mary, da. of James (Compton), 3rd Earl of Northampton* [E.], d. 6 Aug. 1691; *and had issue.*
See the Clarence Volume, Table XX. and pp. 223–227, No. 4502–4613.

2c. *Lady Mary Sackville*, bapt. 11 Feb. 1648; d. 4 Nov. 1710; m. 6 Feb. 1665, *Roger (Boyle), 2nd Earl of Orrery* [I.], d. 29 Mar. 1682; *and had issue.*
See p. 342, Nos. 58418–59088.

3a. *Lady Cecily Sackville*, d. (–); m. *the Hon. Sir Henry Compton, K.B.; and had issue (with 3 sons who d. unm.) 1b to 3b.*

1b. *Cecily Compton*, b. c. 1608; d. 21 Mar. 1675; m. 1st, *Sir John Fermor of Somerton, co. Oxon.*, d.v.p.s.p. 1625; 2ndly, a. 18 May 1629, *Henry (Arundell), 3rd Baron Arundell of Wardour* [E.] *and Count Arundell* [H.R.E.], P.C., K.B., d. 28 Dec. 1694; *and had issue (by 2nd husband).*
See the Clarence Volume, Table LVI. and pp. 462–471, Nos. 20243–20851.

2b. *Mary Compton*, d. (–); m. *the Hon. John Lumley,* d.v.p. Oct. 1658; *and had issue 1c to 2c.*

1c. *Richard (Lumley), 2nd Viscount Lumley* [I.] *and* (10 Ap. 1689) *1st Earl of Scarbrough* [E.], b. c. 1650; d. 17 Dec. 1721; m. 17 Mar. 1685, *Frances, da. and h. of Sir Henry Jones of Aston, co. Oxon.*, d. 7 Aug. 1722; *and had issue 1d to 3d.*

1d. *Richard (Lumley), 2nd Earl of Scarbrough* [E.], &c., K.G., d. unm. 29 Jan. 1740.

2d. *Thomas (Lumley, afterwards (A.P. 1723) Lumley-Saunderson), 3rd Earl of Scarbrough* [E.], &c., K.B., b. c. 1690; d. 15 Mar. 1752; m. 27 June 1724, *Lady Frances, da. of George (Hamilton), 1st Earl of Orkney* [S.], d. 27 Dec. 1772; *and had issue.*
See p. 377, Nos. 62521–62625.

3d. *Lady Mary Lumley*, d. 10 Dec. 1726; m. *as 2nd wife, George (Montague), 1st Earl of Halifax* [E.], K.B., d. 9 May 1739; *and had issue.*
See the Clarence Volume, Table LXXVI. and pp. 615–619, Nos. 26908–27008.

2c. *Elizabeth Lumley*, d. (–); m. *Richard Cotton of Water Gates, co. Essex.*

3b. *Margaret Compton*, d (–); m. *Col. Thomas Sackville of Selscombe, co. Sussex.*[1]

4a. *Lady Anne Sackville*, d. (–); m. 1st, 21 June 1609, *the Hon. Sir Edward Seymour, K.B.* [gd.-son and h.-app. of Edward, 1st Earl of Hertford [E.]], d.s.p.s. Sept. 1618; 2ndly, 7 Oct. 1622, *Sir Edward Lewes.* [Nos. 82309 to 83906.

256. Descendants of Lady JANE HOWARD (Table XXI.) *d.* 1593; *m. a.* 1564, CHARLES (NEVILL), 6th EARL OF WESTMORLAND [E.], K.G., *d.* 16 Nov. 1601; and had issue.

See the Exeter Volume, Table XXII. and pp. 333–338, Nos. 24284–24614.
[Nos. 83907 to 84237.

257. Descendants of GEORGE (BERKELEY), 1st EARL OF BERKELEY [E.], P.C., F.R.S. (see Table XXI.), *b. c.* 1627; *d.* 14 Oct. 1698; *m.* 11 Aug. 1646, ELIZABETH, da. and co-h. of John MASINGBERD of London, Treasurer of the East India Coy., *bur.* 10 Dec. 1708; and had issue 1*a* to 6*a*.

1a. *Charles (Berkeley), 2nd Earl of Berkeley* [E.], K.B., b. 8 Ap. 1649; d. 24 Sept. 1710; m. (lic. dated 16 Aug.) 1677, *the Hon. Elizabeth, da. of Baptist (Noel), 3rd Viscount Campden* [E.], d. 30 July 1719; *and had issue 1b to 3b.*

---

[1] Berry's "Sussex Genealogies," p. 300.

The Plantagenet Roll

1b. *James* (Berkeley), 3rd Earl of Berkeley [E.], K.G., d. at *Aubigny Castle,* near La Rochelle, Aug. 1736; m. Lady Louisa, da. of Charles (Lennox), 1st Duke of Richmond [E.] and Lennox [S.], d. 15 *June* 1717; and had issue.
See the Exeter Volume, pp. 482–487, Nos. 42058–42430.

2b. Hon. *Henry Berkeley,* M.P., Col. 4th Foot, b. 1690; d. May 1736; m. *Mary,* da. of Henry Cornwall of Bredwardine Castle, co. Hereford, d. 25 Ap. 1741; and had issue (with a son and 3 das. who d.s.p.) 1c to 3c.

1c. *Lionel Spencer Berkeley,* d. (–); m. *Margaret,* da. of James Whitefield of Twickenham, co. Midx.; and had issue (with 2 sons d. young) 1d to 4d.

1d. *Velters Cornwall Berkeley,* Capt. R.N.
2d. *Henry Nicholas Lionel Berkeley.*
3d. *James Berkeley.*
4d. *George Berkeley.*

2c. *Mary Berkeley,* d. 10 *Mar.* 1755; m. *Charles Morton,* M.D., F.S.A., Sec. to the Royal Society, Keeper of MSS. and Medals at the British Museum.

3c. *Elizabeth Berkeley,* d. (–); m. (—) *Martin.*

3b. Lady *Mary Berkeley,* d. (–); m. *Thomas Chambers* of *Hanworth,* co. Midx.

2a. Rev. the Hon. *George Berkeley,* Prebendary of Westminster, d. Oct. 1694; m. 4 *Mar.* 1689, *Jane,* da. of George Cole of co. Devon, d. (–); and had issue 1b.

1b. *Elizabeth Berkeley,* da. and h., bapt. 22 *Mar.* 1691; d. 8 Ap. 1730; m. *John Brome* of *Tuppinden,* co. Kent, d. 22 Feb. 1747; and had issue[1] (Thomas, Elizabeth, Maria, Arethusa, William, and Jane, of whom only 2 das. survived, viz.) 1b to 2b.

1b. [da.] *Brome,* m. (—) *Clarke,* M.D.
2b. [da.] *Brome,* m. *John Hamond,* Surgeon H.M. Dockyard at Chatham, d. Jan. 1774; and had issue who inherited Tuppinden.

3a. Lady *Elizabeth Berkeley,* d. c. 1681; m. *William Smith,* of the Inner Temple; and had issue (a da.).

4a. Lady *Theophila Berkeley,* b. 1650; d. 26 *Jan.* 1707; m. 1st, 14 May 1668, Sir *Kingsmill Lucy,* 2nd Bt. [E. 1618], F.R.S., D.C.L., M.P., b. c. 1649; bur. 20 Sept. 1678; 2ndly, 23 Nov. 1682, *Robert Nelson,* the well-known author of "Festivals and Feasts of the Church," d. 16 *June* 1715; and had issue 1b to 2b.

1b. Sir *Berkeley Lucy,* 3rd Bt. [E.], F.R.S., b. c. 1672; d. 19 Nov. 1759; m. *Catherine,* da. of Charles Cotton of Beresford, co. Stafford; bur. 22 *June* 1740; and had issue 1c to 2c.

1c. *Mary Lucy,* da. and co-h., bapt. 9 Nov. 1709; d. (–); m. 14 Aug. 1727, the Hon. *Charles Compton,* M.P., d. 20 Nov. 1755; and had issue.
See the Clarence Volume, Table XX. and pp. 199–219, Nos. 3458–4434.

2c. *Elizabeth Lucy,* da. and co-h., d. (–); m. *William Thompson* of *Leicester Square, London,* d. (–); and had issue (at least) 1d.

1d. *Lucy Thompson,* d. 4 *July* 1765; m. 20 *July* 1755, *Edmund Plowden* of *Plowden,* co. Salop, d. 9 *Jan.* 1768; and had issue.
See the Exeter Volume, Table XVI. and pp. 274–280, Nos. 10900–11110.

2b. *Theophila Lucy,* b. 24 *Jan.* 1671; d. 30 *July* 1721; m. 27 Oct. 1691, Sir *William Ingoldsby,* 3rd Bt. [E.], d. 25 Ap. 1726; and had issue 1c.

1c. *Elizabeth Ingoldsby,* had admon. to father 10 May 1726; and then wife of the Hon. Col. *Thomas Fowkes.*

5a. Lady *Mary Berkeley,* d. 19 May 1719; m. 1st, *Ford* (Grey), 3rd Baron Grey of Werke [E.] and (11 *June* 1695) 1st Earl of Tankerville [E.], P.C., d. 24 *June* 1701; 2ndly, (—) *Booth* of *Epsom,* co. Surrey; and had issue 1b.

[Nos. 84238 to 85798.]

---

[1] Hasted's "Kent," i. 115.

# of The Blood Royal

1b. **Lady Mary Grey**, d. 31 May 1710; m. 3 July 1695, Charles (Bennet), 3rd Baron Ossulston [E.] and (19 Oct. 1714) 1st Earl of Tankerville [G.B.], b. 1674; d. 21 May 1722; and had issue 1c to 4c.

1c. Charles (Bennet), 2nd Earl of Tankerville [G.B.], 4th Baron Ossulston [E.], K.T., d. 14 Mar. 1753; m. a. Nov. 1715, Camilla, da. of Edward Colville of Whitehouse, co. Durham, d. 8 Oct. 1775; and had issue 1d to 3d.

1d. Charles (Bennet), 3rd Earl of Tankerville [G.B.], 5th Baron Ossulston [E.], b. 6 Sept. 1716; d. 27 Oct. 1767; m. 23 Sept. 1742, Alicia, da. and co-h. of Sir John Astley, 2nd Bt. [E.], bur. 7 Mar. 1791; and had issue 1e to 4e.

1e. Charles (Bennet), 4th Earl of Tankerville [G.B.], 6th Baron Ossulston [E.], b. 15 Nov. 1743; d. 10 Dec. 1822; m. 7 Oct. 1771, Emma, da. and co-h. of Sir James Colebrooke, 1st Bt. [G.B.], d. 20 Nov. 1836; and had issue 1f to 4f.

1f. Charles Augustus (Bennet), 5th Earl of Tankerville [G.B.], 7th Baron Ossulston [E.], b. 28 Ap. 1776; d. 25 June 1859; m. 28 July 1806, Corisande Armandine Sophie Léonice Etienne, da. of Anthony Louis Marie (de Gramont), 8th Duke of Gramont [F. 1643], d. 23 Jan. 1865; and had issue 1g.

1g. Charles Augustus (Bennet), 6th Earl of Tankerville [G.B.], 8th Baron Ossulston [E.], P.C., b. 10 Jan. 1810; d. 18 Dec. 1899; m. 29 Jan. 1850, Lady Olivia [descended from George, Duke of Clarence, K.G.], da. of George (Montagu), 6th Duke of Manchester [G.B.]; and had issue.

See the Clarence Volume, pp. 242–243, Nos. 5312–5319.

2f. Hon. Henry Grey Bennet, b. 2 Dec. 1777; d. 29 May 1836; m. 15 May 1816, Gertrude Frances, da. of Lord William Russell [Duke of Bedford Coll., a descendant of King Henry VII. (see Tudor Roll, p. 360)], d. 23 Jan. 1841; and had issue 1g to 2g.

1g. Charlotte Emma Georgiana Bennet, m. 20 Nov. 1839, the Right Hon. Patrick FitzStephen French, P.C., M.P. [brother of Arthur, 1st Baron De Freyne, &c.], d. 4 June 1873; and had issue 1h to 2h.

1h. Louisa Emma Corisande French, m. 18 June 1868, Capt. George H. Bridges, A.D.C.

2h. Augusta Sarah French.

2g. Gertrude Frances Bennet, m. 1 Aug. 1839, Hamilton Gorges of Kilbrew, co. Meath, d. 1860.

3f. **Lady Caroline Bennet**, b. 2 Oct. 1772; d. 7 Mar. 1818; m. as 1st wife, 23 June 1795, John (Wrottesley), 1st Baron Wrottesley [U.K.], d. 16 Mar. 1841; and had issue.

See the Tudor Roll, pp. 333–334, Nos. 26544–26576.

4f. **Lady Anna Bennet**, b. 28 Ap. 1774; d. Sept. 1836; m. 19 July 1804, Rev. the Hon. William Beresford [3rd son of William, 1st Baron Decies [I.], Archbishop of Tuam], d. 27 June 1830; and had issue 1g to 2g.

1g. William Henry Beresford, Capt. Rifle Brigade, b. 1810; d. 26 Feb. 1875; m. 10 July 1850, Emma Catherine [da. of (—)] Lawrence of Montreal, Canada; and had issue 1h.

1h. Henrietta Beresford.

2g. Alicia Beresford, d. 27 Mar. 1882; m. 12 Sept. 1834, Horace Hamond, K.H., Consul at Cherbourg, d. (–); and had issue (a son and 2 das.).

2e. Hon. Henry Astley Bennet, Lieut.-Gen. and Lieut.-Col. 85th Foot, b. 3 Ap. 1757; d. (? s.p.) 1815.

3e. **Lady Camilla Elizabeth Bennet**, b. 22 Mar. 1747; d. 2 Sept. 1821; m. 1st, 5 Sept. 1764, Count Dunhoff, of Poland, d. 25 Sept. 1764; 2ndly, 1778, Robert Robinson.

4e. **Lady Frances Alicia Bennet**, d. (–); m. 1st, William Aslong; 2ndly, 1781, the Rev. Richard Sandys [eldest son of Richard Sandys of Northborne Court, co. Kent]; 3rdly, the Rev. Edward Beckingham Benson, Rector of Deal.

[Nos. 85799 to 85844.

The Plantagenet Roll

2d. Hon. *George Bennet*, a godson of George II., b. 1727; d. (? s.p.) 1799.

3d. *Lady Camilla Bennet*, d. 7 Feb. 1785; m. 1st, 11 Jan. 1754, *Gilbert Fane Fleming*; 2ndly, 9 Oct. 1779, (—) *Wake of Bath*; and had issue (by 1st marriage).

2c. *Lady Bridget Bennet*, d. 12 Oct. 1738; m. as 1st wife, 20 Jan. 1716, *John (Wallop), 1st Earl of Portsmouth* [G.B.], d. 23 Nov. 1762; and had issue.

See the Essex Volume, pp. 237–240, Nos. 30015–30098.

3c. *Lady Annabella Bennet*, d. 27 Nov. 1769; m. Feb. 1721, *William Paulet*, M.P. [D. of Bolton Coll.], d. (–); and had issue.

See the Exeter Volume, Table XXXVII.; the Essex Volume Supplement, p. 638; and the Essex Volume, p. 239, Nos. 30085–30098.

4c. *Lady Mary Bennet*, d. 24 May 1729; m. 6 Aug. 1729[1] or 1720,[2] *William Willmer of Sywel Park, co. Notts*, M.P.

6a. *Lady Arethusa Berkeley*, d. 11 Feb. 1743; m. as 2nd wife, *Charles (Boyle), 3rd Baron Clifford of Lanesborough* [E.], styled Viscount Dungarvan [I.], d.v.p. 12 Oct. 1794; and had issue 1b.

1b. Hon. *Arethusa Boyle*, m. *James Younger*. [Nos. 85845 to 85942.

258. Descendants, if any surviving, of the Hon. MARY BERKELEY (Table XXI.), d. (–); m. Sir JOHN ZOUCH of Codnore, co. Derby, who was knighted 23 Ap. 1604 and was living 1615; and had issue[1] 1a to 3a.

1a. *John Zouch*, son and h.-app., joined father in sale of Codnore, m. *Isabella, da. of Patrick Lowe of Denby*.

2a. *Maria Zouch*.

3a. *Isabella Zouch*.

259. Descendants of the Hon. FRANCES BERKELEY (Table XXI.), b. c. 1564; d. 29 Dec. 1595; m. as 1st wife (settl. 21 Feb.), 1587, Sir GEORGE SHIRLEY, 1st Bt. [E. 22 May 1611], d. 27 Ap. 1622; and had issue 1a to 2a.

1a. Sir *Henry Shirley*, 2nd Bt. [E.], b. c. 1588; d. 8 Feb. 1633; m. 1 Aug. 1616, *Lady Dorothy, da. of Robert (Devereux), 2nd Earl of Essex* [E.] (who m. 2ndly, 1634, *William Stafford of Blatherwick, co. Northants*, and) d. 30 Mar. 1636; and had issue.

See the Essex Volume, Table III. and pp. 36–88, Nos. 4544–6687.

2a. Sir *Thomas Shirley of Botolph Bridge, co. Hants, the Antiquary*, bur. at St. Peter's, Paul's Wharf, London, 4 Feb. 1654; m. *Mary, da. of Thomas Harpar of Rushall, co. Stafford*, living Sept. 1650; and had issue (all living Sept. 1650) 1b to 7b.

1b. *Henry Shirley*, b. a. 1629.

2b. *George Shirley*.

3b. *John Shirley*.

4b. *Francis Shirley*.

5b. *Thomas Shirley*, probably the Capt. Thomas Shirley living 1669, and then next h. to the Baronetcy.

6b. *Mary Shirley*.

7b. *Anne Shirley*. [Nos. 85943 to 88086.

---

[1] Brydge's "Collins," iii. 130.   [2] Burke's "Peerage," 1907, p. 1620.

of The Blood Royal

260. Descendants of Lady MARGARET HOWARD (Table XXI.), *bapt.* 30 Jan. 1543; *d.* 17 Mar. 1590; *m.* as 2nd wife, HENRY (SCROPE), 9th BARON SCROPE of Bolton, K.G., *d.* 10 May 1591; and had issue, which became extinct 30 May 1630.

261. Descendants, if any, of the Hon. DOUGLAS HOWARD (Table XXIV.), *bapt.* at Stratford-le-Bow 29 Jan. 1572; *d.* (-); *m.* as 1st wife, Sir ARTHUR GORGES of Chelsea, *d.* 1625; and had (with possibly other [1]) issue 1*a*.

1*a. Dudley Gorges,* d. (*will proved 17 Sept.*) 1667; m. *at Chelsea 12 Aug.* 1619, *Sir Robert Lane,* d. (*will proved 2 Oct.*) 1624.

262. Descendants of THOMAS (THYNNE), 1st VISCOUNT WEYMOUTH [E. 11 Dec. 1682] (Table XXIV.), *b. c.* 1640; *d.* 28 July 1714; *m.* Lady FRANCES, da. of Heneage (FINCH), 3rd Earl of Winchilsea [E.], *d.* 17 Ap. 1712; and had issue.

See the Tudor Roll, Table XXIV. and pp. 186–240, Nos. 20946–22550.
[Nos. 88087 to 89691.

263. Descendants of THOMAS THYNNE of Old Windsor (Table XXIV.), *d.* 24 Ap. 1710; *m.* 1709, Lady MARY, da. of Edward (VILLIERS), 1st Earl of Jersey [E.] (who *m.* 2ndly, 1711, GEORGE (GRANVILLE), 1st BARON LANSDOWNE [G.B.] and) *d.* 17 Jan. 1735; and had issue.

See p. 377, Nos. 61798–62166.   [Nos. 89692 to 90060.

264. Descendants of DOROTHY THYNNE (Table XXIV.), *bapt.* 21 Sept. 1692; *d.* 14 Feb. 1777; *m.* JOHN (HOWE), 1st BARON CHEDWORTH [G.B.], *d.* Ap. 1742; and had issue 1*a* to 5*a*.

1*a. John Thynne (Howe), 2nd Baron Chedworth [G.B.],* b. 18 *Feb.* 1714; d.s.p. 9 *May* 1762.
2*a. Henry Frederick (Howe), 3rd Baron Chedworth [G.B.],* b. 17 *Feb.* 1715; d. *unm.* 7 *Oct.* 1781.
3*a. Rev. the Hon. Thomas Howe, Rector of Wishford, co. Wilts,* d. (-); m. *Frances, da. of Thomas White of Tattingstone Place, co. Suffolk; and had issue* 1*b.*
1*b. John (Howe), 4th and last Baron Chedworth [G.B.],* b. 22 *Aug.* 1754; d. *unm.* 29 *Oct.* 1804.

---

[1] Sir Arthur Gorges had, in addition to the da. named above: (1) Sir Arthur, whose only son *d.s.p.* 1668; (2) Elizabeth (by 2nd wife), who *m.* 1st, Sir Robert Stanley, and 2ndly, Theophilus, 4th Earl of Lincoln [E.]; (3) Timoleon; (4) Egremont; (5) Carew; and (6) Henry—but, with the exception of the da. Elizabeth, it does not appear clear whether they were the issue of the Howard marriage or of his 2nd wife, Lady Elizabeth Clinton.

The pedigree given in Berry's "Buckingham Genealogies," deducing the Ouseleys from this Sir Arthur, is incorect.

The Plantagenet Roll

4a. Hon. *Mary Howe*, da. and in her issue, if any (1804), co-h., d. (-) ; m. *Alexander Wright*.

5a. Hon. *Anne Howe*, da. and in her issue (1804) h. or co-h., d. (-) ; m. *Roderick Gwynne of Glanbrâne, co. Brecon* ; and had (with possibly other) issue [1] 1b to 2b.

1b. *Sackville Gwynne of Glanbrâne*, d. 1794 ; m. 1st, *Catherine*, da. of (—) *Prytherch* ; and had issue 1c to 5c.

1c. *Sackville Frederick Henry Gwynne of Glanbrâne*, b. 14 Aug. 1778 ; d. (-) ; m. twice ; and had issue.

2c. *John Gwynne of Gwernvale House, co. Brecon*, J.P., D.L., High Sheriff co. Brecon 1819, d. (? s.p.) ; m. *Arabella* [da. of (—)] *Gorges of Alscott Manor, co. Oxon*.

3c. *David Gwynne*, d. (-) ; m. *Catherine*, d. of *Humphrey Jones*.

4c. }
5c. } 2 das.

2b. *Thomas Howe Gwynne of Buckland, co. Brecon*, d. (-) ; m. (—), da. and h. of C. *Matthew of Lundock Castle, co. Glamorgan* ; and had (with possibly other) issue 1c.

1c. *Roderick Gwynne*, son and h., d.v.p. ; m. *Eliza Ann*, da. and co-h. of (—) *Hughes of Tregunter* ; and had issue 1d.

1d. *Anna Maria Eleanor Gwynne*, d. 7 Aug. 1881 ; m. 4 Sept. 1830, *James Price Holford of Kilgwyn, co. Carmarthen*, J.P., and High Sheriff co. Brecknock 1840, Lieut.-Col. in the Army, b. 25 Sept. 1791 ; d. Aug. 1846 ; and had issue 1e to 3e.

1e. *James Price William Holford*, now *Gwynne-Holford, of Kilgwyn and Buckland*, J.P., D.L., M.P. for Brecon 1870–1880, and High Sheriff 1857, formerly 16th Lancers (*Kilgwyn, co. Carmarthen* ; *Buckland, Bwlch* ; *Tre Holford, co. Brecon* ; *Carlton*), b. 25 Nov. 1833 ; m. 14 Ap. 1891, *Mary Eleanor*, da. of Captain *Patrick Robert Gordon-Cumming of Hartpury, co. Glouc.* ; and has issue 1f.

1f. *Eleanor Maria Gwynne-Holford*, b. 18 Nov. 1899.

2e. *Jane Eliza Anna Maria Holford*.

3e. *Louisa Mary Ermine Eleanor Holford*, d. 10 Jan. 1876 ; m. as 1st wife, 21 Oct. 1865, Major *Edmund Philip Herbert* (R.L. 27 Sept. 1848), formerly Jones, of *Llansanffraed Court, Chief Constable co. Monmouth* [descended from George, Duke of Clarence, K.G., brother of King Edward IV. (see Clarence Volume, p. 456)] (*Llansanffraed Court, Abergavenny*) ; and had issue 1f.

1f. *Edmund Arthur Herbert*, M.V.O., Lieut.-Col. Comdg. 6th Inniskilling Dragoons, b. 5 Aug. 1866 ; m. 8 Jan. 1898, *Ethel*, da. of *John Pickersgill Rodger of Hadlow Castle, co. Kent* ; and has issue 1g to 2g.

1g. *Eleanora Herbert*.

2g. *Mary Catherine Herbert*. [Nos. 90061 to 90066.

265. Descendants, if any surviving, of the Hon. MARY LOWTHER (Table XXIV.), d. (-) ; m. Sir JOHN WENTWORTH.

266. Descendants of the Hon. ELIZABETH LOWTHER (Table XXIV.), bur. 9 Oct. 1764 ; m. 6 Aug. 1696, Sir WILLIAM RAMSDEN, 2nd Bt. [E.], bapt. 22 Oct. 1672 ; d. 27 June 1736 ; and had issue 1a to 4a.

1a. Sir *John Ramsden, 3rd Bt.* [E.], M.P., bapt. 21 Mar. 1699 ; d. 10 Ap. 1769 ; m. (lic. dated 8 Aug.) 1748, *Margaret*, widow of *Thomas Bright*, formerly *Liddell of Badsworth, co. York*, da. and h. of *William Norton of Sawley*, bur. 7 June 1775 ; and had issue 1b to 2b.

---

[1] Burke's " Royal Families, i.-cxxix.

of The Blood Royal

1*b*. Sir John Ramsden, 4th Bt. [*E.*], bapt. 1 *Dec.* 1755; d. 15 *July* 1839; m. 5 *June* 1787, *the Hon. Louisa Susan, da. of Charles Ingram (Shepherd), 10th Viscount Irvine* [*S.*], d. 21 *Nov.* 1857; *and had issue.*
See the Essex Volume, pp. 151–152, Nos. 17244–17285.

2*b*. Elizabeth Ramsden, d. (-) ; m. 1771, *William Weddell of Newby, M.P.*

2*a*. Robert Ramsden *of Osberton, co. Notts, an Officer in the Army,* b. 1708; d. 9 *Feb.* 1769; m. 13 *Jan.* 1753, *Elizabeth, da. and event. h. of John Smyth of Heath Hall, co. York; and had issue* 1*b* to 4*b*.

1*b*. Robert Ramsden *of Carlton Hall, co. Notts,* bapt. 22 *Nov.* 1753; d. 27 *Ap.* 1830; m. 1783, *Flizabeth, widow of Abel Smith of Wilford, co. Notts, M.P., da. of Charles Appleby of Wooton, co. Linc.,* d. 21 *Nov.* 1807; *and had (with other) issue* 1*c*.

1*c*. Robert Ramsden *of Carlton Hall, J.P., elder son,* b. 29 *Mar.* 1784; d. 1865; m. 29 *July* 1816, *Frances Matilda, da. of John Plumptre,* d. 22 *Ap.* 1837; *and had issue* 1*d* to 5*d*.

1*d*. Robert John Ramsden *of Carlton Hall, J.P.,* b. 12 *June* 1817; d. 20 *Mar.* 1892; m. 10 *Dec.* 1844, *Mary Matilda, da. of the Rev. Henry Gipps of Elmley,* d. 4 *July* 1874; *and had issue* 1*e* to 8*e*.

1*e*. Robert Henry Ramsden, b. 10 *Sept.* 1845; d.v.p. 19 *May* 1874; m. 31 *May* 1871, *Francesca Romana Maria, da. of Charles William Jebb of Clifton, co. Glouc.; and had issue* 1*f* to 2*f*.

1*f*. Robert Charles Plumptre Ramsden of Carlton Hall, J.P., LL.B., B.A. (Camb.), Bar.-at-Law *(Carlton Hall, Worksop; Oxford and Cambridge Club),* b. 9 Feb. 1874; *unm.*

2*f*. Frances Alice Mary Ramsden, *m.* 16 Ap. 1896, the Rev. John Alfred James, Rector of Dodington, *d.* 21 Jan. 1910; *and has issue* 1*g* to 3*g*.

1*g*. Robert Charles Patrick James, *b.* 17 Mar. 1898.
2*g*. George Herbert Gladwyn James, *b.* 13 Jan. 1901.
3*g*. John Cecil James, *b.* 2 Mar. 1904.

2*e*. Edward Plumptre Ramsden *(Croyde, Cape Patton, Australia),* b. 21 Mar. 1848; *m.* 3 Sept. 1875, Frances Elizabeth, da. of William Kelly of Blackheath; and has issue 1*f* to 7*f*.

1*f*. John Edward Cecil Ramsden, *b.* 5 July 1881.
2*f*. William Eustace Ramsden, *b.* 4 July 1882.
3*f*–7*f*. 5 das.

3*e*. Charles Arthur Ramsden, b. 4 *Ap.* 1849; d. 3 *Jan.* 1902; m. 15 *Sept.* 1875, *Elizabeth Mary (Harkaway, Berwick, Melbourne), da. of John Leckenby of Scarborough; and had issue* 1*f* to 3*f*.

1*f*. Edith Elizabeth Mary Ramsden, *m.* 14 Ap. 1897, Walter Henry Fossey *(Melbourne)*; and has issue.

2*f*. Emily Gertrude Ramsden, *m.* 21 Dec. 1899, Albert Walter Chartress *(Melbourne)*; and has issue.

3*f*. Maud Ramsden, *unm.*

4*e*. Algernon Feilden Ramsden *(Dunmore, 9 Avenue Victoria, Scarboro'),* b. 11 Sept. 1850; *m.* 4 May 1892, Mary Smith, da. of Thomas Purdom of Hawick; and has issue 1*f*.

1*f*. Edward Feilden Ramsden, *b.* 29 May 1893.

5*e*. John Pemberton Ramsden, B.A. (Camb.) *(Fridhem, Bath),* b. 28 Jan. 1854; *m.* 23 Aug. 1883, Alice Louisa, da. of Arthur Malet, Bombay C.S. [Bt. Coll.]; and has issue 1*f* to 7*f*.

1*f*. Arthur Amherst Ramsden, *b.* 11 Feb. 1889.
2*f*. Ralph Western Ramsden, *b.* 10 Oct. 1890.
3*f*. Evelyn Charlotte Ramsden.
4*f*. Alice Frida Ramsden.
5*f*. Guendolen Ebba Ramsden.
6*f*. Frances Teresa Ramsden.
7*f*. Monica Hilda Ramsden.

[Nos. 90067 to 90129.

The Plantagenet Roll

6e. Mary Emma Frances Ramsden, m. 16 Nov. 1876, Thomas Eadie Purdom, M.D. (*Ellerslie, Park Hill Road, Croydon*); and has issue.

7e. Elizabeth Emily Cecilia Ramsden
8e. Frances Eleanor Matilda Ramsden } (16 *West Mall, Clifton, Bristol*).

2d. Rev. Charles Henry Ramsden, M.A., *Vicar of Chilham, co. Kent*, b. 6 *June* 1818; d. 18 Mar. 1893; m. 24 *May* 1846, *Mary Hamilton, da. of the Rev. Henry Hamilton Beamish of Mount Beamish, co. Cork*, d. 14 Aug. 1902; *and had issue* 1e to 7e.

1e. Charles Hamilton Ramsden, b. 27 Mar. 1847; m. 1873, Caroline Augusta, da. of James McEwen of San Francisco; and has issue 1f to 2f.

1f. Charles Harold Lowther Ramsden, B.Sc., b. 1883.

2f. Percival Scott Webber Ramsden, b. 1886.

2e. Rev. Henry Plumptre Ramsden, B.A. (Oxon.), *Rector of Cottingham*, b. 7 *Ap.* 1848; d. 6 Dec. 1901; m. 26 *July* 1887, *Ethel Frances Alice* (*Heathfield, Weston, Bath*), *da. of William Henry Havelock, Bombay C.S.*; *and had issue* 1f to 2f.

1f. William Havelock Chaplin Ramsden, b. 3 Oct. 1888.

2f. Elaine Margaret Frecheville Ramsden.

3e. Francis Edward Ramsden *of Colorado, U.S.A., Comm. R.N.*, b. 24 *July* 1849; d. 2 *Ap.* 1882; m. 7 *June* 1879, *Emma Elizabeth, da. of Col. F. W. Birch*; *and had issue* 1f.

1f. Francis Charles **Home** Ramsden (*Seattle, Washington, U.S.A.*), b. 3 Dec. 1880.

4e. Herbert Frecheville Smyth Ramsden, Col. Indian Army (*Stone Cross House, Wadhurst, Sussex*), b. 6 Mar. 1856; m. 20 Aug. 1889, the Hon. Edwyna Susan Elizabeth, da. of John Fiennes (Twisleton-Wykeham-Fiennes), 14th Baron Saye and Sele [E.]; and has issue 1f to 2f.

1f. Geoffrey Charles Frecheville Ramsden, b. 21 Ap. 1893.

2f. Mary Edwyna Ramsden.

5e. Ernest Western Ramsden (*Port Darwin, Northern Territory, S. Australia*), b. 27 Jan. 1863.

6e. Frances Matilda Anne Ramsden, d. 31 Dec. 1909; m. 19 *Ap.* 1876, *Stafford O'Brien Hoare of Turville Park, co. Bucks, J.P., D.L.*, d. 9 Sept. 1906; *and had issue* 1f.

1f. Lilias Hoare, sometime (D.P. 1897) Stafford O'Brien Hoare, of Turville Park, co. Bucks, m. 23 Jan. 1908, Major Edward Spencer Nairne, now (D.P. Mar. 1910) Hoare-Nairne, R.A. (*Turville Park, Henley-on-Thames*); and has issue 1g.

1g. Lilias Hoare-Nairne, b. 6 June 1909.

7e. Gertrude Mary Ramsden (*The Rookery, Yarlington, Wincanton*), m. 1887, the Rev. Arthur Johnson Rogers, Rector of Yarlington, d. 15 Ap. 1908; and has issue 1f.

1f. Mary Ramsden Rogers.

3d. Rev. Frederick Selwyn Ramsden, M.A., b. 12 *July* 1830; d. 17 *Jan.* 1865; m. 23 *Ap.* 1862, *Mary Jane, da. of the Rev. Joseph Parker, M.A., Rector of Wyton*; *and had issue* 1e.

1e. Frederick Plumptre Ramsden, B.A. (Oxon.), b. 1863; m. Mar. 1906, Norah, da. of (—) White.

4d. Emma Louisa Ramsden, d. 8 Oct. 1901; m. 29 *Sept.* 1853, *the Rev. Henry Gladwin Jebb of Firbeck Hall, co. Yorks*, d. 19 *Ap.* 1898; *and had issue* 1e to 3e.

1e. Henry Scrope Frecheville Jebb, J.P., *formerly Lieut. 3rd Hussars* (*Tullich Lodge, Ballater, Aberdeen; Athenæum*), b. 17 July 1867; m. 1st, 11 Aug. 1888, Evelyn Lucy, widow of Capt. Francis Michael Goold-Adams, R.A., da. of the Rev. Edward Bristow Philips Wynne, d. 2 Mar. 1907; 2ndly, 25 Ap. 1908, Winifred, da. of Thomas Marriott Dodington of Horsington House, co. Som.; and has issue 1f to 2f. [Nos. 90130 to 90148.

of The Blood Royal

1f. Henry Cecil Edward Jebb, b. 14 July 1889.
2f. Samuel Henry Jebb, b. 12 Mar. 1909.

2e. Florence Emily Dorothy Jebb (*East Liss, Hants*).

3e. Edith Fanny Maud Jebb, m. 25 Ap. 1889, John Sydney Burton Borough of Chetwynd Park, M.A. (Oxon.), J.P., High Sheriff co. Salop 1901 (*Chetwynd Park, Newport, Salop; Carlton*); and has issue 1f to 4f.
1f. John George Burton Borough, b. 13 Sept. 1890.
2f. Alaric Charles Henry Borough, b. 9 Ap. 1892.
3f. Elizabeth Honora Borough.
4f. Cynthia Mabel Borough.

5d. Emily Anna Ramsden (*North House, Carlton, Worksop*).

2b. Rev. *John Ramsden, Rector of Crofton and Vicar of Arksey*, d. 12 Oct. 1807; m. 8 Oct. 1790, *Frances Elizabeth, da. of Sir George Cooke, 7th Bt.* [E.], d. 13 Dec. 1847; *and had issue* 1c *to* 2c.
1c. *John Ramsden*, b. 3 Jan. 1793; d. 19 Mar. 1861; m. 28 Oct. 1828, *Maria, da. of* (—) *Jackman*, d. July 1859; *and had issue* 1d.
1d. William John Plantagenet Ramsden, b. 30 Sept. 1837; m. 2 July 1861, Emma Mary, da. of Thomas Fairland, d.s.p. 9 Sept. 1878.
2c. *George Ramsden*, b. 13 Jan. 1796; d. (-); m. 6 Jan. 1825, *Anna, da. of John Fullerton of Thriberg*, d. 3 Jan. 1837; *and had issue* 1d.
1d. *Rev. Frederick John Ramsden, M.A.* (Oxon.), *Rector of Uffington*, b. 5 Aug. 1836; d. 26 Nov. 1903; m. 22 Aug. 1865, *Anna Cassandra, da. of Rear-Adm. the Hon. Major Jacob Henniker*, d. 5 May 1906; *and had issue* 1e *to* 4e.
1e. Frederick Frank Ramsden (*Bishop Thornton Grove, Ripley, Yorks*), b. 8 Dec. 1867; m. 1893, Selina Lucinda, da. of Capt. Edmund Mackinnon, 2nd Life Guards.
2e. Cassandra Ramsden, m. 14 Ap. 1898, George William Staunton.
3e. Julia Selina Ramsden
4e. Frances Georgiana Ramsden } (58 *Cornwall Gardens, S.W.*).

3b. Catherine Ramsden.
4b. Charlotte Ramsden.

3a. *Thomas Ramsden, Latin Sec. in the Office of Sec. of State*, bapt. 22 July 1709; d. (*will dated* 2 *Sept.* 1785, *pr.* 31 *May*) 1791; m. 14 July 1743, *Anne, da. of Sir Philip Medowes, Knight Marshal.*
4a. *Frecheville Ramsden, Lieut.-Col. Grenadier Guards, Lieut.-Gov. of Carlisle*, bapt. 11 Ap. 1715; d. 24 Dec. 1804; m. 17 Mar. 1761, *Isabella* [*descended from the Lady Isabella Plantagenet*], *da. of Col. Charles Ingram* [*Vt. Irvine Coll.*], d. 25 Feb. 1762; *and had issue* 1b.
1b. *George Ramsden, Capt. 15th Light Dragoons*, b. c. 1761; d. 1793; m. *Lucy, da. and co-h. of Gen. Bryn Carpenter*, d. 17 Aug. 1842; *and had issue* (*with a younger son d.s.p.*) 1c *to* 2c.
1c. George Ramsden, Lieut.-Col. 1st Foot Guards, d. (? s.p.) 9 Oct. 1820.
2c. *Rev. William Ramsden, Rector of Ashurst, Kent, and Linwood, co. Linc.*, b. 1787; d. 4 Nov. 1860; m. 5 Ap. 1815, *Elizabeth Jane, da. of Richard Bell of Selby, co. Yorks*, d. 11 Ap. 1888; *and had issue* (*with* 2 *sons and a da.* d. unm.) 1d.
1d. *Arthur Charles Ramsden of Stoneness, co. Kent, J.P., Hon. Col. 2nd Vol. Batt. The Buffs*, b. 1 Ap. 1825; d. 11 Dec. 1891; m. 21 Jan. 1853, *Frances Elizabeth, da. of John Deacon of Mabledon, co. Kent*, d. 8 Oct. 1892; *and had issue* 1e *to* 3e.
1e. Arthur John Ramsden, J.P., *formerly* Capt. and Hon. Major 1st Vol. Batt. Queen's Own (*Great Bidlake, Bridstowe, Devon*), b. 10 June 1855; m. 26 Ap. 1883, Elizabeth Alice, da. of Henry William Hawkins of Martinstown, Dorset; and has issue 1f to 4f. [Nos. 90149 to 90165.

The Plantagenet Roll

1*f.* Arthur Geoffrey Francis Ramsden, *b.* 13 Aug. 1887.
2*f.* John Hope Frecheville Ramsden, *b.* 26 July 1896.
3*f.* Elizabeth Joan Ramsden, *m.* 12 Oct. 1910, Julian Baring-Gould [2nd son of the Rev. Sabine Baring-Gould and a descendant of Lady Isabel Plantagenet (see Essex Volume, p. 127)].
4*f.* Frances Honor Ramsden.

2*e.* Rev. William Frecheville Ramsden, M.A. (Oxon.), Vicar of St. Saviour's, Scarborough (*St. Saviour's Parsonage, Scarborough*), *b.* 16 July 1857; *unm.*
3*e.* Rev. George Ramsden, Chaplain of Walmsgate (*The Priory, Burwell, Louth, Lincoln*), *b.* 8 Mar. 1862; *m.* 27 Sept. 1886, Elizabeth Jane, da. of John Wykes of Daventry, *d.s.p.* 8 Oct. 1905. [Nos. 90166 to 90171.

267. Descendants of the Hon. MARGARET LOWTHER (Table XXIV.), *d.* 15 Sept. 1738; *m.* 20 Mar. 1706, Sir JOSEPH PENNINGTON, 2nd Bt. [E.], *d.* 3 Dec. 1744; and had issue.

See the Exeter Volume, pp. 536–537, Nos. 49016–49258.
[Nos. 90172 to 90414.

268. Descendants, if any, of ELIZABETH THYNNE (Table XXIV.), *d.* (–); *m.* Sir THOMAS NOTT of Richmond, co. Surrey.

269. Descendants, if any, of the Hon. GRACE HOWARD (Table XXIV.), *d.* (–); *m.* JOHN [son and h. of Sir John] HORSEY of Clifton, co. Dorset.

270. Descendants of HENRY (NEVILL), 5th EARL OF WESTMORLAND [E.], K.G. (Table XXV.), *b.* 1525; *d.* Aug. 1563; *m.* 1st, 3 July 1538, Lady ANNE, da. of Thomas (MANNERS), 1st Earl of Rutland [E.]; 2ndly, JANE, da. of Sir Roger CHOLMELEY; 3rdly, MARGARET, widow of Sir HENRY GASCOIGNE, da. of Sir Roger CHOLMELEY, *bur.* 2 Ap. 1570; and had issue 1*a* to 5*a*.

1*a.* Charles (*Nevill*), 6*th Earl of Westmorland* [E.], K.G., *b.* 1543; *d.* 16 *Nov.* 1601; *m. a.* 1564, *Lady Jane, da. of Henry* (*Howard*), *Earl of Surrey* [E.], K.G., *d. c.* 1593; *and had issue.*
See the Exeter Volume, Table XXII. and pp. 333–338, Nos. 24284–24614.

2*a.*[1] *Lady Eleanor Nevill,* m. *as 1st wife, Sir William Pelham, P.C., d.* 1587; *and had issue.*
See the Exeter Volume, Table XXIII. and pp. 339–346, Nos. 24615–25204.

3*a.*[1] *Lady Katherine Nevill,* d.s.p.; m. *Sir John Constable of Kirby Knowle, co. York.*
4*a.*[2] *Lady Margaret Nevill.*
5*a.*[2] *Lady Elizabeth Nevill.* [Nos. 90415 to 91535.

271. Descendants of Lady KATHERINE DE VERE (Table XXV.), *d.* 17 Jan. 1599; *m.* EDWARD (WINDSOR), 3rd BARON WINDSOR [E.], *d.* 24 Jan. 1575; and had issue 1*a* to 6*a*.

1*a.* Frederick (*Windsor*), 4*th Baron Windsor* [E.], *b.* 1559; *d. unm.* 24 *Oct.* 1585.
2*a.* Henry (*Windsor*), 5*th Baron Windsor* [E.], *b.* 1562; *d.* 6 *Ap.* 1605; m.

440

of The Blood Royal

1590, *Anne, da. and co-h. of Sir Thomas Revett of London,* d. 27 *Nov.* 1615; *and had issue* 1b *to* 3b.

1b. *Thomas (Windsor), 6th Baron Windsor* [E.], K.B., b. 29 *Sept.* 1591; d.s.p. 6 *Dec.* 1642.

2b. *Hon. Elizabeth Windsor, da. and co-h.,* d. (-); m. 24 *July* 1616, *Dixie Hickman of Kew, co. Surrey; and had issue* 1c *to* 3c.

1c. *Thomas (Hickman), 7th Baron Windsor and* (6 *Dec.* 1682) 1st *Earl of Plymouth* [E.], d. 3 *Nov.* 1687; m. 1st, 12 *May* 1656, *Anne, da. of Sir William Savile of Thornhill, 3rd Bt.* [E. 1611], d. 22 *Nov.* 1666; 2ndly, 9 *Ap.* 1668, *Ursula, da. and co-h. of Sir Thomas Widdrington of Sherburne Grange, co. Northbd.,* d. 22 *Ap.* 1717; *and had issue* 1d *to* 3d.

1d.[1] *Other Hickman, Lord Windsor,* b. 12 *Sept.* 1659; d.v.p. 11 *Nov.* 1684; m. 20 *Oct.* 1673, *Elizabeth, da. and h. of Thomas Turvey of Walcote, co. Worc.* [*who* m. 2*ndly, Edward Wyke and was*] bur. 29 *Jan.* 1688; *and had issue.*

See the Exeter Volume, Table XXI. and pp. 321-333, Nos. 23949-24283.

2d.[2] *Thomas (Hickman), 1st Viscount Windsor* [I.], *so cr.* 19 *June* 1699, *and Baron Mountjoy* [G.B.], *so cr.* 1 *Jan.* 1712, d. 8 *June* 1738; m. 28 *Aug.* 1703, *Charlotte, widow of John (Jeffreys), 2nd Baron Jeffreys* [E.], *da. and h. of Philip (Herbert), 7th Earl of Pembroke* [E.], d. 13 *Nov.* 1733; *and had issue* 1e *to* 5e.

1e. *Herbert (Hickman), 2nd Viscount Windsor* [I.] *and Baron Mountjoy* [G.B.], d. 25 *Jan.* 1758; m. 12 *Aug.* 1735, *Alice, sister and co-h. of Sir James Clavering, 4th Bt.* [E.], d. 24 *Nov.* 1776; *and had issue* 1f.

1f. *Hon. Charlotte Jane Hickman, da. and* (11 *Nov.* 1772) *sole h.,* d. 28 *Jan* 1800; m. *as* 1st *wife,* 12 *Nov.* 1766, *John (Stuart), 4th Earl* [S.] *and* (27 *Feb.* 1796) 1st *Marquis* [G.B.] *of Bute,* d. 16 *Nov.* 1814; *and had issue.*

See the Exeter Volume, pp. 294-297, Nos. 14681-14791.

2e. *Hon. Ursula Hickman,* d. (-); m. *as* 1st *wife,* 20 *Mar.* 1736, *John Wadman of Imber, co. Wilts,* d. 1793; *and had issue* 3 *children who* d.s.p.[1]

3e. *Hon. Charlotte Hickman,* d. (-); m. 18 *Ap.* 1736, *John Kent of Salisbury.*

4e. *Hon. Catherine Hickman,* b. *in London* 1716; d.s.p. *at Frankfort-on-Main* 26 *May* 1742; m. *as* 1st *wife,* 10 *Feb.* 1741, *Matthews Lestevenon, Lord of Berkenrode and Strijen, in Holland,* LL.D., *Secretary to the City of Amsterdam* 1729-1745, *and Sheriff* 1745-1748, *and Ambassador to France* 1749-1792, d. *at the Hague* 13 *Jan.* 1797.

5e. *Hon. Elizabeth Hickman.*

3d. *Lady Ursula Hickman,* d. 20 *Aug.* 1737; m. 28 *Mar.* 1703, *Thomas Johnson.*

2c. *Mariana Hickman,* b. 1620; bur. *at Worcester* 7 *Feb.* 1670; m. 1st, *June* 1644, *Sir Henry Hunloke,* 1st Bt. [E. 28 *Feb.* 1642], d. 13 *Jan.* 1647; 2ndly, 25 *May* 1655, *Col. William Michell,* d. c. (*will proved* 26 *June*) 1673; *and had issue* (*with a da. by* 2nd *husband who* d.s.p.) 1d.

1d. *Sir Henry Hunloke,* 2nd Bt. [E.], b. 20 *Nov.* 1645; d. 3 *Jan.* 1714; m. 28 *Jan.* 1674, *Katherine, da. and h. of Francis Tyrwhitt of Kettleby, co. Linc.; and had issue.*

See the Exeter Volume, Table II., and pp. 77-78, Nos. 1-106.

3c. *Catherine Hickman,* d. (-); m. *John Columbine.*[2]

3b. *Hon. Elizabeth Windsor, da. and co-h.,* m. 1st, *Sir Andrew Windsor;* 2ndly, *Sir James Ware, Auditor-Gen. of Ireland; and had issue, of whom descendants of the name of Ware survived in Ireland in the eighteenth century.*[3]

[Nos. 91336 to 91887.

---

[1] Hoare's "Wilts," I. ii. 165.

[2] Not mentioned in the Columbine pedigree in Carthew's "West and East Bradenham," p. 160.

[3] Brydge's "Collins," iii. 682.

The Plantagenet Roll

3a. Hon. *Edward Windsor*, m. *Elizabeth [da. of (—)] Ardington*.
4a. Hon. *Andrew Windsor*, m. *Anne [da. of (—)] Peche*.
5a. Hon. *Margaret Windsor*, d.s.p.[1]; m. *as 2nd wife, John Talbot of Grafton, co. Worc.*
6a.[1] Hon. *Catherine Windsor*, b. c. 1568; d. 15 Dec. 1641; m. *Robert Audley of Berechurch, co. Essex*, b. 14 Mar. 1556; d. 27 Sept. 1624; *and had issue* 1b to 5b.[2]

1b. *Sir Henry Audley of Berechurch*, aged 19 and over 1624, m. *Anne, da. of Humphrey Porkington of Horvington, co. Worc.; and had issue (at least 2 sons)*[3] 1c to 2c.

1c. *Thomas Audley of Berechurch*, d.s.p. 1697.
2c. *Henry Audley*, d. 1 Sept. 1714, *after having sold his estates*.
2b. *Robert Audley of Colchester*, living 1634.
3b. *Richard Audley*.
4b. *Catherine Audley*, m. *John Thatcher*.
5b. *Mary Audley*.

272. Descendants, if any, of Lady MARY NEVILL (Table XXV.), d. 14 Mar. 1596; m. Sir THOMAS DANBY of Farnley, co. York, knighted Sept. 1547, d. 13 Sept. 1590; and had issue (with others who all app. d.s.p.) 1a.

1a. *Thomas Danby of Farnley, &c., co. York*, d.v.p. 3 Jan. 1581; m. *Elizabeth, da. of Thomas Wentworth of Wentworth Woodhouse*, d. 1629; *and had issue* 1b.
1b. *Christopher Danby of Farnley and Leighton*, d. 18 July 1624; m. *the Hon. Frances, da. of Edward (Parker), 6th Baron Morley [E.] (who* re-m. *2ndly, William Richards and)* d. 20 Sept. 1654; *and had issue* 1c to 2c.
1c. *Sir Thomas Danby of Farnley and Leighton, High Sheriff co. York* 1625, *and a Col. in the Royal Army*, d. 5 Aug. 1660; m. *Katherine, da. of Christopher Wandesford, Lord-Deputy of Ireland*, d. 22 Sept. 1645[4]; *and had issue* 1d to 3d.
1d. *Thomas Danby of Farnley, 1st Mayor of Leeds*, d. 1667, *leaving issue, which became extinct* 1683.
2d. *Christopher Danby of Farnley*, d. Nov. 1689; m. *Anne, da. of Col. Edward Colepepper; and had issue* 1e to 4e.
1e. *Sir Abstrupus Danby, J.P., D.L., co. York*, b. 1655; d. 24 Mar. 1727; m. *and had issue, which became extinct in or about* 1792.
2e. *Wandesforde Danby*.
3e. *Francelia Danby*.
4e. *Eleanor Danby*.
3d. *Katharine Danby*, d. 1688; m. *Henry Best of Gray's Inn*.

2c. *Katharine Danby*, bapt. *at Leeds* 29 Nov. 1612; bur. 13 Jan. 1666; m. 1629, *Sir Francis Armytage of Kirklees, 1st Bt.* [E. 15 Dec. 1641], d.v.p. (bur. 12 June) 1644; *and had issue* 1d to 5d.
1d. *Sir John Armytage, 2nd Bt.* [E.], bapt. 15 Dec. 1629; bur. 9 Mar. 1677; m. c. 1651, *Margaret, da. of Thomas Thornhill of Fixby, co. York*, bur. 10 Feb. 1695; *and had issue* 1e to 6e.
1e. *Sir Thomas Armytage, 3rd Bt.* [E.], bapt. 10 May 1652; d. unm. 1694.

---

[1] Brydge's "Collins," iii. 36.   [2] Berry's "Essex Pedigrees," p. 134.
[3] Morant's "Essex," ii. 205.
[4] Whitaker's "Richmond," ii. 98. In Thoresby's *Ducatus Leodiensis* (p. 202), however, she is said to have died of her fifteenth child in the thirtieth year of her age, 1629.

# of The Blood Royal

2e. Sir *John Armytage*, 4th Bt. [E.], bapt. 14 *Ap*. 1653; d. *unm*. 2 Dec. 1732.

3e. *Christopher Armytage of Hartshead Hall, whose only son* d.s.p. 1732.

4e. Sir *George Armytage*, 5th Bt. [E.], bapt. 23 *Aug*. 1660; d. *unm*. (bur. 24 *Ap*.) 1736.

5e. *Margaret Armytage*, bapt. 24 *Sept.* 1650; d. (–); m. 27 *May* 1672, *Francis Neville of Chevet, co. York,* bur. 5 *June* 1707; *and had issue, which became extinct* 1765.

6e. *Catherine Armytage*, bapt. 7 *Ap.* 1654; d. (–); m. *as 1st wife,* 19 Nov. 1679, *Christopher Tancred of Whexley, co. York, M.P., High Sheriff* 1685, d. 21 Nov. 1705; *and had issue.*

See the Exeter Volume, pp. 551–553, Nos. 49618–49656.

2d. *Francis Armytage of South Kirby, co. York,* bapt. 3 *Jan.* 1632; d. *between* 1695 *and* 1728; m. *Mary, da. of Robert Trappes of Nidd, co. York; and had issue* 1e.

1e. Sir *Thomas Armytage*, 6th *and last* Bt. [E.], bapt. 31 *July* 1673; d. *unm.* 12 *Oct.* 1737.

3d. *William Armytage of Killinghall, co. York, living* 1660, m. *Elizabeth, da. of Robert Trappes.*

4d. *Anne Armytage,* m. (—) *Smith of London.*

5d. *Winifred Armytage,* m. *Thomas Lacy.*   [Nos. 91888 to 91926.

273. Descendants of Lady MARGARET NEVILL (Table XXV.), *d.* 13 Oct. 1559; *m.* as 1st wife, 3 July 1536, HENRY (MANNERS), 2nd EARL OF RUTLAND [E.], K.G., *d.* 17 Sept. 1563; and had issue.

See the Exeter Volume, Table II., and pp. 77–159, Nos. 1–2470; and Essex Volume Supplement, pp. 606–613, Nos. 2470/1–183.   [Nos. 91927 to 94580.

274. Descendants of JOHN (VERNEY, *afterwards c.* 1772 PEYTO-VERNEY), 14th BARON WILLOUGHBY DE BROKE [E.] (Table XXV.), *b.* 1738; *d.* 15 Feb. 1816; *m.* 8 Oct. 1761, Lady LOUISA, da. of Francis (NORTH), 1st Earl of Guildford [G.B.], *b.* 23 Mar. 1737; *d.* 2 Ap. 1798; and had issue 1*a* to 3*a*.

1a. *John Peyto* (*Verney*), 15*th Baron Willoughby de Broke* [E.], b. 28 *June* 1762; d.s.p. 1 *Sept.* 1820.

2a. *Henry* (*Verney*), 16*th Baron Willoughby de Broke* [E.], b. 5 *Ap.* 1773; d.s.p. 16 *Dec.* 1852.

3a. *Hon. Louisa Verney,* b. 20 *June* 1769; d. 3 *Feb.* 1835; m. 31 *Oct.* 1793, *the Rev. Robert Barnard, Preb. of Winchester,* d. 25 *Feb.* 1835; *and had issue* 1b.

1b. *Robert John* (*Barnard, afterwards* (R.L. 17 *May* 1853) *Verney*), 17*th Baron Willoughby de Broke* [E.], b. 7 *Oct.* 1809; d. 5 *June* 1862; m. 25 *Oct.* 1842, *Georgiana Jane, da. of Major-Gen. Thomas William Taylor of Ogwell, co. Devon, C.B.,* d. 7 *Mar.* 1889; *and had issue* 1c *to* 6c.

1c. *Henry* (*Verney*), 18*th Baron Willoughby de Broke* [E.], b. 14 *May* 1844; d. 19 *Dec.* 1902; m. 17 *Oct.* 1867, *Geraldine, da. of James Hugh Smith-Barry of Marbury Hall, co. Chester,* d. 21 *Dec.* 1894; *and had issue* 1d *to* 3d.

1d. Richard Greville (Verney), 19th Baron Willoughby de Broke [E.] and also *de jure* Baron Latimer [E. 1299], J.P., D.L., &c. (*Kineton House, Warwick; Compton Verney, Warwick; Woodley House, Kineton; Carlton*), b. 29 Mar. 1869; *m.* 2 July 1895, Marie Frances Lisette, da. of Charles Addington Hanbury; *s.p.s.*
[No. 94581.

443

The Plantagenet Roll

2*d*. Hon. Blanche Verney, *m*. 13 Ap. 1898, Richard Granville Lloyd Baker, J.P. [eldest son and h. of Granville Edward Lloyd Baker of Hardwicke Court] (*The Cottage, Hardwicke, Glos.*); and has issue 1*e* to 3*e*.

1*e*. Hylda Blanche Lloyd Baker.
2*e*. Olive Katharine Lloyd Baker.
3*e*. Audrey Pamela Lloyd Baker.

3*d*. Hon. Patience Verney, *m*. 4 June 1896, Basil Hanbury (*The Lodge Farm, Compton Verney, Warwick*); and has issue 1*e*.

1*e*. Harold Greville Hanbury, *b*. 1898.

2*c*. Rev. the Hon. Walter Robert Verney, M.A. (Oxon.), Vicar of Chesterton, late Rector of Lighthorne (*Lighthorne, Warwick; Junior Carlton*), *b*. 18 Mar. 1846; *m*. 5 June 1879, Elizabeth Georgina, da. of Major Robert Wilberforce Bird of Barton House, Shipston-on-Stour; and has issue 1*d* to 3*d*.

1*d*. Robert Barnard Verney, *b*. 5 Nov. 1882.
2*d*. Reynell Henry Verney, *b*. 12 Jan. 1886.
3*d*. Clare Verney.

3*c*. Hon. Margaret Louisa Verney (23 *Hans Place, S.W.; Sandwell, S. Devon*), *m*. 30 Sept. 1874, Jervoise Smith, M.P.; *d*. 21 July 1884; and has issue 1*d*.

1*d*. Dorothy Anne Smith.

4*c*. Hon. Alice Jane Verney, *b*. 3 Feb. 1849; *d*. 8 *Jan*. 1882; *m*. 20 Sept. 1874, *Edward William Tritton*, d. *Jan*. 1902; *and had issue* 1*d to* 4*d*.

1*d*. Oswald Tritton, Officers' Reserve Territorial Force.
2*d*. Louis Tritton.
3*d*. *John Tritton, I.C.S.*, d. *in India*.
4*d*. Claude Tritton.

5*c*. Hon. Susan Emma Verney (*Banks Fee, Moreton-in-Marsh*), *m*. 11 June 1885, Edmund Temple Godman of Banks Fee, co. Glos., J.P., D.L., High Sheriff for that co. 1882, *d*. 22 Mar. 1894; and has issue 1*d*.

1*d*. John Godman, Lieut. 15th Hussars, *b*. 9 May 1886.

6*c*. Hon. Mabel Verney (*Craddocks, Kineton, Warwick*).

[Nos. 94582 to 94599.

275. Descendants, if any, of the Hon. MARY VERNEY (Table XXV.), *d*. (–); *m*. SAMUEL DAVENPORT of Calverley, co. Cheshire.

276. Descendants of the Hon. DIANA VERNEY (Table XXV.), *d*. 28 Sept. 1725; *m*. as 2nd wife (lic. dated 26 Oct.), 1684, Sir CHARLES SHUCKBURGH, 2nd Bt. [E. 1660], M.P., *b*. Nov. 1659; *d*. 2 Sept. 1705; and had issue 1*a* to 4*a*.

1*a*. *Charles Shuckburgh of Longborough, co. Glos.*, b. 1694; d. 1752; m. 1718, *Sarah, da. of Col. Henry Hunt; and had issue* 1*b to* 2*b*.

1*b*. *Sir Charles Shuckburgh, 5th Bt.* [*E.*] *on the death of his cousin* 1759, d.s.p. 10 *Aug.* 1773.

2*b*. *Richard Shuckburgh, Lieut.-Col. in the Army*, b. 1727; d. 3 *Sept.* 1772; m. 1750, *Sarah, widow of Edward Bate, da. of Capt. Hayward, R.N.; and had issue* 1*c to* 3*c*.

1*c*. *Sir George Augustus William Shuckburgh, afterwards (A.P.* 1794) *Evelyn, 6th Bt.* [*E.*], *M.P., a distinguished scientist*, b. c. 1752; d. 11 *Aug.* 1804; m. 2*ndly*, 6 *Oct.* 1785, *Julia Annabella, da. and h. of James Evelyn of Felbridge, co. Surrey*, bur. 23 *Sept.* 1797; *and had issue* 1*d*.

1*d*. *Julia Evelyn Medley Shuckburgh-Evelyn*, b. 6 *Oct.* 1790; d. 8 *Ap.* 1814; m. 19 *July* 1810, *Charles Cecil Cope (Jenkinson), 3rd Earl of Liverpool and Baron*

of The Blood Royal

Hawkesbury [*G.B.*], *&c., G.C.B., Lord Steward of the Household,* d. 3 *Oct.* 1851; *and had issue (with an elder son who* d.s.p.) 1e *to* 2e.

1e. *Lady Selina Charlotte Jenkinson,* b. 3 *July* 1812; d. 24 *Sept.* 1883; m. 1st, 15 *Aug.* 1833, *William Charles Wentworth-Fitzwilliam, Viscount Milton* [s. *and h. of Charles,* 5th *Earl Fitzwilliam* [*I. and G.B.*], *K.G., and a descendant of the Lady Anne, sister of King Edward IV.*], d.v.p. 8 *Nov.* 1835; 2ndly, *as* 2nd *wife,* 28 *Aug.* 1845, *George Savile Foljambe of Osberton and Aldwarke* [*also descended from the Lady Anne, sister of King Edward IV.*], d. 18 *Dec.* 1869; *and had issue* 1f *to* 6f.

1f-2f. Sons by 2nd husband. See the Exeter Volume, p. 673, Nos. 57148-57160.

3f. Da. by 1st husband. See the Exeter Volume, p. 253, Nos. 9608-9631.

4f-6f. Das. by 2nd husband. See the Exeter Volume, p. 674, Nos. 57161-57172.

2e. *Lady Louisa Harriet Jenkinson,* b. 28 *Mar.* 1814; d. 5 *Feb.* 1887; m. 5 *Sept.* 1839, *John Cotes of Woodcote Hall, co. Salop, M.P.*, d. 1874; *and had issue.* See the Tudor Roll, pp. 324-325, Nos. 26303-26318.

2c. *Sir Stewkley Shuckburgh,* 7th *Bt.* [*E.*], b. c. 1760; d. 21 *July* 1809; m. 5 *Sept.* 1786, *Charlotte Catherine, da. of Thomas Tydd,* d. 8 *Feb.* 1837; *and had issue (with* 2 *sons and* 8 *das.* d.s.p.) 1d *to* 3d.

1d. *Sir Francis Shuckburgh,* 8th *Bt.* [*E.*], *F.R.S.*, b. 12 *Mar.* 1789; d. 29 *Oct.* 1876; m. 27 *Oct.* 1825, *Anne Maria Draycott, da. of Peter Denys of Chelsea* [*by his wife Lady Charlotte,* née *Fermor*], d. 8 *Nov.* 1846; *and had issue* 1e *to* 2e.

1e. *Sir George Thomas Francis Shuckburgh,* 9th *Bt.* [*E.*], *J.P., D.L., Major Scots Guards,* b. 23 *July* 1829; d. 12 *Jan.* 1884; m. 24 *June* 1879, *Ida Florence Geraldine, da. of the Rev. Frederick William Robertson* [*who* m. 2ndly, 25 *Nov.* 1886, *Major Henry James Shuckburgh* (*eldest son of Col. Henry Adolphus Shuckburgh,* see below), *who* d.s.p., *and*] d. 12 *Jan.* 1906; *and had issue* 1f *to* 2f.

1f. Sir Stewkley Frederick Draycott Shuckburgh, 10th Bt. [E.] (*Shuckburgh, near Daventry*), b. 20 June 1880.

2f. Gerald Francis Stewkley Shuckburgh, b. 28 Feb. 1882, m. 2 Mar. 1909, Honor Zoë, da. of Neville Thursby of Harleston, co. Northants; and has issue 1g.

1g. Evelyn Honor Shuckburgh, b. 21 Feb. 1910.

2e. *Charlotte Georgiana Amelia Shuckburgh,* b. 21 *Aug.* 1826; d. 11 *June* 1902; m. 24 *Ap.* 1860, *the Rev. John Richard Errington, M.A., Rector of Ladbrooke and Hon. Canon of Worcester,* d. 4 *Oct.* 1882; *and had issue (with a son* d. *young)* 1f *to* 4f.

1f. Frederick Francis Errington, b. 30 July 1861.
2f. *Wilfred John Errington,* b. 10 *Aug.* 1865; d. (?).
3f. Walter Alfred Errington, b. 24 Feb. 1868.
4f. Eliza Margaret Errington.

2d. *Henry Adolphus Shuckburgh, Col.* 40th *Bengal N.I.*, b. 25 *Nov.* 1800; d. 22 *Dec.* 1860; m. 2ndly, 5 *May* 1854, *Catherine Dorothy, da. of Daniel J. Cloete, High Sheriff of Cape Town,* d. 17 *Ap.* 1866; *and had issue (with a son and da.* d.s.p.) 1e *to* 2e.

1e. George Stewkley Shuckburgh, Capt. R.N. (*Falmouth*), b. 5 Aug. 1860; m. 9 Sept. 1898, Amy Mary, da. of John Robertson of Cororooke, Colac, Victoria; and has issue 1f to 2f.

1f. Mabel Evelyn Shuckburgh.
2f. Lorna May Shuckburgh.

2e. Caroline Emma Shuckburgh (36 *Lexham Gardens, W.*).

3d. *Mary Amelia Shuckburgh,* b. 17 *Ap.* 1793; d. 19 *Feb.* 1858; m. 1820, *Thomas Lamb Polden Laugharne, Comm. R.N.; and had issue* 1e *to* 2e.

1e. *Rev. Thomas Robert John Laugharne, Vicar of Rhayader, co. Radnor,* b. 24 *Mar.* 1821; d. 8 *July* 1891; m. 1st, 1 *Mar.* 1859, *Ellen Maria, da. of* (—) *Wilkes,* d. 10 *Aug.* 1868; 2ndly, *Easter Tuesday,* 1873, *Elizabeth Emily, widow* (*with issue*) *of Henry Campbell of Dunmorn, da. of William Henry Cooke of Darfield, co. Yorks,* d. 12 *Jan.* 1906; *and had issue* 1f *to* 4f. [Nos. 94600 to 94674.

The Plantagenet Roll

1*f*. Roland Lamb Polden Laugharne, *b.* 10 June 18—; *m.* 9 June 1890, Alexandra Beatrix, da. of (—) Cox; and has issue 1*g* to 3*g*.
    1*g*. Ronald Hugh Polden Laugharne, Mid. R.N.
    2*g*. Knightley Owen Shuckburgh Laugharne.
    3*g*. Beatrix Laugharne, *unm.*

2*f*.[1] Ellen Mary Julia Laugharne, *m.* 8 Nov. 1888, William Arthur Allen of Gosport House, Laugharne, co. Carmarthen, Manager North and South Wales Branch of London City and Midland Bank, Ltd. (100 *South Road, Waterloo, Liverpool, W.*); and has issue 1*g* to 5*g*.
    1*g*. Cyril Allen, *b.* Dec. 1896.
    2*g*. Arthur Allen, *b.* Aug. 1898.
    3*g*. Ruth Allen.
    4*g*. Barbara Allen.
    5*g*. Gladys Allen.

3*f*.[1] Margaret Maria Meliora Laugharne, *unm.*

4*f*.[2] Emily Ruth Laugharne, *m.* 20 June 1904, Daniel Howell Roland Thomas of Parke, Whitland, co. Carmarthen, Solicitor (*Blaencorse, St. Clears, S. Wales*); and has issue 1*g*.
    1*g*. Elizabeth Orpah Gwenneth Thomas.

2*e*. *Julia Charlotte Laugharne,* b. 18 Feb. 1829; d. 4 Mar. 1905; m. 9 Ap. 1863, *the Rev. Percival Alfred Fothergill, B.A., F.R.A.S., Rector of South Heighton with Tarring Neville, co. Sussex, Dom. Chaplain to the Earl of Limerick, previously R.N.,* d. 24 Aug. 1888; *and had issue (with a son and da. d. unm.)* 1*f* to 4*f*.
    1*f*. Percival Guy Laugharne Fothergill,
    2*f*. Frederick Henry Gaston Fothergill,
    3*f*. Henryetta Mary Bertha Fothergill, } *unm.*
    4*f*. Ernestine Gertrude Frances Fothergill,

3*c*. *Sarah Shuckburgh,* d. (-); m. *John Cleveland of Tapley, co. Devon, M.P. for Saltash* 1761, *for Barnstaple* 1766.

2*a*. *Grace Shuckburgh,* d. (-); m. *the Rev.* (—) *Crabb.*
3*a*. *Sophia Shuckburgh,* d. *Mar.* 1739; m. *Francis Loggin.*
4*a*. *Diana Shuckburgh,* d. (-); m. *the Rev. Nicholas Webb.*
[Nos. 94675 to 94691.]

277. Descendants, if any, of ELIZABETH VERNEY (Table XXV.), *d.* (-); *m.* WILLIAM PEYTO of Chesterton, co. Warwick.

278. Descendants, if any, of GEORGE VERNEY (Table XXV.), *d.* (-); *m.* Lady TRYPHENA, da. of Edmund (SHEFFIELD), 1st Earl of Mulgrave [E.]

279. Descendants of Sir THOMAS SAMWELL of Upton and Gayton, 1st Bt. [E. 1675], M.P. (Table XXV.), *bur.* 3 Mar. 1694; *m.* 1st, 1673, ELIZABETH, da. and h. of George GOODAY of Bowerhall, co. Essex, *bapt.* 3 Mar. 1651; living 1678; 2ndly, 1685, ANNE, da. and h. of Sir John GODSCHALK of Atherston, co. Warwick; and had issue 1*a* to 3*a*.

1*a*. *Sir Thomas Samwell, 2nd Bt.* [*E.*], *M.P.,* bapt. 14 Ap. 1687; d. 16 Nov. 1757; m. 1st, 22 Mar. 1710, *Millicent, da. and h. of the Rev. Thomas Fuller, D.D.,*

# of The Blood Royal

Rector of Hatfield, co. Herts, bur. 11 May 1716; 2ndly, 26 Jan. 1721, Mary, da. of Gilbert Clarke of Chilcot, co. Derby, d. 1 Aug. 1758; and had issue 1b to 4b.

1b. Sir Thomas Samwell, 3rd Bt. [E.], b. 28 May 1711; d.s.p. 3 Dec. 1779.

2b. Sir Wenman Samwell, 4th and last Bt. [E.], b. 24 Oct. 1728; d.s.p. 18 Oct. 1789.

3b. Mary Samwell, da. and in her issue (1789) co-h., bapt. 28 Oct. 1715; d. (-); m. 24 July 1739, the Rev. Stephen Langham, Rector of Cottesbrook (see below), d. 1 Mar. 1755; and had issue (with a son and da. known to have d.s.p.) 1c to 3c.

1c. Millicent Langham, da. and co-h., d. at Northampton 8 Ap. 1808; m. William Drought of Oxford; and had issue 1d to 3d.

1d. Thomas Fuller Drought of Oxford.

2d. Frances Drought.

3d. Juliana Drought.

2c. Frances Anne Langham, da. and co-h.[1]

3c. Phillis Langham, da. and co-h.[1]

4b. Catherine Samwell, da. and co-h. b. 27 May 1724; d. 25 July 1790; m. 6 Mar. 1754, Thomas Atherton Watson of Bedlington, co. Northbd., b. 18 Aug. 1714; d. 1 Oct. 1793; and had issue 1c to 3c.

1c. Thomas Samwell Watson, afterwards (Act. of Parl. 1790) Samwell of Upton, d.s.p. 15 Jan. 1831.

2c. Wenham Langham Watson, afterwards (Act. of Parl. 1832) Samwell of Upton, d.s.p.

3c. Charlotte Felicia Watson, d. (-); m. at Chesterfield 14 Aug. 1792, the Rev. Benjamin Tinley of Whissendine, co. Rutland, B.D., d. 27 Jan. 1804; and had issue 1d to 3d.

1d. Clarissa Felicia Tinley, b. 27 June 1795.

2d. Frances Anne Tinley, b. 3 May 1798.

3d. Charlotte Henrietta Tinley, b. 3 Ap. 1800.

2a. Elizabeth Samwell, bapt. 24 Mar. 1674; d. 1715; m. as 1st wife, 11 June 1691, Sir John Langham, 4th Bt. [E.], d. May 1747; and had (with other) issue 1b to 3b.

1b. Sir James Langham, 5th Bt. [E.], d.s.p. 12 Aug. 1749.

2b. Sir John Langham, 6th Bt. [E.], d.s.p. Sept. 1766.

3b. William Langham of Rance, co. Northants, d. (-); m. Mary, da. of Anthony Drought; and had issue 1c to 2c.

1c. Sir James Langham, 7th Bt. [E.], M.P., b. 31 Jan. 1736; d. 7 Feb. 1795; m. 2 June 1767, Juliana, sister and h. of Thomas Musgrave of Old Cleve, co. Som., d. 21 Mar. 1810; and had issue 1d to 3d.

1d. Sir William Langham, 8th Bt. [E.], b. 10 Feb. 1771; d. 8 Mar. 1812; m. 1st, 20 Aug. 1795, Henrietta Elizabeth Frederica, da. and h. of the Hon. Charles Vane [B. Barnard Coll.], d. 11 Nov. 1809; and had issue.

See the Clarence Volume, Table LXXIII. and pp. 585–586, Nos. 24544–24573.

2d. Sir James Langham, 10th Bt. [E.], M.P., b. 21 Aug. 1776; d. 14 Ap. 1833; m. 26 May 1800, Elizabeth, sister of Sir Francis Burdett, 5th Bt. [E.], da. of Francis Burdett, d. 30 Nov. 1855; and had issue 1e to 3e.

1e. Sir James Hay Langham, 11th Bt. [E.], b. 13 Nov. 1802; d.s.p. 13 Dec. 1893.

2e. Herbert Langham, b. 12 June 1804; d. 27 Feb. 1874; m. 25 June 1839, Laura Charlotte, da. of Nathaniel Micklethwait of Taverham Hall, co. Norfolk [by his 2nd wife Lady Charlotte, née Rous], d. 3 Sept. 1861; and had issue (with a son and 2 das. d.s.p.) 1f to 2f.

1f. Sir Herbert Hay Langham, 12th Bt. [E.], J.P., D.L., late Lieut. 1st Life
[Nos. 94692 to 94721.

---

[1] Baker's "Northants," i. 224.

The Plantagenet Roll

Guards, b. 28 Ap. 1840; d. 13 Dec. 1909; m. 25 Aug. 1868, *the Hon. Anna Maria Frances* [*descended from the Lady Isabel Plantagenet* (see the Essex Volume, p. 143)], da. of *Arthur Marcus Cecil (Sandys), 3rd Baron Sandys* [*U.K.*]. *P.C.*, d. 27 May 1876; and had issue 1g to 2g.

1g. Sir Herbert Charles Arthur Langham, 13th Bt. [E.] (*Cottesbrooke Park, Northampton; Tempo Manor, co. Fermanagh*), b. 24 Mar. 1870; m. 1 June 1893, Ethel Sarah, da. of Sir William Emerson-Tennent, 2nd Bt. [U.K.]; and has issue 1h.

1h. John Charles Patrick Langham, b. 30 June 1894.

2g. Cecily Langham.

2f. Francis Nathaniel Langham (*Spratton, Northampton*), b. 9 June 1841.

3e. Henrietta Langham, d. 25 Mar. 1909; m. 16 Sept. 1851, *the Right Hon. Sir Arthur John Otway, 3rd Bt.* [*U.K.*], *P.C.*, *formerly an M.P. and* (1868–1871) *Under-Sec. of State for Foreign Affairs* (34 *Eaton Square, S.W.*); and had issue 1f.

1f. Henrietta Evelyn Otway, m. 18 Nov. 1880, Edward Garrow-Whitby, d. 1900; and has issue 1g to 2g.

1g. Humphrey Otway Garrow-Whitby, b. 1883.

2g. Phœbe Eleanora Otway.

3d. Charlotte Langham, m. Capt. P. R. Minster, R.N.

2c. Sir William Langham, afterwards Jones, 1st Bt. [G.B. 1774], d.s.p. 3 May 1791.

3a. Frances Samwell, bapt. 5 Dec. 1676; d. 4 Dec. 1730; m. *Sir Richard Newman of Fifehead Magdalen, co. Dorset, 1st Bt.* [*E.* 20 *Dec.* 1699], d. 30 Dec. 1721; and had issue which became extinct 25 Aug. 1775.   [Nos. 94722 to 94729.

280. Descendants, if any surviving, of MARGARET SAMWELL (Table XXV.), bapt. 6 Oct. 1640; d. 12 Jan. 1727; m. 1665, THOMAS CATESBY of Ecton and Whiston, d. 20 Feb. 1700; and had issue.[1]

281. Descendants, if any, of PENELOPE SAMWELL (Table XXV.), bapt. 4 Sept. 1641; d. (–); m. 1678, Sir WILLIAM YORKE of Lessington, co. Lincoln.[2]

282. Descendants of AGNES SAMWELL (Table XXV.), d. 25 Oct. 1717; m. ROBERT CODRINGTON of Codrington, co. Gloucester, d. 11 June 1717; and had issue.[3]

283. Descendants of Sir WALTER WAGSTAFFE BAGOT, 5th Bt. [E.], LL.D., M.P. (Table XXV.), b. 3 Aug. 1702; d. 20 Jan. 1768; m. 27 July 1724, Lady BARBARA, da. of William (LEGGE), 1st Earl of Dartmouth [G.B.], d. 29 Aug. 1765; and had issue 1a to 5a.

1a. William (Bagot), 1st Baron Bagot [G.B.], so cr. 17 Oct. 1780, b. 28 Feb. 1728; d. 22 Oct. 1798; m. 20 Aug. 1760, *the Hon. Elizabeth Louisa, da. of John (St. John), 2nd Viscount St. John* [*G.B.*], d. 4 Feb. 1820; *and had issue.*

See the Clarence Volume, pp. 492–493, Nos. 21328–21515.

[Nos. 94730 to 94917.

---

[1] Baker's "Northants," i. 224.   [2] Ibid.   [3] Ibid.

of The Blood Royal

2a. Charles Bagot, afterwards (Act of Parl.) Chester of Chicheley, co. Bucks, b. 1 Sept. 1730; d. 2 Ap. 1792; m. 3 Oct. 1765, Catherine, da. of the Hon. Heneage Legge, d. 29 Oct. 17—; and had issue 1b to 5b.

1b. Anthony Chester-Bagot, Capt. 13th Regt., b. 5 May 1773; killed in Egypt 1802; m. 1799, Anne Eliza, da. of Hamlet Obins of Castle Obins, co. Armagh, d. 1867; and had issue 1c.

1c. Rev. Anthony Chester-Bagot of Chicheley Hall, co. Bucks, b. 1800; d. 10 Dec. 1858; m. 1834, Henrietta, da. and h. of William Brown of Lisbon, d. Oct. 1854; and had issue 1d.

1d. Henrietta Mary Chester-Bagot, d. 15 May 1895; m. 16 Ap. 1861, Richard Purefoy FitzGerald of North Hall, Preston Candover, J.P., Hon. Col. Bucks Yeo., b. 7 Jan. 1837; d. 28 Feb. 1895; and had issue 1e to 6e.

1e. Richard Purefoy FitzGerald, now (R.L. 26 Dec. 1899) Purefoy of Shalstone, M.V.O., J.P., Capt. R.N. (Shalstone Manor, Buckingham), b. 26 May 1862; m. 23 Dec. 1895, Mary Lillias, da. of the Rev. Francis Gordon Sandys-Lumsdaine of Lumsdaine, J.P.; and has issue 1f.

1f. Mary Lillias Geraldine Purefoy, b. 27 Mar. 1897.

2e. Rev. Henry Purefoy FitzGerald (Lidwells, Goudhurst, co. Kent), b. 27 May 1867; m. 16 Ap. 1895, Lilian Mary, da. of Walter Langton of Gatcombe Park, I.W.; and has issue 1f to 4f.

1f. Knightley Purefoy FitzGerald, b. 12 July 1899.
2f. Cicely Purefoy FitzGerald, b. 4 Jan. 1897.
3f. Marjorie Purefoy FitzGerald, b. 11 Ap. 1898.
4f. Geraldine Purefoy FitzGerald, b. 14 July 1901.

3e. Mary Frances Purefoy FitzGerald, unm.
4e. Laura Purefoy FitzGerald, unm.
5e. Catharine Purefoy FitzGerald, unm.
6e. Mabel Purefoy FitzGerald, unm.

2b. Rev. William Chester, M.A., Rector of Denton, b. 27 May 1775; d. 22 Nov. 1838; m. 1810, the Hon. Elizabeth, da. of Henry (Wilson), 4th Baron Berners [E.], d. 10 Feb. 1865; and had issue 1c to 3c.

1c. Charles Montague Chester of Chicheley Hall, co. Bucks, J.P., D.L., Lieut.-Col. in the Army, b. 18 Jan. 1815; d. 17 Nov. 1879; m. 7 Sept. 1843, Maria, da. of Major Sandham, R.A., d. 8 Ap. 1895; and had issue 1d to 7d.

1d. Rev. John Greville Chester, M.A., Vicar of Gilling (Gilling Vicarage, Richmond, Yorks), b. 15 May 1852; m. 26 Sept. 1883, Amy, da. of Arthur Hughes; and has issue 1e to 7e.

1e. Greville Arthur Bagot Chester, b. 3 Ap. 1891.
2e. Anthony James Bagot Chester, b. 29 Dec. 1892.
3e. George Bagot Chester, b. 6 Sept. 1894.
4e. Henry Montagu Bagot Chester, b. 31 July 1896.
5e. Lewis Charles Bagot Chester, b. 29 Aug. 1898.
6e. Dorothy Mary Bagot Chester.
7e. Kathleen Agnes Bagot Chester.

2d. Rev. Algernon Stewart McKenzie Chester, Rector of Elford and Rural Dean (Elford Rectory, Tamworth), b. 30 Dec. 1853; m. 11 June 1884, Emily Mary, da. of the Rev. Edward Manners Dillman Pyne; and has issue (with a son and da. d. unm.) 1e to 2e.

1e. Walter Greville Chester, Cadet Royal Mil. Coll., b. 15 Mar. 1887.
2e. Muriel Bagot Chester.

3d. Fanny Maria Chester, m 19 Sept. 1876, Lieut.-Col. Charles William Selby-Lowndes [descended from George, Duke of Clarence, K.G., and entitled to quarter the Royal Arms (see the Clarence Volume, p. 476)] (The Limes, Bexhill-on-Sea); and has issue 1e to 5e.   [Nos. 94918 to 94940.

The Plantagenet Roll

1*e*. Charles Henry Chester Selby-Lowndes, *formerly* Lieut. 4th Batt. Bedfordshire Regt., has S. African Medal with 3 Clasps, *b*. 17 Oct. 1880.
2*e*. Rev. George Noel Selby-Lowndes, *b*. 25 Dec. 1886.
3*e*. Laura Fanny Maria Selby-Lowndes.
4*e*. Ella Louisa Selby-Lowndes.
5*e*. Mary Isabella Selby-Lowndes.
4*d*. Louisa Grace Chester.
5*d*. Mary Isabella Chester.
6*d*. Catherine Chester.
7*d*. Margaret Isabel Chester.

2*c*. Fanny Chester, d. 30 *July* 1890 ; m. 2 *June* 1840, *the Rev. Francis Edward Paget, Rector of Elford* [*E. of Uxbridge Coll.*], d. 4 *Aug*. 1882 ; *and had issue.*
See the Clarence Volume, p. 493, Nos. 21499–21515.

3*c*. Charlotte Chester, d. 1887 ; m. 1836, *the Rev. Salisbury Everard, Rector of Burgate, co. Norfolk, Hon. Canon of Norwich ; and had issue* (5 *sons and* 4 *das.*).

3*b*. John Chester *of Ashstead, co. Surrey, a Lieut.-Gen. in the Army*, b. 3 *Aug.* 1779 ; d. 19 *May* 1857 ; m. 17 *May* 1821, *Sophia Elizabeth, da. of Charles Stuart of Airdroch*, d. 19 *May* 1879 ; *and had issue* 1*c to* 5*c*.

1*c*. John Chester, *afterwards* (R.L. 1 *Ap*. 1863) *St. Leger, of Park Hill, co. York, J.P., D.L., Col.* 53*rd and* 85*th Regts.*, b. 6 *May* 1823 ; d. 9 *Aug*. 1905 ; m. 8 *Ap*. 1858, *Philippa, da. of John Bonfoy Rooper of Abbot's Ripton Hall, M.P.*, d. 27 *Dec*. 1909 ; *and had issue* 1*d to* 6*d*.

1*d*. Arthur John Bonfoy St. Leger of Park Hill, *formerly* Capt. King's Royal Rifle Corps (*Park Hill, Rotherham*), *b*. 25 Nov. 1859 ; *m*. 8 Ap. 1896, Hilda Geraldine, da. of Col. Sir Gerard Smith, K.C.M.G., *late* Gov. of West Australia ; and has issue 1*e* to 2*e*.
1*e*. Brenda Mary St. Leger, *b*. 11 July 1897.
2*e*. Vera St. Leger, *b*. 29 July 1900.

2*d*. Henry Berners St. Leger, Bengal Police, *b*. 26 Oct. 1861.
3*d*. Reginald Warham Anthony St. Leger, *b*. 15 Feb. 1868.
4*d*. Gwendolene Mary Hope St. Leger, *m*. 9 Ap. 1885, Frederic William Brooke of Glenbrook, *formerly* Capt. 3rd Batt. Suffolk Regt. (*Glenbrook, Shanklin, I.W.*) ; and has issue 1*e* to 3*e*.
1*e*. Gerald Douglas Brooke, *b*. 20 Mar. 1891.
2*e*. Gladys Beatrice Brooke.
3*e*. Dulce Brooke.

5*d*. Georgiana Harriet St. Leger, *m*. 1888, John Walter Parry-Crooke of Darsham House, co. Suffolk, J.P. (*Carlton, Bournemouth*) ; and has issue 1*e* to 3*e*.
1*e*. Douglas John Parry-Crooke, *b*. 1889.
2*e*. Lionel Walter Parry-Crooke, *b*. 1891.
3*e*. Charles Philip Parry-Crooke, *b*. 1896.

6*d*. Ursula Beatrice Philippa St. Leger, *m*. 19 Dec. 1888, Frances Egbert Hollond, J.P. (*Satis House, Yoxford, Suffolk*) ; and has issue 1*e* to 5*e*.
1*e*. Raymond Claude Hollond, *b*. 1891.
2*e*. George Egbert Hollond, *b*. 1895.
3*e*. Hugh Ernest Hollond, *b*. 1897.
4*e*. Marjorie Hollond.
5*e*. Nancy Ursula Hollond.

2*c*. Heneage Charles Bagot-Chester, Col. Reserve Forces, served throughout Indian Mutiny, has Medal with Clasps (*Zetland House, Maidenhead ; Centre Cliff, Southwold, &c.*), *b*. 12 Feb. 1834 ; *m*. 11 Mar. 1865, Madeline Elizabeth, widow of T. B. Sheriffe of Henstead Hall, co. Suffolk, da. of Richard Mansel Oliver Massey of Tickford Abbey, co. Bucks ; and has issue 1*d* to 2*d*. [Nos. 94941 to 94986.

of The Blood Royal

1*d*. Greville John Massey Bagot-Chester, *formerly* Capt. 1st Scots Guards, has S. African Medals and Clasps, *b.* 20 Oct. 1866.

2*d*. Hugh Augustus Bagot-Chester, *formerly* Capt. 3rd Batt. Royal Lancaster Regt., has S. African Medal and Clasps, *b.* 21 Ap. 1871 ; *m.* 13 Jan. 1895, Margaret Kathleen Juliana (who obtained a div. 1908), da. of Col. R. E. Oakes, B.S.C.

3*c*. Sophia Elizabeth Chester, d. 20 *Sept.* 1892 ; m. 5 *Aug.* 1845, *Lord Alfred Hervey,* d. 15 *Ap.* 1875 ; *and had issue.*
See p. 335, Nos. 55583-55586.

4*c*. *Mary Chester,* d. 15 *Ap.* 1899 ; m. 18 *Feb.* 1846, *her cousin the Rev. Charles Walter Bagot, Chancellor of Bath and Wells,* d. 10 *Sept.* 1884 ; *and had issue.*
See the Tudor Roll, p. 369, Nos. 27951-27963.

5*c*. Barbara Frances Wilhelmina Chester (*Roydsmoor, East Molesley*), *m.* 12 Feb. 1862, Rev. the Hon. William Howard [E. of Effingham Coll.], *d.s.p.* 12 May 1881.

4*b*. *Barbara Chester,* b. 28 *Feb.* 1769 ; d. 9 *Aug.* 1832 ; m. *John Drummond,* d. 28 *May* 1833.

5*b*. *Frances Chester,* b. 26 *Oct.* 1770 ; d. (-) ; m. 6 *Aug.* 1803, *Thomas Richmond-Gale-Braddyll of Highhead Castle, and Conishead Priory, co. Lancaster, J.P., D.L.,* b. 14 *Nov.* 1776 ; d. (-) ; *and had issue* 1*c to* 2*c.*

1*c*. *Edward Stanley Bagot Richmond-Gale-Braddyll of Highhead Castle and Conishead Priory,* d. 2 *Sept.* 1874 ; m. 7 *Dec.* 1837, *Sophia Frances Anne, da. of William Hulton of Hulton Park, co. Lanc. ; and had issue* 1*d to* 3*d.*

1*d*. *Henry John Richmond-Gale-Braddyll of Highhead Castle,* b. 29 *Oct.* 1837 ; d.s.p. 24 *Dec.* 1886 ; m. 2 *June* 1875, *Mary (Amberwood, Christchurch, Hants), da. of William Birch of Barton-under-Needwood, co. Stafford.*

2*d*. *Edward Sotheron Richmond-Gale-Braddyll of Southport,* b. 3 *Jan.* 1839 ; d. 26 *Nov,* 1882 ; m. 21 *Feb.* 1861, *Anna Cecilia, da. of Edward Willis of Cleevemount, co. Glouc.,* d. 1874 ; *and had issue* 1*e to* 6*e.*

1*e*. Hubert Edward Richmond-Gale-Braddyll (*East Court, Oxton, Cheshire*), *b.* 20 Nov. 1861 ; *m.* 1884, Mary, da. of H. M. Lennard of Leven House, co. York ; and has issue 1*f* to 3*f*.

1*f*. Hubert Stanley Richmond-Gale-Braddyll, R.N., *b.* 25 Aug. 1886.

2*f*. Edward Clarence Richmond-Gale-Braddyll, 19th Lancers, *b.* 18 Oct. 1888.

3*f*. Mary Alice Richmond-Gale-Braddyll.

2*e*. Florence Richmond-Gale-Braddyll.

3*e*. Maude Richmond-Gale-Braddyll, *m.* William Rampling Rose.

4*e*. Ethel Marguerite Richmond-Gale-Braddyll, *m.* 31 July 1890, Sir William Rothwell Hulton, 2nd Bt. [U.K.] (*Worden Lodge, Leyland, near Preston*) ; and has issue 1*f* to 2*f*.

1*f*. Roger Braddyll Hulton, *b.* 30 Mar. 1891.

2*f*. Leslie Florence Hulton.

5*e*. Evelyn Cecilia Richmond-Gale-Braddyll, *m.* 30 Mar. 1892, Edward Dennison Hargreaves (*Achnasgiach, N.B. ; Harefield, near Romsey, Hants*) ; and has issue 1*f* to 3*f*.

1*f*. Dennison Braddyll Hargreaves, *b.* 5 Ap. 1893.

2*f*. John Dennison Hargreaves, *b.* 5 Nov. 1905.

3*f*. Audrey Dennison Hargreaves, *b.* 20 Feb. 1898.

6*e*. Lilian Richmond-Gale-Braddyll, *m.* 1 Nov. 1893, Llewellyn Caradoc Picton-Jones [4th son of G. T. Picton-Jones of Yoke House, co. Carnarvon] ; and has issue 1*f*.

1*f*. Esmé Doris Picton-Jones, *b.* 30 Sept. 1896.

3*d*. Harriet Georgiana Richmond-Gale-Braddyll (5 *Albert Road, Birkdale*).

2*c*. *Clarence Richmond-Gale-Braddyll, for whom King William IV. was sponsor.*

[Nos. 94987 to 95022.

The Plantagenet Roll

3a. Rev. Walter Bagot of Pipe Hall, co. Stafford, b. 2 Nov 1731; d. 1806; m. 1st, 7 Sept. 1773, Anne, da. of William Swinnerton of Butterton, co. Stafford; 2ndly, Mary [da. of (—)] Ward; and had issue 1b to 8b.

1b.[2] Rev. Ralph Bagot, Vicar of Erdington, d. 20 July 1866; m. 3 Sept. 1845, Mary [da. of (—)] Adams, d. 8 Mar. 1890; and had issue 1c.

1c. William Walter Bagot of Pipe Hayes Hall, b. 21 Jan. 1847; d. 23 Jan. 1893; m. 4 Feb. 1868, Lucy Matilda, da. of the Rev. Robert Loftus Tottenham, d. 1895; and had issue 1d.

1d. Frances Anna Mary Bagot (Chambers' Court, Tewkesbury), m. 25 Mar. 1890, Henry Richard Reginald Bagot [B. Bagot Coll.], d.s.p. 17 July 1908.

2b.[1] Honora Bagot, b. 20 June 1775; d. 2 Oct. 1863; m. 15 Dec. 1795, Rev. the Hon. Augustus George Legge, Preb. of Winchester [E. of Dartmouth Coll.], d. 21 Aug. 1828; and had issue (with 4 sons who d.s.p.) 1c to 4c.

1c. Rev. Henry Legge of Mareland, co. Surrey, and Bramdean, co. Hants, b. 29 June 1803; d. 8 Nov. 1879; m. 4 May 1830, Elizabeth Louisa, da. of Rear-Adm. Stair Douglas [M. of Queensberry Coll.], d. 28 Oct. 1840; and had issue 1d to 2d.

1d. Rev. Augustus George Legge, M.A. (Oxon.), Vicar of North Elmham, co. Norfolk, b. 20 Jan. 1835; d. 9 Jan. 1906; m. 25 Aug. 1864, Alice Mary, da. of John Greenwood of Broadhanger, co. Hants, Q.C., d. 21 Feb. 1885; and had issue 1e to 5e.

1e. Walter Douglas Legge (Hove Lawn, Hove, Sussex), b. 31 Oct. 1865; m. 24 Sept. 1907, Rebecca Lang, da. of Theophilus Hoskin of Calstock, co. Cornwall.

2e. Honora Alice Charlotte Legge
3e. Beatrice Louisa Legge
4e. Frances Mary Legge
5e. Alice Georgina Legge
(Littledean, Bramdean, Alresford).

2d. Charles Egerton Legge, J.P., D.L., High Sheriff co. Sussex 1901 (Ashling House, Chichester), b. 22 May 1840; unm.

2c. Charlotte Anne Legge, b. 5 June 1799; d. 21 June 1856; m. 15 Dec. 1825, Rev. the Hon. Arthur Philip Perceval [E. of Egmont Coll.], d. 11 June 1853; and had issue.

See the Clarence Volume, pp. 203-204, Nos. 4024-4049.

3c. Honora Augusta Legge, b. 1 May 1816; d. 27 Dec. 1897; m. 12 Ap. 1855, Gen. William Cowper Coles, d. 27 Aug. 1867.

4c. Louisa Frances Catherine Legge, b. 14 July 1817; d. 4 June 1893; m. 4 Ap. 1866, the Rev. Alfred Bishop, Rector of Martyr-Worthy, co. Hants, d. 29 Sept. 1885.

3b.[1] Elizabeth Bagot, b. 25 May 1780; d. 24 Feb. 1855; m. 19 Mar. 1807, Joseph Phillimore of Shiplake House, D.C.L., M.P., Regius Professor of Civil Law in the University of Oxford, Chancellor of the Dioceses of Oxford, Worcester, and Bristol, b. 14 Sept. 1775; d. 24 Feb. 1855; and had issue 1c to 3c.

1c. John George Phillimore of Shiplake House, Q.C., M.P., b. 5 Jan. 1808; d. 27 Ap. 1865; m. 1 Aug. 1839, Rosalind Margaret, da. of the Right Hon. Sir James Lewis Knight Bruce, Vice-Chancellor of England and Lord Justice of the Court of Appeal, d. 22 Sept. 1871; and had issue 1d.

1d. Egerton Grenville Bagot Phillimore of Shiplake House (Shiplake House, Oxon.), b. 20 Dec. 1856; m. 22 Jan. 1880, Susan Eliza, da. of Richard Barnes Roscow of Church, near Accrington, M.R.C.S.; and has (with other) issue 1e to 2e.

1e. John George Phillimore, B.A. (Oxon.), b 24 Oct. 1880.

2e. Margaret Phillimore, b. 24 Nov. 1881.

2c. Sir Robert Joseph Phillimore, 1st Bt. [U.K. 21 Dec. 1881], P.C., M.P., D.C.L., b. 5 Nov. 1810; d. 4 Feb. 1885; m. 19 Dec. 1844, Charlotte Anne, sister of John Evelyn, 1st Viscount Ossington [U.K.], da. of John Denison of Ossington Hall, co. Notts, M.P., d. 19 Jan. 1892; and had issue 1d to 3d.

[Nos. 95023 to 95058.]

of The Blood Royal

1*d*. Sir Walter George Frank Phillimore, 2nd Bt. [U.K.], D.C.L., Hon. LL.D. (Edin.), a Judge of the High Court of Justice (Queen's Bench Div.), Bencher of the Middle Temple, *formerly* Chancellor of Lincoln and Fellow of All Souls' Coll., Oxon., Mayor of Kensington 1910, &c. (*The Coppice, Henley-on-Thames; Cam House, Campden Hill, W.*), *b.* 21 Nov. 1845; *m.* 26 July 1870, Agnes, da. of Charles Manners Lushington, M.P.; and has issue 1*e* to 6*e*.

1*e*. Robert Charles Phillimore, B.A. (Oxon.), Bar. M.T., J.P. (*Radlett, St. Albans*), *b.* 19 Aug. 1871; *m.* 12 Dec. 1895, Lucy, da. of William FitzPatrick.

2*e*. Godfrey Walter Phillimore, M.A. (Oxon.), *b.* 29 Dec. 1879; *m.* 5 July 1905, Dorothy Barbara, da. of Lieut.-Col. Arthur Balfour Haig, C.V.O., C.M.G.; and has issue 1*f*.

1*f*. Anthony Francis Phillimore, *b.* 2 Feb. 1907.

3*e*. Stephen Henry Phillimore, M.A. (Oxon.), *b.* 14 Dec. 1881.

4*e*. Eleanor Mary Phillimore, *m.* 17 Sept. 1895, Francis John Kynaston Cross, J.P., Bar.-at-Law (*Aston Tirrold Manor, Wallingford*); and has issue 1*f* to 5*f*.

1*f*. Philip Kynaston Cross, *b.* 3 Jan. 1898.
2*f*. Michael Robert Cross, *b.* 8 Ap. 1899.
3*f*. Christopher Francis Cross, *b.* 7 Mar. 1902.
4*f*. Geoffrey John Cross, *b.* 2 Feb. 1910.
5*f*. Hannah Margaret Cross, *b.* 25 Ap. 1908.

5*e*. *Margaret Blanche Phillimore*, d. 19 *Oct.* 1904; m. 29 *July* 1899, *Eustace Gilbert Hills, Bar.-at-Law* (22 *Cheyne Gardens, S.W.; Library Chambers, Temple, E.C.*); *and had issue 1f to 2f.*

1*f*. Elizabeth Anna Hills, *b.* 9 Nov. 1900.
2*f*. Katharine Agnes Hills, *b.* 11 June 1902.

6*e*. Grace Agnes Phillimore.

2*d*. Catherine Mary Phillimore } (*Shiplake House, Henley-on-Thames*).
3*d*. Lucy Phillimore

3*c*. *Sir Augustus Phillimore*, K.C.B., Admiral R.N., b. 24 *May* 1822; d. 25 *Nov.* 1897; m. 29 *Mar.* 1864, *Harriet Eleanor* (*Shedfield House, Botley, Hants*), *da. of the Hon. George Matthew Fortescue* [*descended from King Henry VII.* (see Tudor Roll, p. 282)]; *and had issue 1d to 7d.*

1*d*. Richard Fortescue Phillimore, M.V.O., R.N., Capt. H.M.S. *Aboukir* (*Portsmouth; United Service*), *b.* 23 Dec. 1864; *m.* 21 Dec. 1905, Violet Gore, da. of Henry Hobhouse Turton; and has issue 1*e* to 2*e*.

1*e*. Richard Augustus Phillimore, *b.* 9 Jan. 1907.
2*e*. John Gore Phillimore, *b.* 16 Ap. 1908.

2*d*. George Grenville Phillimore, M.A. (Oxon.), Bar. M.T., is an Assist. Charity Commr. (*Maplecroft, Wargrave; Marlborough House, Tunbridge Wells;* 1 *Mitre Court Buildings, Temple*), *b.* 28 Oct. 1867; *m.* 30 Aug. 1893, May Melba, da. of Henry William Franklyn of Shedfield Lodge, co. Hants; and has issue 1*e* to 3*e*.

1*e*. Henry Augustus Grenville Phillimore, *b.* 31 July 1894.
2*e*. Matthew Arden Phillimore, *b.* 17 Mar. 1896.
3*e*. Hester Mary Melba Phillimore, *b.* 7 Oct. 1900.

3*d*. Charles Augustus Phillimore, M.A. (Oxon.), a partner in Coutts' Bank (*Oxford and Cambridge*), *b.* 11 Aug. 1871; *m.* 8 Dec. 1908, Alice (see p. 513), da. of William Henry Campion of Danny, C.B.; and has issue 1*e*.

1*e*. Violet Alice Valentine Phillimore, *b.* 10 Dec. 1909.

4*d*. John Swinnerton Phillimore, M.A. (Oxon.), Professor of Humanity in Glasgow University (5 *The College, Glasgow*), *b.* 26 Feb. 1873; *m.* 26 July 1900, Margaret Cecily, da. of the Rev. Spencer Compton Spencer-Smith [Bt. Coll.]; and has issue 1*e* to 2*e*.

1*e*. John Michael Fortescue Phillimore, *b.* 9 Sept. 1903.
2*e*. Cynthia Mary Louisa Phillimore, *b.* 18 May 1901. [Nos. 95059 to 95086.

The Plantagenet Roll

5*d*. Valentine Egerton Bagot Phillimore, D.S.O., Comm. R.N., *b*. 14 Feb. 1875; *m*. 16 June 1908, Mary Kathleen, da. of George Robinson of Overdale, Shipton-in-Craven, *d*. 23 Mar. 1909.

6*d*. Rev. Edward Granville Phillimore, B.A. (Oxon.), is Priest in Charge of Kingsley (*Kingsley, Hants*), *b*. 7 Sept. 1876; *m*. 14 July 1903, Mabel von Essen, da. of William Henry Moberly of Beechwood, Bitterne; and has issue 1*e* to 2*e*.
    1*e*. Barbara Louisa Agnes Phillimore, *b*. 27 Mar. 1906.
    2*e*. Audrey Magdalen Dominica Gwladys Phillimore.

7*d* Violet Elizabeth Annie Phillimore, *m*. 1 June 1893, John Edward Arthur Willis-Fleming of Chilworth and Stoneham, J.P., D.L., High Sheriff co. Hants 1901 (*Chilworth Manor, Romsey; Stoneham Park, Southampton*); and has issue 1*e* to 5*e*.
    1*e*. John Baynes Phillimore Willis-Fleming, *b*. 2 June 1895.
    2*e*. Richard Thomas Cyril Willis-Fleming, *b*. 3 Aug. 1896.
    3*e*. Edward Charles Augustus Willis-Fleming, *b*. 22 Ap. 1903.
    4*e*. Ida Harriet Willis-Fleming.
    5*e*. Elizabeth Katherine Willis-Fleming.

4*b*.[1] Louisa Bagot, *d. Mar.* 1864; m. 16 *Jan.* 1804, *the Rev. Richard Levett of Milford Hall, co. Stafford*, *b*. 17 Nov. 1772; *d*. 25 Aug. 1843; *and had issue* 1*c*.

1*c*. Richard Byrd Levett of Milford Hall, J.P., D.L., Lieut.-Col. Comdg. 3rd Batt. Staffordshire Rifles, *b*. 24 Nov. 1810; *d*. 8 *July* 1887; m. 1 *Aug*. 1848, Elizabeth Mary, da. of John Mirehouse of Brownslade, co. Pemb., Common Sergeant of London [by Elizabeth, da. of the Right Rev. John Fisher, D.D., Bishop of Salisbury]; *and had issue* 1*d* to 7*d*.

1*d*. Richard Walter Byrd Mirehouse, *formerly* (R.L. 17 Mar. 1865) Levett of Angle, C.M.G., J.P. and High Sheriff co. Pembroke 1886, Hon. Col. and Lieut.-Col. Comdg 4th North Stafford Regt. (*The Hall, Angle, co. Pemb.; Junior Carlton*), *b*. 5 May 1849; *m*. 22 June 1881, Mary Beatrice, da. of Thomas Entwisle of Wolhayes, co. Hants; and has issue 1*e* to 3*e*.
    1*e*. Gladys Sybil Evelyn Mirehouse, *b*. 18 Ap. 1882.
    2*e*. Ruth Violet Esther Mirehouse, *b*. 5 June 1883; *m*. (—).
    3*e*. Cecil Elinor Mirehouse, *b*. 7 Ap. 1886.

2*d*. William Swinnerton Byrd Levett of Milford Hall, J.P., D.L., *late* Capt. Royal Inniskilling Fusiliers (*Milford Hall, Stafford*), *b*. 22 Jan. 1856; *m*. 8 July 1896, Maud Sophia [descended from the Lady Isabel Plantagenet (see Essex Volume, p. 338)], da. of Major Edward Levett, 10th Hussars; and has issue 1*e* to 2*e*.
    1*e*. Richard William Byrd Levett, *b*. 30 May 1897.
    2*e*. Dyonèse Levett, *b*. 13 Ap. 1900.

3*d*. Egerton Bagot Byrd Levett Scrivener (D.P. 6 Ap. 1889), *formerly* Levett of Sibton, J.P., Comm. R.N. (ret.), *formerly* Bursar Keble Coll. (Oxon.) (*Sibton Abbey, Yoxford, Suffolk*), *b*. 11 Feb. 1857; *m*. 1st, Mar. 1884, Mabel Desborough, da. of Sir Harry Smith Parkes, G.C.M.G., K.C.B., *d*. May 1890; 2ndly, 3 Sept. 1891, Mary, da. of Henry John Mirehouse of St. George's Hill, co. Somerset; and has issue 1*e* to 5*e*.
    1*e*. Evelyn Harry Byrd Levett Scrivener, *b*. 11 Dec. 1884.
    2*e*. Alaric Parkes Levett Scrivener, *b*. 12 Ap. 1886.
    3*e*.[2] Iris Theodora Levett Scrivener.
    4*e*.[2] Winifred Violet Levett Scrivener.
    5*e*.[2] Pamela Levett Scrivener.

4*d*. Walter Leveson Byrd Levett, J.P. (*Orleton, Wellington, Salop*), *b*. 1 Aug. 1859; *m*. Oct. 1884, Helen, da. of Charles Lambert of Park Lane, London; and has issue 1*e* to 3*e*.
    1*e*. Richard Walter Levett, *b*. 19 Jan. 1890.

[Nos. 95087 to 95111.

# of The Blood Royal

2*e.* Mary Beatrice Levett, *b.* 28 June 1886; *m.* Jan. 1909, John Benson [son of the Rev. George Riou Benson]; and has issue 1*f.*

1*f.* John Benson.

3*e.* Rachel Helen Levett, *b.* 13 Mar. 1900.

5*d.* Louisa Mary Levett.

6*d.* Evelyn Honora Levett.

7*d.* Isabel Mary Levett, *m.* 6 July 1898, Harry Robert Bruxner (*Chartley Castle, co. Stafford*); and has issue 1*e* to 2*e.*

1*e.* George Mervyn Bruxner, *b.* 4 June 1899.

2*e.* Alistair Egerton Bruxner, *b.* 11 Feb. 1905.

5*b.*² *Caroline Bagot*, b. c. 1797; d. 5 Feb. 1886; m. 1828, *Edmund R. Daniel, Bar.-at-Law.*

6*b.*² *Charlotte Bagot*, d. 24 Feb. 1865; m. 5 May 1830, *Rev. the Hon. William Somerville*, d. 6 July 1857; *and had a son who d. unm.*

7*b.*² *Jane Margaret Bagot*, d. 24 Sept. 1889; m. 1826, *the Right Hon. Sir Edward Vaughan Williams, Judge of the Court of Common Pleas,* d. 1875; *and had issue.*

8*b.*² *Agnes Bagot*, d. (–); m. *John Farquhar Fraser.*

4*a. Barbara Bagot,* b. 29 Mar. 1725; d. 1797; m. 1749, *Ralph Sneyd of Keele*, d. 10 Dec. 1793; *and had issue.*

See the Essex Volume Supplement, pp. 476–479, Nos. 27542/1–27542/116.

5*a. Maria Bagot,* d. (–); m. *Rowland Wingfield.* [Nos. 95112 to 95235.

284. Descendants of ANNE NEALE, Maid-of-Honour to Queen Caroline (Table XXV.), *b.* Feb. 1721; *d.* 1 Dec. 1747; *m.* as 1st wife, *c.* 1744, the Rev. Sir JAMES STONEHOUSE, 10th (1628) and 7th (1670) Bt. [E.], *b.* 9 July 1716; *d.* 8 Dec. 1795; and had issue 1*a* to 2*a.*

1*a. Sir Thomas Stonehouse,* 11*th and* 8*th Bt.* [E.], b. 1744; d. *unm.* 1810.

2*a. Sarah Stonehouse,* d. 1819; m. 24 Oct. 1767, *George Vansittart of Bisham Abbey, co. Berks, J.P., D.L., M.P., a Member of the Supreme Council of Bengal,* b. 15 Sept. 1745; d. 20 June 1825; *and had issue* 1*b* to 4*b.*

1*b. George Henry Vansittart, Gen. in the Army, D.C.L.,* b. 16 July 1768; d.v.p. 4 Feb. 1824; m. 29 Oct. 1818, *Anna Maria, da. and co-h. of Thomas Copson of Sheppey and Sutton, co. Leic.,* d. 1874; *and had issue two sons who both* d. *unm.*

2*b. Rev. Edward Vansittart, afterwards* (R.L. 14 Oct. 1805) *Vansittart-Neale, M.A., B.C.L., Rector of Taplow,* bapt. 4 Nov. 1769; d. 21 Jan. 1850; m. 2*ndly,* 3 Jan. 1809, *Anne, da. of Isaac Spooner of Elmdon, co. Warw.; and had issue.*

See the Essex Volume Supplement, p. 661, Nos. 56226/253–271.

3*b. Henry Vansittart of Eastwood, Woodstock, Canada, Vice-Admiral of the Blue,* b. 7 Ap. 1777; d. 14 Mar. 1842; m. 1st, 15 May 1809, *Mary Charity, da. of the Rev. John Pennefather, D.D.,* d. 2 July 1834; *and had issue.*

See p. 357, Nos. 59776–59821.

4*b. Laura Vansittart,* d. 8 Feb. 1844; m. 26 Nov. 1809, *Fulwar Craven of Brockhampton, co. Glouc.* [B. Craven Coll.], d. 14 Ap. 1860; *and had issue* 1*c* to 2*c.*

1*c. Fulwar William Craven,* b. 12 Sept. 1810; d. 7 Mar. 1844; m. 11 Nov. 1831, *Louisa, da. of the Rev. John Orde,* d. 19 Ap. 1856; *and had issue* 1*d* to 3*d.*

1*d.* Edmund Filmer Craven, a Police Magistrate and J.P. for Queensland, *formerly* R.N. (*The Oasis, Hughenden, viâ Townsville, Queensland*), *b.* 21 Nov. 1836; *m.* 10 Mar. 1866, Caroline, da. of William Smith of Bedford; and has issue 1*e* to 10*e.*

1*e.* Fulwar Craven, *b.* 26 May 1873. [Nos. 95236 to 95302.

The Plantagenet Roll

2e. Edmund Cecil Codrington Craven, served in South Africa 1901–1902 with Queensland Mounted Inf., b. 2 Ap. 1875.

3e. Ethel Laura Craven, m. 1889, John Cowper Linedale, Mining Registrar (*Paradise, Bundaberg, Queensland*); and has issue 1f.

1f. [da.] Linedale, b. 1890.

4e. Georgiana Louisa Craven.

5e. Evelyn Caroline Jocelyn Craven.

6e. Constance Lilian Craven.

7e. Florence Lucy Craven, m. 1899, Edward Goddard Blume (*Bexley, Longreach, Queensland*); and has issue 1f to 2f.

1f. Edward Craven Blume, b. 1900.

2f. [son] Blume, b. 1905.

8e. Beatrice Violet Craven, m. Dec. 1905, Eldred Pringle; and has issue (a da.).

9e. Mabel Carleton Craven, m. Dec. 1909, the Rev. Ernest Clarence Sandeman.

10e. Blanche Guendolene Craven.

2d. Laura Louisa Craven (*27 Pen-y-wern Road, Earl's Court, S.W.*), m. 7 Jan. 1862, Major Edmund Garland Horne, 25th Regt., d. 15 Oct. 1905; and has issue 1e to 2e.

1e. Beatrice Charlotte Maria Horne, m. 2 Dec. 1886, Alfred Harry Veitch, Paymaster R.N. (*Hartland, Victoria Road North, Southsea*); and has issue 1f to 3f.

1f. Harry Cecil Craven Veitch, b. 5 June 1891.

2f. Hyacinth Laura Guendalyn Veitch.

3f. Nesta Phyllis Alfreda Veitch.

2e. Amelia Eliza Eleanor Gwendoline Horne, m. 13 Ap. 1889, Grismond Philipps (*20 Victoria Road, Tenby*); and has issue 1f.

1f. Frances Gwendoline Horne.

3d. Georgina Craven, d. 15 Jan. 1887; m. as 2nd wife, 28 July 1863, the Rev. Thomas Grey Clarke, Vicar of Oldham; and had issue 1e to 2e.

1e. William Edmund Grey Clarke (*61 Manor Park, Lee, S.E.*), b. 4 Ap. 1864; m. 19 Dec. 1886, Emily, da. of Charles Frewen Lord, of Clifford's Inn, Solicitor; and has issue (with a son d. young) 1f to 3f.

1f. Edmund Frewen Grey Clarke, b. 25 Feb. 1892.

2f. Charlotte Phyllis Georgina Clarke, b. 26 June 1888.

3f. Enid Jocelyn Clarke, b. 11 Dec. 1895.

2e. Evelyn-Georgiana Maria Clarke, m. 10 Jan. 1897, the Baron Arturo Lombardi (*Via Aracœli 3, Palazzo Muti, Rome*); and has issue 1f to 2f.

1f. Baron Achille Grey Lombardi, b. 4 Sept. 1897.

2f. Baroness Georgina Amelia Lombardi, b. 14 June 1903.

2c. Georgina Maria Craven, d. 10 Ap. 1878; m. 17 June 1841, Goodwin Charles Colquitt, sometime (R.L. 10 Feb. 1842) Goodwin and finally (R.L. 12 Dec. 1860) Colquitt-Craven of Brockhampton Park, co. Glos., J.P., D.L., d. 29 Jan. 1899; and had issue 1d to 3d.

1d. Fulwar John Colquitt-Craven, Capt. Grenadier Guards, J.P., b. 19 Sept. 1849; d.v.p. 1890; m. 23 Jan. 1873, Sarah Llewellyn, da. of Lewis Llewellyn Dillwyn of Hendrefoilan, M.P., d. 1893; and had issue 1e to 5e.

1e. Lewis Fulwar George Colquitt-Craven of Admington and Burton (*Admington Hall, Shipton-on-Stour; Burton Hall, Cheshire*), b. 14 Nov. 1873; m. 2 Oct. 1900, Rose Macey, widow of (—) Freeman, da. of Richard Taylor.

2e. George Fulwar Llewellyn Colquitt-Craven, b. Jan. 1875; m. in Australia.

3e. Nigel Fulwar de la Beche Colquitt-Craven, b. 6 Nov. 1881; m. 1909.

4e. Arabel Laura Colquitt-Craven, m. 23 Ap. 1902, Llewellyn H. Prichard (*Penmaen House, Penmaen, Glamorgan*); and has issue (a da.).

[Nos. 95303 to 95332.

of The Blood Royal

5e. Hilda Charlotte Colquitt-Craven, m. 10 Sept. 1900, Robert Picton-Warlow [descended from the Lady Isabel Plantagenet (see the Essex Volume, p. 384)] (*Coity Maur, Talybout-on-Usk, Brecon*); and has issue 1f to 2f.

    1f. John Fulwar Picton-Warlow, b. 30 Jan. 1903.

    2f. Robert Wallace Picton-Warlow, b. 13 Oct. 1904.

2d. Leila Louisa Colquitt-Craven, d. 9 Oct. 1899; m. 21 Ap. 1868, *the Rev. Henry William Coventry* [*E. Coventry Coll.*], *Rector of Severn Stoke and Hon. Canon of Worcester, J.P.* (*Severn Stoke Rectory, Worcester*); and had issue 1e to 4e.

    1e. Fulwar Cecil Ashton Coventry, b. 14 July 1874.

    2e. Blanche Katherine Adine Coventry, m. 6 Jan. 1904, the Rev. George Le Strange Amphlett, Rector of Earl's Croome and Hill Croome (*Earl's Croome Rectory, co. Worcester*); and has issue 1f to 3f.

        1f. Leila Blanche Amphlett.

        2f. Ann Elizabeth Amphlett.

        3f. Justina Alice Amphlett.

    3e. Sybil Augusta Coventry, m. 3 Feb. 1904, Capt. Ferdinando Dudley William Lea-Smith [descended from King Henry VII., whose arms he is entitled to quarter (see the Tudor Roll, p. 313)] (*Halesowen Grange, Worcester*); and has issue 1f.

        1f. Barbara Amy Felicity Lea-Smith.

    4e. Winifred Leila Coventry, m. 14 Nov. 1906, the Rev. Francis Herbert Horne, Rector of Beyton (*Beyton Rectory, Bury St. Edmunds*); and has issue 1f.

        1f. Henry Francis Coventry Horne, b. 22 Aug. 1908.

3d. Arabella Catherine Colquitt-Craven (*Court House, Malvern*), m. 9 Feb. 1873, Sir James Buchanan, 2nd Bt. [U.K.], Comm. R.N. [eldest son of the Right Hon. Sir Andrew Buchanan, 1st Bt. [U.K.], G.C.B., H.B.M. Ambassador at Vienna], d.s.p. 14 Oct. 1901. [Nos. 95333 to 95345.

285. Descendants of FRANCES NEALE (see Table XXV.), b. 1723; d. 7 Mar. 1748; m. 17 Oct. 1742, Sir JOHN TURNER of Warham, 3rd Bt. [G.B. 1721], M.P. in six Parliaments 1739–1774 and a Lord of the Treasury 1762–1765, b. 1712; d. 4 June 1780; and had issue 1a to 2a.

1a. Ann Turner, da. and co-h., b. c. 1747; d. 26 *July* 1822, aged 75; m. 27 *July* 1772, Robert Hales, Collector of Customs at King's Lynn, d. 12 *Sept.* 1789, aged 48; *and had issue* (*with 2 elder sons who d.s.p.*) 1b.

1b. James Hales of Norwich, Solicitor, b. 11 Ap. 1785; d. 6 Ap. 1831; m. 13 *June* 1810, Barbara, da. of John Greene Baseley, Mayor of Norwich, d. 9 Dec. 1850; *and had issue* (*with 4 sons and 3 das. who d. unm.*) 1c to 6c.

1c. John Hales, afterwards (Ap. 1892) Hales-Tooke of Copdock and Washbrook, co. Suffolk, and of Holt, co. Norfolk, M.R.C.S.E., b. 26 Sept. 1820; d. 7 Mar. 1899; m. 1st, 16 *Sept.* 1846, Sarah, da. and h. of John Clark of Holt, d. 8 Aug. 1895; *and had issue* 1d to 2d.

1d. John Baseley Tooke Hales of Copdock and Washbrook, B.A. (Camb.) (*The Close, Norwich*), b. 9 Dec. 1849; m. 19 Ap. 1888, Elizabeth Blanche Mary, da. of the Rev. William Bagnall-Oakeley of Newland, co. Glouc.; and has issue 1e to 2e.

    1e. John Baseley Hales, B.A. (Camb.), b. 23 Jan. 1889.

    2e. Mary Barbara Hales.

2d. Robert Turner Hales, M.D., O.M., M.R.C.S.E. (*Holt, Norfolk*), b. 1 Sept. 1853; m. 26 Sept. 1889, Alice Mary, da. of Henry Ward of Rodbaston, co. Stafford; and has issue 1e to 4e.

    1e. Henry Ward Hales, b. 11 Nov. 1890.

    2e. Robert Neale Hales, b. 7 Nov. 1894.

    3e. Margaret Frances Turner Hales, b. 22 Mar. 1893.

    4e. Mabel Alice Jane Hales, b. 9 Jan. 1904. [Nos. 95346 to 95353.

The Plantagenet Roll

2c. Rev. George Hales, LL.B. (Camb.), *late* Rector of Rickinghall (6 *Westgate, Bury St. Edmunds*), b. 15 Ap. 1827; m. 1st, 18 Aug. 1851, Ann Holt, da. of James Horrox, d. 2 Feb. 1892; 2ndly, 26 Oct. 1892, Mary Seton, da. of John Dury; and has issue (by 1st wife) 1d to 10d.

1d. Rev. George Henry Hales, B.A. (Camb.), Rector of Stickney (*Stickney Rectory, Lincolnshire*), b. 20 May 1854.

2d. Herbert Martyn Hales (*Carshalton*), b. 16 Mar. 1856; m. 3 Feb. 1887, Marion Barrow, da. of W. Barrow Simonds of Abbots Barton, Winchester, J.P., D.L.; and has issue 1e to 2e.

1e. Helen Barbara Hales, b. 22 Jan. 1888.

2e. Rhona Brunwin Hales, b. 19 Ap. 1894.

3d. Rev. Canon Greville Turner Hales, now (1905) Brunwin-Hales, of Bradwell, near Braintree (*St. Mary's Rectory, Colchester*), b. 23 Nov. 1859; m. 30 Nov. 1886, Eva Caroline, da. of John Oxley Parker of Woodham Mortimer, co. Essex; and has issue 1e to 3e.

1e. Greville Oxley Brunwin-Hales, b. 21 Nov. 1889.

2e. Henry Tooke Brunwin-Hales, b. 12 Nov. 1892.

3e. Eva Elizabeth Brunwin-Hales, b. 8 June 1888.

4d. Rev. James Tooke Hales, Chaplain, served in S. Africa 1901-1902, Medal and 3 Clasps (*Tientsin*), b. 7 Sept. 1863; *unm.*

5d. Ernest Baseley Hales, Major Durham Light Infantry, served in South Africa, Medal and 2 Clasps, b. 2 Feb. 1867; *unm.*

6d. Rev. John Percy Hales, Rector of Cotgrave (*Cotgrave Rectory, Nottingham*), b. 7 Oct. 1870; m. 8 July 1898, Augusta Margaret, da. of Col. Albert Cantrell Cantrell-Hubbersty; and has issue 1e to 3e.

1e. George Frederick Hales, b. 21 Mar. 1901.

2e. Aline Holt Hales, b. 10 Jan. 1900.

3e. Helen Margaret Hales, b. 2 Nov. 1907.

7d. Caroline Durnford Hales, m. 31 Mar. 1880, the Rev. Harry Edward Beck, M.A. (Camb.), Rector of Harpley, *formerly* a Bar.-at-Law (*Harpley Rectory, King's Lynn*); and has issue 1e to 5e.

1e. Anthony Horace Beck, b. 3 Nov. 1884.

2e. Annie Caroline Beck,
3e. Mabel Constance Beck,
4e. Amy Sybil Beck,
5e. Charlotte Herris Beck,
} *unm.*

8d. Amy Wilson Hales, m. 1 June 1882, Rowland Holt Wilson, Solicitor (see p. 459) (*Bury St. Edmunds*); and has issue 1e to 3e.

1e. Thomas Wilson, Solicitor, b. 12 July 1883.

2e. George Wilson, Lieut. R.N., b. 12 May 1885.

3e. Edward Rowland Wilson, Indian Army, b. 13 June 1887.

9d. Annie Maud Hales, *unm.*

10d. Mary Hales, *unm.*

3c. Barbara Hales, b. 16 *June* 1812; d. 13 *Jan.* 1875; m. 26 *Nov.* 1839, *the Rev. Thomas Daniel Holt Wilson, M.A., Rector of Redgrave* [*2nd son of George Wilson of Redgrave Hall, co. Suffolk, Admiral of the Red*], d. 4 *Jan.* 1881; *and had issue* 1d *to* 5d.

1d. Rev. Charles Holt Wilson, M.A., Vicar of Dilton Marsh and Rural Dean of Heytesbury (*Dilton Marsh Rectory, Wilts*), b. 2 Dec. 1841; m. 12 Jan. 1871, Catharine Ellen, da. and co-h. of the Rev. Thomas Thorogood Upwood of Lovell's Hall, Lynn, J.P., D.L.

2d. Rev. Thomas Holt Wilson, M.A. (Camb.), Rector of Brayesworth 1904-1909, *formerly* of Redgrave and Botesdale (*Briarfield, Great Malvern*), b. 4 June

[Nos. 95354 to 95382.

# of The Blood Royal

1843; *m*. 1st, 13 Sept. 1870, Helen Emily [herself a descendant of King Edward III. through the Mortimer-Percy marriage (see p. 127)], da. of Edward Greene of Nether Hall, M.P., *d*. 25 Oct. 1880; 2ndly, 29 Aug. 1882, Alice Bertha, widow of Henry John Smith [Bt. Coll.], da. of the Rev. Edmund Dawe Wickham, *d*. 5 Mar. 1883; 3rdly, 8 July 1890, Mary Isabella, da. and h. of the Rev. Michael Turner, Rector of Cotton; and has issue 1*e* to 8*e*.

    1*e*. Eric Edward Boketon Wilson, now Holt Wilson, D.S.O., Capt. R.E., Instructor at the Royal Military Academy, Woolwich, *b*. 26 Aug. 1875; *m*. 19 Jan. 1903, Susannah Mary, da. of Charles George Shaw of Ayr; and has issue 1*f* to 2*f*.

        1*f*. Daniel Shaw Holt Wilson, *b*. 10 Dec. 1903.

        2*f*. Charles George Holt Wilson, *b*. 12 July 1905.

    2*e*. Michael Carlyon Holt Wilson, *b*. 19 Sept. 1892.

    3*e*. Algernon Charles Winstanley Wilson, *b*. 3 Jan. 1896.

    4*e*.[1] Muriel Barbara Wilson, *m*. 9 Feb. 1897, Robert Purdon Robertson-Glasgow of Craigmyle, co. Aberdeen, J.P., D.L. co. Ayr, *late* Lieut.-Col. 2nd Vol. Batt. Royal Scots Fusiliers [descended from the Lady Isabel Plantagenet (see the Essex Volume, p. 180)] (*Craigmyle, Aberdeen*); and has issue 1*f* to 2*f*.

        1*f*. Robert Wilson Robertson-Glasgow, *b*. 7 Nov. 1899.

        2*f*. Raymond Charles Robertson-Glasgow, *b*. 15 July 1901.

    5*e*.[1] Helen Ursula Wilson, *m*. 5 June 1900, Philip Armstrong Shaw (*Hemington Hall, Derby*); and has issue 1*f* to 3*f*.

        1*f*. Eric Charles Holt Shaw, *b*. 6 June 1903.

        2*f*. Alexander Armstrong Shaw, *b*. 7 Sept. 1907.

        3*f*. Ursula Flora Shaw, *b*. 12 Mar. 1901.

    6*e*.[2] Amica Nelson Washington Wilson.

    7*e*.[2] Joyce Philippa Turner Wilson.

    8*e*.[2] Rachel Edmunda Holt Wilson.

  3*d*. Algernon George Wilson, *b*. 25 *July* 1844; *d*. (? s.p.) *at Melbourne*, 7 *Sept*. 1877; m. *Mar.* 1872, *Charlotte, da. of* (—) *Parsons*, d. 1879.

  4*d*. Edward Hales Wilson, C.B., Col. Indian Army (*Junior United Service*), *b*. 17 Sept. 1845; *m*, at Agra, Ap. 1874, Rose Mackenzie, da. of John Alone; and has issue 1*e* to 5*e*.

    1*e*. Geoffrey Edward Holt Wilson, Capt. 34th Pioneers, *b*. 27 Ap. 1879.

    2*e*. William Holt Wilson, *b*. 27 July 1888.

    3*e*. Barbara Emily Holt Wilson, *unm*.

    4*e*. Cicely Catherine Wilson, *m*. Oct. 1901, Capt. John Ovans, King's Own Scottish Borderers; and has issue 1*f* to 5*f*.

        1*f*. John Malcolm Ovans, *b*. 21 Dec. 1905.

        2*f*. David Lambert Ovans, *b*. 29 June 1908.

        3*f*. Geoffrey Hornby Ovans, *b*. 26 Aug. 1909.

        4*f*. Joyce Rosemary Ovans, *b*. 14 Oct. 1904.

        5*f*. Katherine Mary Ovans, *b*. 16 Feb. 1907.

    5*e*. Rose Marion Wilson, *unm*.

  5*d*. Rowland Holt Wilson, Solicitor (*Bury St. Edmunds*), *b*. 4 Nov. 1846; *m*. 1 June 1882, Amy Wilson (see p. 458), da. of the Rev. George Hales, LL.B.; and has issue.

    See p. 458, Nos. 95376–95378.

  4*c*. Fanny Hales, b. 12 Dec. 1813; d. 23 *July* 1879; m. 28 Aug. 1834, *the Rev. Charles Herbert Jenner, M.A., Rector of Wenvoe* [2nd *son of the Right Hon. Sir Herbert Jenner-Fust, P.C., LL.D.*], *b*. 26 *July* 1809; d. 6 *Oct*. 1891; *and had issue* (*with* 5 *others who* d. *young*) 1*d to* 3*d*.

    1*d*. Henry Augustus Jenner, District Probate Registrar H.M. High Court of Justice, Chester (11 *Whitefriars, Chester*), *b*. 15 Nov. 1846; *unm*.

[Nos. 95383 to 95413.

The Plantagenet Roll

2d. *Edwin Arthur Jenner of the Bank of England*, b. 3 Dec. 1850; d. 22 Feb. 1908; m. 8 *May* 1879, *Edith Sarah, da. of Frederick Halsey Janson of Chislehurst; and had issue* 1e *to* 6e.

1e. Montague Arthur Jenner, b. 17 Oct. 1883.
2e. Charles Herbert Jenner, b. 31 Oct. 1888.
3e. Violet Edith Jenner.
4e. Muriel Agnes Jenner.
5e. Cicely Frances Jenner, m. 14 July 1908, Sidney Preston (*Wallington, Surrey*).
6e. Evelyn Mary Jenner.

3d. Rev. George Herbert Jenner, M.A. (Oxon.), Rector of Wenvoe (*Wenvoe Rectory, Glamorgan*), b. 17 Aug. 1852; m. 1st, 25 Sept. 1877, Mary Hales (see p. 461), da. of the Rev. William Grigson, d. 11 June 1905; 2ndly, 9 Ap. 1907, Julia, da. of the Rev. Arthur Thomas Whitmore Shadwell; and has issue 1e to 6e.

1e. Herbert Lancelot Jenner, b. 9 Sept. 1885.
2e. Raymund Francis Jenner, b. 30 Aug. 1890.
3e. Caroline Elizabeth Mary Jenner.
4e. Fanny Jenner, m. 19 Ap. 1906, Lancelot Horace Augustus Shadwell (*Durban, Natal*).
5e. Norah Margaret Jenner.
6e. Hilda Mary Lascelles Jenner.

5c. *Margaret Hales*, b. 25 Nov. 1817; d. 26 *Jan.* 1887; m. 9 *July* 1844, *the Rev. William Grigson, M.A., Rector of Whinburgh, co. Norfolk*, d. 6 Oct. 1879; *and had issue* (*with das. who* d. *young*) 1d *to* 7d.

1d. Rev. William Shuckforth Grigson, M.A. (Camb.), *formerly* Scholar Ch. Coll., 2nd Cl. Trip. 1867, Vicar of Pelynt (*Pelynt Vicarage, Duloe, S.O., Cornwall*), b. 15 Ap. 1845; m. 1st, 31 July 1873, Charlotte, da. of John Neve of Wolverhampton, d.s.p. 25 Feb. 1884; 2ndly, 21 June 1886, Mary, da. of Hugh Stott of Lewisham, d.s.p.s. 10 Feb. 1889; 3rdly, 10 Sept. 1890, Mary Beatrice, da. of the Rev. John Simon Boldero, M.A., Vicar of Amblecote; and has issue 1e to 7e.

1e. John William Boldero Grigson, Eastern Telegraph Coy., b. 26 Jan. 1893.
2e. Kenneth Walton Grigson, b. 29 June 1895.
3e. Wilfrid Vernon Grigson, b. 11 Oct. 1896.
4e. Lionel Henry Shuckforth Grigson, b. 25 Jan. 1898.
5e. Claude Vivian Grigson, b. 12 Jan. 1900.
6e. Aubrey Herbert Grigson, b. 22 Feb. 1901.
7e. Geoffrey Edward Harvey Grigson, b. 2 Mar. 1905.

2d. Rev. Edward Grigson, B.A. (Camb.), *late* Rector of Northchurch 1897–1909, &c. (*West Lodge, Aylsham, Norfolk*), b. 2 Sept. 1846; m. 1st, 3Oct. 1872, Eleanor Edith, da. of John Sunley of London, d. 6 Aug. 1904; 2ndly, 16 Jan. 1906, Emma Sara Louisa, da. of Thomas Abraham Rawlinson of Lincoln's Inn; and has issue 1e to 3e.

1e. James Edward Grigson, b. 25 July 1873; *unm.*
2e. Francis Charles William Grigson, b. 16 Aug. 1875; *unm.*
3e.[1] Edith Margaret Grigson, *unm.*

3d. *Francis Grigson*, b. 4 Aug. 1852; d. 25 *Sept.* 1886; m. 2 *Aug.* 1881, *Anna* (*Whinburgh, Musgrave Road, Durban, Natal*), *da. of John Edward Alsebrook of Worthing, co. Norfolk; and had issue* 1e.

1e. Katharine Marion Grigson, b. 1 May 1884.

4d. Rev. Baseley Hales Grigson, B.A. (Camb.), Rector of East Harling (*East Harling Hall, Thetford*), b. 26 Mar. 1856; m. 5 Oct. 1881, Annette Hammond, da. and h. of Grigson Heyhoe Wigg of Swanton, Morley, co. Norfolk, d. 15 July 1903; and has issue 1e to 2e.

1e. Pawlet St. John Baseley Grigson, B.A. (Camb.), now of the Bombay and Burma Trading Corporation, b. 12 June 1882.
2e. Olive Vivia Grigson, *unm.*

[Nos. 95414 to 95442.

of The Blood Royal

5*d*. Robert John Hales Grigson, *b*. 20 Mar. 1858; *m*. 20 July 1897, Dora Anne, da. of the Rev. John William Hunt of St. James', Hull; *s.p.*

6*d*. Barbara Lucy Grigson, *m*. 8 June 1871, Francis Bowman Turner (*Westgate-on-Sea*); and has issue 1*e* to 2*e*.

1*e*. Katharine Mary Turner, *unm*.

2*e*. Mabel Frances Turner, *m*. 24 June 1902, Laurence Rea; *s.p.*

7*d*. *Mary Hales Grigson*, b. 21 Nov. 1849; d. 11 *June* 1905; m. *as* 1*st wife*, 25 *Sept*. 1878, *the Rev. George Herbert Jenner, M.A. (Oxon.), Rector of Wenvoe; and had issue.*

See p. 460, Nos. 95421–95426.

6*c*. Mary Anne Hales.

2*a*. *Fanny Turner*, da. and co-h., d. 30 Nov. 1813; m. 28 Dec. 1777, *Sir Martin Browne ffolkes of Hillington*, 1st Bt. [G.B. 26 *May* 1774], F.R.S., d. 11 Dec. 1821; *and had issue* 1*b* to 3*b*.

1*b*. *Sir William John Henry Browne ffolkes*, 2nd Bt. [G.B.], F.R.S., b. 30 Aug. 1786; d. 24 *Mar*. 1860; m. 21 *Ap*. 1818, *Charlotte Philippa, sister of Dominick*, 1st *Lord Oranmore* [I.], da. *of Dominick Geoffrey Brown of Castle MacGarrett*, d. 23 Dec. 1882; *and had issue* 1*c* to 5*c*.

1*c*. *Martin William Browne ffolkes*, b. 16 *Jan*. 1819; d.v.p. 23 *July* 1849; m. 30 *Mar*. 1843, *Henrietta Bridget*, da. *of Gen. Sir Charles Wale of Shelford, co. Camb., K.C.B*., d. 14 Nov. 1855; *and had issue* 1*d* to 3*d*.

1*d*. Sir William Hovell Browne ffolkes of Hillington, 3rd Bt. [G.B.], K.C.V.O., J.P., D.L., High Sheriff co. Norfolk 1876 and Chairman and Alderman of Norfolk C.C., and Chairman Quarter Sessions, Hon. Major *late* 2nd Brigade Eastern Division R.A., M.P. for King's Lynn 1880–1885 (*Hillington Hall, Lynn*), *b*. 21 Nov. 1847; *m*. 6 Ap. 1875, Emily Charlotte, da. of Robert Elwes of Congham House, co. Norfolk; and has issue 1*e*.

1*e*. Dorothy ffolkes, *m*. 24 July 1902, Capt. the Hon. John Dawnay, D.S.O. [son and h.-app. of Hugh Richard, 8th Viscount Downe [I.], K.C.V.O., &c., descended from King Henry VII. (see Tudor Roll, p. 370)] (*Wykeham, Yorkshire*); and has issue 1*f* to 3*f*.

1*f*. Richard Dawnay, *b*. 16 May 1903.

2*f*. George William ffolkes Dawnay, for whom H.R.H. the Prince of Wales was sponsor, *b*. 20 Ap. 1909.

3*f*. Ruth Mary Dawnay.

2*d*. *Martin William Browne ffolkes*, C.E., b. 19 *July* 1849; d. 3 *Nov*. 1901; m. 28 *Jan*. 1882, *Wilhelmine Mary Emily [descended from George, Duke of Clarence, K.G. (see Clarence Volume, p. 417)] (Heacham, Norfolk), da. of Col. John Davy Brett of Dersingham, co. Norfolk; and had issue* 1*e* to 3*e*.

1*e*. Audrey ffolkes.

2*e*. Barbara ffolkes.

3*e*. Cynthia Mary ffolkes.

3*d*. Etheldreda Isabella ffolkes (*Poringland, Norwich*), *m*. as 2nd wife, 26 Sept. 1871, Henry Birkbeck of Stoke Holy Cross, J.P., High Sheriff co. Norfolk 1860, *b*. 10 Feb. 1821; *d*. 1 Feb. 1895; and has issue 1*e* to 2*e*.

1*e*. Martin Birkbeck, *b*. 10 Nov. 1873.

2*e*. Geoffrey Birkbeck, *b*. 12 Oct. 1875; *m*.

2*c*. Rev. Henry Edward ffolkes, heir-presumptive to Baronetcy, M.A. (Oxon.), Rector of Hillington and Rural Dean of Lynn (*Hillington Rectory, near Lynn*), *b*. 20 Dec. 1823; *m*. 24 Ap. 1860, Sophia Louisa, da. of the Rev. Edward Brown Everard, Rector of Burnham Thorpe; and has issue 1*d* to 9*d*.

1*d*. William Everard Browne ffolkes, *formerly* Lieut. 4th Batt. Suffolk Regt. (8 *Upton Park, Slough*), *b*. 15 Feb. 1861; *m*. 21 Ap. 1896, Sybil Compton, da. of the Rev. Richard Compton Maul; and has issue 1*e*.

1*e*. William Rupert Compton ffolkes, *b*. 7 Aug. 1898. [Nos. 95443 to 95467.

The Plantagenet Roll

2*d*. Edward George Everard ffolkes (*Indian Road, Toronto*), *b.* 24 Jan. 1862; *m.* 4 Aug. 1891, Agnes, da. of A. Strachan of Toronto.

3*d*. Rev. Francis Arthur Stanley ffolkes, M.V.O., J.P., Rector of Wolferton and a Chaplain in Ordinary to H.M. the King, *formerly* Hon. Chaplain to Queen Victoria (*Wolferton Rectory, Norfolk*), *b.* 8 Dec. 1863; *m.* 27 Sept. 1893, Isabel Laura Newbery, da. of John Newbery Boschetti of Eccles, co. Lancaster; and has issue 1*e* to 2*e*.

1*e*. Edward John Patrick Boschetti ffolkes, *b.* 16 Jan. 1899.

2*e*. Philippa Frances Boschetti ffolkes, *b.* 12 June 1896.

4*d*. Robert Walling Everard ffolkes, *b.* 1 Feb. 1865; *m.* 20 July 1884, Ada, da. of Col. Brierley; and has issue 1*e* to 4*e*.

1*e*. Mary Emily Margaret ffolkes.

2*e*. Ethel Christobel Frances ffolkes.

3*e*. Evelyn Maud ffolkes.

4*e*. Muriel Everard ffolkes.

5*d*. Geoffrey Charles Hovell ffolkes, Private Secretary to Hon. Joseph Baynes of Natal, C.M.G. (*Hillington, Norfolk*), *b.* 3 Aug. 1867; *m.* 27 Jan. 1897, Edith Louisa Pollen, widow of the Rev. Charles E. Cummings, da. of Frederick Haworth.

6*d*. Margaret Louisa Everard ffolkes, *m.* Jan. 1888, the Rev. John Erasmus Philipps, M.A., Rector of Cockfield and Vicar of Staindrop (*Staindrop Vicarage, Darlington*); and has issue 1*e*.

1*e*. Edward James Tracy Philipps, *b.* 20 Nov. 1888.

7*d*. Helen Sophia Everard ffolkes.

8*d*. Charlotte Philippa Everard ffolkes, *m.* 25 Oct. 1894, Sir Augustus Vere Foster of Glyde, 4th Bt. [U.K.], J.P., D.L. [descended from George, Duke of Clarence, K.G., brother of King Edward IV. (see Clarence Volume, p. 593)]; and has issue 1*e* to 3*e*.

1*e*. Anthony Vere Foster, *b.* 21 Feb. 1908.

2*e*. Philippa Eugenia Vere Foster.

3*e*. Dorothy Elizabeth Charlotte Vere Foster.

9*d*. Mabel Olive Emily ffolkes.

3*c*. George Howe Browne ffolkes, M.A., J.P. (*Wolferton Manor House, near Lynn*), *b.* 16 Feb. 1834.

4*c*. Margaret Charlotte ffolkes, d. 23 *May* 1899; m. 8 *July* 1847, *Francis Hay Gurney of North Runcton, Norfolk, J.P., D.L.* [*descended from the Lady Anne, sister to King Edward IV.*], d. 1 Dec. 1891.

See the Exeter Volume, p. 684, Nos. 57430–57442.

5*c*. Fanny Louisa ffolkes (*Wolferton Manor House, near Lynn*).

2*b*. *Fanny Mary ffolkes*, b. 1778; d. *Ap.* 1813; bur. *at West Wickham*; m. 1799, *Gilbert Harvey West of H.M. Treasury*, b. 1780; d. 13 *Feb*. 1861; bur. *at Corfe; and had issue* (*with* 4 *other sons and* 2 *das. who* d.s.p.) 1*c to* 3*c*.

1*c*. *Martin John West*, 1*st Lieut.-Gov. of Natal*, b. 1800; d. *at Pietermaritzburg*, 1849; m. 1830, *Albina, da. of* (—) *Sullivan; and had issue* 1*d to* 3*d*.

1*d*. Isabel Caroline West, *m.* 18 July 1854, Major-Gen. Frederick Charles D'Epinay Barclay [2nd son of Sir David William Barclay, 10th Bt. [S.]], *d.s.p.* 28 Dec. 1890.

2*d*. Charlotte Maria West, d. (–); m. (—) *Willock; and had issue* 1*e*.

1*e*. Isabel Willock, *m.* William Wellington Sandeman, Major *late* 78th Highlanders; and has issue 1*f*.

1*f*. William Alastair Sandeman.

3*d*. Albina West, *m.* Capt. Robson; and has issue (2 sons and a da.).

2*c*. *Caroline Elizabeth West*, b. 1805; d. 1897; m. *the Rev. Henry Vyvyan Luke, Rector of Thulbear, Stoke St. Mary, and Thurloxton; and had issue* 1*d to* 4*d*.

[Nos. 95468 to 95504.

# of The Blood Royal

1d. Walter Luke (*Virginia, U.S.A.*), b. (—); m. (—), da. of (—) Pigott; and has issue 1e to 2e.

1e. Vyvyan Luke, b. (—); m. (—), da. of (—) Douglas.

2e. Caroline Luke, m. Frederick Arthur Berkeley Portman [son of the Rev. Henry Fitzharding Berkeley Portman, Rector of Thulbear, Taunton, co. Som.].

2d. Henry Edward Luke (*New Zealand*), b. (—); m. (—); s.p.

3d. Emma Fanny Luke, b. 1844; d. 1864; m. 186–, the Rev. (—) *Henry Ewen*; and has issue 1e.

1e. Fanny Ewen.

4d. Caroline Harriet Luke, d. 1893; m. *Major Burridge*; and had issue (1 son and 2 das).

3c. Maria West, b. 16 *July* 1811; d. 17 *Feb.* 1892; m. 12 *Ap.* 1842, *the Rev. William Hulme, Rector of Brampton Abbotts, co. Hereford*, d. 4 *Jan.* 1890; *and had issue* (with a son and da. who d. unm.) 1d.

1d. Frances Maria Hulme, m. 4 July 1872, Capt. Evans Mynde Allen, J.P., High Sheriff co. Hereford 1910, *late* 1st Batt. Royal Scots Fusiliers (*Manor House, Upton Bishop, Ross, Hereford*); and has issue 1e.

1e. Robert William Allen, M.A. (Oxon.), Bar.-at-Law I.T., and Capt. 8th V.B.T. Hussars, b. 14 Mar. 1873; *unm*.

3b. Lucretia Georgiana ffolkes, b. 1795; d. *in childbirth at Bombay* 4 *Sept.* 1828; m. 26 *Aug.* 1822, *Sir Edward West, Chief Justice of Bombay*, d. *there* 18 *Aug.* 1828; *and had issue* 1c.

1c. Fanny Anna West, b. *May* 1826; d. *at Shelford* 6 *Mar.* 1869; m. *at Hillington as* 1st *wife*, 1849, *Robert Gregory Wale of Shelford, J.P., D.L., Hon. Col. Cambridgeshire Militia, formerly 33rd Regt.* [6th *son of the above-mentioned Sir Charles Wale, K.C.B.*], b. 14 Aug. 1820; d. 17 *Ap.* 1892; *and had issue* 1d to 7d.

1d. Robert ffolkes Wale of Shelford, Capt. 4th Batt. Suffolk Regt., b. 17 May 1863; d. *unm*. 5 *Sept.* 1894.

2d. Fanny Lucretia Wale of Shelford, da. and co-h. (*Little Shelford, Cambridge*), b. in Rome; *unm*.

3d. Mildred Wale of Shelford, da. and co-h., m. Mar. 1909, Col. Wood, R.H.A.

4d. Cecil Henrietta Wale, da. and co-h., m. 8 Oct. 1884, the Rev. Harcourt Morley Isaac Powell, Vicar of Wollaston (*Wollaston Vicarage, Northants*); and has issue 1e to 4e.

1e. Vernon Harcourt de Butts Powell, B.A. (Keble Coll., Oxon.), b. 23 Jan. 1886.

2e. Robert Desmond Fitzgerald Powell, b. 31 July 1892.

3e. Edward Blennerhassett Selwyn Powell, b. 5 Feb. 1897.

4e. Norah Cecil Wale Powell, b. 6 May 1888.

5d. Anna Charlotte Wale, b. Oct. 1856; d. 7 Aug. 1891; m. *Mar.* 1883, *Robert Henry Willis; and had issue* (a da., Mildred Mary, b. 22 *Jan.* 1884; d. *Mar.* 1908).

6d. Georgiana Isabella Wale, da. and co-h., m. 10 June 1880, the Rev. Arthur Charles Jennings, Rector of King's Stanley [grandson of Adm. Sir Edward Hamilton, K.C.B., R.N., descended from James I., King of Scotland, by his Queen, Joan of Beaufort, grandda. of John (of Gaunt), Duke of Lancaster, K.G., in right of which he took his degree as of Founder's Kin at Cambridge] (*King's Stanley Rectory, Gloucester*); and has issue 1e to 3e.

1e. Arthur Richard Jennings, B.A. (Jesus Coll., Camb.), a Medical Student, b. 6 May 1886.

2e. Richard William Jennings (Jesus Coll., Camb.), a Law Student, b. 6 Mar. 1889.

3e. Hermione Louisa Fanny Jennings.

7d. Frederica Wale of Shelford, da. and co-h. (*Little Shelford, Cambridge*), *unm*.

[Nos. 95505 to 95523.

The Plantagenet Roll

286. Descendants of FRANCIS SAMWELL of Upton (Table XXV.), *bapt.* 15 Sept. 1616; *d.* 1657; *m.* REBECCA, da. of Robert SELSBY of Duston, *bur.* 23 May 1708; and had issue (with a son and da. *d.* unm.) 1*a* to 5*a*.

1*a. William Samwell of Gayton,* b. c. 1649; d. 25 Feb. 1706; m. 20 Feb, 1684, *Agnes, da. of Edward Dry of Milton,* d. 21 *Jan.* 1687; *and had issue.*[1]

2*a. Mary Samwell,* bapt. 16 *May* 1651; d. (-); m. *John Goodier of Cransley, Bar.-at-Law; and had issue.*[1]

3*a. Elizabeth Samwell,* bur. 20 *Ap.* 1675; m. *John Robinson of Great Wymondham,* co. *Leic.*

4*a. Jane Samwell,* bapt. 24 *May* 1660; d. (-); m. *W. Knight of London.*

5*a. Frances Samwell, living* unm. 1682.

287. Descendants of HENRY (NEVILL), 6th Lord ABERGAVENNY [E.] (Table XXVI.), *d.* 10 Feb. 1587; *m.* 1st, Lady FRANCES, da. of Thomas (MANNERS), 1st Earl of Rutland [E.], *bur.* Sept. 1576; and had issue.

See the Exeter Volume, Table XXIV. and pp. 347-374, Nos. 25205-26746; and the Essex Volume Supplement, pp. 625-637, Nos. 26240/1-393.

[Nos. 95524 to 97458.

288. Descendants of JOHN (GRANVILLE), 1st EARL OF BATH [E. 20 Ap. 1661] (Table XXVI.), *b.* 29 Aug. 1628; *d.* 22 Aug. 1701; *m. c.* Oct. 1652, JANE, da. of Sir Peter WYCHE of London, Comptroller of the Royal Household; and had issue 1*a* to 5*a*.

1*a. Charles (Granville), 2nd Earl of Bath* [E.], *1st Count Granville* [H.R.E. 27 *Jan.* 1684], bapt. 31 *Aug.* 1661; d. 4 *Sept.* 1701; m. 2*ndly, Feb.* 1691, *Countess Isabella, da. of Count Henry of Nassau, Lord of Auverquerque,* d. 30 *Jan.* 1692; *and had issue* 1*b.*

1*b. William Henry (Granville), 3rd Earl of Bath* [E.], *&c.,* b. 30 *Jan.* 1692; d. unm. 17 *May* 1711.

2*a. John (Granville), 1st Baron Granville* [E. 1703], bapt. 12 *Ap.* 1665; d.s.p. 3 Dec. 1707.

3*a. Lady Jane Granville, da. and in her issue* (1711) *co-h.,* d. 27 Feb. 1696; m. Sir *William Leveson-Gower, 4th Bt.* [E. 1620], *M.P.,* d. Dec. 1691; *and had issue* 1*b* to 3*b.*

1*b. John (Leveson-Gower), 1st Baron Gower* [E. 16 *Mar.* 1703], b. 7 *Jan.* 1675; d. *Sept.* 1709; m. *Sept.* 1692, *Lady Catherine, da. of John (Manners), 1st Duke of Rutland* [E.], d. 7 *May.* 1722; *and had issue.*
See the Exeter Volume, Table VIII. and pp. 172-187, Nos. 3846-6776.

2*b. Katherine Leveson-Gower,* b. c. 1670; d. 14 *Mar.* 1704; m. 16 *May* (? *June*) 1687, Sir *Edward Wyndham of Orchard Wyndham, 2nd Bt.* [E. 1661], bur. 29 *June* 1695; *and had issue* 1*c.*

1*c. Sir William Wyndham, 3rd Bt.* [E.], *P.C., Chancellor of the Exchequer,* b. 1687; d. 17 *June* 1740; m. 1*st,* 1708, *Lady Catherine, da. of Charles (Seymour), 6th Duke of Somerset* [E.], *K.G.; and had issue.*
See the Tudor Roll, Table L. and pp. 263-292, Nos. 24402-25349.

3*b. Jane Leveson-Gower,* d. 24 *May* 1725; m. (*lic.* 2 *Mar.*) 1692, *Henry (Hyde),*
[Nos. 97459 to 101337.

---
[1] Baker's "Northants," i. 225.

of The Blood Royal

4th *Earl of Clarendon* and 2nd *Earl of Rochester* [E.], d. 10 Dec. 1753; and had issue.

See pp. 132-133, Nos. 15257-15469.

4a. *Lady Catherine Granville*, d. (–); m. *Craven Peyton*.

5a. *Grace*, suo jure 1st *Countess Granville* [G.B. 1 Jan. 1715], b. c. 1667; d. 18 Oct. 1744; m. (*lic.* 15 Mar.) 1675, *George (Carteret)*, 1st Baron Carteret [E. 19 Oct. 1681], d. 22 Sept. 1695; and had issue 1b.

1b. *John (Carteret)*, 2nd *Baron Carteret* [E.] and (1744) 2nd *Earl Granville* [G.B.], K.G., Principal Sec. of State to George I., b. 22 Ap. 1690; d. 2 Jan. 1763; m. 1st, 17 Oct. 1710, *Frances*, da. of Sir Robert Worsley, 4th Bt. [E.], d. 20 June 1743; and had issue.

See the Tudor Roll, Table XXXII. and pp. 201-240, Nos. 21378-22550.

[Nos. 101338 to 102723.

289. Descendants of BERNARD GRANVILLE, M.P., Gentleman of the Horse and Groom of the Bedchamber to King Charles II. (Table XXVI.), d. 1701; m. ANNE, da. and h. of Cuthbert MORLEY of Hornby, co. York; and had issue 1a to 3a.

1a. *Sir Bevil Granville, M.P., Major-Gen. and Governor of Barbados*, d.s.p. 1706.

2a. *George (Granville)*, 1st *Baron Lansdowne* [G.B.], so cr. by Anne 1 Jan. 1712, and *Duke of Albemarle* [E.], so cr. by James III. in exile 3 Nov. 1721, P.C., b. 1667; d. 30 Jan. 1735; m. 1711, *Lady Mary*, widow of Thomas Thynne of Old Windsor, da. of Edward (Villiers), 1st Earl of Jersey [E.], d. 17 Jan. 1735; and had issue.

See p. 377, Nos. 62167-62469.

3a. *Bernard Granville of Buckland, co. Glos., Lieut.-Gov. of Hull, M.P.*, d. 1723; m. *Mary*, da. of Sir Martin Westcombe, 1st Bt. [E. 1699]; and had issue 1b to 4b.

1b. *Bernard (Granville)*, 2nd *Duke of Albemarle* [E.] as above, d.s.p. 2 July 1776.

2b. *Rev. Bevil Granville*, d.s.p. in Carolina 1736.

3b. *Mary Granville*, so well known for her literary acquirements, b. 14 May 1770; d.s.p. 15 Ap. 1788; m. 1st, 1717, *Alexander Pendarves of Roscrow*; 2ndly, 1743, the *Very Rev. Patrick Delany*, D.D., Dean of Down.

4b. *Anne Granville*, da. and in her issue (1788) sole h., b. 1707; d. 16 July 1761; m. Aug. 1740, *John D'Ewes of Wellesbourne, co. Warwick*; d. 30 Aug. 1780; and had issue 1c to 2c.

1c. *Bernard D'Ewes of Wellesbourne*, b. 1743; d. 1780; m. 1777, *Anne*, da. of John Delabere of Cheltenham, d. 1780; and had issue 1d to 2d.

1d. *Court D'Ewes, afterwards* (1826) *Granville of Wellesbourne*, b. 1779; d. 16 July 1848; m. 1803, *Maria*, da. of Edward Ferrers of Baddesley Clinton, co. Warwick, d. 16 Nov. 1852; and had issue 1e to 3e.

1e. *Bernard Granville of Wellesbourne, J.P., D.L.*, b. 4 Feb. 1804; d. 6 Jan. 1869; m. 1st, 28 Jan. 1828, *Mathewana Sarah*, da. of Capt. Mathew Richard Onslow, Coldstream Guards [Bt. Coll.], d. 3 Aug. 1829; 2ndly, 27 Oct. 1830, *Anne Catherine*, da. of Admiral Sir Hyde Parker [Bt. Coll.], d. 17 Dec. 1895; and had issue 1f to 9f.

1f. *Bevil Granville of Wellesbourne, J.P., formerly Major Royal Welsh Fusiliers* and (1863-1887) one of H.M.'s Hon. Corps of Gentlemen-at-Arms, b. 20 Jan. 1834; d. 8 Mar. 1909; m. 12 Oct. 1865, *Alice Jane*, da. of the Rev. Nathaniel Wodehouse, Vicar of Worle and Dulverton [E. of Kimberley Coll.], by his wife Georgiana [descended from the Lady Anne, sister of King Edward IV. (see the Exeter Volume, p. 379)], da. of Rev. the Hon. William Capel, d. 21 Oct. 1901; and had issue 1g to 6g.

[Nos. 102724 to 103026.

The Plantagenet Roll

1g. Bernard Granville, Capt. 3rd King's Own Hussars (*Wellesbourne Hall, near Warwick*), b. 21 July 1873; m. 13 Jan. 1903, Edith [descended from the Lady Isabel Plantagenet (see the Essex Volume, p. 282)], da. of the Right Hon. Thomas Frederick Halsey of Gaddesden, P.C., M.P.; and has issue 1h to 3h.

    1h. Bevil Granville, b. 26 Dec. 1904.
    2h. Richard St. Leger Granville, b. 24 Ap. 1907.
    3h. Mary Granville, b. 19 Ap. 1910.

2g. Violet Granville, m. 7 May 1889, Walter Henry Maudslay (69 *Cadogan Gardens, W.*); s.p.s.

3g. Mary Olive Granville, m. Dec. 1893, Arthur Hubert Edward Wood of Sudbourne Hall, co. Suffolk, J.P., D.L. (*Browhead, Windermere*); and has issue 1h to 4h.

    1h. Edward Guy Wood, b. 30 Oct. 1894.
    2h. Richard Oliver Wood, b. 26 Mar. 1896.
    3h. Evelyn Sybil Wood.
    4h. Alice Ava Wood.

4g. Muriel Granville, m. 14 Feb. 1895, Frederick Blomfield (*Netherwylde Farm, St. Albans*); and has issue 1h to 4h.

    1h. Valentine Blomfield, b. 1898.
    2h. Christopher Blomfield, b. 1900.
    3h. Peter Blomfield, b. 1903.
    4h. David Blomfield, b. 1908.

5g. Grace Granville, m. 15 Nov. 1893, Harold M'Corquodale (*Forest Hall, Ongar*); and has issue 1h to 5h.

    1h. Kenneth M'Corquodale.
    2h. Hugh M'Corquodale.
    3h. Donald M'Corquodale.
    4h. Angus M'Corquodale.
    5h. Janet M'Corquodale.

6g. Morwenna Granville, m. 24 Jan. 1905, Capt. Lionel Halsey, R.N. [descended from the Lady Isabel Plantagenet (see the Essex Volume, p. 282)].

2f. George Hyde Granville, H.E.I.C.S., b. 27 Feb. 1837; d. 13 Dec. 1902; m. 18 June 1862, Henrietta, da. of Edward Bolton King of Chadshunt, co. Warwick; and had issue (*with a son d. unm.*) 1g to 2g.

1g. Dennis Granville, M.V.O., Chief Constable of Dorsetshire, Capt. *late* Royal Warwick Regt. (*Shirley House, Dorchester*), b. 14 Ap. 1863; m. 31 July 1895, Margaret Beatrice (see p. 536), da. of Major-Gen. Sir George Henry Waller, 3rd Bt. [U.K.]; and has issue 1h.

    1h. Judith Margaret Granville, b. 14 June 1896.

2g. Mabel Georgiana Lucy Granville, m. 4 Aug. 1897, Major Henry Clerk, *late* Queen's Bays (*The Grange, Wellesbourne, Warwick*); and has issue 1h to 4h.

    1h. Mary Conyers Clerk, b. 5 Aug. 1898.
    2h. Valmai Clerk, b. 11 Oct. 1899.
    3h. Letitia Clerk, b. 29 Aug. 1904.
    4h. Georgiana Clerk, b. 26 July 1909.

3f. Frederic John Granville, b. 14 Oct. 1839; d. 15 Feb. 1883; m. 2 July 1864, Cecilia Anne, da. of Robert Hook, d. 7 Feb. 1877; and had issue 1g to 3g.

    1g. Charles Delabere Granville, Adm. R.N., b. 21 June 1865; unm.
    2g. Cecil Horace Plantagenet Granville, settled in Australia, b. 2 Jan. 1877.
    3g. Marian Florence Granville, unm.

4f. Rev. Roger Granville, Sub-Dean of Exeter, Rector of Bideford 1878–1896 (*Pilton House, Pinhoe, Exeter*), b. 6 Feb. 1848; m. 20 Sept. 1870, Matilda Jane

[Nos. 103027 to 103059.

of The Blood Royal

[descended from George, Duke of Clarence, K.G., brother of King Edward IV. (see the Essex Volume Supplement, p. 530)], da. of Alexander Liebert of Swinton Hall, Lancaster ; and has issue 1g to 2g.

1g. Court Granville, Capt. 3rd Batt. Devonshire Regt. (4 *Cyril Mansions, Battersea Park*), b. 6 May 1872 ; m. 11 Aug. 1879, Beatrice Mabel [descended from the Lady Isabel Plantagenet (see the Essex Volume, p. 205)], da. of Major-Gen. Henry William Hart Davies Dumaresq ; and has issue 1h to 2h.

1h. Roger Francis Granville, b. 23 June 1909.

2h. Barbara Granville, b. 25 Ap. 1899.

2g. Eleanor Morwenna Granville, m. 2 Aug. 1902, Col. George Reginald FitzRoy Talbot, R.A. [descended from George, Duke of Clarence, K.G. (see Clarence Volume, p. 337)] (*Buckerell Lodge, Exeter*) ; and has issue 1h to 2h.

1h. Granville FitzRoy Talbot, b. 3 Mar. 1908.

2h. Gwendoline Betty Alice Talbot, b. 6 June 1905.

5f.[1] Joan Frederica Mathewana Granville (*Field Place, Horsham*), m. as 2nd wife, 10 Aug. 1850, the Rev. Lord Charles Paulet, Preb. of Salisbury [2nd son of Charles, 13th Marquis of Winchester [E.]], d. 23 July 1870 ; and has issue 1g.

1g. Eleanor Mary Paulet, m. 1 June 1889, Lieut.-Gen. Sir Edward Thomas Henry Hutton, K.C.M.G., C.B., Col. Comdt. King's Royal Rifle Corps (*Field Place, Horsham*).

6f.[2] Fanny Granville (*twin*), d. 1 *May* 1897 ; m. *as 2nd wife,* 22 *Ap.* 1858, *the Rev. Wellesley Pole Pigott, M.A., Rector of Fugglestone-cum-Bemerton and Fovant* [*4th son of Sir George Pigott,* 1st *Bt.* [*U.K.*]], d. 27 *Feb.* 1890 ; *and had issue* 1g *to* 2g.

1g. Wellesley George Pigott, J.P., *Capt. late* Rifle Brigade (*Blackmore House, Essex*), b. 20 Ap. 1861 ; m. 7 July 1891, Helen Louise, widow of Capt. Frederick W. Ind, R.A., da. of Capt. Thomas Donaldson, 3rd Hussars ; and has issue 1h.

1h. Gerald Wellesley Pigott, b. 3 Sept. 1896.

2g. Fanny Ada Pigott (*Greenoaks, Brockenhurst, Hants*), m. 25 May 1886, Lieut.-Col. Charles Berkeley Pigott, C.B., D.S.O. [eldest son of Sir Charles Robert Pigott, 3rd and present Bt. [U.K.], J.P., D.L.], d.v.p. 12 Sept. 1897 ; and has issue 1h to 2h.

1h. Berkeley Pigott, b. 21 May 1894.

2h. Florence Ada Cecile Pigott.

7f.[2] Louisa Granville (*Moreton, Bideford*), m. as 2nd wife, 31 Jan. 1872, Sir George Stucley Stucley, 1st Bt. [U.K.], M.P., d. 13 Mar. 1900 ; and has issue.

See p. 483, Nos. 103415–103418.

8f.[2] Amy Granville (*Marham House, Downham Market*), m. 4 Dec. 1861, Capt. Henry Bathurst, 23rd Royal Welsh Fusiliers, d. 5 Sept. 1886 ; and has issue 1g to 7g.

1g. Henry Villebois Bathurst of Marham, Lord of the Manor of Old Hall and Westacre (*Marham House, Downham Market*), b. 30 Oct. 1862.

2g. Granville Frederick Villebois Bathurst, b. 5 Feb. 1864.

3g. Launcelot Villebois Bathurst, b. 23 Ap. 1870.

4g. Laurence Charles Villebois Bathurst, M.A. (Oxon.), b. 4 June 1871 ; m.

5g. Emily Villebois Bathurst.

6g. Finetta Villebois Bathurst.

7g. Amy Villebois Bathurst.

9f.[2] *Harriet Granville,* d. 18 *Mar.* 1909 ; m. 28 *Dec.* 1869, *Henry Compton of Minstead Manor House, co. Hants, and Mapperton House, co. Dorset, J.P., D.L.,* d. 5 *July* 1877 ; *and had issue* 1g *to* 5g.

1g. Henry Francis Compton of Minstead and Mapperton, J.P., D.L., *formerly* M.P. New Forest Div., co. Hants (*The Manor House, Minstead, Lyndhurst ; Mapperton House, Dorset*), b. 16 Jan. 1872 ; m. 12 June 1895, Dorothy Ann [herself a [Nos. 103060 to 103086.

The Plantagenet Roll

descendant of King Edward III. through Mortimer-Percy], da. of Sir Richard Courtenay Musgrave, 11th Bt. [E.]; and has issue.
See p. 199, Nos. 29580–29582.

2g. George Compton, b. 4 Feb. 1873.

3g. Edward Bathurst Compton, Lieut. (ret.) R.N., b. 14 Aug. 1875; m. 23 June 1900, Bertha Alice [descended from the Lady Isabel Plantagenet (see Essex Volume, p. 112)], da. of the Hon. William Sydney Hylton Joliffe [B. Hylton Coll.]; and has issue 1h to 2h.

1h. Sydney Henry Compton, b. 25 Aug. 1901.

2h. Oliver Compton, b. 28 Nov. 1905.

4g. Harriet Compton, m. 17 Nov. 1900, Algernon Charles Wyndham Dunn-Gardner of Chatteris House, co. Camb., and Denton Hall, co. Suffolk, M.A. (Oxon.) (*Dullingham House, Newmarket*); and has issue 1h.

1h. [da.] Dunn-Gardner, b. 28 Sept. 1904.

5g. Eleanor Compton, m. 8 Ap. 1896, Henry Martin Powell of Wilverley, J.P. [eldest son of Lieut.-Col. William Martin Powell of Brooklands, co. Hants, J.P.] (*Wilverley Park, Lyndhurst, Hants*); and has issue 1h.

1h. Henry Weyland Martin Powell, b. 1902.

2e. *Rev. Granville John Granville, Vicar of Stratford-on-Avon*, b. 1807; d. 26 Ap. 1871; m. 16 Ap. 1839, Marrianne [descended from the Lady Anne, sister of King Edward IV.], da. of Sir Grey Skipwith, 8th Bt. [E.], d. 21 Oct. 1878; and had issue.
See the Exeter Volume, p. 328; Nos. 24139–24151.

3e. Mary Granville, d. (? s.p.) 28 Oct. 1886; m. 1856, Col. David Forbes, 91st Regt., d. 1885.

2d. Anne Granville, d. (-); m. 1805, *George Frederick Stratton of Great Tew, co. Oxon*.

2c. Mary D'Ewes, b. 22 Feb. 1746; d. 15 June 1814; m. Dec. 1770, *John Port, previously Sparrow, of Ilam Hall, co. Stafford, J.P.*, b. 1730; d. 9 Aug. 1801; *and had issue (with 3 sons and a da. d.s.p.)* 1d to 4d.

1d. *John Port of Ilam House, which he sold 1807*, b. 1773; d. 1 Mar. 1837; m. c. 1795/7, Mary, da. of Capt. Parke, H.E.I.C.S., d. July 1837; *and had issue (with 2 sons and a da. d. unm.)* 1e to 4e.

1e. *Rev. George Richard Port, B.A. (Oxon.), Rector of Oxenton, co. Glos, 1838–1855, and of Grafton-Flyford, co. Worc., 1855–1875*, b. 23 Dec. 1800; d. 28 Dec. 1882; m. 2ndly, 15 Dec. 1859, Frances Elizabeth Ann, da. of George Syers of Boughton House, co. Chester, b. 19 Mar. 1824; d. 1 Dec. 1909; *and had issue* 1f.

1f. George Brodie MacFarlan Port, b. 12 Mar. 1863; m. 23 Oct. 1888, Frances Emma Annie, da. of Edward Elliot Chambers of Crow Park and Fosterstown, co. Meath, M.A. (Oxon.), Bar.-at-Law, and sister of Richard Edward Elliott Chambers of the same; and has issue 1g to 2g.

1g. Francis George Richard Port, b. 10 Oct. 1892.

2g. Frances Dorothea Mary Port, b. 6 Jan. 1890.

2e. Georgina Port, d. (-); m. 23 Sept. 1830, *Charles Penny of Weymouth, J.P.*, d. (-); *and had issue (with 3 das. d. unm.)* 1f.

1f. *Charles Brodie Footman Penny, Gen. R.E.*, d. (-); m. Mary, da. of (—) Lord; *and had issue (with other sons)* 1g to 2g.

1g. Arthur Taylor Penny, Capt. Hants Regt., b. 17 Ap. 1871.

2g. Alice Penny.

3e. Louisa Port, d. *at Versailles* 1858; m. *at Marylebone*, 20 Sept. 1820, *the Rev. William Webster, M.A., Rector of Church Preen and Easthope, co. Salop, formerly Light Dragoons*, d. 17 Sept. 1844; *and had issue* 1f to 3f.

1f. Frederick Taylor Webster (*Huntington House, Holmer, near Hereford*), b. 10 Ap. 1827; m. 30 Ap. 1853, Mary Ann, da. of George Peach Aston of Newton, co. Salop; and has issue 1g to 4g. [Nos. 103087 to 103116.

of The Blood Royal

1g. Frederick Granville Port Webster, b. 10 Sept. 1863 ; m. 1 Feb. 1888, Anne, da. of (—) Hargrave of co. Warwick ; and has issue 1h.

1h. Frederick Hargrave Webster, b. 4 Jan. 1889.

2g. Mary Louisa Webster, m. Charles Frederick Deaken (Canada); and has issue 1h to 9h.

1h. Robert Frederick Deaken, bapt. 20 Nov. 1881.
2h. Charles Keeliege Deaken, } bapt. 21 Nov. 1882.
3h. Guy Barton Deaken,
4h. George Francis Deaken, bapt. at Bockleton 1 July 1887.
5h. Bickerton Aston Deaken, bapt. there July 1889.
6h. Reginald Grenville Deaken, bapt. there 1892.
7h. Mary Wilhelmina Deaken, bapt. 25 Oct. 1884.
8h. Elsie Winifred Deaken, bapt. 23 Nov. 1885.
9h. Vera Dorothy Deaken, bapt. at Bockleton 14 July 1890.

3g. Emma Elizabeth Webster, unm.

4g. Edith Minna Webster, m.

2f. Mary Webster, unm.

3f. Edith Webster, m. Major Collins, R.M., d. (–); and has issue (6 children, 4 abroad and 2 in England) 1g to 6g.

1g. Garnet Wolseley Collins, b. 23 May 1883.
2g. Francis Le Hardi Collins, b. 5 Mar. 1885.
3g. Edith Muriel Collins, b. 23 Oct. 1880.
4g. Kathleen Maud Wolseley Collins, b. 7 Nov. 1881.
5g. Ethel Gwendoline Collins, b. 1887.
6g. (—) Collins.

4e. *Harriet Port*, d. at Brighton after 1876; m. Sept. 1840, the Rev. Henry Robert Fowler of Felton, co. Glos.; and had issue 1f.

1f. Augusta Fowler, da. and h., d. 15 Mar. 1905; m. 11 July 1867, John Ashfordby-Trenchard of Stanton House (Stanton Fitzwarren, near Highworth); and had issue (with 3 sons d. young) 1g to 2g.

1g. John Henry Mohun Ashfordby-Trenchard, b. 4 May 1868.
2g. Stephen Granville Ashfordby-Trenchard, now (R.L. 1 Aug. 1905) Fowler (Vista Linda, Torquay), b. 21 July 1872.

2d. *Georgina Mary Ann Port*, b. 16 Sept. 1771; d. 19 Jan. 1850; m. 1789, Benjamin Waddington of Llanover, co. Monmouth; and had issue 1e to 3e.

1e. Frances Waddington, da. and co-h., b. 4 Mar. 1791; d. at Karlsruhe Mar. 1876; m. 1 July 1817, Christian Charles Josias (Bunsen), 1st Baron Bunsen (Freiherr von Bunsen) [Prussia], so cr. for life 3 Oct. 1857, for many years Prussian Min. Plen. to the Court of St. James', d. at Bonn 29 Nov. 1860; and had issue (with a son and 3 das. d. unm.) 1f to 8f.

1f. Rev. Henry George de Bunsen, Rector of Donington, naturalised in the United Kingdom 22 Ap. 1842; b. in Rome 2 Ap. 1818; d. 19 Mar. 1885; m. 15 Ap. 1847, Mary Louisa, da. of Abraham Harford-Battersly, formerly Harford, of Stoke House, co. Glos., d. 20 Ap. 1906; and had issue 1g to 2g.

1g. Elizabeth Frances de Bunsen, da. and co-h., m. 14 Jan. 1880, the Rev. William Archibald Sheringham, Rector of Donington (Donington Rectory, Wolverhampton, co. Salop); and has issue 1h to 2h.

1h. Charles John de Bunsen Sheringham, b. 12 Feb. 1883.
2h. Mary Alsager Sheringham.

2g. Louisa Emily de Bunsen, da. and co-h., b. 18 Mar. 1749; d. 22 Ap. 1887; m. as 2nd wife, 8 July 1886, Thomas Cheney Garfit of Kenwick Hall, J.P., D.L., High Sheriff co. Linc. 1897, formerly Capt. Royal North Lincoln Militia (Kenwick Hall, Louth, co. Linc.; Carlton); and has issue 1h.

1h. Henry de Bunsen Cheney Garfit, b. 9 Ap. 1887. [Nos. 103117 to 103144.

The Plantagenet Roll

2*f*. *Ernest Christian Louis de Bunsen of Abbey Lodge, Regent's Park*, b. 19 *Mar.* 1885; d. 13 *May* 1903; m. 5 *Aug.* 1845, *Elizabeth, da. of John Gurney of Ham House, co. Essex*, d. 19 *Jan.* 1903; *and had issue* 1*g* to 3*g*.

1*g*. Sir Maurice William Ernest de Bunsen, P.C., G.C.V.O., K.C.M.G., now H.B.M.'s Ambassador to the Court of Madrid (*British Embassy, Madrid; 2 Whitehall Court, S.W.; St. James'; Travellers'*), b. 8 Jan. 1852; m. 2 May 1899, Berta Mary, da. of Armar Henry Lowry-Corry [E. of Belmore Coll.]; and has issue 1*h* to 3*h*.

   1*h*. Hilda Violet Helena de Bunsen, *b*. 3 Ap. 1900.
   2*h*. Elizabeth Cicely de Bunsen, *b*. 30 Jan. 1902.
   3*h*. Rosalind Margaret de Bunsen, *b*. 25 July 1903.

2*g*. Hilda Elizabeth de Bunsen (8 *Chester Street, Grosvenor Place, S.W.; Bendeleben Castle, Sondershausen*), *m*. 1st, at the Chapel Royal, St. James', 17 Ap. 1873, Hugo von Krause, Fideicommiss-Besitzer of Bendeleben, near Sondershausen, Councillor of the German Embassy, *d*. in London 26 Mar. 1874; 2ndly, 20 Sept. 1877, Adolph Wilhelm Conrad Rudolph (Deichmann), 1st Baron Deichmann (Freiherr von Deichmann) [Prussia 11 June 1888], *d*. 12 Nov. 1907; and has issue 1*h* to 4*h*.

   1*h*. Wilhelm von Krause, Fideicommiss-Besitzer of Bendeleben (*Bendeleben Castle, near Sondershausen*), Diplo. Ser., now Councillor German Imperial Legation at Athens, *b*. 10 Feb. 1874; *unm*.

   2*h*. Baroness Hilda Eveline Marie von Deichmann, *m*. 5 Ap. 1905, Karl Bernhard (von Bismarck), 1st Count of Bismarck-Osten (Graf von Bismarck-Osten) [Prussia 19 Dec. 1906] (*Schloss Plathe, Pomerania, Prussia*); and has issue 1*i* to 2*i*.

      1*i*. Karl Ulrich von Bismarck-Osten, *b*. at Rathe 13 July 1908.
      2*i*. Ferdinand Otto Bernhard Wilhelm von Bismarck-Osten, *b*. 20 Dec. 1909.

   3*h*. Baroness Elsa Olga von Deichmann, *m*. 8 June 1910, Baron Walter von Ruxleben (*Schloss Rottleben, Schwarzburg-Sondershausen*).

   4*h*. Baroness Marie Therese von Deichmann, *unm*.

3*g*. Marie de Bunsen (67 *Eaton Terrace, S.W.*), *unm*.

3*f*. *Carl von Bunsen of Mein Genügen, Biebrich, Germany*, German Diplo. Service, b. 4 *Nov.* 1821; d. 12 *Mar.* 1887; m. *Jan.* 1856, *Mary Isabel (Castle Townshend, co. Cork), da. of Thomas Waddington; and had issue* 1*g*.

1*g*. Beatrice Margaret von Bunsen, da. and h., *m*. 27 Ap. 1895, Charles Loftus Uniacke Townshend of Castle Townshend, *late* Capt. 5th Batt. Royal Irish Rifles (*Castle Townshend, co. Cork;* 46 *Lansdowne Road, Dublin*); and has issue 1*h* to 6*h*.

   1*h*. Charles Richard de Bunsen Loftus Townshend, *b*. 4 Ap. 1896.
   2*h*. Frederick William Chisholm Loftus Townshend, *b*. 19 Nov. 1897.
   3*h*. Charles Maurice Waddington Loftus Townshend, *b*. 31 Jan. 1899.
   4*h*. Edward Arthur Penderell Loftus Townshend, *b*. 20 June 1901.
   5*h*. Walter Bevil Granville Loftus Townshend, *b*. 8 Nov. 1902.
   6*h*. Bernard Hugo Uniacke Loftus Townshend, *b*. 19 Dec. 1905.

4*f*. *Georg Friedrich von Bunsen, Member of the Imperial German Reichstag*, b. 7 *Nov.* 1824; d. *in London* 22 *Dec.* 1896; m. 21 *Dec.* 1854, *Emma, sister of Sir Edward Birkbeck*, 1st Bt. [*U.K.*], *da. of Henry Birkbeck of Keswick Old Hall, co. Norfolk*, d. 25 *July* 1899; *and had issue* (*with an elder son, Carl,* d. *unm.*) 1*g* to 7*g*.

1*g*. Lothar Henry George de Bunsen (*The Abbey, Knaresborough*), *b*. in England 31 Oct. 1858; *m*. 1st, 6 Jan. 1887, Mary Anna, da. of Sir Alexander Kinloch of Gilmerton, 10th Bt. [S.], *d*. 22 Feb. 1898; 2ndly, 25 June 1904, Victoria Alexandrina [descended from George, Duke of Clarence, K.G. (see Clarence Volume, p. 292)], da. of Sir Thomas Fowell Buxton, 3rd Bt. [U.K.], G.C.M.G., by his wife, Lady Victoria, *née* Noel; and has issue 1*h* to 5*h*.

   1*h*. Arnold George de Bunsen, *b*. 15 Dec. 1887.
   2*h*. Eric Henry de Bunsen, *b*. 24 Sept. 1889.
   3*h*. Carl de Bunsen, *b*. 13 Oct. 1905.
   4*h*. Bernard de Bunsen, *b*. 24 July 1907.
   5*h*. Ronald Lothar de Bunsen, *b*. 19 Feb. 1910.   [Nos. 103145 to 103169.

# of The Blood Royal

2g. Waldemar von Bunsen (*Haus Leppe, Rheinland, Prussia*), b. 11 June 1872; m. 15 Aug. 1903, Marie, da. of Geheimer Hofjustizrah Paul Fleischhammer of Berlin; s.p.

3g. Marie von Bunsen, *unm.*

4g. Else von Bunsen, *unm.*

5g. Emma von Bunsen, *unm.*

6g. Hildegard von Bunsen, *unm.*

7g. Berta von Bunsen, *m.* 3 Aug. 1889, Ernest Flagg Henderson, Historian (1 *Mercer Circle, Cambridge, Mass., U.S.A.*); and has issue 1h to 6h.

1h. Gerard Henderson, b. 13 Aug. 1891.

2h. George Henderson, b. 27 June 1894.

3h. Ernest Henderson, b. 7 Mar. 1897.

4h. Hildegard Henderson.

5h. Edith Henderson.

6h. Frances Henderson.

5f. Theodore von Bunsen, b. (*twin*) 3 *Jan.* 1832; d. *at Heidelberg* 1892; m. 1st, c. 1876, Norah, da. of Thomas Hill; *and had issue* 1g to 2g.

1g. Harald von Bunsen, b. 1877; m.

2g. Moritz von Bunsen, b. 1878; m. and has issue.

6f. Emilia von Bunsen (*Carlsruhe, Germany*), *unm.*

7f. Mary Charlotte Elizabeth von Bunsen (*Blaise Castle, Henbury, Bristol*), m, 4 Ap. 1850, John Battersby Harford of Falcondale, co. Cardigan, and Blaise Castle. co. Glos., M.A., J.P., D.L., High Sheriff co. Glos., 1855; d. 11 Feb. 1875; and has issue 1g to 8g.

1g. John Charles Harford of Falcondale and Blaise Castle, Lord of the Manor of Lampeter, J.P., D.L., High Sheriff co. Cardigan 1885 (*Falcondale, Lampeter, South Wales; Blaise Castle, Henbury, Bristol*), b. 28 July 1860; m. 11 Ap. 1893, Blanche Amabel, da. of the Right Hon. Henry Cecil Raikes of Llwynegrin, co. Flint, P.C., d. 28 Aug. 1904; and has issue 1h to 3h.

1h. John Henry Harford, b. 7 Feb. 1896.

2h. George Arthur Harford, b. 29 Dec. 1897.

3h. Mary Amabel Harford.

2g. Frederic Dundas Harford of Holme Hall, C.V.O., J.P., D.L., Councillor of Embassy, Diplo. Service (*Holme Hall, E. R. Yorks; British Legation, Darmstadt*), b. 8 Feb. 1862; m. 29 Sept. 1896, Amy Mary Josephine, Lady of the Manor of Holme [descended from George, Duke of Clarence, K.G. (see Clarence Volume, p. 367)], da. and co-h. of Henry Joseph Stourton of Holme Hall, J.P. [Baron Stourton [E.] Coll.]; and has issue 1h.

1h. Joan Mary Harford.

3g. Alice Mary Elizabeth Harford (*Blaise Castle, Henbury, Bristol*).

4g. Constance Emilia Harford (*Hythe House, Staines*), m. 23 Ap. 1878, John Baird of Lochwood, M.P., J.P., D.L., d. 8 July 1900; and has issue 1h to 3h.

1h. James Alexander Baird, b. 15 Feb. 1879.

2h. Jean Edith Baird, m. 30 Aug. 1906, Thomas Algernon Raikes [4th son of the Right Hon. Henry Cecil Raikes of Llwynegrin, P.C., and a descendant of George, Duke of Clarence, K.G. (see Clarence Volume, p. 407); and has issue 1i to 2i.

1i. Thomas Hugh Cecil Raikes, b. 13 Ap. 1908.

2i. Douglas Charles Gordon Raikes, b. 26 Jan. 1910.

3h. Margaret Ina Baird.

5g. Mary Edith Harford (1 *Funchal Villas, Clifton, Bristol*), m. 13 July 1878, Alban Gwynne of Monachty, co. Cardigan, J.P., D.L., d. 20 Feb. 1904; and has issue (a son and 2 das.) 1h to 3h. [Nos. 103170 to 103199.

The Plantagenet Roll

1*h*. Alban Lewis Gwynne, Lieut. R.N., *b*. 15 Sept. 1880.

2*h*. Dorothy Mary Gwynne.

3*h*. Gladys Evelyn Gwynne.

6*g*. Charlotte Louisa Harford, *unm*.

7*g*. Agnes Clementina Harford, *unm*.

8*g*. Eleanor Dorothy Harford, *m*. 23 Ap. 1889, John Iltyd Dillwyn Nicholl of Merthyr Mawr, J.P., D.L., High Sheriff co. Glam. 1899 [descended from the Lady Anne, sister of Kings Edward IV. and Richard III. (see Exeter Volume, p. 651)] (*Merthyr Mawr, Bridgend, Glamorgan*); and has issue 1*h* to 5*h*.

1*h*. John William Harford Nicholl, *b*. 24 Oct. 1892.

2*h*. Robert Iltyd Nicholl, *b*. 29 Dec. 1896.

3*h*. Gladys Mary Nicholl.

4*h*. Olive Eleanor Nicholl.

5*h*. Rachel Charlotte Nicholl.

8*f*. Theodora Maria Wilhelmine von Bunsen, *b*. (*twin*) *at Rome* 3 *Jan*. 1832; *d. at Karlsruhe* 26 *Mar*. 1862; m. 12 *Sept*. 1855, *August Johann Paul Friedrich, Baron von Ungern-Sternberg* [H.R.E. 16 *July* 1531 *and Sweden* 27 *Oct*. 1653], d. *at Karlsruhe* 20 *Mar*. 1895; *and had issue* (*a son and* 4 *das.*) 1*g* to 5*g*.

1*g*. Reinhold Joseph Christian Ernst Jacob, Baron von Ungern-Sternberg [H.R.E.], Major German Imperial Army, Master of the Household and Chamberlain to the Grand Duke of Hesse (*Darmstadt*), *b*. at Heidelberg 25 Sept. 1860; *m*. at Darmstadt 21 Sept. 1897, Marion Louisa [descended from George, Duke of Clarence, K.G., brother of King Edward IV. (see Clarence Volume, p. 511)], da. of Col. Emilius Charles Delmé-Radcliffe; and has issue 1*h* to 2*h*.

1*h*. Baron Reinhold August Emil Ludwig von Ungern-Sternberg, *b*. 29 May 1909.

2*h*. Baroness Alix Luisa Emilia Marion Hedwig von Ungern-Sternberg, *b*. 7 July 1898.

2*g*. Baroness Elisabeth Rosalie Franzisca von Ungern-Sternberg, *m*. at Karlsruhe 29 July 1882, Lieut.-Col. Karl von Reuterswärd, Swedish Life Hussars, *formerly* A.D.C. and a Chamberlain to H.M. the King of Sweden (*Stockholm*); and has issue 1*h* to 4*h*.

1*h*. Patrick Karl Reinhold von Reuterswärd, an Attaché in the Swedish Legation at Paris, *b*. 2 Feb. 1885.

2*h*. Gösta August Cecil von Reuterswärd, Lieut. Swedish Life Hussars, *b*. 4 Ap. 1887.

3*h*. Viktoria Augusta Fedora von Reuterswärd, *unm*.

4*h*. Margareta Frances Anna von Reuterswärd, *unm*.

3*g*. Baroness Theodora Amélie Helen von Ungern-Sternberg, *m*. at Karlsruhe 27 Sept. 1878, Gen. Friedrich Ludwig Georg von Klöden (*Wiesbaden*); and has issue 1*h* to 3*h*.

1*h*. Thilo George Ludwig August von Klöden, Lieut. Prussian Army, *b*. at Karlsruhe 21 Ap. 1881.

2*h*. Wilhelm von Klöden, Lieut. 109th Regt. German Army, *b*. at Berlin 22 Sept. 1888.

3*h*. Theodora Elisabeth Emelie Franziska Viktoria von Klöden.

4*g*. Baroness Marie Hildegard von Ungern-Sternberg (*Potsdam*), *m*. at Karlsruhe 22 Oct. 1879, Gen. Bernhard von Lippe, A.D.C. to the Emperor, &c., *d*. at Dresden 20 Dec. 1896; and has issue 1*h* to 2*h*.

1*h*. Albrecht von Lippe, *b*. 24 Ap. 1885.

2*h*. Daisy von Lippe.

5*g*. Baroness Aga Theodora Luise Emma Franziska von Ungern-Sternberg, *m*. at Herrenalb 14 June 1893, Major Heinrich Wilhelm Friedrich von Bodelschwingh, 20th Regt. German Imp. Army (*Karlsruhe*); *s.p.*   [Nos. 103200 to 103226.

of The Blood Royal

2e. *Augusta Waddington, da.* and co-h., b. 21 Nov. 1802 ; d. 17 *Jan.* 1896 ; m. 4 *Dec.* 1823, *Benjamin (Hall),* 1st *and only Baron Llanover* [U.K. 27 *June* 1859], P.C., &c., b. 8 *Nov.* 1802; d. 27 *Ap.* 1867; *and had issue (with* 2 *sons* d. *young)* 1*f.*

1*f.* Hon. *Augusta Charlotte Elizabeth Hall,* d. (-) ; m. 12 Nov. 1846, *John Arthur Edward Jones, afterwards* (R.L. 27 *Nov.* 1848) *Herbert, of Llanarth Court,* co. *Mon.,* J.P., D.L., d. 18 Aug. 1895 ; *and had issue.*

See the Clarence Volume, pp. 455-456, Nos. 19659-19679.

3e. *Emily Waddington, da.* and co-h., *d.s.p.* 1817 ; *m.* as 1st wife, George (Manley), 1st Count de Manley [P.S. 184-], of Buckland, co. Som., Adj.-Gen. Papal Army.

3d. *Louisa Port,* b. 7 *Ap.* 1778 ; d. 3 *July* 1817 ; m. 6 *Oct.* 1803, *the Rev. Brownlow Villiers Layard,* M.A., *Rector of Uffington,* co. *Linc., and Chaplain to the Duke of Kent, &c., previously Lieut.* 7*th Fusiliers and* A.D.C. *to the Duke of Kent,* b. 19 *Jan.* 1779 ; d. 26 *Mar.* 1861 ; *and had issue (with* 2 *sons* d.s.p.) 1*e to* 5*e.*

1e. *Brownlow Villiers Layard, Lieut.-Col.* 9*th Regt.,* M.P. *for Carlow,* b. 14 *July* 1804 ; d. 7 *Dec.* 1853 ; m. 14 *July* 1835, *Elizabeth, da. of Capt. John Deane Digby,* 5*th Royal Irish Dragoons ; and had issue* 1*f.*

1*f.* Brownlow Villiers Layard, F.R.G.S., Lieut.-Col. *formerly* Gloucester Regt. *(Riversdale, Vesuvius Bay, British Columbia),* b. 3 Jan. 1838; *m.* 4 Nov. 1882, Clara, da. of Robert John Lattey, J.P. ; and has issue 1g to 3g.

1g. Brownlow Villiers Layard, Lieut. R.N., b. 24 Aug. 1884.

2g. Henry Campville Layard, *b.* 24 Jan. 1886.

3g. Arthur Raymond Layard, *b.* 22 Sept. 1888.

2e. *John Beville Layard, Capt.* 22*nd Madras* N.I., b. 21 *Sept.* 1809 ; d. 12 *Feb.* 1846 ; m. *Harriette Cobbe, da. of Brig.-Gen. Thomas Henry Somerset Conway,* C.B., b. 30 *Nov.* 1821 ; d. 12 *Ap.* 1907 ; *and had issue* 1*f to* 2*f.*

1*f.* Beville Brownlow Edward Layard *(Para Para, near Pungarehu, Taranaki, New Zealand),* b. 3 June 1845 ; *m.* Aug. 1881, Ann, da. of George Poynter Betts of New Plymouth, Taranaki ; and has issue 1g to 2g.

1g. Beville Anthony Layard, *b.* 13 June 1882.

2g. Catherine Louisa Gwladys Layard, *m.* Samuel Russell Feaver, Pharmaceutical Chemist *(Opunaki, Taranaki,* N.Z.); and has issue 1*h* to 2*h.*

1*h.* Mary Catherine Feaver, *b.* 6 Oct. 1906.

2*h.* Helena Jessica Feaver, *b.* Jan. 1909.

2*f.* Harriette Caroline Layard *(Para Para, near Pungarehu, Taranaki, New Zealand).*

3e. *Bernard Granville Layard, Lieut.-Col. in the Army,* b. 10 *Mar.* 1813 ; d. 22 *Sept.* 1872 ; m. 1st, 10 *Aug.* 1841, *Mary Anne, widow of* (—) *Dowker, da. of* (—) *Clarke,* d. (-) ; 2*ndly,* 21 *Oct.* 1847, *Anna Maria, da. of John Knowles; and had issue* 1*f to* 4*f.*

1*f.* John Granville Layard, b. 11 *Dec.* 1851 ; d. (-) ; m. 1 *Jan.* 1879, *Gertrude, da. of Thomas* W. *Phipson,* Q.C. ; *and had issue* 1g.

1g. Violet Layard.

2*f.*[1] Mary Ann Elizabeth Layard, *b.* 4 Oct. 1842 ; *m.* Major Frederick George Pym, R.M., C.B. ; and has issue 1g to 3g.

1g. Charles Brownlow Pym, *b.* 6 Feb. 1864.

2g. John Beville Pym, Capt. R.M., *b.* 16 Nov. 1866 ; *m.* (—), da. of Col. Hope.

3g. Marianne Pym.

3*f.*[2] Maria Louisa Layard (11 *Henrietta Street, Bath).*

4*f.*[2] Georgiana Edith Layard *(Harepath Croft, Colyford, Devon).*

4e. *Frederick Louis Layard,* b. 20 *July* 1815 ; d. (-) ; m. (—), *da. of* (—); *and had issue* 1*f.* [Nos. 103227 to 103265.

The Plantagenet Roll

1*f*. Bertie Layard, b. (—); m. (—), da. of (—); and has issue 1g.

1*g*. Anna L. Layard (*Mitchell Street, Bourke, Australia*).

5*e*. Rev. Charles Clement Layard, b. 25 *Ap*. 1817; d. 1 *Nov*. 1895; m. 3 *June* 1847, Sarah, da. of Samuel Somes, d. 22 *May* 1886; and had issue 1*f* to 5*f*.

1*f*. Abel John Layard, b. 20 *May* 1855; d. 17 *Aug*. 1890; m. 8 *Oct*. 1884, Catherine (*East Hayes House, Bath*), da. of the Rev. Thomas Hayes; and had issue 1g to 2g.

1*g*. Ruth Sidney Layard, b. 2 Jan. 1887.

2*g*. Nora Margaret Layard, b. 16 Mar. 1890.

2*f*. George Somes Layard, Bar.-at-Law, Author and Reviewer (*Bull's Cliff, Felixstowe*), b. 4 Feb. 1857; m. 8 Oct. 1885, Eleanor Byng, da. of Thomas Gribble; and has issue 1g to 3g.

1*g*. John Willoughby Layard, b. 28 Nov. 1891.

2*g*. Peter Clement Layard, b. 7 June 1896.

3*g*. Nancy Layard, b. 8 Sept. 1886.

3*f*. Sarah May Louisa Layard, m. 6 Sept. 1876, the Rev. Henry Robert Whytehead, M.A. (Camb.), Vicar of Warminster (*The Vicarage, Warminster*); and has issue.

See p. 314, Nos. 42373–42375.

4*f*. Nina Frances Layard, F.L.S. (*Rookwood, Ipswich*).

5*f*. Annie Jane Layard, m. 6 Sept. 1881, Evelyn Gordon Reeves (*Wiltshire, Matale, Ceylon*); and has issue 1g to 3g.

1*g*. Frederick Layard Reeves (*Weharegama, Matale, Ceylon*).

2*g*. Margaret Layard Reeves, m. Jan. 1908, the Rev. Archibald Leslie Keith, B.A. (Camb.), Chaplain of Dimbula Planting Dist. (*Talawakella, Ceylon*).

3*g*. Enid Sarah Layard Reeves, *unm*.

4*d*. Frances Anne Port, b. 18 *Ap*. 1783; d. 4 *Nov*. 1860; m. 11 *Aug*. 1803, Abel John Ram of Clonatin, co. Wexford, d.v.p. 3 *Nov*. 1823; and had issue (with 2 das. d. unm.) 1e.

1*e*. Rev. Abel John Ram of Clonatin, Hon. Canon of Rochester, b. 30 *May* 1804; d. 18 *Aug*. 1883; m. 11 *Ap*. 1833, Lady Jane, da. of James George (*Stopford*), 3rd Earl of Courtown [*I*.], K.P., d. 28 Dec. 1873; and had issue.

See the Tudor Roll, pp. 166, Nos. 20048–20068. [Nos. 103266 to 103302.

290. **Descendants** of Sir EDMUND PRIDEAUX of Netherton, 5th Bt. [E.] (Table XXVI.), b. 13 Nov. 1675; d. 26 Feb. 1729; m. 1st (settl. dated 20/21 Feb.), 1710, MARY, da. of Samuel REYNARDSON, d. 12 Aug. 1712; 2ndly (lic. dated 6 May), 1714, ANNE, da. of Philip HAWKINS of Pennans, co. Cornwall, d. 10 May 1741; and had issue 1*a* to 2*a*.

1*a*. Mary Prideaux, da. and in her issue sole h., d. 1758;[1] m. James Winstanley of Braunston, High Sheriff co. Leic. 1748, d. *Mar*. 1770; and had issue 1b to 3b.

1*b*. Clement Winstanley of Braunston, High Sheriff co. Leic. 1774; d. 1808; m. Jane, sister of Thomas Boothby, 1st Baron Rancliffe [*I*.], da. of Sir Thomas Parkyns, 3rd Bt. [*E*.]; and had issue 1c to 2c.

1*c*. Clement Winstanley of Braunston, J.P., D.L., d. *unm*. 1855.

2*c*. Rev. George Winstanley, Rector of Glenfield, co. Leic., d. 1846; m. Mary Frances, da. of the Rev. William Birch of Rugby; and had issue 1d to 4d.

1*d*. James Beaumont Winstanley of Braunston, d. *unm*. 7 July 1862.

---

[1] Fletcher's " Leicestershire Pedigrees and Royal Descents," p. 40.

# of The Blood Royal

2*d.* Anna Jane Winstanley *of Braunston, co. Leicester*, b. *c.* 1825 ; d. 30 *Ap.* 1910 ; m. 18 *Oct.* 1855, *Comm. Ralph George Pochin, R.N., J.P.* [5*th son of George Pochin of Barkby Hall, co. Leic.*], d. 7 *Oct.* 1897 ; *and had issue* (*with* 3 *sons and a da.* d. *unm.*) 1*e to* 4*e.*

1*e.* Richard Norman Pochin, now (20 Nov. 1905) Winstanley, Lord of the Manor of Braunston and Patron of the Living of Glenfield, Major *late* E. Surrey Regt. (*Braunston Hall, Leicester*), b. 19 Ap. 1864 ; *m.* 22 Aug. 1907, Kathleen Rachel Dubois, da. of (—) Phillips ; and has issue 1*f.*

1*f.* Pamela Mary Winstanley, b. 25 Jan. 1910.

2*e.* Francis William Birch Pochin (*Duntroon, Oamaru, New Zealand*), b. 9 Nov. 1865 ; *m.* Alice Josephine, da. of John Borton of Casa Nuova, N.Z.

3*e.* Edward Carlyon Pochin, M.A. (Camb.), b. 1869.

4*e.* Emily Georgiana Pochin.

3*d.* Mary Elizabeth Winstanley, *m.* Charles James Walker (*Newbold Grange, Clarence River, New South Wales*).

4*d.* Frances Winstanley.

2*b.* Mary Winstanley, b. 6 May 1734; d. 17 *Ap.* 1818 ; m. 7 *Ap.* 1763, *the Rev. John Carlyon of Bradwell, co. Essex, LL.B., Rector of St. Mary's, Truro* [3rd *son of Thomas Carlyon of Tregrehan, co. Cornwall*], d. 21 *Sept.* 1798 ; *and had issue* 1*c to* 3*c.*

1*c.* Rev. Thomas Carlyon, *Rector of St. Mary's, Truro, and Vicar of Probus, Cornwall*, M.A., *Fellow and Tutor of Pembroke Coll., Camb.*, b. 12 May 1765 ; bur. 5 Feb. 1826 ; m. 22 *Jan.* 1801, *Mary, da. of William Stackhouse of Trehane, co. Cornwall*, bur. 24 *Mar.* 1843 ; *and had issue* 1*d to* 4*d.*

1*d.* Rev. Thomas Stackhouse Carlyon, *Rector of St. Mary's, Truro, and afterwards of Glenfield, co. Leic.*, M.A. (Camb.), b. 15 *June* 1802 ; d. 15 *Mar.* 1877 ; m. 28 *Feb.* 1832, *Emily, da. of Clement Carlyon, M.D.*, d. 23 *June* 1891 ; *and had issue* 1*e.*

1*e.* Charles Alfred Carlyon, B.A. (Camb.), b. 5 *Sept.* 1838 ; d. 26 *July* 1887 ; m. 3 *Nov.* 1863, *Betsey Green, da. of Isaac Squires of Woodhouse Eaves, co. Leic.* ; *and had issue* 1*f to* 3*f.*

1*f.* Thomas Alfred Carlyon (*Connemara, Darracott Road, Boscombe Park, Bournemouth*), bapt. 5 May 1865 ; *m.* 17 Ap. 1888, Gertrude Elizabeth, da. of George William Mitchell [by his wife Eliza Lilian, da. of Rear-Adm. Robert Sharpe, R.N.] ; and has issue 1*g.*

1*g.* Thomas Clement Winstanley Carlyon, b. 2 Nov. 1890.

2*f.* Agnes Cassandra Carlyon, *m.* 8 Sept. 1886, Philip William Poole Britton, now (R.L. 29 Ap. 1897) Carlyon-Britton, J.P., D.L., F.S.A., Lord of the Manor of Hanham Abbots, co. Glos., President of the British Numismatic Society, *formerly* Capt. 3rd Batt. Royal Inniskilling Fusiliers (*Hanham Court, Bitton, Glos.; 43 Bedford Square, W.C.; Junior Carlton*) ; and has issue 1*g* to 4*g.*

1*g.* Winstanley Carlyon-Britton, b. 25 July 1887.

2*g.* Henry Courtenay Carlyon-Britton, Sub-Lieut. R.N., b. 21 June 1891.

3*g.* Raymond Carlyon Carlyon-Britton, b. 16 Sept. 1893.

4*g.* Ella Carlyon Poole Carlyon-Britton, *m.* and has issue.

3*f.* Ellen Gertrude Carlyon, *m.* as 2nd wife, Major Arthur Henry Daniel Britton, *formerly* Royal Dublin Fusiliers.

2*d.* John Carlyon of Truro, M.A. (Camb.), *Coroner for Cornwall*, b. 2 Dec. 1804 ; d. 30 Dec. 1892 ; m. 8 Dec. 1840, *Jane, da. of Capt. Edward Lawrance, R.N.*, d. 21 Oct. 1890 ; *and had issue* 1*e.*

1*e.* Julia Carlyon, b. 6 Aug. 1842 ; d. (–) ; m. 16 *Ap.* 1863, *Robins Foster of Truro* ; *and had issue.*

3*d.* Rev. Edward Carlyon, B.A. (Oxon.), *Rector of Dibden, co. Hants*, b. 4 Oct. 1808 ; d. 28 *June* 1897 ; m. 1st, 15 Nov. 1832, *Ann Helen, da. of Thomas Harvey of Overross, co. Hereford*, d. 18 *Jan.* 1866 ; *and had issue* 1*e to* 9*e.*

[Nos. 103303 to 103317.

The Plantagenet Roll

1e. Gerald Winstanley Carlyon (*Lyndhurst, Hants*), b. 8 Dec. 1845; m. in Ceylon 27 Ap. 1879, Laura Theresa, da. of the Rev. Llewellyn Lloyd Thomas, Rector of Newport, co. Mon.; s.p.

2e. Rev. Henry Chichele Carlyon, M.A. (Camb.), a Missionary at Delhi, b. 6 Oct. 1847.

3e. Anna Stackhouse Carlyon, m. 1 June 1865, the Rev. Percy Phillipson Izard, B.A. (Camb.), *formerly* Rector of Morstead (*Deepdale, Surrey Road, Bournemouth*); s.p.s.

4e. Augusta Hopton Carlyon, *unm.*

5e. Jessie Carlyon, *unm.*

6e. Louise Carlyon, *unm.*

7e. Mary Evelyn Carlyon, m. 6 Nov. 1895, the Rev. Henry Churton, Vicar of Corkhampton (*Corkhampton Vicarage, Bishop's Waltham*); s.p.

8e. Helen Bionda Carlyon, m. 25 Sept. 1878, Charles Frank Lucas, Solicitor (*Glynavon, Carshalton, Surrey*); s.p.

9e. Caroline Susan Carlyon, *unm.*

4d. Charlotte Carlyon (*Lemon Street, Truro*), b. 6 Feb. 1815; *unm.*

2c. Rev. Philip Carlyon, M.A. (Camb.), Rector of St. Mawgan in Pydar, co. Cornwall, b. 15 May 1769; d. 21 Mar. 1846; m. 27 Oct. 1808, Mary, da. of (—) Phear, d. 25 Oct. 1854; *and had issue 1d to 3d*.

1d. Rev. Philip Carlyon of Pennance House, Falmouth, M.A. (Camb.), Rector of Wisbeach 1869–1882 (*Pennance House, Falmouth, Cornwall*), b. 30 Dec. 1811; m. 31 July 1845, Grace Julia, da. of Col. Keith Young, 71st Highlanders, d. 22 Mar. 1895; *and had issue 1e to 6e*.

1e. Philip Carlyon, b. 1846.

2e. Alexander Keith Carlyon of Mount Park, co. Midx., J.P., D.L., and High Sheriff for that co. 1906, Bar.-at-Law (*Mount Park, Harrow-on-the-Hill; Junior Carlton*), b. 30 Ap. 1848; m. 24 Ap. 1873, Julia Ann Augusta, da. of Major Thomas Tristram Spry Carlyon of Tregrehan, J.P., D.L.; *and has issue 1f to 6f*.

1f. Tristram Carlyon, B.A. (Oxon.), Lieut. R.F.A., b. 4 Aug. 1877.

2f. Julia Maria Violet Carlyon.

3f. Ada Mary Morison Carlyon.

4f. Dorothy Mary Carlyon.

5f. Mabel Young Carlyon.

6f. Millicent Spry Carlyon.

3e. Harold Baird Carlyon, M.A. (Oxon.) (*Falmouth*), b. 1849; *unm.*

4e. Jessie Morison Carlyon, m. 1878, Charles Nicholl, F.R.C.S., d. 1881; *and has issue*.

5e. Katharine Ogilvie Carlyon, m. 1883, the Rev. Joseph Chapman, M.A., Incumbent of Post Bridge (*Post Bridge, Devon*).

6e. Julia Winstanley Carlyon, m. 1884, Major Henry MacLeod Young, Inniskilling Fusiliers, d. 1899; *and has issue*.

2d. Edmund Carlyon of St. Austell, Solicitor, b. 1819; m. (—), sister of the Right Hon. Sir John Robert Mowbray, 1st Bt. [U.K.], P.C., da. of Robert Stribbing Cornish.

3d. Mary Ann Carlyon, m. the Rev. Michael Turner, Rector of Cotton (*Cotton Rectory, Suffolk*); *and has issue*.

3c. Clement Carlyon, M.D., M.A., and Fellow of Pembroke Coll., Camb., b. 22 Ap. 1777; d. 5 Mar. 1864; m. 22 Ap. 1806, Eliza, da. of Thomas Carlyon of St. Just and Tregrehan, d. 17 Sept. 1861; *and had (with other) issue 1d*.

1d. Emily Carlyon, b. 23 June 1891; m. 28 Feb. 1832, the Rev. Thomas Stackhouse Carlyon of Glenfield, co. Leic., d. 15 Mar. 1877; *and had issue*.

See p. 475, Nos. 103310–103317.

3b. Anne Winstanley, bapt. 4 Mar. 1741; d. 22 Aug. 1814; m. 1 Dec. 1766,
[Nos. 103318 to 103342h.

of The Blood Royal

Leonard Fosbrooke of Shardlow, co. Derby, and Ravenstone, co. Leic., High Sheriff co. Derby, 1764, b. 9 June 1732; d. 8 Dec. 1801; and had issue 1c to 2c.

1c. Leonard Fosbrooke of Shardlow and Ravenstone, b. 28 Mar. 1773; d. 26 Mar. 1830; m. 8 June 1801, Mary Elizabeth, da. of the Rev. Philip Story of Lockington Hall, d. 5 July 1838; and had issue 1d to 4d.

1d. Leonard Fosbrooke of Ravenstone, J.P., D.L., Bar.-at-Law, b. 29 Ap. 1804; d. 30 Dec. 1892; m. 3 Sept. 1859, Eliza Ann, da. of John Lewin of Ravenstone, d. 8 Ap. 1909; and had issue 1e to 5e.

1e. Leonard Fosbrooke of Ravenstone (Ravenstone, Ashby-de-la-Zouch), b. 6 June 1860.

2e. Thomas Henry Fosbrooke (Rothley, co. Leicester), b. 21 Mar. 1862; m. 17 May 1894, Edith Mary Elizabeth, da. of Thomas William Parker of Killarmarsh, co. Derby; and has issue 1f.

1f. Mary Cecily Fosbrooke, b. 9 Dec. 1900.

3e. Francis Nathaniel Fosbrooke (Assam, India), b. 5 Mar. 1864.

4e. William Arthur Fosbrooke, served with 57th Coy. Imp. Yeo. in South Africa, b. 4 Sept. 1870.

5e. Elizabeth Anne Fosbrooke, m. as 2nd wife, 23 Oct. 1890, Capt. Palmer Kingsmill Smythies, R.N., J.P., has Zulu Medal and Clasp, and Sudan (1884-1885) Medal and Star (The Turrets, Colchester; Junior United Service); and has issue (with a son, Yorick Palmer Fosbrooke, d. young) 1f.

1f. Frances Palmer Smythies, b. 20 Ap. 1900.

2d. Edmund Fosbrooke, Capt. 56th Regt., b. 18 July 1813; d. at Sorel, Quebec, 16 Sept. 1869; m. 25 May 1841, Augustine Adèle, da. of Thomas Penton of Pentonville, Canada, d. 11 Mar. 1887; and had issue (with 2 sons and a da. d.s.p.) 1e to 7e.

1e. Leonard George James Fosbrooke (Sorel, Quebec), b. 19 Nov. 1850; m. Sept. 1877, Mary Susan (Minnie), da. of (—) Crebassa of Sorel afsd.; and has issue 1f to 5f.

1f. Philip Fosbrooke, b. 1878; m.

2f. Frederick Charles Fosbrooke, b. 1883; m.

3f. [son] Fosbrooke.

4f. Annie Fosbrooke, b. 1881.

5f. [da.] Fosbrooke.

2e. Henry Fosbrooke, b. 17 Dec. 1857.

3e. William Anderson Fosbrooke, b. 9 Sept. 1861; m. Seymour Catharine, da. of (—) Irvine of Bootle; and has issue (with 2 elder das.) 1f to 2f.

1f. Henry Fosbrooke.

2f. Doris Fosbrooke.

4e. Augustine Adella Fosbrooke, b. 15 Jan. 1845.

5e. Frances Fosbrooke, m. at Christ Church, Sorel afsd., 9 June 1881, Edward Dudley Montgomery (Beaumont, near Quebec); and has issue.

6e. Sybilla Fosbrooke.

7e. Ann Fosbrooke, m. Norman Massie; and has issue (2 children).

3d. Henry Nathaniel Fosbrooke of Leeds, b. 1 Ap. 1817; d. 15 Ap. 1880; m. 13 May 1841, Sarah, da. of Thomas Jacobson of Sleaford; and had issue (with a son and da. d. unm.) 1e to 9e.

1e. John Henry Fosbrooke, b. 19 Feb. 1842.

2e. Philip Laycock Fosbrooke, b. 18 Dec. 1845; m. twice, and d.s.p. in America.

3e. Charles Edward Fosbrooke, b. 25 Jan. 1847.

4e. Leonard Fosbrooke, b. 27 Oct. 1848; m. 21 Mar. 1883, Alice Georgiana [da. of (—)] Parker of London; and has issue 1f to 4f.

1f. Herbert Henry Fosbrooke, b. 12 Feb. 1884.

2f. Leonard Sidney Fosbrooke, b. 20 July 1886.

3f. Charles Lewis Fosbrooke, b. 1896.

4f. Gladys Mary Fosbrooke.

[Nos. 103343 to 103371.

The Plantagenet Roll

5e. Arthur Sydney Fosbrooke of Roundhay Road, Leeds, b. 15 Nov. 1850; m. 18 Dec. 1880, Alice [da. of (—)] Parker of Hull; and has issue 1f to 4f.

1f. William Henry Fosbrooke, b. 11 Oct. 1881.
2f. Philip Fosbrooke.
3f. Frances Lilian Fosbrooke, b. 21 Mar. 1883.
4f. Ada Mary Fosbrooke, b. 8 Feb. 1885.

6e. Sarah Fosbrooke (12 *Grange Terrace, Leeds*).
7e. Sibella Frances Fosbrooke.
8e. Annie Mabel Fosbrooke.
9e. Jane Diana Fosbrooke.

4d. Frances Sarah Fosbrooke, b. 29 *May* 1807; d. 11 *Nov.* 1896; m. 14 *Jan.* 1836, *Thomas Rossell Potter of Wymeswold, F.R.S.L., the Antiquary, Author of "Charnwood Forest," &c.*, b. 7 *Jan.* 1799; d. 19 *Ap.* 1873; *and had issue (with 2 sons and 3 das. d. unm.)* 1e to 4e.

1e. *Henry Rossell Potter of Lyonsdown, East Barnet, J.P.*, b. 5 *Ap.* 1840; d. 16 *Sept.* 1907; m. 16 *Ap.* 1879, *Susanne Elizabeth, da. of Thomas Higgs of Chipping Barnet; and had issue* 1f to 4f.

1f. Charles Fosbrooke Potter, b. 16 Aug. 1883.
2f. Leonard Fosbrooke Potter, b. 6 Aug. 1885.
3f. Beryl Rosa Potter, m. 12 Ap. 1909, Arthur E. Ware of New Zealand.
4f. Sybella Frances Potter, m. 25 Ap. 1906, Hermann Tom Schött (*Burna Esperanza, Argentina*).

2e. Charles Neville Potter, *formerly* Assist. Accountant-Gen. H.M. Customs (*Fernwood, Plaistow Lane, Bromley, Kent*), b. 24 Nov. 1842; m. 23 Sept. 1883, Emma, widow of Albert Dean of Esher, da. of William Ward of Belton, co. Rutland; and has issue 1f.

1f. Gladys Ward Potter.

3e. Rev. Herbert Edward Potter, *formerly* Minister of the Bass, Victoria, 1888-1898, &c. (*San Remo, Victoria, Australia*), b. 10 Dec. 1846; m. 1st, Sophia, widow of T. Hemsley of Hemmington, da. and h. of Thomas Eames of Leicester, d. 6 Ap. 1877; 2ndly, 13 Aug. 1884, Mary, da. of Thomas Anderson; and has issue 1f to 3f.

1f. Thomas Rossell Fosbrooke Potter.
2f. Frances Sophia Potter.
3f. Edith Potter.

4e. Ada Mary Potter, b. 29 Mar. 1844; *unm.*

2c. *Frances Fosbrooke*, b. 23 *Nov.* 1772; d. 2 *Jan.* 1850; m. *John Buckley of Chester*.

2a.² *Anne Prideaux*, d. (–); m. 1737, *John Pendarves Basset of Tehidy*, b. 1713; d. 19 *Sept.* 1739; *and had issue* ¹ 1b.

1b. *John Prideaux Basset of Tehidy*, b. 22 *May* 1740; d. 28 *May* 1756.

[Nos. 103372 to 103391.

291. Descendants of PETER PRIDEAUX (Table XXVI.), *d. a.* 1729; *m.* 1st, SUSANNA, widow of RICHARD COFFIN, da. of (—) LELLOND; 2ndly (—); and had issue 1a.

1a. *Susanna Prideaux, da. and h.*, d. (–); m. *Charles Evelyn of Yarlington, co. Som.* [*2nd son of Sir John Evelyn,* 1st *Bt.* [*G.B.*]], b. 1708; d. *Jan.* 1748; *and had issue* 1b.

---

¹ The statement in various works that he was the grandfather of Francis Basset of Tehidy, cr. Lord de Dunstanville 17 June 1796, is incorrect.

of The Blood Royal

1b. *Charles Evelyn*, d. 1781; m. *Philadelphia*, da. *of Fortunatus Wright of Liverpool, Capt. of the "Fane" and "King George" privateers; and had issue* 1c to 6c.

    1c. *Sir John Evelyn, 4th Bt. [G.B.]*, b. c. 1758; d. *unm.* 14 May 1833.

    2c. *Sir Hugh Evelyn, 5th Bt. [G.B.]*, b. 31 *Jan.* 1769; d.s.p. 28 *Aug.* 1848.

    3c. *Susanna Evelyn*, da. *and in her issue co-h.*, d. (–); m. *John Ellworthy Fortunatus Wright, Lieut. R.N.; and had issue* (2 *sons and* 4 *das.*).[1]

    4c. *Martha Boscawen Evelyn*, da. *and in her issue co-h.*, b. 1759; d. 1794; m. *Nicholas Vincent; and had issue* 1d *to* 2d.

        1d. *Nicholas Vincent,* } *settled in America.*[1]
        2d. *Hugh Vincent,*

    5c. *Philippa Evelyn*, da. *and in her issue co-h.*, b. 1760; d. (–); m. 1st, *Major Daniel Francis Haughton*, 69th *Regt.*; 2ndly, *Wilbraham Liardet; and had issue*[1] 1d *to* 6d.

        1d. *Charles Evelyn Daniel Francis Poplet Haughton*, b. 1784.
        2d. *Frederick Hugh Evelyn Haughton.*
        3d. [*son*] *Liardet.*
        4d. *Philippa Haughton.*
        5d. [*da.*] *Liardet.*
        6d. [*da.*] *Liardet.*

    6c. *Frances Louisa Evelyn*, da. *and in her issue co-h.*, b. 1767; d. (–); m. *the Rev. John Griffith of Manchester; and had issue* (2 *das.*).[1]

292. Descendants of Sir JOHN PRIDEAUX, 6th Bt. [E.] (Table XXVI.), b. 17 June 1695; bur. 29 Aug. 1766; m. 4 Feb. 1719, the Hon. ANNE, da. of John (VAUGHAN), 1st Viscount Lisburne [I.], d. 5 Dec. 1767; and had issue 1a to 3a.

    1a. *John Prideaux, Brigadier-Gen.*, d. (*being killed* v.p. *at the siege of Niagara*) 19 *July* 1759; m. *Elizabeth, sister of Sir Edward Bayntum-Rolt, 1st Bt. [G.B.* 1762], da. *of Col. Edward Rolt; and had issue* 1b *to* 3b.

        1b. *Sir John Wilmot Prideaux, 7th Bt.* [E.], b. 13 *Feb.* 1748; d. 4 *Mar.* 1826; m. 2ndly, 28 *Jan.* 1791, *Anne Phœbe*, da. *of William Priddle of Farway*, d. 2 *Sept.* 1793; *and had issue* 1c *to* 2c.

            1c. *Sir John Wilmot Prideaux, 8th Bt.* [E.], b. 29 *Sept.* 1792; d. *unm.* 13 May 1833.

            2c. *Sir Edmund Saunderson Prideaux, 9th Bt.* [E.], b. 23 *Jan.* 1793; d.s.p.s. 11 *Feb.* 1875.

        2b. *Edward Bayntum Edmund Prideaux*, d. (? s.p.).
        3b. *Elizabeth Prideaux*, d. (? *unm.*).

    2a. *Elizabeth Prideaux*, d. (–); m. *Edward Chichester of Northover, co. Somerset.*

    3a. *Anne Prideaux*, d. (–); m. *the Rev. William FitzThomas, Rector of Arrow and Beaudesart, co. Warwick; and had issue.*

293. Descendants, if any, of SUSANNA PRIDEAUX (Table XXVI.), d. (–); m. PHINEAS CHEEK.

---

[1] Betham's "Baronetage," iii. 165. Wheatley's "Diary of John Evelyn," vol. i., folding pedigree.

The Plantagenet Roll

294. Descendants of GRACE FORTESCUE (Table XXVI.), *bur.* 22 Mar. 1694; *m. c.* 1671, Sir HALSWELL TYNTE, 1st Bt. [E. 1673], M.P., *bur.* 9 Ap. 1702; and had issue 1*a* to 2*a*.

1*a*. Sir John Tynte, 2nd Bt. [E.], M.P., bapt. 4 Mar. 1683; d. 5 Mar. 1710; m. 1704, Jane, da. and h. of Sir Charles Kemeys, 3rd Bt. [E.], M.P., bur. 16 Oct. 1747; and had issue.
See p. 184, Nos. 28552–28572.

2*a*. Anne or Grace Tynte, d. (–); m. Arthur Tremayne of Sydenham, co. Devon; and had (with possibly other) issue 1b.

1*b*. Arthur Tremayne of Sydenham, whose only child d.s.p. Dec. 1808.

[Nos. 103392 to 103412.

295. Descendants, if any surviving, of BRIDGET GRANVILLE (Table XXVI.), *b.* 1629; *d.* 1692; *m.* 1st, Sir SIMON LEACH of Cadeleigh, co. Devon; 2ndly (lic. dated 11 Nov.), 1661, Sir THOMAS HIGGONS, M.P., Diplomatist and Author, *b.* 1624; *d.* 24 Nov. 1691; and had issue 1*a* to 7*a*.[1]

1*a*. Sir Simon Leach of Cadeleigh, K.B., d.s.p. July 1708.[2]
2*a*. George Higgons.
3*a*. Sir Thomas Higgons, Secretary of State to King James III. and VIII., in exile Dec. 1713 to July 1715.[3]
4*a*. Bevil Higgons, Historian and Poet, b. 1670; d. unm. 1 Aug. 1735.
5*a*. Grace Higgons, m. the Rev. Sir George Wheeler of Sherfield, co. Hants, Preb. of Durham 1719, d. there 22 Jan. 1724; and had issue "many children"[4] of whom 1b.
1*b*. (—) Wheeler, son and h., d. Oct. 1716; m. (—).
6*a*. Jane Higgons.
7*a*. Bridget Higgons.

296. Descendants, if any surviving, of Sir RICHARD GRANVILLE, "the King's General in the West" (Table XXVI.), *d.* at Ghent soon after 10 May 1659; *m.* MARY, widow of the Hon. Sir CHARLES HOWARD and *previously* of the Hon. THOMAS DARCY and the Hon. Sir ALAN PERCY, da. and h. of Sir John FITZ of Fitzford, near Tavistock, *d.* 17 Oct. 1671; and had issue 1*a*.

1*a*. Elizabeth Granville, living a widow 1664/5, when she petitioned the King for a Privy Purse Pension for herself and her infant son,[5] m. Capt. William Lennard, Capt. of the Block Houses at Tilbury and Gravesend 1660; and had issue.

297. Descendants of GERTRUDE DENYS (Table XXVI.), *d.* 1675; *m.* NICHOLAS GLYNN of Glynn, M.P., *d.* 26 Mar. 1697; and had issue.

See Supplement.

---

[1] "D.N.B.," ix. 826. [2] Le Neve's "Knights," p. 35.
[3] Ruvigny's "Jacobite Peerage," pp. 199, 215.
[4] Le Neve's "Knights," p. 366.
[5] R. Granville's "History of the Granville Family," p. 335.

of The Blood Royal

298. Descendants of BRIDGET GRANVILLE (Table XXVI.), *bur.* in Bristol Cathedral 14 Feb. 1627 ; *m.* 1st [? as 2nd wife¹], Sir CHRISTOPHER HARRIS of Radford, co. Devon, M.P., *d.s.p.s.* 25 Jan. 1625; 2ndly, as 1st wife, the Rev. JOHN WEEKS, Preb. of Bristol.

299. Descendants, if any surviving, of MARY GRANVILLE (GREENFIELD) (Table XXVI.), *bur.* at Lamerton 25 Mar. 1608 ; *m.* at Kilkhampton 2 June 1586, ARTHUR TREMAYNE of Collacombe, co. Devon, *bapt.* at Kilkhampton 4 Ap. 1553 ; *bur.* at Lamerton 4 Feb. 1635 ; and had issue (with 3 sons and 3 das. known to have *d.s.p.*) 1*a* to 11*a*.²

1*a. Edmund Tremayne of Collacombe*, bapt. *at Bideford* 17 *Oct.* 1587; bur. *at Lamerton* 25 *Sept.* 1667; m. (*lic.* 26 *May*) 1615, *Bridget, da. of Sir John Cooper*, bur. *at Lamerton* 17 *Sept.* 1670; *and had issue (with* 4 *sons and* 3 *das.* d.s.p.) 1*b*.

1*b. Arthur Tremayne, a Colonel in the Army*, bapt. 10 *Sept.* 1627; bur. *at Lamerton* 20 *July* 1710; m. *Bridget, da. of Nicholas Hatherleigh of Lamerton,* bur. *there* 12 *Oct.* 1659; *and had issue (with* 2 *sons* d.s.p.) 1*c*.

1*c. Edmund Tremayne*, bapt. 14 *Ap.* 1649; bur. *at Lamerton* 20 *Oct.* 1698; m. *at Exeter* 28 *Jan.* 1674, *Arabella, da. and h. of Sir Edward Wise of Sydenham, co. Devon, K.B.*, bur. 12 *Feb.* 1697; *and had (with other children whose issue failed* 3 *Jan.* 1809) 1*d*.

1*d. Arabella Tremayne,* bapt. *at Lamerton* 27 *Ap.* 1681; d. (? s.p.); m. *at Maristowe,* 18 *Dec.* 1704, *John Harris of Manadon.*

2*a. Digorie Tremayne*, bapt. *at Lamerton* 22 *Jan.* 1589; bur. *there* 22 *Mar.* 1670; m. 1*st*, 9 *Dec.* 1613, *Mary, da. of William Addington of Bideford*, bur. *at Bundstock* 23 *Oct.* 1621; *and had issue* 1*b* to 2*b*.

1*b. Grenfield (Granville) Tremayne*, bapt. *at Lamerton* 2 *Oct.* 1614,
2*b. Arthur Tremayne*, b. 1617,
} living and aged 5 and 3 respectively 1620.

3*a. Richard Tremayne*, bapt. *at Lamerton* 1 *June* 1600, *living* 1629.
4*a. Roger Tremayne,* bur. (? *unm.*) *at Lamerton* 5 *Jan.* 1677.
5*a. Mary Tremayne*, bapt. *at Marhamchurch* 27 *Jan.* 1591.
6*a. Ulalia (Eulalia) Tremayne*, bapt. *at Sydenham Damerell* 14 *Oct.* 1593; m. (*lic.* 13 *Oct.*) 1613, *Thomas Lower of Trelaske, co. Cornwall ; and had issue*³ (*with a son and da.* d. *unm.*) 1*b to* 2*b*.

1*b. Thomas Lower of Trelaske,* bur. *at Lewannick* 1687; m. (*settl.* 3 *May*) 1653, *Anne, da. of John Roberts of Lanrake ; and had issue* 1*c to* 7*c*.

1*c. Thomas Lower of Trelaske, which he sold to John Addis* 22 *July* 1703.

2*c. John Lower,*
3*c. Nicholas Lower,*
4*c. George Lower,*
5*c. Maurice Lower,*
6*c. Elizabeth Lower,*
7*c. Mary Lower,*
} all living and mentioned in father's will 11 *Feb.* 1686.

2*b. Mary Lower,* bapt. *at Lewannick* 3 *Oct.* 1616; *living, aged* 3, 1620.

---

¹ This marriage is not mentioned in Vivian's " Devonshire Pedigrees," p. 448.
² Vivian's " Visitations of Devon," p. 731.   ³ Ibid., p. 299.

The Plantagenet Roll

7*a.* Elizabeth Tremayne, *living* 1659 ; m. *at Lamerton* 24 *Aug.* 1615, Baldwin Acland *of Hawkridge, co. Devon, admon.* 8 *Oct.* 1659 ; *and had issue* 1*b* to 5*b.*

    1*b.* Arthur Acland, *son and h., aged* 4, 1620.

    2*b.* Mary Acland, bapt. *at Lamerton* 1617.

    3*b.* Anne Acland.

    4*b.* Elizabeth Acland, bapt. *there* 9 *May* 1621.

    5*b.* Martha Acland, bapt. *there* 29 *Sept.* 1624.

8*a.* Mary Tremayne, bapt. *at Lamerton* 4 *Sept.* 1603.

9*a.* Margaret Tremayne, bapt. *there* 18 *Nov.* 1604, *living* 1629 ; m. *at Chittlehampton,* 5 *Ap.* 1638, George Slee.

10*a.* Catherine Tremayne, m. 1*st at Lamerton,* 26 *July* 1627, Roger Edgcumbe *of Lamerton, co. Devon* ; bapt. *there* 18 *May* 1595 ; bur. *there* 28 *Oct.* 1643 ; 2*ndly, at the same place* 27 *Sept.* 1651, *Humphrey Arundell* ; *and had issue (with* 4 *das. known to have d. unm.)* 1*b* to 2*b.*

    1*b.* Mary Edgcumbe, bapt. *at Lamerton* 25 *June* 1628; m. *John Wallis of Tremin, co. Cornwall.*

    2*b.* Jane Edgcumbe, bapt. *there* 14 *Ap.* 1638 ; m. *John Merrit of Probus, co. Cornwall.*

11*a.* Rebecca Tremayne, m. *there* 21 *Jan.* 1636, John Edgcumbe [*younger brother of Roger Edgcumbe, aforesaid*].

300. Descendants, if any surviving, of Sir THOMAS STUCLEY of Affeton, co. Devon (Table XXVI.), b. 1620 ; d. 20 Sept. 1663 ; m. ELIZABETH, da. of Sir Ralph SYDENHAM of Yolston (who m. 2ndly, 29 Oct. 1677, the Rev. JOHN DODDERIDGE) ; and had issue (with 2 sons *d.s.p.*)[1] 1*a* to 4*a.*

    1*a.* Frances Stucley, *da. and co-h.,* m. *the Rev. Anthony Gregory.*

    2*a.* Margery Stucley, *da. and co-h.*

    3*a.* Mary Stucley, *da. and co-h.,* m. 1*st, the Rev. Thomas Colley ;* 2*ndly, at Braunton,* 9 *Aug.* 1685, *Michael Arundell.*

    4*a.* Honor Stucley, *da. and co-h.*

301. Descendants of LEWIS STUCLEY of Affeton, co. Devon, Chaplain to Oliver Cromwell (Table XXVI.), *bur.* at Worlington 21 July 1687 ; *m.* 1673, SUSANNAH, da. of (—) DENNIS, *d.* 1692 ; and had issue 1*a.*

    1*a.* Sarah Stucley, *da. and in her issue* (29 *Dec.* 1755) *sole h., d. at Bideford* 4 *Feb.* 1742 ; m. 4 *May* 1697, George Buck, *J.P., seven times Mayor of Bideford,* b. *there* 14 *Dec.* 1671 ; *d.* 7 *Ap.* 1743 ; *and had issue* 1*b.*

        1*b.* John Buck *of Bideford, M.P., three times Mayor of that place,* bapt. 30 *Dec.* 1703 ; *d.* 13 *Ap.* 1745 ; m. 1*st,* 19 *Sept.* 1729, *Judith, da. and h. of William Pawley* (*or Hawley*) *of Bideford, d.* 24 *Oct.* 1739 ; *and had issue* 1*c.*

        1*c.* George Buck *of Affeton, J.P.,* b. 7 *July* 1731 ; *d.* 26 *Jan.* 1794 ; m. 6 *May* 1754, *Anne, da. of Paul Orchard of Hartland Abbey, d.* 11 *Feb.* 1820 ; *and had issue* 1*d.*

        1*d.* George Stucley Buck *of Affeton,* bapt. 8 *Mar.* 1755 ; *d.* 30 *Nov.* 1791 ; m. 8 *Ap.* 1780, *Martha, da. of the Rev. Richard Keats, Master of Tiverton School and Rector of Bideford, &c.* (*who* m. 2*ndly,* 1801, *Lieut.-Col. James Kirkman*), *d.* 30 *Nov.* 1833 ; *and had issue* 1*e* to 3*e.*

---

[1] Vivian's "Visitations of Devon," p. 722.

# of The Blood Royal

1e. Lewis William Buck of Affeton, M.P., b. 25 Ap. 1784; d. 25 Ap. 1858; m. 18 Ap. 1808, Ann, da. of Thomas Robbins of Roundhams, co. Berks, d. 12 Ap. 1879; and had issue 1f to 2f.

1f. Sir George Stucley Stucley (R.L. 27 July 1858), previously Buck, of Affeton, 1st Bt. [U.K.], so cr. 26 Ap. 1859, M.P., J.P., D.L., and High Sheriff (1863) co. Devon, Col. Comdg. Devonshire Artillery, b. 17 Aug. 1812; d. 13 Mar. 1900; m. 1st, 22 Dec. 1835, Lady Elizabeth (see p. 368), da. and co-h. of William (O'Brien), 2nd Marquis of Thomond [I.], K.P., d. 9 May 1870; 2ndly, 31 Jan. 1872, Louisa (see p. 467) (Moreton, Bideford), da. of Bernard Granville of Wellesbourne Hall, co. Warwick; and had issue 1g to 4g.

1g. Sir (William) Lewis Stucley, 2nd Bt. [U.K.], J.P., D.L., late Lieut.-Col. Grenadier Guards (Hartland Abbey, Bideford; Affeton Castle, Devonshire; Carlton), b. 27 Aug. 1836; m. 1st, 15 Ap. 1869, Rosamund Head, da. of Head Pottinger Best of Donnington Grove, co. Berks, d. 29 Sept. 1877; 2ndly, 5 Feb. 1879, Marion Elizabeth, da. of Lieut.-Col. Henry Edward Hamlyn Fane [descended from King Henry VII. (see Tudor Roll, p. 286)].

2g. Edward Arthur George Stucley, Major late 1st South Australian Regt. (Thomond, Pitt Park Road, Guildford), b. 12 Feb. 1852; m. 29 Dec. 1892, May, da. of the Hon. Thomas King, Minister of Education, S. Australia.

3g. Hugh Nicholas Granville Stucley, J.P., C.A., late Lieut. R.N. (Pillhead, Bidehead), b. 22 June 1873; m. 6 Feb. 1902, Gladys, da. and h. of Wynne Albert Bankes of Wolfeton House, Dorchester; and has issue 1h to 2h.

1h. Dennis Frederick Bankes Stucley, b. 1907.

2h. Elizabeth Florence Stucley.

4g. Humphrey St. Leger Stucley, Capt. Grenadier Guards, served at Omdurman and in South Africa 1900–1902, b. 7 June 1877; m. 22 Oct. 1908, Dorothy Beatrice Ross, da. and h. of Francis Harry Carew of Collipriest, Tiverton.

2f. Louisa Buck, d. 11 Ap. 1880; m. as 2nd wife, 9 June 1840, Samuel Trehawke Kekewich of Peamore, co. Devon, M.P., J.P., D.L., d. 1 June 1873; and had issue 1g to 4g.

1g. Sir George William Kekewitch, K.C.B., J.P., D.C.L., M.P. for Exeter 1906, formerly Sec. Educational Dept., &c. (St. Albans, Feltham, Midx.), b. 1 Ap. 1841; m. 1866, (—), da. of (—); and has (with other) issue 1h.

1h. Winifred Kekewich, m. 1900, the Rev. Richard Valpy French, LL.D., Canon of Llandaff, d. (–).

2g. Emma Kekewich.

3g. Louisa Kekewich, m. 6 Oct. 1874, George John Moore of Appleby, J.P., D.L. [descended from King Henry VII. (see the Tudor Roll, p. 485)] (Appleby Hall, near Atherstone; Carlton); and has issue 1h to 4h.

1h. Charles Louis George Moore, b. 3 Mar. 1876.

2h. Gerald Henry Moore, b. 16 May 1877.

3h. Lanuld Geoffrey Moore, b. Feb. 1886.

4h. Elsie Louise Moore.

4g. Anna Maude Kekewich.

2e. Richard Buck of Bideford, Capt. R.N., b. 23 Oct. 1785; d. 7 Aug. 1830; m. at Algiers and again at Bideford, Angelina, da. of Hugh McDonald, Consul General at Algiers, b. at Niagara, Canada, 13 Nov. 1800; d. 11 Dec. 1879; and had issue (see Appendix).

3e. Elizabeth Buck, b. 8 May 1787; d. 29 Ap. 1831; 31 Aug. 1816, Col. Zachary Clutterbuck Bayley, R.A., d. 25 Nov. 1855. [Nos. 103413 to 103428.

302. Descendants, if any, of HONOR STUCLEY (Table XXVI.), m. (—) LUTTRELL.

The Plantagenet Roll

303. Descendants of FRANCES STUCLEY (Table XXVI.), *d.* (–) ; *m.* at Morval 22 Nov. 1635, PHILIP MAYOW of Bray, co. Cornwall, *d.* Oct. 1697 ; and had issue 1*a* to 5*a*.

1*a*. *Philip Mayow of Polgover*, bapt. *Jan.* 1639 ; *d.* 31 *July* 1710 ; m. 1669, *Ursula, da. of Alexander Rolle of Parkgate, co. Devon ; and had issue* 1*b*.

1*b*. *Ursula Mayow, da. and in her issue event.* (1786) *sole h.*, b. 1685 ; d. 14 *July* 1734 ; m. 16 *Mar.* 1711, *her cousin John Wynell* (see p. 486) ; *and had issue* 1*c*.

1*c*. *Philip Wynell, afterwards Wynell-Mayow, of Bray and Polgover*, b. *Jan.* 1716 ; d. 1781 ; m. 1741, *Betty, da. and co-h. of George Salt of Betley, co. Staff.*, d. 1774 ; *and had issue* 1*d to* 4*d*.

1*d*. *John Salt Wynell-Mayow of Bray and Saltash*, b. 1747 ; d. 1802 ; m. 12 *May* 1769, *Mary, da. of Robert Doughty of Hanworth, co. Norfolk*, d. 1820 ; *and had issue* 1*e to* 4*e*.

1*e*. *Philip Wynell-Mayow of Bray, co. Cornwall, and Hanworth Hall, co. Norfolk*, b. 17 *Mar.* 1771 ; d. 28 *Dec.* 1844 ; m. 22 *July* 1806, *Elizabeth, da. of Gen. Charles Deare, H.E.I.C.S.*, d. 10 *Aug.* 1844 ; *and had issue* 1*f to* 3*f*.

1*f*. *George Wynell-Mayow of Bray, &c., C.B., K.L.H., Major-Gen. in the Army*, b. 31 *Aug.* 1808 ; d.s.p. 1 *Jan.* 1873.

2*f*. *Rev. Mayow Wynell-Mayow of Bray, M.A., Rector of Southam*, b. 8 *July* 1810 ; d. 26 *Feb.* 1895 ; m. 14 *July* 1846, *Caroline Kate, da. of the Rev. Alfred Smith of Old Park, Devizes ; and had issue* 1*g to* 4*g*.

1*g*. Mayow Wynell-Mayow of Bray, Major *late* R.A. (*Bray Manor House, St. German's, Cornwall*), *b.* 13 Jan. 1850 ; *unm.*

2*g*. *Rev. Arthur Wynell-Mayow, formerly Vicar of Dunster*, b. 23 *Dec.* 1853 ; d. 4 *Aug.* 1903 ; m. 1 *July* 1890, *Ellen Mary, da. of Lieut.-Col. William Cloves Pamplin of Brighton ; and had issue* 1*h to* 3*h*.

1*h*. Philip Arthur Claude Wynell-Mayow.
2*h*. Ursula Mary Elaine Wynell-Mayow.
3*h*. Betty Mabel Courtenay Wynell-Mayow.

3*g*. Charles Ernest Wynell-Mayow, Capt. Border Regt., *b.* 28 Ap. 1857.

4*g*. Elizabeth Ursula Wynell-Mayow, *m.* 14 Jan. 1869, the Rev. Francis Maundy Gregory, Vicar of St. Michael's, Southampton ; and has issue 1*h* to 3*h*.

1*h*. Edward Denys Wynell Gregory.
2*h*. Arthur John Maundy Gregory.
3*h*. Stephen Ernest Vincent Gregory, *m.* 27 Nov. 1906, Dorothy, da. of W. S. Bernard Bryan of Southsea ; and has issue 1*i* to 2*i*.

1*i*. Harolde Francis Maundy Gregory.
2*i*. Cecil Stephen S. Bernard Gregory.

3*f*. *Rev. Philip Wynell-Mayow of Shortwood, Wells, co. Som., M.A., Vicar of Easton*, b. 16 *May* 1813 ; d. 9 *July* 1890 ; m. 10 *July* 1839, *Mary, da. of the Rev. Benjamin George Heath, Rector of Cresting*, d. 22 *Sept.* 1892 ; *and had issue* 1*g to* 7*g*.

1*g*. Philip Herbert Wynell-Mayow, Capt. R.N. (1 *South Summerlands, Heavitree Road, Exeter*), *b.* 20 Oct. 1841.

2*g*. Rev. Herbert Wynell-Mayow, Rector of Plumstead (*The Ark, Plumstead, Hanworth, Norfolk*), *b.* 13 June 1855 ; *m.* 6 Jan. 1891, Mary, da. of W. Dowling of Easton, co. Som. ; and has issue 1*h*.

1*h*. Philip John Wynell-Mayow, *b.* 13 Aug. 1894.

3*g*. Mary Wynell-Mayow.
4*g*. Margaret Ursula Wynell-Mayow (*Shortwood, Wells*).
5*g*. Fanny Louisa Wynell-Mayow.
6*g*. Edith Wynell-Mayow.
7*g*. Emily Wynell-Mayow (*Shortwood, Wells*). [Nos. 103429 to 103447.

of The Blood Royal

2*e*. Rev. Robert Wynell-Mayow, b. Oct. 1777; d. Jan. 1817; m. Oct. 1805, Elizabeth, da. of William Harding of Liverpool, Merchant (who m. 2ndly, the Rev. John Marrall, and) d. 13 Dec. 1862; *and had issue (with a son, Robert, d. unm.)* 1*f* to 2*f*.

1*f*. John Harding Wynell-Mayow, Lieut.-Col. H.E.I.C.S., b. 20 June 1808; d. 5 Nov. 1876; m. 1st, July 1840, Mary Jane, da. of James Willasey of Allerton Hall, near Liverpool, d. Jan. 1857; 2ndly, 1 June 1859, Theodosia, da. of (—) Lee, d. (-); *and had issue (with a da. by 1st marriage d.s.p.)* 1*g* to 4*g*.

1*g*. John Harding Wynell-Mayow of Haputale, Ceylon, Proprietary Tea and Coffee Planter, b. 2 Mar. 1847; d. 26 Ap. 1905; m. 14 Nov. 1874, Helen Mary (Arthur's Seat, Dimbulla, Ceylon), da. of William Copeland of Staindrop, co. Durham, M.D.; *and had issue (with a son d. young)* 1*h* to 11*h*.

1*h*. John Harding Wynell-Mayow (New Forest, Galaha, Ceylon), b. 16 Oct. 1876; m. 22 May 1900, Eliza Marie, da. of Shelton Agar; *and has issue* 1*i* to 3*i*.

1*i*. Cecil John Shelton Wynell-Mayow, b. Ap. 1902.
2*i*. Moira Betty Shelton Wynell-Mayow, b. 8 May 1901.
3*i*. Bridget Ida Shelton Wynell-Mayow, b. June 1907.

2*h*. Edward Wyllasey Wynell-Mayow, b. 17 Sept. 1879.
3*h*. Gerald Wynell-Mayow, b. 20 Oct. 1888.
4*h*. Charles Eric Wynell-Mayow, b. 12 Ap. 1890.
5*h*. Kenneth Wynell-Mayow, b. 12 Sept. 1891.
6*h*. Reginald Wynell-Mayow, b. 4 June 1893.
7*h*. Ida Helen Wynell-Mayow, m. 15 Oct. 1898, Thomas Scovell [son of Col. Edward Whitmore Scovell, 96th Regt.] (Morval, Warren Edge Road, Southbourne, Christchurch); *and has issue* 1*i* to 4*i*.

1*i*. Hugh Edward Scovell, b. 25 Sept. 1901.
2*i*. George Francis Scovell, b. 9 Jan. 1903.
3*i*. Grace Helen Scovell, b. 25 July 1899.
4*i*. Dorothy Gertrude Scovell, b. 2 Jan. 1904.

8*h*. Flora Wynell-Mayow, m. 6 Sept. 1899, Lionel Charles Maudslay (Glenholm, Sea View, I.W.); *and has issue* 1*i* to 2*i*.

1*i*. Philip Charles Maudslay, b. 4 Aug. 1901.
2*i*. Gerald Wynell Maudslay, b. 8 Dec. 1907.

9*h*. Constance Wynell-Mayow, m. 25 Sept. 1906, Lawrence Anderson Ewart; *and has issue* 1*i*.

1*i*. Phyllis Wynell-Mayow Ewart, b. 18 Ap. 1909.

10*h*. Evelyn Wynell-Mayow, unm.
11*h*. Grace Marian Wynell-Mayow, unm.

2*g*.[2] Robert Sandilands Lawrence Wynell-Mayow, Major *late* North Lancashire Regt. (95 Sydney Place, Bath), b. 7 July 1861.
3*g*.[2] Edith Vyvyan Wynell-Mayow, unm.
4*g*.[2] Helen Stuart Wynell-Mayow, unm.

2*f*. Catherine Anne Wynell-Mayow, b. at Lathom, co. Lancs, 30 Aug. 1815; d. 7 Sept. 1878; m. 1st, at Meerut, 16 Mar. (? Ap.) 1844, Edward Salusbury Lloyd, Lieut.-Col. 49th Regt. H.E.I.C.S. [3rd son and in his issue sole h. of Richard Hughes Lloyd of Plymog, co. Denbigh, Gwerclas, co. Merioneth, and Bashall Hall, co. York], d. at Nakodah, India, 24 Jan. 1851; 2ndly, at Weston, 3 Jan. 1860, the Rev. Edward Deacon Girdlestone, B.A., d. 26 Feb. 1909; *and had issue* 1*g* to 2*g*.

1*g*. Edward Wynell-Mayow Lloyd, M.A. (St. John's Coll., Camb.) (Hartford House, Winchfield, co. Hants), b. 19 Mar. 1845; m. 31 Dec. 1879, Eleanor Elizabeth, da. of the Rev. John Parsons Hastings, M.A., Rector of Martley, co. Worc.; *and has issue (with a son, Charles Hastings Armitage, R.N., b. 12 Jan. 1887; d. 25 July 1902)* 1*h* to 8*h*.

1*h*. Rev. John Hastings Lloyd, M.A. (Queen's Coll., Oxon.), b. 11 Oct. 1881.

[Nos. 103448 to 103473.]

The Plantagenet Roll

2h. Arthur Wynell Lloyd (*Rand and Athenæum Clubs, Johannesburg, S.A.*), b. 4 Ap. 1883.
3h. Edward Mayow Hastings Lloyd, C.C.C. (Oxon.), b. 30 Nov. 1889.
4h. Wynell Hastings Lloyd, b. 19 Nov. 1904.
5h. Robert Aubrey Hastings Lloyd, b. 26 Oct. 1899.
6h. Catherine Constance Lloyd.
7h. Eleanor Margaret Lloyd.
8h. Gladys Mary Lloyd.

2g. Edward Lloyd, Lieut.-Col. 5th Punjab Cavalry (*Culver House, Bedford*), b. 24 Sept. 1848; m. 31 Dec. 1878, Mary Katharine, da. of the Rev. John Wingfield Harding, M.A., Vicar of Cheswardine, co. Salop; and has issue (with a 2nd son d. young) 1h to 5h.
1h. Hugh Salusbury Lloyd, Capt. R.M.L.I., b. 29 Sept. 1879; m. 22 Ap. 1903, Mary Hilda, da. of William Square of Plymouth, M.D.; and has issue (with a son, Ferrers Tudor Walmesley Lloyd, b. 19 Ap. 1904; d. 10 Feb. 1908) 1i to 2i.
1i. Patience Hilda Lloyd, b. 11 Dec. 1905.
2i. Felicity Mary Lloyd, b. 29 Jan. 1909.
2h. Edward Raymond Lloyd, Lieut. Roy. Inniskilling Fusiliers, b. 13 Nov. 1882.
3h. Robin Wynell-Mayow-Lloyd, Lieut. R.N., b. 14 Feb. 1884.
4h. Irene Catherine Lloyd.
5h. Dorothy Cecilia Lloyd.

3e. *Mary Wynell-Mayow*, b. 1774; d. (–); m. 19 *Sept.* 1799, *the Rev. John Richards*.
4e. *Catherine Anne Wynell-Mayow*, b. 1780; d. 1823; m. *the Rev. John Lukin*.
2d. *Mayow Wynell-Mayow of Sydenham, co. Kent*, b. 1753; d. 1807; m. 1776, *Mary, da. of Thomas Paulin; and had issue* 1e *to* 3e.
1e. *Elizabeth Wynell-Mayow*, d. (–); m. 1804, *William Dacres Adams of Bowden; and had issue*.
2e. *Anne Wynell-Mayow*, d. Dec. 1860; m. 5 *Ap*. 1805, *the Right Hon. Thomas Peregrine Courtenay, P.C.,'M.P. [E. of Devon Coll.]*, d. 7 *July* 1841; *and had issue*. See the Exeter Volume, pp. 109–110, Nos. 1240–1263.
3e. *Caroline Wynell-Mayow*, d. (–); m. *the Rev. H. T. Wharton*.
3d. *Ursula Anne Wynell-Mayow*.
4d. *Mary Wynell-Mayow*.

2a. *Lewis Mayow*, b. 1644.
3a. *John Mayow of Bath, Physician*, b. 1645; d. 1679.
4a. *Edith Mayow*, b. Oct. 1637; d. (–); m. *June* 1664, *Nicholas Leigh of Quethiock, co. Cornwall; and had issue a da. d. in infancy*.[1]
5a. *Francis Mayow*, b. Oct. 1647; d. 1724; m. 4 *May* 1671, *the Rev. Philip Wynell, Rector of Landrake, co. Cornwall*, d. 1732; *and had issue* 1b *to* 8b.
1b. *John Wynell*, b. 1674; d. (–); m. 16 *Mar*. 1711, *Ursula, da. and event. sole h. of Philip Mayow of Polgover*, d. 14 *July* 1734; *and had issue*. See p. 484, Nos. 103429–103512.
2b. *Lewis Wynell*, b. 1676.
3b. *Bassett Wynell*, b. 1678.
4b. *Philip Wynell*, b. 1681; m. 1710, *Susanna, da. of Philip Mayow of Polgover; and had a da., Ursula*, b. 1714; d. 1786.
5b. *William Wynell*, b. 1684; d. 1723.
6b. *Frances Wynell*, b. 1687.
7b. *Anne Weynell*, b. 1689.
8b. *Mary Wynell*, b. 1694.   [Nos. 103474 to 103596.

---

[1] Vivian's "Visitations of Cornwall."

of The Blood Royal

304. Descendants, if any, of MARY STUKELEY (Table XXVI.), *m.* JOHN COURTENAY of Molland, co. Devon [apparently the John Courtenay of Molland, *b.* 1630; *d.* 24 Ap. 1684; who *m.* "MARY, da. of (—)";[1] and had issue (with a da., Grace, *bapt.* at Molland 8 May 1667; others known to have *d.s.p.*) 1a.

1a. *John Courtenay of Molland*, b. 28 *Sept.* 1659; d. 14 *Sept.* 1724; m. *(lic.* 3 *Oct.*) 1681, *the Hon. Amy, da. of Thomas (Clifford)*, 1st *Baron Clifford* [*E.*], bur. *at Molland* 7 *Dec.* 1693; *and had issue (with several others who* d.s.p.) 1b.
    1b. *Mary Courtenay, da. and* (11 *Dec.* 1732) *event. sole h.,* b. 1 *Feb.* 1687; *living* 1716; m. *William Paston of Horton, co. Glouc.; and had issue* 1c.
    1c. *Anna Maria Paston of Molland, da. and h.,* d. (-); m. *George Throckmorton, afterwards Courtenay-Throckmorton* [*son and h. of Sir Robert Throckmorton, 4th Bt.* [*E.* 1642], d.v.p. 30 *Aug.* 1767; *and had issue*].

305. Descendants, if any surviving, of HUGH STUKELEY (Table XXVI.), living 1611; *m.* (lic. 17 Aug.) 1621, ARMINELLA (see p. 488), da. of Simon WEEKS of Bideford; and had issue.[2]

306. Descendants of LEWIS STUKELEY (Table XXVI.), living 1611; *m.* 12 Ap. 1627, MARGERY, da. of William COODE of Morval, co. Devon; and had issue 1a.

1a. *Rev. Lewis Stukeley or Stucley of Plymouth*, d. 22 *Aug.* 1693; m. *at St. Andrew's, Plymouth,* 5 *Feb.* 1671, *Elizabeth, da. of* (—) *Alsopp of Plymouth,* d. 16 *Feb.* 1702; *and had issue (with* 3 *sons and* 3 *das.* d.s.p.) 1b *to* 3b.
    1b. *Charles Stucley of Plymouth,* bapt. 8 *Mar.* 1677; bur. 6 *Ap.* 1720; m. *at Kingsweare* 20 *Aug.* 1709, *Anna, da. of John Fownes of Whitley, M.P.; and had issue* 1c.
    1c. *Anne Stucley, da. and h.,* m. *at Kingsweare* 3 *Jan.* 1730, *Francis Luttrell of Venn, co. Som.*
    2b. *Judith Stucley,* bapt. *at St. Andrew's, Plymouth,* 3 *July* 1673.
    3b. *Elizabeth Stucley.*

307. Descendants, if any, of FRANCES STUKELEY (Table XXVI.), *d.* (-); *m.* ROBERT DILLON.

308. Descendants of MARY STUKELEY (Table XXVI.), *bur.* at Bideford 26 Oct. 1632; *m.* SIMON WEEKES of Brodhurst Kelley, co. Devon, *bur.* 14 Feb. 1626; and had issue (with others known to have *d.s.p.*) 1a to 8a.

1a. *Francis Weekes,* b. *c.* 1590; d. 28 *Mar.* 1637; m. 8 *Ap.* 1617, *Wilmot, da. of Richard Coffin of Portlinch; and had issue (with others known to have* d.s.p.) 1b *to* 7b.
    1b. *Simon Weekes,* bapt. 20 *Sept.* 1618; m. *and had issue a son who* d.s.p. 1680.
    2b. *John Weekes,* bapt. 13 *July* 1623; *living* 1637.

---

[1] Vivian's "Visitations of Devon," p. 251.
[2] Vivian's "Visitations of Cornwall," p. 722.

The Plantagenet Roll

3b. *Richard Weekes of Hatherleigh, a Gentleman Pensioner of King Charles II.*, d. *in the King's Bench Prison 5 Feb.* 1671; m. *Dorothy, da. of Philip Catlyn of Wolverston Hall, co. Suffolk; and had issue* 1c.

1c. *Richard Weekes of Northwyke*, bapt. 4 *Aug.* 1656; bur. 28 *Mar.* 1696; m. 11 *Ap.* 1681, *Elizabeth, da. of John Northmore of Well, in South Tawton*, bur. 30 *Mar.* 1706; *and had issue (with* 3 *sons* d.s.p.*)* 1d *to* 3d.

1d *Elizabeth Weekes, da. and event.* co-h., m. 1st *(lic. Aug.)* 1705, *Tapper Langdon of North Bovey*, d.s.p.; 2ndly, *George Hunt of North Bovey; and had issue.*[1]

2d. *Mary Weekes, da. and event.* co-h., bapt. 13 *Nov.* 1638; d. (–); m. *(lic.* 21 *Mar.)* 1707, *Richard Risdon of Spreyton; and had issue.*[1]

3d. *Martha Weekes, da. and event.* co-h., bapt. 25 *Mar.* 1690; d. (–); m. *Robert Hole of Zeal Monachorum; and had issue.*[1]

4b. *William Weekes,*
5b. *Ferdinand Weekes,* } *living* 1637.
6b. *Francis Weekes,*

7b. *Mary Weekes*, bapt. at *Bideford* 20 *Sept.* 1619.

2a. *John Weekes.*

3a. *Grenvil (Granville) Weekes, living* 1637; m. 2ndly *(lic.* 17 *Sept.)* 1628, *Elizabeth, da.* (—) *of Pomeroy of Exeter; and had issue.*[2]

4a. *Simon Weekes.*

5a. *Mary Weekes*, m. *(lic.* 31 *Oct.)* 1621, *Thomas Taylor.*

6a. *Arimell Weekes*, m. *(lic.* 17 *Aug.)* 1621 *Hugh Stukeley; and had issue* (see p. 487).

7a. *Katherine Weekes.*

8a. *Arabella Weekes, living* 1620.

309. Descendants of GERTRUDE STUKELEY (Table XXVI.), living 20 Feb. 1632; *m.* HUMPHREY BURY of Colliton, co. Devon (will dated 2 Sept. 1631, proved 20 Feb. 1632); and had issue (with a son *d.* young) 1*a* to 2*a*.

1a. *John Bury of Colliton*, b. c. 1590; *living, aged* 30, 1620; m. *Mary, da. of Arthur Arscott of Tetcott, co. Devon; and had issue* 1b *to* 4b.

1b. *John Bury.*

2b. *Humphrey Bury*, m. *and had issue (with an elder son who* d.s.p.*)* 1c *to* 2c.

1c. *Arthur Bury of Colliton*, d. *(coticil to will* 29 *Mar.* 1675 *proved* 26 *Nov.)* 1675; m. *Mary, da. of* (—) *Clotworthy*, d. 1673; *and had issue* 1d *to* 2d.

1d. *Humphrey Bury of Colliton, son and h.*, m. *(lic.* 13 *Dec.)* 1679, *Johanna, da. of Thomas Bere of Huntsham; and had issue (with a younger son* d.s.p.*)* 1e.

1e. *Humphrey Bury of Colliton, son and h.*,[3] m. *Anne, da. of John Cutcliffe.*

2d. *John Bury, to have the Barton of Stonegate, in parish of Barnstaple, under father's will.*

2c. *Martha Bury, living* 1675.

3b. *Mary Bury.*

4b. *Gertrude Bury*, m. *the Rev. Hugh Shortridge, Rector of Asgreigny; and had issue, named in the will of her nephew John Bury, dated* 8 *Mar.* 1667.

2a. *Gertrude Bury.*

---

[1] Vivian's "Visitations of Devon," p. 777. [2] Ibid.
[3] Ibid., p. 124.

of The Blood Royal

310. Descendants, if any surviving, of EULALIA ST. LEGER (Table XXVI.), *d.* (–); *m.* 1st at Lamerton, 26 Sept. 1576, EDMUND TREMAYNE, Cadet of Collacombe, Clerk of the Privy Council to Elizabeth, *bur.* at Lamerton 20 Sept. 1582; 2ndly (lic. 7 Oct.) 1583, TRISTRAM ARSCOTT of Annery, co. Devon, *d.* 7 Ap. 1621; and had issue (with 2 sons by 1st husband, *d.* young) 1*a* to 6*a*.[1]

 1*a*. *John Arscott, son and h., aged 30 and more 7 Ap.* 1621; *m. at Exeter 21 Dec.* 1605, *Alice, da. of Thomas Southcot of Bovey (who* m. *2ndly at Islington, 9 Jan.* 1649, *John Pynsent); and had issue (with 2 sons and a da. known to have* d. *young)* 1*b*.
  1*b*. *Elizabeth Arscott, bapt. at Monkleigh* 1611, *living and aged* 9, 1620.
 2*a*. *Tristram Arscott, named in Inq. taken on his father's death.*
 3*a*. *Elizabeth Tremayne, bapt. at Lamerton* 3 *Dec.* 1577; *living* 1600.
 4*a*. *Philippa Tremayne, b. posthumous; living* 1600.
 5*a*. *Mary Arscott, living* 20 *May* 1631; *m. at Monkleigh* 29 *Ap.* 1611, *Edward Trelawny of Menheniot, co. Cornwall, will dated* 29 *Nov./*19 *Dec.* 1625; *prov.* 28 *May* 1631; *and had issue (with three other das. known to have* d.s.p.)[2] 1*b to* 5*b*.
  1*b*. *Robert Trelawney, son and h., a minor* 1621, *living* 1691.
  2*b*. *Anne Trelawney,* ⎫
  3*b*. *Mary Trelawney, bapt. at Pelynt* 24 *Jan.* 1620, ⎬ *named in father's will* 29 *Nov.* 1625, *and then living.*
  4*b*. *Elizabeth Trelawney, bapt. there* 29 *Feb.* 1623, ⎪
  5*b*. *Dorothy Trelawney,* ⎭
 6*a*. *Katherine Arscott,* m. *at Monkleigh* 17 *June* 1604, *Humphrey Prouse of Chagford, co. Devon, bur. there* 24 *Ap.* 1648; *and had issue (with 4 sons and 1 da. known to have* d.s.p.)[3] 1*b to* 2*b*.
  1*b*. *Elizabeth Prouse, da. and co-h.,* m. *at Chagford* 1 *Jan.* 1635, *William Sandford.*
  2*b*. *Philippa Prouse, da. and co-h.,* m. *there* 6 *Jan.* 1638, *Richard Courtenay.*

311. Descendants of Sir FRANCIS COPPINGER of St. Giles-in-the-Fields (Table XXVI.), *b.* 1579, will dated 15 Oct. 1626; *m.* the Hon. FRANCES, da. and co-h. of Robert (DE BURGH), 5th Baron Burgh of Gainsborough [E.], K.G.; and had issue 1*a* to 2*a*.

 1*a*. *Nicholas Coppinger of Ratcliffe, Stepney, Mariner,* d. *c.* 1685; m. *at Stepney* 10 *Feb.* 1658, *Elizabeth, da. of* (—) *Anderson; and had issue* 1*b to* 5*b*.
  1*b*. *Francis Coppinger of Lincoln's Inn, b.* 14 *Mar.* 1671; *d. Dec.* 1759; m. *at St. James', Westminster,* 28 *Ap.* 1696, *Jane, da. of the Rev. Hervey Garnet, Rector of Kilham; and had issue* 1*c to* 3*c*.
   1*c*. *John Coppinger of Linc In's Inn, b.* 2 *Aug.* 1697; *d.v.p.* 9 *Nov.* 1758; m. *at Abchurch, Cannon Street,* 3 *Dec.* 1724, *Katherine, da. and co-h. of Timothy Fysh of Scarborough, d.* 16 *Ap.* 1763; *and had issue* 1*d to* 8*d*.
    1*d*. *Fysh Coppinger, afterwards (R.L.* 30 *Mar.* 1779) *De Burgh, of West Drayton, co. Midx., b.* 26 *Aug.* 1732; *d.* 1790; m. 8 *Oct.* 1765, *Easter, da. of Cornelius Burgh of Scarborough; and had issue* 1*e to* 2*e*.

---

[1] Vivian's "Visitations of Devon," pp. 16, 731.
[2] Vivian's "Visitations of Cornwall," p. 480.
[3] Vivian's "Visitations of Devon," p. 626.

The Plantagenet Roll

1e. *Fysh Coppinger, Capt. in the Guards*, unm. 23 *Jan*. 1793.

2e. *Catherine Coppinger, da. and event. sole h.*, b. 4 *Dec*. 1767; d. 20 *Sept*. 1809; m. 22 *May* 1794, *James Godfrey Lill, afterwards* (R.L. 11 *Feb*. 1800) *De Burgh, of Gaulstown, co. Westmeath*, d. 7 *Mar*. 1832; *and had issue* 1f *to* 2f.

1f. *Hubert de Burgh of West Drayton, J.P., D.L.*, b. 15 *Nov*. 1799; d. 1875; m. 6 *Sept*. 1827, *Marianne* [descended from King Henry VII. (see the Tudor Roll, p. 210)], *da. of Adm. John Richard Delap Tollemache* [by his wife Lady Elizabeth, née Stratford], d. 1880; *and had issue* (with another son and da. who d.s.p.) 1g *to* 3g.

1g. *Frances de Burgh of West Drayton*, d.s.p. 1874.

2g. Edith de Burgh, a co-h. to the Barony of Burgh of Gainsborough [E. 1487] (*West Drayton Manor, Uxbridge*), m. 2 Nov. 1867, Ralfe Oswald Leycester of Toft Hall, co. Chester [descended from King Henry VII. (see the Tudor Roll, p. 209)], d.s.p. 1907.

3g. Eva de Burgh, a co-h. to the Barony of Burgh of Gainsborough [E. 1487] (*West Drayton Manor, Uxbridge*).

2f. Rev. *Robert Lill de Burgh*.

2d. *John Coppinger, Registrar of the Court of Chancery*, b. 2 *Oct*. 1734; d. (*will dated* 4 *Ap*. 1800, *prov. June*) 1809; m. 31 *Dec*. 1764, *Dorothy, da. of Joshua Peale, Solicitor in Chancery; and had issue*[1] 1e *to* 8e.

1e. *Joshua Coppinger*, b. 5 *Jan*. 1766.
2e. *John Coppinger*, b. 6 *May* 1770.
3e. *Henry Coppinger*, b. 20 *Oct*. 1773.
4e. *Elizabeth Coppinger*, d. 26 *July* 1767; m. (—) *Brolland*.
5e. *Easter Coppinger*, b. 3 *Nov*. 1772; m. (—) *Heys*.
6e. *Dorothy Coppinger*, b. 15 *Ap*. 1776.
7e. *Marianna Coppinger*, b. 22 *Oct*. 1777.
8e. *Louisa Coppinger*, b. 1 *Jan*. 1781.

3d. *William Coppinger*.
4d. *Nicholas Coppinger*.
5d. *Henry Coppinger*.
6d. *Anne Coppinger*.
7d. *Elizabeth Coppinger*, b. 2 *June* 1743; m. 3 *Nov*. 1767, *Allaston Burgh, of the Pipe Office, London*.
8d. *Lettice Coppinger*, b. 2 *May* 1745.

2c. *Mary Coppinger*, m. *Peter Pierson*.
3c. *Susanna Coppinger*, m. *David Thomas, Pwllywrach, co. Glamorgan*.

2b. *Barnabas Coppinger*.
3b. *Elizabeth Coppinger*.
4b. *Mary Coppinger*.
5b. *Katherine Coppinger*.

2a. *Lettice Coppinger*, m. 1st, *Paul Barnaby, of Greenwich*; 2ndly, *Sir William Hooker, Sheriff of London, knighted* 1 *Feb*. 1666. [Nos. 103597 to 103599.

312. Descendants of the Hon. JANE NEVILL (Table XXVI.), *d*. (-); *m. c*. 1513, HENRY (POLE), 11th Lord MONTAGU [E.], K.G., beheaded on Tower Hill 9 Jan. 1539; and had issue.

See the Clarence Volume, Table II. and pp. 71-533, Nos. 1 to 22807.
[Nos. 103600 to 126406.

---

[1] History of the Family of Copinger or Coppinger.

# of The Blood Royal

313. Descendants of MARY ST. LEGER (Table XXVII.), d. (will dated 8 July and proved 13 Dec.) 1669; m. as 3rd wife, 21 Feb. 1661, ROBERT (SUTTON), 1st BARON LEXINTON of Aram [E. 21 Nov. 1645], d. 13 Oct. 1668 ; and had issue 1a to 2a.

1a. *Robert (Sutton), 2nd Baron Lexinton [E.], Ambassador to Spain for the Treaty of Ryswick, d.* 19 *Sept.* 1723 ; m. *(lic.* 24 *Sept.)* 1691, *Margaret, da. and h. of Sir Giles Hungerford of Coulston, co. Wilts,* d. *c.* 1712 ; *and had issue* 1b.

1b. *Hon. Bridget Sutton, da. and event. h.,* b. 1699; d. 16 *June* 1734; m. 27 *Aug.* 1717, *John (Manners), 3rd Duke of Rutland [E.], K.G.,* d. 29 *May* 1779 ; *and had issue.*

See the Exeter Volume, Table VII., pp. 159-163, Nos. 2471-2912 ; also Exeter Supplement, 2913-2922/1, and Exeter Volume, 2923-3430.

2a. *Hon. Bridget Sutton,* b. 1662/3 ; *living* 1710; m. *the Hon. John Darcy [son. and h. of Conyers, 2nd Earl of Holderness [E.], &c.],* bapt. 5 *Nov.* 1659 ; d.v.p. 6 *Jan.* 1689 ; *and had issue.*

See the Clarence Volume, Table LXXVIII. and pp. 626-637, Nos. 28040-28849. [Nos. 126407 to 128177.

314. Descendants of DUDLEY ST. LEGER of St. John, Thanet (Table XXVII.), d. 1642; m. ANNE, da. of (—) (who m. 2ndly, 1644, SAMUEL HUSSEY of Ulcombe, co. Kent, and) d. 1646 ; and had issue (with a son, Warham, d. young) 1a to 3a.

1a. *Anthony St. Leger,* b. 1637.

2a. *Dudley St. Leger of Maidstone in* 1663 *and Deal* 1694, b. 1639; d. (-) ; m. 1st, 1663/4, *Winifred* [*da. of* (—)] *Horne of Deal; 2ndly,* 1694, *Mary, widow of* (—) *Weller of Deal; and had issue* 1b *to* 2b.

1b. *Edward St. Leger of Deal, Surgeon,* b. 1665 ; d. 1729 ; m. 1702, *Elizabeth, da. of Charles Bargrave of Eastry; and had issue (with* 4 *other children* d.v.p.) 1c *to* 2c.

1c. *Edward St. Leger.*

2c. *Mary St. Leger,* m. *John Cannon, and was ancestress of* 1d.

1d. *Edward St. Leger Cannon of the Glen, Walmer, Admiral R.N., living* 1867.[1]

2b. *John St. Leger, living* 28 *June* 1711.

3a. *Anne St. Leger,* b. 1641 ; d. (-) ; m. 1666, *the Rev. Nicholas White, Vicar of St. Peter's, Thanet.*

315. Descendants of WARHAM ST. LEGER of Heyward's Hill, co. Cork (Table XXVII.), living Oct. 1691 ; m. 1677, MARY, da. and h. of GILES GREGORY of Thurlesbeg, co. Tipperary ; and had issue 1a to 5a.

1a. *Heyward St. Leger of Heyward's Hill,* d. 10 *June* 1754 ; m. 1704, *Elizabeth, da. of* (—) *Godken, or Gooken, of Courtmasherry ; and had issue* 1b *to* 2b.

1b. *Warham St. Leger of Heyward's Hill,* d. 1784; m. *(settl.* 12 *Feb.)* 1742, *Margaret, da. and h. of Robert Atkins of Waterpark; and had issue* 1c *to* 8c.

1c. *Heyward St. Leger of Heyward's Hill,* d. 1792; m. *Anne, da. and co-h. of Noblett Johnson of Cork; and had issue (with* 4 *other sons* d. unm.) 1d *to* 2d.

1d. *Heyward St. Leger of Heyward's Hill, J.P., D.L., Capt. Glanmire Cav.,* b. 1771 ; d. 1847 ; m. 27 *Nov.* 1797, *Matilda, da. of Noblett Rogers of Lota,* d. 1852 ; *and had issue (with* 2 *younger sons and a da. of whom no issue survives)* 1e *to* 3e.

---

[1] *Stemmata St. Leodegaria,* by E. F. St. Leger, 1867.

The Plantagenet Roll

1e. *Anthony Butler St. Leger of Heyward's Hill, which he sold* 1852, b. 1803; d.s.p. 1866.

2e. *Heyward John St. Leger, of London,* 1867, b. 1805; d. (–); m. 1837, *Sarah* (see below), *da. and co-h. of Michael Busted Westrop; and had issue* (with 2 elder sons d. young) 1f to 3f.

    1f. Anthony Marcus St. Leger
    2f. Noble Edward St. Leger   } (twins), b. 1844.
    3f. Isabella Georgina St. Leger.

3e. *Cornelia Matilda St. Leger,* b. 1809; d. 1867;[1] m. *Edward Galwey of Lota, near Cork, Bar.-at-Law* [*nephew of Vice-Admiral Galwey of Lota*[2]], *last of the Galweys of Lota; and had issue* (with a son, John Edward, b. 1838; d. 1840) 1f to 3f.[3]

    1f. *Matilda Ann Galwey,* m. *Edward Murphy of Streamhill, co. Cork.*
    2f. *Isabella Miranda Galwey,* m. *H. C. Herbert, M.D., 40th Regt.*
    3f. *Cornelia Letitia Galwey.*

2d. *Frances Anne St. Leger,* m. *R. Spread.*

2c. *Robert St. Leger, afterwards Atkins of Waterpark, co. Cork,* d. 1796; m. *Jane, da. and co-h. of Philip Lavallin of Waterstown, co. Cork; and had issue* (with 3 sons known to have d.s.p.) 1d to 4d.

1d. *Warham Atkins of Waterpark,* b. 1780; d. 1830; m. 1800, *Mary, da. of Denis MacCarthy of Macksgrove, co. Cork; and had issue* (with a da. d. unm.) 1e.

1e. *Robert St. Leger Atkins of Waterpark, Major 60th Rifles,* b. 6 Mar. 1802; d. 26 Aug. 1858; m. 3 Dec. 1840, *Sarah Elizabeth, da. of James Penrose of Woodhill, co. Cork,* d. (–); *and had issue* 1f to 4f.

    1f. *Robert St. Leger Atkins of Waterpark,* b. 12 Nov. 1842.
    2f. *Louisa Petitot St. Leger Atkins,*[4] m. *George Moore, R.N., M.D.*
    3f. *Mary Elizabeth St. Leger Atkins,* m. 12 Sept. 1874, *Vice-Admiral John Borlase Warren, R.N.,* has Crimean and Chinese Medals [2nd son of Sir John Borlase Warren, 4th Bt. [I.] (*United Service*); *and has issue* 1g to 3g.

1g. *Bessie Geraldine Gundrida Warren,* m. 20 Nov. 1906, Sir John Scarlett Walsham, 3rd Bt. [U.K.] [also a descendant of King Edward III. through Mortimer-Percy (see p. 287)] (*Knill Court, Kington, Hereford; Germiston, Transvaal*); *and has issue* 1h.

    1h. *Barbara Walsham.*

2g. *Mary Detta St. Leger Warren.*
3g. *Louisa Ursula St. Leger Warren.*

4f. *Henrietta Geraldine St. Leger Atkins.*

2d. *Joseph Atkins.*
3d. *Sarah Atkins,* m. *Robert Berkeley.*
4d. *Jane Atkins,* m. *Michael Bustead Westropp* [*cadet of Westropp, of Attyflin, co. Limerick*], b. 1779; d. (–); *and had issue* 1e to 2e.

1e. *Sarah Westropp,* d. (–); m. 1837, *Heyward St. Leger of London; and had issue.*

See above, Nos. 128178–128180.

2e. *Julia Westropp,* m. *R. Wilkinson.*

3c. *Warham St. Leger,* d. *before* 1847, *probably s.p.*
4c. *Chichester St. Leger,* d. *before* 1847.
5c. *Mary St. Leger,* b. 1746; d. 1807; m. *Thomas Follett of Lyme Regis, co. Dorset; and had issue.*   [Nos. 128178 to 128190.

---

[1] *Stem. St. Leodegaria.*
[2] Burke's " Landed Gentry," 1846, ii. 1176.
[3] " The Galweys of Lota," by C. J. B. Bennett, Dublin 1909, pp. 17, 18.
[4] Burke's " Landed Gentry," 1886, p. 53.

of The Blood Royal

6c. *Barbara St. Leger*, b. 1749; d. 21 *Sept.* (*and* bur. *at Clonegal* 24 *Sept.*) 1820; m. (*lic. from St. Peter's, Dublin,* 21 *Feb.*) *as* 4*th wife, Ap.* 1768, *Alexander Durdin of Shanagarry Castle, co. Cork, and Huntington Castle, co. Carlow, J.P.,* b. 1712; d. 20 *Feb.* 1767; *and had issue* (*with* 3 *sons and* 4 *das. who* d.s.p.) 1*d to* 7*d.*

1d. *Warham Durdin of Shanagarry Castle, &c.,* b. 18 *Feb.* 1769; d. 21 *May* 1823; m. 7 *June* 1792, *Anne, da. of Thomas Garde of Ballindiness, co. Cork,* d. 9 *Jan.* 1847; *and had issue* (*with* 4 *sons and* 4 *das. of whom no issue survives*) 1e *to* 2e.

1e. *Charles Durdin of Shanagarry Castle,* d. 24 *Dec.* 1875; m. *Anne, da. of* (—) *Bowles; and had issue* 1*f to* 5*f.*

1*f.*
2*f.*
3*f.*   } Alive and living in Australia 1886, when they shared in the property of
4*f.*   their uncle, Warham St. Leger Durdin.
5*f.*

2e. *Louisa Durdin,* d. *in Australia* 1844; m. *William Garde of Bilberry, co. Cork,* d. 5 *Oct.* 1895; *and had issue* 1*f to* 2*f.*

1*f.* William Henry Garde, Lieut.-Col., A.M.S., has Medal and Khedive's Star and Clasp for relief of Khartoum 1884-1885 (2 *Sidmonton Square, Bray*), b. 2 Mar. 1842; *m.* 25 June 1891, Fanny Nina Hampton, da. of Edwin Hampton Downs; and has issue 1*g.*

1*g.* Violet Nina Hampton Garde, b. 1892.

2*f.* Annie Winifred Garde, m. 11 Ap. 1871, St. Helier Philip Peard of Cool Abbey, Fermoy (*Glenbrook, Lismore, Richmond River, N.S.W.*); and has issue 1*g* to 6*g.*

1*g.* Ernest St. Helier Peard, b. 24 Dec. 1873.

2*g.* Percy Garde Peard, b. 17 Jan, 1880; *m.* 30 Dec. 1908, Ada Maude, da. of (—) Grisdale.

3*g.* Louisa Alice Peard, *m.* 28 June 1898, Harold T. Carter; and has issue 1*h.*

1*h.* Annie Jean Carter, b. 6 May 1903.

4*g.* Mabel Minnie Peard, *m.* 22 Dec. 1900, Edward R. J. Rohan; and has issue 1*h* to 2*h.*

1*h.* Norman Livesey Rohan, b. 19 Feb. 1905.

2*h.* Dulcie Garde Rohan, b. 7 Feb. 1903.

5*g.* Florence Victoria Peard, *m.* 23 Dec. 1903, Charles Sidney Dunlop; and has issue 1*h* to 3*h.*

1*h.* Douglas Victor Dunlop, b. 23 Dec. 1904.

2*h.* Neville Redmond Dunlop, b. 12 Jan. 1910.

3*h.* Norma Peard Dunlop, b. 14 May 1908.

6*g.* Laura Lily Peard, *unm.*

2d. *Alexander Durdin,* b. 26 *June* 1772; d. 19 *May* 1829; m. *Mary, da. of Thomas Rhames of co. Wicklow* [*who* m. 2*ndly,* 1840, *William Drury and*] d. 21 *Jan.* 1875; *and had issue* 1e.

1e. *Alicia Harriet Durdin,* b. 14 *Mar.* 1823; d. 18 *Ap.* 1908; m. 1 *Sept.* 1840, *William Whitton of Dublin, Solicitor,* d. 10 *Aug.* 1895; *and had issue* 1*f.*

1*f.* Mary Alicia Whitton (*Glenvar, Howth Road, Dublin*), *m.* 28 Sept. 1864, William Blood Smyth of 29 Lower Gardiner Street, Dublin, Solicitor, d. 3 Ap. 1905; and has issue (with 2 others d. young) 1*g* to 11*g.*

1*g.* William Smyth, b. 23 Aug. 1877.

2*g.* John Blood Smyth, Solicitor (29 *Lower Gardiner Street, Dublin; Glenvar, Howth Road, Dublin*), b. 14 Oct. 1880.

3*g.* Charles Whitton Smyth, b. 19 July 1882.

4*g.* Henry Blood Smyth   }
5*g.* FitzGerald Blood Smyth } (twins), b. 21 May 1884.

6*g.* Alice Mary Smyth, *umn.*

[Nos. 128191-128212.

The Plantagenet Roll

7g. Annie Emily Smyth, *unm.*
8g. Florence Smyth, *m.* 8 July 1909, Edward Hartrick Bailey; and has issue 1h.
1h. Edward Hartrick Bailey, *b.* 5 Ap. 1910.
9g. Dora Smyth, *m.* 3 Feb. 1910, Joseph Watson Connell (*Bank House, Talbot Street, Dublin*).
10g. Eleanor Susannah Smyth, *m.* 22 Ap. 1909, the Rev. Matthew Tobias, Chaplain to the Forces at Bulford Camp, Salisbury.
11g. Irene Mary Smyth, *unm.*

3d. Robert Atkins Durdin *of Cranmore House, Kildavin, co. Carlow, J.P.,* b. 16 *Oct.* 1777; d. 5 *Jan.* 1841; m. *Nov.* 1809, *Elizabeth, da. of Thomas Garde of Ballindiness, co. Cork,* d. 11 *Feb.* 1852; *and had issue (with* 2 *sons d.s.p.)* 1e *to* 2e.

1e. Rev. Thomas Garde Durdin, *b.* 18 *Feb.* 1813; d. 27 *Oct.* 1902; m. 28 *Feb.* 1843, *Charlotte, da. of Anthony Browne of Rathgar, Dublin, J.P.,* d. 23 *Dec.* 1904; *and had issue (with a da.,* Mrs. *Singleton, d.s.p.)* 1f *to* 2f.

1f. Robert Charles Garde Durdin, M.D. (T.C.D.) (7 *Frankfort Place, Upper Rathmines, Dublin*), *b.* 27 Jan. 1850; *unm.*

2f. Adelaide Durdin, *m.* 27 Sept. 1888, James Love of Clonkeefy, co. Meath, and Kenwick Hall, co. Norfolk, *d.* 21 Sept. 1904.

2e. Robert Garde Durdin *of Dublin, Solicitor, Lord Mayor of Dublin* 1872, b. 22 *Dec.* 1817; d. 19 *Oct.* 1878; m. *a.* 1847, *Fidelia* (see *p.* 495), *da. of (his uncle) William Leader Durdin of Huntington Castle,* d. 17 *Oct.* 1896; *and had issue* 1f.

1f. Fidelia Barbara Durdin, *m.* 17 Ap. 1884, William Francis Cooke of Kingstown (5 *Morehampton Road, Dublin*); and has issue 1g.

1g. Francis William St. Leger Durdin Cooke, Trinity College, Dublin, *b.* 18 June 1885.

4d. William Leader Durdin *of Huntington Castle, co. Carlow, M.D.* (T.C.D.), b. 10 *Dec.* 1778; d. 1 *Jan.* 1849; m. *Ap.* 1820, *Mary Anne, da. of William Drury of Ballinderry, co. Wicklow,* d. 13 *Ap.* 1883; *and had issue* 1e *to* 2e.

1e. Alexander Durdin *of Huntington Castle, LL.D.* (T.C.D.), *J.P. cos. Carlow and Wicklow,* b. 6 *Mar.* 1821; d. 4 *Jan.* 1892; m. 6 *Sept.* 1851, *Melian Jones, da. of Matthew Hayman of South Abbey, Youghal, co. Cork, J.P.,* d. 12 *Feb.* 1904; *and had issue* 1f *to* 4f.

1f. Helen Alexandrina Melian Durdin, *m.* 1 Jan. 1880 (Thomas) Herbert Robertson of Huntington Castle, co. Carlow, and 36 Bedford Square, co. Midx., J.P. cos. London and Carlow, and Barrister-at-Law of Lincoln's Inn, *formerly* M.P. for Hackney (*Huntington Castle, Clonegal, co. Carlow; 36 Bedford Square, W.C.; 8 Stone Buildings, Lincoln's Inn; Carlton; Athenæum*); and has issue 1g to 4g.

1g. Manning Durdin Robertson, Eton and Magd. Coll., Oxon., *b.* 29 May 1887.
2g. Nevill Warham Robertson, Eton and St. John's Coll., Oxon., *b.* 27 May 1890.
3g. Magnus Storm Robertson, Eton Coll., *b.* 11 Oct. 1893.
4g. Helen Manning Robertson, *unm.*

2f. Florence Amy Durdin, *m.* at St. Paul's, Ivy, Virginia, 14 Feb. 1893, Alexander Ferrier Beasley of Newstead, co. Devon (*Robert's Creek, Vancouver, B.C.*); and has issue 1g to 2g.

1g. William Alexander Ferrier Beasley, *b.* at Vancouver 13 Oct. 1898.
2g. Winifred St. Leger Ferrier Beasley, *b.* at Los Angeles, California, 11 May 1894.

3f. Melian Lucy Anne Durdin, b. 17 *Feb.* 1861; d. 3 *Nov.* 1899; m. 16 *Sept.* 1886, *Walter Henry Benjamin Holloway* (*Ivy House, Charlbury, Oxon.*); *and had issue* 1g.

1g. Melian Eileen Jane Holloway, *m.* 9 Jan. 1908, Charles Cheesman, R.I.C. (*The Barracks, Killarney*); and has issue 1h.

1h. Winifred Melian Anne Cheesman, *b.* 28 Dec. 1908.

[Nos. 128213 to 128232.

# of The Blood Royal

4*f*. Harriette Emily Hayman Durdin, b. 7 Dec. 1862; d. 13 Dec. 1894; m. 25 *Ap*. 1891, Richard William Brockfield Frizell of Clonogan, co. Carlow, and Charlottesville, Virginia; and had issue 1g to 2g.

1*g*.. Richard Alexander Fraser Frizell, *b*. at Charlottesville 26 Jan. 1894.
2*g*. Ethel Melian Frizell, *b*. at Charlottesville 26 Jan. (sic) 1892.

2*e*. Fidelia Durdin, b. 1 *May* 1823; d. 17 *Oct*. 1896; m. *a*. 1847, *Robert Garde Durdin of Dublin, Solicitor,* d. 19 *Oct*. 1878; *and had issue.*
See p. 494, Nos. 128221–128222.

5*d*. Michael Durdin, b. 22 Mar. 1782; d. after 1840; m. Sarah, widow of John Harris, da. of (—), d. 18 Aug. 1835; *and had issue* 1e to 4e.

1*c*. Michael St. Leger Durdin, living at Port Alma, Canada, 22 Aug. 1897.
2*e*. Alexander Durdin, *bapt*. 22 Jan. 1828,⎫
3*e*. Barbara Durdin,   ⎬ living in Canada 1882.
4*e*. Eliza Durdin,   ⎭

6*d*. Sarah Durdin, b. 20 Aug. 1773; d. (–); m. *John Revell of Ardoyne, co. Wicklow; and had issue* 1e.

1*e*. *William Revell*, b. at Huntington Castle 23 Aug. 1805; d. in Australia 1882; m. *Jane, da. of* (—) *Ivors of Castle Ivors, co. Limerick*; *and had issue* 1*f* to 2*f*.

1*f*. John Revell, living at or near Brisbane, Queensland.

2*f*. Eliza Revell, *m*. George Harden of Menai Cottage, Anglesea, and both emigrated to Australia with William Revell and his wife 1862.

7*d*. Barbara Durdin, b. 9 Dec. 1785; d. (–); *m*. 1824, *Henry Beere of Black Castle, co. Kildare*; *and had issue* 2 das. who both apparently d. young.

7*c*. Margaret St. Leger, *b*. Feb. 1828; m. *Ap*. 1768, *William Leader of Mount Leader, co. Cork, J.P.*, b. 1743; *d. Ap.* 1828; *and had issue* 1d to 4d.

1*d*. Nicholas Philpot Leader of Dromagh Castle, co. Cork, M.P., Kilkenny, d. 1836; m. *Margaret, da. of Andrew Nash of Nashville, co. Cork*, d. 8 Oct. 1858; *and had issue* 1e to 5e.

1*e*. Nicholas Philpot Leader of Dromagh Castle, co. Cork, M.P., J.P., b. 1811; d. *unm*. 31 Mar. 1880.

2*e*. *William Leader of Rosnalee, formerly Nashville, Banteer, co. Cork, J.P.*, d. 1860; m. 29 *June* 1847, *Dorothea* (see p. 499), *da. of Richard M'Gillicuddy of the Reeks, co. Kerry, J.P., D.L.*, d. 1897; *and had issue* 1*f* to 4*f*.

1*f*. William Nicholas Leader of Rosnalee, Dromagh Castle, J.P., D.L., B.A. (Camb.), *formerly* Lieut. Scots Guards, High Sheriff co. Cork 1908 (*Dromagh Castle, Banteer, co. Cork; Carlton*), b. 1853; *m*. 21 June 1881, the Hon. Eleanor Burke, da. of Edmund (Roche), 1st Baron Fermoy [I.].

2*f*. Francis Henry Mowbray Leader of Classas, *formerly* Lieut. R.A. (*Classas, Coachford, co. Cork*), *b*. 1855; *m*. Nov. 1879, Agnes, da. of Thomas Brodrick of Leemount, co. Cork; and has issue 1g to 4g.

1*g*. Francis William Mowbray Leader, Lieut. 2nd Batt. Connaught Rangers, *b*. 1881.

2*g*. Thomas Henry Mowbray Leader, *b*. 1885.

3*g*. Mary Gwendoline Leader, *m*. 3 Feb. 1903, Henry Jellett, M.D. [son of the Very Rev. Henry Jellett, D.D., Dean and Ordinary of St. Patrick's Cathedral, Dublin] (34 *Merrion Square North, Dublin*); and has issue 1*h* to 2*h*.

1*h*. Francis Henry Leader Jellett, *b*. 28 Feb. 1904.
2*h*. Gwendoline Stella Leader Jellett.

4*g*. Aileen Agnes Mowbray Leader.

3*f*. Dorothea Margaret Leader, *m*. 1872, George Ware (*Woodfort, Mallow, co. Cork*); and has issue 1g to 5g.

1*g*. George William Webb Ware, M.B., Capt. R.A.M.C., *b*. 9 Sept. 1879.
2*g*. Denis Ware.
3*g*. Ruth Ware.
4*g*. Audrey Ware.   [Nos. 128233 to 128256.
5*g*. Frances Ware.

The Plantagenet Roll

4*f*. Margaret Leader, *m*. 14 Nov. 1883, Henry Bruce Wright-Armstrong of Killylea, co. Armagh, J.P., D.L., High Sheriff co. Armagh 1875, and co. Longford 1894, &c. [descended from the Lady Anne, sister of King Edward IV.] (*Killylea Castle, co. Armagh; Dean's Hill, Armagh*); and has issue.
See the Essex Volume Supplement p. 623, Nos. 9890/92–99.

3*e*. Henry Leader, b. Mar. 1815; d. 10 *July* 1887; m. 1*st*, *June* 1841, *Maria Winifred*, *da. of John Birmingham Miller*, Q.C., d. 14 Oct. 1862; *and had issue* (*with* 3 *sons* d.s.p.) 1*f* to 3*f*.

1*f*. Charles Robert Leader, M.B. (*The Old Hall, Wem, Salop*), b. at Clonmoyle, co. Cork, 5 Sept. 1862; *m*. 7 Jan. 1891, Louisa, da. of James Lowe Holmes of Carrigmore, co. Cork; and has issue 1*g* to 2*g*.

1*g*. Stephen Henry Claude Leader, b. 26 Dec. 1896.
2*g*. Norah Lillie Leader, b. 30 Jan. 1895.

2*f*. *Maria Winifred Leader*, d. 1885; m. 2 *June* 1864, *the Rev. Edward Lavillan Puxley*, *Vicar of Steep, formerly Lieut*. 4*th Dragoons*, d. *June* 1909; *and had issue* (*with* 1 *son* d. *unm.*) 1*g* to 5*g*.

1*g*. Frank Lavallin Puxley (*Carmarthen*), b. 6 May 1868; *m*. Sept. 1903, (—), da. of (—); *s.p.*
2*g*. Greville Lavallin Puxley, b. 19 Jan. 1876; *m*. Sept. 1907, (—-), da. of (—); and has issue (1 child, b. 1908).
3*g*. Frances Kate Puxley } (*Steep, Petersfield, Hants*), *unm*.
4*g*. Winifred Emily Puxley }
5*g*. Florence Lavallin Puxley, m. (—).

3*f*. Ada Henrietta Leader, *m*. 19 Aug. 1889, Rev. Ralph Allan Cumine, M.A. and Scho. (1869) T.C.D., Vicar of Dunmow (*Little Dunmow Vicarage, Chelmsford, Essex*); and has issue 1*g* to 4*g*.

1*g*. Ada Isabel Cumine, b. 4 July 1890.
2*g*. Eveleen Maud Eleanor Cumine, b. 27 Dec. 1891.
3*g*. Florence Mary Cumine, b. 3 Mar. 1894.
4*g*. Cecily Diana Cumine, b. 10 Dec. 1897.

4*e*. Margaret Leader, d. 12 Dec. 1884; m. *John Newman* [*son and h.-app. of Adam Newman of Dromore, co. Cork*], d.v.p. 13 *Aug*. 1844; *and had issue* 1*f* to 3*f*.

1*f*. John Adam Richard Newman of Dromore, J.P., D.L., High Sheriff co. Cork 1874, B.A. (Camb.), b. 5 Aug. 1844; d. 14 Oct. 1893; m. 17 Aug. 1870, Elizabeth Matilda, da. of Lieut.-Col. Robert Bramston Smith of Pencraig, co. Anglesey, D.L. [by his wife Elizabeth Charlotte, da. of Sir Richard John Griffin, 1st Bt.]; and had issue 1*g* to 3*g*.

1*g*. John Robert Bramston Newman of Newberry (Dromore) Manor, &c., J.P., D.L., High Sheriff co. Cork 1898, B.A. (Camb.), *late* Capt. 5th Royal Munster Fusiliers (*Newberry Manor, near Mallow, co. Cork;* 84 *Cadogan Place, S.W.*), b. 22 Aug. 1871; *m*. 1st, 24 Aug. 1895, the Hon. Olivia Anne, da. of the Most. Rev. William Conyngham (Plunket), 4th Baron Plunket [U.K.], Archbishop of Dublin, d.s.p. 24 Jan. 1896; 2ndly, 8 Sept. 1898, Geraldine Amelia (see p. 497), da. of Col. William Pretyman.

2*g*. Richard Griffith Oliver Newman, Capt. 7th Dragoon Guards, b. 19 Jan. 1876.

3*g*. Grace Frances Newman, *m*. 20 Aug. 1895, Henry Charles Villiers-Stuart of Dromana-within-the-Decies, J.P., D.L., High Sheriff co. Waterford 1898, *formerly* Capt. Waterford Art., has S. African Medal (*Dromana, Cappoquin, co. Waterford*); and has issue 1*h* to 3*h*.

1*h*. Ian Henry FitzGerald Villiers-Stuart, b. 23 Nov. 1900.
2*h*. Geraldine Mary Villiers-Stuart, b. 7 June 1896.
3*h*. Nesta Mona Villiers-Stuart, b. 17 Nov. 1897.

2*f*. Frances Dorothea Newman, *m*. 22 Feb. 1870, Capt. Henry E. Bridges, *late* 4th Royal Irish Dragoon Guards. [Nos. 128257 to 128285.

# of The Blood Royal

3f. Geraldine Elizabeth Newman, m. Ap. 1865, Col. William Pretyman, formerly 60th Rifles, b. 5 Ap. 1822; d. 5 Oct. 1894; and has issue 1g.

1g. Geraldine Amelia Pretyman, m. as 2nd wife, 8 Sept. 1898, John Robert Bramston Newman of Dromore, D.L. (see p. 496) (*Newberry Manor, Mallow*).

5e. *Elizabeth Leader*, d. 19 *Aug.* 1903; m. 14 *Ap.* 1849, *Sir George Richard Waldie-Griffith, 2nd Bt.* [U.K.], D.L., b. 31 Jan. 1820; d. 8 *May* 1889; *and had issue* 1f *to* 3f.

1f. Sir Richard John Waldie-Griffith, 3rd Bt. [U.K.], J.P., D.L., Hon. Col. *formerly* Comdg. 1st Roxburgh and Selkirk Vol., *previously* Capt. 2nd Dragoon Guards, Chairman Roxburgh Territorial Force Asso., &c. (*Hendersyde Park, Kelso; Oakfield, Newmarket, co. Camb.*), b. 24 Ap. 1850; m. 11 Ap. 1877, Mary Nena, da. of Col. William Irwin of St. Catherine's Park, Leixlip.

2f. Maria Mona Waldie-Griffith, m. 23 Feb. 1880, Thomas Taylor of Chipchase Castle and Widdrington, J.P., High Sheriff co. Northumberland (*Chipchase Castle, Wark-on-Tyne, R.S.O.; The Cottage, Widdrington*); and has issue 1g to 4g.

1g. Hugh Taylor, B.A. (Oxon.), Lieut. Scots Guards, b. 24 Dec. 1880.
2g. Thomas George Taylor, Lieut. Gordon Highlanders, b. 1 Mar. 1885.
3g. Margaret Taylor.
4g. Violet Mona Taylor.

3f. Mary Isabel Gwendoline Waldie-Griffith (*Trefusis, Falmouth*), m. 22 July 1886, Thomas Turner-Farley of Wartnaby Hall, co. Leicester, d. 13 Mar. 1901; and has issue 1g to 2g.

1g. Dorothy Gladys Turner-Farley.
2g. Olivia Anne Turner-Farley.

2d. *Henry Leader of Mount Leader, co. Cork*, d. 5 *Ap.* 1868; m. *Aug.* 1830, *Elizabeth Anna, da. of the Rev. Charles Eustace of Robertstoun, claimant to the Viscounty of Baltinglass* [I. 1542], d. 1858; *and had issue* 1e.

1e. *Henry Eustace Leader of Mount Leader, J.P., Capt. 16th Lancers,* b. 1833; d. 1 *June* 1876; m. 1 *Oct.* 1868, *Helen Augusta, da. of Lieut.-Col. Williamson of Carrow-Keal, co. Cork* (*who* m. 2ndly, 1878, *Charles Arthur Duncan, Bar.-at-Law*); *and had issue* 1f *to* 3f.

1f. Henry Williamson Leader of Mount Leader, J.P. (*Mount Leader, co. Cork*), b. 18 July 1869; m. 28 July 1900, Maud St. Leger, da. of George Maurice Ievers of Inchera, co. Cork; and has issue 1g to 2g.

1g. Maud Ievers Leader.
2g. Violet Eustace Leader.

2f. Lionel Frederic Leader, Capt. 8th King's (Liverpool) Regt., b. 10 Sept. 1870; m. 2 Oct. 1897, Mabel Campbell, da. of E. Butler Rowley of Manchester; and has issue 1g to 2g.

1g. Eustace Lionel Leader, b. 1 Oct. 1898.
2g. Marvella Hilda Leader, b. 12 Dec. 1892.
3f. Roland William Leader.

3d. *Eliza Leader*, d. (−); m. 17 *July* 1800, *the Rev. Matthew Purcell of Burton Park, co. Cork, Rector of Churchtown and Dungourney*, d. 1845; *and had issue* (*with 3 das. who d.s.p. and one whose issue is extinct*) 1e *to* 5e.

1e. *John Purcell of Burton Park, D.L.*, b. 1801; d. 5 *Jan.* 1853; m. 14 *May* 1850, *Anna Moore, da. of M. K. Dempsey of Kildare*, d. 1872; *and had issue* 1f.

1f. Mathew John Purcell of Burton Park, J.P. (*Burton Park, Churchtown, Buttevant, co. Cork*), b. 30 Nov. 1852; m. 29 Aug. 1882, Annie Marie, da. of Peter Paul Daly of Daly's Grove, co. Galway; and has issue 1g to 7g.

1g. Raymond John Purcell, Lieut. 9th Batt. Royal Rifle Corps, b. 13 May 1885.
2g. Charles Francis Purcell, b. 23 Ap. 1891.
3g. Annie Louisa Purcell.
4g. Margaret Mary Purcell.
5g. Elizabeth Mary Purcell.
6g. Louisa Caroline Purcell.
7g. Angela Mary Purcell. [Nos. 128286 to 128311.

The Plantagenet Roll

2e. Henrietta Purcell, d. (-) ; m. 1st, 1836, Richard Labarte of Springfield, co. Tipperary ; 2ndly, (—) Townsend, d.s.p. ; and had issue (2 das.).

3e. Margaret Purcell, d. (-) ; m. 1st, 1832, William Purcell of Altamira, co. Cork, d. 2 Jan. 1837 ; 2ndly, 1838, Richard Harris Purcell (see below), Bar.-at-Law ; and had issue 1f to 3f.

1f.² Albert Purcell.
2f.² Matthew Purcell.

3f.¹ Eliza Augusta Purcell of Highfort, co. Cork, d. (-) ; m. 30 Ap. 1857, Henry Longfield of Sea Court, co. Cork, b. 1828 ; d. 16 Feb. 1871 ; and had issue 1g to 4g.

1g. Alfred Purcell Longfield, Major R.F.A., b. 6 Dec. 1862 ; m. 12 Ap. 1898, Constance Ada, da. of Professor James Saunders of Edinburgh ; and has issue 1h.

1h. Ada Kathleen Longfield, b. 27 Oct. 1899.

2g. Mountifort Longfield, J.P. (Sea Court, Timoleague, co. Cork), b. 12 Feb. 1866 ; m. 6 Jan. 1891, Geraldine Spencer (see p. 339), da. of Henley J. Edwards, Ind. Navy.

3g. Mary Longfield, m. 1885, Capt. Stuart Banks Roupell, R.N.

4g. Kathleen Augusta Longfield, m. 1889, Alfred Robinson McMullen.

4e. Emily Purcell, d. (-) ; m. Francis Sandys Bradshaw of Tipperary ; and had issue 1f.

1f. Rev. Sandys Ynyer Burges Bradshaw, Vicar of Holy Trinity, South Shore, Lancashire, 1882-1905 (Mossley, Manchester).

5e. Octavia Purcell, b. 1816 ; d. Dec. 1836 ; m. as 1st wife, May 1834, Richard Gibbings of Gibbings Grove, co. Cork, b. 1 Jan. 1813 ; d. 1 Aug. 1876 ; and had issue 1f to 2f.

1f. Rev. Richard Gibbings of Gibbings Grove, D.D., M.A. (Dublin), Rector of Llanmerewig (Gibbings Grove, Charleville, co. Cork ; Llanmerewig Rectory, Abermule, co. Montgomery), b. 16 Ap. 1835 ; m. 14 Jan. 1864, Elizabeth Rebecca, da. of William Ware, Clerk of the Peace, co. Cork ; s.p.

2f. Octavia Mary Emily Purcell Gibbings, d. 7 Ap. 1882 ; m. 24 Sept. 1859, James Denis Foley Cronin, M.D., Fleet Surgeon, R.N., d. 8 Feb. 1909 ; and had issue (with others who d.s.p.) 1g.

1g. John Joseph Cronin, Lieut.-Col. Indian Army, formerly Midx. Regt., since 26 July 1886 attached to Civil Service, and now Dep. Commr., Burma, b. 25 Sept. 1860 ; m. 1st, Daisy, da. of J. T. Pennefather of Ballylanigan Hall, co. Tipperary, d. 4 Aug. 1904 ; 2ndly, Geraldine Frances, da. of J. E. Fottrell of Clonskeagh, co. Dublin.

4d. Louise Leader, d. 1878 ; m. 1812, Richard Harris Purcell of Annabella, near Mallow, and Burnfort Park, co. Cork, d. 1849 ; and had (with others who d.s.p.) issue 1e to 9e.

1e. Richard Harris Purcell of Annabella and Burnfort Park, Bar.-at-Law, d. 3 Sept. 1888 ; m. 1838, Margaret, widow of William Purcell of Altamira, da. of the Rev. Mathew Purcell of Burton House, co. Cork ; and had issue.

See above, Nos. 128312-128318.

2e. John Harris Purcell of Copeswood, co. Cork, d. (-) ; m. Louisa, da. of Thomas Leader of Spring Mount, co. Cork ; and had issue 1f to 3f.

1f. Isabel Purcell, m. Charles J. Starkey of Woodville, Ballyhooley, co. Cork.
2f. Harriet Purcell.
3f. Florence Meta Purcell.

3e. Pierce Harris Purcell of Shanghai, b. 29 Ap. 1830 ; d. at Cork 29 Ap. 1910 ; m. Singa Choy of Canton ; and had issue (4 sons and 6 das., one of the latter m.) (see Appendix).

4e. Augustus Harris Purcell of Annabella, Windsor, Australia, and Brighton, co. Sussex, b. 12 Aug. 1833 ; m. Emma Elizabeth, da. of (—) Hodges of Newton, co. Montgomery ; and has issue 1f.

1f. Ruth Louisa Purcell, m. Alfred Warre Clarke of Australia.

[Nos. 128312 to 128332.

# of The Blood Royal

5e. William Charles Harris Purcell (*Bendigo, Victoria*), b. 3 Aug. 1835; m. Annie, da. of Angus Cornish of Castlemaine, Victoria; and has issue 1f.

1f. Ethel Purcell (*Melbourne*).

6e. Thomas Lyndhurst Leader Purcell, b. 14 Oct. 1836; m. s.p.

7e. Elizabeth Anne Harris Purcell, m. as 2nd wife, 8 May 1873, Thomas Harriott Fuller of Glashnacree, co. Kerry, d. (s.p. by her) 29 Nov. 1886.

8e. Harriet St. Leger Purcell (*Rochestownwood, Rochestown, co. Cork*), m. 18 July 1874, George Roch of Woodbine Hill, co. Waterford, and Rochestown, co. Cork, J.P., D.L., d.s.p. 3 July 1894.

9e. Emily Harris Purcell, m. at St. John's Church, Buenos Ayres, 5 (—) 1872, Thomas Parsons Riggs Boland [son of Thomas Parsons Boland of Pembroke Passage West, co. Cork, J.P.], d. at Ballinahina House 10 Mar. 18—.

8c. Dorothea St. Leger, m. *James Bennett of Cork, M.D.*; *and had issue 1d to 2d.*

1d. (—) *Bennett, Recorder of Cork;* m. *and had issue.*

2d. *Margaret Bennett,* d. 2 Feb. 1849; m. *as 1st wife, Richard M'Gillicuddy of the Reeks, J.P., D.L., High Sheriff co. Kerry 1823,* b. 1 *Jan.* 1790; d. 6 *June* 1866; *and had issue 1e.*

1e. *Dorothea M'Gillicuddy,* d. 1897; m. *1st, 29 June 1847, William Leader of Rosnalie,* d. 1860; *2ndly, at St. George's, Hanover Square, London, 30 Ap. 18—, the Rev. John MacEwan, D.D., Rector of Drumtariffe, Procurator of Ardfort and R.D.; and had issue.*

See p. 495, Nos. 128243–128265.

2b. Elizabeth St. Leger, m. (—) Archer.

2a. Thomas St. Leger, Barrack Master at Newmarket, co. Cork, m. 1 Nov. 1707, Gertrude, da. of Chichester Fortescue of Dromiskin.

3a. William St. Leger of Kilmurray, co. Limerick, d. 1753.

4a. Andrew St. Leger of Ballyvoholane, murdered 1731.

5a. Barbara or Elizabeth St. Leger, m. 25 Aug. 1696, Richard Roffen.

[Nos. 128333 to 128361.

316. Descendants of JOHN ST. LEGER of Cork (Table XXVII.), d. 1730; m. (—); and had issue (with an elder da. d.s.p.) 1a to 4a.

1a. Elizabeth St. Leger, da. and co-h.

2a. Barbara St. Leger, da. and co-h., m. George Lyndon of the Treasury.

3a. Gertrude St. Leger, da. and co-h., m. William O'Brien of Aghacrois.

4a. Mary St. Leger, da. and co-h., m. John Copley of Springfield, co. Limerick.

317. Descendants of MARY ST. LEGER (Table XXVII.), d. 25 Ap. 1718; m. 28 June 1679, JOHN GILLMAN of Curraheen, co. Cork, bapt. 20 Jan. 1645; d. 12 Feb. 1725; and had issue 1a to 4a.[1]

1a. *Heywood Gillman of Curraheen,* d. 1753; m. 1727, *Hannah, da. of the Rev. Edward Sayers of Doneraile;* *and had issue 1b to 2b.*

1b. *St. Leger Heywood Gillman of Curraheen,* d. 4 Nov. 1757; m. 1751, *Eliza Anne, da. of Harding Parker of Hillbrook, co. Cork* [*who* m. *2ndly, 26 Nov. 1761, Sir Henry Martin, 1st Bt. [G.B.] and*] d. 6 *Mar.* 1808; *and had issue 1c.*

1c. *Sir John St. Leger Gillman of Curraheen, 1st Bt.* [*I.*], *so cr.* 1 *Oct.* 1799, b. 21 *Nov.* 1756; d. 1815; m. 10 *June* 1790, *Susanna* [*descended from George,*

---

[1] The statement in Burke's "Landed Gentry," 1871, under O'Callaghan, that there was another da., Ellen, who m., 1713, Roger O'Callaghan, is incorrect.

The Plantagenet Roll

Duke of Clarence, K.G. (see Clarence Volume, p. 507)], *da. of Sir Thomas Miller*, *5th Bt.* [E.], d. 30 May 1803; *and had issue (with 2 das. d. unm.)* 1d to 2d.

1d. *Hannah Elizabeth Gillman, da. and co-h.*, b. 1795; d. *June* 1837; m. as 2nd wife, 30 Aug. 1853, *the Rev. John D'Arcy Jervis Preston of Askham Bryan*, J.P., M.A., d. 7 Aug. 1867; *and had issue* 1e.

1e. Hannah Elizabeth Preston, *m.* 12 Oct. 1870, the Rev. Edward Barber, Vicar of Carleton 1870–1895 (15 *Abbey Terrace, Whitby*); and has issue (with a da., Winifred Hough, d. unm. 29 July 1888) 1f to 3f.

    1f. Charles Edward Gillman Barber, b. 12 Oct. 1871.
    2f. Frances Mary Barber, b. 7 Ap. 1874.
    3f. Constance Elizabeth Barber, b. 18 June 1877.

2d. *Margaret Emily Gillman, da. and co-h.*, b. Nov. 1798; d. Aug. 1881; m. as 2nd wife, 16 June 1832, *William Henry Blaauw of Beechland, co. Sussex*, J.P., D.L., *and High Sheriff* (1859), F.S.A., M.A., b. 25 May 1793; d. 26 Ap. 1870; *and had issue* 1e to 2e.

1e. *Thomas St. Leger Blaauw of Beechland*, J.P., b. 1 July 1839; d. 11 Sept. 1893; m. 6 June 1867, *Fanny Alice, da. of Charles John Bigge of Linden, co. Northbd.;* and had issue 1f to 5f.

    1f. Henry Thomas Gillman Blaauw of Beechland (*Beechland, Newick, Lewes*), b. 4 July 1874.
    2f. Bertram William St. Leger Blaauw, b. 16 May 1876.
    3f. Alice Agneta Emily Mitford Blaauw.
    4f. Frances Catherine Blaauw.
    5f. Margaret Louisa Blaauw.

2e. Emily Hannah Blaauw (*Cissbury, Ascot Heath*), m. 30 Oct. 1860, Capt. the Hon. Charles Cornwallis Chetwynd [4th son of Richard Walter, 6th Viscount Chetwynd [I.]], d. 31 Mar. 1884; and has issue 1f to 5f.

    1f. Emily Mary Frances Chetwynd.
    2f. Margaret Adelaide Chetwynd, *m.* 5 June 1890, Frank Bousfield Hudson (*Oakwood, Roundhay, Leeds*); and has issue 1g to 3g.
        1g. Edwin Chetwynd Hudson, b. 13 Mar. 1892.
        2g. Margaret Elsie Hudson.
        3g. Laura Harland Hudson.
    3f. Louisa Charlotte Chetwynd.
    4f. Julia Alice Chetwynd.
    5f. Katherine Philippa Chetwynd, *m.* 1 Sept. 1908, the Rev. Knowlton Harold Hampshire, M.A. (Oxon.) (*Chiddingfold, Surrey*).

2b. *Elizabeth Gillman*, m. *Jasper Lucas of Richfordstown, co. Cork; and were probably parents of* 1c.

1c. *Thomas Lucas of Richfordstown*, d. (–); m. *Dorothy, da. of* (—) *Evans*; *and had issue.*[1]

2a. *Mary Gillman*, m. *Rowland de la Hide*.
3a. *Barbara Gillman*.
4a. *Ursula Gillman*.   [Nos. 128362 to 128379.]

318. Descendants, if any surviving, of URSULA ST. LEGER, d. 1672; m. 1627, the Rev. DANIEL HORSMANDEN, Rector of Ulcombe, d. 1655; of KATHERINE ST. LEGER, m. 1628, THOMAS CULPEPPER; and of MARY ST. LEGER, b. 1612; d. (–); m. 1632, WILLIAM CODD of Pelicans, Wateringbury (Table XXVII.).

---

[1] Burke's "Landed Gentry."

of The Blood Royal

319. Descendants of AGNES or ANNE ST. LEGER (Table XXVII.), b. 1555; d. 1636; m. THOMAS DIGGES of Barham and Wooton, co. Kent., M.P., Mathematician, Muster-Master-Gen. of the Forces in the Netherlands 1586–1594, d. in London 24 Aug. 1595; and had issue (with a son and da. d. young) 1a to 4a.

1a. *Sir Dudley Digges of Chilham Castle, co. Kent., M.P., Diplomatist and Judge, Master of the Rolls 1636–1639*, b. 1583; d. *at Chilham* 18 *Mar.* 1639; m. *Mary, hss. of Chilham, da. of Sir Thomas Kemp of Ottanleigh, co. Kent*, d. a. 1620; *and had issue (with 4 sons d.v.p. and one other da.*[1]*)* 1b to 6b.

1b. Thomas Digges of Chilham Castle, d. 1687; m. 17 Nov. 1631, *Mary, da. of Sir Thomas Abbot, Lord Mayor of London* 1638; *and had issue (with 4 other sons who d.s.p.)* 1c to 8c.

1c. *Sir Maurice Digges of Chilham Castle, 1st Bt.* [E. 6 *Mar.* 1666], b. c. 1633; d.s.p., v.p. 1672.

2c. *Leonard Digges of Chilham Castle*, b. 1651; m. 1717, *Elizabeth, da. of Sir John Osborne of Chicksand ; and had issue* [1] 1d to 3d.

1d. *John Digges of Chilham Castle*, d.s.p. 1720.

2d. *Thomas Digges of Chilham Castle, a Col. in the Army, sold Chilham, and* d. (–); m. Aug. 1724, *the Hon. Elizabeth, da. of John (West), 6th Baron De La Warr* [E.]; *and is said to have had issue* 1e.

1e. *West Digges, the Player*, d. 10 Nov. 1786.

3d. *Elizabeth Digges*, d. 1746; *m. Lieut.-Gen. Adam Williamson, Gov. of Gravesend and Tilbury ; and had issue* [2] 1e.

1e. *Elizabeth Caroline Williamson*, m. *Daniel Fox of the Six Clerks Office*.

3c. *Mary Digges*, m. 1656, *Sir William Brodnax of Godmersham, co. Kent*, d. 1673 ; *and had issue* 1d.[3]

1d. *William Brodnax of Godmersham*, d. 1726; m. 2ndly, *Mary, da. of* (—) *May ; and had issue* 1e to 2e.

1e. *Thomas Brodnax, afterwards* (1727) *May, and finally* (1738) *Knight, of Godmersham*, d. 1781; m. 11 *July* 1729, *Jane, da. and co-h. of William Monk of Buckingham, in Shoreham, co. Sussex; and had issue 10 children, who were all apparently dead* s.p. *by* 1794.

2e. *Anne Brodnax*, m. *Jacob Sawbridge of Canterbury ; and had issue* 1f to 2f.

1f. *Jacob Sawbridge.*

2f. *Catherine Sawbridge*, m. (—) *M'Caulay, M.D. ; and had issue.*[4]

4c. *Margaret Digges*, m. *the Rev. John Castilion, D.D., Dean of Rochester ; and had issue* [5] 1d.

1d. *Mary Castilion*, m. *Herbert Randolph of Canterbury ; and had issue* 1e.

1e. *Herbert Randolph of Canterbury, F.A.S.*, 1717; m. *and had issue* 1f.

1f. *Herbert Randolph of C.C.C.*, 1765.

5c.–8c. *4 other das.*

2b. *John Digges of Faversham.*

3b. *Dudley Digges, M.A. (Oxon.) and Fellow of All Souls, a Royalist political writer*, b. at *Chilham* 1613 ; d. *at Oxford* 1 *Oct.* 1643.

4b. *Edward Digges of Virginia*, in 1684.

5b. *Anne Digges*, m. 1st *at Chilham*, 6 *July* 1633, *William Hammond of St. Albans Court, co. Kent*, b. 1608 ; d. *at Wilberton, Ely*, 24 *Sept.* 1661 ; 2ndly, *Sir*

---

[1] Hasted's "Kent," iii. 130.
[2] Burke's "Extinct Baronetcies," p. 160; Berry's "Kent Genealogies," p. 143, &c.
[3] Berry's "Kent Genealogies," p. 126.
[4] *Stemmata Chicheleana*, Table 251.   [5] Ibid., Table 264.

The Plantagenet Roll

George Juxon of Canterbury, knighted 1 June 1663; and had issue (with a son and 3 das. known to have d. unm.) 1c to 8c.

1c. *William Hammond of St. Albans Court*, d. 6 May 1685; m. 1st, Elizabeth, widow of Stephen Penkhurst of Buxted Place, co. Sussex, da. of Sir John Marsham, 1st Bt. [E.], d. 1675; and had issue (with 2 other sons s.p.) 1d to 3d.

1d. *William Hammond of St. Albans Court*, b. 12 Aug. 1664; d. 1717; m. 1st, 1692, Elizabeth, da. of John Kingsford, d. 1702; and had issue 1e.

1e. *Anthony Hammond of St. Albans Court*, b. 1693; d. 1723; m. his cousin-german, Catherine, da. of (—) Kingsford, d. 1722; and had issue 1f.

1f. *William Hammond of St. Albans Court*, b. 19 Ap. 1721; d. May 1773; m. 1745, Charlotte [descended from King Henry VII.], da. and co-h. of the Rev. William Egerton, LL.D. [E. of Bridgwater Coll.], d. 1770; and had issue.

See the Tudor Roll, pp. 391-397, Nos. 29467-29687, and Tudor Supplement, 29570/1-16.

2d. *Elizabeth Hammond*, b. 1645; d. (—); m. (lic. London dated 6 Aug.) 1680, Oliver St. John of the Inner Temple [3rd son of Chief Justice Oliver St. John, and only son by his 2nd wife, Elizabeth, da. of Henry Cromwell], b. c. 1643; d. (—); and had issue [1] 1e.

1e. *Oliver St. John.*

3d. *Anne Hammond*, b. 1670; m. the Rev. William Wotton, D.D., Rector of Newport-Pagnell, co. Bucks, the Critic, b. at Wrentham 13 Aug. 1666; d. at Buxted 13 Feb. 1726; and had issue 1e.

1e. *Anne Wotton*, b. June 1700; d. 11 July 1783; m. a. 1724, the Rev. William Clarke, M.A. and Fellow of St. John's, Camb., Chancellor of Chichester, &c., the Antiquary, d. 21 Oct. 1771; and had issue (with 2 others d.s.p.) 1f.

1f. *Rev. Edward Clarke*, M.A. and Fellow of St. John's College, Camb., Rector of Buxted, Traveller and Author, b. 16 Mar. 1730; d. Nov. 1786; m. 1763, Anne, da. of Thomas Grenfield of Guildford, co. Surrey; and had issue 1g to 4g.

1g. *Rev. James Stanier Clarke*, LL.B., LL.D., Canon of Windsor, Domestic Chaplain and Librarian to the Prince of Wales (George IV.), sometime Chaplain R.N., &c., Author, b. at Minorca 1765; d. 4 Oct. 1834.

2g. *Rev. Edward Daniel Clarke*, LL.D., M.A. (Camb.), Traveller, Antiquary, and Mineralogist, b. 5 June 1769; d. 9 Mar. 1822; m. 25 Mar. 1806, Angelica, da. of Sir William Beaumaris Rush, Bt. ; and had issue (5 sons and 2 das.).

3g. *George Clarke*, R.N., drowned in the Thames 1805.

4g. *Anne Clarke*, m. Capt. Parkinson, R.N., who was with Nelson at Trafalgar.

2c. *Dudley Hammond*, m. and had issue 1d.

1d. *(—) Hammond*, m. and had issue 1e.

1e. *William Hammond*, living 1719.[2]

3c. *Anthony Hammond of Somersham Place*, co. Hunts, b. 1641; d. 1681; m. Amy, da. of (—) Browne of co. Glos., d. 1693; and had issue 1d.

1d. *Anthony Hammond of Somersham Place*, F.R.S., M.P., Poet and Pamphleteer, son and h., b. Sept. 1668; d. in the Fleet 1738; m. at Tunbridge Wells, 14 Aug. 1694, Jane, da. of Sir Walter Clarges, 1st Bt. [E.], M.P.; and had issue 1e to 3e.

1e. *Thomas Hammond of Somersham Place*, d.s.p.[3] c. 1758; m. 1742, Elizabeth, da. of (—) Adams, d. c. 1759.

2e. *James Hammond*, M.P. for Truro, the Poet, b. 22 May 1710; d. at Stowe 7 June 1742.

3e. *Amy Hammond*, d. 1754; m. 1st, as 2nd wife, 1719, William Dowdeswell of Pull Court, co. Hereford, M.P., d. 1728; 2ndly, 7 May 1730, Noel Broxholme, M.D., M.A., F.R.C.P., d. by his own hand at Hampton, co. Midx., 8 July 1748; and had issue 1f to 2f. [Nos. 128380 to 128616.

---

[1] Noble's "House of Cromwell," ii. 29.
[2] Ibid., p. 95.
[3] D.N.B., viii. 1124.

of The Blood Royal

1f. Right Hon. *William Dowdeswell* of Pull Court, P.C., M.P., Chancellor of the Exchequer, d. at Nice 6 Feb. 1775; m. 1747, *Bridget*, da. of Sir *William Codrington*, 1st Bt. [G.B.]; and had issue.
See p. 79, Nos. 9460–9556.

2f. *George Dowdeswell*, M.P., d. (–); m. 1760, *Elizabeth*, da. of *Richard Buckle* of Chaceley; and had issue 1g to 4g.

1g. *William Dowdeswell*.
2g. *Charles Dowdeswell*.
3g. *George Dowdeswell*.
4g. *Frances Dowdeswell*.

4c. *Anne Hammond*, m. *Henry Twyman* of Canterbury.

5c. *Elizabeth Hammond*, m. 1st (—) *Snow* of London; 2ndly, as 2nd wife, *John Thomson* of Kenfield, b. c. 1630; d. 1712; and had (with possibly other) issue 2 children by 2nd marriage who d. young.[1]

6c. *Jane Hammond*, m. the Rev. *Isaac Drayton* of Little Chart.

7c. *Phœbe Hammond*, b. 1646; d. 11 July 1713; m. 1st, *Thomas Thomson* of Chartham [younger brother of *John Thomson* above], d. 15 Oct. 1683; 2ndly, the Rev. *Anthony Middleton*; and had issue (with possibly others by 2nd husband) 1d.[2]

1d. *Martha Thomson*, b. c. 1692; d. 26 July 1756; m. *Benjamin Maccaree* of Canterbury; and had issue 1e.

1e. *John Maccaree*.

8c. *Margaret Hammond*.

6b. *Elizabeth Digges*.

2a. *Leonard Digges*, M.A. (Oxon.), Poet and Translator, b. 1588; d. at Oxford 7 Ap. 1635.

3a. *Margaret Digges*, } both living 24 Aug. 1595, and one of whom m. Sir
4a. *Ursula Digges*, } *Anthony Palmer*, K.B., d. 1630, to whom *Leonard Digges* dedicated one of his translations.[3]

[Nos. 128617 to 128713.

320. Descendants of Thomas (Lennard), 15th Baron Dacre and 1st Earl of Sussex (so cr. 5 Oct. 1674) [E.] (Table XXVIII.), b. c. 1653; d. 30 Oct. 1715; m. 16 May 1674, Lady Anne Palmer alias Fitzroy, da. of King Charles II. by Barbara, Duchess of Cleveland [E.], d. 16 May 1722; and had issue 1a.

1a. *Anne* (Lennard), suo jure 16th Baroness Dacre [E.] (see p. 511), d. 26 June 1755; m. 1st, 15 July 1716, *Richard Barrett-Lennard* of Belhouse, co. Essex, d.v.p. Dec. 1716; 2ndly, as 3rd wife, Mar. 1718, *Henry* (Roper), 8th Baron Teynham [E.], d. 16 May 1723; and had issue 1b to 3b.

1b. *Thomas* (Barrett-Lennard), 17th Baron Dacre [E.], b. Ap. 1717; d.s.p.s.l. 3 Jan. 1786.

2b. Hon. *Charles Roper*, d.v.p. 4 Feb. 1754; m. 27 June 1744, *Gertrude*, da. and event. co-h. of *John Morley Trevor* of Glynde, co. Sussex, d. 13 July 1780; and has issue.
See the Clarence Volume, Tables XLV. and LXXVI., and pp. 400–404, Nos. 15196–15382.

3b. Rev. the Hon. *Henry Richard Roper*, b. Nov. 1723; d. Nov. 1810; m. 2ndly, 1760, *Mary*, da. of Col. *Thomas Tenison* of Finglass, co. Dublin, d. 16 Feb. 1795; and had issue.
See the Clarence Volume, Table XLVI. and pp. 404–413, Nos. 15383–15641.

[Nos. 128714 to 129159.

---

[1] Berry's "Kent Genealogies," p. 16.
[2] Ibid., pp. 17–95/6.   [3] D.N.B., v. 976.

The Plantagenet Roll

321. Descendants, if any surviving, of the Hon. HENRY LENNARD (Table XXVIII.), b. posthumous 1662/3; d. 1703; m. MARY, da. of (—) HADDOCK, d. 1709; and had issue [1] 1a to 3a.

1a. *Margaret Lennard*, m. *Col. Lanoye.*
2a. *Catherine Lennard*, m. (—) *Jones.*
3a. *Ann Lennard*, m. *Jerome Tully.*

322. Descendants of Lady CHARLOTTE ANTOINETTE MARIE SEPTEMANIE O'BRIEN (Table XXVIII.), d. at Anteuil, Paris, 4 May 1808; m. 22 Aug. 1775, ANTOINE CÉSAR (DE CHOISEUL), 3rd DUKE OF PRASLIN (DUC DE PRASLIN) [F. 1762], K.C.L.H., Deputy of the Nobility of the Maine to the States General (1789), Maréchal de Camp (1788), &c., b. at Paris 6 Ap. 1756; d. there 28 Jan. 1808; and had issue 1a.

1a. Claude Raynauld Laure Félix (de Choiseul), 4th Duke of Praslin (Duc de Praslin [F.], 1st Count of Choiseul [F.É. 31 Jan. 1810], Peer of France (4 June 1814), Chamberlain to the Emperor Napoleon I., O.L.H., b. at Paris 24 Mar. 1778; d. there 28 June 1841; m. there 12 Ap. 1803, Charlotte Laure Olympe, da. of Claude Stanislaus (de Tonnelier), Viscount de Breteuil [F.], K.M., d. there 6 Ap. 1861; and had issue 1b to 6b.

1b. Charles Laure Hughes Theobald (de Choiseul), 5th Duke of Praslin (Duc de Praslin [F.], and a Peer (1842), &c., b. at Paris 29 June 1805; d. there 23 Aug. 1847; m. there 18 Oct. 1824, Fanny Altarice Rosalba, da. and h. of Horace François Bastien (Sébastiani), 1st Count Sébastiani della Porta [F.É. 31 Dec. 1809], G.C.L.H., K.S.L., Marshal of France, d. at Paris 17 Aug. 1847; and had issue 1c to 9c.

1c. Gaston Louis Philippe (de Choiseul), 6th Duke of Praslin (Duc de Praslin) [F.] (Menton, Alpes Maritimes), b. at Paris 7 Aug. 1834; m. at Geneva, 17 Dec. 1874, Marie Elizabeth, da. of (—) Forbes of New York; and has issue 1d to 7d.

1d. Marie Jean Baptiste Gaston de Choiseul, Marquis of Choiseul (Marquis de Choiseul) (Rue Bayard 7 (VIIIe) Paris; Château du Bois-le-Houx, par Fougères (I. et V.)), b. at Ryde, I.W., 13 Nov. 1876; m. at Paris, 18 Dec. 1901, Jeanne, da. of Georges Baconnière de Salverte.

2d. Count (Marie Cesar) Gabriel de Choiseul, b. at Ryde, I.W., 20 Sept. 1879.

3d. Count (Marie Charles Arnaud Raynald) Gilbert de Choiseul, *styled* Viscount de Choiseul, b. at Paris 20 May 1882.

4d. Count (Marie Jean Horace) Claude de Choiseul, b. at Ryde, I.W., 20 Oct. 1883.

5d. Count (Marie Auguste Eustache) Hughes de Choiseul, b. at Paris 3 June 1885.

6d. Marie Lætizia de Choiseul.

7d. (Marie Marthe) Nicolette de Choiseul.

2c. Count (Eugene Antoine) Horace de Choiseul, K.L.H., Chevalier du Mérite Agricole, Councillor-Gen. and Deputy for the Seine et Marne 1869–1871 and 1885 (Av. Montaigne 57 (VIIIe) Paris; Viry-Chatillon (S. et O.)), b. at Paris 23 Feb. 1837; m. 22 Oct. 1864, the Princess Beatrix Jeanne Marie Josephine, da. of Prince Charles de Beauvau [H.R.E. (1722) Coll.], d. 28 Feb. 1895.

3c. Count (François Hector) Raynald de Choiseul, b. 29 June 1839.

4c. *Marie Laure Isabelle de Choiseul*, b. *at Paris* 19 *Sept.* 1826; d *at Turin,*
[Nos. 129160 to 129169.

---

[1] Nichol's "Topographer and Genealogist," iii. 217.

504

of The Blood Royal

28 Nov. 1878; m. 18 Sept. 1845, Hermann (de Cordero), Marquess of Roburent and Pamparato.

5c. Charlotte Louise Cécile de Choiseul, b. at Paris 15 May 1828; d. there 11 Mar. 1902; m. 21 Nov. 1848, Gen. Count Alfred de Gramont, G.O.L.H. [3rd son of Antoine, 9th Duke of Gramont [F. 1643], G.O.L.H., K.S.L.], d. 18 Dec. 1881; and had issue 1d.

1d. Count Antoine Alfred Arnaud Xavier Louis de Gramont, now (Decree, 26 June 1901) de Gramont-de-Coigny, Dr. ès-sciences, Lt. de rès. d'état-major franc (Paris, 179 rue de L'Université; Le Vignal, Pau, Basses Pyrénées), b. at Paris 21 Ap. 1861; m. at Angers, 2 Oct. 1886, Anne Marie, da. of Paul Émile (Brincard), 1st Baron Brincard [F.É. 31 Mar. 1866]; and has issue 1e to 2e.

1e. Antoine (Louis Marie Arnaud Sanche) de Gramont-de-Coigny, b. at Paris 2 July 1888.

2e. Diane (Antoinette Corisande Anne Marie Louise) de Gramont-de-Coigny.

6c. Fanny Césarine Berthe de Choiseul, b. 18 Feb. 1830; d. at Viry 1 Aug. 1897; m. 29 July 1852, Albert (Robert), —th Count of Robersart (Comte de Robersart) [F.].

7c. Alice Jeanne Slanie de Choiseul, b. 22 Aug. 1831; d. at Paris 28 Feb. 1877; m. June 1851, Count (Antoine Edmond) Eugène de Chabannes [M. of Chabannes du Verger [F.] Coll.].

8c. Marie Marthe de Choiseul (Alassio, Genoa), m. 13 Sept. 1852, Artus Louis Jacques Henri (de Montalembert), 1st Marquis of Montalembert d'Essé (Marquis de Montalembert d'Essé) [F.], b. 14 July 1824; d. 29 Jan. 1887; and had issue 1d to 3d.

1d. Charles Laurent Godefroy (de Montalembert), 2nd Marquis of Montalembert d'Essé (Marquis de Montalembert d'Essé) [F.], b. 1854; m. July 1883, Gratienne Constance Agnes, da. of (—) Loppin de Montmort.

2d. Count Raoul de Montalembert d'Essé (Château de Ménilles, Eure), b. (—); m. 1 Feb. 1888, Alix, da. of Marie Joseph Gabriel Xavier (de Choiseul), —th Marquis of Choiseul-Beaupré [F.]; and has issue 1e to 7e.

1e. Jehan de Montalembert d'Essé, b. 20 Jan. 1890.
2e. Jacques de Montalembert d'Essé.
3e. Xavier de Montalembert d'Essé.
4e. Alix de Montalembert d'Essé, b. 17 Dec. 1888.
5e. Lyna de Montalembert d'Essé.
6e. Nelly de Montalembert d'Essé.
7e. Marie Magdalene de Montalembert d'Essé.

3d. Caroline de Montalembert d'Essé.

9c. Leontine Laure Augustine de Choiseul, m. 22 July 1858, Louis, Marquis d'Adda de Salvaterra (Inverigo, Como, Italy).

2b. Count Edgard Laure Charles Gilbert de Choiseul-Praslin, b. 28 Oct. 1806; d. at Paris 5 Feb. 1887; m. 1852, Georgina Elizabeth Angelina, da. of (—) Schickler, d. 12 Jan. 1849; and had issue 1c.

1c. Alix Eugénie Davida de Choiseul, m. 21 May 1863, Count Charles Henri François Marie de Mercy-Argenteau [2nd son of Charles François Joseph (d'Argenteau), 3rd Count of Mercy-Argenteau [Netherlands]]; and had issue 1d.

1d. Countess Georgina Davida Adelaïde Françoise Marie de Mercy-Argenteau, Lady of the Order of Theresa (D. hon. de l'O bav. de Thérèse), m. at Paris 29 Jan. 1885, Duke Claude Emmanuel Henri Marie de Rarécourt de La Vallée de Pimodan, styled Count de Pimodan, formerly Lieut.-Col. of Cavalry in the French service [younger brother of Gabriel, 1st Duke of Rarécourt (Herzog von Rarécourt) [Bavaria, 29 Feb. 1904], and Duke of Rarécourt de La Vallée de Pimodan (Duca di Rarécourt della Vallée di Pimodan) [P.S. 31 Oct. 1860], —th Marquis of Pimodan (Marquis de Pimodan) [F. 18 Aug. 1766], 2nd Count of Pimodan (Graf von Pimodan) [Austria, 13 Aug. 1852], &c., &c.] (Paris, rue de L'Université, 98 (VIIe); Château d'Ochain, par Clavier, Belgium ; Cercle de L'Union ; Jockey Club); and has issue 1e to 6e. [Nos. 129170 to 129186.

505

The Plantagenet Roll

1*e*. Duke Pierre (Georges Henri Laure Claude) de Rarécourt, *b*. at the Château de Bezy, near Vernon, Eure, 3 Oct. 1886.

2*e*. Duke Henri (Fernand François Gabriel Marie) de Rarécourt, *b*. at Amiens 7 Dec. 1887.

3*e*. Duke Georges (Robert Florimond Claude) de Rarécourt, *b*. at Paris 7 Dec. 1892.

4*e*. Duke Louis (Gaston Philippe Marie Isabella) de Rarécourt, *b*. at Thours 10 July 1899.

5*e*. Marguerite (Leontine Emma Alix Marie) de Rarécourt, *b*. at Abbeville 30 Ap. 1889.

6*e*. Jeanne (Marie Louise Claude) de Rarécourt, *b*. at Boulogne 12 Aug. 1895.

3*b*. *Césarine Charlotte Laure Slanie de Choiseul*, b. 19 Oct. 1807; d. 29 Nov. 1843; m. 30 Nov. 1829, *Henri Marie Nicholas Charles, Marquis of Harcourt (Marquis d'Harcourt) [son and h.-app. of François Eugène Gabriel, 7th Duke of Harcourt [F. 1700), and a Peer, O.L.H.], b. at Paris, 14 Nov. 1808; d.v.p. at Metz-sur-Seine 29 Sept. 1846; and had issue* 1*c* to 4*c*.

1*c*. *Charles François Marie (d'Harcourt), 8th Duke of Harcourt (Duc d'Harcourt) [F.], Deputy for the Calvados* 1871 *and* 1876–1881, *&c.*, b. at Paris 21 June 1835; d. *there* 5 Nov. 1895; m. 27 May 1862, *Countess Marie Ange Thérèse Caroline Alénie (Paris*, 11 *rue Vaneau), da. of Charles Joseph François (d'Argenteau), 3rd Count of Mercy-Argenteau [Netherlands]; and had issue* 1*d* to 2*d*.

1*d*. *Eugène François Marie Henri (d'Harcourt), 9th Duke of Harcourt (Duc d'Harcourt) [F.], K.L.H., Capt. of Chasseurs-à-pied*, b. *at Argenteau* 15 Aug. 1864; d. *at Paris* 17 May 1908; m. 2 *Sept.* 1896, *Amelie Françoise Henriette Marie (Paris,* 47 *rue de Varennes; Château d'Harcourt, Calvados), da. of Marie Charles Gabriel Sosthènes (de La Rochefoucauld), 4th Duke of Doudeauville [F.* 1817]; *and had issue* 1*e* to 3*e*.

1*e*. François (d'Harcourt), 10th Duke of Harcourt (Duc d'Harcourt) [F.] (*Château d'Harcourt, Calvados, &c.*), *b*. 12 July 1902.

2*e*. Lydie Françoise Marie d'Harcourt, *b*. at Paris 28 Oct. 1898.

3*e*. Elisabeth Françoise Marie d'Harcourt, *b*. at Paris 12 Mar. 1901.

2*d*. Count Charles (Félix Marie) d'Harcourt, Capt. rés du 12e bat. de Chass.-à-pied (*Paris*, 57 *Av. Montaigne; Château du Champ de Bataille, Neubowg, Eure*), *b*. in Paris 18 Ap. 1870; *m*. there 2 Sept. 1896, the Princess Henriette Marie Lucie Victurnieune, da. of Marc (de Beauvau), Prince of Beauvau-Craon [H.R.E. 1722], —th Marquis of Beauvau [F. 1664], &c.; *s.p.s.*

2*c*. *Count Louis Marie d'Harcourt, d.* (? s.p.).

3*c*. Count (Charles Marie) Pierre d'Harcourt, ancien capit. d'état-major (*Paris,* 11 *rue Vaneau; Château de Grosbois, Côte d'Or*), *b*. at Paris 25 Oct. 1842; *m*. there 29 Ap. 1874, Alix Adelaide [descended from Kings Henry VII. and Edward IV. (see the Essex Volume, Tudor Supplement, p. 465)], da. of Adrien (de Mun), 13th Marquis of Mun [F. 1588]; and has issue 1*d* to 4*d*.

1*d*. Count Joseph d'Harcourt (*Paris*, 134 *rue de Grenelle*), *b*. at Lumigny 20 Dec. 1879; *m*. at Paris 1 June 1904, Blanche Anne Marie Josephe, da. of Guillaume Charles Joseph Marie (de Melun), 3rd Viscount [F. 1819] and Baron [F. E. 1811] de Melun; and has issue 1*e* to 3*e*.

1*e*. Bernard Joseph Marie Pierre d'Harcourt, *b*. at Paris 1 Mar. 1905.

2*e*. Jean Guillaume Marie d'Harcourt, *b*. at Paris 6 Sept. 1906.

3*e*. Guillemette Josephe Marie d'Harcourt, *b*. at Brumetz 23 Aug. 1908.

2*d*. Count Robert d'Harcourt (*Paris*, 11 *rue de Vaneau*), *b*. at Lumigny 23 Nov. 1881.

3*d*. Slanie Françoise Marie d'Harcourt, *m*. at Paris 5 Ap. 1894, Alexandre Marie Jean Potier de Courcy (Vicomte Potier de Courcy), chef de bat. à l'état-major du IVe corps d'armée franç. (*Le Mans; Paris,* 113 *rue de Grenelle*); and has issue 1*e* to 3*e*.

[Nos. 129187 to 129203.]

# of The Blood Royal

1*e*. Viscount Alfred Pierre Potier de Courcy, b. 16 Feb. 1895.
2*e*. Viscount Xavier René Potier de Courcy, b. 18 May 1898.
3*e*. Claire Potier de Courcy.

4*d*. Adrienne Élisabeth Jeanne Marie d'Harcourt, *m*. at Paris 23 Feb. 1899, Maurice Charles Marc René (de Voyer) — Marquis of Argenson (Marquis d'Argenson) [F.] (*Paris, 117 rue Barbet de Jouy; Château des Ormes, Dépt. de la Vienne*); and has issue 1*e*.
   1*e*. Charlotte de Voyer d'Argenson, b. 1 Mar. 1902.

4*c*. Ernestine Jeanne Maria d'Harcourt, b. *at Paris* 25 *Mar*. 1840; d. (–); m. 15 *Ap*. 1864, *Henri, Count de La Tour du Pin-Chambly de la Charce*.

4*b*. *Laure Régine de Choiseul*, b. *at Dieppe* 2 *Oct*. 1810; d. *at Narbonne* 14 *Feb*. 1855; m. *at Paris* 12 *Feb*. 1833, *Marc Edouard (de Pontevès-Bargème), 1st Duke of Sabran (Duc de Sabran)* [*F*. 18 *July* 1828], d. *at the Castle du Lac, Aude*, 5 *Sept*. 1878; *and had issue* 1*c to* 5*c*.
   1*c*. *Elzéar Charles Antoine (de Pontevès), 2nd Duke of Sabran (Duc de Sabran)* [F.], K.L.H., b. *at Marseilles* 19 *Ap*. 1840; d. *at the Castle of Csicso, Hungary*, 6 *Ap*. 1894; m. 1st, *at Paris*, 3 *June, Marie Julie, da. of Honoré Louis Joseph Marie (d'Albert de Luynes) — Duke of Chevreuse* [F. 1667], d. *at the Castle du Lac* 15 Nov. 1865; *and had issue* 1*d*.
      1*d*. Louise Delphine Marie Valentine de Pontevès, *m*. 1st, at Paris, 10 June 1885, Jules Jean Marie (de Baillardel de Lareinty) — Marquis of Tholozan [F.], d. 25 May 1900; 2ndly, at Hyères, 1 Dec. 1904, Joseph (Horschel), 1st Marquis d'Horschel de Valleford [P.S.] (*Paris*).

   2*c*. *Marie Zozime Edmond (de Pontevès), 3rd Duke of Sabran (Duc de Sabran)* [F.], b. *Marseilles* 16 *Sept*. 1841; d. *at the Château de Magnanne* 17 *Nov*. 1903; m. 1st, *at Ménil, Mayenne*, 9 *Feb*. 1870, *Charlotte Cécile, da. of Jules Joseph de la Tullaye*, d. *at Magnanne* 19 *Dec*. 1884; *and had issue* 1*d to* 3*d*.
      1*d*. Hélion Louis Marie Elzéar (de Pontevès) [de Sabran] (Duc de Sabran) [F.] (*Château de Magnanne, Mayenne*), b. there 9 Nov. 1873.
      2*d*. Count Amic (René Louis Marie Elzéar) de Sabran-Pontevès, b. at Magnanne 13 Sept. 1879; *m*. at Paris 27 Nov. 1909, Marguerite, da. of François Felix Augustin Juhel, Marquis de Lamote-Baracé.
      3*d*. Alyette Léonide Élisabeth Régine Marie Delphine de Sabran-Pontevès.

   3*c*. Delphine Laure Gersinde Eugénie de Sabran-Pontevès (*Château de Buisson Rond, Chambéry, Savoy*), m. at Narbonne 24 June 1852, Ernest Paul Marie (Le Borgne), 3rd Count of Boigne (Conte di Boigne) [Sardinia, 7 June 1816], Member of the Sardinian Parliament, and afterwards Conseiller-général for Savoy, b. at Chambéry 7 Dec. 1829; d. at the Castle of Buisson, Savoy, 26 Nov. 1895; and has issue (with 2 das. d. unm.) 1*d* to 6*d*.
      1*d*. Benoît (Le Borgne), 4th Count of Boigne (Conte di Boigne) [Sardinia] (*Château de Buissonrond, Chambéry, Savoy*), b. 31 July 1854; *m*. Marie Louise, da. of (—) Perquer, *d.s.p*. 2 Aug. 1891.
      2*d*. *Count Élzéard Germain Joseph Le Borgne de Boigne, Officer of Cuirassiers in the French Army*, b. 12 *Feb*. 1865; d. *at Alençon* 27 *Ap*. 1902; m. 18 *Nov*. 1895, *Hélène Pauline, da. of* (—) *de Mandat Grancey; and had issue* 1*e to* 2*e*.
         1*e*. François Le Borgne de Boigne.
         2*e*. Jean Le Borgne de Boigne.
      3*d*. Edmée Le Borgne de Boigne, *m*. 11 June 1873, Eugène Courtois d'Arcollières (*Château de Marterey Morestel, Isère*).
      4*d*. Marthe Le Borgne de Boigne, *m*. 2 Feb. 1884, René, Count de Calonne (*Château de Nyon, près St. Leger-sur-Dheune, Saône et Loire; Château de Paradis, Davayé, Saône et Loire*).
      5*d*. Monique Le Borgne de Boigne, } Religieuses. [Nos. 129204 to 129220.
      6*d*. Inès-Marie Le Borgne de Boigne, }

The Plantagenet Roll

4c. Anne Marie Inés de Sabran-Pontevès, b. at Marseilles 30 Nov. 1836; d. at Chambéry 18 Jan. 1874; m. 1 Aug. 1855, Charles Felix, Marquis Trédicini de Boffalora.

5c. Marie Victorienne Charlotte de Sabran-Pontevès, b. at Paris 27 Mar. 1838; d. at the Castle of Roches, Drôme, 18 July 1867; m. 25 Oct. 1865, Marie Louis Joseph Alfred de Geoffre de Chabrignac.

5b. Laure Geneviève Marie de Choiseul, b. at Dieppe 12 Sept. 1813; d. 14 Dec. 1873; m. 1833, Charles François Marie Anne Joseph, Marquis of Calvière.

6b. Alix Laure Marguerite de Choiseul, b. 4 Aug. 1820; d. at the Castle of Clères 30 Jan. 1891; m. as 2nd wife, 18 June 1833, Louis Hector (de Galard de Béarn), —th Marquis of Brassac [F.], 1st Count of Béarn [F. E.,1811], a Senator of the Empire (4 Dec. 1854) and Min. Plen. (1853), d. 26 Mar. 1871; and had issue 1c to 4c.

1c. Laure Henri Gaston (de Galard-Béarn), —th Marquess of Brassac [F.], 2nd Count of Béarn [F. E. 1811] and (9 July 1868) 1st Prince of Béarn and Viana [Spain], K.L.H., b. 1840; d. 25 June 1893; m. at Paris 10 May 1873, Cécile Charlotte Marie, 13th Princess of Chalais (1450), 9th Marchioness of Excideuil (1713), and 10th Countess of Grignols (1713) [F.], 6th Princess of Chalais and Grandee of the 1st Class [Sp. 1 Oct. 1714], da. and h. of Count Augustin René Adalbert Paul de Talleyrand-Périgord, and niece and h. of Elie Louis Roger (de Talleyrand-Périgord), 3rd and last Duke of Périgord [F. 26 Dec. 1818], 12th Prince of Chalais, &c., d. at Pau 11 Dec. 1890; and had issue 1d to 6d.

1d. Louis Hélie Joseph Henri (de Galard-Béarn), 14th Prince of Chalais (1450), 10th Marquis of Excideuil (1713), and —th Marquis of Brassac (17—), and 11th Count of Grignols (1713) (Prince de Chalais, Marquis d'Excideuil et de Brassac et Comte de Grignols) [F.], 3rd Count of Béarn (Comte de Béarn) [F. E. 1811], 8th Prince of Chalais and a Grandee of the 1st Class (1714, confirmed 23 Nov. 1904), 2nd Prince of Béarn and Viana (1868) (Prince de Chalais y Grande de España de Primera Clase, Prince de Béarn y de Viana) [Spain], &c., styled Prince of Béarn and Chalais (Paris, rue de Commaille 2 (VIIe); Société Hippique), b. at Paris 3 May 1874; m. there 23/24 June 1905, Beatrice, da. of (—) Wynans of Baltimore, d. at St. Petersburg 17 Oct. 1907; and has issue 1e to 2e.

1e. Count Gaston (Ross Joseph Henri) de Galard-Béarn, b. at St. Petersburg 11 Oct. 1907.

2e. (Cecile Nèva Marie) Beatrice de Galard-Béarn, b. at St. Petersburg 17 Ap. 1906.

2d. Count (Centule Edmond) François de Galard-Béarn (Château d'Eslayou, par Lescar, Basse Pyr.), b. 1875.

3d. Count Bernard (Étienne Raymond) de Galard-Béarn (Château de Couloutre, par Donzy, Nièvre; Château de Parenchères par Sainte-Foy-la-Grand, Gironde), b. 1879.

4d. Count Pierre (Paul Albert Pierre Arnaud) de Galard-Béarn (Châlet Périgord, à Arcachon, Gironde), b. 1881.

5d. Count (Étienne Gabriel) Odon de Galard-Béarn (Châlet Périgord, à Arcachon, Gironde), b. 1882.

6d. Blanche Marie Pauline de Galard-Béarn.

2c. Count Jean (Casimir Alexandre Gontran) de Galard-Béarn, an Officer in the French Army (Château de Clères, S.-Inf.; Palais Valéry, à Bastia, Corse), b. 20 Mar. 1852; m. 24 June 1880, Marie Antoinette, da. of Joseph, Count Valéry, a Senator; and has issue 1d to 6d.

1d. Count Centule de Galard-Béarn, Officier de Cavalerie de Reserve, b. 5 Jan. 1883.

2d. Count Hector de Galard-Béarn, Ensigne de vaisseau de 1er classe, b. 19 June 1886.

3d. Count Sanche de Galard-Béarn, b. 31 Jan. 1888.

4d. Jeanne de Galard-Béarn. [Nos. 129221 to 129233.

# of The Blood Royal

5*d*. Sabine de Galard-Béarn, *m*. 26 Ap. 1910, J. Salomon Koechlin, Capitaine d'Artillerie.

6*d*. Pauline de Galard-Béarn.

3*c*. Count (Louis Jean Sanche) Arsieu de Galard-Béarn, Attaché d'Ambassade, *b*. 1863.

4*c*. Blanche de Galard-Béarn, Religieuse. [Nos. 129234 to 129237.

323. Descendants of Lady ELIZABETH BRABAZON (Table XXVIII.), *d*. 1725 ; *m*. 1st, as 2nd wife, Sir PHILIPS COOTE of Mount Coote, co. Limerick, *bapt*. 10 Mar. 1685 ; *d*. 1715 ; 2ndly, the Hon. PHILIP BERTIE, *d.s.p*. 1728 ; and had issue 1*a* to 3*a*.

1*a*. Charles Coote of Mount Coote, d. 1761 ; m. *Catherine, da. of Sir Robert Newcomen, 6th Bt*. [*I*. 1625] ; *and had issue* 1*b*.

1*b*. *Chidley Coote of Mount Coote*, d. 24 *Jan*. 1764 ; m. *Jane, da. of Sir Ralph Gore, 4th Bt*. [*I*. 1622], *M.P*. ; *and had issue* 1*c to* 2*c*.

1*c*. *Charles Coote of Mount Coote*, d. 17 *Sept*. 1792 ; m. 1775, *Elizabeth, da. and co-h. of Philip Oliver of Altamira, M.P*. ; *and had issue* 1*d to* 3*d*.

1*d*. *Chidley Coote of Mount Coote*, b. 14 Feb. 1776 ; d. 11 *July* 1843 ; m. 24 *July* 1797, *Ann, da. and co-h. of the Hon. William Williams Hewitt* [*B. Lifford Coll*.], *d*. 11 Dec. 1842 ; *and had issue (with* 4 *sons* d.s.p.) 1*e to* 3*e*.

1*e*. *Charles Eyre Coote*, b. 5 *June* 1801 ; d. 12 *Mar*. 1858 ; m. 8 *Jan*. 1828, *Catherine Dillon, da. of Major Crofton Croker*, d. 4 *Mar*. 1878 ; *and had issue (with an elder da*. d.s.p.) 1*f to* 2*f*.

1*f*. Mary Anne Coote, da. and co-h., *m*. 5 Feb. 1856, William Uniack Townsend, *d*. 1888 ; and has issue.

2*f*. Caroline Alicia Coote, da. and co-h., *m*. 26 June 1866, Walter James Cummins ; and has issue.

2*e*. *Charles James Coote, Lieut.-Col*. 18*th Royal Irish Regt*., b. 1818 ; d. (–) ; m. *Anne, da. of Thomas Stewart of Limerick*, d. 24 *May* 1853 ; *and had issue (with a son and da*. d.s.p.) 1*f to* 3*f*.

1*f*. Charles James Coote of Mount Coote, *formerly* Capt. 18th Royal Irish Regt. (*Mount Coote, Limerick*), *b*. 19 Aug. 1837 ; *m*. 6 June 1867, Emily, da. of Very Rev. the Hon. Henry Pakenham [E. of Longford Coll.], *d.s.p*. 23 May 1896.

2*f*. Anne Hewitt Coote, *m*. 20 Dec. 1866, Henry John Norman of Gadesden, Hayes, Kent ; and has issue.

3*f*. Ada Coote (*Bel Air, Dinard, France*), *m*. 17 Nov. 1868, the Hon. Henry Leslie Pepys [E. of Cottenham Coll., &c., descended from the Lady Isabel Plantagenet (see Essex Volume, p. 163)], *d*. 18 Mar. 1891 ; and has issue 1*g* to 3*g*.

1*g*. Arthur Guy Leslie Pepys, Capt. Essex Regt. and Adj. 5th Batt. Royal Warwickshire Regt., *b*. 24 Aug. 1875.

2*g*. Gerald Leslie Pepys, Capt. 57th Wildes Rifles (Indian Frontier Force), *b*. 30 Jan. 1879 ; *m*. 20 June 1907, Charlotte Helen, da. of Charles W. Lambe Forbes of Auchrannie, co. Forfar ; and has issue 1*h* to 2*h*.

1*h*. Charles Donald Leslie Pepys, *b*. 25 Sept. 1909.

2*h*. Geraldine Mary Leslie Pepys, *b*. 26 Aug. 1908.

3*g*. Evelyn Pepys, *m*. 3 June 1902, Col. John Monteith, C.B., *formerly* 32nd Bombay Lancers (*Les Rochers, Dinard, France*).

3*e*. *Alicia Coote*, b. *in Bath* 8 *June* 1808 ; d. 14 *Sept*. 1855 ; m. *as* 1*st wife*, 14 *June* 1831, *John Wingfield King* [*son of Lieut.-Gen. the Hon. Sir Henry King, K.C.B*., 4*th son of Robert*, 2*nd Earl of Kingston* [*I*.]], d. 19 *Sept*. 1868 ; *and had issue* 1*f to* 8*f*. [Nos. 129238 to 129247.

The Plantagenet Roll

1*f.* **Henry Edward King**, *late* Speaker of the Legislative Assembly, Queensland (*Raymond Terrace, S. Brisbane, Queensland*), *b.* 9 June 1832; *m.* 1 June 1858, Harriette, da. of J. A. Armstrong; and has issue 1*g* to 8*g*.
    1*g.* Harry Edward Wingfield King, *b.* 4 Aug. 1869.
    2*g.* John Robert Fitzgerald King, *b.* 27 Jan. 1871.
    3*g.* Wyndham Grey Fitzgerald King, *b.* 23 Sept. 1872.
    4*g.* Gerald Coote King, *b.* 9 May 1874.
    5*g.* Maurice James King, *b.* 31 Jan. 1879.
    6*g.* Alice Caroline King, *m.* 1886, Edward Hubert Waring (*Macknade Mill, Herbert River, N. Queensland*); and has issue 1*h* to 5*h*.
        1*h.* John King Waring, *b.* 1888.
        2*h.* Hubert Parker Waring, *b.* 1889.
        3*h.* Frank Jocelyn Waring, *b.* 1893.
        4*h.* Lavinia Katherine Waring, *b.* 1891.
        5*h.* Alicia Armstrong Waring, *b.* 1898.

    7*g.* Katherine Anne King, *m.* 1885, William Howe.
    8*g.* Ethel Coote King.

2*f.* **John Robert King**, *Col. R.A.*, *b.* 13 Nov. 1837; d. (–); *m.* 26 Sept. 1872, Kate Elizabeth, da. of Lieut.-Gen. John Henry Francklyn, R.A., C.B.; and had issue 1*g* to 3*g*.
    1*g.* Robert Alen King, *b.* 1874.
    2*g.* Robert Guy Cecil King, *b.* 1877.
    3*g.* [da.] King, *b.* 1880.

3*f.* **Mary Anne Alicia King**, *m.* 20 July 1859, the Rev. Matthew Kerr, a Presbyterian Minister; and has issue 1*g* to 3*g*.
    1*g.* John Robert King Kerr, *b.* 30 July 1861.
    2*g.* Alicia Coote Kerr.
    3*g.* Mary King Kerr.

4*f.* **Caroline King**.
5*f.* **Anne Katherine King**.
6*f.* **Marian Alice King**, *m.* 1st, 1870, Charles James Buckland, d. (–); 2ndly, James Green Davis.
7*f.* **Isabella King**, *m.* 12 Nov. 1870, William Macdonald Browne; and has issue 1*g* to 2*g*.
    1*g.* William Coote Browne, *b.* 4 Feb. 1874.
    2*g.* Jessie Alicia Browne.

8*f.* **Louisa Augusta King**.

2*d.* **Rev. Charles Philips Coote**, *Rector of Doon, Limerick*, d. 1838; *m. Anne*, da. of Charles Atkinson of Rehins, co. Mayo; and had issue (with 2 elder sons known to have d.s.p.) 1*e* to 6*e*.
    1*e.* Chidley Oliver Coote.
    2*e.* William Philip Oliver Coote.
    3*e. Mary Coote*, *m.* 1838, *Thomas Lloyd*; and had issue.
    4*e.* Eliza Coote, *m.* Richard Lloyd.
    5*e.* Ann Coote, *m.* Capt. Stack.
    6*e.* Harriet Lucinda Coote, *m.* John Tennant.

3*d.* **Elizabeth Coote**, *m.* Major Caleb Barnes.

2*c.* **Elizabeth Coote**, m. *James King of Gola*.

2*a.* **Cecilia Coote**.
3*a.* **Elizabeth Coote**.   [Nos. 129248 to 129281.

# of The Blood Royal

324. Descendants of Lady CATHERINE BRABAZON (Table XXVIII.), *d.* (-) ; *m.* ALONZO VERE ; and had issue (with 2 sons, Thomas and William, who *d.* unm.[1]) 1*a*.

1*a*. Mary Vere, m. (—) Usher.

325. Descendants of the Hon. RICHARD LENNARD, *afterwards* (1644) Barrett, of Horsford, co. Norfolk, and Bellhouse, co. Essex (Table XXVIII.), *d.* 1696 ; *m.* ANNE, da. of the Hon. Sir Robert LOFTUS [V. Loftus Coll.] ; and had issue 1*a* to 2*a*.

1*a. Dacre Barrett-Lennard of Bellhouse, co. Essex, High Sheriff for the co.* 1706, d. 1723 ; m. 1*st, Lady Jane, da. of Arthur (Chichester), 2nd Earl of Donegal* [*I.*]; 2*ndly, Elizabeth, da. and co-h. of Thomas Moore of co. Monaghan ; 3rdly, Sarah, widow of Richard Saltonstall of Groves, co. Essex, da. of Sir Capel Luckyn, 2nd Bt.* [*E.* 1629]; *and had issue* 1*b to* 3*b*.
  1*b*.[1] *Richard Barrett-Lennard*, d.v.p. Dec. 1716; m. 15 *July* 1716, *Anne* (*Lennard*), suo jure 16*th Baroness Dacre* [*E.*]*, d.* 26 *June* 1755 ; *and had issue.*
See p. 503, Nos. 128714-129159.

  2*b*.[1] *Dorothy Barrett-Lennard*, m. 1722, *Hugh Smith of Weald Hall, co. Eseex ; and had issue* 1*c to* 2*c*.
  1*c. Dorothy Smith, da. and co-h.,* m. 1746, *the Hon. John Barry* [*E. of Barrymore Coll.*]; *and had issue* 2 *sons who* d.s.p.l.
  2*c. Lucy Smith*, d. 7 Feb. 1759 ; m. 17 *Mar.* 1747, *James Stanley, afterwards Smith-Stanley, Lord Strange* [*son and h.-app. of Edward*, 11*th Earl of Derby* [*E.*]], d.v.p. 1 *June* 1771 ; *and had issue*.
See the Exeter Volume, Table XLIII. and pp. 509-513, Nos. 44310-44711.

  3*b. Catherine Barrett-Lennard,* m. *Sir Philip Hall of Upton, co. Essex, High Sheriff for that co.* 1726 ; *and had issue* (*with* 3 *das.*)[2] 1*c*.
  1*c. Philip Hall.*

2*a. Anne Barrett-Lennard,* d. *Jan.* 1718; m. *Carew Hervey Mildmay of Marks, co. Essex, High Sheriff* 1712, b. 1658 ; d. 1743 ; *and had issue* 1*b to* 2*b*.
  1*b. Carew Hervey Mildmay of Marks, &c.,* M.P., d.s.p.s. 16 *Jan.* 1784.
  2*b. Humphrey Hervey Mildmay,* b. 1692 ; d. 9 *July* 1761 ; m. 20 *Aug.* 1706, *Letitia, da. and h. of Halliday Mildmay of Shawford House, co. Hants,* and *Stoke Newington,* d. *Oct.* 1749 ; *and had issue.*
See the Exeter Volume, Table XXXI. and pp. 413-416, Nos. 34237-34434.
[Nos. 129282 to 130327.

326. Descendants of the Hon. CATHERINE LENNARD (Table XXVIII.), *d.* (-) ; *m.* CHALONER CHUTE of The Vine, co. Hants ; and had issue 1*a* to 3*a*.

1*a. Edward Chute of the Vine,* m. *and had issue which became extinct* 1776.
2*a. Thomas Chute of Pickenham Hall, co. Norfolk, after* 1700, d. (-) ; m. *Elizabeth, da. of* (—) *Rivett ; and had issue which became extinct* 23 *Sept.* 1885.
3*a. Elizabeth Chute,* m. *Sir Charles Cotterell, Bt.*[3] (sic.).

---

[1] Playfair's "Peerage," iv. 207.
[2] Collins, 1779, vi. 388.
[3] Burke's "Commoners," i. 634.

The Plantagenet Roll

327. Descendants, if any surviving, of the Hon. MARGARET LENNARD (Table XXVIII.), m. Sir ANNESLEY WILDEGOSS [son of Sir John Wildegoss of Iridgcourt, co. Sussex], d.v.p.; and had issue 1a.

    1a. *Robert Wildegoss*, a student at Leyden, aged 19 in 1634; only son.[1]

328. Descendants of GEORGE PARKER of Ratton, co. Sussex (Table XXVIII.), bapt. at Willingdon, June 1620; d. 2 July 1673; m. MARY, da. of Sir Richard NEWDIGATE of Arbury, 1st Bt. [E. 1677]; and had issue 1a to 2a.

    1a. *Sir Robert Parker of Ratton*, 1st Bt. [E. 22 May 1674], M.P., b. c. 1655; d. 30 Nov. 1691; m. 5 Feb. 1674, Sarah, da. of George Chute of Brixton Causeway, d. 2 Aug. 1708; and had issue 1b to 2b.
    1b. *Sir George Parker*, 2nd Bt. [E.], M.P., b. 1677; d. 18 June 1726; m. 25 Feb. 1692, Mary, da. of Sir Walter Bagot, 3rd Bt. [E. 1627], d. 14 May 1727; and had issue 1c to 5c.
    1c. *Sir Walter Parker*, 3rd Bt. [E.], b. c. 1700; d. unm. 19 Ap. 1750.
    2c. *Sarah Parker*, m. Thomas Luxford of Laming, co. Sussex.
    3c. *Anne Parker*.
    4c. *Jane Parker*.
    5c. *Philadelphia Parker*, m. Nathaniel Trayton of Lewes, and apparently had issue 1d.
    1d. (—) *Trayton*, m. John Lidgiter; and had issue 1e.
    1e. *Eleanor Lidgiter*, who succeeded to the Parker estates, 1750, as heiress of the Traytons, bur. at Waldron 7 Feb. 1770; m. Thomas Fuller [7th son of John Fuller of Brightling, co. Sussex, J.P.]; and had issue[2] 1f to 2f.
    1f. *John Fuller*, m. Ann, da. of Sir George Elliot.
    2f. *Rose Fuller*, Merchant.
    2b. *Philadelphia Parker*, b. 1704[3]; m. Col. Piper of Essex.[4]

    2a. *Richard Parker of Hedson*, co. Bucks, m. Sarah, da. and co.-h. of Robert Chilcot of Isleworth, co. Midx.; and had issue 1b to 3b.[5]
    1b. *Jeffrey Parker*.
    2b. *Juliana Parker*, m. Cecil Bowyer.
    3b. *Elizabeth Parker*, m. William Bowyer.

329. Descendants of WILLIAM CAMPION of Combwell Priory, co. Kent, and Danny, co. Sussex (Table XXVIII.), d. (—); m. FRANCES, da. of Sir John GLYNDE, Sergeant-at-Law to King Charles II.; and had issue 1a to 2a.

    1a. *Henry Campion of Danny*, co. Sussex, and Combwell Priory, co. Kent, d. (—); m. Barbara, da. and h. of Peter Courthope of Danny aforesaid; and had issue 1b to 2b.
    1b. *William Campion of Danny*, bapt. at Hurstpierspoint 1700; d. 1771; m. Elizabeth, da. of Edward Parteriche of Ely, co. Camb., d. 1768; and had issue 1c to 3c.

---

[1] Berry's "Sussex Pedigrees," p. 10.
[2] Berry's "Sussex Genealogies," p. 279.
[3] Ibid., p. 228.
[4] Burke's "Extinct Baronetcies," p. 401.
[5] Ibid.

# of The Blood Royal

1c. *Henry Courthope Campion of Danny*, b. 1734; d. *July* 1811; m. *Henrietta*, da. of Sir John Heathcote, 2nd Bt. [G.B. 1733], M.P., d. 6 Feb. 1771; *and had issue* 1d.

1d. *William John Campion of Danny, High Sheriff co. Sussex* 1820, b. 19 *July* 1770; d. 20 *Jan.* 1855; m. 10 Jan. 1797, *Jane, da. of Francis Motley Austen of Kippington, co. Kent*, d. 1857; *and had issue* 1e *to* 3e.

1e. *William John Campion of Danny, J.P., D.L.*, b. 16 Nov. 1804; d. 27 *June* 1869; m. 17 *Jan.* 1829, *Harriet, da. of Thomas Read Kemp of Kemptown, Brighton*, d. 3 *Jan.* 1900; *and had issue* 1f *to* 5f.

1f. William Henry Campion of Danny, C.B., J.P., Hon. Col., *late* Lieut.-Col. Comdg. 2nd Vol. Batt. Royal Sussex Regt., *formerly* Capt. 72nd and 53rd Regts. (*Danny, Hurstpierspoint, Sussex*), b. 1 Ap. 1836; m. 2 Sept. 1869, the Hon. Gertrude [descended from George, Duke of Clarence, K.G. (see Clarence Volume, p. 401)], da. of Henry Bouverie William (Brand), 1st Viscount Hampden [U.K.]; and has issue (with a son, Charles, killed in action in South Africa 29 May 1901, and a da. *d.* young) 1g to 6g.

1g. William Robert Campion, b. 3 July 1870; *m.* 5 July 1894, Katherine Mary [descended from the Lady Anne, sister of Edward IV. (see Exeter Volume, p. 317)], da. of Rev. the Hon. William Byron; and has issue 1h to 4h.

1h. William Simon Campion, b. 1895.
2h. [son] Campion.
3h. Dorothy Campion.
4h. [da.] Campion.

2g. Frederick Henry Campion, b. 8 Sept. 1872.
3g. Edward Campion, Lieut. Seaforth Highlanders, b. 17 Dec. 1873.
4g. Mary Gertrude Campion, *unm.*
5g. Alice Campion, *m.* 8 Dec. 1908, Charles Augustus Phillimore, M.A.; and has issue.

See p. 453, No. 95083.

6g. Joan Campion, *unm.*

2f. Charles Walter Campion, B.A. (Oxon.), Bar.-at-Law of Lincoln's Inn, and Examiner of Standing Orders, House of Commons (52 *Lennox Gardens, S.W.*), b. 10 Nov. 1839; *m.* 27 May 1879, Charlotte Susan [descended from George, Duke of Clarence, K.G. (see Clarence Volume, p. 128)], da. of Hugh Horatio Seymour.

3f. Caroline Florence Campion (16 *Prince's Gardens, S.W.*), m. 3 Jan. 1856, John George (Dodson), 1st Baron Monk-Bretton [U.K. 4 Nov. 1884], P.C., Chancellor of the Duchy of Lancaster 1882–1884, Pres. of the Local Govt. Board 1880–1882, &c., b. 18 Oct. 1825; d. 25 May 1897; and had issue 1g to 3g.

1g. John William (Dodson), 2nd Baron Monk-Bretton [U.K.], C.B., J.P., D.L., Capt. Sussex Yeo., Private Sec. to Sec. of State for Colonies (Rt. Hon. Joseph Chamberlain, M.P.) 1900–1903, &c. (*Conyboro, Lewes; Travellers'; Brooks'*), b. 22 Sept. 1869.

2g. Hon. Ethel Millicent Dodson.
3g. Hon. Mildred Augusta Dodson.

4f. Frances Campion, *m.* 17 June 1857, John George Blencowe of Bineham, co. Sussex, M.P., J.P., D.L., b. 28 Feb. 1817; d. 28 Ap. 1900; and has issue 1g to 8g.

1g. Robert Campion Blencowe of Bineham, &c., J.P. (*Bineham, Chailey, near Lewes; Skippetts House, Basingstoke*), b. 16 May 1858; m. 28 Oct. 1886, Augusta Frederica, da. of Frederick Boughton Newton Dickenson of Syston Court, Bath, d.s.p. 13 Ap. 1905.

2g. John Ingham Blencowe, b. 14 Dec. 1860; *m.* 21 Feb. 1889, Mabel, da. of James Ingram of Ades, Chailey, co. Sussex; and has issue 1h.

1h. Margaret Blencowe.

3g. *William Poole Blencowe*, b. 6 Feb. 1869; d. 14 *Dec.* 1900; m. 21 *June* 1900, *Muriel, da. of Henry Courage of Gravenhurst, Bolney, Sussex; and had issue* 1h.

1h. Deborah Blencowe. [Nos. 130328 to 130349.

The Plantagenet Roll

4g. Florence Charlotte Blencowe, m. 25 Feb. 1886, Major John William Ainslie Drummond, formerly Scots Guards; and has issue (5 children).

5g. Harriet Blencowe, m. 19 Oct. 1892, Col. Richard Woodford Deane, Lancashire Fusiliers; and has issue 2 sons and 2 das.

6g. Frances Isabel Blencowe, unm.

7g. Mary Blencowe, m. 29 Ap. 1905, W. H. Edwards; and has issue (1 child).

8g. Elizabeth Penelope Blencowe, m. 19 Jan. 1898, the Rev. Arthur Hamilton Boyd, Rector of Slaugham [5th son of Sir John Boyd of Maxpoffle, Lord Provost of Edinburgh] (*Slaugham Rectory, Sussex*); and has issue 1h to 2h.

1h. William Arthur Hamilton Boyd, b. 29 Jan. 1901.

2h. James Hamilton Boyd, b. 18 Jan. 1903.

5f. *Mary Georgina Campion*, d. 26 Nov. 1874; m. 3 Oct. 1861, *the Rev. Ferdinand Ernest Tower* [cadet of Tower of Huntsmoor Park, co. Bucks], b. 4 Oct. 1820; d. 21 Jan. 1885; and had issue (with a son d. unm.) 1g to 7g.

1g. Rev. Henry Tower, M.V.O., M.A. (Oxon.), Rector of Holy Trinity, Windsor, Acting Chaplain to the Forces (*Holy Trinity Rectory, Windsor*), b. 15 July 1862; m. 4 June 1901, Kate Theresa, widow of S. F. Gedge, da. of the Right Hon. H. Escombe, Prime Minister of Natal; and has issue 1h to 2h.

1h. Ernest Conyers Tower, b. 28 Feb. 1904.

2h. Cicely Tower, b. 9 July 1902.

2g. Rev. Frederick Tower, M.A. (Oxon.), Vicar of Badminton (*Badminton Vicarage, Glos.*), b. 10 Dec. 1863; m. 4 Dec. 1894, Katrine Amy, da. of the Hon. G. C. Hawker of the Briars, Adelaide, S.A.

3g. William Tower, b. 27 Sept. 1866.

4g. David Eric Tower, b. 1 Mar. 1870.

5g. Walter Ernest Tower (*Old Place, Lindfield, Hayward's Heath, Sussex*), b. 9 Mar. 1873; m. 12 July 1902, Marion Lindsay, da. of Æneas Ranald Macdonell, Chief of Glengarry; and has issue 1h to 3h.

1h. Anthony Paschal Tower, b. 13 Ap. 1903.

2h. Barbara Tower, b. 28 Sept. 1905.

3h. Cecilia Tower, b. 15 May 1909.

6g. Agatha Tower, unm.

7g. Mary Tower, unm.

2e. *Rev. Charles Heathcote Campion*, B.A. (Oxon.), Rector of Westmeston, co. Sussex, and Prebendary of Chichester Cathedral, b. 14 Feb. 1814; d. 8 Oct. 1888; m. 16 May 1842, Cecil Lydia, da. of James Henry Sclater of Newick Park, co. Sussex, d. 26 Dec. 1872; and had issue (with 2 sons d.s.p.) 1f to 4f.

1f. Heathcote Francis George Campion, Lieut.-Col. *late* Connaught Rangers (*Beacon Nursery, Ditchling, Hassock, Sussex*), b. 12 Sept. 1853; unm.

2f. Charles Cecil Campion (*Castle Gate, Lodge, Lewis*), b. 20 Sept. 1848; unm.

3f. Jane Cecil Campion, m. 28 Sept. 1892, the Rev. Walter Lock, D.D., Warden of Keble College (*Keble College, Oxford*); and has issue 1g to 5g.

1g. Walter Heathcote Lock, b. 5 Dec. 1900.

2g. Cecil May Lock.

3g. Elizabeth Jessie Lock.

4g. Lucy Austen Lock.

5g. Mildred Susan Lock.

4f. Selina Letitia Campion, unm.

3e. *Frances Henrietta Campion*, b. 2 Mar. 1809; d. *at San Remo*, 15 Feb. 1878; m. 1 Nov. 1843, *the Rev. Augustus Packe*, Rector of Walton, co. Leic., d. Feb. 1861; and had issue 1f.

1f. Georgiana Frances Packe (*Asherne, Dartmouth, Devonshire*), unm.

2c. *William Campion of Lewes*, co. Sussex, d. there 1818; m. 2ndly, 5 Sept. 1774, Priscilla, da. of John Page of Oporto; and had issue 1d to 2d.

[Nos. 130350 to 130378.

# of The Blood Royal

1*d*. Henrietta Campion, da. and event. co-h., b. at Oporto 16 July 1778; d. 13 Mar. 1813; m. 20 Jan. 1820, the Rev. P. G. Crofts, Rector of St. John's, Lewes.

2*d*. Amelia Campion, da. and event. co.-h., b. 26 Feb. 1787; d. 10 July 1849; m. 20 Jan. 1808, George Courthope of Bedford Square, London, and Whiligh, co. Sussex (see p. 517), b. Sept. 1767; d. 13 Jan. 1835; and had issue (with 2 das. d. unm.) 1e to 4e.

1*e*. George Campion Courthope of Whiligh, co. Sussex, J.P., D.L., High Sheriff for that co. 1850, b. 22 Feb. 1811; d. 7 Sept. 1895; m. 15 Jan. 1841, Anna, da. of John Deacon of Mabledon, Tonbridge, d. 12 Dec. 1897; and had issue (with a son and 2 das. d. unm.) 1f to 5f.

1*f*. George John Courthope of Whiligh, co. Sussex, and Sprivers, co. Kent, M.A. (Oxon.), J.P., D.L., Bar.-at-Law, &c. (Whiligh, Sussex; St. Stephens), b. 3 Nov. 1848; m. 21 Sept. 1876, Elinor Sarah, da. of Lieut.-Col. Edward Loyd of Lillesden Hawkhurst, co. Kent, J.P., D.L., d. 25 Dec. 1895; and has issue (with 2 sons and a da. d. young) 1g to 5g.

1*g*. George Loyd Courthope, M.P. Rye Div. of Sussex 1906, J.P., Bar.-at-Law, Capt. 5th Batt. (Cinque Ports) Royal Sussex Regt. (Fairview, Hawkhurst, Kent; Carlton; Constitutional, &c.), b. 12 June 1877; m. 14 June 1899, Hilda Gertrude, da. of Major-Gen. Henry Pelham Close, B.S.C.; and has issue 1h to 2h.

1*h*. Hilda Beryl Courthope, b. 2 Nov. 1900.

2*h*. Elinor Daphne Courthope, b. 11 Oct. 1902.

2*g*. John Edward Courthope, b. 28 Jan. 1882.

3*g*. Robert Courthope, b. 15 Mar. 1891.

4*g*. Barbara Frances Courthope.

5*g*. Elinor Joan Courthope.

2*f*. William Francis Courthope, b. 2 June 1850.

3*f*. Alexander Courthope, b. 20 Jan. 1852.

4*f*. Emily Mary Courthope.

5*f*. Frances Albinia Courthope.

2*e*. Rev. William Courthope, Vicar of South Malling, Sussex, b. Jan. 1816; d. 7 Mar 1849; m. 29 Sept. 1841, Caroline Elizabeth, da. of John Ryle of Henbury Hall, co. Chester, M.P., d. 6 June 1857; and had issue 1f to 3f.

1*f*. William John Courthope, C.B., M.A. (Oxon.), Hon. D. Lit. (Durham), Hon. LL.D. (Edin.), Hon. Fellow of New College, Oxon., Professor of Poetry, Oxford, 1895-1900, and 1st Civil Service Commissioner 1892-1907, is a Fellow of British Academy of Letters, Editor of Pope's Works and Author of "A History of English Poetry," "The Paradise of Birds," &c. (The Lodge, Wadhurst; Athenæum), b. 17 July 1842; m. 2 Nov. 1870, Mary, da. of John Scott, Inspector-Gen. of Hospitals, Bombay; and has issue 1g to 6g.

1*g*. William George Courthope, b. 28 Nov. 1871.

2*g*. John Courthope, b. 15 Mar. 1876.

3*g*. Edward Arthur Courthope, b. 28 Nov. 1879.

4*g*. Richard Alan Courthope, b. 8 Oct. 1882.

5*g*. Katherine Courthope, m. 1897, the Rev. Charles Fiennes Cholmondeley, Rector of Little Sampford [descended from King Henry VII. (see Tudor Roll, p. 154)] (Little Sampford Rectory, Essex).

6*g*. Emily Mary Dorothea Courthope, unm.

2*f*. Frederic George Courthope, J.P. (Southover, Lewes), b. 26 Nov. 1845; m. 14 Sept. 1869, Lucy, da. of William Smith Uppleby of Bonby, co. Linc.; and has issue (with 2 elder sons d. young) 1g to 4g.

1*g*. Ronald Frederic Courthope, b. 18 Jan. 1881.

2*g*. Wilfred Herbert Frederic Courthope, b. 28 Oct. 1883.

3*g*. Margaret Esther Lucy Courthope.

4*g*. Caroline Hilda Courthope, m. 19 Nov. 1903, John Grahame Slee (Oceanside, S. California). [Nos. 130379 to 130402.

The Plantagenet Roll

3*f*. Caroline Susan Courthope, d. 22 Mar. 1896; m. 15 Sept. 1864, Vice-Adm. George Stanley Bosanquet, R.N. (see below) (*Bitchet Wood, Sevenoaks*); *and had issue* 1*g to* 2*g*.

1*g*. William Cecil Bosanquet, M.A., M.D., F.R.C.P., *late* Fellow of New College, Oxford, *b*. 12 Oct. 1866.

2*g*. Ethel Bosanquet, *m*. 23 June 1896, the Rev. Horace Ricardo Wilkinson, B.A., Vicar of Stoke by Nayland [son of Horace Wilkinson of Frankfield, Seal, Chart] (*Stoke-by-Nayland Vicarage, Colchester*), *d*. 1908; and has issue 1*h* to 3*h*.

1*h*. Horace Norman Stanley Wilkinson.
2*h*. Kathleen Courthope Wilkinson.
3*h*. Naomi Wilkinson.

3*e*. Emily Courthope, d. 1 Jan. 1869; m. 4 Feb. 1830, *Samuel Richard Bosanquet of Dingestow Court, co. Monmouth*, J.P., D.L., *Chairman Quarter Sessions*, b. 1 Ap. 1800; d. 27 Dec. 1882; *and had issue* (*with a son and da*. d.s.p.) 1*f to* 10*f*.

1*f*. Samuel Courthope Bosanquet of Dingestow, M.A. (Oxon.), J.P., D.L., Chairman of Quarter Sessions and High Sheriff (1898) co. Monmouth (*Dingestow Court, co. Monmouth*), *b*. 2 Oct. 1832; *m*. 7 Aug. 1862, Mary [descended from George, Duke of Clarence, K.G. (see Clarence Volume, p. 111)], da. of John Arkwright of Hampton Court, co. Hereford; and has issue 1*g* to 3*g*.

1*g*. Samuel Ronald Courthope Bosanquet, LL.B. (Camb.), J.P., co. Monmouth, *b*. 6 Sept. 1868.

2*g*. Vivian Henry Courthope Bosanquet, H.B.M.'s Vice-Consul at Moscow, *b*. 13 Ap. 1872.

3*g*. Maud Bosanquet.

2*f*. Rev. *Claude Bosanquet*, M.A. (*Oxon*.), *Vicar of Christchurch, Folkestone*, *b*. 8 Nov. 1833; d. 3 June 1897; m. 22 May 1861, his cousin-german Amelia Eleanor, da. of Vice-Adm. Charles John Bosanquet, R.N.; *and had issue* (*with a son d. young*) 1*g to* 4*g*.

1*g*. Rev. Claude Charles Courthope Bosanquet, M.A. (Oxon.), Vicar of Linkinhorne (*Linkinhorne Vicarage, Callington, Cornwall*), *b*. 19 Dec. 1862; *m*. 9 Feb 1892, Millicent Percy, da. of Gen. Percy Smith, R.E.; and has issue 1*h* to 4*h*.

1*h*. Armytage Percy Bosanquet, *b*. 1893.
2*h*. Claude Henry Bosanquet, *b*. 1896.
3*h*. Lancelot Stephen Bosanquet, *b*. 1903.
4*h*. Hilda Mary Bosanquet.

2*g*. Charles Richard Bosanquet, *b*. 21 Ap. 1865.

3*g*. Rev. Reginald Albert Bosanquet, M.A. (Oxon.), Chaplain in the Scilly Isles (*The Chaplaincy, Scilly Isles*), *b*. 14 June 1867.

4*g*. Eustace Fulcrand Bosanquet, J.P. co. Wilts, *b*. 20 Ap. 1871; *m*. 6 June 1894, Harriet Maria, da. of Frederic W. Moore of Buenos Ayres, *d*. 1901; and has issue 1*h* to 2*h*.

1*h*. Nancy Bosanquet.
2*h*. Inez Bosanquet.

3*f*. George Stanley Bosanquet, Rear-Adm. R.N. (*Bitchet Woods, Sevenoaks*), *b*. 18 Ap. 1835; *m*. 15 Sept. 1864, Caroline Susan, da. of the Rev. William Courthope, *d*. 22 Mar. 1896; and had issue.

See above, Nos. 130403–130407.

4*f*. Sir Frederick Albert Bosanquet, M.A., K.C., J.P., Common Serjeant for the City of London since 1900, *formerly* Recorder of Wolverhampton 1891 and 1900, and of Worcester 1879–1891, &c. (12 *Grenville Place, S.W.; Cobbe Place, Lewes*), *b*. 8 Feb. 1837; *m*. 1st, 22 Aug. 1871, Albinia Mary, da. of John Curtis Hayward of Quedgeley House, co. Glouc., *d*. (–); 2ndly, 12 Aug. 1885, Philippa Frances, da. of William Bence-Jones of Lisselan, co. Cork; and has issue 1*g* to 6*g*.

1*g*. Rev. Bernard Hugh Bosanquet, M.A. (Camb.), Vicar of Thames Ditton (*Thames Ditton Vicarage*), *b*. 21 Nov. 1872.

2*g*. Geoffrey Courthope Bosanquet, *b*. 26 Dec. 1876.   [Nos. 130403 to 130430.

# of The Blood Royal

3g. William Sydney Bence Bosanquet, b. 9 May 1893.
4g.[1] Lilian Bosanquet.
5g.[1] Nora Margaret Bosanquet.
6g.[2] Edith Madeline Bosanquet.

5f. *Walter Henry Bosanquet of Hope Park, Bromley*, b. 10 Jan. 1839; d. 9 Oct. 1904; m. 5 Ap. 1866, Penelope Eliza, da. of the Rev. Stewart Forster of Southend, Lewisham; and had issue 1g to 3g.

1g. Henry Stewart Bosanquet, b. 29 Jan. 1867.
2g. Evelyn Mabel Bosanquet, m. 18 Oct. 1900, the Rev. William Shuckford Flynn, A.K.C. London Univ. (*The Rosary, Heath Road, Hayward's Heath*); and has issue 1h.

1h. John Henry Flynn, b. 13 Ap. 1903.

3g. Florence Mary Bosanquet, m. 23 July 1902, the Rev. Bertie Phelps, M.A. (Oxon.), Vicar of Smalley (*Smalley Vicarage, Derby*) [son of Major-Gen. Robert Hoskyns Phelps, descended from George, Duke of Clarence, K.G. (see Clarence Volume, p. 112)] (*Church View, Heanor, Derby*); and has issue 1h to 2h.

1h. Beryl Penelope Phelps } (twins), b. 31 Aug. 1903.
2h. Edith Mary Phelps

6f. *Edmund Fletcher Bosanquet* (*The Court, Wotton-under-Edge*), b. 2 Sept. 1840; m. 20 Jan. 1876, Louisa, da. of Major Henry Christopher Marriott of Avonbank, co. Worc.; and has issue (with a son and da. d. unm.) 1g to 3g.

1g. Edmund Marriott Bosanquet, Lieut. R.A., b. 24 Mar. 1878.
2g. Ernest Courthope Bosanquet, Lieut. R.N., b. 11 June 1879.
3g. Catherine Marriott Bosanquet, m. 28 Jan. 1904, Francis Anthony Cedric Wright [son of Philip Wright of Mellington, co. Montgomery] (*West Summerland, British Columbia*); and has issue 1h to 3h.

1h. Noel Nithsdale Wright, b. 23 Dec. 1904.
2h. Rupert Anthony Wright, b. 31 Aug. 1906.
3h. Basil Owen Wright, b. 10 July 1909.

7f. William David Bosanquet, b. 4 June 1849; m. 7 Aug. 1872, Elinor, da. of George Hamilton Verity; and has issue 1g.

1g. Mabel Bosanquet, m. Edward Alexander, Ceylon C.S.

8f. Richard Arthur Bosanquet (*Bank House, Windsor*), b. 25 May 1852; m. 15 Nov. 1888, Ruth Rivers, da. of Sir Augustus Rivers Thompson, Lieut.-Gov. of Bengal 1862-1867; and has issue 1g to 3g.

1g. Arthur Rivers Bosanquet, b. 12 July 1890.
2g. Raymond Francis Bosanquet, b. 3 Sept. 1895.
3g. Cicely Ruth Bosanquet.

9f. *Emily Letitia Bosanquet*, d. 19 May 1898; m. 3 Oct. 1861, the Rev. John Lloyd, M.A., Rector of Llanvapley, co. Mon.; and had issue 1g to 2g.

1g. Emily Mary Edith Lloyd, m. 26 Aug. 1891, Charles John Bosanquet, Electrical Engineer; and has issue 1h to 2h.

1h. Sydney Courthope Bosanquet, b. 15 July 1894.
2h. Leslie Frederick Ives Bosanquet, b. 17 June 1900.

2g. Violet Amy Lloyd.

10f. Fanny Elizabeth Bosanquet, *unm.*

4e. Frances Courthope, d. Jan. 1841; m. the Rev. Henry Watkins.

3c. Frances Barbara Campion, d. (-); m. 1766, George Courthope of Bedford Square, London, and Whiligh, co. Sussex, d. 1828; and had issue 1d to 2d.

1d. *George Courthope of Bedford Square, London, and Whiligh, co. Sussex*, b. Sept. 1767; d. 13 Jan. 1835; m. 20 Jan. 1808, Amelia, da. of William Campion of Lewes, d. 10 July 1849; *and had issue.*

See p. 515, Nos. 130379–130458. [Nos. 130431 to 130538.

The Plantagenet Roll

2*d*. Rev. *William Henry Courthope of St. John's College, Cambridge, Vicar of Whiligh*, m. Mary, da. and co-h. *of William Peckham of Arches, co. Sussex*.[1]

2*b*. *Catherine Courthope*, d. (-) ; m. 11 Nov. 1735, *George Courthope of Whiligh, co. Sussex*, d. Ap. 1793 ; *and had (with other) issue* 1*c*.

1*c*. *George Courthope of Whiligh, and Bedford Square, London*, b. 22 Nov. 1737 ; d. 1828 ; m. 1766, *Frances Barbara*, da. *of William Campion of Danny Place* ; *and had issue*.

2*a*. *Francis Campion*, d. (-) ; m. (—) *Clutterbuck of Southampton*.

330. Descendants of PHILADELPHIA PARKER (Table XXVIII.), *d*. (-) ; *m*. at Willingdon 1 Feb. 1649, SAMUEL BOYS of Hawkhurst, co. Kent, *b*. 1617 ; *d*. 3 June 1688 ; and had issue [2] 1*a* to 7*a*.

1*a*. *William Boys of Hawkhurst*, d. 1698 ; m. *Elizabeth*, da. *of Sir Anthony Shirley*, 1st Bt. [E. 1665] ; *and had issue (with a son and* 6 *das. who all apparently* d.s.p.) 1*b to* 3*b*.

1*b*. *Samuel Boys of Hawkhurst*, d. 1753 ; m. *Jane*, da. *of Sir Richard Newdigate*, 2*nd Bt*. [E. 1677], M.P. ; *and had issue (with* 4 *sons and* 3 *das. who all apparently* d.s.p.) 1*c*.

1*c*. *Samuel Boys of Hawkhurst*, d. 16 *May* 1772 ; m. *Elizabeth*, da. *and co-h. of Thomas Hicks of Mountfield, co. Sussex* ; *and had issue (with* 2 *das*. d. unm.) 1*d* to 3*d*.

1*d*. *Samuel Boys of Hawkhurst, High Sheriff co. Kent* 1782, d. *at Hawkhurst* 1 *May* 1795 ; m. *Elizabeth*, da. *of Henry Gatland of Cuckfield, co. Sussex* ; *and had issue* 1*e*.

1*e*. *Elizabeth Boys*, da. *and h.*, b. 1 Feb. 1762 ; d. (-) ; m. 16 *Jan*. 1786, *Charles Lamb of Higham, co. Sussex* ; *and had issue* 1*f*.

1*f*. *Elizabeth Dorothy Lamb*, da. *and h.*, d. (-) ; m. *at Salehurst, co. Sussex*, 13 Dec. 1809, *the Rev. Thomas Ferris of Hawkhurst, Thackham, and Clothall's, Grinstead, co. Sussex* [*eldest son of the Very Rev. Thomas Ferris, Dean of Battle*] ; *and had issue (with* 3 *sons and* 2 *das. who* d.s.p.) 1*g* to 4*g*.

1*g*. *Rev. Thomas Boys Ferris, Rector of Guiseley*, b. 1 *Nov*. 1810 ; d. 2 *Sept*. 1878 ; m. 13 *Aug*. 1842, *Hannah*, da. *of William Barraclough of Leeds, Manufacturer*, d. 22 (?) *Mar*. 1902 ; *and had issue (with* 2 *sons* d. unm.) 1*h* to 4*h*.

1*h*. Rev. Thomas Boys Barraclough Ferris, M.A., *and sometime* (1868–1870) *Fellow of Durham, Rector of Gonalston and Canon of Southwell* (*Gonalston Rectory, Notts*), b. 1 Ap. 1845 ; *m*. 28 Dec. 1870, Maria Teresa, da. of William Edward Swaine of York, M.D. ; and has issue (with 2 sons, Arthur Henry and Wilfred, and a da., Mabel Teresa, all *d*. unm.) 1*i* to 10*i*.

1*i*. Rev. Thomas Edward Swaine Ferris, M.A., Curate of Dunham, Notts, b. 2 Oct. 1871.

2*i*. William Arthur Boys Ferris, Manager and Traveller (*Sherwood, Nottingham*), b. 23 Oct. 1872 ; m. 18 May 1901, Nellie, da. of William Hutchinson Farmer of Nottingham, Lace Manufacturer ; and has issue 1*j* to 2*j*.

1*j*. Joan Farmer Ferris, b. 22 Ap. 1902.

2*j*. Mary Boys Ferris, b. 24 July 1906.

3*i*. Godfrey Francis Ferris, Assist. Sec. to Jesuit Fathers' Apostolic Mission House, Washington, U.S.A., b. 13 Dec. 1873.

4*i*. Cecil Ernest Ferris, Assist. Master Southport High School (*Southport, Queensland*), b. 9 Mar. 1877.   [Nos. 130539 to 130545.

---

[1] Hasted's " Kent," ii. 375.

[2] Dallaway's " Sussex," II. ii. 245 ; also Berry's " Sussex Genealogies," 1830, p. 318.

# of The Blood Royal

5*i*. Rev. Hermann Boys Ferris, L.Th. Durham Univ., Curate of Holy Trinity, Stockton (1 *Laurence Street, Stockton-on-Tees*), *b.* 6 May 1881.

6*i*. Andrew Octavius Ferris, settled in Canada, *b.* 30 Nov. 1883.

7*i*. Nowell Swaine Ferris, Organist and Choir Master, St. Matthew's, Winnipeg, *b.* 21 Dec. 1884.

8*i*. Ernest Hugh Ferris, Lace Buyer, St. Gall, *b.* 22 Sept. 1886.

9*i*. Dora Christiana Ferris, *m.* 2 July 1907, Cyril Horner Bearder [son of William Corthan Bearder, Lace Manufacturer] (*Nottingham*); and has issue 1*j*.

1*j*. Teresa Joyce Ferris Bearder, *b.* 23 Sept. 1908.

10*i*. Ernestine Emily Ferris, *b.* 12 Mar. 1888.

2*h*. William Godfrey Ferris (*Roseneath, Terrace Road, Dulwich Hill, N.S.W.*), *b.* 16 July 1853; *m.* Emily Eleanor, da. of Thomas Chilton, Station Manager, N.S.W.; and has issue (see Appendix).

3*h*. Elizabeth Martha Ferris, *b.* 15 Oct. 1846; *m.* 4 Nov. 1876, the Rev. Oscar Dan Watkins, M.A. (Oxon.), Vicar of Holywell, *formerly* Archdeacon of Lucknow (*Holywell Vicarage, Oxford*); and has issue (with 4 other sons, Basil Henry, Clement Reginald, Cuthbert Thomas, and Noel Christopher, who all *d.* young) 1*i* to 3*i*.

1*i*. Oscar Ferris Watkins, M.A. (Oxon.), Assist. District Commr. at Mombasa, British East Africa, *b.* 23 Dec. 1877.

2*i*. Laurence Theodore Watkins, B.A. (Camb.), Assist. Master, King William's College, Isle of Man, *b.* 6 July 1887.

3*i*. Dorothy Anne Watkins, *unm*.

4*h*. Cordelia Frances Ferris, *m.* 12 Sept. 1883, Herbert Glanville South (*62 Leyham Vale, Streatham*); and has issue 1*i* to 2*i*.

1*i*. Algernon Cedric South, *b.* 18 Oct. 1885.

2*i*. Bertha Winifred South, *b.* 29 Sept. 1887.

2*g*. *William Ferris*, Indigo Merchant, b. 1 *Aug.* 1814; d. 23 *May* 1864; m. *at Calcutta* 10 *Jan.* 1844, *Georgina, da. of S. Robinson of Islington Square, London,* d. 17 *Dec.* 1873; *and had issue (with 2 sons and 2 das. d. unm.)* 1*h to* 3*h*.

1*h*. Georgina Emily Ferris, *m.* 31 Jan. 1901, Cyril Ward Perkins [son of the Rev. B. R. Perkins, B.C.L. (Oxon.), Vicar of Wotton-under-Edge] (*The Brands, Wotton-under-Edge, Glos*); *s.p.*

2*h*. Gertrude Cecilia Ferris, *m.* 30 Sept. 1879, the Rev. William Clarke Leeper, M.A. (T.C.D.), Rector of Mellis [son of the Rev. William Leeper, Rector of All Saints, Lynn] (*Mellis Rectory, Eye, Suffolk*); and has issue 1*i* to 7*i*.

1*i*. Leonard Leeper, B.E. (Royal Univ. Irel.), A.M.I.C.E., Borough Surveyor's Office, Great Yarmouth, *b.* 10 Dec. 1880.

2*i*. Rev. Clement Leeper, B.A., Curate of Retford, Notts, *b.* 9 Feb. 1882.

3*i*. Alban Leeper, Prudential Assurance Co., High Holborn, *b.* 25 Jan. 1883.

4*i*. Bernard Leeper, National Provincial Bank, Ipswich, *b.* 29 May 1887.

5*i*. Bertha Mary Leeper, *unm*.

6*i*. Dorothy Leeper, *unm*.

7*i*. Mildred Leeper, *unm*.

3*h*. Beatrice Alice Ferris, d. 27 *May* 1887; m. 6 *Ap.* 1880, *Edward Henry Toulmin* [son of *Samuel Toulmin, Bar.-at-Law*], d. 22 *Mar.* 1909; *and had issue* 1*i* to 4*i*.

1*i*. Harold Edward Toulmin, } settled in New Zealand.
2*i*. Vincent Ferris Toulmin, }

3*i*. Dora Agnes Toulmin.

4*i*. Edith Alice Toulmin.

3*g*. *Edward Fiott Ferris, Commandant Forces of Nawab of Rampur,* b. 20 *June* 1819; d. *May* 1892; m. *Laura, da. of* (—) *Evans; and had issue* 1*h to* 2*h*.

1*h*. Charles Ferris.

2*h*. *Edward Ferris,* b 28 *Oct.* 18—; d. 23 *Aug.* 1892; m. *Emma S.* (*42 Sussex Road, Norwich*), *da. of* (—) *Camplin; and had issue (a son and 5 das.).*

[Nos. 130546 to 130574.

The Plantagenet Roll

4g. *Godfrey Richard Ferris*, b. 8 *Jan*. 1825 ; d. (-) ; m. *Emily* (7 *Matlock Road, Torquay*), *da. of* (—) *Kenny of Halifax, M.D. ; and had issue* 1h *to* 4h.

1h. Amy Ferris.
2h. Kate Ferris.
3h. Susan Ferris.
4h. Louisa Ferris.

2d. *William Boys*, d. (-) ; m. 1777, *Elizabeth, da. and co-h. of Richard Harcourt of Wigsell, co. Sussex ; and had issue (with a son and da. d. young)* 1e.

1e. *William Hooper Boys*, d. (-) ; m.[1] *Sarah, da. of Sir Barry Collis Meredyth, 7th Bt.* [*I.*] ; *and had issue*[1] 1f *to* 3f.

1f. *William Boys, Consul at Hamburg and* (?) *Hobartown*, m. 1855, *Catherine, da. of Frederic Roper ; and had issue.*

2f. *Corima Boys*, m. 1st, 8 *Oct.* 1851, *Ambrose Crawley, H.E.I.C.S ;* d. 1849 (*sic* 1859) ; 2ndly, 7 *Sept.* 1861, *the Chevalier Vigliani, Prefect of Naples.*

3f. *Lydia Boys*, m. 1st, 8 *Oct.* 1851, *the Chevalier de Letterstedt ;* 2ndly, 18 *Aug.* 1864, *Paul de Juvencel ; and had issue* 1g.

1g. Corima de Letterstedt, *m.* 30 June 1879, Viscount J. de Manmorte.

3d. *Anne Boys, living unm.* 1745.

2b. *Anne Boys*, m. *Benjamin Day of Ticehurst ; living* 1745.

3b. *Elizabeth Boys*, m. 1st, *John Morton ;* 2ndly, *John Sparrow of Beaumaris, co. Anglesey.*

2a. *Grace Boys.*
3a. *Cordelia Boys*, m. *Henry Apsley of Ticehurst.*
4a. *Margaret Boys*, m. *Richard Banks of Storrington.*
5a. *Mary Boys*, m. *William Simons of Marden.*
6a. *Bridget Boys*, m. *John* [*son of Walter*] *Roberts.*
7a. *Philadelphia Boys.* [Nos. 130575 to 130579.

331. Descendants of RACHEL PARKER (Table XXVIII.), *bapt.* at Wellingdon 13 Oct. 1631 ; *d.* 22 Mar. 1650 ; *m.* as 1st wife, 20 Jan. 1645, WILLIAM GEE of Bishop Burton, co. York, *b.* 1625 ; *d.* 30 Aug. 1678 ; and had issue[2] 1a.

1a. *William Gee of Bishop Burton*, b. 1648; bur. 15 *Oct.* 1718; m. 1st, 23 *Feb.* 1664, *Elizabeth, da. and h. of Sir John Hotham, 3rd Bt.* [*E.* 1661], bur. 24 *Mar.* 1684; 2ndly (*settlement dated* 8 *Oct.*), 1685, *Elizabeth, widow of John Elleker of Risby, da. of Charles Cracroft of Louth, co. Lincoln,* bur. 1 *Dec.* 1726; *and had issue (with others known to have* d.s.p.*)* 1b *to* 5b.

1b. *Thomas Gee of Bishop Burton*, bapt. 4 *Nov.* 1673 ; bur. 28 *July* 1750 ; m. 1st, *Elizabeth, da. of* (—), bur. *at Belfreys* 29 *June* 1730 ; *and had issue* 1c *to* 5c.

1c. *William Gee of Bishop Burton, Col. 20th Foot,* d.v.p. (*being killed at Fontenoy*) 30 *Ap.* 1745 ; m. 1st (*settlement dated* 30 *Mar.*), 1725, *Philippa, da. of Sir Charles Hotham, M.P.,* bur. s.p.s. 26 *Sept.* 1728 ; 2ndly (*settlement dated* 2 *May*), 1735, *Elizabeth, da. and event. h. of Roger Talbot of Woodend, living a widow* 1765 ; *and had issue* 1d.

1d. *Roger Gee of Bishop Burton*, d. 9 *Dec.* 1778 ; m. *Caroline* [*descended from the Lady Anne, sister of King Edward IV.* (*see the Essex Volume Supplement,* p. 666)], *da. and co-h. of Sir Warton Pennyman, 5th Bt.* [*E.*] [*who* m. 2ndly, 29 *Nov.* 1779, *Peter Acklam, by whom she also had issue, and*] d. 24 *Mar.* (*Dec.*) 1811 ; *and had issue* 1e *to* 2e.

---

[1] MS. additions in Berry's " Kent Genealogies," p. 453.
[2] Foster's " Yorkshire Pedigrees."

of The Blood Royal

1e. *Sarah Elizabeth Gee, da. and co-h.*, bapt. *at York* 14 *June* 1770; d. 28 *Nov.* 1832; m. 23 *Ap.* 1788, *Henry Boldero Barnard of Cave Castle, co. York*, d. 6 *Feb.* 1815; *and had issue* (*with a 2nd son, Charles Lewyns, Capt. Scots Greys, killed unm. at Waterloo*) 1*f to* 3*f*.

1*f.* Henry Gee Boldero Barnard *of Cave Castle, Capt. Scots Greys.* b. 22 *Feb.* 1789; d.s.p. 23 *Ap.* 1858.

2*f. Rev. Edward William Barnard of Brantingham Thorpe, Vicar of South Cave*, b. 16 *Mar.* 1791; d. 10 *Jan.* 1828; m. 25 *Ap.* 1821, *Philadelphia Frances Esther* [*descended from the Lady Anne, sister of King Edward IV.* (see the Essex Volume Supplement, p. 676)], *da. of the Ven. Frances Wrangham, Archdeacon of the West Riding; and had issue* 1g *to* 3g.

1g. *Charles Edward Gee Barnard of Cave Castle, J.P.*, b. 23 *Mar.* 1822; d. 14 *Aug.* 1894; m. 5 *June* 1862, *Sophia Letitia, da. of the Hon. Andrew Godfrey Stuart* [*E. of Castle Stewart* [*I.*] *Coll.*]; *and had issue* 1h.

1h. Ursula Mary Florence Boldero Barnard of Cave Castle (*Cave Castle, Brough, Yorks*), b. 4 July 1869; *unm.*

2g. Rosamond Barnard.

3g. Caroline Barnard.

3*f. Sarah Elinor Barnard*, b. 11 *Aug.* 1810; d. 7 *Jan.* 1852; m. 10 *Oct.* 1832, *Joseph* [*only surviving son of Samuel Delpratt of Jamaica; and had issue* (2 *sons and* 8 *das.*).

2e. *Caroline Gee, da. and co-h.*, bapt. *at Bishop Burton* 19 *Oct.* 1774; d. 23 *Dec.* 1811; m. *as* 1*st wife, Mar.* 1792, *Lieut.-Col. George Hotham* [*Bt. Coll.*], d. 24 *Dec.* 1823; *and had issue.*

See the Essex Volume Supplement, pp. 666-670, Nos. 57622/591-735.

2c. *Thomas Gee*, bapt. 3 *Oct.* 1700.

3c. *Bridget Gee*, bapt. 27 *Nov.* 1701; d. (–); m. 1*st*, 14 *Oct.* 1721, *James Taylor*, bur. 28 *Sept.* 1754; 2*ndly, Ralph Pennyman* [*youngest son of Sir James Pennyman, 3rd Bt.* [*E.*]], b. *c.* 1696; d. 1762; *and had issue by both husbands.*

See the Essex Volume, Exeter Supplement, p. 671, for issue by second.

4c. *Ann Gee*, bapt. 31 *Aug.* 1703.

5c. *Catherine Gee*, bapt. 23 *Dec.* 1707.

2b. *Matthew Gee*, bapt. 17 *Aug.* 1675.

3b. *William Gee*, bapt. 11 *Sept.* 1676; d. *a.* 1717, *when his widow was living*.

4b.[2] *James Gee of Beverley*, bapt. 15 *Aug.* 1636; d. (*will proved* 26 *Nov.*) 1751; m. 7 *Nov.* 1727, *Constance, da. of John Moyser of Beverley; and had issue* (*with* 2 *sons d. in infancy*) 1c *to* 2c.

1c. *William Gee*, b. 26 *Ap.* 1735, *living and then a ward of Richard Burton*, 1751.

2c. *Rev. Richard Gee, Vicar of North Cave and Rector of Leven*, bapt. 10 *Feb.* 1742; d.s.p.s.

5b. *Bridget Gee*, bapt. 28 *Sept.* 1671; d. (–); m. *at Bishop Burton as* 1*st wife*, 9 *Sept.* 1690, *Sir Charles Hotham*, 4*th Bt.* [*E.* 1622], *M.P. for Beverley* 1703, d. *Jan.* 1723; *and had issue* 1c *to* 4c.

1c. *Sir Charles Hotham*, 5*th Bt.* [*E.*], *M.P.*, d. 15 *Jan.* 1739; m. 1724, *Lady Gertrude, da. of Philip* (*Stanhope*), 3*rd Earl of Chesterfield* [*E.*], d. 12 *Ap.* 1775; *and had issue* 1d.

1d. *Sir Charles Hotham*, 6*th Bt.* [*E.*], d.s.p. *Dec.* 1767.

2c. *Sir Beaumont Hotham*, 7*th Bt.* [*E.*], d. 29 *Aug.* 1771; m. *Frances, da. and co-h. of Stephen Thompson of Welton, co. Yorks*, d. 18 *Nov.* 1771; *and had issue* 1d *to* 5d.

1d. *Sir Charles Hotham, afterwards Hotham-Thompson*, 8*th Bt.* [*E.*], *K.B.*, b. *May* 1729; d.s.p. 15 *Jan.* 1794. [Nos. 130580 to 130727.

The Plantagenet Roll

2d. Right Rev. Sir John Hotham, 9th Bt. [E.], Lord Bishop of Ossory 1779-1782 and of Clogher 1782-1795, b. Feb. 1735; d. 3 Nov. 1795; m. 11 Ap. 1765, Susan, da. of Herbert Mackworth, M.P.; and had issue 1e.

1e. Sir Charles Hotham, 10th Bt. [E.], b. 24 May 1766; d.s.p. 18 July 1811.

3d. William (Hotham), 1st Baron Hotham [I.], so cr. 7 Mar. 1797 with rem. to the heirs male of his father, 11th Bt. [E.], Admiral of the White, b. 8 Ap. 1736; d. unm. 2 May 1813.

4d. Beaumont (Hotham), 2nd Baron Hotham [I.], 12th Bt. [E.], a Baron of the Exchequer, b. 5 Aug. 1737; d. 4 Mar. 1814; m. 6 June 1767, Susannah, widow of Sir James Norman, da. of Sir Thomas Hankey, d. 1 Aug. 1799; and had issue 1e to 6e.

1e. Beaumont Hotham, Col. Coldstream Guards, b. 30 Ap. 1868; d. Aug. 1799; m. 20 May 1790, Philadelphia, da. of Sir John Dixon Dyke, 3rd Bt. [E.], d. 20 May 1808; and had issue 1f to 2f.

1f. Beaumont (Hotham), 3rd Baron Hotham [I.], 13th Bt. [E.], b. 9 Aug. 1794; d. unm. 12 Dec. 1870.

2f. Hon. (R.W. 1 Sept. 1835) George Frederick Hotham, Rear-Adm. R.N., b. posthumous 20 Oct. 1799; d. 19 Oct. 1856; m. 12 Aug. 1824, Lady Susan Maria, da. and co-h. of William (O'Brien), 2nd Marquis of Thomond [I.], d. 25 Mar. 1857; and had issue.

See p. 368, Nos. 60088-60089.

2e. Rev. the Hon. Frederick Hotham, Prebendary of Rochester, b. 16 June 1774; d. 10 Oct. 1854 (?); m. 23 Nov. 1802, Anne Elizabeth, da. of Thomas Hallett Hodges of Hemstead Place, co. Kent, d. 28 Jan. 1862; and had issue (with 4 elder sons and 3 das. who d.s.p.) 1f to 3f.

1f. Rev. William Francis Hotham, M.A., Rector of Buckland, Surrey, b. 28 Mar. 1819; d. 10 Sept. 1883; m. 31 Jan. 1855, Emma, da. of John Carbonell, d. 28 May 1909; and had issue 1g to 2g.

1g. Frederick William (Hotham), 6th Baron Hotham [I.], 16th Bt. [E.] (Bereleigh, Petersfield, Hants; Automobile and Junior Constitutional), b. 19 Mar. 1863; m. 9 July 1902, Benita, da. of Thomas Sanders of Sanders Park, Charleville, co. Cork; and has issue 1h to 2h.

1h. Hon. Sylvia Benita Frances Hotham, b. 19 Sept. 1903.

2h. Hon. Jocelyne Mary Emma Hotham, b. 18 Ap. 1908.

2g. Frances Emma Hotham, m. 8 Oct. 1889, the Very Rev. Edward Reid Currie, D.D., Dean of Battle (The Deanery, Battle, Sussex).

2f. Louisa Hotham, b. 1807; d. 1894; m. 12 Mar. 1844, Lieut.-Col. Patrick Grieve, 75th Regt., d. 11 Jan. 1853.

3f. Frederica Hotham, d. 1 Sept. 1843; m. 12 Mar. 1840, the Rev. Charles Montagu Doughty of Theberton Hall, co. Suffolk, d. 23 Ap. 1850; and had issue 1g to 2g.

1g. Henry Montagu Doughty of Theberton, co. Suffolk, J.P., formerly R.N., Bar.-at-Law (Theberton Hall, near Leiston, Suffolk), b. 15 Mar. 1841; m. 21 Aug. 1860, Edith Rebecca, da. of D. Cameron, Chief Justice of Vancouver Island [and niece of Sir James Douglas, K.C.B., Governor of Vancouver and British Columbia], d. 4 Sept. 1870; and has issue 1h to 6h.

1h. Charles Hotham Montagu Doughty, now [D.P. 1904] Doughty-Wylie, C.M.G., Maj. Royal Welsh Fusiliers (Lavrock, Grange Road, Eastbourne), b. 23 July 1868; m. 1904, Lily, widow of Henry Adams-Wylie, Lieut. I.M.S., da. of John Wylie of West Cliffe Hall, Hants.

2h. Henry Montagu Doughty, Capt. R.N., b. 4 Sept. 1870.
3h. Edith Amelia Mary Doughty.
4h. Katharine Frances Doughty.
5h. Gertrude Millicent Doughty.
6h. Frederica Helen Doughty.

[Nos. 130728 to 130740.]

# of The Blood Royal

2g. Charles Montagu Doughty, Hon. Litt. D. (Oxon.), b. 19 Aug. 1843; m. 7 Oct. 1886, Caroline Amelia, da. of Gen. Sir William Montagu Scott McMurdo, G.C.B.; and has issue 1h to 2h.

1h. Susan Dorothy Doughty.
2h. Frederica Gertrude Doughty.

3e. Sir Henry Hotham, G.C.M.G., K.C.B., Vice-Adm. of the Red, b. 19 Feb. 1777; d. at Malta 19 Ap. 1833; m. 6 July 1816, Lady Frances Anne Juliana, da. of John (Rous), 1st Earl of Stradbroke [U.K.], d. 31 Jan. 1859; and had issue.
See the Exeter Volume, p. 543, Nos. 49448–49476.

4e. Frances Hotham, d. 1836; m. Sir John Sutton, K.C.B.
5e. Amelia Hotham, d. 1804; m. John Woodcock; and had issue.
6e. Louisa Hotham, b. 9 Oct. 1778; d. 30 Aug. 1840; m. 1st, as 2nd wife, 5 Dec. 1804, Sir Charles Edmonstone, 2nd Bt. [G.B. 1774], M.P., b. 10 Oct. 1764; d. 1 Ap. 1821; 2ndly, Jan. 1832, Charles Woodcock of Park Crescent, Portland Place, London; and had issue by 1st husband (with 3 sons and 1 da. d.s.p.) 1f to 2f.

1f. Sir William Edmonstone, 4th Bt. [G.B.], C.B., D.L., Adm. R.N. (ret.), formerly Naval A.D.C. to Queen Victoria and M.P. for Stirling, b. 29 Jan. 1810; d. 18 Feb. 1888; m. July 1841, Mary Elizabeth, da. of Lieut.-Col. Parsons, C.M.G., d. 11 Aug. 1902; and had issue 1g to 9g.

1g. Sir Archibald Edmonstone, 5th Bt. [G.B.], C.V.O., D.L., a Groom-in-Waiting to H.M. King Edward VII. (Duntreath Castle, Blanefield, near Glasgow; 6 Lancaster Gate Terrace, W.; Marlborough), b. 30 May 1867; m. 30 Nov. 1895, Ida Agnes, da. of George Stewart Forbes [Bt. Coll.]; and has issue 1h to 3h.

1h. William George Edmonstone, b. 20 Oct. 1896.
2h. Archibald Charles Edmonstone, b. 16 June 1898.
3h. Edward St. John Edmonstone (for whom H.M. the King stood sponsor in person), b. 3 Nov. 1901.

2g. Louisa Anne Edmonstone, m. 12 Oct. 1872, Major-Gen. Henry Pipon, R.H.A. (ret.), C.B. (King's House, Tower of London, E.C.); and has issue 1h to 5h.

1h. Mary Elizabeth Pipon, m. 14 Sept. 1899, Capt. Cecil Toogood, D.S.O., Lincolnshire Regt. (see Appendix); and has issue 1i to 3i.

1i. Alexander Henry Cecil Toogood, b. 26 Aug. 1900.
2i. Harry Reginald George Cecil Toogood, b. 29 Feb. 1904.
3i. Georgiana Natalie Toogood.

2h. Emma Philippa Pipon, m. 1908, Maurice William Clifford, Lieut. Indian Army Reserve, Deputy Examiner of Accounts, P.W.D., India; and has issue (a da).
3h. Georgina Helen Pipon, m. 1901, Herbert Graham Stainforth, Major 4th Indian Cav. (see p. 570); and has issue 1i to 2i.

1i. Graham Henry Stainforth, b. 3 Oct. 1906.
2i. Madeleine Susan Stainforth.

4h. Evangeline Aimee Pipon.
5h. Geraldine Maria Pipon.

3g. Charlotte Henrietta Edmonstone (Carbeile Torpoint, R.S.O., Cornwall), m. 9 June 1866, the Rev. John Francis Kitson, Vicar of Antony, d. 1907; and has (with other) issue (see Appendix) 1h to 2h.

1h. Antony Buller Kitson, b. 1890.
2h. Dorothy Euphemia Kitson.

4g. Jessie Edmonstone, m. 3 June 1884, Edward John Winnington Ingram, Major Royal Warwickshire Regt. [Bt. Coll.], d.s.p.s. 5 Aug. 1892.

5g. Frances Euphemia Edmonstone, m. 3 June 1873, Alexander Robert Duncan of Parkhill, co. Forfar, Advocate; and has issue (see Appendix) 1h.

1h. John Alexander Duncan, b. 22 Mar. 1878. [Nos. 130741 to 130793.

The Plantagenet Roll

6g. Sophia Edmonstone, m. 1 June 1880, James Edward Hope [Bt. Coll.] (*Belmont, Murrayfield, Midlothian*), b. 6 Nov. 1852; and has issue 1h to 4h.
 1h. James Horatio Hope, Lieut. Highland L.I., b. 12 Mar. 1881.
 2h. Reginald John Hope, b. 1884.
 3h. William Douglas Hope, b. 1886.
 4h. Vera Mary Hope.

7g. *Susanna Emily Edmonstone*, d. 9 *May* 1886; m. 16 *Feb.* 1885, *Jonathan Bucknill*, d. *Ap.* 1898; *and had issue* 1h.
 1h. Susanna Mary Frances Bucknill.

8g. Mary Clementina Edmonstone, m. 1 Oct. 1874, Andrew Graham (Murray), 1st Baron Dunedin [U.K.], P.C., K.C.V.O., Lord Justice-General and President of the Court of Session in Scotland (7 *Rothesay Terrace, Edinburgh; Stenton, Dunkeld, Perthshire*), b. 21 Nov. 1849; and has issue 1h to 4h.
 1h. Hon. Ronald Thomas Graham Murray, Capt. 3rd Batt. Black Watch, b. 1 Aug. 1875; m. 19 Feb. 1903, Evelyn, da. of Sir David Baird, 3rd Bt. [U.K.].
 2h. Mary Caroline Murray.
 3h. Gladys Esme Murray.
 4h. Marjorie Murray.

9g. Alice Frederica Edmonstone, m. 1 June 1891, Capt. the Hon. George Keppel, M.V.O. [3rd son of William Coates, 7th Earl of Albemarle [I.] and a descendant of George, Duke of Clarence, K.G. (see Clarence Volume, p. 250)] (30 *Portman Square, W.; Marlborough*); and has issue 1h to 2h.
 1h. Violet Keppel.
 2h. Sonia Rosemary Keppel.

2f. *Louisa Henrietta Edmonstone*, d. 14 *Mar.* 1840; m. 15 *Dec.* 1829, *John Kingston of London; and had issue* (1 *son and* 3 *das.*).

5d. *George Hotham*, General in the Army, b. 7 *Jan.* 1741; d. 7 *Feb.* 1805; m. 16 *Dec.* 1769, *Diana, da. and co-h. of Sir Warton Pennyman-Warton, 5th Bt.* [E.], d. 17 *July* 1817; *and had issue.*
 See the Essex Volume, Exeter Supplement, pp. 666–671, Nos. 57622/591–751.

3c. *Elizabeth Hotham*, bapt. 10 *Jan.* 1694; d. 25 *Oct.* 1737; m. *Sir Thomas Style, 4th Bt.* [E. 1627], d. 11 *Jan.* 1769; *and had issue* 1d *to* 2d.
 1d. *Sir Charles Style, 5th Bt.* [E.], d. 18 *Ap.* 1774; m. 7 *Mar.* 1770, *the Hon. Isabella, da. of Richard (Wingfield), 1st Viscount Powerscourt* [I.], d. 24 *Sept.* 1808; *and had issue* 1e *to* 2e.
  1e. *Sir Charles Style, 6th Bt.* [E.], d. 5 *Sept.* 1804; m. 29 *Mar.* 1794, *Camilla, da. of James Whatman of Vintners, co. Kent*, d. 17 *Sept.* 1829; *and had issue (with* 2 *das.* d.s.p.) 1f *to* 2f.
   1f. *Sir Thomas Style, 7th Bt.* [E.], d. unm., *in Spain,* 5 *Nov.* 1813.
   2f. Sir Thomas Charles Style, 8th Bt. [E.], J.P., D.L., M.P., b. 21 *Aug.* 1797; d.s.p.s. 23 *July* 1879.
  2e. Dorothy Style, m. John Larking.
 2d. *Rev. Robert Style, Vicar of Wateringbury and Rector of Mereworth*, d. (–); m. *Priscilla, da. of the Rev. John Davis*, d. 18 *June* 1832; *and had issue (with* 1 *son and* 1 *da.* d. unm.) 1e *to* 6e.
  1e. *Charles Style of Stranorlar, co. Donegal*, b. 1777; d. 21 *Dec.* 1853; m. *Apr.* 1812, *Frances, da. of John Cochrane of Edenmore, co. Donegal*, d. 20 *Jan.* 1875; *and had issue (with* 2 *sons and* 3 *das.* d.s.p.) 1f *to* 3f.
   1f. *Anna Maria Style*, d. 3 *Dec.* 1902; m. 1838, *Lieut.-Col. John Pitt Kennedy*, d. 28 *June* 1879; *and had issue (with a da., Mrs. Martin of Cleveragh, who* d.s.p.) 1g.
    1g. Charles Napier Kennedy, b. 1852; m. 1882, Lucy, da. of George Marwood.
   2f. *Elizabeth Style*, m. 1850, *John James Hamilton Humphreys, Bar.-at-Law*, d. 1890; *and had issue* 1g *to* 5g.
    1g. John Bayfield Humphreys, b. 1854.
    2g. Charles Style Humphreys, b. 1858.

[Nos. 130794 to 130972.

524

# of The Blood Royal

3g. Alice Rachel Humphreys, m. 1876, Robert Jocelyn Alexander, H.M.'s Inspector of Schools.

4g. Ethel Humphreys, m. 1879, Albert Crease Coxhead.

5g. Rosamond Humphreys, m. 1904, Col. William Francis Henry Style Kincaid, C.B., R.E. *(United Service)*.

3f. *Isabella Style*, d. *Aug.* 1867; m. *Sept.* 1858, *John Henry Kincaid of Dublin*, d. *Aug.* 1867; *and had issue* 1g *to* 2g.

    1g. Charles Style Kincaid.

    2g. William Henry Kincaid.

2e. *William Style of Bicester House, Oxfordshire*, b. 12 *Ap.* 1785; d. 24 *Feb.* 1868; m. 22 *Dec.* 1814, *Louisa Charlotte, da. of the Hon. Jacob Marsham*, d. 25 *Oct.* 1866; *and had issue (with* 2 *das.* d.s.p.) 1f *to* 3f.

1f. *Sir William Henry Marsham Style, 9th Bt.* [*E.*], *J.P., D.L., High Sheriff co. Donegal* 1856, *M.A. (Oxon.)*, b. 3 *Sept.* 1826; d. 31 *Jan.* 1904; m. 1*st*, 18 *Dec.* 1848, *the Hon. Rosamond Marion, da. of Charles (Morgan), 1st Lord Tredegar* [*U.K.*], d. 15 *Jan.* 1883; 2*ndly*, 2 *June* 1885, *Ellen Catharine (The Firs, Crowborough, Sussex), widow of Henry Hyde Nugent Bankes, and previously of the Rev. Charles Henry Barham of Trecwn, da. of Edward Taylor Massy of Cottesmore; and had issue* 1g *to* 7g.

1g. Sir Frederick Montague Style, 10th Bt. [E.] *(Glenmore, Cloghan, co. Donegal)*, b. 10 May 1857; m. 14 Oct. 1886, Caroline, da. of Frederick Schultz; and has issue 1h to 2h.

    1h. William Frederick Style, b. 11 July 1887.

    2h. Louise Violet Style.

2g. Henry Albert Glenmore Style, b. 11 June 1862; m. 5 May 1886, Annie Lydia, da. of Samuel Fletcher Goldsmith; and has issue 1h to 4h.

    1h. Glenmore Rodney Style, b. 29 June 1887.

    2h. Rosamond Lydia Style.

    3h. Brenda Helen Style.

    4h. Viola Style.

3g. Rodney Charles Style, Lieut.-Col. Comdg. 1st Batt. Queen's Own, b. 4 May 1864.

4g. *Rosamond Louisa Style*, d. 21 *June* 1899; m. 8 *Ap.* 1872, *Henry Price Holford, 10th Hussars*, d. 21 *June* 1899; *and had issue* 1h *to* 4h.

    1h. George Holford, b. 1872.

    2h. Arthur Holford, b. 1873.

    3h. Alfred Holford, b. 1876.

    4h. Frederick Holford, b. 1881.

5g. Selina Isabella Style.

6g. *Lydia Frances Style*, d. 23 *June* 1900; m. 12 *Jan.* 1875, *Benjamin Francis Meynell Bloomfield of Castle Caldwell, co. Fermanagh, D.L.*, d.v.p. 26 *Nov.* 1886; *and had issue* 1h *to* 3h.

1h. Meynell Caldwell Egerton Rodney Bloomfield of Castle Caldwell *(Castle Caldwell, Belleek, co. Fermanagh)*, b. 12 Dec. 1882.

2h. Marian Blanche Bloomfield, m. 3 June 1903, the Rev. Benjamin James du Boe, M.A. (T.C.D.), Incumbent of Ballintemple *(Dundrum, Tipperary)*; and has issue 1i.

    1i. Rodney Benjamin du Boe, b. 11 Mar. 1904.

3h. Grace Maria Bloomfield, m. 6 Dec. 1898, Arthur Francis Forster [eldest son of William Stewart Forster of Rumwood, Maidstone] (24 *Portland Place, W.*).

7g. Mary Louisa Style, m. 24 Ap. 1884, the Rev. Thomas Thornhill Peyton, Rector of St. Mary, March, co. Cambridge *(St. Mary's Rectory, March, Ely)*, b. 8 Dec. 1856; and has issue 1h.

    1h. Rosamond Lucy Peyton.

[Nos. 130973 to 130997.

The Plantagenet Roll

2*f.* Rev. Charles Montague Style, D.D., M.A. (Oxon.), *formerly* Fellow of St. John's Coll., Oxon., Rector of Warnborough (*South Warnborough Rectory, Winchfield, Hants*), *b.* 21 Aug. 1830; *m.* 24 Sept. 1867, Jessie Elizabeth, da. of Robert Bullock Marsham, D.C.L. [E. Romney Coll.]; and has issue 1*g*.
    1*g.* Richard Charles Montague Style, *b.* 20 Sept. 1870.

3*f. Albert Frederick Style*, b. 20 *May* 1837; *d.* 28 *Dec.* 1895; *m.* 30 *Ap.* 1868, *Eliza, da. of Henry Tubb of Bicester, d.* 30 *Ap.* 1898; *and had issue (with* 1 *da. d. young)* 1*g to* 4*g.*
    1*g.* George Montague Style, B.A. (Oxon.), Capt. W. Kent Yeo. (*Pickwell Manor, Braunton, N. Devon*), *b.* 7 Mar. 1869; *m.* 7 Ap. 1896, Eleanora Morrison, da. of James Morrison Kirkwood of Yeo Vale Bideford, co. Devon; and has issue 1*h* to 3*h*.
        1*h.* Oliver George Style, *b.* 1 Feb. 1897.
        2*h.* Priscilla Style.
        3*h.* Patience Paulina Style.

    2*g.* Charles Humphrey Style, Major Royal E. Kent Yeo. (*Crouch House, Boro' Green, Kent*), *b.* 8 May 1877; *m.* 15 Nov. 1899, Annie Maud Harriet, da. of Gen. Sir Hugh Henry Gough, G.C.B., V.C.; and has issue 1*h* to 5*h*.
        1*h.* Charles Richard Style, *b.* 13 Ap. 1901.
        2*h.* Humphrey Bloomfield Style, *b.* 12 Nov. 1902.
        3*h.* Hubert Anthony Style, *b.* 9 Jan. 1910.
        4*h.* Barbara Ann Style.
        5*h.* Camilla Style.

    3*g.* Robert Henry Style, Lieut. Royal E. Kent Yeo. (*Boxley House, near Maidstone*), *b.* 20 Oct. 1881; *m.* 15 Feb. 1905, Grace Winifred, da. of John Bazley-White; and has issue (with 1 son *d. young*) 1*h* to 2*h*.
        1*h.* John Peter Style, *b.* 1908.
        2*h.* Betty Winifred Style.

    4*g.* Florence Louisa Style (*Heathfield House, Bletchington, Oxford*), *m.* 22 Nov. 1898, Charles Stratton, *d.* 1907; and has issue 1*h* to 3*h*.
        1*h.* John Humphrey Stratton, *b.* 1900.
        2*h.* Charles Michael Stratton, *b.* 1906.
        3*h.* Ida Rosemary Stratton.

3*e. Margaretta Style, d. Sept.* 1863; *m. John Johnston, d. July* 1859; *and had issue.*

4*e. Henrietta Style, d.* (–); *m. June* 1808, *John Francis Norris*, d. 2 *Nov.* 1854; *and had issue.*

5*e. Elizabeth Style, d.* 4 *Dec.* 1854; *m. Adm. John Drake, d.* 6 *Aug.* 1864.

6*e. Clara Style, d.* 31 *Dec.* 1861; *m. July* 1845, *Col. Wilson.*

4*c. Charlotte Hotham*, d. 7 *June* 1771; *m.* 31 *Mar.* 1725, *Sir Warton Pennyman-Warton*, 5*th Bt.* [*E.*], *d.* 14 *Jan.* 1770; *and had issue.*

See the Essex Volume, Exeter Supplement, p. 666, Nos. 57622/551-751.
                                                                                   [Nos. 130998 to 131217.

332. Descendants of PHILADELPHIA NUTT (Table XXVIII.), *d.* after 1706; *m. c.* 1695, Sir THOMAS DYKE of Horeham, 1st Bt. [E. 3 Mar. 1677], *d.* 31 Oct. 1706; and had issue 1*a* to 3*a*.

    1*a. Sir Thomas Dyke*, 2*nd Bt.* [*E.*], b. *c.* 1700; *d.* 20 *Aug.* 1756; *m.* 23 *May* 1728, *Anne, widow of John Bluet of Holcombe Regis, co. Devon, da. and h. of Percival Hart of Lullingstone Castle, co. Kent*, d. 24 *Nov.* 1763; *and had issue* 1*b* to 2*b*.
        1*b. Sir John Dixon Dyke*, 3*rd Bt.* [*E.*], b. 23 *Nov.* 1732; *d.* 6 *Sept.* 1710; *m.*

# of The Blood Royal

3 *May* 1756, *Philadelphia Payne, da. of George Horne of East Grinstead, co. Sussex,* d. 31 *Jan.* 1781 ; *and had issue* 1c *to* 2c.

1c. Sir Thomas Dyke, 4th Bt. [E.], b. 23 Dec. 1763 ; d. *unm.* 22 Nov. 1831.

2c. Sir Percival Hart Dyke, 5th Bt. [E.], *a co-h. of the Barony of Braye* [E.], *which he successfully claimed,* b. 27 Dec. 1767 ; d. 4 Aug. 1846 ; m. 26 *July* 1798, *Anne, da. of Robert Jenner of Chislehurst, co. Kent,* d. 27 Dec. 1847 ; *and had issue* 1d *to* 6d.

1d. Sir Percyvall Hart Dyke, 6th Bt. [E.], b. 9 *June* 1799 ; d. 12 Nov. 1875 ; m. 25 *June* 1835, *Elizabeth. da. of John Wells of Bickley, co. Kent,* d. 10 *July* 1888 ; *and had issue (with a son d. in the Crimea)* 1e *to* 7e.

1e. Right Hon. Sir William Hart Dyke, 7th Bt. [E.], P.C., J.P., D.L., co. Kent, M.A. (Oxon.), M.P. for West Kent 1865-1868, for Mid. Kent 1868-1885, and for N.W. Kent 1885-1906, Vice-President of the Committee of Council on Education 1887-1892, Chief Sec. to the Lord-Lieutenant of Ireland 1885-1886, and Joint-Sec. of the Treasury 1874-1880 (*Lullingstone Castle, Dartford, Kent ; Carlton, &c.*), b. 7 Aug. 1837 ; m. 30 May 1870, Lady Emily Caroline [descended from the Lady Anne, sister of King Edward IV., &c. (see the Exeter Volume, p. 363)], da. of John William (Montagu), 7th Earl of Sandwich [E.] ; *and has issue (with a son d. young)* 1f *to* 5f.

1f. Percyvall Hart Dyke, J.P., B.A. (Camb.), Bar.-at-Law (*Lullingstone Castle, Eynsford, Kent ; Carlton*), b. 27 Oct. 1871 ; m. 15 Aug. 1908, Edythe, da. of W. G. Harrison, Q.C. ; *and has issue* 1g.

1g. Edythe Frediswide Hart Dyke, b. 18 July 1909.

2f. Oliver Hamilton Hart Dyke, b. 4 Sept. 1885.

3f. Lina Mary Hart Dyke, m. 10 Feb. 1902, Alexander John Scott Scott-Gatty [son of Sir Alfred Scott Scott-Gatty, Garter King of Arms] (18 *Buckingham Gate, S.W.*) ; and has issue 1g.

1g. Edward Comyn Scott-Gatty, b. 1903.

4f. Hon. Mary Hart Dyke, *formerly* Maid-of-Honour to H.M. Queen Alexandra, m. 11 July 1905, Capt. Matthew Gerald Edward Bell of Bourne Park, co. Kent, 116th (Reserve) Batt. (*formerly* 3rd Batt.) Rifle Brig. (105 *Cadogan Gardens, S.W. ; Bourne Park, Canterbury*) ; and has issue 1g.

1g. Matthew Alexander Henry Bell, b. 1909.

5f. Sydney Margaret Eleanor Hart Dyke, *unm.*

2e. George Augustus Hart Dyke (1 *Grosvenor Place, S.W. ; Wellington*), b. 27 Sept. 1847.

3e. Reginald Charles Hart Dyke (*Dacre Lodge, Cockfosters, New Barnet*), b. 1 May 1852 ; m. 1st, 22 Oct. 1891, Guinevere Eva, da. of Gen. Lord Alfred Paget, C.B. [descended from the Lady Isabel, aunt of King Edward IV. (see Essex Volume, p. 107)], d. 26 Feb. 1894 ; 2ndly, 10 June 1897, Millicent Ada [descended from George, Duke of Clarence, K.G. (see Essex Volume Supplement, p. 516)], da. of Robert Cooper Lee Bevan of Trent Park, co. Herts, and Fosbury House, co. Wilts ; and has issue 1f to 2f.

1f.¹ Wyndham Douglas Hart Dyke, b. 13 Aug. 1892.

2f.² Ashley Francis Hart Dyke, b. 16 Oct. 1899.

4e. Frances Julia Hart Dyke (*Crowbury, Watton, Herts*), m. 24 July 1877, Abel Smith of Woodhall Park, Herts, M.P. [descended from the Lady Isabel Plantagenet (see Essex Volume, p. 303)], d. 30 May 1898 ; and has issue 1f.

1f. Rachel Caroline Smith.

5e. Eleanor Laura Hart Dyke.

6e. Sybella Catherine Hart Dyke.

7e. Gertrude Hart Dyke, m. as 3rd wife, 19 June 1894, the Hon. Reynolds Moreton [brother of 3rd Earl of Ducie [U.K.]] (*St. John's, Bishopstoke, Hants*).

2d. Rev. Thomas Hart Dyke, *Rector of Long Newton, co. Durham, and Lulling-*
[Nos. 131218 to 131235.

The Plantagenet Roll

stone, co. Kent, b. 11 Dec. 1801; d. 25 June 1866; m. 4 Feb. 1833, Elizabeth [*descended from the Lady Anne, sister of King Edward IV., &c.* (see the Exeter Volume, p. 536)], *da. of Thomas Fairfax of Newton Kyme*, d. 6 Oct. 1893; *and had issue* 1e *to* 2e.

1e. Thomas Dyke of Beaumaris, *Clifton, Bristol*, M.I.C.E., J.P., b. 1 Ap. 1834; d. 6 Aug. 1906; m. 26 Feb. 1863, Georgina Isabella Russell (9 *York Crescent Road, Clifton, Bristol*), *da. of Robert Edward Fullerton of Shuthonger Manor, near Tewkesbury; and had issue* 1f *to* 4f.

1f. Percyvall Hart Dyke, Capt. Indian Army, served in Uganda 1897–1898 (Despatches, Medal with 2 Clasps) and with Zakka Khel Exped. 1908 (Despatches, Medal with Clasp), b. 24 Aug. 1872; m. 10 Oct. 1900, Louisa Catherine, *da. of Adm. John Halliday Cave*, C.B., R.N.; *and has issue* 1g *to* 3g.

1g. Trevor Hart Dyke, b. 19 Feb. 1905.
2g. Eric Hart Dyke, b. 28 July 1906.
3g. Cicely Hart Dyke.

2f. Ethel Frances Hart Dyke.
3f. Winifred Evelyn Hart Dyke.
4f. Theophania Louisa Hart Dyke.

2e. Rev. Percival Hart Dyke, Hon. Canon of Salisbury (*Lullingstone, Wimborne*), b. 1 June 1835; m. 12 Jan. 1864, Margaret Isabella, *da. of Robert John Peel of Burton-on-Trent*, d. 10 Ap. 1909; *and has issue* 1f *to* 3f.

1f. Robert Percyvall Hart Dyke (20 *Pembridge Mansions, W.*), b. 3 Nov. 1864; m. 30 Sept. 1908, Mary Harriette Theodora, *da. of the Rev. John Shephard (formerly Vicar of Eton)*, Hon. Canon of Christ Church, Oxford, of 39 Princes Square, W.; *and has issue* 1g.

1g. Michael Percyvall Hart Dyke, b. 10 Sept. 1909.

2f. Mabel Louisa Hart Dyke, m. 11 Feb. 1892, Harold Gordon (*Meddecombra, Watagoda, Ceylon*).

3f. Maud Cecilia Hart Dyke, m. 16 Ap. 1891, the Rev. Walter Basil Broughton, M.A., Vicar of Brackley, Northants; *and has issue* 1g *to* 2g.

1g. Stephen Percyvale Hart Broughton, b. 26 Dec. 1897.
2g. Olive Irene Broughton, b. 22 June 1892.

3d. John Dixon Dyke, Lieut.-Col. H.E.I.C.S., b. 6 Jan. 1803; d. 1 Aug. 1885; m. 10 Feb. 1836, Millicent, *da. of Isaac Minet of Baldwins, co. Kent*, d. 5 Aug. 1901; *and had issue* 1e *to* 8e.

1e. Rev. John Dixon Dyke, Vicar and Rural Dean of St. James' Camberwell (30 *Crowhurst Road, Brixton, S.W.; Union*), b. 31 Oct. 1836.

2e. Edward Hart Dyke, *formerly* Col. R.A., served in Indian Mutiny (Medal with Clasp) (*Leavers, Hadlow, Tonbridge*), b. 11 Nov. 1837; m. 23 Mar. 1893, Elizabeth Grace, *da. of Col. Thomas Stannard MacAdam of Blackwater, co. Clare*; *and has issue* 1f *to* 5f.

1f. Francis Hart Dyke, b. 20 Jan. 1898.
2f. Edward Hart Dyke, b. 24 Oct. 1899.
3f. Charles Hart Dyke, b. 27 May 1901.
4f. Percyvall Hart Dyke, b. 15 Dec. 1902.
5f. Millicent Grace Hart Dyke.

3e. Frederick Hotham Dyke, Lieut.-Col. *late* 69th Regt., Professor of Military Studies at Camb. Univ. since 1904, served in Canada 1870 (Medal with Clasp) and in Egypt 1884 (43 *Morshead Mansions, Maida Vale, W.; Junior United Service*), b. 6 Feb. 1840; m. 20 Ap. 1871, Emily, *da. of the Rev. Charles Faunce Thorndike*; *and has issue* 1f *to* 2f.

1f. Agnese Millicent Dyke, m. 16 Dec. 1893, Richard Thomas Nicholson (M.A.) (*The Mount, Loughton, Essex*).

2f. Winifred Amy Dyke. [Nos. 131236 to 131259.]

of The Blood Royal

4*e*. George Hart Dyke, *formerly* Lieut.-Col. Comdg. 2nd Batt. Northbd. Fus., served in Afghan War 1878-1879 (Medal) (*Army and Navy*), *b.* 21 Jan. 1847; *m.* 25 July 1895, Edith Louise, da. of Thomas William Kinder, Master of Mints of Hong Kong and Japan; and has issue 1*f*.

1*f*. Helen Sandra Millicent Dyke.

5*e*. Henry Hart Dyke, Adm. R.N. (ret.), has Abyssinian Medal (*Sphinx, Banbury; Junior United Service*), *b.* 26 Mar. 1848; *m.* 1st, 10 Feb. 1886, Louisa, da. of William Covey of Lee, Kent, *d.s.p.* 10 Dec. 1886; 2ndly, 3 July 1900, Mary Blanche, da. of the Rev. Thomas Prater of Farnborough, Banbury, *d.s.p.* 8 June 1905.

6*e*. Millicent Dyke } (*Camoys Court, Barcombe, near Lewes*).
7*e*. Julia Dyke

8*e*. Matilda Dyke (20 *Dartmouth Row, Blackheath, S.E.*).

4*d*. Francis Hart Dyke, Queen's Proctor, *b.* 28 *Nov.* 1803, *d.* 17 *July* 1876; m. 1 Dec. 1835, Charlotte Lascelles, da. of the Right Hon. Sir Herbert Jenner Fust, P.C., d. 17 Dec. 1899; *and had issue* 1*e* to 3*e*.

1*e*. Rev. Edwin Francis Dyke, Rector of Mersham, Kent, Hon. Canon of Canterbury and Rural Dean (*Mersham Rectory, Kent*), *b.* 27 Sept. 1842; *m.* 22 Nov. 1870, Katharine Louisa, da. of Sir Frederick Currie, 1st Bt. [U.K.].

2*e*. Evelyn Ellen Dyke.

3*e*. Alice Frances Dyke (*Bark Hart, Wokingham, Berks*).

5*d. Harriet Jenner Dyke*, d. *Nov.* 1883; m. 11 *June* 1835, *the Rev. Nicholas Fiott, afterwards* (R.L. 4 *Oct.* 1816) *Lee, Vicar of Edgeware, M.A. and Fellow of St. John's Coll., Camb.* (see p. 530), d. 1858; *and had issue* (with a da., Mrs. Luard, who d.s.p.) 1*e* to 3*e*.

1*e*. Edward Dyke Lee of Hartwell, co. Bucks, and Totteridge Park, co. Herts, J.P., Lieut.-Col. and Hon. Col. 3rd Batt. Oxfordshire L.I. (*Hartwell House, Aylesbury; Totteridge Park, Barnet; Carlton, &c.*), *b.* 16 Sept. 1844.

2*e*. Philadelphia Bruce Lee, *m.* 24 Oct. 1876, Liebert Edward Goodall, J.P., D.L., Major and Hon. Lieut.-Col. Royal N. Gloucester Militia, *formerly* Capt. 59th Regt. (*Dinton Hall, Aylesbury*).

3*e*. Fanny Charlotte Lee.

6*d. Laura Dyke*, d. 28 *Feb.* 1900; m. 9 *Feb.* 1847, *the Rev. Thomas Prankerd Phelps, M.A., Hon. Canon of Rochester, Rural Dean and Rector of Ridley* (*Ridley Parsonage, Wrotham, Kent*); *and had issue* 1*e* to 3*e*.

1*e*. Henry George Hart Phelps (*Great Comp, Sevenoaks*), *b.* 17 Nov. 1849; *m.* 1886, Joyce, da. of J. Hassell of Clock House, Darenth, Kent; and has issue 1*f* to 2*f*.

1*f*. Henry Dampier Phelps, *b.* 1889.

2*f*. Vera Laura Phelps.

2*e*. Herbert Dampier Phelps, Sub-Lieut. (ret.) R.N. (*Belle Vue, Fowey, Cornwall*), *b.* 24 July 1851.

3*e*. Rev. Lancelot Ridley Phelps, M.A., Fellow of Oriel Coll., Oxford, and Vice-Principal of St. Mary Hall, Oxford, 1889-1893 (*Oriel College, Oxford*), *b.* 3 Nov. 1853.

2*b*. *Philadelphia Dyke*, b. *c.* 1730; d. 5 *Mar.* 1799; m. *at Lullingstone, William Lee of Totteridge, co. Herts, M.A.* [*son of the Right Hon. Sir William Lee, P.C., K.B., Lord Chief Justice of England* 1738 *and Chancellor of the Exchequer* 1754], bur. 12 *Aug.* 1778; *and had issue* (*with a son, William Lee, afterwards Antoine of Colworth, co. Beds., M.P.*, d.s.p. *Sept.* 1825, *and* 2 *das.* d. *unm.*[1]) 1*c* to 3*c*.

1*c*. *Harriet Lee, da. and in her issue* (1825) *co-h.*, d. 25 *July* 1794; m. 19 *July* 1782, *John Fiott of London* [5*th son of Nicholas Fiott of St. Helier's, Jersey, Lord of the Fee and Seigniory of Melesches*]; *and had issue*[2] (*with a son and* 4 *das.* d. *unm.*) 1*d* to 4*d*. Nos. 131260 to 131276.

---

[1] Lipscomb's " Bucks," ii. 308.   [2] Ibid.

The Plantagenet Roll

1*d*. *John Fiott, afterwards* (R.L. 4 Oct. 1816) *Lee of Colworth, co. Bucks, M.A., LL.D.* (*Camb.*), b. 28 *Ap*. 1783; d. (? s.p.); m. 25 *Oct*. 1833, *Cecilia, da. of* (—) *Rutter*.

2*d*. *William Edward Fiott, Lieut. R.N.*, b. 28 *July* 1786; d. (? s.p.).

3*d*. *Rev. Nicholas Fiott, afterwards* (R.L. 4 Oct. 1816) *Lee, M.A., Fellow of St. John's Coll., Camb., Vicar of Edgware*, b. 5 *June* 1794; d. 1858; m. 11 *June* 1835, *Harriet Jenner, da. of Sir Percival Hart Dyke, 5th Bt.* [E.]; *and had issue.*
See p. 529, Nos. 131269-131271.

4*d*. *Philadelphia Fiott*, b. 10 *May* 1784; d. (—); m. *John Ede of London, Merchant; and had issue.*[1]

2*c*. *Louisa Lee, da. and either herself or in her issue, if any, co.-h.*, d. (—); m. *Edward Arrowsmith of Totteridge, co. Herts.*

3*c*. *Sophia Lee.*

2*a*. *Philadelphia Dyke*, m. *Lewis Stephens, D.D., Rector of Droxford, co. Hants, Archdeacon of Barnstaple and Exeter and Canon Residentiary of York and Southwark.*

3*a*. *Elizabeth Dyke*, d. *Sept*. 1739; m. *as 2nd wife, John Cockman of Kent, M.D.* [*brother of* (—) *Cockman, D.D., Master of University College, Oxon.*].[2]
[Nos. 131277 to 131279.

333. Descendants of CATHERINE NUTT (Table XXVIII.), *b*. 1662; *d*. 24 June 1708; *m*. ANTHONY BRAMSTON of Skreens, co. Essex, *d*. 26 Jan. 1722; and had issue 1*a* to 10*a*.

1*a*. *John Bramston of Chigwell, co. Essex*, b. c. 1683; d.v.p. 17 *Aug*. 1718; m. *and had issue 3 das. who all* d.s.p.

2*a*. *Thomas Bramston of Skreens*, d. 1769; m. *2ndly, Elizabeth, da. of Richard Berney, Recorder of Norwich*, d. 1769; *and had issue* 1*b to* 2*b*.

1*b*. *Thomas Berney Bramston of Skreens, M.P. co. Essex*, b. 7 *Dec*. 1733; d. 7 *Mar*. 1813; m. 10 *Jan*. 1764, *Mary, da. and h. of Stephen Gardiner*, d. 25 *Nov*. 1805; *and had issue* 1*c to* 3*c*.

1*c*. *Thomas Gardiner Bramston of Skreens, M.P. co. Essex*, b. 24 *July* 1770; d. 3 *Feb*. 1831; m. 1*st*, 6 *Feb*. 1796, *Mary Anne, da. of William Blaauw of Queen Anne St., London*, d. *Feb*. 1821; *and had issue* 1*d to* 4*d*.

1*d*. *Thomas William Bramston of Skreens, M.P., J.P., D.L.*, b. 30 *Oct*. 1796; d. 21 *May* 1871; m. 12 *Aug*. 1830, *Eliza* [*also a descendant of Edward III. through Mortimer-Percy*], *da. and co-h. of Adm. Sir Eliab Harvey of Rolls Park, co. Essex, G.C.B., M.P.*, d. 11 *Oct*. 1870; *and had issue* 1*e to* 6*e*.

1*e*. Thomas Harvey Bramston of Skreens, J.P., D.L., *formerly* Lieut.-Col. Grenadier Guards (20 *Old Burlington Street, London, W.; Travellers'*), *b*. 11 May 1831; *m*. 7 Ap. 1864, Honoria Louisa, da. of Thomas Thornhill of Fixby Hall, co. York; *s.p.*

2*e*. Sir John Bramston, G.C.M.G., C.B., D.C.L., Fellow of All Souls' College, Oxon., Assist. Under-Sec. of State Colonial Dept. 1876-1897 and Registrar Order of St. Michael and St. George 1892-1907, *formerly* Attorney-Gen. of Hong-Kong and *previously* of Queensland, &c. (18 *Berkeley Place, Wimbledon; Travellers'*), *b*. 14 Nov. 1832; *m*. 14 Dec. 1872, Eliza Isabella, da. of the Rev. Harry Vane Russell; *s.p.*

3*e*. Rev. William Mondeford Bramston, M.A., Rector of Willingale Doe with
[Nos. 131280 to 131281.

---

[1] Lipscomb's "Bucks," ii. 308.

[2] In Betham's "Baronetage," iii. 4, they are said to have had issue a da., wife of Nicholas Toke, Bar.-at-Law; but the wife of Nicholas Toke, who was of Godington, co. Kent, was Eleanor, da. and h. of John Cockman, M.D., by Margaret, his 1st wife, da. and h. of Sir Felix Wilde, 2nd Bt.

# of The Blood Royal

Shellow Bowels, co. Essex, b. 3 Feb. 1835; d. 9 *Jan.* 1892; m. 7 *July* 1868, Hyacinth Laura, da. of the Rev. George Chetwode; and had issue 1f to 2f.

1f. Mabel Charlotte Bramston, *m*. 3 Jan. 1893, Robert George Baird [Bt. of Newbyth [U.K. 1809] Coll.] (*Holmleigh, Granville Road, Sevenoaks*); and has issue 1g to 3g.

    1g. Robert Douglas Baird, *b*. 19 Dec. 1893.
    2g. George Henry William Baird, *b*. 10 Jan. 1903.
    3g. Elizabeth Mabel Baird.

2f. Eleanor Hyacinth Bramston, *m*. 6 Ap. 1904, Oswald Francis Massingberd-Mundy [3rd son of Charles Francis Massingberd-Mundy of Ormsby, J.P., D.L., and a descendant of the Lady Anne, sister of Edward IV. (see the Exeter Volume, p. 552)] (*Iddesleigh, Granville Road, Sevenoaks*); and has issue 1g to 2g.

    1g. Francis Massingberd-Mundy, *b*. 1 Sept. 1905.
    2g. John Massingberd-Mundy, *b*. 5 Feb. 1907.

4e. Georgina Bramston, *unm*.

5e. Eliza Harriet Bramston, *m*. 26 Oct. 1875, Robert Little (*Whytecliffe, Brisbane, Queensland*); and has issue 1f.

    1f. Marcus Charles Herbert Little, *b*. 6 June 1881.

6e. Emma Alice Bramston, *m*. 28 Ap. 1864, Major Edward Clerk [5th son of the Right Hon. Sir George Clerk, 6th Bt. [S.], P.C., M.P.] (*Travellers'*); and has issue 1f to 4f.

    1f. William Henry Clerk, *b*. 19 Sept. 1867.
    2f. Herbert Edward Clerk, *b*. 15 Ap. 1871; *m*. 1908, Helen, da. of Jules A. Heuer.
    3f. Florence Eliza Clerk.
    4f. Maud Alice Clerk.

2d. Very Rev. *John Bramston, Dean of Winchester*, b. 12 *May* 1802; d. 13 *Nov.* 1889; m. 1*st*, 1832, *Clarissa Sandford*, da. of Sir Nicholas Trant, d. Ap. 1844; 2*ndly*, Sept. 1846, *Anna*, da. of Osgood Hanbury of Holfield Grange, co. Essex, d. 26 Dec. 1897; and had issue 1e to 4e.

1e. Rev. John Trant Bramston, M.A. (Oxon). (*St. Nicholas, St. Cross, Winchester*), *b*. 3 Feb. 1843; *m*. 29 Dec. 1875, Jane, da. of the Ven. William Brice Ady, Archdeacon of Colchester; and has issue 1f.

    1f. Margaret Clarissa Bramston; *m*. Aug. 1904, Robert Douglas Beloe, M.A., Assist. Master Winchester College (*Kingscote House, Winchester*); and has issue 1g to 3g.

        1g. Robert Beloe, *b*. 14 May 1905.
        2g. John Douglas Beloe, *b*. 9 Mar. 1907.
        3g. Isaac William Trant Beloe, *b*. 9 Dec. 1909.

2e.[1] *Clara Isabella Sandford Bramston*, b. *Oct.* 1833; d. 28 *Mar.* 1907; m. 13 *Sept.* 1860, *the Rev. Bixby Garnham Luard, Rector of Birch, Colchester*, d. 27 *Mar.* 1907; and had issue (with a son and da. d. unm.) 1f to 11f.

1f. Frederick Bramston Luard, Capt. (ret.) West India Regt., *b*. 3 Nov. 1861; *unm*.

2f. Hugh Bixby Luard, M.B. (Camb.), F.R.C.S., D.P.H., Capt. (ret.) Indian Medical Service (*Osmotherly, Yorks*), *b*. 13 Oct. 1862; *m*. 13 Ap. 1905, Flora Anne Phœbe, da. of Colin Alexander McVean of the Isle of Mull, J.P.; and has issue 1g to 2g.

    1g. John McVean Luard, *b*. 2 Mar. 1906.
    2g. Mary Clarissa Luard, *b*. 19 Dec. 1908.

3f. Frank William Luard, Lieut.-Col. R.M.L.I., *b*. 15 Jan. 1865; *m*. 1896, Eloine Beatrice, da. of Walter Perkins; and has issue 1g to 2g.

    1g. Betty Frances Clare Luard, *b*. 1897.
    2g. Joan Anstace de Beauregard Luard, *b*. 1899.

4f. Rev. Edwin Percy Luard, M.A. (Camb.), Curate of Birch, *b*. 13 Oct. 1869.

[Nos. 131282 to 131309.

The Plantagenet Roll

5f. Trant Bramston Luard, Capt. R.M.L.I., b. 5 Nov. 1873.
6f. Clara Georgina Luard, b. 28 Feb. 1866.
7f. Annette Jane Luard, b. 29 Aug. 1868.
8f. Helen Lucy Luard, b. 17 July 1871 ; m. 1898, M. Douglass Round.
9f. Kate Evelyn Luard, b. 29 June 1872.
10f. Rose Mary Luard, b. 22 Ap. 1876.
11f. Margaret Annie Luard, b. 10 Mar. 1880.

3e.[1] Mary Eliza Bramston, unm.
4e.[2] Anna Rachel Bramston, unm

3d. *Charlotte Bramston*, b. 11 Nov. 1799 ; d. 1841 ; m. the Rev. *John Davidson*, Rector of East Harptree, co. Somerset ; and had issue (with a da., Elibabeth, who d. unm. 20 Oct. 1909) 1e.

1e. Anna Davidson (1 *Montpelier Terrace, Braddons Hill Road West, Torquay*), m. 1889, the Rev. (—) Wilmot ; d.s.p. 1890.

4d. *Elizabeth Bramston*, b. 25 *May* 1801 ; d. 6 *July* 1839 ; m. 1831, Lieut. *William Hooper, R.N.* ; and had issue 1e to 2e.

1e. Rev. William Hooper, M.A., D.D. (Oxon.), Boden Sanskrit Sch. 1857, Hon. Canon of Lucknow Cath. 1906, *formerly* Vicar of Cressing, co. Essex, 1870-1872, Minister of Mt. Auckland, N.Z., 1889-1891, Principal of St. Paul's Div. Sch., Allahabad, 1881-1887, author of the Hebrew-Urdu Dict., Greek-Hindi Dict., and many other works (*Mussoorie, U.P., India*), b. 27 Sept. 1837 ; m. 1st, 10 Dec. 1862, Charlotte Elizabeth, da. of the Rev. George Candy, Vicar of South Newington, co. Oxon., d. 15 Aug. 1886 ; 2ndly, 17 Nov. 1891, Mary Priscilla, da. of William Robins Matthews of Newport, co. Mon. ; and has issue,(with 2 sons. d. unm.) 1f to 6f.

1f. Joseph Hayward Hooper, Dentist (*Feilding, New Zealand*), b. 10 Ap. 1864 ; m. 1892, Flora, da. of (—) Sheddan ; and has issue 1g to 5g.

1g. Howard Henry Hooper, b. 16 June 1893.
2g. Victor Candy Hooper, b. 2 Mar. 1895.
3g. William Rowlands Hooper, b. 22 Ap. 1900.
4g. Ruth Charlotte Hooper, b. 26 Oct. 1896.
5g. Flora Mackenzie Hooper, b. 8 Sept. 1898.

2f. Richard Henry Hooper, Govt. C.E. (*Fernside, Wadestown, Wellington, New Zealand*), b. 27 Nov. 1868 ; m. 1893, Sophia, da. of R. A. Hould of the N.Z. Justice Dept. ; and has issue 1g to 3g.

1g. Richard Kevin Hooper, b. 11 May 1908.
2g. Kate Challis Excelsa Hooper, b. 25 June 1894.
3g. Estelle Mary Hooper, b. 9 Dec. 1900.

3f. Frederick Kay Hooper (*Savu Savu Central, Fiji*), b. 9 Mar. 1871 ; m. 1902, Alice, da. of Gideon von Vecsey ; and has issue (with 2 sons d. young) 1g to 2g.

1g. Basil Frederick Hooper, b. 29 June 1905.
2g. Madeline Christina Anna Bramston, b. 6 Nov. 1909.

4f. John Edward Hooper, Schoolmaster (*Herbertville, N.Z.*), b. 30 Sept. 1872 ; m. 30 Mar. 1910, Kate, da. of (—) Ensor of Wellington, N.Z.

5f. Basil Bramston Hooper, A.R.I.B.A. (*Dunedin, New Zealand*), b. 17 Ap. 1876 ; m. 29 Ap. 1909, Jessie Edith, da. of Frederick Henry Seldon of Nelson, N.Z., C.E. ; and has issue 1g.

1g. Aston Seldon Hooper, b. 30 June 1910.
6f. Susan Elizabeth Hooper, Teacher (*Nelson, N.Z.*), unm.

2e. Jane Hooper, m. 6 Oct. 1864, Capt. John Alves Low, R.N. [brother of Sir Robert Cunliffe Low, G.C.B.](*Jerusalem*) ; and has issue (with a da., Augusta Jane, d. young) 1f.

1f. Charlotte Low, m. 30 Aug, 1894, Frank T. Ellis, Head Master Bishop Gobat Boarding School for Native Boys, C.M.S., Jerusalem (*Jerusalem*) ; s.p.

2c. Rev. *John Bramston, afterwards Stane of Forest Hall, co. Essex*, b. 21 *May* 1773 ; d. (—) ; m. 20 *June* 1801, *Mary Elizabeth, da. of William Newton*, d. (—) ; and had issue (with a son d. unm.) 1d. [Nos. 131310 to 131337b.]

532

of The Blood Royal

1*d*. Maria Elizabeth Bramston Stane, b. 15 *June* 1802; d. 27 *July* 1890; m. 12 *Jan*. 1822, *William Beckford of Hatchford House, co. Surrey* [*also descended from Edward III.*], b. 23 *Mar*. 1790; d. at Rome 21 *Jan*. 1859; *and had issue* (*with* 2 *das. d. unm.*) 1*e* to 2*e*.

1*e*. Francis Bramston Beckford (*Witley, Parkstone, Dorset*), b. 2 Feb. 1842; *m*. 1st, 8 July 1868, Harriett Lucy, da. of Capt. Richard Octavius Ward, 10th Hussars, *d*. 19 Ap. 1907; 2ndly, 20 Ap. 1909, Dorothea Faith, da. of Henry Forde of Luscombe, Parkstone; and has issue 1*f* to 2*f*.

1*f*. Francis William Beckford (*Lypiatt Cottage, Broadstone, Dorset*), b. 1 Feb. 1873; *m*. 18 Sept. 1907, Maud, da. of Charles Fletcher of Bournemouth; *s.p.*

2*f*. Lucy Helen Beckford, *m*. 30 Ap. 1908, Henry John Alexander Kirby [youngest son of T. F. Kirby, Burser of Winchester Coll.] (*Winchester*).

2*e*. Harriette Marianne Beckford, *unm*.

3*c*. Mary Anne Bramston, b. *c*. 1777; d. 4 *Ap*. 1865; m. 29 *July* 1797, *John Archer Houblon of Hallingbury Place, co. Essex, and Welford Park, co. Berks, M.P.*, d. 1 *June* 1831; *and had issue*.

See the Exeter Volume, p. 344, Nos. 25121–25163.

2*b*. Mary Bramston, d. 26 *June* 1792; m. 1758, *William Deedes of St. Stephens, Canterbury, Chairman East Kent Quarter Sessions*, d. 16 Nov. 1793; *and had issue* 1*c* to 3*c*.

1*c*. *William Deedes of Sandling, M.P.*, b. *June* 1761; d. 1834; m. 27 Dec. 1791, *Sophia, da. of Sir Brook Bridges, 3rd Bt.* [*G.B.*], d. 1844; *and had issue* (*with* 4 *sons who app. all d.s.p., and* 2 *das. d. unm.*) 1*d* to 9*d*.

1*d*. *William Deedes of Sandling, M.P., J.P., D.L.*, b. 17 Oct. 1796; d. 30 *Nov*. 1862; m. 30 May 1833, *Emily Octavia, da. of Edward Taylor of Bifrons, co. Kent*, d. 19 Feb. 1871; *and had issue* (*with* 2 *sons and* 2 *das. d. young*) 1*e* to 8*e*.

1*e*. *William Deedes of Sandling, M.P., J.P., D.L.*, b. 11 Oct. 1834; d.s.p. 27 May 1887.

2*e*. *Herbert George Deedes of Sandling Park and Saltwood Castle, co. Kent, J.P., Col.* 60*th Rifles and Assist. Under-Sec. of State for War* 1878, b. 28 *Sept.* 1836; d. 5 May 1891; m. 5 Dec. 1870, *Rose Elinor, da. of Major-Gen. L. Barrow, C.B., Chief Commr. for Oudh*; *and had issue* 1*f* to 4*f*.

1*f*. Herbert William Deedes of Saltwood, Lieut. 1st Batt. 60th Rifles (*Saltwood Castle, Hythe, co. Kent*; 4 *Lyall Street, Belgrave Square, W.*), b. 27 Oct. 1881; *unm*.

2*f*. Wyndham Henry Deedes, Lieut. 3rd Batt. 60th Rifles, *b*. 10 Mar. 1883.

3*f*. Dorothy Mary Deedes.

4*f*. Marjorie Constance Deedes.

3*e*. Rev. Brook Deedes, M.A. (Oxon.), Vicar of Hampstead since 1900 (*The Vicarage, Hampstead*), b. Jan. 1847; *m*. Feb. 1889, Mary Caroline, da. of Maynard Brodhurst, I.C.S.

4*e*. Louisa Deedes.

5*e*. Mary Deedes.

6*e*. Margaret Deedes, *m*. 5 Jan. 1871, Halifax Wyatt.

7*e*. Charlotte Deedes.

8*e*. Jessy Deedes.

2*d*. *Rev. Julius Deedes, Rector of Witlersham, co. Kent*, bapt. 25 *May* 1798; d. 24 *Oct*. 1879; m. 14 *May* 1829, *Henrietta Charlotte* [*descended from the Lady Anne, sister of Edward IV.* (see the Exeter Volume, p. 608)], *da. of Edward Dering* [*and grand-da. of Sir Edward Dering, 7th Bt.* [*E.*], d. 1 Dec. 1904; *and had issue* (2 *sons and* 4 *das.*).

3*d*. Edward Deedes, H.E.I.C.C.S., bapt. 20 *Jan*. 1802; d. *at Poona* 26 *May* 1848; m. 1846, *Emily, da. of* (—) *Cheek of Calcutta, M.D.*; *and had issue*.

4*d*. *Rev. Charles Deedes, Rector of West Carmel, co. Somerset*, b. 9 Oct. 1808;

[Nos. 131338 to 131394.

The Plantagenet Roll

d. 25 Dec. 1875; m. 29 Nov. 1843, *Letitia Anne*, da. of the Hon. Philip Pleydell-Bouverie [*E. of Radnor Coll. and a descendant of George, Duke of Clarence, K.G.* (see Clarence Volume, p. 505)], d. 1887; *and had issue.*

5d. *Rev. Lewis Deedes M.A., Rector of Branfield.* b. 13 *Jan* 1811; d. *Nov.* 1888; m. 4 *Oct.* 1838, *Augusta*, da. *of George Smith of Selsdon, co. Surrey; and had issue.*

6d. *Edmund Deedes, settled in Canada,* b. 1812; d. (–); m. 1846, *Annie*, da. of (—) *Kelly of Toronto.*

7d. *Fanny Deedes,* d. *Jan.* 1869; m. *May* 1831, *Charles Andrew* [son of Archdeacon Andrew], d. *June* 1871; *and had issue.*

8d. *Isabella Deedes,* d. 26 Oct. 1870; m. 4 Aug. 1830, *George Warry of Shapwick, co. Somerset, J.P., Bar.-at-Law,* d. 29 *Mar.* 1883; *and had issue (with others d.s.p.) le to 4e.*

1e. *George Deedes Warry of Shapwick, J.P., M.A., K.C., Recorder of Portsmouth, &c.,* b. 7 *June* 1831; d. 4 *May* 1904; m. 23 Oct. 1860, *Catherine Emily,* da. of *John Clitsome Warren of Taunton; and had issue (with others d.s.p.) 1f to 3f.*

1f. *Bertram Arthur Warry of Shapwick, J.P., Capt. formerly Essex Regt. (Shapwick House, Bridgwater; United Service),* b. 22 Sept. 1864; *unm.*

2f. Ernest Gerald Warry, b. 14 May 1874; *unm.*

3f. Gertrude Florence Warry, *unm.*

2e. *William Taylor Warry, I.S.O., B.A. (Oxon.),* b. 4 Dec. 1836; d. (–); m. *and had issue* (see Appendix).

3e. Georgiana Sophia Warry, *m.* 23 Oct. 1866, Capt. Alexander Decimus Toogood, Bengal Fusiliers, one of H.M. Corps of Gentlemen-at-Arms, *d.* 4 Dec. 1874; and has issue (see Appendix)].

4e. Anna Maria Warry.

9d. *Marianne Deedes,* b. 31 *Jan.* 1817; d. *Feb.* 1867; m. 26 *Oct.* 1842, *the Rev. Gordon Frederic Deedes, Vicar of Netherbury, and afterwards* (1856–1898) *of Heydour,* b. 1 *May* 1814; d. 9 *Aug.* 1898; *and had issue 1e to 5e.*

1e. Gordon Frederic Deedes (*West Coker, Yeovil*), b. 1 Jan. 1848; *m.* 1st, 27 June 1878, Emily Rosa, da. of Col. George Augustus Sullivan, *d.* 18 Mar. 1881; 2ndly, 3 July 1890, the Hon. Alice Fanny Catherine, da. of Florance George Henry (Irby), 5th Baron Boston [G.B.]; and has issue 1f to 3f.

1f. John Gordon Deedes, b. 22 Mar. 1892.
2f. Bertram Gordon Deedes } (twins), b. 2 July 1899.
3f. Percy Gordon Deedes }

2e. Walter Gordon Deedes (*Lympstone, Devon*), b. 28 July 1856; *m.* 24 Oct. 1895, Florence, da. of Col. H. R. Salusbury Trelawny; and has issue 1f.

1f. Phœbe Trelawny Deedes, b. 9 May 1899.

3e. Rev. Arthur Gordon Deedes, St. John the Divine, Kennington, b. 4 Feb. 1861.

4e. Agnes Sophia Deedes } (*Bourne Corner, Farnham*).
5e. Isabella Mary Deedes }

2c. *Rev. John Deedes,* b. Dec. 1768; d. 2 *July* 1843; m. 18 *Sept.* 1798, *Sophia,* da. of *Gen. Gordon Forbes,* d. *Feb.* 1846; *and had issue.*

3c. *Mary Deedes,* d. 1830; m. 1799, *Robert Montague Wilmot, M.D.; and had issue.*

3a. *Theodosia Bramston.*
4a. *Catharine Bramston.*
5a. *Alice Bramston,* m. *Thomas*[1] *or John Williams.*[2]
6a. *Mary Bramston.*
7a. *Elizabeth Bramston.*
8a. *Grace Bramston.*
9a. *Sarah Bramston.*
10a. *Philadelphia Bramston.*   [Nos. 131394 to 131408.

---

[1] Berry's "Essex Genealogies," p. 50.   [2] Burke's "Commoners," ii. 432.

of The Blood Royal

334. Descendants of the Hon. ANNE LENNARD (Table XXVIII.), d. (–); m. HERBERT MORLEY of Glynde, co. Sussex, d. 1611; and had issue 1a to 3a.

 1a. *Margaret Morley*, da. and co-h., d. c. 1667, *will proved that year*; m. Sir Humphrey Tufton *of the Mote and Bobbing Court, co. Kent, 1st Bt. [E. 24 Dec. 1641] [2nd brother of Nicholas, 1st Earl of Thanet [E.]], d. Oct. 1659; and had issue 1b to 2b.*

  1b. *Sir John Tufton, 2nd Bt.* [E.], b. 1663; d.s.p. 11 *Oct.* 1685.

  2b. *Olympia Tufton, in her issue sole h.*, d. *Sept.* 1680; m. c. 1652, Sir William Wray *of Ashby, 1st Bt.* [E. 1660], M.P., d. 17 *Oct.* 1669; *and had issue.*

See the Clarence Volume, Table LXX. and p. 551; and the Essex Volume (Clarence Supplement), pp. 571–575, Nos. 23486/1–100.

 2a. *Anne Morley*, da. and co h., m. (–) *Houghton*.[1]

 3a. *Chrisogan Morley, da and co-h.*, m. Richard Tufton *of Tothill Street, Westminster* [4th brother of Nicholas, 1st Earl of Thanet [E.]], d. 4 *Oct.* 1631; *and had issue 1b to 3b.*

  1b. *John Tufton*, son and h., d. 24 *Jan.* 1649, *father of Sir Richard Tufton, who* d.s.p.[2]

  2b. *Mary Tufton*.

  3b. *Christian Tufton*, m. as 2nd wife, Sir Robert Huddleston *of Salston, co. Camb.*, d.s.p.   [Nos. 131409 to 131508.

335. Descendants of the Hon. MARY LENNARD (Table XXVIII.), d. (–); m. Sir RALPH BOSVILLE of Bradborne, co. Kent, living 1619; and had issue[3] 1a.

 1a. *Leonard Bosville*, son and h., m. Anne, da. of Sir Thomas Ridley, LL.D.

336. Descendants of KATHERINE WALLER (Table XXIX.), d. (–); m. as 2nd wife, RICHARD COURTENAY [4th son of Sir William Courtenay of Powderham, 1st Bt. [E.]], d. 1696; and had issue.

See the Essex Volume (Exeter Supplement), p. 601, Nos. 1618/1–154.
              [Nos. 131509 to 131662.

337. Descendants of THOMAS WALLER of South Lambeth (Table XXIX.), d. 1731; m. Anne, da. of George SMYTH of Beverley, co. York, d. 1781; and had issue (with a son, James, who d.s.p. 1802) 1a to 2a.

 1a. *Anne Waller*, da. and event. h., b. 1713; d. 1801; m. 1st, *John Allen of London*, d. 1760; 2ndly, *Jonathan Wathen of East Acton, co. Middx.*; *and had issue 1b.*

  1b. *Mary Allen*, da. and h., d. (–); m. *Joshua Phipps of London* [2nd son of Robert Phipps *of Walthamstow, co. Essex*]; *and had issue 1c to 2c.*

   1c. Sir *(Jonathan) Wathen Phipps, afterwards (R.L. 7 Mar. 1814) Waller,*

---

[1] Berry's "Sussex Genealogies," 175.

[2] Brydges' "Collins," iii. 440; see also Pocock's "Memorials of the Tuftons," 1800, p. 38 *et seq.*

[3] Berry's "Kent Genealogies," p. 481.

The Plantagenet Roll

1st Bt. [U.K. 30 May 1815], G.C.H., b. 6 Oct. 1769; d. 1 Jan. 1853; m. 1st, 23 Feb. 1793, Elizabeth, da. of Thomas Slack of Braywick Lodge, co. Berks, d. 20 Jan. 1809; and had issue 1d to 4d.

1d. Sir Thomas Wathen Waller, 2nd Bt. [U.K.], b. 24 June 1805; d. 29 Jan. 1892; m. 20 Oct. 1836, Catherine, da. of the Rev. Henry Wise of Offchurch, co. Warwick, d. 24 July 1861; and had issue 1e to 5e.

1e. Sir George Henry Waller, 3rd Bt. [U.K.], Major-Gen. and Col. 7th Fusiliers, b. 2 Sept. 1837; d. 9 Oct. 1892; m. 21 June 1870, Beatrice Katherine Frances [descended from King Henry VII. (see the Tudor Roll, p. 384)], da. of Christopher John Hume Tower of Huntsmore Park, co. Bucks, J.P., D.L. [by his wife, Lady Sophia Frances, née Cust], d. 7 Dec. 1898; and had issue 1f to 4f.

1f. Sir Francis Ernest Waller, 4th Bt. [U.K.], Capt. Special Reserve of Officers, formerly Royal Fusiliers, served in S. Africa 1899–1902 (Woodcote, Warwick), b. 11 June 1880.

2f. Wathen Arthur Waller, formerly Lieut. Northumberland Fusiliers, b. 6 Oct. 1881; m. 1904, Viola, da. of Henry Le Súeúr of La Plaisance, Wynberg, Cape Colony, I.S.O., J.P.

3f. Margaret Beatrice Waller, m. 31 July 1895, Capt. Denis Granville, M.V.O., Chief Constable co. Dorsetshire (Shirley House, Dorchester); and has issue. See p. 466, No. 103050.

4f. Edith Sophia Waller, unm.

2e. Rev. Adolphus Waller, M.A., Vicar of Hunstanton, Norfolk, b. 8 Oct. 1838; d. 16 July 1890; m. 19 July 1866, Jamesina (Hunstanton Cottage, King's Lynn), da. of Henry L'Estrange Styleman-Le Strange of Hunstanton, J.P., D.L.; and had issue.
See p. 412, No. 79922.

3e. Katherine Mary Waller, d. 1 May 1884; m. as 2nd wife, 10 Mar. 1868, James Sydney Stopford [E. of Courtown Coll.], d. 8 July 1885; and had issue.
See the Tudor Roll, p. 185, Nos. 20925-931.

4e. Sophia Harriett Waller, m. 9 Oct. 1866, Arthur Thomas (Liddell), 5th Baron Ravensworth [U.K.], &c. [descended from George, Duke of Clarence, K.G. (see the Clarence Volume, p. 91)] (Ravensworth Castle, Gateshead; Eslington Park, Whittingham S.O); and has issue 1f to 5f.

1f. Hon. Gerald Wellesley Liddell (Rooksbury, Weybridge, Surrey; Wellington, &c.), b. 21 Mar. 1869; m. 11 Oct. 1899, Isolde Blanche [descended from George, Duke of Clarence, K.G. (see the Clarence Volume, p. 516)], da. of Charles Glynn Prideaux-Brune of Prideaux Place; and has issue 1g to 3g.

1g. Robert Arthur Liddell, b. 2 Jan. 1902.
2g. Ellen Isolda Liddell, b. 5 July 1905.
3g. Beatrice Sophia Liddell, b. 23 Sept. 1906.

2f. Hon. Cyril Arthur Liddell, J.P. (Wellington; Durham County, &c.), b. 22 June 1872.

3f. Hon. Athol Robert Henry Liddell (30 Ebury St., S.W.; Garrick), b. 2 Feb. 1881.

4f. Hon. Emily Agnes Liddell.
5f. Hon. Catherine Anna Liddell.

5e. Charlotte Louisa Waller (69 Warwick Square, S.W.).

2d. Rev. Ernest Adolphus Waller, for whom T.R.H. the Dukes of Cumberland and Cambridge and the Princesses Sophia and Mary stood sponsors, b. 11 Dec. 1807; d. 20 Ap. 1845; m. 15 Jan. 1835, Louisa, da. of the Rev. Henry Wise of Offchurch, d. 22 Oct. 1874; and had issue 1e to 3e.

1e. Rev. Ernest Alured Waller, M.A., Rector of Packington, Hon. Canon of Worcester, Proctor in Convocation, and Rural Dean of Kenilworth (Little Packington Rectory, Coventry), b. 6 Jan. 1836; m. 12 Jan. 1864, Mary Louisa, da. of Henry Barton of Rangemore, co. Staff.; and has issue (with an eldest son, Ernest Henry, Lieut. R. Fusiliers, d. unm.) 1f to 8f. [Nos. 131663 to 131686.

# of The Blood Royal

1*f*. Edmund Waller, *b.* 24 Oct. 1871; *m.* 14 June 1906, Muriel Grace [descended from King Henry VII. (see the Tudor Roll, p. 153)], da. of the Hon. Henry Arden Adderley, J.P., D.L. [B. Norton Coll.].

2*f*. Richard Alured Waller, *b.* 1884.

3*f*. Louisa Jane Marion Waller.

4*f*. Ella Nutcombe Waller.

5*f*. Margaretta Waller.

6*f*. Katherine Louisa Waller, *m.* 5 Jan. 1899, Henry Arthur Heywood [Bt. Coll.] (*Christleton Lodge, Chester*); and has issue 1*g* to 2*g*.

1*g*. Geoffrey Henry Heywood, *b.* 1903.

2*g*. Charles Richard Heywood, *b.* 1908.

7*f*. Beatrice Mary Waller.

8*f*. Constance Harriett Waller, *m.* 1907, Frederick Wyldbore Digby Pinney.

2*e*. Stanier Waller, C.V.O., Hon. M.A. (Oxon.), Col. (ret.) R.E. and a Military Member Oxford Territorial Force Ass., an Hon. Equerry to H.R.H. the Duchess of Albany, *formerly* Extra Equerry to Queen Victoria, has Egyptian Medal with Clasp and Bronze Star and 4th Class Midjidie, &c. (28 *Bardwell Road, Oxford*), *b.* 13 Aug. 1844; *m.* 23 Ap. 1879, Sophia Louisa, da. of William Willes of Astrop House, co. Northants, *d.* 25 June 1893; and has issue 1*f* to 5*f*.

1*f*. Stanier Edmund William Waller, *formerly* Lieut. Royal Fusiliers, *b.* 15 Aug. 1881.

2*f*. Wathen Ernest Waller, *b.* 1886.

3*f*. Michael Henry Waller, *b.* 1888.

4*f*. Louisa Waller.

5*f*. Dorothy Waller.

3*e*. Louisa Mary Waller, *m.* 30 Sept. 1869, the Rev. Daniel Goddard Compton, M.A. (Oxon.), Rector of Barnsley 1874–1901, &c. (*The Downs, Clifton Road, West Southbourne, Bournemouth*); and has issue 1*f* to 4*f*.

1*f*. John Henry Compton, *b.* 1875.

2*f*. William Edmund Compton, *b.* 1883.

3*f*. Mary Goddard Compton.

4*f*. Rose Waller Compton.

3*d*. Georgiana Waller, d. 11 *Ap.* 1871; m. 6 *July* 1830, *the Rev. Sainsbury Langford-Sainsbury of Froyle, co. Hants, Rector of Beckington-cum-Standerwick,* d. 5 *Sept.* 1849 *or* 1857; *and had* (*with a son and da. who d.s.p.*) *issue* 1*e to* 3*e*.

1*e*. Rev. Sainsbury Langford-Sainsbury, Rector of Beckington, *b.* 29 *June* 1831; d. 7 *July* 1892; m. 3 *Aug.* 1864, *Mary* [descended *from the Lady Anne, sister of King Edward IV., &c.* (see the Exeter Volume, p. 522)], *da. of John Blandy-Jenkins of Kingston House, co. Berks,* d. 5 *Nov.* 1870; *and had issue* 1*f to* 4*f*.

1*f*. Rev. Thomas Hugh Langford-Sainsbury, M.A. (Oxon.), Rector of Beckington (*Beckington Rectory, Bath*), *b.* 23 Sept. 1869; *m.* 2 Dec. 1896, Emma Harriot [descended from King Henry VII. (see the Tudor Roll, p. 350), da. of Arthur Harvey Thursby, J.P., D.L.; and has issue 1*g* to 2*g*.

1*g*. Thomas Audley Langford-Sainsbury, *b.* 23 Nov. 1897.

2*g*. Hugh Waller Langford-Sainsbury, *b.* 31 Dec. 1902.

2*f*. Grace Mary Langford-Sainsbury, *m.* 17 Ap. 1895, the Rev. Walter Errington, Rector of Hunsdon (*Hunsdon Rectory, Ware, Herts*); and has issue 1*g* to 3*g*.

1*g*. John Errington, *b.* Feb. 1899.

2*g*. George Errington, *b.* 1902.

3*g*. Mary Errington, *b.* 29 Ap. 1903.

3*f*. Katherine Langford-Sainsbury, *unm.*

4*f*. Mary Langford-Sainsbury, *unm.*

2*e*. *Waller Langford Sainsbury,* b. 18 *May* 1838; d. 5 *Sept.* 1898; m. (—), *da. of* (—); *and had issue* 1*f*.

1*f*. Georgina Langford Sainsbury. [Nos. 131687 to 131717.

The Plantagenet Roll

3e. Georgina Catherine Louisa Langford Sainsbury, *unm.*

4d. Anna Eliza Waller, d. 26 Mar. 1868; m. 15 *July* 1823, John Jarrett of Camerton Court, *J.P., D.L.,* High Sheriff co. Somerset 1840, b. 4 *July* 1802; d. 25 *Ap.* 1863; *and had issue* 1e *to* 2e.

1e. Anna Mary Jarrett, Lady of the Manor of Camerton, b. 25 *Jan.* 1838; d. *unm.* 8 Dec. 1893.

2e. Emily Elizabeth Jarrett, Lady of the Manor of Camerton (*Camerton Court, near Bath*), b. 4 Dec. 1840.

2c. Mary Phipps, d. (-); m. *Thomas Blunt of Chelsea.*

2a. Jane Waller, d. (-); m. *Enos Coope; and had issue.*[1]

[Nos. 131718 to 131719.

338. Descendants of MARGARET WALLER (Table XXIX.), *bur.* 9 Jan. 1694; *m. c.* 1643, Sir WILLIAM COURTENAY of Powderham, 1st Bt. [E. Feb. 1644], *d.* 4 Aug. 1702; and had issue.

See the Exeter Volume, Table V., pp. 102-128, Nos. 900-1645, and the Essex Volume (Exeter Supplement), pp. 601-606, Nos. 1618/1-154.

[Nos. 131720 to 132619.

339. Descendants of SIMON (HARCOURT), 1st VISCOUNT HARCOURT [G.B.], P.C., Lord High Chancellor of Great Britain 1712-1714 (Table XXIX.), *b.* 1661; *d.* 29 July 1727; *m.* 1st, 18 Oct. 1680, REBECCA, da. of the Rev. Thomas CLARK, M.A., *bur.* 16 May 1687; and had issue 1*a* to 3*a*.

1a. Hon. Simon Harcourt, *M.P.,* b. 1685; d.v.p. 1 *July* 1720; m. *Elizabeth, da. of John Evelyn of Wotton, co. Surrey; and had issue* 1b *to* 2b.

1b. Simon (Harcourt), 2nd Viscount and (21 Dec. 1749) 1st Earl of Harcourt [G.B.], Viceroy of Ireland, b. c. 1712; d. 16 *Sept.* 1777; m. 16 Oct. 1735, *Rebecca, da. and h. of Charles Samborne Le Bas of Pipwell Abbey, co. Northants,* d. 16 *Jan.* 1765; *and had issue (with a da., Lady Lee, whose issue failed)* 1c *to* 2c.

1c. George Simon (Harcourt), 2nd Earl of Harcourt [G.B.], b. 1 Aug. 1736; d.s.p. 20 *Ap.* 1809.

2c. William (Harcourt), 3rd Earl of Harcourt [G.B.], Field-Marshal, G.C.B., b. 20 Mar. 1743; d.s.p. 18 *June* 1830.

2b. Martha Harcourt, a co-h. to the Barony of Fitzalan [E. 1295], d. 8 *Ap.* 1794; m. as 3rd wife, 10 *Ap.* 1844, *George (Venables-Vernon), 1st Baron Vernon* [G.B. 1762], d. 21 Aug. 1780; *and had issue* 1c *to* 2c.

1c. Henry (Venables-Vernon), 3rd Baron Vernon [G.B.], b. 18 *Ap.* 1747; d. 20 Mar. 1829; m. 1st, 14 Feb. 1779, *Elizabeth Rebecca Anne, da. of Sir Charles Sedley, 2nd Bt.* [E. 1702], d. 16 Aug. 1793; 2ndly, 29 Nov. 1795, *Alice Lucy, da. and co-h. of Sir John Whitefoord, 3rd Bt.* [S. 1701], d. 1 Aug. 1827; *and had issue* 1d *to* 2d.

1d. George Charles (Venables-Vernon), 4th Baron Vernon [G.B.], b. 4 Dec. 1779; d. 18 Nov. 1835; m. 5 Aug. 1802, *Frances Maria, da. and h. of Adm. the Right Hon. Sir John Borlase Warren, 1st Bt.* [G.B. 1775], d. 17 *Sept.* 1837; *and had issue.*

See the Exeter Volume, pp. 90-92, Nos. 509-574.

2d. Hon. Henry Sedley Venables-Vernon, *Lieut.-Col. Grenadier Guards,* b 1796; d. 12 Dec. 1845; m. 29 Aug. 1822, *Eliza Grace, da. of Edward Coke of Longford Court, co. Derby [niece of Thomas William (Coke), 1st Earl of Leicester* [U.K.]]; *and had issue* 1e. [Nos. 132620 to 132685.

---

[1] Berry's "Buckinghamshire Genealogies," p. 5.

# of The Blood Royal

1*e.* **Edward Henry Venables-Vernon**, *Lieut. R.N.*, b. 5 *July* 1823; d. 7 *Jan.* 1856; m. 21 *Jan.* 1851, ⟨*Louisa Sophia Charlotte*, da. of the *Ven. J. G. de Joux, Archdeacon of Mauritius*, d. 1895; *and had issue* 1*f.*

1*f.* Sir **William Henry Venables-Vernon**, *Bailiff of Jersey, formerly Attorney-Gen. for that Island, &c.* (*St. Peter's House, Jersey; Travellers'*), b. 1 Jan. 1852; m. 18 Dec. 1880, Julia Matilda, da. and h. of Philip Gossett of Bagot Manor, Jersey.

2*c.* Right Rev. the Hon. **Edward Venables-Vernon**, *afterwards* (*R.L.* 15 *Jan.* 1831) **Harcourt**, *D.D., Lord Archbishop of York*, b. 10 *Oct.* 1757; d. 5 *Nov.* 1847; m. 5 *Feb.* 1784, *Lady Anne, da. of Granville (Leveson-Gower), 1st Marquis of Stafford* [*G.B.*], d. 16 *Nov.* 1832; *and had issue.*
See the Tudor Roll, pp. 380-383, Nos. 28983-29129.

2*a.* Hon. **Anne Harcourt**, d. (-); m. *John Barlow of Alebeak, co. Pembroke.*
3*a.* Hon. **Arabella Harcourt**, d. (-); m. *Herbert Aubrey of Clayhanger.*

[Nos. 132686 to 132833.

340. Descendants, if any, of ELIZABETH WALLER, wife of Sir FRANCIS BARNHAM (*sic*), and of BRIDGET WALLER, wife of Sir THOMAS MORE (Table XXIX.).

341. Descendants of the Hon. ELIZABETH LENNARD (Table XXVIII.), d. (-); *m.* 1599, Sir FRANCIS BARNHAM of Boughton Monchelsea, co. Kent, *d.* 1646; and had issue (15 children of whom) 1*a* to 11*a*.

1*a.* **Dacres Barnham**, d.s.p.

2*a.* Sir **Robert Barnham**, *1st Bt.* [*E.* 1663], *M.P.*, b. 1606; d. *apparently* s.p.m.s. *May or June* 1685; m. 1*st, c.* 1636, *Elizabeth or Anne, da. of Robert Henley of Henley, co. Som.*; 2*ndly* (*lic.* 18 *Aug.*), 1663, *Hannah, widow of* (—) *Lowfield, da. of* (—) *Nichols of London*, d. 1686; *and had issue* 1*b to* 5*b*.

1*b.* **Francis Barnham**, *only son living* 1664, *and then unm*,[1] d.v.p. 1668.
2*b.*[1] **Mary Barnham**.
3*b.*[1] **Elizabeth Barnham**,[2] m. *as 1st wife, Sir Nathaniel Powell, 2nd Bt.* [*E.*], d. *c.* 1707; *and had issue* (*with a son, Nicholas, who* d.s.p. *and das.*) 1*c*.
1*c.* **Barnham Powell**, d.v.p.; m. *Elizabeth, da. of James Clitherow of Boston House, Brentford, co. Midx.; and had issue* 1*d to* 3*d*.
1*d.* Sir **Nathaniel Powell**, *3rd Bt.* [*E.*], b. *c.* 1688; d. *unm.* 1708.
2*d.* **James Powell**, d. *unm.*

---

[1] Visitation of Kent. See the "Complete Baronetage," iii. 285. In Le Neve's MS. "Baronetage" he is said to have *m.* 1st, a lady unnamed; 2ndly, the widow of Lowfield (by whom he had issue a da. and h.); and 3rdly, Anne, widow of John Shirley. The last was the da. of Sir Philip Parker, and the licence is dated 12 Sept. 1667. In the Waller pedigree (see Table XXIX.) Elizabeth (a cousin-german of this Francis Barnham) is said to have married a Sir Francis Barnham, and she may perhaps have been the first wife. The second is clearly a mistake for his father's second marriage. A very confused genealogy is given in Burke's "Extinct Baronetcies," and also in Berry's "Hants Pedigrees" (p. 167). There he is said to have *m.* Anne Shirley, and to have been father of Sir Robert Barnham, 2nd Bt., who *d.* 1728, leaving issue a da. and h., who *m.* Thomas Rider (see above). As Sir Robert, if he ever existed, cannot have been born before 1668, and as Sir Barnham Ryder (son of the above-named Thomas Rider and Philadelphia Barnham) was knighted 1714, this descent is impossible.

[2] In Berry's "Hants Pedigrees" (p. 167) she is made the daughter of her nephew, Sir Barnham Rider.

The Plantagenet Roll

3*d.* Sir *Christopher Powell*,[1] 4th Bt. [E.], M.P., b. *c.* 1690; d.s.p. 5 *July* 1742.
4*b.*[1] *Annie Barnham.*
5*b.*[2] *Philadelphia Barnham,* b. 1664; m. *Thomas Rider;* and had issue 1*c.*
1*c.* Sir *Barnham Rider of Kent, knighted* 20 *Oct.* 1714; m. 1717, (—), da. of Adm. *Littleton;* and had issue 1*d.*
1*d.* Sir *Thomas Rider of Boughton Monchelsea, knighted* 13/21 *Mar.* 1744.
3*a. Edward Barnham.*
4*a.* Francis *Barnham of Maidstone, will dated* 1677, *said to have* m. Margaret (—), *and to have had issue (Francis, Robert, Edward, Frances, Grace, and Margaret).*

5*a. William Barnham.*[1] 6*a. Dudley Barnham.*
7*a. Martin Barnham.* 8*a. Margaret Barnham.*
9*a. Judith Barnham.* 10*a. Elizabeth Barnham.*
11*a. Frances Barnham.*

342. Descendants, if any surviving, of the Hon. FRANCES LENNARD (Table XXVIII.), *d.* (–); *m.* Sir ROBERT MORE of Losely, co. Surrey, M.P., *b.* 21 May 1581; *d.* 2 Feb. 1626; and had issue 1*a* to 4*a*.

1*a.* Sir *Poynings More,* 1st Bt. [E. 18 *May* 1642], M.P., b. 13 *Feb.* 1606; d. 11 *Ap.* 1649; m. *Elizabeth, widow of Christopher Rous of Henham, co. Suffolk, da. of Sir John Fytch of Woodham Walter, co. Essex,* d. 13 *Sept.* 1666; *and had issue* 1*b.*
1*b.* Sir *William More,* 2nd Bt. [E.], M.P., b. 1644; d.s.p. 24 *July* 1684.
2*a.* Rev. *Nicholas More of Loseley, d.* 22 *Dec.* 1684; m. *Susan, da. of Richard Saunders; and had issue (with Robert,* d.s.p. 1689, *and Elizabeth,* d. *unm.* 13 *Feb.* 1692) 1*b.*
1*b. Margaret More,* d. 14 *Sept.* 1704; m. Sir *Thomas Molyneux; and had issue (with a da.)* 1*c.*
1*c.* Sir *More Molyneux of Loseley,* d. (–); m. 1 *Mar.* 1722, *Casandra, da. and co-h. of Francis Cornwallis of Abermarles, co. Caermarthen; and had issue.*
3*a. Robert More, Major in the Army,* m. *and had issue* 1*b.*
1*b. Frances More,* d.s.p. 1680; *m. as* 1st *wife, John Latton of Esher Place, co. Surrey,* bur. 23 *Nov.* 1727.
4*a. Anne More,* m. *John Gresham.*

343. Descendants of Lady MARY FITZALAN (Table II.), *b. c.* 1540; *d.* 25 Aug. 1557; *m.* as 1st wife, 1556, THOMAS (HOWARD), 4th DUKE OF NORFOLK [E.], K.G., *b.* 10 Mar. 1536; *d.* 2 June 1572; and had issue.

See Section 199, p. 331, Nos. 52611–55452. [Nos. 132834 to 133675.

344. Descendants of Lady ANNE WENTWORTH (Table XXX.), *b.* 8 Oct. 1629; *bur.* 8 Jan. 1696; *m.* 13 Nov. 1654, EDWARD (WATSON), 2nd LORD ROCKINGHAM [E.], *bapt.* 30 June 1630, *d.* 22 June 1689; and had issue.

See the Exeter Volume, Table XIII. and pp. 243–261, Nos. 8843–9890, and Supp., 9763/1–13. [Nos. 133676 to 134736.

---

[1] Berry and Burke confuse him with a William Barnham, Mayor of Norwich 1652, and make him marry three times and have numerous descendants. See, however, Henry Woodds' " Family of Woodds," p. 48.

of The Blood Royal

345. Descendants of Sir WILLIAM WENTWORTH (Table XXX.), d. (−); m. ELIZABETH, da. and co-h. of Thomas SAVILE of Hasseldon Hall, co. York; and had issue.

See the Mortimer-Percy Volume, Part II.

346. Descendants of the Hon. ANNE HOWARD (Table XXXI.), d. 12 Sept. 1775; m. as 2nd wife, 14 Sept. 1729, the Right Hon. Sir WILLIAM YONGE of Colyton, 4th Bt. [E. 1661], K.B., P.C., M.P., b. c. 1693; d. 10 Aug. 1755; and had issue 1a to 7a.

1a. *Right Hon. Sir George Yonge, 5th Bt. [E.], K.B., P.C., M.P., Governor of the Cape, &c.,* b. 1731; d.s.p. 25 *Sept.* 1812.
2a. *Anne Yonge.*
3a. *Louisa Yonge,* m. *the Very Rev. Charles Howard, D.D., Dean of Exeter.*
4a. *Charlotte Yonge,* m. *James Stuart Fulk.*
5a. *Amelia Yonge,* d. *in or before* 1831; m. *as* 2nd *wife,* 3 *July* 1774, *Sir Edward Lloyd of Pengwern, co. Flint,* 1st *Bt.* [G.B. 29 *Aug.* 1778], d.s.p. 26 *May* 1795.
6a. *Juliana Yonge,* m. *as* 3rd *wife, Henry William Sanford of Walford, co. Som.* (see the Essex Volume, p. 335).
7a. *Sophia Yonge.*

347. Descendants of GEORGE (VERNON), 2nd BARON VERNON [G.B.] (Table XXXI.), b. 9 May 1735; d. 18 June 1813; m. 2ndly, 25 May 1786, GEORGIANA, da. of William FAUQUIER, d. 31 May 1823; and had issue 1a.

1a. *Hon. Georgiana Vernon,* b. 9 *Jan.* 1788; d. 13 *Sept.* 1824; m. 19 *Sept.* 1809, *Edward (Harbord), 3rd Baron Suffield* [G.B. 1786], d. 6 *July* 1835; *and had issue* 1b *to* 2b.
1b. *Edward Vernon (Harbord), 4th Baron Suffield* [G.B.], b. 19 *June* 1813; d. unm. 22 *Aug.* 1853.
2b. *Hon. Georgiana Mary Harbord* (see p. 555), b. 23 *June* 1816; d. 13 *Nov.* 1903; m. 1st, 2 Oct. 1837, *George Edward Anson, C.B.,* d. 8 *Oct.* 1849; 2ndly, 22 *Oct.* 1855, *Charles Edward Boothby, Ranger of Needwood Forest* [*Bt. Coll.*]; *and had issue* 1c.
1c. Mary Anson, m. 13 Sept. 1877, the Rev. Robert Digby Ram, M.A., Vicar of Hampton and Preb. of St. Paul's [descended from King Henry VII., &c. (see the Tudor Roll, p. 166)]; and has issue 1d to 3d.
1d. George Edward Ram, b. 1879.
2d. Frederick Montagu Anson Ram, b. 1885.
3d. Emily Jane Ram, m. 1 Oct. 1901, Sir John Home-Purves-Hume-Campbell, 8th Bt. [S.] (*Marchmont, Greenlaw, S.O.*); and has issue 1e to 2e.
1e. Mabel Jane Home-Purves-Hume-Campbell.
2e. Elsie Barbara Home-Purves-Hume-Campbell.   [Nos. 134737 to 134742.

348. Descendants of THOMAS (ANSON), 1st VISCOUNT ANSON [U.K. 17 Feb. 1806] (Table XXXI.), b. 14 Feb. 1767; d. 31 July 1818; m. 15 Sept. 1794, Lady ANNE MARGARET, da. of Thomas William (COKE), 1st Earl of Leicester [U.K.], d. 23 May 1843; and had issue 1a to 6a.

1a. *Thomas William (Anson), 2nd Viscount Anson and* (15 *Sept.* 1831) 1*st Earl of Lichfield* [U.K.], b. 20 *Oct.* 1795; d. 18 *Mar.* 1854; m. 11 *Feb.* 1819, *Louisa Catherine, da. of Nathaniel Philips of Slebech Hall, co. Pembroke,* d. 20 *Aug.* 1879; *and had issue* 1b *to* 5b.

The Plantagenet Roll

1b. Thomas George (Anson), 2nd Earl of Lichfield [U.K.], b. 15 Aug. 1825; d. 7 Jan. 1892; m. 10 Ap. 1855, Lady Harriet Georgiana Louisa, da. of James (Hamilton), 1st Duke of Abercorn [I.], K.G., P.C.; and had issue.
See the Tudor Roll, pp. 482-483, Nos. 33440-33475.

2b. Lady Louisa Mary Anne Anson, b. 6 Dec. 1819; d. 27 Aug. 1882; m. 26 Nov. 1838, Edward King Tenison of Kilronan Castle, co. Roscommon, Lt. and Custos Rotulorum and M.P. for that co., &c., b. 21 Jan. 1805; d. 19 June 1878; and had issue 1c to 2c.

1c. Louisa Frances Mary Tenison, d. 9 Sept. 1868; m. as 1st wife, 14 June 1866, John Baptiste Joseph (Dormer), 12th Lord Dormer [E.], d. 22 Dec. 1900; and had issue.
See the Exeter Volume, pp. 275-276, Nos. 10944-10947.

2c. Florence Margaret Christina Tenison, d. 18 Oct. 1907; m. 23 Jan. 1872, Henry Ernest Newcomen (King, afterwards R.L. 10 Mar. 1883, King-Tenison), 8th Earl of Kingston [I.], d. 13 Jan. 1896; and had issue 1d to 2d.

1d. Henry Edwyn (King-Tenison), 9th Earl of Kingston [I.], late Irish Guards (Kilronan Castle, Keadue; Oakport, Boyle, both co. Roscommon; Carlton; Guards, &c.), b. 19 Sept. 1874; m. 3 Feb. 1897, Ethel Lisette, da. of Sir Andrew Barclay Walker, 1st Bt. [U.K.]; and has issue 1e to 4e.

1e. Robert Henry Ethelbert (King-Tenison), Viscount Kingsborough, b. 27 Nov. 1897.

2e. Lady Sheelah Florence Lizette King-Tenison.
3e. Lady Honor Bridget King-Tenison.
4e. Lady Doreen Kara King-Tenison.

2d. Lady Edith Charlotte Harriet King-Tenison, m. 11 Sept. 1907, Capt. George Ivor Patrick Poer O'Shee, Prince of Wales' Leinster Regt. (see below) (26 Hans Crescent, S.W.); and has issue 1e to 2e.

1e. Patrick Ivor Rivallon O'Shee, b. 18 Feb. 1910.
2e. Christine O'Shee.

3b. Lady Anne Frederica Anson, b. 22 Feb. 1823; d. 22 July 1896; m. as 1st wife, 29 Aug. 1843, Francis (Wemyss-Charteris-Douglas), 10th Earl of Wemyss and 6th Earl of March [S.], 3rd Baron Wemyss [U.K.] (Gosford, Longniddry; Elcho Castle, co. Perth, &c.); and had issue.
See the Clarence Volume, pp. 253-254, Nos. 6095-6116.

4b. Lady Harriet Frances Maria Anson, b. 26 Dec. 1827; d. 15 Feb. 1898; m. 7 June 1851, Augustus Henry (Venables-Vernon), 6th Baron Vernon [G.B.], d. 1 May 1883; and had issue.
See the Exeter Volume, pp. 90-91, Nos. 509-525.

5b. Lady Gwendoline Isabella Anna Maria Anson (Gardenmorris, Kilmacthomas, co. Waterford), m. 19 Ap. 1865, Nicholas Richard Power O'Shee of Gardenmorris, co. Waterford, J.P., D.L., d. 30 Mar. 1902; and has issue 1c to 5c.

1c. Richard Alfred Poer O'Shee of Gardenmorris, &c., Major R.E., and Commr. Brito-French Boundary Commission, W. Africa, has Benin Exped. Medal and Clasp 1897 and West Africa Clasp 1897-1898 (Gardenmorris, Kill, Piltown; Sheestown, near Kilkenny), b. 6 Aug. 1867.

2c. John Marcus Poer O'Shee, Dep. Inspector R.I.C., b. 1869; m. 22 Sept. 1900, Myrtle Constance, da. of Col. Ynyr Henry Burges of Parkanaur, co. Tyrone; and has issue 1d.

1d. [da.] O'Shee, b. 19 Ap. 1903.

3c. George Ivor Patrick Poer O'Shee, Capt. Royal Canadians (Leinster Regt.) and Adj. 5th Batt. Rifle Brig. (26 Hans Crescent, S.W.), b. 4 June 1873; m. 11 Sept. 1907, Lady Edith Charlotte Harriet (see above), da. of Henry Ernest Newcomen (King-Tenison), 8th Earl of Kingston [I.]; and has issue.
See above, Nos. 134789-134790.

4c. Gwendolen O'Shee.
5c. Aline Angela O'Shee.

[Nos. 134743 to 134838.

# of The Blood Royal

2a. Hon. George Anson, Major-Gen. and Com.-in-Chief in India, b. 13 Oct. 1797; d. in India 27 May 1857; m. 30 Nov. 1830, the Hon. Isabella Elizabeth Annabella [descended from King Henry VII., &c.], da. of Cecil Weld (Forrester), 1st Baron Forrester [U.K.], d. 29 Dec. 1858; and had issue.
See the Tudor Roll, p. 302, Nos. 25625-25654.

3a. Hon. Anne Margaret Anson, b. 3 Oct. 1796; d. 19 Aug. 1882; m. as 2nd wife, Archibald John (Primrose), 4th Earl of Rosebery [S.], 1st Baron Rosebery [U.K.], K.T., P.C., d. 4 Mar. 1868; and had issue 1b.

1b. Lady Anne Primrose, b. 22 Aug. 1820; d. 17 Sept. 1862; m. as 3rd wife, 30 May 1848, the Right Hon. Henry Tufnell, P.C., M.P., d. 15 June 1854; and had issue 1c.

1c. Henry Archibald Tufnell, M.A. (Oxon.), b. 15 May 1854; d. (? s.p.) 21 Sept. 1898.

4a. Hon. Frances Elizabeth Anson, b. 9 Jan. 1810; d. 25 Dec. 1899; m. 1st, 12 Sept. 1835, the Hon. Charles John Murray [2nd son of David William, 3rd Earl of Mansfield [G.B.], K.T.], d. 1 Aug. 1851; 2ndly, 10 Sept. 1853, Ambrose Isted of Ecton, co. Northants, d.s.p. 13 May 1881; and had issue 1b to 2b.

1b. Charles Archibald Murray of Taymount (Taymount, Stanley, Perthshire), b. 10 Oct. 1836; m. 1st, 27 Ap. 1865, Lady Adelaide Emily [descended from King Henry VII. (see Tudor Roll, p. 270)], da. of William Basil Percy (Feilding), 7th Earl of Denbigh [E.] and Desmond [I.], d. 24 May 1870; 2ndly, 11 June 1878, Blanche, da. of Sir Thomas Moncreiffe, 7th Bt. [S.] [by his wife Lady Louisa, née Hay]; and has issue 1c to 6c.

1c. Ronald William Murray (Homefield, Fishponds, Bristol), b. 10 May 1866; m. 16 Feb. 1904, Constance Mary Jane [descended from King Henry VII., &c. (see Tudor Roll, p. 477)], da. of Gen. Sir Richard Chambre Hayes-Taylor, G.C.B. [M. of Headford Coll.].

2c. Archibald John Percy Murray (Logie House, Methven, Perth), b. 16 July 1867; m. 9 Ap. 1907, Dulcibella, da. of Collingwood Lindsay Wood of Freeland, Forgandenny.

3c. Charles John Murray, Lieut. Coldstream Guards and A.D.C. to Gov. of British East Africa (Bachelors'; Guards, &c.), b. 1 Dec. 1881.

4c.[1] Margaret Frances Murray, m. 10 July 1902, Arthur Holford, late 19th Hussars; and has issue 1d.

1d. Violet Adelaide Margaret Holford, b. July 1905.

5c.[2] Gertrude Blanche Murray, m. 12 June 1907, Alasdair Ronald Macgregor of Macgregor (The Hermitage, Rothesay, Isle of Bute); and has issue 1d to 2d.

1d. Malcolm Findanus Macgregor, b. 2 Mar. 1908.

2d. Dorviegelda Malvina Macgregor, b. 5 Ap. 1910.

6c.[2] Edith Lilian Murray.

2b. Frederick John George Murray, Col. formerly 3rd Dragoon Guards (Dedington, Oxford; Junior United Service; Travellers', &c.), b. 18 May 1839.

5a. Hon. Frederica Sophia Anson, b. 24 Aug. 1814; d. 11 Oct. 1867; m. 21 Ap. 1838, Lieut.-Col. the Hon. Bouverie Francis Primrose, C.B. [2nd son of Archibald John, 4th Earl of Rosebery [S.], K.T.], d. 20 Mar. 1898; and had issue.
See the Clarence Volume, p. 467, Nos. 20762-20779.

6a. Hon. Elizabeth Jane Anson, b. 26 Feb. 1816; d. 15 Sept. 1894; m. 18 July 1837, Henry Manners (Cavendish), 3rd Baron Waterpark [I.], b. 8 Nov 1793; d. 31 Mar. 1863; and had issue 1b to 3b.

1b. Henry Anson (Cavendish), 4th Lord Waterpark [I.] and 5th Bt. [G.B.], J.P., D.L. (Doveridge, Derby), b. 14 Ap. 1839; m. 1873, Emily, da. of John Stenning; and has issue 1c to 4c.

1c. Hon. Charles Frederick Cavendish, Lieut. R.N., b. 11 May 1883.

2c. Hon. Mary Cavendish.   [Nos. 134839 to 134900.

The Plantagenet Roll

3c. Hon. Winifred Cavendish, *m.* 8 Mar. 1904, George Ashton Strutt (*Rock House, Cromford, near Matlock*).

4c. Hon. Norah Lilian Cavendish.

2b. Hon. Eliza Anne Cavendish, *m.* 12 July 1859, Haughton Charles Okeover of Okeover, J.P., D.L., High Sheriff co. Derby 1862 (see p. 548) (*Okeover Hall, Ashbourne*); and has issue 1c to 8c.

1c. Haughton Ealdred Okeover, M.V.O., Capt. 7th Batt. King's Royal Rifle Corps, *b.* 10 May 1875.

2c. Mabel Alice Okeover.

3c. Hon. Maude Okeover, *formerly* (1884-1887), Maid of Honour to H.M. Queen Victoria, *m.* 1st as 2nd wife, 11 Oct. 1887, Sir Andrew Barclay Walker of Osmaston, 1st Bt. [U.K.], J.P., *d.* 27 Feb. 1893; 2ndly, 30 July 1895, John Frederick Lort Phillips of Laurenny, J.P. [descended from the Lady Anne, sister to King Edward IV. (see Exeter Volume, p. 115)] (*Laurenny Park, Pembroke*).

4c. Ruth Isabel Okeover, *m.* 3 Nov. 1903, Capt. Hervey Ronald Bruce, Irish Guards [son and h. of Lieut.-Col. Sir Hervey Jacke Lloyd Bruce, 4th Bt. [U.K.], J.P., D.L. (*Downhill, Coleraine, co. Londonderry*).

5c. Edith Mary Okeover, *m.* 11 Aug. 1891, Capt. the Hon. Herbert Tongue Alsopp, J.P., *late* 10th Hussars [descended from the Lady Anne, sister of King Edward IV. (see Exeter Volume, p. 446)] (*Walton Bury, near Stafford*); and has issue 1d.

1d. Cynthia Bridget Allsopp.

6c. Ethel Blanche Okeover, *m.* 30 May 1899, Sir Peter Carlaw Walker of Osmaston, 2nd Bt. [U.K.], D.L., Lieut.-Col. Comdg. Derbyshire Yeo. (*Osmaston Manor, Ashburne, Derby; Junior Carlton, &c.*); and has issue 1d to 2d.

1d. Ian Peter Anthony Monro Walker, *b.* 30 Nov. 1902.

2d. Enid Walker.

7c. Mercy Lilian Okeover, *m.* 20 July 1897, the Hon. Assheton Nathaniel Curzon [4th son of Alfred Nathaniel Holden, 4th Baron Scarsdale [G.B.], and a descendant of the Lady Anne, sister of King Edward IV. (see the Exeter Volume, p. 455)] (34 *Stanhope Gardens, S.W.*); and has issue 1d to 4d.

1d. Ralph Okeover Nathaniel Curzon, *b.* 24 July 1904.

2d. Joan Doreen Curzon, *b.* 13 June 1898.

3d. Rhona Lilian Curzon, } twins.
4d. Vera Lilian Curzon, }

8c. Victoria Alexandrina Okeover.

3b. Hon. Adelaide Cavendish (10 *Egerton Place, S.W.*), *m.* as 2nd wife, 3 Dec. 1863, Samuel William Clowes of Broughton Hall and Norbury, M.P., J.P., D.L. [descended from the Lady Isabel Plantagenet, aunt of King Edward IV.], *d.* 31 Dec. 1898; and had issue.

See the Essex Volume, p. 358, Nos. 35369-35378.   [Nos. 134901 to 134929.

349. **Descendants** of Sir GEORGE ANSON, G.C.B., K.T.S., M.P., Gen. in the Army and Col. 4th Dragoon Guards, Equerry to H.R.H. the Duchess of Kent, Groom of the Bedchamber to H.R.H. the Prince Consort, and finally Governor of Chelsea Hospital (Table XXXI.), *b.* 12 Aug. 1769; *d.* 4 Nov. 1849; *m.* 27 May 1800, FRANCES, sister of Sir Frederick Hamilton, 5th Bt. [S. 1646], da. of Capt. John William HAMILTON, *d.* 24 Feb. 1834; and had issue (with 2 elder sons who *d.s.p.*) 1a to 10a.

1a. Frederic Walpole Anson, *Major H.E.I.C.S.*, *b.* 21 *May* 1806; *d.* 12 *Nov.* 1848; m. 25 *July* 1827, *Catherine, da. of* (—) *Hanson*, b. 11 *June* 1880; *and had issue* (*with an elder son who d. young*) 1b *to* 3b.

of The Blood Royal

1b. Frederick William Norgate Hamilton Anson, b. (—).
2b. Thomas Anson, b. (—); m. in New Zealand; and has issue.
3b. Frances Anson, d. c. 1846; m. Major Wilkie.

2a. Talavera Vernon Anson, Adm. R.N., b. 26 Nov. 1809; d. (–); m. 1st, 13 June 1843, Sarah Anne, da. of Richard Potter, M.P. for Wigan, d. 5 May 1846; 2ndly, 24 Aug. 1847, Caroline Octavia Emma, da. of Major-Gen. William Staveley, Com.-in-Chief of Madras; and had issue (with 2 sons who d.s.p.) 1b to 5b.

1b. Charles Vernon Anson, Com. R.N., b. 4 Feb. 1846; m. 1 Jan. 1874, Louisa Augusta Anne, da. of the Hon. Robert Hare [E. Listowel Coll.], d. 1898; and had issue (Kathleen Louisa Anson, b. 23 Dec. 1874; d. 26 Feb. 1880).
2b. Edward Harcourt Anson, b. 7 Feb. 1858.
3b.[2] Sarah Constance Anson.
4b.[2] Charlotte Rose Anson.
5b.[2] Adelaide Frances Mary Anson.

3a. Octavius Henry St. George Anson, Major 9th Lancers, served throughout Indian Mutiny, b. 28 Sept. 1818; d. 14 Jan. 1859; m. 1st, 20 Feb. 1845, Katherine Harriette, da. of James Wemyss of Cawnpore, H.E.I.C.S. [E. Wemyss Coll.], d. 17 May 1849; 2ndly, 12 Dec. 1850, Frances Elizabeth, da. of Major-Gen. James Manson of London, d. 19 Feb. 1901; and had issue 1b to 7b.

1b. George Wemyss Anson, J.P., Lieut.-Col. (ret.) Indian Army (Garvock, Kippington, Sevenoaks), b. 30 Nov. 1848; m. 28 Nov. 1878, his cousin, Katherine Harriette, da. of Sir William Muir, K.C.S.I., LL.D.; and has issue (with a son, Octavius Muir Hamilton Anson, Indian Army, previously Dorset Regt., b. 13 Nov. 1879; d. unm. 29 Aug. 1905; and a da. d. young) 1c to 4c.

1c. George Frank Wemyss Anson, Capt. Indian Army, b. 22 Mar. 1881.
2c. Katharine Wemyss Anson.
3c. Mabel Wemyss Anson.
4c. Maud Vernon Anson.

2b. Henry Brooke Anson, Capt. R.N. (48 St. Edward's Road, Southsea), b. 7 Dec. 1852; m. 19 Aug. 1891, Mary, da. of Col. Hall; and has issue.

3b. James Okeover Anson, of the Land Survey Dept., New Zealand (King's Road, Lower Hutt, Wellington), b. 7 Ap. 1854; m. 7 Mar. 1900, Rebekah Midgley, da. of James Naylor of Bradford, co. York; and has issue 1c to 5c.

1c. James Midgley Anson, b. at Wellington Prov., N.Z., 15 Ap. 1901.
2c. Victor Hamilton Anson, b. there 17 Aug. 1902.
3c. Robert Alexander Anson, b. there 30 Sept. 1903.
4c. Charles Okeover Anson, b. there 27 Mar. 1905.
5c. Mabel Alice Anson, b. there 25 Mar. 1908.

4b. Rev. Harcourt Suft Anson, Rector of Southover (Southover Rectory, Lewes), b. 24 Oct. 1857; m. 1 July 1886, Edith, da. of Edward Thomas Busk; and has issue (with a da. d. young) 1c to 6c.

1c. Wilfrid Gordon Anson, b. 14 Sept. 1890.
2c. Arthur Harcourt Busk Anson, b. 28 June 1895.
3c. Cyril Okeover Anson, b. 29 July 1899.
4c. Dorothy Susan Anson.
5c. Edith Rowena Anson.
6c. Frances Grace Anson.

5b. Octavius Henry St. George Anson (X 1229 E. Johnson Street, Madison, Wis., U.S.A.), b. 8 Ap. 1859; m. at Milwaukee 3 Mar. 1902, Charlotte Elizabeth, da. of Daniel Andreas Whit Beck.

6b.[1] Fanny Caroline Anson, m. 3 July 1866, William Coldstream, H.E.I.C.S. (69 West Cromwell Road, S.W.); and has issue 1c to 6c.

1c. William Menzies Coldstream, Maj. R.E., b. 19 Feb. 1869; m. 29 July 1897, Adèle Margaret Edith, da. of Sir John Foster Stevens; and has issue 1d to 2d.

1d. William John Anson Coldstream, b. 15 July 1901.
2d. Margaret Anson Coldstream, b. 24 May 1898. [Nos. 134930 to 134960.]

The Plantagenet Roll

2c. George Probyn Coldstream, M.B., C.M. (Edin.), b. 16 Aug. 1870; m. 25 Ap. 1895, Susan Jane Lilian Mercer, da. of Major Mercer Tod, late 43rd Regt.; and has issue 1d to 5d.
    1d. George Anson Probyn Coldstream, b. 20 July 1899.
    2d. William Menzies Coldstream, b. 28 Feb. 1908.
    3d. Winifred Mercer Muir Coldstream, b. 12 Mar. 1896.
    4d. Enid Lilian Wemyss Coldstream, b. 13 Aug. 1897.
    5d. Kathleen Nancy Coldstream, b. 5 Aug. 1900.
3c. John Coldstream, I.C.S., b. 23 Dec. 1877; unm.
4c. Margaret Muir Coldstream, m. 4 Oct. 1890, Thomas Wistar Brown of Philadelphia; and has issue 1d to 6d.
    1d. Moses Brown, b. 6 Nov. 1892.
    2d. William Wistar Brown, b. 29 Jan. 1896.
    3d. Margaret Coldstream Brown, b. 4 Aug. 1891.
    4d. Frances Mary Brown, b. 4 Dec. 1894.
    5d. Rhoda Menzies Brown, b. 15 Dec. 1901.
    6d. Lydia Wistar Brown, b. 16 Ap. 1903.
5c. Katherine Harriette Coldstream, m. 25 Ap. 1893, Major Ernest Moncrieff Paul, R.E.,; and has issue 1d to 6d.
    1d. Henry William Moncrieff Paul, b. 20 Jan. 1894.
    2d. George Anson Moncrieff Paul, b. 31 July 1895.
    3d. Ernest Kenneth Moncrieff Paul, b. 17 July 1897.
    4d. Cedric Stewart.Toller Paul, b. 6 Mar. 1905.
    5d. James Stewart Moncrieff Paul, b. 22 Feb. 1908.
    6d. Emily Moncrieff Paul, b. 8 Aug. 1901.
6c. Elizabeth Huntly Muir Coldstream, m. 22 Oct. 1901, Reginald Fendale Lowis, Assist. Comr. Port Blair; and has issue 1d to 4d.
    1d. John William Anson Lowis, b. 27 Sept. 1908.
    2d. Elizabeth Evelyn Lowis, b. 30 June 1903.
    3d. Janet Marion Lowis, b. 27 Oct. 1904.
    4d. Mary Hope Wemyss Lowis, b. 8 Mar. 1907.

7b.[2] *Henrietta Constance Anson*, b. 5 Nov. 1855; d. 22 Mar. 1886; m. 5 July 1877, *Thomas Duncan* (183 *Portsdown Road, Maida Vale, N.W.*); *and has issue* 1c *to* 5c.
    1c. Ernest Anson Duncan, a Clerk in the Bank of England, b. 22 July 1882.
    2c. Emmeline Ella Duncan.
    3c. Frances Christine Duncan.
    4c. Lilian Mary Duncan.
    5c. Henrietta Constance Duncan.

4a. *Rev. Thomas Anchitel Anson, M.A., Rector of Longford and Rural Dean*, b. 14 Oct. 1818; d. 3 Oct. 1899; m. 5 Aug. 1846, *Anne Jane* [*herself descended from Edward III. through the Mortimer-Percy marriage*], da. *of Henry Packe of Twyford Hall, co. Norfolk, Lieut.-Col. Grenadier Guards*, b. 19 Oct. 1822; d. 4 *Sept.* 1897; *and had issue* (*with a da., Emily Mary, who d. unm.* 27 *Aug.* 1864) 1b *to* 8b.
  1b. Walter Hamilton Anson (*Harkaway, Stanley Avenue, Mosman, N.S.W.*), b. 19 Aug. 1849; m. Annie Augusta, da. of Robert Wesley Sherlock of Port Luis, Mauritius; and has issue (with a son, Archibald Vernon, d. young) 1c to 4c.
    1c. Beatrice Kate Hamilton Anson, b. 21 Jan. 1879.
    2c. Madeline Anson, b. 31 July 1880.
    3c. Marjorie Doris Anson, b. 4 Mar. 1892.
    4c. Olive Audrey Okeover Anson, b. 9 June 1894.

  2b. Henry Vernon Anson (*Brookholme, Vanbrugh Park, Blackheath, S.E.*), b. 20 Feb. 1852; m. 10 Mar. 1875, Frances Elizabeth, da. of John Taylor Gorle, Capt. late 40th Regt.; and has issue 1c to 7c.
    1c. John Anchitel Anson, b. 16 May 1876.   [Nos. 134961 to 134998.

# of The Blood Royal

2c. Henry Percy Richmond Anson, Capt. Middlesex Regt., b. 20 Oct. 1877; m. 28 July 1909, Lilian Mary, da. of Capt. Thomas Daw, Middlesex Regt.

3c. George Okeover Anson, b. 8 Aug. 1880.

4c. Archibald Anson, a Clerk in the London and Westminster Bank, b. 8 Mar. 1882; m. 24 Dec. 1907, Mabel, da. of Charles Henry Walker Biggs of Glebe Lodge, Champion Hill, S.E.; and has issue 1d to 2d.

1d. Donald Archibald Vernon Anson, b. 5 Ap. 1910.

2d. Dahlia Anson, b. 23 Sept. 1908.

5c. Frances Octavia Anson.

6c. Mildred Anson.

7c. Mabel Muriel Gladys Anson.

3b. Charles George Archibald Anson of the Chartres, West Falkland, Falkland Islands, and of Meadow Hurst, Slinfold, co. Sussex, a J.P. for the Falklands (*Meadow Hurst, Slinfold, Sussex*), b. 22 Oct. 1858; m. 7 Ap. 1885, Mabel, da. of Thomas Kerr, C.M.G., sometime (1880–1891) Governor and Chief Justice of the Falkland Islands; and has issue (with 2 sons: Philip Thomas Archibald, b. 23 June 1886; d. 26 Oct. 1890; and Walter Vernon, b. 26 Ap. 1890; d. 22 Oct. following) 1c.

1c. Philip Archibald Noël Primrose Anson, b. 29 Dec. 1903.

4b. Henrietta Maria Anson (*Bear Wood, Wokingham, Berks*), m. 15 Oct. 1872, Arthur Fraser Walter of Bear Wood, J.P., D.L., co. Berks, High Steward of Wokingham and one of H.M.'s Lieuts. for City of London, d. Feb. 1910; and has issue 1c to 4c.

1c. John Walter, M.A. (Oxon.), Capt. and Hon. Major 4th Batt. Royal Berks Regt., Chairman *The Times* Publishing Coy. (*Bear Wood, Wokingham, Berks*), b. 8 Aug. 1873; m. 7 Nov. 1903, Charlotte Hilda, da. of Col. C. E. Foster; and has issue 1d to 2d.

1d. John Walter, b. 31 Oct. 1908.

2d. Pamela Mary Walter, b. 24 Ap. 1907.

2c. Stephen Walter (49 *Cornwall Gardens, S.W.*), b. 16 June 1878; m. 16 July 1904, Beatrice Mary, da. of James Henry Coleman of Napier, N.Z.; and has issue 1d to 2d.

1d. Arthur Ewart Stephen Walter, b. 11 May 1905.

2d. Eileen Beryl Stephen Walter, b. 18 Ap. 1908.

3c. Dorothy Walter, m. 15 Sept. 1898, Arthur Edmund Gill (*Chenies, Oakwood Hill, Ockley; Oxford and Cambridge*); and has issue (with a son, Arthur Charles, b. 22 July 1899; d. Dec. 1901) 1d to 4d.

1d. Humphrey Clarendon Gill, b. 31 July 1903.

2d. Geoffrey Walter Gill, b. 3 Dec. 1905.

3d. Edmund Benedict Gill, b. 27 June 1907.

4d. Margery Gill, b. 21 Oct. 1901.

4c. Olive Walter.

5b. Constance Louisa Anson.

6b. Charlotte Isabella Anson, m. 16 Aug. 1876, the Rev. Henry Major Walter, Rector of St. Paul's (*St. Paul's Rectory, Wokingham*); and has issue 1c to 3c.

1c. Elwyn Henry Walter, b. 6 Sept. 1885.

2c. Maud Isabel Walter.

3c. Rachel Walter, m. 5 Ap. 1904, Frederick Thomas Henry Henlé (9 *Radnor Place, Hyde Park, W.*); and has issue 1d to 2d.

1d. Nevil Frederick Henlé, b. 14 Feb. 1905.

2d. Cordelia Rachel Henlé, b. 14 Nov. 1907.

7b. Madeline Anson.

8b. Ethel Grace Anson, m. 30 Sept. 1885, the Rev. Egerton Corfield, M.A. (Camb.) (*Kirkley*, 15 *Willis Road, Cambridge*); and has issue 1c to 5c.

1c. Egerton Anson Frederick Corfield, b. 3 Dec. 1887.

2c. Bernard Conyngham Corfield, b. 22 May 1890. [Nos. 134999 to 135032.

The Plantagenet Roll

3c. Conrad Lawrence Corfield, b. 15 Aug. 1893.
4c. Hubert Vernon Anchitel Corfield, b. 21 Dec. 1895.
5c. Ethel Marjorie Corfield, b. 30 Oct. 1891.

5a. Edward Hamilton Anson, *late* Bengal C.S. and *formerly* Gentleman Usher to Queen Victoria (*57 Cambridge Terrace, Hyde Park, W.*), b. 2 Dec. 1821; *m.* 1st, 4 Jan. 1843, Louisa, da. of George Bunter Clapcott of Reynstone, co. Dorset, *d.* 25 Sept. 1868; 2ndly, 5 June 1872, Virginia Arnold, widow of George C. Tugwell, da. of Major-Gen. Mackie, C.B.; and has issue (with others who d.s.p.) 1b to 3b.
1b. Edward Rosebery Anson, b. 25 Aug. 1855; *m.* and has issue.
2b. Frank Charles Montresor Anson, b. 18 Aug. 1857; *m.*
3b.¹ Grace Etta Anson.

6a. *Mary Ann Anson*, d. 1875; m. 1st, 17 *Sept.* 1823, *the Rev. Charles Gregory Okeover of Okeover*, b. 11 *May* 1792; d. 2 *Aug.* 1826; 2ndly, 14 *Feb.* 1833, *Robert Plumer Ward of Gilston Park,* co. *Herts,* d. (-); *and had issue (with possibly others by 2nd husband)* 1b.
1b. Haughton Charles Okeover of Okeover, J.P., D.L., High Sheriff co. Derby 1862 (*Okeover Hall, Ashbourne, Derby*), b. 13 Nov. 1825; *m.* 12 July 1859, the Hon. Eliza Anne Cavendish [also descended from Edward III. through Mortimer-Percy], da. of Henry Manners (Cavendish), 3rd Baron Waterpark [I.]; and has issue.
See p. 544, Nos. 134904–134918.

7a. *Charlotte Isabella Anson*, d. 18 *Jan.* 1842; m. *as* 1st *wife*, 29 *Mar.* 1828, *Edward Richard Northey of Woodcote, co. Surrey, and Box, co. Wilts, J.P., D.L., High Sheriff co. Surrey* 1856, *sometime 3rd Guards and 52nd Foot, served in the Peninsular War, Waterloo, &c.*, b. 8 *Feb.* 1795; d. 2 *Dec.* 1878; *and had issue (with a son killed in action in South Africa* 6 *Ap.* 1879) 1b to 4b.
1b. Rev. Edward William Northey of Woodcote, M.A. (Oxon.), J.P., Lord of the Manors of Cheam, Ewell, and Cuddington, co. Surrey, and Joint Lord of the Manor of Box, co. Wilts, *formerly* Vicar of Chaddesden, &c. (*Woodcote House, Epsom*), b. 23 Ap. 1832; *m.* 22 Aug. 1867, Florence Elizabeth [descended from the Lady Anne, sister of King Edward IV., &c.], da. of Sir John Edward Honywood, 6th Bt. [E.]; and has issue.
See the Exeter Volume, p. 103, Nos. 930–940.

2b. George Wilbraham Northey *of Ashley Manor, co. Wilts, J.P., D.L., Lieut.-Col. Cameronians*, b. 28 *Jan.* 1835; d. 12 *Mar.* 1906; m. 20 *Sept.* 1859, *Louisa, da. of Arthur James S. Barrow, 23rd and 30th Regts.; and had issue* 1c to 12c.
1c. George Edward Northey of Ashley Manor, J.P., Lord of the Manors of Box, Ashley, and Ditteridge, and Patron of one Living, *late* Governor of H.M. Prison, Manchester (*Ashley Manor, Wilts; Cheney Court, Box, Chippenham*), b. 4 July 1860; *m.* 10 June 1885, Mabel Beatrice Helen, da. of Capt. F. Hunter of Killylung, co. Dumfries, and Weston Park, Bath; and has issue 1d to 3d.
1d. George Evelyn Anson Northey, Lieut. 3rd Batt. Essex Regt., b. 10 Nov. 1886.
2d. Armand Hunter Kennedy Northey, b. 16 Jan. 1897.
3d. Vere Wilbraham Northey, *m.* Sept. 1910, Austin Gardner.

2c. *Francis William Northey, Capt.* 36th *Regt.*, b. 5 *Jan.* 1862; d. 9 *Aug.* 1898; m. *Sept.* 1888, *Beatrice, da. of Capt. T. Robinson, Indian Army; and had issue* 1d.
1d. Eileen Northey.

3c. Herbert Hamilton Northey, Capt. Royal Scots Fusiliers, b. 27 June 1870; *m.* 27 Jan. 1903, Elizabeth, da. of Neale Thompson of Strathdoon, co. Ayr; and has issue 1d.
1d Herbert Wilbraham Hamilton Northey, b. 23 Nov. 1906.

4c. Percy Wilbraham Northey, b. 31 Jan. 1872; *m.* 11 Mar. 1896, Rosalie, da. of John Roupell; and has issue. [Nos. 135033 to 135075.

# of The Blood Royal

5c. Arthur Cecil Northey, Capt. Scottish Rifles, b. 11 Nov. 1873; m. 20 Dec. 1905, Madeleine, da. of Col. Arthur Allen Owen, Royal Bodyguard, *late* 88th Regt. ; and has issue 1d.

    1d. Peter Arthur Owen Northey, b. 19 Nov. 1906.

6c. Cyril Brook Northey (*Ditteridge House, Wilts*), b. Oct. 1877; m. 1 May 1899, Elsa, da. of C. Thiedemann ; and has issue 1d.

    1d. Rosemary Northey.

7c. Constance Fanny Northey, m. 5 Sept. 1888, the Rev. Walter Barlow, M.A., Rector of St. Mary Magdalene, Bridgnorth (*St. Mary Magdalene's Rectory, Bridgnorth*); and has issue 1d to 2d.

    1d. Walter Northey Cecil Barlow.
    2d. Percy Arthur Northey Barlow.

8c. Mary Louisa Northey.

9c. Alice Northey, m. Ap. 1885, George Jones Mitton of Mitton, Major 3rd Batt. S. Staffordshire Regt. [descended from King Henry VII. (see Tudor Roll, p. 319), George, Duke of Clarence, K.G. (see Clarence Volume, p. 310), &c.] (*Mitton Manor, Penkridge, Stafford ; Beamish Hall, Allrighton, Salop*); and has issue 1d to 4d.

    1d. George Henwayn Northey Mitton, b. 25 Oct. 1895.
    2d. Gladys Marjorie Alice Mitton.
    3d. Phyllis May Northey Mitton.
    4d. Muriel Enid Mitton.

10c. Mabel Charlotte Northey, m. Sept. 1902, Reginald Granville; and has issue 1d.

    1d. Robert Northey Granville.

11c. Lilian Beatrice Northey, m. Oct. 1904, Capt. Douglas Hunter, R.A. ; and has issue 1d to 2d.

    1d. Elizabeth Hunter.
    2d. Pamela Hunter.

12c. Evelyn Marion Northey, m. Ap. 1910, Capt. Cyril Gepp, King's African Rifles.

3b. Harriet Elizabeth Northey, m. 20 Sept. 1855, Capt. George Ross, R.E. [son and h. of Field-Marshal Sir Hew Dalrymple Ross, G.C.B.].

4b. Agnes Constance Northey.

8a. Constantia Anson, d. 28 *Nov.* 1842; m. 6 *Oct.* 1831, *Sir Robert North Collie Hamilton of Silverton, 6th Bt.* [S.], *K.C.B., Member of the Supreme Council of India* 1859, *who received the thanks of Parliament for his services during the Mutiny*, b. 7 *Ap.* 1802 ; d. 31 *May* 1887 ; *and had issue* 1b *to* 5b.

    1b. Sir Frederick Harding Anson Hamilton of Silverton, 7th Bt. [S.], *formerly* Major 60th Royal Rifles (*Avon Cliffe, Stratford-on-Avon*), b. 24 Sept. 1836 ; m. 28 Sept. 1865, Mary Jane, da. of H. Willan ; and has issue 1c to 6c.

    1c. Robert Caradoc Hamilton, Lieut. 2nd Batt. Norfolk Regt., b. 22 Mar. 1877 ; m. July 1907, Irene [descended from King Henry VII. (see the Tudor Roll, p. 154)], da. of Sir Osbert L'Estrange Mordaunt, 11th Bt. [E.].

    2c. Frank Hamilton, b. 12 Feb. 1878.
    3c. Constance Ida Hamilton.
    4c. Mary Louisa Hamilton.
    5c. Cerise Hamilton, m.
    6c. Ann Eileen Hamilton, m. 10 Mar. 1906, Edward Cowan [2nd son of Capt. Cowan of Alveston].

    2b. *Francis Henry Hamilton, Capt. 5th Lancers*, b. 7 *Ap.* 1840 ; d. 29 *Nov.* 1891 ; m. 12 *Ap.* 1867, *Maria Theresa, widow of Major George Ernest Rose, da. of Charles Crosbie of Northlands, co. Sussex ; and had issue* 1c *to* 3c.

[Nos. 135076 to 135103.

The Plantagenet Roll

1*c*. Francesca Teresa Hamilton, *m*. Feb. 1894, Capt. Victor Bitossi, 2nd Italian Grenadiers; and has issue 1*d* to 2*d*.
  1*d*. Pier Francesco Bitossi, *b*. 1895.
  2*d*. Graziella Bitossi.

2*c*. Pyne Hamilton, *m*. 18 Aug. 1890, Morris Wickersham Cowen of Philadelphia, U.S.A.

3*c*. Ruby Hamilton, *m*. 1895, Alfred Wilson Hamilton Barrett (*Pebworth House, Pebworth, Warwickshire*); and has issue 1*d*.
  1*d*. Adrian Barrett, *b*. 1896.

3*b*. Constance Eliza Anne Hamilton (*Tiddington House, Stratford-on-Avon*), *m*. 19 Mar. 1853, Major-Gen. Alexander Ross Eliot Hutchinson, Indian Army, *d*. 19 Oct. 1908; and has issue 1*c* to 10*c*.

1*c*. *Alexander John Ross Hamilton Hutchinson, Capt. B.S.C.*, *b*. 20 Sept. 1857; (? d.s.p.) 27 *Feb*. 1891.

2*c*. Rev. Robert Hamilton Hutchinson, M.A. (Oxon.), Vicar of St. Anselm's, Kennington Cross (*St. Anselm's Vicarage, Kennington Cross, S.E.*), *b*. 13 Jan. 1867; *m*. 2 Jan. 1895, Alice Amelia, da. of William Hornby.

3*c*. Anson Vernon Mackenzie Hutchinson (*Robin Hood, Little River*), *b*. 11 Oct. 1869; *m*. 1896, Helen, da. of H. Buchanan of Little River, Canterbury, N.Z.; and has issue 1*d* to 2*d*.
  1*d*. Alexander Anson Hutchinson, *b*. 24 Oct. 1901.
  2*d*. William John Buchanan Hutchinson, *b*. 24 Feb. 1904.

4*c*. *James William Hutchinson*, b. 21 *Feb*. 1876; d. (–).

5*c*. Constance Caroline Hutchinson, *m*. 6 Nov. 1879, Major Arthur James Lushington, *formerly* Dorsetshire Regt. (*Waldo House, Beckenham, Kent*); and has issue 1*d* to 2*d*.
  1*d*. Arthur Edmund Godfrey Hamilton Lushington, *b*. 11 Sept. 1883.
  2*d*. Cecil Henry Gosset Lushington, *b*. 16 Dec. 1884.

6*c*. *Louisa Catherine Hutchinson*, d. 10 *Ap*. 1893; m. 27 *Jan*. 1886, *George William Caldwell Hutchinson; and had issue* 1*d* to 3*d*.
  1*d*. Becher Alexander Colin Hutchinson, *b*. 6 Oct. 1889.
  2*d*. Phyllis Irene Constance Hutchinson, *b*. 8 Jan. 1887.
  3*d*. Enid Frances Caldwell Hutchinson, *b*. 16 Ap. 1891.

7*c*. Frances Eliza Hutchinson.

8*c*. Isabella Harriet Hutchinson, *m*. 24 June 1896, Arthur Robert Johnston Dewar, Lieut. 5th Batt. Warwickshire Regt. and Assist. Sup. of Police, Straits Settlements.

9*c*. Georgina Maud Hutchinson, *m*. 21 Oct. 1903, William Alleyne Paxton Wayte (*Buston, Wilts*); and has issue 1*d* to 3*d*.
  1*d*. William Guy Alexander Wayte, *b*. 4 Ap. 1907.
  2*d*. Robert Thomas Humphrey Wayte, *b*. 28 Dec. 1908.
  3*d*. Cicely Maud Wayte.

10*c*. Mildred Irene Hutchinson, *m*. 30 Ap. 1902, Cornelius Cecil Morley (*St. Ann's, Milford Haven*); and has issue 1*d* to 3*d*.
  1*d*. Cornelius William Morley, *b*. 22 Feb. 1904.
  2*d*. Dorothy Constance Morley.
  3*d*. Violet Irene Morley.

4*b*. *Isabella Frances Hamilton*, d. (–); m. 8 *June* 1854, *Capt. William Ross Shakespear, Madras Cav.*, d. 31 *May* 1861; *and had issue* 1*c* to 2*c*.
  1*c*. Robert Henry Shakespear, *b*. 17 Mar. 1856.
  2*c*. William Frederick Shakespear, *b*. 21 Mar. 1861.

5*b*. Louisa Catherine Emma Hamilton (*2 Hobart Place, S.W.*), *m*. 26 July 1864, Charles Raymond Pelly of Plashet, co. Essex [Bt. of Upton Coll.], *d*. 12 June 1879; and has issue 1*c* to 4*c*. [Nos. 135104 to 135133.]

# of The Blood Royal

1*c*. Charles Hamilton Raymond Pelly, Major and Hon. Lieut.-Col. R.F.A. (*Aveley, Romford; 2 Hobart Place, S.W.*), *b.* 24 Ap. 1867; *m.* 1907, Mary Elizabeth, widow of Capt. E. Trevitt of Haslemere.

2*c*. Constance Louisa Pelly, *m.* 1st, 21 Sept. 1882, Richard Davis Matthey (who obtained a divorce 1895); 2ndly, 1895, Lloyd Harry Baxendale, J.P. (*Greenham Lodge, Newbury, Berks*); and has issue 1*d* to 2*d*.

1*d*. George Cowper Hugh Matthey, *b.* 1883.
2*d*. Constance Joyce Matthey.

3*c*. Ethel Henrietta Pelly, *m.* 21 Aug. 1889, Charles Edward Grey Hatherell (*Radford House, near Leamington; Bolas Parva, near Wellington, co. Salop; Charlton King's, Cheltenham*); and has issue 1*d* to 3*d*.

1*d*. James Hamilton Grey Hatherell, *b.* 8 May 1894.
2*d*. Rita Constance Ellen Hatherell.
3*d*. Sylvia Adelaide Anna Hatherell.

4*c*. Adelaide Pelly (2 *Hobart Place, S.W.*).

9*a*. Sophia Anson, d. 18 *Ap.* 1864; m. 11 *June* 1836, *James John Kinloch of Keir, co. Kincardine*, d. 27 Dec. 1877; *and had issue (with 2 other sons and 3 other das.*[1]) 1*b* to 6*b*.

1*b*. George Hibbert Anchitel Kinloch, Lieut.-Col. (ret.) *late* Somersetshire L.I., *b.* 4 June 1841; *m.* 1st, 7 Ap. 1874, Margaret Emma, da. of John Thomas White of Cashiobury, co. Herts, *d.* 30 July 1884; 2ndly, 20 Jan. 1886, Frances Jane, widow of Francis Plunket Dunne of Brittas, da. of the Rev. Robert Hedges Dunne; and has issue 1*c* to 2*c*.

1*c*.[1] Victoria Frances Emma Kinloch, *m.* 10 Mar. 1897, Henry Arthur Shuckburg Upton of Coolatore, co. Westmeath (*Coolatore, Moate, Westmeath*); *s.p.*

2*c*.[2] Grace Theodosia Farquhar Kinloch, *unm.*

2*b*. Victoria Charlotte Isabella Kinloch, *m.* 1859, Sir Lesley Charles Probyn, K.C.V.O., Auditor of the Duchy of Cornwall and a Member of Council of H.R.H. the Prince of Wales, Dep.-Chairman Great Northern Railway (79 *Onslow Square, S.W.*).

3*b*. Theodosia Frances Mary Anne Kinloch, *m.* 11 Jan. 1859, Gen. Charles Raper Stainforth, Ind. Army, *d.* 4 Feb. 1883; and has issue (see Appendix).

4*b*. Constance Helen Sarah Kinloch, *m.* 26 Aug. 1861, Lieut.-Col. Frederick Morris Alexander, Ind. Army; and has issue (see Appendix).

5*b*. *Susan Ferrier Kinloch*, d.s.p. 25 *July* 1906; m. *as 2nd wife*, 10 *Oct.* 1882, *Chester Workman-Macnaghten, M.A.*, *Principal Rajkumar Coll., Bombay* [*Bt. Coll.*], d.s.p. 1896.

6*b*. Julia Catharine Kinloch, *m.* 27 Ap. 1878, John Fortune of Bengairn (*Bengairn, Castle Douglas, Kirkcudbrightshire*); and has issue 1*c* to 5*c*.

1*c*. Victor Morven Fortune, Lieut. Black Watch, *b.* 21 Aug. 1883.

2*c*. Lilian Forrester Fortune, *m.* 8 Dec. 1898, Major-Gen. John Archibald Henry Pollock, C.B., Indian Army [Pollock of the Khyber Pass, Bt. [U.K. 1872] Coll.] (*East India United Service*); and has issue 1*d* to 3*d*.

1*d*. Frederick Arthur Pollock, *b.* 25 Aug. 1899.
2*d*. Justina Lilian Pollock.
3*d*. Daphne Victoria Catherine Pollock.

3*c*. Mildred Sophia Fortune, *m.* Feb. 1902, David Landale (*Shanghai*); and has issue 1*d* to 2*d*.

1*d*. David Fortune Landale, *b.* 9 Nov. 1905.
2*d*. Margaret Landale.

4*c*. Mary Forrester Fortune, *unm.*
5*c*. Julia Violet Macnaghten Fortune, *unm.*

10*a*. Hon. *Julia Henrietta Anson, Maid of Honour to Queen Victoria*, d. 27 Dec. [Nos. 135134 to 135159.

---

[1] Foster's "Peerage," 1880, p. 385.

The Plantagenet Roll

1886; m. 15 Dec. 1841, Sir Arthur Brinsley Brooke of Colebrooke, 2nd Bt. [U.K.], M.P., b. 1797; d. 21 Nov. 1854; and had issue 1b to 4b.

1b. Sir Victor Alexander Brooke, 3rd Bt. [U.K.], D.L., a Godson of Queen Victoria, b. 5 Jan. 1843; d. 23 Nov. 1891; m. 28 July 1864, Alice Sophia (Villa Jouvence, Pau), da. of Sir Alan Edward Bellingham, 3rd Bt. [G.B.]; and had issue 1c to 8c.

1c. Sir Arthur Douglas Brooke, 4th Bt. [U.K.], J.P., D.L., b. 7 Oct. 1865; d. 27 Nov. 1907; m. 28 July 1887, Gertrude Isabella [descended through three lines from King Henry VII. (see Tudor Roll, p. 261, &c.)] (Colebrooke Park, co. Fermanagh), da. of Stanlake Ricketts Batson of Horseheath, co. Camb.; and had issue 1d to 5d.

1d. Sir Basil Stanlake Brooke, 5th Bt. [U.K.], Lieut. Royal Fusiliers (Colebrooke Park, co. Fermanagh), b. 9 June 1888.

2d. Victor Mervyn Brooke, b. 8 June 1893.

3d. Arthur Francis Brooke, b. 24 Sept. 1896.

4d. Sylvia Henrietta Brooke, b. 17 Feb. 1890.

5d. Sheelah Brooke, b. 9 Jan. 1895.

2c. Ronald George Brooke, D.S.O., formerly Major and Brevet Lieut.-Col. 11th Hussars, served in S. Africa as D.A A.G., &c., 1899-1902, Nile Expedition 1898, &c. &c., b. 25 Sept. 1866; m. 6 May 1908, Haller, da. of Orville Howitz of Baltimore.

3c. Butler Brooke, b. 2 May 1870; m. 2 June 1910, Mary Viva, da. of Cyril Earle Johnston of 4 Boulevard du Midi, Pau.

4c. Victor Reginald Brooke, D.S.O., Lieut.-Col. 9th Lancers and Mil. Sec. to Viceroy of India (Lord Minto), b. 22 Jan. 1872.

5c. Alan Francis Brooke, Lieut. R.F.A., b. 23 July 1883.

6c. Alice Mildred Brooke, m. 28 Sept. 1896, Lieut.-Col. James Ramsay Campbell, formerly Shropshire L.I. [Bt. of Succoth Coll.] (Ardachie, Fort Augustus).

7c. Kathleen Mary Brooke.

8c. Hylda Henrietta Brooke, m. 5 July 1899, Capt. Frederick Henry Arthur Des Vœux [son and h.-app. of Sir Charles Champagné Des Vœux, 6th Bt. [I.]] (31 North Audley Street, W.).

2b. Harry Vesey Brooke, J.P., D.L., Capt. formerly 92nd Highlanders (Fairley, Countesswells, co. Aberdeen), b. 23 Sept. 1845; m. 9 Dec. 1879, Patricia, da. of James Gregory Moir Byres of Tonley, co. Aberdeen; and has issue 1c to 6c.

1c. James Anson Otho Brooke, Lieut. 2nd Batt. Gordon Highlanders, b. 3 Feb. 1884.

2c. Arthur Brooke, Lieut. Indian Army, b. 13 Feb. 1886.

3c. Henry Brian Brooke, b. 9 Dec. 1889.

4c. Patrick Harry Brooke, b. May 1895.

5c. Constance Geraldine Brooke.

6c. Alice Irene Brooke.

3b. Arthur Basil Brooke, R.N., b. 1847; d. 3 Aug. 1884; m. 11 Sept. 1869, Alice Georgina (33 Egerton Gardens, S.W.), widow of J. Shirley Ball of Abbeylara, co. Longford, da. of the Rev. William Norton of Baltinglas; and had issue 1c to 4c.

1c. Harry Brinsley Brooke, 2nd Sec. Diplo. Ser. (British Legation, Berne; Travellers'), b. 30 June 1872; m. 10 Jan. 1907, Hilda Gertrude, da. of Henry Tootal Broadhurst.

2c. Basil Vernon Brooke, Comm. R.N., b. 9 Mar. 1876.

3c. Bertram Norman Brooke, Capt. Grenadier Guards, b. 20 July 1880.

4c. Norah Mary Brooke.

4b. Constance Henrietta Brooke, m. 1st, 3 Oct. 1872, Colin John Campbell, younger, of Colgrain, Royal Scots Greys, d.v.p. 6 Aug. 1880; 2ndly, 24 Sept. 1883,

[Nos. 135160 to 135183.

of The Blood Royal

Col. Robert Henry Patrick Doran, *formerly* 1st Queen's Own Royal West Kent Regt. (*Lurganbrae, Brookeborough, co. Fermanagh*); and has issue 1*c*.

1*c*. Alice Constance Campbell, *m*. 23 Oct. 1895, Col. Charles Edward Lefroy, *formerly* Comdg. 6th Batt. Rifle Brig. [4th son of Thomas Paul Lefroy of Carrigglas, Q.C.] (*Monkstown House, co. Dublin*); and has issue 1*d* to 4*d*.

1*d*. Theodore Charles Geoffrey Lefroy, *b*. 25 Jan. 1900.
2*d*. Aileen Muriel Lefroy.
3*d*. Constance Elizabeth Lefroy.
4*d*. Gladys Mary Lefroy   [Nos. 135784 to 135188.

350. Descendants of Gen. Sir WILLIAM ANSON, 1st Baronet [U.K. 1831], K.C.B. (Table XXXI.), *b*. 13 Aug. 1772; *d*. 13 Jan. 1847; *m*. 26 Jan. 1815, LOUISA FRANCES MARY, da. and h. of John DICKENSON of London [by his wife, Mary, da. and h. of Lord Archibald Hamilton], *d*. 30 July 1831; and had issue 1*a* to 5*a*.

1*a*. Sir John William Hamilton Anson, 2nd Bt. [*U.K.*], b. 26 Dec. 1816; d. 2 Aug. 1873; m. 27 *July* 1842, *Elizabeth Catherine* [*descended from Lady Isabel Plantagenet*], *da. of Major-Gen. Sir Denis Pack, K.C.B.*, d. 3 *July* 1903; *and had issue*.
See the Essex Volume, p. 159, Nos. 19054–19078.

2*a*. Sir Archibald Edward Harbord Anson, K.C.M.G., J.P. Major-Gen. (ret.) R.A., was Lieut.-Gov. of Penang 1867–1882 and Acting Gov. Straits Settlements 1871–1872, 1877, 1879, &c. (*Southfield, Silverhill, St. Leonard's-on-Sea*), b. 16 Ap. 1826; m. 1st, 9 Jan. 1851, Elizabeth Mary, da. of Richard Bourchier, d. 23 Sept. 1891; 2ndly, 15 May 1906, Isabella Jane, da. of Robert Armitstead of Dunscar; and has issue 1*b* to 2*b*.

1*b*. Archibald John George Anson, *b*. 4 Nov. 1851.
2*b*. Elizabeth Mary Louisa Anson.

3*a*. *Mary Louisa Anson*, d. 15 *Nov*. 1856; m. as 2nd *wife*, 8 *July* 1848, *the Rev. Matthew Thomas Farrer of Ingleborough, co. York, M.A., Vicar of Addington and P.C. of Shirley, co. Surrey*, b. 3 *Feb*. 1816; d. 14 *July* 1889; *and had issue* 1*b* to 4*b*.

1*b*. James Anson Farrer of Ingleborough, J.P., Bar.-at-Law, High Sheriff co. Yorks 1897 (*Ingleborough, viâ Lancaster; 50 Ennismore Gardens, Prince's Gate, S.W.*), *b*. 24 July 1849; *m*. 1 Mar. 1877, Elizabeth Georgiana Anne [descended from the Lady Isabel Plantagenet (see the Essex Volume, p. 158)], da. of Col. Arthur J. Reynell Pack, C.B.; and has issue 1*c* to 2*c*.

1*c*. Reginald John Farrer, *b*. 17 Feb. 1880.
2*c*. Sydney James Farrer, *b*. 19 Jan. 1888.

2*b*. Rev. William Farrer, M.A. (Oxon.) (*Bisham Vicarage, Marlow*), *b*. 11 Nov. 1850; *m*. 17 July 1879, Edith Sophia, da. of Frederick Boyd Marson; and has issue 1*c*.

1*c*. Harold Marson Farrer, *b*. 20 Ap. 1882.

3*b*. Matthew George Farrer (*The Elms, Mortimer, Berks*), *b*. 14 Feb. 1852; *m*. 26 Jan. 1884, Caroline Rachel [descended from the Lady Isabel Plantagenet (see Essex Volume, p. 305)], da. of Robert Culling Hanbury of Poles, M.P., J.P.; and has issue (5 sons and 1 da.).

4*b*. Mary Charlotte Farrer, *m*. 9 *Dec*. 1890, the Rev. Charles Augustus Whittuck, M.A. (Oxon.), Vicar of St. Mary's, Oxford (*St. Mary's Vicarage, Oxford*)

4*a*. Anne Georgiana Frances Anson (*Kingsthorpe Hall, near Northampton*), *m*. 19 Feb. 1846, the Rev. William Thornton of Kingsthorpe Hall, M.A. [2nd son
[Nos. 135189 to 135224.

The Plantagenet Roll

of Thomas Reeve Thornton of Brockhall, J.P., D.L.], b. 22 July 1806; d. 20 May 1881; and has issue 1b to 5b.

 1b. Thomas William Thornton of Brockhall, J.P., High Sheriff co. Northants 1886, *formerly* Capt. Northants and Rutland Militia (*Brockhall, near Weedon, Northants*), b. 26 July 1850; m. 6 Sept. 1883, Evelyn Margaret, da. of Edmund Charles Burton of Daventry; and has issue 1c to 5c.

  1c. Thomas Anson Thornton, Lieut. 7th Hussars, b. 5 Jan. 1887.
  2c. Ronald Edmund Thornton, b. 13 Ap. 1889.
  3c. John Burton Thornton, b. 19 Nov. 1891.
  4c. Rosamond Fremeaux Thornton.
  5c. Violet Eleanor Thornton.

 2b. Frances Hugh Thornton, LL.B. (Camb.), J.P., Bar.-at-Law (*Kingsthorpe Hall, near Northampton*), b. 8 Oct. 1853; m. 19 Aug. 1886, Adelaide Ethel, da. of W. Burchell, d. 10 May 1903; and has issue 1c to 2c.

  1c. Henry Gerard Thornton, b. 23 Jan. 1892.
  2c. Peter Fremeaux Thornton, b. 23 Ap. 1903.

 3b. Bertha Anne Thornton, m. 31 Jan. 1884, the Rev. Charles Brooke [descended from King Henry VII. (see Tudor Roll, p. 325)], Vicar of Grendon (*Grendon Vicarage, Northants*).

 4b. Anne Letitia Thornton, m. 1 Sept. 1891, the Rev. Edmund Milnes Ellerbeck, *formerly* Vicar of Chipperfield, Herts (3 *Park Avenue, Bedford*); and has issue 1c to 4c.

  1c. Ernest Alfred Victor Ellerbeck, b. 26 June 1897.
  2c. Bertram John James Ellerbeck, b. 18 July 1899.
  3c. Mabel Mary Ellerbeck.
  4c. Bertha Lilian Ellerbeck.

 5b. Mabel Thornton, m. 1893, James Joseph Maclaren (*Ratho Park, Midlothian*).

 5a. Louisa Frances Maria Anson, d. 14 *Jan*. 1904; m. 16 *Ap*. 1857, Major *Francis Du Cane, R.E.* [*younger brother of Sir Charles Du Cane of Braxted, K.C.M.G.*], d. 4 *Oct*. 1880; *and had issue* 1b to 6b.

  1b. Francis Charles John Du Cane, b. 7 Jan. 1862; m. 1891, Gwendolene, da. of the Rev. Jonathan Harvard Jones.
  2b. Louisa Frances Du Cane.
  3b. Katherine Christabel Du Cane.
  4b. Frances Anne Du Cane.
  5b. Mary Du Cane.
  6b. Caroline Anne Bella Du Cane. [Nos. 135225 to 135246.

351. Descendants of Capt. EDWARD ANSON (Table XXXI.), b. 28 Ap. 1775; d. 18 Mar. 1837; m. Jan. 1808, HARRIOTT, da. of James RAMSBOTTOM, d. 14 Ap. 1858; and had issue 1a to 2a.

 1a. Charles Anson, b. 20 *Oct*. 1813; d. 26 *May* 1854, m. 22 *Ap*. 1844, *Louisa, da. of Joseph Collings of Guernsey* [*re-m*. 9 *Jan*. 1873, *William Tombs Dewé of Coates, co. Glouc.*]; *and had issue* 1b *to* 3b.

  1b. William Charles Collings Anson, b. 18 Ap. 1845; m. 27 Aug. 1878, Eleanor Jane, da. of Willoughby Wood of Hollyhurst, co. Staff.

  2b. Edith Elizabeth Anson, m. 5 Ap. 1865, the Rev. Marcus Samuel Cam Rickards of Clifton, M.A., F.L.S.; and has issue 1c to 3c.

   1c. Robert Hillier Traherne Rickards, b. 20 May 1874.
   2c. Marcus Cecil Anson Rickards, b. 22 Mar. 1878.
   3c. Louisa Caroline Anson Rickards. [Nos. 135247 to 135251.

Of The Blood Royal

3b. Rosalie Harriott Anson, m. 18 Ap. 1878, Capt. Edward Maunsell, 13th Hussars.

2a. Harriott Anson, b. 19 Aug. 1811; d. (? s.p.); m. as 2nd wife, 14 Aug. 1855, Capt. William Dalgairns, 7th Fusiliers, d. 26 Feb. 1869. [No. 135252.

352. Descendants of Lieut.-Col. SAMBROKE ANSON, 1st Foot Guards (Table XXXI.), b. 18 Feb. 1778; d. 10 Oct. 1846; m. ELIZABETH [da. of (—)] HAWKINS of co. Stafford, d. 22 Mar. 1866; and had issue 1a.

1a. Elizabeth Grace Anson, d. (? s.p.); m. 1st, 29 Mar. 1831, Thomas King of Alvediston House, co. Wilts, d. 23 Dec. 1863; 2ndly, 22 Nov. 1867, Thomas Jarvis Bennett of Wilton, co. Wilts, M.D.

353. Descendants of the Rev. FREDERICK ANSON, D.D., Dean of Chester and Preb. of Southwell (Table XXXI.), b. 23 Mar. 1779; d. 8 May 1867; m. May 1807, MARY ANNE, da. of the Rev. Richard LEVETT of Milford, co. Staff., d. (–); and had issue 1a to 6a.

1a. Frederick Anson, M.A., Canon of Windsor, Rector of Sudbury 1836–1876, b. 28 Mar. 1811; d. 9 Sept. 1885; m. 7 May 1845, the Hon. Caroline Maria [descended from the Lady Anne, sister of King Edward IV.], da. of George John (Venables-Vernon), 5th Baron Vernon [G.B.]; and had issue.

See the Exeter Volume, pp. 91–92, Nos. 533–565.

2a. George Edward Anson, C.B., Priv. Sec. to H.R.H. the Prince Consort and Keeper of the Privy Purse to Queen Victoria, and Treasurer and Cofferer to King Edward VII. when Prince of Wales, b. 14 May 1812; d. 8 Oct. 1849; m. 20 Oct. 1837, the Hon. Georgiana Mary, da. of Edward (Harbord), 3rd Baron Suffield [G.B.] [re-m. 2ndly, 22 Oct. 1855, Charles Edward Boothby, Ranger of Needwood Forest [Bt. Coll.] and] d. 13 Nov. 1903; and had issue.

See p. 541, Nos. 134737–134742.

3a. Rev. Arthur Henry Anson, Rector of Potter Hanworth and Dean of Chester, b. 10 Aug. 1817; d. 24 Nov. 1859; m. 18 Feb. 1851, Augusta Theresa, da. of the Right Hon. Henry Tuffnell, P.C., M.P.; d. (–); and had issue 1b to 5b.

1b. Hugh Anson, b. 1853.
2b. Arthur Anson, b. (posthumous) 20 Jan. 1860.
3b. Anne Anson.
4b. Alice Anson.
5b. Lucy Anson.

4a. Ellen Anne Anson, d. (–); m. 24 Aug. 1837, the Rev. Temple Hillyard, Canon of Chester and Rector of Oakford, co. Devon; and had issue 1b to 6b.

1b. Frederick Temple Hillyard, b. 18 Aug. 1838; d. (? s.p.) 8 Nov. 1877.
2b. George Anson Hillyard, Capt. Rifle Brigade, b. 7 Nov. 1841; m. 20 Nov. 1878, Grace, da. of the Rev. Thomas Colville of Rougham.
3b. Arthur Anson, b. 16 Jan. 1845.
4b. Henry Anson, b. 2 Oct. 1850.
5b. Rev. Walter Anson, Incumbent of Doddington, b. 6 Ap. 1853; d. 21 July 1881; m. 29 Jan. 1879, Ursula Mary, da. of the Right Rev. George Edward Lynch Cotton, D.D., Lord Bishop of Calcutta [Bt. Coll.] [re m. 2ndly, 1884, the Rev.

[Nos. 135253 to 135299.

The Plantagenet Roll

Arthur Atkinson, Hon. Canon of Chester (Highfield, Northop, Flints)]; and had issue 1c.
    1c. George Walter Hillyard, b. 1880.
    6b. Ellen Anson.
    5a. Lucy Frederica Anson.
    6a. Georgiana Frances Anson, m. 9 Oct. 1866, the Rev. Adam Charles Gordon, M.A., Rector of Dodlestone; d.s.p.   [Nos. 135300 to 135303.

354. Descendants of MARY ANSON (Table XXXI.), b. 8 Dec. 1763; d. (−); m. 22 Jan. 1785, Sir FRANCIS FORD, 1st Bt. [G.B. 1793], M.P., a Member of the Council of Barbados, b. 15 Nov. 1758; d. in Barbados 17 June 1801; and had issue 1a to 6a.

    1a. Sir Francis Ford, 2nd Bt. [G.B.], b. 15 Feb. 1787; d. 13 Ap. 1839; m. 4 Sept. 1817, Eliza, da. of Henry Brady of Limerick, d. 29 May 1875; and had issue 1b to 5b.
    1b. Sir Francis John Ford, 3rd Bt. [G.B.], b. 14 Aug. 1818; d. 26 Nov. 1850; m. 31 Oct. 1846, Cornelia Maria, da. of Gen. Sir Ralph Darling, G.C.B., d. 21 May 1896; and had issue 1c.
    1c. Sir Francis Colville Ford, 4th Bt. [G.B.], b. 4 June 1850; d. 16 Nov. 1890; m. 25 Mar. 1873, Frances Colville (see below), da. of William Ford, C.S.I.; and had issue 1d to 5d.
    1d. Sir Francis Charles Rupert Ford, 5th Bt. [G.B.] (30 Bedford Row, W.C.), b. 5 Ap. 1877.
    2d. Rev. Francis Walter Barton Ford, M.A. (Durham), formerly Vicar of Dunton Green (2 Cumberland Gardens, Tunbridge Wells), b. (twin) 5 Ap. 1877; m. 12 Sept. 1909, Louisa Gann, da. of Robert McKenzie Nish.
    3d. Frances Elsie Ford, m. 10 Sept. 1900, Raymond Carpmael, A.M.I.C.E. (Beechcroft, Shrewsbury).
    4d. Helena Blanche Colville Ford ⎫
    5d. Cornelia Caroline Ford   ⎭ (Shamrock Cottage, Lymington, Hants).

    2b. William Ford, C.S.I., B.C.S. 1842–1869, had Bar and Medal for services at Delhi during the Mutiny, b. 29 Nov. 1821; d. 18 June 1905; m. 27 Oct. 1845, Catherine Margaret, da. of Major-Gen. John Anthony Hodgson, H.E.I.C.S., d. 23 Oct. 1869; and had issue 1c to 4c.
    1c. Frances Colville Ford (Shamrock Cottage, Lymington, Hants), m. 25 Mar. 1873, Sir Francis Colville Ford, 4th Bt. [G.B.], d. 16 Nov. 1900; and had issue.
    See above, Nos. 135304–135308.
    2c. Helen Mowbray Ford (Canna Park, North Bovey, Moretonhampstead).
    3c. Edith Mary Ford, m. 26 Aug. 1875, Edward Penrose Arnold-Forster of Cathedine, J.P., D.L. (Cathedine, Burley-in-Wharfedale, Yorks); and has issue 1d to 5d.
    1d. Forster Delafield Arnold-Forster, Comm. R.N., b. 27 Aug. 1876; m. 2 Ap. 1907, Georgina Mary, da. of Alfred Tucker of Forthampton, Orangia; and has issue 1e.
    1e. Georgina Margaret Arnold-Forster.
    2d. William Howard Arnold-Forster, Capt. 4th W. Riding Howitzer Brig., R.F.A. (Weetwood, Shenston, Yorks), b. 30 Aug. 1882; m. 4 July 1909, Angela Mary Wharfedale, da. of Harry Wharfedale Tennant Garnett of Wharfeside, Otley, co. York; and has issue 1e.
    1e. Michael Garnett Arnold-Forster, b. 28 May 1910.   [Nos. 135304 to 135320.

of The Blood Royal

3*d*. Edward Trevenen Arnold-Forster (*Wharfedale Farm, Newcastle, Ontario, Canada*), *b*. 16 Sept. 1885.

4*d*. Francis Anson Arnold-Forster, Lieut. 4th W. Riding Howitzer Brig., R.F.A., *b*. 20 Mar. 1890.

5*d*. Iris Mary Arnold-Forster.

4*c*. Kate St. Clair Ford (*Canna Park, North Bovey, Moretonhampstead*).

3*b*. St. Clair Ford, Capt. Bombay S.C., b. 6 *Jan*. 1830; d. 31 *Jan*. 1896; m. 27 *Nov*. 1862, Eliza Jane (*Zeelugt, Cheltenham*), *da. of* Thomas Smalley Potter *of East Court, co. Glouc.; and had issue* 1*c to* 5*c*.

1*c*. Anson St. Clair Ford, *b*. 7 Oct. 1864; *m*. 18 Feb. 1903, Isabel Maria Frances, da. of Francis Adams of Llyfnant, Cheltenham; and has issue 1*d* to 3*d*.

1*d*. Aubrey St. Clair Ford, *b*. 29 Feb. 1904.
2*d*. Peter St. Clair Ford, *b*. 25 Nov. 1905.
3*d*. Drummond St. Clair Ford, *b*. 16 Dec. 1907.

2*c*. Beauchamp St. Clair Ford, Major E. Yorks Regt., *b*. 7 Ap. 1867.

3*c*. Leicester St. Clair Ford, *b*. 30 July 1879; *m*. 12 June 1906, Hildred Carlyle, da. of Rowland Ticehurst of 15 Royal Crescent, Cheltenham.

4*c*. Eva St. Clair Ford (*Cheltenham*), *m*. 21 July 1898, Henry Cecil Donald, *d*. 27 Oct. 1904.

5*c*. Ada St. Clair Ford, *m*. 29 July 1893, Archibald Hamilton Donald, Solicitor, a Member of H.M.'s Body Guard for Scotland, *formerly* Major and Hon. Lieut.-Col. (V.D.) 1st Lanarkshire Vol. Rifle Corps (33 *Lynedoch Street, Glasgow*); and has issue 1*d* to 3*d*.

1*d*. Colin George Hamilton Donald, *b*. 8 May 1899.
2*d*. Eva St. Clair Donald.
3*d*. Helen Hamilton Donald.

4*b*. Eliza Caroline Ford, d. (? s.p.) 5 *Jan*. 1879; m. 1*st*, 28 *Sept*. 1849, Lieut.-Col. Christopher Simpson Maling, 68th Regt., d. *Mar*. 1860; 2*ndly*, 12 Feb. 1866, Lieut.-Col. William Charles Newhouse, late 5th Fusiliers.

5*b*. Anna Maria Ford, d. 14 Feb. 1881; m. *as* 1*st wife*, 13 *Aug*. 1851, Gen. Sir David Scott Dodgson, K.C.B., *Bengal Army*, d. 26 *May* 1898; *and had issue* 1*c to* 5*c*.

1*c*. St. Clair Scott Dodgson, b. 18 *June* 1852; d. (? *s.p.*).

2*c*. Gerald Colville Dodgson (7 *Court Road, West Norwood*), *b*. 23 May 1855.

3*c*. Rev. Francis Vivian Dodgson, M.A., Vicar of Ellacombe (*Ellacombe Vicarage, Torquay*), *b*. 21 Jan. 1859.

4*c*. Harcourt Leicester Dodgson, Major 2nd "Queen's Own" Rajput Light Infantry, b. 14 *July* 1864; *d*. (*at Alipore, India*) 7 *May* 1904; m. 26 *Mar*. 1889, Agnes Mary (*Gatteridge Manor, Denton, Canterbury*), *da. of* Capt. John Millar-Mitchell, R.N.; *and had issue* (*with a son and da. d. young*) 1*d*.

1*d*. Alice May Dodgson.

5*c*. Ethel Ada Dodgson, *m*. Claud Hamilton (*Galtrim Road, Bray, Wicklow*).

2*a*. George Ford, d. (? s.p.).

3*a*. Rev. Charles Ford, M.A., *Rector of Billingford and Postwick*, d. 9 *May* 1863; m. 9 *May* 1839, Catharine Juliana, *da. of* Henry Stuart *of Sidmouth* [*? niece of Viscount Anson*], d. 30 *Nov*. 1879; *and had issue* 1*b to* 3*b*.

1*b*. Henry Stuart Ford *of Florida, U.S.A., formerly* Lieut. *R.A.*, *b*. 1 Oct. 1843; *d*. 8 *Oct*. 1895; m. 2*ndly*, 8 *Sept*. 1883, Mary, *da. of* Thomas Wells; *and had issue* 1*c*.

1*c*. Reginald Severne Ford, *b*. 4 *June* 1888; d. (-).

2*b*. Rev. Charles Primrose Ford, B.A. (Camb.), Rector of St. Michael's, Stone (*The Rectory, Stone, Staffs*), *b*. 27 May 1849; *m*. 2 Sept. 1875, Mary Jane, da. of the Rev. I. B. Turner; and has issue 1*c* to 4*c*.

1*c*. Rev. Roger Anson Ford, *b*. 5 July 1878.
2*c*. Charles Stuart Ford, *b*. 7 Oct. 1879. [Nos. 135321 to 135342.

The Plantagenet Roll

3*c*. Margaret Vernon Ford, *m*. 1 Sept. 1904, Reginald Tavernor Johnson (*Oaklands, Barlaston, Stafford*).
4*c*. Alice Constance Ford, *m*. 17 July 1907, Cuthbert Bailey (*Godolphin, Wolstanton, Staffs*); and has issue 1*d* to 2*d*.
1*d*. Helen Mowbray Bailey, *b*. 5 Ap. 1909.
2*d*. Barbara Vernon Bailey, *b*. 27 June 1910.
3*b*. Catherine Mary Ford, d.s.p. 27 *Oct*. 1900; m. 12 *Ap*. 1864, *Henry Prescott Green*, d. 11 *Jan*. 1892.
4*a*. Mary Ford, b. 1786; d. 12 *May* 1872; m. 1*st*, 24 *Feb*. 1807, *Peter Touchet*, d. (–); 2nd*ly*, 20 *July* 1816, *Capt. Henry Elton, R.N.* [3rd son of Sir Abraham Elton, 5th Bt. [G.B.], d. 10 Nov. 1858; *and had issue* (*with possibly others by 1st marriage*, 2 das. by 2nd who both d. unm.).
5*a*. Georgina Ford, d.s.p. *Ap*. 1879; m. 4 *Mar*. 1816, *I. W. F. Welch of Ebworth Park*, co. *Glouc*.
6*a*. Caroline Ford, d. 24 *Sept*. 1882; m. 26 *Oct*. 1822, *John Hyde of Ardwick*, co. Lancaster, d. 25 *Mar*. 1848; *and had issue* 1*b*.
1*b*. Francis Colville Hyde *of Syndale, Ospringe, co. Kent, J.P., Capt. East Kent Yeo.*, b. 24 *July* 1826; d. 9 *Mar*. 1892; m. 19 *June* 1850, *Charlotte Amelia* (*Wilderton, Branksome Park, Bournemouth*), *da. of Gen. Sir Ralph Darling, G.C.H.*; *and had issue* (*with others who* d.s.p.) 1*c* to 8*c*.
1*c*. John Colville Hyde, *b*. 11 Mar. 1853; *unm*.
2*c*. Francis Frederick Musgrave Hyde, *late* Lieut. East Surrey Regt., *b*. 16 June 1861; *m*. 26 Jan. 1907, Mary Jane, widow of Capt. Frederick Bults, *late* 77th Regt., da. of the Rev. James Briggs; *s.p.*
3*c*. Bertram Charles Anson Hyde, *b*. 2 June 1863; *unm*.
4*c*. Arthur Colville Hyde, *late* Major York and Lancaster Regts., *b*. 9 Sept. 1866; *m*. 1901, Lilian Amelia, da. of (–) Todd; and has issue 1*d*.
1*d*. Arthur Frederick Colville Hyde, *b*. 24 Dec. 1901.
5*c*. Isabel Anne Hyde, *unm*.
6*c*. Evelyn Elizabeth Hyde, *m*. 18 Oct. 1893, the Rev. Cyril Eden Fawcett, *d*. 29 Aug. 1894.
7*c*. Emily Mabel Hyde, *m*. 1 Aug. 1894, the Rev. William Jacob; and has issue 1*d* to 4*d*.
1*d*. Isabel Frances Jacob, *b*. 28 May 1895.
2*d*. Evelyn Mary Jacob, *b*. 14 Nov. 1897.
3*d*. Constance Kathleen Jacob, *b*. 6 Oct. 1900.
4*d*. Lois Amelia Jacob, *b*. 27 Nov. 1904.
8*c*. Dorothy Frances Hyde, *unm*. [Nos. 135343 to 135359.

355. Descendants of ANNE ANSON (Table XXXI.), *b*. 22 Feb. 1768; *d*. 25 May 1822; *m*. 20 Dec. 1792, BELL LLOYD [Baronet [G.B. 1778] Coll., 2nd son of Bell Lloyd of Bodfach, co. Montgomery, brother of Edward Pryce (Lloyd), 1st Baron Mostyn [U.K.]], *d*. July 1845; and had issue 1*a* to 2*a*.

1*a*. Edward Bell Lloyd, *Lieut. 16th Lancers*, b. 3 *May* 1794; d. 8 *May* 1864; m. 1819, *Lowry*, da. of Robert Morris, d. 14 Feb. 1878; *and had issue* 1*b* to 2*b*.
1*b*. William Lloyd, *of the General Post Office for 37 years*, b. 7 *Jan*. 1824; d. 28 Nov. 1878; m. 21 *Mar*. 1854, *Anne*, da. of Charles Stück, b. 31 Dec. 1837; d. *in America* 11 *Sept*. 1908; *and had issue* (*with other sons and a da., Mrs. Davy, of whom no issue survives*) 1*c* to 8*c*.
1*c*. William Anson Lloyd, b. 27 *Ap*. 1859; d. 1890; m. 5 *Sept*. 1881, *Elizabeth*, da. of George Wheeler; *and had issue* 1*d* to 2*d*.
1*d*. Ernest William Lloyd.
2*d*. Violet Anson Lloyd. [Nos. 135360 to 135361.

# of The Blood Royal

2c. Edward Bell Lloyd (47 *Ravensdale Road, Stamford Hill, W.*), b. 22 Dec. 1862; m. May 1888, Alice Maud Mary, da. of George Aubrey; and had issue 1d to 3d.

    1d. Alice Anson Lloyd.

    2d. Beatrice Alice Lloyd.

    3d. Clarice Audrey Lloyd.

3c. Thomas Mostyn Lloyd, b. 1865.

4c. Frederick Victor Lloyd, b. 14 Feb. 1867; m. Oct. 1901, Dorothy, da. of (—) Omagh; and has issue 1d to 2d.

    1d. James Mostyn Lloyd, b. 1906.

    2d. Gladys Anson Lloyd, b. 1903.

5c. Constantine Cynric Lloyd, b. 1874.

6c. Constance Ellen Lloyd, m. 27 Sept. 1887, the Rev. James Silvester, M.A. (Oxon.), Vicar of Great Clacton (*Great Clacton Vicarage, Clacton-on-Sea*); and has issue 1d to 2d.

    1d. Anson Lloyd Silvester, b. 11 Dec. 1888.

    2d. James Mostyn Silvester, b. 20 Feb. 1891.

7c. Laura Letitia Lloyd.

8c. Eleanor Arabella Lloyd.

2b. Anne Anson Lloyd, *unm.*

2a. Ven. William Henry Cynric Lloyd, M.A. (Oxon.), *Archdeacon of Durban*, b. 13 Jan. 1802; d. 3 Jan. 1882; m. 1st, 3 July 1832, Lucy Anne [*descended from George, Duke of Clarence, K.G.* (see Essex Volume Supplement, p. 574)], da. of the Rev. John Jeffreys, d. 14 Feb. 1843; 2ndly, 23 May 1844, Ellen, da. of the Rev. Henry Norman; and had issue 1b to 12b.

1b. William Henry Anson Lloyd, b. 26 Feb. 1848.

2b. Albert Charles George Lloyd, b. 5 June 1851; m. 1882, Eleanor (divorced 1904), da. of Swainston Harrison.

3b. Alfred Norman Mostyn Lloyd (*430 Burger Street, Pietermaritzburg*), b. 28 Sept. 1868; m. 29 Ap. 1895, Harriet, da. of the Rev. Canon Crompton, d. 28 Feb. 1904; and has issue 1c to 2c.

    1c. Theodora Cynric Lloyd, b. 24 Mar. 1901.

    2c. Gwynedd Lloyd, b. 18 July 1899.

4b.[1] Frances Anne Lloyd (*Knesebeck-strasse 9, Charlottenburg, Berlin*).

5b.[1] Lucy Catherine Lloyd.

6b.[1] Jemima Charlotte Lloyd, m. at Cape Town, 22 Nov. 1862, Dr. Wilhelm Heinrich Emmanuel Bleek, Librarian Grey's Library, Cape Town; and has issue 1c to 4c.

    1c. Edith Mabel Bleek.

    2c. Mabel Augusta Lucy Bleek, m. 4 May 1899, Karl Albert Jaeger; and has issue 1d to 2d.

        1d. Wilhelm Heinrich Immanuel Friedrich Jaeger, b. 21 May 1903.

        2d. Johanna Maryanthe May Jaeger.

    3c. Dorothea Frances Bleek.

    4c. Wilhelmine Henriette Anna Bleek.

7b.[1] *Julia Elizabeth Lloyd*, d. (*unm.*) 1 Jan. 1909.

8b.[2] Ellen Lloyd,
9b.[2] Henrietta Lloyd,   } *unm.*
10b.[2] Victoria Hope Natalia Lloyd,

11b.[2] *Adelaide Octavia Susan Lloyd*, d. 22 May 1908; m. *Feb.* 1883, Robert Trelss Nimmo *of Durban*; and has issue.

12b.[2] Isabella Lloyd, *unm.*   [Nos. 135362 to 135394.

The Plantagenet Roll

356. Descendants of COLUMBUS INGILBY of Clapdale Hall and Austwick, co. York, *afterwards* of Lawkland Hall (Table XXXII.), bapt. 28 Sept. 1642; bur. at Clapham 15 May 1716; m. at Leeds Parish Church, 9 Dec. 1676, ANNE, sister of Joseph Proctor of Leeds, Clothworker, da. of (—) PROCTOR, bur. at Clapham 25 May 1737; and had issue 1a to 6a.

1a. *John Ingilby of Lawkland*, bapt. 25 Mar. 1679; d. 1746, *leaving issue which became extinct before* 1800.

2a. *Thomas Ingilby of Austwick, co. York*, bapt. at Clapham 21 Dec. 1685; bur. *there* 17 Oct. 1765; m. *(bond dated at Lancaster* 19 *June* 1723*)*, *Agnes, da. of Thomas Foster of Austwick and Clapham*, bur. *at Clapham* 28 *July* 1766; *and had issue* 1b.

1b. *Columbus Ingilby of Clapdale Hall and afterwards of Lawkland*, bapt. 5 Dec. 1724; bur. 19 Nov. 1801; m. *Ellen, da. and co-h. of Thomas Abbotson of Kilnsey Hall, co. York*, bur. 12 Ap. 1795; *and had issue* 1c.

1c. *John Abbotson Ingilby of Lawkland, Lord of the Manor of Lawkland*, bapt. 16 Jan. 1764; d. 21 Oct. 1831; m. *at Thornton* 19 *June* 1787, *Margaret, da. of Richard Hodgson of West House, Thornton-in-Londale*, d. 26 *Mar.* 1824; *and had issue* 1d *to* 3d.

1d. *Thomas Ingilby of Lawkland, J.P.*, bapt. 8 Ap. 1788; d. 6 Dec. 1846; m. 1 June 1813, *Margaret, da. of Christopher Brown of Stainforth, co. York*, d. 26 Feb. 1852; *and had issue* (with 2 *sons and* 3 *das.* d.s.p.) 1e *to* 3e.

1e. *Christopher Ingilby of Lawkland, J.P., b.* 17 *Mar.* 1824; *d.* 1 *Nov.* 1889; m. 4 Dec. 1849, *Anne, da. of Thomas Watters of Kendal, co. Westmorland*, d. 13 Ap. 1891; *and had issue* 1f.

1f. Rev. Arthur Ingilby of Lawkland Hall, co. York, J.P., B.A. (Camb.), *formerly* Rector of St. John's Episcopal Church at Oban *(Harden, Austwick, Yorks)*, b. 9 Dec. 1852; m. 7 Sept. 1880, Constance Alice Ynyr, da. of the Rev. Edward Cadogan, Rector of Wicken; and has issue 1g.

1g. Alice Ynyr Christobel Ingilby, b. 6 Aug. 1881.

2e. *Elizabeth Ingilby*, b. 12 *July* 1815; d. 20 *Sept.* 1878; m. 28 Ap. 1841, *Thomas Bairstow of Royd Hall, near Kildwick, co. York*, b. 7 Ap. 1808; d. 2 Dec. 1867; *and had issue* (with 3 *sons and* 3 *das.* d. *young*) 1f *to* 2f.

1f. Walter Bairstow, J.P., High Sheriff co. Northants 1908 *(The Lodge, Towcester)*, b. 2 Sept. 1857; m. 13 Sept. 1882, Marion, da. of Alfred Sharp of Bingley; and has issue (with a da. d. young) 1g to 4g.

1g. Geoffrey Walter Ingilby Bairstow, b. 1 Aug. 1891.

2g. Cyril Thomas Alfred Bairstow, b. 2 July 1903.

3g. Agnes Irene Bairstow, m. 20 Feb. 1908, Harold Edward Cherry *(Geary House, Bretty, Burton-on-Trent)*.

4g. Marjorie Victoria Bairstow.

2f. *Ellen Bairstow*, m. 1 June 1881, Joshua Robert Jennings *(Ormonderley Close, Ripon)*; and has issue (with a son d. young) 1g to 2g.

1g. Rev. Robert Ingilby Jennings, b. 12 June 1882.

2g. Agnes Ellen Jennings.

3e. *Anne Ingilby*, b. 20 Feb. 1823; d. 10 Jan. 1910; m. 16 June 1842, *John William Foster of Clapham and Horton-in-Ribblesdale, co. York, D.L.*, b. 16 July 1812; d. 18 Oct. 1879; *and had issue* 1f to 6f.

1f. *Thomas Foster, Lieut. 63rd Regt.*, b. 9 Ap. 1843; d. *in Canada* 10 Ap. 1880; m. 21 Nov. 1866, *Leila [da. of (—)] Nowell of London*, d. 15 *May* 1885; *and had issue* 1g *to* 5g.

1g. Bryan Nowell Foster *(Cross Roads, Upper Skwiache, Nova Scotia)*, b.

[Nos. 135395 to 135405.

# of The Blood Royal

27 Jan. 1870; m. 1 May 1894, Elizabeth, da. of David Johnson of Upper Skwiache; and had issue 1h to 3h.
  1h. Francis Ingleby Foster, b. in Canada 6 Dec. 1897.
  2h. Thomas Hesleden Foster, b. in Canada 6 Dec. 1899.
  3h. Hilda Jane Foster, b. in Canada 28 Feb. 1903.
 2g. Herbert Ingleby Foster (*Silchester, near Reading*), b. 20 Feb. 1874; *unm.*
 3g. Thomas William Foster (*Johannesburg*), b. 5 Dec. 1879; *unm.*
 4g. Jessie Maud Foster, m. 10 Mar. 1892, Walter Vavasour Hemingway (*Poplar Grove, Wapella, Canada*); and has issue 1h to 2h.
  1h. Dorothy Hemingway.
  2h. Mabel Hemingway.
 5g. Alice Blanche Foster, m. 1 Oct. 1894, John Godfrey Beedie (*Parkin, Assa, Canada*); and has issue 1h to 4h.
  1h. Reginald Beedie, b. 17 Jan. 1898.
  2h. Violet Beedie, b. 7 Sept. 1897.
  3h. Doris Marion Beedie, b. 30 Dec. 1901.
  4h. Margaret Anne Beedie, b. 15 July 1906.
2f. Bryan Hesleden Foster, Major 44th Regt., b. 1 Aug. 1845; d. 20 Mar. 1889; m. 8 Sept. 1875, Isabel, da. of Henry Robinson of The Cliff, Wensleydale; and had issue 1g to 3g.
 1g. John Foster (*Burnside, Horton-in-Ribblesdale*), b. 11 Nov. 1877; *unm.*
 2g. Alice Foster, m. 20 Aug. 1901, Mark Feetham [son and h. of John Feetham of Whinfield, J.P.] (*Whinfield, Darlington, Durham*); and has issue 1h.
  1h. Margaret Isabel Feetham.
 3g. Mabel Foster, m. 15 Sept. 1909, Arthur Feetham [5th son of John Feetham aforesaid].
3f. John Foster (*Douk Ghyll, Horton-in-Ribblesdale, Settle*), b. 22 Aug. 1849; m. 4 Sept. 1876, Ethel Anne, da. of the Rev. Thomas James Clark of Horncastle, co. Linc., M.A.; *s.p.*
4f. William Foster (*Beechwood, Iffley, Oxon.*), b. 19 Aug. 1851; m. 2 Dec. 1874, Martha Rebecca Margaret, da. of William Lister Marriner of Keighley, co. York; and has issue 1g to 8g.
 1g. Charles Alban Foster, Lieut. Worcestershire Regt., b. 14 May 1883.
 2g. William Gerald Marriner Foster, b. 22 Feb. 1885.
 3g. Margaret Rebecca Foster.
 4g. Aveline Ingleby Foster.
 5g. Alice Joan Foster.
 6g. Ruth Anne Lister Foster.
 7g. Rhoda Mary Foster.
 8g. Maud Mael Foster.
5f. Alice Foster, m. 9 May 1876, Thomas Theophilus Secundus Metcalfe, Capt. 2nd West York Mil. (*Claydon House, Lechlade, co. Gloucester*); and has issue 1g.
 1g. Geoffrey Bryan Theophilus Metcalfe, *formerly* Lieut. 8th Hussars, b. 23 May 1878; m. 26 Sept. 1907, Agnes Maletta, da. of Charles O'Keeffe, *formerly* of Marble Hill, co. Cork.
6f. Florence Foster, m. 13 June 1882, William Herbert Lister Marriner, M.B. (Lond.) [son and h. of William Lister Marriner of Keighley, co. York] (*Craig Vaen, Poole Road, Bournemouth*); and has issue (with a da. *d.* young) 1g to 3g.
 1g. Bryan Lister Marriner, Lieut. R.A., b. 22 Ap. 1888.
 2g. Humphrey Ingilby Marriner, b. 12 Aug. 1892.
 3g. Alice Audrey Marriner.

2d. Arthur Ingilby (or Ingleby) of Lancaster, Lieut. 1st Dragoons, bapt. 18 Mar.
[Nos. 135406 to 135438.

The Plantagenet Roll

1794; d. 10 Ap. 1824: m. Jan. 1813, Bessy, da. of James Proctor of Lancaster, d. 18 Jan. 1857; and had issue 1e to 4e.

1e. William Ingleby of Douglas, Isle of Man, sometime 11th Hussars, b. 7 July 1817; d. 21 Nov. 1883; m. at Nottingham, 31 Jan. 1852, Margaret Gilbert, da. of Gabriel Brittain of Butterley Park, co. Derby, d. 26 July 1885; and had issue (with 2 das. d. young) 1f to 3f.

1f. Arthur Ingleby, Shore Superintendent, Liverpool (6 Spellow Lane, Kirkdale, Liverpool, N.), b. 21 Jan. 1854; m. 1st, 17 May 1876, Elizabeth Jane, da. of Richard Wilkinson of Liverpool, d. 15 July 1888; 2ndly, 19 July 1890, Sophia Amelia, younger da. of the said Richard Wilkinson; and has issue 1g to 7g.

    1$g.^1$ Arthur Gilbert Ingleby (440 Stanley Road, Bootle, Liverpool, W.), b. 11 Oct. 1878; m. 30 July 1904, Agnes, da. of George Taylor of Liverpool.

    2$g.^1$ Richard Henry Ingleby, b. 20 Aug. 1885.

    3$g.^2$ John Ingleby, b. 22 Ap. 1900.

    4$g.^1$ Elizabeth Ann Ingleby, b. 15 Ap. 1877.

    5$g.^2$ Emily Ada Ingleby, b. 11 Feb. 1891.

    6$g.^2$ Eleanor Ingleby, b. 11 Oct. 1892.

    7$g.^2$ Florence Ingleby, b. 22 Sept. 1896.

2f. Fred Holland Ingleby, in Garrison Artillery, b. 15 Sept. 1868; unm.

3f. Charles Ingleby, b. 1 Nov. 1857; m. 24 Mar. 1881, Annie, da. of Philip Draper of Liverpool, d. 24 Dec. 1892; and has issue 1g to 3g.

    1g. Philip Draper Ingleby, b. 26 Ap. 1886.

    2g. Annie Ingleby, b. 13 Ap. 1884.

    3g. Lizzie Ingleby, b. Oct. 1890.

2e. Bessie Ingleby, b. 23 Dec. 1815; d. 5 July 1882; m. at Lancaster, 14 Feb. 1834, Edward Cox of Lancaster, b. 10 Dec. 1799; d. 30 Mar. 1849; and had issue.

3e. Agnes Ingleby, b. 18 May 1822; d. 4 Nov. 1859; m. 1st, 4 June 1842, John Miller of Lancaster, d. Feb. 1852; 2ndly, Sept. 1855, George Reginald Kemp of Lancaster; and had issue (by 1st husband).

4e. Margaret Ingleby, b. 5 Feb. 1842; d. 17 May 1886; m. at Barnes, co. Surrey, 23 Feb. 1854, John Palmer of Liverpool, b. 15 Feb. 1817; d. (–); and had issue.

3d. Robert Ingleby of Austwick, co. York, bapt. 29 Ap. 1795; d. 24 Ap. 1863; m. 13 Sept. 1826, Mary, da. of William King of Austwick Hall, d. 21 June 1897; and had issue 1e to 2e.

1e. John Ingleby of Austwick, Major North Craven Rifles (Austwick, Clapham, co. York), b. 22 Sept. 1829; unm.

2e. Margaret Ingleby (Standard House, Northallerton), m. at Clapham, Yorks, 23 Nov. 1852, William Thrush Jefferson of Northallerton, co. York, Solicitor, b. 30 Mar. 1820; d. 13 Ap. 1891; and had issue 1f to 10f.

1f. John Ingleby Jefferson of Messrs. W. T. Jefferson & Son of Northallerton, Solicitors (Standard House, Northallerton), b. 1 Sept. 1853.

2f. William Dixon Jefferson (North House, Ripon), b. 30 May 1855; m. 23 Feb. 1892, Mary Stuart, da. of the Rev. Samuel Gray; and had issue 1g to 2g.

    1g. Ingleby Stuart Jefferson, b. 7 Jan. 1893.

    2g. Julian Jefferson, b. 10 July 1899.

3f. Robert Ingleby Jefferson, Manager Skipton Branch Bank of Liverpool (Skirton, Skipton), b. 13 Feb. 1857; m. 30 Aug. 1899, Arabella Florence, da. of the Rev. John Meire Ward, M.A., Rector of Clapham; s.p.

4f. Arthur Jefferson, b. 2 Sept. 1859; d. 15 Ap. 1892; m. 15 Dec. 1886, Georgina, da. of William Peareth, d. 3 Ap. 1891; and had issue 1g.

    1g. Dorothy Margaret Lennox Jefferson (Campsie, Stirling), b. 4 Aug. 1888; m. 7 Oct. 1909, Edmund Gilling Hallewell of Schenectady, N.Y.; and has issue 1h.

        1h. John Lennox Hallewell, b. 15 Aug. 1910. [Nos. 135439 to 135460.

of The Blood Royal

5f. Charles Wilkin Jefferson (*Schenectady, U.S.A.*), b. 8 July 1863; m. 7 Nov. 1889, Margaret A., da. of Charles Dyer, d. 16 May 1906; and has issue (with an elder son, Jack, d. 18 Jan. 1891) 1g to 2g.
    1g. Charles Wilson Jefferson, b. 15 Jan. 1895.
    2g. Margaret Elizabeth Jefferson, b. 26 Jan. 1892.

6f. Mary Jefferson, m. as 2nd wife, 28 Jan. 1886, Sylvester Richmond, M.D. [descended from the Lady Isabel Plantagenet (see the Essex Volume, p. 130)] (*Greenhithe, Kent*); and has issue 1g to 2g.
    1g. Arnold Ingleby Richmond, b. 3 Aug. 1887.
    2g. Sylvia Richmond, b. 19 Mar. 1892.

7f. Annie Jefferson, m. 23 Jan. 1890, Arthur Dewhurst (*Sunnybank, Otley Road, Skipton*); and has issue 1g to 3g.
    1g. Godfrey Jefferson Dewhurst, b. 2 Mar. 1894.
    2g. Joan Ingleby Dewhurst, b. 7 Nov. 1890.
    3g. Nancy Stevenson Dewhurst, b. 16 May 1900.

8f. Cicely Jefferson, m. 2 June 1892, George James Ernest Gardner (*South Parade, Northallerton*); and has issue 1g to 2g.
    1g. George Dudley Gardner, b. 29 July 1896.
    2g. Grace Ingleby Gardner, b. 27 Aug. 1893.

9f. Margaret Elizabeth Jefferson, m. 5 Jan. 1897, Harry Yeoman (*The Green, Brompton, near Northallerton*); and has issue (with a son, Henry Dixon, d. in infancy) 1g to 3g.
    1g. Philip Yeoman, b. 10 Feb. 1901.
    2g. Antony Yeoman, b. 8 Mar. 1907.
    3g. Ruth Yeoman, b. 29 Oct. 1897.

10f. Florence Jefferson, m. 12 Ap. 1898, the Rev. Stewart Dalrymple Crawford, B.A. (*Masham, Yorks*); and has issue 1g to 2g.
    1g. Frazer Stewart Crawford, b. 13 Sept. 1901.
    2g. David Stewart Crawford, b. 24 Feb. 1904.

3a. *Mary Ingilby*, bapt. 8 Nov. 1677.
4a. *Margery Ingilby*, bapt. 29 May 1681.
5a. *Margaret Ingilby*, bapt. 5 Aug. 1683; m. 27 Oct. 1705, Christopher Procter.
6a. *Elizabeth Ingilby*, bapt. 19 Ap. 1689.   [Nos. 135461 to 135480.

357. Descendants of Sir CHARLES INGILBY of Austwick Hall, co. York, one of the Barons of the Exchequer [E.] (Table XXXII.), *bapt.* at Clapham, co. York, 20 Feb. 1644; *bur.* there 6 Aug. 1719; *m.* ALATHEA, da. of Richard EYSTON of East Hendred, co. Berks, *bur.* at Clapham 19 Sept. 1715; and had issue (with a da., Anne, *d.* unm. at Liége) 1a to 4a.

1a. *Thomas Ingilby of Austwick Hall, Sergeant-at-Law*, bapt. *at Clapham* 15 May 1684; bur. *there* 13 Feb. 1729; m. *at Bentham* 11 *Aug.* 1717, *Elizabeth, da. of William Husband of Bentham Hall, co. York; and had issue* (*with a son and da.* d.s.p.) 1b *to* 4b.

1b. *Charles Ingilby of Austwick Hall*, bapt. *at Clapham* 22 *Aug.* 1724; bur. *there* 14 *Sept.* 1773; m. *there* 11 *Aug.* 1756, *Agnes, widow of* (—) *Armistead, da. of George Jackson of Far End, Austwick*, bur. 15 *Feb.* 1806; *and had issue which became extinct* 14 *Ap.* 1844.

2b. *Elizabeth Ingilby*, bapt. *at Clapham* 4 *Mar.* 1718; bur. *at Halifax* 1755; m. *Jan.* 1747, *James Carr of Giggleswick, a Solicitor in Halifax and afterwards in Preston*, bapt. 14 *Ap.* 1715; d. 1794; *and had issue* 1c.

1c. *William Carr of Preston, Solicitor*, b. 3 *July* 1747; d. 1799; m. *Fidelia, da. of John Bulcock of Langroyd, near Colne*, d. 1819; *and had issue* (*with 3 sons and* 3 *das. who* d.s.p.) 1d *to* 2d.

563

The Plantagenet Roll

1*d*. **George Thomas Carr**, b. 1791; d. 17 *Jan*. 1828; m. *Sarah, da. of William Midgley of Colne, co. Lanc.*, d. 9 *Ap*. 1848; *and had issue (with a son, George Thomas*, d. *unm*. 29 *Nov*. 1908) 1*e* to 2*e*.

1*e*. **William James Carr** *of Langroyd, Solicitor*, b. 1823; d. 24 *May* 1882; m. *Martha Joanna, da. of Henry Binns of Ripponden, co. Yorks*, d. 14 *July* 1898; *and had issue* 1*f* to 5*f*.

1*f*. **James Carr** of Colne, Solicitor, Registrar of Colne and Nelson County Court (*Thornton House, Thornton-in-Craven, Yorks*), b. 5 Oct. 1850; *m*. 29 Ap. 1882, Mary Ellen, da. of James Spencer; and has issue 1*g* to 5*g*.

    1*g*. William James Carr, *b*. 30 Jan. 1883.
    2*g*. Muriel Carr, *b*. 29 May 1884.
    3*g*. Winifred Carr, *b*. 16 June 1887.
    4*g*. Elsie Mary Carr, *b*. 23 Aug. 1890.
    5*g*. Doris Noel Carr, *b*. 25 Dec. 1893.

2*f*. Rev. **William Henry Carr**, M.A. (Oxon.), Vicar of St. Peter's, Westleigh (*Westleigh Vicarage, Lancashire*), b. 1 Feb. 1854; *unm*.

3*f*. **Edward Carr**, J.P. (*Langroyd, Colne*), b. 11 Aug. 1867; *m*. 14 June 1900, Ann Mabel, da. of Joseph Henry Threlfall of Moorlands, Foulridge; and has issue 1*g* to 3*g*.

    1*g*. Edward Ridehalgh Carr, *b*. 27 Ap. 1907.
    2*g*. Evelyn Carr, *b*. 5 Oct. 1902.
    3*g*. Joan Carr, *b*. 29 Oct. 1905.

4*f*. Mary Ada Carr, *unm*.

5*f*. **Helen Carr**, d. 5 *Oct*. 1899; m. 1*st*, 4 *Oct*. 1883, *Francis Benjamin Brodribb of Colne, Surgeon*, d. 17 *Nov*. 1893; 2*ndly*, 1897, *William Lyons Lovett of the same, Surgeon; and had issue* 1*g* to 5*g*.

    1*g*. William Carr Brodribb, *b*. 22 June 1886.
    2*g*. Francis George Brodribb, *b*. 8 Sept. 1890.
    3*g*. Frederick Lyons Lovett, *b*. 3 Mar. 1898.
    4*g*. Helen Margaret Brodribb, *b*. 4 May 1885.
    5*g*. Edith Mary Brodribb, *b*. 6 Oct. 1888.

2*e*. **Mary Carr** (*Colne, Lanc*.), *b*. 30 *Ap*. 1821; *m*. 16 *July* 1844, *John Joseph Ayre* of Colne; *and has issue* (*with a son d.s.p.*) 1*f* to 2*f*.

    1*f*. Eleanor Eames Ayre.
    2*f*. Georgina Birdsworth Ayre.

2*d*. **Elizabeth Carr**, d. (–); m. *John Birdsworth of Preston*, d. 1816; *and had issue* 2 *sons who* d. *unm*.

3*b*. **Dorothy Ingilby**, bapt. *at Clapham, co. York*, 19 *Feb*. 1722; bur. *there* 29 *May* 1765; m. *at Lancaster* 28 *Ap*. 1742, *Thomas Armistead of Austwick; and had issue*.

4*b*. **Mary Ingilby**, bapt. 12 *July* 1723, *living a widow* 14 *May* 1755; m. *James Bond of Stainforth, co. York, and Bury St. Edmunds, a non-juror* [*grandson of Thomas Bond by his wife the Hon. Henrietta, da. and co-h. of Thomas (Jermyn), 2nd Baron Jermyn* [*E*.]], b. 1724; d. (–); *and had issue*.

2*a*. **Dorothea Ingilby**, bapt. *at Clapham, co. York*, 27 *Ap*. 1681.

3*a*. **Mary Ingilby**, bapt. *at Clapham, co. York*, 25 *Ap*. 1683; d. (–); m. *William Estcourt of Bremellham and Cowitch, co. Wilts, of which latter he was life tenant under the terms of his marriage settlement* [*son of Sir Thomas Estcourt of Pinkney Park, co. Wilts*], bur. *at Clapham* 29 *Aug*. 1727; *and had issue* (*with 2 sons and 2 das*. d. *young, and* bur. *at Clapham*) 1*b* to 6*b*.

    1*b*. *William Estcourt*, b. *at Lawkland Hall and* bapt. *at Clapham* 21 *Jan*. 1709.
    2*b*. *Mary Estcourt*, bapt. *at Clapham* 5 *Jan*. 1711.
    3*b*. **Elizabeth Estcourt** *of Austwick*, bapt. *at Clapham* 7 *Feb*. 1716; m. (*lic. York dated Feb*.) 1746, *Charles Harrison of Ripon*, d. (–); *and had issue* 1*c*.

[Nos. 135481 to 135500.

# of The Blood Royal

1c. **Charles Harrison** of Newbridge, Nidderdale, co. York, Lawyer, bapt. in Ripon Cathedral 6 June 1758; d. 8 Dec. 1823; m. 1st, (—), da. of (—); 2ndly, Isabella, da. of Charles Charnock of Leeds, d. 15 June 1864; and had issue 1d to 4d.

1d.[1] **Charles Harrison**, afterwards (R.L. 10 May 1822) Harrison-Batley, M.P. for Beverley 1824–1830, Recorder of Ripon 1816–1833, b. c. 1786; d. 1 Aug. 1835; m. May 1822, Anna, widow of John Lodge Batley of Masham, co. Yorks, da. of (—); and had issue (1 son and 1 da.).

2d.[2] Rev. **William Estcourt Harrison**, Vicar of Sturton, co. Notts, b. 13 Ap. 1809; d. 17 Oct. 1887; m. 6 July 1859, Margaret (1 St. Peter's Grove, York), da. of William Battye of Skelton Hall, co. York; and had issue 1e to 3e.

1e. **Arthur Estcourt Harrison**, Major Royal Artillery (Chargrove House, Shurdington, near Cheltenham), b. 21 Jan. 1865; m. 7 Oct. 1897, Mabel, da. of George Clark of Sunderland; and has issue 1f to 2f.

1f. Margaret Estcourt Harrison.
2f. Rachel Estcourt Harrison.

2e. **Richard Scholefield Estcourt Harrison** (Canada), b. 19 June 1867; unm.

3e. Margaret Gertrude Estcourt Harrison, unm.

3d.[2] **Charnock Ingleby Harrison**, Capt. 65th Regt., H.E.I.C.S., bapt. 25 Aug. 1810; d. 6 Nov. 1848; m. 10 Mar. 1838, Mary Ann, da. of Capt. John Tritton, 24th Light Dragoons, d. 10 Sept. 1872; and had issue 1e to 2e.

1e. **Charles William Ingleby Harrison**, Col. R.E., late Chief Engineer of the United Provinces and Oude, and Sec. to the Govt. of India, presented with a Sword of Honour at Addiscombe 1858 (Court Royal, Dehra, Dun, India), b. 28 June 1839.

2e. Marion Ellen Harrison, now (D.P. 1909) Oswald (2 Park Avenue, Dover), m. 20 Dec. 1862, Col. James Williamson, formerly Oswald, 26th Punjaub Infantry [son of James Oswald of Shieldhall, M.P., who had three lines of descent from King Edward III.], d. 16 June 1877; and had issue (with a son, Charnock Ingleby Harrison, Lieut. 26th Punjaub Infantry, b. 13 Nov. 1864; d. unm. 14 Jan. 1892) 1f to 4f.

1f. **Oswald Charles Williamson**, now (D.P. 8 Mar. 1910) Williamson Oswald, F.R.G.S., Major R.A., served in Burma 1887–1889 (Medal and 2 Clasps), Waziristan Exp. 1894–1895 (Clasp), Chitral with relief force 1895, Tochi Field Force, N.W. Frontier 1897–1898 (Medal with Clasp), and South Africa 1901 (Medal with 4 Clasps), J.P., b. 20 Sept. 1863; m. 9 Oct. 1908, Margaret Malcolm, da. of William Carson of Carnalea House, co. Down; and has issue 1g.

1g. Praxeda Estcourt Isabella Emily Williamson Oswald.

2f. **Noel Williamson**, now (D.P. 1 Oct. 1910) Williamson Oswald, F.R.G.S., Assist. Political Officer at Sadiya, Assam, formerly Lieut. 4th Batt. West York Regt., b. 27 Oct. 1868.

3f. Theodora Williamson, m. 29 Sept. 1898, Major Kenneth Combe, R.H.A. (Ryston Lodge, Newbridge, co. Kildare).

4f. Agnes (Nancy) Williamson, M.B. (Lond.), who has now (D.P. 18 Jan. 1909) with her mother reverted to the name of Oswald.

4d.[2] **John James Harrison**, Chaplain R.N., b. 15 Feb. 1818; d. 17 Mar. 1888; m. 3 Oct. 1866, Louisa Edith (Barn Park, Boscastle, Cornwall), da. of the Rev. Frederick William Darwall of Sholden; and had issue 1e to 8e.

1e. **John Frederick Harrison**, b. 26 Jan. 1868; d. 11 Aug. 1904; m. 1 Aug. 1901, Ruth (52 Goldstone Villa, Hove), da. of the Rev. Frederick King of South Molton; and had issue 1f.

1f. Richard Ingleby Harrison, b. 14 Aug. 1903.

2e. Charles Ingleby Harrison, b. 2 Jan. 1876; unm.
3e. James Ingleby Harrison, Lieut. R.N., b. 3 June 1881; unm.
4e. Francis Ingleby Harrison, b. 27 Ap. 1883; unm.
5e. Janet Frances Harrison.
6e. Isabella Louisa Harrison.
7e. Mary Ingleby Harrison.
8e. Margaret Anne Ingleby Harrison.   [Nos. 135501 to 135520.

The Plantagenet Roll

4b. *Katherine Estcourt*, bapt. *at Clapham, co. Yorks*, 18 *Nov.* 1720.

5b. *Dorothy Estcourt*, bapt. *at Clapham* 4 *Dec.* 1725, *confirmed in Lawkland Hall Chapel* 14 *May* 1755 *by the Right Rev. Francis Petre, Lord Bishop of Amorium.*

6b. *Anne Estcourt*, b. *at Lawkland Hall, and* bapt. *at Clapham* 26 *Dec.* 1721.

4a. *Alethea Ingleby*, bapt. *at Clapham* 23 *Feb.* 1685; bur. *at Giggleswick* 17 *July* 1770; m. (—) *Fell of London, Apothecary.*

358. Descendants of ISABEL INGILBY (Table XXXII.), *d.* 16 Ap. 1793; *m.* RICHARD SHERBURN of Stonyhurst, co. Lancaster; and had issue.

See the Mortimer-Percy Volume, Part II.

APPENDIX

PAGE 37.—Though it is probable that descendants of Lady Elizabeth Woodroffe may still exist, they have not up till now been satisfactorily traced. Burke ("Peerage," *sub* Northumberland) says that her "descendant and sole heiress *m.*, 1719, Aaron Scales of Ranskill, co. Notts, and is now represented by Edward Peacock of Bottisford. By this "descendant and sole heiress" is presumably meant the "Elizabeth, sister and h. of Samuel Woodroffe, the last male heir of the Woodroffes of Ranskill, a branch of the Woodroffes of Wolley, co. York," who in the Peacock pedigree, printed in "English Church Furniture" (edited by the above-named Edward Peacock, 1866, p. 78), is there stated to have married Aaron Scales of Ranskill. One of their [? daughters and] co-heirs, Mary [? Scales], is further stated to have *m.* Robert Shaw of Bawtry, and to have had issue, a da. and co-h., Martha, who *m.* at Coopersall Church, co. Essex, 3 Ap. 1790, Thomas Peacock (*b.* at Northorpe, 21 Nov. 1766; *d.* 1 June 1824), grandfather of the said Edward Peacock. A further descent would also appear to be indicated, since the father of Thomas Peacock, another Thomas Peacock (*b.* at Scotter, 10 Mar. 1738; *bur.* at Northorpe, 27 Ap. 1782), *m.* Abigail (*bur.* at Northorpe, 24 Feb. 1772, aged forty), da. and co-h. (with her sister Keturah, *bur.* at Northorpe, 10 Ap. 1808, aged seventy-eight) of an Aaron Scales of Ranskill, though it is not stated whether the last-named Aaron Scales was identical with the first, or if he were, whether the mother of Abigail and Keturah was the said Elizabeth Woodroffe. Inasmuch, however, as the Woodroffes of Ranskill, though they may have been a branch of the Wolley family, were certainly not descended from the above Richard Woodroffe of Wolley, no descent from, or representation of, Lady Elizabeth can be vested in the Scales or Peacock families.

Of Maximilian Woodroffe, the eldest son, Banks (*Baronia Anglica Concentrata*, i. 369) says that he went to Virginia, where his cousin, the Hon. George Percy, had previously gone; and that in a MS. entitled "Indigested Chronology" among the Stirling papers in the Historical Library at New York, he is said to have planted Virginia and to have discovered Powhattan, now called James, River; that he *d.* 1652, having *m.* Mabel, da. and h. of Arthur Paver of Wetherby, and had issue a son and h., Maximilian, who *d.v.p.* 1644, leaving by his wife Eleanor, da. of William Paver of Braham Hall, an only child Milliana, who *m.* John Paver of St. Nicholas House, York, and was ancestress of Percy Woodroffe Paver, *b.* 1829, living 1843. This descent, which was printed in *Notes and Queries*, 6th S. vii. 29, wants proof, which the Editor has been unable to obtain.

Page 86.—The children of Georgina Fanny, *née* Bourchier, and her husband, Edward Raven Priest, are as follows, viz. 1g to 4g.

    1g. Edward Raven Priest, Electrician, *b.* 12 June 1880; *m.* May, da. of (—) Chapman of Brisbane.

    2g. Ella Constance Priest, *b.* 5 Jan. 1869; *unm.*

    3g. Jessie Beatrice Priest, *b.* 29 Sept. 1872; *m.* Richard Cheriton of Waul, West Australia, Farmer.

    4g. Janet Mary Priest, *b.* 10 Mar. 1875; *m.* Arthur O'Connor of Perth, West Australia, Journalist.

Page 156, line 26. 3c. *d.* 6 Ap. 1910.

Page 319, line 1. 2i. (Malcolm Orton) has two younger children, viz. :—

    7j. Constance Orton.

    8j. Nattie Charlotte Orton, *b.* 20 Nov. 1907.

Appendix

4*i*. (Allan Orton) has issue 1*j* to 3*j*.
1*j*. Allan Orton, *b*. 9 Sept. 1906.
2*j*. Reginald Bruce Orton, *b*. 6 May 1908.
3*j*. Elizabeth Jean Orton, *b*. 19 May 1910.
5*i*. (Mrs. Mee) has two younger children, viz.:—
3*j*. Caroline Jeannie Mee, *b*. 21 Nov. 1898.
4*j*. Bowery Bradley Mee, *b*. 1 July 1900.
8*i*. (Mrs. Whittaker) has issue 1*j*.
1*j*. Orton Whittaker, *b*. 6 Dec. 1906.
10*i*. (Mrs. Nixon) has issue 1*j* to 2*j*.
1*j*. Jack Orton Nixon, *b*. 24 Jan. 1907.
2*j*. Reginald Orton Nixon, *b*. 8 Mar. 1908.
11*i*. (Mrs. Hintz) has issue 1*j*.
1*j*. Orton Sutherland Hintz, *b*. 15 Nov. 1907.

Page 326. 4*d*. (Mrs. Smallpiece, *née* Frances Molineux) had issue (with 3 other sons and 2 das. who *d.s.p.*) 1*e* to 2*e*.
    1*e*. George Molineux Smallpiece, *b*. 21 Ap. 1841; *d*. (−); *m*. 12 Oct. 1869, *Beatrice Mary, da. of A. Savory of Potters Park, Chertsey; and had issue* 1*f* to 2*f*.
        1*f*. George Albert Molineux Smallpiece, *b*. 12 Feb. 1872.
        2*f*. Frances Molineux Smallpiece, *m*. Capt. Frank Arthur Horridge, *late Duke of Cornwall's Light Infantry; s.p.*
    2*e*. Robinson Smallpiece (*Merry Hills, Loxwood, Billingshurst*), *b*. 29 Aug. 1850; *m*. 1st, Annie Rachel, da. of Adolphus Marx of Nottingham; 2ndly, Sarah Rose, da. of Samuel Muggeridge of London; *s.p.*
    3*e*. Cordelia Molineux Smallpiece, *unm*.

Page 370, line 25 (Mrs. Fuhrhop, *née* Hoare) has issue 1*f* to 3*f*.
    1*f*. Otto Fritz Fuhrhop, *b*. 1 Ap. 1907.
    2*f*. Helen Mary Fuhrhop, *b*. 4 Dec. 1902.
    3*f*. Daisy Wilhelmina Fuhrhop, *b*. 1 Jan. 1908.

Page 483. 2*e* (Richard Buck of Bideford) had issue 1*f* to 3*f*.
    1*f*. *Rev. Richard Hugh Keats Buck, B.A.* (*Camb.*), *Rector of St. Dominick, co. Cornwall, and Hon. Canon of Truro Cathedral*, *b*. 4 *Mar*. 1815; *d*. 15 *Dec*. 1893; *m*. 29 *Jan*. 1852, *Mary, da. of the Rev. Joseph Bradshaw, d*. 19 *Jan*. 1893; *and had issue* 1*g* to 2*g*.
        1*g*. Rev. Richard Eustace Stukeley Buck, Rector of St Alban's (*St. Alban's Rectory, Cornwall*), *b*. 4 Nov. 1853; *m*. 7 Jan. 1891, Mary Constance, da. of John Richards Paull of Bosvigs, Truro; and has issue 1*h* to 4*h*.
            1*h*. Richard Vivian Stukeley Buck, *b*. 14 Oct. 1891.
            2*h*. Constance Angelina Mary Buck.
            3*h*. Veronica Charlotte McDonald Buck.
            4*h*. Ida Alexandra Amelia Buck.
        2*g*. Ida Frances Harriet Buck, *m*. in Rome, Oct. 1902, Capt. Luigi Falchotti; *s.p.*
    2*f*. Lewis William Buck, Major-Gen. M.C.S. (3 *Cavendish Place, Bath*), *b*. 13 Jan. 1824; *m*. at Wattaer, East Indies, 19 May 1854, Henrietta Jane, da. of Col. David Archer; and has issue (with 2 sons *d*. unm.) 1*g* to 6*g*.
        1*g*. Lewis Archer Buck, F.R.C.S., *b*. 1855; *unm*.
        2*g*. William Tennant Buck, Major (ret.) Durham L.I., *b*. 23 May 1862;

Appendix

m. in Bombay Cathedral 1898, Beatrice de la Poer, da. of Charles de la Poer Beresford; and has issue 1h to 4h.
1h. William Stuckley de la Poer Beresford Buck, b. 1 Feb. 1903.
2h. Reginald Claude de la Poer Beresford Buck, b. 31 Mar. 1905.
3h. Grace Eileen Joly de la Poer Beresford Buck, b. 30 Jan. 1899.
4h. Kathleen Manners de la Poer Beresford Buck, b. 22 June 1900.
3g. Walter Keats Buck, m.s.p.
4g. Harriette Grace Buck, m. 1880, Col. George Godfrey, Madras S.C., d.s.p. 1890.
5g. Annie Mary Buck.
6g. Ethel Maude Buck (3 *Cavendish Place, Bath*).
3f. Martha Buck, d. (-); m. *Major Oliver D'Arcy, 18th Regt.*, d. 3 Feb. 1880.

Page 498, line 50. The issue of 3e (Pierce Harris Purcell) is as follows, viz. 1f to 10f.
1f. George Harris Purcell.
2f. William Harris Purcell.
3f. Charles Harris Purcell.
4f. Richard Harris Purcell.
5f. Henrietta Harris Purcell.
6f. Rosina Harris Purcell, m. Arnold Köbler (*Walsrode, Hanover*).
7f. Louisa St. Leger Harris Purcell.
8f. Eva St. Leger Harris Purcell.
9f. Minnie Harris Purcell.
10f. Amy Harris Purcell.

Page 519, line 11. 2h. (W. G. Ferris) has issue (besides a da., Olive Mary, d. young) 1i to 5i.
1i. William Thomas Chilton Ferris, b. 29 May 1890.
2i. Arthur Guiseley Ferris, b. 11 June 1891.
3i. Ronald Boys Ferris, b. 29 Jan. 1899.
4i. Eric Charles Ferris, b. 15 May 1900.
5i. Leslie Francis Ferris, b. 15 Jan. 1907.

Page 523, line 45. 3g. (Mrs. Kitson) has issue 1h to 9h.
1h. William Edmonstone Kitson, b. (—); m. Muriel Lindsay, da. of Collingwood Lindsay Wood of Freeland, co. Perth, J.P., D.L.
2h. Rev. John Archibald Kitson, Rector of Brechin (*The Rectory, Brechin*), b. (—); m. Mary Catherine (see below), da. of Alexander Robert Duncan of Parkhill; and has issue 1i to 3i.
1i. John Duncan Kitson.
2i. Alexander Frederick Kitson.
3i. Joan Frances Kitson.
3h. Charles Kitson, b. (—).
4h. Robert Kitson, b. (—).
5h. Frederick Kitson, b. (—).
6h. Antony Buller Kitson, b. (—).
7h. Geraldine Kitson, m. the Rev. Lewis Evans, Vicar of Eton (*Eton Vicarage, Windsor*); s.p.
8h. Rosamond Kitson, *unm*.
9h. Dorothy Euphemia Kitson.

Appendix

Line 52. (Mrs Duncan) has issue 1h to 4h.
- 1h. John Alexander Duncan, b. 22 Mar. 1878; m. Dorothy, da. of (—) Weston; and has issue (a da.).
- 2h. Basil W. Duncan, b. (—); unm.
- 3h. William E. Duncan, b. (—); unm.
- 4h. Mary Catherine Duncan, m. the Rev. John Archibald Kitson (*Brechin*); and has issue.

See above.

Page 534, line 20. 2e. (William Taylor Warry) had issue 1f to 2f.
- 1f. Richard Arthur Warry, b. 6 Aug. 1886.
- 2f. Muriel Joan Warry, b. 4 Jan. 1888.

3e. (Mrs. Toogood) has issue 1f to 4f.
- 1f. Cecil Toogood, D.S.O., Capt. Lincolnshire Regt., b. 31 Mar. 1870; m. 14 Sept. 1899, Mary Elizabeth (see p. 523), da. of Major-Gen. Henry Pipon; and has issue.
  See p. 523, Nos. 130779–130781.
- 2f. Ella Georgina Toogood.
- 3f. Dora Isabel Toogood.
- 4f. Evelyn Maud Toogood.

Page 551, line 30. 3b. (Mrs. Stainforth) has issue 1c to 4c.
- 1c. Lesley Charles Stainforth, Col. Indian Army, b. 23 June 1860; m. Helen, da. of (—) Bell.
- 2c. Herbert Graham Stainforth, Major 4th Indian Cavalry, b. 18 May 1865; m. 1901, Georgina Helen (see p. 523), da. of Major-Gen. Henry Pipon; and has issue 1d to 2d.
  - 1d. Graham Henry Stainforth, b. 3 Oct. 1906.
  - 2d. Madeline Susan Stainforth, b. 26 July 1902.
- 3c. Douglas Anson Stainforth, R.N., b. 12 Aug. 1874.
- 4c. Edith Vernon Stainforth, b. 9 Oct. 1890, Charles Frederick Cross (53 *Chepstow Place*, W.); and has issue 1d to 3d.
  - 1d. Charles Ralli Cross, b. 30 Sept. 1893.
  - 2d. Lionel Lesley Cross, b. 7 June 1899.
  - 3d. Daisy Marion Cross, b. 4 Sept. 1891.

Page 551, line 32. 4b. (Mrs. Alexander) has issue 1d to 2d.
- 1d. Ernest Vernon Alexander, b. 13 Sept. 1863; m. 1883, Ina, da. of (—) Giles; and has issue 1e to 2e.
  - 1e. Lelia Constance Alexander.
  - 2e. Mary Helen Alexander.
- 2d. Eva Constance Alexander, m. 12 Sept. 1895, the Rev. Frederick Ball, M.A. (Oxon.), Chaplain Royal Navy (7 *Naval Terrace, Sheerness*); and has issue 1e to 2e.
  - 1e. Vernon Frederick Ball, b. 19 Oct. 1899.
  - 2e. David Herbert Alexander Ball, b. 5 Mar. 1903.

INDEX OF NAMES

Compound surnames are indexed under the first name. The numbers refer to the descents. Thus any one having two numbers after their name has two descents from the Lady Elizabeth Mortimer and her husband Henry, Lord Percy; any one having three, has three descents, and so on.

ABRAHAM, C. C., p. 274, 38512; D. M., p. 274, 38514; G. A., p. 274, 38513; Mrs. M. H., p. 274, 38511
Acland, Rt. Hon. A. H. D., p. 410, 79863; Sir (C.) T. D., 12th Bt., p. 410, 79862; F. D., p. 410, 79864; M. A., p. 410, 79865
Adair, Lieut. D., p. 178, 27232; Mrs. G. S., p. 178, 27231
Adams, A. B., p. 70, 888, 57307; A. C. P., p. 287, 39001; A. D., p. 355, 59723; A. St. G., p. 70, 887, 57306; C., p. 399, 77254; Mrs. C. M., p. 329, 43213; E., p. 399, 77250; E. A., p. 355, 59728; Mrs. E. A. I., p. 69, 884, 57303; E. J. P., p. 69, 879, 57298; Mrs. E. M., p. 69, 872, 57291; Mrs. E. R., p. 287, 38996; Mrs. E. W., p. 158, 16859; F. W., p. 158, 16860; G. R., p. 287, 39002; H., p. 69, 875, 57294; H. G., p. 355, 59726; H. G. C., p. 69, 878, 57297; H. L. E., p. 69, 885, 57304; Rev. H. T., p. 69, 873, 57292; L, p. 69, 876, 57295; Lieut. J. C., p. 69, 877, 59296; J. H. S., p. 355, 59721; J. P. F., p. 69, 886, 57305; J. S. L., p. 69, 874, 57293; M., p. 399, 77252; M., p. 399, 77255; M. G., p. 287, 39003; M. H., p. 70, 889, 57308; M. H. M., p. 355, 59725; N. R., p. 70, 890, 57309; O. M., p. 355, 59724; R., p. 287, 38998; R. S., p. 287, 38997; S., p. 399, 77253; Lieut. S. A., p. 355, 59720; S. A., p. 355, 59722; U., p. 287, 39000; W., p. 287, 38999; W., p. 399, 77251
Adda de Salvaterra, Leontine L. A., Mohss. of, p. 505, 129184.
Addley, Mrs. L. E., p. 211, 30012
Aglionby, Capt. A. C., p. 207, 29884; A. H., p. 208, 29890; A. M., p. 208, 29893; Lieut. C.

E., p. 208, 29888; C. M., p. 207, 29885; F. B., p. 208, 29887; Rev. F. K., p. 207, 29886; J. E., p. 208, 29895; J. O., p. 208, 29889; J. O., p. 208, 29894; R. F., p. 208, 29892; W. H., p. 208, 29891; Aitken, Mrs. G. E. F., p. 371, 60161, 64365
Alexander, Mrs. A. R., p. 525, 130973; B., p. 192, 28891, 29162; Mrs. C. H. S., p. 551, 135148; Mrs. E. D., p. 247, 37460; E. M., p. 191, 28886, 28925, 29157; E. V., p. 570 (App.); H., p. 191, 28888, 29159; Rev. J. B., p. 191, 28885, 29156; L. C., p. 570 (App.); Mrs. M., p. 517, 130449, 130529; M. H., p. 570 (App.); Mrs. M. C. F., p. 286, 38969; N. L., p. 191, 28887, 28926, 29158; P., p. 192, 28892, 29163; P. J., p. 247, 37461; R. D., p. 192, 28889, 29160; W., p. 192, 28890, 29161
Alington, Mrs. M., p. 200, 29592; N. S., p. 200, 29593; U. M., p. 200, 29594
Alison, C. H., p. 267, 38289; E. I. J., p. 267, 38293; Mrs. E. T., p. 267, 38288; G. R., p. 267, 38291; L. H., p. 267, 38292; Lieut. R. V., p. 267, 38290
Allen, A., p. 446, 94681; B., p. 446, 94683; C., p. 446, 94680; Mrs. E. M. J., p. 446, 94679; Mrs. F. M., p. 463, 95510; Mrs. G., p. 85, 9798, 9982; G., p. 446, 94684; Mrs. I. M., p. 51, 335; R., p. 446, 94682; Capt. R. W., p. 463, 95511
Allgood, Mrs. I. E., p. 43, 115
Allsopp, C. B., p. 544, 134909, 135046; Hon. Mrs. E. M., p. 544, 134908, 135045
Amphlett, A. E., p. 417, 80038; A. E., p. 457, 95339; Mrs. B. K. A., p. 457, 95337; Maj. C. G., p. 416, 80035; Rev.

G. Le S., p. 416, 80036; J. A., p. 417, 80039; J. A., p. 457, 95340; L. B., p. 416, 80037; L. B., p. 457, 95338
Anderson, A. B., p. 63, 658; Mrs. A. L. H., p. 58, 5 5; B., p. 214, 30111; B. S., p. 214, 30097; D. W., p. 214, 30115; E., p. 190, 28860; E. F., p. 63, 659; Mrs. E. L., p. 102, 10221, 41397; Mrs. F., p. 63, 657; F. O., p. 58, 513; F. W., p. 214, 30099; H. E., p. 63, 660; J. B., p. 63, 662; Maj. J. D., p. 190, 28858; J. F. S., p. 214, 30098; Maj. J. H., p. 190, 28859; L. S., p. 214, 30096; M. D., p. 63, 661; Maj. R. D. A., p. 190, 28857
Angus, A. F., p. 231, 36554; E. E. F. D., p. 231, 36556; Lieut.-Col. J., p. 231, 36555; Lieut. W. J., p. 231, 36557
Anson, A., p. 547, 135001; A., p. 555, 135293; A., p. 555, 135294; A., p. 555, 135295; A., p. 555, 135298; Maj.-Gen. Sir A. E. H., p. 553, 135214; A. F. M., p. 545, 134936; Mrs. A. H., p. 410, 79875; A. H. B., p. 545, 134951; A. J. G., p. 553, 135215; B. K. H., p. 546, 134993; C. G. A., p. 547, 135007; C. L., p. 547, 135022; C. O., p. 545, 134947; C. O., p. 545, 134952; C. R., p. 545, 134935; Com. C. V., p. 545, 134932; D., p. 547, 135003; D. A. V., p. 547, 135002; D. S., p. 545, 134953; E., p. 556, 135301; E. H., p. 545, 134933; E. H., p. 548, 135036; E. M. L., p. 553, 135216; E. R., p. 545, 134954; E. R., p. 548, 135037; F. C. M., p. 548, 135038; F. G., p. 410, 79877; F. G., p. 545, 134955; F. O., p. 547, 135004; F. W. N. H., p. 545, 134930; G. E., p. 548, 135039; Capt.

G. F. W., p. 545, 134938; G. O., p. 547, 135000; Lieut.-Col. G. W., p. 545, 134937; H., p. 555, 135292; H., p. 555, 135299; Capt. H. B., p. 545, 134942; Capt. H. P. R., p. 547, 134999; Rev. H. S., p. 545, 134949; H. V., p. 546, 134997; J. A., p. 546, 134998; J. M., p. 545, 134994; J. O., p. 545, 134943; K. W., p. 545, 134939; L., p. 555, 135296; L. F., p. 556, 135302; M., p. 546, 134994; M., p. 547, 135005; M., p. 547, 135029; M. A., p. 410, 79876; M. A., p. 545, 134948; M. D., p. 546, 134995; M. M. G., p. 547, 135006; M. V., p. 545, 134941; M. W., p. 545, 134940; O. A. O., p. 546, 134996; O. H. St. G., p. 545, 134956; P. A. N. P., p. 547, 135008; R. A., p. 545, 134946; S. C., p. 545, 134934; T., p. 545, 134931; V. H., p. 545, 134945; W. C. C., p. 554, 135247; W. G., p. 545, 134950; W. H., p. 546, 134992
Anstruther, Capt. P. G., p. 279, 38740; R. A. A., p. 279, 38741
Antoniadi, H. E. R. F. A. M., p. 283, 38896; Mrs. V. J. H., p. 283, 38895
Appleford, D. L., p. 144, 16325; Mrs. M., p. 144, 16323; W. A. N., p. 144, 16324
Appleton, Mrs. F. M., p. 280, 38799.
Appletree, F. R., p. 217. 30319
Archdale, A. M., p. 134, 15998; B. M., p. 134, 16001; E., p. 134, 15994; E. P., p. 134, 16010; Capt. G., p. 134, 16003; G. M., p. 134, 15999; G. M., p. 134, 16005; H. A., p. 134, 16006; H. B., p. 134, 15997; H. D., p. 134, 15995; J., p. 134, 16009; Maj. J. B., p. 134, 15996; M., p. 134, 16002; M. B., p. 134, 16007; M. H.,

Index

p. 134, 16000 ; M. H., p. 134, 16012 ; M. H. D., p. 134, 16004 ; R. M., p. 134, 16013 ; Mrs. S. E., p. 134, 15993 ; S. M., p. 134, 16008

d'Arcollières, Mrs. E. Le B., p. 507, 129217

Argenson, Adrienne E. G. M., Mchss. of, p. 507, 129207

d'Argenson, C. de V., p. 507, 129208

Arnold-Forster, Mrs. E. M., p. 556, 135316 ; E. T., p. 557, 135321 ; Lieut. F. A., p. 557, 135322 ; Com. F. D., p. 556, 135317 ; G. M., p. 556, 135318 ; I. M., p. 557, 135323 ; M. G., p. 556, 135320 ; Capt. W. H., p. 556, 135319

Ashbrook, 8th Vct., p. 103, 10226, 10325, 41402, 41501 ; Gertrude S., Vctss., p. 108, 10359, 41535

Ashburner, Mrs. A., p. 64, 705 ; A., p. 64, 708 ; C. E., p. 64, 706 ; L., p. 64, 707 ; V., p. 64, 709

Ashford, C. L., p. 309, 41917, 43110 ; Mrs. M. E., p. 309, 41916, 43109

Ashfordby-Trenchard, J. H. M., p. 469, 103139

Aspinall, Mrs. F. A., p. 104, 10255, 10354, 41431, 41530

Asquith, H. F., p. 394, 72237 ; Mrs. K. F., p. 394, 72236

Astell, C. E. V., p. 40, 48 ; L. A., p. 40, 47 ; R. J. V., p. 40, 46

Astley, Hon. A. R., p. 422, 80168, 80312 ; B. A. F., p. 422, 80179, 80323 ; B. L'E., p. 422, 80178, 80322 ; Hon. C. M., p. 422, 80167, 80311 ; C. M., p. 422, 80175, 80319 ; Maj. D. G. L'E., p. 422, 80176, 80320 ; D. L., p. 424, 80210, 80354 ; E., p. 424, 80209, 80353 ; E. H. N., p. 422, 80174, 80318 ; F. J. L'E., p. 422, 80173, 80317 ; Hon. H., p. 422, 80169, 80313 ; Rev. H. D., p. 422, 80184, 80328 ; Hon. H. E. D., p. 422, 80165, 80309 ; H. J. D., p. 422, 80182, 80326 ; J. D., p. 422, 80177, 80321 ; Lieut. the Hon. J. J., p. 422, 80166, 80310 ; L. A. M., p. 422, 80180, 80324 ; O. J., p. 422, 80183, 80327 ; P. R., p. 422, 80185, 80329 ; R. B., p. 422, 80187, 80331 ; R. C., p. 422, 80186, 80330 ; W. H. L'E. M., p. 424, 80208, 80352

Atherstone, A. A., p. 418, 80070 ; Mrs. A. H. J., p. 418, 80068 ; R., p. 418, 80069

Atholl, 7th D. of, p. 66, 749, 57168

Atkins, H. G. St. L., p. 492, 128188 ; R. St. L., p. 492, 128181

Atkinson, A. M., p. 250, 37555 ; D. M., p. 250, 37557 ; E. H. T., p. 250, 37553 ; E. K., p. 250, 37556 ; E. M., p. 250, 37554 ; Mrs. M. A., p. 250, 37552

Attwood, Hon. Mrs. H. E., p. 108, 10324, 41500

Atty, D. F., p. 152, 16679, 72491 ; E. p. 152, 16682, 72494 ; E. M., p. 152, 16675, 72487 ; F., p. 152, 16674, 72486 ; G., p. 152, 16694, 72506 ; G. C., p. 152, 16673, 72485 ; J. E., p. 152, 16672, 72484 ; R., p. 152, 16676, 72488 ; W., p. 152, 16677, 72489 ; W. J. W., p. 152, 16678, 72490

Auckland, Edith, Dow. Bnss., p. 271, 38415

Ayre, E. E., p. 564, 135499 ; G. B., p. 564, 135500 ; Mrs. M., p. 564, 135498

BAGNALL, Mrs. E. D., p. 82, 9731 ; Mrs. N. J., p. 82, 9733

Bagnell, Mrs. E. D., p. 305, 40315 ; M. D., p. 305, 40317 ; R. D., p. 305, 40316

Bagot, Mrs. C. C., p. 112, 10587, 41763 ; C. E., p. 112, 10588, 41764 ; Mrs. F. A. M., p. 452, 95023

Bagot-Chester, Capt. G. J. M., p. 451, 94987 ; Capt. H. A., p. 451, 94988 ; Col. H. C., p. 450, 94986

Bailey, Mrs. A. C., p. 558, 135344 ; Hon. B. M., p. 423, 80197, 80341 ; B. V., p. 558, 135346 ; C. E., p. 51, 352, 381 ; Hon. D. E., p. 423, 80198, 80342 ; Mrs. E., p. 355, 59718 ; E. H., p. 494, 128215 ; Mrs. E. L. M., p. 51, 350, 379 ; Mrs. F., p. 494, 128284 ; Hon. G. S., p. 423, 80196, 80340 ; H. M., p. 558, 135345 ; T. N. A., p. 51, 351, 380 ; Hon. W. R., p. 423, 80195, 80339

Baillie-Hamilton, C. R., p. 238, 37217 ; Capt. G. D., p. 238, 37215 ; Col. Sir W. A., p. 238, 37214 ; W. S., p. 238, 37216

Baily, B. E. V., p. 239, 37223 ; M. H. H., p. 239, 37222 ; Mrs. V. M., p. 239, 37221

Baines, Mrs. C. A., p. 46, 222 ; E. R., p. 47, 224 ; F. J. T., p. 47, 223 ; H. W., p. 47, 225 ; S. M. T., p. 47, 226

Baird, Mrs. C. E., p. 471,

103193 ; E. M., p. 531, 131285 ; F. H., p. 232, 36597, 36611 ; G. H. W., p. 531, 131284 ; J. A., p. 471, 103194 ; Capt. J. H. G., p. 232, 36595, 36609 ; M. I., p. 471, 103198 ; Mrs. M. C., p. 531, 131282 ; R. D., p. 531, 131283 ; Lieut. W. F. G., p. 232, 36596, 36610 ; Lieut.-Col. Sir W. J. G., 8th Bt., p. 232, 36594, 36608

Bairstow, Capt. C. T. A., p. 560, 135399 ; G. W. I., p. 560, 135398 ; M. V., p. 560, 135401 ; W., p. 560, 135397

Baker, A. P. L., p. 444, 94585 ; Hon. Mrs. B., p. 444, 94582 ; Mrs. F. L., p. 367, 60036, 60087, 62520, 64240 ; H. B., p. 444, 94583 ; H., p. 103, 10223, 41399 ; H. M., p. 103, 10224, 41400 ; O. K. L., p. 444, 94584 ; T. N., p. 103, 10222, 41398

Baker-Cresswell, Capt. A. F., p. 60, 580, 17559 ; A. J., p. 60, 582, 17561 ; C. M., p. 60, 583, 17562 ; Capt. H., p. 60, 584, 17563 ; J., p. 60, 581, 17560

Baldwin, Mrs. C. M., p. 289, 39054

Balfour, P. M., p. 64, 697 ; R. H., p. 64, 698

Ball, Mrs. E. C., p. 570 (App.) ; D. H. A., p. 570 (App.) ; Mrs. P. L., p. 570 (App.)

Bandon, Georgiana D. H., Ctss. of, p. 164, 17503

Bannatyne, Mrs. E. G., p. 172, 17845 ; J. F., p. 172, 17846 ; M. S., p. 172, 17847 ; V. V., p. 172, 17848

Barber, C. E., p. 500, 128365 ; C. E. G., p. 500, 128363 ; F. M., p. 500, 128364 ; Mrs. H. E., p. 500, 128362

Barclay, Mrs. I. C., p. 462, 95501 ; Mrs. M., p. 125, 11581

Baring-Gould, Mrs. E. J., p. 440, 90168

Barker, E., p. 63, 684 ; E. H., p. 64, 704 ; E. L., p. 63, 678 ; E. Y., p. 63, 680 ; F. B., p. 63, 676 ; F. G., p. 63, 683 ; G. L., p. 63, 681 ; G. M., p. 64, 693 ; H., p. 64, 702 ; H. Y., p. 63, 675 ; L. R., p. 63, 682 ; P. L., p. 64, 691 ; P. S., p. 64, 692 ; R. L., p. 64, 690 ; R. V., p. 64, 695 ; U. G., p. 64, 694 ; W. H., p. 63, 677 ; W. M., p. 63, 677

Barkley, Mrs. F. P., p. 154, 16747 ; G. H., p. 154, 16746 ; Mrs. K. H., p. 154, 16745 ; L. K., p. 154, 16748

Barlow, A. E., p. 60,

574, 17553 ; Anna M. H., Hon. Lady, p. 60, 570, 17549 ; Mrs. C. F., p. 549, 135080 ; H. A. N., p. 549, 135082 ; J. D., p. 60, 571, 17550 ; N. M. E., p. 60, 573, 17552 ; T. B., p. 60, 572, 17551 ; W. N. C., p. 549, 135081

Barnard, C., p. 521, 130582 ; R., p. 521, 130581 ; U. M. F. B., p. 521, 130580

Barnes, Mrs. E., p. 510, 129281

Barnett, A. M., p. 95, 10049 ; B. S., p. 95, 10050 ; J. C. L, p. 95, 10048 ; Mrs. M., p. 95, 10047 ; Mrs. S. E., p. 60, 585, 17564

Barratt, C. F. T., p. 156, 16788 ; L., p. 156, 16790 ; Mrs. L. H., p. 156, 16787 ; N. C., p. 156, 16789

Barretts, A., p. 289, 39031 ; A., p. 550, 135109 ; B. de C., p. 289, 39039 ; C., p. 289, 39032 ; C. R., p. 289, 39034 ; D. M., p. 289, 39038 ; E., p. 289, 39033 ; E. C. G., p. 215, 30137 ; H. E., p. 289, 39042 ; K. D., p. 289, 39036 ; L. A., p. 289, 39037 ; Mrs. M. A, p. 215, 30136 ; M. D., p. 289, 39043 ; Mrs. R., p. 550, 135108 ; R. B., p. 289, 39040 ; R. C., p. 289, 39041 ; R. S., p. 289, 29035 ; V. D. M., p. 289, 39044

Barry, Mrs. p. 339, 56016

Bartels, Mrs. B. H., p. 237, 36890

Barton, A. G., p. 396, 72274 ; B. C. L., p. 396, 72273 ; Mrs. E., p. 277, 38697 ; N. J. K., p. 396, 72276 ; R. H., p. 396, 72275 ; Mrs. S. T., p. 396, 72272 ; Mrs. W., p. 50, 303

Barttelot, I. M. M., p. 199, 29567, 29807 ; Lieut. N. K. W., p. 198, 29566, 29806 ; Sir W. B., 3rd Bt., p. 198, 29563, 29803 ; W. F. G. N., p. 198, 29565, 29805 ; W. de S., p. 198, 29564, 29804

Basevi, Mrs. C. L., p. 257, 37990 ; Rev. C. L., p. 257, 37994 ; D. F., p. 257, 37993 ; I. D., p. 257, 37992 ; Maj. W. H., p. 257, 37991

Bassett, Rev H. J., p. 171, 17808 ; I. E., p. 171, 17810 ; K. P., p. 171, 17811 ; R. P. H., p. 171, 17809

Bastard, R., p. 73, 9367, 43467 ; V. L., p. 73, 9368. 43468

Bateson, A., p. 54, 407 ; A., p. 54, 413 ; A. C., p. 53, 399 ; A. W., p. 53, 390 ; D., p. 54, 412 ; E., p. 53, 400 ; E., p. 53, 405 ; E., p. 54, 408 ; F., p. 54, 410 ;

Index

F. N. W., p. 54, 414; G., p. 53, 404; G., p. 54, 409; G., p. 54, 411; H. G., p. 53, 391; J., p. 53, 402; M., p. 53, 403; R. G., p. 54, 415; W., p. 53, 401
Bathurst, Mrs. A., p. 467, 103078; A. V., p. 467, 103085; E., p. 467, 103083; F. V., p. 467, 103084; G. F. V., p. 467, 103080; H. V., p. 467, 103079; L. C. V., p. 467, 103082; L. V., p. 467, 103081
Battiscombe, Maj. C., p. 136, 16060; C. F., p. 135, 16049; C. R., p. 136, 16061; C. W., p. 135, 16048; E. H., p. 135, 16052; G. A., p. 135, 16022, 16044; Mrs. H. B. A., p. 135, 16020; M. A., p. 136, 16062; M. E., p. 135, 16050; P. F., p. 135, 16042; P. R., p. 135, 16021, 16043; R. C. T., p. 135, 16023, 16045; S., p. 135, 16025, 16047; V., p. 135, 16024, 16046
Baxendale, Mrs. C. L., p. 551, 135135
Bayles, M., p. 316, 42483
Bayley, Mrs. B. B. O., p. 319, 42578; C. C., p. 319, 42579
Baynes, Capt. H. C. A., p. 168, 17677
Beall, A. E., p. 209, 29936; E., p. 428, 80460; G. B., p. 209, 29925; G. W., p. 209, 29928; H., p. 209, 29924; J. L., p. 209, 29937; J. Y., p. 209, 29927; L., p. 428, 80461; L. A., p. 209, 29930; M. Y., p. 209, 29931; M. Y. K., p. 209, 29938; R. E., p. 209, 29929; W. W., p. 209, 29926
Beamish, A. D., p. 247, 37482; C. H., p. 247, 37484; Rev. C. N. B., p. 247, 37481; E. P. F., p. 247, 27480; F. C., p. 247, 37478; L., p. 247, 37479; O. M., p. 247, 37483
Bearder, Mrs. D. C., p. 519, 130550; T. J. F., p. 519, 130551
Beasley, Mrs. F. A., p. 494, 128228; W. A. F., p. 494, 128229; W. St. L. F., p. 494, 128230
Beattie, Mrs. J. C., p. 232, 36562; L. B., p. 232, 36564; Rev. W. R. J., p. 232, 36563
Beatty, Mrs. A. G. E., p. 169, 17705; H. L., p. 169, 17706
Beavan, Mrs. G. A. M., p. 373, 60191, 64395
Beck, A. C., p. 458, 95371; A. H., p. 458, 95370; A. S., p. 458, 95373; Mrs. C. D., p. 458, 95369; C. H., p. 458, 95374; M. C., p. 458, 95372
Beckford, F. B., p. 533, 131338; F. W., p. 533, 131339; H. M., p. 533, 131341
Bedford, M. B., p. 87, 9840
Beedie (———), p. 561, 135418; Mrs. A. B., p. 561, 135414; D. M., p. 561, 135417; R., p. 561, 135415; V., p. 561, 135416
Beisiegel, Mrs. E. M., p. 192, 28898, 29169; L. M., p. 192, 28900, 29171; W. K., p. 192, 28899, 29170
Belcher, F. H. B., p. 198, 29543, 29783; M. V. G., p. 198, 29544, 29784; Lieut. R. G. H., p. 198, 29542, 29782
Bell, C. L., p. 286, 38970; D. M., p. 286, 38978; F., p. 286, 38980; I. E., p. 286, 38981; M., p. 288, 39029; M. A. H., p. 527, 131225; Hon. Mrs. M. H., p. 527, 131224; R. M., p. 288, 39030; W., p. 286, 38979; W. M., p. 286, 38971
Bell-Irving, A., p. 90, 9932; D. E., p. 90, 9933; D. P., p. 90, 9930; Mrs. E., p. 90, 9929; R., p. 90, 9931
Beloe, I. W. T., p. 531, 131301; J. D., p. 531, 131300; Mrs. M. C., p. 531, 131298; P., p. 531, 131299
Bence-Jones, C. W. W., p. 395, 72250; P. R., p. 395, 72251; R., p. 395, 72249
Benjamin, Mrs. E. M., p. 113, 10636, 11081, 41812, 42142
Bennet, B. M., p. 41, 82; Mrs. C. G., p. 41, 80; J. H., p. 41, 81
Benson, Mrs. C. G. J. E., p. 106, 10295, 41471; Mrs. F. C. A., p. 165, 17521, 17804; J., p. 455, 95113; Mrs. M. B., p. 455, 95112
Bentinck, 7th Ct., p. 382, 64175; Lieut. Ct. A. W. D., p. 382, 64165; Ct. C. A. R. W. G. A., p. 383, 64184; Ct. C. H., p. 382, 64163; Capt. Ct. C. R. A., p. 383, 64181; Ctss. E. M. R. S. L., p. 383, 64188; Ct. F. G. U. W., p. 383, 64177; Ct. G. A. H. J., p. 383, 64185; Ct. G. J. G. C., p. 383, 64183, Lieut. Ct. H. D., p. 382, 64164; Ct. I. A. M. C., p. 383, 64180; Ct. J. V. R. R., p. 383, 64186; Ctss. M. A. M. A., p. 383, 64182; Ctss. N. M. H., p. 382, 64174; Lieut. Ct. R. O., p. 382, 64162; Ctss. U. V. H., p. 382, 64173; Ct. V. M. F. M., p. 383, 64189; W. F. C. H., Hered. Ct., p. 382, 64176; Ct. W. H. F. G., p. 383, 64187

Bentley, A. M., p. 51, 334; Mrs. E. K., p. 51, 331; F. M., p. 51, 333; S. R., p. 51, 332
Berens, R., p. 79, 9461, 128618
Beresford, B. C., p. 239, 37239; H., p. 433, 85844; Maj. M. J. B., p. 239, 37233
Beresford-Ash, D., p. 239, 37232; Maj. W. R. H., p. 239, 37231
Berners, Mrs. E. M. G., p. 199, 29571, 29811
Bertie-Roberts, C., p. 181, 27336 : Rev. R. H., p. 181, 27335
de Bertouch, 2nd B., p. 41, 59; Bn. E. R. A. G., p. 41, 61; Bn. E. R. F. J., p. 41, 60
Best, D. M., p. 117, 10722, 11167, 37648, 41898, 42228; F. B., p. 117, 10721, 11166, 37647, 41897, 42227; J. E., p. 117, 10719, 11164, 37645, 41895, 42225; Mrs. R. L., p. 116, 10718, 11163, 37644, 41894, 42224; V. R., p. 117, 10720, 11165, 37646, 41896, 42226
Bethell, Mrs. A., p. 52, 369; R. P., p. 52, 371; V. L. S., p. 52, 370
Bethune, Maj. H. A., p. 242, 37326; J. M., p. 242, 37332; Mrs. M. L., p. 242, 37325; M. S., p. 242, 37327
Bevan, E., p. 416, 80012; Von. E. L., p. 415, 80004; W. A., p. 415, 80003
Biber-Erskine, G. O. H. E., p. 221, 36519; M. E., p. 221, 36306
Bickham, Mrs. E. F. M., p. 160, 17022; R. H. S., p. 160, 17023
Bigg-Wither, J. G., p. 116, 10693, 11138, 41869, 42199; Mrs. M. F., p. 116, 10691, 11136, 41867, 42197; O. M., p. 116, 10692, 11137, 41868, 42198
Billings, Mrs. A. M. L., p. 230, 36515
Bindley, H. D., p. 312, 42334; M. D., p. 312, 42335; Mrs. M. S., p. 312, 42333
Birkbeck, Mrs. E. I., p. 461, 95462; G., p. 461, 95464; M., p. 461, 95463
Birkett, Mrs. F. H., p. 116, 10695, 11140, 41871, 42201; F., p. 116, 10699, 11144, 41875, 42205; L., p. 116, 10698, 11143, 41874, 42204; M., p. 116, 10697, 11142, 41873, 42203; T., p. 116, 10696, 11141, 41872, 42202
Bisdee, Mrs. G. T., p. 351, 59515
Bishop, Mrs. E. L., p. 359, 59814, 95293
von Bismarck-Osten, F. O.

B. W., p. 470, 103153; Hilda E. M., Ctss., p. 470, 103151; K. U., p. 470, 103152
Bitossi, Mrs. F. T., p. 550, 135104; G., p. 550, 135106; P. F., p. 550, 135105
Blaauw, A. A. E. M., p. 500, 128368; B. W. St. L., p. 500, 128367; F. C., p. 500, 128369; H. T. G., p. 500, 128366; M. L., p. 500, 128370
Blacker (———), p. 163, 17108
Blair, A. M. M., p. 156, 16811; F., p. 156, 16810; F., p. 156, 16812; G., p. 156, 16809
Blake, Lieut. C. P., p. 41, 73; E. G., p. 41, 83; E. J. P., p. 42, 86; Col. G. P., p. 42, 85; J. P., p. 41, 78; H. L. G., p. 41, 84; M. A. T., p. 41, 79; M. L., p. 41, 75; N. P., p. 42, 87; Sir P. J. G., 5th Bt., p. 41, 72; V., p. 41, 74; V. H., p. 42, 88
Blakeney, E. C. C., p. 103, 10235, 10334, 41411, 41510; F. A., p. 103, 10236, 10335, 41412, 41511; F. R., p. 103, 10234, 10333, 41410, 41509; H. R., p. 103, 10233, 10332, 41409, 41508
Blakiston, C., p. 424, 80232, 80376; Mrs. G. H., p. 424, 80229, 80373; J. F., p. 424, 80230, 80374; M., p. 424, 80231, 80375; M. H., p. 424, 80233, 80377
Blanshard, E., p. 268, 38296; F. J., p. 268, 38297; H. E., p. 268, 38294
Bleek, D. F., p. 559, 135389; E. M., p. 559, 135385; Mrs. J. C., p. 559, 135384; W. H. A., p. 559, 135390
Blencowe, D., p. 513, 130349; Mrs. F., p. 513, 130345; F. I., p 514, 130352; J. I., p. 513, 130347; M., p. 513, 130348; R. C., p. 513, 130346
van Blokland, H. J. Jkvr. V. J. G. B., p. 379, 64113; Jkr. V. P. A. B., p. 379, 64114
Blomfield, C., p. 466, 103039; D., p. 466, 103041; Mrs. M., p. 466, 103037; P., p. 466, 103040; V., p. 466, 103038
Bloomfield, M. C. E. R., p. 525, 130992
Blume (———), p. 456, 95311; E. C., p. 456, 95310; Mrs. F. S., p. 456, 95309
Blundell, B. D., p. 301, 40184; Mrs. H., p. 301, 40183
Blythswood, Augusta C.,

Index

Hon. Bnss., p. 175, 27081
du Boe, Mrs. M. B., p. 525, 130993 ; R. B., p. 525, 130994
von Bodelschwingh, A. T. L. E. F., p. 472, 103226
Bohm, Mrs. H. C., p. 212, 30046 ; J. R. F., p. 212, 30047
Boigne, 4th Ct. of, p. 507, 129214 ; Delphine L. G. E., Ctss. of, p. 507, 129213
de Boigne, F. Le B., p. 507, 129215 ; I. M. Le B., p. 507, 129220 ; J. Le B., p. 507, 129216 ; M. Le B., p. 507, 129219
Bolam, Rev. C. E., p. 266, 38236 ; Mrs. C. M., p. 266, 38235 ; J. H., p. 266, 38237 ; K. M., p. 266, 38240
Boland, Mrs. E. H., p. 499, 128338
Bolitho, Mrs. A. J., p. 172, 17844
Bolton, Maj. R. G. I., p. 52, 365
Bond, Capt. A. A. G., p. 114, 10667, 11112, 41843, 42173 ; E. C. G., p. 115, 10669, 11114, 41845, 42175 ; L. M. G., p. 115, 10670, 11115, 41846, 42176 ; Mrs. M. C., p. 114, 10666, 11111, 41842, 42172 ; M. H. G., p. 115, 10671, 11116, 41847, 42177 ; W. R. G., p. 115, 10668, 11113, 41844, 42174
Bonham, F. W., p. 205, 29742, 30001 ; G. M., p. 205, 29744, 30003 ; Col. H. W. M., p. 197, 29535, 29775 ; J. W., p. 205, 29743, 30002 ; M. A., p. 205, 29745 ; M. L., p. 205, 29746, 30005
Booth, Mrs. C. L. A., p. 420, 80142 ; Mrs. F. J. W., p. 428, 80459 ; V. I. M., p. 420, 80143
Born, Mrs. T. H., p. 424, 80217, 80361
Borough, A. C. H., p. 439, 90154 ; C. M., p. 439, 90156 ; Mrs. E. F. M., p. 439, 90152 ; E. H., p. 439, 90155 ; J. G. B., p. 439, 90153
Bosanquet, A. P., p. 516, 130413, 130493 ; A. R., p. 517, 130451, 130531 ; Rev. B. H., p. 516, 130429, 130509 ; Rev. C. C. C., p. 516, 130412, 130492 ; C. H., p. 516, 130414, 130494 ; C. R., p. 516, 130417, 130497 ; C. R., p. 517, 130453, 130533 ; Lieut. E. C., p. 517, 130443, 130523 ; E. F., p. 516, 130419, 130499 ; E. F., p. 517, 130441, 130521 ; E. M., p. 395, 72261 ; E. M., p. 517, 130434, 130514 ; Lieut. E. M., p. 516, 130442, 130522 ; Mrs. E. M. E., p. 517, 130454, 130534 ; Sir F. A., p. 516, 130428, 130508 ;

F. E., p. 517, 130458, 130538 ; G. C., p. 516, 130430, 130510 ; Rear-Adm. G. S., p. 516, 130422, 130502 ; H. M., p. 516, 130416, 130496 ; H. S., p. 517, 130435, 130515 ; I., p. 516, 130421, 130501 ; L., p. 517, 130432, 130512 ; L. F. I., p. 517, 130456, 130536 ; L. S., p. 516, 130415, 130495 ; M., p. 516, 130411, 130491 ; N., p. 516, 130420, 130500 ; N. M., p. 517, 130433, 130513 ; Philippa F., Lady, p. 395, 72259 ; Rev. R. A., p. 516, 130418, 130498 ; R. A., p. 517, 130450, 130530 ; R. F., p. 517, 130452, 130532 ; S. C., p. 516, 130408, 130488 ; S. C., p. 517, 130455, 130535 ; S. R. C., p. 516, 130409, 130489 ; V. H. C., p. 516, 130410, 130490 ; W. C., p. 516, 130403, 130423, 130483, 130503 ; W. D., p. 517, 130448, 130528 ; W. S. B., p. 395, 72260 ; W. S. B., p. 517, 130431, 130511
Bounds, C. H., p. 209, 29935 ; Mrs. E. W., p. 209, 29932 ; K., p. 209, 29933 ; T. A., p. 209, 29934
Bourchier, A., p. 84, 9776 ; A., p. 86, 9823, 9881 ; A. C. F., p. 83, 9769 ; A. E., p. 87, 9838 ; A. G., p. 86, 9812 ; A. U., p. 87, 9824 ; Rev. B. G., p. 87, 9845 ; C., p. 86, 9826 ; C. H. J., p. 84, 9782 ; Capt. C. L. J., p. 84, 9781 ; E., p. 83, 9765 ; E. A., p. 87, 9836 ; E. D., p. 84, 9789 ; E. H., p. 83, 9768 ; E. M., p. 86, 9810 ; F., p. 83, 9766 ; G. L., p. 83, 9767 ; H. E., p. 83, 9770 ; Comm. H. E., p. 86, 9813, 9871 ; H. E. L., p. 84, 9777 ; H. J., p. 84, 9783 ; Lieut.-Col. H. S., p. 86, 9825 ; I. M. M., p. 83, 9771 ; J. R., p. 87, 9842 ; L. E., p. 86, 9828 ; L. McD., p. 86, 9814, 9872 ; M. E. S., p. 86, 9811 ; M. F., p. 84, 9788 ; M. J., p. 86, 9815, 9873 ; M. J., p. 86, 9827 ; O. L., p. 86, 9809 ; P. C. W., p. 87, 9846 ; R. L., p. 84, 9772 ; R. W. H., p. 84, 9774 ; S. L., p. 86, 9808 ; W., p. 87, 9841 ; Rev. W., p. 87, 9843 ; W. J. M., p. 87, 9844 ; W. T., p. 87, 9837
Bourke, A. J. H., p. 345, 59497 ; A. M., p. 345, 59502 ; Ven. C. F. J.,

p. 345, 59489 ; C. H., p. 345, 59494 ; D., p. 339, 56021 ; D. S. R., p. 345, 59493 ; E. L., p. 345, 59498 ; E. M., p. 345, 59500 ; F. A. D., p. 346, 59506 ; Col. G. D., p. 346, 59503 ; Lieut.-Col. H. B., p. 345, 59499 ; Lieut. H. E. M., p. 345, 59492 ; L. J. M., p. 345, 59490 ; L. M. J., p. 345, 59501 ; M. A. D., p. 346, 59507 ; M. J. D., p. 346, 59508 ; P., p. 339, 56020 ; R. J., p. 346, 59505 ; Lieut. S. G. T., p. 345, 59491 ; Lieut. U. J. D., p. 346, 59504 ; V. M. N., p. 345, 59495
Bourne, Mrs. C. M. G., p. 113, 10627, 11072, 41803, 42133 ; C. R., p. 113, 10629, 11074, 41805, 42135 ; H. C., p. 316, 42490 ; J. P., p. 316, 42489 ; R. C., p. 113, 10628, 11073, 41804, 42134
Bovill, Mrs. C. E., p. 56, 471 ; D., p. 56, 472 ; G., p. 56, 473 ; Mrs. V. E. J., p. 350, 59594
Bowen, Mrs. A., p. 417, 80045
Bower, A. E. C., p. 255, 37974 ; A. W. C., p. 255, 37972 ; B. L. C., p. 255, 37977 ; M. C., p. 255, 37976 ; E. A. C., p. 255, 37975 ; E. T. C., p. 255, 37969 ; F. C., p. 255, 37971 ; G. C., p. 255, 37970
Bowles, C. E., p. 359, 59817, 95296 ; Mrs. G., p. 359, 59816, 95295 ; M. I., p. 359, 59821, 95300
Bowling, C. R., p. 140, 16165 ; E. R., p. 140, 16166 ; C. R., p. 140, 16168 ; H. R., p. 140, 16167 ; M. M., p. 140, 16170 ; Mrs. R. C., p. 140, 16164 ; R. M., p. 140, 16169
Bowring, A. C., p. 264, 38199 ; Mrs. E., p. 264, 38198
Bowring-Hanbury, V., p. 264, 38200
Bowser, H. M., p. 192, 28919, 29190
Bowyer, G. P., p. 387, 71764 ; Rev. G. E. W., p. 386, 71753 ; G. E. W., p. 386, 71748 ; Sir G. H., 9th Bt., p. 385, 71732 ; H. G., p. 386, 71735 ; H. G., p. 386, 71755 ; H. M., p. 386, 71751 ; J. F., p. 386, 71750 ; M. E., p. 386, 71752 ; M. F., p. 387, 71763 ; R. G., p. 386, 71749 ; Lieut.-Col. W. G., p. 386, 71747
Boyd, Mrs. E. P., p. 514, 130354 ; J. H., p. 514, 130356 ; Mrs. M., p.

242, 37333 ; M. C., p. 242, 37344 ; W. A. H., p. 514, 130355
Boyle, Mrs. B. E. M., p. 426, 80281, 80425 ; D. H. M., p. 56, 466 ; Mrs. E. C., p. 56, 465
Bradburne, C. W., p. 400, 77831, 79340 ; F. A., p. 400, 77828, 79337 ; H. H. B., p. 400, 77829, 79338 ; J. E., p. 400, 77830, 79339
Bradford, Mrs. E. F., p. 30, 315
Bradshaw, Rev. S. Y. B., p. 498, 128319
Bradshaw-Isherwood, C. W., p. 127, 11624 ; Mrs. K. M., p. 127, 11623
Bramston, A. R., p. 532, 131318 ; G., p. 531, 131289 ; Sir J., p. 530, 131281 ; Rev. J. T., p. 531, 131297 ; M. E., p. 532, 131317 ; Lieut.-Col. T. H., p. 530, 131280
Bree, A. S., p. 101, 10180, 41356 ; B. S., p. 102, 10202, 41378, C. H., p. 101, 10178, 41354 ; E. H., p. 101, 10179, 41355 ; E. M., p. 101, 10186, 41362 ; E. N. S., p. 102, 10204, 41380 ; J., p. 101, 10181, 41357 ; M., p. 101, 10188, 41364 ; M. E., p. 101, 10185, 41361 ; R., p. 101, 10187, 41363 ; R. N. S., p. 102, 10203, 41379
Breed, Mrs. G. E., p. 109, 10398, 41574 ; N. G., p. 109, 10399, 41575
Bridges, Mrs. F. D., p. 496, 128285 ; L. E. C., p. 433, 85808
Brierley, Mrs. E. T., p. 135, 16051
Bright, A. H., p. 58, 514 ; E. H., p. 58, 515 ; Rev. H., p. 58, 518 ; H., p. 59, 546 ; H. Y., p. 58, 516 ; H. E. Y., p. 58, 517 ; M. H., p. 58, 522 ; S., p. 58, 524 ; U. D. E., p. 58, 523
Briscoe, Mrs. E., p. 217, 30318
Britton, Mrs. E. G., p. 475, 103317, 103342 h
Brocklebank, E. J. I., p. 248, 37500 ; Mrs. H. C., p. 248, 37497 ; M. P., p. 248, 37499 ; T. A., p. 248, 37498
Brodribb, E. M., p. 564, 135497 ; F. G., p. 564, 135494 ; H. M., p. 564, 135496 ; O. A. K., p. 354, 59710, 59752 ; W. C., p. 564, 135493
Broke, H., p. 429, 80470
Bromley, Mrs. E. M. T., p. 309, 41910, 43103
Broock, Mrs. R. G. E., p. 359, 59818, 95297
Brooke, Lieut. A., p. 552, 135174 ; A. F., p. 552, 135162 ; Lieut. A. F., p. 552, 135168 ; A. I., p. 552, 135178 ; A. T., p. 62, 653 ; B., p. 552, 135166 ; Mrs. B. A., p. 554, 135234 ; Capt.

574

Index

B. N., p. 552, 135181; Lieut. Sir B. S., 5th Bt., p. 552, 135160; Comm. B. V., p. 552, 135180; C. G., p. 552, 135177; D., p. 450, 94975; E. M., p. 552, 655; Elfrida M., Lady, p. 270, 38402; G. B., p. 450, 94974; G. D., p. 450, 94973; Mrs. G. M. H., p. 450, 94972; H. B., p. 552, 135175; H. B., p. 552, 135179; Capt. H. V., p. 552, 135172; Lieut. J. A. O., p. 552, 135173; K. M., p. 552, 135170; Mrs. L., p. 62, 652; M., p. 63, 667; N. M., p. 552, 135182; P. H., p. 552, 135176; Maj. R. G., p. 552, 135165; R. H., p. 62, 654; S., p. 552, 135164; S. H., p. 552, 135163; V. M., p. 552, 135161; Lieut.-Col.V.R., p.552, 135167
Brooker, Mrs. M. C., p. 289, 39060
Brooksbank, Mrs. B., p. 180, 27323; Maj. E. C., p. 240, 37283; E. Y., p. 240, 37285; H. E., p. 262, 38118, 38147; H. G., p. 240, 37286; H. L., p. 262, 38126, 38155; J. L, p. 262, 38116, 38145; K., p. 262, 38141, 38170; K. D. A., p. 262, 38117, 38146; L. H., p. 240, 37291; M. G., p. 240, 37287; M., P., p. 262, 38119, 38148; P., p. 240, 37288; S., p. 240, 37284; S. P., p. 262, 38125, 38154; T., p. 180, 27324; U. F. H., p. 262, 38120, 38149; W. L., p. 262, 38115, 38144
Broughall, D., p. 246, 37445; G., p. 246, 37448; J., p. 246, 37447; Mrs. L. M., p. 246, 37444; S., p. 246, 37446
Broughton, Mrs. M. C., p. 359, 59804, 95283; Mrs. M. C. H., p. 528, 131247; O. I., p. 528, 131249; S. P. H., p. 528, 131248
Brown, Mrs. A. M., p. 284, 38934; Mrs. C. C., p. 87, 9847; C. J., p. 145, 16353; F. H. M., p. 145, 16352; F. M., p. 546, 134972; G. N., p. 145, 16356; H. N., p. 145, 16355; L., p. 145, 16357; L. W., p. 546, 134974; M., p. 145, 16350; M., p. 546, 134969; M. C., p. 546, 134971; Mrs. M. M., p. 546, 134968; N. E., p. 145, 16351; R. M., p. 546, 134973; S., p. 144, 16348; S. M., p. 144, 16349; W. W., p. 546, 134970
Browne, Mrs. A. C. B., p. 395, 72256; Mrs. A. M. E., p. 159, 17002; C. B. E., p. 233, 36606; Hon. Mrs. C. G., p. 233, 36604; C. M. H., p. 233, 36605; G. C. J., p. 233, 36607; Mrs. I., p. 510, 129272; J. A., p. 510, 129274; M. D., p. 159, 17005; M. E., p. 159, 17004; P. R. E., p. 395, 72257; R. C., p. 347, 59540; R. M., p. 159, 17003; W. C., p. 510, 129273
Browne-Clayton, A. C., p. 347, 59527; A. M., p. 347, 59522; J. H. V., p. 347, 59538; K. O. L., p. 347, 59532; L. D., p. 347, 59523; M. E., p. 347, 59533; M. F., p. 347, 59528; Maj. R. C., p. 347, 59520; W. P., p. 347, 59521
Brownlow, N. F, p. 349, 59569; Maj.-Gen. W. V., p. 349, 59570
Bruce, Mrs. A., p. 295, 39484; E. M., p. 169, 17690; M. M., p. 169, 17687; Mrs. M. O., p. 169, 17686; M. R., p. 295, 39486; M. W. J., p. 295, 39485; N. M., p. 169, 17689; Mrs. R. I., p. 544, 134907, 135044; R. M., p. 169, 17688
Brunwin-Hales, Rev. Canon G. T., p. 458, 95359
Bruxner, A. E., p. 455, 95119; G. M., p. 455, 95118; Mrs. I. M., p. 455, 95117
Bryans, E. A., p. 64, 714; E. de V., p. 64, 716
Bryant, Mrs. P. M., p. 244, 37381
Buchan, 14th E. of, p. 221, 36307
Buchanann, Arabella C., Lady, p. 457, 95345; A. V., p. 147, 16569; E. T., p. 241, 37313; Mrs. F. E. C., p. 241, 37312; G. H., p. 147, 16571; J. H., p. 241, 37314; Mrs. L., p. 147, 16568; M. L., p. 147, 16572; N. L., p. 64, 717; W. L., p. 147, 16570
Buck, A. M., p. 569 (App.); C. A. M., p. 568 (App.); E. M., p. 568 (App.); G. E. J. de la P. B., p. 569 (App.); I. A. A., p. 568 (App.); K. M. de la P. B., p. 569 (App.); L. A., p. 568 (App.); Maj.-Gen. L. W., p. 568 (App.); R. C. de la P. B., p. 569 (App.); Rev. R. E. S., p. 568 (App.); R. V. S., p. 568 (App.); V. C. M., p. 568 (App.); W. K., p. 569 (App.); W. S. de la P. B., p. 569 (App.); Maj. W. T., p. 568 (App.)

Bucknill, Mrs. M. S., p. 146, 16423; S., p. 524, 130799
Budd, E. E., p. 254, 37890; M. E., p. 254, 37889
de Bunsen, A. G., p. 470, 103165; B., p. 470, 103171; C., p. 470, 103167
von Bunsen, E., p. 471, 103172; E., p. 471, 103173; E., p. 471, 103184
de Bunsen, E. C., p. 470, 103147; E. H., p. 470, 103166
von Bunsen, H., p. 471, 103174; H., p. 471, 103182
de Bunsen, H. V. H., p. 470, 103146; L. H. G., p. 470, 103164; M., p. 470, 103156
von Bunsen, M., p. 471, 103171; M., p. 471, 103183
de Bunsen, Sir M. W. E., p. 470, 103145; R. L., p. 470, 103169; R. M., p. 470, 103148
von Bunsen, W., p. 471, 103170
Burdon, E. A., p. 245, 37402; E. A. B., p. 244, 37401; F. M., p. 244, 37395; J., p. 244, 37396; J., p. 244, 37400; J. G., p. 244, 37398; L., p. 244, 37397; Lieut.-Col. R. p. 244, 37393; N. E., p. 244, 37399; R., p. 244, 37394
de Burgh, R., p. 490, 103598; Rev. R. L., p. 490, 103599
Burghley, Lord, p. 150, 16644, 72456
Burke, A. L., p. 359, 59799, 95278; J. L., p. 359, 59800, 95279; Mrs. M. A., p. 358, 59797, 95276; N. H. M., p. 359, 59798, 95277; Y. L. G., p. 359, 95801, 95280
Burnaby, H. A. G., St. V., p. 226, 36409; K. R. W., p. 225, 36385
Burnett, Mrs. E. A., p. 102, 10208, 41384; M., p. 84, 9778
Burr, F. M. D., p. 239, 37227; Mrs. K. D., p. 239, 37225; K. V. M., p. 239, 37226
Burrell, Hon. C., p. 175, 27088
Burroughs, Mrs. E. C., p. 353, 59689
Burrows, H. M., p. 46, 221
Burton, A. M., p. 57, 499; K. V., p. 57, 492; M., p. 57, 498; Mrs. M. V., p. 57, 491
Bury, W. P., p. 360, 59832
Bushell, M. D., p. 425, 80264, 80408
Butler, Mrs. A., p. 288, 39025; C. F., p. 288, 39026; Hon. P. H. A., p. 143, 16302
Buxton, A. L., p. 425,

80265, 80409; Mrs. M., p. 425, 80262, 80406; Capt. W. L. G., p. 425, 80263, 80407
Byng, G. S., p. 178, 27224; Hon. Mrs. L. M., p. 178, 27222; W. H. S., p. 178, 27223
Byrom, E. L. G., p. 193, 28982, 29063, 29253; Mrs. F. M., p. 193, 28981, 29062, 29252; R. E. J., p. 193, 28983, 29064, 29254
Callender, Mrs. E. H., p. 211, 30010; F. J., p. 223, 36337, 36422; G. F. W., p. 223, 36335; H. B., p. 223, 36336; Mrs. M. F., p. 211, 30011
Calonne, Marthe Le B., Ctss., p. 507, 129218
Cameron, Mrs. A. A., p. 4289; C. H. H., p. 175, 27127; Lieut. C. P. G., p. 175, 27128; E. P. B., p. 175, 27129
Campbell, A. G., p. 412, 79933; Mrs. A. L. B., p. 247, 37463; A. C. S., p. 412, 79931; Mrs. A. M., p. 552, 135160; A. P., p. 247, 37464; Mrs. C. C., 275, 38649; Maj. C. L. K., p. 340, 56044; Mrs. D. E., p. 282, 38876; D. F., p. 412, 79930; D. F. L., p. 213, 30084; E. A., p. 223, 36341, 36426; Hon. Mrs. E. E., p. 189, 28831; Mrs. F. M., p. 213, 30082; Capt. H. H., p. 223, 36360; Mrs. H. M., p. 223, 36359; H. P., p. 213, 30086; I., p. 282, 38879; J. D., p. 247, 37465; J. F., p. 412, 79928; J. L., p. 213, 30085; Jane S., Lady, p. 223, 36339, 36424; K. G., p. 412, 79932; K. L., p. 213, 30083; M., p. 282, 38878; Mrs. M. A., p. 340, 56043; Mrs. M. A. S., p. 184, 28558, 103398; M. V., p. 282, 38880; N. D., p. 223, 36340, 36425; R. H., p. 282, 38877; W. McL., p. 412, 79929
Campbell-Davys, E. G., p. 167, 17613; G. E., p. 167, 17614; Mrs. G. H., p. 167, 17611; I. E., p. 167, 17612; L. E., p. 167, 17615
Campbell-Lambert, E. K., p. 152, 16681, 72493; J. V., p. 152, 16680, 72492
Campion (——), p. 513, 130331; (——), p. 513, 130333; C. C., p. 514, 130370; C. W., p. 513, 130340; D., p. 513, 130332; Lieut. E., p. 513, 130335; F. H., p. 513, 130334; Lieut.-Col. H. F. G., p. 514, 130369; J., p. 513, 130339; M. G., p. 513,

Index

130336 ; L. L., p. 514, 130377 ; Col. W. H., p. 513, 130328 ; W. R., p. 513, 130329 ; W. S., p. 513, 130330
Cann, Mrs. C. G. R., p. 140, 16187 ; C. N. C., p. 140, 16189 ; H. J., p. 140, 16188
Carbery, 10th B., p. 204, 29727, 29986
Carden, E. E., p. 204, 29713, 29972 ; H. C., p. 204, 28712, 29971 ; Winifred M., Lady, p. 204, 29711, 29970
Cardross, Lord, p. 221, 36308
Carey, E. B., p. 180, 27322 ; E. J., p. 180, 27325 ; Mrs. F. A., p. 266, 38243 ; G. W., p. 107, 10315, 41491 ; H. S., p. 180, 27319 ; M. D., p. 180, 27321 ; W. S., p. 180, 27320
Carington, Lieut.-Col the Hon. R. C. G., p. 174, 27079 ; R. V. J., p. 174, 27080 ; Capt. the Hon. Sir W. H. P., p. 174, 27078
Carlyon, A. H., p. 476, 103321 ; A. K., p. 476, 103330 ; A. M. M., p. 476, 10333 ; C., p. 476, 103327 ; C. S., p. 476, 103326 ; D. M., p. 476, 103334 ; E., p. 476, 103341 ; G. W., p. 476, 103318 ; H. B., p. 476, 103337 ; Rev. H. C. p. 476, 103319 ; J., p. 476, 103322 ; J. M. V., p. 476, 103323 ; M. S., p. 476, 103336 ; W. V., p. 476, p. 476, 103328 ; P., p. 476, 103328 ; P., p. 476, 103329 ; Lieut. T., p. 476, 103331 ; T. A., p. 475, 103310, 103342 a ; T. C. W., p. 475, 103311, 103342 b
Carlyon-Britton, Mrs. A. C., p. 475, 103312, 103342 c ; E. C. P., p. 475, 103316, 103342 g ; H. C., p. 475, 103314, 103342 e ; R. C., p. 475, 103315, 103342 f ; W., p. 475, 103313, 103342 d
Carpenter, Mrs. E. M., p. 328, 43197
Carpmael, Mrs. F. E., p. 556, 135306, 135312
Carr, D. N., p. 564, 135486 ; E., p. 564, 135488 ; E., p. 564, 135490 ; E. M., p. 564, 135485 ; E. R., p. 564, 135489 ; J., p. 564, 135481 ; J., p. 564, 135491 ; M., p. 564, 135483 ; M. A., p. 564, 135492 ; W., p. 564, 135484 ; Rev. W. H., p. 564, 135487 ; W. J., p. 564, 135482
Carré, Mrs. C., p. 50, 305 ; F. B. C., p. 50, 309
Carrington, 1st B., p. 174, 27067
Carter, A. J., p. 493, 128197 ; Mrs. E., p.

302, 40201 ; Mrs. L. A., p. 493, 128196 ; S., p. 302, 40202
Cary, B. P., p. 328, 43201 ; Lieut, the Hon. B. P., p. 329, 43202 ; Hon. C. M., p. 329, 43204 ; Hon. L., p. 329, 43206 ; L. H. C. P., p. 328, 43200 ; Hon. M. S., p. 329, 43205 ; Hon. P. P., p. 329, 43203
Castell, Mechtild C. R. M., p. 383, 64178 ; Hered. Ctss. of, p. 383, 64178 ; Ctss. M. E. A. V. E. C. M. of, p. 383, 64179
Cator, Mrs. J. L., p. 346, 59516
Cavaye, Mrs. A. M., p. 199, 29573, 29813
Cavendish, Lieut. the Hon. C. F., p. 543, 134899 ; E. G., p. 38, 9 ; E. J., p. 38, 8 ; Lucy C., Hon. Lady, p. 47, 233 ; Hon. M., p. 543, 134900 ; Hon. N. L., p. 544, 134902
Cavendish-Bentinck, Lord F. M. D., p. 226, 36412 ; Lady, V. A. V., p. 226, 36413
Cawdor, Edith G., Ctss., p. 130, 12196, 71998, 81029
Cazenove, Mrs. G., p. 54, 426 ; P., p. 54, 428 ; R., p. 54. 427
Cecil, Lady L. S. W., p. 150, 16645, 72457
Chadwick, Mrs. A. L., p. 85, 9807, 9991 ; E. F., p. 84, 9787
Chalais, 14th Pr. of, p. 508, 129221
Chaloner, C. E. S., p. 255, 37934 ; C. W., p. 254, 37931 ; H. E., p. 254, 37933 ; J. E., p. 254, 37932
Chamberlain, Mrs. R. T., p. 294, 39476
Chambers, Mrs. L. B. H., p. 63, 656
Chambres, A. D., p. 54, 419 ; B. G., p. 55, 442 ; C. L., p. 55, 440 ; C. L., p. 55, 445 ; D. G., p. 55, 439 ; E., p. 54, 423 ; E., p. 55, 438 ; E. L., p. 55, 437 ; G., p. 56, 475 ; Rev. G. C., p. 55, 449 ; G. M. G., p. 54, 418 ; G. M. L., p. 55, 443 ; H. C., p. 54, 429 ; H. C., p. 55, 450 ; H. G., p. 55, 436 ; H. L., p. 55, 444 ; J., p. 55, 430 ; J. H., p. 55, 434 ; L., p. 54, 421 ; M., p. 54, 420 ; M., p. 55, 431 ; M., p. 55, 441 ; M., p. 55, 446 ; M. A., p. 56, 474 ; P., p. 55, 433 ; P., p. 55, 453 ; Hon. Maj. R. G., p. 54, 417 ; R. N., p. 55, 432 ; W., p. 55, 435
le Champion, Mrs. G., p. 374, 60237, 64441
Chaplin, H., p. 204, 29737, 29996 ; Mrs. E. M., p. 204, 29735, 29994 ; S., p. 204, 29736, 29995

Chapman, Caroline M., Lady, p. 278, 38739 ; E. J. L., p. 278, 38734 ; F. L., p. 278, 38736 ; F. V., p. 278, 38738 ; J. M., p. 322, 42664 ; Mrs. K. M., p. 322, 42662 ; Mrs. K. O., p. 476, 103339 ; M. C., p. 278, 38737 ; R. I., p. 278, 38735 ; T. R. T., p. 278, 38733 ; W. M., p. 322, 42663
Charles, Mrs. M. L., p. 395, 72258
Charlesworth, F. R., p. 127, 11619 ; Mrs. H. L. R., p. 127, 11618 ; J. B., p. 127, 11620 ; K. A., p. 127, 11621
Charlton, E. F. B., p. 296, 39503 ; F. J. L., p. 296, 39507 ; G. V. B., p. 296, 39506 ; O. J., p. 296, 39505 ; W. L. S., p. 296, 39504
Charrington, Mrs. D., p. 95, 10051 ; J. A. P., p. 95, 10053 ; L. M., p. 95, 10054 ; R. L., p. 95, 10052 ; S. A., p. 95, 10055
Chartress, Mrs. E. G., p. 437, 90118
Chauncy, Maj. A. C., p. 364, 59937 ; A. F., p. 365. 59942 ; C. F., p. 365, 59940 ; Capt. C. H. K., p. 365, 59943 ; E. A. M., p. 365, 59950 ; Mrs. F. A., p. 364, 59936 ; F. C. M., p. 364, 59938 ; H. C., p. 365, 59945 ; J. B. W., p. 365, 59939 ; J. F., p. 365, 59946 ; K. I., p. 365, 59951 ; L., p. 365, 59944 ; R. A., p. 365, 39941
Cheesman, Mrs. M. E. J., p. 494, 128231 ; W. M. A., p. 494, 128232
Cheriton, Mrs. J. B., p. 567 (App.)
Cherry, Mrs. A. I., p. 560, 135400
Chester, A. J. B., p. 449, 94931 ; Rev. A. S. M., p. 449, 94937 ; C., p. 450, 94948 ; D. M. B., p. 449, 94935 ; G. A. B., p. 449, 94930 ; G. B., p. 449, 94932 ; H. M. B., p. 449, 94933 ; Rev. J. G., p. 449, 94929 ; K. A. B., p. 449, 94936 ; L. C. B., p. 449, 94934 ; M. G., p. 450, 94946 ; M. B., p. 449, 94939 ; M. I., p. 450, 94947 ; M. I., p. 450, 94949 ; W. G., p. 449, 94938
Chestney, F. E., p. 147, 16565 ; Mrs. H. E., p. 147, 16564 ; J., p. 147, 16566 ; M. E., p. 147, 16567
Chetwynd, Hon. Mrs. E. H., p. 500, 128371 ; E. M. F., p. 500, 128372 ; J. A., p. 500, 128378 ; L. C., p. 500, 128377
Chevallier, Mrs. M., p. 257, 38012

Chisholm, Mrs. J. F., p. 247, 37462
Chisholme, Mrs. E. M. E., p. 228, 36485, 36534, 36577
Chitty, Mrs. G. M., p. 113, 10630, 11075, 41806, 42136 ; J. M., p. 113, 10631, 11076, 41807, 42137 ; M. H., p. 113, 10632, 11077, 41808, 42138 ; V. A. P., p. 113, 10633, 11078, 41809, 42139
Choiseul, Marquis of, p. 504, 129161
de Choiseul, Ct. E. A. H., p. 504, 129168 ; Ct. F. H. R., p. 504, 129169 ; Ct. M. A. E. H., p. 504, 129165 ; M. C. A. R. G., Vct., p. 504, 129163 ; Ct. M. C. G., p. 504, 129162 ; Ct. M. J. H. C., p. 504, 129164 ; M. L., p. 504, 129166 ; M. M. N., p. 504, 129167
Cholmeley, L. S., p. 295, 39487 ; Capt. H. J., p. 295, 39483
Cholmondeley, Mrs. K. p. 515, 130396, 130476
Christian, Mrs. E., p. 351, 59614
Christie, Mrs. F. M., p. 202, 29694
Churton, Mrs. M. E., p. 476, 103324
Clark, G., p. 338, 55981 ; Mrs. H., p. 337, 55979 ; R. F., p. 338, 55980
Clarke, C. P. G., p. 456, 95324 ; E. F. G., p. 456, 95323 ; E. J., p. 456, 95325 ; Mrs. I., p. 123, 11512 ; Mrs. R. L., p. 498, 128332 ; W. E. G., p. 456, 95322
Clay, E. E., p. 302, 40186
Clayton, D. P., p. 43, 111 ; E., p. 43, 110 ; Mrs. E., p. 100, 10167, 41343 ; Maj. E. F., p. 43, 112 ; G. S., p. 43, 113 ; Mrs. I., p. 43, 109
Clerk, Mrs. I. E. A., p. 531, 131292 ; F. E., p. 531, 131225 ; G., p. 466, 103055 ; H. E., p. 531, 131294 ; L., p. 466, 103054 ; M. A., p. 531, 131296 ; M. C., p. 466, 103052 ; Mrs. M. G. L., p. 466, 103051 ; V., p. 466, 103053 ; W. H., p. 531, 131293
Cleveland, B. S., p. 261, 38101 ; E. E., p. 261, 38102 ; Mrs. E. H., p. 261, 38098 ; H. W., p. 261, 38099 ; E. M. W., p. 261, 38100
Cliffden, Mary, Vctss., p. 394, 72217, 72322
Clifford, Mrs. E. P., p. 523, 130782
Cloete, Mrs. E. H., p. 203, 29700
Clowes, Hon. Mrs. A., p. 544, 134919
Cobb, A., p. 388, 71783
Cobbe, Mrs. E. C., p. 300, 40157
Cobbold, C. F., p. 176, 27131 ; M. R. J. C., p. 176, 27132 ; N. E., p.

Index

284, 38933; Mrs. S. W. S., p. 175, 27130
Cobham, 8th Vct., p. 45, 185
Cochrane, Lady A. C., p. 198, 29557, 29797
Cockayne-Cust, Mrs. E. M. E., p. 48, 249
Cockburn, Mrs. A. B., p. 414, 79968; A. F., p. 414, 79965; A. M., p. 414, 79969; E. L. M., p. 414, 79971; F. A., p. 414, 79970; Mrs. I. M., p. 414, 79964; I. S., p. 414, 79966; L. A., p. 414, 79967
Cocks, A. C. S., p. 408, 79742; A. E., p. 408, 79746; C. J. S., p. 408, 79743; C. R., p. 408, 79745 D. E. W., p. 408, 79741; E. B., p. 408, 79737; E. M. S., p. 408, 79739; F. A., p. 408, 79740; H. B., p. 408, 79735; Mrs. H. E., p. 408, 79732; H. L. M., p. 408, 79750; H. M., p. 408, 79738; J. R., p. 408, 79736; K. A., p. 408, 79751; M., p. 408, 79752; Rev. P. J., p. 408, 79734; P. S., p. 408, 79744; R. W., p. 408, 79733
Codrington, Maj.-Gen. A. E., p. 77, 9414; A J., p. 76, 9389; F. C., p. 76, 9387; G. R., p. 76, 9388; Lieut. G. R., p. 77, 9415; J. A., p. 77, 9417; M. A., p. 77, 9418; W. M., p. 77, 9416; Capt. Sir W. R., 6th Bt., p. 76, 9385; W. R., p. 76, 9386
Coghill, Elizabeth H. A., Lady, p. 366, 59980; J. A. C., p. 367, 59983; K. A. H., p. 367, 59984; M. N. P. S., p. 367, 59981; N. H. K. A., p. 367, 59982
Coke, Mrs. C. E. H., p. 336, 55935
Coldstream, E. L. W., p. 546, 134965; Mrs. F. C., p. 545, 134957; G. A. P., p. 546, 134962; G. P., p. 546, 134961; J., p. 546, 134967; K. N., p. 546, 134966; M. A., p. 545, 134960; W. J. A., p. 545, 134959; Maj. W. M., p. 545, 134958; W. M., p. 546, 134963; W. M. M., p. 546, 134964
Cole, A. A., p. 207, 29880; D. G., p. 207, 29883; Mrs. E. M., p. 164, 17510, 17793; Mrs. H., p. 207, 29879; H. P., p. 207, 29881; H. T. S., p. 164, 17512, 17795; L. A. S., p. 164, 17511, 17794; U., p. 207, 29882
Colegrave, Mrs. V. L. H., p. 164, 17514, 17797
Coleridge, C. E., p. 141, 16200; E. J., p. 141, 16198; F. A. T., p. 140, 16186; F. R. C., p.

141, 16193; Rev. G. F., p. 140, 16183; Lieut.-Col. H. F., p. 140, 16184; Mrs. H. G., p. 140, 16182; J., p. 141, 16191; J. D. C., p. 140, 16185; P., p. 141, 16192; Mrs. S. A., p. 141, 16190
Collins (——) p. 469, 103138; Mrs. E., p. 469, 103132; E. G., p. 469, 103137; E. M., p. 469, 103135; F. Le H., p. 469, 103134; G. W., p. 469, 103133; K. M. W., p. 469, 103136; Mrs. M., p. 272, 38474
Colquitt-Craven, G. F. L., p. 456, 95330; L. F. G., p. 456, 95329; N. F. de la B., p. 456, 95331
Colvile, A. L., p. 429, 80468; C. H. E., p. 429, 80469
Colvin, A. M. M., p. 198, 29562, 29802; Lady G. A. A. B., p. 198, 29560, 29800; R. B. R., p. 198, 29561, 29801
Combe, C. D., p. 159, 17008; E. D., p. 159, 17007; R. T., p. 159, 17006; Mrs. T., p. 565, 135511
Compton, D., p. 199, 29582, 103089; Mrs. D. A., p. 199, 29579; Lieut. E. B., p. 468, 103091; G., p. 468, 103090; H. F., p. 467, 103086; H. R., p. 199, 29580, 103087; J. H., p. 537, 131704; Mrs. L. M., p. 537, 131703; M. G., p. 537, 131706; O., p. 468, 103093; P. D., p. 199, 29581, 103088; R. W., p. 537, 131707; S. H., p. 468, 103092; W. E., p. 537, 131705
Connell, Mrs. D., p. 494, 128216
Conner, D. H., p. 360, 59834; E., p. 360, 59838; H., p. 360, 59836; K. L., p. 360, 59839; Maj. R., p. 360, 59835; S., p. 360, 59837; W., p. 360, 59840
Constantine, Mrs. M., p. 195, 29032, 29113, 29303
Cook, Mrs. G., p. 318, 42527; P., p. 318, 42528
Cooke, Mrs. A. M., p. 248, 37515; C. E. D., p. 239, 37243; C. E. L., p. 248, 37518; C. H. E., p. 248, 37516; Mrs. E. C. L., p. 239, 37236; Mrs. F. B., p. 494, 128221, 128235; F. C., p. 239, 37242; F. W. St. L. D., p. 494, 128222, 128236; J. S. F., p. 239, 37241; L. M. E., p. 248, 37517; Mrs. M. E., p. 239, 37240
Cooper, Mrs. C. M., p.

157, 16837; F. A., p. 63, 688; J., p. 63, 689; Mrs. M. E., p. 63, 687
Coote, Capt. C. J., p. 509, 129240; C. O., p. 510, 129276; W. P. O., p. 510, 129277
Copley, A. W., 256, 37982
Corfield, B. C., p. 547, 135032; C. L., p. 548, 135033; E. A. F., p. 547, 135031; Mrs E., G., p. 547, 135030; E. M., p. 548, 135035; H. V. A., p. 548, 135034
Cornewall, Sir G., 6th Bt., p. 401, 78060, 79569; M. L., p. 401, 78062, 79571; W. F., p. 401, 78061, 79570
Cotton-Watson, Capt. A., p. 116, 10690, 11135, 41866, 42196
Coulson, A. A., p. 316, 42415; F. L., p. 315, 42412; H. J. W., p. 315, 42411; M. A., p. 316, 42416; M. L., p. 316, 42420; M. M. L., p. 316, 42419; T. H., p. 316, 42418
Couper, A. E., p. 289, 39052; A. L., p. 106, 10296, 41472; Caroline P., Lady, p. 105, 10282 41458; D. H., p. 106, 10294, 41470; D. M., p. 289, 39059; Mrs. E., p. 106, 10286, 41462; Lieut.-Col. E. E., p. 106, 10288, 41464; G. p. 106, 10284, 41460; G. R. O., p. 106, 10291, 41467; I. C. B., p. 289, 39050; J. C., p. 289, 39049; J. E., p. 106, 10292, 41468; J. R., p. 106, 10290, 41466; J. R., p. 106, 10293, 41469; Mrs. J. S., p. 289, 39048; J. V. H., p. 106, 10289, 41465; M. J., p. 289, 39051; M. M., p. 106, 10297, 41473; Lieut. Sir R. G. H., p. 106, 10283, 41459; S., p. 106, 10285, 41461; S. B., p. 289, 39053; Lieut.-Col. V. A., p. 106, 10287, 41463
Courthope, A., p. 515, 130388, 130468; B. F., p. 515, 130385, 130465; E. A., p. 515, 130394, 130474; E. D., p. 515, 130382, 130462; E. J., p. 515, 130386, 130466; E. M., p. 515, 130389, 130469; E. M. D., p. 515, 130397, 130477; F. A., p. 515, 130390, 130470; F. G., p. 515, 130398, 130478; G. J., p. 515, 130379, 130459; Capt. G. L., p. 515, 130380, 130460; H. B., p. 515, 130381, 130461; J., p. 515, 130393, 130473; J. E., p. 515, 130383, 130463; M. E. L., p. 515, 130401, 130481; M. P., p. 515, 130384, 130464; R. A., p. 515, 130395, 130475; R. F., p. 515, 130399,

130479; W. F., p. 515, 130387, 130467; W. G., p. 515, 130392, 130472; W. H. F., p. 515, 130400, 130480; W. J., p. 515, 130391, 130471
Coventry, F. C. A., p. 457, 95336
Covey, E., p. 263, 38185; M. J., p. 264, 38192
Cowan, Mrs. A. E., p. 549, 135103;
Cowen, Mrs. P., p. 550, 135107
Cox, A. C., p. 281, 38855; A. E. G., p. 237, 36903; A. F., p. 237, 36899; C. L. H., p. 237, 36900; C. M., p. 237, 36902; Mrs. E., p. 146, 16421; E. M., p. 112, 10582, 41758; E. P., p. 237, 36896; F., p. 281, 38856; G. N., p. 237, 36901; H. A., p. 237, 36897; H. A., p. 281, 38854; H. P., p. 237, 36898; I. V., p. 281, 38857; Mrs. L., p. 276, 38667; Mrs. M. H., p. 112, 10581, 41757; M. H., p. 112, 10583, 41759; M. H., p. 281, 38859; R. H., p. 281, 38853; Mrs. S., p. 146, 16422
Coxhead, Mrs. E., p. 525, 130974
Cradock-Hartopp, Mrs. E. A. M., p. 412, 79940; G. M., p. 412, 79941
Craik, Mrs. S. M., p. 64, 696
Craufurd, Capt. A. G., p. 257, 38003; A. J. F., p. 39, 36, 65; Lieut. C. E. V., p. 40, 37, 66; Capt. C. Q., p. 257, 38006; Sir C. W. F., 4th Bt., p. 41, 62; E. K. G., p. 257, 38005; E. M. D., p. 40, 41, 70; Capt. G. S. G., p. 39, 34, 63; H. J. L., p. 40, 38, 67; H. R. G., p. 257, 38001; Isolda C., Hon. Lady, p. 39, 33; J. G., p. 257, 38004; L. I., p. 49, 39, 68; M. E. M., p. 40, 42, 71; Lieut. Q. C. A., p. 39, 35, 64; Q. G., p. 257, 38007; Capt. R. Q. G., p. 257, 38002
Craven, B. G., p. 456, 95314; C. L., p. 456, 95308; E. C. C., p. 456, 95303; E. C. J., p. 456, 95307; E. F., p. 455, 95301; F., p. 455, 95302; G. L., p. 456, 95306
Crawford, Mrs. C. M., p. 268, 38295; D., p. 365, 59949; D. S., p. 563, 135480; Mrs. E. J. F. R., p. 365, 59947; Mrs. F., p. 563, 135478; F. S., p. 563, 135479; G. O., p. 365, 59948
Creery, Mrs. A., p. 90, 9934; C. J., p. 90, 9936; I. A., p. 90, 9940; K. A., p. 90, 9935; L. C., p. 90, 9938; R. H., p. 90,

577

Index

9937; W. B., p. 90, 9939
Cremers, Jkvr. A., p. 381, 64151
Crewe-Read, E. C., p. 225, 36402; Mrs. G. M., p. 225, 36399; R. O., p. 225, 36401
Croft, C., p. 113, 10622, 11067, 41798, 42128; E., p. 113, 10623, 11068, 41799, 42129; F. E., p. 113, 10620; 11065, 41796, 42126; Sir F. L., 3rd Bt., p. 113, 10619, 11064, 41796, 42125; L. M., p. 113, 10621, 11066, 41797, 42127; M. J. G., p. 113, 10642, 11087, 41818, 42148; P. H., p. 113, 10625, 11070, 41801, 42131; T. R., p. 113, 10626, 11071, 41802, 42132; W. G., p. 113, 10624, 11069, 41800, 42130
Cronin, Lieut.-Col. J. J., p. 498, 128321
Cropper, A., p. 168, 17657; A. W., p. 168, 17663; C. F. J., p. 168, 17660; C. H. E., p. 168, 17655; C. L., p. 168, 17656; D. A. D., p. 168, 17653; E. G., p. 168, 17654; E. P., p. 168, 17647; E. W., p. 168, 17668; Mrs. F., p. 167, 17644; F. A., p. 168, 17649; Rev. F. W., p. 168, 17659; Rev. J., p. 168, 17645; J., p. 168, 17651; M. E., p. 168, 17658; M. P., p. 168, 17650; P., p. 168, 17646; R. A., p. 168, 17648; T. A., p. 168, 17652; V. G., p. 168, 17661
Cross, C. F., p. 453, 95067; C. R., p. 570 (App.); D. M., p. 570 (App.); Mrs. E M., p. 453, 95064; Mrs. E. V., p. 570 (App.); G. J., p. 453, 95068; H. M., p. 453, 95069; L. I., p. 570 (App.); M. R., p. 453, 95066; P. K., p. 453, 95065
Crosthwaite, Mrs. B. M., p. 266, 38242
Crouch, D. E., p. 388, 71793; Mrs. E. C., p. 388, 71791; H. W., p. 388, 71792
Crum, Mrs. E. V., p. 113, 10634, 11079, 41810, 42140; J. M. C., p. 113, 10635, 11080, 41811, 42141
Cubitt, A., p. 264, 38207; A. B., p. 424, 80214, 80358; B. B., p. 424, 80212, 80356; E. J., p. 424, 80222, 80366; Capt. F. A., p. 424, 80211, 80355; Maj. F. A., p. 424, 80216, 80360; F. L., p. 424, 80213, 80357; J. F., p. 424, 80215, 80359; L., p. 424, 80221, 80365; Rev. S. H., p. 424, 80218, 80362
Cuffe-Knox, Mrs. V. I.

C., p. 114, 10652, 11097, 41828, 42158
Cull, Mrs. A., p. 245, 37423; E., p. 245, 37425; H., p. 245, 37424
Cumberland, A. G., p. 182, 27334; A. M., p. 181, 27356; A. M., p. 182, 27391; A. M., p. 183, 27411; A. R., p. 182, 27381; A. R., p. 182, 27401; B. L., p. 182, 27373; C. B., p. 182, 27387; Maj.-Gen. C. E., p. 181, 27363; C. G., p. 182, 27389; C. R., p. 182, 27379; Maj. C. S., p. 182, 27403; C. T., p. 181, 27370; D. R., p. 182, 27383; E. A., p. 181, 27369; F. L., p. 182, 27377; Lieut.-Col. G. B. M., p. 182, 27402; G. L., p. 181, 27371; J. B., p. 182, 27380; J. L., p. 182, 27375; Capt. L. B., p. 181, 27365; M., p. 182, 27385; M. F., p. 183, 27410; M. G. L., p. 182, 27374; M. L., p. 182, 27376; N. H., p. 181, 27367; P. B., p. 182 27386; P. M. E., p. 181, 27368; R. G., p. 182, 27388; R. L., p. 181, 27372; R. L., p. 182, 27378; V. B., p. 182, 27390; Maj.-Gen. W. B., p. 181, 27364; W. B., p. 182, 27382
Cumine, Mrs. A. H., p. 496, 128274; A. I., p. 496, 128275; C. D., p. 496, 128278; E. M. E., p. 496, 128277; F. M., p. 496, 128277
Cummins, Mrs. C. A., p. 509, 129239
Cunard ( ), p. 96, 10081; Mrs. C. M., p. 96, 10080
Cunliffe-Owen, Mrs A., p. 264, 38201; A. R., p. 264, 38204; D. M., p. 264, 38205; E., p. 264, 38202; F. E., p. 264, 38203; S., p. 264, 38206
Cure, Mrs, F. M., p. 104, 10240, 10339, 41416, 41515
Currie, B. F. G., p. 406, 79681; D. M., p. 406, 79683; E. C., p. 406, 79682; Mrs. F. E., p. 522, 130733; L., p. 406, 79680
Curwen, E. M. S., p. 42, 102
Curzon, J. P., p. 544, 134915, 135052; Hon. Mrs. M. L., p. 544, 134913, 135050; R. L., p. 544, 134914, 135053; R. O. N., p. 544, 134914, 135051; V. L., p. 544, 134917, 135054
D'AGUILAR, E. G., p. 70, 952, 57371; Emily P., Lady, p. 70, 951, 57370
Dallas, E., p. 212, 30059;

Mrs. E. M., p. 212, 30057; J., p. 212, 30058
Dalton, A., p. 123, 11511; H., p. 123, 11509; O., p. 123, 11519; W., p. 123, 11510
Daniel, Mrs. A. E., p. 210, 29954; A. L., p. 210, 29958; E. J., p. 210, 29959; F. W., p. 210, 29957; J. M., p. 210, 29956; M. M., p. 210, 29960; W. A., p. 210, 29955
Daniell, Mrs. B., p. 100, 10174, 41350; C. J. W., p. 125, 11567; Mrs. C. S., p. 395, 72252; G. E. S., p. 125, 11564; G. F. B., p. 395, 72253; H. E. B., p. 395, 72255; J. S., p. 125, 11566; Mrs. M. E., p. 125, 11563; M. S., p. 125, 11570; Capt. W. A. B., p. 395, 72254; Capt. W. R., p. 125, 11565
Daniels, Mrs. F., p. 193, 28927, 29198
D'Arcy, Mrs. M., p. 483, 103428
Dasent, Ellen, Lady, p. 77, 9431; Lieut. M., p. 78, 9432; Lieut. W., p. 78, 9433
Dashwood, A. K., p. 409, 79833; E. C., p. 409, 79834; F., p. 409, 79831; L. B., p. 409, 79835; M., p. 409, 79830; Mrs. M. G., p. 257, 38008; R., p. 409, 79832; T. H. K., p. 409, 79824
Daukes, Mrs. G. I., p. 314, 42387, 42459
Daunt, Mrs. M. E., p. 360, 59828, 59895
Davey, Mrs. M. E., p. 61, 610, 17589
David, H. E., p. 201, 29670; Mrs. L. G., p. 201, 29669; R. F. A., p. 201, 29671
Davidson, L. H., p. 388, 71805
Davie, Mrs. B. P. M., p. 78, 9452; E. M., p. 78, 9454; P. C., p. 78, 9453
Davies, Mrs. F. E., p. 416, 80011; Mrs. F. H., p. 151, 16654, 72466; H. E. T., p. 65, 734; K. M., p. 65, 736; Mrs. M. M., p. 65, 733; M. P., p. 65, 735
Davis, Mrs. M. A., p. 510, 129271
Dawdney, Hon. Mrs. B. E. P., p. 185, 28571, 103411
Dawkins, Mrs. M. H., p. 223, 36338, 36423
Dawnay, Hon. Mrs. D., p. 461, 95455; G. W. ff., p. 461, 95467; R., p. 461, 95456; R. M., p. 461, 95458
Dawson, A. D. M., p. 301, 40170; A. M., p. 301, 40175; A. M., p. 301, 40172; A. P., p. 300, 40147; Rev A. P., p.

301, 40174; A. R., p. 301, 40178; C. E. C., p. 301, 40173; C. J., p. 301, 40167; C. P., p. 306, 40146; E. P., p. 301, 40180; G. C., p. 301, 40172; G. J. C., p. 301, 40171; G. M., p. 415, 80007 H. C., p. 415, 80006; H. M., p. 301, 40177; H. P., p. 301, 40176; L. M. P., p. 300, 40150; Mrs. M. L., p. 415, 80005; M. L. P., p. 300, 40149; M. P., p. 301, 40179; R. C., p. 301, 40165; R. C., p. 301, 40168; R. I., p. 301, 40181; R. P., p. 300, 40144; R. P., p. 301, 40166; Mrs. S. F., p. 409, 79799; F. S. P., p. 300, 40148; W. C., p. 301, 40169; W. P., p. 300, 40145
Day, A. M. M., p. 418, 80088; B. M., p. 171, 17813; J. L'E., p. 418, 80087
Dayrell, F. W., p. 182, 27335; M. A., p. 305, 40314; Mrs. V. E., p. 182, 27394; V. E. M., p. 182, 27396
Deaken, B. A., p. 469, 103124; C. K., p. 469, 103121; E. W., p. 469, 103127; G. B., p. 469, 103122; G. F., p. 469, 103123; Mrs. M. L., p. 469, 103119; M. W., p. 469, 103126; R. F., p. 469, 103120; R. G., p. 469, 103125; V. D., p. 469, 103128
Dean, Mrs. C. B., p. 277, 38681
Deane, Mrs. H., p. 514, 130351
Decies, Mrs. A. H., p. 414, 79972
Deedes, Rev. A. G., p. 534, 131406; A. S., p. 533, 131389; B. G., p. 534, 131402; C., p. 533, 131393; D. M., p. 534, 131400; Lieut. I. M., p. 534, 131408; J., p. 533, 131394; J. G., p. 534, 131401; L., p. 533, 131390; M. C., p. 533, 131388; P. G., p. 534, 131403; P. T., p. 534, 131405; W. G., p. 534, 131404; Lieut. W. H., p. 533, 131386
Deichmann, Hilda E., Bnss., p. 470, 103149 von Deichmann, Bnss., M. T., p. 470, 103155
Delille, Mrs. E. A., p. 276, 38659
Denman, 3rd B., p. 60, 566, 17545; A., p. 166, 17591; Hon. A. J., p. 60, 568, 17547; C. A., p. 166, 17606, 38808; F. E., p. 166, 17604, 38806; G. L., p. 166, 17590; J. A., p. 166, 17602, 38804; J. E. T., p. 60, 577, 17556;

Index

Comm. L. B., p. 166, 17595; L. W. E., p. 166, 17601, 38803; M. C., p. 60, 578, 17557; R. C., p. 60, 576, 17555; Hon. R. D., p. 60, 569, 17548; Hon. T., p. 60, 567, 17546; T. H. A., p. 60, 575, 17554; T. L., p. 166, 17605, 38807; T. V., p. 166, 17603, 38805

Dent, M. M., p. 160, 17025

Denton, Capt. Sir G. C., p. 215, 30139; G. C., p. 216, 30140; J. M. M., p. 216, 30141

Deramore, 3rd B., p. 95, 10036

Des Vœux, Mrs. H. H., p. 552, 135171

Dew, Maj. A. B., p. 413, 79957; A. H., p. 413, 79955; A. R., p. 413, 79958; A. T., p. 413, 79944; E. M., p. 413, 79949; Rev. E. N., p. 413, 79945; F. E. M. M., p. 414, 79962; G. R., p. 414, 79960; H. E. le S., p. 413, 79946; H. F., p. 413, 79954; H. M., p. 413, 79943; J. B., p. 413, 79950; Mrs. L. E., p. 417, 80040; M. L. A., p. 414, 79961; Rev. R., p. 414, 79959; R. C., p. 413, 79942; S. G. A. T., p. 413, 79948; W. F., p. 413, 79947

Dewar, Mrs. I. H., p. 550, 135122

Dewhurst, Mrs. A., p. 563, 135467; G. J., p. 563, 135468; J. I., p. 563, 135469; N. S., p. 563, 135470

Dibben, A. D. H., p. 373, 60194, 64398; E., p. 373, 60195, 64399; Mrs. L. L., p. 373, 60193, 64397; M., p. 373, 60196, 64400

Dibblee, D. L., p. 215, 30132; M. E., p. 215, 30133; Mrs. V. A., p. 215, 30151

Dick-Cunyngham, Mrs. E. P., p. 183, 27404; Capt. G. A., p. 183, 27405; K. M. D., p. 183, 27406; M. I. A., p. 183, 27407

Dickenson, C., p. 337, 55969; C., p. 337, 55970; E. N., p. 337, 55968; L., p. 337, 55971; Mrs. M. D., p. 337, 55967

Dickinson, A., p. 393, 72208, 72313; E., p. 394, 72227, 72332; F., p. 393, 72212, 72317; Capt. F., p. 393, 72209, 72314; G. B., p. 393, 72206, 72311; H. C., p. 393, 72205, 72310; J. M., p. 393, 72204, 72309; O. E., p. 394, 72230, P. F., p. 394, 72229; R., p. 393, 72207, 72312 R. E., p. 394, 72228; S. C., p. 393, 72210,

72315; S. C., p. 393, 72211, 74316; V. M., p. 394, 72231; W., p. 393, 72202, 72307; W. F., p. 393, 72203, 72308

D'Iffanger, Mrs. M. M., p. 86, 9829

Digby, Emily, B. S., Bnss. p. 142, 16236; Hon. E. K., p. 143, 16237; Hon. G. M., p. 143, 16240; Hon. L. T., p. 143, 16239; Hon. R. H., p. 143, 16238; Hon. V. J., p. 143, 16241

Divett, Mrs. M., p. 215, 30122; R., p. 215, 30123

Dobson, Mrs. L. A., p. 176, 27147; S. C. C., p. 176, 27148

Dodgson, A. D., p. 135, 16034; A. M., p. 557, 135338; C. C., p. 135, 16036; Rev. F. V., p. 557, 135337; G. C., p. 557, 135336; Mrs. H. C., p. 135, 16030; J. H., p. 135, 16032; R. C., p. 135, 16033; R. H., p. 135, 16035; Lieut. W. L., p 135, 16031

Dodson, Hon. E. M., p. 513, 130343; Hon. M. A., p. 513, 130344

Donald, Mrs. A. St. C., p. 557, 135332; C G. H., p. 557, 135333; D. A., p. 246, 37437; Mrs. E. St. C., p. 557, 135331; E. St. C., p. 557, 135334; Mrs. F. E., p. 246, 37436; H. H., p. 557, 135335; I. S., p. 246, 37438; M. T., p. 246, 37439

Don-Wauchope, A. R., p. 233, 36599; B. H., p. 233, 36602; Sir J. D., 9th Bt., p. 233, 36598; P. G., p. 233, 36601; P. H., p. 233, 36600

Donovan, Lieut. E. H. P., p. 391, 71078

Doran, Mrs. C. H., p. 552, 135183

Dougall, E. M., p. 373, 60214, 64418; Mrs. E. R. B., p. 373, 60212, 64416; F. M., p. 373, 60213, 64417

Doughty, C. M., p. 523, 130741; E. A. M., p. 522, 130737; F. G., p. 523, 130743; F. H., p. 522, 130740; G. M., p. 522, 130739; H. M., p. 522, 130734; Capt. H. M., p. 522, 130736; K F., p 522, 130738; S. D., p. 523, 130742

Doughty-Wylie, Maj. C. H. M., p. 522, 130735

Douglas, S. O. G., p. 237, 36889

Douglas-Pennant,Hon. C., p. 44, 154; Hon. E., p. 44, 149; Capt. the Hon. G. H., p. 44, 153; Hon. L., p. 44, 159; Hon. N., p. 44, 162; Hon. W., p. 44. 160

Dowdeswell, Rev. E. R., p. 79, 9460, 128617

Draper, M. D., p. 166, 17596

Drew,Mrs. A. A. S., p. 357, 59770; A. E. M., p. 357, 59774; A. J., p. 357, 59773; D. M. C., p. 45, 183; F. W. M., p. 357, 59771; Mrs. M., p. 45, 182; R. C. W., p. 357, 59772

Drummond, Mrs. E., p. 256, 37980, 38395; Mrs. F. C., p. 514, 130350

Drury, Mrs. A. E., p. 88, 9870; J., p. 361, 59859; Mrs. L. M., p. 420, 80126; R. W., p. 361, 59860; Mrs. S. L. C., p. 361, 59858

Du Cane, C. A. B., p. 554, 135246; F. A., p. 554, 135244; F. C. J., p. 554, 135241; K. C., p. 554, 135243; L. F., p. 554, 135242; M., p. 554, 135245

Duff-Gordon, A. M., p. 282, 38886; C. L., p. 282, 38885; D. F., p. 282, 38884; Mrs. M. E., p. 282, 38883

Dugmore, H. N. P., p. 427, 80296, 80440

Duncan, B. W., p. 570 (App.); D. L. C., p. 146, 16432; Mrs. E., p. 204, 29731, 29990; E. A., p. 546, 134987; E. E., p. 546, 134988; Mrs. E. M., p. 146, 16430; F. C., p. 546, 134989; Mrs. F. E., p. 523, 130792; H. C., p. 546, 134991; J. A., p. 523, 130793; J A., p. 570 (App.); J. H. B., p. 146, 16431; L. M., p. 546, 134990; W. E., p. 570 (App.)

Duncombe-Anderson, A. J., p. 58, 507; Mrs. M. L., p. 58, 506; R. F., p. 58, 508

Dunedin, Mary C., Bnss., p. 524, 130800

Dunlop, D. V., p. 493, 128202; Mrs. F. V., p. 493, 128201; N. P., p. 493, 128204; N. R., p. 493, 128203

Dunluce, Margaret I., Vctss., p. 47, 231

Dunn-Gardner (——), p. 468, 103095; Mrs. H., p. 468, 103094

Dunsterville, Mrs. G. M., p. 62, 649; M. I., p. 62, 650

Dunwich, Vct., p. 197, 29537, 29777

Dupuis, Mrs. J. M., p. 206, 29872

Durand, Maude E., Lady, p. 68, 840, 57259

Durant, C. F., p. 100, 10176, 41352; N. H. C. F., p. 100, 10177, 41353

Durdin, A., p. 495, 128238; B., p. 495, 128239 E., p. 495, 128240; M. St. L., p. 495, 128237; R. C. G., p. 494, 128236

von Düring, A. H. G. L. C. J., p. 228, 36475,

36567; I. U. C., p. 228, 36477, 36569; L. C. H., p. 228, 36476, 36568; Mrs. L. L., p. 228, 36474, 36566

Durnford, Mrs. J. E. S., p. 100, 10170, 41346

Duthy, A. E. D. C., p. 82, 9747; C. A., p. 83, 9761; G., p. 82, 9751; H. W. G., p. 82, 9749; J. W. B., p. 82, 9750; R. E. A., p. 82, 9748; Rev. R. H., p. 82, 9752

Dyas, Mrs. E. F. G., p. 138, 16105; E. J. S., p. 138, 16107; J. H., p. 138, 16106

Dyke, A. F., p. 529, 131268; A. F. H., p. 527, 131230; C. H., p. 528, 131239; C. H., p. 528, 131239; E. E., p. 529, 131267; Rev. E. F., p. 529, 131266; E. F. H., p. 527, 131220; E. F. H., p. 528, 131240; E. H., p. 528, 131238; Col. E. H., p. 528, 131251; E. H., p. 528, 131253; E. L. H., p. 527, 131233; F. H., p. 528, 131252; Lieut.-Col. F. H., p. 528, 131257; G. A. H., p. 527, 131227; Lieut.-Col. G. H., p. 529, 131260; Adm. H. H., p. 529, 131262; H. S. M., p. 529, 131261; J., p. 529, 131264; Rev. J. D., p. 528, 131250; M., p. 529, 131263; M., p. 529, 131265; M.G.H.,p. 528, 131256; M. P. H., p. 528, 131245; O. H. H., p. 527, 130221; P. H., p. 527, 131219; Capt. P. H., p. 528, 131236; Rev. P. H., p. 528, 131243; P. H., p. 528, 131255; R. C. H., p. 527, 131228; R. P. H., p. 528, 131244; S. C. H., p. 527, 131234; S. M. E. H., p. 527, 131226; T. H., p. 528, 131237; T. L. H., p. 528, 131242; W. A., p. 528, 131259; W. D. H., p. 527, 131229; W. E. H., p. 528, 131241; Rt. Hon. Sir W. H., 7th Bt., p. 527, 131218

Dyson, Rev. F. L., p. 109, 10400, 41576

Eade, A., p. 172, 17855; Mrs. C., p. 172, 17852; C., p. 172, 17854; J., p. 172, 17853

Eagle, C. M., p. 42, 99; E. G. W., p. 42, 100; Maj. F. E. B., p. 42, 93; E. K. L., p. 42, 98; L. D., p. 42, 97; M. C., p. 42, 94; R., p. 42, 95; V., p. 42, 96

Earle, Mrs. M., p. 77, 9420; R. M., p. 77, 9421

Index

Eden, A. p., 271, 38422, 38519; A. F., p. 279, 38785; A. G., p. 271, 38421; A. J., p. 281, 38851; A. N., p. 284, 38926; A. Y., p. 284, 38927; B. Y., p. 284, 38928; C., p. 284, 38921; C., p. 284, 38923; C. A. M., p. 285, 38946; C. F., p. 279, 38783; C. H., p. 279, 38792; C. H. H., p. 279, 38793; C. W. G., p. 271, 38426; D., p. 279, 38795; D. F., p. 279, 38790; D. F., p. 284, 38930; E. E., p. 285, 38944; E. G., p. 280, 38835; E. L. C., p. 273, 38487; F., p. 281, 38852; F. A. M., p. 271, 38420; F. C., p. 271, 38418, 38518; F. C., p. 279, 38794; F. C., p. 285, 38937; F. E. M., p. 273, 38490; Capt. F. M., p. 271, 38416; Maj. F. M., p. 281, 38843; Rev. F. N., p. 280, 38796; F. S., p. 273, 38478; G. B., p. 279, 38788; Lieut. G. H., p. 281, 38844; Right Rev. G. R., p. 279, 38786; G. W., p. 279, 38782; H., p. 271, 38424; H., p. 284, 38925 Rev. H. C., p. 280, 38797; Maj. H. H. F., p. 280, 38801; H. M., p. 281, 38845; J., p. 270, 38398; J. A. M., p. 285, 38938; J. Hon. Mrs. J. E., p. 154, 16727; Lieut.-Col. J. H., p. 279, 38780; J. R., p. 279, 38787; L. E. E., p. 284, 38929; M., p. 271, 38417, 38517; M., p. 272, 38477; M., p. 284, 38922; M. A., p. 279, 38789; M. C., p. 279, 38791; M. D., p. 280, 38800; M. E., p. 285, 38940; M. F., p. 273, 38486; M. W., p. 285, 38943; N., p. 284, 38924; N. M., p. 279, 38784; R. A., p. 270, 38400; Rev. R. A., p. 271, 38427; R. C., p. 285, 38839; R. F., p. 271, 38419; R. G. R., p. 280, 38798; R. H. S., p. 285, 38941; R. J. P., p. 279, 38781; R. Y., p. 285, 38942; S. C., p. 285, 38945; Capt. S. H., p. 271, 38425; T. C., p. 270, 38399; Col. Sir W., 7th Bt., p. 270, 38397; Col. W. A., p. 271, 38428; Lieut. W. G., p. 284, 38920; W. N., p. 270, 38401; Col. W. T., p. 281, 38842
Eden-Perkins, Mrs. E. A., p. 284, 38936
Edge, A., p. 290, 39062; E., p. 290, 39063; Mrs. M. B., p. 289, 39061

Edmonds, Mrs. M. M., p. 266, 38238; W. M., p. 266, 38239
Edmonstone, Sir A., 5th Bt., p. 523, 130773; A. C., p. 523, 130775; E. St. J., p. 523, 130776; W. G., p. 523, 130774
Edwards (——), p. 339, 56012; (——), p. 339, 56013; A., p. 339, 56011; A. C., p. 318, 42546; A. O., p. 318, 42547; G., p. 339, 56014; K., p. 318, 42548; Mrs. M., p. 514, 130353; Mrs. M. A., p. 370, 60149, 64353
Egerton, Mrs. N. F., p. 153, 16701, 72513
Eldon, Harriet M., Ctss. of, p. 392, 72018
Elkington, Mrs. E., p. 151, 16655, 72467
Ellerbeck, Mrs. A. L., p. 554, 135235; B. J. J., p. 554, 135237; B. L., p. 554, 135239; E. A. V., p. 554, 135236; M. M., p. 554, 135238
Ellis, A. E. P., p. 332, 55462, 55485; A. F. G., p. 332, 55464; A. L. M., p. 333, 55474; Hon. Mrs. A. M., p. 333, 55484; Mrs. C., p. 532, 131337 b; Hon. E. H., p. 332, 55461; F. B., p. 332, 55457; Capt. G. M. A., p. 333, 55472; H. A. A., p. 332, 55471; H. C., p. 332, 55456; H. C., p. 332, 55460; H. G. B., p. 332, 55455; L. E. M., p. 332, 55470; M., p. 332, 55463, 55486; R. A., p. 332, 55458; Rev. the Hon. W. C., p. 332, 55454
Embrey, Mrs. A. B., p. 208, 29905; A. E., p. 208, 29908; A. W., p. 208, 29906; S. J., p. 208, 29909; W. S., p. 208, 29907
English, Mrs. E. F., p. 315, 42398, 42470; G. W., p. 315, 42400, 42472; M., p. 315, 42402, 42474; M. C., p. 315, 42399, 42471; O., p. 315, 42403, 42475; P., p. 315, 42404, 42476; R. W., p. 315, 42401, 42473
van Ericksen, Mrs. M. L., p. 208, 29910; M. L., p. 208, 29911
Errington, E. M., p. 445, 94670; F. F., p. 445, 94668; G., p. 537, 131713; Mrs. G. M. L., p. 537, 131711; J., p. 537, 131712; M., p. 537, 131714; W. A., p. 445, 94669
Erskine, 5th B., p. 224, 36371; 2nd B., p. 226, 36405; A. A., p. 225, 36389; Capt. the Hon. A. M. S., p. 222, 36315; Mrs. C. E., p. 302, 40187; C. E. E., p. 225, 36404; C. M., p.

227, 36458; D., p. 227, 36471; D. F. C., p. 224, 36373; D. I., p. 227, 36464; D. M., p. 226, 36373; E. J., p. 227, 10467; Hon. E. S., p. 224, 36377; G. B., p. 227, 36459; Hon. H., p. 227, 36472; Lieut.-Col. H. A., p. 227, 36455; H. D., p. 227, 36456; H. H., p. 225, 36388; Bnss. H. M., p. 226, 36406; J. S., p. 227, 36462; Hon. M., p. 224, 36372; Lady M. G. S., p. 222, 36312; M. H., p. 227, 36457; M. R. H., p. 227, 36463; R. A., p. 224, 36374; R. H., p. 225, 36390; R. S., p. 227, 36466; S. E., p. 227, 36468; S. G., p. 227, 36469; Hon. (S. J.) R., p. 224, 36376; S. T., p. 225, 36386; St. V. W., p. 225, 36387; T., p. 227, 36461; T. E., p. 227, 36460; V. A., p. 227, 36465; V. E., p. 224, 36375
Estcourt, Margaret M., Lady, p. 100, 10173, 41349
Eustace, Mrs. G. A., p. 69, 848, 57267
Evans, Mrs. G., p. 569 (App.)
Evans-Freke, Hon. Mrs. E., p. 340, 56055; M. C., p. 340, 56056; Hon. R., p. 204, 29728, 29987
Evans-Gordon, Mrs. H. F., p. 110, 10464, 41640; J., p. 110, 10468, 41644; J. P., p. 110, 10469, 41645; K. A. G., p. 110, 10465, 41641; M., p. 110, 10466, 41642; M., p. 110, 10467, 41643
Every, A. M., p. 105, 10270, 10389, 41446, 41565; A. V., p. 105, 10264, 10383, 41440, 41559; C. M., p. 105, 10266, 10385, 41442, 41561; C. V., p. 105, 10280, 41456; E., p. 105, 10271, 41447; Right Rev. E. F., p. 105, 10260, 10379, 41436, 41555; E. H., p. 105, 10261, 10380, 41437, 41556; E. H., p. 105, 10262, 10381, 41438, 41557; E. M., p. 105, 10265, 10384, 41441, 41560; Sir E. O., 11th Bt., p. 105, 10259, 10378, 41435, 41554; F. F., p. 105, 10275, 41451; J., p. 105, 10274, 41450; M., p. 105, 10281, 41457; Mary I., Lady, p. 108, 10377, 41553; Lieut. O., p. 105, 10272, 41448; P., p. 105, 10263, 10382, 41439, 41558; V. G., p. 105, 10273, 41449
Ewart, Mrs. C., p. 485, 103465, 103549; C. G., p. 364, 59925; C H., p. 364, 59926; E., p.

326, 43155; E. F., p. 326, 43156; I. K., p. 364, 59927; J. A., p. 64, 712; J. M., p. 64, 711; Mrs. M., p 64, 710; M. G., p. 364, 59928; M. M., p. 64, 713; Mary W., Lady, p. 364, 59923; P. W.-M., p. 485, 103466, 103550; R. H., p. 364, 59924
Ewen, F., p. 463, 95509
Exeter, 5th M. of p. 150, 16643, 72455; Isabella, Dow. Mchss. of, p. 150, 16642, 72454
Eyre, C. O., p. 260, 38072; Lieut. E. B., p. 260, 38071; Lieut.-Col. G. S., p. 260, 38069; H., p. 260, 38073; L. M., p. 260, 38070; M. L., p. 260, 38086; S. F., p. 260, 38074
Eyton, A. C., p. 182, 27393; A. M., p. 374, 60244, 64448; C. S. W., p. 374, 60241, 64445; D. E., p. 374, 60242, 64446; E. M., p. 182, 27400; I. G., p. 182, 27399; J K., p. 374, 60243, 64447; L. A. C., p. 182, 27398; R. A. R., p. 182, 27397; J. R. M., p. 374, 60240, 64444; W. C. C., p. 182, 27392

Falchotti, Mrs. I. F H., p. 568 (App.)
Falkland, 12th Vct., p. 328, 43198; Master of, p. 328, 43199
Fane, Lady A. F., p. 198, 29553, 29793; C. G. C., p. 198, 29554, 29794; J. L. R., p. 198, 29555, 29795
Fardell, Mrs. J C., p. 171, 17812
Farmer, C. G. E., p. 139, 16157; Mrs. E. A., p. 139, 16156; H. G., p. 139, 16158; H. R. M., p. 139, 16159; O. A. E., p. 139, 16160; R. A., p. 139, 16161
Farnell, Mrs. E. M., p. 373, 60192, 64396
Farquharson, E. C. L., p. 144, 16331; Mrs. M., p. 144, 16329; M., p. 199, 29584; S., p. 199, 29585; W. J., p. 144, 16330; Mrs. Z. C., p. 199, 29583
Farquhar - Spottiswood, Lieut. A. E., p. 229, 364981, 36590; H. A., p. 229, 36497, 36589; M. G., p. 229, 36501, 36593; T. W., p. 229, 36500, 36592; V. D., p. 229, 36499, 36591
Farrer, H. M., p. 553, 135221; J. A., p. 553, 135217; M. G., p. 553, 135222; R. J., p. 553, 135218; S. J., p. 553, 135219; Rev. W., p. 553, 135220
Fasken, D., p. 427, 80303, 80447; Mrs. E., p. 427, 80302, 80446; G. E., p.

Index

427, 80304, 80448; M. A., p. 427, 80305, 80449
Fawcett, Mrs. E. E., p. 558, 135353
Fawssett, E. M. H., p. 327, 43184; F. W., p. 327, 43183; J. L., p. 327, 43182; R. M., p. 327, 43181
Feaver, Mrs. C. L. G., p. 473, 103255; H. J., p. 473, 103257; M. C., p. 473, 103256
Feetham, Mrs. A., p. 561, 135420; Mrs. M., p. 561, 135422; M. I., p. 561, 135421
Fellowes, Mrs. E. F. A., p. 219, 30336; R. W. L., p. 219, 30337
Fendall, C. J., p. 162, 17073
Fenwick, Mrs. A. K., p. 43, 118; Mrs. M. S., p. 43, 114
Ferguson, Hon. Mrs. E. A., p. 329, 43207; E. N., p. 329, 43209
Ferris, A., p. 520, 130575; A. G., p. 569 (App.); A. O., p. 519, 130547; C., p. 519, 130574; C. E., p. 518, 130545; E. C., p. 569 (App.); E. E., p. 519, 130552; E. H., p. 519, 130549; G. F., p. 518, 130544; Rev. H. B., p. 519, 130546; J. F., p. 518, 130542; K., p. 520, 130576; L., p. 520, 130578; L. F., p. 569 (App.); M. B., p. 518, 130543; N. S., p. 519, 130548; R. B., p. 569 (App.); S., p. 520, 130577; Rev. T. B. B.. p. 518, 130539; Rev. T. E. S., p. 518, 130540; W. A. B., p. 518, 130541; W. G., p. 519, 130553; W. T. C., p. 569 (App.)
Festing, Comm. H. M. C., p. 93, 10014; M. C., p. 93, 10016; M. G., p. 93, 10018; Capt. M. M. M., p. 93, 10015; M. V., p. 93, 10017
ffolkes, A., p. 461, 95459; B., p. 461, 95460; C. M., p. 461, 95461; C. F., p. 462, 95474; E. G. E., p. 462, 95468; E. J. P. B., p. 462, 95470; E. M., p. 462, 95475; Rev. F. A. S., p. 462, 95469; F. L., p. 462, 95500; G. C. H., p. 462, 95477; G. H. B., p. 462, 95486; Rev. H. E., p. 461, 95465; H. S. E., p. 462, 95480; M. E., p. 462, 95476; M. E. M., p. 462, 95473; M. O. E., p. 462, 95485; P. F. B., p. 462, 95471; R. W. E., p. 462, 95472; Lieut. W. E. B., p. 461, 95466; Sir W. H. B., 3rd Bt., p. 461, 95454; W. R. C., p. 461, 95467
Ffrench, Mrs. C. H., p. 144, 16347; N. G., p. 145, 16358
Fiennes-Clinton, C. W., p. 51, 328; E. C., p. 51, 330; E. H., p. 51, 327;

Rev. H., p. 51, 325; H., p. 51, 329; Rev. H. G., p. 51, 326
Fife, D. F., p. 204, 29733, 29992; Mrs. F. J., p. 204, 29732, 29991; M. A., p. 204, 29734, 29993
Figulelli, F. M. S., p. 100, 10175, 41351
Fillingham, Mrs. E. G., p. 41, 76; G. A., p. 41, 77
Finch, Mrs. M. B., p. 276, 38657
Finch-Hatton, Hon. D. G., p. 77, 9429, 12180; Lady G. M., p. 77, 9430, 12181
Fischer, D. T., p. 267, 38273; E., p. 267, 38270; E. G., p. 267, 38272; Mrs. F. E., p. 267, 38269; M. E., p. 267, 38274; N. M., p. 267, 38271
Fisher, A. W., p. 271, 38436; Mrs. C., p. 271, 38435; Capt. C. S. D., p. 271, 38437; E. M., p. 272, 38446; F. A'C., p. 272, 38438; Mrs. F. M., p. 408, 79747; H. M., p. 408, 79748; M. A., p. 124, 11561; M. A., p. 408, 79749; M. E., p. 124, 11562; Mrs. M. R., p. 124, 11560
FitzGerald, A., p. 338, 55988; A., p. 338, 55989; A., p. 339, 56028; C., p. 338, 55995; C. H., p. 338, 55994; C. L., p. 339, 56022; C. P., p. 449, 94922; C. P., p. 449, 94927; D., p. 337, 55972; D., p. 338, 55984; D., p. 338, 55987; D., p. 339, 56030; D. G., p. 338, 55990; E., p. 337, 55974; E. C., p. 338, 55993; E. W., p. 338, 55983; F., p. 338, 55985; F., p. 339, 56031; G., p. 339, 55992; G., p. 339, 56032; G. P., p. 449, 94924; G. T. M., p. 186, 28640; H., p. 337, 55973; H., p. 339, 56025; H., p. 339, 56026; H., p. 339, 56029; Rev. H. P., p. 449, 94920; K. P., p. 449, 94921; L. P., p. 449, 94926; M., p. 338, 55986; M. F. P., p. 338, 55988; M. P., p. 449, 94925; M. P., p. 449, 94923; M. P., p. 449, 94928; O., p. 339, 56023; O., p. 339, 56024; O. E., p. 338, 55927; O. E., p. 338, 55982; R. G., p. 338, 55991; S. N., p. 338, 56000; S. S., p. 337, 55996
FitzGerald-Wilson, W. H., p. 171, 17826
Fitzherbert, A. V., p. 276, 38663; Mrs. M. E., p. 276, 38662
Fitzmaurice, C. E., p. 367, 60035, 60086, 62519, 64239; C. H., p. 367,

60034, 60085, 62518, 64238
Fleming, Mrs. M. E., p. 359, 59819, 95298
Flood, Mrs. C. V., p. 106, 10312, 41488
Flower, Hon. E. C. G., p. 103, 10231, 10330, 10364, 41407, 41506, 41539; Hon. G., p. 103, 10232, 10331, 10365, 41408, 41507, 41540; Hon. L. R., p. 103, 10227, 10326, 10360, 41403, 41502, 41535; Hon. R. H., p. 103, 10228, 10327, 10361, 41404, 41503, 41536
Flowerdew, Mrs. A. D., p. 322, 42665; G. D. H., p. 322, 42666
Flynn, Mrs. E. M., p. 517, 130436, 130516; J. H., p. 517, 130437, 130517
Foley, P. H., p. 40, 58
Foote, Mrs. A. M., p. 242, 37346; Lieut. A. W. B., p. 243, 37347; Lieut. P. W. B., p. 243, 37348; R. C. B., p. 243, 37349; S. M. B., p. 243, 37350
Forbes, A., p. 194, 29008, 29089, 29279; A. D. M., p. 228, 36479, 36528, 36571; A. E. B., p. 228, 36478, 36527, 36570; A. M., p. 231, 36536; C., p. 194, 29007, 29088, 29278; C. J., p. 231, 36541; Maj.-Gen. C. F., p. 230, 36526; D. A., p. 231, 36537; D. J., p. 231, 36544; E. B. C., p. 228, 36480, 36529, 36572; Rev. E. E., p. 228, 36483, 36532, 36575; E. M. L., p. 228, 36481, 36530, 36573; H. D. E., p. 228, 36482, 36531, 36574; H. J., p. 231, 36545; J., p. 231, 36535; K. E., p. 231, 36542; M., p. 194, 29009, 29090, 29280; M. D., p. 231, 36538; M. M., p. 231, 36539; M. T. L., p. 228, 36484, 36533, 36576; R. H., p. 231, 36546; Capt. W. A., p. 231, 36543; W. H., p. 231, 36540
Forbes-Gordon, Mrs. D. I. H., p. 271, 38423
Forbes-Mitchell, M. I., p. 228, 36473, 36565
Ford, A. E., p. 47, 239; A. St. C., p. 557, 135325; A. St. C., p. 557, 135326; Maj. B. St. C., p. 557, 135329; C. C., p. 556, 135308, 135314; Rev. C. P., p. 557, 135340; C. S., p. 557, 135327; D. St. C., p. 557, 135328; Francis C., Dow. Lady, p. 556, 135309; Sir F. C. St. C., 5th Bt., p. 556, 135304, 135310; Rev. F. W. B., p. 556, 135305, 135311; H. B. C., p. 556, 135307, 135313; H. M., p. 556, 135315; K. St. C., p. 557, 135324; L. St. C., p. 557, 135330; Mrs. M.

C., p. 47, 238; N. M., p. 47, 240; P. St. C., p. 557, 135327; Rev. R. A., p. 557, 135341; R. L., p. 47, 241
Fordham, A. S., p. 200, 29598; Mrs. C. A., p. 200, 29597; J. M., p. 200, 29599
Formby, Mrs. A. J., p. 205, 29756
Forster, Lieut.-Gen. B. L., p. 177, 27203; E. B., p. 178, 27225; Mrs. G. M., p. 525, 130995; G. N. B., p. 177, 27206; I. G., p. 177, 27208; L. M. J., p. 178, 27226; L. W. G., p. 177, 27207; P. H., p. 177, 27209; S. B. E. D., p. 177, 27205; W. A. M. P., p. 177, 27204
Forsyth, A. C. N., p. 368, 60099, 64303; A. H. O'B., p. 368, 60103, 64307; Comm. D. M., p. 368, 60101, 64305; D. W. O'B., p. 368, 60102, 64306; K. M. O'B., p. 368, 60104, 64308; M. B., p. 368, 60100, 64304; R. G. H., p. 368, 60097, 64301; Col. T. H., p. 368, 60096, 64300; T. H., p. 368, 60098, 64302
Fortune, Mrs. J. C., p. 551, 135149; J. V. M., p. 551, 135159; M. F., p. 551, 135158; Lieut. V. M., p. 551, 135150
Fosberry, Mrs. W. M., p. 64, 699
Fosbrooke (——), p. 477, 103353; (——), p. 477, 103355; A. p. 477, 103354; A. A., p. 477, 103360; A. M., p. 478, 103376; A. M., p. 478, 103379; A. S., p. 478, 103372; C. E., p. 477, 103366; C. L., p. 477, 103370; D., p. 477, 103359; F. C., p. 477, 103352; F. L., p. 478, 103375; F. N., p. 477, 103346; G. M., p. 477, 103371; H., p. 477, 103356; H., p. 477, 103358; H. H., p. 477, 103368; J. D., p. 478, 103380; J. H., p. 477, 103364; L., p. 477, 103343; L., p. 477, 103367; L. G. J., p. 477, 103350; L. S., p. 477, 103369; M. C., p. 477, 103345; P., p. 478, 103374; P. L., p. 477, 103365; S., p. 477, 103362; S., p. 478, 103377; S. F., p. 478, 103378; T. H., p. 477, 103344; W. A., p. 477, 103347; W. A., p. 477, 103357; W. H., p. 478, 103373
Fossey, Mrs. E. E. M., p. 437, 90117
Foster, A. I., p. 561, 135428; A. J., p. 561, 135429; A. V., p. 462, 95482; B. N., p. 560, 135405; Lieut. C. A.,

Index

p. 561, 135425; Charlotte P. E., Lady, p. 462, 95481; D. E. C. V., p. 462, 95484; F. I., p. 561, 135406; H. I., p. 561, 135409; H. J., p. 561, 135408; J., p. 561, 135419; J., p. 561, 135423; M. M., p. 561, 135432; M. R., p. 561, 135427; P. E. V., p. 462, 95483; R. A. L., p. 561, 135430; R. M., p. 561, 135431; T. H., p. 561, 135407; T. W., p. 561, 135410; W., p. 561, 135424; W. G. M., p. 561, 135426
Fothergill, C. F., p. 200, 29610; E. G. F., p. 446, 94691; F. H. G., p. 446, 94689; H. M. B., p. 446, 94690; M. H. S., p. 200, 29611; P. G. L., p. 446, 94688; R., p. 200, 29609; Mrs. W. S., p. 200, 29608
Fowell, Mrs. E. L. F., p. 165, 17543
Fowler, Capt. C. W. H., p. 50, 306; C. W., p. 50, 308; F. B., p. 50, 307; F. M., p. 118, 10745, 10767; G. S., p. 118, 10744, 10766; M., p. 118, 10746; S. G., p. 469, 103140
Fox, A. L., p. 238, 36915; A. S., p. 329, 43211; B. E., p. 238, 36916; C. D., p. 238, 36913; C. D., p. 238, 36914; D., p. 329, 43212; K., p. 238, 36918; M. C., p. 238, 36917; Hon. Mrs. S. C., p. 329, 43210; Mrs. S. K., p. 415, 79996
Francis, A. C., p. 165, 17528; Mrs. E. C., p. 165, 17527; H., p. 165, 17532; H. V., p. 165, 17529; Mrs. S. G., p. 65, 737
Frankland, B. C., p. 300, 40158; K. M. C., p. 300, 40156; M. A. M., p. 321, 42625; Mrs. M. A. P., p. 321, 42624; Mrs. M. J., p. 300, 40153; M. O. E., p. 300, 40159; Lieut. R. C. C., p. 300, 40154; R. L. S., p. 321, 42626; Lieut. T. H. C., p. 300, 40155
Fraser, E., p. 230, 36520
Freeman, Mrs. C., p. 146, 16545, 79883; E. S., p. 146, 16548, 79886; H. A., p. 146, 16546, 79884; K. M., p. 146, 16547, 79885
French, A. J. P., p. 149, 16616; A. M., p. 149, 16622; A. S., p. 316, 42484; A. S., p. 433, 85809; Mrs. C. E. G., p. 433, 85807; D., p. 149, 16613; D. M., p. 348, 59567; E. B., p. 316, 42491; E. F., p. 316, 42492; F. C., p. 149, 16611; H. N., p. 316, 42485; H. O'D., p. 149, 16620; Mrs.

H. S., p. 149, 16610; I. H., p. 149, 16615; L. S., p. 149, 16621; M. A., p. 316, 42488; M. D., p. 149, 16618; M. M., p. 316, 42493; Mrs. R., p. 348, 59566; R. E., p. 316, 42486; R. M., p. 316, 42487; R. S., p. 149, 16612; R. W., p. 149, 16617; S. O'M., p. 149, 16619; T. F., p. 149, 16614; Mrs. W., p. 483, 103420
Frizell, E. M., p. 495, 128234; R. A. F., p. 495, 128233
Fry, B. H., p. 127, 11627; Rev. C. E. M., p. 127, 11626; Mrs. J. I., p. 127, 11625
Fuhrhop, D. W., p. 568 (App.); Mrs. E. M., p. 370, 60136, 64340; H. M., p. 568 (App.); O. F., p. 568 (App.)
Fuller, Mrs. A. L., p. 407, 79714; Mrs. E. A. H., p. 499, 128336; G. R., p. 364, 59931
Fulton, Mrs. A. G., p. 103, 10225, 40401; B. S., p. 212, 30043; E. A., p. 212, 30045; E. M. W., p. 212, 30037; F., p. 211, 30019; F. R., p. 211, 30026; G., p. 211, 30022; G. S., p. 211, 30028; G. W. W., p. 211, 30027; H., p. 211, 30024; H. A., p. 212, 30044; Major H. T., p. 212, 30042; J. O., p. 211, 30021; L. H. W., p. 212, 30038; N., p. 211, 30025; O. H. C., p. 212, 30041; P. J., p. 212, 30039; Col. R., p. 211, 30020; R. R., p. 389, 71810; S. A. W., p. 212, 30036; S. W., p. 212, 30035; W. M., p. 212, 30040; W. W., p. 211, 30023
Furley, Mrs. R. M., p. 149, 16631
Furlonge, A., p. 417, 80050; Mrs. A., p. 413, 79951; A. S., p. 417, 80052; C. G. H., p. 417, 80045; C. G. H. de L., p. 417, 80047; Lieut. C. le S., p. 413, 79953, 80058; E. A., p. 417, 80053; C. G. R., p. 417, 80054; Lieut. G. H. S., p. 413, 79952, 80057; G. Le S., p. 417, 80048; Col. G. W., p. 417, 80056; I. A. R., p. 417, 80055; L. E. A., p. 417, 80046; M. E., p. 417, 80051

GAGE, 5th Vct., p. 38, 1; B. E. F., p. 39, 16; C. W., p. 40, 56; E. F. F., p. 39, 17; Maj. E. M. B., p. 38, 12; F., p. 40, 57; F. E., p. 38, 11, 51; G. E., p. 39, 21, 55; Hon. H. R., p. 38, 2; Hon. I. A., p. 38, 3; J. F. B., p. 38, 13; J. S. D., p. 39, 14; Maj. M. F., p. 39, 15;

Hon. V. B., p. 38, 4; W. H. St. Q., p. 38, 10, 50; Hon. Y. R., p. 38, 5
de Galard-Béarn, B., p. 509, 129237; Ct. B. E. R., p. 508, 129225; B. M. P., p. 508, 129228; Ct. C., p. 508, 129230; Ct. C. E. F., p. 508, 129224; C. N. M. B., p. 508, 129223; Ct. E. G. O. p. 508, 129227; Ct. G. R. J. H., p. 508, 129222; Ct. H., p. 508, 129231; J., p. 508, 129233; Ct. J. C. A. G., p. 508, 129229; Ct. L. J. S. A., p. 509, 129236; P., p. 509, 129235; Ct. P. P. A. P. A., p. 508, 129226; Ct. S., p. 508, 129232
Gallwey, Fanny C., Lady, p. 225, 36391
Garbett, B. M., p. 177, 27212; Rev. C. F., p. 177, 27211; C. S., p. 177, 27213; E. M. K., p. 177, 27215; L. G., p. 177, 27214; Mrs. S. C., p. 177, 27210
Garde, V. N. H., p. 493, 128192; Lieut.-Col. W. H., p. 493, 128191
Gardener, B. A., p. 214, 30114; Mrs. B. W., p. 214, 30112; V. A., p. 214, 30113
Gardner, Mrs. C., p. 563, 135471; D. F., p. 418, 80080; Mrs. F. N., p. 418, 80077; G. D., p. 563, 135472; G. I., p. 563, 135473; G. M., p. 418, 80081; N. P. E., p. 418, 80079; R. L., p. 418, 80078; Mrs. V. W., p. 548, 135071
Garfit, A., p. 268, 38301; H. de B. C., p. 469, 103144; M., p. 268, 38303; M. L., p. 268, 38304; S. F., p. 268, 38302; Capt. W., p. 268, 38298
Garrow-Whitby, Mrs. H. E., p. 448, 94726; H. O., p. 448, 94727
Garth, A. D., p. 109, 10452, 41628; C., p. 110, 10457, 41633; C. D., p. 109, 10451, 41627; H., p. 109, 10453, 41629; M., p. 109, 10454, 41630; P., p. 109, 10450, 41626; W., p. 110, 41631
Gataker, A. M., p. 81, 9720; C. F., p. 81, 9716; C. J., p. 81, 9722; D. M., p. 81, 9724; Lieut. F. A., p. 81, 9727; G. G. O., p. 81, 9715; G. W. F., p. 81, 9721; K. E., p. 81, 9726; L. S., p. 81, 9729; M. E. G., p. 81, 9712; M. L., p. 81, 9717; M. L., p. 81, 9718; M. L. S., p. 81, 9719; M. W., p. 81, 9710; R. H. W., p. 81,

9713; R. M. G., p. 81, 9714; V. L. de M., p. 81, 9711; W. R., p. 81, 9723
Gayer, Rev. A. C. S., p. 150, 16637; C. M. A., p. 150, 16638; D. M., p. 150, 16639; E. M., p. 150, 16641; E. H. T., p. 150, 16635; Mrs. E. M., p. 148, 16580; E. P., p. 150, 16636; Rev. E. R., p. 149, 16633; L. H., p. 150, 16640; Capt. H. W., p. 150, 16634
Geach, G. C., p. 84, 9780; Mrs. J., p. 84, 9779
Geddes, A. J. W., p. 215, 30127; D. C., p. 215, 30130; Capt. E. D. E., p. 215, 30125; E. L. L., p. 215, 30128; Mrs. E. J., p. 215, 30124; G. O., p. 215, 30138; Capt. M. H. B., p. 215, 30126
Gepp, Mrs. E. M., p. 549, 135094; M. H., p. 415, 80000; Mrs. M. N., p. 415, 79999
de Gex, R. G., p. 105, 10276, 41452
Gibbings, Rev. R., p. 498, 128320
Gifford, C. M. E., p. 310, 41942, 43135; D. F., p. 310, 41943, 43136; J., p. 310, 41944, 43137; Hon. Mrs. M., p. 310, 41941, 43134; V. M., p. 310, 41945, 43138
Gilbert-Cooper, A. D., p. 165, 17523, 17806; A. E., p. 164, 17518, 17801; Mrs. C. L., p. 164, 17517, 17800; M. F., p. 164, 17520, 17803; W. N. R., p. 164, 17519, 17802
Gilbertson, Mrs. I. de W., p. 280, 38837; M. D. F., p. 280, 38838
Gill, B. E., p. 105, 10279, 41455; Mrs. D., p. 547, 135019; E. E., p. 105, 10277, 41453; G. W., p. 547, 135018; H. C., p. 547, 135017; Mrs. M., p. 547, 135020; O. T. E., p. 105, 10278, 41454
Gillett, Lieut. C. R., p. 366, 59962; Mrs. E. M., p. 193, 28946, 29217; Hon. Mrs. E. M. G., p. 366, 59960; G. M., p. 366, 59965; G. M. G., p. 366, 59963; H. V., p. 366, 59961; S. E., p. 366, 59964
Gillies-Smith, A. C., p. 289, 39047; C. B., p. 289, 39046; M., p. 289, 39045
Girdlestone, C., p. 417, 80064; Mrs. C. W., p. 417, 80059; H. C., p. 417, 80060; H., p. 417, 80065; H. B., p. 417, 80062; L'E., p. 417, 80061; N. S., p. 417, 80063; V. M., p. 417, 80066; R., p. 417, 80067
Gladstone, 1st Vct., p. 44,

Index

175; A. C., p. 44, 168; A. S., p. 59, 551; C., p. 44, 172; C. A., p. 44, 169; Mrs. C. E. W., p. 39, 18, 52; C. G., p. 44, 166; E., p. 44, 173; E. C., p. 44, 165; E. S., p. 59, 554; E. S., p. 59, 558; F. S., p. 59, 557; H., p. 45, 184; H. N., p. 44, 174; H. S., p. 59, 560; Lieut. H. S., p. 200, 29606; J., p. 200, 29607; J. S., p. 59, 552; K. M., p. 39, 20, 54; K. S., p. 59, 556; L. S., p. 59, 561; M. E., p. 59, 555; M. S., p. 59, 559; R., p. 59, 553; Mrs. S., p. 200, 29605; S. D., p. 44, 170; Rev. S. E., p. 44, 167; T. H., p. 39, 19, 53; W. G. C., p. 44, 164; W. H., p. 44, 171; W. L., p. 59, 550
Glanusk, Edith E., Bnss., p. 423, 80194, 80338
Glenny, Mrs. A. G., p. 255, 37938; A. H., p. 255, 37940; H. W., p. 255, 37939
Glossop, A. E. H., p. 400, 77847, 79356; Rev. A. G. B., p. 400, 77836, 79345; Rev. C. H. J., p. 400, 77833, 79342; Mrs. E. M., p. 400, 77832, 79341; E. M., p. 400, 77846, 79355; Maj. F. E., p. 400, 77835, 79344; G. C. W., p. 400, 77834, 79343; Lieut. H. A. P., p. 401, 77839, 79348; Comm. J. C. T., p. 400, 77838, 79347; W. R. N., p. 400, 77837, 79346
Glyn, Hon. Mrs. C. H., p. 242, 37335; C. P. R., p. 242, 37339; Frances G., Lady, p. 336, 55952; F. M. G., p. 242, 37340; G., p. 337, 55955; Maj. G. C., p. 242, 37336; L. G., p. 242, 37337; Lieut. M. G. C., p. 242, 37338; M. St. L., p. 242, 37341; Lieut. R. F., p. 337, 55953; R. H., p. 337, 55954
Glynne, M., p. 44, 151
Godfrey, E. L., p. 143, 16305; E. M. A., p. 143, 16308, Mrs. H.G., p. 569 (App.); V. L., p. 143, 16307
Godman, Lieut. J., p. 444, 94598; Hon. Mrs. S. E., p. 444, 94597
Going, A. J., p. 355, 59719; B., p. 355, 59717
Goldney, Mrs. L. A., p. 387, 71773
Gooch, B. M., p. 62, 628; Mrs. E. C. E., p. 62, 627; Mrs. M. C., p. 112, 10586, 41762
Goodall, Mrs. P. B., p. 529, 131270, 131278
Goodhart, A. H., p. 147, 16575; Mrs. A. K., p. 147, 16573; H. A., p. 147, 16574
Gooding, Mrs. L. F., p. 239, 37230

Goodlake, Mrs. L. E., p. 202, 29695
Gordon, Mrs. A. A., p. 260, 38075; Mrs. A. J. E., p. 222, 36330; A. M., p. 231, 36547; Lieut. A. R. G., p. 260, 38076; B. I., p. 222, 36321; C. G., p. 195, 29020, 29101, 29291; C. G S., p. 249, 37538; C. S., p. 222, 36322; D. B., p. 222, 36319; Capt. D. F., p. 231; 36549; E., p. 260, 38077; Rev. E. C., p. 195, 29019, 29100, 29290; E. O., p. 260, 38079; E. P., p. 260, 38081; F., p. 195, 29021, 29102, 29292; F., p. 195, 29022, 29103, 29293; Mrs. F. E. M., p. 153, 16705, 72517; F. W., p. 153, 16707, 72519; Mrs. G. F., p. 556, 135303; G. M. H., p. 222, 36326; H., p. 222, 36327; H., p. 260, 38084; Maj. H. E., p. 222, 36316; H. E. M., p. 195, 29023, 29104, 29294; H. G., p. 260, 38080; H. W. F., p. 222, 36324; I. D. C., p. 260, 38082; J. C. H., p. 153, 16706, 72518; J. de la H., p. 260, 38078; J. M., p. 231, 36553; J. S., p. 222, 36323; J. V., p. 249, 37539; J. V. C. E., p. 222, 36317; L. B., p. 195, 29025, 29106, 29296; M. A., p. 260, 38085; M. F., p. 260, 38083; M. H., p. 231, 36548; M. I. E., p. 222, 36325; Mrs. M. L. H., p. 528, 131246; M. V., p. 153, 16709, 72521; N. A., p. 222, 36318; Mrs. N. M., p. 249, 37537; S. M., p. 153, 16708, 72520; V. E., p. 222, 36320
Gore-Langton, Lieut. F. W., 391, 71980; Lieut. G. W., p. 391, 71981; Mrs. L., p. 391, 71979; Lieut. M. V., p. 391, 71982
Gorges, Mrs. G. F., p. 433, 85810
Gort, 6th Vct., p. 39, 22 9962
Gott, Mrs. M. G., p. 91, 9962
Govan, A. M., p. 267, 38268; Lieut. D. M., p. 267, 38266; E. F., p. 267, 38264; Mrs. F. M., p. 267, 38262; Rev. G. W., p. 267, 38263; H. M., p. 267, 38265
Gower, A. L., p. 230, 36525; Mrs. E. E., p. 230, 36522; H. D., p. 230, 36524; J. F., p. 230, 36523
Graham, A., p. 187, 28650, 28813; A. M., p. 200, 29600; Lieut. C., p. 187, 28647, 28810; Lieut. C. E., p. 187, 28648, 28811; E. R., p. 200, 29601; Rev. I. C.,

p. 200, 29602; Maj.-Gen. J. G., p. 187, 28644, 28807; Mrs. L., p. 113, 10641, 11086, 41817, 42147; M. A., p. 200, 29604; M. H., p. 187, 28646, 28809; M. T., p. 187, 28651, 28814; R. A., p. 187, 28652, 28815; S. A., p. 200, 29603; V., p. 187, 28649, 28812; Lieut. W. F., p. 187, 28645, 28808
de Gramont-de-Coigny, Ct. A. A. A. X. L., p. 505, 129170; A. L. M. A. S., p. 505, 129171; D. A. C. A. M. L., p. 505, 129172
Grant, Mrs. E. M., p. 145, 16420; F. A., p. 157, 16838; J. E., p. 157, 16839
Grant-Thorold, R. S., p. 157, 16833
Granville, Capt. B., p. 466, 103027; B., p. 466, 103028; B., p. 467, 103062; Capt. C., p. 467, 103060; Adm. C. D., p. 466, 103056; C. H. P., p. 466, 103057; Capt. D., p. 466, 103049; J. M., p. 466, 103050, 131666; M., p. 466, 103030; Mrs. M. B., p. 536, 131665; Mrs. M. C., p. 549, 135089; M. F., p. 466, 103058; Rev. R., p. 466, 103059; R. F., p. 467, 103061; R. N., p. 549, 135090; R. St. L., p. 466, 103029
Gray, Eveleen, Lady, p. 188, 28829; Capt. J. M. S., p. 188, 28830; Hon. K. E. M., p. 189, 28833; Hon. T. Z. G., p. 189, 28832
Greathead, Mrs. A. M., p. 178, 27219; E. S., p. 178, 27220
Greaves, H. G. L., p. 387, 71758
Green, A. D., p. 248, 37512; Mrs. B. R. D., p. 422, 80181, 80325; C. A. M., p. 160, 17019; Rev. C. E. M., p. 160, 17018; E. C., p. 248, 37513; E. R. M., p. 160, 17021; F. E., p. 249, 37519; Mrs. F. G., p. 248, 37502; Mrs. F. M. T., p. 168, 17662; G. P., p. 248, 37514; G. R., p. 248, 37504; H., p. 248, 37509; H. C. M., p. 160, 17020; J., p. 248, 37510; Capt. J. F. E., p. 248, 37508; Mrs. L. A., p. 420, 80145; M. L., p. 248, 37520; M. M., p. 248, 37505; N. L., p. 248, 37506; R. H., p. 248, 37503; R. M., p. 248, 37507; W. L., p. 248, 37511
Greene, A. M., p. 126, 11601; Rev. C., p. 126, 11595; C. R., p. 126, 11599; E. A., p. 125, 11571; Lieut. E. A., p. 126, 11607; E. W.,

p. 126, 11592; Sir (E.) W., 1st Bt., p. 126, 11605; F. C., p. 126, 11596; H. G., p. 126, 11600; J. C. W., p. 126, 11590; J. W., p. 126, 11589; K. W., p. 126, 11591; M. C., p. 126, 11602; Mrs. M. R., p. 126, 11597; N. C., p. 126, 11603; R. W., p. 126, 11594; W. H., p. 126, 11598; Lieut. W. R., p. 126, 11606
Greenly, E. M., p. 178, 27221; J. H. M., p. 178, 27218; Mrs. S. C., p. 177, 27216; Maj. W. H., p. 178, 27217
Greenwell, Mrs. A. I., p. 119, 10770; A. S. G., p. 119, 10771; E. E. M., p. 119, 10774; H. S., p. 119, 10769; L. W., p. 119, 10768; O. W., p. 119, 10773; Lieut. W. B., p. 119, 10772
Gregory, A. J. M., p. 484, 103436, 103520; C. S. S. B., p. 484, 103439, 103523; E. D. W., p. 484, 103435, 103519; Mrs. E. U., p. 484, 103434, 103518; Maj. F. H., p. 143, 16249; F. S., p. 284, 38912; Mrs. J. C., p. 284, 38910; H. F. M., p. 484, 103438, 103522; Mrs. J. C., p. 350, 59588; J. S., p. 284, 38913; M. N., p. 284, 38915; R. H., p. 284, 38911; S. E. V., p. 484, 103437, 103521; V. E., p. 284, 38914
Grenfell, Mrs. H. M., p. 45, 197
Gresley, D., p. 312, 42332; F., p. 312, 42331; Mrs. R. S., p. 312, 42330
Greville (——), p. 256, 37981, 38396; C., p. 256, 37978, 38393
Griffiths, Rev. E. S. M., p. 110, 10470, 41646; I. H., p. 110, 10472, 41648; J. M., p. 110, 10473, 41649; R. E., p. 110, 10471, 41647
Grigson, A. H., p. 460, 95433; Rev. B. H., p. 460, 95440; C. V., p. 460, 95432; Rev. E., p. 460, 95438; F. C. W., p. 460, 95437; G. E. H., p. 460, 95434; J. E., p. 460, 95436; J. W. B., p. 460, 95439; K. M., p. 460, 95429; K. W., p. 460, 95429; L. H. S., p. 460, 95431; O. V., p. 460, 95442; P. St. J. B., p. 460, 95441; R. J., p. 460, 95443; Rev. W. S., p. 460, 95427; W. V., p. 460, 95430
Grimston, Rev. A., p. 194, 28998, 29079, 29269; A. M., p. 194, 29001, 29082, 29272; B. L., p. 194, 28990, 29071,

583

Index

29261; C. D., p. 194, 28994, 29075, 29265; C. E., p. 194, 29000, 29081, 29271; O. J., p. 194, 28987, 29068, 28258; C. M., p. 194, 29004, 29085, 29275; E. M., p. 194, 28999, 92080, 29270; E. M. C., p. 194, 28988, 29069, 29259; E. W., p. 194, 28986, 29067, 29257; F. B., p. 194, 29003, 29084, 29274; F. N., p. 196, 29055, 29136, 29326; G. M., p. 194, 28997, 20978, 29268; G. S., p. 196, 29054, 29135, 29325; H., p. 194, 29002, 29083, 29273; H. L., p. 196, 29057, 29138, 29328; H. W., p. 194, 28989, 29070, 29260; J., p. 195, 29018, 29099, 29289; J. M. W., p. 194, 28996, 29077, 29267; L. A., p. 196, 29056, 29137, 29327; L. M., p. 194, 28995, 29076, 29266; Col. O. J. A., p. 196, 29051, 29132, 29322; P., p. 196, 29059, 29140, 29330; Lieut.-Col. R. E., p. 196, 29052, 29133, 29323; Maj. S. B., p. 196, 29053, 29134, 29324; S. G., p. 194, 28993, 29074, 29264; V. A., p. 194, 28991, 29072, 29262; Col. W. H., p. 194, 28992, 29073, 29263

Guerin, E. M., p. 165, 17539; J., p. 165, 17538; J. A., p. 165, 17537

Guildford, 8th E. of, p. 285, 38955

Guinness, B. W., p. 222, 36314; E. F., p. 286, 38976; Lady Evelyn H. S., p. 222, 36313; H. P., p. 286, 38977; Mrs. I. G., p. 286, 38975

Gurdon, A. E. P., p. 136, 16069; E. J., p. 136, 16068; J., p. 136, 16066; P., p. 136, 16065; Maj. W., p. 136, 16070; W. N., p. 136, 16067

Gurney, Mrs. A. A., p. 425, 80244, 80388; C., p. 425, 80247, 80391; J., p. 425, 80245, 80389; J. E., p. 425, 80246, 80390; R. A., p. 425, 80248, 80392

Gwydyr, 5th B., p. 175, 27083

Gwynne, Lieut. A. L., p. 472, 103200; D. M., p. 472, 103201; G. E., p. 472, 103202; Mrs. M. E., p. 471, 103199

Gwynne-Holford, E. M., p. 436, 90062; J. P. W., p. 436, 90061

Hale, A. F., p. 350, 59606; A. V. D., p. 241, 37319; Rev. B. G. R., p. 243, 37374; C. E. B., p.

350, 59595; C. M., p. 241, 37320; Mrs. E. A., p. 356, 59743; E. A. A., p. 241, 37321; E. A. F., p. 241, 37316; E. C., p. 241, 37311; E. F., p. 242, 37322; E. J., p. 241, 37306; Comm. E. M., p. 350, 59597; E. N., p. 350, 59605; Capt. E. R., p. 241, 37307; F. A., p. 241, 37308; F. A., p. 243, 37355; G., p. 349, 59587; G. C., p. 243, 37352; G. D., p. 244, 37387; H., p. 243, 37354; H., p. 350, 59600; H. J., p. 241, 37310; H. M. O., p. 350, 59601; I. M. A., p. 244, 37391; J., p. 243, 37351; J., p. 244, 37390; J., p. 245, 37422; J. B. W., p. 243, 37375; J. J., p. 241, 37309; L. H., p. 244, 37389; M., p. 242, 37323; M. A. M., p. 244, 37392; M. B., p. 350, 59598; M. C., p. 350, 59604; M. G., p. 350, 59603; M. G. F., p. 241, 37317; M. H., p. 349, 59571; M. S., p. 241, 37318; R. B., p. 350, 59602; R. D., p. 350, 59596; R. E., p. 244, 37388; T., p. 349, 59586; T., p. 350, 59599; W. A., p. 241, 37315; W. E., p. 244, 37386

Hales, A. H., p. 458, 95367; A. M., p. 458, 95379; Capt. E. B., p. 458, 95364; E E., p. 458, 95362; Rev. G., p. 458, 95354; G. F., p. 458, 95366; Rev. G. H., p. 458, 95355; G. O., p. 458, 95360; H. B., p. 458, 95357; H. M., p. 458, 95356; H. M., p. 458, 95358; H. T., p. 458, 95361; H. W., p. 457, 95350; J. B., p. 457, 95347; J. B. T., p. 457, 95346; Rev. J. P., p. 458, 95365; Rev. J. T., p. 458, 95363; M., p. 458, 95380; M. A., p. 461, 95453; M. A. J., p. 457, 95353; M. B., p. 457, 95349; M. F. T., p. 457, 95352; R. B., p. 458, 95358; R. N., p. 457, 95351; R. T., p. 457, 95349

Hall, A. N., p. 144, 16317; A. W., p. 144, 16316; Mrs. A. W., p. 165, 17534; A. W., p. 144, 16337; B. A. E. M., p. 159, 16998; Mrs. C. Z., p. 347, 59539; F. C., p. 144, 16346; F. C., p. 280, 38802; Rev. G. C. M., p. 159, 16997; H., p. 144, 16334; H. F. G., p. 144, 16335; H. L., p. 144, 16333; H. N., p. 144, 16336; H. S., p. 144, 16332; K. F., p. 165, 17536;

K. J. M., p. 159, 17000; M. D. M., p. 159, 16999; M. H. C., p. 159, 17001; R. D., p. 165, 17535; R. E., p. 144, 16318

Hall-Dare, D. A., p. 276, 38665; Mrs. E. C., p. 276, 38664; I. C., p. 276, 38666

Hallewell, Mrs. D. M. L., p. 562, 135459; J. L., p. 562, 135460

Halliwell, Mrs. E. M., p. 145, 16359; E. O., p. 145, 16360; M., p. 145, 16361

Hallowell-Carew, Mrs. A. R., p. 125, 11582; Mrs. E. M. I., p. 124, 11543; M., p. 125, 11586; M. M., p. 124, 11545, 11585; R. G., p. 125, 11583; Lieut. R. R., p. 124, 11544, 11584

Hallward, A. W., p. 137, 16100; B. L., p. 137, 16081; B. M., p. 137, 16091; C. G., p. 137, 16085; C. J., p. 137, 16093; C. J., p. 137, 16096; C. M., p. 137, 16086; C. R., p. 137, 16089; D., p. 137, 16087; F. M., p. 137, 16097; H. R., p. 137, 16083; I. L., p. 137, 16092; K. L., p. 138, 16101; L., p. 138, 16134; L. B., p. 138, 16108; Rev. L. W., p. 137, 16084; M., p. 137, 16088; M., p. 138, 16102; N. L., p. 137, 16080; P. E. G. J., p. 137, 16099; P. N. R., p. 137, 16098; P. N. R., p. 137, 16082; R. F., p. 137, 16094; R. M. B., p. 137, 16095; W. L., p. 137, 16090

Halsey, Mrs. M., p. 466, 103048

Hamilton, A. H., p. 363, 59911; A. W., p. 363, 59908; C., p. 549, 135102; C. I., p. 549, 135100; Mrs. E. A., p. 557, 135339; Mrs. E. L., p. 351, 59630, 60229, 64433; F., p. 549; 135099; F. A., p. 363, 59913; Maj. Sir F. H. A., p. 549, 135097; J. B. W., p. 363, 59909; Mrs. M., p. 363, 59907; M. L., p. 549, 135101; Lieut. R. C., p. 549, 135098; R. S., p. 363, 59910; S., p. 108, 10358, 41534

Hamilton-Russell, Mrs. A. G. L., p. 290, 39075; E. C., p. 290, 39076; J. K., p. 290, 39077; Hon. Mrs. M. L., p. 290, 39074

Hammersley, A. C., p. 281, 38850; C. E., p. 282, 38867; C. R., p. 82, 9744, 38862; D., p. 282, 38868; D. F., p. 82, 9745, 38863; G. F., p. 282, 38871; H. C., p. 281, 38861; H. G., p. 282, 38870; M. V., p. 82, 9746,

38869; S., p. 282, 3888; Mrs. V. M., p. 82, 9743

Hammick, Elinor, Lady, p. 402, 78119, 79628

Hammond, Rev. A., p. 387, 71775; A., p. 387, 71776; C. M., p. 387, 71777; E. D., p. 387, 71778; H. E. D., p. 387, 71779; I. B., p. 387, 71782; M. K., p. 387, 71781; R. F. F., p. 387, 71780; Hampshire, Mrs. K. P., p. 500, 128379

Hanbury, H. G., p. 444, 94587; Hon. Mrs. P., p. 444, 94586

Hanham, E. H. E., p. 110, 10481, 41657; Mrs. G., p. 110, 10480, 41656; P. J., p. 110, 10482, 41658

Hankey, D., p. 388, 71803; E. M., p. 388, 71804

Hanmer, A. H., p. 153, 16713, 72525; Mrs. C., p. 153, 16717, 72529; D. H., p. 153, 16714, 72526; E. H. J., p. 153, 16718, 72530; E. M. H., p. 153, 16720, 72532; F. C. A., p. 153, 16721, 72533; G., p. 153, 16710, 72522; H. G., p. 153, 16711, 72523; H. R., p. 153, 16719, 72531; J. P., p. 153, 16712, 72524; M. C., p. 153, 16716, 72528; M. R., p. 153, 16715, 72527; N. G. W., p. 153, 16704, 72516; T. A., p. 153, 16722, 72534

Hannay, Mrs. D., p. 96, 10067

Hanning-Lee, Col. E., p. 143, 16297; Lieut. C., p. 143, 16299; H., p. 143, 16300; S., p. 143, 16304; Comm. V. H., p. 143, 16298; Col. W., p. 143, 16303

Harberton, 6th Vct., p. 108, 10320, 41496

Harcourt, 10th D. of, p. 506, 129193

d'Harcourt, B. J. M. P., p. 506, 129199; Capt. the Ct. C. F. M., p. 506, 129196; Ct. C. M. P., p. 506, 129197; E. F. M., p. 506, 129195; G. J. M., p. 506, 129201; Ct. J. G. M., p. 506, 129198; J. G. M., p. 506, 129200; L. F. M., p. 506, 129194; Ct. R., p. 506, 129202

Harden, Mrs. E., p. 495, 128242

Hardinge, Sir A. H., p. 333, 55482; Alexandra M., Lady, p. 333, 55475; H. A. M., p. 333, 55476, 55483; Mary G. F., Hon. Lady, p. 333, 55481

Hardy, Mrs. E. R., p 363, 59868

Hare, E. G., p. 159, 17010; M. H., p. 159, 17011; R., p. 159, 17013; Lieut.-Col. R. P.,

Index

p. 159, 17012 ; Lieut.-Col. R. T., p. 159, 17009 ; S., p. 159, 17014
Harford, A. C., p. 472, 103204 ; A. M. E., p. 471, 103192 ; C. L., p. 472, 103203 ; F. D., p. 471, 103190 ; G. A., p. 471, 103188 ; J. C., p. 471, 103186 ; J. H., p. 471, 103187 ; J. M., p. 471, 103191 ; M. A., p. 471, 103189 ; Mrs. M. C. E., p. 471, 103185
Hargreaves, A. D., p. 451, 95019 ; D. B., p. 451, 95017 ; Mrs. E. C., p. 451, 95016 ; J. D., p. 451, 95018
Harington, E. H. V., p. 391, 71974 ; Mrs. L. M., p. 391, 71973
Harling, H. M., p. 247, 37477 ; K. E., p. 247, 37476 ; Mrs. M. B., p. 247, 37475
Harrington, Eva E., Hon. Ctss. of, p. 175, 27082
Harris, Mrs. C. A., p. 302, 40199 ; Mrs. M., p. 52, 368
Harrison, Mrs. A., p. 144, 16326 ; Maj. A. E., p. 565, 135501 ; B., p. 287, 39009 ; Mrs. C. E. Le S., p. 419, 80111 ; C. I., p. 565, 135514 ; Col. C. W. I., p. 565, 135506 ; Mrs. D. C. L., p. 387, 71759 ; E., p. 287, 39007 ; E., p. 287, 39008 ; F. I., p. 565, 135516 ; H., p. 287, 39005 ; H. D., p. 419, 80112 ; I. L., p. 565, 135518 ; J., p. 287, 39004 ; J. F., p. 565, 135517 ; Lieut. J. I., p. 565, 135515 ; M. A. I., p. 565, 135520 ; M. E., p. 565, 135502 ; M. G. E., p. 565, 135505 ; M. I., p. 505, 135519 ; R. E., p. 565, 135503 ; R. I., p. 505, 135513 ; R. S. E., p. 565, 135504 ; R. V., p. 144, 16327
Hart-Davis, A. C., p. 410, 79871 ; D., p. 410, 79870 ; H. V., p. 410, 79867 ; H. V., p. 410, 79873 ; K. L., p. 410, 79868 ; M., p. 410, 79869 ; Mrs. M. L., p. 410, 79866 ; S. C., p. 410, 79874 ; S. F., p. 410, 79872
Hasell, D., p. 205, 29754 ; D. J., p. 205, 29749 ; E. F. H., p. 205, 29750 ; E. J., p. 205, 29755 ; E. W., p. 205, 29752 ; F. A., p. 205, 29759 ; Rev. G. E., p. 205, 29751 ; G. S., p. 205, 29753 ; J. E., p. 205, 29748
Hassard, D. V., p. 265, 38232 ; E. H., p. 265, 38230 ; G. E., p. 266, 38245 ; H. E., p. 265, 38231 ; H. H., p. 266, 38246 ; Rev. R. S., p. 266, 38247

Hassell, A. B., p. 55, 448 ; Mrs. M., p. 55, 447
Hastings, 21st B., p. 422, 80164, 80308
Haszard, Mrs. C. G., p. 280, 38832 ; G. F., p. 280, 38833 ; G. G., p. 280, 38834
Hatchell, Mrs. E. D'A., p. 390, 71832 ; E. W., p. 390, 71833 ; S. D'A., p. 390, 71834
Hatfield, C. J., p. 293, 39468 ; J. R., p. 293, 39467 ; L., p. 293, 39469
Hatherell, Mrs. E. H., p. 551, 135138 ; J. H. G., p. 551, 135139 ; R. C. E., p. 551, 135140 ; S. A. A., p. 551, 135141
Haughton, F. P. A., p. 49, 299 ; Capt. H. L., p. 50, 302 ; J. A., p. 49, 300 ; J. W., p. 49, 297 ; M. P., p. 49, 301 ; Mrs. P., p. 49, 296 ; W. J., p. 49, 298
Havelock-Allan, Edith M., Lady, p. 172, 17841
Hawkesworth, C. E. M., p. 83, 9763 ; Mrs. E. M., p. 83, 9762 ; T. A. F., p. 83, 9764
Hawkins, B., p. 245, 37418 ; Capt. C. F., p. 245, 37416 ; C H., p. 271, 38431 ; E. R., p. 271, 38429 ; G. L., p. 271, 38434 ; H. E., p. 271, 38430 ; Mrs. K. E., p. 118, 10741 ; M. E., p. 270, 38432 ; M. M., p. 271, 38433 ; O., p. 245, 37421 ; R. M., p. 245, 37417 ; Rev. W. W., p. 245, 37415
Haworth, C. F. R., p. 215, 30134 ; R. L. G., p. 215, 30135
Hay, S., p. 222, 36328
Hayes, A. E., p. 91, 9965 ; Mrs. C. A., p. 91, 9964 ; H. L., p. 62, 642 ; J. D., p. 62, 643 ; Mrs. M. K., p. 62, 640 ; T. S., p. 62, 641
Heard, A. D., p. 364, 59921 ; A. R., p. 364, 59922 ; E. M. W., p. 364, 59919 ; K. V. F. S., p. 364, 59920 ; M. M. A., p. 364, 59918 ; R. H. W., p. 364, 59917
Heathcote - Drummond - Willoughby, C. P., p. 222, 36310 ; Hon. Lady Muriel A. S., p. 222, 36309 ; R., p. 222, 36311
Heaton, Hon. Mrs. C. M. S., p. 175, 27084 ; J. V. P. H., p. 175, 27085 ; M. A. H., p. 175, 27087 ; P. J. H., p. 175, 27086
Heaven, B. M. J., p. 255, 37947 ; E. J., p. 255, 37946 ; E. J. B., p. 255, 37944 ; M. J. R. S., p. 255, 37945 ; M. M. T., p. 255, 37948 ; Mrs. O. M. E., p. 255, 37943
Heaviside, Lady S. E., p. 198, 29556, 29796
Heber-Percy, Capt. A., p.

68, 810, 57229 ; A. C., p 68, 814, 57233 ; A. G. W., p. 68, 812, 57231 ; Lieut. A. H., p. 68, 811, 57230 ; A. J., p. 68, 823, 57242 ; A. K., p. 68, 839, 57258 ; A. W., p. 68, 826, 57245 ; B., p. 68, 828, 57247 ; C. E., p. 68, 832, 57251 ; C. H. R., p. 68, 813, 57232 ; D. J. A., p. 67, 770, 816, 57189, 57235 ; H. A., p. 68, 827, 57246 ; H. B., p. 68, 825, 57244 ; H. C., p. 68, 822, 57241 ; H. L., p. 68, 819, 57238 ; Rev. H. V., p. 68, 820, 57239 ; I. M., p. 68, 831, 57250 ; J. R., p. 68, 815, 57234 ; Mrs. K. L. V., p. 67, 769, 57188 ; M. E., p. 68, 830, 57249 ; M. K. V., p. 67, 771, 817, 57190, 57236 ; N. H., p. 68, 821, 57240 ; P., p. 68, 829, 57248 ; Lieut.-Col. R. J., p. 68, 818, 57237 ; R. J., p. 68, 824, 57243
Hedley, A., p. 349, 59583 ; Mrs. E. A., p. 349, 59580 ; M. S., p. 349, 59582 ; R. H., p. 349, 59581
van Heeckeren van Keil, Bnss. A. R. A. H. M. O., p. 382, 64169 ; Bn. A. W. H. W., p. 382, 64167 ; Bnss. H., p. 382, 64171 ; Bn. H. R., p. 382, 64168 ; Bnss. L. G. J. M., p. 382, 64172 ; Renira C., p. 382, 64166, Bnss.; Bnss. R. S. L. R., p. 382, 64170
Heitland, Mrs. M., p. 53, 406
Hellicar, M. G., p. 155, 16786 ; Mrs. S. H., p. 155, 16785
Hemingway, D., p. 561, 135412 ; Mrs. J. M., p. 561, 135411 ; M., p. 561, 135413
Henderson, Mrs. A. O., p. 209, 29939 ; Mrs. B., p. 471, 103178 ; Mrs. E., p. 209, 29940 ; E., p. 471, 103178 ; F., p. 471, 103180 ; G., p. 471, 103181 ; G., p. 471, 103176 ; H., p. 471, 103177 ; H., p. 471, 103179
Henlé, C. R., p. 547, 135028 ; N. F., p. 547, 135027 ; Mrs. R., p. 547, 135026
Henley, 4th B., p. 283, 38897 ; Hon. A. E., p. 283, 38898 ; Capt. the Hon. A. M., p. 283, 38900 ; B. M., p. 284, 38916 ; C. B., p. 284, 38909 ; E. M., p. 284, 38917 ; Hon. F. R., p. 283, 38901 ; Hon. G. A., p. 283, 38899 ; M. A., p. 284, 38919 ; M. C., p. 284, 38918 ; Rev. the Hon. R., p. 284,

38907 ; Rev. R. E., p. 284, 38908
Hennell, Lieut.-Col. A. R., p. 319, 42587 ; A. S., p. 319, 42588 ; E. B., p. 320, 42591 ; F. A. E., p. 320, 42592 ; F. J., p. 319, 42589 ; J. R., p. 320, 42590 ; K. R., p. 320, 42593 ; L. A., p. 320, 42594 ; M. E., p. 320, 42595
Henry, B., p. 110, 10477, 41653 ; C. C., p. 110, 10475, 41651 ; Mrs. E., p. 110, 10474, 41650 ; J. C., p. 110, 10476, 41652 ; M. M., p. 110, 10478, 41654
Hensley, Mrs. J. C., p. 243, 37353
Henty, Mrs. A. C., p. 280, 38840 ; R. I., p. 280, 38841
Herbert, E., p. 436, 90065 ; Lieut.-Col. E. A., p. 436, 90064 ; M. C., p. 436, 90066
Herington, Mrs. M. A., p. 266, 38241
Hermelin, Bnss. B., p. 251, 37580 ; Bnss. B. H. E., p. 251, 37577 ; Jane M., Bnss., p. 251, 37575 ; Bnss. K. E. S., p. 251, 37578 ; Bnss. N. J. I., p. 251, 37579 ; Bn. P. F. S. A., p. 251, 37576
Herne, C. G., p. 289, 39056 ; D., p. 289, 39058 ; D. J., p. 289, 39057 ; Mrs. E. J., p. 289, 39055
Herrick, Capt. J. E. H., p. 363, 59889 ; J. R. W., p. 363, 59891 ; Mrs. M., p. 363, 59888 ; R. L. W., p. 363, 59892 ; R. W., p. 363, 59890
Herring, A. B. Le S., p. 419, 80107 ; A. H. Le S., p. 419, 80110 ; E. le S., p. 418, 80086 ; Capt. H. Le S., p. 419, 80106 ; Lieut. H. W., p. 419, 80109 ; M. S., p. 418, 80085 ; S. P. B. Le S., p. 419, 80108 ; Lieut.-Col. W., p. 418, 80084
Hervey, A. C. C., p. 334, 55531 ; A. C. G., p. 334, 55585, 94991 ; A. E., p. 334, 55529 ; A. F., p. 334, 55527 ; A. L., p. 335, 55584, 94990 ; A. L. P., p. 334, 55543 ; C. A., p. 334, 55525 ; C. A., p. 335, 55557 ; Col. C. R. W., p. 334, 55542 ; D. G., p. 334, 55536 ; E. G., p. 334, 55524 ; E. V., p. 334, 55540 ; Rev. F. A. J., p. 335, 55583, 94989 ; G. A., p. 334, 55537 ; G. E., p. 334, 55538 ; Lieut. G. E. W., p. 334, 55522 ; G. H. W., p. 334, 55535 ; G. M., p. 334, 55539 ; Sir G. W., p. 334, 55521 ; Rev. J. A., p. 334, 55544 ; Rev. J. F. A., p. 334, 55530 ; L. A., p. 334, 55528 ;

Index

M. C., p. 334, 55532; M. E. E., p. 334, 55533; M. F. S., p. 335, 55586, 94992; P. G., p. 334, 55534; P. H. C., p. 334, 55523; Lieut. R. G., p. 334, 55526; Rev. S. H. A., p. 334, 55541; T. A. P., p. 334, 55545
Hewat, D. L., p. 102, 10199, 41375; F., p. 102, 10200, 41376
Hewer, J. A. L. W., p. 213, 30081
Hewetson, D., p. 241, 37305; Mrs. H., p. 241, 37302; M., p. 241, 37304; R. S., p. 241, 37303
Hewett, Eleanor M., Lady, p. 169, 17700; G. N., p. 169, 17703; H., p. 169, 17701; J. G., p. 169, 17702; M., p. 169, 17704
Hext, A., p. 273, 38504; Mrs. A. H., p. 273, 38500; M., p. 273, 38503; R. M., p. 273, 38501; S. M., p. 273, 38502
Heywood, C. R., p. 537, 131694; G. H., p. 537, 131693; Mrs. K. L., p. 537, 131692
Heywood-Jones, C. E., p. 57, 488; C. L., p. 57, 489; M. H., p. 57, 486; V. M., p. 57, 487
Higham, G. L., p. 217, 30316; H., p. 217, 30317
Hilbers, A. M., p. 151, 16668, 72480; D. F. T., p. 151, 16652, 72464; Rev. G. C., p. 151, 16649, 72461; H. G., p. 151, 16651, 72463; L., p. 151, 16653, 72465; W., p. 151, 16650, 72462
Hildyard, B. R., p. 155, 16772; C., p. 155, 16777, 41903, 43096, 43113; C. C., p. 155, 16769, 16794; C. F., p. 244, 37385; C. G., p. 154, 16757; C. G. O., p. 155, 16779; C. J. R. T. D'A., p. 309, 41912, 43105; C. M. T., p. 309, 41908, 43101; C. T., p. 309, 41901, 41918, 43094, 43111; Mrs. D. A. F. T., p. 309, 41902, 41919, 43095, 43112; D. L., p. 155, 16773; E. C., p. 310, 41931, 43124; E. D., p. 244, 37377; E. F., p. 154, 16763; E. M., p. 155, 16765; E. M., p. 244, 37382; E. S., p. 310, 41947, 43140; F., p. 154, 16758; F. E., p. 155, 16775; F. W., p. 155, 16770, 16795; G. G., p. 155, 16766, 16791; G. I., p. 244, 37384; H., p. 154, 16755; Maj. H. C. T., p. 309, 41907, 43100; Col. Sir H. J. T., p. 309, 41906, 43099; J., p. 154, 16760; J. A., p. 244, 37376; J. G. B.,

p. 309, 41929, 43122; J. H., p. 155, 16774; K., p. 154, 16754; K., p. 309, 41905, 41922, 43098, 43115; Rev. L. D'A., p. 155, 16776; L. M., p. 155, 16782; L. R., p. 155, 16781; L. V. M., p. 155, 16780; M., p. 310, 41930, 43123; M. A., p. 310, 41932, 43125; M. L., p. 154, 16761; N. F. D., p. 155, 16778, 41904, 43097, 43114; O., p. 154, 16762; P., p. 154, 16759; P. G. D'E., p. 155, 16768, 16793; R., p. 154, 16756; Capt. R. J. T., p. 309, 41909, 43102; R. S., p. 155, 16767, 16792; R. V. S. D'A., p. 309, 41911, 43104; Lieut. T. B. T., p. 308, 41900, 43093; V. D., p. 244, 37383; Rev. W., p. 155, 16771
Hill, B. E., p. 170, 17718; Col. C., p. 313, 42358, 42430; C. R., p. 170, 17715; C. V., p. 313, 42359, 42431; Mrs. E., p. 207, 29878; H. I. S., p. 170, 17721; H. R., p. 170, 17714; J. D., p. 170, 17720; L. R., p. 170, 17717; M., p. 170, 17719; M., p. 313, 42360, 42432; Mrs. M. E. B., p. 170, 17712; O. C. R., p. 170, 17716; R. A. E., p. 170, 17713
Hillersdon, Mrs. K., p. 156, 16841
Hills, E. A., p 453, 95070; K. A., p. 453, 95071
Hill-Walker, Maj. A., p. 313, 42355, 42427; C. A., p. 313, 42353, 42356, 42425, 42428; Mrs. M. L., p. 313, 42352, 42424; T. H., p. 313, 42354, 42357, 42426, 42429
Hillyard, Capt. G. A., p. 555, 135297; G. W., p. 556, 135300
Hinds, Mrs. C. D., p. 246, 37452; Mrs. H., p. 157, 16840; N., p. 246, 27453
Hintz, Mrs. C. E. M., p. 319, 42576; O. S., p. 568 (App.)
Hippisley, Mrs. C. A., p. 165, 17530; J. P., p. 165, 17531
Hoare, A., p. 369, 60119, 64323; A. C. D., p. 370, 60142, 64346; A. H., p. 335, 55548; B. E., p. 370, 60150, 64354; B. O'B., p. 371, 60152, 64356; C. B. E., p. 371, 60158, 64362; C. C. W., p. 370, 60147, 64351; C. F., p. 370, 60148, 64352; Capt. C. H., p. 335, 55547; C. S., p. 335, 55552; D., p. 370, 60125, 64329; D. O'B., p. 369, 60121, 64325; E. C., p. 369, 60117, 64321; E. O'B., p.

369, 60108, 60091, 64295, 64312; G. H., p. 335, 55549; G. R. O'B., p. 371, 60154, 64358; H. S. O'B., p. 371, 60159, 64363; J., p. 370, 60122, 64326; J. M., p. 370, 60124, 64328; J. O'B., p. 370, 60123, 64327; Rev. J. O'B. D. R., p. 369, 60118, 64322; K. A., p. 335, 55553; K. H., p. 369, 60110, 64314; Mrs. K. P. G., p. 334, 55546; L., p. 370, 60135, 64339; M., p. 370, 60127, 64331; Mabel O'B., Lady, p. 368, 60090, 64294; M. V., p. 370, 60137, 64341; N. C. H., p. 369, 60111, 64315; N. T. O'B., p. 370, 60126, 64330; O. G. St. C., p. 371, 60151; P., p. 369, 60120, 64324; P. M., p. 335, 55551; R. H., p. 335, 55550; Lieut. Sir S. J. O'B., 6th Bt., p. 369, 60107, 64311; T. O'B., p. 369, 60109, 60092, 64296, 64313; W. J., p. 371, 60153, 64357
Hoare-Nairne, Mrs. L., p. 438, 90143; L., p. 438, 90144
Hobart, A. B. S. E., p. 194, 28985, 29066, 29256; Mrs. R. A. F., p. 194, 28984, 29065, 29255
Hodge, Mrs. H. S. A., p. 145, 16366
Hodgson, C. M., p. 388, 71796; D. B., p. 388, 71795; F. C. D., p. 168, 17669; G. H., p. 388, 71797; Rev. H. A., p. 388, 71794; J. T., p. 168, 17676; J. V., p. 168, 17670; L. V., p. 168, 17673; M. F., p. 168, 17675; M. V., p. 168, 17671; N. W., p. 388, 71800; R. C., p. 388, 71798; S. B., p. 168, 17672; Mrs. V. M., p. 99, 10156, 41332; W. M., p. 388, 71799
Hogarth, Mrs. C., p. 256, 37979, 38394
Holdsworth, A. M., p. 169, 17708; Mrs. F. A., p. 169, 17707; F. E., p. 169, 17710; F. J. C., p. 169, 17709; J., p. 169, 17711
Hole, Mrs. A. M., p. 320, 42608, 42651; B. M., p. 320, 42609, 42652
Holford, A., p. 525, 130988; A., p. 525, 130990; F., p. 525, 130989; J. E. A. M., p. 525, 130987; J. E. A. M. F., p. 436, 90065; Mrs. M. F., p. 543, 134873; V. A. M., p. 543, 134874
Holland, A., p. 170, 17725; A. S., p. 170, 17726; C., p. 170, 17727; C., p. 418, 80076; D., p.

418, 80075; E., p. 170, 17722; Mrs. E. S., p. 165, 17522, 17805; F., p. 418, 80073; F. A., p. 170, 17723; G. G., p. 418, 80072; L., p. 418, 80074; R. L., p. 170, 17724; T. C., p. 170, 17728
Holland, C. A. S., p. 108, 10370, 41546; E. R., p. 108, 10366, 41542; G. E., p. 450, 94982; H. E., p. 450, 94983; J. R., p. 108, 10367, 41543; M., p. 108, 10376, 41552; M., p. 450, 94984; M. B., p. 108, 10374, 41550; N. U., p. 450, 94985; R. C., p. 450, 94981; R. E., p. 108, 10368, 41544; Capt. S. E., p. 108, 10369, 41545; Mrs. U. B. P., p. 450, 94980
Holmes, Mrs. M. V., p. 144, 16328
Holmgren, Noble A. M. E., p. 251, 37581
Holt, Mrs. E., p. 59, 544; E. G., p. 59, 545
Home - Purves - Hume - Campbell, E. B., p. 274, 38522, 134742, 135291; Emily J., Lady, p. 541, 134740, 135289; Capt. Sir J., 8th Bt., p. 274, 38520; M. J., p. 274, 38521, 134741, 135290
Homfray, F. R., p. 48, 270; G. M., p. 48, 271; H. C. R., p. 48, 268; Lieut.-Col. H. R., p. 48, 267; Capt. J. G. R., p. 48, 266; J. R., p. 48, 269
Hood, 5th Vct., p. 142, 16217; Hon. A., p. 142, 16229; A. E., p. 142, 16234; Capt. A. F., p. 142, 16233; Hon. F., p. 142, 16243; Lieut. A. O., p. 142, 16231; Hon. D. V., p. 142, 16228; Hon. Mrs. E. C., p. 68, 833, 57252; E. R., p. 142, 16220; F. B., p. 142, 16222; Hon. F. G., p. 142, 16221; Capt. the Hon. H. L. A., p. 142, 16218; M. J., p. 143, 16242; Capt. the Hon. N. A., p. 142, 16219; R. V., p. 142, 16235; S. W. H., p. 142, 16230
Hooper, A. S., p. 532, 131336; B. B., p. 532, 131335; B. F., p. 532, 131329; E. M., p. 532, 131330; F. K., p. 532, 131331; F. M., p. 532, 131326; H. H., p. 532, 131322; J. E., p. 532, 131334; J. H., p. 532, 131321; M. C. A. B., p. 532, 131333; M. E. G., p. 225, 36394; R. C., p. 532, 131325; R. H., p. 532, 131327; R. K., p. 532, 131328; S. E., p. 532, 131337; Mrs. S. F., p. 225,

Index

36393; V. C., p. 532, 131323; Rev. W., p. 532, 131320; W. R., p. 532, 131324
Hope, Rev. A. S., p. 258, 38026; B. S. L., p. 258, 38029; C. E. W., p. 258, 38025; C. K. M., p. 258, 38018; D. K. E., p. 258, 38022; Mrs. F., p. 112, 10585, 41761; G. D. T., p. 258, 38020; I. R. D., p. 258, 38030; J. G. A., p. 258, 38021; Lieut. J. H., p. 524, 130795; J. L. A., p. 258, 38017; Mrs. K. E., p. 258, 38016; M. C. A., p. 258, 38024; M. K. S.. p. 258, 38028; N. E., p. 258, 38027; R. H. W., p. 258, 38023; R. J., p. 524, 130796; R. O. M., p. 258, 38019; Mrs. S., p. 524, 130794; V. M., p. 524, 130798; W. D., p. 525, 130797
Hopkins, J. M. A., p. 78, 9459; S. G. A., p. 78, 9458; Mrs. S. M., p. 78, 9456; W. S. A., p. 78, 9457
Hopper, A. M., p. 218, 30330; A. S., p. 218, 30329; C., p. 218, 30331; E. C., p. 218, 30328
Hornby, Mrs. M., p. 406, 79678
Horne, F. G., p. 456, 95321; H. F. C., p. 457, 95344; Mrs. L. L., p. 456, 95315; Mrs. W. L., p. 457, 95343
Horner, A. M., p. 394, 72248; B. S., p. 394, 72241; C. S., p. 394, 72247; D. S., p. 394, 72243; E. G., p. 394, 72245; E. W., p. 394, 72233; Rev. G. W., p. 394, 72238; Sir J. F. F., p. 394, 72232; J. S., p. 394, 72240; M., p. 394, 72239; M., p. 394, 72246; M. S., p. 394, 72242; O. S., p. 394, 72244
Horridge, Mrs. F. M., p. 568 (App.)
Horschel de Valleford, Louise D. M. V., Mchss. of, p. 507, 129209
Horton, D. M., p. 306, 40340; F. H. Le G., p. 306, 40339; Rev. Le G. G., p. 306, 40337; Le G. G. W., p. 306, 40338
Hoskins, A., p. 300, 40151; Mrs. A., p. 339, 56017; F. D., p. 339, 56019; N., p. 339, 56018
Hotham, 6th B., p. 522, 130730; D. J., p. 171, 17823; G., p. 235, 36622, 72426; Mrs. G. M., p. 171, 17822; Hon. J. M. E., p. 522, 130732; L., p. 235, 36624, 72428; M., p. 171, 17824; M., p. 235, 36623, 72427; Hon. S. B. F., p. 522, 130731

Howard, A., p. 226, 36407; Mrs. A. C., p. 139, 16149; A. E., p. 136, 16073; Capt. A. G. M. F., p. 129, 12173, 81006; Mrs. B. F. W., p. 451. 95006; Lady C. E. C., p. 129, 12169, 81002; C. M., p. 137, 16079; C. W., p. 137, 16075; H. B., p. 137, 16076; G. F. H. C., p. 129; 12170, 81003; Mrs. H. L., p. 136, 16072; J. A. F. C., p. 129, 12172, 81005; K. S., p. 137, 16077; K. P., p. 137, 16078; M. H. G., p. 129, 12171, 81004; T., p. 136, 16074
Howard de Walden, 8th Bn., p. 332, 55453
Howe, Mrs. K. A., p. 510, 129260
Hudson, C. L., p. 192, 28896, 29167; E. C., p. 500, 128374; E. M., p. 192, 28902, 29173; F. D., p. 192, 28895, 29166; G. E., p. 192, 28901, 29172; L. H., p. 500, 128376; Mrs. M., p. 192, 28893, 29164; Mrs. M. A., p. 500, 128373; M. E., p. 500, 128375; M. J., p. 192, 28903, 29174; N. B., p. 192, 28904, 29175; N. M., p. 192, 28905, 29176; R. D., p. 192, 28897, 29168; W. A., p. 192, 28894, 29165
Hughes, K. C., p. 65, 738; M. H., p. 65, 739; Mrs. S. M., p. 65, 732
Hulbert, A., p. 90, 9928; A. I., p. 89, 9916; A. M. E., p. 89, 9915; C., p. 89, 9918; C. E., p. 90, 9944; C. G. K., p. 89, 9919; E., p. 90, 9941; Mrs. E. F., p. 89, 9917; F., p. 90, 9942; F., p. 91, 9972; F. S. N., p. 89, 9927; G. D., p. 89, 9911; H., p. 89, 9913; H. B., p. 89, 9920; J., p. 89, 9923; J. E. B., p. 89, 9914; Maj. J. G., p. 89, 9924; M. J., p. 89, 9922; O. M., p. 90, 9945; R. C., p. 63, 664; R. C., p. 90, 9925; Capt. T. E., p. 90, 9927; W., p. 89, 9910; W. B. A., p. 89, 9912; W. H., p. 90, 9926
Hull, Mrs. A. R., p. 51, 341
Hulton, Ethel M., Lady, p. 451, 95013; L. F., p. 451, 95015; R. B., p. 451, 95014
Humphreys, C. S., p. 524, 130972; Mrs. E., p. 524, 130970; F. S., p. 230, 36518; J. B., p. 524, 130971; M., p. 230, 36519; Mrs. O. H., p. 36517
Hunt, A. K., p. 91,

9969; E. C., p. 91, 9970; H. L., p. 91, 9968; Rev. H. de V., p. 91, 9967; Mrs. M. H., p. 274, 38505; V. M., p. 91, 9971
Hunter, A. C., p. 318, 42539; B. D'A., p. 318, 42536; D., p. 318, 42541; E., p. 549, 135092; E. W. B., p. 318, 42534; Mrs. F. L., p. 318, 42529; H. A., p. 318, 42530; H. M., p. 318, 42537; K. A., p. 318, 42538; Mrs. L. B., p. 549, 135091; L. L., p. 318, 42540; L. M., p. 318, 42533; M. C. I., p. 318, 42535; M. E., p. 318, 42532; Mrs. M. I. G., p. 237, 36894; O., p. 318, 42531; F., p. 549, 135093
Hunter-Blair, C. E., p. 374, 60239, 64443; Mrs. M., p. 374, 60238, 64442
Hussey, E. B., p. 427, 80301, 80445; Mrs. L. L., p. 427, 80299, 80443; Mrs. M. R., p. 279, 38742; W. J., p. 427, 80300, 80444
Hutchinson, A. A., p. 550, 135113; Mrs. A. M., p. 253, 37866; A. V. M., p. 550, 135112; B. A. C., p. 550, 135118; B. L. M., p. 419, 80102; Mrs. C. E. A., p. 550, 135110; C. H., p. 419, 80100; Mrs. E. A., p. 419, 80099; E. F. C., p. 550, 135120; F. E., p. 550, 135121; H. S., p. 419, 80101; P. I. C., p. 550, 135119; Rev. R. H., p. 550, 135111; W. J. B., p. 550, 135114
Hutt, Mrs. C. M., p. 255, 37935; J. C., p. 255, 37936; M. G., p. 255, 37937
Hutton, Eleanor M., Lady, p. 467, 103067
Hyde, Maj. A. C., p. 558, 135350; A. F. C., p. 558, 135351; B. C. A., p. 558, 135349; D. F., p. 558, 135359; Lieut. F. F. M., p. 558, 135348; I. A., p. 558, 135352; J. C., p. 558, 135347
IDDESLEIGH, Elizabeth L., Ctss. of, p. 114, 10662, 11107, 41838
Imlach, B. D., p. 246, 37449; E. C., p. 246, 37454; G. H., p. 246, 37455
Ince, B. R., p. 88, 8856; C. W. G., p. 88, 9860; D. E., p. 88, 9862; E. G. G., p. 88, 9869; G. B., p. 88, 9865; Rev. H. G., p. 88, 9859; H. M., p. 88, 9861; Rev. J. B. C., p. 88, 9864; M. C., p. 88, 9867; N. S., p. 88, 9863; V. B., p. 88, 9868
Ind, Mrs. M., p. 111, 10575, 41761
Ingilby, Rev. A., p. 560,

135395; A. Y. C., p. 560, 135396; Mrs. S., p. 287, 39010
Ingleby, A., p. 562, 135439; A. S., p. 562, 135450; A. G., p. 562, 135440; C., p. 562, 135448; C. H. E., p. 192, 28915, 29186; E., p. 562, 135445; E. A., p. 562, 135443; E. A., p. 562, 135444; E. M. R., p. 192, 28916, 29187; F., p. 562, 135446; F. H., p. 562, 135447; J., p. 562, 135442; Maj. J., p. 562, 135452; L., p. 562, 135451; Mrs. M. P., p. 192, 28913, 29184; P. D., p. 562, 135449; R. A. O., p. 192, 28914, 29185; R. H., p. 562, 135441
Ingram, Mrs. J., p. 523, 130791
Inman, B., p. 318, 42545; Mrs. I. L., p. 315, 42414; M. C., p. 317, 42511
Irwin, A., p. 309, 41915, 43108; C., p. 309, 41913, 43106; F., p. 309, 41914, 43107
Isaac, E. S. W., p. 408, 79728; G. H., p. 408, 79730; G. L., p. 408, 79729; Mrs. L. A., p. 407, 79727; M. C. L., p. 408, 79731
Ives, Mrs. (——), p. 397, 72303
Izard, Mrs. A. S., p. 476, 103220

JACKSON, A. F. C., p. 368, 60089, 64293, 130729; B. H., p. 136, 16064; Maj. C. W., p. 52, 362; Mrs. E. M., p. 52, 361; H. N., p. 136, 16063; Mrs. R., p. 387, 71757; Hon. Mrs. S. F., p. 368, 60088, 64292, 130728; Mrs. V. E. C., p. 52, 367
Jacob, C. K., p. 558, 135357; Mrs. E. M., p. 558, 135354; E. M., p. 558, 135356; I. F., p. 558, 135355; L. A., p. 558, 135358
Jaeger, J. M. M., p. 559, 135388; Mrs. M. A. L., p. 559, 135386; W. H. I. F., p. 559, 135387
James, A. H. E., p. 414, 79981; D. G., p. 241, 37297; E. J., p. 414, 79980; Mrs. F. A. M., p. 437, 90110; Hon. Mrs. F. M., p. 405, 79657; G. H. G., p. 437, 90112; J. C., p. 437, 90113; J. M., p. 241, 37299; Mrs. K., p. 414, 79979; Hon. Mrs. L. G., p. 241, 37295; M. B., p. 241, 37298; O. M., p. 405, 79659; R. C. F., p. 437, 90111; T., p. 405, 79658; W. E. C., p. 241, 37296
Jarrett, E. E., p. 538, 131719
Jarvis, R. G. E., p. 253,

Index

37878; Capt. C. F. C., p. 253, 37877; Mrs. C. O. M. V., p. 253, 37876
Jay, G. H. B., p. 373, 60206, 64410; G. M. B., p. 373, 60209, 64413; H. B., p. 373, 60205, 64409; J. M. B., p. 373, 60207, 64411; M. G. B., p. 373, 60208, 64412; M. K., p. 373, 60210, 64414
Jebb, F. E. D., p. 439, 90151; H. C. E., p. 439, 90149; Lieut. H. S. F., p. 438, 90148; S. H., p. 439, 90150
Jefferson, C. W., p. 563, 135461; C. W., p. 563, 135462; I. S., p. 562, 135456; J., p. 562, 135457; J. I., p. 562, 135454; Mrs. M., p. 562, 135453; M. E., p. 563, 135463; R. I., p. 562, 135458; W. D., p. 562, 135455
Jellett, F. H. L., p. 495, 128248, 128344; G. S. L., p. 495, 128249, 128345; Mrs. M. G., p. 495, 128247, 128343
Jenner, C. E. M., p. 460, 95423, 95449; C. H., p. 460, 95415; E. M., p. 460, 95419; G., p. 203, 29703; G. F. B., p. 203, 29702; Rev. G. H., p. 460, 95420; H. A., p. 459, 95413; H. L., p. 460, 95421, 95447; H. M. L., p. 460, 95426, 95452; M. A., p. 460, 95414; M. A., p. 460, 95417; N. M., p. 460, 95425, 95451; R. F., p. 460, 95422, 95448; V. E., p. 460, 95416
Jennings, A. D., p. 300, 40152; A. E., p. 560, 135404; A. R., p. 463, 95520; Mrs. E., p. 560, 135402; Mrs. G. I., p. 463, 95519; H. L. F., p. 463, 95522; Rev. R. I., p. 560, 135403; R. W., p. 463, 95521
Jermyn, Mrs. S. H., p. 43, 108
Jewitt, D. J. B., p. 112, 10594, 41770; Mrs. E. A., p. 112, 10593, 41769
Jodrell, Sir A., 4th Bt., p. 111, 10573, 41749
Johansson, Noble N. F. H., p. 251, 37574
Johnson, C. H., p. 154, 16724; E. D., p. 154, 16726; F. L., p. 210, 29963; J. P., p. 210, 29962; Mrs. M., p. 154, 16723; M. A., p. 210, 29964; M. H., p. 154, 16725; Mrs. M. V., p. 558, 135343; W. R., p. 210, 29961
Johnston, Mrs. F. H., p. 347, 59529; F. W., p. 347, 59530; P. J., p. 347, 59531
Johnstone, Rev. C. V. B., p. 304, 40298; C. V. B., p. 304, 40302; L. G. V. B., p. 304, 40299

Jones, Mrs. A. C., p. 62, 630; A. H., p. 57, 501; B. N. H., p. 58, 504; B. W., p. 62, 633; C., p. 57, 484; C. D., p. 61, 619; C. K. D., p. 61, 620; D. C., p. 356, 59733; D. C., p. 356, 59734; E., p. 57, 500; E. C., p. 195, 29038, 29119, 29309; Mrs. E. F., p. 356, 59735; E. N., p. 356, 59737; H. C. V., p. 62, 631; J. H. C., p. 355, 59731; K., p. 57, 490; L. E., p. 62, 626; L. H., p. 58, 503; L. P., p. 418, 80083; Mrs. L. R. M., p. 418, 80082; Mrs. M. A., p. 355, 59729; M. E. D., p. 61, 622; Mrs. M. G., p. 195, 29037, 29118, 29308; Capt. O. G. D., p. 61, 623; O. H., p. 57, 502; O. H., p. 61, 39481; P. J. C., p. 355, 59730; P. K. D., p. 61, 621; P. S., p. 62, 632; R. E., p. 61, 624; S. F., p. 356, 39736; W. A. C., p. 356, 59732; Capt. W. E., p. 62, 625
Jordan, Mrs. E. B., p. 102, 10205, 41381
Judkin-FitzGerald, E. C. H., p. 356, 59740; Sir J. C., p. 356, 59738; R. U., p. 356, 59741; T. J., p. 356, 59739

Kay, A. E. I., p. 52, 374; Emily, Lady, p. 52, 372; Capt. W. A. I., p. 52, 373
Kaye, A. M., p. 89, 9902
Keale, Mrs. H. M. De la P., p. 356, 59744
Keane, H. L., p. 147, 16559; Mrs. H. M., p. 147, 16557; M. W., p. 147, 16558
Keates, B. C., p. 86, 9832; C. C., p. 86, 9831; Mrs. F. A., p. 86, 9830
Keays, A. M., p. 165, 17542; F. E., p. 165, 17540; H. G., p. 165, 17541; M. E., p. 165, 17544
Keith, Mrs. M. L., p. 474, 103280
Kekewitch, A. M., p. 483, 103427; E., p. 483, 103421; Sir G. W., p. 483, 103419
Kemeys-Tynte, Capt. A. M. P., p. 185, 28563, 103403; B. M. G. C., p. 185, 28567, 103407; C. J. H., p. 184, 28553, 55479, 103393; Lieut. C. T. H., p. 184, 28552, 103392; Mrs. D., p. 333, 55478; E., p. 184, 28555, 103395; E. D., p. 184, 28554, 55480, 103394; Capt. E. P., p. 185, 28565, 103405; E. V. R., p. 184, 28557, 103397; F. T. F., p. 185, 28564, 103404; G., p. 184, 28560, 103400; Lieut. J. B., p. 184, 28561, 103401; M. L. F., p. 185, 28569,

103409; M. V. B. E., p. 185, 28566, 103406; N. H., p. 184, 28556, 103396; R. E. H., p. 184, 28559, 103399; Lieut. St. D. M., p. 184, 28562, 103402; V. M. A., p. 185, 28568, 103408
Kemmis, Capt. A. H. N., p. 185, 28572, 103412
Kendall, A. M. M., p. 263, 38183; A. J., p. 263, 38182; E. H., p. 263, 38181; M. L., p. 263, 38184; T. C. J., p. 263, 38180
Kennedy, C. N., p. 524, 130969; D., p. 93, 10008; Mrs. E. E., p. 93, 10006; G. L., p. 92, 10003; H. T., p. 92, 10005; Lieut. J. P., p. 92, 10004; Mrs. L. S., p. 92, 10002; M., p. 93, 10009; T. G., p. 93, 10007; V., p. 93, 10010
Keppel, Hon. Mrs. A. F., p. 524, 130805; S. R., p. 524, 130807; V., p. 524, 130806
Ker, D., p. 212, 30055; E., p. 212, 30052; Mrs. G. F., p. 212, 30048; H., p. 212, 30054; J., p. 212, 30051; M., p. 212, 30050; P., p. 212, 30053; R., p. 212, 30056; T. M., p. 212, 30049
Kerr, A. C., p. 510, 129267; Mrs. E. M., p. 333, 52477; Mrs. F., p. 152, 16693, 72505; J. R. K., p. 510, 129266; Mrs. M. A. A., p. 510, 129265; M. K., p. 510, 129268
Keys-Wells, Mrs. M. C., p. 288, 39023; W. Y., p. 288, 39024
Kimberley, 2nd E. of, p. 404, 79649
Kincaid, C. S., p. 525, 130976; Mrs. K., p. 525, 130975; W. H., p. 525, 130977
King, (——), p. 510, 129264; Mrs. A., p. 409, 79800; A. C., p. 195, 29030, 29111, 29301; A. K., p. 510, 129270; C., p. 510, 129269; Mrs. E., p. 195, 29026, 29107, 29297; E. C., p. 195, 29028, 29109, 29299; C., p. 510, 129261; F. M., p. 195, 29031, 29112, 29302; G. C., p. 510, 129252; H. C., p. 195, 29029, 29110, 29300; Mrs. H. L., p. 510, 129248; H. E. W., p. 510, 129249; H. F. M., p. 239, 37224; H. L., p. 239, 37228; J. R. F., p. 510, 129250; L. A., p. 510, 129275; L. B., p. 239, 37229; M. J., p. 510, 129253; Rev. M. J. G., p. 195, 29027, 29108, 29298; M. R., p. 364, 55929; R. A.,

p. 510, 129262; R. G. C., p. 510, 129263; W. G. F., p. 510, 129251
Kingsborough, Vct., p. 542, 134784
Kingston, 9th E. of, p. 542, 134783
King-Tenison, Lady D. K., p. 542, 134787; Lady H. B., p. 542, 134786; Lady S. F. L., p. 542, 134785
Kinloch, Lieut.-Col. G. H. A., p. 551, 135143; G. T. F., p. 551, 135145
Kirby, Mrs. L. H., p. 533, 131340
Kirkpatrick, C. E. C., p. 176, 27139; Mrs. E. G., p. 176, 27138; Hon. Mrs. M., p. 333, 55437
Kirwan, Maj. B. R., p. 389, 71824; C., p. 340, 56058; Rev. E. C., p. 389, 71819; F. S. B., p. 390, 71838; Lieut. F. V. B., p. 390, 71830; G. B., p. 390, 71829; G. W. C., p. 389, 71827; H. E., p. 389, 71823; K. H., p. 389, 71826; L. E., p. 389, 71820; M. F., p. 340, 56057; N. G. B., p. 390, 71831; P. L., p. 389, 71821; R. B., p. 389, 71822; R. C. H., p. 389, 71825; Rev. R. M., p. 389, 71818
Kitson, A. B., p. 523, 130789; A. F., p. 569 (App.); C., p. 569 (App.); Mrs. C. H., p. 523, 130788; D. E., p. 523, 130790; F., p. 569 (App.); Rev. J. A., p. 569 (App.); J. D., p. 569 (App.); J. F., p. 569 (App.); Mrs. M. C., p. 570 (App.); R., p. 569 (App.); R., p. 569 (App.); W. E., p. 569 (App.)
von Klöden, Bnss. T. A. H., p. 472, 103219; T. E. E. F. V., p. 472, 103222; Lieut. T. G. L. A., p. 472, 103220; Lieut. W., p. 472, 103221
Knapp, Rev. A. H. A., p. 373, 60200, 64404; C. C., p. 373, 60198, 64402; F. H., p. 373, 60199, 64403; G. A. A., p. 373, 60203, 64407; R. V. O. p. 373, 60204, 64408
Knaresborough, 1st B., p. 114, 10644, 11089, 41820, 42150; Ethel A., Bnss., p. 218, 30321
Knight, Mrs. C. L., p. 394, 72214, 72319; K. L., p. 394, 72216, 72321; R. C. D., p. 394, 72215, 72320; S. M., p. 146, 16429
van Knobelsdorff, 3rd B., p. 379, 64116; Bnss, A. H., p. 379, 64115
Knox, Maj. A. R., p. 51, 344; Rev. C. W., p. 51, 345; Maj. E. F.,

Index

p. 321, 42657; E. M., p. 322, 42659; G. D., p. 322, 42661; H. F. C., p. 51, 343; J., p. 321, 42656; Katharine A. L., Lady, p. 321, 42653; K. N., p. 322, 42660; M. F. C., p. 51, 340, 346; Mrs. M. I., p. 51, 339; R. W., p. 322, 42658; Maj. S. G., p. 321, 42654; S. G. E. I., p. 321, 42655; W. F., p. 51, 342
von Koch, Noble A. L. A. A., p. 251, 37586; Noble C. F. R., p. 250, 37570; Noble C. W. G., p. 251, 37573; Noble F. M., p. 251, 37584; Noble F. W., p. 250, 37569; Noble G. M. R., p. 251, 37585; Noble H. A., p. 250, 37564; Noble H. E., p. 251, 37592; Noble H. S. E., p. 250, 37572; Noble I. H. F. W., p. 250, 37568; Noble J. B. N., p. 250, 37563; Noble L. I., p. 250, 37566; Noble M. M., p. 250, 37565; Noble N. A., p. 251, 37589; Noble N. F. H., p. 251, 37583; Noble N. R., p. 251, 37591; Noble N. T. G., p. 250, 37560; Noble N. T. M., p. 250, 37562; Noble N. T. V., p. 250, 37561; Noble O. F., p. 251, 37597; Noble R. G. H., p. 251, 37588; Noble R. S. V., p. 251, 37590; Lieut.-Col. Noble R. V., p. 251, 37582; Noble S. F. R., p. 250, 37571; Noble S. J., p. 250, 37567; Noble S. M., p. 251, 37587
Koechlin, Mrs. S., p. 509, 129234
Koenig, Mrs. E. H. A., p. 228, 36486, 36578; P. F. L. G., p. 228, 36487, 36579
Köhler, Mrs. R. H., p. 569 (App.)
von Krause, W., p. 470, 103150
Kulenkampff-Pauli, Mrs. M., p. 420, 80141
Kynnersley, Mrs. F. G., p. 301, 40163

Lacon, Hon. Mrs. M., p. 224, 36378
Lahusen, A. A. C., p. 421, 80163; Mrs. A., p. 421, 80155; A. T. M., p. 420, 80144; (C. F. G.) C., p. 421, 80156; C. H., p. 420, 80133; D. (D.), p. 421, 80157; D. H. F. G., p. 420, 80137; F. G. H. D., p. 420, 80136; F. (J.) p. 421, 80161; (F. M.) A., p. 421, 80162; H. (L.), p. 421, 80160; Mrs. I., p. 420, 80132; I. L., p. 420, 80135; J. (C.), p. 421, 80159; J. G. L., p. 420, 80134;

(J. H.) G., p. 421, 80158
Lake, B. V., p. 125, 11579; E. C., p. 125, 11577; H. M. B., p. 125, 11576; Capt. J. S. R., p. 125, 11573; K. M., p. 125, 11580; M. E., p. 125, 11578; Mrs. M. B., p. 125, 11572; M. N., p. 125, 11575; Lieut. R. St. G., p. 125, 11574
Lamb, A. M., p. 315, 42397, 42469; C. E., p. 315, 42390, 42462; F. M., p. 315, 42391, 42463; Rev. G. H., p. 314, 42389, 42461; H. V., p. 315, 42393, 42465; J., p. 315, 42394, 42466; Mrs. J. M., p. 319, 42574; Mrs. L. F., p. 314, 42388, 42460; L. W., p. 315, 42395, 42467; M., p. 315, 42396, 42468; P. H., p. 315, 42392, 42464
Lambarde, B. A. T., p. 134, 16015; Rev. C. J., p. 135, 16041; D. S. F., p. 134, 16016; E. G., p. 134, 16018; E. G., p. 135, 16029; F., p. 135, 16037; F. E., p. 135, 16040; Capt. F. F., p. 135, 16038; H., p. 136, 16059; J. B., p. 135, 16039; M. E., p. 135, 16019; W. G., p. 134, 16014
Lambert, A. E., p. 183, 27408; Mrs. E., p. 183, 27407
Lambton, Hon. Mrs. C. M., p. 394, 72234; J., p. 394, 72235
Lampen, Mrs. E. M., p. 267, 38267
L'Amy, Mrs. A., p. 152, 16683, 72495
Lancaster-Lucas, F., p. 285, 38949; M. H. U., p. 285, 38948; Mrs. M. Y., p. 285, 38947
Landale, D. F., p. 551, 135156; M., p. 551, 135157; Mrs. M. S., p. 551, 135155
Langham, C., p. 448, 94724; F. N., p. 448, 94725; Sir H. C. A., 13th Bt., p. 448, 94722; J. C. P., p. 448, 94723
de La Pryme, A. G., p. 424, 80224, 80368; H., p. 424, 80228, 80372; L., p. 424, 80227, 80371; Capt. P. C., p. 424, 80225, 80369; Mrs. S. A., p. 424, 80223, 80367; Lieut. W. H. A., p. 424, 80226, 80370
Laugharne, B., p. 446, 94678; K. O. S., p. 446, 94677; M. M. M., p. 446, 94685; R. H. P., p. 446, 94676; R. L. P., p. 446, 94675
Law, A. D. H., p. 423, 80207, 80351; A. P. A., p. 423, 80205,

80349; C. L. G., p. 176, 27135; H. H. B., p. 423, 80206, 80350; H. M. B., p. 176, 27134; Mrs. M. F. L., p. 176, 27133; M. F. W., p. 176, 27137; M. G. C., p. 176, 27136
Lawford, Mrs. L., p. 406, 79677
Lawton, Mrs. I. E. L., p. 161, 17054; J. C., p. 161, 17056; J. W. E., p. 225, 36397; M. E., p. 225, 36400; R. L. E., p. 225, 36398; S. C., p. 161, 17055
Layard, A. L., p. 474, 103266; A. R., p. 473, 103252; B. A., p. 473, 103254; B. B. E., p. 473, 103253; Lieut.-Col. B. V., p. 473, 103249; Lieut. B. V., p. 473, 103250; G. E., p. 473, 103265; G. S., p. 474, 103269; H. C., p. 473, 103251; H. C., p. 473, 103258; J. W., p. 474, 103270; M. L., p. 473, 103264; N., p. 474, 103272; N. F., p. 474, 103277; N. M., p. 474, 103268; P. C., p. 474, 103271; R. S., p. 474, 103267; V., p. 473, 103269
Leader, A. A. M., p. 495, 128250, 128346; C. R., p. 496, 128266; E. L., p. 497, 128301; Lieut. F. H. M., p. 495, 128244, 138340; Lieut. F. W. M., p. 495, 128245, 128341; H. W., p. 497, 128297; Capt. L. F., p. 497, 128300; M. H., p. 497, 128302; M. I., p. 497, 128298; N. L., p. 496, 128268; R. W., p. 497, 128303; S. H. C., p. 496, 128267; T. H. M., p. 495, 128246, 128342; V. E., p. 497, 128299; Lieut. W. N., p. 495, 128243, 128339
Leake, Mrs. G. M. B., p. 112, 10590, 41766; M. A., p. 112, 10591, 41767; M. G., p. 112, 10592, 41768
Lea-Smith, B. A. F., p. 457, 95342; Mrs. S. A., p. 457, 95341
Leavell, E. H., p. 209, 29942; W. T., p. 209, 29941
Le Blond, Mrs. E. A. F., p. 226, 36408
Lee, Lieut.-Col. E. D., p. 529, 131269, 131277; F. C., p. 529, 131271, 131279
Leeper, A., p. 517, 130565; B., p. 519, 130566; B. M., p. 519, 130567; Rev C., p. 519, 130564; D., p. 519, 130568; Mrs. G. C., p. 519, 130562; L., p. 519, 130563; M., p. 519, 130569
Lee-Warner, Rev. A., p. 425, 80238, 80382; A., p. 425, 80261, 80405; B. M., p. 425, 80251,

80395; C., p. 425, 80240, 80384; E., p. 425, 80237, 80381; E., p. 425, 80252, 80396; E., p. 425, 80267, 80411; E. H., p. 425, 80253, 80397; G., p. 425, 80235, 80379; G., p. 425, 80236, 80380; G. C., p. 425, 80250, 80394; H., p. 425, 80241, 80385; Lieut. H. G., p. 425, 80243, 80387; I. E., p. 425, 80257, 80401; Rev. J., p. 424, 80234, 80378; J., p. 425, 80239, 80383; J., p. 425, 80242, 80386; L., p. 425, 80260, 80404; M. G., p. 425, 80254, 80398; P. H., p. 425, 80256, 80400; R. P., p. 425, 80259, 80403; R. V., p. 425, 80249, 80393; Sir W., p. 425, 80255, 80399; W. H., p. 425, 80258, 80402
Le Fleming (——), p. 104, 10252, 10351, 41428, 41527; Mrs. A. A. C., p. 104, 10249, 10348, 41425, 41524; M. G., p. 104, 10250, 10349, 41426, 41525; R. C., p. 104, 10251, 10350, 41427, 41526
Lefroy, Mrs. A. C., p. 552, 135184; A. M., p. 553, 135186; C. E., p. 553, 135187; F. K., p. 246, 37443; G. M., p. 553, 135188; H. C., p. 246, 37441; L. D., p. 246, 37442; Mrs. M. T., p. 246, 37440; T. C. G., p. 553, 135185
Legard, Mrs. A. M., p. 288, 39028; Sir A. W., 12th Bt., p. 191, 28879, 29150; Rev. C. H., p. 191, 28880, 29151; D. A. H., p. 191, 28881, 29152; G. C., p. 191, 28884, 29155; J. D'A., p. 191, 28883, 29154; T. D., p. 191, 28882, 29153
Legge, A. G., p. 452, 95028; B. L., p. 452, 95026; C. E., p. 452, 95029; Hon. E., p. 174, 27075; F. M., p. 452, 95027; H. A. C., p. 452, 95025; Hon. M. C., p. 174, 27074; W. D., p. 452, 95024
Legh, Mrs. E. S., p. 38, 7
Leishman, G., p. 373, 60188, 64392; G. A. B., p. 373, 60190, 64394; H. A., p. 373, 60186, 64390; H. J. C., p. 372, 60185, 64389; L., p. 373, 60187, 64391; R. E. A., p. 373, 60197, 64401; S. B., p. 373, 60189, 64393
Leman, A. T. J. O., p. 170, 17783; B. A. E., p. 170, 17785; E. H. M., p. 170, 17786; H. E. F., p. 170, 17784; N. R. T. O., p. 170, 17781; R. N. O., p. 170, 17782

589   4 F

Index

Le Page, E. M. B. De J., p. 316, 42496; F. B. L. De W., p. 316, 42495; Mrs. L. C., p. 316, 42494; W. M. M. d'E., p. 316, 42497
Leslie, A. I., p. 369, 60115, 64319; Capt. A. T. O'B., p. 369, 60113, 64317; Rev. E. C., p. 369, 60112, 64316; F. E. C., p. 369, 60116, 64320; H. E. J., p. 369, 60114, 64318
Lethbridge, A. M. S., p. 95, 10045; E., p. 95, 10056; J., p. 95, 10046; R., p. 95, 10060; T. C., p. 95, 10044
Levett, D., p. 454, 95103; E. H., p. 455, 95116; L. M., p. 455, 95115; R. H., p. 455, 95114; R. W., p. 454, 95111; R. W. B., p. 454, 95102; W. L. B., p. 454, 95110; Capt. W. S. B., p. 454, 95101
Lewin (——), p. 249, 37530; A. H., p. 249, 37542; A. W. W., p. 261, 38105; C. E. C., p. 261, 38109; Comm. C. L., p. 248, 37496; Capt. C. M., p. 249, 37529; D. B., p. 247, 37468; E. C., p. 250, 37548; Mrs. E. C., p. 261, 38104; E. G. A., p. 250, 37558; Capt. E. H., p. 248, 37492; F. A. W., p. 261, 38106; F. D., p. 248, 37490; F. G. M., p. 261, 38107; F. H., p. 250, 37549; Lieut. F. H. L., p. 248, 37491; G. B. J., p. 261, 38110; G. E. de M., p. 261, 38108; H. C., p. 250, 37547; Capt. H. F. E., p. 248, 37495; J. B., p. 247, 37485; J. E., p. 248, 37501; M., p. 247, 37466; M. D., p. 250, 37546; M. H., p. 250, 37550; M. T., p. 250, 37551; P. M., p. 250, 37545; R. A. H., p. 250, 37544; T. D. W., p. 261, 38111; Col. T. H., p. 249, 37528; Col. W. H., p. 249, 37543; Rev. W. G., p. 248, 37493; Comm. W. H., p. 248, 37494; W. M., p. 247, 37467
Lewis, Sir H. E. F., 4th Bt., p. 402, 78117, 79626; M. A., p. 402, 78118, 79627
Lewisham, Ruperta, Vetss., p. 174, 27073
Ley, Capt. A. E. H., p. 350, 59590; Rev. E. H. B., p. 350, 59589; L. H., p. 350, 59591; M. J., p. 350, 59593; R. H., p. 350, 59592
Leycester, Mrs. E., p. 490, 103597
Liddell, Hon. A. R. H., p. 536, 131682; B. S., p. 536, 131680; Hon. C. A., p. 536, 131681; Hon. C. A., p. 536, 131684; Hon. E. A., p. 536, 131683; E. I., p. 536, 131679; Hon. G. W., p. 536, 131677; R. A., p. 536, 131678
Liddon, Mrs. E. I., p. 136, 16071
von Lilienæron, Cecilia, Bnss., p. 405, 79663
Ling, D. E., p. 225, 36396; Mrs. G. K., p. 225, 36395
Linedale, (——), p. 456, 95305; Mrs. E. L., p. 456, 95304
Linton, Mrs. J. G., p. 50, 323
von Lippe, A., p. 472, 103224; D., p. 472, 103225; Bnss. M. H., p. 472, 103223
Lipscombe, A., p. 198, 29552, 29792; Mrs. E. A. A. B., p. 198, 29545, 29785; E. C., p. 198, 29550, 29790; E. M., p. 198, 29549, 29789; F. E., p. 198, 29548, 29788; G., p. 198, 29546, 29786; M., p. 198, 29551, 29791; W. H., p. 198, 29547, 29787
Lisle, 6th B., p. 352, 59634
De L'Isle and Dudley, 3rd B., p. 234, 36612, 72416; Elizabeth, H., Hon. Bnss., p. 40, 45
Little, D., p. 388, 71790; Mrs. E. H., p. 531, 131290; K. M., p. 388, 71789; M. C. H., p. 531, 131291
Littlejohn, Mrs. M. J., p. 321, 42631
Livingstone, Mrs. F. I. L., p. 358, 59778, 95257; G., p. 203, 29705; H. A. A., p. 203, 29704; I. K., p. 358, 59781, 95260; J. P., p. 358, 59779, 95258; M. V., p. 359, 59780, 95295
Lloyd, A. C., p. 559, 135363; A. A., p. 559, 135376; A. C. G., p. 559, 135378; A. M., p. 96, 10075; A. M., p. 354, 59711, 59753; A. N. M., p. 559, 135379; A. W., p. 486, 103474, 103588; B. A., p. 559, 135364; Mrs. C., p. 355, 59713, 59846; C. A., p. 559, 135365; C. C., p. 486, 103478, 103562; C. C., p. 559, 135370; C. D., p. 96, 10073; C. G., p. 96, 10070; C. G., p. 253, 37859; C. H., p. 253, 37857; C. R. F., p. 354, 59705, 59747; C. W. R., p. 253, 37852; D. C., p. 486, 103488, 103572; D. M. V., p. 253, 37856; D. S., p. 253, 37858; Lieut.-Col. E., p. 476, 103481, 103565; Mrs. E., p. 510, 129278; E., p. 559, 135391; E. A., p. 559, 135375; E. B., p. 559, 135362; Mrs. E. C., p. 202, 29692; Mrs. E. E. M., p. 69, 880, 57299; E. M., p. 486, 103479, 103563; E. M. H., p. 486, 103475, 103559; Lieut. E. R., p. 486, 103485, 103569; E. W., p. 558, 135360; E. W.-M., p. 485, 103472, 103556; F. A., p. 252, 37847; F. A., p. 252, 37848; F. E. A., p. 252, 37849; F. M., p. 354, 59709, 59751; F. M., p. 486, 103484, 103568; F. O., p. 253, 37853; F. V., p. 559, 135367; G., p. 559, 135381; G. A., p. 252, 37850; G. A., p. 559, 135369; G. E. M., p. 354, 59706, 59748; G. M., p. 486, 103480, 103564; G. W., p. 96, 10068; G. W., p. 253, 37871; H., p. 559, 135392; H. D., p. 253, 37860; H. G., p. 96, 10072; Maj. H. J. G., p. 96, 10069; Mrs. H. M. J., p. 271, 38412; Capt. H. S., p. 486, 103482, 103566; I., p. 559, 135394; I. C., p. 486, 103487, 103571; J. C., p. 354, 59707, 59749; Rev. J. H., p. 485, 103473, 103557; J. M., p. 559, 135368; J. P. A., p. 253, 37873; J. R., p. 96, 10071; K. A., p. 96, 10074; K. R., p. 253, 37867; L. C., p. 559, 135383; L. E. J., p. 253, 37875; L. L., p. 559, 135374; L. R., p. 253, 37869; L. S., p. 202, 29693; L. S., p. 253, 37855; M. A., p. 253, 37879; M. B., p. 253, 37868; M. E. V., p. 253, 37874; O. J. M., p. 354, 59708, 59750; P. A., p. 253, 37872; P. H., p. 486, 103483, 103567; R., p. 253, 37865; R. A. H., p. 486, 103477, 103561; R. L., p. 271, 38413; Col. R. O., p. 252, 37861; Lieut. R. W.-M., p. 486, 103486, 103570; S. H. E., p. 271, 38414; T. C., p. 559, 135380; T. M., p. 559, 135366; U. M. V., p. 253, 37854; V. A., p. 253, 37870; V. A., p. 558, 135361; V. A., p. 517, 130457, 130537; V. H. N., p. 559, 135393; Capt. W., p. 354, 59703, 59745; W. H., p. 354, 59704, 59746; W. H., p. 486, 103476, 103560; W. H. A., p. 559, 135377; W. O., p. 354, 59712, 59714, 59847
Lloyd-Anstruther, Lieut. F. R. H., p. 175, 27090; Maj. R. H., p. 175, 27089; R. H., p. 175, 27091
Lloyd-Greame, E., p. 96, 10066; N., p. 96, 10064; P., p. 96, 10065; Lieut. Y., p. 96, 10062; Y. D., p. 96, 10063; Lieut.-Col. Y. G., p. 96, 10061
Loch, C. W., p. 321, 42635; E. E., p. 321, 42637; F. P., p. 321, 42634; F. S., p. 321, 42636; K. M., p. 321, 42633; P. G., p. 321, 42632
Lock, C. M., p. 514, 130373; E. J., p. 514, 130374; Mrs. J. C., p. 514, 130371; L. A., p. 514, 130375; M. S., p. 514, 130376; W. H., p. 514, 130372
Lockhart, E. E., p. 186, 28643; M. T., p. 186, 28641; Sir S. M., 5th Bt., p. 186, 28639
Loftus, A., p. 52, 366; A. M. K., p. 149, 16609
Logan, C. R., p. 420, 80125; G. L'E., p. 420, 80124; R. H., p. 420, 80123; Mrs. S. C., p. 420, 80122
Lomas, A., p. 328, 43193; E. M., p. 328, 43196; H., p. 328, 43194; V. W., p. 318, 43195
Lombardi, Baron A. G., p. 456, 95327; Evelyn G. M., Bnss., p. 456, 95326; Bnss. G. A., p. 456, 95328
Long, Mrs. C. M., p. 276, 38668; D. M., p. 111, 10567, 41743; Mrs. F., p. 275, 38650; F. K. R., p. 111, 10565, 41741; M. E., p. 111, 10566, 41742; Mrs. L., p. 276, 38668; Mrs. M. M., p. 111, 10564, 41740; W. V., p. 275, 38651
Longfield, A. K., p. 498, 128315, 128325; Maj. A. P., p. 498, 128314, 128324; Mrs. G. S., p. 339, 55015; M., p. 498, 128316, 128326
Longley, C. R., p. 147, 16561; Mrs. I. K., p. 147, 16560; J. M., p. 147, 16562
Longueville, A. M., p. 57, 481, 674; Lieut. E., p. 57, 478, 671; E., p. 57, 482; F., p. 57, 479, 672; M. M. A. I., p. 57, 480, 673; Maj. R., p. 57, 477, 670; T., p. 56, 476, 669
van Loon, Jkvr. A. C., p. 381, 64154; Bnss. C., p. 381, 64152; Jkr. L. C., p. 381, 64153
Lopdell, E., p. 390, 71836; H., p. 390, 71837; Mrs. K. B., p. 390, 71835
Love, Mrs. A., p. 494, 128220
Lovett, F. L., p. 564, 135495
Low (——), p. 353, 59673; Mrs. A. K. S., p. 353, 59672; Mrs. J., p. 532, 131337 a
Lowis, E. E., p. 546,

Index

134984 ; Mrs. E. H. M., p. 546, 134982 ; J. M., p. 546, 134985 ; J. W. A., p. 546, 134983 ; M. H. W., p. 546, 134986
Lowndes, J., p. 66, 747 ; Sub. Lieut. M., p. 66, 748 ; T., p. 66, 746
Lowry, C., p. 200, 29591
Loy, Mrs. E., p. 192, 28906, 29177 ; M. I. A., p. 192, 28909, 29180 ; W. A., p. 192, 28907, 29178 ; Z. G. A., p. 192, 28908, 29179
Luard, A. J., p. 532, 131312 ; B. F. C., p. 531, 131307 ; C. G., p. 532, 131311 ; Rev. E. P., p. 531, 131309 ; Capt. F. B., p. 531, 131302 ; Lieut.-Col. F. W., p. 531, 131306 ; Capt. H. B., p. 531, 131303 ; J. A. de B., p. 531, 131308 ; J. McV., p. 531, 131304 ; K. E., p. 532, 131314 ; M. A., p. 532, 131316 ; M. C., p. 531, 131305 ; R. M., p. 532, 131315 ; Capt. T. B., p. 532, 131310
Lucas, Mrs. H. B., p. 476, 103325 ; Mrs. L., p. 427, 80307, 80451
Luke, H. E., p. 463, 95508 ; V., p. 463, 95506 ; W., p. 463, 95505
Lushington, A. E. G. H., p. 550, 135116 ; Mrs. C. C., p. 550, 135115 ; C. H. G., p. 550, 135117
Luther, Capt. A. C. G., p. 388, 71808 ; Capt. G. F., p. 388, 71807 ; J. W., p. 388, 71809 ; Mrs. M., p. 388, 71806
Lynch-Staunton, A., p. 115, 10688, 11133, 41864, 42194 ; C. R., p. 115, 10687, 11132, 41863, 42193
Lysaght, A. A., p. 352, 59638 ; Lieut. the Hon. F., p. 352, 59640 ; F. E. J., p. 352, 59641 ; Rev. the Hon. H., p. 352, 59642 ; Hon. H. G., p. 352, 59635 ; H. J. W., p. 352, 59637 ; Rev. J. A. C., p. 352, 59643 ; J. N. H., p. 352, 59636 ; Hon. K. E., p. 352, 59639 ; K. M., p. 352, 59645 ; R. F., p. 352, 59646 ; W. J., p. 352, 59644
Lyttleton, Rt. Hon. the Hon. A., p. 46, 207 ; Lieut. A. G., p. 46, 200 ; Rev. the Hon. A. V., p. 45, 194 ; Hon. C. F., p. 45, 189 ; C. J., p. 45, 187 ; D., p. 46, 206 ; Rev. the Hon. E., p. 46, 204 ; Hon. F. H., p. 45, 192 ; Hon. G. W., p. 45, 188 ; Hon. G. W. S., p. 46, 199 ; Hon. J. C., p. 45, 186 ; M. F., p. 46, 209 ; M. H., p. 45, 198 ; M. L., p. 46, 202 ; Hon. Sir N. G., p. 45, 195 ; N. J., p. 46, 205 ; O., p. 46, 208 ; Hon. R. B., p. 45, 193 ; Hon. R. G., p. 45, 190 ; Hon. R. H., p. 46, 203 ; Sub. Lieut. S. C., p. 46, 201
Lyveden, 3rd B., p. 366, 59956

M'ALPINE, C. M., p. 290, 39080 ; H. C., p. 290, 39081 ; Mrs. J. C., p. 290, 39079 ; K., p. 290, 39083 ; M. L., p. 290, 39084 ; Adm. R. K., p. 290, 29082
MacCarthy, Mrs. E. D., p. 168, 17674
Macartney, Mrs. M. L., p. 88, 9895
Macaulay, A. B., p. 169, 17683 ; A. J. D., p. 169, 17680 ; E., p. 169, 17684 ; E. J., p. 169, 17685 ; Lieut. H. D., p. 169, 17678 ; J. B., p. 169, 17682 ; L., p. 169, 17691 ; T. C. E. C., p. 169, 17681 ; W. E. B., p. 169, 17679
Macbean, A. C., p. 272, 38444 ; Mrs. A. C. A., p. 272, 38441 ; I. G., p. 272, 38443 ; M. J., p. 272, 38445 ; R. E., p. 272, 38442
McClintock, Mrs. C. E. C., p. 355, 59727
M'Corquodale, A., p. 466, 103046 ; D., p. 466, 103045 ; J., p. 466, 103047 ; Mrs. G., p. 466, 103042 ; H., p. 466, 103044 ; K., p. 466, 103043
McCullagh, Lieut. A., p. 193, 28921, 29192 ; A. C. H., p. 193, 28923, 29194 ; Mrs. C., p. 192, 28920, 29191 ; F. D., p. 193, 28924, 29195 ; H. R., p. 193, 28922, 29193
Macdonald, A. F., p. 319, 42565 ; E. F., p. 301, 40162 ; Mrs. E. H. G., p. 249, 37531 ; Rev. F. W., p. 301, 40160 ; J. W., p. 319, 42567 ; Mrs. M. J., p. 319, 42564 ; M. K., p. 301, 40164 ; R., p. 319, 42566 ; R. E., p. 301, 40161
McDonald, A. W., p. 210, 29946 ; A. Y., p. 210 29951 ; E. L., p. 210, 29944 ; F. L., p. 210, 29950 ; J. T., p. 210, 29952 ; Mrs. J. Y., p. 209, 29943 ; J. Y., p. 210, 29949 ; M. A., p. 210, 29953 ; M. W., p. 210, 29948 ; N. T., p. 210, 29947 ; W. T., p. 210, 29945
McDonnell, Hon. R. G. L., p. 47, 232
Macfie, Mrs. E. C., p. 66, 744 ; E. L. J., p. 66, 745
McGachen, Mrs. K., p. 273, 38485, 80044 ; Mrs. L., p. 273, 38484 ; Rev. N. H., p. 417, 80042 ; Comm. W. N., p. 417, 80043
Macgregor, D. M., p. 543, 134877 ; Mrs. G. B., p. 543, 134875 ; M. F., p. 543, 134876
McHardy, E. L., p. 89, 9907 ; E. M., p. 89, 9908 ; G. G., p. 89, 9905 ; Mrs. M., p. 89, 9903 ; M. A., p. 89, 9906 ; R. P., p. 89, 9904
Machin, Mrs. L. A., p. 242, 37324
MacIver, Mrs. A. F., p. 65, 741 ; E. A. G., p. 65, 743 ; P. G., p. 65, 742
Mackay, C. L., p. 359, 59811, 95290 ; E. M., p. 359, 95808, 95287 ; E. V., p. 359, 59809, 95288 ; E. V., p. 359, 95810, 95289 ; L. M., p. 359, 95813, 95292 ; S. E., p. 359, 59806, 95285 ; V. M. V., p. 359, 59812, 95291 ; W. p. 359, 59807, 95286
McKean, Mrs. G. E., p. 371, 60157, 64361
MacKenzie, J. W., p. 317, 42504 ; Mrs. L. I., p. 317, 42503
Mackinlay, Mrs. E. E., p. 138, 16103 ; M., p. 138, 16104
Mackinnon, A. A., p. 153, 16698, 72510 ; A. E. H., p. 153, 16699, 72511 ; A. H., p. 153, 16697, 72509 ; C. E., p. 153, 16702, 72514 ; Capt. F. A., p. 153, 16696, 72508 ; Mrs. M. S., p. 152, 16695, 72507 ; S. L., p. 153, 16703, 72515 ; Lieut.-Gen. Sir W. H., p. 153, 16700, 72512
Macky, Mrs. E. C., p. 239, 37234 ; E. C., p. 239, 37238 ; G. K., p. 239, 37237 ; Lieut. J. B. B., p. 239, 37235 ;
Maclaren, Mrs. M., p. 554, 135240
Macleod, A., p. 213, 30077 ; A. J., p. 213, 30076 ; D. C., p. 338, 55998 ; D. H. G., p. 338, 55999 ; Mrs. E. L. H., p. 338, 55997 ; M. C. W., p. 213, 30079 ; Morgiana L., Lady, p. 213, 30072 ; M. L. C., p. 213, 30078 ; N. B. W., p. 213, 30075 ; R. T. W., p. 213, 30074 ; Lieut. W. B., p. 213, 30073
McMullen, Mrs. K. A., p. 498, 128318, 128328
M'Neill, B. M. A., p. 198, 29559, 29799 ; R. F. R., p. 198, 29558, 29798
Maconchy, Mrs. E. M., p. 242, 37328
Maddison, A. J. G., p. 162, 17067 ; Rev. A. R., p. 161, 17057 ; A. R., p. 162, 17060 ; A. W., p. 162, 17071 ; C.
C., p. 161, 17052 ; E., p. 161, 17053 ; E. M., p. 160, 17016 ; F. E. T., p. 161, 17051 ; F. T., p. 161, 17057 a ; G. E., p. 162, 17072 ; G. I., p. 162, 17070 ; G. L. F., p. 160, 17015 ; G. M., p. 160, 17017 ; Lieut. H., p. 161, 17050 ; H. F., p. 162, 17066 ; H. G., p. 161, 17049 ; I. A., p. 162, 17064 ; J. S., p. 162, 17058 ; M., p. 162, 17069 ; M. I., p. 162, 17061 ; M. M., p. 162, 17065 ; M. T., p. 162, 17059 ; R. J. G., p. 162, 17063 ; T. E., p. 162, 17062 ; W. W., p. 162, 17068
Mahon, Mrs. G. A., p. 213, 30080
Maidstone, Vct., p. 77, 9428, 12179
Maister, Rev. A. G., p. 119, 10760 ; G. S., p. 118, 10759 ; H. G., p. 119, 10761 ; O. L., p. 119, 10762 ; R. H., p. 118, 10758
Maitland, D. B., p. 179, 27289 ; Col. E., p. 179, 27290 ; E., p. 179, 27293 ; E. L. K., p. 179, 27292 ; E. T., p. 179, 27291 ; Adm. H. A. L., p. 177, 27202 ; H. V. A., p. 179, 27294 ; M. E., p. 179, 27288
Maitland-Kirwan, A. M., p. 340, 56037 ; E. V., p. 340, 56040 ; G., p. 340, 56041 ; G., p. 340, 56042 ; J. D., p. 340, 56038 ; L., p. 340, 56034 ; Lieut. L. F., p. 340, 56035 ; M. D., p. 340, 56039 ; M. R., p. 340, 56036 ; Capt. W. F., p. 340, 56033
Majendie, Mrs. D. M. D., p. 290, 39091, 31937
Major, Mrs. F. H., p. 418, 80089
Malan, F., p. 93, 10024 ; Mrs. F. E., p. 93, 10023 ; L. de M., p. 93, 10025
Malcolm, A. E. W., p. 152, 16686, 72498 ; A. W. A., p. 152, 16690, 72502 ; B. V., p. 152, 16692, 72504 ; Lieut. C. E., p. 152, 16689, 72501 ; E. M. I., p.152, 16687, 72499 ; G. H. A., p. 152, 16688, 72500 ; H. A., p. 152, 16691, 72503 ; Sir J. W., 9th Bt., p. 152, 16684, 72496 ; M. A. J., p. 152, 16685, 72497
Malet, Col. C. St. L., p. 270, 38404 ; Sir E. St. L., 5th Bt., p. 270, 38403 ; E. V. St. L., p. 270, 38407 ; W. St. L., p. 270, 38406 ; H. A. H., p. 271, 38411 ; Capt. H. C., p. 270, 38405
de Manley, Emily, Ctss., p. 473, 103248
Manmorte, Corima, Vctss. of, p. 520, 130579

591

Index

Mansel, Mrs. H. C., p. 233, 36603
Mansergh, (——), p. 361, 59842; (——), p. 361, 59843; (——), p. 361, 59844; H E. F., p. 361, 59845
Mansfield, Annie E. M., Lady, p. 333, 55488; F. H. E., p. 333, 55491; J. C., p. 333, 55490; Maj.-Gen. J. C. E., p. 333, 55489; M. M. B., p. 333, 55492
Margetts, Mrs. C. C., p. 176, 27140; D. L. C, p. 176, 27144; G. C., p. 176, 27142; J. T. C., p. 176, 27141; M. C. B., p. 176, 27146; M. G. L., p. 176, 27145
Marriner, A. A., p. 561, 135438; Lieut. B. L., p. 561, 135436; Mrs. F., p. 561, 135435; G. M. M., p. 266, 38244; H. I., p. 561, 135437
Marris, D. M., p. 158, 16863; D. S., p. 158, 16853; E. H., p. 157, 16843; E. H., p. 157, 16844; E. L., p. 158, 16854; H. A., p. 158, 16861; H. E., p. 158, 16855; H. E., p. 158, 16857; H. W., p. 158, 16850; J. A., p. 158, 16858; L. P., p. 158, 16851; M. I., p. 157, 16845; N. L., p. 158, 16852; R. W., p. 158, 16846; R. W., p. 158, 16849; W. C., p. 158, 16848; W. H., p. 157, 16842; W. J., p. 158, 16856
Marsh, Col. H. C., p. 250, 37559
Marshall, Rev. C. C., p. 102, 10215, 41391; C. C., p. 141, 16196; Mrs. E. E., p. 406, 79679; Mrs. E. L. M., p. 42, 101; G. H. L., p. 102, 10212, 41388; Mrs. H. G., p. 141, 16195; H. S., p. 100, 10171, 41347; Lieut. J., p. 102, 10211, 41387; Lucy M., Lady, p. 102, 10209, 41385; M. A. C., p. 141, 16197; M. H., p. 102, 10216, 41392; R., p. 102, 10213, 41389; R., p. 102, 10214, 41390; Maj. T. E., p. 102, 10210, 41386
Martin, A. M., p. 364, 59916; C. A., p. 364, 59914; Lieut.-Col. D. N., p. 361, 59849; J. M. W., p. 361, 59852; J. W., p. 361, 59851; R. M., p. 361, 59848; V., p. 361, 39850; W., p. 361, 59853; W. J. B., p. 364, 59915
Martin-Edmunds, C. E. M., p. 255, 37941
Marton, A. C., p. 104, 10256, 10355, 41432, 41531; A. E., p. 104, 10257, 10356, 41433, 41532; Hon. Mrs. C.

G., p. 104, 10242, 10341, 41418, 41517; G. B. H., p. 104, 10246, 10345, 41422, 41521; G. H. P., p. 104, 10243, 10342, 41419, 41518; G. M., p. 104, 10258, 10357, 41434, 41533; Lieut. L., p. 104, 10248, 10347, 41424, 41523; Rev. L. E., p. 104, 10247, 10346, 41423, 41522; O. E. C., p. 104, 10245, 10344, 41421, 41520; Capt. R. O., p. 104, 10244, 10343, 41420, 41519
Marwood, Lieut. A. H. L., p. 352, 59648; A. P., p. 92, 9996; C. C., p. 93, 10011; Lieut. C. P. L., p. 352, 59649; E. M., p. 92, 9995; E. M. L., p. 352, 59650; F. M., p. 92, 9997; G. H., p. 92, 9994; Lieut.-Col. H., p. 92, 9993; L., p. 93, 10012; Hon. Mrs. P. C., p. 352, 59647; R., p. 93, 10013; W. F., p. 92, 9992
Mason, A. D. H., p. 145, 16417; A. I., p. 208, 29915; Mrs. A. P., p. 257, 37995; A. S., p. 145, 16413; Rev. C. A., p. 145, 16412; Mrs. C. W. S., p. 335, 55556; E. A. P. M., p. 257, 37998; E. M. M., p. 257, 37999; Rev. F. W. R., p. 145, 16410; G. F., p. 145, 16414; H. F., p. 145, 16419; J. O. I., p. 145, 16415; Mrs. L. A. H., p. 266, 38248; M. D., p. 208, 29916; Mrs. M. E., p. 427, 80306, 80450; Mrs. O. L., p. 208, 29914; Capt. R. H. M., p. 257, 37996; R. L., p. 145, 16411; T. G. M., p. 257, 37997; V. S., p. 208, 29917; W. A. M., p. 257, 38000; W. K., p. 145, 16416; W. R., p. 145, 16418
Massey, Mrs. E., p. 64, 703
Massie, Mrs. A., p. 477, 103363
Massingberd-Mundy, Mrs. E. H., p. 531, 131286; F., p. 531, 131287; J., p. 531, 131288
Massy, A., p. 364, 59935; H. H., p. 364, 59932; J. W., p. 364, 59933; R. C., p. 364, 59934
Masterman, Mrs. L. B., p. 45, 196
Matchett, A. C., p. 62, 636; C. P. T., p. 62, 638; E. S., p. 62, 639; Rev. J. T., p. 62, 637; Mrs. S. E., p. 62, 635
Mather, Mrs. A. E. J., p. 70, 892, 57311; M. H., p. 70, 893, 57312; P., p. 70, 894, 57313
Mathias, Mrs. A., p. 420, 80146; D. L'E., p. 420, 80127; G., p. 420, 80128; G., p. 420,

80130; G. E., p. 420, 80117; G. H. D., p. 420, 80129; H., p. 420, 80119; J. A. D., p. 420, 80148; L. A., p. 420, 80147; Lieut.-Col. L. J., p. 420, 80115; Mrs. L. S., p. 419, 80105; L. W. H., p. 420, 80116; M. E., p. 420, 80131; P. G., p. 420, 80118
Matthey, C. J., p. 551, 135137; G. C. H., p. 551, 135136
Maturin, Mrs. A. C., p. 237, 36891
Maude, Mrs. R., p. 294, 39478
Maudslay, C. C., p. 223, 36366; Mrs. E. E., p. 223, 36365; Mrs. F., p. 485, 103462, 103546; G. W., p. 485, 103464, 103548; I. I., p. 223, 36369; M. E., p. 223, 36368; P. C., p. 485, 103463, 103547; R. V., p. 223, 36367; V. S., p. 223, 36370
Maudsly, Mrs. V., p. 466, 103031
Maugham, Mrs. H. W., p. 126, 11593
Maule, E. M. St. J., p. 281, 38849; Mrs. F. C., p. 281, 38846; H. N. St. J., p. 281, 38847; W. J., p. 281, 38848
Maunsell, Mrs. J., p. 357, 59775; Mrs. R. H., p. 555, 135252
Maxwell, C. L., p. 229, 36507; C. L., p. 340, 56047; Lieut. D., p. 340, 56048; Mrs. D. F., p. 340, 56045; I. M., p. 229, 36506; J. H., p. 340, 56049; J. H., p. 340, 56051; K. I., p. 229, 36508; Mrs. M. E., p. 48, 265; M. E., p. 229, 36504; Mrs. E., p. 340, 56050; R., p. 229, 36505; V., p. 340, 56052; W. G., p. 229, 36502; W. J., p. 229, 36503; Lieut. W. J. H., p. 340, 56046
Mee, A. R., p. 319, 42563; B. B., p. 568 (App.); Mrs. C. A., p. 319, 42561; C. J., p. 568 (App.); W. T., p. 319, 42562
Meek, F. F. O'B., p. 370, 60134, 64338; Mrs. H. S. K., p. 370, 60132, 64336; J. W., p. 370, 60133, 64337
Mellish, D. K., p. 180, 27329; E. A., p. 180, 27328; J. S., p. 180, 27326; P. B., p. 180, 27327
Melly, A. J. M., p. 59, 529; D. H., p. 59, 536; E. M., p. 59, 532; F. E., p. 59, 538; F. H., p. 59, 535; G. H., p. 58, 526; H. M., p. 58, 527; H. P. E. M., p. 59, 528; J. M., p. 59, 531; M. E., p. 59, 537; M. M., p. 59, 530; Mrs. S. E. M., p. 58, 525;

S. H., p. 59, 534; W. R., p. 59, 533
Menzies, A. N., p. 212, 30060
Mercer, E. A. V., p. 351, 59632, 60231, 64435; Mrs. E. E., p. 351, 59631, 60230, 64434; O. M. N., p. 351, 59633, 60232, 64436
de Mercy-Argenteau, Alix E. D., Ctss., p. 505, 129185
Merivale, A., p. 58, 520; Mrs. E. P., p. 58, 519; H. C., p. 82, 9734; P., p. 58, 521
Merriman, Mrs. L. M., p. 359, 59820, 95299
Metcalfe, A., p. 94, 10034; Mrs. A., p. 561, 135433; A. E. G., p. 419, 80095; A. F., p. 429, 80464; Rev. A. G., p. 419, 80094; A. G., p. 419, 80103; A. G., p. 428, 80457; A. H., p. 91, 9958; C., p. 429, 80467; C. B., p. 428, 80458; C. K., p. 429, 80463; C. Le S., p. 419, 80091; C. W., p. 91, 9963; D. C., p. 90, 9952; D. E. W., p. 428, 80456; D. G. D., p. 419, 80093; E. M., p. 90, 9950; E. M., p. 91, 9960; F. C., p. 91, 9966; F. H., p. 94, 10029; F. M., p. 429, 80465; F. S., p. 428, 80455; G., p. 429, 80466; Lieut. G. B. T., p. 561, 135434; G. H., p. 90, 9949; G. H. P., p. 428, 80453; H., p. 94, 10035; H. C., p. 94, 10028; Capt. H. C., p. 428, 80090; H. C., p. 428, 80452; H. E., p. 90, 9948; H. G., p. 419, 80096; H. H., p. 90, 9947; H. H., p. 93, 10027; H. P., p. 429, 80462; H. W., p. 419, 80097; I. B., p. 90, 9956; J. G., p. 90, 9954; J. J., p. 428, 80454; K. A. M., p. 419, 80104; K. M., p. 94, 10031; Mrs. M., p. 90, 9946; M. S., p. 90, 9951; N. W., p. 419, 80098; P., p. 90, 9953; P. H., p. 90, 9957; S., p. 94, 10030; V., p. 91, 9961; V. B. A., p. 419, 80092; Capt. W. M., p. 93, 10026
Metheun, Rev. P. E. O'B., p. 368, 60095, 64299
Meyer-Lahuson, G. R., p. 420, 80139; I. M. H., p. 420, 80140; Mrs. V. F. A., p. 420, 80138
Meyrick, M. C., p. 61, 588, 17567; Mrs. M. E., p. 60, 586, 17565; P. E., p. 61, 589, 17568; T. F., p. 61, 587, 17566
Meysey-Thompson, A. A., p. 115, 10672, 11117, 41848, 42177; A. De

Index

C. C., p. 114, 10651, 11096, 41827, 42157; Lieut. A. H., p. 114, 10655, 11100, 41831, 42161; A. H. E., p. 114, 10661, 11106, 41837, 42167; Lieut. the Hon. C. H. M., p. 114, 10645, 11090, 30322, 41821, 42151; D. E., p. 114, 10658, 11103, 41834, 42164; Hon. D. M. P., p. 114, 10648, 11093, 30325, 41824, 42154; Elizabeth A. C., Lady, p. 114, 10643, 11088, 41819, 42149; Maj. E. C., p. 114, 10659, 11104, 41835, 42165; Hon. G. C., p. 114, 10649, 11094, 30326, 41825, 42155; G. H., p. 114, 10656, 11101, 41832, 42162; H. C., p. 114, 10653, 11098, 41829, 42159; Capt. H. J., p. 114, 10654, 11099, 41830, 42160; Hon. H. W., p. 114, 10647, 11092, 30324, 41823, 42153; O. V. C., p. 114, 10660, 11105, 41836, 42166; Lieut. Col. R. F., p. 114, 10650, 11095, 41826, 42156; S. D., p. 114, 10657, 11102, 41833, 42163; Hon. V. E., p. 114, 10646, 11091, 30323, 41822, 42152; Michael, Mrs. M. A. E., p. 196, 29060, 29141, 29331; M. D., p. 196, 29061, 29142, 29332; Middleton, D. M., p. 242, 37331; Mrs. L. C., p. 242, 37329; R. C., p. 242, 37330; Miers, Mrs. S. A., p. 87, 9848; Miéville, A. D., p. 416, 80020; C. A., p. 416, 80014; C. E., p. 416, 80017; E. A., p. 416, 80013; E. C., p. 416, 80019; E. F., p. 416, 80018; G., p. 416, 80021; H. Le S., p. 416, 80022; O. V., p. 416, 80015; Sir W. F., p. 416, 80016; Milbank, Mrs. H. A. D., p. 171, 17819; J. G. F., p. 171, 17821; M. V., p. 171, 17820; Milbanke, Elizabeth M., Lady, p. 61, 590, 17569; Maj. Sir J. P., 10th Bt., p. 61, 591, 17570; J. P. C., p. 61, 592, 17571; M. R., p. 61, 594, 17573; R. M., p. 61, 593, 17572; Mills, A. E., p. 147, 16553, 79891; A. F. H., p. 147, 16551, 79889; Rev. B. R. V., p. 146, 16550, 79888; Col. D. A., p. 147, 16555, 79893; D. R. P., p. 314, 42384, 42456; E. M., p. 146, 16544, 79882; F., p. 146, 16540, 79878; F., p. 146, 16549, 79887; G. H. M., p. 314, 42383, 42455; G. R. A., p.

147, 16552, 79890; H. V., p. 146, 16541, 79879; Mrs. I. F., p. 314, 42382, 42454; I. I., p. 314, 42385, 42457; M. F., p. 146, 16542, 79880; P., p. 146, 16543, 79881; V. E., p. 147, 16554, 79892; Milman, F., p. 353, 59682; H., p. 353, 59687; H. A., p. 353, 59686; Katherine G., Lady, p. 353, 59681 Lieut. L. C. P., p. 353, 59684; S. W., p. 353, 59685; V. G., p. 353, 59688; W. E., p. 353, 59683; Milne, Mrs. M. L., p. 189, 28843; E. M., p. 189, 28845; R. H. J., p. 189, 28844; Milne-Home, C. A., p. 332, 55466; Mrs. M. P., p. 332, 55465; Minster, Mrs. C., p. 448, 94729; Mirehouse, C. E., p. 454, 95100; G. S. E., p. 454, 95098; R. V. E., p. 454, 95099; Col. R. W. B., p. 454, 95097; Mitton, Mrs. A., p. 549, 135084; G. H. N., p. 549, 135085; G. M. A., p. 549, 135086; M. E., p. 549, 135088; P. M. N., p. 549, 135087; Moberly, Mrs. B. M., p. 370, 60144, 64348; B. W., p. 370, 60145, 64349; Modlin, Mrs. C. A., p. 319, 42577; Monckton, Mrs. E. M., p. 69, 853, 57272; Moneypenny, Mrs. K. A., p. 194, 29005, 29086, 29276; Monk-Bretton, 2nd B., p. 513, 130342; Caroline F., Bnss., p. 513, 130341; Molineux, Rev. A. E., p. 325, 43144; A. I., p. 325, 43145; A. R., p. 325, 43152; Rev. C. H., p. 325, 43142; C. H., p. 327, 43173; D. E., p. 325, 43150; E. M., p. 325, 43146; F., p. 327, 43192; F. M. P., p. 327, 43175; G. B., p. 327, 43171; Rev. G. E. F., p. 327, 43170; G. F., p. 325, 43141; Lieut. G. K., p. 325, 43148; G. W., p. 327, 43180; H., p. 325, 43154; H. E., p. 325, 43149; Maj. H. P., p. 325, 43147; L. P., p. 327, 43172; M. B., p. 327, 43176; M. C., p. 325, 43153; M. E. S., p. 327, 43174; P. H., p. 325, 43143; W. F. P., p. 327, 43169; W. P., p. 327, 43168; Molony, Capt. A. D., p. 149, 16629; A. H., p. 148, 16582; A. W., p. 148, 16585; C. B., p. 148, 16600; C. B., p. 148, 16597; C. E. G., p. 149, 16624; Capt.

C. V., p. 148, 16603; D. K., p. 148, 16587; E. A., p. 148, 16578; E. F., p. 148, 16586; E. P., p. 149, 16623; F. A., p. 148, 16579; Maj. F. A., p. 148, 16584; Rev. H. J., p. 148, 16589; H. J. C., p. 149, 16627; I., p. 147, 16577; J. A., p. 147, 16563; J. C., p. 149, 16628; J. R. H., p. 148, 16593; J. R. P., p. 149, 16625; K. G., p. 149, 16632; L. E., p. 148, 16583; L. S., p. 148, 16581; M. E., p. 148, 16588; M., p. 149, 16626; M. S., p. 148, 16590; M. V., p. 148, 16595; N., p. 148, 16601; P., p. 148, 16602; P. W., p. 149, 16630; R. H., p. 148, 16596; Maj. T. C. W., p. 148, 16598; T. J., p. 148, 16594; T. St P., p. 148, 16599; Capt. W. B., p. 147, 16556 Monson, Augusta L. C., Bnss., p. 353, 55493 de Montalembert d'Essé, 2nd M., p. 505, 129174; A., p. 505, 129179; C., p. 505, 129183; J., p. 505, 129176; J., p. 505, 129177; L., p. 505, 129180; Marie M., Mchss., p. 505, 129173; M. M., p. 505, 129182; N., p. 505, 129181; Ct. R., p. 505, 129175; X., p. 505, 129178 Monteith, Mrs. E., p. 509, 129247 Montgomery, Mrs. A. S. E., p. 329, 43208; E. C., p. 237, 36949; Mrs. F., p. 477, 103361; G. L. J., p. 237, 36905; Mrs. M. H. C., p. 107, 10313, 41489 Moor, Rev. C., p. 195, 29011, 29092, 29282; C., p. 195, 29012, 29093, 29283; F., p. 195, 29013, 29094, 29284; Mrs. F. D., p. 194, 29010, 29091, 29281; O., p. 195, 29014, 29095, 29285; R., p. 195, 29015, 29096, 29286; S. M., p. 195, 29017, 29098, 29288; V., p. 195, 29016, 29097, 29287 Moore, C. H. A., p. 353, 59678; C. L. G., p. 291, 39135; E. L., p. 483, 103426; Mrs. F. M., p. 374, 60236, 64440; G. E., p. 353, 59674; G. H., p. 483, 103424; Mrs. L., p. 483, 103422; L. G., p. 483, 103425; Mrs. L. P. St. L., p. 492, 128182; R. A., p. 353, 59677; Lieut. R. K., p. 353, 59670 Morant, E. J. H. E., p. 286, 38967; F. G., p.

286, 38968; Mrs. F. J., p. 286, 38966 Moray, 17th E. of, p. 189, 28834; Edith D., Ctss. of, p. 190, 28867 Mordaunt (———), p. 201, 29643, 79895; C., p. 201, 29647, 79899; F. L., p. 201, 29644, 79896; H., p. 201, 29646, 79898; H. I., p. 201, 29650, 79902; J., p. 201, 29645, 79897; Lieut.-Col. J. S., p. 201, 29642, 79894; K., p. 201, 29651, 79903; M., p. 201, 29649, 79901; P. M., p. 201, 29648, 79900 More, Mrs. A. de M., p. 360, 59823; D. P. T., p. 360, 59824 Moreton, Hon. Mrs. G. H., p. 527, 131235 Morgan, Mrs. A. C., p. 415, 80008; J., p. 415, 80009; Mrs. M., p. 393, 72029; S., p. 415, 80010 Morgan-Owen, Mrs. M. S., p. 86, 9820, 9878 Morland, Hon. Mrs. A. C., p. 329, 43214 Morley, C. W., p. 550, 135128; D. C., p. 550, 135129; Mrs. M. I., p. 550, 135127; V. I., p. 550, 135130 Morison, A. E. F., p. 231, 36551; I. G., p. 231, 36552; Mrs. J. F., p. 231, 36550 Morris, A. R., p. 201, 29662; C. A. S., p. 202, 29680; C. L., p. 202, 29685; Lieut. C. L., p. 202, 29698; C. S., p. 202, 29679; D. E., p. 201, 29657; D. E. S., p. 202, 29682; Maj. F., p. 202, 29697; F. H., p. 202, 29691; G. C., p. 201, 29661; Lieut. G. L., p. 202, 29684; H., p. 201, 29663; H. G., p. 201, 29665; Lieut.-Col. J., p. 201, 29659; J. B., p. 201, 29664; J. H., A. B., p. 201, 29660; J. T., p. 201, 29654; K. D., p. 201, 29666; L. G., p. 201, 29655; L. G., p. 203, 29701; L. M., p. 202, 29683; M., p. 202, 29688; M. D., p. 370, 60141, 64345; M. E., p. 202, 29666; Mrs. M. M., p. 185, 28570, 103410; M. T., p. 202, 29681; N., p. 202, 29687; Mrs. O. B., p. 370, 60138, 64342; P. B., p. 202, 29669; Sir R. A., 4th Bt., p. 201, 29652; R. B., p. 202, 29690; R. H., p. 202, 29696; R. T., p. 202, 29678; S. R., p. 201, 29658; T. B., p. 202, 29689; T. R. A., p. 201, 29653; V. E., p. 201, 29656; W. A., p. 370, 60139, 64343; W. G., p. 370, 60140, 64344 Morrison, F. B., p. 118,

Index

10757 ; H. O. E., p. 118, 10755 ; J. W. S., p. 118, 10754 ; Mrs. L. E., p. 118, 10751 ; M. J., p. 118, 10753 ; R. J. M., p. 118, 10752 ; R. S. M., p. 118, 10756
Morritt, C. G., p. 311, 42320 ; F. C., p. 311, 42321 ; Lieut. H. E., p. 311, 42319 ; H. M., p. 311, 42322 ; L. B., p. 311, 42323
Mosley, A. E., p. 106, 10300, 41476 ; Maj. A. R., p. 106, 10298, 41474 ; Maj. G., p. 106, 10299, 41475 ; J. A. M., p. 106, 10305, 41481 ; M. I., p. 106, 10303, 41479 ; S. G. R., p. 106, 10304, 41480 ; T. J., p. 106, 10302, 41478 ; W. R., p. 106, 10301, 41477
Mountgarret, Robinia M., Vctss., p. 143, 16301
Mundy, Mrs. G. H., p. 365, 59954
Murray, A. J. P., p. 543, 134871 ; C. A., p. 543, 134869 ; C. F., p. 66, 756, 57175 ; Lieut. C. J., p. 543, 134872 ; E., p. 187, 28660, 28823 ; E. J., p. 187, 28657, 28820 ; E. L., p. 543, 134878 ; E. M., p. 156, 16807 ; F., p. 187, 28659, 28822 ; Col. F. J.G., p. 543, 134879 ; G. E., p. 524, 130803 ; Mrs. G. H., p. 187, 28653, 28816 ; H., p. 187, 28661, 28824 ; J. M., p. 156, 16805 ; M. C., p. 524, 130802 ; M. E., p. 156, 16806 ; M. E., p. 187, 28655, 28818 ; M. G., p. 187, 28658, 28821 ; M., p. 524, 130804 ; Capt. the Hon. R. T. G., p. 524, 130801 ; R. W., p. 543, 134870 ; V., p. 187, 28656, 28819 ; W., p. 187, 28654, 28817
Murton, E., p. 245, 37428 ; Mrs. F., p. 245, 37426 ; N., p. 245, 37427
Musgrave, A. F., p. 217, 30313 ; C., p. 199, 29576 ; C., p. 217, 30306 ; C. B., p. 217, 30314 ; E. H., p. 217, 30309 ; E. M., p. 217, 30307 ; G. A., p. 217, 30310 ; H. A. F., p. 217, 30311 ; H. E., p. 216, 30305 ; N. C., p. 199, 29575 ; Lieut. P. C., p. 217, 30308 ; Lieut. P. R., p. 199, 29577 ; Sir R. G., 12th Bt., p. 199, 29574 ; R. R., p. 217, 30312 ; T. C., p. 199, 29578

Nash, G. C., p. 214, 30105 ; Mrs. M., p. 214, 30103 ; M. E. V., p. 214, 30106 ; T. S., p. 214, 30104
Naylor, Mrs. (——), p. 57, 485 ; M., p. 157, 16832
Neave, D. F., p. 276, 38673 ; E. A., p. 276, 38670 ; E. H., p. 276, 38676 ; Mrs. E. J., p. 276, 38669 ; E. L. S., p. 276, 38675 ; G. M., p. 276, 38672 ; G. V., p. 276, 38671 ; H. A., p. 276, 38674
Neville, Mrs. F., p. 393, 72027
Newcombe, A. P. L., p. 387, 71761 ; H. V. M. L., p. 387, 71762 ; Mrs. M. B. M. L., p. 387, 71760
Newenham, Rev. A. O'B., p. 372, 60182, 64380 ; E. B., p. 372, 60176, 64380 ; E. F., p. 372, 60180, 64384 ; F. A. J., p. 372, 60178, 64382 ; F. G., p. 372, 60181, 64385 ; G. A. B., p. 372, 60183, 64387 ; I. A., p. 372, 60184, 64388 ; R. O'B., p. 372, 60179, 64383 ; W. E. B., p. 372, 60177, 64381
Newhouse, C. M., p. 124, 11558 ; Mrs. K. E., p. 124, 11556 ; K. R., p. 124, 11557 ; M. P., p. 124, 11559
Newman, E., p. 246, 37451 ; Mrs. G. A., p. 497, 128287 ; Capt. J. R. B., p. 496, 128279 ; Capt. R. G. O., p. 496, 128280
Newton, A. E., p. 163, 17086 ; B., p. 162, 17075 ; B. E., p. 162, 17081 ; D. F., p. 162, 17078 ; E. M., p. 163, 17084 ; F. J., p. 163, 17087 ; G. F., p. 162, 17080 ; Mrs. H., p. 162, 17074 ; L. H., p. 163, 17085 ; M. G., p. 162, 17077 ; M. T., p. 163, 17095 ; R., p. 162, 17076 ; R., p. 163, 17094 ; W. L., p. 162, 17079
Nicholetts, Mrs. E. F., p. 108, 10371, 41547 ; G. E., p. 108, 10372, 41548 ; N. J., p. 108, 10373, 41549
Nicholl, Mrs. E. D., p. 472, 103205 ; G. M., p. 472, 103208 ; Mrs. J. M., p. 476, 103338 ; J. W. H., p. 472, 103206 ; O. E., p. 472, 103209 ; R. C., p. 472, 103210 ; R. I., p. 472, 103207
Nicholson, Mrs. A. M., p. 528, 131258
Nimo, D., p. 357, 59767 ; K., p. 357, 59766 ; W. P., p. 357, 59765
Nixon, J. O., p. 568 (App.) ; Mrs. L. E., p. 319, 42575 ; R. O., p. 568 (App.)
Norbury, C. P., p. 261, 38096 ; Lucy H. K., Ctss. of, p. 332, 55459 ; Mrs. R. A. A., p. 261, 38095
Norman, Mrs. A. H., p. 509, 129341
van Norman, Mrs. E., p. 88, 9886

Norris, Mrs. E. M., p. 362, 59881
North, Lord, p. 285, 38956 ; Charlotte M., Dow.-Lady, p. 285, 38954 ; Lieut. D. J., p. 285, 38959 ; H. G. M., p. 285, 38960 ; Hon. J. M., p. 285, 38957 ; Lady M. E., p. 285, 38958 ; R., p. 285, 38961
Northcote, Lady E. M., p. 114, 10665, 11110, 41841, 42171 ; Lady R. L., p. 114, 10664, 11109, 41840, 42170
Northey, Capt. A. C., p. 549, 135076 ; A. C., p. 549, 135096 ; A. H. K., p. 548, 135070 ; C. B., p. 549, 135078 ; E., p. 548, 135072 ; Rev. E. W., p. 548, 135068 ; G. E., p. 548, 135068 ; Lieut. G. E. A., p. 548, 135069 ; Capt. G. H., p. 548, 135073 ; H. W. H., p. 548, 135074 ; M. L., p. 549, 135083 ; P. A. O., p. 549, 135077 ; P. W., p. 548, 135075 ; R., p. 549, 135079
Northmore, G., 51, 349, 378 ; J., p. 51 353, 382 ; J., p. 52, 354, 383 ; J. M., p. 52, 356, 385 ; J. G. L., p. 52, 355, 384 ; T. W., p. 51, 347, 376 ; T. W. W., p. 51, 348, 377
Northumberland, 7th D. of, p. 67, 757, 57176
Nowell-Usticke C. de V., p. 101, 10198, 41374 ; C. M., p. 101, 10197, 41373 ; C. S., p. 101, 10195, 41371 ; G. W., p. 101, 10194, 41370 ; Mrs. J., p. 101, 10182, 41358 ; M. S., p. 101, 10192, 41368 ; P. E., p. 101, 10191, 10184 ; 41360, 41367 ; Capt. R. S., p. 101, 10190, 10183, 41359, 41366 ; R. S., p. 101, 10196, 41372 ; W. G. S., p. 101, 10193, 41369
Nunburnholme, Marjorie C., Bnss., p. 174, 27069

Oakes, E. A. M., p. 270, 38408 ; Mrs. E. St. L., p. 270, 38408 ; M. J., p. 270, 38410
O'Connor, Mrs. J. M., p. 567 (App.)
Oddin-Taylor, Mrs. C. M. P., p. 116, 10708, 11153, 37634, 41884, 42214
O'Donovan, M., p. 52, 360, 389 ; N. K., p. 52, 359, 388 ; Mrs. O., p. 52, 357, 386 ; T., p. 52, 358, 387
Ogilby, A. C., p. 237, 36908 ; B. E. E., p. 237, 36910 ; E. S., p. 237, 36912 ; I. C., p. 237, 36909 ; J. D., p. 237, 36907 ; L., p. 237, 36911 ; Mrs. E. F., p. 148, 16591
Ogle, A. C., p. 43, 107 ;
B. C., p. 43, 106 ; H. M., p. 43, 105 ; J. F. C., p. 43, 104 ; N. C., p. 43, 103
Okeover, Hon. Mrs. E. A., p. 544, 134903 ; H. C., p. 548, 135040 ; Capt. H. E., p. 544, 134904, 135041 ; M. A., p. 544, 134905, 135042 ; V. A., p. 544, 134918, 135055
Oldfield, H., p. 340, 56054 ; Mrs. M. D., p. 340, 56053
Olivier, A. C. S., p. 272, 38464 ; A. E., p. 272, 38462 ; A. F., p. 272, 38465 ; E. M., p. 272, 38475 ; E. M., p. 272, 38476 ; G. E., p. 272, 38471 ; Rev. H. E., p. 272, 38460 ; J. E., p. 272, 38469 ; J. G., p. 272, 38461 ; L. R., p. 272, 38470 ; M. J., p. 272, 38463 ; R. E., p. 272, 38472 ; Capt. R. H., p. 272, 38473 ; R. H. D., p. 272, 38467 ; S. J., p. 272, 38468 ; Comm. S. R., p. 272, 38466
Oram, E. M., p. 317, 42514 ; G. M., p. 317, 42513 ; Rev. R. A., p. 317, 42512
O'Reilly, E. P., p. 246, 37457 ; Mrs. E. S. D., p. 246, 37456 ; L. H., p. 247, 37458
Orlebar, C. K., p. 243, 37371 ; C. M., p. 243, 37366 ; D. E., p. 243, 37367 ; F. H., p. 243, 37373 ; H., p. 243, 37372 ; Rev. H. A., p. 243, 37364 ; J. A., p. 243, 37369 ; Rev. J. E., p. 243, 37368 ; M. E. M., p. 243, 37370 ; R. C., p. 243, 37365
Orpen, D. E. P., p. 116, 10705, 11150, 37631, 41881, 42211 ; Mrs. R. C., p. 116, 10704, 11149, 37630, 41880, 42210
Orton, A., p. 319, 42560 ; A., p. 568 (App.) ; B., p. 319, 42559 (App.) ; E. J., p. 568 (App.) ; E. L., p. 319, 42557 ; H., p. 319, 42558 ; I. J., p. 318, 42550 ; K., p. 319, 42554 ; K., p. 319, 42556 ; M., p. 319, 42551 ; M. M., p. 319, 42553 ; N. C., p. 567 (App.) ; R., p. 318, 42549 ; R. B., p. 568 (App.) ; R. H., p. 319, 42552 ; S., p. 319, 42555
Osborne, F. D'A. G., p. 282, 38873 ; Mrs. M. D., p. 282, 38872 ; M. G., p. 282, 38875 ; S. H. G., p. 282, 38874
O'Shee (——), p. 542, 134833 ; A. A., p. 542, 134838 ; C., p. 542, 134790, 134836 ; Lady E. C. K., p. 542, 134788 ; G., p. 542, 134837 ; Lady G. I. A. M., p. 542,

Index

134830; Capt. G. I. P. P., p. 542, 134834; J. M. P., p. 542, 134832; P. I. R., p. 542, 134789, 134835; Maj. R. A. P., p. 542, 134831
Oswald, A., p. 565, 135512; Mrs. M. E., p. 565, 135507; Lieut. N. W., p. 565, 135510; Maj. O. C. W., p. 565, 135508; P. E. I. E. W., p. 565, 135509
Oswell, Mrs. M., p. 417, 80041
Otway, P. E., p. 448, 94728
Ovans, Mrs. C. C., p. 459, 95402; D. L., p. 459, 95404; G. H., p. 459, 95405; J. M., p. 459, 95403; J. R., p. 459, 95406; K. M., p. 459, 95407
Owen, Mrs. C. A., p. 400, 77849, 79358
Oyles, Mrs. I., p. 371, 60155, 64359

PACK-BERESFORD, A. L., p. 348, 59551; A. R., p. 347, 59547; Maj. C. G., p. 347, 59542; D. J., p. 347, 59544; D. R., p. 347, 59541; E. H., p. 348, 59550; Capt. H. J., p. 347, 59543; H. de la P., p. 348, 59549; J. A., p. 347, 59548; R. J., p. 347, 59546; T. A., p. 347, 59545
Packe, Lady A., p. 405, 79655; E. H., p. 405, 79656; G. F., p. 514, 130378; S. A., p. 405, 79660
Paget, A. S., p. 129, 12177, 81010; Muriel E. V., Lady, p. 129, 12174, 81007; Mrs. F., p. 110, 10479, 41655; F. M. E., p. 110, 10483, 41659; Mrs. G. M., p. 337, 55956; P. W., p. 129, 12176, 81009; S. M., p. 129, 12175, 81008
Pain, Mrs. A. B., p. 225, 36392; A. B., p. 260, 38068; C. M., p. 260, 38065; H. M., p. 260, 38067; J. C., p. 260, 38064; M. H., p. 260, 38066
Paine, Mrs. G. C., p. 273, 38483
Pakenham, C. S., p. 375, 60261, 64465; F. E. S., p. 375, 60256, 64460; F. H. G., p. 375, 60258, 64462; H. R., p. 375, 60260, 64464; I. C., p. 375, 60255, 64459; M. C. S., p. 375, 60257, 64461; R. S., p. 375, 60259, 64463; W. H. V., p. 375, 60254, 64458; Lieut.-Col. W. W. V., p. 375, 60253, 64457
van Pallandt, Bn. A. L. A., p. 378, 64093, 64106, 64118; Bnss. A. W., p. 379, 64126; Bnss. A. W. C., p. 379,

64117; Bnss. A. W. C. W., p. 378, 64097, 64110, 64122; Bnss. C. E. L., p. 378, 64091, 64104; Bnss. C. L. W., p. 379, 64123; Bn. E. J., p. 378, 64094, 64107, 64119; Bn. E. J., p. 379, 64111; Bn. F. J., p. 379, 64112; Bn. F. J. W., p. 378, 64086, 64099; Bn. H. H. A., p. 378, 64088, 64101; Bnss. H. J. A., p. 378, 64096, 64109, 64121; Bnss. H. S. C., p. 378, 64090, 64103; Bn. K. W., p. 378, 64095, 64108, 64120; Bn. R. J. C., p. 378, 64087, 64100; Bn. W. F. T., p. 378, 64089, 64102; Bn. W. K., p. 378, 64092, 64105
Palliser (——), p. 75, 9382; F., p. 75, 9384; Rev. M., p. 75, 9383
Palmer, Mrs. D. G., p. 65, 726; Mrs. E., p. 190, 28862; F. R., p. 65, 729; G., p. 65, 727; G. D., p. 190, 28863; Maj. H. D., p. 190, 28864; H. M., p. 65, 728; R. H., p. 65, 730
Palmer-Douglas, A., p. 190, 28856; Mrs. M., p. 190, 28855
Palmer-Morewood, Mrs. P. M., p. 335, 55554; R. C. A., p. 335, 55555
Palmes, B. W., p. 96, 10079; E. W. E., p. 96, 10078; Mrs. G. R., p. 96, 10076; G. St. M., p. 96, 10077; J. M. G., p. 96, 10082
Park, Mrs. A. E., p. 272, 38439; F. I. A., p. 272, 38440
Parke, A. F. W., p. 88, 9891; A. L., p. 88, 9883; C., p. 88, 9884; E., p. 88, 9882; E. R., p. 88, 9890; F., p. 88, 9885; G., p. 88, 9888; G. M., p. 88, 9893; G. M., p. 88, 9894; L., p. 88, 9887; R. P. W., p. 88, 9892; W., p. 88, 9889
Parker, A. H., p. 274, 38510; Mrs. C., p. 57, 483; D. B. H., p. 273, 38498; Capt. E. H., p. 273, 38495; F. L., p. 274, 38527; H. H., p. 273, 38493; J. B., p. 273, 38499; L. H., p. 273, 38496; Mrs. M., p. 205, 29757; M. H., p. 273, 38497; M. S. H., p. 273, 38494; S. H., p. 274, 38509; Rev. Sir W. H., 10th Bt., p. 273, 38491; W. S. H., p. 273, 38492
Parry, E. J. G., p. 166, 17600; Mrs. E., p. 166, 17597; M. D. G., p. 166, 17598; R. G., p. 166, 17599
Parry-Crooke, C. P., p. 450, 94979; D. J., p. 450, 94977; Mrs. G.

H., p. 450, 94976; L. W., p. 450, 94978
Partridge, Mrs. E. M., p. 81, 9728
Paul, C. S. T., p. 546, 134979; E. K. M., p. 546, 134978; E. M., p. 546, 134981; G. A. M., p. 546, 134977; H. W. M., p. 546, 134976; J. S. M., p. 546, 134980; Mrs. K. H., p. 546, 134975
Paulet, Joan F. M., Lady, p. 467, 103066
Payne, E. E., p. 362, 59885; J. C. W., p. 362, 59884; M. W., p. 362, 59886; Capt. R. L., p. 362, 59883; S. H., p. 362, 59882
Pearce-Serocold, (——), p. 241, 37301; Mrs. B. L., p. 241, 37300
Peard, Mrs. A. W., p. 493, 128193; E. St. H., p. 493, 128194; L. L., p. 493, 128205; P. G., p. 493, 128195
Pearson, Mrs. I., p. 424, 80219, 80363; Mrs. M. G., p. 102, 10201, 41377
Pease, D. V., p. 347, 59535; L. M., p. 347, 59536; Mrs. L. V., p. 347, 59534; O. M. C., p. 347, 59537
Peirse-Duncombe, Mrs. A. G., p. 312, 42324; C. S., p. 312, 42325; E. S., p. 312, 42327; E. S., p. 312, 42329; R. S., p. 312, 42328; R. S., p. 312, 42326; W. S., p. 312, 42336
Pell, A. L. A., p. 127, 11616; B. K., p. 127, 11617; Mrs. C. M., p. 127, 11615
le Pelley, A. M., p. 180, 27309; C. M., p. 180, 27307; E. B., p. 180, 27305; E. C., p. 180, 27306; Mrs. F., p. 180, 27304; F. E., p. 180, 27308
Pelly, A., p. 551, 135142; Maj. C. H. R., p. 551, 135134; Mrs. L. C. E., p. 550, 135133
Pemberton, C. L., p. 95, 10059; C. L., p. 110, 10459, 41635; D. L., p. 110, 10463, 41639; E. M., p. 100, 10165, 41341; G. L., p. 110, 10462, 41638; H. L., p. 110, 10461, 41637; J. S. G., p. 100, 10162, 41338; L. F., p. 100, 10169, 41345; M. A. S., p. 95, 10058; Mrs. M. E., p. 110, 10458, 41634; M. L., p. 100, 10168, 41344; N. L., p. 110, 10460, 41636; N. P., p. 100, 10164, 41340; Mrs. R., p. 95, 10057; R. H., p. 100, 10166, 41342; R. L. S., p. 100, 10163, 10220, 41339, 41396
Pennefather, A., p. 353, 59695; A. L., p. 354, 59701; C., p. 356, 59764; C., p. 356,

59763; C., p. 356, 59758; C. E. de F., p. 356, 59756; D. F., p. 353, 59692; De F., p. 356, 59760; E., p. 356, 59759; E., p. 356, 59761; F., p. 356, 59762; H. L., p. 354, 59700; J., p. 356, 59755; J., p. 356, 59757; J., p. 357, 59768; M., p. 353, 59694; M. E., p. 354, 59699; M. E. de M., p. 360, 59825; R., p. 353, 59693; R., p. 354, 59697; R. D., p. 354, 59698; W., p. 354, 59702; Rev. W. de M., p. 360, 59822; W. V., p. 354, 59696
Penny, A., p. 468, 103115; Capt. A. T., p. 468, 103114
Penrhyn, Gertrude J., Lady, p. 44, 152
Pepys, Mrs. A., p. 509, 129242; Capt. A. G. L, p 509, 129243; C. D. L, p. 509, 129245; Capt. G. L., p. 509, 129244; G. M. L., p. 509, 129246
Perceval, Mrs. E. M. B., p. 133, 15986; Mrs. H. M. M. p. 426, 80282, 80426; M. P., p. 133, 15988; R. J., p. 133, 15987
Percy, Earl, p. 67, 758, 57177; Capt. Lord A. I., p. 67, 759, 57178; Lord A. M. A., p. 67, 767, 57186; Lieut. A. W., p. 67, 768, 57187; C., p. 69, 871, 960, 57290, 57378; Lady E. E., p. 67, 762, 57181; E. G. H., p. 69, 866, 57285; E. J., p. 70, 891, 57310; Lord E. S. C., p. 67, 761, 57180; Lieut.-Col. G. A., p. 67, 772, 57191; Mrs. G. A., p. 70, 956, 57375; H., p. 69, 864, 57283; H. E., p. 69, 868, 957, 57287, 57375; Capt. J. H. P., p. 69, 867, 57286; J. R., p. 69, 869, 958, 57288, 57376; Lady M., p. 67, 763, 57182; Lady M., p. 67, 765, 57184; M., p. 69, 865, 57284; M., p. 69, 870, 959, 57289, 57377; Lady M. E. N., p. 67, 766, 57185; Lord E. W. R., p. 67, 760, 57179; Lady V. A., p. 67, 764, 57183
Perkins, Mrs. G. E., p. 519, 130561
Perret, Mrs. (——), p. 388, 71787
Perrott, Mrs. E. M., p. 360, 59841
Perry, A. S. R., p. 123, 11522; Rev. C. R., p. 123, 11521; Mrs. E. B., p. 123, 11520; E. J. St. C., p. 123, 11523; W. E. V., p. 123, 11524
Peyton, Mrs. M. L., p. 525, 130996; R. L., p. 525, 130997

Index

Phelips, B. P., p. 517, 130439, 130519 ; E. M., p. 517, 130440, 130520 ; Mrs. F. M., p. 517, 130438, 130518
Phelps, Mrs. A. S., p. 362, 39861 ; H. D., p. 529, 131273 ; Sub.-Lieut. H. D., p. 529, 131275 ; H. G. H., p. 529, 131272 ; Rev. L. R., p. 529, 131276 ; V. L., p. 529, 131274
Philipps, Mrs. A. E. E. G., p. 456, 95320 ; E. J. T., p. 462, 95479 ; Mrs. I. F., p. 315, 42413 ; Mrs. M. L. E., p. 462, 95478
Philips, A. A., p. 104, 10238, 10254, 10337, 10353, 41414, 41430, 41513, 41529 ; Lieut.-Col. B. H., p. 104, 10237, 10336, 41413, 41512 ; B. M., p. 104, 10241, 10340, 41417, 41516 ; J. A., p. 104, 10239, 10338, 41415, 41514 ; Mrs. L. M., p. 104, 10253, 10352, 41429, 41528
Phillimore, Mrs. A., p. 513, 130337 ; A. F., p. 453, 95062 ; A. M. D. G., 454, 95090 ; B. L. A., p. 454, 95089 ; C. A., p. 453, 95082 ; C. M., p. 453, 95073 ; C. M. L., p. 453, 95086 ; Rev. E. G., p. 454, 95088 ; E. G. B., p. 452, 95056 ; G. A., p. 543, 95072 ; G. G., p. 453, 95078 ; G. W., p. 453, 95061 ; H. A. G., p. 453, 95079 ; H. M. M., p. 453, 95081 ; J. G., p. 452, 95057 ; J. G., p. 453, 95077 ; J. M. F., p. 453, 95085 ; J. S., p. 453, 95084 ; L., p. 453, 95074 ; M., p. 452, 95058 ; M. A., p. 453, 95080 ; R. A., p. 453, 95076 ; R. C., p. 453, 95060 ; Capt. R. F., p. 453, 95075 ; S. H., p. 453, 95063 ; V. A. V., p. 453, 95083 ; Comm. V. E. B., p. 454, 95087 ; Sir W. G. F., 2nd Bt., p. 453, 95059
Phillip, Mrs. M. L., p. 237, 36892
Phillips, G. O'B., p. 370, 60129, 64333 ; Mrs. J., p. 370, 60128, 64332 ; Hon. Mrs. M., p. 544, 134906, 135043 ; M. O'B., p. 370, 60130, 64334
Picton-Jones, E. D., p. 451, 95021 ; Mrs. L., p. 451, 95020
Picton-Warlow, Mrs. H. C., p. 457, 95333 ; J. F., p. 457, 95334 ; R. W., p. 457, 95335
Pigott, B., p. 467, 103071 ; Mrs. F. A., p. 467, 103070 ; F. A. C., p. 467, 103069 ; Capt. W. G., p. 467, 103068

Pilkington, Mrs. E. F., p. 389, 71811 ; E. M., p. 389, 71813 ; U. W., p. 389, 71812
Pillans, D. C., p. 257, 38011 ; E. K., p. 257 38013 ; Mrs. E. K. G., p. 257, 38009 ; R., p. 257, 38010
de Pimodan, Ctss. G. D. A. F. M., p. 505, 129186
Pine-Coffin, E. C., p. 240, 37245 ; G. B., p. 240, 37247 ; G. M., p. 240, 37248 ; Mrs. L. G. D., p. 239, 37244 ; R. G., p. 240, 37246
Pinney, Mrs. C. H., p. 537, 131696
Pinwill, Mrs. A. E., p. 419, 80113
Pipon, E. A., p. 523, 130786 ; G. M., p. 523, 130787 ; Mrs. L. A., p. 523, 130777
Platt, Mrs. A. B., p. 102, 10217, 41393 ; Mrs. C. Le G., p. 306, 40334 ; E. G., p. 102, 10219, 41395 ; L. S., p. 102, 10218, 41394
Plestow, C. J. B., p. 217, 30315
Plumer, Mrs. E. A. M., p. 389, 71828
Pochin, E. G., p. 475, 103306 ; E. G., p. 475, 103307 ; F. W. B., p. 475, 103305
Polignano, 6th D. of, p. 91, 9973
Pollard, Capt. A. E. St. V., p. 226, 36417 ; A. R. E., p. 226, 36416 ; G. E., p. 226, 36421 ; H. H. W., p. 226, 36415 ; Maj. J. H. W., p. 226, 36414 ; L. C., p. 226, 36419 ; R. E., p. 226, 36418 ; S. F., p. 226, 36420
Pollard-Urquhart, Rev. A. de C. B., p. 229, 36510 ; A. L., p. 229, 36514 ; Lieut.-Col. F. E. R., p. 229, 36509 ; L. A. M. H., p. 230, 36516 ; M. A., p. 229, 36512 ; Lieut. M. B., p. 229, 36511 ; W. E., p. 229, 36513
Pollock, A. M. S., p. 320, 42607, 42650 ; A. W. S., p. 320, 42606, 42649 ; D. V. C., p. 551, 135154 ; Mrs. E. M., p. 320, 42604, 42647 ; E. R. S., p. 320, 42605, 42648 ; F. A., p. 551, 135152 ; J. L., p. 551, 135153 ; Mrs. L. F. p. 551, 135151
Pomeroy, Capt. the Hon. E. A. G., p. 108, 10321, 41497 ; Capt. the Hon. R. L., p. 108, 10322, 41498 ; H. R. M., p. 108, 10323, 41499
Port, F. D. M., p. 468, 103113 ; F. G. R., p. 468, 103112 ; G. B. M., p. 468, 103111
Portal-Turner, Mrs. C. G., p. 156, 16808
Portland, 6th D. of, p. 226, 36410

Portman, Mrs. C., p. 463, 95507
Post, C. A., p. 282, 38866 ; Mrs. G. M., p. 281, 38864 ; P., p. 282, 38865
Potier de Courcy, Vct. A. P., p. 507, 129204 ; C., p. 507, 129206 ; Slanie F. M., Vctss., p. 506, 129203 ; Vct. X. R., p. 507, 129205
Potter, A. M., p. 478, 103391 ; C. F., p. 478, 103381 ; C. N., p. 478, 103385 ; E., p. 478, 103390 ; F. S., p. 478, 103389 ; G. W., p. 478, 103386 ; Rev. H. E., p. 478, 103387 ; L. F., p. 478, 103382 ; T. R. F., p. 478, 103388
Poulton, Mrs. S. E., p. 415, 79997
Powell (——), p. 338, 56002 ; A. F., p. 338, 56005 ; Maj. A. L., p. 415, 79985 ; Mrs. C. H., p. 463, 95514 ; D., p. 110, 10488, 41664 ; E., p. 468, 103096 ; E. B. S., p. 463, 95517 ; E. D., p. 338, 56007 ; E. E., p. 415, 79987 ; F. E., p. 415, 79988 ; G., p. 110, 10487, 41663 ; H., p. 338, 56006 ; H., p. 339, 56009 ; H. I. F., p. 339, 56010 ; H. W. M., p. 468, 103097 ; I., p. 110, 10486, 41662 ; J. A. L., p. 415, 79986 ; J. E., p. 338, 56001 ; L., p. 338, 56004 ; M., p. 338, 56008 ; Mrs. M. E. M., p. 110, 10485, 41661 ; N. C. W., p. 463, 95518 ; Mrs. P. O. B., p. 414, 79983 ; R., p. 338, 56003 ; R. D. F., p. 463, 95516 ; Capt. R. M., p. 415, 79989 ; V. H. de B., p. 463, 95515
Powles, F. B., p. 262, 38124, 38153 ; Lieut. J. C., p. 262, 38122, 38151 ; Mrs. M. E. A., p. 262, 38121, 38150 ; Rev. R. C., p. 262, 38123, 38152
Poyser, Mrs. A., p. 314, 42379, 42451 ; A. H. R. W., p. 314, 42380, 42452 ; A. I., p. 314, 42381, 42453 ; I. G., p. 314, 42386, 42458
Praed, Mrs. M., p. 138, 16135
Praslin, 6th D. of, p. 504, 129160
Pratt, A., p. 427, 80294, 80438 ; A. M., p. 426, 80278, 80422 ; B. E., p. 426, 80280, 80424 ; C. A., p. 426, 80277, 80421 ; Rev. D., p. 427, 80295, 80439 ; D. L., p. 426, 80272, 80416 ; E. L., p. 427, 80291, 80435 ; E. R., p. 425, 80269, 80413 ; Col. E. R. M., p. 426, 80268, 80412 ; G. H., p. 426,

80279, 80423 ; H., p. 427, 80298, 80442 ; Col. H. M., p. 427, 80289, 80433 ; H. R., p. 426, 80276, 80420 ; Capt. H. R. M., p. 427, 80293, 80437 ; H. S. A., p. 427, 80297, 80441 ; J. H., p. 426, 80270, 80414 ; L. H., p. 426, 80271, 80415 ; P. M. M., p. 427, 80290, 80434 ; R. H. M., p. 426, 80275, 80419 ; U. F., p. 426, 80273, 80417 ; W. D., p. 427, 80292, 80436 ; W. J. M., p. 426, 80274, 80418 ; W. R., p. 426, 80288, 80432
Prescott, A. R., p. 89, 9897 ; B. J., p. 89, 9909 ; C. A., p. 89, 9901 ; C. C., p. 89, 9898 ; H. C., p. 89, 9896
Preston, Mrs. C. F., p. 460, 95418
Pretyman, Mrs. G. E., p. 497, 128286
Price, A. M. F., p. 133, 15991 ; C. A., p. 133, 15990 ; C. W. B., p. 133, 15984 ; Rev. E. H. B., p. 133, 15985 ; F. W., p. 133, 15989 ; Brevet-Major J. N. B., p. 133, 15983 ; M G., p. 133, 15992
Prichard, Mrs. A. L., p. 456, 95332
Priday, Mrs. E. E., p. 416, 80029 ; J., p. 416, 80030
Priest, Capt. C. F., p. 567 (App.) ; E. R., p. 567 (App.)
Pringle, Mrs. B. V., p. 456, 95312 ; Mrs. M., p. 391, 71975
Probyn, M. E., p. 168, 17667 ; E. A., p. 168, 17666 ; Mrs. E. M., p. 168, 17664 ; Victoria C. I., Lady, p. 551, 135146
Prothero, Mrs. C., p. 237, 36906 ; Mrs. M. C., p. 237, 36893
Pryor, A. V., p. 414, 59974 ; B. E. M., p. 414, 79978 ; E., p. 414, 79982 ; J. A., p. 414, 79977 ; K., p. 415, 80002 ; P., p. 414, 79976 ; R., p. 414, 79975
Puckle, B. H., p. 254, 37882 ; E. H., p. 254, 37887 ; F. H., p. 254, 37881 ; G. H., p. 254, 37883 ; G. H., p. 254, 37888 ; L. H., p. 254, 37886 ; M. H., p. 254, 37885 ; P. H., p. 254, 37884 ; S. H., p. 254, 37880
Pulling, Mrs. E. A., p. 151, 16665, 72477 ; J. B., p. 151, 16666, 72478 ; V. E., p. 151, 16667, 72479
Purcell, A., p. 498, 128312, 128322 ; A. H., p. 498, 128331 ; A. H., p. 569

Index

(App.); A. L., p. 497, 128307; A. M., p. 497, 128311; C. F., p. 497, 128306; C. H., p. 569 (App.); E., p. 498, 128334; E. M., p. 497, 128309; E. St. L. H., p. 569 (App.); F. M., p. 498, 128330; G. H., p. 569 (App.); H., p. 498, 128329a; H. H., p. 569 (App.); L. C., p. 497, 128310; L. St. L. H., p. 569 (App.); M., p. 498, 128313, 128323; M. H., p. 569 (App.); M. J., p. 497, 128304; M. M., p. 497, 128308; R. H., p. 569 (App.); Lieut. R. J., p. 497, 128305; T. L., p. 498, 128335; W. C. H., p. 498, 128333; W. H., p. 569 (App.)
Purchas, A. F. E., p. 309, 41927, 43120; D. M., p. 309, 41928, 43121; Mrs. F. S. A., p. 309, 41926, 43119
Purdon, Mrs. M. E. F., p. 438, 90130
Purefoy, M. L. G., p. 449, 94919; Capt. R. P., p. 449, 94918
Purves, A. H., p. 317, 42507; A. L. H., p. 274, 38525; A. M. C., p. 274, 38526; C. E., p. 317, 42510; D. B. J., p. 84, 9785; E. M., p. 317, 42809; H. G. J., p. 84, 9786; Mrs. L. W., p. 317, 42506; Mrs. M. G. J., p. 84, 9784; T. B., p. 317, 42508
Puxley, Mrs. D. F. M., p. 204, 29708, 29967; F. K., p. 496, 128271; F. L., p. 496, 128269; F. L., p. 496, 128273; G. L., p. 496, 128270; W. E., p. 496, 128272
Pyke, E., p. 160, 17024
Pym, C. B., p. 473, 103261; G., p. 106, 10309, 41485; G. W. E., p. 106, 10308, 41484; J., p. 106, 10310, 41486; Capt. J. B, p. 473, 103262; M., p. 473, 103263; Mrs. M. A. E., p. 473, 103260; Mrs. M. G., p. 106, 10306, 41482; P. J. E., p. 106, 10307, 41483; V., p. 106, 10311, 41487

QUILTER, Hon. Mrs. G., p. 44, 155; G. E. C., p. 44, 156; I., p. 44, 158; J. R., p. 44, 157

RADCLIFFE, Mrs. A., p. 111, 10557, 41733; A. E., p. 111, 10563, 41739; C. A., p. 111, 10561, 41737; J. N. A., p. 111, 10559, 41735; M. M., p. 111, 10562, 41738; R. E. L., p. 111, 10558, 41734; Maj. W. S. W., p. 111, 10560, 41736

Radclyffe, Mrs. T. C., p. 186, 28642
Radmall, Mrs. V. M., p. 319, 42586
Ragg, B. L. V., p. 180, 27332; Mrs. L. M., p. 180, 27331
Raikes, D. C. G., p. 471, 103197; E. B., p. 154, 16753; Mrs. H., p. 154, 16749; Mrs. J. E., p. 471, 103195; R. B., p. 154, 16751; R. M. B., p. 154, 16752; T. B., p. 154, 16750; T. H. C., p. 471, 103196
Rainsford, Mrs. C. R., p. 397, 72299
Ram, A., p. 105, 10269, 10388, 41445, 41564; A. J., p. 105, 10268, 10387, 41444, 41563; Mrs. C. H., p. 105, 10267, 10386, 41443, 41562; F. M. A., p. 541, 134739, 135288; G. E., p. 541, 134738, 135287; Mrs. M., p. 541, 134737, 135286
Ramsay, Caroline C., Lady, p. 52, 375
Ramsden, A. A., p. 437, 90123; A. F., p. 437, 90120; A. F., p. 437, 90126; A. G. F., p. 440, 90166; Capt. A. J., p. 439, 90165; C., p. 439, 90163; C., p. 439, 90164; C. H., p. 438, 90133; C. H. L., p. 438, 90134; E. A., p. 439, 90157; E. C., p. 437, 90125; E. E. C., p. 438, 90131; E. M. F., p. 438, 90137; E. P., p. 437, 90114; E. W., p. 438, 90142; F. C. H., p. 438, 90138; F. E. M., p. 438, 90132; F. F., p. 439, 90159; F. G., p. 439, 90162; F. H., p. 440, 90169; F. P., p. 438, 90147; F. T., p. 437, 90128; Rev. G., p. 440, 90171; G. C. F., p. 438, 90140; G. E., p. 437, 90127; Col. H. F. S., p. 438, 90139; J. E. C., p. 437, 90115; J. H. F., p. 440, 90167; J. P., p. 437, 90122; J. S., p. 439, 90161; M., p. 437, 90119; M. E., p. 438, 90141; M. H., p. 437, 90129; P. S. W., p. 438, 90135; R. C. P., p. 437, 90109; R. W., p. 437, 90124; W. E., p. 437, 90116; Rev. W. F., p. 440, 90170; W. H. C., p. 438, 90136; W. J. P., p. 439, 90158
Randolph, A. E., p. 140, 16178; Col. A. F., p. 139, 16147; A. M., p. 139, 16162; A. S., p. 141, 16215; B. M., p. 141, 16208; B. N., p. 141, 16211; Rev. B. W., p. 141, 16209; Rev. C., p. 141, 16201; C. E., p. 139, 16141; C. F. M., p. 139, 16169; Rev.

C. G., p. 141, 16203; C. J., p. 139, 16145; E. S. F., p. 140, 16180; Rev. E. S. L., p. 139, 16139; F. E., p. 140, 16176; F. M., p. 141, 16216; G. A., p. 139, 16143; G. B., p. 140, 16172; G. F., p. 141, 16213; G. W., p. 139, 16140; H. L., p. 141, 16210; H. M., p. 139, 16144; J. C., p. 139, 16148; J. H., p. 141, 16202; Right Rev. J. H. G., p. 140, 16173; J. M., p. 140, 16174; L. F. A., p. 140, 16181; M. A., p. 140, 16175; M. C., p. 140, 16177; M. F. E., p. 141, 16205; M. I., p. 141, 16207; P. J. C., p. 140, 16179; Rev. R. G., p. 140, 16163; R. S., p. 141, 16212; S. C., p. 141, 16214; S. E., p. 141, 16206; T. B., p. 141, 16204; T. G., p. 139, 16142; V. M., p. 140, 16171; Rev. W. F. H., p. 139, 16146
Rankin, A. C., p. 351, 59611; Mrs. A. H., p. 350, 59610; J. M., p. 351, 59612
Ranking, Mrs. V. E., p. 110, 10484, 41660
de Rarécourt, Duke G. R. F. C., p. 505, 129189; J. M. L. C., p. 506, 129192; Duke L. G. P. M. I., p. 506, 129190; M. L. E. A. M., p. 506, 129191; Duke P. G. H. L. C., p. 506, 129187
Ravensworth, Emma, Ctss. of, p. 60, 579, 17558; Sophia H., Bnss., p. 536, 131676
Rawson, A. E. G., p. 302, 40190; A. J. S., p. 302, 40193; C. D., p. 302, 40194; C. S., p. 302, 40192; D. A. J., p. 302, 40195; E. B., p. 302, 40200; E. F., p. 302, 40198; H. E., p. 302, 40188; H. E., p. 312, 40189; J. S., p. 302, 40191; M. S., p. 302, 40197; S., p. 302, 40196
Rawstorne, Mrs. A. F., p. 306, 40341; F. M., p. 306, 40345; G. S., p. 306, 40343; J., p. 306, 40346; M. E., p. 306, 40347; R. A., p. 306, 40342; R. G., p. 306, 40344
Raymond, A. L., p. 124, 11538; A. M., p. 124, 11553; C., p. 124, 11533; Rev. C. A., p. 124, 11547; E. C., p. 124, 11534; E. G., p. 124, 11529; Mrs. F. E. R., p. 126, 11604; H. M., p. 124, 11550; H. P., p. 124, 11532; H. T., p. 124, 11537; J., p. 123 11527; J., p. 125, 11587; K. M., p. 124, 11528; L. C., p. 124, 11535; L. C., p. 124,

11540; M., p. 124, 11551; M. L., p. 124, 11546; M. M., p. 124, 11539; N. M., p. 124, 11552; O. C., p. 124, 11541; Rev. O. E., p. 123, 11525; O. J., p. 123, 11526; O. M., p. 123, 11530; O. W. E., p. 124, 11549; P. A., p. 124, 11536; Rev. P. F., p. 124, 11531; R. L., p. 124, 11542; S. P. St. C., p. 123, 11508; Rev. W. M., p. 124, 11548
Rea, Mrs. M. F., p. 461, 95446
Reed, C. L., p. 283, 38905; Hon. Mrs. E., p. 283, 38903; E. L., p. 283, 38906; Mrs. P. F. E., p. 348, 59554; H. L., p. 283, 38904
Rees, Mrs. M. A. F., p. 418, 80071
Reeves, Mrs. A. J., p. 474, 103278; E. S. L., p. 474, 103281; F. L., p. 474, 103279
Reid, Mrs. S. M., p. 240, 37282
Rennie, Mrs. F. M., p. 204, 29710, 29969
Renny, A. G. L., p. 232, 36560; Mrs. M. F., p. 231, 36558; P. C. F. N., p. 232, 36559; S. A., p. 232, 36561
van Rensselaer, C. A., p. 337, 55977; Mrs. C. E., p. 337, 55976; S., p. 337, 55978
von Reuterswärd, Bnss. E. R. F., p. 472, 103214; Lieut. G. A. C., p. 472, 103216; M. F. A., p. 472, 103218; P. K. R., p. 472, 103215; V. A. F., p. 472, 103217
Revell, J., p. 495, 128241
Revoil, Mrs. C., p. 345, 69496
Reynard, C. E., p. 96, 10084; C. F., p. 96, 10085; Mrs. E. M. G., p. 96, 10083
Reynolds, E. O., p. 319, 42584; R. H., p. 319, 42585
Riach, Mrs. M. A. G., p. 144, 16319; N., p. 144, 16322; R., p. 144, 16321; S. M. A., p. 144, 16320
Riccardi-Cubitt, 1st Ct., p. 264, 38193; C. C., p. 264, 38194; M. Y., p. 264, 38197; T. F. M., p. 264, 38196; V. A. M., p. 264, 38195
Rice, Lieut. A., p. 240, 37294; Mrs. C. M., p. 96, 10086; Mrs. C. M. D. P., p. 240, 37292; D. T., p. 96, 10089; H. T., p. 96, 10087; J. A. T., p. 96, 10088; Mrs. L. M., p. 240, 37293
Rice-Wiggin, C. F. S., p. 64, 701; Mrs. H., p. 64, 700
Richardson, D. C., p. 276, 38654, 38730; E. W. R., p. 278, 38725; G.,

Index

Richmond, p. 326, 43158; J. C., p. 278, 38727; K. D., p. 276, 38655, 38731; Mrs. K. T., p. 276, 38653; L. G., p. 278, 38726; M. E., p. 276, 38656, 38732; Mrs. M. R., p. 326, 43157; R. E. R., p. 278, 38729; R. E. Y. S., p. 278, 38728; Mrs. T. E., p. 278, 38724
Richmond, A. I., p. 563, 135465; Mrs. C. C., p. 302, 40185; Mrs. M., p. 563, 135464; S., p. 563, 135466
Richmond-Gale-Braddyll, E. C., p. 451, 95009; F. R., p. 451, 95011; H. E., p. 451, 95007; H. G., p. 451, 95022; H. S., p. 451, 95008; M. A., p. 451, 95010
Rickards, Mrs. E. E., p. 554, 135248; Mrs. K. M., p. 42, 90; L. C. A., p. 554, 135251; M. C. A., p. 554, 135250; R. H. T., p. 554, 135249; T. M., p. 42, 91
Ricketts, Mrs. M. M. C., p. 21, 30095
Riddell, C. E., p. 359, 59802, 95281; E. A. B., p. 358, 59792, 95271; E. J., p. 359, 59805, 95284; Capt. E. V. D., p. 358, 59791, 95270; F. A. L, p. 359, 59803, 95282; Capt. J. B., p. 358, 59793, 95272; L. A., p. 358, 59796, 95275; Capt. R. B., p. 358, 59790; 95269; Col. R. V., p. 358, 59789, 95268
Riley, A. M., p. 146, 16428; D. L. B., p. 146, 16427; Mrs. E. M., p. 146, 16425; E. M., p. 146, 16429; Lieut. G. B., p. 146, 16426
Ringrose, Mrs. B., p. 244, 37378; C. H., p. 244, 37379; E. B., p. 244, 37380
Ripley, D. A. S., p. 321, 42630; H. E., p. 321, 42629
Rivers, Emmeline L., Bnss., p. 73, 9369, 43469
Robbins, Mrs. C. J., p. 364, 59930
Roberts, E., p. 63, 668; Mrs. E., p. 90, 9943; Mrs. E. A., p. 356, 59742; E. D., p. 180, 27333; G., p. 51, 338; H. A., p. 62, 629; Rev. H. B., p. 180, 27334; H. M., p. 180, 27330; K. H. T., p. 51, 337; M. A., p. 62, 651; S. C. C., p. 51, 336; W., p. 62, 634; Mrs. W. C., p. 190, 28861
Robertson, A. K. A., p. 202, 29675; C. A. B., p. 202, 29672; Mrs. H. A. M., p. 494, 128223; Mrs. H. C. M., p. 214, 30100; H. M., p. 404, 128227; L. G., p. 214, 30101; M. D., p. 494, 128224; M. M. S. G., p. 214, 30102; M. S., p. 494, 128226; N. M., p. 202, 29676; N. M., p. 494, 128225; P. R. M., p. 202, 29673; R. L., p. 202, 29677; T. P. M., p. 202, 29674
Robertson-Glasgow, Mrs. M. B., p. 459, 95388, 11631; R. C., p. 459, 95390, 11633; R. W., p. 459, 95389, 11632
Robeson, Mrs. C., p. 278, 38723
Robins, A. M. M., p. 409, 79828; A. P. T., p. 409, 79827; H. D. G. D., p. 409, 79826; Mrs. M. S., p. 409, 79825; S. R., p. 409, 79829
Robinson, A. C., p. 55, 458; A. F., p. 56, 463; B. B. T., p. 56, 462; Mrs. D. M., p. 215, 30121; Mrs. E., p. 55, 454; E., p. 56, 470; Mrs. E. F., p. 275, 38652; F., p. 56, 461; F. H., p. 56, 460; Lieut. Sir F. V. D., 10th Bt., p. 52, 9730; H. F., p. 56, 464; H. G., p. 55, 466; H. G., p. 55, 457; H. M., p. 55, 455; M. J., p. 56, 469; M. S., p. 82, 9732; Lieut.-Col. Sir R. H., 5th Bt., p. 107, 10314, 41490; W. C., p. 56, 459
Robson, Mrs. A., p. 462, 95504; Mrs. F., p. 309, 41925, 43118
Roch, Mrs. H. St. L., p. 499, 128337
Rochfort, Mrs. H. C., p. 144, 16338
Rogers, Mrs. G. M., p. 438, 90145; M. R., p. 438, 90146
Roger-Smith, B., p. 109, 10397, 41573; B. H., p. 109, 10396, 41572; Mrs. D. E., p. 109, 10394, 41570; R., p. 109, 10395, 41571
Rogerson, E. M., p. 63, 686; Mrs. M., p. 63, 685
Rohan, D. G., p. 493, 128200; Mrs. M. M., p. 493, 128198; N. L., p. 493, 128199
Rooke, Mrs. A., p. 267, 38287; Mrs. E. E., p. 281, 38850
Roper, Mrs. E. H., p. 336, 55931; G. D., p. 336, 55933; G. F., p. 336, 55932; I. K., p. 336, 55934;
Rose, Mrs. E., p. 113, 10639, 11084, 41815, 42145; Mrs. M., p. 451, 95012; R. P. L., p. 113, 10640, 11085, 41816, 42146
Ross, Mrs. H. E., p. 549, 135095; Mrs. M. E., p. 549, 39477
Rosser, Mrs. L., p. 394, 72213, 72318
Rosmore, Mittie, Bnss., p. 157, 16828

Round, Mrs. H. L., p. 532, 131313
Roundell, C. F., p. 235, 36621, 72425; D. G. A., p. 235, 36619, 72423; N. L., p. 235, 36620, 72424; Capt. R. F., p. 235, 36617, 72421; R. H. S., p. 235, 36618, 72422
Roupell, Mrs. M., p. 498, 128317, 128327
Rous, Lady B. H. J., p. 197, 29541, 29781; Lady C. C., p. 197, 29540, 29780; Lady P. E., p. 197, 29539, 29779; Hon. W. K., p. 197, 29538, 29778
Rouse-Boughton-Knight, Mrs. I. H., p. 69, 860, 57279
Routh, Mrs. B. P., p. 219, 30340
Rowden, D., p. 116, 10706, 11151, 37632, 41882, 42212; E., p. 116, 10707, 11152, 37633, 41883, 42213; F. C. B., p. 116, 10702, 11147, 37628, 41878, 42208; Mrs. L. C., p. 116, 10701, 11146, 37627, 41877, 42207; L. E., p. 116, 10703, 11148, 37629, 41879, 42209
Rowland, Mrs. C. I., p. 189, 28846; E. M., p. 189, 28848; F. E., p. 189, 28849; G. E., p. 189, 28851; H. I., p. 189, 28850; W. G. S., p. 189, 28847
Rowley, C., p. 224, 36379; D. T. C., p. 388, 71802; Mrs. M. A., p. 388, 71801
Roxby, C. W., p. 263, 38178; Rev. E. L., p. 263, 38177; Capt. H., p. 263, 38179
Rudstow-Read, Mrs. L., p. 281, 38858
Ruggles-Brise, Lady D. L., p. 66, 753, 57172
Rushworth, E. H., p. 115, 10673, 11118, 41849, 42179; W. A., p. 115, 10674, 11119, 41850, 42180
Russell, A. J. G., p. 143, 16306
Ruttledge, E. P. K., p. 389, 71817; J. F., p. 389, 71815; Mrs. M. C., p. 347, 59524; Mrs. M. O., p. 389, 71814; R. F., p. 347, 59525; R. T., p. 389, 71816; W., p. 347, 59526
Ruxleben, Bnss. E. O., p. 470, 103154
Ryan, C. A., p. 357, 59769; Mrs. S. B., p. 134, 16011
Ryde, A. J., p. 228, 36489, 36581; A. M., p. 229, 36496, 36588; C. A., p. 229, 36493, 36585; C. E., p. 229, 36495, 36587; Maj. F. E., p. 229, 36491, 36583; H. F., p. 229, 36494, 36586; H. G., p. 229, 36492, 36584; Rev. L.

F., p. 229, 36490, 36582; W. E. C., p. 228, 36488, 36580
SABRAN, 4th D. of, p. 507, 129210
de Sabran-Pontevés, A. L. E. R. M. D., p. 507, 129212; Ct. A. R. L. M. E., p. 507, 129211
Safford, Capt. C. J., p. 111, 10577, 41753; Mrs. E. N., p. 111, 10576, 41752; J. C., p. 112, 10579, 41755; Mrs. L. M., p. 413, 79956; Capt. N. E. F., p. 112, 10578, 41754; S. F., p. 112, 10584, 41760; V. H. D., p. 112, 10580, 41756
Sainsbury, G. C. L. L., p. 538, 131718; G. L., p. 537, 131717; H. W. L., p. 537, 131710; K. L., p. 537, 131716; M. L., p. 537, 131715; T. A., p. 537, 131709; Rev. T. H. L., p. 537, 131708
St. Clair, A. J., p. 53, 396; C., p. 53, 395; Mrs. C. A., p. 53, 392; J. S., p. 53, 393; L., p. 53, 397; N. G., p. 53, 398; P. R., p. 53, 394
St. Cyres, Vct., p. 114, 10663, 11108, 41839, 42169
St. John, G. R., p. 242, 37343; Mrs. M. L., p. 242, 37342; M. O., p. 242, 37344; U. M., p. 242, 37345
St. Leger, Capt. A. J. B., p. 450, 94967; A. M., p. 492, 128178, 128188; B. M., p. 450, 94968; H. B., p. 450, 94970; I. G., p. 292, 128180, 128190; N. E., p. 492, 128179, 128189; R. W. A., p. 450, 94971; V., p. 450, 94969
de Salis, Mrs. E. E., p. 215, 30129
Salmond, F., p. 206, 29871; F. M., p. 206, 29867; H. B., p. 206, 29869; H. M., p. 206, 29868; I. F. F., p. 206, 29870
Salvin, Mrs. P. B., p. 262, 38142, 38171; P. M., p. 262, 38143, 38172
Sanctuary, A. G. E., p. 400, 77842, 79351; C. T., p. 400, 77841, 79350; H. N., p. 400, 77843, 79352; I. G., p. 400, 77845, 79354; Mrs. M. E., p. 400, 77840, 79349; M. F. A., p. 400, 77844, 79353
Sandbach, Mrs. A. M., p. 115, 10677, 11122, 41853, 42183; C. D. A., p. 115, 10678, 11123, 41854, 42184; E. S., p. 115, 10679, 11124, 41855, 42185; G. R., p. 115, 10676, 11121, 41852, 42182; Mrs. H. J., p. 115, 10675, 11120, 41851, 42181; M. E.,

Index

p. 115, 10681, 11126, 41857, 42187; V. M., p. 115, 10680, 11125, 41856, 42186
Sanderman, Mrs. I., p. 462, 95502; Mrs. M. C., p. 456, 95313; W. A., p. 462, 95503
Sandford, A., p. 204, 29730, 29989; C., p. 204, 29729, 29988; F. G. M., p. 187, 28665, 28828; Mary, Lady, p. 204, 29726, 29985; Capt. W. G., p. 187, 28664, 28827
Sandford-Wills, E., p. 351, 59624, 60223, 64427; L. E., p. 351, 59625, 60224, 64428; M. G., p. 351, 59626, 60225, 64429
Sandham, A. M., p. 199, 29572, 29812; C. H., p. 199, 29570, 29810; Mrs. E. F., p. 199, 29569, 29809
Sandys, E. M., p. 145, 16363; Mrs. H. K. E., p. 145, 16362; H. M., p. 145, 16365; S. E., p. 145, 16364
Saunders, A. L., p. 138, 16137; C. I., p. 196, 29049, 29130, 29320; F. M., p. 196, 29048, 29129, 29319; G. H., p. 196, 29046, 29127, 29317; Mrs. H. C., p. 138, 16136; H. S., p. 196, 29042, 29123, 29313; M. I., p. 196, 29044, 29125, 29315; Mrs. O., p. 195, 29041, 29122, 29312; O. E., p. 196, 29050, 29131, 29321; R. P., p. 196, 29045, 29126, 29316; U. M. J., p. 196, 29043, 29124, 29314; V. C., p. 196, 29047, 29128, 29318; Capt. W. St. L., p. 138, 16138
Saurin, J., p. 369, 60105, 64309; M. A., p. 369, 60106, 64310
Savile, B. A. L., p. 353, 59691; Capt. J. H. D., p. 353, 59690
Sawer, Mrs. E. C., p. 319, 42580; E. R., p. 319, 42581; K. M., p. 319, 42582; R. H., p. 319, 42583
Sawyer, A. E., p. 386, 71742; B. H., p. 214, 30110; C., p. 386, 71745; D. A., p. 386, 71744; D. M. A., p. 214, 30109; E., p. 214, 30108; E. C., p. 386, 71738; Mrs. F. W., p. 214, 30107; Rev. G. H. p. 386, 71736; G. H., p. 386, 71741; H. W., p. 386, 71739; M. H., p. 386, 71743; W. E., p. 386, 71740; Rev. W. G., p. 386, 71737
Saxton, Mrs. A. E., p. 318, 42542; D. J., p. 318, 42544; W. T., p. 318, 42543
Schimmelpennick van der Oye, 3rd B., p. 380, 64130; Bnss. C. E. A., p. 380, 64141; Bnss. C. M. H. A. G., p. 380, 64140; Bn. F. C., p. 380, 64136; Bnss. F. M., p. 380, 64139; Bn. H. F. M., p. 380, 64137; Bn. H. N., p. 380, 64134; Bnss. I. H., p. 380, 64142; Bn. L. F. C., p. 380, 64132; Bnss. L. H., p. 380, 64133; Bnss. M. C. A., p. 380, 64138; Bn. R. H., p. 380, 64135; Bn. W. A. A. J., p. 380, 64131
Scholefield, Mrs. A. L. S., p. 102, 10206, 41382; J. H. B., p. 102, 10207, 41383
Schomberg, Mrs. V. L., p. 99, 10157, 41333
Schött, Mrs. S. F., p. 478, 103384
Sclater, Mrs. E. H., p. 199, 29568, 29808
Scott, Mrs. F. A., p. 141, 16194
Scott-Gatty, E. C., p. 527, 131223; Mrs. L. M. H., p. 527, 131222
Scott-Murray, Mrs. M. M. J., p. 255, 37942
Scougall, C., p. 93, 10021; H., p. 93, 10019; H. B. W., p. 93, 10022; J. H., p. 93, 10020
Scovell, D. G., p. 485, 103461, 103545; G. F., p. 485, 103459, 103543; G. H., p. 485, 103460, 103544; H. E., p. 485, 103458, 103542; Mrs. I. H., p. 485, 103457, 103541
Scrivener, A. P. L., p. 454, 95106; Comm. E. B. B. L., p. 454, 95104; E. H. B. L., p. 454, 95105; I. T. L., p. 454, 95107; P. L., p. 454, 95109; W. V. L., p. 454, 95108
Scrivenor, P., p. 161, 17035; T. V., p. 161, 17034; Mrs. V., p. 161, 17033
Seale, Adela, Lady, p. 111, 10574, 41750
Seely, Mrs. G. F., p. 396, 72277; S. K., p. 396, 72278
Seemann, E. D. C., p. 421, 80150; Mrs. G. E., p. 421, 80149; I. G. C., p. 421, 80154; J. A. H. A., p. 421, 80151; M. A. I., p. 421, 80152; M. O. G., p. 421, 80153
Selby-Lowndes, Lieut. C. H. C., p. 450, 94941; E. L., p. 450, 94944; Mrs. F. M., p. 449, 94940; Rev. G. N., p. 450, 94942; L. F. M., p. 450, 94943; M. H., p. 450, 94945
Senior, Mrs. M. B., p. 282, 38881; O. N., p. 282, 38882
Sergison, C. M., p. 423, 80193, 80337; Capt. C. W., p. 423, 80191, 80335; P. I. E., p. 423, 80192, 80336

Seton, A. H., p. 320, 42597, 42640; Maj. B. G., p. 320, 42596, 42639; E. L., p. 320, 42598, 42641; C. B., p. 320, 42618, 42622; Lieut. C. C., p. 320, 42620; C. H., p. 321, 42621; C. M., p. 320, 42601, 42644; Mrs. E. E., p. 321, 42638; Maj. H. J., p. 321, 42627; J. G., p. 320, 42599, 42642; J. P., p. 320, 42619, 42623; K. M., p. 320, 42603, 42646; M., p. 321, 42628; M. de S., p. 320, 42600, 42643; Mrs. V. A., p. 320, 42617; W. W., p. 320, 42602, 42645
Shadwell, Mrs. F., p. 460, 95424, 95450
Shafto, C. M. F. D., p. 290, 39090, 39136
Shakespear, R. H., p. 550, 135131; W. F., p. 550, 135132
Shann, A., p. 265, 38210; Rev. C. B., p. 265, 38218; C. D., p. 265, 38214; E. K., p. 265, 38221; E. W., p. 265, 38212; F., p. 265, 38209; F., p. 265, 38227; G., p. 265, 38208; G. D., p. 265, 38213; H., p. 265, 38225; H. C., p. 265, 38211; K., p. 265, 38224; L. H., p. 265, 38228; L. J., p. 265, 38229; L. M., p. 265, 38220; M. G., p. 265, 38226; Rev. R., p. 265, 38217; R. A., p. 265, 38219; R. M., p. 265, 38216; T. L., p. 265, 38223; V. F., p. 265, 38215; W. A., p. 265, 38222
Shaw, A. A., p. 459, 95393, 11636; Mrs. B. M., p. 386, 71733; C. H., p. 386, 71734; E. C. P., p. 459, 95392, 11635; Mrs. H. U., p. 459, 95391, 11634; P., p. 54, 425; U. F., p. 459, 95394, 11637
Shea, Mrs. E. C. H., p. 266, 38249
Shelley, Mrs. E. E., p. 158, 16847
Shenstone, A., p. 373, 60202, 64406; Mrs. A. E. G., p. 373, 60201, 64405
Sheringham, C. J. de B., p. 469, 103142; Mrs. E. F., p. 469, 103141; M. A., p. 469, 103143
Sherlock, Mrs. D. H., p. 274, 38515; H., p. 274, 38516
Sherrard, Mrs. A. L., p. 284, 38931; A. W. E., p. 284, 38932
Sherwood, Mrs. A., p. 349, 59572; A. A. F., p. 349, 59578; A. J. H., p. 349, 59579; A. R., p. 349, 59576; F. H., p. 349, 59575; R. G., p. 349, 59574; T. E.,

p. 349, 59573; T. M., p. 349, 59577
Shipperdson, I. H., p. 218, 30327; T. H., p. 218, 30320
Shore, H. A., p. 207, 29875; Lieut. L. H. P., p. 207, 29876; Hon. Mrs. M. A., p. 207, 29874; N. B. P., p. 207, 29877
Short, A. H., p. 266, 38253; Lieut. A. L. H., p. 265, 38233; C. M., p. 266, 38254; D. B., p. 267, 38261; Capt. F. H., p. 266, 38251; Rev. F. W. H., p. 266, 38252; J. H., p. 267, 38257; J. H., p. 267, 38258; J. L. B., p. 266, 38255; K. R. B. H., p. 266, 38234; M., p., 267, 38259; V., p. 267, 38260; W. H., p. 267, 38256; W. J., p. 266, 38250
Shuckburgh, C. E., p. 445, 94674; E. H., p. 445, 94667; G. F. S., p. 445, 94666; Capt. G. S., p. 445, 96471; L. M., p. 445, 94673; M. E., p. 445, 94672; Sir S. F. D., 10th Bt., p. 445, 94665
Shuldham, Lieut.-Col. A. I., p. 165, 17525; D. F. M. B., p. 164, 17513, 17796; E. D., p. 164, 17504, 17787; F. N. Q., p. 164, 17515, 17798; H. L. D., p. 164, 17506, 17789; M. C. D., p. 164, 17505, 17788; S. A. N., p. 164, 17507, 17790; V. L., p. 164, 17508, 17791; W. F. Q., p. 164, 17516, 17799
Shuldham-Lye, Capt. H., p. 165, 17524, 17807
Sidney, Lieut.-Col. the Hon. A., p. 235, 36613, 72417; M. O., p. 235, 36616, 72420; Hon. W., p. 235, 36614, 72418; W. P., p. 235, 36615, 72419
Sillifant, B. C., p. 83, 9760; C. H., p. 83, 9754; E., p. 83, 9759; E. H., p. 83, 9756; Mrs. G. C., p. 82, 9753; G. C. E., p. 83, 9755; G. F., p. 83, 9757; M., p. 83, 9758
Silvester, A. L., p. 559, 135372; Mrs. C. E., p. 559, 135371; J. M., p. 559, 135373
Sinclair, C. G., p. 167, 17640; J. H., p. 167, 17642; T. A., p. 167, 17643; Mrs. T. H., p. 167, 17639; W. F., p. 167, 17641
Sitwell, Lieut.-Col. F. H., p. 371, 60165, 64369; Lieut. W. H., p. 371, 60163, 64367; W. H., p. 371, 60164, 64368; W. G. H., p. 371, 60162, 64366
Skipwith, E. K., p. 69, 883, 57302; G. H., p.

Index

69, 882, 57301; Mrs. K. A. G., p. 69, 881, 57300
Slater, Mrs. F. H., p. 158, 16862
Slee, Mrs. C. H., p. 515, 130402, 130482
Slingsby, H., p. 240, 37290; T., p. 240, 37289
Smallpiece, A., p. 326, 43166; C. M., p. 568 (App.); F., p. 326, 43159; F. W., p. 326, 43160; G., p. 326, 43167; G. A. M., p. 568 (App.); H., p. 326, 43163; J., p. 326, 43165; L., p. 326, 43161; R., p. 568 (App.); R. A., p. 326, 43162; S., p. 326, 43164
Smith(——), p. 176, 27153; (——), p. 176, 27154; (——), p. 176, 27155; A., p. 179, 27300, 27315; A., p. 213, 30091; A., p. 258, 38015; Lieut. A. W., p. 176, 27151; B. E. R., p. 59, 543; B. G. O., p. 275, 38638; C., p. 179, 27295, 27310; C. E., p. 179, 27299, 27314; C. H. C., p. 115, 10684, 11129, 41860, 42190; C. I., p. 176, 27152; C. M., p. 176, 27159; Mrs. C. M., p. 187, 28662, 28825; C. W., p. 176, 27150; C. W., p. 213, 30090; D. A., p. 444, 94593; Mrs. E. B., p. 59, 539; Lieut. E. C., p. 115, 10683, 11128, 41859, 42189; E. G., p. 176, 27158; E. R., p. 59, 542; Mrs. E. S., p. 127, 11622; Mrs. F. J. H., p. 527, 131231; G., p. 179, 27301, 27316; G., p. 258, 38014; G. C. B., p. 176, 27157; G. F. R., p. 59, 540; J. C., p. 179, 27298, 27313; J. L. A., p. 163, 17083; J. W. C., p. 176, 27149; L. K. C., p. 115, 10686, 11131, 41862, 42192; M., p. 179, 27302, 27317; M., p. 213, 30092; M., p. 213, 30093; Mrs. M. C., p. 163, 17082; M. C., p. 179, 27297, 25312; M. C., p. 187, 28663, 28826; Hon. Mrs. M. L., p. 444, 94592; M. O., p. 275, 38641; N. O., p. 275, 38639; R. C., p. 527, 131232; Mrs. R. L., p. 115, 10682, 11127, 41858, 42188; R. M. C., p. 115, 10685, 11130, 41861, 42191; R. O., p. 275, 38640; R. P. C., p. 179, 27296, 27311; R. Z., p. 213, 30094; S. C., p. 179, 27303, 27318; W. H. R., p. 59, 541; W. L., p. 176, 27156
Smith-Wright, E. G., p. 305, 40308; H. G., p. 305, 40310; Mrs. I. M., p. 305, 40307; J. E., p. 305, 40309; J. M., p. 305, 40311
Smyth, A. E., p. 494, 128213; A. M., p. 493, 128212; B. L., p. 317, 42518; C., p. 318, 42523; O. I., p. 317, 42516; C. M., p. 318, 42521; C. W., p. 493, 128209; D., p. 318, 42526; F. B., p. 493, 128211; H. B., p. 493, 128210; I. M., p. 494, 128218; J., p. 318, 42525; J. B., p. 493, 128208; J. F., p. 318, 42520; K. B. I., p. 317, 42517; Mrs. M. A., p. 493, 128206; R., p. 318, 42524; R. M., p. 317, 42515; S., p. 318, 42522; S. F., p. 318, 42519; W., p. 493, 128207
Smythies, Mrs. E. A., p. 477, 103348; F. P., p. 477, 103349; Maj. R. H. R., p 126, 11588
Snell, Mrs Y. C., p. 112, 10589, 41765
Sneyd, Mrs. M. E., p. 333, 55473
Snouckaert van Schauburg, Bnss. E. S., p. 379, 64124; Bn. W. C., p. 379, 64125
Solger, Mrs. H. B., p. 370, 60143, 64347
Solms-Wildensfels, Hereditary Ct. of, p. 382, 64157
von Solms - Wildenfels, Ctss. A., p. 382, 64140; Ctss. G. C. C. C., p. 382, 64161; Ctss. J. C. A., p. 381, 64156; Ctss. M. M. A. A., p. 382, 64159; Ctss. S., p. 382, 64158
Solomon, A. F. W., p. 50, 311; C. W., p. 50, 312; H. W., p. 50, 313; Mrs. K., p. 50, 310; M. J., p. 50, 314
Somerville, Capt. A. C., p. 366, 59972; B. A., p. 366, 59969; D. H. S., p. 366, 59973; D. M., p. 366, 59971; E. A. Æ., p. 366, 59979; E. G. A., p. 366, 59976; G. M. H., p. 366, 39975; H., p. 367, 59985; Capt. H. B. T., p. 366, 59967; Capt. H. G. C., p. 366, 59978; Maj. J. A. C., p. 366, 59977; M. F., p. 366, 59970; R. T., p. 366, 59968; Col. T. C. F., p. 366, 59974; T. H. G., p. 366, 59974
Sotheby, A. F., p. 346, 59514; C. E., p. 346, 59517; E. C., p. 346, 59515; H. G., p. 346, 59513; L. F. S., p. 346, 59511; N. W. A., p. 346, 59512; W. E., p. 346, 59510; Rev. W. E. H., p. 346, 59509
South, A. C., p. 519, 130559; B. W., p. 519, 130560; Mrs. C. F., p. 519, 130558
Sowerby, Capt. C. F., p. 172, 17832; E. C., p. 172, 17835; Lieut. G., p. 172, 17838; G. F. A., p. 172, 17839; G. S., p. 172, 17834; H. D., p. 219, 30334; Lieut.-Col. H. J., p. 219, 30335; L. M., p. 219, 30338; Capt. M. E., p. 172, 17837; M. F., p. 172, 17840; M. G., p. 172, 17842; R. T. R., p. 219, 30333; Maj. T. G., p. 219, 30332; T. M., p. 172, 17836; V. F., p. 219, 30339; W. B., p. 172, 17833
Spalding, A. F. M., p. 283, 38894
Sparke, A. V. L'E. A., p. 423, 80204, 80348; E. A., p. 423, 80203, 80347; H. B., p. 423, 80200, 80344; M. E. B., p. 423, 80201, 80345; R. C. B., p. 423, 80202, 80346
Speck, G. L., p. 263, 38175; J., p. 263, 38174; Rev. J. H., p. 263, 38173; S., p. 263, 38176
Spencer, E. A., p. 157, 16836; Mrs. E. H. C., p. 387, 71774; Mrs. H., p. 157, 16834; Lieut. R. A., p. 157, 16835
Stack, Mrs. A., p. 510, 129279
Staley, Mrs. E. G. T., p. 349, 59584; E. V., p. 349, 59585
Stafford, Mrs. M. L., p. 414, 79973
Stainforth, D. A., p. 570 (App.); Mrs. G. H., p. 523, 130783; G. H., p. 523, 130784; H. G., p. 570 (App.); Col. L. C., p. 570 (App.); M. S., p. 523, 130785; Mrs. T. F. A., p. 551, 135147
Stanley, A. W. W., p. 215, 30117; B. C. W., p. 215, 30120; Mrs. C., p. 199, 29586; C. M., p. 200, 29596; C. S. B. W., p. 215, 30119; E. N., p. 199, 29590; Mrs. H. M., p. 215, 30118; Mrs. L. C., p. 214, 30116; L. M., p. 200, 29595; N. A., p. 199, 29589; P., p. 199, 29588; Mrs. R. M., p. 359, 59815, 95294; Capt. W., p. 199, 29587
Stansfeld, Mrs. K. G., p. 78, 9455
Staples-Browne, M. F., p. 327, 43179; Mrs. M. J., p. 327, 43177; R. C., p. 327, 43178
Stapylton, A., p. 117, 10732; A., p. 118, 10737; A. M., p. 118, 10743, 10765; E., p. 117, 10729; E., p. 117, 10730; E. M., p. 118, 10739; E. O., p. 99, 10160, 41336; H., p. 99, 10161, 41337; H., p. 99, 10159, 41335; H. M., p. 117, 10731; J., p. 99, 10158, 41334; J. M., p. 117, 10725; M., p. 117, 10733; M., p. 117, 10735; M., p. 117, 10736; M. D., p. 118, 10740; M. F., p. 99, 10153, 41329; M. G., p. 118, 10738; M. H., p. 99, 10150, 41326; Maj. M. J., p. 99, 10149, 41325; M. J., p. 118, 10742; N. C., p. 99, 10152, 41328; O. H., p. 117, 10726; O, L, p. 99, 10154, 41330; R., p. 117, 10734; Rev. R. M., p. 117, 10724; R. M., p. 117, 10728; S. M. R., p. 100, 10172, 41348; U. E. M., p. 99, 10151, 41327
Starkey, Mrs. I., p. 498, 128329
Starkie, Capt. E. A. Le G., p. 306, 40331; F. C. Le G., p. 306, 40333; Rev. H. A., p. 306, 40336; Lieut. P. C. Le G., p. 306, 40332; S. K. Le G., p. 306, 40335
Starr, Mrs. K. M., p. 89, 9899; M. C., p. 89, 9900
Statham, C. O., p. 123, 11515; Mrs. M., p. 123, 11513; M. L., p. 123, 11516; P. B., p. 123, 11514
Staunton, Mrs. C., p. 439, 90160
Steengracht, Jhr. Mr. H. A., p. 381, 64155; Jhr. H. A. A. G., p. 380, 64128
Steengracht van Moyland, 2nd B., p. 380, 64127
von Steengracht-Moyland, Jhr. G. A., p. 380, 64129
Stephenson, A. W., p. 47, 230; Mrs. G., p. 47, 229
Sterne, Mrs. K. A., p. 259, 38061
Stevens, Mrs. M., p. 110, 10489, 43665
Stevenson, Mrs. C. H., p. 371, 60156, 64360; E. K. I., p. 249, 37541; H. M., p. 249, 37540; Mrs. I. C., p. 249, 37536
Steward, Mrs. S. H. G., p. 353, 59676
Stewart, F. E. K., p. 277, 38700; F. L. M., p. 332, 55469; Mrs. F. M., p. 277, 38698; Mrs. H. L. G., p. 332, 55467; Lieut. H. W. V., p. 277, 38704; J. C. G., p. 332, 55468; J. C. K., p. 277, 38701; Capt. J. M. K., p. 277, 38699; Capt. J. M. V., p. 277, 38703; Capt. P. A. V., p. 277, 38702
Stewart-Murray, Lady E., p. 66, 755, 57174; Capt. Lord G., p. 66, 751, 57170; Lady H., p. 66, 754, 57173; Lieut.

Index

Lord J. T., p. 66, 752, 57171
Stock, B. M., p. 262, 38133, 38162; C. E., p. 262, 38131, 38160; C. H., p. 262, 38130, 38159; Mrs. E., p. 262, 38127, 38156; E. M., p. 262, 38132, 38161; G. M., p. 262, 38134, 38163; H. R., p. 262, 38128, 38157; K. M., p. 262, 38135, 38164; R. W., p. 262, 38129, 38158
Stockdale, D. H., p. 258, 38036; E. H., p. 259, 38045; E. V. M., p. 259, 38040; G. E. C. S.,p. 258, 38035; Col. G. H. W., p. 258, 38034; H., p. 259, 38042; H. C. M., p. 259, 38039; Maj. H. E., p. 259, 38044; Capt. H. M., p. 259, 38037; Maj. H. M., p. 259, 38038; K. F., p. 259, 38043; M. K. M., p. 259, 38046; M. L., p. 258, 38033; 'Rev. R. W., p. 259, 38041; R. W. D., p. 258, 38032
Stone, A., p. 416, 80025; D., p. 416, 80031; Lieut. E., p. 416, 80024; Mrs. E. F., p. 416, 80023; E. W., p. 416, 80034; F. le. S., p. 416, 80027; M. A., p. 416, 80032; Lieut. R. G., p. 416, 80026; W. N., p. 416, 80028
Stoney, A. V., p. 149, 16607; J. B., p. 149, 16606; Mrs. L., p. 149, 16605; M. E., p. 149, 16608; Mrs. P. E., p. 107, 10317, 41493; R. V., p. 107, 10319, 41495; T. S. V., p. 107, 10318, 41494
Stradbroke, 3rd E. of, p. 197, 29536, 29776
le Strange, Rev. A., p. 411, 79908; Hon. Mrs. A. F. D., p. 422, 80170, 80314; B., p. 411, 79907, 80172; C. A., p. 411, 79906, 80171; D., p. 411, 79911; E., p. 411, 79912; G., p. 411, 79913; G., p. 412, 79920; H., p. 411, 79904; M., p. 411, 79909; M., p. 411, 79918; Lieut. R., p. 411, 79905; S., p. 411, 79919; V., p. 411, 79910
Strathy, D., p. 245, 37431; E., p. 246, 37433; H., p. 245, 37430; H., p. 246, 37434; H. E. B., p. 246, 37435; P., p. 245, 37432
Stratten, Mrs. G. F., p. 414, 79963
Stratton, C. M., p. 526, 131015; Mrs. F. L., p. 526, 131013; I. R., p: 526, 131016; J. H., p. 526, 131014
Streatfield, M. A., p. 306, 40353; R. H. A., p. 306, 40354
Street, J. N. E., p. 273, 38489; Mrs. V. C., p. 273, 38488
Strutt, Mrs. F. N., p. 108, 10375, 41551; Hon. Mrs. W., p. 544, 134901
Stuart, A. E., p. 183, 27413; A. R. B., p. 183, 27416; C. B. G., p. 183, 27412; Mrs. F. W., p. 412, 79938; F. E. A. A., p. 183, 27414; H. C., p. 412, 79935; J. D., p. 412, 79939; Mrs. M., p. 230, 36521; M. B., p. 412, 79936; M. E. E., p. 183, 27415; M. W., p. 412, 79937
Stuart-Gray, Hon. A. J. M., p. 189, 28836, 28869; Hon. F. D., p. 189, 28835, 28868; Lady H. M., p. 189, 28838, 28871; Hon. J. G., p. 189, 28837, 28870
Stucley, Louisa, Dow. Lady, p. 467, 103073; D. F. B., p. 483, 103416, 103075; Maj. E. A. G., p. 483, 103414, 60094, 64298; E. F., p. 483, 103417, 103076; Lieut. H. N. G., p. 483, 103415, 103074; Capt. H. St. L., p. 483, 103418, 103077; Lieut.-Col. Sir (W.) L., 2nd Bt., p. 483, 103413, 60093, 64297
Studdy, A. R., p. 169, 17698; E., p. 169, 17696; H., p. 169, 17695; Capt. H. E. M., p. 169, 17694; J., p. 169, 17697; M., p. 169, 17699
Style, B. A., p. 526, 131008; B. H., p. 525, 130984; B. W., p. 526, 131012; C., p. 526, 131009; Maj. C. H., p. 526, 131004; Rev. C. M., p. 526, 130998; C. R., p. 526, 131005; Sir F. M., 10th Bt., p. 525, 130978; Capt. G. M., p. 526, 131000; G. R., p. 525, 130982; H. A., p. 526, 131007; H. A. G., p. 525, 130981; H. B., p. 526, 131006; J. P., p. 526, 131011; L. V., p. 525, 130980; O. G., p. 526, 131001; P., p. 526, 131002; P., p. 526, 131003; Lieut.-Col. R. C., p. 525, 130986; R. C. M., p. 526, 130999; Lieut. R. H. 526, 131010; R. L., p. 525, 130983; S. J., p. 525, 130991; V., p. 525, 130985; W. F., p. 525, 130979
Sufferin, Mrs. L. F., p. 363, 59912
Sulivan, Mrs. K. A., p. 325, 43151
Summers, Mrs. A. M. E., p. 169, 17693; Mrs. D. H., p. 141, 16199
Sunderland, M., p. 320, 42615; P. J., p. 320, 42616; Mrs. R. M., p. 320, 42614
Sutton, C. O., p. 118, 10750; E. J. S., p. 118, 10749; Mrs. E. L., p. 415, 79990; F. A., p. 415, 79994; F. R. H., p. 58, 510, 79991; G. W., p. 118, 10748; J. S., p. 118, 10747; Mrs. K. H., p. 58, 509; O. K., p. 58, 512, 79993; O. M., p. 58, 511, 79992
Swayne, Mrs. M., p. 267, 38286
Sweet, B., p. 138, 16129; C. V. L., p. 138, 16123; D. M. W., p. 78, 9451; E. H., p. 138, 16130; Mrs. E. M., p. 78, 9448; E. M., p. 138, 16131; G. C. W., p. 78, 9449; G. H. L., p. 138, 16122; J., p. 138, 16127; J. L., p. 138, 16120; J. L. L., p. 138, 16121; L. H. W., p. 78, 9450; M. B., p. 138, 16133; M. L., p. 138, 16124; R. M., p. 138, 16128; W. M., p. 138, 16126; W. M. L., p. 138, 16125
Swinburne, A., p. 296, 39539; Mrs. A. P., p. 43, 116; Capt. H., p. 294, 39471; I., p. 294, 39480; I., p. 296, 39541; Capt. Sir J., 7th Bt., p. 294, 39470; J., p. 43, 117, 39472; J., p. 296, 39538; Lieut. J., p. 296, 39543; M., p. 294, 39475; M., p. 296, 39542; M. F. T., p. 296, 39537; R., p. 294, 39474; S. C., p. 296, 39540; T., p. 297, 39554; Lieut. T. A. S., p. 296, 39536; Maj. T. R., p. 296, 39535; U. P., p. 294, 39473
Sykes, A. F. S., p. 320, 42611; C. M., p. 320, 42612; Mrs. E., p. 320, 42610; E. M., p. 320, 42613
Syngo, Mrs. A. F., p. 148, 16592

Talbot, A. M., p. 46, 219; B., p. 46, 215; Mrs. B. C., p. 273, 38479; C. I., p. 273, 38482; E., p. 47, 228; E. A. C., p. 46, 217; Rev. E. K., p. 47, 235; Mrs. E. M., p. 467, 103063; B. A., p. 467, 103065; G. F., p. 467, 103064; G. J., p. 46, 211; G. W. L., p. 47, 237; J. A., p. 46, 220; J. A., p. 273, 38481; J. B., p. 46, 212; J. E., p. 46, 216; Hon. Mrs. L., p. 47, 234; L. C., p. 47, 242; M. G., p. 46, 214; M. L., p. 47, 227; Hon. Mrs. M. S., p. 46, 210; Rev. N. S., p. 47, 236; R. C., p. 273, 38480; R. E., p. 46, 218; T. G., p. 46, 213
Tate, H. R., p. 155, 16783; J. G., p. 155, 16784
Taverner, Mrs. W. W., p. 176, 27143
Taylor, A., p. 127, 11612; A., p. 127, 11613; Mrs. A. H., p. 274, 38525; C., p. 127. 11611; Mrs. E. A., p. 423, 80199, 80343; F. M. J. du P., p. 274, 38524; Mrs. G., p. 262, 38136, 38165; G. F., p. 262, 38139, 38168; Lieut. H., p. 497, 128290; J. W., p. 127, 11610; M., p. 497, 128292; Mrs. M. M., p. 497, 128289; N., p. 262, 38140, 38169; P. M., p. 127, 11614; Lieut. R. B., p. 262, 38138, 38167; Rev. S., p. 262, 38137, 38166; Lieut. T. G., p. 497, 128291; V. M., p. 497, 128293
Tell, V. B., p. 387, 71756
Templetown, Evelyn G., Vctss., p. 130, 12212, 81045
Tennant, Mrs. H. L., p. 510, 129280
Tennent, C. H. M., p. 243, 37361; F. M., p. 243, 37360; I. V., p. 98, 10108; J. B. H., p. 243, 37357; M. A., p. 243, 37363; Mrs. M. C. P., p. 243, 37356; Mrs. M. L., p. 98, 10103; M. L., p. 98, 10104; M. I., p. 98, 10106; M. P. C., p. 243, 37359; O. C., p. 98, 10107; O. M., p. 243, 37358; S. M., p. 243, 37362; V. F., p. 98, 10105
Terrill, J. L., p. 210, 29965
van Tets, Jkvr. D. H., p. 380, 64146; Jhr. G. C. W., p. 380, 64144; Jkvr. H., p. 380, 64145; Bnss. H. M. S., p. 380, 64143
Thackeray, B. J. M., p. 111, 10571, 41747; C. M. C., p. 111, 10570, 41746; Mrs. E. M., p. 111, 10568, 41744; G. St. V. R., p. 111, 10569, 41745; U. M. A., p. 111, 10572, 41748
Tharp, Mrs. M. J., p. 112, 10595, 41771
Thomas, D., p. 87, 9835; D. I., p. 280, 38839; Mrs. E. E., p. 119, 10763; H. E. E., p. 119, 10764; E. O. G., p. 446, 94687; Mrs. E. R., p. 448, 94686; Mrs. G., p. 42, 92; I. E., p. 280, 38836; L., p. 87, 9834; Mrs. L. J., p. 391, 71977
Thompson, A. E., p. 248, 37487; Maj. A. H., p. 247, 37470; Mrs. A. H., p. 248, 37486; A. M., p. 70, 955, 57374; C., p. 70, 962, 57381; Mrs. C. A., p. 70, 953, 57372; D. B., p. 248, 37485; G., p. 70, 961, 57380; Lieut. H., p. 70, 954, 57373; Mrs. M. H., p. 247, 37469; M. H., p.

Index

247, 37473 ; N. G., p. 247, 37474 ; O., p. 247, 37472 ; Mrs. V., p. 65, 740 ; V. I., p. 248, 37489 ; Capt. W. M., p. 247, 37471
Thomson, Mrs. M. A., p. 353, 59675
Thorley, Mrs. M. U., p. 117, 10727
Thornburgh-Cropper, E. D., p. 169, 17692
Thorne, Hon. Mrs. M., p. 44, 161
Thornhill, Mrs. A. M., p. 353, 59679 ; C., p. 353, 59680 ; Mrs. F. A., p. 288, 39018 ; H., p. 288, 39019 ; K., p. 288, 39020 ; P., p. 288, 39021 ; S., p. 288, 39022
Thornton, A. F., p. 396, 72285 ; Mrs. A. G. F., p. 554, 135224 ; A. N., p. 396, 72290 ; A. R., p. 396, 72295 ; B. G., p. 396 ; 72284 ; C. A. M., p. 396, 72281 ; Rev. C. C., p. 395, 72266 ; Rev. C. C., p. 396, 72279 ; C. Du F., p. 396, 72280 ; C. E. C., p. 405, 79665 ; C. M., p. 396, 72291 ; C. S., p. 397, 72305 ; D. M., p. 396, 72293 ; E. C., p. 396, 72289 ; E. L. R., p. 396, 72292 ; E. M., p. 396, 72286 ; E. M., p. 397, 72306 ; F. H., p. 554, 135231 ; F. R., p. 397, 72298 ; G. H., p. 395, 72262 ; Rev. G. R., p. 397, 72297 ; Capt. G. St. L., p. 396, 72268 ; H. E., p. 395, 72263 ; H. G., p. 395, 72264 ; H. G., p. 554, 135232 ; J. B., p. 554, 135228 ; Rev. J. G., p. 396, 72269 ; K. E. C., p. 396, 72287 ; Rev. L. S., p. 396, 72283 ; Mrs. M. D., p. 405, 79664 ; M. L. R., p. 397, 72300 ; M. R., p. 396, 72296 ; P. C., p. 396, 72267 ; P. F., p. 554, 135233 ; P. S., p. 395, 72265 ; R. C., p. 396, 72282 ; R. E., p. 554, 135227 ; R. F., p. 554, 135229 ; R. H., p. 396, 72270 ; S. R., p. 396, 72294 ; Lieut. T. A., p. 554, 135226 ; Capt. T. W., p. 554, 135225 ; V. E., p. 554, 135230 ; W. M., p. 396, 72288
Thornewill, A. B., p. 60, 564 ; E. N., p. 60, 562 ; H. M., p. 60, 565 ; H. P., p. 60, 563
Thorold, E. M., p. 310, 41946, 43139 ; F. H., p. 157, 16827 ; Sir J. H., 12th Bt., p. 310, 41933, 43126 ; M. G., p. 310, 41940, 43133
Threlfell, C. R. M., p. 355, 59716 ; Mrs. M. A., p. 355, 59715
Thumann, Mrs. J., p. 294, 39479

Thwaites, Mrs. M., p. 424, 80220, 80364
Timberlake, Mrs. F. S., p. 208, 29899 ; W. B., p. 208, 29900
Tinne, Mrs. L. B., p. 203, 29706
Tisdall, Mrs. B. T., p. 195, 29024, 29105, 29295
Titchfield, M. of, p. 226, 36411
Tobias, Mrs. E. S., p. 494, 128217
Todd, Mrs. C., p. 63, 665 ; D. A., p. 63, 666
Tollemache, A. H. W., p. 223, 36362 ; E. L. C., p. 223, 36363 ; H. E. A., p. 223, 36364 ; Mrs. S. E., p. 223, 36361
Tomlin, Mrs. H., p. 249, 37533 ; H. G., p. 249, 37534 ; L. J., p. 249, 37535
Toogood, A. H. C., p. 523, 130779 ; Capt. D. I., p. 570 (App.) ; D. I., p. 570 (App.) ; E. G., p. 570 (App.) ; E. M. p. 570 (App.) ; G. N., p. 523, 130781 ; Mrs. G. S., p. 534, 131398 ; H. R. G. C., p. 523, 130780 ; Mrs. M. E., p. 523, 130778
Torck van Pallandt, 8th B., p. 378, 64085, 64098
Torkington, Capt. A., p. 85, 9796, 9980 ; Capt. C., p. 85, 9790, 9974 ; C., p. 85, 9805, 9989 ; C. C., p. 85, 9792, 9976 ; C. R., p. 85, 9804, 9988 ; D. M., p. 85, 9794, 9978 ; E., p. 85, 9803, 9987 ; G., p. 85, 9806, 9990 ; G. S., p. 85, 9791, 9975 ; Lieut.-Col. H., p. 85, 9799, 9983 ; I., p. 85, 9797, 9981 ; J. É. B., p. 85, 9793, 9977 ; M. C., p. 85, 9802, 9986 ; M. D., p. 85, 9795, 9979 ; Capt. O. M., p. 85, 9801, 9985 ; R. H., p. 85, 9800, 9984
Torry, J. S. A., p. 373, 60211, 64415
Tottenham, Mrs. C., p. 195, 29033, 29114, 29304 ; E. L., p. 195, 29039, 29120, 29310 ; F. L., p. 195, 29035, 29116, 29306 ; G. M., p. 195, 29040, 29121, 29311 ; P. M., p. 195, 29034, 29115, 29305
Toulmin, C. M., p. 205, 29739, 29998 ; D. A., p. 519, 130572 ; E. A., p. 519, 130573 ; Mrs. E. L., p. 204, 29723, 29982 ; Mrs. E. V., p. 415, 80001 ; G. M., p. 205, 29740, 29999 ; H. E., p. 519, 130570 ; H. W., p. 204, 29724, 29983 ; I. M., p. 205, 29741, 30000 ; L., p. 204, 29738, 29997 ; M., p. 204, 29725, 29984 ; V. F., p. 519, 130571
Tower, A., p. 514, 130367 ; A. P., p. 514, 130364 ;

B., p. 514, 130365 ; C., p. 514, 130359 ; C., p. 514, 130366 ; D. E., p. 514, 130362 ; E. C., p. 514, 130358 ; Rev. F., p. 514, 130360 ; Rev. H., p. 514, 130357 ; M., p. 514, 130368 ; W., p. 514, 130361 ; W. E., p. 514, 130363
Towler, C. J., p. 327, p. 509, 129238
Townley, Mrs. A. R. M., p. 426, 80283, 80427 ; C. E., p. 426, 80284, 80428 ; G. M., p. 426, 80285, 80429 ; R. C., p. 426, 80286, 80430 ; S. G., p. 426, 80287, 80431
Townsend, Mrs. M. A., p. 509, 129238
Townshend, B. H. U. L., p. 470, 103163 ; Mrs. B. M., p. 470, 103157 ; C. M. W. L., p. 470, 103160 ; C. R. de B. L., p. 470, 103158 ; E. A. F. L., p. 470, 103161 ; F. W. C. L., p. 470, 103159 ; Capt. H. de B. F., p. 365, 59953 ; M. F. S., p. 365, 59952 ; W. B. G. L., p. 470, 103162
Traill, C. J., p. 136, 16054 ; J. M., p. 136, 16057 ; J. W., p. 136, 16053 ; M. H., p. 136, 16058 ; Rev. R. R. W., p. 136, 16056 ; S. G., p. 136, 16055
Trappes, Mrs. F. L., p. 372, 60175, 64379
Treherne, Mrs. B., p. 282, 38887
Trench, S. G. B., p. 130, 12210, 72012, 81043 ; T. C., p. 130, 12211, 72013, 81044 ;
Trenow, Mrs. S. H. L., p. 65, 731
Trevor, Mrs. F., p. 127, 11608 ; Mrs. H., p. 206, 60131, 64336 ; R. S. R., p. 127, 11609
Trew, Mrs. A. M., p. 327, 43185 ; B. M., p. 327, 43187 ; J. M'C., p. 327, 43186 ; M., p. 327, 43191
Tritton, C., p. 444, 94596 ; L., p. 444, 94595 ; O., p. 444, 94594
Trollope, Rev. C. H. B., p. 401, 77850, 79359 ; C. W. A., p. 401, 77853, 79362 ; C. Z., p. 400, 77827, 79336 ; D. M. A., p. 401, 77856, 79365 ; E. M., p. 401, 77851, 79360 ; F. W., p. 401, 77852, 79361 ; H. B. A., p. 401, 77854, 79363 ; H. L., p. 400, 77848, 79357 ; L. E. A., p. 401, 77855, 79364 ; M. E. A., p. 400, 77826, 79335
Troyte-Bullock, A. C., p. 49, 283 ; Capt. C. J., p. 49, 280 ; C. V., p. 49, 277 ; Lieut.-Col. E. G., p. 49, 273 ; E. G., p.

49, 275 ; E. M., p. 49, 282 ; G. V., p. 49, 274 ; H. A., p. 49, 278 ; M., p. 49, 279 ; M. G., p. 49, 281 ; M. W., p. 49, 276
Troyte - Chafyn - Grove, Mrs. A., p. 49, 272
Truell, C. E., p. 189, 28854 ; Lady C. S., p. 189, 28839 ; E. G. S., p. 189, 28841 ; G. M., p. 189, 28853 ; K. A., p. 189, 28852 ; L. A., p. 107, 10316 41492 ; R. H. S., p. 189, 28840 ; W. H. S., p. 189, 28842
Tryon, J., p. 152, 16671, 72483 ; M., p. 151, 16659, 72481 ; S., p. 152, 16670, 72482
Tuckey, Mrs. A. K. R., p. 125, 11568 ; Mrs. F. J., p. 361, 59833 ; R. E. O., p. 125, 11569
Tudor, Mrs. B., p. 196, 29058, 29139, 29329
Tufnell, F. E. S., p. 224, 36382 ; Mrs. G. A., p. 224, 36380 ; R. E., p. 224, 36381
Tugwell, Rev. G., p. 94, 10032 ; H. W., p. 94, 10033
Tullibardine, Capt. the M. of, p. 66, 750, 57169
Tupper, Sir (C.) L., p. 348, 59563 ; F. G., p. 348, 59565 ; G., p. 348, 59564 ; Capt. R. G. O., p. 348, 59568
Turnbull, A. E., p. 253, 37862 ; Col. C. F. A., p. 178, 27227 ; D. R., p. 178, 27228 ; Mrs. M. H., p. 253, 37861 ; M. H., p. 253, 37863 ; M. R., p. 253, 37864 ; S. N. E., p. 178, 27229
Turner, Mrs. B. L., p. 461, 95444 ; Mrs. E. I., p. 211, 30018 ; J. E. U. P., p. 371, 60160, 64364 K. M., p. 461, 95465 ; Mrs. M. A., p. 476, 103342
Turner-Farley, D. G., p. 497, 128295 ; Mrs. M. I. G., p. 497, 128294 ; O. A., p. 497, 128296
Turnor, A., p. 130, 12183, 71985, 81016 ; A. B., p. 130, 12187, 71989, 81020 ; B. K., p. 130, 12194, 71996, 81027 ; B. K., p. 130, 12209, 72011, 81042 ; C., p. 392, 72015 ; C. H., p. 130, 12182, 71984, 81015 ; C. R., p. 130, 12185, 71987, 81018 ; C. O., p. 130, 12193, 71995, 81026 ; C. Y., p. 130, 12192, 71994, 81025 ; E., p. 130, 12190, 71992, 81023 ; E., p. 130, 12195, 71997, 81028 ; E. C., p. 130, 12191, 71993, 81024 ; G. A., p. 130, 12189, 71991, 81022 ; H. B., p. 130, 12184, 71986, 81017 ; J., p. 392, 72017 ; M. C. I., p. 130, 12186, 71988, 81019 ; R., p. 393, 72016 ; Maj.

Index

R. C., p. 392, 72014;
V. H., p. 130, 12188,
71990, 81021
van Tuyll van Serooskerken, Bnss. A. T. A.,
p. 381, 64150; Cornelia
M., Bnss., p. 381, 64147;
Bn. J. W. G., p. 381,
64148; Bnss. M. C., p.
381, 64149
Twedale, Mrs. D. T., p.
362, 59569
Twiss, A. Q., p. 264,
38187; E. F., p. 264,
38188; H. W., p. 264,
38186; M. C., p. 264,
38191

UNDERWOOD, Mrs. E.
J., p. 135, 16026; G.
J., p. 135, 16027; K.
S., p. 135, 16028
von Ungern-Sternberg, B.,
p. 472, 103211; Bnss.
A. L. E. M. H., p. 472,
103213; Bn. R. A. E.
L., p. 472, 103212
Uniacke - Penrose - FitzGerald, Jane E., Lady,
p. 77, 9419
Unwin, Mrs. C. K., p. 165,
17526; Mrs. F. J. W.,
p. 316, 42417; M., p.
165, 17533
Upton, Lieut. the Hon.
E. M. J., p. 130, 12213,
81046; Hon. H. A. G.
M. H., p. 130, 12214,
81047; Hon. M. E., p.
130, 12215, 81048; Mrs.
V., p. 551, 135144
Urquhart, C. F., p. 309,
41924, 43117; Mrs. M.,
p. 309, 41923, 43116

VAISEY, A. W., p. 160,
17027; A. W., p. 160,
17029; Mrs. E., p. 160,
17026; E. A., p. 161,
17048; F. D., p. 161,
17044; G. M., p. 161,
17046; H. B., p. 160,
17028; I., p. 161,
17040; J. C., p. 161,
17042; J. E. D., p. 161,
17041; J. M., p. 161,
17030; L., p. 161,
17036; M., p. 160,
17032; M., p. 161,
17038; M., p. 161,
17045; M., p. 161,
17047; O., p. 161,
17039; R. M., p. 160,
17031; T. L., p. 161,
17043; V., p. 161,
17037
Vallack-Tom, Mrs. N. C.,
p. 155, 16764
Vallado, 9th M. of, p. 78,
9434
Vallings, D. G., p. 62, 646;
G. C., p. 62, 647; G.
M., p. 62, 648; Maj.
H. A., p. 62, 645; Mrs.
M., p. 62, 644
Valpy, Mrs. E. A., p. 295,
39482
Vandeleur, Mrs. M., p. 148,
16604
Vansittart, A., p. 278,
38707; A. B., p. 275,
38644; A. G., p. 277,
38682; A. M., p. 277,
38688; A. M., p. 277,
38693; B., p. 276,
38660; C., p. 277,

38690; Capt. C. E. B.,
p. 276, 38678; C. H.
M. B., p. 276, 38679;
C. I., p. 358, 59777,
95256; Lieut. C. N.,
p. 277, 38683; D. M.,
p. 277, 38691; E., p.
277, 38689; Col. E.,
p. 277, 38695; E. C.,
p. 277, 38686; F. de
M., p. 277, 38684; G.
E., p. 358, 59776, 95255;
G. N., p. 274, 38645;
Lieut. H., p. 277, 38687;
H., p. 277, 38692;
H. E., p. 275, 38647;
H. F., p. 277, 38694;
M., p. 358, 59782,
95261; M. B., p. 276,
38680; M. M., p. 275,
38648; R., p. 277,
38705; Capt. R. A., p.
275, 38642; R. G., p.
275, 38643; S. A., p.
275, 38646; S. N., p.
278, 38706; V., p. 277,
38685; V. M. E., p.
277, 38696; W. H., p.
276, 38677
Vaughan, M. C., p. 83,
11518; Mrs. V., p. 123,
11517
Veitch, Mrs. B. C. M., p.
456, 95316; H. C. C.,
p. 456, 95317; H. L.
G., p. 456, 95318; N.
P. A., p. 456, 95319
Venables-Vernon, Sir W.
H., p. 539, 132686
Vereker, Hon. C. J., p.
40, 49; F. G. P., p. 39,
27; I. M., p. 39, 31;
Major the Hon. J. E. P.,
p. 39, 32; Lieut. L.
G. P., p. 39, 25; L. I.,
p. 39, 29; Hon. L. M.,
p. 40, 44; M. A., p. 39,
30; M. C. P., p. 39,
26; Hon. M. E., p. 40,
43; S. H. P., p. 39,
24; Hon. S. R. G. F.,
p. 39, 23; V. E., p. 39,
28
Verey, Mrs. H. M., p. 205,
29758
Verney, C., p. 444, 94591;
Hon. M., p. 444, 94599;
R. B., p. 444, 96589;
R. H., p. 444, 94590;
Rev. the Hon. W. R.,
p. 444, 94588
Vernon, Hon. Mrs. A. G.,
p. 365, 59955; A. L.,
p. 390, 71950; B. W.,
p. 391, 71970; C. C. W.,
p. 391, 71964; C. P., p.
390, 71957; D., p. 390,
71951; E., p. 390,
71959; E. C. W., p.
391, 71965; Rev. E.
H., p. 391, 71969; E.
H. S., p. 391, 71976;
G. B., p. 391, 71972;
H. A., p. 391, 71971;
H. C., p. 390, 71954;
H. W., p. 390, 71956;
I. A., p. 391, 71968;
Mrs. I. C. E., p. 386,
71746; L. G., p. 391,
71966; M. E., p. 390,
71962; M. I., p. 391,
71983; P. W., p. 390,
71961; R., p. 390,
71960; R. F., p. 390,
71958; Hon. R. F. C.,
p. 366, 59957; R. L.,

p. 390, 71953; Hon.
S. C. F., p. 366, 59959;
S. M., p. 390, 71955;
S. R. W., p. 391, 71967;
Hon. V. W. D., p. 366,
59958; W. B. W., p.
390, 71952; Rev. W.
G., p. 391, 71963;
Verschoyle, F. H. H. S.,
p. 156, 16814; H. C.
G., p. 156, 16815; Mrs.
H. C. H., p. 156, 16813;
M. H., p. 156, 16816
Villiers, A. H., p. 77,
9423; Mrs. G. E., p. 77,
9422; J. M., p. 77,
9425; R. M., p. 77,
9426; W. E., p. 77,
9424
Villiers-Stuart, Mrs. G.
F., p. 496, 128281; G.
M., p. 496, 128283; I.
H. F., p. 496, 128282;
N. M., p. 496, 128284
Vincent, A. F., p. 222,
36332; E. J., p. 222,
36334; Lieut. F. E.,
p. 222, 36331; V. N.
E., p. 222, 36333
Viner, Mrs. F. E. C., p.
138, 16132
Wachtmeister, Ctss. E.
F. A., p. 251, 37594;
Frances A., Ctss., p.
251, 37593; Ctss. S.
A., p. 251, 37595;
Ctss. S. R., p. 251,
37596
Waddington, Mrs. E. M.,
p. 420, 80120; G. O'N.
p. 420, 80121
Waggett, Mrs. A. C., p.
264, 28189; J. B., p.
264, 38190
Wagner, Mrs. J. B., p.
208, 29913
Wake, B. C., p. 261,
38112; Rev. B. E., p.
261, 38087; G. F., p.
261, 38093; G. M., p.
261, 38113; G. M. M.,
p. 261, 38097; H. B.
L., p. 261, 38089; Rev.
H. E., p. 261, 38094;
L. J., p. 261, 38103;
M. G. H., p. 261,
38092; T. M., p. 261,
38090; T. M., p. 261,
38091
Waldie-Griffith, Col. Sir
R. J., 3rd Bt., p. 497,
128288
Waldy, Mrs. C., p. 163,
17088; C. T., p. 163,
17091; D. E., p. 163,
17093; J. N., p. 163,
17089; R. G., p. 163,
17090; V. M., p. 163,
17092
Wale, F., p. 463, 95523;
F. L., p. 463, 95512;
Walker, A. J., p. 304,
40300; Mrs. B., p. 52,
364; C. H., p. 313,
42350, 42422; E., p.
544, 134912, 135049;
Ethel B., Lady, p. 544,
134910, 135047; F., p.
192, 28911, 20182; F.
E., p. 304, 40301; Mrs.
G. M., p. 164, 17509,
17792; H. B., p. 192,
28912, 29183; H. C.,
p. 192, 28917, 29188;
I. P. A. M., p. 544,

134911, 135048; Mrs.
M. E., p. 475, 103308;
N., p. 192, 28918,
29189; R. A., p. 192,
28910, 29181; V. E.,
p. 313, 42349, 42421
Wallace, C. W., p. 211,
30030; Mrs. E. C., p.
211, 30029; H. C., p.
211, 30032; J. H., p.
211, 30034; R., p. 211,
30031; T., p. 211,
30033
Waller, B. M., p. 537,
131695; C. L., p. 536,
131685; D., p. 537,
131702; E., p. 537,
131687; Rev. E. A.
p. 536, 131686; E. N.
p. 537, 131690; E. S.,
p. 536, 131667; Capt.
Sir F. E., p. 536,
131663; Mrs. J. S.,
p. 412, 79921; L. J. M.,
p. 537, 131701; L. J. M.,
p. 537, 131689; M.,
p. 537, 131691; M. H.,
p. 537, 131700; R. A.,
p. 537, 131688; Col.
S., p. 537, 131697;
Lieut. S. E. W., p. 537,
131698; Lieut. W. A.,
p. 536, 131664; W. E.,
p. 537, 131699; Rev.
W. H., p. 412, 79922,
131668
Walrond, B. M., p. 78,
9442; C. M., p. 78,
9446; E. A., p. 78,
9436; E. H., p. 78,
9437; F. A., p. 78,
9440; F. H., p. 78,
9439; G. O., p. 78,
9438; G. S. B., p. 78,
9447; H. H., p. 78,
9435; H. H. R. M., p.
78, 9441; H. W. J., p.
78, 9445; I. F. M., p.
78, 9443; M. J. M.,
p. 78, 9444
Walsham, B., p. 288,
39012, 59904, 128185;
Bessie G., Lady, p.
363, 59903; F. M., p.
288, 39015; G. N., p.
288, 39016; J. C., p.
288, 39017; Sir J. S.,
3rd Bt., p. 287, 39011;
P. R., p. 288, 39013;
P. R. S., p. 288, 39014
Walter, A. E. S., p. 547,
135014; Mrs. C. I., p.
547, 135023; E. B. S.,
p. 547, 135024; E. H.,
p. 547, 135015; E. H.,
H. M., p. 547, 135009;
Capt. J., p. 547, 135010;
J., p. 547, 135011;
M. I., p. 547, 135025;
O., p. 547, 135021;
P. M., p. 547, 135012;
S., p. 547, 135013
Wanklyn, Mrs. L. M., p.
99, 10155, 41331
Warburton, Mrs. A., p.
52, 363; Mrs. S. J. F.,
p. 370, 60146, 64350
Warde, D., p. 56, 468;
Mrs. G., p. 56, 467
Ware, A., p. 495, 128256,
128352; Mrs. B. R., p.
478, 103383; D., p.
495, 128254, 128350;
Mrs. D. M., p. 495,
128251, 128347; F.,
p. 495, 128253, 128349;

603

Index

Mrs. G., p. 246, 37450;
Capt. G. W., p. 495, 128252, 128348; R., p. 495, 128255, 128351
Waring, A. A., p. 510, 129259; Mrs. A. C., p. 510, 129254; F. J., p. 510, 129257; H. P., p. 510, 129256; J. K., p. 510, 129255; L. K., p. 510, 129258
Warner, A. C. F., p. 252, 37610; A. E. C., p. 252, 37612; B. H., p. 252, 37614; G. E. M., p. 252, 37618; J., p. 252, 37611; J., p. 252, 37615; J. T., p. 252, 37613; L. D., p. 252, 37619; L. O., p. 252, 37609; M., p. 252, 37621; Mrs. M. J. H., p. 252, 37608; O. M. W., p. 252, 37617; R. C., p. 252, 37616; W. A., p. 252, 37620
Warren, A. G. D., p. 363, 59901; A. J., p. 360, 59829, 59896; A. J., p. 361, 59855; A. L. W., p 362, 59880; Sir A. R., 5th Bt., p. 363, 59809; Lieut. A. R. J. B., p. 363, 59900; C. F., p. 360, 59830, 59897; E. C. L. L., p. 362, 59864; E. R., p. 362, 59866; G. I., p. 361, 59856; G. M., p. 362, 59877; H. C. H., p. 362, 59867; H. H., p. 362, 59872; Vice-Adm. J. B., p. 363, 59902; K. P. L., p. 362, 59865; L. U., p. 363, 59906, 128187; M., p. 362, 59869; M. A., p. 362, 59871; M. D. St. L., p. 363, 59905, 128186; Mrs. M. E. St. L., p. 492, 128183; M. F., p. 361, 59867; M. J., p. 362, 59878; Lieut.-Col. P. B., p. 362, 59874; R., p. 360, 59827, 59894; R., p. 361, 59854; Maj. Gen. R., p. 362, 59863; R. A., p. 362, 59873; R. C., p. 362, 59875; V. L., p. 360, 59831, 59898; W. L., p. 362, 59870; W. P., p. 360, 59826, 59893; W. W., p. 362, 59879
Warry, A. M., p. 534, 131399; Capt. B. A., p. 534, 131395; E. G., p. 534, 131396; G. F., p. 534, 131397; M. J., p. 570 (App.); R. A., p. 570 (App.)
Waterfield, Mrs. C. L., p. 98, 10109; H. G. O., p. 98, 10110
Waterhouse, Mrs. A. H., p. 249, 37532
Waterpark, 4th Lord, p. 543, 134898
Waterton, A. M. P., p. 97, 10096; B. R., p. 98, 10101; C., p. 97, 10091; C., p. 98, 10100; E., p. 97, 10092; E. M. P., p. 97, 10099; Rev. Canon G. W., p.

98, 10102 ; J., p. 97, 10090; J., p. 97, 10093; J. M. E. P., p. 97, 10097; M. M. C. P., p. 97, 10098; M. P. P., p. 97, 10095; T. M. M. J. P., p. 97, 10094
Wathen, Mrs. M. L., p. 425, 80266, 80410
Watkins, D. A., p. 519, 130557; Mrs. E. M., p. 519, 130554; L. T., p. 519, 130556; O. F., p. 519, 130555
Watson, A. C. R., p. 116, 10694, 11139, 41870, 42200; Rev. A. H., p. 286, 38982; B. H. F., p. 286, 38986; Mrs. C., p. 415, 79998; C. E., p. 287, 39988; C. H., p. 287, 38992; C. J. T., p. 287, 38990; Sir C. R., 3rd Bt., p. 115, 10689, 11134, 41865, 42195; D. H., p. 286, 38974, 38994; E. F. K., p. 287, 38991; Mrs. E. G., p. 287, 39006; E. S., p. 286, 38983; G. C., p. 286, 38973, 38993; G. I. A., p. 388, 71785; G. L. P., p. 287, 38989; Mrs. I. M. E. W., p. 314, 42368, 42440; J. A., p. 314, 42369, 42441; J. M. L., p. 286, 38987; L. C., p. 388, 71786; L. J., p. 287, 38995; Mrs. M. E., p. 286, 38972; Mrs. M. K., p. 388, 71784; M. Y., p. 286, 38985; O. A., p. 286, 38984; Mrs. O. F., p. 415, 79995
Watt, Mrs J. S., p. 216, 30142 ; Mrs. W. M., p. 362, 59870
Wauchope, A. J., p. 179, 27286; A. M., p. 179, 27284; C., p. 179, 27287; Rev. D. M. D., p. 179, 27283; O. S., p. 179, 27285
Wayte, G. M., p. 550, 135126; Mrs. G. M., p. 550, 135123; R. T. H., p. 550, 135125; W. G. A., p. 550, 135124
Weaver, Mrs. H. C., p. 147, 16576
Webb, Mrs. E. J., p. 296, 39508; Mrs. H. B., p. 247, 37459; Mrs. R. F., p. 167, 17610
Webber, A. R., p. 280, 38829; G. J., p. 280, 38830; G. R., p. 280, 38828; Lieut. H. A. W., p. 201, 29668; Mrs. H. E., p. 201, 29667; H. K., p. 280, 38831
Webster, Mrs. (——), p. 397, 72304; C. F. S., p. 317, 42500; E. E., p. 469, 103129; E. M., p. 469, 103130; E. O., p. 317, 42502; F. G. F., p. 469, 103117; F. H., p. 469, 103118; F. T., p. 468, 103116; H. B., p. 317, 42499; J. M., p. 207, 29873; M., p. 469, 103131; M. G., p. 317, 42501; M. G.

A., p. 317, 42505; W. P., p. 317, 42498
Weigall, Mrs. C. E. C., p. 252, 37622; D. H., p. 252, 37625; G. S. C., p. 252, 37624; R. E. C., p. 252, 37623
Weir, Capt. G. A., p. 59, 458; H. B., p. 59, 549; H. H., p. 59, 547
Welby, Lieut.-Col. A. C. E., p. 48, 261; A. E., p. 49, 287; A. M., p. 48, 263; C. E., p. 50, 321; C. E., p. 48, 259; Capt. C. E., p. 49, 285; C. E., p. 49, 288; Sir C. G. E., 5th Bt., p. 47, 243; D. G., p. 48, 246; E., p. 50, 304; E. D., p. 48, 264; E J., p. 49, 284; E. M. E., p. 48, 252; F. A., p. 48, 251; F. T. G. E., p. 49, 292; G., p. 49, 295; G. E., p. 50, 317; Capt. G. E. E., p. 48, 257; G. H. F. E., p. 50, 320; H. B., p. 49, 290; H. E., p. 49, 284; H. R. E., p. 48, 258; I. F., p. 50, 318; J. M., p. 48, 248; K. A., p. 48, 247; M., p. 49, 291; M., p. 50, 319; M. C., p. 49, 293; M. S., p. 48, 260; O. C. E., p. 48, 245; R. A. E., p. 48, 262; Capt. R. E., p. 50, 322; R. W. G., p. 48, 244; S. E., p. 50, 316; S. W. M., p. 50, 324; T. E., p. 49, 289; Rev. W. H. E., p. 48, 250
Welby-Everard, C. E., p. 48, 255; C. P. O., p. 48, 256; E. E. E., p. 48, 253; P. H. E., p. 48, 254
Wells, B. M. F., p. 259, 38057; C. E., p. 259, 38063; E. E., p. 259, 38062; E. K., p. 259, 38054; E. R., p. 259, 38053; H. L., p. 259, 38058; K. E., p. 259, 38059; L. B., p. 259, 38047; L. F., p. 259, 38048; M. B., p. 259, 38055; M. D., p. 259, 38052; R. A. G., p. 113, 10638, 11083, 41814, 42143; T. B., p. 259, 38060; V. H., p. 259, 38056; Y. H. F. G., p. 113, 10637, 11082, 41813, 62143
Wendover, Vct., p. 174, 27068
Werninck, A. M. W., p. 358, 59988, 95267; Mrs. F. G., p. 358, 59783, 95268; H. F. G., p. 358, 59787, 95266; H. V. W., p. 358, 59785, 95264; K. M. W., p. 358, 59786, 95265; P. V. W., p. 358, 59784, 95263
Wetenhall, W., p. 245, 37429
Wethered, Mrs. E., p. 276, 38661

West, Mrs. C. C., p. 305, 40314
Westenra, Hon. M., p. 157, 16831; Hon. R., p. 157, 16830; Hon. W., p. 157, 16829
Whateley, A., p. 79, 9556, 128713
Wheeler, Mrs. (——), p. 393, 72028; C. P., p. 348, 59559; Lieut.-Col. E., p. 348, 59558; J.W., p. 348, 59561; M., p. 348, 59562; P. G. L., p. 348, 59560
Wheeler-Cuffe, Maj. Sir C. F. D., 2nd Bt., p. 348, 59552; Lieut. O. F. L., p. 348, 59553
Whichcote, Sir G., 9th Bt., p. 151, 16646, 72458; H. C., p. 151, 16647, 72459; L. M. p. 151, 16648, 72460
White, Mrs. B. A., p. 319, 42568; Mrs. E. C., p. 225, 36403; Hon. Mrs. F. M., p. 103, 10229, 10328, 10362, 41405, 41504, 41537; L. O., p. 319, 42569; R. L., p. 103, 10230, 10329, 10363, 41406, 41505, 41538; Mrs. S. E., p. 38, 6; U. K., p. 319, 42570; Z. M., p. 319, 42571
Whittaker, Mrs. M. A., p. 319, 42572; O., p. 319, 42573; O., p. 568 (App.)
Whittall, Mrs. K. E., p. 259, 38049; K. M., p. 259, 38051; L. H., p. 259, 38050
Whittington-Ince, A. C., p. 87, 9858; A. L., p. 87, 9856; C. H., p. 87, 9852; E. G., p. 87, 9855; Rev. E. J. C., p. 87, 9849; E. W., p. 87, 9850; N. M., p. 87, 9857; W. B., p. 87, 9853; W. B., p. 87, 9854
Whittuck, Mrs. M. C., p. 553, 135223
Whytehead, C. J. W., p. 314, 42364, 42436; C. L. H. D., p. 314, 42370, 42442; D. H., p. 314, 42378, 42450; E. F. D., p. 314,42366, 42438; G. H., p. 314, 42377, 42449; Mrs. H. E., p. 245, 37419; H. H., p. 314, 42376, 42448; H. L., p. 314, 42373, 42445, 103274; Rev. H. R., p. 314, 42372, 42444; H. R. A., p. 314, 42363, 42435; J. L., p. 314, 42374, 42446, 103275; L. W. W., p. 314, 42365, 42437; M. A. B., p. 314, 42367, 42439; N. B., p. 245, 37420, 42362, 42434; Rev. R. L., p. 314, 42375, 42447, 103276; Mrs. S. M. L., p. 474, 103277; T. B. H., p. 314, 42361, 42433; W. W., p. 314, 42371, 42443

Index

Wickers, Mrs. C. R., p. 261, 38114
Wickham, Mrs. A., p. 45, 176; C. M. L., p. 45, 179; C. T., p. 65, 722; Rev. E. S. G., p. 45, 178; H. C., p. 65, 721; H. T., p. 65, 723; J. H. T., p. 65, 724; L. C., p. 45, 180; L. T., p. 65, 719; M. A., p. 45, 181; P. L., p. 65, 725; R. G., p. 65, 720; R. T., p. 65, 718; W. G., p. 45, 177; Capt. W. W., p. 245, 37403
Wilberforce, Mrs. A. M., p. 61, 595, 17574
Wild, Mrs. F. M. M., p. 86, 9833
Wilder, A. B., p. 343, 59447; A. H. M., p. 343, 59442; A. M., p. 343, 59448; A. V., p. 343, 59443; E., p. 344, 59451; E. I., p. 343, 59450; F. E., p. 343, 59446; F. L., p. 343, 59444; F. W., p. 343, 59441; G., p. 344, 59452; H. A. J., p. 343, 59440; Rev. H. C., p. 343, 59439; H. M., p. 343, 59449; J. C., p. 343, 59445
Wilkinson, Mrs. A., p. 350, 59607; C., p. 351, 59613; Mrs. E., p. 516, 130404, 130424, 130484, 130504; G. J., p. 350, 59609; H. N. S., p. 516, 130405, 130425, 130485, 130505; K. C., p. 516, 130406, 130426, 130486, 130506; M. H., p. 350, 59608; N., p. 516, 130407, 130427, 130487, 130507
Wilding-Jones, C., p. 57, 494, 613; C. L., p. 57, 495, 614; O. W., p. 61, 612; D. A., p. 57, 497, 616; Mrs. F., p. 57, 493; M. W., p. 61, 617; R. M., p. 57, 496, 615; V. M., p. 61, 618; W., p. 61, 611
Williams, Mrs. A. S., p. 419, 80114; C. D., p. 358, 59795, 95274; C. W. H., p. 387, 71768; D., p. 387, 71770; Mrs. E., p. 358, 59794, 95273; E., p. 387, 71769; E. A., p. 387, 71771; E. F. M., p. 267, 38276; F. W., p. 267, 38278; G., p. 267, 38277; G., p. 267, 38279; G., p. 267, 38284; G., p. 267, 38285; H. L., p. 387, 71767; J., p. 267, 38281; J. K., p. 267, 38283; J. W., p. 409, 79801; L., p. 267, 38282; Mrs. L. A., p. 267, 38275; Mrs. M. G., p. 194, 29006, 29087, 29277; P., p. 387, 71772; V. L., p. 267, 38280
Williams-Freeman, A. C., p. 82, 9742; C., p. 82, 9740; D. F., p. 82, 9739; Mrs. I. F., p. 82, 9735; Rev. L. P., p. 82, 9736; M. L., p. 82, 9738; V., p. 82, 9741; W. P., p. 82, 9737
Williamson, A. M., p. 86, 9822, 9880; C. D., p. 86, 9821, 9879; Mrs. E., p. 54, 416; Mrs. H. C., p. 86, 9816, 9874; J. C. B., p. 86, 9818, 9876; K. B., p. 86, 9819, 9877; Mrs. K. E., p. 285, 38950; K. E., p. 285, 38952; O. McD., p. 86, 9817, 9875; R. M. F., p. 285, 38953; R. W. B. R., p. 285, 38951
Willis-Fleming, E. C. A., p. 454, 95094; E. K., p. 454, 95096; I. H., p. 454, 95095; J. B. P., p. 454, 95092; R. T. C., p. 454, 95093; Mrs. V. E. A., p. 454, 95091
Willoughby, A. M., p. 139, 16153; B. D., p. 139, 16154; C. J., p. 225, 36384; K. M. S., p. 139, 16155; Hon. Mrs. M. C., p. 224, 36383; Mrs. M. E., p. 139, 16151; R. J. E., p. 139, 16152
Willoughby de Broke, 19th B., p. 443, 94581
Wills-Sandford, A. M., p. 351, 59627, 60228, 64432; A. P., p. 374, 60233, 64437; C. J., p. 374, 60245, 64449; G. M., p. 374, 60235, 64439; G. R., p. 351, 59627, 60226, 64430; M. A., p. 351, 59623, 60222, 64426; R., p. 374, 60234, 64438; T. E., p. 351, 59628, 60227, 64431; T. G., p. 351, 59626, 60215, 64419; W. R., p. 351, 59617; 60216, 64420
Wilmer, Lieut. S. T., p. 353, 59671
Wilmot, Mrs. A., p. 532, 131319
Wilson, A. C. W., p. 459, 95387 A. H., p. 172, 17850; A. N. W., p. 459, 95395; Mrs. A. W., p. 458, 95375; B. E. H., p. 459, 95401; B. F., p. 171, 17831; C. G. H., p. 459, 95385, 11630; Rev. C. H., p. 458, 95381; Hon. C. J., p. 174, 27070; Hon. C. M., p. 174, 27071; D. B., p. 172, 17849; Capt. D. D., p. 171, 17817; D. S. H., p. 459, 95384, 11629; Mrs. E. D., p. 190, 28865; Capt. E. E. B. H., p. 459, 95383, 11628; Col. E. H., p. 459, 95398; E. R., p. 458, 95378, 95412; Mrs. F. M., p. 268, 38299; Lieut. F. O'B., p. 171, 17818; G., p. 171, 17825; Lieut. G., p. 458, 95377, 95411; Capt. G. E. H.,

p. 459, 95399; G. E. M., p. 171, 17815; G. S. F., p. 172, 17851; Mrs. I. M. C., p. 40, 40, 69; Mrs. I. S. F., p. 237, 36895; J., p. 397, 72302; J. P. T., p. 459, 95396; K. M., p. 171, 17816; L., p. 172, 17856; L. G., p. 268, 38300; M. C. H., p. 459, 95386; M. F., p. 171, 17829; M. F. J., p. 171, 17814; M. L., p. 172, 17843; Mrs. M. H., p. 362, 59887; R. E. H., p. 459, 95397; R. H., p. 459, 95409; R. M., p. 459, 95408; S. D., p. 190, 28866; T., p. 458, 95376, 95410; Rev. T. H., p. 458, 95382; W. H., p. 459, 95400; Lieut. W. T. P., p. 397, 72301
Wilson-FitzGerald, F. W., p. 171, 17827; O. C., p. 171, 17828
Winchilsea, 13th E. of, p. 129, 12178, 81011; Anne, Ctss. of, p. 77, 9427
Winstanley, F., p. 475, 103309; P. M., p. 475, 103304; Maj. R. N., p. 475, 103303
Wodehouse, Lord, p. 404, 79650; Col. A., p. 405, 79662; A. F. B., p. 405, 79674; A. G., p. 406, 79694; Lieut. A. P., p. 407, 79710; Col. A. P., p. 407, 79725; Lady C., p. 405, 79661; C. F. B., p. 405, 79670; C. G., p. 407, 79706; C. J. D'E., p. 405, 79671; C. L., p. 407, 79708; C. M., p. 405, 79710; Hon. E., p. 404, 79652; E. A., p. 407, 79722; Maj. E. C. F., p. 407, 79713; E. G. S., p. 406, 79695; E. H., p. 409, 79798; Rt. Hon. E. R., p. 408, 79795; Rev. F. A., p. 407, 79715; F. A., p. 407, 79717; F. A., p. 409, 79797; Maj. F. W., p. 407, 79709; H., p. 406, 79675; H., p. 406, 79676; H. E., p. 407, 79720; H. M., p. 407, 79707; Lady J., p. 404, 79663; Lieut.-Gen. Sir J. H., p. 406, 79693; K. D. B., p. 405, 79673; K. D. L., p. 407, 79711; Col. K. R. B., p. 405, 79666; L. J., p. 407, 79726; L. M. K., p. 405, 79669; M. E., p. 407, 79719; M. J. G. B., p. 405, 79672; Lieut. N. A., p. 407, 79718; Hon. P., p. 404, 79651; P. E. B., p. 405, 79668; Lieut. P. G., p. 407, 79705; P. G., p. 407, 79723; Rev. P. J., p. 407, 79704; P. P. J., p. 407, 29721; R., p. 405, 79654; R. B., p.

405, 79667; R. L. D., p. 407, 79724; S. M., p. 407, 79712
Wolley, A. L., p. 256, 37983; E. E., p. 256, 37987; G. L. I., p. 258, 38031; Rev. H. F., p. 256, 57984; Lieut. H. S., p. 256, 37985; M. K., p. 256, 37986; M. L., p. 256, 37987; M. S., p. 256, 37988
Wonnacott, Mrs. F. J., p. 313, 42351, 42423
Wood, A. A., p. 466, 103036; A. N. L., p. 290, 39068; Mrs. B., p. 64, 715; B. H., p. 411, 79917; C. E. S., p. 351, 59621, 60220, 64424; Mrs. C. G., p. 351, 59618, 60217, 64421; C. L., p. 290, 39070; D. G., p. 411, 79916; D. M., p. 290, 39064; Mrs. E., p. 178, 27230; E., p. 290, 39065; Mrs. E., p. 411, 79914; E. E. L., p. 290, 39078; E. G., p. 466, 103033; E. H., p. 411, 79915; E. M. S., p. 351, 59620, 60219, 64423; E. S., p. 466, 103035; Mrs. F., p. 54, 422; F. M., p. 55, 452; H., p. 290, 39072; H. L., p. 290, 39069; I. L., p. 290, 39071; J., p. 290, 39066; J. C., p. 55, 451; J. K. S., p. 351, 59622, 60221, 64425; M., p. 290, 39067; Mrs. M., p. 463, 95513; Mrs. M. O., p. 466, 103032; P. B. S., p. 351, 59619, 60218, 64422; R. L., p. 290, 39073; R. O., p. 466, 103034
Woodd, Lieut. B. A., p. 109, 10391, 41567; E. A., p. 109, 10393, 41569; Mrs. E. H., p. 109, 10390, 41566; E. J., p. 109, 10392, 41568
Woods, Mrs. N. K., p. 396, 72271
Woodyatt, B. H., p. 116, 10713, 11158, 37639, 41889, 42219; E., p. 116, 10711, 11156, 37637, 41887, 42217; E. B., p. 117, 10723, 11168, 37649, 41899, 42229; F., p. 116, 10717, 11162, 37643, 41893, 42223; Capt. G. E. S., p. 116, 10714, 11159, 37640, 41890, 42220; G. Y., p. 116, 10712, 11157, 37638, 41888, 42218; H. C., p. 116, 10716, 11161, 37642, 41892, 42222; H. L. B., p. 116, 10715, 11160, 37641, 41891, 42221; Col. N. G., p. 116, 10709, 11154, 37635, 41885, 42215; R. N. G., p. 116, 10710, 11155, 37636, 41886, 42216
Woollcombe, E. M., p. 284, 38935
Woolley, H., p. 249, 37525;

Index

H. M., p. 249, 37527; L. S., p. 249, 37526; M. F., p. 249, 37524; Mrs. M. H., p. 249, 37521; P., p. 249, 37523; S., p. 249, 37522

Worlledge, Rev. A. J., p. 315, 42405, 42477; A. M., p. 315, 42407, 42479; E. C., p. 315, 42408, 42480; E. W., p. 315, 42406, 42478; Lieut. J. P. G., p. 315, 42410, 42482; O. M., p. 315, 42409, 42481

Worsley, Mrs. M. L. J., p. 112, 10596, 41772

Wrenford, Mrs. A. M., p. 124, 11554; C. R. B., p. 124, 11555

Wright, A. D., p. 167, 17626; B. O., p. 517, 130447, 130527; B. T., p. 166, 17609; Capt. C. B., p. 166, 17607; Mrs. C. M., p. 517, 130444, 130524; E. G. S., p. 167, 17620; E. H. S., p. 167, 17619; E. J., p. 167, 17637; E. M., p. 167, 17625; E. T., p. 167, 17629; F., p. 167, 17627; F. A., p. 167, 17631; F. D., p. 167, 17628; G D. L., p. 167, 17636; Rev. G. H., p. 167, 17635; G. L. S., p. 167, 17618; Capt. H. A. S., p. 167, 17617; H. D., p. 167, 17633; H. G. S., p. 167, 17622; H. S., p. 167, 17616; J. E. S., p. 167, 17621; J. H., p. 167, 17624; J. M. S., p. 167, 17623; M. F. B., p. 167, 17634; M. J., p. 167, 17632; M. N., p. 167, 17630; N., p. 166, 17608; N. N., p. 517, 130445, 130525; R. A., p. 517, 130446, 130526; T. A. E., p. 167, 17638

Wright-Armstrong, Mrs. M., p. 496, 128257, 128353

Wroughton, Lieut. A. C., p. 204, 29718, 29977; Capt. A. O. B., p. 213, 30071; B. C., p. 205, 29747, 30006; C., p. 213, 30089; C. F. M., p. 211, 30007; C. M., p. 204, 29721, 29980; C. W., p. 213, 30088; D., p. 213, 30070; D. M., p. 204, 29722, 29981; E. H., p. 204, 29717, 29976; E. M. G., p. 213, 30065; E. N. M., p. 213, 30063; F. B., p. 211, 30008; Capt. H. B., p. 211, 30014; H. B., p. 213, 30017; H. W. F., p. 213, 30062; J., p. 213, 30068; Capt. J. B., p. 204, 29716, 29975; J. H. T., p. 213, 30064; L., p. 211, 30015; L. C., p. 211, 30009; M. C., p. 204, 29720, 29979; M. E. M., p. 204, 29709, 29968; M. St. Q. M., p. 204, 29715, 29974; P. M. N., p. 204, 29707, 29966; R. C., p. 211, 30013; R. L., p. 211, 30016; S. A., p. 213, 30087; T. A., p. 213, 30066; V. B. M., p. 204, 29714, 29973; W. E., p. 213, 30069; W. H., p. 213, 30067; W. M., p. 204, 29719, 29978; Col. W. N., p. 212, 30061

Wyatt, Mrs. M., p. 533, 131392

Wylie, Mrs. A. M., p. 195, 29036, 29117, 29307

Wyndham, Mr. p. 337, 55962; B., p. 337, 55963; C. H., p. 337, 55959; E., p. 337, 55964; Mrs. E. G., p. 337, 55957; E. J. E., p. 337, 55958; E. W., p. 388, 71788; F. W., p. 337, 55960; G., p. 337, 55966; I., p. 337, 55965; J. F., p. 337, 55961; Hon. Mrs. M. M., p. 45, 191

Wynell-Mayow, B. I. S., p. 485, 103451, 103536; B. M. C., p. 484, 103432, 103516; Capt. C. E., p. 484, 103433, 103517; C. E., p. 485, 103454, 103538; C. J. S., p. 485, 103449, 103533; E., p. 484, 103446, 103530; E., p. 484, 103447, 103531; E., p. 485, 103467, 103551; E. V., p. 485, 103470, 103554; E. W., p. 485, 103452, 103536; F. L., p. 484, 103445, 103529; G., p. 485, 103453, 103537; G. M., p. 485, 103468, 103552; Rev. H., p. 484, 103441, 103525; H. S., p. 485, 103471, 103555; J. H., p. 485, 103448, 103532; K., p. 485, 103455, 103539; Maj. M., p. 484, 103429, 103513; M., p. 484, 103443, 103527; M. B. S., p. 485, 103450, 103534; M. U., p. 484, 103444, 103528; P. A. C., p. 484, 103430, 103514; Capt. P. H., p. 484, 103440, 103524; P. J., p. 484, 103442, 103526; R., p. 485, 103456, 103540; Maj. R. S. L., p. 485, 103469, 103553; U. M. E., p. 484, 103431, 103515

Wynkoop, A. G., p. 209, 29919; B. L., p. 209, 29921; F. Y., p. 209, 29920; J. Y., p. 209, 29923; Mrs. M. B., p. 209, 29918; S. V., p. 209, 29922

Wynn-Carrington, Lady A. A., p. 174, 27072; Lady J. S. M., p. 174, 27076; Lady V. A., p. 174, 27077

Wynne-Finch, A., p. 92, 9999; Mrs. E. C., p. 92, 9998; Lieut. G., p. 92, 10000; H., p. 92, 10001; H., p. 412, 79923

DE YARBURGH-BATESON, Hon. E., p. 95, 10041; Hon. G. N., p. 95, 10038; J. K., p. 95, 10040; Hon. K. H., p. 95, 10043; Hon. M. F. L., p. 95, 10037; Hon. M. L., p. 95, 10042; S. N., p. 95, 10039

Yates, A. B., p. 208, 29903; B. M., p. 208, 29902; F., p. 208, 29896; J. K., p. 208, 29897; L. B., p. 208, 29904; L. C., p. 208, 29898; M. H., p. 208, 29901; S. M., p. 208, 29912

Yeoman, A., p. 563, 135476; Capt. C. L., p. 116, 10700, 11145, 37626, 41876, 42206; Mrs. M. E., p. 563, 135474; P., p. 563, 135475; R., p. 563, 135477

York, B. P. L., p. 240, 37280; C., p. 240, 37275; Capt. E., p. 240, 37274; E. A., p. 240, 37279; F. S., p. 240, 37278; L. V. D., p. 240, 37276; M. R., p. 240, 37281; R. L., p. 240, 37277

Yorke, Mrs. F., p. 288, 39027

Young, C. R., p. 151, 16660, 72472; D. F. M., p. 305, 40313; E. G., p. 305, 40305; E. H., p. 151, 16661, 72473; E. H., p. 151, 16663, 72475; E. V., p. 151, 16664, 72476; G. F., p. 305, 40306; Mrs. G. M., p. 305, 40312; Mrs. I. J., p. 305, 40303; I. M., p. 305, 40304; J. H. E., p. 222, 36329; Mrs. J. W., p. 476, 103340; K. M., p. 151, 16662, 72474; L. L., p. 151, 16657, 72469; Mrs. M., p. 151, 16656, 72468; Mrs. M. T. L., p. 134, 16017; N. B., p. 151, 16659, 72471; R. H., p. 151, 16658, 72470

ZERFFI, H. G. W., p. 387, 71766; Mrs. L., p. 387, 71765

INDEX OF NUMBERS IN THE TUDOR, CLARENCE, EXETER, AND ESSEX VOLUMES WHICH REPEAT IN THE PRESENT.

OWING to the very great number, it has been found impossible to include in the Index to the present volume the names of those persons descended from Edward III. through the Lady Elizabeth Percy, *née* Mortimer, who at the same time have a senior descent from her brother, the Earl of March, which has been set out fully in one of the four preceding volumes. In order, however, that any person whose name appears in any of these preceding volumes may at once be able to discover whether he or she is also descended through the Mortimer-Percy line, an index to those numbers in the Tudor, Clarence, Exeter, and Essex Volumes is here given, with their equivalent number in the present book.

In order to make this quite clear, the following example may be given. If the name of Lieutenant Alexander Hood is referred to in the index to the Tudor Volume, it will be seen that his descent is through the families of Percy (Smithson), Seymour, Thynne, Finch, Seymour, Gray, Brandon, and Tudor, to Edward IV., and so to Edward III., his number being 21015. Glancing down the following index of numbers, it will be found that this number (21015) = Nos. 834, 16244, 55253, and 88156, which shows that he has, besides the descent through the Tudor line (and any other descent which can be found in the Clarence, Exeter, and Essex Volumes), four other lines of descent from Edward III. through the Mortimer-Percy marriage. These other four lines of descent can be traced by referring to the numbers in the present volume.

No. 834 occurs on page 68, and by following the line there given back to pages 68 and 67 and Table III., it will be found that the two lines merge by the marriage in 1715 of Algernon, 7th Duke of Somerset (a descendant of Edward III. through Mortimer-Percy), with Frances Thynne, a descendant of Edward III. through the Tudor line (see the Tudor Roll, Table XXIV., &c.).

No. 16244 occurs on page 143, where the paternal descent of the said Lieutenant Alexander Hood from Edward III. through Mortimer-Percy is given, the two preceding descents being through his mother, *née* Percy, the three now merging in his person.

No. 55253 occurs on page 231, and to follow this up it will be necessary to refer to the Clarence and Exeter Volumes, the said Lieutenant Hood being also descended from Edward III. through both George, Duke of Clarence, and his sister, the Duchess of Exeter; and by following the same plan it will be found that the descents are traced out until they all finally unite in the Tudor line before mentioned.

No. 88156 occurs on page 455, where the descent is traced, through the Mortimer-Percy marriage, to Thomas (Thynne), 1st Viscount Weymouth (died 1714), who married Lady Frances Finch, a Tudor descendant (see Tudor Volume, Table XXIV.).

This may sound complicated, but it is inevitable when one is dealing with thousands of persons, many of whom have a great many lines of descent. A little trouble, however, will enable any who find their names in one of the previous volumes, followed by a number which repeats below, to trace at once their line or lines of descent through the Mortimer-Percy marriage.

Index of Numbers

TUDOR ROLL

Tudor Nos.	Mortimer-Percy Nos.
19862–19899	= 39097–39134.
20048–20068	= 103282–103302.
20337–20447	= 71839–71949.
20925–20931	= 131669 = 131675.
20946–21014	= 88087–88155.
21015–21019	= 834–838, 16244–16248, 57253–57257, 88156–88160.
21020–21021	= 88161–88162.
21022–21028	= 841–847, 57260–57266, 88163–88169.
21029	= 88170.
21030–21033	= 849–852, 57268–57271, 88172–88174.
21034	= 88175.
21035–21040	= 854–859, 57273–57278, 88176–88181.
21041	= 88182.
21042–21044	= 861–863, 57280–57282, 88183–88185.
21045–21072	= 88186–88213.
21073–21075	= 895–897, 57314–57316, 88214–88216.
21076–21121	= 898–943, 57317–57362, 88217–88262.
21122	= 88263.
21123–21129	= 944–950, 57363–57369, 88264–88270.
21130–21140	= 88271–88281.
21141–21168	= 963–990, 57382–57409, 88282–88309.
21169–21176	= 991–998, 57410–57417, 79696–79703, 88310–88317.
21177–21184	= 999–1006, 57418–57425, 88318–88325.
21185–21229	= 1007–1051, 57426–57470, 88326–88370.
21230–21273	= 88371–88414.
21274–21294	= 12231–12251, 81064, 81084, 88415–88435.
21295–21326	= 88436–88467.
21327–21341	= 12216–12230, 81049–81063, 88468–88482.
21342–21377	= 88483–88518.
21378–21513	= 88519–88654, 101551–101686.
21514–21530	= 27050–27066, 88655–88671, 101687–101703.
21531–21553	= 88672–88694, 101704–101726.
21554–21653	= 88695–88794, 101727–101826.
21654–21734	= 61798–61878, 88795–88875, 101827–101907.
21735–21746	= 12197–12208, 61879–61890, 71999–72010, 81030–81041, 88876–88887, 101908–101919.
21747–22022	= 61891–62166, 88888–89163, 101920–102195.
22023–22550	= 89164–89691, 102195–102723.
22551–23254	= 13476–14179.
23255–23494	= 14180–14419, 59089–59328.
23495–23604	= 59329–59438.
23605–24117	= 14420–14932, 15470–15982.
24118–24401	= 12252–12535, 81085–81368.
24402–24519	= 1052–1169, 57471–57588; 100390–100507.
24520–24544	= 1170–1194, 28614–28638, 57589–57613, 100508–100532.
24545–25349	= 1195–1999, 57614–58418, 100533–101337.
25350–25459	= 12536–12645, 81369–81478.
25460–25479	= 12646–12665, 55501–55520, 81479–81498.
25480–25624	= 12666–12810, 81499–81643.
25625–25654	= 12811–12840, 81644–81673, 134839–134868.
25655–26006	= 12841–13192, 81674–82025.
26303–26318	= 94694–94664.
26544–26576	= 85811–85843.
27543–27950	= 17857–18264, 61128–61535.
27951–27963	= 18265–18277, 61536–61548, 94993–95005.
27964–28029	= 18278–18343, 61549–61614.
28030–28982	= 18344–19296.
28983–29129	= 19297–19443, 132687–132833.
29130–29173	= 19444–19487.
29174–29190	= 19488–19504, 78063–78079, 79572–79588.
29191–29198	= 19505–19512.
29199–29203	= 19513–19517, 78080–78084, 79598–79593.
29204–29381	= 19518–19695.
29382–29406	= 19696–19720, 36625–36649, 72429–72453.
29407–29466	= 19721–19780.
29467–29687	= 19781–20001, 128380–128600.
29688–29803	= 20002–20117.
29804–29823	= 20118–20137, 27337–27356.
29824–30219	= 20138–20533.
30220–30323	= 20534–20637, 75564–75667.
30324–30994	= 20638–21308, 58418–59088, 75668–76338, 82421–83091.
30995–31676	= 21309–21990.
31677–31702	= 21991–22016, 79836–79861.
31703–31824	= 22017–22138.
31825–31829	= 16223–16227, 22139–22143.
31830–32740	= 22144–23054.
32741–32797	= 23055–23111, 37157–37213.
32798–32923	= 23112–23237.
32924–32941	= 23238–23255, 27233–27250.
32942–32963	= 23256–23277, 27251–27272.
32964–32973	= 23278–23287 = 27273–27282.
32974–33060	= 23288–23374.
33061–33065	= 23375–23379, 40348–40352.
33066–33415	= 23380–23729.
33416–33558	= 23730–23872, 37006–37148.
33559–34121	= 23873–24435.
34122–34143	= 24436–24457, 36984–37005.
34144–35119	= 24458–25433.
35120–35139	= 25434–25453, 37949–37968.
35140–35148	= 24454–24462.
35149–35173	= 25463–25487, 55558–55582.
35174–35195	= 25488–25509.
35196–35336	= 25510–25650, 28666–28806.
35337–35705	= 25651–26019.
35706–35742	= 26020–26056.
35743–36735	= 26057–27049.

TUDOR SUPPLEMENT (ESSEX VOLUME)

Tudor Supp. Nos.	Mortimer-Percy Nos.
27542/1–27542/116	= 95120–95235.
29570/1–29570/16	= 128601–128616, 20001/1–20001/16.
34307–34310/3	= 29814–29820.

Index of Numbers

CLARENCE VOLUME

Clarence Nos.	Mortimer-Percy Nos.
1– 1502	=103600–105101.
1503– 1544	=27160–27201, 105102–105143.
1545– 1800	=105144–105399.
1801– 1807	=55587–55593, 105400–105406.
1808– 1809	=105407–105408.
1810– 1814	=55594–55598, 105409–105413.
1815– 2096	=105414–105695.
2097– 2105	=60166–60174, 64370–64378, 105696–105704.
2106– 2468	=105705–106067.
2469– 2487	=59651–59669, 106068–106086.
2488– 2599	=106087–106198.
2600– 2608	=16797–16805, 106199–106207.
2609– 3042	=106208–106641.
3043– 3058	=55936–55951, 106642–106657.
3059– 3130	=106658–106729.
3131– 3176	=29821–29866, 106730–106775.
3177– 3457	=106776–107056.
3458– 3997	=84611–85150, 107057–107596.
3998– 4019	=9345–9366, 43445–43466, 85151–85172, 107597–107618.
4020– 4023	=85173–85176, 107619–107622.
4024– 4049	=85177–85202, 95030–95055, 107623–107648.
4050– 4434	=85203–85587, 107649–108033.
4435– 4501	=108034–108100.
4502– 4613	=82309–82420, 108101–108212.
4614– 4816	=108213–108415.
4817– 4865	=10401–10449, 41577–41625, 108416–108464.
4866– 5311	=108465–108910.
5312– 5319	=86799–85806, 108911–108918.
5320– 5866	=108919–109465.
5867– 5886	=78120–78139, 79629–79648, 109466–109485.
5887– 6094	=109486–109693.
6095– 6116	=109694–109715, 134791–134812.
6117– 7787	=109716–111386.
7788– 7799	=40355–40366, 111387–111398.
7800– 8365	=111399–111964.
8366– 8393	=59453–59480, 111965–111992.
8394– 9082	=111993–112681.
9083– 9214	=35958–36089, 78140–78271, 112682–112813.
9215– 9225	=39646–39656, 77256–77266, 112814–112824.
9226– 9240	=39657–39671, 39703–39717, 77267–77281, 77313–77327, 112825–112839.
9241	=39677, 39718, 77287, 77328, 112840.
9242– 9266	=39678–39702, 77288–77312, 112841–112865.
9267– 9505	=39905–40143, 77515–77753, 112866–113104.
9506–10872	=113105–114471.
10873–10881	=36975–36983, 114472–114480.
10882–11285	=114481–114884.
11286–11289	=79924–79927, 114885–114888.
11290–11570	=114889–115169.
11571–11594	=9390–9413, 115170–115193.
11595–12328	=115194–115927.
12329–12372	=30143–30186, 115928–115971.
12373–12724	=115972–116323.
12725–12739	=29520–29534, 29760–29774, 116324–116338.
12740–14420	=116339–118019.
14421–14617	=7773–7969, 118020–118216.
14618–14628	=7970–7980, 39509–39519, 118217–118227.
14629–14643	=7981–7995, 39488–39502, 39520–39534, 118228–118242.
14644–15000	=7996–8352, 118243–118599.
15001–15122	=61006–61127, 118600–118721.
15123–15195	=118722–118794.
15196–15382	=118795–118981, 128714–128900, 129282–129468.
15383–15641	=118982–119240, 128901–129159, 129469–129727.
15642–16288	=119241–119887.
16289–16303	=38708–38722, 119888–119902.
16304–19066	=119903–122665.
19067–19104	=10111–10148, 122666–122703.
19105–19658	=122704–123257.
19659–19679	=103227–103247, 123258–123278.
19680–20242	=123279–123841.
20243–20761	=83092–83610, 123842–124360.
20762–20779	=83611–83628, 134880–134897, 124361–124378.
20780–20851	=83629–83700, 124379–124450.
20852–21327	=124451–124926.
21328–21498	=94730–94900, 124927–125097.
21499–21515	=94901–94917, 94950–94966, 125098–125114.
21516–22807	=125115–126406.
22808–23151	=43482–43825.
23152–23282	=43826–43956, 77857–77987, 79366–79496.
23283–23354	=43957–44028, 77754–77825, 77988–78059, 79263–79334, 79497–79568.
23355–23486	=44029–44160, 72535–72666.
23487–24240	=44161–44914.
24241–24443	=10775–10977, 44915–45117.
24444–24543	=45118–45217.
24544–24573	=45218–45247, 94692–94721.
24574–25395	=45248–46069.
25396–26138	=27417–28159, 46070–46812.
26139–26185	=9509–9555, 28160–28206, 46813–46859, 128666–128712.
26186–26281	=28207–28302, 46860–46955.
26282–26530	=28303–28551, 46956–47204.
26531–26757	=47205–47431.
26758–26762	=17499–17503, 47432–47436.
26763–26862	=47437–47536.
26863–26865	=17592–17594, 47537–47539.
26866–26907	=47540–47581.
26908–27008	=47582–47682, 83806–83906.
27009–27995	=47683–48669.
27996–28039	=48670–48713, 65210–65253.
28040–28053	=40446–40459, 48714–48727, 65254–65267, 127368–127381.
28054–28117	=38574–38637, 40460–40523, 48728–48791, 65268–65331, 127382–127445.
28118–28836	=40524–41242, 48792–49510, 65332–66050, 127446–128164.
28837–28849	=41243–41255, 49511–49523, 66051–66063, 71045–71057, 128165–128177.
28850–30078	=49524–50752.
30079–30087	=50753–50761, 72218–72226, 72323–72331.
30088–31936	=50762–52610.

CLARENCE SUPPLEMENT (ESSEX VOLUME)

Clarence Supp. Nos.	Mortimer-Percy Nos.
1324/209–1324/291	=72333–72415.
9240/1–9240/5	=39672–39676, 39717/1–39717/5, 77282–77286, 77327/1–77327/5, 112839/1–112839/5.
21679/53–21679/62	=16818–16827.
23486/1–23486/100	=131409–131508.

Index of Numbers

EXETER VOLUME

Exeter Nos.	Mortimer-Percy Nos.
1– 106	= 91782–91887, 91927–92032.
107– 145	= 92033–92071.
146– 177	= 119–150, 92072–92103.
178– 508	= 92104–92434.
509– 525	= 92435–92451, 132620–132636, 134813–134829.
526– 532	= 92452–92458, 132637–132643.
533– 565	= 92459–92491, 132644–132676, 135253–135285.
566– 574	= 92492–92500, 132677–132685.
575– 899	= 92501–92825.
900– 929	= 92826–92855, 131720–131749.
930– 940	= 92856–92866, 131750–131760, 135057–135067.
941– 1239	= 92867–93165, 131761–132059.
1240– 1263	= 93166–93189, 103489–103512, 103573–103596, 132060–132083.
1264– 1454	= 93190–93380, 132084–132274.
1455– 1497	= 16367–16409, 93381–93423, 132275–132317.
1498– 1618	= 93424–93544, 132318–132438.
1619– 1645	= 93545–93571, 132593–132619.
1646– 1974	= 93572–93900.
1975– 1980	= 27357–27362, 93901–93906.
1981– 2470	= 93907–94396.
2471– 2900	= 126407–126836.
2901– 2903	= 80188–80190, 80332–80334, 126837–126839.
2904– 2912	= 126840–126848.
2923– 3430	= 126860–127367.
3846– 5448	= 97459–99061.
5449– 5574	= 11991–12116, 80824–80949, 99062–99187.
5575– 6401	= 99188–100014.
6402– 6413	= 9370–9381, 43470–43481, 100015–100026.
6414– 6637	= 100027–100250.
6638– 6645	= 37149–37156, 100251–100258.
6646– 6776	= 100259–100389.
7100– 7110	= 16109–16119.
7263– 7269	= 16309–16315.
7271– 7277	= 16339–16345.
7652– 7738	= 11904–11990, 60736–60822, 64940–65026, 71058–71144, 80737–80823.
7739– 8318	= 71145–71724.
8448– 8702	= 55676–55930.
8843– 9108	= 11638–11903, 80471–80736, 133676–133941.
9109– 9115	= 17110–17116, 55494–55500, 133942–133948.
9116– 9155	= 17117–17156, 133949–133988.
9156– 9207	= 11729–11780, 17157–17208, 42230–42281, 133989–134040.
9208– 9244	= 17209–17245, 42282–42318, 134041–134077.
9245– 9497	= 17246–17498, 134078–134330.
9498– 9607	= 134331–134440.
9608– 9631	= 13193–13216, 82026–82049, 94613–94636, 13441–13464.
9632– 9688	= 13217–13273, 82050–82106, 134465–134521.
9689– 9730	= 13274–13315, 37650–37691, 82107–82148, 134522–134563.
9731– 9740	= 13316–13325, 37598–37607, 37691–37700, 82149–82158, 134564–134573.
9741– 9763	= 13326–13348, 37701–37724, 82159–82181, 134574–134596.
9764– 9778	= 13349–13363, 37725–37739, 40203–40217, 82182–82196, 134610–134624.
9779– 9798	= 13364–13383, 36656–36675, 37740–37759, 82197–82216, 134625–134644.
9799– 9885	= 13384–13470, 37760–37846, 82217–82303, 134645–134731.
9886– 9890	= 13472–13475, 82304–82308, 134732–134736.

Exeter Nos.	Mortimer-Percy Nos.
10900–10943	= 85588–85631.
10944–10947	= 85632–85635, 134779–134782.
10048–11110	= 85636–85798.
11625–11646	= 10597–10618, 11042–11063, 41773–41794, 42103–42124.
11740–13755	= 52611–54626, 132834–133675/1174.
13756–13799	= 54627–54670, 78705–78748, 133675/1175–133675/1218.
13800–14581	= 54671–55452, 133675/1219–133675/2000.
14681–14791	= 91671–91781.
14808–14882	= 55601–55675.
15216–15243	= 36427–36454.
19416–19439	= 38313–38336.
19440–19444	= 38337–38341, 39092–39096, 39138–39142.
19445–19495	= 38342–38392.
23949–23984	= 91336–91371.
23985–24031	= 16250–16296, 91372–91418.
24032–24138	= 91419–91525.
24139–24151	= 91526–91538, 103098–103110.
24152–24283	= 91539–91670.
24284–24535	= 35706–35957, 90415–90666.
24536–24543	= 38305–38312, 40367–40374, 90667–90674.
24544–24569	= 40375–40400, 90675–90700.
24570–24614	= 39601–39645, 40401–40445, 90701–90745.
24615–25120	= 90746–91251.
25121–25163	= 91252–91294, 131342–131384.
25164–25204	= 91295–91335.
25205–25860	= 95524–96179.
25861–25927	= 10490–10556, 41666–41732, 96180–96246.
25928–26240	= 96247–96559.
26241–26746	= 96953–97458.
26747–26852	= 2000–2105, 63560–63665, 72667–72772.
26853–26874	= 2106–2127, 63666–63687, 72773–72794, 79802–79823.
26875–27057	= 2128–2310, 15257–15439, 61615–61797, 63688–63870, 72795–72977.
27058–27087	= 2311–2340, 15440–15469, 63871–63900, 72978–73007.
27088–27271	= 2341–2524, 63901–64084, 73008–73191.
27272–28169	= 2525–3422, 66064–66961, 73192–74089, 76352–77249.
32552–33268	= 56186–56902.
33269–33303	= 27092–27126, 56903–56937.
33304–33533	= 56938–57167.
34237–34434	= 130130–130327.
34734–34997	= 11244–11507.
34998–35014	= 36342–36358.
35653–35677	= 37249–37273.
36503–36558	= 36919–36974.
36724–37038	= 36090–36404, 78272–78586.
41433–41753	= 60262–60582, 64466–64786.
41754–41759	= 12143–12148, 60583–60588, 64787–64792, 80976–80981.
41760–41780	= 60608–60628, 64812–64832.
42058–42430	= 84238–84610.
44310–44711	= 129728–130129.
44910–44914	= 38889–38893.
48488–48739	= 78915–79166.
48740–48777	= 39548–39585, 79167–79204.
48778–48820	= 79205–79247.
48821–48835	= 39586–39600, 79248–79262.
48976–48993	= 36676–36693, 37891–37908, 39143–39160.
48994–49004	= 36694–36704, 37404–37414, 37909–37919, 39161–39171.
49005–49015	= 36705–36715, 37920–37930, 39172–39182.
49016–49258	= 90172–90414.
49448–49476	= 130744–130772.
49541–49561	= 9615–9635, 9662–9682.

Index of Numbers

Exeter Nos.	Mortimer-Percy Nos.
49562–49564	= 9636–9638, 9683–9685, 39545–39547.
49565–49587	= 9639–9661, 9686–9708.
49588–49617	= 41256–41285.
49618–49656	= 41286–41324, 91888–91926.
49657–49683	= 41948–41974.
49684–49747	= 10978–11041, 41975–42038, 42039–42102.
49748–49773	= 39739–39764, 77349–77374, 78749–78774.
49774–49891	= 30187–30304, 39765–39882, 77375–77492, 78587–78704, 78775–78892.
49892–49913	= 39883–39904, 77493–77514, 78893–78914.
50255–50274	= 42667–42686.
50275–50080	= 42687–43092.
51408–51415	= 72019–72026.
51968–52174	= 30341–30547.
52175–52180	= 30548–30553, 36650–36655.
52181–52197	= 30554–30570.
52198–52203	= 30571–30676, 41934–41939, 43127–43132.
52204–53021	= 30577–31394.
53022–53040	= 28573–28591, 31395–31413.
53041–53043	= 28592–28594, 31414–31416, 59555–59557.
53044–53062	= 28595–28613, 31417–31435.
53063–53562	= 31436–31935.
53563–53667	= 31936–32040, 62521–62625.
53668–54165	= 32041–32538.

Exeter Nos.	Mortimer-Percy Nos.
54166–54395	= 9115–9344, 32539–32768, 43215–43444.
54396–55516	= 32769–33889.
55517–55597	= 8353–8433, 33890–34069.
55598–55673	= 8434–8509, 33971–34046, 36813–36888.
55674–55762	= 8510–8598, 34047–34135.
55763–55769	= 8599–8605, 28872–28878, 29143–29149, 34136–34142.
55770–56278	= 8606–9114, 34143–34651.
56279–57147	= 34652–35520.
57148–57160	= 35521–35533, 94600–94612.
57161–57172	= 35534–35545, 94637–94648.
57173–57241	= 35546–35614.
57242–57295	= 35615–35668, 40218–40271.
57296–57321	= 35669–35694, 40272–40297.
57322–57332	= 35695–35705.
57387–57391	= 39085–39089, 79753–79757.
57392–57428	= 79758–79794.
57430–57442	= 95487–95499.
57567–57600	= 28947–28980, 29218–29251.
57769–57862	= 29333–29426.
57863–57876	= 28928–28941, 29199–29212, 29427–29440.
57877–57893	= 29441–29457.
57894–57897	= 29842–29845, 29213–29216, 29458–29461.
57898–57955	= 29462–29519.
58067–58078	= 42337–42348.
58308–58527	= 39719–39738, 77329–77348.
58365–58390	= 12117–12142, 80950–80975.

EXETER SUPPLEMENT (ESSEX VOLUME)

Exeter Supp. Nos.	Mortimer-Percy Nos.
1618/1 – 1618/154	= 93544/1–93544/154, 131509–131662, 132439–132592.
2470/1 – 2470/183	= 94397–94679.
2913 – 2922/1	= 126849–126859.
9763/1 – 9763/13	= 13349/1–13349/13, 37724/1–37724/13.
9890/92 – 9890/99	= 13475/92–13475/99, 128285–128265, 128354–128361.
52020/1 – 52020/58	= 9557–9614.
56226/216–56226/229	= 596–609, 9062/216–9062/229, 17575–17588, 34599/216–34599/229.

Exeter Supp. Nos.	Mortimer-Percy Nos.
56226/230–56226/252	= 9062/230–9062/252, 34599/230–34599/252.
56226/253–56226/271	= 9062/253–9062/271, 34599/253–34599/271, 95236–95254.
57522/1 – 57522/9	= 79664–79692.
57622/551–57622/590	= 131017–131056.
57622/591–57622/753	= 130583–130727, 130808–130952, 131057–131201.
57622/736–57622/751	= 130953–130968, 131202–131217.

EXETER SUPPLEMENT (MORTIMER-PERCY VOLUME —PART I.)

Exeter Supp. Nos.	Mortimer-Percy Nos.
1263/1 –1263/84	= 93189/1–93189/84, 132084/1–132084/84.
1263/85–1263/86	= 93189/85–93189/86, 93189/135–93189/136, 132084/85–132084/86.
1263/87–1263/147	= 93189/87–93189/147, 132084/87–132084/147.

Exeter Supp. Nos.	Mortimer-Percy Nos.
1263/148–1263/149	= 9453–9454, 93189/148–93189/149, 132084/148–132084/149.
1263/150–1263/223	= 93189/150–93189/223, 132084/150–132084/223.

ESSEX VOLUME

Essex Nos.	Mortimer-Percy Nos.
4544– 5512	= 85943–86911.
5513– 5619	= 16433–16539, 86912–87018.
5620– 5713	= 56092–56185, 87019–87112.
5714– 6482	= 87113–87881.
6483– 6489	= 60246–60252, 64450–64456, 87882–87888.
6490– 6687	= 87889–88086.

Essex Nos.	Mortimer-Percy Nos.
9363– 9375	= 3423–3435, 76339–76351.
9376–13712	= 3436–7772.
15509–15556	= 59986–60033, 60037–60084, 62470–62517, 64190–64237, 64241–64288.
15690–15702	= 38447–38459, 38506–38508j.
16037–16055	= 38809–38827.

Index of Numbers

Essex Nos.	Mortimer-Percy Nos.
16212–16318	= 60629–60735, 64833–64939.
16461–16490	= 29612–29641.
17211–17243	= 56059–56091, 11169–11201.
17244–17285	= 90067–90108, 11202–11243.
18189–19053	= 62670–63534.
19054–19078	= 63535–63559, 135189–135213.
20495–20541	= 9462–9508, 128619–128665.
21135–22907	= 66962–68734.
22908–23662	= 68735–69489, 74090–74844.
23663–23795	= 16865–16997, 69490–69622, 74845–74977.
23796–24012	= 69623–69839, 74978–75194.
24013–24014	= 55599–55600, 69840–69841, 75195–75196.
24015–24381	= 69842–70208, 75197–75563.
24382–25217	= 70209–71044.
26449–26468	= 14933–14952.
26506–26809	= 14953–15256.

Essex Nos.	Mortimer-Percy Nos.
29531–29713	= 60823–61005, 65027–65209.
30015–30084	= 85845–85914.
30085–30098	= 85915–85928, 85929–85942.
30328–30364	= 773–809, 57192–57228.
30974–31025	= 72132–72183.
32334–32338	= 40326–40330.
32716–32817	= 72030–72131.
33109–33254	= 62167–62312, 102724–102869.
33255–33266	= 17097–17108, 62313–62324, 102870–102881.
33267–33411	= 62325–62469, 102882–103026.
33493–33589	= 36716–36812.
35486–35502	= 38528–38544.
35503–35519	= 16728–16744, 38545–38561.
35520–35531	= 38562–38573.
35574–35605	= 78085–78116, 79594 79625.
36474–36480	= 71725–71731.

ESSEX SUPPLEMENT (MORTIMER-PERCY VOLUME—PART I.)

Essex Supp. Nos.	Mortimer-Percy Nos.
32817/24–32817/27	= 80200–80203.
32817/85	= 11588.

The Exeter Volume

SUPPLEMENT

SUPPLEMENTARY TABLE OF EXETER AND ESSEX DESCENTS CONTAINED IN SUPPLEMENT

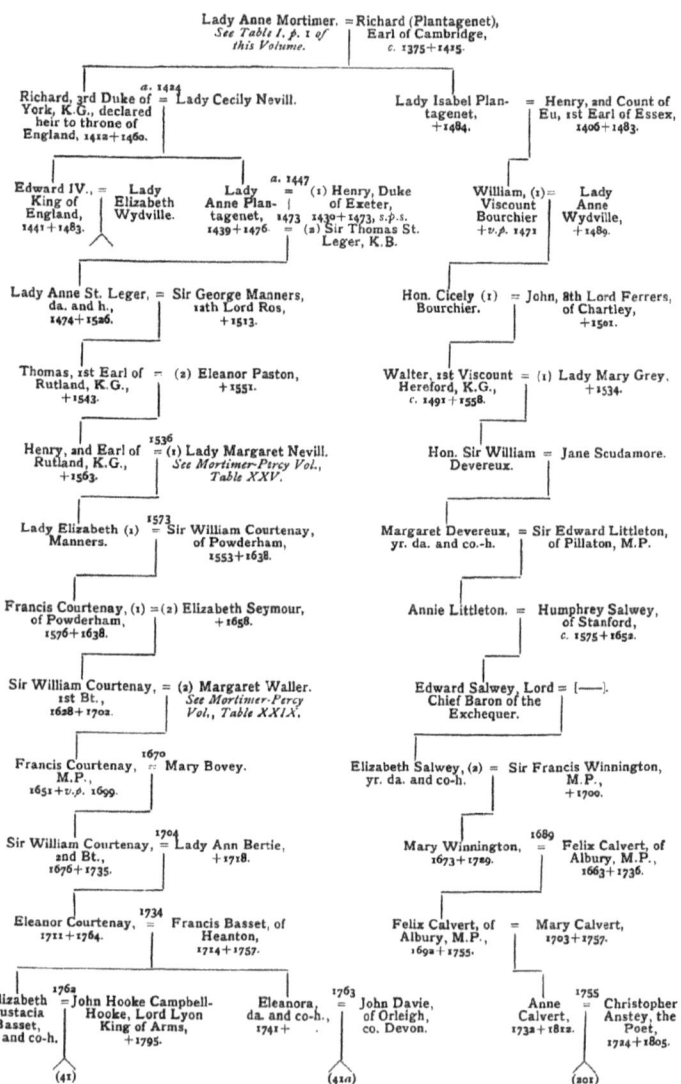

THE EXETER VOLUME

SUPPLEMENT

Pages 110-112. Delete Section 41 and in place thereof read—

41. Descendants of ELIZABETH EUSTACIA BASSET (Supplementary Table), *d.* (-); *m.* 31 July or 1 Aug. 1762, JOHN HOOKE CAMPBELL, *afterwards* CAMPBELL-HOOKE, of Bangeston, co. Pembroke, Lord Lyon King of Arms 1754–1795 [E. of Argyll Coll. and uncle of John, 1st Lord Cawdor [G.B.]], *d.* 1 Sept. 1795; and had issue (with 2 sons and a da. who *d.s.p.*) 1*a* to 2*a*.

    1*a. Charlotte Campbell-Hooke, da. and co-h.,* b. *c.* 1768; d. 8 *Jan.* 1849; m. *as 2nd wife,* 22 *Sept.* 1796, *Sir Thomas Gage of Hengrave,* 6*th Bt.* [*E.*], d. 1 *Dec.* 1798; *and had issue* 1*b to* 2*b.*
    1*b.* Lucy Gage.
    2*b. Emma Gage,* d. 17 *June* 1845; m. 31 *July* 1826, *John Collett, M.P.* [*son of Ebenezer John Collett of Locker's House, Hemel Hempstead*]; *and had issue* 1*c.*
    1*c.* Charlotte Eustacia Collett.

    2*a. Louisa Caroline Hooke Campbell, da. and co-h.,* b. 18 *Sept.* 1773; d. *at Manchester* 31 *Mar.* 1863; m. 25 *Aug.* 1798, *Henry Hulton, Lieut.-Col. Comdg. Blackburne Mil.* [3*rd son of William Hulton of Hulton Park, co. Lanc.*], b. 27 *Nov.* 1765; d. *Sept.* 1831; *and had issue (with* 3 *sons and* 3 *das.* d.s.p.) 1*b to* 4*b.*
    1*b. William Adam Hulton of Hurst Grange, Preston, J.P., D.L., Bar.-at-Law, Judge of County Courts,* b. 18 *Oct.* 1802; d. 3 *Mar.* 1887; m. 15 *Sept.* 1832, *Dorothy Anne, da. of Edward Gorst of Preston,* d. 1 *May* 1886; *and had issue* 1*c to* 5*c.*
    1*c.* Rev. Henry Edward Hulton, M.A. (Oxon.), Rural Dean of Chelmsford (1886) and Hon. Canon of St. Albans (1900), *formerly* Vicar of Great Waltham 1876–1906 (*Boreham Manor, Chelmsford*), *b.* 21 June 1839; *unm.*
    2*c.* Frederick Campbell Hulton, Clerk of the Peace, co. Lancaster, *b.* 23 June 1841.
    3*c.* George Eustace Hulton, *b.* 14 July 1842.
    4*c.* Alyne Louisa Elizabeth Hulton (*Catisfield Lodge, Fareham*), *m.* 6 Aug. 1874, James Mathias [son of Lewis Mathias of Lamphey Court, Pembrokeshire], *d.* 3 June 1886; and has issue 1*d* to 4*d.*
    1*d.* William Delamotte Mathias, *b.* 29 May 1877.
    2*d.* James Herbert Mathias, *b.* 8 Sept. 1881.
    3*d.* Maria Frederica Mathias.
    4*d.* Dorothy Alyne Louisa Mathias.
    5*c.* Mary Caroline Hulton.
    2*b.* Rev. Campbell Bassett Arthur Grey Hulton, *Hulme Exr., Oxford, Ellerton* [Nos. 1263/1 to 1263/10.

The Plantagenet Roll

Prize, 2nd Class, Rector of Emberton, co. Bucks, 1860–1878, b. 3 May 1813; d. 30 Ap. 1878; m. 27 Mar. 1845, Sarah Stokes, da. of Samuel Fletcher of Manchester, d. 4 July 1876; and had issue 1c to 13c.

    1c. Campbell Arthur Grey Hulton of Manchester, Merchant (*Hotel Metropole, London*), b. 16 Mar. 1846; m. 21 Ap. 1875, Florence, da. of James Burton of Tyldesley, d. 12 Ap. 1898; and has issue 1d to 3d.

    1d. Rev. Campbell Blethyn Hulton, Rector of Turvey (*Turvey Rectory, Beds*), b. 30 May 1877; m. 5 Aug. 1903, Dorothy, da. of John Heelis of Manchester, s.p.

    2d. Roger Adam Hulton, b. 29 July 1878.

    3d. John Meredith Hulton, Lieut. Royal Sussex Regt., b. 8 Jan. 1882.

    2c. Jessop Henry Fletcher Hulton, of Messrs. Fullager, Hulton, Bailey & Co. of Bolton, Solicitors (*Astley House, Bolton*), b. 17 Oct. 1848; m. 1st, 16 Aug. 1875, Eleanor Brada, da. of the Rev. Samuel Simpson of Lancaster, d. 4 Feb. 1887; 2ndly, 2 July 1895, Blanche, da. of Simon Martin, B.C.S.; and has issue 1d to 3d.

    1d. Jessop Arthur Hulton, served in South African War as Lieut. Railway Staff Corps, b. 3 Aug 1878; m. Anabel, da. of (—) Jones of Birmingham.

    2d. Charles Edward Hulton, Solicitor, b. 26 Ap. 1881.

    3d.[1] Brada Hulton, m. 15 Aug. 1901, Spencer Hogg, Bar.-at-Law (*Orchard House, Altrincham*); and has issue 1e to 2e.

    1e. Jessop Martin Spencer Hogg, b. 3 Dec. 1903.

    2e. Brada Elizabeth Spencer Hogg.

    3c. William Stokes Hulton, Artist (6383 *Calle della Testa, SS. Giovanni e Paolo, Venice*), b. 23 Oct. 1852; m. 1886, Constanza Maria Orsola, da. of Vincenzo Mazini; and has issue 1d to 2d.

    1d. Gioconda Hulton, b. 5 Oct. 1887.

    2d. Edith Teresa Hulton, b. 6 Aug. 1890.

    4c. Henry Hulton, of the Fiji Islands, Planter, b. 5 Feb. 1854; d. unm. 9 Dec. 1883.

    5c. Reginald Edward Hulton, Engineer (*Brynhir, Tenby*), b. 10 June 1857; m. 16 Sept. 1886, Sydney Alice, da. of the Rev. E. Cadogan; and has issue 1d to 2d.

    1d. Edward Campbell Hulton, b. 19 Sept. 1898.

    2d. Mary Hulton.

    6c. Charles Copley Hulton, b. 12 Jan. 1860; unm.

    7c. Samuel Fletcher Hulton, Bar.-at-Law, Author of *Rixæ Oxoniensis*, &c. (10 *King's Bench Walk, Temple, E.C.*), b. 20 Feb. 1862; unm.

    8c. Frederick Courtenay Longuet Hulton, Major 1st King's Dragoon Guards, b. 14 Mar. 1864; m. 16 June 1895, Nelly, da. of (—) Darvel; and has issue 1d.

    1d. Rowena Hulton.

    9c. Mary Louisa Hulton (40 *Cadogan Place, S.W.*), m. 14 Ap. 1869, William Clarence Watson, Ottoman Vice-Consul in London, d. 7 Feb. 1906; and has issue 1d to 9d.

    1d. William Donald Paul Watson, b. 19 Ap. 1872.

    2d. Hugh Gordon Watson, b. 13 Ap. 1874.

    3d. Edith Campbell Watson.

    4d. Margaret Louisa Watson.

    5d. Evelyn Mary Watson.

    6d. Sylvia Maud Watson.

    7d. Helen Lilias Watson

    8d. Cicely Cunninghame Watson.

    9d. Violet Watson.

    10c. Sarah Beatrice Hulton, m. 9 Jan. 1878, the Rev. George Frederick Sams, M.A. (Camb.), Rector of Emberton (*Emberton Rectory, Newport-Pagnell, Bucks*); and has issue 1d to 7d.   [Nos. 1263/11 to 1263/41.

# of The Blood Royal

1*d*. Frederick Edward Barwick Hulton Sams, *b.* 22 Nov. 1881.
2*d*. Cecil Henry Hulton Sams, *b.* 9 Mar. 1883.
3*d*. Kenneth Assheton Hulton Sams, *b.* 26 Oct. 1884.
4*d*. Mona Beatrix Hulton Sams, *m.* 14 Ap. 1909, Henry Johnston Carson (*Belvedere, Upper Drive, Hove*).
5*d*. Elsie Campbell Hulton Sams.
6*d*. Florence Marjorie Hulton Sams, *m.* 16 Sept. 1908, Sir William George Eden Wiseman, 10th Bt. [E.] [see Exeter Volume, p. 397] (*Holyport, Berks*).
7*d*. Sidney Alyne Hulton Sams.

11*c*. Harriet Alyne Hulton, *m.* 7 Aug. 1879, Richard Freer Austin, of Messrs. Austin & Austin of 3 and 4 Clement's Inn, London, Solicitors (6H *Hyde Park Mansions, Marylebone Road, N.W.*), *s.p.*

12*c*. Gertrude Jane Hulton, *m.* 5 June 1888, the Rev. Reginald Illingworth Woodhouse, Rector of Merstham (*Merstham Rectory, Surrey*); and has issue 1*d* to 3*d*.

1*d*. Reginald Courtenay Hulton Woodhouse.
2*d*. Gertrude Helen Hulton Woodhouse.
3*d*. Rosamund Hulton Woodhouse.

13*c*. Edith Helen Hulton, *m.* 10 July 1889, Edward Grant of Lichborough, M.A. (Oxon.), J.P., D.L., High Sheriff of Northants 1893, Alderman of the County Council and Lord of the Manor and Patron of Maidford (*Lichborough Hall, Weedon*); and has issue 1*d* to 3*d*.

1*d*. Edith Muriel Grant, *b.* 21 Aug. 1890.
2*d*. Violet Helen Grant, *b.* 11 Aug. 1891.
3*d*. Frances Enid Grant, *b.* 20 May 1898.

3*b*. *Louisa Caroline Mary Anne Hulton*, b. *at Pembroke* 9 *Aug.* 1799; d. *at Preston* 15 *Aug.* 1825; m. *there* 21 *June* 1823, *John Addison of Preston, Bar.-at-Law, Recorder of Clitheroe and a County Court Judge*, b. 21 *Ap.* 1794; d. *at Preston* 14 *July* 1859; *and had issue* 1*c*.

1*c*. *Anne Agnes Addison, da. and h.*, b. 1 *Aug.* 1824; d. *at 29 Sussex Gardens, London,* 14 *Feb.* 1900; m. *at Preston* 15 *Oct.* 1845, *Gen. John ffolliot Crofton, Col. 6th Reg.* [*Bt. of Mohill* [*U.K.*] *Coll.*], b. 9 *Oct.* 1802; d. *at 29 Sussex Gardens a/sd.* 17 *July* 1885; *and had issue* 1*d* to 4*d*.

1*d*. *Rev. Addison Crofton, M.A.* (Oxon.), b. 13 *July* 1846; d. *at Genoa* 12 *Jan.* 1904; m. 7 *Aug.* 1873, *Mary Pilkington, da. of John Hall of Baldingstone,* d. 7 *May* 1903; *and had issue* 1*e* to 2*e*.

1*e*. Annie Crofton
2*e*. Sydney d'Abzac Crofton } (*Linton Court, Settle, Yorkshire*).

2*d*. Henry Thomas Crofton, Solicitor (*Oldfield, Maidenhead*), *b.* 23 July 1848; *m.* 7 Sept. 1871, Martha Pilling, da. of Joseph M'Keand; and has issue 1*e* to 4*e*.

1*e*. John ffolliott Frederick Crofton, Solicitor, *late* Capt. 3rd Vol. Batt. Cheshire Regt., *b.* 1 Jan. 1877.

2*e*. *Josephine Christie Crofton*, d. 20 *May* 1906; m. 7 *Sept.* 1897, *Herman Barker-Hahlo* (*Foxlease Park, Lyndhurst*); *and had issue* 1*f* to 3*f*.

1*f*. John Francis Crofton Barker-Hahlo, *b.* 2 Oct. 1901.
2*f*. Alice Christine Barker-Hahlo.
3*f*. Frances Natalie Barker-Hahlo.

3*e*. Alice Addison Crofton.
4*e*. Gladys Noelle Crofton.

3*d*. Rev. William d'Abzac Crofton, M.A. (Oxon.), Vicar of Codicote (*Codicote Vicarage, Welwyn, Herts*), *b.* 3 June 1854; *unm.*

4*d*. *Caroline Anne Agnes Crofton*, b. *at 29 Sussex Gardens, London,* 27 *Jan.* 1852; d. *at Liverpool* 2 *Jan.* 1880; m. *at St. James', Paddington,* 21 *Jan.* 1879, *Ralph Cririe Clayton of Liverpool,* d. *in Jermyn Street, London,* 13 *Sept.* 1904; *and had issue* 1*e*.

[Nos. 1263/42 to 1263/67.]

The Plantagenet Roll

1e. Gerald Edward Cririe Clayton, M.A. (Oxon.), Bar.-at-Law (*Pen-ar-wel, Llanbedrog, Wales*), b. at Liverpool 27 Dec. 1879; m. at St. James', Spanish Place, London, 28 Ap. 1908, Violet Alice Ione, da. of Baron Oscar de Satgé de Thoren; and has issue 1f.

1f. Ralph Dominic de Satgé Clayton, b. 18 Feb. 1909.

4b. Anne Beatrice Hulton, b. 1 Sept. 1804; d. at Manchester 19 Sept. 1866; m. at *Moreton-in-Marsh* 21 Ap. 1840, the Rev. Samuel Farmer Sadler, d. at *Blackpool* 31 Oct. 1862; and had issue 1c.

1c. Samuel Campbell Hulton Sadler, Deputy-Clerk of the Peace for co. Lancaster, b. 14 Nov. 1842; d. at Southport 5 Aug. 1904; m. in London 30 Nov. 1867, Annie, da. of Nelson Cain, d. 22 Dec. 1887; and had issue 1d to 8d.

1d. Talfourd Hayes Sadler (*Bronx, New York, U.S.A.*), b. 23 Sept. 1868; *unm.*

2d. Reginald Cobham Sadler (*Mabel Lake, Lumby, British Columbia*), b. 2 Ap. 1874; m. 24 June 1906, Mary, da. of (—) Hanson.

3d. Catherine Annie Sadler, m. at Southport 3 Ap. 1902, Herbert Foyster, of Messrs. Foyster, Waddington & Foyster of Manchester, Solicitors (*Bramcote, Parkfield Road, Didsbury*); and has issue 1e.

1e. Eileen Selma Foyster.

4d. Gertrude Muriel Sadler, m. 15 Feb. 1908, Charles Henry Marriot Wharton, Bar.-at-Law (3 *Wellington Street East, Broughton, Manchester*), s.p.

5d. Edith Beatrix Sadler, m. 10 July 1902, Charles Henry Gardner, Banker (244 *Upper Chorlton Road, Manchester*).

6d. Eleanor Louisa Sadler, *unm.*

7d. Mabel Cecilia Sadler, m. 8 Oct. 1903, the Rev. Edward William Whitley, B.A., Rector of Framilode (*Framilode Rectory, Stonehouse, Glos.*); and has issue 1e.

1e. Edward Campbell Rodbard Whitley.

8d. Florence Winifred Sadler, *unm.* [Nos. 1263/68 to 1263/79.

41a. Descendants of ELEANORA BASSET (Supplementary Table), b. at Heanton Punchardon 9 June 1741; d. (–); m. at Atherington 18 Aug. 1763, JOHN DAVIE of Orleigh, Buckland Brewer, co. Devon, d. (–); and had issue (with 3 other sons and 2 das. who d. unm.) 1a to 9a.

1a. Joseph Davie, afterwards (1803) Basset, of Watermouth and Umberleigh, b. 18 May 1764; d. 10 Dec. 1846; m. 1799, Mary, da. of Christopher Irwin of Barnstaple, d. 21 Ap. 1862; and had issue 1b to 4b.

1b. Arthur Davie Basset of Watermouth, b. 14 May 1801; d. 8 Dec. 1870; m. 4 Dec. 1828, Harriet Sarah, da. of Thomas Smith Crawfurth, b. 14 July 1806; d. 18 Dec. 1863; and had issue 1c to 2c.

1c. Rev. Arthur Crawfurth Davie Basset of Watermouth, M.A., b. 11 Aug. 1830; d. unm. 23 Ap. 1880.

2c. Harriet Mary Basset of Umberleigh and Watermouth (*Watermouth Castle, Ilfracombe; Umberleigh, Atherington, &c.*), m. 7 Jan. 1858, Charles Henry Williams, now (R.L. 11 Oct. 1880) Basset, J.P., D.L., Major N. Devon Hussars [son of Sir William Williams, 1st Bt. [U.K.]], d. 1 Feb. 1908; and has issue 1d to 2d.

1d. Walter Basset, Lieut. R.N., b. 20 Sept. 1863; d. 27 May 1907; m. 18 Nov. 1890, Ellen Caroline Charlotte, da. of Adm. Sir William Montague Dowell, G.C.B.

2d. Edith Basset Basset, m. 18 Oct. 1882, Capt. Ernest Charles Penn Curzon [E. Howe Coll.], *late* 18th Hussars; and has issue 1e to 2e.

1e. Charles Ernest Basset Lothian Curzon, b. 10 May 1885.

2e. Lorna Katherine Curzon, m. 27 Oct. 1908, Capt. Quintin Dick.

2b. Rev. Francis William Davie Basset, Rector of Heanton Punchardon, Devon, m. Mary, da. of William Cartwright of Teignmouth. [Nos. 1263/80 to 1263/84.

# of The Blood Royal

3b. *Augusta Mary Basset*, d. (–); m. 17 *Ap.* 1827, *the Rev. William Bickford Coham of Coham and Dunsland*, LL.B., bapt. 6 *Ap.* 1792; d. 2 *July* 1843; and had issue 1c to 2c.

1c. *William Holland Bickford Coham of Coham and Dunsland*, J.P., D.L., b. 28 *July* 1828; d. 22 *Sept.* 1880; m. 3 *Sept.* 1857, *Dora Elizabeth Louisa* (see p. 620), *da. of Gen. Sir Hopton Stratford Scott*, K.C.B.; and had issue 1d.

1d. Elinor Mary Bickford Coham of Coham, m. 5 June 1883, John Blyth Fleming, now (R.L. 1883) Coham-Fleming, J.P., D.L., High Sheriff co. Devon 1887 (*Coham, co. Devon; Upcot Avenal, Sheepwash, co. Devon*); and has issue 1e.

1e. Blyth Bickford Coham-Fleming, b. 5 Sept. 1884.

2c. *Augusta Christiana Davie Coham of Dunsland and Arscott*, d. 13 *July* 1901; m. 29 *Ap.* 1858, *Major Harvey George Dickinson*, d. Nov. 1866; and had issue 1d to 3d.

1d. Arscott William Harvey Dickinson, M.A. (Oxon.), J.P., Bar.-at-Law (*Dunsland, Brandis-Corner, N. Devon; The Tower, Compton Gifford, S. Devon*), b. 23 Ap. 1859; m. 11 Jan. 1893, Mary, da. of the Rev. Sabine Baring-Gould of Lew Trenchard; and has issue 1e to 3e.

1e. Arscott Sabine Harvey Dickinson, b. 28 Nov. 1893.
2e. Edward Dabernon Dickinson, b. 27 June 1895.
3e. Bickford Holland Coham Dickinson, b. 16 July 1900.

2d. *Augusta Frances Courtenay Dickinson*, d. 14 *Oct.* 1892; m. 3 Nov. 1883, Henry Morton Tudor Tudor, Rear-Adm. R.N.; and had issue 1e to 2e.

1e. Douglas Courtenay Tudor, b. 9 July 1891.
2e. Alice Irene Tudor, m. 12 Dec. 1906, Lieut. John Evelyn Bray, R.N.

3d. Elinor Mary Coham Dickinson, m. 14 Ap. 1884, Capt. William M'Coy FitzGerald Castle, R.N.; and has issue 1e to 2e.

1e. Basil Langford Harvey Castle, b. 13 Sept. 1892.
2e. Violet Eleanor M'Coy Castle, b. 22 Sept. 1888.

4b. *Mary Davie Basset*, d. (–); m. 1826, *Gen. Sir Hopton Stratford Scott of Woodville, Lucan, co. Dublin*, K.C.B.; and had issue (with a da., Augusta, who d. unm.) 1c to 7c.

1c. Hopton Basset Scott, Lieut.-Col., *formerly* 19th Regt. (*Locksley, Shankill, co. Dublin*), b. 22 Mar. 1829; m. 15 Dec. 1865, Alice Jane Blaine, da. of Henry Blaine; and has issue (with 3 sons (Hopton Arthur, b. 1868; d. 1907; Herbert Courtenay, b. 1871; d. 1899; Raynold Woodville, b. 1877; d. 1896) and a da. (Agnes Gertrude, d. 1877), who all d. unm.) 1d to 8d.

1d. Edward Baliol Scott, b. 1872.
2d. Gerald Basset Scott, b. 1875.
3d. George Ernest Blaine Scott, b. 1883.
4d. John Davie Scott, b. 1883.
5d. Alice Mary Scott.
6d. Edith Margaret Scott.
7d. Dora Cecil Scott.
8d. Marjorie Ruth Scott.

2c. Courtenay Harvey Saltren Scott, Col. *formerly* 71st H.L.I. (*Pennant Hall, Abermule, R.S.O., co. Montgomery*), b. 24 June 1833; m. 11 Feb. 1862, Margaret Julia, da. of James Colquhoun; and has issue (with a son who d. young) 1d to 2d.

1d. Eleanor Margaret Scott, m. as 2nd wife, 10 Feb. 1891, Sir Edward Arthur Barry, 2nd Bt. [U.K.], J.P., Major Berks Yeo. (*Ockwells Manor, Bray, Berks; Hill Head House, Hants; Cavalry*); and has issue 1e to 4e.

1e. Edward Courtenay Tress Barry, b. 23 Jan. 1895.
2e. Cicely Eleanor Barry.
3e. Margaret Colquhoun Barry.
4e. Rosamond Barry.

[Nos. 1263/85 to 1263/110.

The Plantagenet Roll

2*d*. Adelaide Louisa Scott, *m.* James Gray Flowerdew-Lowson; and has issue 1*e* to 3*e*.

1*e*. Courtenay Patrick Flowerdew-Lowson, *b.* 4 Ap. 1897.
2*e*. Denis Colquhoun Flowerdew-Lowson, *b.* 20 Jan. 1906.
3*e*. Eleanor Margaret Flowerdew-Lowson, *b.* 9 Ap. 1892.

3*c*. Osmund Walter Scott (*Smytham House, Torrington, Devon*), *b.* 11 Jan. 1837; *m.* 31 May 1864, Julia Georgina, da. of Samuel Brown of Clifton; and has issue 1*d* to 4*d*.

1*d*. Hopton Stratford Scott, *b.* 20 June 1867.
2*d*. Evelyn Mary Scott, *b.* 23 Mar. 1866.
3*d*. Julia Augusta Scott, *b.* 22 Mar. 1870.
4*d*. Florence Adelaide Scott, *b.* 26 Jan. 1873.

4*c*. George Townsend Scott, 52nd Regt., *d.* 21 Feb. 1879; *m. Charlotte, da. of* (—) *Pearse*, *d.* 22 *Sept.* 1900; *and had issue* 1*d to* 2*d*.

1*d*. Violet Ethel Scott, *m.* 17 July 1905, Edward Gordon Stewart McClellan [2nd son of Col. McClellan, 3rd Dragoon Guards] (*East Brook, Wokingham, Berks*); and has issue 1*e* to 2*e*.

1*e*. Greville Alick Stewart McClellan, *b.* 17 Oct. 1906.
2*e*. Dora Violet McClellan, *b.* 8 Feb. 1908.

2*d*. Kathleen Mary Scott, *m.* 17 Jan. 1903, Capt. Ferdinand Ewing M'Clellan, Somersetshire L.I. [eldest son of Col. McClellan afsd.] (*St. Margaret's, Shortlands, Kent*), *s.p.*

5*c*. Adelaide Harriet Scott (*4 Markwich Terrace, St. Leonards-on-Sea*), *m.* 1850, Capt. Edward John Thomas Montrésor, 55th Regt. [son of Gen. Sir Henry Montrésor of Denne Hill, co. Kent], *d.* 1907; and has issue (with 4 sons and a da. who *d. unm.*) 1*d* to 4*d*.

1*d*. Edward Henry Hopton Montrésor, Lieut.-Col. *late* Bengal Lancers, *b.* 8 May 1851; *m.* Bertha, da. of Gen. Hennessy; and has issue 1*e* to 2*e*.

1*e*. Charles Egerton Montrésor, *b.* 22 Dec. 1892.
2*e*. Marion Montrésor, *b.* 21 Jan. 1880.

2*d*. Henry Scott Montrésor, *b.* 18 June 1859; *unm.*
3*d*. Louis Bassett Montrésor, Capt. R.F.A., *b.* 17 Feb. 1874; *unm.*
4*d*. Constance Mary Montrésor, *m.* 8 Oct. 1889, Walter William Gordon Beatson [son of Major-Gen. Beatson, R.E.], *d.* 7 May 1897; and has issue (with a son who *d. unm.*) 1*e* to 3*e*.

1*e*. Roger Stewart Montrésor Beatson, *b.* 20 July 1890.
2*e*. Claude Gordon Beatson, *b.* 13 Jan. 1894.
3*e*. Walter William Gordon Beatson, *b.* 5 Aug. 1897.

6*c*. Dora Elizabeth Louisa Scott, *m.* 3 Sept. 1857, William Holland Bickford Coham of Coham and Dunsland, J.P., D.L. (see p. 619), *d.* 22 Sept. 1880; and has issue.

See p. 619, Nos. 1263/85—1263/86.

7*c*. Susan Agnes Scott (*Suncote, Austen Way, Gerrard's Cross, Bucks*), *m.* 20 Oct. 1864, Major Augustus Leacock Marsh, 55th Regt., *d.* 8 Mar. 1876; and has issue 1*d* to 6*d*.

1*d*. Hopton Elliot Marsh, Major R.G.A., *b.* 6 Nov. 1865; *m.* 30 Dec. 1896, Ethel, da. of Col. Morton Taylor, R.A.; and has issue 1*e*.

1*e*. Kathleen Marsh, *b.* 26 Sept. 1897.

2*d*. Francis Courtenay Marsh, Capt. 2nd Border Regt., *b.* 27 Ap. 1867.
3*d*. Frederick William Marsh, *b.* 20 Nov. 1868.
4*d*. Edward Augustus Marsh, *b.* 29 Jan. 1870.
5*d*. Julia Augusta Marsh, *m.* 25 Jan. 1894, Frederick Feist; and has issue 1*e*.

1*e*. Doris Evelyn Feist.

6*d*. Ada Caroline Mary Marsh, *m.* 17 May 1896, Stanislas Sigismund Zaleski.

[Nos. 1263/111 to 1263/145.

# of The Blood Royal

2a. Rev. Charles Davie, Rector of Heanton Punchardon, Devon, b. 15/18 Aug. 1765; d. 1836; m. 1801, Bridget, da. of (—) Boyfield of Lee, co. Kent; and has issue 1b to 2b.

1b. Charles Christopher Davie, Capt. 67th Regt., b. 1803; d. 1874; m. 1840, Eliza Frances, da. of Capt. (—) White of Barnstaple, d. 1905; and has issue (with others d.s.p.) 1c.

1c. George Christopher Davie, b. 1841; m. 1868, Annie Sarah, da. of Thomas Dickson of Harley Street, London; and has issue (with 2 da͞s. d. unm.) 1d to 3d.

1d. Charles Christopher Davie (21 Selburne Road, Hove), b. 18 Aug. 1869; m. 28 Nov. 1900, Beatrice Paulina Mabel, da. of Henry (Walrond), 9th Marquis of Vallado and a Grandee of the 1st Class [Spain], Lieut.-Col. and Hon. Col. late 4th Batt. Devon Regt.; and has issue.

See Mortimer-Percy Volume, Part I. p. 78, Nos. 9453–9454.

2d. Bertie George Davie (24 Eccleston Square, S.W.), b. 16 Nov. 1874; m. 29 Aug. 1903, Flora Helen Frances [descended from the Lady Anne, sister to King Edward IV., &c. (see Essex Volume Supp., p. 622)], da. of Major Michael M'Creagh Thornhill of Stanton-in-Peak, co. Derby, J.P., D.L.; and has issue 1e.

1e. Humphrey Bache Christopher Davie, b. 1904.

3d. Annie Frances Davie.

2b. Mary Jane Davie, b. 1802; d.s.p. 19 Aug. 1857/8; m. 1st, 1877, Capt. John May of Broadoak, near Barnstaple, J.P., D.L., d. (-); 2ndly, 6 Aug. 1857, Frederick Lee.

3a. John Davie, Post Capt. R.N., in command of the Conqueror at St. Helena, during the imprisonment of the Emperor Napoleon there, b. 1770; d. (-); m. Jemima, da. of (—) Tapper; and had issue which became extinct 4 May 1900.

4a. Peregrine Davie, H.E.I.C.S., d. (-); m. (—), da. of (—), a Gen. in the French Service, d. (-); and had issue (with a son, Calmar, who d. unm. in India) 1b to 2b.

1b. Peregrine Davie.

2b. Eleanora Juliana Davie, b. 1811; d. 11 Oct. 1884; m. 10 Sept. 1828, Capt. John Wynch, Madras Horse Artillery, commanded Artillery with Gen. Lang's Force 1818 [2nd son of George Wynch, Madras C.S. (by his wife Mary, widow of (—) Smyth, da. of John Secker, youngest brother of Thomas, Archbishop of Canterbury 1758–68), who was 5th son of Alexander Wynch, Governor of Madras, 2 Feb. 1772–Dec. 1775, see p. 236], b. at Dindigub 5 June 1796; d. 11 Jan. 1880; and had issue (with a son, George Peregrine, and a da., Eleanor Jane, who both d. unm.) 1c to 7c.

1c. Henry St. Maur Wynch, Col. formerly H.E.I.C.S., b. 23 Dec. 1833; m. 1st, at Greenwich 18 Aug. 1892, Laura Edith, da. of Henry Habbijam, d. 7 Dec. 1894; 2ndly, (—).

2c. Rev. John William Wynch, Assist. Chaplain, Madras Ecclesiastical Estab., 14 Jan. 1861–14 Jan. 1886 (36 The Park, Ealing), b. at St. Thomas' Mount, Madras, 23 Dec. 1835; m. 6 Sept. 1860, Mary Jane, da. of Lieut.-Col. Frederick Minchin, H.E.I.C.S.; and has issue (with 2 das. who d. young) 1d to 3d.

1d. Frederick John Wynch, Lieut.-Col. Comdg. 41st Dogras since 19 Oct. 1907, b. 28 Aug. 1862; m. 1 Mar. 1892, (—), da. of (—) Jones; and has issue 1e to 4e.

1e. Wilfred Alexander Davie Wynch, b. 29 Ap. 1899.

2e. Avice Wynch, b. 19 Dec. 1892.

3e. Phyllis Loveday Wynch, b. 3 Feb. 1895.

4e. Audrey Wynch, b. 24 Mar. 1897.

2d. Eleanora Mary Davie Wynch, m. 1 Mar. 1881, Capt. Charles Brenton Wickham, R.A.; and has issue 1e to 2e.

1e. John Charles Wickham, Lieut. R.E., b. 23 June 1886.

2e. Evelyn Wickham.

3d. Lilian Gordon Wynch, unm.

[Nos. 1263/146 to 1263/163.

The Plantagenet Roll

3c. Alexander Wynch, Lieut.-Col. (ret.) Madras Artillery (105 *Park Street, Grosvenor Square, W.*), b. 1 Aug. 1838 ; m. 1st, 26 Oct. 1865, Mary Jane, da. of Lieut.-Col. Balmain, Royal Madras Artillery, d. 19 Dec. 1867 ; 2ndly, 20 Dec. 1876, Mary, da. of James Hole; and has issue (with a son, Alexander Balmain, b. 21 Sept. 1866 ; d. unm. 20 July 1888) 1d to 2d.

 1d.¹ Mary Balmain Wynch, m. 4 Sept. 1890, William Reid Lewis (*Philadelphia*) ; and has issue (with a da., Denys de Bardt, who d. young) 1e to 2e.

 1e. Eleanor Lewis, b. 14 Aug. 1894.

 2e. Marguerita Balmain Lewis, b. 3 Nov. 1891.

 2d.² Ethel Alexandra Wynch, m. 20 Dec. 1905, Edward John Urwick ; and has issue 1e to 2e.

 1e. Edward Hilary Urwick, b. 4 Oct. 1906.

 2e. Maurice Alexis Urwick, b. 30 Mar. 1909.

4c. Edward James Wynch, Major Madras Army, b. 23 Oct. 1840 ; d.s.p. 7 Sept. 1882.

5c. Mary Jane Wynch, m. 1st, 24 Dec. 1872, Arthur Leared, M.D., F.R.C.P., d. 16 Oct. 1879 ; 2ndly, 16 Sept. 1893, Edmund Philip Carleton, Consular Agent at Alcazar, Morocco (*Tangiers*) ; s.p.

6c. Florentia Sale Wynch, m. 18 June 1874, Robert Edward Master, Madras C.S. (*Hillingdon Furze, Uxbridge*); and has issue 1d.

 1d Eleanora Frances Master, m. 11 Dec. 1901, Walter S. Curtis, Bar.-at-Law (4 *Norfolk Crescent, W.*) ; and has issue 1e to 3e.

 1e. Lilias Marion Curtis, b. 13 Oct. 1902.

 2e. Rosemary Curtis, b. 8 Oct. 1905.

 3e. Adelaide Gabrielle Curtis, b. 31 July 1909.

7c. Julia Charlotte Secker Wynch, b. 26 Dec. 1850 ; unm.

5a. Eleanora Davie, d. 1840 ; m. 22 Sept. 1802, *the Rev. Lewis Lewis of Gwynfé, J.P., D.L., Rector of Clovelly*, d. 1826 ; *and had issue* 1b to 3b.

 1b. Lewis Lewis of Gwynfé, *J.P., D.L.*, b. 23 Dec. 1805 ; d. 8/9 Jan. 1859 ; m. 9 Mar. 1830, *Sarah Simmons, da. of William Colbourne of Colbourne*, d. 19 Feb. 1890 ; *and had issue* 1c to 8c.

 1c. Charles Basset Lewis of Gwinfé, *J.P., D.L., Major late 44th and 25th Regts., &c.*, b. 13 Dec. 1831 ; d. 15 Oct. 1903 ; m. 29 Jan. 1863, *Sarah Amelia, da. of Samuel Brown of Clifton ; and had issue* 1d.

 1d. Eleanora Constance Lewis, m. 9 Feb. 1898, Col. James Henry Worthington Pedder (*Gwinfé House, near Llangadock, co. Carmarthen ; Hillside Hatherley, Cheltenham*) ; and has issue 1e.

 1e. Eleanor Barbara Pedder, b. 27 Nov. 1905.

2c. Lewis Gwyn Lewis, Lieut. Indian Navy, b. 21 Sept. 1834 ; m. 30 Oct. 1872, Blanche Mary, da. of (—) Fitzmaurice ; and has issue 1d to 2d.

 1d. Christine Eola Lewis, m. 6 Jan. 1900, Joseph M. Davey ; s.p.

 2d. Olive Eleanora Lewis, m. 12 Sept. 1899, Harold Ashton Tonge ; s.p.

3c. Edward Studley Lewis (*New Zealand*), m. and has issue (2 das.).

4c. Frank Davie Lewis (*Australia*), b. 31 May 1838 ; m. (—); and has (with possibly other) issue 1d.

 1d. Albert Thomas Lewis.

5c. George Septimus Lewis, b. 21 Sept. 1848 ; m. twice ; and has issue 1d to 2d.

 1d.¹ Studley Lewis, Lieut. 5th Fusiliers.

 2d.¹ George Lewis.

6c. Eleanora Jane Lewis, unm.

7c. Eustatia Harriette Lewis, m. 1875, the Rev. Henry Sylvester Alison (*Barming Heath, Maidstone*) ; and has issue 1d to 5d.

 1d. Henry Lewis Guthrie Alison, b. 1882.   [Nos. 1263/164 to 1263/191.

of The Blood Royal

2*d*. Constance Annie Alison, *m*. 1897, Edward Browne; and has issue 1*e* to 4*e*.
1*e*. Helen Mary Browne, *b*. 1898.
2*e*. Constance Margaret Browne, *b*. 1901.
3*e*. Catherine Alison Browne, *b*. 1905.
4*e*. Elinor Laura Browne, *b*. 1908.

3*d*. Clare Alison.
4*d*. Winifred Bell Alison.
5*d*. Eustatia Violet Alison.

8*c*. *Augusta Blanche Lewis*, d.s.p. 31 Oct. 1890; m. A*p*. 1890, *James Maddan*.

2*b*. *Thomas Lewis*, d. (-); m. 19 A*p*. 1836, *Victoire Maria, da. of the Hon. Andrew Houston of Grenada, W.I.*; and had issue 1*c* to 6*c*.
1*c*. *Andrew Courtenay Lewis*, b. 31 Jan. 1837; d. (-).
2*c*. Charles Houston Lewis, b. 17 Feb. 1844.
3*c*. *Arthur Whalley Lewis*, b. 16 July 1847; d. (-).
4*c*. Alexander Goldwyre Lewis, b. 28 Feb. 1849.
5*c*. William Studley Lewis, b. 30 Mar. 1851.
6*c*. Eleanora Harriette Lewis, *b*. 13 Jan. 1838; *unm*.

3*b*. *Eleanora Elizabeth Lewis*, b. 19 Oct. 1803; d. 13 A*p*. 1866; m. 3 Oct. 1827, *Charles Bishop of Dôlgarreg, co. Carmarthen*, b. 12 Aug. 1799; d. 7 June 1886; and had issue (with a da., Frances Gwenllian, who d. *unm*. 1904) 1*c* to 11*c*.
1*c*. John Bishop, Bar.-at-Law and a County Court Judge (*Dôl-y-garreg, Llandovery, S. Wales*), *b*. 19 Nov. 1828; *m*. 1884, Caroline Florentia Affleck, da. of Morgan Pryse Lloyd of Glansevin; and has issue (with a son, John Ivor Pryse, who d. aged 7, 1892) 1*d*.
1*d*. Frances Gwenllian Enid Bishop.

2*c*. Charles Bishop (*Cwmrhuddan, co. Carmarthen*), *b*. 18 Sept. 1832; *m*. 29 Ap. 1868, Helen Lexey, da. of John Carnegie of Redhall, co. Kincardine; and has issue (with 2 das.: Alice Caroline Ayliffe, *b*. 22 Aug. 1872; *d*. 2 Nov. 1893; and Christine Harriet Sybil, *b*. 17 Sept. 1880; *d*. 8 Ap. 1905, who both *d. unm*.) 1*d* to 2*d*.
1*d*. Lexey Eleanora Edith Bishop, *m*. 30 June 1892, George Maximilian Lindner; and has issue 1*e* to 6*e*.
1*e*. George Austin Carnegie Lindner, *b*. 13 June 1893.
2*e*. Charles Frederick Harold Lindner, *b*. 8 June 1901.
3*e*. Courtenay Peter Lloyd Lindner, *b*. 20 Aug. 1904.
4*e*. Doris Lexey Margaret Lindner, *b*. 8 July 1896.
5*e*. Charlotte Eleanora Rosamond Lindner, *b*. 20 May 1898.
6*e*. Helen Nancy Beryl Lindner, *b*. 25 Mar. 1907.

2*d*. Helen Frances Amy Bishop, *unm*.

3*c*. Arthur Bishop, *b*. 27 Jan. 1837.

4*c*. Edward Bishop, Com. (ret.) R.I.M. (*Bath*), *b*. 7 May 1840; *m*. 15 Feb. 1877, Isabella Jane Eleanor, da. of A. Wilkins, R.I.M.; and has issue 1*e* to 5*e*.
1*e*. Charles Arthur Bishop, Capt. R.M.A., *b*. 22 Feb. 1879; *m*. 1 June 1905, C. M., da of (-) Betham; *s.p*.
2*e*. Alfred Edward Bishop, Capt. Mounted Police, *b*. 8 Jan. 1883; *unm*.
3*e*. Isabel Gwen Bishop, *unm*.
4*e*. Frances Amy Bishop, *m*. 9 July 1897, M. H. Reynolds, Indian P.W.D.; *s.p*.
5*e*. Violet Caroline Bishop, *unm*.

5*c*. Lewis Bishop (*Bryneithen, Llandilo, Carmarthen*), *b*. 10 Jan. 1842; *m*. 27 Ap. 1871, Ramona Jannette, da. of William Poor Neville; and has issue 1*d* to 3*d*.
1*d*. John Walton Bishop, *b*. 1 Dec. 1880; *m*. 27 June 1906, Dorothy Isabel, da. of Malcolm de Saumarez Edye. [Nos. 1263/192 to 1263/223.

The Plantagenet Roll

2*d*. Ramona Isabel Joan Bishop, *m*. 9 Sept. 1903, Capt. Thomas Charles Bedford Holland, Devonshire Regt. (*Hove, Brighton*).

3*d*. Marguerite Muriel Gardner Bishop, *m*. 30 July 1896, Major Alexander John Henry Swiney, R.E.; and has issue 1*e* to 2*e*.

1*e*. George Alexander Neville Swiney, *b*. 10 June 1897.

2*e*. Henry Richard Terence Swiney, *b*. 30 Mar. 1901.

6*c*. Richard Henry Bishop, *b*. 17 May 1843.

7*c*. Rev. Rhys Bishop, Rector of Letton and Willersley (*Letton Rectory, co. Hereford*), *b*. 15 July 1844; *m*. 13 Aug. 1884, Amy, da. of James Crighton Nelson of London; and has issue 1*d* to 2*d*.

1*d*. Rev. Lewis Cornewall Bishop, Curate of St. Philip's, Lambeth, *b*. 23 June 1885; *unm*.

2*d*. Stella Eleanora Bishop, *unm*.

8*c*. Juliana Elizabeth Bishop, *b*. 10 Oct. 1830; *m*. Oct. 1855, the Rev. James Copner of Hartland, co. Devon; and has (with 2 younger sons who *d. unm*.) issue 1*d* to 4*d*.

1*d*. Charles James Copner (*Laston, Ilfracombe*), *b*. 28 July 1856; *m*. 19 Ap. 1883, Hebe Constance, da. of Charles John Down; and has issue 1*e* to 4*e*.

1*e*. Charles John Pomeroy Copner, *b*. 19 Mar. 1891.

2*e*. Mary Constance Copner, *b*. 10 Feb. 1885.

3*e*. Hebe Gwenllian Copner, *b*. 31 Dec. 1887.

4*e*. Alice Marjorie Copner, *b*. 13 July 1889.

2*d*. *Arthur Lewis Copner*, *b*. 28 *Feb*. 1858; *d*. 31 *May* 1894; *m*. 29 *Oct*. 1890, *Margaret Helen, da. of John Michael Blagg; and had issue* 1*e* to 2*e*.

1*e*. Arthur Bruce Copner, *b*. 21 July 1892.

2*e*. Eric Cecil Lewis Copner, *b*. 10 Aug. 1894.

3*d*. Francis John Copner (*Cranmore, Headcorn*), *b*. 30 Ap. 1865; *m*. 30 Dec. 1893, Beatrice Sylvester, da. of William Gill; and has issue 1*e* to 2*e*.

1*e*. James William Francis Copner, *b*. 4 Ap. 1902.

2*e*. Eleanora Aimée Vye Copner, *b*. 6 July 1896.

4*d*. Florence Katherine Copner, *m*. 20 July 1892, Francis Edward Blagg [son of John Michael Blagg of Cheadle, co. Staff.] (*Westmark, Petersfield*); and has issue 1*e* to 3*e*.

1*e*. Francis Osmond Blagg, *b*. 27 Nov. 1893.

2*e*. Claude Edmund Langley Blagg, *b*. 27 Jan. 1895.

3*e*. Raymond Courtenay Blagg, *b*. 29 Ap. 1900.

9*c*. Caroline Eleanora Bishop, *unm*.

10*c*. Harriett Susan Bishop, *m*. 17 Ap. 1883, the Right Rev. John Lloyd, D.D., Lord Bishop of Swansea and Suffragan for the Diocese of St. David's (*Cantref Rectory, Brecon*); and has issue 1*d* to 4*d*.

1*d*. Charles Geoffrey Lloyd, Lieut. Essex Regt., *b*. 12 Mar. 1884.

2*d*. Constance Mary Ethel Lloyd.

3*d*. Eleanor Kathleen Myfanwy Lloyd.

4*d*. Olwen Isabel Lloyd.

11*c*. Mary Augusta Bishop, *m*. 21 July 1875, Thomas Noon Talfourd Strick (*Llanfair, West Cross, R.S.O., Glamorgan*); and has issue 1*d* to 4*d*.

1*d*. Edward Talfourd Strick, *b*. 13 Jan. 1883.

2*d*. Courtenay Charles Strick, *b*. 24 May 1886.

3*d*. Gladys Eleanora Rachael Strick, *m*. 1 Jan. 1907, Bertram Lloyd Meek; and has issue 1*e*.

1*e*. Richard Ombler Meek, *b*. Oct. 1908.

4*d*. Eileen Mary Strick.   [Nos. 1263/224 to 1263/258.

of The Blood Royal

6a. *Julia Davie*, d. (-) ; m. *the Rev. John Beadon of Christian Malford*.
7a. *Eustatia Davie*, d. 11 Nov. 1843 ; m. *at Heanton Punchardon Aug.* 1797, *Major William Shairp of Kirkton*, 29*th Regt.*, *J.P.*, *D.L.*, *co. Linlithgow* [*cadet of Houston, being eldest son of Major William Shairp by his wife Ann Bromley Mordaunt, grandda. of Sir John Mordaunt of Tangiers, K.B., and grandson of Alexander Shairp, for* 34 *years a Director of the Bank of Scotland, and Treasurer of the City of Edinburgh* 1738-39 (b. 25 *May* 1686 ; d. 20 *Feb.* 1775), 2*nd son of Thomas Shairp, Baron of Houston, M.P.*], b. 20 *June* 1775 ; d. *in Jersey* 1840 ; *and had issue (with* 4 *other sons and* 4 *das. who* d. *unm.*) 1b *to* 3b.

1b. *William Joseph Shairp, a Clerk in the Colonial Office, Sydney*, b. 1798 ; d. *at Sydney, N.S.W., Nov.* 1847 ; m. *there* 3 Oct. 1827, *Sophia, da. of James Milson of North Shore, Sydney*, d. 1877 ; *and had issue (with a son and da.* d. *young)* 1c *to* 5c.

 1c. William Milson Shairp, b. 14 May 1829 ; *unm*.
 2c. Alexander Davie Shairp, b. 23 Oct. 1846 ; *unm*.
 3c. Eustatia Elizabeth Shairp, b. 7 Aug. 1830 ; *unm*.
 4c. *Sophia Frances Shairp*, b. 15 Feb. 1832 ; d. 9 *Mar*. 1881.
 5c. Elizabeth Milson Shairp, b. 9 Jan. 1843 ; *m*. 17 July 1861, Henry Hocken Bligh, b. at Bodmin, Cornwall, 19 Oct. 1826 ; *d*. at Sydney 30 July 1904 ; and had issue (with a son and da. *d. young*) 1d to 6d.

  1d. Henry Albury Gaden Bligh, b. 22 Sept. 1862 ; *unm*.
  2d. William Milson Bligh, b. 16 Aug. 1867 ; *m*. 1898, Lilian Mabel, da. of (—) Day.
  3d. Ernest Mordaunt Bligh, b. 11 June 1879 ; *unm*.
  4d. Rose Eustatia Lawry Bligh, b. 23 Ap. 1864 ; *unm*.
  5d. Caroline Ernestine Bligh, b. 3 Mar. 1866 ; *m*. 1898, Charles Thomson ; and has issue 1e to 2e.

   1e. Carl Thomson.
   2e. Jean Thomson.

  6d. Florence Mary Bligh, b. 27 May 1872.

2b. *Alexander Mordaunt Shairp, Lieut. R.N.*, d. (*being killed at sea*) 4 *June* 1848 ; m. 18 *Jan.* 1834, *his cousin Emily, da. of Major Alexander Shairp of Stonehouse, Plymouth*, d. *Sept.* 1895 ; *and had issue (with* 2 *sons who* d.s.p.) 1c.

 1c. Francis Mordaunt Shairp, Lieut.-Col. (ret.) R.M. (*The Bungalow, Hedge End, Botley, Hants*), b. 5 June 1842 ; *m*. 14 Nov. 1877, Elise Mary, da. of Edward La Trobe Budd ; and has issue 1d.

  1d. Mordaunt Douglas Shairp, b. 29 Aug. 1878.

3b. *Stephen Francis Shairp of St. Maur, St. Leonards*, b. 29 *Jan*. 1806 ; d. *at Southsea* 24 *Nov.* 1886 ; m. 26 *Aug.* 1844, *Caroline, da. of Charles Michelmore of Highfield House, Totnes*, d. 29 *Feb.* 1884 ; *and had issue (with* 2 *other sons and* 2 *das. who* d.s.p.) 1c *to* 8c.

 1c. Stuart Courtenay Shairp (1 *Marlborough Gate, Hyde Park, W.*), b. 1 May 1854 ; *m*. 4 Aug. 1885, Marie, da. of Henry Charles Warre Ekins [son of the Rev. Robert Ekins, Vicar of Godalming, by his wife Eliza, a da. of Sir Charles Warre Malet, 1st Bt. [G.B.], F.R.S.] ; and has issue (with a da., Evelyn Mary, who was b. 6 and d. 23 July 1889) 1d to 2d.

  1d. Alexander Mordaunt Shairp, b. 13 Mar. 1887.
  2d. Stephen Francis Shairp, b. 22 June 1892.

 2c. Eustatia Emily Shairp (2 *Mansfield Place, Richmond, Surrey*), *m*. 23 July 1884, Charles George Herring, *d*. 7 June 1882 ; and has issue (with a son, Charles Eustace, who *d. unm.*) 1d to 7d.

  1d. Sydney Herring, b. 14 Sept. 1868 ; *m*. 25 Feb. 1908, Mary, da. of (—) Povall.
  2d. Arthur Grendon Herring, b. 23 Oct. 1869 ; *m*. 15 June 1894, Maude, da. of (—) Ridley ; and has issue 1e.
   1e. Maude Ridley Herring.

[Nos. 1263/259 to 1263/279.

The Plantagenet Roll

3*d*. Stephen Francis Herring, *b*. 1877; *unm*.

4*d*. George Norman Herring, *b*. 19 Ap. 1882; *m*. Feb. 1905, Winifred, da. of (—) Smith; and has issue 1*e*.

1*e*. Charles Norman Herring, *b*. Oct. 1905.

5*d*. Florence Gertrude Herring, *m*. 26 Mar. 1890, Thomson Chiene Shepherd (*Gleghornie, North Berwick*); and has issue 1*e* to 3*e*.

1*e*. Thomson Shepherd, *b*. 14 June 1894.

2*e*. Emily Elizabeth Shepherd.

3*e*. Florence Gertrude Shepherd.

6*d*. Lilian Mary Herring, *m*. 7 Sept. 1894, James Francis Shepherd; and has issue 1*e* to 4*e*.

1*e*. James Chiene Shepherd.

2*e*. George Edward Shepherd.

3*e*. Eileen Shepherd } (twins).
4*e*. Kathleen Shepherd }

7*d*. Lucy Mignon Herring, *m*. 30 Ap. 1903, Douglas Frederick Charrington [son of John Douglas Charrington, by his wife Mary, *née* Herring] (2 *Mansfield Place, Richmond, Surrey*); and has issue 1*e*.

1*e*. Norman Douglas Charrington, *b*. 9 Aug. 1909.

3*c*. Caroline Lucy Shairp, *unm*.

4*c*. Fanny Gertrude Shairp, *unm*.

5*c*. Annie Shairp, *m*. as 2nd wife, 1886, Col. Henry Vansittart Riddell [Riddell of Riddell, Bt. [S. 1628] Coll.], *d.s.p.* by her 1888.

6*c*. Eleanora Beatrice Shairp, *m*. 22 Sept. 1893, Major Philip Sykes Murphy Burlton, I.S.C.; and has issue 1*d*.

1*d*. Henry Lionel Granville Burlton, *b*. 13 June 1896.

7*c*. Edith Shairp, *m*. 18 Sept. 1883, Henry Glennie Reid [son of Lieut.-Gen. C. S. Reid, R.A.]; and has issue (with a da., Nora, who *d*. in infancy) 1*d* to 3*d*.

1*d*. Charles Henry Stuart Reid, *b*. 27 July 1884.

2*d*. Hugh Courtenay Reid.

3*d*. Edith Ivy Reid.

8*c*. Emma Rosalie Pender Shairp, *m*. 30 Nov. 1882, Col. Granville William Vernon, lately Comdg. 2nd Batt. Bedfordshire Regt., and West India Dept., Jamaica [4th son of John Edward Venables Vernon of Clontarf Castle, co. Dublin, J.P., D.L.] (23 *Onslow Square, S.W.*); and has issue (with a younger son who *d*. in infancy) 1*d*.

1*d*. Charles Edward Granville Vernon, *b*. 29 Sept. 1883.

8*a*. *Charlotte Davie*, d. 1847; m. 1802, *Gen. Jasper de Brisay*, 4*th Dragoons*, d. 22 Nov. 1818; *and had issue* 1*b*.

1*b*. *John Theophilus de Brisay*, b. 24 *Jan*. 1804; d. 25 *Sept*. 1846; m. 1828, *Harriette, da. of Capt. Lestock Wilson, Indian Marine*, d. 12 *Nov*. 1855; *and had issue (with a son, George,* d.s.p.) 1*c*.

1*c*. Rev. Henry Delacour de Brisay, M.A., *formerly* Vicar of Gettenhall, co. Stafford (11 *Bradmore Road, Oxford*), *b*. 5 Dec. 1831; *m*. 11 July 1854, Jane Amelia, da. of Philip Marett, *d*. 21 Mar. 1904; and had issue (with a da., Mrs. Baker, who *d.s.p.* 1893) 1*d* to 3*d*.

1*d*. Rev. Henry Lestock Delacour de Brisay, M.A., Rector of Northill (*Northill Rectory, co. Bedford*), *b*. 16 Mar. 1860; *m*. 15 Oct. 1891, Emily, da. of the Very Rev. Robert Forrest, D.D., Dean of Worcester; and has issue 1*e* to 2*e*.

1*e*. Aubrey Cust Delacour de Brisay, *b*. 5 Nov. 1896.

2*e*. Robert Lestock de Brisay, *b*. 27 Nov. 1897.

2*d*. Jane Marguerite de Brisay, *unm*.

3*d*. Beatrice Mary de Brisay, *m*. 3 Dec. 1896, William Priestley Barber, *d.s.p.* 2 Aug. 1908. [Nos. 1263/280 to 1263/310.

# of The Blood Royal

9a. Mary Davie, d. 15 June 1859; m. 1st, 14 Feb. 1811, John Alexander Lumsden, Lieut. 80th Regt., d. 1812; 2ndly, Capt. Michael Jones of Lisgoole Abbey, co. Fermanagh, d. 20 Aug. 1864; and had issue 1b to 3b.

1b. Alexander John Henry Lumsden, b. 24 Mar. 1812; d. 9 Oct. 1894; m. in Bermuda c. 1840, Emma Jane, da. of Capt. N. Skinner of Bermuda, R.N.; and had issue 1c to 4c.

1c. Charles Arthur Lumsden (Ashpringlon, Totnes, Devon), b. 21 Sept. 1841; m. 3 July 1886, Frances Elizabeth, da. of the Rev. C. Penny; and has issue 1d.

1d. Alexander Louis Courtenay Lumsden, b. 18 July 1891.

2c. Richard Francis Hopton Lumsden, b. 14 Jan. 1847; unm.

3c. Mary Elizabeth Lumsden, unm.

4c. Emily Augusta Gordon Lumsden, unm.

2b. William Christopher Jones, b. 30 Mar. 1815; d. c. 1860/1; m. 9 Jan. 1858, Isabella, da of (—) Denham of Fairwood Park, co. Fermanagh; and had issue 1c.

1c. Michael Obins Jones, b. 16 Mar. 1839.

3b. Michael Obins Seely Jones, b. 4 Sept. 1818; d.v.p. 5 Ap. 1860; m. 19 Feb. 1846, Kate, da. of Travers Homan of Colga, co. Sligo, d. 18 Jan. 1847; and had issue 1c.

1c. Kate Mary Barrett Jones (Rosslare, Sligo), m. 24 Aug. 1871, Edward Willoughby Fowler of Cleaghmore, co. Galway, J.P. [grandson of the Right Rev. Robert Fowler, Lord Bishop of Ossory and Ferns, by his wife the Hon. Louisa, née Gardner, and great-grandson of the Most Rev. and Right Hon. Robert Fowler, Archbishop of Dublin, D.D., K.P., P.C.], b. 6 Aug. 1831; d. 17 Jan. 1900; and has issue 1d to 5d.

1d. Willoughby Jones Fowler, Capt. R.G.A., b. 25 Feb. 1873; m. 20 July 1905, Gwendolen Ada, da. of Col. William Barton Wade, C.B.; and has issue 1e.

1e. Kathleen Muriel Fowler, b. 10 Jan. 1908.

2d. Cecil Arthur Fowler, b. 6 Feb. 1876.

3d. Edward Gardiner Fowler, Lieut. R.G.A., b. 2 Dec. 1879.

4d. Charles Knox Fowler, b. 28 Ap. 1882.

5d. Elizabeth Katherine Fowler. [Nos. 1263/311 to 1263/323.

INDEX OF NAMES

SUPPLEMENT TO THE EXETER VOLUME

ALISON, C., p. 623 ; Mrs. E. H., p. 622 ; E. V., p. 623 ; H. L. G., p. 622 ; W. B., p. 623
Austin, Mrs. H. A., p. 617

BARBER, Mrs. B. M., p. 626
Barker-Hahlo, A. C., p. 617 ; F. N., p. 617 ; J. F. C., p. 617
Barry, C. E., p. 619 ; E. C. T., p. 619 ; Eleanor M., Lady, p. 619 ; M. C., p. 619 ; R., p. 619
Basset, Rev. F. W. D., p. 618 ; Mrs. H. M., p. 618
Beatson, C. G., p. 620 ; Mrs. C. M., p. 620 ; R. S. M., p. 620 ; W. W. G., p. 620
Bishop, A., p. 623 ; Capt. A. E., 623 ; C., p. 623 ; C. A., p. 623 ; C. E., p. 624 ; Comm. E., p. 623 ; F. G. E., p. 623 ; H. F. A., p. 623 ; I. G., p. 623 ; J., p. 623 ; J. W., p. 623 ; L., p. 623 ; Rev. L. C., p. 624 ; Rev. R., p. 624 ; R. H., p. 624 ; S. E., p. 624 ; V. C., p. 623
Blagg, C. E. L., p. 624 ; Mrs. F. K., p. 624 ; F. O., p. 624 ; R. C., p. 624
Bligh, Mrs. E. M., p. 625 ; E. M., p. 625 ; F. M., p. 625 ; H. A. G., p. 625 ; R. E. L., p. 625 ; W. M., p. 625
Bray, Mrs. A. I., p. 619
de Brisay, A. C. D., p. 626 ; Rev. H. D., p. 626 ; Rev. H. L. D., p. 626 ; J. M., p. 626 ; R. L., p. 626
Browne, Mrs. C. A., p. 623 ; C. A., p. 623 ; C. M., p. 623 ; E. L. p. 623 ; H. M., p. 623
Burlton, Mrs. E. B., p. 626 ; H. L. G., p. 626

CARLTON, Mrs. M. J., p. 622
Carson, Mrs. M. B. H., p. 617
Castle, B. L. H., p. 619 ; Mrs. E. M. C., p. 619 ; V. E. M'C., p. 619
Charrington, Mrs. L. M., p. 626 ; N. D., p. 626
Clayton, G. E. C., p. 618 ; R. D. de S., p. 618
Coham, Mrs. D. E. L., p. 620
Coham-Fleming, B. B., p. 619 ; Mrs. E. M. B., p. 619
Collett, C. E., p. 615
Copner, A. B., p. 624 ; A. M., p. 624 ; C. J., p. 624 ; C. J. P., p. 624 ; E. A. V., p. 624 ;
E. C. L., p. 624 ; F. J., p. 624 ; H. G., p. 624 ; Mrs. J. E., p. 624 ; J. W. F., p. 624 ; M. C., p. 624
Crofton, A., p. 617 ; A. A., p. 617 ; G. N., p. 617 ; H. T., p. 617 ; Capt. J. ff. F., p. 617 ; S. d'A., p. 617 ; Rev. W. d'A., p. 617
Curtis, A. G., p. 622 ; Mrs. E. F., p. 622 ; L. M., p. 622 ; R., p. 622
Curzon, C. E. B. L., p. 618 ; Mrs. E. B., p. 618

DAVEY, Mrs. C. E., p. 622
Davie, A. F., p. 621 ; B. G., p. 621 ; C. C., p. 621 ; G. C., p. 621 ; H. B. C., p. 621
Dick, Mrs. L. K., p. 618
Dickinson, A. S. H., p. 619 ; A. W. H., p. 619 ; B. H. C., p. 619 ; E. D., p. 619

FEIST, D. E., p. 620 ; Mrs. J. A., p. 620
Flowerdew-Lowson, Mrs. A. L., p. 620 ; C. P., p. 620 ; D. C., p. 620 ; E. M., p. 620
Fowler, C. A., p. 627 ; C. K., p. 627 ; Lieut. E. G., p. 627 ; E. K., p. 627 ; K. M., p. 627 ; Mrs. K. M. B., p. 627 ; Capt. W. J., p. 627
Foyster, Mrs. C. A., p. 618 ; E. S., p. 618

GARDNER, Mrs. E. B., p. 618
Grant, Mrs. E. H., p. 617 ; E. M., p. 617 ; F. E., p. 617 ; V. H., p. 617

HERRING, A. G., p. 625 ; C. N., p. 626 ; Mrs. E. E., p. 625 ; G. N., p. 626 ; M. R., p. 625 ; S., p. 625 ; S. F., p. 626
Hogg, Mrs. B., p. 616 ; B. E. S., p. 616 ; J. M. S., p. 616
Holland, Mrs. R. I. J., p. 624
Hulton, C. A. G., p. 616 ; Rev. C. B., p. 616 ; C. C., p. 616 ; C. E., p. 616 ; E. C., p. 616 ; E. T., p. 616 ; F. C., p. 615 ; Maj. F. C. L., p. 616 ; G., p. 616 ; G. E., p. 615 ; Rev. H. E., p. 615 ; Lieut. J. A., p. 616 ; J. H. F., p. 616 ; Lieut. J. M., p. 616 ; M., p. 616 ; M. C., p. 615 ; R., p. 616 ; R. A., p. 616 ; R. E., p. 616 ; S. F., p. 616 ; W. S., p. 616

JONES, M. O., p. 627

LEWIS, A. G., p. 623 ; A. T., p. 622 ; C. H., p. 623 ; E., p. 622 ; E. H., p. 623 ; E. J., p. 622 ; E. S., p. 622 ; F. D., p. 622 ; G., p. 622 ; G. S., p. 622 ; Lieut. L. G., p. 622 ; Mrs. M. B., p. 622 ; M. B., p. 622 ; Lieut. S., p. 622 ; W. S., p. 623
Lindner, C. E. R., p. 623 ; C. F. H., p. 623 ; C. P. L., p. 623 ; D. L. M., p. 623 ; G. A. C., p. 623 ; H. N. B., p. 623 ; Mrs. L. E. E., p. 623
Lloyd, Lieut. C. G., p. 624 ; C. M. E., p. 624 ; E. K. M., p. 624 ; Mrs. H. S., p. 624 ; O. I., p. 624
Lumsden, A. L. C., p. 627 ; C. A., p. 627 ; E. A. G., p. 627 ; M. E., p. 627 ; R. F. H., p. 627

McCLELLAN, D. V., p. 620 ; G. A. S., p. 626 ; Mrs. K. M., p. 620 ; Mrs. V. E., p. 620
Marsh, E. A., p. 620 ; Capt. F. C., p. 620 ; F. W., p. 620 ; Maj. H. E., p. 620 ; K., p. 620 ; Mrs. S. A., p. 620
Master, Mrs. F. S., p. 622
Mathias, Mrs. A. L. E., p. 615 ; D. A. L., p. 615 ; J. W., p. 615 ; M. F., p. 615 ; W. D., p. 615
Meek, Mrs. G. E. R., p. 624 ; R. O., p. 624
Montrésor, Mrs. A. H., p. 620 ; C. E., p. 620 ; Lieut.-Col. E. H. H., p. 620 ; H. S., p. 620 ; Capt. L. B., p. 620 ; M., p. 620

PEDDER, E. B., p. 622 ; Mrs. E. C., p. 622

REID, C. H. S., p. 626 ; Mrs. E., p. 626 ; E. I., p. 626 ; H. C., p. 626
Reynolds, Mrs. F. A., p. 623
Riddell, Mrs. A., p. 626

SADLER, E. L., p. 618 ; F. W., p. 618 ; R. C., p. 618 ; T. H., p. 618
Sams, C. H. H., p. 617 ; E. C. H., p. 617 ; F. E. B. H., p. 617 ; K. A. H., p. 617 ; S. A. H., p. 617 ; Mrs. S. B., p. 616
Scott, A. M., p. 619 ; Col. C. H. S., p. 619 ; D. C., p. 619 ; E. B., p.
619 ; E. M., p. 619 ; E. M., p. 620 ; F. P., p. 620 ; G. B., p. 619 ; G. E. B., p. 619 ; J. D., p. 619 ; Lieut.-Col. H. B., p. 619 ; H. S., p. 620 ; J. A., p. 620 ; M. R., p. 619 ; O. W., p. 620
Shairp, A. D., p. 625 ; A. M., p. 625 ; C. L., p. 626 ; E. E., p. 625 ; F. G., p. 626 ; Lieut.-Col. F. M., p. 625 ; M. D., p. 625 ; S. C., p. 625 ; S. F., p. 625 ; W. M., p. 625
Shepherd, E., p. 626 ; E. E., p. 626 ; Mrs. F. G., p. 626 ; F. G., p. 626 ; G. E., p. 626 ; J. C., p. 626 ; K., p. 626 ; Mrs. L. M., p. 626 ; T., p. 626
Strick, C. C., p. 624 ; E. M., p. 624 ; E. T., p. 624 ; Mrs. M. A., p. 624
Swiney, G. A. N., p. 624 ; H. R. T., p. 624 ; Mrs. M. M. G., p. 624

THOMSON, C., p. 625 ; Mrs. C. E., p. 625 ; J., p. 625
Tonge, Mrs. O. E., p. 622
Tudor, D. C., p. 619

URWICK, Mrs. E. A., p. 622 ; E. H., p. 622 ; M. A., p. 622

VERNON, C. E. G., p. 626 ; Mrs. E. R. P., p. 626

WATSON, C. C., p. 616 ; E. C., p. 616 ; E. M., p. 616 ; H. G., p. 616 ; H. L., p. 616 ; Mrs. M. L., p. 616 ; M. L., p. 616 ; S. M., p. 616 ; V., p. 616 ; W. D. P., p. 616
Wharton, Mrs. G. M., p. 618
Whitley, E. C. R., p. 618 ; Mrs. M. C., p. 618
Wickham, E., p. 621 ; Mrs. E. M. D., p. 621 ; Lieut. J. C., p. 621
Wisoman, Florence M. H., Lady, p. 617
Woodhouse, G. H. H., p. 617 ; Mrs. G. J., p. 617 ; R. C. H., p. 617 ; R. H., p. 617
Wynch, A., p. 621 ; A., p. 621 ; Lieut.-Col. A., p. 622 ; Lieut.-Col. F. J., p. 621 ; Col. H. St. M., p. 621 ; J. C. S., p. 622 ; Rev. J. W., p. 621 ; L. G., p. 621 ; P. L., p. 621 ; W. A. D., p. 621

ZALESKI, Mrs. A. C. M., p. 620

The Essex Volume

SUPPLEMENT

ANNE, *née* CALVERT, WIFE OF CHRISTOPHER ANSTEY, Esq.
A DESCENDANT OF KING EDWARD III., AND THE COMMON ANCESTRESS OF ALL THOSE WHOSE NAMES APPEAR IN THE ESSEX SUPPLEMENT.

From an Oil Painting in possession of the Corporation of Bath, by William Hoare, R.A.

THE ESSEX VOLUME

SUPPLEMENT

Page 306. Delete lines 23 to 36, and in place thereof read—

201. Descendants of ANNE CALVERT (Supplementary Table, p. 614), b. 7 May 1732; d. 31 Jan. 1812; m. 20 Dec. 1755,[1] CHRISTOPHER ANSTEY of Trumpington, co. Camb., the Poet, Author of the "New Bath Guide," &c., b. 1724; d. 3 Aug. 1805; M.I. in Walcot Church, Bath; Monument in Westminster Abbey; and had issue 1a to 11a.

1a. *Rev. Christopher Anstey, Vicar of Stockton-on-Tees to 1782, and Norton, co. Durham, M.A. (Camb.),* b. 1756; d.s.p. 19 Dec. 1827; m. 8 [*not* 21] *June* 1783, *Elizabeth, da. of William Grey of London,* d. 23 Nov. 1821; 2ndly, 1825, *Elizabeth, da. of John Grey of Norton,* d. 20 Sept. 1876.

2a. *Robert Anstey, Capt. 21st Light Dragoons, Pensioner of St. John's,* 7 July 1799; d. 12 Ap. 1818 [*will dated* 18 Dec. 1817, pr. P.C.C. 20 July 1818]; m. 1st, 21 Ap. 1791, *Lucretia, a Lady of the Holy Roman Empire, widow of William Light,* H.E.I.C.S., *da. of Theodore von Luders, a Hereditary Knight* [H.R.E., 1763], *Chargé d'Affaires and Councillor of the Russian Embassy in London,* d. Ap. 1794; 2ndly, (—); *and had issue* 1b.

1b. *Diana Matilda Anne Anstey,* m. *before* 1817, *the Rev. John Peregrine Lascelles Fenwick.*

3a. *John Anstey, M.A. (Camb.), Bar.-at-Law and Secretary of the Audit Office, and a Commissioner for Auditing Public Accounts, appointed Special Commissioner to investigate claims of American Loyalists, Author of the* "*Pleader's Guide,*" *&c.,* d. 25 Nov. 1819; m.[2] *Helen, da. of Ascanius William Senior of Pilewell,* co. *Hants, and Cannon Hill House,* co. *Berks, a Master in Chancery, by 1st wife,* b. 18 Oct. 1763; d. 3 *Mar.* 1837; *and had issue* 1b *to* 7b.

1b. *Christopher John Anstey of Trumpington,* d. *unm.*

2b. *William Jekyll Anstey, Postmaster-General of Jamaica, and formerly in the Audit Office,* d. (–); m. *Balbina, da. of* (—); *and had issue* 1c *to* 9c.[3]

1c. *William Anstey.*
2c. *Frederick Anstey.*
3c. *Herbert Anstey.*
4c. *Frank Anstey.*
5c. *Emma Anstey.*
6c. *Sofie Anstey,* m. *Castle Smith.*
7c. *Louisa Anstey.*
8c. *Fanny Anstey.*
9c. *Laura Anstey.*

---

[1] *Gentleman's Magazine,* 1756, p. 426. *Notes and Queries* (22 Oct. 1881) gives 20 Jan. 1756.

[2] In *Notes and Queries,* 6th Series, iv. p. 324, he is is incorrectly said to have m. in 1794 the da. of Francis Pierson of Mowthorpe Grange, co. York.

[3] Most, if not all, of the sons emigrated to Canada and U.S.A., and the daughters are now (1909) all dead.

The Plantagenet Roll

3b. *John Thomas Anstey of Bath*, H.E.I.C.S., b. 28 *Ap.* 1795; d. 1 *Oct.* 1885; m. 1823, *Charlotte, sister of Sir Edmund Filmer, 8th Bt.* [E.], *da. of Capt. Edmund Filmer*, d. 10 Dec. 1865; *and had issue* 1c *to* 5c.

1c. Rev. John Filmer Anstey, M.A. (2 *St. James' Terrace, Regent's Park, N.W.*), b. 13 Aug. 1824; *m.* 1st, 25 June 1851, Caroline, da. of the Rev. E. A. Daubeny, d.s.p. 11 Ap. 1864; 2ndly, 17 Nov. 1867, her sister, Annie Daubeny, by whom he has issue 1d.

1d. Caroline Mary Anstey, *m.* as 2nd wife, 27 Oct. 1904, Major Frederick Samborne-Palmer (2 *St. James' Terrace, Regent's Park, N.W.*).

2c. *Edmund Francis Anstey, Capt.* 20*th Regt.*, b. 1825; d. *at Brighton*, 12 *Dec.* 1869; m. *at Weston, near Bath*, 2 *Jan.* 1861, *Charlotte Maria, da. of the Rev. Henry Hodges Mogg of Newbridge Hill House, near Bath; and had issue* (*with an elder da., Mrs. Samborne-Palmer*, d.s.p.) 1d.

1d. *Frances Charlotte Anstey*, b. 14 *Jan.* 1862; d. 17 *Oct.* 1907; m. 7 *June* 1888, *Sidney Whitman, F.R.G.S., Political Writer and Author, represented the* New York Herald *during Armenian Conspiracy Aug.* 1896, *during Greek War* 1897, *and with Turkish Mission through Kurdistan, &c.*, 1897–1898 (6 *Russell Road, Kensington, W.; Junior Athenæum*); *and had issue* 1e *to* 3e.

1e. Herbert Francis Anstey Whitman, b. 15 Jan. 1892.
2e. Sidney Athol Anstey Whitman, b. 20 Jan. 1903.
3e. Eleanor (Elsa) Mary Anstey Whitman, b. 21 Sept. 1889.

3c. *Charlotte Anstey*, b. 12 *July* 1827; d. 7 *Dec.* 1891; m. 8 *Oct.* 1848, *Thomas Bennett of Castle Roe*, d.v.p. 15 *Oct.* 1856; *and had issue* (*with a son* d. *unm.*) 1d to 2d.

1d. Rev. Edmund Thomas Anstey Bennett of Castle Roe, *formerly* Vicar of Littleton, co. Hants, M.A. (Oxon.) (*Castle Roe, Coleraine, co. Londonderry; 43 Stanhope Gardens, S.W.*), b 9 Aug. 1849; *m.* 24 Sept. 1872, Laura Maria, da. of Lieut.-Col. Thomas Edmonds Holmes, Oxfordshire L.I.; and has issue 1e to 3e.

1e. Lionel Edmund Anstey Bennett, *late* Oxfordshire L.I., served in South Africa, was severely wounded 1901, Medal with 3 Clasps (*Arthur's*), b. 18 Ap. 1875; *m.* 19 Ap. 1898, Anna Constance Georgina, da. and h. of Gen. the Hon. Charles Dawson Plunkett [son of 11th Lord Louth]; and has issue 1f.

1f. Constance Evelyn Bennett, b. 10 Feb. 1899.

2e. Eveline Anstey Bennett, *m.* 26 Feb. 1895, Francis Edward Drummond-Hay, M.V.O., Consul for Norway [son of Sir Francis Ringler Drummond-Hay, E. of Kinnoull Coll.] (*British Consulate, Christiania*); and has issue 1f to 2f.

1f. Claude Francis Drummond-Hay, b. 31 July 1898.
2f. Donald Drummond-Hay, b. 28 Oct. 1906.

3e. Muriel Grace Charlotte Anstey Bennett, *m.* 6 July 1908, Thomas Erskine Lambert, *late* 13th Hussars [eldest son of Cowley Lambert of Little Langley, Guildford].

2d. Rev. Thomas John Filmer Bennett, M.A. (Camb.), *formerly* Incumbent of Curzon Chapel, Mayfair, b. 26 July 1854; *m.* 1877, Alice Sarah, da. of Charles Marsh of 34 Grosvenor, Bath; and has issue 1e to 3e.

1e. Maurice Filmer Bennett, Capt. R.M.L.I., b. 2 July 1878; *m.* 11 Sept. 1906, Bianca Rosalie Russell, da. of the Rev. S. Russell Stephens, Vicar and Patron of St. Stephen's, Lewisham.
2e. Harold Filmer Bennett.
3e. Alice Filmer Bennett, *unm.*

4c. *Ellen Anstey*, b. 28 Nov. 1829; d. 9 *Mar.* 1902; m. 28 *May* 1850, *Lieut.-Col. John Marcon of Wallington Hall, co. Norfolk, J.P., formerly* 12*th Regt.*, d. 3 *July* 1883; *and had issue* 1d *to* 8d.

1d. John Marcon, Lord of the Manor of Edgefield, co. Norfolk, and Patron of the Living, J.P., b. 14 Ap. 1855.

2d. Edith Ellen Marcon (*Burgh Heath Lodge, Surrey*), *m.* 14 Ap. 1880, the

[Nos. 32817/1 to 32817/18.

632

of The Blood Royal

Rev. Charles Greenwood Floyd, M.A., Rector of Holme and Runcton [4th son of Major-Gen. Sir Henry Floyd, 2nd Bt. [U.K.]], d. 26 Feb. 1903; and has issue 1e to 3e.

1e. John Marcon Floyd, b. 25 Mar. 1882.

2e. Arthur Bowen Floyd, b. 21 Jan. 1888.

3e. Helena Margaret Floyd, m. 11 July 1906, Cecil James Shuttleworth Holden [descended from King Henry VII., &c. (see Tudor Roll, p. 485)] (*Park Lodge, Ingatestone, Essex*); and has issue 1f.

1f. Richard Arthur Shuttleworth Holden, b. 10 Ap. 1909.

3d. Annie Marcon (*Gunthorpe Hall, Briningham, R.S.O., Norfolk;* 66 *Eaton Square, S.W.*), m. 4 July 1872, Edward Bowyer Sparke of Gunthorpe, J.P., D.L., High Sheriff co. Norfolk 1877 [descended from King Edward III. through Mortimer-Percy], d. 1 June 1910; and has issue.

See the Mortimer-Percy Volume, p. 423, Nos. 80200–80203.

4d. Charlotte Amelia Marcon, m. 6 July 1876, Capt. Ernest de Montesquieu Lacon, Chairman of E. Lacon & Co., Ltd., Mayor of Great Yarmouth 1897, *late* Duke of Cornwall's L.I. [4th son of Sir Edmund Henry Knowles Lacon, 3rd Bt. [U.K.]] (2 *Wilton Terrace, S.W.*); and has issue (with a son d. young) 1e.

1e. Dorothy Mortlock Lacon, m. 30 Ap. 1908, Herbert Kevill-Davies, *late* 7th Hussars (*Croft Castle, Herefordshire*); and has issue 1f.

1f. Geoffrey Somerset Ernest Kevill-Davies, b. 20 Oct. 1909.

5d. Florence Marcon (6 *Ovington Square, S.W.*).

6d. Blanche Marcon ⎫
7d. Eleanor Marcon ⎭ (*Eaton Mansions, S.W.*).

8d. Eveline Marcon.

5c. Caroline Anstey, d.s.p. 9 *Mar.* 1879; m. *as 2nd wife,* 12 *Aug.* 1871, Col. Charles St. Lo Malet [2nd son of Sir Charles Warre Malet, 1st Bt. [G.B.]].

4b. Charles Alleyne Anstey, M.A. (*Trin. Coll., Oxon.*), *for many years* (1819–1864) *a Master at Rugby School and afterwards Rector of Cathorpe, near Rugby, and Vicar of Coggs, near Witney,* b. 25 *May* 1797; d. 19 *Aug.* 1881; m. 1821, *Ann, da. of Thomas Townsend of Rugby,* b. 1803; d. 1861; *and had issue* (with 3 das. d.s.p.) 1c to 8c.

1c. Charles Christopher Anstey, M.A. (*Camb.*), *Rector of St. Levan, Cornwall,* b. 10 *Jan.* 1826; d. 13 *Oct.* 1877; m. 16 *Aug.* 1855, *Frances Mary* (34 *Edith Road, West Kensington, W.*), *da. of Harry Scott Gibb of London, J.P., formerly R.A.; and had issue* 1d to 4d.

1d. Rev. Harry Christopher Scott Anstey, Chaplain Indian Ecclesiastical Establishment, b. 25 Jan. 1864; m. Nov. 1887, Bertha Amelia, da. of Theodore Paul of Thwaite St. Mary, Norfolk; s.p.

2d. Bessie Couper Anstey, m. 10 Jan. 1887, Zuitzen Houkes (*Tarrigindi Road, Annesley, Queensland*); and has issue 1e to 3e.

1e. Zuitzen Houkes.

2e. Frances Maud Houkes, b. 1888.

3e. Ada Houkes.

3d. Maud Lisle Anstey, *unm.*

4d. Amy Townsend Anstey, *unm.*

2c. Rev. Henry Anstey, M.A. (Oxon.), *formerly* Rector of Leighton Buzzard, *previously* Vice-Principal of St. Mary's Hall, Oxford, Author of *Epistolæ Academiæ, Munimenta Academica,* &c. (*St. Levan, Downfield Road, Clifton, Bristol*), b. 23 Sept. 1827; m. 1st, 13 July 1854, Anna Maria, da. of Capt. John Woodford Chase [by his wife Louisa Millicent, *née* Thomas, of Ripple Hall, co. Worc., and Epsom], d. 13 Dec. 1857; and has issue (with a da. d. unm.) 1d to 2d.

1d. John Walter Benjamin Anstey of Swanfels (*Swanfels, Yangan, Queensland*), [Nos. 32817/19 to 32817/43.

The Plantagenet Roll

b. 25 Nov. 1857; *m.* in Australia, (—), da. of Joseph Rigby of Dingle, Yangan; and has (with possibly other) issue 1*e* to 2*e*.
  1*e*. Henry Anstey, *b.* c. 1896.
  2*e*. Eleanor Parkhurst Anstey, *b.* Aug. 1894.

  2*d*. Alice Mary Anstey, b. at Oxford 18 *July* 1856; d. 12 *Dec.* 1895; m. *at Slapton,* 8 *July* 1885, *Henry Cookson of Cotefield, Surgeon-Major Indian Army, F.R.C.S. (Cotefield, Leighton Buzzard, co. Bedford); and had issue* 1*e to* 2*e*.
  1*e*. Henry Anstey Cookson, *b.* 1 July 1886.
  2*e*. John Power Hicks Cookson, *b.* 5 Feb. 1888.

  3*c*. Francis Senior Anstey (*Kamloops, British Columbia*), *b.* 16 Aug. 1830; *m.* at Detroit, Mich., U.S.A., 22 Ap. 1856, Ann, da. of James Doherty, Collector of Customs, Ammersville, Ontario; and has issue (with a son, Walter Herbert, *d.* young) 1*d*.

  1*d*. Charles Townsend Anstey, b. 2 *Feb.* 1857; d. (–) (*having left on a prospecting expedition in 1893, and has not since been heard of*); m. *at Portland, Ore., U.S.A., Georgina Durno (Box* 124, *Seattle, Wash.), da. of Theophilus Thayer of Boston, Mass.; and had issue* 1*e to* 3*e*.
  1*e*. Charles Alleyne Anstey, *b.* 7 Oct. 1880; *m.* at San Francisco, Winifred Mary, da. of Frank Treanor of Sacramento, Cal.
  2*e*. James Durno Anstey, *b.* at Oakland, Cal., 22 June 1883; *m.* Lily Bertine, da. of L. M. Larson of Seattle; and has issue 1*f*.
  1*f*. Georgina Julia Anstey, *b.* at Los Angeles, Cal., 7 Oct. 1909.
  3*e*. George Roy Anstey, U.S. Civil Service (*Seattle, U.S.A.*), *b.* at Oakland afsd. 25 Feb. 1885.

  4*c*. Elizabeth Anstey (*South Leigh, Oxon.*), *m.* 3 July 1855, the Rev. Gerard Moultrie, M.A. (Oxon.), Rector of South Leigh, *d.* 1885; and has issue 1*d* to 8*d*.
  1*d*. Rev. Bernard Moultrie, B.A. (Keble Coll., Oxon.), Rector of Christ Church, St. Leonard's (*Christ Church Rectory, St. Leonards-on-Sea*), *b.* 10 Jan. 1859; *unm.*
  2*d*. Rev. John Moultrie, B.A. (Oxon.), in Holy Orders of the Catholic Church, *b.* 3 Feb. 1860.
  3*d*. Rev. Laurence Gerard Moultrie, Rector of Valley (*Valley Rectory, N. Dakota, U.S.A.*), *b.* 10 Aug. 1866; *m.* at Janeville, Min., 23 Oct. 1895, Carrie Isabella, d. of Brewster Dane of Minnesota, U.S.A.; and has issue 1*e*.
  1*e*. Gerard Earle Moultrie, *b.* 25 Mar. 1898.
  4*d*. Rev. Austin Moultrie, B.A. (Keble Coll., Oxon.), Rector of Matatule, Kaffraria, *formerly* Vicar of St. Saviour's, Leeds (*Matatule Rectory, Kaffraria*), *b.* 4 Dec. 1867; *m.* at Port St. Johns, Kaffraria, 1901, Blanche, da. of (—) Shaw of Cape Colony; and has issue (with a son, Mary, *d.* young) 1*e* to 2*e*.
  1*e*. John Austin Moultrie, *b.* 22 Oct. 1902.
  2*e*. Elizabeth Anstey Moultrie, *b.* 31 July 1906.
  5*d*. Eleanor May Moultrie, *m.* 11 Aug. 1880, the Rev. Walter Edward Wallace, *d.* 9 July 1891; and has issue (with a son *d.* young) 1*e* to 4*e*.
  1*e*. Alexander Moultrie Wallace, *b.* 8 May 1881.
  2*e*. Gerard Percy Wallace, *b.* 29 Mar. 1885.
  3*e*. Cyril Walter Wallace, *b.* 1 Oct. 1890.
  4*e*. Margaret Wallace, *b.* 16 June 1887.
  6*d*. Adela Moultrie, *unm.*
  7*d*. Mary Moultrie, *m.* 13 Ap. 1887, the Rev. Arthur East, B.A. (Camb.), Recto of South Leigh (*South Leigh Rectory, Witney, Oxon.*); and has issue 1*e* to 3*e*.
  1*e*. Arthur Gerard East, *b.* 16 March 1889.
  2*e*. Michael Edmund East, Cadet R.N., *b.* 22 Mar. 1893.
  3*e*. Rupert Moultrie East, *b.* 18 Aug. 1898.
  8*d*. Agatha Moultrie, *unm.* [Nos. 32817/44 to 32817/71.

of The Blood Royal

5c. Emily Caroline Anstey, m. 21 July 1852, Frederick Thomas Haggard, Author of numerous pamphlets on economic subjects, especially Tariff Reform (*Broadwater Down, Tunbridge Wells*); and has issue 1d to 7d.

1d. Frederick Charles Debonnaire Haggard (*Tomlyns, Hutton, near Brentwood, Essex*), b. 8 Oct. 1857; m. 26 June 1890, Grace, da. of Thomas Fairbank of Windsor, M.D.; and has issue 1e.

1e. Victor Ernest Debonnaire Haggard, for whom H.H. the Princess Victoria of Schleswig-Holstein was Sponsor, b. 9 May 1908.

2d. Reginald Anstey Haggard, b. 13 Feb. 1862; m. 3 Sept. 1888, Alice, da. of Alexander James Gibb; and has issue 1e.

1e. Ruth Elsie Haggard, b. 11 July 1889.

3d. Emily Annie Haggard, m. 21 June 1894, William Wolfran Gardner Cornwall, *formerly* Indian Civil Service (*Burford Lodge, Elstead, Surrey*), s.p.

4d. Edith Isabella Ellis Haggard, b. 1855; d. 23 Nov. 1901; m. 1889, *Alfred Baker*; and had issue 1e.

1e. Kenneth Baker, b. 21 Ap. 1890.

5d. Eleanor Haggard, m. 20 Dec. 1894, John Edward Ivor Yale [eldest son of Edward Yale-Jones-Parry of Plas-y-Yale, Denbighshire, and Madryn Castle, co. Carnarvon, J.P., D.L.], d. 1896; and has issue 1e.

1e. Ivor Eleanor Yale.

6d. Mabel Sarah Haggard, m. 18 Sept. 1906, the Rev. Henry James Clayton (*Hillcrest, Mulgrave Road, Croydon*); and has issue 1e.

1e. Henry Richard Michael Clayton, b. 11 Aug. 1907.

7d. Mildred Haggard, *unm.*

6c. Mary Louisa Anstey (16 *Talbot Square, Hyde Park, W.*), m. 11 Oct. 1866, Lieut.-Col. Edward Law, Royal Dublin Fusiliers, *d.s.p.* 10 June 1883; 2ndly, 1 Oct. 1889, *m.* Surg.-Gen. Robert Cockburn, Indian Medical Service, *d.s.p.* 30 Ap. 1899.

7c. Isabella Jane Anstey, b. 5 *Sept.* 1836; d. 28 *July* 1903; m. 1st, at Rugby, 27 Dec. 1859, the Rev. Raymond Brewster Smythies, M.A. (*Emmanuel Coll., Camb.*) [descended from King Edward III. through Mortimer-Percy (see that Volume, p. 126)], d. 19 *Jan.* 1861; 2ndly, at Calcutta, 1868, *Major-Gen. Robert Yeld Chambers;* and had issue 1d to 3d.

1d. Raymond Henry Raymond Smythies, Major (ret.) P.W.V. South Lancashire Regt., author of "Historical Records of the 40th Regt." [descended from King Edward III. through Mortimer-Percy (see that Volume)] (*Army and Navy Club*), b. at Rugby 19 Nov. 1860; *unm.*

2d. Robert Anstey Chambers, *formerly* Lieut. Northumberland Fusiliers (23 *Fitz-George Avenue, W.*), b. at Barrackpore, India, 5 Sept. 1869; m. 4 Aug. 1902, Maud Grace, da. of Patrick Neil Barry of Boston, U.S.A.; and has issue 1e to 3e.

1e. Robert Vyvian Raymond Chambers, b. 16 Mar. 1905.

2e. Vernon Stewart Chambers, b. 7 May 1910.

3e. Isabella Dorothy Anne Chambers, b. 20 May 1903.

3d. David Macdonald Chambers (23 *St. Mary's Mansions, W.*), b. at Dinapore, India, 29 Aug. 1876; m. 30 Oct. 1900, Elizabeth Adelaide, da. of Adam William Black of Edinburgh, and 44 Hyde Park Square, London; and has issue 1e to 2e.

1e. Elizabeth Isabella Macdonald Chambers, b. 20 Nov. 1901.

2e. Margaret Adelaide Irene Chambers, b. 24 Ap. 1905.

8c. Lucy Amelia Anstey (*Wyverstone Rectory, near Stowmarket*), m. 1865, Maj. Justinian Armitage Nutt, 109th and 27th Regts., d. (-); and has issue 1d to 2d.

1d. Ida Cecilia Nutt, m. Nov. 1896, the Rev. Ernest Arthur Milne, M.A. (Oxon.), Rector of Wyverstone (*Wyverstone Rectory, near Stowmarket, Suffolk*), s.p.

2d. Eva Mary Nutt, b. 4 *Jan.* 1874; d. 11 *Ap.* 1902; m. at Plymouth, 2 June 1896, *Capt., now Lieut-Col., Reginald Seward Ruston, the Devonshire Regt.* (*St. Columba's, Killiney, co. Dublin; Army and Navy*); and had issue 1e to 2e.

[Nos. 32817/72 to 32817/93.

The Plantagenet Roll

1e. Sylvia Mary Ruston, b. 1 June 1897.
2e. Margaret Joan Ruston, b. 29 July 1900.
5b. George Anstey, in the Audit Office, d. (? unm.).
6b. Helen Anstey, d. (? unm.) 1880.
7b. Caroline Anstey, d. 1879; unm.
4a. Thomas Anstey, went to India, d. (? s.p.) in Bath.
5a. Arthur Anstey, afterwards Anstey-Calvert, executor to will of brother, 20 July 1818.
6a. William Anstey, 6th son, bur. with father in Walcot Church.
7a. William Thomas Anstey, 7th son, bur. with father in Walcot Church.
8a. [da.] Anstey.
9a. [da.] Anstey.
10a. Caroline Anstey, d. (-); m. 1790, Henry Bosanquet of Clanville, co. Hants, High Sheriff for that co. 1815, d. 29 Jan. 1817; and had issue (with a da. d. unm.) 1b.
1b. Henry Bosanquet of Clanville Lodge, b. 29 Dec. 1793; d. 31 Jan. 1861; m. 6 June 1827, Mary, da. of William Richards of Clatford, co. Hants; and had issue 1c.
1c. Henry Anstey Bosanquet of Clanville, M.A., J.P., Bar.-at-Law (Clanville Lodge, Hants), b. 25 Mar. 1828; m. 4 Sept. 1861, Mary Anne, da. of Lieut.-Col. Francis Luttrell of Kilve Court, co. Som.; and has issue 1d to 3d.
1d. Mary Bosanquet, m. 4 Dec. 1890, Robert Shafto Adair, B.A. (Oxon.), Bar.-at-Law [2nd son of Sir Hugh Edward Adair, 3rd Bt. [U.K.], M.P.] (9 Lower Berkeley Street, W.); and has issue 1e to 2e.
1e. Allan Henry Shafto Adair, b. 3 Nov. 1897.
2e. Camilla Mary Shafto Adair, b. 24 May 1895.
2d. Edith Caroline Bosanquet, unm.
3d. Amy Louisa Bosanquet, m. 23 Oct. 1900, the Rev. James Phlips, Vicar of Yeovil and Prebendary of Wells (Yeovil Vicarage, Somerset); and has issue.
11a. Sarah Anstey, 4th da., bur. with father in Walcot Church; m. as 1st wife, Rear-Adm. Thomas Sotheby [see Mortimer-Percy Volume, p. 346]; and had issue (with a son and da. who d. in infancy) 1b to 2b.
1b. Sarah Sotheby, d.s.p.; m. the Rev. Armytage Gaussen.
2b. Elizabeth Sotheby, d. 1839; m. as 2nd wife, 1829, Capt. Charles Thomas Thruston of Pennal Tower, co. Merioneth, R.N., d, 1858; and had issue 1c.
1c. Clement Arthur Thruston of Pennal Tower, Bar.-at-Law, High Sheriff co. Merioneth 1870, b. 12 June 1837; d. 9 June 1883; m. 2 Oct. 1861, Constance Sophia Margaret, da. of Gen. Lechmere Coore Russell of Ashford Hall, co. Salop, C.B.; and had issue (with a son killed in Uganda, unm.) 1d to 3d.
1d. Edmund Heathcote Thruston of Pennal Tower, J.P., D.L., late Capt. 3rd Batt. Royal Welsh Fusiliers, previously Mid. R.N. (25 Cambridge Road, Hove, Brighton; Pennal Tower, Machynlleth), b. 10 Dec. 1863; m. 8 May 1896, Lucy [descended from King Henry VII. (see Tudor Roll, p. 509)], da. of Sir Wilfrid Lawson, 2nd Bt. [U.K.], M.P.; and has issue 1e to 4e.
1e. Edmund Wybergh Thruston, b. 6 Dec. 1903.
2e. John Wilfrid Russell Thruston, b. 30 Oct. 1910.
3e. Margaret Thruston, b. 1 Aug. 1897.
4e. Hoima Thruston, b. 23 Jan. 1901.
2d. Marion Janet Thruston.
3d. Olwen Millicent Thruston.

[Nos. 32817/94 to 32817/108.

INDEX OF NAMES

SUPPLEMENT TO THE ESSEX VOLUME

ADAIR, A. H. S., p. 636; C. M. S., p. 636; Mrs. M., p. 636
Anstey, A. T., p. 633; C. A., p. 634; E. P., p. 634; F. S., p. 634; G. J., p. 634; G. R., p. 634; Rev. H., p. 633; H., p. 634; Rev. H. C. S., p. 633; J. D., p. 634; Rev. J. F., p. 632; J. W. B., p. 633; M. L., p. 633

BAKER, K., p. 635
Bennett, A. F., p. 632; C. E., p. 632; Rev. E. T. A., p. 632; H. F., p. 632; L. E. A., p. 632; Capt. M. F., p. 632; Rev. T. J. F., p. 632
Bosanquet, E. C., p. 636; H. A., p. 636

CHAMBERS, D. M., p. 635; E. I. M., p. 635; I. D. A., p. 635; M. A. L, p. 635; Lieut. R. A., p. 635; R. V. R., p. 635
Clayton, H. R. M., p. 635; Mrs. M. S., p. 635
Cockburn, Mrs. M. L., p. 635
Cornwall, Mrs. E. A., p. 635
Cookson, H. A., p. 634; J. P. H., p. 634

DRUMMOND-HAY, C. F., p. 632; D., p. 632; Mrs. E. A., p. 632

EAST, A. G., p. 634; Mrs. M., p. 634; M. E., p. 634; R. M., p. 634

FLOYD, A. B., p. 633; Mrs. E. E., p. 632; J. M., p. 633

HAGGARD, Mrs. E. C., p. 635; F. C. D., p. 635; M., p. 635; R. A., p. 635; R. E., p. 635; V. E. D., p. 635
Holden, Mrs. H. M., p. 633; R. A. S., p. 633
Houkes, A., p. 633; Mrs. B. C., p. 633; F. M., p. 633; Z., p. 633

KEVILL-DAVIES, Mrs. D. M., p. 633; G. S. E., p. 633

LACON, Mrs. C. A., p. 633
Lambert, Mrs. M. G. C. A., p. 632

MARCON, B., p. 633; E., p. 633; E., p. 633; F., p. 633; J., p. 632
Milne, Mrs. I. C., p. 635
Moultrie. Rev. A., p. 634; A., p. 634; A., p. 634; Rev. B., p. 634; Mrs. E., p. 634; E. A., p. 634; G. E., p. 634; Rev. J., p. 634; J. A., p. 634; Rev. L. G., p. 634

NUTT, Mrs. L. A., p. 635

PHLIPS, Mrs. A. L., p. 636

RUSTON, M. J., p. 635; S. M., p. 635

SAMBORNE-PALMER, Mrs. C. M., p. 632
Smythies, Maj. R. H. R., p. 635
Sparke, Mrs. A., p. 633

THRUSTON, Capt. E. H., p. 636; E. W., p. 636; H., p. 636; J. W. R., p. 636; M., p. 636; M. J., p. 636; O. M., p. 636

WALLACE, A. M., p. 634; C. W., p. 634; Mrs. E. M., p. 634; G. P., p. 634; M., p. 634
Whitman, E. M. A., p. 632; H. F. A., p. 632; S. A. A., p. 632

YALE, Mrs. E., p. 635; I. E., p. 635

www.ingramcontent.com/pod-product-compliance
Lightning Source LLC
Chambersburg PA
CBHW070905300426
44113CB00008B/936